# DOCUMENTS ON BRITISH FOREIGN POLICY
# 1919–1939

EDITED BY

## W. N. MEDLICOTT, M.A., D.Lit., D.Litt.
*Emeritus Professor of International History*
*University of London*

## DOUGLAS DAKIN, M.A., Ph.D.
*Professor of History, Birkbeck College, University of London*

AND

## M. E. LAMBERT, M.A.

*SECOND SERIES*
*Volume XIII*

LONDON
HER MAJESTY'S STATIONERY OFFICE
1973

362765

PRINTED IN ENGLAND
FOR HER MAJESTY'S STATIONERY OFFICE
BY VIVIAN RIDLER AT THE UNIVERSITY PRESS, OXFORD

Dd 503201 K16 4/73
SBN 11 590188 4*

# DOCUMENTS ON BRITISH FOREIGN POLICY

## 1919–1939

Second Series, Volume XIII

Naval Policy and Defence Requirements
July 20, 1934–March 25, 1936

# PREFACE

THIS volume has two main themes. The first is the debate among the leading naval powers which started in the summer of 1934 and culminated in the second London naval conference (December 1935 to March 1936). The second is the development of Anglo-German relations from mid-April to November 1935, continuing the story in Volume XII of the Series. Here, too, naval questions played an important part.

Chapters I and II describe preliminary discussions which took place in London during the second half of 1934 between British and American, Japanese, French, and Italian representatives as to their governments' respective naval desiderata. The state of the Royal Navy had already figured prominently in the tentative rearmament discussions which had followed the denunciation of the ten-year rule by the Chiefs of Staff in March 1932 and the setting up of the Defence Requirements Committee (D.R.C.) in November 1933. These discussions are summarized in the Introductory Note to Chapter I below. The British Cabinet set up a Naval Ministerial Committee in April 1934 to examine and report on the policy to be followed at the conference, which according to the London Naval Treaty of 1930 was to take place before the end of 1935. The British took the view that naval rearmament was on a somewhat different footing from that of the other two fighting services, both because the level of naval as distinct from air and land armaments was regulated by international treaty with specific time limits, and because the needs of the Royal Navy were considered to be in some respects absolute, that is, not adjustable to the requirements of other powers. Nevertheless, proposals for qualitative limitation (in size and armaments) of warships had been made by His Majesty's Government to the Disarmament Conference in 1932 (cf. Volume III of this Series, p. 610).

The American representatives were somewhat startled to discover at the end of June 1934 that the British Admiralty envisaged a substantial increase in the number of cruisers needed by the United Kingdom, but this difference did not become publicly known, and in a reasonably friendly atmosphere it was agreed to postpone further discussion until the arrival of Japanese representatives in London in October (cf. document No. 1). Mr. R. L. Craigie of the American Department of the Foreign Office argued the British case for revised figures frankly and cogently in a Note on Cruiser Tonnage of July 25 (No. 2).

The desirability of an Anglo-Japanese rapprochement had been very much urged by the D.R.C. in its report of February 28, 1934, and was considered by the Ministerial Committee on Disarmament to which the D.R.C. report was referred. It was again urged by Sir Warren Fisher, Permanent Secretary of the Treasury, in the boldly-worded memorandum

v

for the Cabinet of April 29, 1934, in which he spelled out the argument for action independent if necessary of the United States (Appendix I). To the staff of the Foreign Office, and indeed to most members of the Cabinet, good relations with the United States were paramount (cf. No. 18). The case for an Anglo-Japanese pact continued nevertheless to be aired until late in October, for Sir Warren Fisher had a formidable supporter in his chief at the Treasury, Mr. Neville Chamberlain.

Chapter I includes all the documentation on this interesting Treasury initiative that appears to be available in the Foreign Office archives. Sir John Simon, the Secretary of State for Foreign Affairs, looked hopefully for a time on a rather vague Japanese offer early in July of non-aggression pacts with Great Britain and the United States, and he believed that something of the sort might soften Japanese hostility to the 5-5-3 ratio of the Washington Naval Treaty of 1922. The Foreign Office officials, apart from Mr. Craigie, were, however, more critical (No. 8). Mr. Chamberlain, acting Prime Minister during the holiday season (August 8–September 22), elaborated his arguments in favour of an Anglo–Japanese pact in a letter to Sir J. Simon of September 1, with the comment that if the pact were 'right in our interests we should not be frightened out of it by any fear of American objection' (No. 14). Foreign Office uneasiness about this plan can be seen from Mr. C. W. Orde's weighty memorandum of September 4 (No. 15) which raised doubts about American acceptance but dwelt mainly on the wider disadvantages which might follow a pact on any terms which the Japanese were likely to accept. These doubts evidently led Sir John Simon to seek to dampen some of the Chancellor's ardour, but he was still sufficiently interested in agreement with Japan to secure, against the views of Sir R. Vansittart, the Cabinet's consent to a cautious enquiry as to what the Japanese foreign minister, Mr. Hirota, had had in mind (No. 21). The Cabinet further agreed that Sir John Simon and Mr. Chamberlain should circulate a joint memorandum on the pact proposal. The resulting document (No. 29: cf. No. 28), dated October 16, was drafted in the Foreign Office, and after reinforcing many of the objections earlier outlined by Mr. Orde, proposed a triple Anglo-American-Japanese pact only as a last resort if the Japanese were agreeable and if the naval talks broke down.

This should perhaps be interpreted as the virtual abandonment of any idea of ignoring American reactions, although the memorandum did suggest that if the United States should refuse to contemplate such a pact, it could take 'no reasonable exception to the pursuit of a bilateral Anglo-Japanese agreement'. The Cabinet postponed further action on October 24 and the Japanese attitude thereafter precluded any serious revival of the project, although the Japanese Foreign Office continued to show an elusive and intermittent interest in a political agreement during the next eighteen months (cf. Nos. 590, 591, 608, 638). Sir John Simon's hopes of improved Anglo-Japanese relations remained (Nos. 67, 76, 90).

In the further round of 'exploratory' naval talks in London from late October to December 1934 the British representatives succeeded in maintaining amicable relations with the American and Japanese delegations without removing the basic Japanese-American deadlock. The Japanese would have nothing more to do with the 5-5-3 ratio and asked at the end of October for agreement on a common upper limit of total tonnage for all naval powers and the abolition or reduction of offensive arms, after which each should be free to build within the limit as it deemed fit. There seemed little doubt that the sense of competitiveness of the Japanese was aroused mainly by the United States fleet, and that they were willing to recognize the special position of the United Kingdom with its worldwide responsibilities. But the United States was not prepared to concede parity to Japan.

In the opinion of the British Naval Staff Japan and the United States had each built up naval armaments exceeding its real needs and would be prepared to reduce them in the interests of economy, but for reasons of prestige could not do so without equivalent British reductions. The British, however, steadily maintained that their absolute requirements of imperial defence precluded reductions in any of the categories apart from submarines, and that they needed a substantial increase in cruisers (cf. No. 111). To meet the situation they proposed to the Japanese delegates on November 6 as a compromise or 'middle-way' plan the unreserved recognition of the principle of equality between the signatories of a new naval treaty, combined with a voluntary acceptance by each contracting party of a building programme corresponding to the minimum limits of naval strength required for its security (No. 41). It was hoped that after accepting this plan the Japanese could be induced to leave the existing relative positions substantially unaffected. They preferred to regard it as the ratio system in a disguised form. No compromise proved possible, and the Japanese Government formally announced on December 30 its decision to abrogate the Washington Treaty. The United States delegation reacted 'not unfavourably' to the British proposal about building programmes, and seemed ready to accept what the British regarded as their minimum requirements.

When the talks were adjourned on December 19, 1934, it was evident that quantitative limitation in its old form was probably dead. But it was still hoped that the 'middle way' plan would serve somewhat the same purpose, and that the French and Italians, who had been deadlocked for years over the question of equality, would also find in the plan a way round the problem of prestige (Nos. 1, 4, 7, 32, 48, 108, 111). Qualitative limitation was considered to be in some ways more important as a means of avoiding an armaments race. As the initiative in calling the conference before the end of 1935 had been left in British hands, planning for it in London on the basis of qualitative limitation and the middle-way compromise began almost at once.

But the conference could hardly succeed unless Germany's naval requirements were taken into account. Herr Hitler had already, on November 27 1934 (Volume XII, No. 230), mentioned his desire for a 35 per cent ratio of German to British naval strength. It was evidently felt in London at this point that in view of the timetable imposed by the earlier naval treaties, naval agreements must be discussed and, if necessary, concluded separately from those of air and land armaments, in spite of the British emphasis in the Anglo-French discussions of February 1–3, 1935, on 'the principle of simultaneity' (that is, that negotiations with Germany on the separate issues might take place but that none should be formally concluded until all were complete: cf. Volume XII, No. 400). Naval questions do not appear to have been mentioned in these Anglo-French discussions, and it seemed a reasonable assumption that France had tacitly agreed to separate British naval talks with Germany (cf. Nos. 1 and 114, note 2). Soundings followed in Berlin, and on March 26 Sir John Simon suggested informal Anglo-German naval discussions to Herr Hitler; the suggestion was accepted (Volume XII, No. 651, pp. 728–33).

From this point documents about the planning of the naval conference will be found in Chapters III to VI, which deal in the main with the story of Anglo-German relations from April 18 to early November, 1935. The plans for an all-round agreement with Germany, as embodied in the Anglo-French communiqué of February 3, 1935, had been due to British eagerness to secure such an agreement before rapidly growing self-confidence finally killed any German inclination to compromise. The Foreign Office thoroughly accepted the practical aim embodied in the principle of simultaneity—namely that Germany should pay for concessions by counter-concessions—but was coming by the summer to fear that the rigid French attitude on land armaments was likely to frustrate all chances of progress. Preferring the more pragmatic approach, it wanted to advance step-by-step in negotiation when the chance offered, and it recognized some genuine feeling in German professions of grievance and affronted national dignity. Although the United Kingdom joined with France and Italy at Geneva on April 16, after the Stresa conference, in condemning Germany's declaration of unilateral rearmament of March 16 there were considered to be hopeful prospects of Germany's agreement to an eastern pact on a non-aggression basis (as suggested by the German Foreign Minister on April 13) and to Anglo-German discussions for a naval agreement and air pact. Germany professed not to take British rearmament amiss.

The Foreign Office was entirely in tune with Sir Eric Phipps, the British Ambassador in Berlin, whose caustic and penetrating reports on German policy did not exclude hope of an ultimate Anglo-German agreement. On June 12, commenting on Herr Hitler's fury over the Geneva agreement, and conceding his many breaches of faith in the past, Phipps nevertheless deprecated the view 'that no faith can be attached to his signature'.

His Majesty's Government may decide that it is now undesirable to conclude any convention with this country; they may prefer to maintain their liberty of action. If, however, they feel that advantage should be taken of the presence of M. Laval at the head of the French Government and of his notorious desire to come to some reasonable understanding with Germany, I earnestly hope that they will not allow themselves to be deterred by the mere contemplation of Herr Hitler's past misdeeds or breaches of faith.

He believed that Hitler might, 'like many men, have evolved since the old, somewhat gangsterlike days at Munich . . . And if the worst befall, and Hitler decide to break his freely-given, solemn pledge, surely our battle-ground would be all the firmer for having put him to the test?' (No. 327).

In spite of this cautious encouragement to optimism the Foreign Office remained intensely apprehensive about German rearmament and intentions, keenly aware of the tactical advantages of substantial British rearmament, and worried over its slow progress. In the spring of 1935 an inter-departmental debate on the German air figures, initiated by Herr Hitler's apparently random claim on March 26 to have achieved parity with the United Kingdom, found the Foreign Office supporting the more alarmist interpretation as opposed to the more correct estimate of the Air Ministry (No. 127). On 30 April the Ministerial Committee on Defence Requirements set up a sub-committee on Air Parity which quickly recommended both a bigger air expansion programme to meet the German figures and the announcement of measures which would deter Germany and pacify public opinion at home. The D.R.C., on which the Foreign Office continued to be represented, was then instructed, on July 8, to re-examine the existing Services programme, and on July 24 it presented a second (and interim) report recommending air and naval expansion, a slight later provision for the Field Force, and the plans for industrial mobilization. Influenced no doubt by Sir R. Vansittart's urgent representations (cf. No. 396) the committee rejected the Services' view that Germany would not deliberately launch aggression before 1942 and advanced January 1, 1939, as the latest date compatible with British security. The Ministerial Committee, now known as the Ministerial Committee on Defence Policy and Requirements, then authorized the D.R.C. to work out programmes on this basis which would place each Service in a state of readiness to meet the needs of national defence by the end of the financial year 1938–1939 'within the limits of practicability'. The D.R.C. presented its detailed programme in the following November.

Meanwhile during the summer of 1935 the Foreign Office retained its hopes of the eastern pact. M. Laval continued to receive reminders from London of the desirability of an agreement with Germany about land armaments (cf. Nos. 416, 431, 473, 496), but there seemed no scope for negotiations with Germany about military effectives, and the French and Italians made it clear that they would regard themselves as 'very naive' if, in the circumstances, they were to consider reducing their small lead in heavy war material (cf. No. 134). The prospects of an air pact were more promising: Germany had shown interest in the idea since February, and in May both the French and the Italians agreed that it provided the best hopes of bringing Germany 'back into the collective security ring again' (Nos. 182, 191). Drafts of an air pact had already been exchanged between Britain, France, Italy, and Belgium but had not been shown to the fifth Locarno power,

Germany, who herself presented a draft air pact to the British Government on May 29. This German draft provided for reciprocal aid between the Locarno powers to meet the eventuality of unprovoked air attack by another of the High Contracting Powers. It did not cover air limitation or the outlawing of indiscriminate bombing, which Sir John Simon regarded as essential to a complete air agreement, but the German Government did not dissent at this point from the initiation of discussions for this triple purpose (Nos. 259, 263).

The French feared, or professed to fear, that the British might rapidly lose interest in a united front if their immediate concern over sea and air armaments were removed by Germany. Anxieties on this score were evidently increased by the Anglo-German naval agreement of June 18, 1935, although this had clearly much to recommend it even from the point of view of French interests. But while grudgingly admitting this, M. Laval complained about the 'form and method' of the agreement (No. 363). It could perhaps have been argued that as a preliminary to the all-round settlement of naval questions at the forthcoming conference the agreement did not depart from the 'simultaneity' principle. However, this argument would have been more convincing if the negotiations had taken the course originally anticipated by the Foreign Office. At the opening meeting on June 4 the British negotiators had proposed to put aside the plan for a specific ratio of 35 per cent (which Herr Hitler had repeated in his speech of May 21) on the ground that there was now little hope of progress in quantitative limitation; instead, they wanted the Germans to accept the 'middle way', with minimum building programmes defined in talks between the experts. The chief German delegate insisted, however, that 'Herr Hitler was a very consistent man, and thought in long historical periods, as a result of which he had fixed this ratio'; Germany would proceed on no other basis (No. 289). The British ministers decided to agree on June 5, after a warning from the British delegates that 'if we now refuse to accept the offer for the purpose of these discussions, Herr Hitler will withdraw the offer and Germany will seek to build up to a higher level than 35 per cent' (Nos. 305, 311). The rigid German position undoubtedly gave an appearance of finality to the agreement which the 'middle course' procedure would have avoided. It was still, nevertheless, only the first stage towards a final arrangement: talks between the British and German experts continued for the next nine months (Nos. 348, 488, 490, 526, 561, 573, 575, 588, 621, 635, 647, 674, 678, 679, 682, 688, 691, 693, 703, 705, 710). Germany had still to be brought into a general naval treaty.

The Anglo-German naval agreement is often associated with Sir Samuel Hoare's name, but all the effective steps, including the decision of June 5, fell within Sir John Simon's term of office. He told the Germans on June 6 that the formal acceptance of their proposal must be delayed until the other interested governments had been given a chance to comment. Of these the United States Government greeted the news with 'particular satisfaction' (No. 325); the Japanese Government had no objection, providing no Japanese interest would suffer (No. 328); the Italian Government was non-committal, but not openly hostile (No. 328); the French, however, after being compelled by a domestic crisis to delay any reply until the eve of signature of the agreement on June 18, bluntly deplored it as a unilateral revision of the treaty of Versailles (No. 354).

Sir Samuel Hoare, who became Foreign Secretary on June 7, had had long experience as Air Minister in the nineteen-twenties, and he strove hard for the air pact as the vital step towards a general agreement with Germany. The Cabinet had decided on June 5 that the Air Pact and Air Limitation 'should be taken up as a separate question and no longer be considered to be necessarily linked up with a general settlement' but M. Laval's reaction to the naval agreement convinced the Foreign Office that 'the French must be humoured and not rushed' over the terms of an air agreement with Germany, and that no separate agreement with her on this issue could now be contemplated, although negotiations should proceed (Nos. 330, note 1, 358, 378). The views of the Foreign Office and Air Ministry on all the issues were set out in a Cabinet memorandum of June 26 (No. 364). To retain some elasticity in the discussions with Germany, efforts were made during July to secure a relaxation of M. Laval's conditions, but he insisted that the air pact should be completed by bilateral military agreements which must include one between France and Great Britain, and that neither the air pact nor the limitation agreement should become operative until the completion of all the other projects contemplated in the communiqué of February 3 (Nos. 389, 400, 406, 409, 420, 433, 435). All this was probably a waste of effort. There was no response to Sir Samuel Hoare's appeal to Germany in his Commons speech of July 11 to help on negotiations for the Eastern and Danubian pacts in order to facilitate the air agreement. On July 29 the German Ambassador announced that the German offer of an eastern pact of April 13 had been withdrawn (No. 441). On August 1 Sir John Simon urged the German Government to enter negotiations for the air pact (No. 447). But the German Foreign Office continued to evade proposals for negotiations with bland references to the holiday season. It was now satisfied that the mounting Italo-Ethiopian crisis would disrupt the Stresa front without German intervention (No. 440, note 6).

The final stage of planning for the naval conference was complicated by the French reactions to the Anglo-German naval agreement (No. 362), but after a visit by Captain Danckwerts, R.N., to Paris in August (No. 461), arrangements were completed in London in conversations, conducted mainly by Mr. Craigie, with American (Nos. 498, 507, 511, 513, 520, 527, 540), French (Nos. 524, 546), and Italian (Nos. 531, 552, 554, 555) representatives. Chapters VII and VIII contain the ample correspondence and documentation about the conference preserved in the Foreign Office archives, including Admiralty communications and memoranda, but excluding the minutes of meetings and committees which have been published elsewhere (see Introductory Note to Chapter VII). Although in his opening speech to the conference on December 9 Mr. Baldwin referred to the desirability of both quantitative and qualitative limitation it was already more than probable that the former would have to be abandoned in view of the Japanese proposal for a common-upper-limit which was tabled at the opening of the conference. When the proposal proved unacceptable to all the other delegations, Japan, on January 15, 1936, withdrew her delegation from the conference, leaving observers to watch its progress. The United Kingdom proposals for a 'middle way' also proved to be generally unacceptable, but the conference did achieve in the end a wide measure of agreement on qualitative limitation, together with provision for advance notification of the construction or acquisition of war vessels and the exchange of information as to their principal characteristics. The maximum displacement of 35,000 tons for capital ships had to be accepted in spite of French objections, but there were hopes that a reduction in gun calibre to 14″ would be achieved. The British proposals made to the disarmament conference in 1932 were substantially achieved in respect of aircraft carriers, cruisers, and destroyers. The treaty was signed on March 25, 1936, by the United States, Great Britain, and France and six Commonwealth countries after France for a time had objected to Germany's ultimate accession to the treaty. It was finally ratified by His Majesty's Government on July 9, 1937, twelve days after the German and Soviet Governments had agreed to the provisions for the limitation of naval armaments and exchange of information (cf. No. 711, note 12).

The conditions under which the Editors accepted the task of producing this Collection, namely, access to all papers in the Foreign Office archives and freedom in the selection and arrangement of documents, continue to be fulfilled. The documents printed in this volume are drawn mainly from the files of the American Department (for Chapters I, II, IV, VII, and VIII) and Central Department (for Chapters III, IV, V, and VI). Naval matters were normally handled at this time in the Foreign Office by the American Department, which was closely involved owing to the continuing importance of naval problems in Anglo-American relations; in the process Mr. R. L. Craigie, the head of the department from 1929 to 1936, became the Foreign Office's leading expert on naval affairs. Thus the material for the Anglo-German naval discussions in June 1935 will be found mainly under the file number A22/45. As in previous volumes, documents already published in the Command Papers and elsewhere have normally been excluded. Use has been made where relevant of the personal papers of Viscount Simon (F.O. 800/289–291), Lord Templewood (F.O. 800/295), and Sir Orme Sargent (F.O. 800/272–279).

I must thank Mr. B. Cheeseman, O.B.E., the Head of the Library and Records Department of the Foreign and Commonwealth Office, and his staff for all necessary facilities. This is the last volume in the preparation of which I have had the help of Miss Irene Bains, M.A., who retired in September 1972. Miss Bains joined the editorial team for these documents in November 1953 and worked successively with Professor E. L. Woodward, Mr. R. D'O. Butler, Mr. J. P. T. Bury, and myself. She also compiled the Index, published in 1961, to the Third Series of this Collection, and was responsible for most of the correspondence, sometimes of a very technical character, with our printers and Her Majesty's Stationery Office. She has thus made a valuable contribution over the years to the progress of this Collection, and she takes with her our best wishes for her retirement. I have also to thank Miss Jane Roskill, B.A., for help in the final stages of preparation of this volume.

W. N. MEDLICOTT

*November 1972*

# CONTENTS

# LIST OF ABBREVIATIONS

| | |
|---|---|
| *B.F.S.P.* | *British and Foreign State Papers* (London). |
| Cmd. | Command Paper (London). |
| *D.D.F.* | *Documents Diplomatiques Français 1932–1939* (Paris). |
| *D.G.F.P.* | *Documents on German Foreign Policy 1918–1945*, Series C (1933–37) (London). |
| D.R.C. | Defence Requirements Committee. |
| *F.R.U.S.* | *Papers relating to the Foreign Relations of the United States* (Washington). |
| *Facing the Dictators* | The Earl of Avon, *The Eden Memoirs: Facing the Dictators* (London, 1962). |
| *H.C. Deb. 5 s.* | *Parliamentary Debates (Hansard), Official Report, 5th Series,* House of Commons (London). |
| *H.L. Deb. 5 s.* | *Parliamentary Debates (Hansard), Official Report, 5th Series,* House of Lords (London). |
| *Hitler's Speeches* | *The Speeches of Adolf Hitler, April 1922–August 1939,* edited by Norman H. Baynes, 2 vols (London, 1942). |
| *L/N.O.J.* | *League of Nations Official Journal* (Geneva). |
| *L/N.O.J., S.S.* | *League of Nations Official Journal, Special Supplement* (Geneva). |

An asterisk following the file number of a document indicates that the text has been taken from Confidential Print.

# CHAPTER SUMMARIES

## CHAPTER I

The debate in London on the terms of a naval understanding with the United States and Japan

July 20–October 16, 1934

CHAPTER II

# Further discussion on possible bases of naval limitation and future policy

## October 19, 1934–March 30, 1935

XXV

xxvii

## CHAPTER III

# Questions of German rearmament and of security: proposals for Anglo-German naval conversations

## April 18–May 28, 1935

# CHAPTER IV

## German Government's proposal for an Air Pact: Anglo-German Naval Agreement

### May 29–June 20, 1935

CHAPTER V

# Reactions to Anglo-German Naval Agreement: further discussion on proposed Eastern and Air Pacts

## June 20–July 31, 1935

1

liii

CHAPTER VI

Abortive discussions on proposed Eastern and Air Pacts: preparations for the Naval Conference

August 1–December 3, 1935

lvii

CHAPTER VII

Correspondence relating to the earlier proceedings of the London Naval Conference

December 4, 1935–January 16, 1936

Correspondence relating to the proceedings of the London Naval
Conference after the withdrawal of the Japanese Delegation

January 17–March 25, 1936

# CHAPTER I

## The debate in London on the terms of a naval understanding with the United States and Japan

## July 20–October 16, 1934

### INTRODUCTORY NOTE

ACCORDING to Article 1, Part I, of the London Naval Treaty of April 22, 1930, the High Contracting Parties (the United States, France, Great Britain, Italy, and Japan) agreed 'not to exercise their rights to lay down the keels of capital ship replacement tonnage during the years 1931–1936 inclusive as provided in Chapter II, Part 3 of the Treaty for the Limitation of Naval Armament signed between them at Washington on the 6th February, 1922 . . .' Article 23, Part V, further provided that the 'present Treaty shall remain in force until the 31st December, 1936', and that

> Unless the High Contracting Parties should agree otherwise by reason of a more general agreement limiting naval armaments, to which they all become parties, they shall meet in conference in 1935 to frame a new treaty to replace and to carry out the purposes of the present Treaty, it being understood that none of the provisions of the present Treaty shall prejudice the attitude of any of the High Contracting Parties at the conference agreed to.[1]

During the next five years the theme of naval disarmament remained more or less distinct from the general disarmament discussions, the unsatisfactory course of which can be followed down to April 1935 in Volumes VI and XII, Second Series, of these documents. All the signatory powers had some grounds for dissatisfaction with the London Naval Treaty. But while the United States Government had decided by the beginning of 1934 that it would be content to maintain the 5–5–3 ratio for capital ships as between Great Britain, the United States, and Japan established by the Washington Naval Treaty of 1922, the Japanese Government appeared powerless to resist the demand of the Japanese Navy for parity with the two greater naval powers or, failing that, for the rejection of all limitation on naval construction. At the same time France and Italy, who had been unable to accept certain portions of the London Treaty owing to the French refusal to concede Italian demands for parity, had continued to disagree.

---

[1] The text of the London Naval Treaty is printed as Appendix I in Volume I of the Second Series of *Documents on British Foreign Policy 1919–1939*, and in *British and Foreign State Papers (B.F.S.P.)*, vol. 132, pp. 603 ff.

The British Government's Draft Convention of March 1933[2] contained a Naval Chapter but in the Foreign Office memorandum on disarmament of January 25, 1934 it was questioned whether 'some simpler arrangement' should not be aimed at in view of the forthcoming naval conference.[3] Towards the end of January the British and United States Governments agreed that informal talks on the preparations for the 1935 conference would be desirable as soon as their experts had completed their studies of the technical aspects. The subsequent course of United States policy during the first half of 1934 can be followed in some detail in *Foreign Relations of the United States 1934*, volume i, pp. 217–303. It was desired that the initiative in the discussions should come, as far as possible, from the British.

On the British side the report to the Cabinet and the Committee of Imperial Defence in February 1934 of the Defence Requirements Sub-Committee (D.R.C.) described Germany as the country's 'ultimate potential enemy' and called for a programme of naval expansion, including the restoration of naval stations abroad (particularly at Singapore) and of the target figure of seventy cruisers abandoned under American pressure in 1929–30. In the discussions which preceded the completion of the D.R.C. report it had been recognized that financial considerations made impossible the maintenance of a Two-Power standard fleet (that is, one strong enough to protect British interests, simultaneously, against Japan in the Far East and against the strongest naval power in Europe, hitherto France). The obvious corollary to this was the desirability of a *détente* in Anglo-Japanese relations sufficient to allow the concentration of British naval effort in European and Mediterranean waters if the need arose.[4]

The Cabinet began to discuss the report (C.P. 64(34)) on March 14. After agreeing that no fresh expenditure should be incurred on measures of defence 'to provide exclusively against attack by the United States, France or Italy', it turned to the committee's recommendation that an attempt should be made 'to get back at least to our old terms of cordiality and mutual respect with Japan'. There was ample support for this proposal from certain members, but not from the Prime Minister. Sir John Simon, Secretary of State for Foreign Affairs, said that since the Manchurian crisis he had been doing everything possible in an unspectacular way to improve relations with Japan, although he foresaw serious difficulties at the forthcoming naval conference in view of the American attitude. Mr. Neville Chamberlain, the Chancellor of the Exchequer, warmly supported the policy of the report and emphasized the desirability of restoring Japanese *amour propre* by 'some kind of bilateral understanding'. He put forward 'as a basis for discussion' the view that the British Government should decide not to submit to the limitations of a naval treaty and should say that they did not mind what America chose to build. Japan would then 'be free from the fear that we might be united with America against her'.[5]

---

[2] See Cmd. 4279 of 1933; cf. Volume IV, Appendix IV.    [3] See Volume VI, No. 206.
[4] The committee's proposals will be discussed in vol. i of Professor N. H. Gibbs, *Grand Strategy* (Her Majesty's Stationery Office, London).    [5] Cabinet Conclusions No. 9(34).

The Cabinet resumed the discussion on March 19 on the basis of compendious Foreign Office memoranda, including a cabinet paper of March 16 (C.P. 80 (34)) which found the balance of advantage to be against a bilateral agreement. The Prime Minister asked Sir John Simon for a précis of the contents of these memoranda.[6] This had the effect of postponing further Cabinet discussion of a bilateral understanding until the autumn, although the possibilities of an Anglo-Japanese agreement which might somehow be reconciled with good Anglo-American relations continued to interest Mr. Chamberlain and Sir John Simon.[7] In the meantime Sir Robert Vansittart, Permanent Under-Secretary of State in the Foreign Office, in a memorandum for the Cabinet of April 7, 1934,[8] justified the priority proposed to be given to Germany. In a further memorandum of April 19, circulated to the Cabinet by Mr. Chamberlain on April 23, Sir Warren Fisher, Permanent Secretary to the Treasury and a member of the Defence Requirements Sub-Committee, elaborated the argument that as 'we cannot successfully fight both Japan and Germany at the same time' the prime condition of avoiding war with Japan was 'disentanglement of ourselves from the United States of America'.[9]

The British Government's general aim was to maintain good relations with both Japan and the United States, while supporting the United States' opposition to parity for Japan and insisting on the 70-cruiser strength which the United States Government deplored. In the circumstances the first exchange of views about naval matters in the summer of 1934 was of an extremely tentative character, as will be seen from the summary of the talks given in the first document printed below.

[6] Cabinet Conclusions No. 10 (34).
[7] See especially Nos. 8, 14, 19, and 29 below. American reactions to these discussions are referred to in an essay by Professor D. C. Watt, 'Britain, the United States and Japan in 1934' (*Personalities and Policies*, London 1965, pp. 83–99), based in part on unpublished American material.
[8] See Volume VI, Appendix III.
[9] Sir W. Fisher's memorandum is printed as Appendix I in this Volume.

## No. 1

*Letter from Mr. Craigie[1] to Mr. Osborne[2] (Washington)*

[*A 5167/1938/45*]

*Private and Secret*                    FOREIGN OFFICE, *July 20, 1934*

Dear Osborne,

As our preliminary conversations with the United States representatives on the subject of the 1935 Naval Conference have now concluded with the

[1] Mr. R. L. Craigie, a Counsellor in the Foreign Office, was head of the American Department.
[2] Mr. F. D'A. G. Osborne, H.M. Minister at Washington, was acting as Chargé d'Affaires during the absence on leave of H.M. Ambassador, Sir R. Lindsay.

departure of Mr. Norman Davis[3] yesterday for the United States, you may care to know the history of these conversations and also how matters stand at the moment.

The conversations originated at a lunch given by the United States Ambassador[4] on the 2nd March, at which the Prime Minister[5] and Mr. Norman Davis agreed that a meeting should take place shortly between representatives of the two Governments, with the purpose not of making agreements but of exchanging views and ascertaining their respective positions.[6] A meeting accordingly took place on the 12th April between Mr. Davis and Mr. Bingham, representing the United States, and Vice-Admiral Little[7] and myself, representing the United Kingdom. Views were exchanged on technical and political aspects of the question, and it was provisionally suggested that preliminary conversations might take place between United States and United Kingdom representatives and Japanese and United Kingdom representatives in London at different times, the invitations to be issued simultaneously.[8]

On the 18th May Mr. Atherton[9] and the Japanese Ambassador[10] were accordingly asked to suggest to their Governments that bilateral exchanges of view should take place in London in order to make a preliminary survey of the ground in preparation for 1935. It was felt that bilateral conversations were preferable to a tripartite meeting, since the latter procedure was unlikely to be agreeable to the French and Italian Governments. The invitation to participate in preliminary discussions was accepted by the United States Government and conversations began on the 18th June. On that date and on the 20th June, political questions were discussed and, on the 21st, Vice-Admiral Little and myself explained frankly and in detail the technical requirements of His Majesty's Government which would have to be covered by any treaty arising out of the 1935 Naval Conference. On the 27th the United States representatives furnished us with their views of the arguments put forward by us, and it soon became apparent that little progress was to be expected. The United States representatives expressed surprise that the Admiralty envisaged an increase in the number of cruisers required by the United Kingdom, stating that they wished to preserve the Washington[11] and London Naval Treaties[12] with perhaps a reduction on the figures provided

[3] Chairman of the American delegation to the Disarmament Conference.

[4] Mr. R. W. Bingham.  [5] Mr. J. Ramsay MacDonald.

[6] Cf. Mr. Davis's account of a conversation with Mr. MacDonald before this luncheon printed in *Foreign Relations of the United States* (*F.R.U.S.*), *1934*, vol. i, pp. 225–30.

[7] Deputy Chief of the British Naval Staff.

[8] Reports on this meeting by Vice-Admiral Little and by Mr. Craigie were circulated as N.C.M. (35) 2, not printed. Cf. *F.R.U.S.*, *op. cit.*, p. 232.

[9] Counsellor in the United States Embassy in London.

[10] M. Tsuneo Matsudaira.

[11] For the text of the Treaty for the Limitation of Naval Armament signed at Washington on February 6, 1922, by representatives of the United States, British Empire, France, Italy, and Japan, see *B.F.S.P.*, vol. 117, pp. 453 ff. (also No. 1 in Cmd. 1627 of 1922).

[12] For the London Naval Treaty of April 22, 1930, see Introductory Note to this Chapter, note 1.

4

for by them. But they were unable to furnish either information or figures as to the requirements of the United States in respect of security, and it was therefore impossible at that juncture to seek to reconcile the views of the two Governments.[13]

It was agreed, however, that the differences of opinion which had emerged must not be allowed to become too publicly known, and it was therefore decided to announce that discussions would continue. It was also decided at the meeting on the 27th June that a further meeting should be held after each side had had time to consider the position, but no such meeting was eventually held. Mr. Davis had an interview with Mr. Baldwin on the 4th July and further informal talks took place between Mr. Davis and myself which did not, however, result in any new points being raised.[14]

Mr. Davis took his departure on the 19th instant as there was no suitable sailing for some little time after, and before his departure discussions were held with the American delegation as to whether a joint communiqué should be issued embodying such results as the conversations might have had, but it was found impossible to agree on the precise language which the communiqué should contain. Meanwhile, however, three factors had combined to improve the atmosphere, namely the issue of an Anglo-American-Japanese communiqué[15] stating that further discussions would be postponed until October pending the arrival of the Japanese representatives, the statement by Mr. Hull[16] to the press on the 16th July to the effect that the

[13] Mr. R. MacDonald, Mr. Stanley Baldwin (Lord President of the Council), and Sir J. Simon attended this meeting of June 27. In a private letter to Mr. Baldwin of the same day Sir J. Simon wrote: 'After our extremely ineffective interview with Norman Davis and Co. this afternoon, I feel that the problem of the Naval Conference can be stated in very simple terms, thus: (1) The duties and responsibilities of this country discharged through its navy are necessarily greater and more various than those which fall to be discharged for the United States by the American navy. (Our American friends practically admitted this much this afternoon, and it is manifestly true). (2) We must provide ourselves with a navy sufficient for the discharge of these duties and responsibilities, if we can afford it, treaty or no treaty. (3) Consequently, there are four choices before the United States and four only: (a) To treat our requirements as the contractual standard for themselves as well as for us, but to refrain, if they choose, from building up to this standard. (By "our requirements" I do not necessarily mean figures quite so high as our present proposals). (b) To swallow their pride and admit that in the region of naval responsibilities there is no "parity" between Yankee needs and English ones. (c) To agree to relate their strength to the United Kingdom only, leaving the Dominion quotas out of account. (d) To have no further treaty and leave everybody to build as they please.

'Our American friends may well be sincere in saying that they do not mind how big a navy we have; their real concern is that the British needs should not encourage Japan to build a navy so big as to threaten America. It may be, therefore, that the only hope would be a preliminary Anglo-Japanese negotiation which fixed the Japanese navy at a reasonable level and then to face the Americans with the prospect of losing this advantage if they do not find it possible to agree on the British level. But I doubt very much whether Japan is going to agree with us. All of which shows what a delightful job we have inherited in this naval conundrum.'

[14] For an American account of these discussions see *F.R.U.S.*, *op. cit.*, pp. 259–61, 266–8, 281–2, 287–9.                    [15] See *The Times*, July 17, p. 14.

[16] Mr. Cordell Hull was United States Secretary of State; for his statement to the press on July 16, see *ibid.*

suspension of the talks did not mean that there had been a breakdown, and the report cabled to Washington newspapers stating that Mr. Bingham and Mr. Davis had had a very friendly final talk with the Secretary of State on the 17th. As a result of this improved atmosphere the United States Government felt that the discussions had been adjourned on such a friendly and harmonious note that it would be a pity to take a step which might conceivably provoke a discord. It was therefore agreed that no communiqué should be issued.

In the meantime on the 9th, 10th and 11th July conversations took place with representatives of the French Government headed by M. Piétri, the Minister of Marine.[17] As a result of technical discussions on qualitative limits it was decided that certain questions relative to cruiser categories and to the reduction of the category tonnage of submarines would need further consideration but that otherwise the two countries were in complete agreement on this aspect of the question. The French representatives also gave a full exposition of French naval requirements in relation to Italy and Germany. On the political side both parties agreed that a preliminary five Power talk was necessary in order to see how far those Powers could progress towards agreement before a conference of all Powers was summoned. The French raised the question of German participation and its relation to a possible enlargement of the Conference.

The Italian Government have not yet informed us when they are proposing to send over representatives to take part in bilateral conversations though they have accepted our invitation. The Japanese, as I have mentioned, are expected at the end of September or the beginning of October and, by the end of our conversations with them, we shall presumably know whether and when it will be profitable to resume direct contact with the Americans.

Yours ever,<br>
PHILIP BROAD[18]<br>
(in Mr. Craigie's absence)

[17] Cf. Volume VI, No. 489, note 2, and No. 490.
[18] A member of the American Department of the Foreign Office.

## No. 2

*Letter from Mr. Craigie to Mr. Atherton*[1]

*[A 6144/1938/45]*

Secret                                    FOREIGN OFFICE, *July 26, 1934*

My dear Ray,

On looking through the records of our naval meetings it has occured to me

[1] This letter and the enclosed memorandum (printed also in *F.R.U.S. 1934*, vol. i, pp. 299–303) were circulated by direction of Sir J. Simon on August 2 to the Ministerial Naval Committee: it was numbered N.C.M.(35)16. This Committee had been formed in April 1934 'for the purpose of examining and reporting upon the policy that should be followed at the 1935 Naval Conference'. Its members were the Prime Minister, Lord President of the Council, Chancellor of the Exchequer, Secretary of State for Foreign Affairs,

that a short restatement of the British position and of the reasons for increases in one category might be useful to you. The Prime Minister, before he left,[2] stated the British case in broad outline but did not go into detail. At the experts' meeting Admiral Little gave a full and clear statement of our requirements but this was done particularly from the technical and naval point of view. The enclosed memorandum is an effort to present the two aspects of the case—political and technical—in one document, and to do this as briefly and concisely as possible.

It is our hope that this document, which I send to you privately and unofficially, may fill a gap in our [?your] records.[3]

[Yours sincerely,

R. L. CRAIGIE]

ENCLOSURE IN No. 2

*Secret*                                          FOREIGN OFFICE, *July 25, 1934*

*Note on Cruiser Tonnages by Mr. Craigie*

I. *Possible decrease in total tonnage under method proposed by Great Britain.* Put very shortly the American *desiderata* are stated to be (*a*) a reduction of 20 per cent on the tonnage levels of existing naval treaties or (*b*) failing that, the maintenance of existing treaty levels. Similarly, the statement of British requirements put forward in the recent conversations, by reason of the limitations on the unit size of vessels and the abolition of the submarine which it suggests, would, if adopted in its entirety, permit of a decrease of 10 per cent on the tonnages provided for under existing treaties. Had the British Representatives, paying no regard to the requirements of the United States, put forward a statement of the full qualitative reductions which Great Britain is prepared to advocate, they would have been able to propose an ultimate decrease of 22 per cent on existing treaty tonnages. Any suggestion therefore that the United States stands in general for naval reductions while Great Britain stands in general for naval increases would be incorrect and misleading, particularly when it is remembered that all naval Powers other than the United States are prepared to agree to considerable reductions in the unit size of most categories of ships. Both countries are in fact prepared for reductions, but unfortunately only by methods which, for vital strategical reasons, would be unacceptable to the other. It is felt therefore that the only hope of reaching a solution satisfactory to both Powers is to approach this question from a strictly practical point of view, each country recognising the special difficulties and the strategical problems with which the other is faced

Secretary of State for Dominion Affairs, and the First Lord of the Admiralty: the following officials attended as experts—Permanent Under-Secretary of State for Foreign Affairs, First Sea Lord, Chief of Naval Staff, and Mr. R. L. Craigie (Counsellor, Foreign Office).

[2] Mr. Ramsay MacDonald left London on July 1, on medical advice, for a 3 months' holiday which included a visit to Canada and Newfoundland. He returned on October 4.

[3] In a minute in this file Mr. Craigie remarked that he had attempted in the memorandum to bring out the fact that despite the proposed increase in cruiser tonnage 'our proposals as a whole provide for a nett decrease of 10 per cent'.

and attempting to reach an understanding based upon the political situation as it exists to-day. In such circumstances there seems no reason why the resulting treaty should show more than a slight increase in the undersize [under-age][4] tonnage for all categories, which would be a small price to pay for the resultant political appeasement and the prevention of unrestricted naval competition. Naval limitation cannot be said to serve its full purpose if it leaves behind it a genuine sense of insecurity on the part of one or other of the signatories of the treaty.

II. *Relative sizes of British and other cruisers.* It has been suggested that, because in the London Naval Treaty Great Britain agreed to the United States having 18 8″ gun cruisers to 15 British 8″ gun cruisers (the difference being made good by a larger 6″ gun cruiser allowance to Great Britain), Great Britain is prepared to agree in principle to construct cruisers for trade protection purposes of a smaller displacement than those which are being constructed by other Powers. This is quite incorrect. The arrangement referred to affected the British and United States cruiser strengths only and, as has frequently been stated, a settlement of this cruiser difficulty would be simple enough were it one between the two countries only and were it not that the minimum size of cruiser acceptable to the United States regulates automatically the average size of cruiser to be constructed by other Powers. There has never been any question of Great Britain agreeing to construct cruisers which, when placed upon the trade routes in isolated positions would, ship for ship, be outclassed by the cruisers of a potential adversary. Nor is it believed that the United States would wish to urge upon Great Britain the adoption of such a course.

III. *Why cruiser tonnage figures must automatically increase independently of increase in number of British cruisers.* If Great Britain was able in the London Naval Treaty to agree to the exceptionally low total cruiser tonnage figure of 339,000 tons this was because—

(*a*) the figure was calculated on a basis of 50 cruisers;

(*b*) it was hoped and believed that no other Power would build large 6″ gun cruisers of 9,000 or 10,000 tons displacement, and that, in consequence, no such cruisers would be required by Great Britain, which has indeed since 1930 led the way with smaller ships of Leander class.

(*c*) The international outlook permitted a steady replacement programme of about 3 ships a year, so that during the period of the treaty the small type of cruisers averaging 4,000 to 5,000 tons and designed for North Sea warfare would still be retained in considerable numbers.

(*b*) and (*c*) no longer apply, so that even if the future cruiser figure for Great Britain were to be based on the number of 50 cruisers, it would have to be considerably larger than 339,000 tons. Great Britain cannot be expected to replace her existing small wartime cruisers by ships which will be out-classed from the start by those in other navies, nor is it believed that such a course is seriously suggested by the United States. From this it follows that

4 Wording in printed text of N.C.M.(35)16 and in *F.R.U.S.*, *op. cit.*, see note 1.

8

there must be an automatic increase, without any increase in the number of 50 cruisers, from a tonnage of 339,000 tons to 408,600 tons, which is arrived at as follows:

| | |
|---|---:|
| 15 – 8″ Gun Cruisers   .       . | 146,800 |
| 10 'M' Class 6″ Gun Cruisers | 95,000 |
| 8 LEANDERS (7030 to 7250) | 57,000 |
| 12 new 7,000 tons        .       . | 84,000 |
| 4 ARETHUSAS (5200 tons) | 20,800 |
| 1 new 5,000 tons        .       . | 5,000 |
| 50 | 408,600 |

It will be seen that this figure of 408,600 tons for 50 cruisers is based on the general acceptance of a future limitation of 7,000 tons beyond a specified number of large 6″ gun cruisers. If this limitation of 7,000 tons could not be accepted by other Powers, and the limit remained as at present at 10,000 tons, then the automatic increase of the London Naval Treaty figure would bring the British figure up to 438,600 (in a period of 10 years). In estimating the total tonnage increase consequent on the increased number of cruisers that we require, the figure of 408,600 tons—not the London Naval Treaty figure 339,000 tons—should in all fairness be taken as the point of departure.

IV. *Why an increase in the number of British cruisers is necessary.* In the London Naval Treaty Great Britain accepted a cruiser tonnage figure based on the tonnage of 50 cruisers for the following reasons:

(*a*) The Treaty was for six years only, and under the international conditions existing at that time there was a reasonable assurance that there would be more than six years of peace.

(*b*) It was accepted, subject to the Powers other than the three signatories to Part III of the London Naval Treaty[5] agreeing to corresponding reductions. This has not occurred; on the contrary the Naval Forces in Europe have greatly increased. If the 'escalator' clause[6] has not been invoked, this has not been because the building of other naval Powers did not justify such a step but because it was thought better to await the meeting of the 1935 Conference to explain the grounds on which the cruiser tonnages accepted by Great Britain in 1930 could no longer hold good.

(*c*) In 1930 we were on the eve of the summoning of a General Disarmament Conference from which much was hoped.

(*d*) Owing to the small size and worn out condition of the 14 cruisers that have been, or are being, scrapped since the London Naval Treaty was signed, it would not have been possible to keep those ships as efficient cruisers. Therefore, the number 50 could not in any case have been increased by December 1936 without departing from a steady building programme and providing more new ships.

5 i.e. the United States, British Empire, and Japan.
6 i.e. Article 21 of the London Naval Treaty of 1930.

9

(e) In the process of the steady reconstruction of the Fleet after the war, a halt had been called in cruiser building for some years in the hope of inducing a corresponding halt in the building of foreign cruisers. Thus the curve indicating the number of British under-age cruisers was at its lowest during the period of the Treaty.

It is unfortunately the case that, since the London Naval Treaty was concluded in 1930, a serious deterioration in the international and political outlook has occurred. Furthermore there are not present to-day any of the other conditions that rendered possible the acceptance in 1930 of a cruiser tonnage figure based on 50 ships. That this figure was an exceptional one was made clear during the 1930 Conference and by the Prime Minister and First Lord of the Admiralty in the House of Commons immediately afterwards.[7] Moreover, an allusion to this fact was contained in Article 23 of the London Naval Treaty which states, with reference to the Naval Conference to be held in 1935 that 'none of the provisions of the present Treaty should [shall] prejudice the attitude of any of the High Contracting Parties at the Conference agreed to'.

[7] For these statements by Mr. Ramsay MacDonald and Mr. A. V. Alexander on May 5, 1930, see 238 *H.C. Deb.* 5 *s.*, cols. 2091 and 2195–6 respectively.

## No. 3

*Mr. Osborne (Washington) to Sir J. Simon (Received August 3, 9.30 a.m.)*
*No. 251 Telegraphic [A 6233/1938/45]*

WASHINGTON, *August 2, 1934, 8.5 p.m.*

At press conference yesterday Secretary of the Navy[1] stated that while Washington Treaty ratios should be maintained he advocated a general reduction of 20 per cent in Naval armaments.[2]

Naval Attaché[3] has been informed that Secretary of Navy's views as expressed were entirely personal and by way of a rejoinder to the recent statement of new Japanese Prime Minister.[4]

[1] Mr. C. A. Swanson, born 1862, was United States delegate to the Disarmament Conference in 1932 and had been Secretary of the United States Navy since March 4, 1933.

[2] On May 24, 1934, President Roosevelt had laid down that 'the original platform on which' the United States might stand was 'a willingness to reduce by 25 per cent our total treaty allowance by tonnage and by number'; see *F.R.U.S. 1934*, vol. i, p. 237.

[3] Captain A. R. Dewar.

[4] Admiral Okada, Japanese Prime Minister since July 8, 1934, had been reported in *The Times* of August 1 as having told a press conference on July 31 that Japan 'did not expect to achieve parity with Great Britain and America at the Naval Conference next year, but could not approve of the principle of a ratio, which was incompatible with national self-respect'.

With reference to the alleged personal nature of Mr. Swanson's views, Mr. Gore-Booth, a member of the American Department, wrote in a minute of August 3: 'All the same we know that this *does* in fact represent U.S. policy at present and that it is not calculated to make negotiations any easier.' It was also noted that Mr. Swanson had been reported in the

London press as saying that the United States was planning two 35,000 ton battleships, one to be fitted with 16″ guns and the other with 14″, for when the time came, probably early in 1937, to replace battleships (see *News Chronicle*, July 12; *Daily Telegraph*, August 1).

## No. 4

### *Minute by Mr. Craigie*
### [*A 6484/1938/45*]

FOREIGN OFFICE, *August 7, 1934*

The upshot of the conversations with Captain Biscia on the Italian capital ship question[1] is that Italy remains determined to proceed with the construction of her two 35,000 ton ships[2] but that, *if between now and the autumn* we and the Americans could agree on a maximum gun calibre of 14″ for the capital ship of the future, there is just a chance that Italy might then consent to equip these ships with 14″ guns instead of 15″ guns.

Such a change in gun calibre on the Italian ships is all important, for France would then be freed from the necessity of answering these two ships with ships armed with 15″ or 16″ guns and might even be prepared (in view of her possession of the Dunkerques) to build her next capital ships with a displacement of 30,000 tons instead of 35,000 tons. Thus the risk of all future reduction being barred by Italy's action would have been averted.

But what chance is there of an understanding on this point being reached between the Americans and ourselves by the autumn? As things stand at present, I should say none. Mr. Swanson seems determined to bluster and to use the capital ship displacement question as a lever to force a reduction of our demands for new cruiser construction. The recent Anglo-American conversations proved unsatisfactory for four principal reasons:—

1. Mr. Roosevelt, having only the haziest knowledge of the question, has hitherto looked upon it largely in terms of domestic politics and has consequently laid it down that he will be content with nothing less than an all-round percentage reduction.[3]

2. His principal adviser on naval matters, Mr. Swanson, is a type of diehard big-navyist who believes in bluster and the big stick, and who has had the misfortune to sit for a generation in the United States Senate.

3. Mr. Norman Davis is a politician who draws his main support from peace societies and good-will organisations in the United States, and, as he

[1] Conversations between British and Italian representatives had been held at the Foreign Office on July 30, 1934, at 11 a.m. and 3 p.m. (cf. No. 7 below). The British representatives were Mr. Craigie, Rear-Admiral R. M. Bellairs (British naval representative on the Permanent Advisory Committee of the League of Nations), Captain V. H. Danckwerts (Plans Division, Admiralty), and Commander A. W. Clarke (Assistant Secretary, Committee of Imperial Defence; acting as Secretary). The Italian representatives were Captain G. Raineri Biscia and Acting Commander Count Ferrante Capponi (Naval Attaché at London).

[2] i.e. of two ships up to the limit of standard displacement for capital ships permitted under article V of the Treaty for the Limitation of Naval Armament signed at Washington on February 6, 1922; cf. No. 1, note 11.　　　　[3] Cf. No. 3, note 2.

said to me in a moment of candour, he could not afford to sign an agreement which provided for increases over existing Treaty figures; thus our case for cruiser increases will certainly not have gained in its presentation by Mr. Norman Davis and his influence will have tended to emphasise rather than to moderate Mr. Roosevelt's natural inclination to look at this question through domestic spectacles.

4. Mr. Hull is what the Americans call a 'poor fish', and there is no reason to believe he is friendly to this country.

Mr. Roosevelt personally would like good relations with this country, but he is surrounded by men who try to narrow what would normally be a broad vision in foreign affairs. In his hands is the key to this naval problem and, unless he can be won over first, the conversations in the autumn are likely to fare no better than the last. In fact, with the Japanese and Americans both in London, the 'talks' bid fair to develop into a tripartite wrangle which will finally seal the doom of the naval treaties. It is held in some quarters here that if the United States continues to be uncompromising we might reach some kind of naval understanding with the Japanese. This hope is in my humble opinion quite illusory and, in any case, such a course would be politically dangerous. If matters cannot be improved between the United States and ourselves Japan will have an unrivalled opportunity to fish in troubled waters—a pastime in which she has always shown herself most proficient.

Is there any way by which, before next autumn, Mr. Roosevelt can be brought to a better and more sympathetic view of our case? Sir Ronald Lindsay will be returning to Washington at the end of this month and will, I hope, be able to see the President and discuss these matters with him. But he would obviously be able to carry more conviction if he had with him either myself or a representative of the Admiralty who has participated in the recent naval talks. To me personally, it would be inconvenient to break into my leave and to go to the United States at this time, but I am so apprehensive at the way things are going and at the risks inherent in the meetings next October that I feel no stone should be left unturned to bring the United States Government to a more reasonable frame of mind. As I have shown above, time is an important element and we do not want to find later that we have missed the 'bus. If anyone goes from here it should be laid down that he would go not to *negotiate* (this must be left for the American representatives in October) but merely to present our case before the American representatives sail again. Also it would be well to inform M. Matsudaira frankly of the purpose and scope of any such mission. But it is useless to submit detailed suggestions on these points until it is decided in principle whether, between now and October, an effort should be made to effect a direct presentation of our case to President Roosevelt.[4]

R. L. CRAIGIE

[4] Admiral Sir Ernle Chatfield, the First Sea Lord, declared himself 'strongly opposed to any attempt to gain the ear of the President in the manner suggested by Mr. Craigie' and in particular he 'deprecated any action which might involve the sending of experts to

Washington for the purpose'. Sir R. Vansittart wrote in the course of a minute of August 8: 'I agree that it would be worth while to make an effort to secure Mr. Roosevelt. I am not sure whether it would be good tactics to send Mr. Craigie especially for that purpose. His purpose wd. be obvious. I anticipate that everyone interested wd. be mobilised to interfere with his stalking, before he even got down to it.' No further action was taken on Mr. Craigie's proposal.

## No. 5

*Sir J. Simon to Sir R. Clive[1] (Tokyo) and Mr. Osborne (Washington)*
*No. 128[2] Telegraphic [A 6404/1938/45]*

*Very confidential*                    FOREIGN OFFICE, *August 8, 1934, 5.30 p.m.*

Following from Mr. Craigie.

On the 19th July Mr. Hugh Wilson[3] called on the Lord Privy Seal[4] with a message from Mr. Norman Davis. He said that the Chief Japanese Military Adviser at Geneva, in taking leave of his American colleague there, had stated that Japan henceforth would not be represented on any technical committee in connection with the Disarmament Conference. Mr. Norman Davis had been anxious that we should be informed of this development as soon as possible, since, were the information confirmed, it might constitute an important indication of Japan's future attitude both to the Disarmament Conference itself and to the Naval Conference of 1935.

2. Mr. Wilson added that both he and Mr. Davis felt strongly that if the Naval Conference were to fail, as in view of the attitude of Japan now seemed only too probable, it was very desirable that it should be clear that Japan was in fact the guilty party and that Anglo-American relations should remain unimpaired. In order to ensure this he argued that it was very desirable that the position taken up by this country and the United States should if possible be similar. If we could both demand the maintenance of the position established by the Washington and London Treaties, or even a further reduction below that level, and Japan were to refuse, then it would be quite clear where the onus lay. That was the only reason why he and Mr. Davis were nervous of our demands for increased cruiser tonnage.[5]

---

[1] H.M. Ambassador at Tokyo.                    [2] No. 128 to Tokyo, No. 212 to Washington.
[3] U.S. Minister to Switzerland and delegate to the General Disarmament Conference.
[4] Mr. A. Eden.
[5] Mr. Eden's record of this conversation, written on July 19, here included the following additional paragraph. 'Mr. Wilson went on to say that he fully appreciated the strength of the Admiralty case, which was no doubt based upon our exceptional needs due to our long lines of communication, but he doubted whether it was possible for any Power to make itself impregnable upon the seas in these days. In the light of the anxious situation in the Far East there seemed indeed to be only two courses open: H.M. Government might seek to renew the Anglo-Japanese alliance—as to the practicability or advisability of this they were of course sole judges, or alternatively there might be an Anglo-American alliance, but he feared that the United States opinion would not be eager over this latter course. In the circumstances, therefore, the only course remaining was to seek by our joint efforts to maintain so far as possible a full measure of Anglo-American agreement. This Mr. Wilson emphasised was the only reason for being anxious about the increase in cruiser

tonnage, since of course the United States had no anxieties as to the size of the British Navy.' In a minute of July 20 on this conversation Sir R. Vansittart remarked: 'Unfortunately the American idea of tactics, which is one always inspired by their own internal politics, is not one which could conceivably be adopted by our Admiralty . . . As to Mr. Wilson's panacea, no sane person dreams of renewing the Anglo-Japanese alliance. As to America there is no question of closer relations. These *may* become possible when America realises that she must have a policy. Hitherto she has thought it possible to dispense with the inconvenience . . .'

## No. 6

*Sir J. Simon to Mr. Murray[1] (Rome)*
*No. 260 Telegraphic [A 6501/1938/45]*

FOREIGN OFFICE, *August 14, 1934*

Your despatch No. 665.[2]

It is not proposed that any written reply should be made to the Italian note verbale of the 25th July.[2] You should, however, inform the Italian Government orally in the following sense:

Begins. His Majesty's Government hope that, if the Italian decision as regards the size of the ships is irrevocable, the Italian Government will at all events consider the possibility of reducing the gun calibre from 15″ to 14″, as this would still leave the door open to an ultimate international agreement on a 14″ gun. In spite of the recent public utterances of Mr. Swanson,[3] His Majesty's Government are not without hope, as a result of conversations with representatives of the United States Government, that the United States will eventually agree to a 14″ gun limitation. Ends.

[1] Counsellor in H.M. Embassy at Rome.
[2] This despatch transmitted a note verbale of July 25, not printed, from the Italian Ministry of Foreign Affairs recapitulating the events which led to the Government's decision to construct two new capital ships of 35,000 tons each without awaiting the outcome of preliminary Anglo-Italian naval conversations in London as suggested by His Majesty's Government. Cf. No. 4.　　　　　　　　　　　　　　　　[3] Cf. No. 3, note 4.

## No. 7

*Letter from Mr. Kelly[1] to Mr. Murray (Rome)*
*[A 6483/1938/45]*

*Private and Secret*　　　　　　　　　FOREIGN OFFICE, *August 16, 1934*

My dear Murray,

As Craigie has now gone on leave, I am writing to give you, for your private inf[ormatio]n, a very brief account of our conversations with Captain R. Biscia, which took place on the 30th July.[2]

Captain Biscia explained that he was in London only with the object of exchanging information and that he had no authority to negotiate. He gave

[1] Mr. D. V. Kelly was a First Secretary in the Foreign Office.　　　[2] Cf. No. 4, note 1.

an exposition of the views of the Italian Government on the various questions as to the sizes of ships and as to quantitative limits, but said that he had firm instructions not to discuss the question of the 35,000 ton capital ships, though he was prepared to explain privately the reason which had led Italy to lay down those ships at the present time.

The conversations were satisfactory except on two important points, the insistence of the Italians on building the two new 35,000 ton ships, and the fact that they have no suggestions to make for the solution of the Franco-Italian parity problem. Indeed, Craigie has noticed that since the failure of the recent Franco-Italian discussions[3] the Italians have been in a more unconciliatory mood than he has ever known them.

It may interest you to know that the conversations with the French, which took place from the 9th to the 12th July,[4] were also reasonably satisfactory, and a considerable measure of agreement was found to exist on technical problems, though the French Government were naturally inclined to reserve their attitude in view of the announced intention of the Italians to build the two new ships. In the matter of procedure the French representatives expressed their agreement that a preliminary Five Power Conference should be held with a view to ascertaining how far those Powers could progress towards agreement before a conference of all Powers was summoned.

There is now a complete lull in the discussions, but further conversations with the Italians are anticipated in late September or early October and, as you will have seen, Japanese representatives are expected to arrive about the middle of October.

Yrs ever[5]

[3] In the official record of the Anglo-Italian meeting on July 30, circulated as N.C. (I) 1st Meeting, it was recorded that Captain Biscia 'held forth at some length on the subject of the discussions that had been taking place within the last three months between Italy and France. The Italians were most indignant at the treatment that had been handed to them by France in this matter, and he said that Italy was now no longer prepared to accept proposals for equality in construction programmes with France, in view of the opposition to every Italian suggestion in the past . . . negotiations had consequently been broken off and the construction of two 35,000 ton battleships by Italy put in hand.'
[4] Cf. No. 1, penultimate paragraph.
[5] Signature missing on the filed copy.

## No. 8

*Note by Sir J. Simon to Sir R. Vansittart*[1]

*[A 7695/1938/45]*

MARINE HOTEL, NORTH BERWICK, *August 20, 1934*

1. I do not believe that Japan will accept an inferior ratio imposed by Treaty. Japan feels the impulses of 'equality of status' as much as Germany.

[1] This note was sent in reply to a note of August 17 from Sir R. Vansittart forwarding Tokyo despatch No. 369 of July 5 (received August 7). In this despatch Sir R. Clive expressed (in para. 3) the views that the new Japanese Government under Admiral Okada

But if conceded 'equality of status' as her right, might she not make a *voluntary declaration* of limits accepted by her? Such a voluntary declaration might be annexed to any Treaty, if indeed a Treaty is possible. What do you and Mr. Craigie think of this?

2. As regards 'non aggression' pact, *why not*? We should contract for the whole Empire (or perhaps the Dominions shd sign separately). What would Japan want in return? Something equivalent to recognition of Manchukuo? A freer hand in China would be more difficult. I should like to see the idea of an Anglo-Japanese non-aggression pact worked out on paper. It may be a valuable buffer against Japanese naval liberty. It would please many people, here and in Japan, to have this much of the atmosphere of the Anglo-Japanese treaty revived. And in view of Sir R. Clive's cold douche (para. 8) it is important to get our positive ideas developed quickly.[2]

J. S.

would be unyielding on the 'unrestricted' navy view and that 'to accept a quota for Japan ... might be as much as his [Admiral Okada's] life is worth'. In para. 7 he referred to the Minister for Foreign Affairs' statement that 'to show her good faith Japan would be only too ready to conclude non-aggression pacts with America and Great Britain'. (This statement by Mr. Hirota had been reported to the Foreign Office in Tokyo telegram No. 172 of July 3, not here printed.) Sir R. Clive added: 'I understand that the American and Japanese ideas about a non-aggression pact differ materially in that the American Government would only consider one which comprised non-aggression generally in the Far East.' He continued in para. 8 as follows: 'When Mr. Hirota, in the course of our conversation on the 3rd July, said that Japan would be ready to conclude a non-aggression pact with Great Britain, I was somewhat taken by surprise, as, so far as I know, this is the first time that such a suggestion has ever been put forward. I thought it better therefore to give the impression that I personally considered such a pact entirely unnecessary between our two countries, in view of the traditional friendship between us. But, of course, I have no idea how the proposal will be viewed by His Majesty's Government, and my remarks were merely intended to avoid giving encouragement to a new idea which might not be viewed favourably in London.' Sir R. Clive further reported Mr. Hirota's statements that 'he was convinced that the old spirit of the Anglo-Japanese Alliance remained' and 'that the Emperor was most emphatic in his desire for the friendliest relations with Great Britain'.

[2] In a note of August 22 to the American and Eastern Departments, Sir R. Vansittart asked for comments on these two enquiries from the Secretary of State. The replies by Mr. Craigie and Mr. Orde (head of the Far Eastern Department) are printed as Appendixes to this document.

Sir J. Simon's note also led to minutes by Sir G. Mounsey (an Assistant Under-Secretary of State) on August 28 and by Mr. Eden on September 2. In the course of a minute of August 29 addressed to Sir J. Simon, Sir R. Vansittart stated: '(1) that Mr. Craigie inclines to your suggestion, (2) that I do not think that his minute meets my objections, (3) that Mr. Orde and Sir G. Mounsey agree with my objections, and Mr. Orde reinforces them. I consider that the sum total of these objections as regards any pact of non-aggression easily outweighs any possible advantage to be gained by *a reaffirmation at an inopportune moment of what already exists* for all our intents and purposes.' He concluded that 'a bilateral pact is out of the question; that a tripartite one is not only superfluous ... but dangerous also', and added that he was sorry 'to have reached this conclusion so unavoidably, for, as I mentioned in my minute of August 20, the Chancellor [Mr. N. Chamberlain] has also supported the idea very strongly'. This minute of August 20 has not been traced in Foreign Office archives: for Mr. Chamberlain's views see No. 14 below.

## Note by Mr. Craigie[3]

FOREIGN OFFICE, *August 23, 1934*

(*I*) *Voluntary declaration by Japan.* I have felt for some time that the only possible basis for a naval agreement with Japan in 1935 (at all events as far as cruisers, destroyers and submarines are concerned) is an 'equality of status' declaration followed by a declaration setting forth the quantity of tonnage which each signatory Power will in point of fact require to build in each category over a period of x years. The second declaration could be voluntary in form, but should in practice constitute a treaty obligation (subject to an escalator clause). If even this form of treaty obligation were to prove repugnant to the Japanese Government, it would surely be better to have from Japan a simple voluntary declaration, such as the Secretary of State suggests, than nothing at all. Our task, which should not pass the wit of man, is to help the more moderate elements in Japan to 'save face' in this matter and so overcome the extremist elements who want no naval treaty at all.

The kind of general declaration I have in mind is the following:

'The principle of equality of national status between all the Powers signatories of the present treaty is mutually and unreservedly recognised. The voluntary acceptance by a particular Contracting Party of a specific programme of naval construction over a specific period of years is to be regarded simply as the expression of that country's naval needs of the moment and not as any derogation of the foregoing principle of equality of national status between the parties.'

The form of the declaration relative to construction programmes might be somewhat as follows:

'The Contracting Parties do not anticipate that during the next . . . years their requirements in cruisers, destroyers and submarines will impose on them an average annual construction greater than that shown in the table which follows and, subject to Article . . . below (escalator clause), they accordingly undertake that their naval construction during the period of the treaty shall not exceed the average annual figures shown in the table.'

Some such presentation of future naval relationships is likely to prove more palatable to Japan than the presentation adopted in existing treaties (i.e. definite tonnage levels which may not be exceeded). In practice we should be no worse off than under the present system, for all we should have abandoned would be the pretence that a naval treaty concluded for a limited period of years can impose a permanent inferiority of naval strength on any particular country. The Admiralty would naturally prefer a less cumbersome presentation but would not, I think, object to that which I have suggested above, provided that it enabled the Japanese Government to accept annual construction figures which would not in fact increase their ratio vis-à-vis this country.[4]

---

[3] See note 2 above.

[4] Marginal notes by Sir R. Vansittart and Mr. Craigie at this point read: 'Yes but . . . tout est là! R.V.' 'Yes, but please see the passage marked X in my final paragraph. R.L.C. 27/9.' (The passage referred to was the first sentence of the final paragraph of section (1) of this Appendix.) In a minute of August 25, referring to Mr. Craigie's note and his own

The U.S.A. may be more intractable as they may regard such a phraseology as a first concession to Japan's claim to parity. (It is of course nothing of the kind.) But they would have to agree eventually if we did.

I doubt the utility of taking this matter up at present with the Admiralty, since everyone there connected with the naval negotiations is at present away on leave. I suggest that the matter might be left in abeyance for the moment and discussed, in the first instance orally, with the Admiralty when I return from leave. It would however be well to have Sir W. Malkin's[5] views as to the best form of words to convey the idea suggested in the minutes.

I believe that on this basis and in this form an agreement between the United Kingdom and Japan would be possible without any effective change being made in our existing ratio. The difficulty is that no amount of camouflage is likely to deter Japan from her apparent determination to alter in her favour the actual balance of naval strength as between the U.S.A. and herself. But if the United States continues to show so little comprehension of our naval needs and leaves matters where they were left by the recent Anglo-American naval conversations[6] we may have to consider the relative advantages and disadvantages of a naval agreement with Japan and France (and perhaps Italy on a similar equality of status formula), leaving the United States to build what she wants and leaving Japan to safeguard herself vis-à-vis the United States by means of an escalator clause. From a naval point of view this would suit us admirably, but the risk to our future relations with the United States is obvious.

(*II*) *Non-aggression Pact.* If M. Hirota would like non-aggression pacts with the United States and ourselves, it is obviously because he thinks this would help him overcome the intransigeance [*sic*] of his naval authorities. If from this point of view only, the matter merits sympathetic consideration here.

So much depends on what is meant by a non-aggression pact. The form I have in mind is a bi-lateral pact which would in practice involve no further engagement than that already assumed under the Kellogg Pact[7] and, by leaving the right of self-defence open, would enable us to defend our interests in the Far East to the extent to which the Kellogg Pact still permits us to defend them. This would, in practice, be mere camouflage—but heavy applications of political camouflage may be necessary if we are to prevent naval limitation from going by the board next year.

Would it not be useful, as a first step, to ascertain from the United States Government (when Sir R. Lindsay returns) whether a non-aggression pact with Japan has in fact been definitely and finally refused by the United States Government, and, if so, in what form and on what grounds. It should not be impossible to devise a form of pact which would not hamper our liberty of action in the event of an aggression by Japan against China.

R. L. CRAIGIE

marginal comment, Sir R. Vansittart wrote: 'Why, of course if they will do *that*, there is only one side to the question. Naturally we shd without any question concur in this face-saving camouflage. But I don't think the Japanese are so simple, or that there is any chance whatever of the Japanese failing to estimate their needs at a figure which will entirely alter the status quo. It will be as much as the negotiators' lives will be worth not to do so.'

[5] Legal Adviser to the Foreign Office.

[6] Cf. No. 1.

[7] This International Treaty for the renunciation of war as an instrument of national policy had been signed at Paris on August 27, 1928; see *B.F.S.P.*, vol. 128, pp. 447-9.

*Note by Mr. Orde*[8]

FOREIGN OFFICE, *August 28, 1934*

*I. Voluntary declaration by Japan.* From the Far Eastern Department point of view, I would only say that I feel the greatest doubt as to the Japanese being willing to make any declaration which would be moderate as to figures and of a tolerably binding character. M. Hirota's protestations about not wanting a big navy may be quite sincere, but I have great doubts, nevertheless, as to the civilian element in the Government being able to persuade the higher naval authorities to accept the building programme which such a declaration would represent as the maximum possible, except perhaps for a very short period. Even if they were able to do so, they would still be exposed, together with the naval authorities, to the attacks of fanatics, both on sentimental patriotic grounds and on subjectively valid realist grounds, with backing and inspiration from less responsible naval circles.

*II. Non-aggression Pact.* The objections to a bi-lateral pact with Japan seem to me formidable. Some of them were stated in the memorandum circulated to the Cabinet last March (C.P. 80 (34)).[9] Personally, I feel them even more strongly now. The shock which it would give to the U.S.A. would be all the greater since the United States have rejected with ridicule the idea of a Japanese-American non-aggression pact;[10] we should, in the light of that rejection, seem to be ostentatiously divorcing ourselves from America and following in the Japanese wake. There is no sign of Japan thinking better of her ambitions in China; the April demand of 'hands off China' for other Powers[11] is proof to the contrary, and there has been nothing but the feeblest watering down of that demand in answer to protests. The resentment in China would, I greatly fear, be intense, all the more so in view of the tendency at present in evidence in the United States to liquidate the American position in the Far East, which must enhance our importance in Chinese eyes as a potential brake on Japanese ambitions. The resentment might well take the irrational form of a boycott. It would seem essential, even if active Chinese resentment were to be left out of account, to cover the Chinese problem in some way if a pact were concluded, and I fail to see how it could be done; and, if it *were* done, the pact would be felt by the Japanese to have a negative and not a positive value. We should have scored a victory over them, not given them something of value.

Russia would, no doubt, take a pact amiss, and if, as might conceivably happen, the result of a pact were to encourage Japan to fight Russia, we should see the Russian counterpoise to Germany seriously weakened.

Other not inconsiderable objections already stated are the inconsistency of concluding an apparently superfluous pact after our previously expressed dislike of such things; the possibility of being drawn into a pact involving Russia, Turkey, Persia and Afghanistan; and the horror of the League of Nations Union at the

---

[8] See note 2 above.

[9] See Introductory Note to this Chapter.

[10] Cf. enclosure in No. 14 below, paragraph 5.

[11] The reference is to a statement issued to the Japanese press on April 17, 1934, by Mr. Amau, Chief of the Bureau of Information and Intelligence of the Japanese Foreign Office. Cf. *The Times*, April 19, p. 14, and *F.R.U.S., Japan 1931–1941*, vol. i, pp. 223–5.

implicit condonation of Japanese aggression in Manchuria and encouragement of further aggression.

To all these objections must be added the situation in regard to the Netherland East Indies. I am not particularly an alarmist in regard to this, or in regard to a Russo-Japanese war at an early date, but possible Japanese ambitions in that direction cannot be dismissed as chimerical. A non-aggression pact could hardly be concluded for a short period; it would probably have to be unlimited in duration, for a refusal to renew one on expiry would probably be a serious matter, all the more serious in the very circumstances which might make it necessary. A pact could hardly fail to handicap us seriously in dealing with a Japanese movement against the Netherland East Indies, which would be bound to arouse the liveliest fears in Singapore and India, while Hongkong would clearly be left isolated if the movement were to succeed. Australian and New Zealand feeling, in the event of such a movement developing, need not be described. I am not sure that even now we should find it easy to carry them, any more than Canada, with us in concluding a pact, and imperial solidarity seems essential in such a matter, both formally and materially.

To me personally, the more I reflect on the proposal, the more varied and more considerable the objectionable implications of it seem to be. I cannot help feeling that we are in the position of conducting a long range defensive against Japan and that a non-aggression pact might give her added confidence in her expansionist tendencies and hamper us in resisting them. The more valuable a pact were to appear to Japan, the more serious the dangers indicated above would be proved to be. If the dangers are negligible, it is difficult to see that a pact would be valued by Japan more highly than as a gesture indicating superfluously a certain degree of good will.

American sentiment might possibly be less adverse to a tri-partite than it is to a bi-lateral pact. If this were found to be the case, it would be possible to avoid the bad effect on American opinion which an Anglo-Japanese pact would have, but it would be a delicate matter to handle things so as to distribute Chinese resentment between ourselves and the United States. To escape such resentment altogether seems scarcely possible. The other main objections on the Russian and Dutch East Indies sides would seem to apply with equal, if not with added force, to a tri-partite pact, for a tri-partite pact would encourage Japanese ambitions even more than a bi-lateral would do.

I suggest as an alternative that we might give Japan, at a suitable moment, an assurance that we do not contemplate denouncing the Four Power Pact of Washington of 1921,[12] by which the Contracting Parties (the U.S.A., British Empire, France and Japan) agreed to respect each other's 'rights in relation to their insular possessions and insular dominions in the region of the Pacific Ocean', and to get the United States and France to give Japan a similar assurance. This would presumably involve the maintenance, which is obviously desirable, of the contemporary declaration made by each of the four Parties to the Netherlands and Portugal[13] of their intention to respect the similar rights of those countries in the same region.

C. W. ORDE

[12] For the text of this treaty, signed at Washington on December 13, 1921, see *B.F.S.P.*, vol. 116, pp. 627–30; printed also as No. 7 in Cmd. 1627 of 1922.

[13] For the text of this declaration made to the Netherlands Government on February 4 and to the Portuguese Government on February 6, 1922, see *B.F.S.P.*, *op. cit.*, pp. 623–3 (No. 10 in Cmd. 1627).

## No. 9

*Sir R. Clive (Tokyo) to Sir J. Simon (Received October 1)*
*No. 461 [F 5873/591/23]*\*

CHUZENJI, *August 29, 1934*

Sir,

Some weeks ago a rumour started among the journalists in Tokyo 'that an alliance between Great Britain and Japan was under negotiation' and would shortly be concluded. One enterprising paper went so far as to outline the terms of the alliance.

2. When the now celebrated official spokesman of the Japanese Foreign Office[1] stated on August 20th in reply to enquiries from the journalists that '*so far as he knew*' no conversations were going on between Great Britain and Japan for a political understanding, suspicions that something of the sort was on the tapis, instead of being allayed were only increased in the minds of many of these gentlemen.

3. On August 23rd, however, a telegram to the 'Jiji' from their London correspondent denied the rumour and stated that the British Authorities attributed it to reports in connection with the prospective visit to Japan and Manchuria of the industrial mission headed by Lord Barnby.[2] The 'Jiji' correspondent went on to say that the Foreign Secretary, in spite of opposition from the Liberal and Labour members to his pro-Japanese policy, might even be in favour of a revival of the Anglo-Japanese Alliance and that the only man in the National Government to oppose this would be the Prime Minister, the Conservative members being all in favour of restoring the former British friendship for Japan.

4. After the statement by the Foreign Office spokesman on August 20th, Reuter's correspondent in Tokyo telegraphed that the author of the canard was a certain Fabius, a Dutch journalist, who claimed to have obtained the information from an unimpeachable source and that he had attempted unsuccessfully to sell the information to an American news-agency.

5. A few days ago I met my French colleague[3] who asked me if I could throw any light on this rumour. I said that I gathered the rumour had been in the air for some time and that the announcement of the visit next month of an industrial mission had been taken by most of the journalists as confirming it. There was, as he no doubt realised, not a word of truth in it, in fact some of the stories were so incredible as to make one doubt the sanity of the authors. For instance, it was being said that His Majesty's Embassy had nothing to do with the negotiations which were being conducted by Baron de Bassompierre, the Belgian Ambassador, who was acting as liaison between

---

[1] A reference presumably to Mr. Shiratori, Head of the Press Bureau of the Japanese Ministry of Foreign Affairs. Cf. Volume X, No. 351, note 5.

[2] A mission, under the chairmanship of Lord Barnby, was being sent by the Federation of British Industries: it arrived in Tokyo on September 27 and spent a month in Japan and Manchuria. For its report published in London on December 20, in which 'the entirely unofficial and non-political character of the Mission' was emphasized, see *The Times*, December 21, 1934, pp. 6 and 13.          [3] M. Fernand Pila.

His Majesty's Government and the Japanese Government. Monsieur Pila said that he had also heard this. At the same time the Japanese Press were evidently very exercised over what they considered the growing intimacy between the French and Soviet Governments and being in his view the most irresponsible Press in the world, not even excluding the American, had willingly lent an ear to the canard set going by Fabius.

I have, &c.,

R. H. CLIVE

## No. 10

*Sir R. Clive (Tokyo) to Sir J. Simon (Received August 30, 9 a.m.)*

*No. 209 Telegraphic* [*F 5303/591/23*]

*Confidential*                                                    TOKYO, *August 30, 1934, 12.15 p.m.*

My immediately preceding telegram.[1]

Minister for Foreign Affairs said that there was a growing feeling in Japan in favour of friendliest relations with Great Britain. I assured him that my Government reciprocated this feeling. In the course of conversation the tendency of the Powers to revert to pre-war friendships was discussed and I had definite impression that in view of rapprochement between France and the Soviets Japanese Government wished for more intimate relations with Great Britain. His Excellency twice mentioned desire of Japanese Government that the Japanese representative should have preliminary conversation with British representative and said he hoped that even if general conversation led to no basis of agreement Japanese should remain in touch with us.

[1] No. 11. These two telegrams were despatched in reverse order.

## No. 11

*Sir R. Clive (Tokyo) to Sir J. Simon (Received August 30, 9.30 a.m.)*

*No. 208 Telegraphic* [*A 6932/1938/45*]

TOKYO, *August 30, 1934, 12.27 p.m.*

Your telegram No. 131.[1]

Minister for Foreign Affairs told me yesterday that Japanese representatives to preliminary Naval conversations leave Tokyo for London, September 16th. His Excellency hopes very much that they may have prior meeting with British representatives before general conversations begin. He said that Japanese representatives would bring definite proposals. I asked if these were to replace ratios. He said that instructions had not yet been finally approved by Cabinet and were still secret. His Excellency emphasized desire of Japanese Government for reduction in Naval armaments.

[1] This Foreign Office telegram of August 13 said that it 'is now unlikely that Ministers will be in London before October 15' and asked Sir R. Clive to suggest that Japanese representatives for the naval discussions 'should arrive here at a date slightly subsequent to October 15'.

## No. 12

*Sir J. Simon to Sir R. Clive (Tokyo)*
*No. 145 Telegraphic [A 6932/1938/45]*

FOREIGN OFFICE, *August 31, 1934, 7.50 p.m.*

Your telegram No. 208.[1]

We are not quite clear as to the meaning of the expression 'general conversations' in the second sentence. If, as it appears, it means that the Japanese Government assume that tripartite or multilateral preliminary discussions are contemplated to take place in London, you should inform the Minister for Foreign Affairs that it is not known at what date any United States representatives propose to arrive here, and assure him that even if they should be here at the same time as the Japanese representatives, His Majesty's Government in the United Kingdom still envisage bilateral conversations with the Japanese representatives as originally proposed. (See my telegram No. 91).[2]

You should also enquire which route to England the Japanese representatives are proposing to take, and at what date they expect to arrive. You should add that we would propose to inform the United States Government of the date of arrival of the Japanese representatives unless, of course, the Japanese Government would prefer to convey the information to the United States Government themselves.

[1] No. 11.    [2] Of May 18, 1934; not printed.

## No. 13

*Mr. Osborne (Washington) to Sir J. Simon (Received September 2, 10 a.m.)*
*No. 272 Telegraphic [A 6983/1938/45]*

WASHINGTON, *September 1, 1934, 1.56 p.m.*

Articles in Washington and New York papers yesterday by two reputable correspondents stated in one case that United States Government had already, and in the other that they would shortly, make proposals to His Majesty's Government for agreement on 14 inch maximum guns for battleships. This is said to be a compromise between existing 16 inch limit and maximum of 12 inch favoured by His Majesty's Government. It is also stated that the United States Government will agree to 32,000 tons as maximum size of battleships.

Naval Attaché has enquired of Navy Department if there is anything in these reports and has been told that they are without any official authority and are purely an invention in the minds of writers, being presumably their own opinion.

## No. 14

### Letter from Mr. N. Chamberlain to Sir J. Simon
### [F 6189/591/23]

*Personal. Confidential*    KINLOCH RANNOCH, PERTHSHIRE, *September 1, 1934*

My dear John,

While I have been here I have been thinking a great deal about the European situation, the coming Naval Conference and the position of the Government. It seems to me that some immensely important question, affecting the whole future of G[reat]. B[ritain]. and the Empire, may turn upon the actions we take this autumn, and the more I have turned it over the more convinced I have become that this is one of those crucial points in history which test the statesman's capacity and foresight.

The result of my cogitations has led me to certain conclusions which, as they would require Cabinet authority to carry out, I have embodied in a memorandum to the Cabinet.[1] I propose to circulate this memorandum very soon, as time presses, but I am sending you with this letter an advance copy in the hope that you may have time to consider it before you go to Geneva.[2]

I am sending it to you, not only because you are the Minister most directly concerned, but because I attach particular weight to your cool and analytical judgment. Moreover I can't help reflecting that if you could bring off an agreement with Japan such as I have suggested, it would stamp your tenure of office with the special distinction that is attached to memorable historical events, and, incidentally would add greatly to the prestige of the National Government in the most difficult of all fields.

I have been immensely impressed and confirmed in my views by two things since I wrote this paper. One is the report from Sir R. Clive referred to in the P.S.[3] which relates how he was actually offered a Pact of Non-aggression by Japan and how Hirota impressed upon him the friendliness of the Emperor. The second is more recent, namely the semi-official statement of Japanese ideas about the Naval Conference in which suggestions were made very closely approximating to those I have sketched in my paper. (See *The Times*, August 30th).[4]

---

[1] See enclosure below. The memorandum is briefly outlined in Keith Feiling, *The Life of Neville Chamberlain* (London, 1946), pp. 253–4, with the comment, 'A memorandum, drafted but never used in Cabinet, takes us to the heart of the matter'. Mr. N. Chamberlain was Acting Prime Minister, August 8 to September 22, during the absence abroad of Mr. MacDonald (see No. 2, note 2) and Mr. Baldwin.

[2] Sir J. Simon led the British delegation at the opening meeting in Geneva of the 81st session of the Council of the League of Nations on September 10.

[3] The postscript is not printed: the report there referred to was Tokyo despatch No. 369 of July 5; cf. No. 8, note 1.

[4] According to this report of August 29 from *The Times* correspondent in Tokyo (see *The Times*, August 30, p. 12), a spokesman of the Japanese Foreign Office had stated on that day that 'the Japanese delegates in London will submit a scheme for the limitation of arms which, by providing an alternative ratio system and substitute for the Washington Treaty, will render abrogation unnecessary. The spokesman could not say anything about the

Surely with these two confirmatory bits of evidence I must be on the right tack. But if we neglected even to enquire what were Japan's ideas about a Pact, what might not be said of us by future historians if we drifted into unfriendly relations with Japan, lost our Far Eastern trade to them, had to look on helplessly while she marched from one aggression to another.

As for U.S.A. don't let us be browbeaten by her. She will never repay us for sacrificing our interests in order to conciliate her and if we maintain at once a bold and a frank attitude towards her I am not afraid of the result.

Although Van[sittart] has not seen my paper he knows it is on the stocks, and as a result of some remarks I made when he sent me Clive's report, he has written to me that he was having the whole question of the Pact very carefully examined.[5]

He has therefore begun the good work; I hope you may think sufficiently well of the idea to pursue it and that you will some day be remembered (inter alia!) as the author of the 'Simon-Hirota Pact'.

Yours ever,

N. CHAMBERLAIN

ENCLOSURE IN No. 14

*Draft of a memorandum by Mr. N. Chamberlain on the Naval Conference and relations with Japan*

1. My colleagues will be aware that about the middle of October there will be coming to London representatives of the Japanese Admiralty for the purpose of entering upon discussions preparatory to the Naval Conference. Similar discussions have already taken place between ourselves and the Americans the results of which will be referred to later in this paper (paragraph 10). While the subject of these discussions has been under the consideration of a Cabinet Committee, that Committee has not itself received any instructions from the Cabinet as to the policy to be pursued. But it is already evident that more is at stake than Admiralty programmes or national economy. Grave differences of opinion between the principal nations concerned have already manifested themselves which, if handled without due reflection, may seriously prejudice our good relations with Japan on the one hand or the United States on the other. It seems to me therefore that the Cabinet should lose no time in deciding where our interests lie in the major issues concerned, before we enter upon conversations which may otherwise lead us unwittingly to trammel ourselves in just those directions where in the interest of our own security we ought to be free.

2. I suggest that the paramount consideration in this matter to which

scheme except that its aim was the reduction of armaments. . . . Press reports—on which officials decline a comment—state that the Japanese plan includes: (1) The fixing of total tonnage allotments within which each nation would be free to build whatever kinds of craft it deemed necessary, subject to limitation of the size of capital ships, aircraft carriers, and certain other categories of vessel; (2) curtailment of the strength of heavily armed Powers to the point of rendering attack impossible while guaranteeing defence.'

5 See No. 8, note 2.

everything else, home politics, economy, or desire for disarmament must be subject is the safety, first of this country and then of the British Empire. As an abstract proposition probably this statement would command general assent, but we have to translate it into the concrete and the practical application of it is bound to depend on the conditions of the time and to change as these conditions change. At this moment in the autumn of 1934 there is no immediate threat to our safety. But there is a universal feeling of apprehension about the future, whether it be a matter of 2, 3, 5 or 10 years, that such a threat may materialise and that the quarter from which it will come is Germany. In a recent and extremely interesting survey of affairs and persons in that country Sir E. Phipps summed up his conclusions in a grave warning of the need for a strong, united and watchful Europe.[6]

3. Whatever may be the outcome of the present regime in Germany I do not think we need anticipate that we should have to fight her singlehanded, and although the results of any war between civilised peoples must necessarily result in appalling loss and suffering we might reasonably hope to escape serious disaster if the hostilities were confined to European nations. But if we had to enter upon such a struggle with a hostile instead of a friendly Japan in the East, if we had to contemplate the division of our forces so as to protect our Far Eastern interests while prosecuting a war in Europe, then it must be evident that not only would India, Hong Kong, and Australasia be in dire peril but that we ourselves would stand in far greater danger of destruction by a fully armed and organised Germany.

4. So far I do not anticipate that any of my colleagues will disagree with me, and indeed the Cabinet has already more than once expressed its concurrence with the idea that it is desirable to cultivate the most friendly relations with Japan, although they have not as yet had before them any proposal for a specific agreement with that country. It is true that various circumstances, such as the Japanese action in Manchukuo, her defiant attitude towards the League of Nations and her aggressive export policy, have made her unpopular in Europe and have certainly not rendered it easier to introduce greater cordiality into our own relations with her. Yet it is at least arguable that the Manchukuo affair,[7] except insofar as it served to discredit the League, has not hitherto harmed us and, so long as the open door is maintained, is actually likely to benefit British exporters. Moreover there is a good deal to be said for the view that if Japan had reason to think that she had a special friend in Great Britain she would be likely to try and make her conduct conform more closely to the opinions and advice of this country than it has done of late. Considerations of this kind have led me to the view that whatever difficulties and objections there may be in exploratory discussions with Japan just now they are not so serious as to outweigh the immense advantages which would accrue from a satisfactory outcome. In any case, however, the imminence of the naval discussions and the inevitable repercussions of any action taken by us therein make it essential in my judgment that we should go further than the mere recognition of what is

[6] See Volume XII, No. 5.        [7] Cf. Volumes VIII–XI.

theoretically desirable and at once enter upon active steps with a view at least to the ascertainment of the possibilities of agreement. It is clear that the measures necessary to maintain that safety which is our paramount interest must be affected by any arrangement which gave us not merely a neutral but a benevolent Japan in the East and still more so if we could feel that we had eliminated, so far as that is humanly possible, any cause of difference between Japan and ourselves for a considerable time to come.

5. I come back then to a suggestion which I made to the Cabinet some time ago and in rather different circumstances, namely that we should endeavour to frame a Pact of Non-Aggression with Japan for a period say of ten years. I notice that in a despatch from Washington recently circulated (N.C.M. (35) 17)[8] an account was given of an unofficial or more probably a semi-official statement made by a Japanese spokesman last June in which in effect he offered such a Pact of Non-Aggression to the U.S.A. It appeared from this despatch that the offer had a very bad press in the United States. It was assumed that no conditions were attached to the Pact, which would therefore mean that America was asked to give Japan a blank cheque in the Far East to be filled in as she chose.[9] I confess I find it difficult to accept this view of Japanese intentions. I believe they sent up a ballon d'essai to see how the wind blew towards any sort of rapprochement. When they found it unfavourable they dropped the proposal at once. But I cannot believe that so clever a people thought they could get away with a free hand for nothing. They must have been prepared to discuss the possible conditions of a pact, and although in the end their terms might have been too hard one cannot be sure without having enquired.

6. I have heard it suggested that whatever may have been the case in the past the Japanese are now in so aggressive a mood and so much under the influence of ambitious soldiers and sailors that they would not think of tying their hands by any agreement to keep the peace. This view seems to me to give insufficient weight to their anxieties about the Soviet Government, the only Power which really menaces their present acquisitions or their future ambitions. With Russia on their flank it seems to me that Japan would gladly see any accession of security in other directions. But in any case I wish to submit that in view of the immense importance of the issues involved we have no right to assume the absolute impossibility of finding terms on which we could agree upon a pact of non-aggression with Japan. On the contrary I believe that our proper course would be at once to open conversations with her in order to ascertain what sort of terms she had in mind when approaching America and how far she would be prepared to modify them in deference to any representations we might feel called upon to make. In this connection I would remind the Cabinet of the repeated intimations that have come to us from various sources, all showing the great importance attached to our friendship and the strong desire of influential men in Japan (including the Emperor) to do something to strengthen it.

[8] This despatch was Washington No. 787 of June 27, 1934.
[9] Cf. *F.R.U.S., Japan 1931–1941*, vol. i, pp. 232–9.

27

7. The exploration of Japanese policy in the sense I have mentioned is the only step I propose at the moment. Until it is taken nothing can be done in other directions, but the consequences, if it were successful, would be far reaching and in order to carry forward a little further the line of thought I have been pursuing it is necessary to assume that it will be found possible to conclude such a Pact as I have suggested. In that case there would at once be a great easing of the Australasian situation. I see no reason for not completing the Singapore base; indeed to leave it uncompleted would be to waste money already spent upon it by ourselves and the Dominions. But it is clear that our Naval Programme would be affected; and indeed we should have to approach the Naval Conference from a new angle.

8. For the moment I leave out of account the United States to which however I return later (paragraph 10). But with regard to Japan we might well put to their representatives the question why, in view of the difficulty of arriving in a Naval Conference at an agreement which suits equally the U.S.A., themselves and us, should we not add a gentleman's understanding on naval matters to the agreement we have already made not to fight one another for the next ten years.[10] In view of that agreement our respective needs would depend now on other potential enemies, and on regard for our national prestige, whilst our ability to satisfy them is limited by our financial resources. Why not, then, agree that each of us shall be free to build in future what numbers of each kind of ship we like, subject to such limitations of size and armament as we may agree upon with each other from time to time. And for the purposes of a closer understanding and appreciation of each other's policy let us agree that each year we will communicate to each other the main outlines (or with any details that our naval experts might suggest as useful) of our programme for the next two years.

9. My colleagues will observe that the proposal here tentatively sketched is an alternative to the plan proposed by me in an earlier paper (D.C. (M) (32) 120).[11] If it were possible to conclude such an agreement or understanding with Japan on naval matters, very considerable elasticity would be permissible to the Admiralty in laying out their programmes. Financial limitations would still have to govern our expenditure, but the acutest feature of the present situation would be relieved and with the greater certainty as to the conditions of the future it should be possible to consider the distribution of naval strength among different types of ships with greater confidence.

10. I now return to relations with the United States. In the complications of international discussions it is always extremely difficult to know where to begin, and in the present case I am not sure that we could have avoided beginning with America [? even] if we had wanted to. But the fact remains

[10] Article III of the Quadruple Pacific Treaty of December 13, 1921 (cf. No. 8, note 12) said: 'This Treaty shall remain in force for ten years from the time it shall take effect, and after the expiration of said period it shall continue to be in force subject to the right of any of the High Contracting Parties to terminate it upon twelve months' notice.'

[11] Not traced in Foreign Office archives.

that we entered upon the American conversations without having had any complete examination among ourselves of the full implications of the various alternatives open to us and while we have been unable to come to any agreement we have to some extent tied our hands in future talks. For, as a result of our preliminary talks with Mr. Norman Davis, we have agreed that we will not abate our opposition to any alteration of the ratio 5 : 5 : 3 without first communicating with the Americans.[12] In return for this concession we have received nothing, for Mr. Davis while declaring that he quite understood our reasons for wanting the programme which we disclosed to him was at pains to reiterate that he would be misleading us if he allowed us to think for a moment that it would be accepted by the American Senate.

11. Mr. Davis' attitude is in fact only a repetition of a procedure with which we have become very familiar. American representatives lay stress in private upon the immense advantages which would accrue to the world if only we worked together. In pursuance of this admirable sentiment they invite us to disclose our hand without disclosing their own. When we have laid all our cards on the table they shake their heads sadly and express their regretful conviction that Congress will have nothing to do with us unless we can make an offer that will suit them better. Congress (and in particular the Senate) are the Mr. Jorkins[13] of American representatives.

12. In considering the proposed action with regard to Japan I submit that if it is right in our interests we should not be frightened out of it by any fear of American objection, unless that objection be founded on really solid and reasonable grounds. In the case of the proposed Pact of Non-Aggression the objection could not be merely to our agreeing not to settle differences by force. It could only apply to some condition attached to the Pact and while it is impossible to discuss this question until the conditions have been formulated I see no reason for supposing that they are likely to be prejudicial to America, since our purpose is not to obtain a preferential position but to secure our national and imperial safety.

13. On the other hand with a people so suspicious as the Americans I can quite believe that a perfectly harmless and desirable agreement might be misrepresented in that country as something specially aimed at and harmful to themselves. I would therefore take particular pains to keep the Americans informed of what we were doing and our object in doing it, since I believe that complete frankness is in this case likely to produce the best effect, and so far as the Pact is concerned I cannot imagine that if it were fully understood it would raise any serious concern or anxiety in the U.S.A.

14. On the other hand I am fully aware that any naval understanding with Japan which involved our acquiescence in her building, if she chose, above the Washington ratio would be decidedly distasteful to America. Japan is her only possible foe and it suits her very well to have some other country to keep the claws of the animal well clipped, especially if she herself

---

[12] Cf. No. 1. See also *F.R.U.S. 1934*, vol. i, p. 260.

[13] Mr. Spenlow, in Charles Dickens's novel *David Copperfield*, chapter 23, evaded concessions by saying that his partner, Mr. Jorkins, was immovable.

has nothing to pay for the service. But America can have no reasonable ground of complaint if in this matter we follow our own interests since in that respect we should only be following her example. At the same time I wish to make it clear that I do not anticipate an increase in the Japanese ratio as a consequence of the proposed gentleman's agreement with her. The more intimate footing on which we should be placed would enable us to speak with greater freedom and probably with greater acceptance on the folly of Japan's attempting to compete with the U.S.A. in a race in which the superior resources of the latter must eventually give her the victory.

15. Assuming that everything went 'according to plan' in our discussions first with Japan and then with the U.S.A. there would still remain to be considered our attitude towards European Powers and particularly France. Here I submit that the main point to be kept in mind is that the *fons et origo* of all our European troubles and anxieties is Germany. If that fact be constantly present to the consciousness of our negotiators they will not be too stiff with France or too insistent upon her discarding weapons which she may think essential for her safety. A sympathetic attitude on matters which are really important to her ought to help in making her more accommodating on such subjects as the 35,000 ton battleship which touches her vanity rather than her essential interests.

16. For convenience, I will now sum up the considerations and recommendations I wish to submit to the Cabinet.

To preserve the safety of the country and of the Empire without crippling our financial resources it is essential that we should not find ourselves in a few years time confronted simultaneously with a hostile Germany and an unfriendly Japan. We ought therefore so to direct our policy as to eliminate one of these two dangers.

All our evidence indicates that it would be easier and simpler to come to an agreement with Japan than with Germany. Japan has already semi-officially offered a Pact of Non-Aggression to the United States, but no one knows the conditions which she must have had in her mind. She has however pointed the way to us and

*My first recommendation* is

That conversations be opened with Japan at once in whatever manner may seem to the Foreign Secretary most appropriate with the object of ascertaining

(*a*) Whether she is prepared to make a Pact of Non-Aggression with us;
(*b*) On what terms she would consider such a pact favourably.

Before asking this last question (*b*) it would be necessary for us to consider what assurances we should want to obtain before agreeing to abandon the use of force against Japan during the next ten years.

Until the negotiations involved in this first recommendation are completed no further progress can or should be made with the negotiations on the Naval Conference. If however our efforts should be successful and a Pact concluded then

*My second recommendation* is

That we should follow up the Pact with an attempt to reach an agreement with Japan which would in effect supersede the Naval Conference. Such an agreement would leave each side formally unbound as to numbers and types of ships, but every effort would be made to obtain agreement on limits of size and equipment, and in particular we should undertake to keep each other informed of our respective programmes well in advance of their execution.

*My third recommendation* concerns our relations with the U.S.A. and is as follows:

As regards the proposed Pact the fullest information and explanations should be given to the Americans in order to convince them that the action taken is not against any interests of theirs and is a valuable aid to the preservation of world peace. As regards the Naval Agreement we should remind the Americans that they have found themselves unable to agree to a British programme on which we can make no compromise. Since we have no desire to dictate to them what Navy they shall have we think it better not to discredit international attempts to agree on disarmament further by holding a Naval Conference already clearly doomed to failure. We have therefore chosen the alternative which seems to us most practicable and helpful to others as well as ourselves in the course we have taken.

*My fourth recommendation* is merely that in dealing with European Powers in naval matters we should bear in mind that Germany and not France is our source of anxiety in the future and that we should conduct our negotiations accordingly.

I have only one more observation to make. Whatever be the ultimate decisions of the Cabinet they will have been arrived at after full consideration and discussion of ample materials and with the aid of expert opinion. The public have up to now had no such opportunities and it would hardly be fair to expect them to swallow our conclusions without any preparation.

*My final recommendation* therefore is that as soon as the Government has reached its decision as to the course to be followed careful consideration should be given to the question how best the policy decided on can be explained and commended to the public.

N. C.

## No. 15

*Memorandum by Mr. Orde on Mr. N. Chamberlain's proposals*[1]
[F 6190/591/23]

FOREIGN OFFICE, September 4, 1934

The root idea in the Chancellor's mind seems to be the fear that if we become seriously embroiled with Germany Japan will seize the opportunity

---
[1] See enclosure in No. 14.

to attack our possessions in the Far East. Her apparent willingness to conclude non-aggression pacts with us and with the United States and her anxiety for good relations with us suggests that we could exorcise this danger by means of a pact; and at the same time we might improve the occasion by obtaining a gentleman's agreement not to indulge in immoderate naval construction. It is not, if I understand the Chancellor aright, a question of deciding on a price which it may be worth while to pay in order to strengthen ourselves against Germany, but simply one of the best means of protecting our interests in the Far East and incidentally of reducing our need for new naval construction.

There are a variety of objections to a pact which have been mentioned in a previous minute.[2] Writing in haste I will not repeat them in full. They are to be found in the probable effect of a pact, or rather of its implications, on Japanese ambitions, on China, Russia, the United States of America, the Dutch East Indies, and on our defensive power against Japanese expansion towards the South West. I will endeavour only to supplement what I have already written.

Since the German danger is primary the effect of a pact on Russia is of the first importance. I believe it is agreed to be desirable that Russia should be sufficiently strong to be a potential check on Germany. If so, anything that will weaken Russia may presumably be taken as increasing the danger we have to fear from Germany. An Anglo-Japanese pact I suggest can hardly have any other effect. We are, it must be admitted, in the dark as to Japan's real reasons for wanting to be on specially good terms with us and the United States, but they must be of a shallow and emotional or extremely naive character if they are not to be found in a desire to strengthen herself against Russia. Is she *afraid* of Russia? or is she anxious to try conclusions with her if the rear can be made safe? I find it difficult to believe that Japan in the flush of her success in Manchuria is not confident of her ability to keep Russia at bay. The danger from Russian air power based at Vladivostok is surely what is really exercising Japanese fears, and the removal of this implies an aggressive intention. But Russia, we are told, will fight if Japan attacks her; her resources will be strained and Germany will find herself in a stronger position. It is *after* a successful settling of accounts with Russia and a pause for recovery that Japan may become a real danger to our own possessions in the Far East. Meanwhile, is it not prudent from both points of view not to encourage Japan against Russia, but to keep her nervous as to her position or restrained in any aggressive thoughts she may have? It may be worth while asking Sir R. Clive whether Japan is afraid of Russian aggression. If she is, and the effect of a pact would merely be to relieve her fear in some measure, but not to encourage an aggressive spirit, this particular argument against a pact would be weakened or disappear.

A minor but perhaps not negligible consideration from the Russian aspect is the offence that any encouragement of Japan against Russia would cause to the Soviet Government and the worsening of our relations with them that

[2] See Appendix II to No. 8.

32

would ensue. We have already had to soothe their suspicion that we favour difficulties between them and Japan (see Sir R. Vansittart's conversation with the Soviet Ambassador recorded in the despatch to Moscow No. 352 of July 18th).[3]

A movement by Japan against the East Indies is perhaps the most likely form in which an attack on our own possessions would develop. It would be particularly insidious, for she might reckon on a passive attitude on our part, and if she succeeded in establishing herself in the Dutch East Indies, our own position would have been immensely weakened. But if Japan is *afraid* of Russia, such a movement seems most unlikely. The Russian position at Vladivostok and half enveloping Manchuria must dominate the Japanese conception of policy. If Japan is not afraid, but aggressively minded, a pact will surely bring nearer the day when she will attack Russia and then, after a pause for recovery from the effort, proceed against the East Indies. It may be argued that Japan might come to some understanding with Russia which would leave her free for adventures further south. This seems to me frankly unlikely.

American feeling towards us may be a minor consideration; I am not confident as to this, but I am not competent to discuss the question. It may be possible to explain a pro-Japanese policy to the United States, as the Chancellor suggests in a way to make it acceptable, though I should have thought it unlikely. Even if they are in the mood to clear out of the Far East, I feel doubts as to the permanence of the mood or as to their equanimity if they were to see us apparently follow suit; and can we avoid this appearance unless the pact takes a form in which China is explicitly protected? I submit that it would be very dangerous to conclude a pact without providing for the protection of China. A pact pure and simple could hardly fail to arouse consternation and violent resentment in China, which could only be removed by explanations which would show the Chinese that we were afraid of Japan. This would merely result in increasing Japanese influence and encouraging the Chinese to attack our interests in view of our self-confessed weakness. I see no escape from this dilemma, and I fear that we shall have a big price to pay in China unless we can show that in a pact with Japan we have protected China's own interests. But how can this be done? After the tearing up of the Nine Power Treaty by Japan[4] in defiance of world opinion would a new treaty protecting China against further aggression look like anything but mockery? After the April declaration of Japan's ambition to treat China as her own exclusive province[5] is it conceivable that Japan would be a party to such a treaty in any form sufficient to make it anything but a patent mockery? If it is, Japan must indeed be in a more nervous condition

[3] Volume VI, No. 510.

[4] A reference to Japan's actions in Manchuria, 1931–3; see Volumes VIII–XI. For the text of the Treaty between the United States, Belgium, the British Empire, China, France, Italy, Japan, the Netherlands, and Portugal relating to principles and policies to be followed in matters concerning China, signed at Washington on February 6, 1922, see *B.F.S.P.*, vol. 119, pp. 562–6 (No. 11 in Cmd. 1627).

[5] Cf. No. 8, note 11.

than anyone has dreamt. Are we prepared to conclude a treaty that will be an obvious mockery or to abandon China to Japan, as we shall be taken to do in Japan and everywhere else if we do not get better guarantees than the very explicit Nine Power Treaty seemed to give us? I do not see how such better guarantees can be obtained. If they are obtained, Japan will have suffered a defeat and bear us a grudge. And if they are not, the risks to our trade from Chinese resentment or contempt will be great; at the same time, the League of Nations will have been virtually flouted, and its influence will have suffered a grievous blow from our hands. The real power or powerlessness of the League may not be altered, but we shall be regarded as having taken the Japanese side as against the League and to have demonstrated our belief that the League must be disregarded when real problems arise. We still, I imagine, set store by the influence of the League for the preservation of peace; if so, in order to save its power in Europe, it would seem necessary, if we are to give the impression of abandoning China to Japan, to come out at the same time or previously with a bold policy of altering the constitution of the League by setting up a more effective organisation in Europe while frankly giving up the ideal of a world wide League.

I would try to sum up these rather hurried and, I fear, rather disjointed remarks by saying that the Chancellor's memorandum seems to me to ignore the prime importance of Russia for Japanese policy and the improbability of a Japanese threat to our own possessions coming before she has secured herself against the Russian danger. A pact will increase the chances of a Russo-Japanese war and of a weakening of Russia, and will entail, unless accompanied by unobtainable guarantees for China, violent Chinese resentment against us, a diminution in the authority of the League, and most likely a worsening of our relations with the United States.

C. W. ORDE[6]

[6] On September 4 Sir R. Vansittart gave instructions for the memorandum to be submitted to Sir J. Simon 'with the file which was recently before him'. On September 25 Mr. Seymour noted: 'The S. of S. has seen these papers and used them in the discussions resulting in a draft telegram to Sir R. Clive [cf. No. 21 below], which was prepared to-day. H.J.S. Sept. 25.' Mr. H. J. Seymour was private secretary to Sir J. Simon.

## No. 16

*Report by H.M. Naval Attaché at Tokyo*[1]
*Report No. 6 [A 8247/1938/45]*

Secret                                                          TOKYO, *September 5, 1934*

Sir,

I have the honour to inform Your Excellency that I gave a farewell dinner party for Rear-Admiral Yamamoto and his A.D.C., Lieutenant-Commander Mitsunobu, last night to which I also invited the Vice-Minister of Marine.

2. Rear-Admiral Yamamoto has been Naval Attaché at Washington and was a member of the Japanese naval delegation to the London Conference in 1930.

[1] A copy of this report by Captain Vivian was enclosed in Tokyo despatch No. 494 of September 17 to the Foreign Office.

He has held important appointments in the Naval Air Service.

3. I had not met him before and was astonished to find that the Ministry of Marine had selected an officer of his type to carry out what must be a mission of some importance to his country.

He is far from being the best type of naval officer being, as far as I could gather on short acquaintance, a man of little charm and extremely abrupt manner. He is obviously a hard drinker and is apparently well known as an inveterate gambler; in fact, he stated that his greatest interest is gambling in any form and poker in particular.

It may be that his skill at this game has earned him his present appointment.

4. His A.D.C., Lieutenant-Commander Mitsunobu, is a man of unprepossessing appearance. He speaks good English and French and appears to have a good brain. This officer, again, is devoted to whiskey and is an accomplished after-dinner entertainer.

5. Although a great many Japanese naval officers have the attributes which, to Western minds, are indicative of a 'gentleman', neither of these officers appear[?s] to be of that type.

6. In conversation with Mr. Cunningham, Japanese Counsellor at this Embassy, Captain Iwamura, A.D.C. to the Minister of Marine, stated (i) that the Russians are building submarines at Vladivostok and (ii) that he, Iwamura, fully realised that in the event of a Russo-Japanese war, Japan's international position would be a difficult one.

Captain Iwamura is a man who holds broadminded views and he probably reflects the opinions of the Minister of Marine. The Vice-Minister[2] informed me that Iwamura is an exceptionally able officer.

7. In conversation with me, Admiral Hasegawa said à propos of a possible Russo-Japanese war, 'That is the last thing we want and the Army is not ready', he then hastily changed the subject.

8. Neither Admiral Yamamoto nor his A.D.C. could inform me of their definite date of departure nor of the exact route. Admiral Yamamoto stated that he hoped to go via San Francisco and New York.

I have, &c.,

G. VIVIAN

[2] Admiral K. Hasegawa.

## No. 17

*Sir R. Clive (Tokyo) to Sir J. Simon (Received September 7, 9.30 a.m.)*
*No. 214 Telegraphic [A 7119/1938/45]*

TOKYO, *September 7, 1934, 11.5 a.m.*

Your telegram No. 145.[1]

I have explained situation to Minister for Foreign Affairs in the sense of paragraph one.

Minister for Foreign Affairs has now informed me that Rear Admiral I. Yamamoto will be appointed 'additional representative' and that he and

[1] No. 12.

his party will leave Japan for the United Kingdom on September 20th travelling via Seattle and New York. They are due to arrive in London on October 15th.

Mr. Hirota states that while United States Government will be asked to grant transit facilities Japanese government see no objection to His Majesty's Government informing United States government of date of arrival of party in England.

## No. 18

*Memorandum by Lord Lothian on the Anglo-American Naval Problems*[1]
[*A 7185/1938/45*]

1. The British, American and Japanese governments all want reductions in the size and expense of their fleets. The British want it in the size of battleships and cruisers though they want an increased number of small cruisers. The Americans want it in reduced total tonnage though they want their tonnage in large battleships and large cruisers. The Japanese want reduction provided the U.S.A. and Great Britain reduce more than they do so as to give them a ratio nearer to equality.

2. Agreement about armaments always depend on prior agreement about policy, for armaments are but the instruments of policy.

3. So far as the Pacific is concerned the vital question is security. The main basis of the Washington treaties was twofold, the ratio 5: 5: 3 and the non-fortification of Hong Kong, the Philippines, and the Japanese mandated Islands.[2] Neither Great Britain nor the United States can maintain their full fleets in the Pacific (Great Britain indeed can only maintain a small part of hers). Therefore any increase in the relative offensive power of the Japanese navy means insecurity for Singapore and Hawaii. The existing ratios assure the absolute security of Japan in her own waters, as the Manchukuo incident made clear. If, therefore, the Japanese refuse to be satisfied with her present ratio or something like it Great Britain and U.S.A. ought to make it clear that they will build two ships to one against her. If that is made clear there will probably be no difficulty about the ratio.[3]

4. The other foundation of the Washington treaties was the integrity of China and the open door.[4] It seems quite clear that neither U.S.A. nor Great Britain regard this as a *casus belli*, as they would an attack on Hawaii

---

[1] This undated memorandum by the first editor of *The Round Table* was filed in the Foreign Office on September 10. It was described by Mr. Craigie, in a minute of September 7, as 'a valuable contribution from a representative of that large volume of British opinion which believes in the advantages and feasibility of Anglo-American co-operation'.

[2] See articles IV and XIX of the Treaty for the Limitation of Naval Armament of February 6, 1922; cf. No. 1, note 11.

[3] An undated marginal comment by Sir R. Vansittart here read: 'I wonder if we could really afford to implement this threat, or if we shd feel *strong* enough to implement it till Singapore is ready. RV.' Subsequent marginal comments on this memorandum by Sir R. Vansittart are reproduced below in notes 5–7, 9–12, 14–17, and 19.

[4] Cf. No. 15, note 4.

or Singapore. They will not, in other words, build against Japan in order to ensure the integrity of China. On the other hand any further destruction of Chinese independence or the closing of the open door would produce bitter feeling and might lead to collective action of an economic character by all nations interested in Chinese trade, and if the naval (and air) ratios are maintained for the reasons given in section 3 Japan will probably accept the principle of the integrity of China apart from Manchukuo and the open door, and will not build or threaten war in order to repudiate them, though there will doubtless be instant diplomatic difficulties.

5. Anglo-American agreement about Pacific problems is probably easy on these lines[5] and the present naval programme of President Roosevelt shows that the U.S.A. will live up to it. It is a policy which also respects the reasonable rights and the special position of Japan in the Far East, and it would therefore seem that a friendly agreement would also be reached with Japan on the basis of it,[6] provided it is made clear that the U.S.A. and Great Britain cannot be divided and mean to stand firm on the ratio so far as Hawaii and Singapore are concerned.[7]

6. There are still left, however, two difficult problems as between Great Britain and the U.S.A. The first concerns the reconciliation of the principle of 'parity' with Great Britain's need for large numbers of small cruisers and the United States insistence on large battleships and cruisers on the ground that she has no overseas bases. The second is the old issue of the freedom of the seas (i.e. the interference with neutral trade by belligerents) in the new conditions created by the Covenant of the League of Nations and the Kellogg Pact. The London treaty[8] solved the first of these problems by giving the United States a slightly larger tonnage of 10,000 cruisers and Great Britain a slightly larger total tonnage to be put into a larger number of small cruisers —thus giving Great Britain rather more commerce destroying and protectory power and the United States more battle power.[9] This method is still probably the only basis on which the conflicting naval needs of the two countries can be reconciled with the principle of parity.[10] But it obviously creates difficulties for both sides, as does the question of the number, size and cost of the battleships which are to replace the existing battleships, unless there is a sufficient degree of agreement on policy to convince public opinion on both sides of the Atlantic, that there is no likelihood of the two countries ever having to use their navies against one another;[11] because their international interests and policies are substantially the same.

[5] *Marginal comment*: 'Of course the real doubt here is whether any one can really count on the U.S.A. in any circumstances. RV.'

[6] *Marginal comment*: 'This wd be a friendly agreement reached via the big stick. RV.'

[7] *Marginal comment*: 'There will be some opposition in the Cabinet on this. RV.'

[8] Of April 22, 1930; cf. Introductory Note to this Chapter, note 1.

[9] *Marginal comment*: 'Very true. RV.'

[10] *Marginal comment*: 'The Admiralty will not agree to this basis again, and have given us a quite unanswerable reason for their attitude. RV.'

[11] *Marginal comment*: 'This is already one of the fundamental principles of our calculations. RV.'

7. Assuming agreement about policy in the Pacific, i.e. maintenance of the principles of the Washington treaties on lines set forth above, the only other large question of policy between the United States and Great Britain relates to their attitude to Europe and to the question of the 'freedom of the seas'.[12] There is no other issue—territorial or otherwise—of a character which might give rise to grave complications, which divides them. Is it possible to reach agreement about these issues which might not only remove all possibility of conflict but also make easy a naval agreement on 'tonnage and gunnage'. The situation has been made much easier by the Kellogg Pact and the Stimson and Norman Davis declarations as to the attitude of the United States towards violations of that Pact.[13] When war breaks out it will hardly be possible for either the United States or Great Britain to supply munitions of war, which now include raw materials and food stuffs, to any state which is adjudged to be the aggressor. On the other hand what matters most to Great Britain is that the sea ways should be kept open for her own supplies in the event of her becoming involved in war herself.[14] She needs a navy (or air power) far more for this reason than as an instrument for bringing pressure to bear upon others for blockade is a proverbially slow way of bringing pressure on other states unless it is universally applied.

Is it possible for Great Britain and the United States to agree upon two cardinal principles of policy?

(a) That whenever war breaks out or threatens they will, under the Covenant or the Kellogg Pact, attend a conference of non-belligerents with the object of denying financial resources and munitions of war either to both belligerents or to whoever may be deemed the aggressor,[15] either by embargo or if necessary by blockade, with the object of preventing the war or of bringing it to an end as soon as possible on fair terms.

(b) That except in so far as an embargo or a blockade has been declared against a belligerent under the Covenant or the Kellogg Pact, the seas shall be open to the trade of all countries and that the navies of both the United States and Great Britain will be actively employed to keep them open.[16] This would mean that if ships belonging to an aggressor state began to interrupt trade they would be arrested or sunk.

If such an agreement could be reached it would immensely strengthen the

---

[12] *Marginal comment*: 'This is a favourite topic of Lothian's—also of Hankey's! And they take opposite views. I shd have thought that, in our altered circumstances, Lothian was probably right. But there will be no moving Hankey! RV.' Sir Maurice Hankey was Secretary to the Cabinet.

[13] See, for example, the declarations by the U.S. Secretary of State, Mr. H. Stimson on, January 7 and February 23, 1932; cf. Volume X, No. 9, note 11, and No. 49, note 7; also Volume XI, No. 506.

[14] *Marginal comment*: 'This is the point of divergence. The Prime Minister belongs to the Lothian school. But some of his colleagues—and the Admiralty—will almost certainly dissent strongly. RV.'

[15] *Marginal comment*: 'The U.S.A. are in a very bad mood for any commitment just now, (and might well make play with the old difficulty of defining an aggressor). RV.'

[16] *Marginal comment*: 'I don't think even Roosevelt could get his public, let alone his Senate, thus far. RV.'

power of the collective system, it would be a great re-inforcement to British security, and to a less degree of American security, and it would diminish enormously the risk of conflict between the two countries over interference with neutral trade. It would be in line with the present trend of American policy, which is to boycott belligerents. It is, too, the only way in which the United States can make good her policy of 'keeping out of war', for the really serious risk to the United States is that Great Britain should get into a war, while the United States was a neutral. And the fact that there was, to a considerable extent, a common policy in the two countries towards war, would make agreement about naval and air 'tonnage and gunnage' much easier.[17]

8. There remains the difficult question of Great Britain's commitments in Europe and the attitudes of France and Italy and possibly Germany to naval armaments. The essential attitude of American foreign policy since 1920 has been avoidance of commitment to intervene in the internal affairs of Europe, and any arrangement to consult with Great Britain or other signatories of the Covenant which seemed to imply involvement in the internal affairs of Europe would certainly be rejected by American public opinion. This situation, however, has been greatly simplified by the recent declaration of Sir John Simon in connection with the Barthou proposals for an Eastern Locarno,[18] to the effect that Great Britain's commitments in Europe were strictly limited to those embodied in the Covenant, the Kellogg and the Locarno Pacts and would not be increased, together with his stressing of the importance of maintaining the integrity of Belgium.[19] In other words Great Britain has proclaimed her detachment from any regional security system which may be created in Europe and which must depend upon military and air sanctions, subject only to her vital interest in the independence of Belgium and the permanence of the Franco-German frontiers, and has declared that, apart from this, her interest in Europe is in what can be done under the Covenant and the Kellogg Pact to prevent European war or bring it rapidly to an end before it can spread into a world war. That will make conference about common action under the Kellogg Pact far easier both with the United States and the Dominions.

As regards France and Italy the more they can be convinced that the United States and Great Britain are likely to interest themselves in the prevention of war and in denying the means of prosecuting war to aggressors, the less likely are they to put forward naval demands which will prevent some reduction in existing navies or lead to competition between themselves.[20]

[17] *Marginal comment*: 'Yes, if there *was* this Common Policy. RV.'
[18] A reference presumably to Sir J. Simon's report to the House of Commons, on July 13, 1934, on M. Barthou's visit to London; see 292 *H.C. Deb.* 5 *s.*, cols. 691–9. Cf. Volume VI, Nos. 487–9.     [19] *Marginal comment*: 'Lothian approved this warmly. RV.'
[20] Sir R. Vansittart made the following undated general comment: 'A very interesting paper. I have suggested some difficulties, but it wd be most interesting if Lothian were to try it on the dog, privately, and let us know the result. But the trial will be wasted unless it is on the great man himself and none other. RV.' Other minutes included a comment by Mr. Craigie on September 7 (cf. note 1 above): 'This paper of Lord Lothian's and his article in *The Round Table* [No. 96, September 1934, pp. 693–716] bring out the urgency of

formulating a definite answer to the following question: are we going to steer for the kind of Anglo-American co-operation which Lord Lothian outlines, or are we going to line up with Japan (in other words 'throw up the sponge' in the Far East) and so make further Anglo-American co-operation impossible?'

## No. 19

### Letter from Mr. N. Chamberlain to Sir J. Simon
### [F.O. 800/291]

*Personal and Confidential*  TARLAND, ABERDEENSHIRE, *September 10, 1934*

My dear John,

Many thanks for your letter of the 7th[1] on the subject of my draft memorandum to the Cabinet.[2] You will appreciate that the reason why I was anxious to get this matter before my colleagues as early as possible was the imminence of the Naval conversations the trend of which might be considerably affected if my suggestions were entertained. But I have no idea of trying to force upon you a line of advance which does not commend itself to you and in view of the difficulties you have set out I gladly accept your suggestion that we should discuss the whole matter together before I proceed any further.

I am returning to London at the end of this week and I am spending the following weekend with Sam Hoare.[3] I shall however be back in London on the 24th Monday and if it would suit you we might perhaps have our meeting on that day when you will have left Balmoral. Will you let me know how you are fixed and if the 24th is not available what would be the first day on which we could meet.

In the meantime I make the following brief comments:

Bi-lateral treaties and pacts have a very different significance in the mind of the signatories from multi-lateral pacts and agreements. The responsibilities and obligations of the former are more direct and there is less likelihood of misunderstanding or evasion. That Japan appreciates this is proved by her new enquiries about such Pacts with us or with U.S.A. We may, I think, safely assume that in addition to the Kellogg Pact and the Four Power Treaty she would welcome a bi-lateral Pact and would be willing to pay for it.

No doubt she would like a Free Hand in the Far East, so long as she respects British Possessions there. But I did not suggest that we should give it to her. I tried to make it clear that what I proposed was to find out from her how far she was prepared to go in renouncing a free hand in return for the bi-lateral pact. When we had learned this we should have to consider whether she was going far enough to make the pact worth our while. If you did not understand this my paper has been badly drafted and I must amend it.

---

[1] No copy of this letter has been traced in Foreign Office archives.
[2] Enclosure in No. 14.
[3] Sir Samuel Hoare was at that time Secretary of State for India.

I would like to put to you that in speaking of Japan's 'designs in China' you are assuming that we know what they are. I am not sure that Japan herself knows what they are, but if she does it would surely be well that we should be in the secret and if the conversations revealed that they were such as we could not accept we should then have a new set of data on which to frame our Far Eastern policy.

All this I can elaborate further when we meet. I sincerely hope that we may be able to agree on some course of action that will commend itself to both of us.

Yours ever,
N. Chamberlain

## No. 20

*Sir R. Clive (Tokyo) to Sir J. Simon (Received September 21, 9.30 a.m.)*
*No. 221 Telegraphic [A 7533/1938/45]*

TOKYO, *September 21, 1934, 11.27 a.m.*

My telegram No. 214.[1]

Departure yesterday for London of Admiral Yamamoto was made the occasion of great patriotic demonstration both at Tokyo station and at Yokohama. Numerous patriotic associations of young men assembled while the entire official hierarchy of Japanese Navy were present.

In a final speech to the press on board Admiral is reported as saying 'I firmly believe that public opinion through the world will agree with our proposal. I will fight to the last for that object and my departure today is to me the same as a departure for actual warfare'.

[1] No. 17.

## No. 21

*Sir J. Simon to Sir R. Clive (Tokyo)[1]*
*No. 153 Telegraphic [F 5808/591/23]*

*Very confidential*          FOREIGN OFFICE, *September 25, 1934, 6.55 p.m.*

1. In reading paragraph 8 of your despatch No. 369 of July 5th[2] the tentative suggestion made by the Japanese Minister for Foreign Affairs for

[1] Sir J. Simon secured the agreement of the Cabinet on September 25 to the despatch of this telegram. Mr. Chamberlain, in supporting Sir J. Simon's proposal to this effect, said that he considered it so important 'both in regards the whole future policy of Great Britain and also of the Dominions' that the Cabinet might, before reaching any final decision, like to have a detailed review of the whole problem. The Cabinet accordingly took note that he and Sir J. Simon would circulate a joint memorandum on the Japanese situation with reference to the question of a non-aggression pact. In a minute referring to this decision, Sir R. Vansittart wrote: 'This is the view of the Chancellor and S. of S. *I* feel that enquiries are very dangerous, but that if they are prepared to run the obvious risks, the enquiry can well be made, though I expect nothing of the result.'

[2] See No. 8, note 1.

a bilateral pact of non-aggression with Great Britain was duly noted. In the circumstances your caution in replying was perfectly correct.

2. In connexion, however, with the whole subject of Anglo-Japanese relations it seems desirable to probe this matter somewhat further. This course is timely and prudent both because of possible developments in Europe and because of possible and not improbable obstacles in connexion with the Naval Conference of 1935. You should therefore in an early conversation with Mr. Hirota endeavour to bring the conversation round to this subject taking, however, particular care to give no official colour to your investigations and inquiries. Your action should in fact be strictly unofficial, for the dangers of indiscreet publicity on the Japanese side will of course be obvious to you.

3. What I really wish to know, for the guidance of myself and my colleagues, is this: what exactly have the Japanese in mind in making this suggestion? The Americans have already rejected the proposal of a bilateral pact with Japan and Japan has declined such a proposal when made by the Russians. These facts make the delicacy of your own inquiries very apparent.

4. You will appreciate that a bilateral pact pure and simple without conditions would raise many difficulties for us in connexion, for example, with China and the United States of America. It might even operate to encourage a forward policy in Japan against Russia. The matter might bear a different aspect if the bilateral pact were accompanied by satisfactory assurances of non-aggression in other directions, particularly China. Failing that, we should appear to be giving *carte blanche* to Japan and that would be an impossible position for us. Even the future of the Netherlands East Indies is a matter of vital concern for us.

5. Is it your opinion, or can you discreetly ascertain, whether the Japanese would have it in mind to cover all or any of these problems in a manner satisfactory and reassuring to us? If so, for how long? In a word, are the Japanese really so desirous of such a pact that they would be prepared to pay a reasonable price for it? And if so, how much?

6. There is some apprehension among my advisers that Japan would not be prepared to pay a price high enough to compensate for the dangers of hostility or criticism in other quarters. I have, however, felt that I should not be justified in allowing the opening described in your above-mentioned despatch to remain unexplored. I shall therefore be glad if you will take the course indicated with the greatest possible discretion and let me have your observations as soon as possible.

### No. 22

*Sir R. Clive (Tokyo) to Sir J. Simon (Received September 29, 4.20 p.m.)*
*No. 232 Telegraphic [F 5846/591/23]*

*Very confidential*                    TOKYO, *September 29, 1934, 5.20 p.m.*

Your telegram No. 153.[1]

Minister for Foreign Affairs gave a dinner last night for Industrial Mission.[2]

<hr>

[1] No. 21.                    [2] See No. 9.

Lord Barnby made a friendly and tactful speech which made an excellent impression. Minister for Foreign Affairs expressed his appreciation to me after dinner and the atmosphere seemed favourable for broaching question of Anglo-Japanese relations.

After congratulating His Excellency on prospect of settlement of Chinese Eastern Railway question[3] I referred to unfortunate incident at Mukden mentioned in your telegram No. 151[4] and said I much hoped this would be cleared up before the Mission went to Manchukuo. His Excellency knew vaguely about it and I said I would send him a memorandum.

I then said I felt there had been a slight misunderstanding on the part of Vice Minister for Foreign Affairs when I had suggested that an audience with the Emperor *before* departure of Mission for Manchukuo might re-start misrepresentation in the press and in China as to the real object of the Mission (see my telegram No. 217).[5] I had never meant to oppose audience on return of Mission from Manchukuo. It was so easy for misunderstandings to arise that it was essential to clear them up at once especially when both our countries desired the friendliest relations.

His Excellency cordially agreed and went on to talk of Japan's desire for closer relations of friendship. He recalled your very friendly message communicated last December by Sir F. Lindley.[6] I then referred to suggestion he had made shortly after my arrival of a non-aggression pact. What exactly had His Excellency had in mind? He said that Japanese Government were very anxious in case Naval Conference failed that there should be no break in friendly relations with Great Britain and he would like to see some more definite understanding. This might perhaps take the form of a non-aggression pact. I asked whether he anticipated the failure of the conference. He smiled. Were the proposals of (? Japanese Government)[7] which the Japanese delegates were taking to London unlikely to prove acceptable to us and to America? He replied, 'they will perhaps be acceptable to you but perhaps not to the Americans'. Japan did not want parity with Great Britain which requires a big navy but America had no need whatever for a big fleet. He had sent instructions to Japanese Ambassador to speak very

[3] Sir R. Clive had reported, in his telegram No. 225 of September 25, a press report 'that agreement had been reached for the purchase of Chinese Eastern Railway for 140 million yen and payment of 30 million compensation to employees'. Agreement on the sale of the Chinese Eastern Railway by the U.S.S.R. to Manchukuo was finally reached on March 23, 1935; see *Soviet Documents on Foreign Policy*, selected and edited by Jane Degras, vol. iii (London, 1953), pp. 120–2.

[4] This telegram referred to a reported attack by Japanese in the outskirts of Mukden on August 19 on the British Vice-Consul at Mukden (Mr. Coghill), a British employee of the Asiatic Petroleum Co. (Mr. J. H. Ford), and an American citizen (Mr. Rowsome). Sir R. Clive was instructed to draw Mr. Hirota's attention to the 'one-sided and inaccurate nature of the police report on the case, and request a further investigation'.

[5] Of September 19, not printed.

[6] Sir F. Lindley was H.M. Ambassador at Tokyo from May 1931 to June 1934. Documents relating to British policy in the Far East after June 3, 1933 (see Volume XI) will be printed in subsequent volumes in this Series.

[7] The text was here uncertain.

openly to you and he wanted you to know that Japan would like an understanding in some form with Great Britain.

I hinted that a bilateral agreement was an extremely delicate matter and that we were bound to consider reactions politically in the United States and also elsewhere. He said that he realised this.

Conversation had lasted some time and it would have been inopportune to press His Excellency then to define more closely his idea of a (? non)[7] aggression pact. I am not even convinced he has a definite idea. He repeatedly spoke of some form of understanding.

## No. 23

*Sir R. Clive (Tokyo) to Sir J. Simon (Received October 3, 9.30 a.m.)*
*No. 234 Telegraphic [F 5899/591/23]*

TOKYO, *October 3, 1934, 2.40 p.m.*

I paid courtesy call on the Prime Minister whom I had not yet met. His Excellency began conversation by referring to former (? alliance)[1] and emphasizing desire of Japan for friendliest relations with Great Britain. I said that I knew my Government reciprocated these feelings.

With regard to naval conversations His Excellency said that if it was the wish of every country to reduce naval armaments he hoped Japanese proposals would be accepted.

I mentioned Ministry of War pamphlet referred to in my immediately preceding telegram[2] and said I feared this would have unfortunate effect in some countries. His Excellency at once said he deplored publication which in no way represented the views of Japanese Government.

Japan wanted war with no country. At the same time huge Soviet army along the Manchurian frontier was a menace. When I referred to the sale of Chinese Eastern Railway[3] as likely to relieve tension he said he hoped it would be possible to come to agreement with the Soviets. He ridiculed the idea of war with America.

[1] The text was here uncertain.
[2] Not here printed. The reference was to a pamphlet entitled *The Real Meaning of National Defence and Advocacy of its Strengthening* issued on October 1 by the Press Section of the Japanese Ministry of War; cf. *The Times*, October 3, p. 12. [3] Cf. No. 22, note 3.

## No. 24

*Memorandum recording the results up to date of preliminary conversations relating to preparations for the 1935 Naval Conference held with the United States, Japanese, French, and Italian representatives[1]*

*N.C.M.(35)18 [A 7947/1938/45]*

*October 3, 1934*

For convenience of record this report follows the order of the headings

[1] This memorandum was prepared by Mr. Craigie in consultation with the Admiralty. On October 6 Sir J. Simon authorized its circulation.

adopted in the Draft Report of the Naval Ministerial Committee (N.C.M. (35) 12).[2]

## I. *Ratio*

*United States.*

The United States representatives declared definitely that their Government were not prepared to agree to any change in the Japanese–United States ratio, and they sought to obtain an understanding with the British representatives that both countries would adopt a common attitude of opposition to any increase in the Japanese ratio of naval strength. The British representatives were not prepared to give any hard and fast undertaking to this effect, but it was agreed that neither side would depart from its attitude of opposition without previous consultation with the other.

The question of ratio was not discussed with any of the other foreign representatives, although the impression was gained that France would now be less opposed to accepting a 50 per cent. ratio in relation to the British fleet than she has been in the past.

## *Dominion Quotas*

*United States.*

The proposals set forth in N.C.M. (35) 12 were never put formally before the American representatives. Informally, however, and in answer to American enquiries, the American representatives were informed of the reasons why it would seem equitable that the strength of foreign navies should, in future, be related to the strength of the United Kingdom navy only, and not the sum of the quotas for the several members of the British Commonwealth of Nations. In a similarly informal manner Mr. Norman Davis made it clear that in his opinion no American delegation would ever be able to accept such a proposal, which would be held to be an abandonment by the United States Government of the principle of parity with the British Commonwealth. Mr. Norman Davis held out no hope of accommodation on this point.

The matter was not mentioned in the discussions with any of the other foreign representatives.

## II. *Capital Ships*

*United States.*

*Displacement.* The United States representatives were not in a position to make any positive proposals, but unofficially the United States representatives indicated that the United States Government might eventually agree to a reduction in displacement from 35,000 tons to about 32,500 tons, and to a reduction in the size of guns from 16-inch to 14-inch calibre.

*Replacement and Numbers.* This subject was not discussed in any detail. It was clear that the United States Government do contemplate the replacement of a certain number of capital ships, though no indication was given as to the rate at which this replacement would take place. It was known that the United States Government would welcome a reduction in the number

---

[2] This draft report of June 11, 1934, is not printed.

of capital ships, but no encouragement was given to this idea from the British side.

*France.*

*Displacement.* The French Government would be prepared to agree to our proposal for a capital ship of about 25,000 tons with 12-inch guns. If, however, Italy insists on building the two 35,000-ton 15-inch gun ships, France must likewise build two 35,000-ton capital ships.

*Replacement and Numbers.* The French Government intend to continue the gradual replacement of their capital ships though no definite indication was given as to the rate of replacement or the numbers at which they will eventually aim, both these factors being dependent in the main on what is decided as regards Germany. It was, however, indicated quite unofficially that, if an agreement could be concluded with Italy on a ratio of 3:2 and if Germany remained bound by the Versailles Treaty limitations, France would like seven capital ships of 25,000 tons displacement. France, while considering that parity with Italy in capital-ship construction is inequitable, does not propose to denounce the Washington Treaty[3] unless construction by Germany renders this inevitable.

*Italy.*

The Italian Government insist, despite all arguments to the contrary, on the construction of the two proposed 35,000-ton capital ships. After their construction Italy will be prepared to agree to a reduction in the size of capital ships to any size acceptable to the other naval Powers. Italy desires to maintain the Washington Naval Treaty.

### III. *Cruisers*

*United States.*

*Displacement.* Officially, the United States representatives showed no disposition to accept the British proposals that no further 8-inch gun cruisers should be constructed, that the number of 10,000-ton 6-inch gun cruisers should be numerically limited and that the maximum displacement of all other 6-inch gun cruisers should be 7,000 tons. An agreement on this question of size must, they said, depend on a previous agreement on total tonnage allowances. Unofficially, however, it was indicated by the naval representatives that the Navy Department might not prove irrevocably opposed to adopting these British qualitative proposals, but time must be given for their due consideration in Washington.

*Total Tonnage.* The United States representatives expressed surprise at the increase in total tonnage which would be involved under the British proposals and declared that their instructions were, on the contrary, to press for a 20 per cent. reduction all round in naval strength, or, failing that, for the continuation of the tonnage levels contained in the Washington and London Naval Treaties. They expressed some sympathy with the political difficulties

[3] i.e. the Treaty for the Limitation of Naval Armament of February 6, 1922; cf. No. 1, note 11.

which had obliged Great Britain to contemplate an increase in cruiser tonnage, but declared that their instructions precluded their entering into discussions on the basis of the proposed increases.

*France.*

*Displacement.* The French representatives stated that their Government would like to build two further 8-inch gun cruisers, bringing the total of French 8-inch gun cruisers up to nine, but they did not think that the French Government would necessarily make this a *sine qua non*. They thought that the French Government would probably agree not to build cruisers of greater displacement than 7,000 to 8,000 tons, provided that a numerical limitation of 10,000-ton cruisers, already in existence or projected, as proposed by Great Britain, were to be generally accepted.

*Total Tonnage.* It was indicated quite unofficially that, if an agreement could be concluded with Italy on the basis of a ratio of 3:2, and if Germany were to remain bound by the Versailles Treaty limitations, France would be prepared to accept a total for the combined category of cruisers and destroyers of 341,000 tons. (It will be seen that this tallies very closely with the figure of 342,500 tons allocated to France in the Admiralty table on page 11 of N.C.M. (35) 1.)[4]

*Italy.*

*Displacement.* The Italian representative considered that Italy would agree to no further construction of 8-inch gun cruisers, provided France similarly agreed. As regards the proposal to limit 10,000-ton cruisers numerically and to place a maximum limit of 7,000 tons on all other 6-inch gun cruisers, the Italian representative agreed that a maximum displacement of 7,000 tons would probably be agreeable to Italy, but could not pledge his Government not to build a certain number of larger ships, seeing that the construction of some twenty-six new ships of 9,000 or 10,000 tons, with 6-inch guns, was in progress or contemplated.

*Total Tonnage.* The Italian representative was unable to give any indication as to Italy's quantitative requirements in the combined cruiser and destroyer category, beyond the fact that they were based on the principle of parity with France.

## IV. *Aircraft Carriers*

*United States.*

While it is understood that the United States Government remain satisfied with the displacement, tonnage allowances and maximum gun calibres provided for aircraft carriers in the Washington and London Naval Treaties, it is not thought that they would raise objection to the modifications proposed in N.C.M. (35) 12 (namely, a 22,000-ton limitation, with a 4·7-inch gun and total tonnage reduction from 135,000 tons to 110,000 tons), except to propose a 5·1-inch gun instead of a 4·7-inch.

[4] This memorandum of March 23, 1934, on preparations for the 1935 Naval Conference, compiled by the Admiralty and Foreign Office, is not printed.

*France and Italy.*

No objection was offered to the British proposals by either the French or the Italian representatives.

## V. *Destroyers*

*United States.*

*Displacement.* The United States representatives agreed that the present destroyer qualitative limits of 1,850 tons with 5·1-inch guns should be maintained.

*Total Tonnage.* The United States representatives gave no indication as to what the American requirements would be beyond their general proposal that all levels should be reduced by 20 per cent., or, alternatively, remain as at present.

*France and Italy.*
See under *Cruisers*.

## VI. *Submarines*

*United States.*

*Displacement.* The United States representatives agreed that, failing total abolition, the existing qualitative limitation of 2,000 tons standard displacement with 5·1-inch guns should be maintained.

*Total Tonnage.* No indication was given of the American *desiderata* beyond the general proposal for maintenance at existing levels failing reduction.

*France.*

*Displacement.* France was prepared to abide by the qualitative limits laid down by the London Naval Treaty (namely, 2,000 tons with a 5·1-inch gun).

*Total Tonnage.* The French representatives indicated, privately and unofficially, that provided continental fleets were stabilised at approximately their present levels, France would be able to reduce her submarine tonnage to 80,000 tons. She might contemplate further reductions below this level by scrapping submarines as they became over-age and only building sufficient new ones occasionally to keep the dockyards efficient in this type of construction, but, in that case, France would require compensation in some other category so as to preserve her total tonnage figure for all categories at 640,000 tons.

*Italy.*

*Displacement.* Italy is in favour of a reduction in the size of the submarine to 1,400 tons. If this could not be achieved, the retention of the London Naval Treaty limitations would be satisfactory to Italy.

*Total Tonnage.* Italy aimed at parity with other nations and would be quite satisfied with a parity figure of 52,700 tons. Italy recognises that France cannot reduce abruptly to this figure, and is quite willing to agree to proposals for a gradual French reduction in the submarine arm.

### VII. *Duration of the Treaty*

The United States, French and Italian representatives all appeared favourable to an idea that the period of validity of any treaty should, if possible, be ten years.

### VIII. *Place of Conference*

*United States.* The United States Government favour the Conference being held in London: they do not favour Washington.

*Japan.* The Japanese Government do not wish the Conference to be held in Tokyo. They are also against Washington or London, and would prefer Paris. It is believed that, failing Paris, they might eventually come round to London.

*France.* The French Government do not wish the Conference to be held in Paris and would be agreeable either to London or to the capital of some smaller European Power.

*Italy.* The Italian Government wish that the Conference should be held at some place in Europe and would have no objection to London.

### IX. *Time of Conference*

*The United States Government* would prefer that the Conference should not take place before June 1935, when Congress is normally due to rise.

*Japan* would prefer that the Conference should not start before April 1935, when the Diet is due to rise.

*France and Italy* would be prepared to agree to the British proposal that the Conference should take place as early as possible in 1935, preferably in January.

### X. *Powers to be Invited to the Conference*

*The United States, Japanese and Italian Governments* are all in favour of the Conference, in its initial stages, being confined to the Powers signatory of the Washington and London Treaties. Later the scope of the Conference could be extended as the occasion seems to demand or the Five-Power Conference could be regarded as a preliminary to the summoning of a general Naval Conference. The French representatives indicated that their Government would probably not be opposed to this procedure, but would prefer that the first Conference should be called merely a 'preliminary meeting' or 'causerie' to prepare the way for the general Naval Conference provided for in the British draft for a General Disarmament Convention. The French representatives felt that this nomenclature was desirable in order to soothe the susceptibilities of the other naval Powers.

It was generally agreed that this procedure would not obviate the holding, at some opportune moment before this 'preliminary Five-Power meeting', of bilateral talks with representatives of Powers other than the London Naval Treaty Powers (*e.g.*, Germany).

## XI. *General Conclusions*

*United States.* The conversations with the United States representatives were unsatisfactory because they arrived with instructions which precluded their opening any serious discussions on the basis of an increase in British cruiser strength. Opportunity was, however, taken to give the United States representatives a detailed account of the reasons for this proposed increase and it is to be anticipated that a careful examination of the British *desiderata*, both as regards quantitative and qualitative limitations, will have taken place in Washington since the United States representatives returned to their country. It now remains to be seen whether, as a result of this examination, Mr. Norman Davis will return to this country with instructions which will permit of the Anglo-American conversations being renewed on a more favourable basis.

*France.* The representatives of the Ministry of Marine proved unexpectedly conciliatory and helpful. The exchange of views showed that there are likely to be no serious divergences between the French and ourselves on qualitative questions. As regards total tonnages, the French representatives were able to indicate privately and unofficially that, on certain conditions, France would be agreeable to accept tonnage levels in the various categories which (with the exception of submarines) would not differ greatly from the tonnage figures contemplated for France in N.C.M. (35) 1. It is true that one of the French conditions (a satisfactory agreement with Italy) is difficult of realisation, and the other (that Germany should agree to remain bound by Versailles limits) is impossible of realisation. At all events, we now have a solid basis for further discussions with France, and, if Germany can be induced to be content, for the period of the next treaty, with figures in the various categories not greatly in excess of her Versailles figures, it should not prove impossible to reach a satisfactory agreement with France in regard to the relative strengths of the British and French navies.

*Italy.* The conversations with the Italian representative were satisfactory except on two points: (1) the apparently inflexible decision of the Italians to build two 35,000-ton ships; and (2) the fact that the Italian Government have no suggestion to make for a solution of the Franco-Italian parity problem. The Italian attitude on the latter point has now become exceedingly unconciliatory, and the only hope of agreement on the parity question was that it should form part of a general *entente* between France and Italy and a general settlement of outstanding political questions. Our latest information is that the naval question will not be discussed at Rome in October.[5]

*Japan.* Conversations with Mr. Matsudaira have so far been confined to matters of procedure. The Japanese Government are very insistent that political questions should not be considered in connexion with the naval negotiations. No objection has so far been raised in any quarter to this limitation. By 'political questions' it is understood that the Japanese Government mean, in particular, those questions relating to China which are dealt with in the Nine-Power Treaty.[6]

[5] M. Barthou, French Minister for Foreign Affairs, was expected to visit Italy in October 1934.      [6] Cf. No. 15, note 4.

*Sir R. Lindsay (Washington) to Sir J. Simon (Received October 15)*
*No. 1074 [A 8117/1938/45]*

WASHINGTON, *October 4, 1934*

Sir,

I have the honour to report that it is announced that, when Mr. Norman Davis sails for England next week to attend the naval disarmament talks, he will be accompanied by Admiral Standley, the chief of naval operations. Although Rear-Admiral Leigh,[1] who accompanied Mr. Davis to London earlier in the year, has since retired, the fact that an officer of Admiral Standley's seniority has now been selected is taken in some quarters as a sure indication of the fact that the United States representatives will adhere firmly to the present ratios.

2. At a press conference yesterday Mr. Roosevelt emphasized the fact that the forthcoming conversations would not be of the nature of a formal conference and, for this reason, he is stated to have given Mr. Norman Davis a thoroughly free hand in the conduct of his negotiations.

I have, &c.,
R. C. LINDSAY

[1] Rear-Admiral R. H. Leigh was at that time Chairman of the General Board of the United States Navy.

## No. 26

*Sir J. Simon to Sir R. Clive (Tokyo)*
*No. 624 [F 6050/591/23]*

FOREIGN OFFICE, *October 8, 1934*

Sir,

I asked the Japanese Ambassador to see me to-day, observing that we had not met for some time and that I should like a general talk. We began by referring to the impending discussions with the Japanese delegation in preparation for the Naval Conference. Mr. Matsudaira said that Admiral Yamamoto would be arriving with full details of the Japanese case but that he himself would be head of the delegation. Without being unduly pressing, I got from the Ambassador a general indication of the Japanese view. He referred to an interview which Admiral Yamamoto had had with an American journalist on his way, which had represented the Japanese intention as being to announce forthwith the termination on their part of the Washington Treaty, after which they would discuss new arrangements. Mr. Matsudaira said that this was not the right way to put it. The intention was to put forward the Japanese programme, but only to proceed to give notice of termination in the last resort. As I understood it, this means that Japan's object will be, if possible, to get an agreed termination of the existing treaty and an agreement on new terms rather than brusquely to denounce the treaty. The Ambassador indicated plainly that Japan was not prepared to continue to accept the existing ratio. The Japanese argument was, he said, that even if the Japanese navy was equal in size to the American navy, it could not involve any aggression against the United States. For one thing, Japanese resources for war were so much smaller. Japan could not accept the argument that only a portion of the American fleet was in the Pacific and considered that as between Japan and the United States the whole American navy must be put in the scale. I said that however that might be, a similar argument could hardly be applied to the British navy. Mr. Matsudaira said that he entirely agreed and that Japan raised no objection to the British navy being of superior size. He added that Japan hoped to be able to make important proposals for reducing the size of ships and said that these qualitative limits were an application of the principle that offensive power should be reduced while defensive power should be maintained. For example, aircraft carriers, by being reduced in size, would be reduced in range and offensive power. (He did not, as I understood him, speak of proposing the abolition of aircraft carriers altogether, but he may have been speaking only by way of illustration.)

2. On the subject of procedure he expressed the hope that we could conduct conversations with the Japanese delegation by themselves. He had heard or read of a suggestion from America that when Mr. Norman Davis arrived triangular conversations might be instituted. I said that our intention was to exchange views with the Japanese delegation just as we had previously had conversations with the American delegation. No doubt Mr. Norman Davis would be keeping in touch with both the other parties. We were not contemplating a new procedure now that the Japanese delegation were arriving, though of course there might be occasions when it was convenient for all three to meet together.

3. I asked Mr. Matsudaira whether he had yet received any further instructions which he could communicate to me on this or cognate subjects. We had had a report from you that Mr. Hirota had more than once expressed his great desire to strengthen Anglo-Japanese friendship and I had wondered whether the Ambassador had any communication to make, especially as on one occasion Mr. Hirota, in connexion with the naval conversations, had observed that Japan had no aggressive designs and would be quite prepared to sign non-aggression pacts with England and America.[1] Any observations coming from the Japanese Foreign Minister which dealt with the maintenance and improvement of Anglo-Japanese relations would, of course, receive our closest attention and I had therefore wondered what this observation implied and whether Mr. Hirota's observation represented a considered suggestion. It was obvious, for example, that in any effort to promote Anglo-Japanese friendship and mutual confidence by a defined understanding there were British interests and responsibilities in the Far East that must be recognised and provided for.

4. Mr. Matsudaira said that in fact he had as yet no specific instructions

[1] Cf. No. 8, note 1.

to communicate to me but that a special messenger was on his way via Siberia from the Japanese Foreign Office who was bringing him instructions of an urgent nature. Moreover, Mr. Sugimura, who has recently been appointed Japanese Ambassador to Rome, had instructions to travel via London and was on his way for the purpose of seeing Mr. Matsudaira. He would, however, arrive somewhat later than the special messenger. Mr. Matsudaira would communicate with me as soon as he received any further instructions and he expected this to be in a very few days' time.

5. I told the Ambassador that of course it was impossible to form any view as to the expediency or possibility of any proposal until it was more fully defined. For example, we should have to feel secure as to the position of China, not only because we had ourselves great interests in that country but because respect for the integrity of China was provided for in the Nine-Power Treaty,[2] by which Japan, the United States and ourselves were all bound. Mr. Matsudaira expressed the personal opinion that, putting aside the question of Manchukuo as being a *fait accompli*, assurances on the subject of China inside the Great Wall might reasonably be expected to form part of any new understanding with Japan designed to strengthen Anglo-Japanese relations.

6. This part of the conversation was couched in somewhat general terms, but the result of it was that I conveyed clearly to Mr. Matsudaira that we wanted to know whether there was anything behind Mr. Hirota's observation, and if there was what sort of assurances the Japanese Foreign Minister had in mind, since guarantees on other matters such as the one which I had mentioned would be necessarily involved. We throughout spoke of Mr. Hirota's idea as applying to the United States as well as to this country, and no reference was made to the reported rejection of the suggestion by the American press. On leaving, Mr. Matsudaira repeated that he would ask to see me again as soon as he had anything further to say on this subject.

I am, &c.,
JOHN SIMON

[2] Cf. No. 15, note 4.

## No. 27

*Sir R. Lindsay (Washington) to Sir R. Vansittart (Received November 14)*[1]
[*F 6784/591/23*]

WASHINGTON, *October 12, 1934*

Dear Van:

Lord Lothian has been here and saw the President on October 10th. His conversation seems to me to be so interesting that I asked him to write down a note of it and I enclose it herewith.

Ever yours,
RONALD LINDSAY

[1] Date of filing in the Foreign Office. A minute by Mr. H. J. Seymour records, 'seen by the S. of S. Nov. 9'.

*Lord Lothian's note on his interview with President Roosevelt on October 10, 1934*

*October 11, 1934*

The President showed an active interest in the political situation in England and asked me a number of shrewd questions about personalities and parties. He expressed the view that the Labour Party did not want to have power for another five years. He also discussed economic questions rather vaguely and I detected some combativeness in his attitude to Great Britain about stabilisation and monetary questions. We then turned to the Pacific question. I told him that the British were in a difficult position because the situation had changed from that which existed at the time of the Washington Treaties in two vital respects. On the one hand whereas Japan had willingly accepted the Washington principles in 1922 she was unwilling to do so today and was definitely expansionist. On the other hand Great Britain had to face the fact of a resurgent militarist Germany. Both these Powers and possibly Mussolini had reverted to Power diplomacy. From every point of view it was essential that Great Britain should be able to exercise influence in Europe in the next few years and it was clearly impossible for her to denude the British Isles of her fleet with Europe in its present condition. In these circumstances the alternatives before her in the Far East were:

(*a*) to build a large addition to the Navy to be stationed at Singapore;
(*b*) to have a definite understanding with the United States, or,
(*c*) to come to terms with Japan as she had done in 1904 [? 1902] when the German naval menace had begun.

Great Britain would naturally want to abide by the Washington principles but she had now to face the fact that she was in the front line in Europe and that she could not by herself be in the front line in the Far East also.

The President replied that anything in the nature of a definite commitment on the part of the United States was impossible. He added that, even if an individual President like himself entered into an informal understanding which might be effective during his tenure of power, no one could guarantee that his successor would take the same view. The cooperation between the United States and Great Britain would have to rest on the fundamental identity of their interests and ideals.

I said that I fully understood the necessity of that position but that he would understand how difficult a position it created for Great Britain, which might be confronted with a quarrel with Japan without a certain friend in the Pacific, and without the armament to make good their position. The President replied that in no circumstances would he agree to Japanese parity; that if Japan insisted on parity and denounced the Treaties he would ask Congress for 500 million dollars for naval purposes, and he added that he would have no difficulty in getting it. He said that Norman Davis had instructions not to use threats but to make this clear if necessary to the

British Government in London. The President spent some time in setting forth his view of Japanese policy. He had no illusions about it. They were pursuing a very long distance programme of imperialist expansion in Asia and would use with vigour but discretion the ordinary tactics of power diplomacy. He agreed with me that the immediate object of their diplomacy was to attain such a strategic position in the Pacific, either by means of parity or by means of new bases in the islands or China, or both, as to make it impossible for the United States or Great Britain to interfere with their Asiatic designs. He said that much the best way of dealing with the situation would be for Great Britain and the United States to take firmly the same line. If this were so the Japanese would face the facts and agreement might be possible, possibly under a formula which was based on 'security' rather than ratios. I pointed out the difficulty of Great Britain taking an initiative in circumstances in which she might be left by herself. He repeated that the United States would in no circumstances agree to parity, and if necessary would build. He went on to say that he understood the British position but that he did not believe that Great Britain or the Dominions could face the possibility of Japan having a larger Navy than their own and that if Japan forced the building contest they would have to follow suit. He evidently did not think that in practice it would be possible for Great Britain to come to terms with Japan in her present temper.

I asked the President whether it was the intention of the United States to abandon the naval bases in the Philippines. He said not for ten years but that at the end of ten years it was possible and even probable. So far as the relations between the United States and Great Britain were concerned he did not see why each side should not build the types of ships which suited themselves in friendly consultation. The essence of Anglo-American cooperation was agreement on political objectives rather than on technical questions. He ended the interview by saying emphatically that we ought to stand by the principle of sanctity of treaties, that the war of 1914 had been largely fought on that issue, and seemed to imply that in no circumstances would he agree to the recognition of Manchukuo.

The President's attitude was fundamentally not unlike the attitude which Great Britain takes to France.

I said in conclusion that I thought it essential that the United States and the British Empire should stand together in preventing the dictatorships which lie between the Rhine and Japan from breaking out or establishing bases in the rest of the world, which was still democratic and non-militarist. The danger lay on the 'front', Canada, Hawaii, Philippines, Singapore, and that there the United States must be in the front line as we were elsewhere. The real question was whether the democracies would wake up to the situation in time. The President did not demur to this view though he expressed no consent.

L.[1]

[1] There is a brief reference to Lord Lothian's visit in Sir James Butler, *Lord Lothian* (London, 1960), p. 200.

## No. 28

### Suggestions as to British Attitude in the Forthcoming Anglo-Japanese Naval Discussions[1]

### N.C.M. (35) 19

The Japanese representatives at the forthcoming naval discussions will be Mr. Matsudaira and Rear-Admiral Yamamoto. This officer, of whom little is known in this country, is expected to arrive in London on the 16th instant, and Anglo-Japanese conversations will open shortly after that date. Mr. Norman Davis is expected to arrive in London on the 16th or 17th instant, and it is presumably his intention to carry on simultaneously bilateral conversations both with the Japanese and ourselves. It has been agreed on all sides that these preliminary talks should be bilateral only, but there is nothing to prevent them [sic] being turned at a later stage into tripartite conversations between Great Britain, the United States and Japan should all parties consider this desirable—nothing, that is, provided this can be done without wounding the susceptibilities of France and Italy.

So much has been heard in the press recently about the 'Japanese plan' that our representatives would be justified in opening the proceedings by asking the Japanese representatives whether, in fact, they have a new plan and are prepared to explain it. It is possible that the Japanese representatives may ask that they should first be placed on the same footing as the representatives of other naval Powers by being informed of the British tonnage proposals. Such a request, if made, should presumably be complied with, though it will in the circumstances suffice to give a brief and general outline of our *desiderata*.

Piecing together the numerous Japanese press statements and the declarations made from time to time by Japanese 'official spokesmen,' we may assume with some confidence that the plan to be unfolded by the Japanese representatives will be as follows:—

1. *Guiding Principle.* The Japanese will demand recognition of the principle that all countries have an equal right to armaments necessary for their defence. These should be limited so that, while providing the necessary security, they cannot be taken as a threat to any other Power.

With this end in view, Japan will propose an equal and comparatively small maximum strength which arranges that, whilst defensive requirements are maintained, offensive power is reduced.

2. *Qualitative Proposals.* Japan will suggest the total abolition of aircraft carriers, and also possibly of capital ships.

---

[1] This joint memorandum by the Foreign Office and Admiralty was undated. It appears to have been discussed, on October 16, by the Committee set up by the Cabinet on October 10, 1934 (Cabinet Conclusions 34 (34)). This Committee recommended to the Cabinet on October 17, *inter alia*, that the United Kingdom representatives should ascertain the Japanese proposals and have full discretion to discuss and negotiate on those proposals on the understanding that no final conclusions of major importance would be reached without further reference to the Cabinet. This recommendation was accepted by the Cabinet (Cabinet Conclusions 35 (34) of October 17).

If this meets with no acceptance, then it is likely that, in order to give effect to the principle referred to above, Japan will suggest that an equal total tonnage figure should be arrived at; this figure being a reduction on the present figures for ourselves and the United States. With the particular object of reducing offensive power, reduction should be greatest in the capital ship, aircraft carrier and 8-inch cruiser categories. Japan is likely to insist on parity with the United States in each of these three categories.

3. As stated in the foregoing paragraph, the Japanese proposal will be for a total tonnage figure less than the present figure for ourselves and the United States.

It may be, however, larger than the present figure for Japan, and in these circumstances Japan, whilst at first insisting on the right to build up to the new figure at once, is unlikely to press the point, and would probably finally agree to effect the increase over a number of years.

4. Failing any agreement with the other signatory Powers to terminate the Washington Treaty, the Japanese Government will themselves denounce the Washington Naval Treaty at the end of this year, and they wish to substitute an equitable new convention between the Powers concerned. The Japanese Government are, however, prepared to delay the notice of termination whilst an attempt is being made to secure an arrangement with the interested Powers whereby Japan would go through the formality of denouncing the Treaty during the present year, and all the Powers would thereafter co-operate in working for the conclusion of a new Treaty. Better still, they consider, would be a joint notice by all the Powers to terminate the Treaty as from the end of 1936.

While it is not clear from the above whether the Japanese Government would be prepared to agree that the existing naval ratio should continue as between the British Empire and Japan, we may hope that neither in principle nor in practice will Japan claim parity with the British Empire as she does with the United States. The proposal for the abolition of capital ships (which really means the reduction in their size to 10,000 tons displacement in future ships and which would be to the advantage of Japan) and the abolition of the aircraft carrier is unacceptable to us and will evidently not be put forward by the Japanese with much hope of success. It is also not clear whether, failing abolition of the capital ship and aircraft carrier categories, the Japanese Government will advocate the system of limitation by 'global' tonnage in two divisions instead of by categories, but we believe this to be the Japanese intention. Should proposals on the above lines be made it is suggested that the British representatives should fasten on the guiding principle mentioned under (1) and should state that it is our prin-ciple as well as theirs that the naval armaments of the different Powers should be so related as to increase defensive strength without constituting a menace to other Powers. So far as the British Empire and Japan are concerned this principle could, in our view, best be expressed by agreeing on equal power of defence in the Pacific. Would the Japanese Government be prepared to consider this principle? If the Japanese then propose that their naval strength *vis-à-vis* of the British Empire should be increased, it would be desirable to explain to them as fully as possible why we consider that the existing relationship is a fair one and is in accordance with the guiding principle expressed by the Japanese representatives.

As regards the Japanese claim to parity with the United States, it would seem desirable to suggest that this should be discussed in the first instance with Mr. Norman Davis, while pointing out that we have not the least reason to believe that the United States Government would be prepared to agree to anything of the kind. It would seem desirable to be as non-committal as possible in our first discussions with the Japanese in regard to their ratio with the United States, while at the same time giving the Japanese no encouragement to believe that they may be able to drive a wedge between the Americans and ourselves on this question. We have agreed to parity between the British Empire and the United States so that it will be little help to the negotiation of a new multilateral treaty even if we do discover that Japan is prepared to continue with us on the basis of the existing ratio.

We have reason to believe that the above proposal for immediate parity with the United States of America, which emanates from the Japanese Admiralty, is being put forward against the advice of the Japanese Foreign Office, and that, if it is rejected by the United States, the counter-proposal of the Japanese Foreign Office may be put forward. This provides that Japanese parity with the United States should be achieved over a longer period (say 20 years). From the United States point of view such a proposal is little less objectionable than the first, because it would presumably mean that over a period of 20 years the United States would be asked gradually to reduce the level of their fleet to the Japanese level. As the second proposal, like the first, would presumably be rejected, it is for consideration whether, after the first has been rejected, it would not be desirable to put forward a British compromise proposal, after the necessary consultation with the United States representatives. This matter has been discussed between the Admiralty and the Foreign Office, and the following suggestions for a counter-proposal are now put forward:—

The proposal would take account of the fact that the presentation of the relative strengths of navies contained in the Washington and London Naval Treaties is unacceptable to Japan as appearing to confer some kind of superiority of status upon the Powers with the larger navies. The Japanese representatives might be informed that, while we do not agree that this inference can be drawn from existing treaties, we would be prepared to modify their form so as to take account of Japanese susceptibilities and to conclude a treaty providing for the qualitative limitation of naval armaments in which would be inserted a clause emphasising the equality of national status, which might run as follows:—

The principle of equality of national status between all the Powers signatories of the present treaty is mutually and unreservedly recognised.

58

As regards naval strengths, it is a guiding principle that they should be based on the minimum limits required for the national security of the respective Powers. The voluntary acceptance by a particular contracting party of a specific quota of naval construction over a period of years is to be regarded simply as the expression of that country's naval needs of the moment and not as any derogation of the foregoing principle of equality of national status between the parties.

Having laid down the foregoing principles, we might then enquire whether the Japanese difficulties would not be largely met if, instead of attempting to regulate future naval construction quantitatively by means of a multilateral treaty, we could substitute a series of voluntary declarations by the various Powers as to what it was their intention to construct during a given period of years. These declarations would not be in any contractual form. The declarations would be simply a statement of present intentions and, while this would have to be concerted between the Powers concerned, any Power could at any time modify its declaration on giving notice to the others. From the Japanese point of view this system would have the merit of greater elasticity and greater appearance of equality and from our point of view it would offer a barrier—albeit a somewhat flimsy one—against the renewal of unrestricted naval competition.

The form of such a declaration, which is complicated in detail, requires further careful examination by the Foreign Office and the Admiralty.

While it is difficult to speak with any certainty before the Japanese representatives explain their proposals, it is possible to say that, judging from present indications, such a proposal might serve as a satisfactory basis of agreement between the Japanese and ourselves. It is recognised that this proposal would not in itself solve the American-Japanese difficulty since the Japanese Admiralty are apparently determined to have actual naval parity with the United States quite irrespective of any question of prestige.

Our attitude in regard to this Japanese claim to parity with the United States must, it is suggested, be to a great extent determined by the nature of the instructions which Mr. Norman Davis will bring with him when he returns from Washington. If the American attitude, after Mr. Norman Davis's return, opens the door to an ultimate Anglo-American agreement on the basis of N.C.M. (35) 12,[2] it will presumably be considered desirable that the British representatives should use their best endeavours to dissuade the Japanese Government from engaging on a race with the United States in naval armaments and to bring the two parties together.

If, however, the American attitude remains as unhelpful and as divorced from realities as was their attitude during last summer, then the position will be a very difficult one. Sooner or later, we should be faced by a direct question from Mr. Norman Davis whether, in this matter of the Japanese claim to parity with the United States, Great Britain will continue, as in the past, to use her best endeavours to dissuade Japan from proceeding with the claim

[2] Cf. No. 24, note 2.

and would only continue negotiations with Japan on the basis of the preservation of the existing Japanese ratio, not only to the British Empire but also to the United States. This is the crucial question we shall have to answer.

### SUMMARY OF CONCLUSIONS

(1) There is every reason to suppose that the new Japanese naval proposal will prove unacceptable to this country, and even more so to the United States. In order to gain time, however, it is suggested that, as a first step, the British representatives should enquire whether the principle underlying the Japanese proposals could not be applied so far as the British Empire is concerned by equal defensive strength in the Pacific.

(2) As regards the Japanese claim to parity with the United States, it is suggested that we should in the first instance decline to discuss this and invite the Japanese representatives to take the matter up with Mr. Norman Davis, while at the same time leaving them in no doubt as to its certain rejection and giving them no encouragement to try to drive a wedge on this matter between the Americans and ourselves.

(3) Assuming that the Japanese proposal will ultimately have to be rejected both by ourselves and the Americans, it is suggested that a British compromise should, at the appropriate moment, and after consultation with the Americans, be put forward to the Japanese representatives on the following basis:—

(a) A new multilateral treaty to be concluded maintaining the qualitative provisions in existing treaties, with such expansion of the qualitative definitions (e.g., zones of no construction), and such reductions in the sizes of ships and gun calibres as may prove possible. This treaty would also contain an article laying down the principle of equality of national status between all the signatory Powers;

(b) No provision as regards future naval construction would be inserted in the new treaty. On the other hand, each Power would make a voluntary declaration as to its intentions, which, while not constituting a contractual obligation, would not be departed from without previous notice to other signatories of the multilateral treaty. To serve any useful purpose such declarations, while appearing to be entirely voluntary, would require to have been concerted beforehand between the various signatories of the multilateral treaty.

(4) The crucial question we may be asked by the United States representatives is whether, in the matter of the Japanese claim to parity with the United States of America, Great Britain will continue as in the past to dissuade Japan from proceeding with the claim, and will only continue negotiations with Japan on the basis of the preservation of the existing Japanese ratio, not only to the British Empire but also to the United States. Our answer must be largely determined by the attitude that the United States representatives now take up towards the British proposals already

explained to them. The United States representatives can hardly expect us to fight their battles for them so long as they maintain the same unreasonable attitude towards the British proposals as they adopted last summer.

## No. 29

*Memorandum by the Chancellor of the Exchequer and the Secretary of State for Foreign Affairs on the Future of Anglo-Japanese Relations*[1]

*C.P. 223 (34) [F 6241/591/23]*

FOREIGN OFFICE, *October 16, 1934*

The Cabinet have been promised a paper on the above subject, with special reference to the suggestion that has been put forward of the possibility of negotiating and entering into a non-aggression pact with Japan. This memorandum, after recounting the recent history of the matter, sets out the main considerations which have to be weighed and borne in mind, and indicates the conditions which, it would seem, would have to be fulfilled if the objective of a good and firm understanding with Japan is to be attained by such means, without reactions in other directions so serious as to nullify its good effects.

2. Mr. Hirota, the Japanese Minister for Foreign Affairs, has on several occasions recently dropped the hint that the development of closer relations between Britain and Japan would be welcome. (See Sir Robert Clive's telegrams No. 172[2] of the 3rd July, No. 209[3] of the 30th August, and No. 232[4] of the 29th September.) This last telegram records our Ambassador's attempt to probe Mr. Hirota's meaning when he referred to the willingness of Japan 'to sign non-aggression pacts with England and America.' The enquiry did not produce a useful explanation, and Sir Robert Clive indicates that he thinks this is more likely to be obtained at the London end through Mr. Matsudaira. Discreet steps with this object are being taken (see conversation recorded in despatch to Tokyo, No. 624, of the 8th October).[5] We are still awaiting any further information which Mr. Matsudaira can give us after receiving his special instructions.

3. There can, of course, be no doubt as to the immense advantages which might flow from assured friendship with Japan, so long as the gain is not off-set by very material disadvantages elsewhere. The paramount consideration in this matter, to which everything else—home politics, economy, or desire for disarmament—must be subject, is the safety, first of this country, and then of the British Empire. At this moment, in the autumn of 1934, there is no immediate threat to our safety. But there is the universal feeling

[1] This memorandum was drafted in the Foreign Office in accordance with the Cabinet's agreement of September 25 (cf. No. 21, note 1) and following discussions between Sir J. Simon and Mr. Chamberlain after the receipt of the latter's draft memorandum of September 1 (see No. 14). It came before the Cabinet as C.P. 223 (34) at its meeting on October 24, when it was agreed that consideration of the question should be postponed until further progress had been made in the Anglo-Japanese naval discussions.

[2] Not printed: see No. 8, note 1.      [3] No. 10.      [4] No. 22.      [5] No. 26.

of apprehension about the future, and the near future, that such a threat may materialise, and that the quarter from which it will come is Germany. Whatever may be the outcome of the present régime in Germany, we need not anticipate that we should have to fight her single-handed, and although the results of any war between civilised peoples must necessarily result in appalling loss and suffering, we might reasonably hope to escape ultimate disaster if the hostilities were confined to European nations. But if we had to enter upon such a struggle with a hostile, instead of a friendly, Japan in the East; if we had to contemplate the division of our forces so as to protect our Far Eastern interests while prosecuting a war in Europe; then not only would India, Hong Kong and Australasia be in dire peril, but we ourselves would stand in far greater danger of destruction by a fully armed and organised Germany.

4. There is therefore everything to be said for pursuing such a policy and making such arrangements as will best secure ourselves from attack in the Far East by the Power whose hostility at a difficult time might undermine our whole position. We may anticipate that India, Australia and New Zealand, amongst others, would warmly approve such a course. Mr. Bennett,[6] in recent conversations with Ministers in London, has been expressing the view that Canada also greatly desires to see Anglo-Japanese relations on the best footing. If there was nothing to be set on the other side the gain would be enormous. As against the advantage we have to consider fully and carefully what the disadvantages and dangers may be and whether there is any way of overcoming them.

5. So far as external politics are concerned, the main topics of difficulty in connexion with any Anglo-Japanese non-aggression pact may be grouped under the heads of China, the United States and Russia. There is also to be considered the effect of such an arrangement upon the League of Nations and our attitude at Geneva. This paper, therefore, proposes to examine the above-named topics of difficulty and to enquire whether there are any conditions or guarantees which, if they were associated with the suggested non-aggression pact, would remove manifest objections. It may be said at once that, in relation to all these matters, a pact with Japan which amounted to or could be regarded as giving Japan *carte blanche* so long as she respected her promise not to attack any part of the British Commonwealth, is manifestly impossible. Those who favour the idea of seeking some special compact with Japan do not contemplate anything of the kind. Our obligations under the Nine-Power Treaty, our trading interests in China, our right to the Open Door and our obligations under the Covenant rule out from the start any notion of purchasing a promise from Japan that she will leave us alone at the price of giving her a free hand.

6. As for China, the Nine-Power Treaty (see Appendix)[7] bound the contracting Powers other than China 'to respect the sovereignty, the in-

[6] Mr. R. B. Bennett, Canadian Prime Minister and Minister for External Affairs since 1930, visited England from September 28 to October 12, 1934.

[7] Not printed: for this treaty of February 6, 1922, see No. 15, note 4.

dependence and the territorial and administrative integrity of China' (Article I), and under the Treaty the contracting Powers 'agree not to enter into any treaty, agreement, arrangement, or understanding, either with one another, or, individually or collectively, with any Power or Powers, which would infringe or impair the principles stated in Article I' (Article II). The story of Manchukuo shows how little Japan has observed these stipulations so far as regards the four Chinese provinces outside the Great Wall. That, however, is largely past history, and the important thing, both for China and for ourselves, is that Japanese aggression and penetration should not pass the Great Wall and invade or monopolise China proper. Mr. Matsudaira's reference to this subject in his conversation of the 8th October,[8] though expressing only a tentative and personal view, is not unhopeful. If, indeed, Japan were prepared to enter into a new and specific assurance which would guarantee the integrity of China proper, without prejudice to the position on either side as regards Manchukuo, this might provide in the eyes of China something of real value in a special Anglo-Japanese arrangement which otherwise it would be impossible to justify. While it would be difficult to frame the guarantee in such a way as not to amount to a recognition of Manchukuo and an abandonment of the line hitherto taken by the League of Nations in reference to it, an undertaking which definitely called a halt to Japanese penetration into China, contained in an instrument signed both by Japan and by ourselves (we leave out for the moment the question whether the United States could not also be a party) would be of the greatest practical value to China and to British trade with China, as well as making a material contribution to peace in the Far East. If, when Japan states the conditions which she would be prepared to see attached to the proposed pact, Japan declines terms which would safeguard the interests of China, then this would be fatal to the proposed pact. But if we could secure such conditions, the matter would wear an entirely different and much more hopeful aspect.

7. As regards the United States, there can of course be no doubt that Anglo-Japanese approaches, designed to lead to a bilateral agreement between ourselves and Japan, are calculated, unless most discreetly handled, to arouse suspicion and resentment to a high degree. We set out some of the considerations tending to lead to such a result, for the purpose of seeing how best they might be overcome.

America believes that some day she will have to fight Japan, and throughout the United States the conclusion of an Anglo-Japanese pact (unless accompanied by a simultaneous American-Japanese pact) would tend to be regarded as meaning that when the moment came, our influence and sympathy would be on the side of Japan. It is therefore exceedingly important that the proposal should be in a form which would serve America's interests as well as our own.

The urgency of the matter is bound up with the present state and prospects of the naval discussions. As the result of our preliminary talks with Mr. Norman Davis[9] we have agreed that we will not abate our opposition to any

[8] See No. 26.          [9] Cf. No. 24.

alteration to the ratio 5: 5: 3 without first communicating with the Americans. In return for this concession we have received nothing, for Mr. Davis, while declaring that he quite understood our reasons for wanting the programme which we disclosed to him, was at pains to reiterate that he would be misleading us if he allowed us to think for a moment that it would be accepted by the American Senate. No doubt the attitude which the United States would like best would be that we should make common cause with them in the naval discussions against Japan and meet Japan's refusal to accept the present fractional inferiority by declaring that, in that event, we shall make no agreement, but will join the United States in outbuilding her whatever she does. We shall not be able to gratify American feelings by making such a declaration, and it is therefore very desirable, in American interests as well as our own, to find some other way of curbing Japanese *intransigeance*.

There are strong indications that Japan would prefer to terminate the Washington Treaty if she cannot secure its amendment in her favour. It is a striking fact that both Mr. Hirota and Mr. Matsudaira within the last few days have asserted that Japan has no objection to the greater size of the British navy;[10] what she objects to is that the Japanese navy should be smaller than the American. Since we presumably cannot accept the American invitation to join her in meeting Japan's demands by threatening to lay down two keels for one, the prospect of agreement as regards the size of navies (as distinguished from agreement on qualitative matters) appears far from good.

Yet the prospect of unlimited building, both by Japan and by the United States, is very disturbing. Supposing, then, that the Japanese reply to our enquiry as to the implications of Mr. Hirota's suggestion of a non-aggression pact gave any encouragement to pursue the idea, and supposing that the imminent preliminary discussions on naval problems show that agreement is very unlikely, it might be possible at that stage to approach the United States with the suggestion that Japanese naval claims (which profess to be based on the fear of aggression) would be materially modified if a non-aggression pact could be entered into by Japan with *both* the United States *and* the British Empire—preferably in a single instrument. Such an instrument would have to contain the reaffirmation and, if possible, strengthening of the assurances of the Nine-Power Treaty as regards China proper, as well as the confirmation of the Four-Power Treaty to respect the rights of the respective parties in relation to their insular possessions in the Pacific (see also note to Appendix).[11] This latter treaty (see Appendix) which was negotiated at the same time as the Nine-Power Treaty, is liable to termination by twelve months' notice given by any party, and it would be necessary to stipulate that it should not be terminated during the period of the proposed pact. If the United States were prepared, as a means of reducing Japan's naval demands and as a contribution to peace in the Pacific, to contemplate a tripartite pact of this nature, the difficulties above pointed out would be

[10] Cf. Nos. 22 and 26.     [11] Not printed; for the Four-Power Pact, see No. 8, note 12.

largely removed. If, on the other hand, the United States were to refuse to contemplate such a pact, and, accepting the breakdown, were to insist instead on building a navy without restriction, with Japan following suit, she could take no reasonable exception to our pursuit of a bilateral agreement with Japan, the need for which would be more pressing than ever.

8. As regards Soviet Russia, anything which makes Japan feel more secure tends to encourage her in an aggressive attitude towards Russia. It may well be that Russia's admission to the League of Nations[12] will cause Japan to adopt a less aggressive policy—the settlement of the dispute about the Chinese Eastern Railway, which has occurred since Russia's entry,[13] may be an illustration of this. Japan's attitude in favour of a definite policy of Anglo-Japanese friendship is in part inspired by the desire to secure our benevolence in the event of Soviet-Japanese relations becoming extremely strained. On the other hand, the fact that the relation of Japan and Russia to the League of Nations has now been reversed, Russia coming in and Japan going out,[14] may mean, in the event of a Russo-Japanese war, an increased anxiety for ourselves as a member of the League. Therefore, the creation of especially friendly relations between ourselves and Japan would help to correct the balance and to maintain the neutral attitude which we should beyond question have to adopt. There is always the possibility, though it is only a possibility, that once specially friendly relations have been established with Japan, Japan might consider coming back to the League.

9. It may be objected that, whatever may be the advantages of securing a non-aggression pact between Japan, the British Commonwealth and the United States, Japan might, at a time of special opportunity, be tempted to disregard it—Japan's record in observing her treaty relations in regard to China is not a good one. But the contrast we have to make is between the risks of the position *without* any such specific assurance and the improved situation which would flow from and be backed by such an assurance. Moreover, it is not proposed to substitute mere political assurances for naval limitation in the sense that Japan, after once entering into the pact of non-aggression, would construct an unlimited navy. The idea rather is to use the negotiation of a non-aggression pact as a lever for reducing Japan's naval programme. The Japanese desire to increase their relative naval strength *vis-à-vis* of the United States is dictated mainly by their fear of strained relations developing between their two countries and leading ultimately to war. In the measure that political appeasement can be introduced, Japanese naval pretentions are likely to abate.

For the moment, however, we have to await Mr. Matsudaira's further communication as to any special instructions he may receive.

J. S[IMON].

N. C[HAMBERLAIN].

[12] The Soviet Union had been elected a member of the League of Nations on September 18, 1934; cf. Volume VII, Nos. 630–1.　　　　　　　　　　　　　　[13] Cf. No. 22.
[14] Japan's withdrawal from the League of Nations would become effective in March 1935; cf. Volume XI, No. 465.

# CHAPTER II

## Further discussion on possible bases of naval limitation and future policy

## October 19, 1934–March 30, 1935

### No. 30

*Sir R. Clive (Tokyo) to Sir J. Simon (Received October 19, 9.30 a.m.)*
*No. 255 Telegraphic [F 6221/591/23]*

TOKYO, *October 19, 1934, 3.15 p.m.*

My despatch No. 237.[1]

Two Japanese papers alleged yesterday that conclusion of a non-aggression pact between Great Britain and Japan as an outcome of naval conversations was not improbable.

Yomiuri understands that views have recently been secretly exchanged and that . . .[2] been negotiations have made progress and that Japanese Ambassador will shortly open negotiations with His Majesty's Government.

Jiji states that there must be definite political agreement based on principle of non-aggression and such an agreement between Great Britain and Japan is . . .[3] although it will be difficult to make a non-aggression pact with United States. As informed opinion in England is tending more towards resuscitation of Anglo-Japanese Alliance conclusion of a non-aggression pact would be significant step towards alliance.

Asahi, morning,[4] quotes Foreign Office spokesman as saying that Mr. Hirota considered there should be political diplomatic negotiations between Japan, England and America with a view to establishing between themselves principle of mutual abstention from war and bases upon this creation of a new machinery for world peace. Such an understanding would be in the interests of a new naval treaty but would also serve to preserve world peace should a new naval treaty not materialise.

[1] The reference was evidently to Tokyo telegram No. 237 of October 5, not here printed, in which Sir R. Clive summarized recent examples of Japanese hostility towards British interests and suggested somewhat ambiguously that the 'obvious advantages of an under-standing with Japan should apart from its effect on our international relations also be considered in relation to present Japanese attitude towards British interests generally'.

[2] The text was here uncertain. A printed text read: 'that preliminary negotiations.'

[3] The text was here uncertain. A printed text read: 'is likely.'

[4] It was suggested on the filed copy that the text here should read: 'this morning.'

66

## No. 31

*Sir R. Clive (Tokyo) to Sir J. Simon (Received October 20, 9.30 a.m.)*
*No. 258 Telegraphic [F 6258/591/23]*

TOKYO, *October 20, 1934, 12.35 p.m.*

My telegram No. 255.[1]

Press correspondents questioned the Foreign Office spokesman yesterday as to newspaper reports mentioned. The latter replied that report that Japan wants non-aggression pact originated in London whence it was cabled to America. He added that the Minister for Foreign Affairs is thinking only of concluding Naval Treaty and is doing nothing on the assumption that Naval Conference will fail.

[1] No. 30.

## No. 32

*Record by Mr. Craigie of a conversation with M. Cambon*
*[A 8666/1938/45]*

FOREIGN OFFICE, *October 23, 1934*

M. Cambon, Counsellor of the French Embassy, called to-day to ask whether I would supply him with any information in regard to the naval discussions as the French Ministry of Marine (he did not mention the Quai d'Orsay) were very anxious to keep in close touch with us on this matter. I replied that the obvious desire of M. Piétri and the Minister of Marine to co-operate helpfully in the naval discussions had made an excellent impression here last summer[1] and that it would certainly be our desire to keep the French Government as closely informed as possible.

I briefly outlined developments since our talk with the French representatives but stated that I could not give him details of the Japanese proposals which had just been communicated to us in outline,[2] since it had been decided that it would be for Japan to communicate information on this point to other signatories of the Washington Treaty. I said, however, that the Japanese proposals, so far as they had been disclosed, did not appear

[1] Cf. Volume VI, No. 489, note 2, and No. 490.

[2] A brief press announcement, which appeared in *The Times* on October 24, stated that the first meeting between the Japanese and United Kingdom representatives was held at 10 Downing Street on October 23 and that a general exchange of views had taken place in reference to the future limitation of naval armaments. The British representatives were Mr. Ramsay MacDonald, Sir John Simon, and Sir Bolton M. Eyres Monsell (First Lord of the Admiralty): Japan was represented by Mr. Matsudaira and Rear Admiral I. Yamamoto. British 'advisers' present were Admiral Sir Ernle Chatfield, Sir Warren Fisher (Permanent Secretary, Treasury), Vice-Admiral C. J. C. Little, and Mr. R. L. Craigie. Japanese 'advisers' were Mr. S. Kato (Counsellor of Japanese Embassy in London), Captain Iwashita, and Mr. Mizota (Interpreter). A further full meeting was held on October 26 at 10.30 a.m., and a meeting of technical experts in the afternoon. See No. 37 below for details of the Japanese proposals.

to me to differ much from the published versions made by Japanese spokesmen from time to time. M. Cambon said that, in that case, he would ask their Naval Attaché to get into touch at once with the Japanese and United States technical advisers. He thought that this might be the best channel of communication for purely technical matters but that as regards general questions of policy and procedure the sole channel of communication had better be to M. Cambon from myself. I agreed. I also confirmed the correctness of M. Cambon's assumption that we would let them know as soon as we thought it desirable that the French representatives should pay a further visit to London.

R. L. Craigie

## No. 33

### Note by Mr. Craigie
### [A 8451/1938/45]

FOREIGN OFFICE, October 24, 1934

As a matter of courtesy I informed Mr. Atherton by telephone yesterday evening that yesterday's conversation with the Japanese representatives[1] had not carried us very far; that the Japanese had given a general outline of their proposals and that most of the meeting had been occupied in addressing to them a number of questions to elucidate obscure points. I understood that the Japanese proposals would similarly be communicated to the American representatives at 10.30 this morning and this was confirmed by Mr. Atherton.

To-day Mr. Atherton rang me up to say that the conversations between the Americans and the Japanese this morning[2] had followed much the same line as that I had described to him yesterday, and that only a very general outline of the Japanese proposals had so far been communicated. Before leaving, Mr. Matsudaira had asked to be informed of the nature of any American proposals that may have been made to the British Government last summer. The Americans replied that no very definite American proposals had been made but that, in general, the American view was that limitation should continue to be effected on the basis of the tonnage levels provided for in the Washington and London Naval Treaties.

R. L. Craigie

[1] Cf. No. 32, note 2.
[2] An account of this meeting is printed in *F.R.U.S. 1934*, vol. i, pp. 314–15.


## No. 34

*Sir R. Lindsay (Washington) to Sir J. Simon (Received October 26, 8.30 a.m.)*
*No. 299 Telegraphic [A 8434/1938/45]*

WASHINGTON, October 25, 1934[1]

Naval discussions are given front page prominence throughout press here.

[1] The time of despatch is not recorded.

2. 'New York Times' states that change which Japan is understood to be proposing is known to be unacceptable to United States; but that it seems now doubtful whether Great Britain will, as previously presumed, resist all Japanese proposals. It adds that Mr. Ramsay MacDonald is understood to desire to do something to satisfy Japanese demand, and that while it is to be doubted whether Cabinet and the British delegates to Conference share Mr. Ramsay MacDonald's attitude, your own policy is noticeably pro Japanese. Lack of sympathy shown by Great Britain to United States in January 1932 on Mr. Stimson's protest against Japanese action in China is cited as a parallel.[2] United States, 'New York Times' suggests, are quite likely to be persuaded into acceptance of Japanese proposals as France was at Geneva in connexion with concessions to Germany. Japan is stated to have refused offer of personal mediation by Mr. Ramsay MacDonald.

3. 'New York Tribune' states 'a blunt and uncompromising assertion of Japan's naval demands from an official but undisclosed source[3] has aroused concern in State Department and navy circles'. No details, it says, have yet been received from London regarding United States–Japanese conversations; but Japanese position as set forth here is as follows:

(A) Japan can no longer accept the ratio system and inferiority to the United States and Great Britain.

(B) Japan demands equality based on an equal maximum limitation for each fleet within which global arrangement each nation could build types of ships to meet its needs and desires.

(C) Japan urges within the scope of equality a limitation involving drastic reductions upon offensive weapons, namely battleships and aircraft carriers. Their size and gun calibre as well as numbers would be reduced.

(D) The status quo in fortifications must be maintained. Article adds that Japan suggests as alternative that battleships and airplane carriers should be entirely abolished, leaving only defensive weapons among which they place submarines first. Above attitude is regarded as intolerably uncompromising even though agreement on parity would not necessarily mean building by Japan up to limits allowed. Article concludes that, if this is Japanese position, it is hopelessly at odds with that of United States. Limitation of armaments by global tonnage might be reached according to some officials here, but it would give rise to constant uncertainties and probably be opposed by Great Britain. In insisting on parity, Japan, it is argued, is demanding something that the United States could never concede.

4. Special London correspondent of the Universal Service says that Japan had previously stated her position to His Majesty's Government in similar terms. Conclusion reached is that with views so widely divergent, ultimate

[2] Cf. Volume IX, Nos. 53, 58, 61, 66.

[3] In Washington telegram No. 300 of even date (received October 26 at 9.30 a.m.) Sir R. Lindsay said the official source referred to in this paragraph was the Japanese Naval Attaché. In a minute of October 26 Mr. Craigie wrote: 'The Japanese N.A. at Washington —inspired no doubt by the militarist elements in Japan—is busily nailing Japan's colours to the mast for fear there may be compromise in London.'

agreement looks impossible. Prospect of successful outcome of Conference is similarly doubted throughout press. No optimistic view has been seen.

5. Hearst Press states that Mr. Ramsay MacDonald was asked by Japan to mediate but refused.

## No. 35

*Sir R. Clive (Tokyo) to Sir J. Simon (Received October 26, 12.15 p.m.)*
*No. 265 Telegraphic [A 8448/1938/45]*

TOKYO, *October 26, 1934, 7.5 p.m.*

Your telegram No. 174.[1]

Little comment at present but great prominence in the press to naval discussions. Nippon Yusen Kaisha Dempo telegram of October 24th . . .[2] that Prime Minister will probably come between conflicting American and Japanese views; that Great Britain appears ready to accept Japan's claim to parity provided that she agrees not to build up to it for a fixed period but that as regards the latter point there is some difference of opinion between yourself and the Prime Minister.[3]

London correspondent of Jiji reports that Great Britain appears to sympathize with alleged American proposal to divide vessels into long and short range categories which would adversely affect Japanese strength in long distance submarines.

[1] In this telegram of October 25, not printed, Sir R. Clive was asked to send 'a brief daily telegram summarizing general trend of press comment' on the naval discussions in London, with official reference to press messages from London. An identic telegram was sent to Sir R. Lindsay as Foreign Office telegram No. 257 to Washington.

[2] The text was here uncertain. It was suggested on the filed copy that it should read 'states that'.

[3] In a minute of October 26 Mr. Craigie wrote: 'I don't know how this absurd idea of a difference of opinion between the Prime Minister and the Secretary of State arose (see also Washington telegram No. 299 [No. 34]), but discreet steps will be taken to assure the press that they are barking up the wrong tree.'

## No. 36

*Note by Mr. Craigie on Points for discussion at Meeting with the United States Representatives on 29th October on the naval question*

[A 9052/1938/45]

Secret

FOREIGN OFFICE, *October 27, 1934*

(1) *Anglo-American position.*

In the Foreign Office and Admiralty joint memorandum number N.C.M. (35) 19[1] it was suggested at the bottom of p. 3 that our attitude in regard to

[1] No. 28.

the Japanese claim to parity with the United States should to a great extent be determined by the nature of the instructions which Mr. Norman Davis brings back with him from the United States.

It is therefore desirable to ask the United States representatives at an early stage of the proceedings whether they are now in a position to furnish more detailed observations on our proposals of last summer than has been possible hitherto. If the United States representatives respond, it is possible they may base their reply on the memorandum communicated to Mr. Atherton on July 26th last (Number N.C.M. (35) 16[2] in the file). This memorandum explains in as short a compass as I can put it the main issue between the United States and ourselves.

(2) *New Japanese Proposals.*

Presumably our respective views on these proposals will be exchanged at the meeting. The United States representatives may be expected to adopt an uncompromising attitude, to talk about breaking off the discussions and to maintain that only a firm refusal of these Japanese proposals made by the United Kingdom and United States jointly will bring the Japanese to their senses. We on the other hand will presumably say we believe the Japanese are not bluffing when they say they would rather denounce the Washington Treaty and resume freedom of action than continue under the present ratio system; that an abrupt break now will almost certainly lead to a race in naval armaments after 1936; and that a better course is to handle the Japanese representatives with patience and to see whether, without compromising the naval security of any Power, some method cannot be found of meeting the Japanese on the point of prestige.

You[3] will probably not be proposing at this coming meeting to make any reference to the idea of a political pact with Japan. The composition of the meeting is not suitable for a discussion of this essentially political point, and, from the point of view of avoiding publicity, it is important to be able to tell the press that the naval question only is under discussion at these meetings. For broaching to the Americans the idea of a political pact the most appropriate channel would seem to be Mr. Bingham and Mr. Norman Davis—or better still Mr. Norman Davis and Mr. Atherton. In view of the press rumours that are already circulating about Anglo-Japanese negotiations for a political understanding, the sooner something is said to the Americans on this subject the better.[4]

R. L. Craigie

[2] See No. 2.  [3] i.e. Sir J. Simon, to whom this note was addressed.

[4] A meeting of American and British representatives was held at 3.30 p.m. on October 29 (N.C. (U.S.A.) 5th Meeting). The British representatives were Mr. MacDonald, Sir Bolton Eyres Monsell, and Sir John Simon; Admiral Sir Ernle Chatfield, Sir Warren Fisher, and Vice-Admiral C. J. C. Little were also present. The U.S. representatives were Mr. N. Davis, Admiral W. H. Standley, Mr. H. R. Wilson, Mr. Atherton, and Commander Shuirmann of the U.S. Navy. An American report of this meeting is printed in *F.R.U.S. 1934*, vol. i, pp. 318–21: see also *ibid.*, pp. 317–18 and 323–4 for accounts of meetings between Japanese and American delegates on the morning of October 29 and on October 31.

## No. 37

*Report on the preliminary naval discussions which have taken place with the Japanese representatives*[1]

*N.C.M.* (*35*) *22*

October 27, 1934

At the opening of the proceedings the Japanese representatives read a document setting forth the principles on which their plan is based. The text of this document is as follows:—

'To possess the measure of armaments necessary for national safety is a right to which all nations are equally entitled. In considering the question of disarmament, therefore, due regard must be given to that right in order that the sense of national security of the various Powers might not be impaired; and any agreement for the limitation and reduction of armaments must be based on the fundamental principle of "non-aggression and non-menace".

To that end, we believe that the most appropriate method in the field of naval disarmament is for us, the leading naval Powers, to fix a common upper limit which may in no case be exceeded, but within which limit each Power would be left free to equip itself in the manner and to the extent which it deems necessary for its defensive needs.

It is desirable that this common upper limit should be fixed in the agreement as low as possible, and that offensive arms should be reduced to the minimum or abolished altogether in favour of essentially defensive arms so as to facilitate defence and to render attack difficult.'

At a later stage of the proceedings, the Japanese representatives indicated that the purpose of their formula might be briefly summarised as:

(1) to fix a common upper limit;
(2) to set up the principle of 'non-aggression and non-menace' by the abolition or reduction of offensive arms; and
(3) to leave to each country the right to build within that limit in the manner which it deems most fit.

In the course of the two full meetings and of the sub-committee meeting which have taken place it was established by a process of questioning that the practical application of the above formula is envisaged by the Japanese as follows:—

The most vital and essential point of the plan is the fixing of a common upper limit of total tonnage for all naval Powers, this limit to be determined by the Power which considers itself to be the most vulnerable and therefore to have need of the largest navy. In the Japanese view it is unlikely, if the principle of 'non-aggression and non-menace' is generally accepted, that the less vulnerable Powers would in fact build up to this common upper limit,

---

[1] Cf. No. 32, note 2. This report was circulated to the Cabinet on October 27 and re-issued 'in its finally approved form' as C.P. 238 (34) of October 30. The wording of the report on the naval discussions was unchanged in the Cabinet paper except for the amendments to the text of the 'General Conclusions' set out in note 2 below.

but they are to have the right to do so should they so desire. By way of example, it was made clear that Japan could not in advance limit her navy to a percentage of the total tonnage figure of the British navy. So strongly does Japan feel on this question that she will denounce the Washington Treaty if international agreement on this basis cannot be obtained.

The second vital point is the abolition of the aircraft carrier and, if possible, also of the capital ship; and a drastic reduction in numbers—even abolition—of the 8″ gun cruiser. These three types of vessels are considered to be essentially offensive. Should it be impossible to secure agreement for abolition, it is proposed that these three types of vessels should be drastically reduced in numbers and should be separated by categories as at present. Vessels which the Japanese plan classes as essentially defensive are: the 6″ gun cruiser, the destroyer and the submarine, and these should be merged into a single category with complete liberty for each Power to build as it chooses. Should it prove impossible to secure general agreement for the grouping of these classes in a single category, the Japanese Government would reluctantly agree to the retention of a separate category for submarines but would hope at least to retain a single category for 6″ gun cruisers and destroyers.

As regards sizes of ships and guns, the Japanese representatives gave certain tentative indications as to their attitude, but emphasised that this information was furnished subject to the general adoption of the proposed common upper limit and would no longer hold good if the idea of this common upper limit were to be rejected. The information thus given is to the following effect:—

*Capital Ships.* Failing abolition, 28,000 to 30,000 tons displacement with a 14″ gun.

*Aircraft carrier.* Failing abolition, 20,000 tons with a 6·1″ gun.

*Cruisers.* Would wish to retain a few 8″ gun cruisers if capital ships are abolished or if aircraft carriers are retained; otherwise would agree that this class of ship should be allowed to die out.

*6″ gun Cruisers.* Would agree to numerical limitation of large 6″ gun cruisers. Would put maximum displacement for all other 6″ gun cruisers at 5,000 tons.

*Destroyers and Submarines.* Would agree to maintain London Naval Treaty displacements and gun calibres, if separate categories for these two classes of vessels are retained. It was also ascertained that, if the capital ship and the aircraft carrier are to be retained, Japan would demand 120,000 tons of submarines (as compared with 52,700 tons under the London Naval Treaty).

In the course of the discussion the United Kingdom representatives drew attention to the difficulties inherent in the Japanese plan. They pointed out that the British Empire, with its huge areas to protect, its long lines of communication and its diverse responsibilities, was in an especially vulnerable position. The Japanese representatives had admitted that an equality in security or risk might require some inequality in tonnage yet the Japanese proposals apparently contemplated that a country with world-wide responsibilities would be placed at this common upper limit, whilst other countries, with less wide responsibilities, might build up to the same limit. State A, with her world-wide responsibilities, would have her maximum naval strength fixed at the common upper limit, while State B with admittedly less responsibilities would have latitude of movement to build up, if she thought fit, to the same limit. If State B in fact used her power to build up to the limit, State A, which was debarred from exceeding the limit, could not be indifferent to the action of State B. The Japanese plan, by fixing the limit in the case of State A, fettered the liberty of action of that State while giving liberty of action, within the limit, to State B and other States which may become aggressive to A. In other words, if the British Empire, with world-wide responsibilities, agreed to be fixed at the common upper limit while other States were free to build up their strength to that limit, the safety of the British Empire against attack will no longer exist. The naval needs of any particular Power were both absolute and relative so that the size and composition of one navy must necessarily influence those of another. In the circumstances the United Kingdom representatives enquired whether, once agreement had been reached on general principles, the Japanese plan contemplated that programmes of future naval construction should be exchanged between the various Powers and, if possible, agreed in advance.

The grounds on which the retention of the capital ship has been considered, in relation to the British strategical position, to be an essentially defensive weapon were fully explained to the Japanese representatives, and it was pointed out that the abolition of the capital ship, far from decreasing our vulnerability, would greatly increase it.

The answer given by the Japanese representatives on the above points was to the following general effect:

While it was recognised by Japan that the security of national defence might depend to some degree upon the armed strengths of the various Powers as well as the size of territory and length of coasts and trade routes, it appeared to the Japanese representatives that the state of international relations and such domestic factors as natural resources and industries had an important bearing on the question of security. But these factors were so varied and complicated in the different countries that it would be impossible to convince the Powers of the propriety or advisability of employing such factors as the basis for determining the quantity of arms to be possessed by each. It was for this reason that Japan had finally developed the plan now embodied in her proposals, which contemplated that all naval Powers would have to make sacrifices but naturally the stronger naval Powers (the United Kingdom and the United States of America) would be expected to make larger sacrifices than the weaker naval Powers. In the view of the Japanese delegation the ratio of naval strength fixed by the Washington Treaty was injurious to the prestige of Japan, who objected to the theory that her naval requirements were less than those of other Powers.

Japan fully recognised the special position of the United Kingdom and the reasons, based on her worldwide responsibilities, for the United Kingdom's naval requirements. But Japan's position must be considered in relation to the position of the United States, a highly concentrated, well developed country, with almost inexhaustible resources in regard to raw materials and productive capacity. Japan, on the other hand, consisted of islands spread out over a large area and was dependent in the main for her raw materials on her imports from overseas. If the two countries were compared, the vulnerability of the United States of America was insignificant compared with the vulnerability of Japan.

It was true that the United Kingdom would have little power of movement at the common upper limit, but where that common upper limit was to be fixed was, of course, an entirely separate question and, so far as Japan was concerned, it might be fixed as high as the United Kingdom wished. Japan, however, definitely objected to the continuance of the position of inferiority fixed by the Washington Treaty. If the provisions relating to the abolition or substantial reduction of offensive weapons could be carried out the degree of vulnerability of particular nations would be greatly reduced. On this basis, even if all the more important naval Powers build up to the common upper limit, there should be no question of increasing the vulnerability of any particular Power.

On the question of discussion and agreement upon programmes, the Japanese representatives at one time expressed their belief that agreement on a building programme would in due course be reached in discussions with other interested nations, but at a later stage it was stated that it would be difficult to announce these limitations in advance in every case. Under the Japanese plan individual countries should settle their own tonnage limitations.

*General Conclusions.*[2]

The Japanese attach the utmost importance, as a matter of national prestige, to the fixing of a common upper limit, but they would see no

[2] The following amendments to the 'General Conclusions' appeared in C.P. 238 (34), see note 1 above: *1st para*: 'which entails the abolition of existing ratios' was added after 'common upper limit.' *2nd para*. was reworded to read: 'Even if this upper limit were agreed to, Japan is not prepared in advance voluntarily to limit her navy to a percentage of the total of any other navy, nor is she prepared to discuss a building programme in which her navy would remain inferior to that of another Power. On the other hand, Rear-Admiral Yamamoto mentioned that Japan would not necessarily build up to the upper limit, though she must retain the right to do so.' *4th para*. began: 'Japan also makes it a major point to secure...' The third sentence was reworded to read: 'She will adhere to the category system in these types if their abolition cannot be achieved, but stands for merging all 6" gun cruisers and destroyers into a single category.' The word 'impossible' was omitted from the fourth sentence.

The following paragraph, numbered as conclusion 5, was substituted for the concluding sentence: '5. Japan's proposals in regard to qualitative limitation appear to be close to our own, but it was only under some pressure that she was induced to discuss the technical questions so long as her demand for the *common upper limit* was unsatisfied. She showed a disposition not to press too strongly her wish for global tonnage limitation and accommodation seems possible on this matter.'

objection to the United Kingdom fixing this limit at a point higher than its present requirements, so as to give the British Empire some future latitude of movement.

Even if this upper limit were agreed to, Japan is not prepared in advance to limit her navy to a percentage of the total of any other navy, nor to discuss and agree to a building programme which would be a fraction of the common upper limit, though that would not be precluded.

It will be seen that this does not necessarily exclude the possibility of Japan's ultimately accepting the idea of a 'gentlemen's agreement' or 'voluntary declaration' in relation to future naval construction, once the prestige point has been disposed of to her satisfaction.

Japan is most anxious to secure the abolition of what is to her though not to other differently situated powers, offensive vessels, namely capital ships, aircraft carriers and 8″ gun cruisers, but is evidently not very hopeful that this will be possible. Should it prove impossible, Japan would insist strongly upon a reduction in the numbers of these vessels. She will adhere to the category system, if abolition of the so-called offensive vessels proves impossible, but would probably stand out strongly for the merging of 6″ gun cruisers and destroyers into a single category. In the submarine category Japan proposes the impossible figure of 120,000 tons if capital ships are retained. Subject to agreement upon the idea of a common upper limit and assuming the retention of the category system and an agreement on building programmes, the possibility of which has been hinted at (though two opposites have been taken up), Japan's proposals in regard to qualitative limitation appear to be very close to our own.

### No. 38

*Sir R. Clive (Tokyo) to Sir J. Simon (Received October 29, 9.30 a.m.)*
*No. 270 Telegraphic [A 8527/1938/45]*

TOKYO, *October 29, 1934, 12.50 p.m.*

Naval conversations.

Yamamoto quoted as pleased with technical discussion on Friday[1] and Japanese press correspondents report that British view Japanese proposals with sympathy.

Comment of the week end, reviewing past week is that British are conciliatory but Americans likely to provoke collision.

Press unanimously criticise Japanese Government's alleged policy of secrecy with regard to conversations in contrast to American propaganda which is described as strongly anti-Japanese.

[1] October 26; cf. No. 32, note 2.

# No. 39

*Memorandum by the Chief of the Naval Staff* [1]

*N.C.M.* (*35*) *23*

*October 30, 1934*

It now seems more than probable that we shall fail to induce the Japanese to recede from their main demand, i.e., the right to equality, the right which, if it were granted to Japan, would also have to be granted to the European Signatories of the Washington Treaty and which would inevitably be extended to Russia and Germany. It is therefore necessary to consider in advance what is to be the result if Japan denounces the Washington Treaty. Standing in our mental background is the spectre of an armament race. What is meant by an armament race? There are two ways of increasing your Naval strength over that of another country:—

(*a*) By building more ships.

(*b*) By building larger ships.

Of these two (*b*) is of far more serious consequence.

2. The armament races of the past have been almost entirely because of the building by one nation of a ship that would outclass that of her rival—the principle of going one better. It was this principle that led to the creation of the Dreadnought and then the Super-Dreadnought. It was this principle that during the War led to the building of 16-inch gun ships by the United States, and which, if it had not been for the Washington Treaty, would have led to the building of 18-inch gun ships. The greatest accomplishment of the Washington Treaty was not in limiting numbers or total tonnages but in stopping the principle of going one better.

3. If, therefore, we are to get no treaty and if some measure of competition will consequently be opened, the one thing the interests of this country require is that the competition shall not be in size of ships. If we can avoid this, as it surely can be avoided, then competition can only take place in numbers.

4. Competition in numbers is a far less serious thing. Competition in size of ships allows you to spring a surprise on another country as Italy has recently done to France, a surprise which is exceedingly difficult to meet because the designing of new guns and mountings takes a number of years and once a country has got a start by secret preparations her opponent cannot catch her up at once. Competition in numbers is very different. If your opponent lays down an extra ship or two you can reply at once by a similar action if you wish.

5. Let us take for example the case of the Japanese Battlefleet. If Japan wished to increase the numbers of her Battlefleet so as to force her way up towards equality it would not be very easy for her to do so. Her Battlefleet is already old and she has therefore the prospect of replacing it in front of her which will take her a good many years. She would, therefore, only increase

[1] This memorandum was circulated by direction of the First Lord of the Admiralty.

the numbers of her Battleships by building new ones and retaining the old ones, a step which would cause us little difficulty because we could act in exactly the same manner. The same applies to the question of Aircraft Carriers and large Cruisers. By fixing the maximum size of these vessels an armament race is unlikely to develop.

6. It is therefore, in my opinion, outstandingly necessary that should the Washington Treaty lapse we should induce the United States and Japan to agree to qualitative limitation. It is hardly an exaggeration to say that it would pay us to fix almost any size limit, within reason, so long as it was fixed.

7. Hitherto we have always been afraid that if the negotiations between the United States and Japan broke down American public opinion might lead that country to build very large ships. Mr. Norman Davis, however, gave a fairly clear indication yesterday[2] that that was not their present intention, that they did not want a race with us to ensue, and that they would be satisfied to increase parallel with us the numbers of their ships if Japan's action made it necessary. That was a very important admission and an early opportunity should I think be taken to get it confirmed and to emphasise the importance we attach to it.

8. Another important consideration is what will Japan do, when she denounces the Treaty, as regards the smaller classes of ships. We have had a fairly clear indication from Admiral Yamamoto that they will increase their numbers of destroyers and submarines. I do not think any action they take as regards destroyers need cause us any anxiety. There must be a limit to a race in numbers of destroyers and it is not really a serious problem. The question with regard to submarines is more serious. If Japan builds 120,000 tons of submarines will it have any effect on European nations? I do not see why it should. Undoubtedly the possession of such a powerful force of submarines would greatly increase her defence power in the North West Pacific and increase her dominance in that Area, but I do not feel that such ships would be able to do vital damage to the British Empire in view of the vast distance our main trade routes are from Japan. They would be a serious inconvenience but in view of modern methods of dealing with the submarine I do not think they would be more than that. In fact, for Japan to build a large submarine force may well be looked on as mainly a defensive move on her part, a very different thing from similar action by France, Russia or Germany.

9. I have set down these general strategical Naval views as they may be of assistance in deciding on our line of action in the next stages of discussion.

10. I will sum them up as follows:—

(1) The break up of the Washington Treaty is feared to result in an armament race.

(2) An armament race can be of two natures—

    (*a*) numbers of ships

    (*b*) sizes of ships.

[2] Cf. No. 36, note 3.

(3) Of the above (*b*) is of far more serious consequence than (*a*), which is of lesser consequence both as regards security, surprise, and finance.

(4) It is of outstanding importance to the British Empire to have the sizes of ships fixed as low as possible, but almost any limit is better than none.

(5) We should therefore see the Japanese again and emphasise to them that even should we be unable to get agreement on the question of equality we place the utmost importance on retaining qualitative agreements, which would be greatly to her own interest as well as that of the world.

(6) We should emphasise this point also to the United States.

E[RNLE] C[HATFIELD]

## No. 40

*Sir R. Clive (Tokyo) to Sir J. Simon (Received November 1, 12.30 p.m.)*
*No. 273 Telegraphic [A 8661/1938/45]*

*Confidential*                                    TOKYO, *November 1, 1934, 7.15 p.m.*

Chinese Naval Attaché told Naval Attaché that he regretted that China's friend, America, was being so unyielding to Japan over naval conversations.[1] French Naval Attaché was told by Senior Japanese Officer that he anticipated another May 15th incident i.e. another political assassination before the end of the year.[2]

We are convinced here that Japanese dare not and will not yield over ratio question. United States Ambassador with whom I discussed this today shares this view and tells me he has so informed Washington.[3] But I had the impression from what he said that United States Government, while realising this, consider that during the two years that must elapse before Japanese denunciation of naval treaties takes effect there will be time to reach agreement with Japanese.

At the same time he showed me in strict confidence telegram he sent (about September 17th)[4] embodying a letter from Mr. Yoshida[5]—see my

---

[1] After Mr. Craigie, Mr. Orde, and Sir V. Wellesley had expressed difficulty in understanding the Chinese Naval Attaché's remark, Sir J. Simon minuted: 'I doubt whether there is any misunderstanding. China wants to know *our* position so her representative professes to our Ambassador in Tokio regret at the *American* attitude. If we regret it too, China (1) has found out what she wants to know and (2) has a story to tell America behind our backs. J. S. 3/11.' A telegram, No. 15 Tour of November 5, was despatched at 6.50 p.m. to Sir A. Cadogan (H.M. Minister at Peking) asking him whether the Naval Attaché's remark 'represents the official view of the Chinese Government'.

[2] A marginal note by Mr. Craigie here reads: 'presumably if the Navy does not get what it wants! R.L.C.' For the attack on the Prime Minister, Mr. Inukai, and other outrages on May 15, 1932, see Volume X, Nos. 347–8, 357, 374.

[3] Cf. *F.R.U.S. 1934*, vol. i, pp. 322–3.

[4] Cf. *ibid.*, p. 307.

[5] Mr. S. Yoshida had held no official position since the end of his appointment as Japanese Ambassador at Rome, 1930–2. Cf. No. 67 below, paragraph 6.

telegram No. 251[6]—written he said with obvious concurrence of Minister for Foreign Affairs to the effect that Ambassador must not take too seriously anti-American press articles that Japan could not possibly afford to build up to American navy and leaving impression that if ratios were dropped in principle Japan would be very amenable. Absence of anti-American comment in press appears to be due to Government instructions.

My United States colleague understands that Yoshida when he reaches London will hold watching brief for Japanese Foreign Office with instructions to pour oil when waters get too troubled.

[6] In this telegram of October 12, not printed, Sir R. Clive reported that Mr. Yoshida was leaving for Europe via Siberia on October 14 and would visit London among other capitals.

## No. 41

*Draft statement*[1] *of the British position* vis-à-vis *the Japanese proposals*
*N.C.M.*(*35*) *25* [*A 8864/1938/45*]

FOREIGN OFFICE, *November 6, 1934*

(1) We have no intention of wounding Japanese feelings by insisting on the public expression of a fundamental and permanent ratio nor do we think that insistence on such a course would be helpful to any of the three Powers principally concerned.

(2) On the other hand, it is impossible for this country to accept in its present form the Japanese proposal for a common upper limit of total tonnage because this would involve the nation in constant uncertainty and unsettlement and would, in practice, open the way for a strong militarist propaganda here which it is vital to avoid. We cannot bind ourselves to an arrangement which, if implemented, deprives us of security.

(3) Consequently, we must concentrate on getting an agreement on building programmes, though we would be prepared to subscribe to a general declaration laying down the fundamental principle of equality of national status as between the parties to any future treaty, if this would facilitate agreement on future building programmes. An example of such a declaration is given in Annex I.

(4) If the Japanese Government are unwilling that an agreement in regard to future building programmes should be expressed in treaty form, we should be prepared to accept an arrangement whereby each party to the treaty would make a separate declaration of its intentions in the matter of naval construction over a specific period of years, the terms of such declarations being agreed between the parties beforehand. Each Power would be at liberty to modify the figures contained in its declaration on advance notice to this effect having been given to the other parties to the treaty. A form of draft declaration from which the element of 'ratio' is completely eliminated is contained in Annex II.

[1] This statement was circulated by direction of the Prime Minister.

(5) We should only be prepared to agree to the above measures of quantitative limitation if satisfactory provisions in regard to future qualitative limitation were to be included in a future international treaty.

(6) If the Japanese Government were to accept in principle a plan on the above lines, the next task would be to secure agreement on actual programmes. We are still of opinion that there is no justification for any Japanese claim to a change in relative naval strengths and we should therefore endeavour to persuade Japan to accept a building programme which would in practice leave the present relative positions unaffected.[2]

## ANNEX I TO No. 41

*Form of declaration of equality of national status (for use in any future naval treaty)*[3]
*(Based on the formula contained in N.C.M.(35)19)*[4]

(The principle of equality of national status between all the Powers signatories of the present treaty is mutually and unreservedly recognised. As regards naval strengths, it is a guiding principle that they should be based on the minimum limits required for the national security of the respective Powers, and these limits necessarily vary according to circumstances). The voluntary acceptance by a particular contracting party of a specific amount of naval construction over a period of years is to be regarded simply as the expression of that country's naval needs of the moment and not as any derogation of the (foregoing) principle of equality of national status between the parties.

## ANNEX II TO No. 41

*Form of draft declaration for notifying future building programmes*

The . . . Government, bearing in mind the provisions relating to equality of national status contained in article . . . of the Treaty signed this day, have the honour to make the following declaration:—

They do not anticipate that the needs of their national security will, during the periods (January 1st, 1937–December 31st, 1941, and January 1st, 1942–December 31st, 1946) impose upon them the construction or acquisition of naval tonnage beyond the figures set out, under the different categories of vessels of war, in the Table[5] attached hereto. Accordingly it is not their intention that their construction or acquisition of naval tonnage shall exceed the said figures during the periods stated, and they do not propose to lay down or acquire, in any one year, more than $\frac{2}{5}$ of the total tonnage in any category set out in the Table for the period covering the year in question.

---

[2] The Cabinet, at its meeting on November 7, took note that proposals on these lines would be submitted by the British representatives to the Japanese representatives at a meeting to be held at 4 p.m. that afternoon (Cabinet Conclusions No. 39 (34)).

[3] *Note in original*: 'If a shorter and less emphatic formula is preferred, the words in brackets could be omitted.'                                                                       [4] No. 28.

[5] *Note in original*: 'Table to be agreed between all parties making the Declaration.'

Should any change of circumstances so materially affect the needs of their national security as to necessitate a departure from the figures set out in the Table attached hereto, or the laying down or acquisition in any one year of more than $\frac{2}{5}$ of the total tonnage in any category set out for the period covering the year in question, the . . . Government will at once inform the other Parties to the Treaty signed this day, and will be willing to confer with them on the situation in such manner as may be deemed appropriate in the circumstances.

## No. 42

*Sir J. Simon to Sir R. Lindsay (Washington)*[1]
*No. 265 Telegraphic [F 6420/591/23]*

FOREIGN OFFICE, *November 7, 1934, 6.25 p.m.*

Your despatch No. 787. *Private.*[2]

Have there been any subsequent developments? Presumably pact was not proposed officially and was merely newspaper talk or Japanese ballon d'essai. Without leading Americans to think we attach importance to the matter I should be glad to know exact position.[3]

[1] This telegram resulted from a despatch of October 19 from the British Library of Information in New York reporting a statement in the *New York American*, based on 'the highest authority', that 'Japan has offered a non-aggression pact to Britain' and that a 'secret exchange of views between London and Tokio has been going on for several weeks'. It was thought in the Far Eastern Department that this and similar pronouncements would 'leave no doubt in the American mind that we have been engineering a renewal of the Anglo-Japanese alliance', and that it would be desirable to know whether Japan did actually offer a pact to the United States in the summer of 1934.

[2] Cf. enclosure in No. 14, paragraph 5, and note 8.

[3] Replying in telegram No. 323 of November 9, Sir R. Lindsay said that the Assistant Chief of the Division of Far Eastern Affairs had said in answer to an informal enquiry that Japan had made no proposal of a non-aggression pact to the United States Government during the present naval discussions.

## No. 43

*Sir R. Clive (Tokyo) to Sir J. Simon (Received November 7, 2.5 p.m.)*
*No. 286 Telegraphic [A 8845/1938/45]*

TOKYO, *November 7, 1934, 7.29 p.m.*

Naval conversations.

No comment.

Press reports interview of Yamamoto with United Press in which he scouted the idea of partial agreement and declared that Japan would not enter naval race in the event of failure of negotiations but would abrogate Washington Treaty before the end of the year regardless of developments at London.

## No. 44

*Sir R. Lindsay (Washington) to Sir J. Simon (Received November 9, 9.30 a.m.)*
*No. 319 Telegraphic [A 8866/1938/45]*

WASHINGTON, *November 8, 1934, 5.40 p.m.*

My telegram No. 317.[1]

Associated Press London correspondent telegraphs that although British delegation deny having made specific compromise proposals, he understands that proposals made to Japanese yesterday involve, firstly, recognition of Japan's right to equality of defensive armaments, but statement of that principle in terms milder than in original Japanese proposals; secondly, limitation of navies on maximum tonnage basis urged by Japan, but with addition of categories and number of ships permitted; thirdly, softening of Japanese demand for reduction or abolition of offensive ships.

New York Times correspondent telegraphs that after discussions yesterday deadlock is tighter than before.

Hearst Press continues to attack Norman Davis as inadequate representative of United States Government at discussions.

[1] This telegram of November 7, not printed, summarized recent press reports from London to the effect that the British Government were arranging for renewal of discussions with the Japanese representatives.

## No. 45

*Record by Mr. Craigie of a conversation with Mr. Davis[1]*
*[A 9052/1938/45]*

FOREIGN OFFICE, *November 8, 1934*

I called on Mr. Davis this morning to inform him of what had passed at the meeting with the Japanese yesterday afternoon.[2] Mr. Atherton and Mr. Wilson were also present. I said that Mr. Davis' letter to the Secretary of State expressing doubt as to the advisability of a programme arrangement which would have no contractual force[3] was only received a few minutes before the meeting, and that there had been no time therefore to consider it carefully. Nevertheless, I was able to assure Mr. Norman Davis that, when the idea was under discussion at the meeting, the Japanese were informed that programmes of construction, once agreed between the parties, should, in our view, be collected together and form if possible a single instrument of agreement. Mr. Norman Davis' point, therefore, had, I thought, been safeguarded.

Mr. Davis was sceptical as to the Japanese agreeing to maintain the existing ratio even in the form of an agreed programme, and reverted to the idea of the four other signatories of the Washington Treaty trying to

[1] For Mr. Davis's account of this conversation see *F.R.U.S. 1934*, vol. i, p. 326.
[2] Cf. No. 41, note 2.
[3] This letter has not been traced in Foreign Office archives and is not printed in *F.R.U.S.*

maintain the Treaty as between themselves. I pointed out some of the difficulties about this proposal and in particular:—

(1) That the Washington Treaty, once it was denounced by one Power, could not be prolonged but that a new treaty would have to be negotiated;

(2) That it would seem a risky proceeding to leave Japan her liberty of action even if we introduced into the treaty an elastic 'escalator' clause. The position would, I thought, become quite impossible if Japan did not even agree to be bound by the qualitative limitations of existing treaties;

(3) That there was a danger, under such an arrangement, of giving an impetus to the existing isolationist and nationalistic tendencies in Japan.

The American representatives had not realised that a completely new treaty would have to be negotiated and, when the point had been confirmed by reference to the Treaty, I think they were a little shaken as to the feasibility of this idea.

Before leaving I expressed my personal opinion that, with so many American naval officers collected in London, it was a pity that the technical discussions should remain entirely at a standstill. Mr. Norman Davis replied that if, as he expected, the Japanese proved completely uncompromising on quantitative questions, public opinion in the United States would find it difficult to understand the continuance of talks on qualitative questions between the Americans and the British on one hand, and the British and the Japanese on the other hand. For this reason if there were to be any technical conversations it was desirable that they should not be between the representatives themselves or higher officials, but no objection would be seen to Commander Schuirmann of the American delegation discussing such matters direct with the appropriate representatives of the British Admiralty. If such conversations took place, Mr. Norman Davis would, however, prefer not to be officially aware of their existence. He added that Admiral Standley, much as he would like to see a reduction in the size of the capital ship, did not at present see how this was to be brought about without sacrificing some of its essential characteristics. Admiral Standley would, however, only be too glad to consider any technical arguments on this point which the British Admiralty could put forward.

I said that in that case it seemed very important that such technical discussions should take place before the American representatives returned to Washington, and promised to let him know if the idea of direct private talks between Commander Schuirmann and representatives of the Admiralty was approved here.[4]

R. L. Craigie

[4] In a minute of November 9 Mr. Craigie asked 'whether the Secretary of State would see any objection to the proposal that Commander Schuirmann should start discussions with the representatives of the Admiralty on purely qualitative matters'. He said that on November 8 Mr. MacDonald was 'rather doubtful about discussions between naval repre-

sentatives only at this stage' and thought it better 'for me to undertake such conversations but he had not at that time been informed of Mr. Davis' views as given in this record'.

Mr. MacDonald agreed to the suggested procedure, on the 9th, subject to the approval of Sir J. Simon, who wrote: 'I agree—one reason why N[orman] D[avis] wants to preserve the Treaty even if Japan drops out is, I have no doubt, to try to avoid the need of fresh Senatorial approval.' Mr. Atherton and the Admiralty were informed on November 13 'that conversations with Comm$^r$ Schuirmann may commence'.

## No. 46

*Sir R. Lindsay (Washington) to Sir J. Simon*
*(Received November 10, 9.30 a.m.)*
*No. 324 Telegraphic [A 8907/1938/45]*

WASHINGTON, *November 9, 1934, 6.16 p.m.*

London correspondent New York Times telegraphs that British proposals have been flatly rejected by Yamamoto and received with marked disfavour in Tokyo. He says that when news of proposals spread flurry stirred up was worst since present unhappy naval discussions began. In all three Naval Delegations, but especially in American, Prime Minister's ideas left trail of confusion and suspicion behind them. Disclosures confirmed all rumours of past fortnight, which Norman Davis had been unwilling to believe, that Mr. MacDonald was flirting with Japanese. American's [*sic*] confidence in British has been shattered, perhaps beyond repair. It will be a long time before Americans are as sure as they were last week that British were standing with them for maintenance of Washington Treaty.

London correspondent New York Tribune telegraphs that if by any chance Japanese were to accept British proposals there is every indication that Americans would oppose them. Public are in a maze of uncertainty as to exact position of discussions and it seems fair to assume that there is a certain lack of frankness on British part. Such development has been feared in certain American circles who would have preferred round table conference to bilateral talks.

Associated Press message says that although Japanese are likely to reject British plan they were highly pleased that it had been tendered and were hoping British would yield still more to their demands.

Buell,[1] President, Foreign Policy Association, has issued statement urging American Government to abandon insistence on parity in sea power and to adopt policy based on principle of territorial defence. By this he means maintenance of fleet and naval bases adequate to defend only Atlantic and Pacific coasts including Caribbean area. He has also urged another five year extension of battleship holiday with reduction in tonnage or complete abolition of battleships: secondly agreement not to lay down any new category of vessel: thirdly agreement admitting principle of defensive equality for Japan but providing for approximate maintenance of present tonnages on ground that they are adequate for defence of existing territorial interests.

[1] Mr. R. L. Buell.

Agreement might, he suggests, include right of denunciation when any Power believes its defence needs have changed.

## No. 47

*Sir R. Clive (Tokyo) to Sir J. Simon (Received November 9, 2.30 p.m.)*
*No. 292 Telegraphic [A 8902/1938/45]*

TOKYO, *November 9, 1934, 8.7 p.m.*

Vice Minister for Foreign Affairs asked me to-day if I had news of naval conversations. I replied only what I read in the press. He said that you had suggested to Japanese Ambassador the principle of parity but that relative strength of the three principal navies should remain the same. Vice Minister for Foreign Affairs said that Japanese Government much appreciated the fact that you had proposed the principle. He believed, however, that it would be difficult for Ministry of Marine to accept the proposal in its present form by which the Japanese would be formally bound indefinitely to accept less [? than] parity. Japanese navy wished to look forward to a day when they would be entitled to real parity although this would not necessarily imply that they would build up to it. If you could modify your proposal in this sense, he added, it would be of the greatest help to the Japanese delegates.

## No. 48

*Record by Mr. Craigie of his interviews with M. Cambon and Signor Vitetti*[1]
*N.C.M. (35) 27*

FOREIGN OFFICE, *November 9, 1934*

I have been keeping M. Cambon, Counsellor of the French Embassy, and the Italian Chargé d'Affaires informed of all important developments in the naval discussions. I saw them both on the 31st ultimo, and again to-day. In outlining to them the suggestion now under consideration with the Japanese for an agreement on programmes, I impressed on them the absolute necessity for secrecy; it was bad enough to face the risk of leaks occurring in London, Washington and Tokyo without adding Paris and Rome. In each case I was assured that complete secrecy would be observed and that the efforts which were being made to keep the French and Italian Governments informed of developments were greatly appreciated.

It emerged from one of my talks with M. Cambon that the French Government had been approached by both the Americans and the Japanese in the matter of the denunciation of the Washington Treaty, the Japanese urging the French Government to join them in denouncing the Washington Treaty and the Americans insisting on the importance of the United States, the United Kingdom, France and Italy preserving the Washington Treaty,

[1] This record was circulated by direction of Sir J. Simon.

even if Japan were to retire from it. I suggested to M. Cambon that France's real interest lay, on the contrary, on [?in] lining up with the United Kingdom in this matter, for it was a common interest that there should be no serious estrangement between Japan and the Pacific Powers which might lead in turn to a *rapprochement* between Japan and Germany. For this purpose our best course was to do everything possible to ensure that counsels of moderation ultimately prevailed at Tokyo.

R. L. CRAIGIE

## No. 49

*Note by Mr. Craigie*

[*A 9052/1938/45*]

Secret                                                FOREIGN OFFICE, *November 9, 1934*

Just as a leak has occurred in regard to the 'separate programmes' idea,[1] so one may occur at any moment in regard to the idea of a political pact with Japan. There are already many rumours in press circles. It would be very much better that, before any serious leak occurs, we should have taken the Americans, however slightly, into our confidence over the political pact.

Perhaps the Secretary of State would consider informing Mr. Norman Davis (and preferably Mr. Atherton at the same time)[2] privately and confidentially that Mr. Hirota has, as Mr. Norman Davis will have seen in the press, been throwing out hints about a political pact or political pacts with the United Kingdom and the United States and that we have made enquiry through Mr. Matsudaira to ascertain exactly what Mr. Hirota has in mind.[3] Mr. Davis might be asked whether his Government have been approached on the subject by the Japanese Government.

This would not be saying much more to the Americans than we have been obliged to say in answer to press enquiries (when we admitted interest in Mr. Hirota's public references to this subject). But it would put us right with the Americans when the inevitable leak occurs at Tokyo and would avoid the reproach that we had been negotiating behind their backs.[4]

R. L. CRAIGIE

[1] Cf. No. 44.

[2] A marginal comment by Mr. Craigie at this point reads: 'in order to bring in the U.S. Embassy.'

[3] Cf. No. 26.

[4] Sir J. Simon appended the following undated minute: 'I did this in an interview (which Mr. N[orman] D[avis] insisted should exclude Mr. Craigie and Mr. Atherton!) on, I think, Nov. 13th. J.S.' No further account by Sir J. Simon of this meeting has been found in the Foreign Office archives. For Mr. Davis's account of the interview see *F.R.U.S. 1934*, vol. i, pp. 328 and 331.

## No. 50

*Sir R. Lindsay (Washington) to Sir J. Simon (Received November 11)*
*No. 325 Telegraphic [A 8915/1938/45]*

WASHINGTON, *November 10, 1934*[1]

According to Associated Press telegram it is authoritatively stated that Japanese in notifying their rejection of suggested compromise will invite new proposals going further toward meeting Japanese demands for equality.

United Press telegraphs that impression is rapidly gaining ground that side by side with naval negotiations there is now intense secret activity between British and Japanese on economic and political front. Foreign Office and Board of Trade are said to be considering a Japanese secret offer of concessions in regard to Manchukuo and Japan oil situation. It is also believed that Japanese textile competition is under consideration.[2]

Prime Minister's Guildhall speech[3] is fully reported but there has been no comment as yet.

[1] The time of despatch is not recorded.
[2] In a press statement dated November 12, published in *The Times* of November 13, p. 14, Mr. MacDonald denied there was any truth in the story that there was 'intense secret activity between the British and Japanese on the economic and political fronts', and said that the American and Japanese representatives had each been kept informed of British conversations with the other. Sir Arthur Willert, Press Officer in the Foreign Office, minuted on November 14: 'There is general agreement that the denial has served its purpose and has reassured American opinion without irritating the Japanese.'
[3] At the Lord Mayor's banquet on November 9; see *The Times*, November 10, p. 17.

## No. 51

*Sir R. Lindsay (Washington) to Sir J. Simon*
*(Received November 12, 10.15 a.m.)*

*Unnumbered Telegraphic [A 8926/1938/45]*

WASHINGTON, *November 12, 1934, 12.21 a.m.*

Associated Press London message reports outlook in naval discussions as pessimistic. British officials are said to have scouted yesterday's statements that Britain would put naval armaments on trading basis against commercial concessions.

London correspondent 'New York Times' telegraphs that by latest proposals His Majesty's Government have come into open as willing to concede Japan equality in principle and if necessary in order to conciliate her to scrap system of treaty limitation. Belief that Britain would stand by United States on ratios is shown to have been illusion. From now onwards there will be less talk in Washington of Anglo-American solidarity and more realistic approach to Far Eastern problem. Britain with her interests in Pacific Ocean in mind has chosen less glorious but more practical course. European situation has its effects on British Asiatic policy and British are simply asking Japanese to name their price. Nevertheless Norman Davis and his colleagues can find no anti-American bias behind these efforts to please Japan. They believe in complete sincerity of Britain's readiness to let United States build as many battleships as she likes. In British minds Atlantic will remain undefended boundary like Canada. American naval authorities in London are not too pessimistic about future of Anglo-Americans [*sic*] despite shock caused by British proposals: they feel that Japanese admirals might restore Anglo-American solidarity by being too insistent.

## No. 52

*Sir A. Cadogan (Nanking) to Sir J. Simon (Received November 12, 2.30 p.m.)*
*No. 61 Tour. Telegraphic: by wireless [A 8956/1938/45]*

NANKING, *November 12, 1934*

Your telegram No. 15 Tour.[1]
I have endeavoured to sound Chinese on this subject but have been unable to obtain from them any criticism of American attitude though they have commented on deadlock which appears to exist between America and Japan and express hope that His Majesty's Government might be able, as forecast in the press reports, to find a way round it.
Repeated to Peking.

[1] See No. 40, note 1.

## No. 53

*Sir J. Simon to Sir R. Lindsay (Washington)*
*No. 269 Telegraphic [A 9035/1938/45]*

*Immediate. Secret*      FOREIGN OFFICE, *November 13, 1934, 8 p.m.*

My immediately preceding telegram[1] is sent for your own information only.
Mr. Norman Davis was duly informed before we put forward the tentative suggestion outlined in paragraphs 5 and 6 and we have throughout kept in the closest touch with the United States representatives. Several American newspapers on the other hand (particularly the 'New York Times') have been at pains to give the opposite impression and we have so far been unable to ascertain the actual origin of these mischievous press reports from London. This becomes the more objectionable if, as reported by the 'Times' correspondent in Washington on November 11th,[2] President Roosevelt is basing his opinions not only on official reports but on despatches from American newspaper correspondents, some of whom have shown themselves the reverse of helpful or truthful.
It is obviously undesirable that you should appear to be going behind the

[1] i.e. a repetition of No. 54 below.      [2] See *The Times*, November 12, p. 14.

backs of the American representatives here but at the same time it would be unfortunate if the United States Government were really to gain the impression from American press reports that: (i) we had made our suggestion to the Japanese without the courtesy of first informing the United States representatives; (ii) that the suggestion involved any change in our views on the question of the relative defensive needs of the British and Japanese navies; or (iii) that we were seeking to make a deal with Japan in the matter of our respective naval strengths as a means of furthering some economic deal which we are alleged by the American press, quite falsely, to be negotiating with Japan.

It would help me to decide whether any further communication should be made on this subject to the United States Government if I could know whether you have any reason to think that there is in official quarters any misapprehension on the points mentioned above or other points connected with the naval negotiations.

## No. 54

*Sir J. Simon to Sir R. Clive (Tokyo)*

*No. 187 Telegraphic [A 9035/1938/45]*

*Immediate. Secret*     FOREIGN OFFICE, *November 13, 1934, 10 p.m.*

Your telegram No. 292.[1]

The position here is as follows.

2. The Japanese representatives have laid down as their fundamental principle:—

'To possess the measure of armaments necessary for national safety is a right to which all nations are equally entitled. In considering the question of disarmament, therefore, due regard must be given to that right in order that the sense of national security of the various Powers might not be impaired and any agreement for the limitation and reduction of armaments must be based on the fundamental principle of non-aggression and non-menace.'

3. To put this principle into effect they propose that a 'common upper limit' should be established representing the maximum 'global' tonnage which any Power may attain. They state that Japan will not necessarily build up to this limit, but she must have the right to do so if and when she wishes. The Japanese representatives also propose the abolition of what they term 'offensive' vessels, viz. capital ships, aircraft carriers and 8″ gun cruisers.

4. Confidentially, the Japanese admit freely that by the test of vulnerability which they regard as fundamental the British Empire has greater naval needs than Japan, but they do not admit the validity of the United States' claim to a larger navy than Japan.

5. We have informed the Japanese representatives that the suggestion of a 'common upper limit' is unacceptable and have given full reasons for our

---

[1] No. 47.

view, including in particular the fact that, quite apart from our responsibilities in Asia, the Pacific, and elsewhere in the world, we could not regard it as consistent with our defence requirements if the system of a common upper limit were applicable in the case of all the European navies equally with our own. We have, however, expressed sympathy with the Japanese desire to eliminate from any future treaty the principle of an inferior ratio which, in their opinion, carries with it the implication of inferiority of status. To meet this difficulty we have suggested that the new treaty should contain, in addition to provisions for qualitative limitation, a solemn and explicit declaration as to the equality of national status of all parties to the treaty, including the guiding principle that naval strengths should be based on the minimum limits required for the national security of the respective Powers. The fact that one party accepts for a certain period a programme of construction less than that of another party does not in any way derogate from the principle of equality of national status.

6. As regards future naval construction, we have inquired whether this could be regulated by unilateral declarations by each Power as to its intentions over a given period, such declarations necessarily being agreed between the parties before issue. At the same time we have made it clear that for the reasons given in paragraph 5 we see no justification for any change in the existing relative naval strengths of the British Commonwealth and Japan, so that the programmes contained in the declarations would not, in fact, for the period covered, produce any substantial modification in the existing situation. It is our hope that all these declarations would subsequently be collected together into a single agreed document.

7. The purpose of the above formula is to remove altogether from the proposed treaty the actual formulation of a ratio. It is true that if programmes are agreed which do not substantially modify the present situation, this carries with it the implication that Japan does not intend to increase her relative strength during the period of that programme. On the other hand there is nothing in the proposed arrangement which conflicts with the fundamental principle put forward by the Japanese representatives and quoted in paragraph 2 above.

8. We hope that the Japanese Government will give careful consideration to a suggestion which is made with the sincere desire to take account of the arguments in regard to prestige put forward by their representatives. We have pointed out to the Japanese representatives here how serious the consequences of no quantitative limitation of future naval construction might be, for it is not to be supposed that the United States would hesitate to spend yet more on their navy and British needs are not only absolute but relative.

9. It is of course most undesirable to conduct these negotiations both in London and in Tokio, or even to appear to be going behind the backs of the Japanese representatives here. I gather, however, from your telegram that the Vice-Minister for Foreign Affairs seems to be under some misapprehension as to the actual character of our suggestions and you are authorised, therefore,

if you think fit to correct his impressions by using the above material and to urge that the Japanese Government should give careful consideration to the possibility of a solution on these lines.

Reported to Washington, No. 268.

## No. 55

*Notes of a meeting of representatives of the Dominions, India, and the United Kingdom held on November 13, 1934, at 11 a.m.*[1]

*N.C.(D) 1st Meeting [A 9712/1938/45]*

Present: *United Kingdom*: The Right Hon. J. H. Thomas, Secretary of State for Dominion Affairs (in the Chair); The Right Hon. Sir John Simon; Admiral Sir Ernle Chatfield.

*Dominions and India*: The Hon. G. H. Ferguson (High Commissioner for the Dominion of Canada); The Right Hon. S. M. Bruce (High Commissioner for the Commonwealth of Australia); The Hon. Sir James Parr (High Commissioner for the Dominion of New Zealand); General the Right Hon. J. C. Smuts (Minister of Justice, Union of South Africa); Mr. H. T. Andrews (Union of South Africa); Mr. J. W. Dulanty (High Commissioner for the Irish Free State); Sir H. Wheeler (Member of the Council of India).[2]

MR. THOMAS opened the proceedings by explaining that the meeting was with the object of taking the representatives of the Dominions into their confidence with regard to the negotiations for the limitation of naval armaments that have been in progress in London. That this meeting had not taken place before was due to the difficulty of knowing how matters were shaping, but it was now possible to gauge the opinions of the various Powers concerned. Sir John Simon, he said, was present to give in greater detail what had occurred to-date.

SIR JOHN SIMON said that he would speak with great frankness. Considerable leakage had taken place both in Japan and in the United States of America as regards the proceedings, but His Majesty's Government wished to put before their partners in the British Commonwealth of Nations a confidential statement of the actual position. Japan, he said, had announced that she came to these preliminary negotiations with a plan. On being asked what her plan was, it appeared that it was contained in a very few words.

[1] This meeting was held at the Dominions Office. These notes were circulated to the United Kingdom representatives only and were not distributed to or revised by representatives of the Dominions or India.

[2] The following were also present: Sir E. Harding (Permanent Under-Secretary of State, Dominions Office); Sir H. F. Batterbee (Assistant Under-Secretary of State, Dominions Office); Mr. E. H. Marsh and Mr. E. B. Bowyer (Dominions Office); Mr. R. L. Craigie (Foreign Office); and, as joint secretaries, Commander A. W. Clarke (Assistant Secretary, Committee of Imperial Defence) and Mr. C. R. Price (Dominions Office).

She claimed that all nations had an equal right to possess armaments necessary for their security. Her method of applying this right presented matters of grave difficulty. She had proposed the principle that all the Powers concerned should accept a common upper limit beyond which no Power should build: in other words, she proposed that there should be a single limitation in total global tonnage for all Powers. Below that common upper limit, the extent to which each Power built was left to the discretion of the individual.

The Japanese Delegation had intimated that it was the British Commonwealth of Nations who was entitled to enjoy in practice the full common upper limit and that the level of this limit would, in practice, be based on the requirements of the British Commonwealth and, if desired, that common upper limit could be placed higher than the present figures of the British Empire. But the Japanese Delegation had emphasised that they must not be asked to limit themselves in advance to any particular fraction of the common upper limit. They further expressed a wish for agreement on the abolition or, at any rate, the strict limitation of offensive vessels. Capital ships, aircraft carriers and the bigger class of cruisers were termed 'offensive vessels'. Of these they would like to see the abolition of the two former classes and a strict limitation of the latter. The Japanese representatives had further intimated that, in the event of a non-acceptance of capital ship abolition, Japan would require 120,000 tons of submarines.

Sir John Simon, continuing, said that the United Kingdom representatives had replied to these proposals in the first instance by pointing out that the common upper limit by itself did not provide a satisfactory basis for a naval agreement which would ensure equal security for all parties. The very principle of equality in security made proportions in the size of navies necessary. It had further been explained to the Japanese Delegation that the needs of the British Commonwealth of Nations were not only absolute but relative. A certain number of cruisers, for example, was an absolute requirement in order that the trade routes should be adequately protected, but there was a relative requirement directly dependent upon the forces possessed by other Powers. An acceptance of a common upper limit made security for the British Empire very difficult. The British Empire would be bound by the limit beyond which she could not build, while the other Powers were not bound by any limit other than that which was binding on the British Empire. Consequently, they would be in a position to come up to this limit while the British strength was fixed.

The Japanese, in passing, had been told that Great Britain would be glad to see a reduction in the size of the capital ship. It was then explained to them that the British Empire had a European problem and that it must be clear to the Japanese that in any event only a part of the British Fleet could be put in the Far East. Yet, under the Japanese proposals, Japan would be able to build up to the same limit as the British.

(Mr. Thomas left the meeting at this point, in order to attend a Cabinet Committee).

Sir John Simon said that the Japanese proposals had also been put by Japan to the representatives of the United States of America. There had been no triangular talks between the parties, but each has told the other its views. The Japanese had said to the British representatives that they recognised the claim of Great Britain to a bigger fleet, but they did not recognise the similar claim by the United States of America. Japan argued that the latter had, in practice, the whole of her fleet at her disposal for employment in Far Eastern waters. The Panama Canal was available to provide the means of quick transit and the United States of America need not consider the problem of defending her Atlantic coasts. The Japanese had, in fact, intimated that they considered their claims to naval armaments equal to those of the United States of America. It was clear that if the claim to equality between the United States of America and the British Empire was accepted, and also a similar claim to parity between Japan and the United States of America was accepted, one arrived at the conclusion that Japan must have parity with the British Empire.

In the ensuing discussions it had been put to the Japanese Delegation that the position they had taken up appeared to be due to firstly, feelings of prestige and status, and secondly, a fear of the United States of America, and therefore it had been suggested that something might be done with regard to the first problem by constructing a treaty which threw no doubt on the equality of Japanese prestige and status.

As regards their fear of the United States of America, the Japanese had been told that the British representatives did not think they had any need to fear attack by America. However, if the Japanese objection was to a treaty which stated matters in terms such as 5: 5: 3, would it not be possible to frame a treaty in such a manner as not to expose the Japanese position to home criticism? Surely Japan did not want the disappearance of all agreement which would at once force her to face both American money and British determination. It had, therefore, been suggested that future agreement on limitations should be drawn up in the following form. Firstly, that there should be a declaration of equality of national status, and then that the parties should exchange and agree their proposals for future building over a stated number of years. These declarations of programmes would be unilateral and, naturally as a preliminary, the proposed building programmes would have to be discussed between the Powers.

Sir John Simon then quoted his idea of the form that this arrangement with regard to building programmes might take, as follows:—

'The . . . Government, bearing in mind the provisions relating to equality of national status contained in Article . . . of the Treaty, declare that their programme of building for . . . years will not exceed the figures shown in the table attached, nor do they propose to lay down or require in any one year more than two-fifths of the total tonnage in any category set out in the table, etc., etc.,'[3]

[3] Cf. No. 41, Annex II.

It had been made quite clear, however, to the Japanese Delegation that the British proposals were with the object of maintaining approximately the present proportions in fleets while acknowledging equality in status and that, of course, it would be quite unacceptable if, for example, the Japanese at once prepared a table of future construction which carried them immediately to equality.

Sir John Simon said that the Japanese Delegation had not replied to these suggestions yet and that the matter had been referred to the Japanese Government. It was his impression that Japan was in some doubts as to what to reply. It had been pointed out to the Japanese that the ideas put forward above were not in the form of a firm proposal. It was only that the British were very anxious to find a way to meet the deep feelings of the Japanese consistent with British needs. The common upper limit plan did not provide this and, consequently, the suggestions were in the hope that they might be helpful if the matter was dealt with in the form put forward.

MR. BRUCE asked what had been the reactions of the United States of America to these suggestions to meet the Japanese views.

SIR JOHN SIMON said that the American Delegation had not liked them much, but were not against their being put to the Japanese provided it was made clear that such an arrangement would not permit Japan to do exactly what she liked.

On another point, he said he had enquired with much interest as to the attitude of the Japanese towards the 'fortifications' clause in the Washington Treaty.[4] He pointed out, for example, that at present Japan was unable to erect new fortifications in her island possessions outside Japan itself within a certain radius of that country. It was possible of course, that Japan banked on the fact that when the Washington Treaty no longer held good, the British Empire and the United States of America would not exercise their rights to erect fortifications while Japan, of course, would be perfectly free to do so should she wish. In reply to his enquiry as to whether Japan attached importance to this clause in the Treaty, Mr. Matsudaira had intimated that Japan might be interested in considering the retention of some similar clause limiting fortifications in any new treaty arrived at. This was, however, only Mr. Matsudaira's personal expression of opinion and might not be that of his Government.

SIR JOHN SIMON then continued by referring to the qualitative side of the question. From some points of view qualitative limitation was at least as important as quantitative. A qualitative race involving new types exposed the British Empire to a prodigious burden. If there could be assurance that there would be no race in sizes of ships, the relief from that race would be almost as good as a relief in a race in numbers. The Japanese had taken a curious line in this matter. They had said they were in favour of qualitative limitations, but that such limitations must follow an agreement on a common upper limit; in fact, they had hinted that other parties must agree to the Japanese proposals if they wished Japan to agree to the qualitative proposals.

[4] i.e. Article XIX of the Treaty for Limitation of Naval Armament of February 6, 1922.

Sir Ernle Chatfield amplified this by saying that in his talks with the Japanese Admiral, the latter had said that if the present treaties went by the board, then Japan would not agree to any qualitative limitations as she would wish to build the types of ships best suited for her own defence. Such building would upset the present standard *vis-à-vis* America and the British Empire. It would be very similar to the line that Germany had already taken by building a class of ship which upset France.[5]

Sir John Simon said that finally the Japanese had stated that their instructions were to give notice of the termination of the Five Power Naval Treaty of Washington at the end of this year. If they gave such notice the Treaty would terminate at the end of 1936. This was very serious for the British Empire. France and Italy were both in the Washington Treaty, and account must be taken of the repercussions on the naval situation in Europe.

General Smuts wondered whether the Japanese were not attempting a bluff. He questioned whether they were seriously going to build against the British and the Americans.

Sir John Simon said that, as he read it, Japan did not consider that she was really going to lose much by having no agreement. Should things go badly for her, she would always be able to suggest a return to the treaty later on, because she would assume that such a treaty would always be on offer.

Sir Ernle Chatfield said that Admiral Yamamoto had given him to understand that the Japanese view was that they would be more secure with no treaty than they were at present under existing treaties.

General Smuts said that he viewed a breach at this stage with much concern, and that once a break in the Pacific arrangements had taken place it would never be possible to get back to the same level of agreement again.

Sir John Simon observed that a release from the treaty limitations did not expose Japan to any obvious dangers, and at the same time it made her the dominant Power in the Pacific.

Mr. Bruce observed that the ability of Japan to become dominant rested on the assumption that the British Empire and the United States of America would not be resolute in countering such action.

General Smuts said that if the Washington Treaty went, he could not see in the future the construction of another treaty which would be so pleasant for the British Empire. His feeling was that, rather than let Japan back out at this stage, it was wiser to make an arrangement which would save her face. The Japanese argument with regard to status was not sound, in his view. After all, Great Britain had not felt that its status was affected by accepting an inferior Army under the proposed disarmament treaty.

Sir John Simon remarked that this very point had been put to the Japanese by the Prime Minister.

[5] A reference presumably to the 10,000-ton *Deutschland* type of 'pocket battleship' being built by Germany which, while conforming to tonnage displacement limitations imposed by the Treaty of Versailles, 1919 (Art. 190), mounted six 11-inch guns as compared with the 8-inch guns permitted for vessels of war, other than capital ships, under the Washington Naval Treaty of 1922 (Art. XII). Cf. Volume VI, No. 489 (pp. 820–1) and No. 490.

GENERAL SMUTS, continuing, said that he preferred the course of saving Japan's face plus a non-fortifications clause (to which he attached great importance) and some system of agreement on practical limitations in building from time to time. In fact, he was in favour of the suggestions which had been put to the Japanese, and explained at this meeting by Sir John Simon, always provided that the British Empire kept company with the United States of America in this matter.

SIR JOHN SIMON said that Mr. Norman Davis of the American Delegation had taken a very cool view of the possibility of Japan dropping out of agreement. He had, in fact, suggested that if Japan would not come in it would yet be possible to arrange a Four-Power treaty.[6] This was quite satisfactory probably from the American point of view, but the British Empire did not want to stand in with the United States of America if by so doing she made a certain enemy of Japan.

GENERAL SMUTS observed that there were two policies in Japan—one the civil one and the other the naval one. It was very possible that the naval party would not remain in power and that then a change of attitude for the better might occur. It was possible that Japan was passing through a phase which would improve.

SIR ERNLE CHATFIELD suggested that the word 'prestige' used by the Japanese might be only a means of disguising her real objective.

MR. BRUCE said that the first point that arose was—what would be the general Dominion attitude towards the Japanese proposals that Sir John Simon had put before them? He thought that clearly, it must be the same as that of the United Kingdom, and speaking for Australia, he was sure that this was so. The common upper limit was quite unacceptable. It was most desirable to keep Japan in some arrangement with the other Powers and the best hope for this was in the line that had been taken of suggesting a means of saving her prestige and yet agreeing on building programmes which kept the Powers more or less in their present relative positions. It was a hard fact that the British Empire must build to keep her naval position within recognisable distance of the present position.

GENERAL SMUTS said that the British Empire's weakness lay in the size of her frontiers. He drew a parallel with the Roman Empire. There her concern was her land frontiers. With the British Empire she had a similar concern, although those were sea frontiers. Naval defence went to the roots of her Imperial defence system. If Japan was now out to establish a mastery in the East, and to this end intended to build nearer to the British strength, it became a very serious matter for the Empire. There was then a threat to the whole Imperial system. If the British Empire made concessions to Japan which went too far, then she would become a second rate Power and go the way that the Roman Empire had gone. Therefore, if Japan persists in her present attitude, the British Empire must not fall behind in the race and she must build as Japan builds. The major issue was either a first rate Power at sea or a second rate Power and ultimate extinction.

[6] Cf. No. 45.

Summing up, he said he advocated the maintenance by the British Empire of her position in the race, and at the same time the maintenance of good relations with the United States of America.

Sir John Simon said that friendship with the United States of America was a *sine qua non*, but at the same time one could not be sure that America would always be there when the British wanted her help. That was the difficulty in relying on Anglo-American co-operation.

Sir James Parr said that he could not see any other way of handling the situation except that suggested by Sir John Simon. He agreed with General Smuts that it would be wise to let Japan see that increases by her were a threat to the Empire and that the British Empire would have to regard them as such. It must be made clear to Japan that she would have to face not only American building, but also British building.

Sir Ernle Chatfield said it was sometimes the idea that if the treaties lapsed Japan would set herself to build up to the level of the United States of America, and that, consequently, the British Empire would have to build up as well. He did not think that Japan would do this precisely. All that Japan wanted was to secure her defensive position in the East and so have a free hand with regard to China. She would not rival the United States of America in, for example, battleships or aircraft carriers, but she would build a defensive fleet to cope with those ships in Japanese waters. She would probably build submarines and destroyers and make increases in her shore-based aircraft. She might even build some very fast battle cruisers to be employed in raids on the Pacific coast of America, thereby forcing America to retain a proportion of her battle fleet for defensive measures. Such building by Japan would be very awkward for the British Empire. The British Fleet must be able to meet not only Japanese building, but the possibilities of a different building in Europe. Consequently, the construction of the British Fleet would have to be on lines which permitted that Fleet to compete equally with the different types constructed in the East and the West. The race would be not quite as General Smuts envisaged it; it would be a race in types.

Sir John Simon said that Japan's method was to give herself a free hand in the Far East. In confidence he told the Committee that the Japanese Foreign Minister had thrown out hints of the possibility of a non-aggression pact between Japan and America and the British Empire. Enquiries had been made as to the precise meaning of this suggestion, and to test the sincerity of Japan, she had been informed that nothing of that sort would be possible unless the integrity of China was ensured.[7] No answer had been received from Japan subsequent to this.

As regards the United States of America, Sir John Simon said that there was a feeling by some people that the size of the American Navy was disproportionate *vis-à-vis* Japan.

Sir Ernle Chatfield observed that in the case of the United States of America, their naval strength was a matter of prestige and not of need.

[7] See Nos. 21 and 26.

GENERAL SMUTS suggested that such an American Navy was a comfort and a reserve to the British Empire.

SIR JOHN SIMON, in answer to a question by Mr. Dulanty, read out the proposed form the declarations might take under the treaty proposals put forward by the British to Japan. He explained that these Texts had not been given to anybody.

(These are attached as Annexes I and II to this Record).[8]

He said that the United States representatives were quite aware of the British suggestions to Japan and did not mind attempts being made to obtain Japanese agreement, but the American representatives did not believe that in any case they would be effective.

MR. FERGUSON said that he inclined to the American view that Japan intended to get out of the treaties in order to pursue her own course. She intended to obtain domination in the East and was not going to be obstructed in this intention by anyone.

GENERAL SMUTS said that it was clear to him that if Japan was not prepared to agree to such a loose proposition as had been put up to her, then her policy must be a sinister one. Consequently, the British Empire should be on its guard.

SIR JOHN SIMON referred to the doctrine of what he termed 'Japonism' which was being inculcated in that country. It was very similar to the doctrine in Germany. Japan was carrying out this doctrine with amazing skill. Individualism was suppressed and all worked for the nation. He instanced the girls in the factories who laboured for little or no wages, and the suicide cult. If the Japanese demands were an expression of 'Japonism', then they were certainly very sinister. All this showed the importance of not having to face both Germany and Japan together.

In reply to a question by Sir James Parr, he said that he did not think the United States would fight Japan on the question of China. The benefit of Anglo-American co-operation was not quite the same thing for each party, for our commitments made China of great concern to the British.

On the subject of the Washington Treaty, he pointed out that it contains a clause which makes a meeting between the Signatories necessary in the year following the abrogation by any one party of the Treaty. Consequently, should Japan denounce the Treaty at the end of this year, it would be necessary to have a meeting of all the Powers in 1935. Unfortunately, the London Naval Treaty also provided for a certain amount of scrapping in the last year. It was obvious that it would be folly for the British Empire to carry out this scrapping if, immediately on the conclusion of the year, an unrestricted race in armaments commenced.

SIR ERNLE CHATFIELD suggested that there were means of overcoming this difficulty. The British Empire might claim the retention of those ships which would be scrapped under the 'escalator' clause.

On the subject of qualitative limitations, he said that there was a safeguard in the naval race if the United States of America and Japan would

[8] Not here reprinted. They were the same as Annexes I and II to No. 41.

agree to limitations in the sizes of ships. Races in naval armaments in the past had always been in size. If qualitative restrictions were agreed to it would be difficult for Japan to catch up in naval strength, and the British Empire would be better able to keep the *status quo*. Unfortunately, Japan saw this, and without a qualitative limitation she would undoubtedly take the line of building out-sizes of ships with the purpose of upsetting the existing plans. The Admiralty view was that, if complete agreement could not be reached, it would be better to give Japan everything else she claimed provided qualitative agreement was obtained. There were, however, difficulties not only with Japan in this direction, but in persuading the United States of America to take the same view. He illustrated the difficulties that arise when competition in size takes place by quoting the Italian building of two battleships of 35,000 tons and the effect that that had had on France who was already committed to the construction of a smaller capital ship. He reiterated that the Admiralty's feeling was that a qualitative agreement was the clearest and simplest system of ensuring the maintenance of the British *status quo* at sea and overcoming the difficulties of quantitative agreement between the maritime powers of the world.

## No. 56

*Notes of a conversation between representatives of the United Kingdom and the United States of America on November 14, 1934, at 2.45 p.m.*[1]
*N.C. (U.S.A.) 7th Meeting*

Present: *United Kingdom*: Mr. J. Ramsay MacDonald, Sir J. Simon, and, as advisers, Admiral Sir A. Ernle Chatfield, Sir Warren Fisher, Vice-Admiral C. J. C. Little, and, as secretaries, Commander B. J. Hodsoll (Acting Secretary to the Committee of Imperial Defence) and Commander A. W. Clarke
*United States*: Mr. Norman Davis, Admiral W. H. Standley, Mr. R. Atherton, Commander R. Schuirmann; and Mr. N. H. Field and Mr. S. Reber, secretaries to the American Delegation.

SIR JOHN SIMON explained to the American Delegation the purpose of the meeting and amplified the information which he had already given privately to Mr. Norman Davis as regards the recent meeting between the United Kingdom and Japanese Delegations on November 7th.[2] The Japanese Delegation had noted what had been said and intimated that they would have to consult their Government before returning any answer. There seemed to be, however, indications that Japan was about to denounce the Washington Treaty, which would mean, in addition, that the prospects of the London Naval Treaty would be fatally prejudiced, and the United Kingdom had therefore been considering, on a purely hypothetical basis,

[1] This meeting was held in the Prime Minister's Room at the House of Commons. For the record made by the Secretary of the United States delegation see *F.R.U.S. 1934*, vol. i, pp. 334–50.     [2] Cf. No. 45.

what would be the position in the event of this denunciation taking place and how to deal with this situation.

Continuing, he suggested that, for purposes of this examination, we should assume that, even though the Washington Treaty had been denounced, it would be possible to get agreement with Japan by which she would observe in practice the existing ratio of strengths; in other words, that Japan would take no definite step to modify the present proportions. During the conversations held with the United States Delegation in the summer,[3] we had informed them of certain adjustments for which we desired their help. The United States Delegation then had told the United Kingdom that they appreciated the reasons for British anxieties but also felt that there might be certain difficulties of a political character. The American Delegation had since had an opportunity of discussing these points with their Government, and he was anxious that, basing what they had to say on the above assumption, they should inform the United Kingdom Delegation of their definite views. Continuing, he said he understood the United States Delegation thought it might be possible for the United Kingdom to have more cruisers provided the increase in tonnage in this category was made by an adjustment elsewhere within the total tonnage. He was anxious to know the present feeling of the United States Delegation on that point which was a quantitative point.

The other matter was concerned with qualitative limitation. Let us now take the opposite hypothesis that it proves impossible for us to secure a general international agreement on quantitative limits: did the United States appreciate how important it was for us to secure agreement as to qualitative limits even if it was impossible to get agreement on quantitative limits? Could the United States Delegation give the views of their Government on these points?

In answer to a question from Mr. Norman Davis, he emphasized that he did not mean to raise the question of Anglo-American agreement. His point was that if it was possible to secure from Japan, even though she had denounced the Washington Treaty, an assurance that she would not exceed existing ratios, would that be sufficient to enable the United States to help to get agreement with us over, say, cruisers?

MR. NORMAN DAVIS then explained that neither his Government nor his Delegation had given any consideration to the question of a limited agreement with Japan. They had taken into account only the following two alternatives: either that the present Treaty bases would remain, or that there would be no agreement of any sort with Japan.

Continuing to expand these views, he said that in the event of a complete collapse of all the treaties, it would surely be possible for the United Kingdom and the United States Governments to reach agreement on the principle of parity and also on the naval programmes which would meet their requirements. To do this would, first of all, avoid a race between the two countries and would also discourage a general naval race. The question of qualitative agreement with Japan if all else failed had not, however, been

[3] June 18–27; cf. No. 1.

envisaged. He then referred to the Memorandum which had been communicated to the United States Embassy by Mr. Craigie last July[4] and emphasised that the United States fully appreciated the United Kingdom's particular need which resulted in a demand for increased cruiser tonnage, and were disposed to try and meet that claim, provided that no increase in the total tonnage was involved.

In answer to a question from Sir John Simon, he added that the assumptions he had made were on the basis that the Washington Treaty remained, and that if it was denounced, then the question of parity between the United Kingdom and the United States became entirely academic. Action might in the latter hypothesis be quite different and if there was to be agreement between the two countries to maintain parity, it would be perfectly logical to get an agreement on naval programmes and his Government would be very willing to do so.

THE PRIME MINISTER then explained in some detail to the American Delegation our need for relative and absolute requirements in cruisers, with particular reference to the political situation in the Pacific. He emphasised the difference in the situation now to what it was when the London Naval Treaty was negotiated, and he drew particular attention to the fact that we had got a certain minimum requirement in numbers of vessels and their capacity for carrying out the work which was entrusted to them.

MR. NORMAN DAVIS, referring to the position if there was no Treaty, when all countries would be free to do what they pleased and assuming the United Kingdom and United States were desirous of salvaging what they could from the wreck, suggested that mutual agreement might be got on programmes in order to avoid competition and also a race. He was not at all sure how his Government would feel if Japan was unwilling to come to any agreement. He emphasised that the Japanese question was not solely a naval one and that when the naval limitations were established, it was on the basis of certain political agreements and a collective system to co-operate in the maintenance of peace. He added that if Japan was going to say that she would have nothing to do with the collective system, the whole problem was changed.

THE PRIME MINISTER emphasised the fact that there would be no competition so far as this country was concerned and that our only object was to co-operate and to use such co-operation to terrorise the rest of the world by[5] giving moral answers to big moral issues. He again emphasised our pre-occupations in the Pacific and the fact that if our risks and needs could be reduced, then we should be perfectly willing to reduce the size of our Fleet in proportion. He was trying to make sure that the needs of Great Britain were fully appreciated and to make it clear that there was a definite point below which it was not possible for us to go.

[4] A reference to enclosure in No. 2.

[5] In the record made by the United States delegation (see note 1) the text here read: 'to terrorize the rest of the world into giving great moral answers to great moral issues, rather than to use guns'.

MR. NORMAN DAVIS again emphasised the sympathy he felt for our needs but reiterated that President Roosevelt felt quite unable to sign any treaty on the existing bases which provided for an increase in total tonnage. While emphasising that he thought it should still be possible to find a solution within these limitations, he said that if there was no renewal of the treaty, it was possible that his Government might look more leniently on our situation.

SIR JOHN SIMON said he understood the United States' position was as follows. If the Washington Treaty was continued, there would be great difficulty in making such change in its terms as would increase the total of British tonnage in the existing Treaties, on the ground, firstly, that there was a strong sentiment in favour of a reduction of naval armaments; and, secondly, the historic political difficulty with the Senate. He then reiterated what he understood was the American proposal to meet the increase in cruiser tonnage he required.

Continuing, he said he understood Mr. Norman Davis had not considered what he might call 'the middle position'—if the Washington Treaty disappeared. Was it not perhaps desirable to consider this middle situation? It was true that the existing naval treaties would not be renewed but it might be possible to secure an assurance from Japan in respect of her building programme, which would mean that she would not, in practice, differ from the existing proportions. If this situation arose, would it be possible for the United States to meet our difficulties?

MR. NORMAN DAVIS emphasised that he had said that either the existing system must be preserved or, failing that, the United States and the United Kingdom ought to reach agreement to prevent competition between themselves.

Mr. Norman Davis, referring to previous conversations, understood that we had always attached the greatest importance to maintaining the present treaty bases and that there had also been agreement that if any change in these bases was proposed, then consultations would take place. He now understood the United Kingdom Delegation to say that, as Japan was apparently unwilling to continue under the present naval treaty system, would it not be better to try and reach a limited naval agreement with Japan which would have nothing to do with the political foundations on which the original treaties had been based? This represented such a tremendous come down from the whole structure that it would want the most careful thought. This middle course which had been proposed seemed to him very dangerous because it completely ignored the question of the naval bases in the Pacific. He repeated the conditions of the Washington Treaty and remarked that if the Washington Treaty disappeared, all these safeguards would go and very much bigger problems would be presented.

SIR JOHN SIMON said, speaking without any particular knowledge and as his own personal opinion, he would have thought that the right course would be to try and get a renewal of the non-fortification clause.[6] What was necessary was to consider what choice lay before us. He entirely agreed that the

[6] i.e. Article XIX.

first consideration was to get the treaties renewed if this was possible, but if this proved impossible, was the middle course, or some other course which might be put forward, better than nothing at all?

MR. NORMAN DAVIS again emphasised that he had not put this point up to his Government because they had all been waiting patiently for the Japanese in an attempt to solve the situation. He referred again to the importance of the non-fortification agreement in the Pacific and expressed the opinion that if the naval treaties went overboard, the policy on which they were founded would also suffer the same fate. He would much deplore reducing the existing Treaties to an agreement in respect of a few naval vessels.

SIR JOHN SIMON remarked that there were three matters which could be considered outside the question of a quantitative limit expressed in the form of a ratio. First of all, there was agreement not to fortify naval bases in the Pacific. It might be quite possible to get this arrangement renewed. Secondly, there was the question of trying to achieve a qualitative limitation; and, thirdly, to get agreement in respect of programmes of future construction. If it was possible to get agreement on these three points, it would certainly be better than nothing.

MR. NORMAN DAVIS, reiterating the political consequences of no Treaty agreement, emphasised the question of the Open Door in China. He then put forward the suggestion that the situation might perhaps be easier once Japan had denounced the Treaty. Japan had announced that she was in any case going to denounce the Treaty and, therefore, discussions when this event had taken place would be on a far more realistic basis.

THE PRIME MINISTER remarked that this was, perhaps, a matter of judgment and he was not sure if he agreed with Mr. Norman Davis.

Continuing, he thought it would be very necessary for the United States and the United Kingdom to have an understanding as to how their minds were working if the Treaty denunciation took place. If there was trouble in the Pacific it would inevitably involve both countries, which was one of the first points raised to-day. We were entirely concerned with our defences and would keep quietly pressing Japan to tell us what she proposed to do, and he would emphasise that we would regard the denunciation of the Treaty as a most serious matter. He was not suggesting there should be joint pressure on Japan by the two countries but there should be separate pressure, although the United States and the United Kingdom ought to know what was in each other's minds. He then suggested that there might be some value in continuing contacts by the experts in regard to the cruiser question.

MR. NORMAN DAVIS agreed that we were faced with a most difficult and important question. He thought that our wisest course up to the present was patiently to try and find out Japan's ultimate position. He thought, however, that if we both accepted the fact that Japan had denounced the Treaty in the first instance, it might make the situation easier and more realistic.

(THE PRIME MINISTER left the meeting at this point and Sir John Simon took his place in the Chair, and there was a short interval for private discussion.)

SIR JOHN SIMON, when the meeting resumed, raised first of all the question of the non-fortification clause. He remarked that so long as the agreement existed, none of the signatories to the Treaty could build fortifications. On the other hand, if all were free, he would like to know who would build fortifications. He had a suspicion that it might only be Japan. He wondered if the Americans had found out anything on this point from the Japanese in their talks.

MR. NORMAN DAVIS said that this particular point had not been discussed at all and that he had no information from the Japanese.

There was some further discussion on this point, during the course of which it was pointed out that the non-fortification clause was inserted in the Washington Treaty in order to help Japan to accept the 5:5:3 ratio. Further, that Mr. Matsudaira, during the Anglo-Japanese conversations, had not excluded the possibility of agreement to continue the non-fortification arrangements, even though the Washington Treaty had been denounced.

MR. NORMAN DAVIS then said that, in fact, the non-fortification clause gave Japan a definite feeling of security, but the other agreements operated so as to make the United States and the United Kingdom feel that they would not have to use their Navies in the Far East. He found great difficulty in answering the question in regard to qualitative limitation. This matter had not been considered by his Government and he had no authority to negotiate on any such basis.

SIR JOHN SIMON said he was not sure that he had ever informed the United States Delegation that in the view of the United Kingdom advisers qualitative limitation was so important. Broadly speaking, it was a historical fact that naval races began because of lack of limitation in regard to size. He referred to the advent of H.M.S. 'Dreadnought'[7] which had started a new level which had eventually spread all round the world. A second example he thought he might quote now as it was ancient history was the 8″ cruiser.[8] As a general principle, once a country was free and chose to bring out a new type, then it was liable to throw out the whole programme of other Powers. A good example of this was the 'Deutschland',[9] the construction of which had thrown the French programme into confusion. Therefore, assuming that we did not succeed in getting agreement in any form in respect of quantitative limitation, a situation of great danger would, in our view, arise if there was complete freedom of construction as regards new types. It might well be that Japan, instead of building an orthodox programme, would construct special types which would place us in a position of great difficulty. Those were the broad reasons why so much importance was attached by us to qualitative limitation, why we regarded it as a big matter.

[7] In 1906.

[8] For discussions on the cruiser question in the Tripartite Naval Conferences of 1927, *Records of the Conference for the Limitation of Naval Armament Held at Geneva from June 20th to August 4th, 1927* (Geneva, 1927); cf. Series IA, Volume III, Chapter III. For discussions in the London Naval Conference of 1930, see Second Series, Volume I, Chapters I and III. [9] Cf. No. 55, note 4.

Sir Ernle Chatfield, in amplification of Sir John Simon's speech, said it was felt that when the Washington Conference was started, it was not to prevent a race in numbers so much as a race in size, and he quoted examples of the types of vessels which countries were building and laying down. He also referred to Geneva where Mr. Gibson[10] had subscribed to the idea of trying to get qualitative agreement. If there was to be a new race numbers were of comparatively small importance because for Japan it would be a long race and a stern chase, and she would find it extremely difficult to upset the countries in front. All those countries would have to do would be to lay down another vessel. Then there was always the question of replacements which was another reason which would make it very difficult for Japan to catch up. But suppose Japan was to start on a new type, for example, instead of the 35,000 ton battleship with 14″ or 16″ guns she was to build very fast battle cruisers, the situation would be made very difficult because it might quite easily start the same sort of construction in Europe. Japan might even contemplate building 16,000 ton cruisers. There would be no limit at all, and a race would be started at once in many types. It would be a great thing to try and avoid such a race, and qualitative limitation was, therefore, the best way of preserving the present position.

He mentioned as a further example the construction by Italy of 2 35,000 ton battleships and the reactions on France.[11]

Continuing, he pointed out that it was possible to produce secretly, if there was no qualitative limitation, guns and mountings which had taken two or three years to design, and then these could be sprung on the unsuspecting rival. An advantage gained in this way would be extremely difficult to catch up. Therefore, from the technical point of view, the question of size was very important and it also had a bearing on preventing the whole naval situation being upset.

Sir John Simon emphasised that this explanation was purely theoretical and was not intended in any way as a lever for reducing the tonnage of some particular unit.

Mr. Norman Davis agreed that there was a good deal to be said for this argument. He reverted to his point that naval agreements had only been reached in the past because agreement had been achieved on political questions. He was anxious to clear up the position as to whether the United Kingdom thought it advisable to have qualitative limitation without political agreement.

Sir John Simon said that the more agreements that would be possible the better we should be pleased, but he felt bound to envisage the position where the choice lay between nothing or something, and qualitative limitation would certainly be a great deal better than nothing.

Mr. Norman Davis said that this was a very serious question even from

[10] Mr. Hugh Gibson, United States Ambassador at Brussels, had been head of the United States delegation to the Tripartite Conference for the Limitation of Naval Armament held at Geneva in 1927, and Chairman of the Plenary Sessions. Cf. Series Ia, Volume III, Chapter III.  [11] Cf. Volume VI, No. 490.

the purely naval point of view, but the Navy were, after all, only the instrument of the foreign policy of nations. The nations were not in the least anxious to have a naval race and were very keen on achieving comprehensive naval agreements on the present status. He still felt that it might be much easier to come to grips with the naval aspect after the political aspect had been successfully dealt with.

SIR JOHN SIMON agreed with Mr. Norman Davis that navies were instruments of policy. He reminded him, however, that the Nine Power Treaty was not going to end and that nothing Japan did would affect its existence because it was not terminable. The Four Power Treaty, on the other hand, was terminable at some notice, and it had always been assumed that if any agreement was achieved in regard to the naval side of the question a stipulation would be included whereby the Four Power Treaty would be prolonged for the period of the agreed programme and that the parties thereto would not denounce this Treaty.

As regards the fundamental political frame-work, it would not, therefore, be altered in the respects he had mentioned, although there might be a big disappointment as to the ultimate result. The relation of the political to the naval side of the Washington Treaty must be clearly understood, and notice to terminate the naval side did not affect the political side.

MR. NORMAN DAVIS then reverted to the question of the United Kingdom and the United States navies. He thought the problems between them were far more simple because neither wanted competition or suspected each other or wanted new types. He wondered if it might not be better for the United States and the United Kingdom to reach agreement between themselves. It might be a more effective way of preventing Japan from building new types because, having reached this agreement, we might then invite Japan to be a party.

SIR JOHN SIMON thought that both the United States and the United Kingdom felt that very shortly Japan would announce her denunciation of the Washington Treaty, and it was very necessary to consider how best to make use of the situation which would then arise. There seemed to him to be two ways. First of all, Japan was bound to be a little apologetic about the action which she was taking, especially in view of the great patience which we had shown with her. He suggested that that might be a good psychological moment to say to Japan how sorry we were that she felt she must denounce the Treaty, but to point out to her that the Treaty also made provision for a meeting to discuss the situation. We might then go on and suggest that at least Japan should discuss qualitative limitation. He felt that Japan might not like twice running to refuse proposals put forward. It would not, in fact, be a very good moment for Japan, and it might be a moment when the Japanese might be more forthcoming. Such action could not be taken unless previous discussions had taken place, and he understood the United States had received no instructions. Would it be worth while the United States delegation representing to their Government that both the United States and the United Kingdom representatives felt there was strong indication that Japan would give notice to terminate the Washington Treaty? The United Kingdom felt Japan might be apologetic about this and that it might be a good moment to tackle the Japanese there and then in regard to qualitative limitation. If the United States Delegation had received instructions from their Government that they agreed in this course, it would be a help. If something was not done, then he felt there was a danger of Japan running right out. Also, there would be the non-fortification point which he had in mind.

SIR ERNLE CHATFIELD said that in the Washington Treaty there was also a very important clause whereby countries agreed to give notice in respect of the ships that they were laying down. It was very important that this practice should be continued.

SIR WARREN FISHER made the point that we were most anxious to get any qualitative agreement as general as possible in view of our European situation.

MR. NORMAN DAVIS agreed, and said that he understood that any agreement for the United Kingdom would have to be contingent on the situation in Europe, and for both the United Kingdom and the United States on the situation *vis-à-vis* Japan. As regards the method, there might be two ways of proceeding. First of all, the United States and the United Kingdom might agree what they proposed to do, conditional of course with what other countries did, and secondly they might then decide if they wished to ask other countries to come in, or they might announce that the United Kingdom and the United States proposed to adhere to the present treaties unless some other country took action which affected their position. He then wondered whether, assuming Japan was not willing to reach agreement, it might not be better to wait until the meeting which would have to be arranged in accordance with the provisions of the Washington Treaty. Once the ghost of denunciation was laid, then it might be much easier to discuss the other questions. In fact, he had information that the Japanese themselves felt it would be easier for them once this situation had arisen. He was rather afraid that if we showed too much keenness to get the Japanese to agree to anything, they would get the impression of weakness and would, therefore, increase their price. He thought this was a point which must be taken into account.

SIR JOHN SIMON pointed out that there were two considerations, however, which must weigh on the other side. In forming judgment it was necessary to balance everything. The first point was that once a country had been in treaty relations and had broken away from these relations, there would be some difficulty in getting them back again. There might be a tendency for their price of return to rise. Secondly, there was a practical point. It was not specifically stated in the Washington Treaty exactly what time the meeting should take place, but whenever it was held it would need preparation, and might it not be a good moment, while both the Japanese and the Americans were in this country, to start this preparatory work?

MR. NORMAN DAVIS realised this point, but felt bound to admit doubts as to the wisdom of going so far with Japan at the present time. He did not think the case was altogether a parallel one with Germany. He thought that it might, in a perfectly friendly way, be intimated that it was realised that Japan's primary purpose at the present moment was to denounce the Washington Treaty, and to assure her that this action did not arouse any suspicions, and to agree to maintain an entirely friendly atmosphere until fresh negotiations could be opened. He thought, speaking quite personally and not for his Government, that it might be agreed to face the fact that if Japan denounced the Washington Treaty it would be necessary to have time to consider what the next steps were and to meet again perhaps after three months' interval in order to hold preliminary conferences with a view to preparing the way for the conference which must be held within twelve months of the denunciation of the Treaty.

He reiterated again that he thought this would be easier for Japan. He added that he felt the Japanese Delegation had no freedom to negotiate today.

In answer to a question from Sir Warren Fisher who emphasised that no risk ought to be taken of giving Japan the impression of concerted action, he said he had not contemplated anything of this kind and did not wish for a combination against anyone.

Sir John Simon said he understood Mr. Davis to be proposing a pause in the conversations when both delegations would return to their own countries. He outlined what he thought was likely to happen when the Japanese delegation arrived in Japan, and felt very doubtful if, after the reception which he thought they would receive, they would be likely to agree to come back in three months time to open negotiations on other matters.

Mr. Norman Davis, in answer to various questions as to his opinion on the via media proposed, emphasised again that to accept this procedure would mean giving up all hope of a comprehensive naval agreement.

Sir Ernle Chatfield said there seemed to be three possible courses. First of all, to accept the situation that there was nothing to be done at all; secondly, to ask Japan whether she would be prepared to consider qualitative limitation and to ask for an answer; and thirdly to put the suggestions about qualitative limitation to Japan but not to request an answer at the present time. If both the United States and the United Kingdom were agreed on the question of qualitative limitation, it might be possible during the interval, if his third course was adopted, by means of propaganda, to put the Japanese in a difficult position finally to resist this proposal.

Mr. Norman Davis suggested putting the two first suggestions together. Assuming that Japan was going to denounce the Treaty, it would be necessary to face the fact that in two years there would be no naval limitation; or within twelve months to hold a conference under the Washington Treaty in order to see if it was possible to negotiate a new treaty. Would the Japanese prefer to go ahead and discuss the pro's and con's of that preparatory to a conference under the Washington Treaty or would it be better to adjourn the discussions and meet within some fixed time which could be agreed upon?

He wanted to know whether the British Government were ready to go on that basis.

SIR JOHN SIMON said there were two questions involved. First of all, how much importance the United States Government attached to achieving qualitative limitation combined with other matters if the bigger objective failed; and secondly if this matter was worth raising and, if so, when would be the moment to raise it. This was a question of judgment and tactics.

MR. NORMAN DAVIS emphasised that this was an extremely difficult question which his Delegation and Government had not envisaged. He added that he realised that this question was, perhaps, of more importance to the United Kingdom than to the United States, but for this reason the United States would be anxious to help the United Kingdom if they could.

There was some discussion then on the question of mutually considering programmes and also the political difficulties which might arise on the denunciation of the Washington Treaty. Attention was again drawn to the firm conviction held by President Roosevelt that any increases in total tonnages under present agreements would have a very bad effect on the world.

SIR JOHN SIMON agreed that there would be a moral reaction and that if the Treaties went by the board the situation might be very difficult. He was encouraged to hear that the technical conversations which had taken place had been of value and he was very willing that they should continue.

As regards the middle course, he wished to emphasise that the United Kingdom were not advocating this course in preference to the present treaties, but they were trying to look ahead and were basing these proposals on the view that Japan was going to terminate the Washington Treaty. He thought it was wise to think out the situation in advance. He agreed that the middle course which he had suggested was less valuable than a combination of the present agreements, but it was certainly better than having nothing at all. If it was not possible to reach agreement to the extent we wanted, might it not be possible to hope to get agreement which would include some or all of the following points:—

(a) agreement on programmes;
(b) agreement to preserve non-fortification of bases in the Pacific;
(c) the preservation of qualitative limitation;
(d) the preservation of the provision for notification to be given of laying down new ships.

The value of the conversations, he thought, was the explanation which the United Kingdom had been able to make of their view that if the treaties did go there might still be some objective worth pursuing. He was anxious to know first of all what importance the United States attached to the middle course, and secondly, when might be the appropriate time to raise this course.

SIR ERNLE CHATFIELD reminded the Committee that Italy and France had been kept in touch with the present negotiations and would be anxious to know what was happening. It would be impossible to break off the present conversations without informing them of the position. What would they do when they heard that Japan proposed to denounce the Washington Treaty?

MR. NORMAN DAVIS said that there were really two questions to be decided. First of all, was primary importance to be given to even a restricted naval agreement dealing primarily with categories, or would still more determined efforts be made to preserve the real fundamentals? Did the United Kingdom Delegation attach primary importance to reaching agreement with Japan on any terms that could be obtained or to co-operating with a view to preserving the principles and policies on which the existing treaties were based and, of course, including France and Italy? Either it would be necessary to continue, in effect, the existing treaties or to try and get Japan to come in on some basis of that kind.

Sir John Simon thought that the view in this country was that we must use every method open to us to secure that there will not be unrestricted competition from Japan. It was a very important matter to us, more serious really to the United Kingdom than to the United States because of our European position. It was not conceivable that this country could sit down in [*sic*] any unrestricted building by Japan. Therefore, it was our object to try and avoid such a result, first of all by trying to preserve the present treaties and if that failed, by trying to find any means based on the two principles of close and friendly co-operation, which would not leave out Japan, or give her the impression of a combination against her but would bind her within some voluntary and effective limits.

Mr. Norman Davis said that supposing the United States and the United Kingdom, Italy and France all said they did not wish to forego the existing treaty benefits and were willing to continue in these treaties whether Japan did so or not, would it make it easier for Japan to give in? Would the fact that there was going to be no building against Japan encourage her to maintain the existing status?

Sir Warren Fisher wondered whether the effect of any arrangements of this kind might not be to make Japan feel that she was being formally ostracised.

Mr. Norman Davis suggested that perhaps Japan might be made to feel that she had ostracised herself and that the effect would, therefore, be good and helpful.

Sir John Simon said that this was an interesting suggestion. He felt that the whole question wanted more careful thinking over and he again emphasised the dangers of leaving Japan unbound as regards qualitative limitation.

The meeting adjourned at that point.

## No. 57

*Sir J. Simon to Sir R. Lindsay (Washington)*

*No. 272 Telegraphic [A 9000/1938/45]*

FOREIGN OFFICE, *November 15, 1934, 12.30 p.m.*

The following notice was issued to the press at 11 p.m. yesterday.

It is stated officially at Foreign Office that reports circulated this evening that British representatives at to-day's naval talks[1] criticized attitude

[1] See No. 56.

of American representatives in naval conversations are totally untrue and pure invention. The object of the meeting was not to discuss Japanese proposals, and they were not discussed. Indeed, no further discussion of them can usefully be undertaken until replies are received from Tokyo to certain questions put to Japanese representatives by British representatives. The meeting was held to continue conversations which took place this summer between British and American Delegations on certain points of special common interest to them, and has served to clear the air. The meeting was of a very friendly character, and any report to the contrary is sheer fabrication.

The United States representatives stated that they would associate themselves with the above.
Please inform Mr. Fletcher.[2]

[2] Mr. A. Fletcher was a Director of the British Library of Information at New York.

## No. 58

*Sir R. Lindsay (Washington) to Sir J. Simon (Received November 16, 9.30 a.m.)*
*No. 332 Telegraphic [A 9264/1938/45]*

*Personal and Secret*            WASHINGTON, *November 15, 1934, 6.11 p.m.*

Following for Sir R. Vansittart:
See your telegram No. 269[1] paragraph 2 sub-paragraph 1 and my immediately preceding telegram.[2]
I said to Phillips[3] that according to press telegrams here British suggestion to Japanese Government had come as a great shock to United States delegation.
Surely, I said, it must have been communicated previously if privately to the latter. He said that he would answer quite frankly. Part of suggestion had been communicated to the delegation by Mr. Craigie and two days later the remainder was communicated by Secretary of State himself who had expressed surprise that United States delegation had not been made aware of the whole.
This was meant as a reflexion on Mr. Craigie. Just as I am aware of a certain feeling in London that Mr. Norman Davis is not always exactly helpful so I am conscious of a similar feeling here in regard to Mr. Craigie though I do not know what its nature or cause may be as I have never responded to the slight hints of its existence that have been given to me.[4]

[1] No. 53.
[2] No. 60. These two telegrams were despatched in reverse order.
[3] Mr. William Phillips, United States Under-Secretary of State.
[4] In a minute of November 17 Mr. Craigie said that as he was 'completely at a loss to understand the allegation' in this paragraph. He had, with Sir Victor Wellesley's authority, discussed the matter privately with Mr. Atherton, who 'explained that the difficulty had arisen as follows: On November 7th there had been a formal meeting between the Japanese and ourselves at which our "tentative suggestions" had been put forward. On the following

day I had called on Mr. Davis to tell him what had passed at the meeting with the Japanese and indicated that I had informed the Americans of all that had passed [cf. No. 45]. On the 13th instant Mr. Davis had called on the Secretary of State and, at the former's request, Mr. Atherton and I had remained in the waiting-room [cf. No. 49, note 4]. At this interview the Secretary of State had expressed surprise that I had not already informed Mr. Norman Davis of the "political" conversations with the Japanese (i.e. the question of a tripartite pact) and proceeded to give him an outline of what had passed between us and the Japanese on the subject.' Sir John Simon underlined the phrase 'had expressed surprise that I had not already' in the minute, and added the marginal comment: 'I did nothing of the sort and I never mentioned Mr. C's name.' Cf. No. 66 below.

## No. 59

*Sir R. Clive (Tokyo) to Sir J. Simon (Received November 15, 12.45 p.m.)*
*No. 301 Telegraphic [A 9065/1938/45]*

TOKYO, *November 15, 1934, 7.30 p.m.*

Naval conversations.
Press messages report you as having appealed to American delegation to adopt more conciliatory attitude in order to permit continuation of conversations on compromise basis.
No comment.

## No. 60

*Sir R. Lindsay (Washington) to Sir J. Simon (Received November 16, 9.30 a.m.)*
*No. 331 Telegraphic [A 9190/1938/45]*

Secret                                WASHINGTON, *November 15, 1934, 7.35 p.m.*
Your telegram No. 269.[1]
Today being diplomatic reception day I called on Under Secretary of State and said that I had been greatly disturbed at press accounts of London Naval conversations. I had no official information as to their course and still less any instructions and the last thing I desired was to interfere in a negotiation which is being conducted at other end, but to judge from some of the press telegrams attitude of Americans towards British delegation had at times been one almost of suspicion, and could he reassure me personally.
Phillips answered that he was very pleased indeed at the manner in which London discussions as between British and Americans had developed. United States delegation had approached negotiation with a feeling not of suspicion but of apprehension that His Majesty's Government should show a marked tendency to embark on schemes of agreement with Japan in which United States Government could take no part at all. So far he felt perfectly satisfied with the course of discussions. He completely accepted Prime Minister's disavowal of any secret bargain and in reply to my question he agreed that suggestion made to the Japanese Government was not inconsistent with principle that existing ratios met Japanese defensive requirements. As to the press he said it had approached London meetings with spirit

[1] No. 53.

of apprehension which inspired the United States delegation but in more acute form, and that it had drawn its fears and suspicions from atmosphere in London but he did not think that its tone here had been bad on the whole.

He then went on to talk about process of ending the present conversations. He said that you seemed inclined to play for time and to try further to spin discussions out while he rather preferred to end the present phase fairly soon, but he was anxious to avoid any abrupt termination and to make it clear that there was no breach but that further talks might be possible. On this I made no comment.

## No. 61

*Record by Mr. Craigie of a conversation with Mr. Kato on November 15*[1]
*N.C.M.(35)28 [A 9225/1938/45]*

FOREIGN OFFICE, *November 15, 1934*

Mr. Kato called here to-day at my request and I gave him a general outline of yesterday afternoon's discussions between the Americans and ourselves.[2] I said that the idea behind the meeting had been that we should occupy the interval while we were awaiting a reply from Tokyo with discussions of some problems which were of particular concern to the Americans and ourselves, e.g. the problem of our own need for numbers and of the American need for size. This problem had been discussed on the assumption that some satisfactory arrangement would ultimately be reached between the three countries—Japan, the United Kingdom and the United States—and, while it was not possible to say that much progress had been made, nevertheless I did not personally feel that the Anglo-American problem would present insuperable difficulties once our problem with Japan had been solved. I said that the question of qualitative limitation had also been discussed, though not in great detail, and that our representatives had expressed the hope that, should it unfortunately prove quite impossible to get international agreement on quantitative limitation, an effort should at least be made to prevent future competition in the evolution of new types of ship. The discussions had been of a rather discursive nature and no conclusions or agreements had been reached, but I thought that the talk had been definitely helpful and that we were moving in the right direction. I told Mr. Kato that he might discount entirely the press reports about 'marked divergences and plain speaking' at the discussions. On the contrary the discussions had been perfectly friendly throughout.

Mr. Kato expressed his thanks and said that his Ambassador would be interested to learn what had happened yesterday.

In the course of the interview Mr. Kato stated, for my private and very confidential information, that Mr. Matsudaira thought that at Tokyo the omens were on the whole favourable to the suggested compromise.[3] The

[1] This record was circulated by direction of Sir J. Simon.
[2] See No. 56.      [3] See No. 54.

Government were doing their best to work out an understanding on the lines proposed but they were meeting with strong resistance from the extremists in the navy, and it was now just a question of which side would win. At all events we might be sure that our suggestions were receiving the most careful consideration in responsible quarters.

R. L. CRAIGIE

## No. 62

*Record by Mr. Craigie of a conversation with Mr. Kato on November 15*
*[A 9571/1938/45]*

FOREIGN OFFICE, *November 15, 1934*

In the course of an interview to-day Mr. Kato, Counsellor of the Japanese Embassy, stated that he had been asked by his Ambassador to make the following communication:

During conversations which he had had with the Secretary of State, Mr. Matsudaira had mentioned the intention of the Japanese Government to denounce the Washington Treaty before the end of the present year.[1] They were most anxious that this step should not have an unsettling effect on public opinion generally, and it was accordingly their hope that the denunciation might, by arrangement between the signatory Powers, be a joint denunciation. Mr. Matsudaira had now received instructions to enquire whether His Majesty's Government would be prepared to join with the Japanese Government, and with any other Power which might be so disposed, in making a joint denunciation.

I replied that I would submit this enquiry to the Secretary of State, but that I feared I could not hold out any hope that it would be answered in the affirmative. If it were possible during the present year to work out a new basis of agreement acceptable to all the Powers which would take the place of the existing treaties, clearly there would be more to be said for the idea of joint denunciation; unfortunately, up to the present we had not made much progress in this direction. As things stand I thought His Majesty's Government would regard the denunciation of the Washington Treaty as a very unfortunate step, for which they could hardly be expected to share responsibility. On the other hand, I thought there would be every disposition in official circles here to exercise a soothing influence on public opinion in this country should the Japanese Government unfortunately be compelled to take this step, and this would be particularly the case if there were at the time some hope of reaching a friendly settlement on the tentative suggestions now under consideration.

Mr. Kato appeared to agree with my observations which I emphasised were of a preliminary character, and I promised to let him have an official reply to his question as soon as possible.[2]

R. L. CRAIGIE

[1] Cf. No. 26.
[2] A note of November 30 by Mr. Craigie on the filed copy of this paper reads: 'the

Secretary of State has informed Mr. Matsudaira orally that we are unable in present circumstances to associate ourselves with Japan in terminating the Washington Treaty, though we might be able to do so if agreement were first to be reached on various matters so as to constitute a new treaty (see last paragraph of despatch to Tokyo No. 729 of November 21st)' [No. 76 below].

## No. 63

*Sir R. Clive (Tokyo) to Sir J. Simon (Received November 16, 12.30 p.m.)*
*No. 302 Telegraphic [A 9191/1938/45]*

TOKYO, *November 16, 1934, 6.55 p.m.*

Your telegram 187.[1]

In my temporary absence Counsellor handed to Vice Minister for Foreign Affairs yesterday aide mémoire embodying British proposals. Vice Minister for Foreign Affairs seemed genuinely grateful for statement of British proposals but still expressed doubt as to Navy being satisfied with anything less than real parity. Counsellor did his utmost to convince Vice Minister for Foreign Affairs of need to take broader view and give careful consideration to British proposals. He contested as illogical attitude of Japanese Navy when they admitted our need for larger fleet.

Conversation was very friendly and it was agreed that it was outside the negotiation which neither of them was empowered to conduct.

[1] No. 54.

## No. 64

*Record by Mr. Craigie of a conversation with Mr. Kato on November 17*
*[A 9226/1938/45]*

Secret                                        FOREIGN OFFICE, *November 17, 1934*

I asked Mr. Kato to call this morning with reference to the misleading telegram from Washington in today's 'Times'[1] to the effect that, as a result of the last Anglo-American meeting, the United States representatives had asked their Government for instructions as to the form which an Anglo-American naval agreement might take in the event of a breakdown of the present negotiations. I said that the United States delegation, with whom I had communicated, agreed that it was quite incorrect to suggest either that the idea of a bilateral agreement had been under discussion or that we had been contemplating the breakdown of the negotiations. What we had, amongst other things, considered was the form of a multilateral naval agreement in the event of the breakdown of the system established by the Washington Naval Treaty. As I had informed Mr. Kato when he last called,[2] one possibility mooted was the conclusion of an agreement which would at least prevent competition in types and sizes of ships, but the question of a limited

[1] *The Times*, November 17, p. 12.                    [2] See No. 61.

116

agreement of this character was really an academic one so long as the hope remained of reaching an understanding on quant[it]ative limitation as well.

Mr. Kato was glad to receive this assurance because public opinion, if not official opinion, was so quickly led astray by such misleading messages.

He then said that the reply of the Japanese Government had been received to the suggestions in regard to the form of a future naval agreement put forward at the last Anglo-Japanese meeting. Unfortunately this reply was not so favourable as the Ambassador had hoped it would be. Similarly the Japanese Government's reply on the subject of a possible political pact was too vague. Nevertheless it would be a mistake to be too pessimistic yet. The Japanese Government had a formidable task to overcome the resistance of the leaders of naval opinion and great patience would be necessary if a satisfactory solution were to be found. Before suggesting that another Anglo-Japanese meeting should be summoned, Mr. Matsudaira would like to talk over the position with the Secretary of State and it was arranged that this interview should, if possible, take place on Monday.[3]

R. L. CRAIGIE

[3] November 19.

## No. 65

*Sir R. Lindsay (Washington) to Sir J. Simon (Received November 19, 9 a.m.)*
*No. 339 Telegraphic [A 9128/1938/45]*

WASHINGTON, *November 18, 1934, 10.2 p.m.*

Kuhn[1] telegraphing to 'New York Times' after reporting outline of Japanese reply said to have been given to Craigie yesterday declares it is apparent that British have failed in their effort to achieve compromise. Japan's price is too high for Britain to pay and certainly more than America will pay. British and Americans may be compelled to discuss their future procedure following Japanese denunciation of Washington Treaty. Message then outlines Lord Lothian's article in 'Observer'.[2]

Selden[3] telegraphs that British people, parliament and many members of government have taken General Smuts' words[4] to heart as their best guide in present crisis. Financiers also declare that he voiced overwhelming sentiment of city.

[1] Mr. Ferdinand Kuhn, Jnr., a London correspondent of the *New York Times*.
[2] Of November 18, 1934.
[3] Mr. Charles A. Selden, a London correspondent of the *New York Times*.
[4] In an address on the international outlook delivered on November 12 at a dinner arranged by the Royal Institute of International Affairs at the Savoy Hotel, London, and reported fully in *The Times*, November 13, pp. 15–16.

## No. 66

### Sir J. Simon to Sir R. Lindsay (Washington)
### No. 276 Telegraphic [A 9264/1938/45]

*Personal and private*      FOREIGN OFFICE, *November 19, 1934, 9.45 p.m.*

Your telegram No. 332.[1]

1. I never expressed surprise as suggested and never mentioned Mr. Craigie's name at all. Mr. Craigie has acted perfectly properly throughout and the explanation seems to be that Mr. Norman Davis, who insisted on seeing me without Mr. Atherton,[2] did not quite gather the right impression. For example, he was wrong in supposing that the political enquiry addressed to Mr. Matsudaira was made at the meeting of the Delegations about which Mr. Craigie had informed him. In any case, it is not my habit to criticise Foreign Office officials to foreigners and I trust you expressed your disbelief in the suggestion that I did.

2. The whole of this business is due to a complete misunderstanding, assisted by the unfortunate American propensity of suggesting that there is something secretive in our proceedings. I have no doubt that this unfortunate attitude is sometimes prominent in American press messages and you should not place too much reliance on them.

3. I have seen Mr. Atherton and cleared up the misunderstanding. He tells me that Mr. Davis much regrets that he gave the wrong impression and that he is writing to Mr. Phillips.

4. You will of course understand that the above comments are exclusively for your own use, but I suggest that you might tell Mr. Phillips that it is now ascertained that the impression he conveyed to you is based on a misunderstanding, that the American delegation has complete confidence in Mr. Craigie's accuracy and candour, and that Mr. Davis is writing to him. There is, in fact, the closest co-operation between us all and all reports to the contrary should be scouted as preposterous.

[1] No. 58.        [2] See No. 49, note 4.

## No. 67

### Sir J. Simon to Sir R. Clive (Tokyo)
### No. 720 [A 9235/1938/45]

*Secret*      FOREIGN OFFICE, *November 19, 1934*

Sir,

Mr. Matsudaira saw me late this afternoon to communicate the views of his Government on the enquiries and suggestions we had addressed to Japan in our efforts to find a basis for a further naval agreement and to promote good understanding between our two countries. The Ambassador's instructions were contained in a very long telegram and, owing to the lateness of the hour and the complexity of the subject, it was not possible to do more last night than to receive his communication and indicate that I should like to see him again.

2. Mr. Matsudaira divided his remarks into two parts, the first, which he called 'the political part', dealing with my enquiries of October 8th (see my despatch to you No. 624 of that date)[1] on the subject of Mr. Hirota's statement to you in July last that Japan would be quite prepared to sign non-aggression pacts with America and ourselves; and the second, dealing with our suggestions made at the meeting of the United Kingdom and Japanese representatives on November 7th when we put before him and Admiral Yamamoto the idea of meeting Japan's claim by a clause which would fully satisfy Japan's feelings as to prestige, combined with the negotiation between all parties of voluntary unilateral declarations as regards their proposed future building programme over a suitable number of years.[2]

3. As regards the first topic, the Ambassador said that Mr. Hirota assumed that political matters would be treated independently of the naval problem. It had not been the intention of Japan that they should be connected. (I reminded Mr. Matsudaira at this point that Mr. Hirota's original observation to you had been made in connexion with the naval conversations, and indicated that we felt that both sides of the problem should be considered in relation to one another.) Mr. Matsudaira went on to say that the Four Power Treaty of 1922[3] was based on the principle of non-aggression in the Pacific, and he enquired whether, instead of a special non-aggression pact being entered into at the present moment, the same purpose might not be served by securing the continuance of the Four Power Treaty. That Treaty came into force in August 1923 and after ten years any party can give a year's notice to terminate it. Mr. Matsudaira's suggestion therefore amounted to a proposal that the parties to the Four Power Treaty should now enter into a covenant not to denounce it for a number of years ahead. (This would mean the continuation of the agreement to respect each other's rights in relation to insular possessions and dominions in the Pacific, and presumably would carry with it the continuation of corresponding assurances given to Holland and Portugal.) The Ambassador said that Mr. Hirota had mentioned this to you as a possible method of carrying out the purpose he had in mind. But he added that Mr. Hirota had never made any definite proposal of a political character; it was merely a suggestion.

4. Before Mr. Matsudaira passed to the next subject I said, in reply to the above communication, that the success or failure of the Naval Conference depended on reaching a position in which every Power concerned might feel that it was safe from attack, and consequently there was a connexion between the political and technical side of our discussion. Mr. Matsudaira indicated that he personally agreed with this view, and I rather inferred that he might communicate further with Tokyo to put this consideration before his Government.

5. The Ambassador next took up the enquiry I had made on October 8th (see paragraph 5 of my despatch No. 624)[1] as to the future position of China

[1] No. 26.   [2] Cf. No. 41, note 2, and No. 54.   [3] Cf. No. 8, note 12.

and as to the possibility of assurances from Japan which would form part of any new understanding. He said that Japan did not like the idea of mentioning this specific subject now, 'for fear of confusion'—this was his phrase, but he indicated that this part of his instructions was in very vague terms—but he threw out the idea that the United Kingdom and Japan might concert together, not only in relation to China, but in relation to any other question also which called for treatment, freely and in the most friendly fashion, for the general adjustment of the interests of the two countries. Could a general arrangement of this sort be made between us? If we had any apprehension of Japan's infringing the rights or interests of British subjects in China, he could assure me that they were without foundation. Japan, he said, had no intention whatever of invading China. The Nine Power Treaty[4] was not terminable, and Japan would continue to observe it. It was the Naval Treaty which Japan would have to abrogate, and American comment which he had seen that the whole series of Washington Treaties fell together, was wrong. He wished to remind me that Japan did not desire China to be a subject of discussion at the Naval Conference, if it took place, next year.

6. I made a few comments on this part of his communication, while reserving for a future occasion its fuller discussion. I asked whether what he had now been instructed to say had reached him owing to the arrival in this country of Mr. Yoshida, reminding him that he had previously told me of a special messenger being on the way from Japan. He said no; what he had said was the effect of telegraphic instructions which had just reached him. Mr. Yoshida, as I understood him, was not a special envoy for this purpose, but was an ex-Ambassador who was making a tour of a number of European capitals. He had already been in Berlin and Paris and would very shortly be going, for example, to Italy and Turkey. He hoped that Mr. Yoshida would be coming back to this country a little later on.

7. I next pointed out that the proposal now made to us by Mr. Hirota did not cover the same ground as my previous enquiry. Mr. Hirota had suggested an Anglo-American-Japanese pact; what was now put forward was a bilateral arrangement between ourselves and Japan. Moreover, as I had previously explained to the Ambassador, our concern was not confined to the interests of British subjects in China (see paragraph 5 of my despatch No. 624).[1] It was the integrity of China under the Nine Power Treaty which we had to bear in mind, and that was an interest which did not affect limited and special British interests alone. I noted the assurance that it was Japan's intention to continue to observe the Nine Power Treaty, but his Excellency was well aware of the difficulty in that connexion which had arisen in relation to Manchukuo.[4] I said that I made these observations on the spur of the moment so that he might reflect on them, but I was careful not to use language which treated the Japanese response as putting the question beyond discussion.

8. As regards the second topic, viz., our suggestions on November 7th[5] for finding a means of agreement on naval limitation, the Ambassador said

<hr/>

[4] Cf. No. 15, note 4.          [5] Cf. No. 45.

that Japan greatly appreciated our efforts to find a way of settlement. But proposals according to which satisfaction would be given to Japan's sense of prestige but the actual right to build up to the 'common upper limit' would not be conceded (though Japan might not use that right) would not meet the strong desire of Japan to have actual liberty. The Japanese Government had received the impression that our view was that there was no justification for any change in relative naval strengths between Britain and Japan. This view amounted to preserving the idea of inferiority, and Japan could not accept it. The Ambassador said that he had gathered the impression from his private talk with me on October 30th (see my despatch No. 672)[6] that the 'Gentleman's Agreement' as to respective naval strengths would not amount to fixing definite ratios. I said that this was correct, but that I had indicated that the object would be to attain a result which would roughly maintain existing proportions. Even in the formal meeting of November 7th, Mr. Matsudaira went on, the language used did not seem to be quite so definite as the impression which the Japanese Government had now received. Nominal equality combined with a binding obligation to preserve existing ratios was a thing which the Japanese Government could not accept. Mr. Matsudaira indicated, with great politeness, that he felt that the Japanese Government had perhaps received an impression of our attitude which made it out to be more stiff and unyielding on the subject of actual proportionate strength than he himself had gathered was our real point of view.

9. At this point we had to break off our interview owing to the lateness of the hour, and I indicated that I should like to resume it as soon as possible. I gathered the strong impression from the interview as a whole that Mr. Matsudaira was most anxious to do his utmost to bring about agreement, and that he felt there was a danger that the authorities in Japan, and perhaps especially the naval authorities, would regard us as offering the shadow without the substance. He spoke of the difficulty of his own position in trying to find a way of adjustment, and I told him how deeply we appreciated the service which he was rendering to his own country and how completely we had confidence in the way in which he was endeavouring to act as the means of communication of our own point of view.

I am, &c.,
JOHN SIMON[7]

[6] This despatch of October 30 is not printed.
[7] This despatch was circulated by direction of Sir J. Simon: it was numbered N.C.M. (35)31.

### No. 68

*Sir J. Simon to Sir R. Clive (Tokyo)*
*No. 191 Telegraphic [A 9135/1938/45]*

FOREIGN OFFICE, *November 20, 1934, 4 p.m.*

Your telegram No. 305.[1]

Report in Nippon Dempo that British representatives have rejected the

[1] This telegram of November 19, not printed, briefly reported comments in the Japanese press on the naval conversations.

idea of an Anglo-American accord if the conversations break down and that this was emphasised in conversation with Japanese Counsellor on November 17th[2] is incorrect. What we denied was accuracy of a press report from Washington that we had been discussing the form of an Anglo-American agreement in the event of a breakdown in the present negotiations. After consultation with the American delegation, press here were informed that one of the matters discussed with the American representatives has been the possible form which a general international naval agreement might take in the event of a breakdown of the present naval treaty system.

In other words our denial related to a question of fact and was not intended in any way to relate to matters of future policy.

Repeated to Washington, No. 278.

[2] Cf. No. 64.

## No. 69

### Sir J. Simon to Sir R. Clive (Tokyo)
#### Unnumbered Telegraphic [A 9191/1938/45]

*Private and Secret*          FOREIGN OFFICE, *November 20, 1934, 6.30 p.m.*

1. I was very much concerned to learn from your telegram No. 302[1] that in your temporary absence Counsellor had 'handed to Vice Minister for Foreign Affairs yesterday an *aide mémoire* embodying British proposals'. The purpose of my telegram No. 187[2] had been to inform you of the position so that you might be equipped to deal verbally with any misapprehension in the mind of the Japanese Foreign Office which might emerge in the course of further conversations and, in view of my express statement in paragraph 9 that it was undesirable to conduct negotiations both in London and in Tokyo, it never occurred to me that any written communication would be made to the Japanese Government.

2. I now learn from Mr. Matsudaira that the Japanese Government have based their reply to us not on the conversations which have been taking place here but on the terms of the Embassy's *aide mémoire* and that this explains in some measure the somewhat uncompromising character of the Japanese reply. You will appreciate that while the necessarily short summary of the position contained in my telegram No. 187 might have been sufficient for you to sustain a conversation with the Vice Minister for Foreign Affairs it was not sufficient to form the basis of a written communication, even if it were authorised.

3. Mr. Matsudaira has repeated to me textually the contents of paragraph 4 of my telegram which began 'Confidential'. I must presume, therefore, that this confidential paragraph was also included in the *aide mémoire*. This puts the Ambassador in a particularly difficult position, as he pointed out to me, and must cast doubt on my willingness to respect his confidence.

[1] No. 63.          [2] No. 54.

122

Another point which does not seem to have been considered is the risk of publication of a document which was communicated without any previous consultation with the United States representatives. This may be decidedly embarrassing for me and for all concerned.

4. In these circumstances I should be glad, unless you see really serious objection, if you would explain to the Vice-Minister for Foreign Affairs that the *aide mémoire* was communicated under a misapprehension; and that we should be glad if it could be returned to you and regarded as *non avenu*. You could explain that the telegram you received was a summary to enable you to deal with oral enquiries which might be addressed to you by the Japanese Foreign Office and that you had asked for it because the Vice-Minister had addressed a general enquiry to you as to whether you had news of naval conversations in London.

5. We have avoided putting anything in writing up to date and it is most undesirable while these delicate discussions are going on in London that there should be any change in this method.

6. Please also report to me whether the *aide-mémoire* had any, and if so, what heading.

## No. 70

*Sir R. Lindsay (Washington) to Sir J. Simon (Received November 21, 8.30 a.m.)*
*No. 345 Telegraphic [A 9236/1938/45]*

WASHINGTON, *November 20, 1934*[1]

Associated Press telegraphs that while rejecting suggested compromise Matsudaira urged British to consider new way of granting Japan full equality. British regard this as hopeful sign of eventual compromise.

Selden telegraphing to 'New York Times' says it was disclosed in British official quarters yesterday that Japanese naval delegates had admitted they would be willing to have future ratio of five four four in favour of Britain. This proposal has never been put by Japanese to American delegates but latter have heard of it from British. This is doubtless one of major factors to account for pessimism that has occasionally crept into attitude of American representatives since futile talks began. Proposal was evidently designed as wedge between British and Americans but redeeming feature of situation from American viewpoint is that wedge has made no headway. British also intimated yesterday that they repudiated role of mediator between Japan and America. Rejection of Japan's common upper limit theory is one of cardinal points on which Britain and America are agreed as are also Dominions.

'New York Tribune' correspondent telegraphs that it was intimated in British circles last night that door was still open. Japanese quarters were adamant on common upper limit but hoped that future discussions might lead to better comprehension of Japanese standpoint.

[1] The time of despatch is not recorded.

## No. 71

*Sir R. Clive (Tokyo) to Sir J. Simon (Received November 21, 10.20 a.m.)*
*No. 309 Telegraphic [A 9262/1938/45]*

TOKYO, *November 21, 1934, 4.10 p.m.*

Your private and secret telegram of November 20th.[1] Following is text of informal document handed by Counsellor to Vice Minister for Foreign Affairs and headed Aide-Mémoire November 15th.

'We have informed Japanese representatives that suggestion of a "Common upper limit" is unacceptable and have given full reasons for our view. We have however expressed sympathy with Japanese desire to eliminate from any future treaty principle of an inferior ratio which in their opinion carries implication of inferior status. To meet this difficulty we have suggested that new treaty should contain in addition to provisional qualitative limitation, solemn and explicit declaration as to equality of national status of all parties to the treaty, including guiding principle that naval strengths . . .[2] required for national security of the respective powers. Fact that one party accepts for certain period agreed programme of construction less than that of another party does not in any way derogate from the principle of equality of national status.

'As regards future naval construction we have suggested that this could be regulated by unilateral declarations by each power as to its intentions over a given period, such declarations necessarily being agreed to between two parties before issue. At the same time we have made it clear that owing to our minimum defensive requirement we see no justification of any change in existing relative naval strengths of the British Commonwealth and Japan; so that programmes contained in declarations would not in fact for period covered produce any substantial modification in the existing situation. It is our hope that all these declarations would subsequently be collected together into a single agreed document.

'Purpose of above formula is to remove altogether from proposed treaty actual formulation of a ratio and there is nothing in proposed arrangement which conflicts with fundamental principle contested by Japanese representative(s).'

I will ask Vice Minister for Foreign Affairs to return aide-mémoire.

[1] No. 69.      [2] The text was here uncertain.

## No. 72

*Sir R. Clive (Tokyo) to Sir J. Simon (Received November 21, 12.45 p.m.)*
*No. 310 Telegraphic [A 9262/1938/45]*

TOKYO, *November 21, 1934, 7.40 p.m.*

My telegram No. 309.[1] Paragraph 4 of your telegram No. 187[2] as decyphered began:—

'Confidentially Japanese admitted'. It could not be decyphered as 'Con-

[1] No. 71.      [2] No. 54.

fidential' in which form it is quoted in your private and secret telegram of November 20th.[3]

Aide-mémoire did not reproduce that paragraph but in view of above reading, Counsellor saw no harm in quoting the first half in conversation. To the best of his recollection he was careful not to quote second part viz 'but they do not admit etc.'.

Vice Minister for Foreign Affairs has promised to return aide-memoire to-morrow.[4]

[3] See No. 69.
[4] Mr. Craigie minuted this telegram on November 24: 'No further action is, I think, necessary.'

## No. 73

*Sir R. Clive (Tokyo) to Sir J. Simon (Received November 21, 1.45 p.m.)*
*No. 313 Telegraphic [A 9263/1938/45]*

TOKYO, *November 21, 1934, 7.50 p.m.*

Naval conversations.

According to local press, authorit[i]es at Ministry of Foreign Affairs and Ministry of Marine deny that Japanese delegation have admitted that Great Britain needs larger navy than Japan or have in any way changed their attitude.

Your statement to press[1] is fully reported but Foreign Office spokesman questions accuracy of report on the ground that it had been agreed that nothing should be given to the press beyond official communiqués. Asahi urges Japanese Government to elucidate Japan's proposals instead of talking about guiding principle. Article urges Japan to agree to discuss political questions in connexion with naval question which is itself a political issue.

Latest Rengo message reports Japanese Ambassador refused to entertain your proposal for new pact to guarantee peace in the Pacific area if conference fails on the ground that political questions were not at present under discussion and adds that with Japan's rejection of British compromise early collapse of negotiations is predicted.

[1] A reference presumably to the report on the naval conversations in *The Times*, November 20, p. 14.

## No. 74

*Mr. Patteson (Geneva) to Sir J. Simon (Received November 22)*
*No. 70 Saving: Telegraphic [A 9305/1938/45]*

GENEVA, *November 21, 1934*

Following from Mr. Eden.

M. Litvinov asked to see me this afternoon . . .[1]

*Far East.* M. Litvinov then went on to speak of the Far East. He

[1] The paragraphs here omitted dealt with European affairs and have been printed as No. 199 in Volume XII. M. Litvinov was Soviet Commissar for Foreign Affairs.

asked whether I had any information as to the progress of the naval conversations. I replied that while I had no personal information to give him, since I had not taken part in them myself, I understood that the negotiations were presenting considerable difficulties. M. Litvinov said that the correspondents of the Soviet papers in London were usually exceptionally well-informed and they had stated that there was a project between us and Japan for the conclusion of a non-aggression pact, and that Japan had offered as an inducement to the signature of such a pact that she should undertake to respect special British interests in China. I said that I was confident that this information was incorrect. We had been engaged in naval negotiations and I thought that in respect of them we had sought to satisfy Japanese prestige in so far as Japan's demand for equality was a matter of prestige. It must surely be quite clear that our interest in the Far East was much wider than any special British interest in China. Our desire was for peace in the Pacific, and in my view this would not be secured by such an agreement as he had outlined. M. Litvinov said that he felt sure we would not make with Japan the mistake that Poland was making vis-à-vis Germany. I trust that my answer was correct, but I felt it necessary to reassure M. Litvinov as far as I could. He seemed to have a surprising amount of information on the subject. If there is anything further that you would wish me to say to M. Litvinov perhaps I could be told as M. Litvinov will be here for some days.[2]

Copy to Paris. Not repeated elsewhere.

[2] No further instructions appear to have been sent to Mr. Eden at this time.

## No. 75

*Summary of meeting held on November 21, 1934, between Admiral Sir A. Ernle Chatfield and Admiral William H. Standley*

### N.C. (U.S.A.) 9th Meeting

Admiral Standley agreed that the chances of reaching quantitative agreement were now very slender, and said that the Japanese would go back with their new toy of equality, but after a time they would find it very difficult to know what to do with it. He thought that next year they would be in a better mood and would be more likely to come in a reasonable frame of mind to make a new Treaty of some kind.

2. As regards the fortifications and the 'Status Quo' question, Admiral Standley thought that, on the whole, the situation was still as it was in 1922, viz., that the clause was a concession to Japan by Great Britain and the United States. If the clause were abandoned it was possible that the United States of America might consider building a base in some of the Southern Islands.

3. As regards qualitative questions, Admiral Standley said they had considered carefully our proposal for the 25,000 ton capital ship but could not see their way to agree to it. On the contrary, their tendency at Washington at the present time was to have a 35,000 ton ship with 16" guns. Personally,

he thought some compromise might be possible. He agreed that there was no advantage, from a fighting point of view, in both sides having 16″ guns rather than 12″ or 14″ guns, and said that he himself would be willing to come down to a 14″ gun ship of 32,000 or 33,000 tons. The First Sea Lord has no doubt, from what he said, that the American return to the larger size of ship is partly due to the old thesis that the great Maritime Powers were those who were willing to put forth great efforts on the sea and so deter lesser Powers from challenging them, and that this would be an influence on the Japanese who could not afford to undertake a financial race with the United States of America.

4. Admiral Standley agreed that, in order to give meaning and force to a cruiser qualitative limitation, it was necessary to have a minimum size for battleships as well as a maximum, but he gave the impression that the Navy Board at Washington are definitely governed by the idea of outbuilding Japan in whatever type of ship she chose; for instance, he suggested that if the Japanese built outsize ships, such as 20,000 ton cruisers, the Americans would reply by building double the number with larger guns. He said that he wished us to understand that the Japanese abrogation of the Treaty had had a far more profound effect at Washington than it had had over here.

5. On the question of cruisers, Admiral Standley entirely agreed that the big 6″ gun cruiser was a mistake, and that he had told Admiral Yamamoto that Japan had started this race by laying down the 'MOGAMI' class with 5–6″ guns. Personally Admiral Standley believed in a light cruiser with combined high angle and low angle armament for fleet work.

### No. 76

*Sir J. Simon to Sir R. Clive (Tokyo)*

*No. 729 [A 9297/1938/45]*

Secret                                 FOREIGN OFFICE, *November 21, 1934*

Sir,

Mr. Matsudaira came this afternoon to complete the conversation which we had begun two days ago (see my despatch No. 720[1] of November 19th). He had really finished his own statement at the earlier interview, and the present occasion was chiefly taken up with comments and enquiries of my own, as to some of which the Ambassador gave answers of considerable importance, and as to others he proposed to consult his Government. The main points dealt with were as follows:

2. I began by observing that the Washington Naval Treaty contained a number of provisions in addition to the quantitative limits put to the various navies. The question therefore arose whether, even if the treaty came to an end so far as naval proportions are concerned, these other provisions were also to be terminated, or whether it was the intention in any case to preserve them. First, as to the non-fortification clause[2]: Could the Ambassador tell me the view of his Government as to the preservation, in any event, of this provision?

[1] No. 67.                [2] Cf. No. 56, note 6.

Mr. Matsudaira replied that his Government had found the clause useful, and that his information was that, if the other parties to the Washington Treaty agreed, Japan would be willing to negotiate for the purpose of preserving the effects of the clause. I said that we attached value to the clause, both as a means of reducing expenditure which we would otherwise have to incur and as contributing to a sense of confidence in the Pacific. We should therefore be willing to co-operate with Japan so as to secure that the provisions of the clause continued unimpaired whatever happened to some other parts of the Treaty. I hinted to the Ambassador that we should like a definite answer on the point, and that he might consult his Government, if his instructions were not sufficiently definite, so as to be able to give it. Mr. Matsudaira, however, conveyed to me the view that he was sure that Japan was favourable to our view, and would be ready to negotiate for the purpose of preserving the effects of the clause. I laid stress on the importance, from the political point of view, of working for a conclusion which would in any event be something better than a mere denunciation of the Treaty. For instance, a positive and prompt agreement as to preserving the non-fortification clause in all events would have an excellent effect all round.

3. Next we took up the clause in the Washington Treaty which binds the signatories to inform one another of the details of ships which they lay down. This clause has operated in the past from time to time under the London Treaty, but I urged that the principle of it was valuable and should be preserved whatever happened. Otherwise, there was the suspicion and possible exaggeration which arose from building in the dark. Mr. Matsudaira did not dissent, and, indeed, seemed disposed to approve; but he said that, on this point, he would like Admiral Yamamoto to be consulted, as technical questions were involved.

4. Next, I referred to what Mr. Matsudaira had said two days ago about securing the continuance of the Four-Power Treaty (see paragraph 3 of my despatch No. 720).[1] He took the opportunity of explaining that Mr. Hirota's reference to this matter should be regarded as a suggestion rather than a definite proposal. I said that we, too, favoured the continuance in operation of the Four-Power Treaty, guaranteeing rights in relation to insular possessions and dominions in the Pacific from infringement, and that I assumed that the continuation of the Four-Power Treaty would carry with it the continuation of the assurances annexed to it which were given to Holland and to Portugal. Was this the Japanese view? I had no doubt of it, but would like to have it affirmed as soon as possible, as once this matter became the subject of public notice we should all be approached with enquiries from the Dutch and Portuguese Governments. Mr. Matsudaira promised to enquire as to this and let me know.

5. I then referred to the importance of securing agreement about qualitative limitation even though we might fail to establish quantitative limits. We were very far from abandoning hope of agreement on a quantitative basis, but it would be a great mistake to regard quantitative limits as the only limits that were of value. Was Japan prepared, in any event, to work

with us and the others to fix maximum sizes, &c., for individual units, as this was a most important aspect of naval limitation? Mr. Matsudaira drew a distinction between the possibility of establishing qualitative limits if agreement was reached on quantitative matters, and the difficulty of settling qualitative limits if the main negotiation broke down. He again referred to Admiral Yamamoto as the person to give an authoritative reply on such technical matters, but himself advanced the argument that qualitative limitation might be difficult for Japan if there were no treaty as to quantities, for in that event the Powers with the biggest navies might maintain their superiority in numbers so that Japan would need to reserve the right to build any sort of ship she liked in order to compensate for her numerical inferiority. The argument about qualitative limitation was, however, left entirely open, Mr. Matsudaira indicating that it should be raised in a fuller meeting between the Delegations, when he expected that Admiral Yamamoto would be the person to deal with it on the side of Japan.

6. Having thus far cleared the ground in respect of other matters, I returned to the main subject of our earlier interview and asked Mr. Matsudaira if he could explain to me more fully what there was in the suggestions we had made to Japan for voluntary unilateral declarations of programme which was 'more stiff and unyielding' (see paragraph 8 of my despatch No. 720) than he had hoped or expected. Where did the real difficulty lie, and could he tell me in what direction adjustment was, in his view, needed in order to bring about agreement? Was the plan of arranging programmes by the method of mutual discussion objectionable? Or did the difficulty arise in his mind because we had said that all we visualised would be a series of programmes which would more or less maintain in practice the existing proportions? Or was it a difficulty that the programmes resulting from the negotiation would have in effect a contractual consequence, so that a State would be committed to its programme and unable to alter it after due notice? Mr. Matsudaira conveyed to me that it was the last of these features which constituted the main stumbling-block. Japan, he thought, felt that the version of our suggestions which she had been considering gave her the shadow without the substance. Japan did not want to build up to some unnecessary maximum, but she wanted the right to build, if and when she wished, as large a navy as anybody else. He added, with great earnestness, that the concession of this latitude to Japan would, he was convinced, change the whole atmosphere. At present the sense of inferiority due to the knowledge that limits were sought to be put on Japan which did not apply to some others roused Japanese feeling, so that the Big Navy people were very powerful. But if Japan once received the right to have a navy as big as that of anyone else, she would be content with the recognition which that grant involved, her whole outlook would be changed, and she would not seek to build up to the full exercise of her rights, but would be perfectly prepared to use her new-found liberty moderately. This was an expression of Mr. Matsudaira's personal opinion, and I gathered from this interview, as I did from the last, that he is, in fact, anxious to do everything he can to bring

about an agreement, but that he feels that there are elements in Japan which will pursue a more reckless course if the party of moderation is not sufficiently encouraged.

7. Mr. Matsudaira mentioned one other matter as to which the Japanese Counsellor had already communicated with this Office.[3] Would His Majesty's Government be willing to join with Japan in terminating the Washington Naval Treaty? The Ambassador said that Japan quite realised that by acting alone in this matter Japan would incur grave criticism, and that good relations between her and others might be jeopardised. Japan, however, was absolutely determined that the Washington Treaty must be ended by notice—he said 'by the end of the year'. In order to avoid these serious reactions and the threat to amicable relations, the Japanese Government ventured to ask whether we, recognising that the Treaty would be terminated in any case, would not consent to be party to its termination.

8. I pointed out, in reply, that there was nothing in the Washington Treaty which required notice of termination to be given by the end of the present calendar year if a signatory desired to see the Treaty brought to an end. The Treaty merely provided that this was the earliest date at which such a notice could be effectively given. It was equally possible to give the notice, if necessary, later on, and the only difference would be that the actual termination would operate from a correspondingly later date two years later. If agreement was reached, as we still hoped it might be reached, on various matters so as to constitute a new treaty, we should certainly be ready to associate ourselves with Japan in notice to terminate the old treaty. But, as matters stood at present, if the old treaty was terminated by notice, what was there to put in its place? Our view, therefore, was that we should devote ourselves to reaching an agreement which would provide for the future, and we could not lend ourselves to the termination of the existing Treaty by sharing in a notice which we were bound to feel was premature. Mr. Matsudaira obviously expected this reply, and said that in these circumstances it was hardly worth while asking America whether she would join Japan in giving notice. I did my best to frame my answer in such a way as not to provoke Japan into giving her notice forthwith, and that is the reason why I have noted Mr. Matsudaira's phrase that Japan would have to give the notice single-handed 'by the end of the year'.

I am, &c.,

JOHN SIMON[4]

[3] Cf. No. 62.

[4] This despatch was circulated by direction of Sir J. Simon: it was numbered N.C.M. (35)32.

## No. 77

*Record of a meeting of representatives of the United Kingdom and the United States on November 23, 1934, at 10.15 a.m.*[1]

*N.C. (U.S.A.) 8th Meeting*

Present: *United Kingdom*: Mr. J. Ramsay MacDonald, Sir J. Simon, Mr. R. L. Craigie

*United States of America*: Mr. Norman Davis, Mr. R. Atherton, Mr. N. H. Field

SIR JOHN SIMON opened the meeting by outlining that part of his interview with Mr. Matsudaira on 21st November which dealt with the naval question proper.[2]

MR. NORMAN DAVIS had no comments to offer on this record of the interview but proceeded at once to read out extracts from telegrams which he had exchanged with Washington. He said he had, after the last formal meeting with the United Kingdom representatives,[3] put forward our suggestions as to the proposed 'middle course', a course which it was suggested should be taken once the denunciation of the Washington Treaty had been got out of the way.[4] The reply he had received from his Government indicated some concern at this suggestion: his Government, in fact, considered it inadvisable to proceed with the setting up of a substitute for the Washington Treaty while this sword of Damocles hung over our heads. If Japan were to take this serious step it seemed to the United States Government that we should take the matter rather less calmly than His Majesty's Government seemed disposed to do, since such an attitude amounted almost to tacit acquiescence in upsetting the whole collective system in the Pacific. The problem was, in fact, so difficult a one that it appeared to the United States Government that the only hope of solution lay in close Anglo-American co-operation. After all, there would be a period of two years for negotiation after the Japanese Government had denounced the Washington Treaty, and this would give us time to test the real temper of Japan. The United States Government felt that, if, on top of denunciation of the Treaty, we allowed the Japanese representatives here to go home with some definite achievement in their pocket (such as the 'middle course'), this would be a great help to the militarists in Japan who would claim a diplomatic victory. On the contrary, the Anglo-American attitude should be to state how deeply we deplored Japan's action in this matter.[5]

In his reply to his Government Mr. Norman Davis had agreed that co-operation between the United States and the United Kingdom was more

[1] This meeting was held in the Prime Minister's Room at the House of Commons. A note on the circulated record read: 'The meeting was originally arranged as a result of a request by Mr. Norman Davis to see the Prime Minister and the Secretary of State for Foreign Affairs.' For the United States delegation's record of the meeting see *F.R.U.S. 1934*, vol. i, pp. 368–74.

[2] No. 76.

[3] See No. 56.

[4] Cf. *F.R.U.S.*, *op. cit.*, pp. 351–3.

[5] Cf. *ibid.*, pp. 353–4.

important than the salvaging of something from the wreck of the Naval Treaties. Nevertheless, there was something to be said for continuing to explore every possibility and to leave finally to Japan the responsibility of turning down every proposal for a compromise that was made. Mr. Davis had pointed out that British opinion would be more likely to come round to the idea of Anglo-American co-operation if this course of pursuing to the end every possibility of compromise were to be followed. Mr. Davis had declared his firm belief that the British Government had no intention of making any agreement with Japan separately from the United States. In fact, the United States and the United Kingdom were agreed on principles and objectives and the divergence of view related purely to questions of 'time and approach': the Americans considered it advisable to bring conversations to a close now: the British hoped to keep the conversations going. Mr. Davis accordingly expressed his hope that his Government would further examine the 'middle course' which had been submitted to them.[6]

As regards qualitative limitation, the reaction of the United States Government had not been good; probably, Mr. Davis thought, owing to a misunderstanding. The United States Government remained of opinion that Japan should be given no encouragement and that there should be no further appearance of solicitude for Japan's action either in the British or the American camp. They considered that the tactics we favoured were bad from the point of view of politics in the Far East and of domestic politics in the United States. They considered, in particular, that it would be very bad to continue the conversations after the denunciation of the Washington Treaty had taken place: that it would be better to leave to Japan the responsibility of initiating fresh conversations. Even if Japan did not take the initiative, we should have two years in which to consider our course. The United States Government considered that the continuation of conversations now would have no practical value except for the purposes of filling in time and the objection was that they gave to Japan the idea of undue perturbation on our part.[7]

THE PRIME MINISTER and SIR JOHN SIMON agreed that Mr. Norman Davis had correctly summarised our view as to the desirability of continuing the present conversations.

SIR JOHN SIMON then informed the American representatives privately and confidentially of the enquiry made by the Japanese Government as to whether His Majesty's Government would be willing to join with Japan in terminating the Washington Naval Treaty. He summarised paragraphs 7 and 8 of his despatch to Tokyo No. 729[8] of the 21st instant, pointing out that, in existing circumstances, with nothing to replace the present treaties, we could not lend ourselves to the termination of the Washington Treaty by sharing in a notice which we were bound to feel was premature; the position might be different if agreement could be reached on various matters so as to constitute a new treaty, and His Majesty's Government would certainly be

[6] Cf. *ibid.*, pp. 356–8.    [7] Cf. *ibid.*, pp. 364–5.
[8] No. 76.

ready then to associate themselves with Japan in a notice to terminate the Treaty.

Mr. NORMAN DAVIS stated that one of their difficulties was the attitude of the Hearst press in the United States; the United States representatives were being accused of having surrendered the whole ratio system. They felt that they must convince public opinion in the United States that neither they nor the British had given way on the ratio question. He suggested accordingly that we should point out to the Japanese Representatives that, since they said their decision to denounce the Washington Treaty was irrevocable, no basis really existed for the continuance of the collective system and that in destroying the Washington Treaty they were destroying much more than the purely technical provisions in that Treaty. They hoped, therefore, that the British representatives would consider the issue of a joint United States–United Kingdom statement showing that both were agreed on the seriousness of the step to be taken by Japan.

SIR JOHN SIMON agreed that the problem between us was now one of method, and Mr. Davis had been quite right to say to his Government that in view of the state of public opinion here, it would be difficult for us to depart from the method which we had advocated, namely, to continue the conversations as long as there was any hope of a settlement satisfactory to all the parties.

THE PRIME MINISTER said that we must bear in mind the effect on the military mind of the announcement of a failure of the conversations at this stage. The public mind in Japan was already inflamed and the military element would claim that, if the Japanese representatives returned after breaking up the Treaties and making no concessions whatever as to the system to be put in their place, this represented a victory by the military who would declare that they had obtained everything they wanted. When denunciation actually took place we should have to consider whether this made it impossible to continue the purely naval side of the talks. Proceeding, the Prime Minister enquired how, in view of all the perplexities and difficulties with which we were going to be faced in the Far East, the United States, while recognising the seriousness of these problems, could simultaneously be urging the British Government to reduce the size of the British Fleet. We were in the front line and it was impossible for us to reduce our naval strength on purely theoretical considerations.

MR. DAVIS replied that he had never before received from Washington such a categorical statement about the desire of his Government for Anglo-American co-operation. He believed that something really worth while would come out of all this if only the situation were properly handled. The fact was that neither country could afford to allow anything to happen to the other country. Once the Washington Treaty disappeared, it would be found that the United States Government would take an even more reasonable view of British naval requirements than they did at present and, in the altered circumstances, he did not believe that there would be the slightest difficulty in reaching an agreement on matters relating to future naval construction.

THE PRIME MINISTER said there was much in Mr. Norman Davis' statement with which he could agree; we must see that Anglo-American relations were always cordial—even affectionate, if he might use such a word—and co-operative. But we must take account of public opinion here as it was to-day. It must be stated frankly that it would be the simplest thing in the world, as things stood, to re-establish the Anglo-Japanese Treaty.

MR. NORMAN DAVIS finally indicated that one of our difficulties here was the limited authority enjoyed by Admiral Yamamoto, and this was also a reason for terminating the discussions. He added that he thought the talk between Admiral Chatfield and Admiral Standley[9] had been most useful and that, in the long run, the United States would come round to the idea of a treaty based on qualitative limitation if quantitative limitation proved quite impossible.

[9] See No. 75.

## No. 78

*Sir R. Lindsay (Washington) to Sir J. Simon (Received November 25, 10 a.m.)*
*No. 353 [A 9358/1938/45]*

WASHINGTON, *November 24, 1934, 12.54 p.m.*

Secretary of State issued following statement here yesterday afternoon.

I have read the newspaper accounts of Sir John Simon's speech in the House of Commons yesterday with particular interest. His statement on the naval conference[1] is a lucid exposition of the difficulties facing the conferees at the London naval talks. One of the bright spots of the negotiations has been the close and friendly relationship existing between the delegations and I should like to pay tribute to the fair and cooperative attitude which has been shown by the British Delegates throughout.

I should like also in passing to mention my gratification at the general tenor of Sir John's speech on the armaments industry,[2] a speech which was both friendly and courageous.

When Mr. MacDonald states that 'The British Government always attaches the highest value to close friendship and cooperation[3] between Great Britain and the United States' I can assure him that this Government wholeheartedly reciprocates.[4]

[1] See 295 *H.C. Deb.* 5 *s.*, cols. 292–6.
[2] See *ibid.*, cols. 296–303.
[3] A marginal note here reads: 'collaboration (see Hansard 22/10)'; see *ibid.*, col. 252.
[4] Sir J. Simon's despatch No. 1022 of November 27 (see Volume XII, No. 223) records his request to Mr. Bingham 'to send a personal message from me to Mr. Cordell Hull expressing my gratitude for his kind references the other day'.

## No. 79

*Sir R. Lindsay (Washington) to Sir J. Simon (Received November 25, 9.30 a.m.)*
*No. 356 Telegraphic [A 9360/1938/45]*

WASHINGTON, *November 25, 1934, 8.45 p.m.*

My telegram No. 353.[1]

This unusually friendly statement corresponds in my opinion to feelings genuinely entertained by administration. It is doubtless also intended to dissipate atmosphere of suspicion with which the press here surrounded proceedings in London, to express gratification of the United States Government at the outcome of those proceedings so far, and to ensure that as far as possible present favourable course of events may continue.

Finally no doubt it is meant as answer to deplorable attack on yourself printed by Krock in the 'New York Times' and telegraphed, I believe, to London 'Morning Post'.[2] Secretary of State on November 22nd took the initiative of speaking to me about this article which he reprobated very severely. On this I have reported by bag which left yesterday.[3]

[1] No. 78.

[2] An article dated November 21 from 'our own correspondent' in New York, printed in the *Morning Post* of November 22, began: 'The *New York Times* this morning gives prominence to the report of its chief Washington correspondent, Mr. Arthur Krock, that as a result of the failure of Great Britain to align herself with the United States on the naval problem the "highest American officials are privately revealing impatience with the British, particularly with Sir John Simon".'

[3] No relevant despatch has been traced in Foreign Office archives. Cf. *F.R.U.S. 1934*, vol. i, p. 363.

## No. 80

*Sir R. Clive (Tokyo) to Sir J. Simon (Received November 26, 9.30 a.m.)*
*No. 323 Telegraphic [A 9353/1938/45]*

*Immediate*                                              TOKYO, *November 26, 1934, 10 a.m.*

Naval conversations.

Ministry of Foreign Affairs spokesman referring to press reports from London denies that political questions had been discussed between you and Japanese Ambassador and added that the Japanese government had no political proposals to offer. He further said that reason for Japanese demand for equality was that existing naval agreement neither satisfied Japanese prestige nor gave sense of security. Press expects Minister for Foreign Affairs to speak in the Diet on November 30th on foreign affairs including naval conversations and to give notice of abrogation of Washington Treaty by December 10th.[1]

[1] Mr. R. Craigie minuted on November 26: 'We must take the same line with the press about rumoured political talks.'

## No. 81

*Mr. Craigie's record of a conversation with Mr. Davis on November 26, 1934*[1]
*N.C.M.(35)35 [A 9542/1938/45]*

FOREIGN OFFICE, *November 26, 1934*

Mr. Norman Davis asked me to call at Claridge's to-day to inform me of what had passed between Mr. Matsudaira and himself.[2] I gathered that most of the talk had occurred during a game of golf yesterday and that the interview to-day had been arranged mainly for the sake of appearances because there had been no American-Japanese contacts for some time.

Mr. Matsudaira had spoken very frankly of his own feelings in the matter and had informed Mr. Norman Davis that as he did not agree with his own Government on many points, he had at the outset asked that someone else should be appointed in his place. The Japanese Government had, however, insisted on his taking charge of the discussions. Mr. Matsudaira had then spoken of the difficulties between the moderates and the extremists in Japan and expressed the opinion that in about a year's time the internal political situation would be easier and Japan's attitude on questions of foreign policy correspondingly less rigid. In reply to Mr. Norman Davis' enquiry whether, from the point of view of the moderates in Japan, it would not be a mistake to permit the extreme element to come back from London with something which they would regard as a diplomatic victory, Mr. Matsudaira had said that the point was worth considering. I did not, however, gather that Mr. Matsudaira had shown much enthusiasm for Mr. Norman Davis' suggestion for an early adjournment.

Mr. Norman Davis then reverted to his idea that once the Japanese denounced the Washington Treaty it would be a mistake to continue the conversations here. Japan would have taken a most serious step and it was necessary to indicate to her in no uncertain terms how strongly her action was deprecated in the United Kingdom and United States. I said that the divergence of opinion on this question of method appeared to me to be as follows: while the Americans attached great importance to 'registering moral indignation' when something of this kind occurred, we felt it more important to get on with the business of finding some practical means of preventing things from going from bad to worse. I felt convinced myself that the only effect on Japan of our expressions of moral indignation would be to strengthen her determination to cut adrift from anything in the nature of naval limitation and to pursue a completely isolationist policy. Mr. Norman Davis agreed that we should not break off the conversations here while there was a chance of their leading to anything, but he thought that, once the Japanese had actually denounced the Treaty, it would be very difficult for the American Government to continue negotiations with the Japanese.

R. L. CRAIGIE

[1] This record was circulated by direction of Sir J. Simon.
[2] Cf. *F.R.U.S. 1934*, vol. i, pp. 374-5.

## No. 82

*Mr. Craigie's record of a conversation with M. Cambon on November 27, 1934*[1]
*N.C.M.(35)36 [A 9543/1938/45]*

Secret                                    FOREIGN OFFICE, *November 27, 1934*

M. Cambon called to-day and I informed him of the present position, adding that we had not yet entirely given up hope of reaching some form of quantitative limitation of naval armaments.

M. Cambon then referred to a chance remark I had made one day to the French Naval Attaché suggesting that, as the French Government were apparently in agreement with us that it would be disastrous for the Naval Treaties to disappear until we had something to put in their place, they might perhaps help us by impressing this view on the Japanese. M. Piétri had been informed of this suggestion but had felt that as the French Government was not at present taking part in the conversations it might be difficult for them to intervene officially. I said that my idea had been, not that there should be any official intervention by the French Government but that members of the Embassy here might find an opportunity of conveying their personal views to the Japanese representatives here—views which they would know to be in accordance with the French Government's policy. I knew that the Japanese would be prone to pay attention to any advice coming from French sources. M. Cambon thought this a good idea and said he would mention it to his Ambassador.[2]

He confirmed what the French Naval Attaché had told me on the occasion referred to, that the French Government considered it as of the utmost importance to retain the qualitative provisions of existing naval treaties should it prove impossible to secure any form of quantitative limitation.

R. L. CRAIGIE

[1] This record was circulated by direction of Sir J. Simon.        [2] M. Corbin.

## No. 83

*Mr. Murray (Rome) to Sir J. Simon (Received November 28, 3.5 p.m.)*
*No. 371 Telegraphic [A 9507/1938/45]*

ROME, *November 28, 1934, 2.40 p.m.*

Press announces that Japanese Government have officially suggested to the French and Italian Governments that they should join them in denouncing Washington Treaty.[1]

[1] This information was received in the Foreign Office at 11.30 a.m. on November 28 in Tokyo telegram No. 328, which read: 'Minister for Foreign Affairs yesterday invited French and Italian representatives to urge their Governments to join Japan in abrogating Washington Treaty. Press messages from Rome and Paris indicate that neither country is likely to comply. Rengo referred to your latest conversation with Japanese Ambassador, latter's desire for some agreement, and your reported view that there was little use in continuing present conversations.'

Ministry of Foreign Affairs on the other hand state that, according to your[2] information from Tokyo, whereas Japanese Minister for Foreign Affairs informed Italian Ambassador that Japan intended to denounce Treaty he did not make any suggestion to Italian Ambassador but merely enquired what the point of view of Italy was.

Repeated to Tokyo.

[2] This word is queried on the filed copy.

## No. 84

*Mr. Campbell*[1] *(Paris) to Sir J. Simon (Received December 3)*
*No. 326 Saving: Telegraphic [A 9577/1938/45]*

PARIS, *December 2, 1934*

Naval Disarmament

It is announced in the press from Tokyo that the French Ambassador has informed the Ministry of Foreign Affairs that the French Government are unable to accept the Japanese suggestion that they should join in the denunciation of the Washington Treaty.[2]

[1] Mr. R. H. Campbell was Minister in H.M. Embassy at Paris.
[2] Cf. No. 83. Paris telegram No. 332 Saving of December 3 to the Foreign Office said: 'Ministry confirm that press report is correct.'

## No. 85

*Notes of a conversation between representatives of the United Kingdom and the United States on December 4, 1934, at 4 p.m.*[1]
*N.C. (U.S.A.) 10th Meeting*

Present: *United Kingdom*: Mr. J. Ramsay MacDonald, Sir J. Simon, Sir B. M. Eyres Monsell, Admiral Sir A. Ernle Chatfield, Sir Warren Fisher, Vice-Admiral C. J. C. Little, Mr. R. L. Craigie, Mr. Howorth and Commander E. J. Hodsoll.

*United States*: Mr. N. Davis, Admiral W. H. Standley, Mr. R. Atherton, Mr. E. H. Dooman (of the Division of Far Eastern Affairs), Commander R. Schuirmann, Mr. N. H. Field (Secretary).

MR. NORMAN DAVIS said he had asked for a meeting on information which he had received, that the denunciation of the Washington Treaty by Japan might take place sooner than was expected. This denunciation would raise a number of very serious complications. He thought the United Kingdom and the United States Delegations had been agreed, in principle, as to the objects to be pursued, although there had been some difference as to the

[1] This meeting was held in the Prime Minister's Room at the House of Commons. For the record made by the Secretary of the United States delegation see *F.R.U.S. 1934*, vol. i, pp. 381–8.

methods and tactics used. The United States Delegation had done their best to co-operate and assist in conducting the conversations so long as the United Kingdom Delegation thought that the continuance of these conversations was desirable and that Japan was willing that they should go on. But all this was on the basis that the situation remained as it was at present. The denunciation of the Washington Treaty, however, would, in his opinion, entirely change the whole status of the situation which formed the basis of the present conversation. The United States Government felt that if and when Japan did announce the termination of the Washington Treaty, that was tantamount to terminating also the conversations, and that the Japanese action would cause a clean break, and that any further continuance of conversations would have to be on the entirely new basis which had been created. He wondered whether there was anything that could be done with a view to persuading Japan to postpone her denunciation.

In answer to various questions, he said that Mr. Kato had informed Mr. Dooman yesterday morning that it appeared Japan was likely to announce her denunciation of the Washington Treaty on December 12th.

In answer to a question from the First Lord of the Admiralty, he said that he thought the fact of denunciation would create a different situation for both the United Kingdom and the United States. The United Kingdom had invited Japan and the United States to discuss a certain Agenda for the purpose of renewing the Naval Treaties. He agreed that it was already known before Japan arrived that she intended to denounce the Washington Treaty but, on her arrival here, it was discovered that this decision was apparently irrevocable. The complications which would ensue from denunciation had been recognised but the United Kingdom Government had suggested that an attempt should be made to try and find some face-saving formula in order to help Japan. The United States had agreed, provided this did not involve any fundamental change of policy. Preliminary indications from Japan when the conversations had first begun were not very hopeful, but at the last full meeting[2] the United Kingdom had informed the United States that they had worked out an idea of a 'middle course' with which they would try and make a further effort towards agreement. He had explained at the time that he had no authority from his Government and had submitted the proposal accordingly to Washington. As a result, he had explained, at the private meeting held the other day,[3] that apart from any merits or demerits of the 'middle course' the United States Government felt it would be bad tactics to attempt to reach agreement on the basis of the 'middle course' in face of the denunciation of the Washington Treaty by Japan. In other words, it was felt that it would be advisable to have a break and to take the matter up afresh later on. If the Japanese were anxious to keep the conversations in being and really wanted an agreement, the easiest thing for them to do would be to postpone their denunciation of the Washington Treaty.

SIR JOHN SIMON thought it must be taken, not only as the fixed, but also the declared, intention of Japan to terminate the Washington Treaty before

2 See No. 56.          3 See No. 77.

the end of the present calendar year. He had grave doubts as to whether they would be persuaded to alter in any way that decision, but giving notice earlier in the month was a different matter.

MR. NORMAN DAVIS said that, if Japan originally had told the United Kingdom and the United States that, to satisfy her public opinion, it would be necessary to try and obtain some modification to the Treaty and that if such modification was not possible, then she would have to denounce the Washington Treaty, it might have been much easier to negotiate; but the United States felt that the position was that if Japan, without any preliminary discussions, decided arbitrarily to denounce the Washington Treaty and thereby to destroy the whole peace structure of these Treaties and the collective system in the Far East, then so many difficult questions would be raised that if negotiations were to continue after the formal notice to denounce had been given, it might be very difficult for the United Kingdom and the United States to escape being charged with having given their tacit approval to such a course; in fact, it might almost be said that they were parties to this denunciation. He recalled that the Prime Minister, at an earlier meeting,[4] had attached great importance to the maintenance of the Washington Treaty which he considered should be a cardinal point of policy and that everything should be done to discourage such denunciation.

THE PRIME MINISTER agreed that that had been his feeling but unfortunately it had not been possible to persuade Japan to do otherwise. He wondered if Mr. Norman Davis had been studying the Japanese Press recently. There was no sign, so far as he could see, of any particular jubilation in Japan over events in connection with the conversations. In fact, he would judge that the Japanese were not really getting any particular satisfaction out of their position.

SIR JOHN SIMON said he saw quite clearly that if Japan gave premature notice to terminate the Washington Treaty, difficulties would be raised. At the same time, he was not yet satisfied that every possible avenue had been explored with them. He had not either any particular feeling that we had been in a position of weakness on account of the impending denunciation of the Washington Treaty. This fact had been known for some time and actually, he thought, the United States had given us the first hint. He did not like the idea of letting the Japanese go away because it might only be a case of the Sibylline books[5] all over again.

In answer to a question from Mr. Norman Davis, he suggested it might be a good thing to take up this denunciation question with Japan.

MR. NORMAN DAVIS said that in spite of all the efforts which the United Kingdom Government had made in every direction, efforts for which he could have nothing but praise, he thought it was hardly possible to construe the act of denunciation of the Washington Treaty into anything except the desire to terminate the present conversations. The United Kingdom

4 The record in *F.R.U.S.* (cf. note 1) here reads: 'At the first meeting last summer': cf. No. 1.

5 i.e. delay might mean that the same price had to be paid for a diminished return.

Government was the host and had invited the United States and Japan to hold conversations on a specific basis, and the position appeared to him to be that one of the parties contemplated taking action which would break up such conversations.

In answer to a question from the First Lord, he said that the question of when conversations could be re-opened if Japan went away would have to be considered. It might be that an adjournment would be arranged with no particular agreement to meet again, but on the understanding that if one Power was anxious to resume the conversations, then the others would be willing, provided the basis seemed satisfactory.

THE PRIME MINISTER said that if, as the result of Japan's denunciation of the Washington Treaty, the conversations were brought to an end, he would find the very greatest difficulty in asking Japan to come back again. He thought to do this would be to play straight into the hands of Japan and would give her every justification to be pleased with her efforts. If the conversations were to be resumed in such circumstances, they could only be started on Japanese initiative.

MR. NORMAN DAVIS said he would be quite willing to tell the Japanese that we still hoped to find a basis of agreement, but if they intended to denounce the Washington Treaty, then it would be necessary to work very quickly and to delay the actual act of denunciation. He reiterated his opinion that the act of denunciation was tantamount to termination of the conversations by Japan.

THE PRIME MINISTER said that we had done our best to get Admiral Yamamoto to be reasonable and to visualise the terrible situation which would arise if no agreement was reached. Although his first impression of Admiral Yamamoto had been not very happy from the point of view of negotiation, he was inclined now to modify his opinion and to think that in his heart he really was anxious to get agreement, and that Admiral Yamamoto, having done his best to bluff both the United States and the United Kingdom, and having so far had no success in these tactics, that it might now be possible to get something from him. He would very much like to have Admiral Standley's opinion, because he was quite sure that Admiral Yamamoto preferred private conversations with sailors.

ADMIRAL STANDLEY said he had had several conversations with Admiral Yamamoto and had found him very human. He had also formed the impression that although he was the spokesman of the Japanese Delegation, he was not a free agent and he was bound to his Navy by instructions he had been given before he left. Admiral Yamamoto, at one meeting, had explained very frankly and freely to him why in Japanese opinion conditions had changed and Japanese security had been jeopardised. He had formed the opinion that Japan was really anxious to reach some form of understanding, but that the Japanese Government was committed to a policy of denunciation.

MR. NORMAN DAVIS wondered whether the United Kingdom had got the impression that Admiral Yamamoto thought he must get something which he could take back to help him to convince his own Navy afterwards.

THE PRIME MINISTER said he had asked this question, because he thought that Admiral Yamamoto was inclined to speak more frankly to sailors and because he was anxious to know whether the United States had formed any opinion as to the usefulness of continuing with the conversations.

ADMIRAL STANDLEY said he had received distinctly the impression that the Japanese Delegation would have been happier if things had been otherwise. The Japanese thought that after denunciation the whole situation would be thrown open and they would welcome this situation.

THE PRIME MINISTER said there were two things which he thought were extremely serious. His whole aim was to get peace and to try and keep peace, and if peace was broken with the world in its present state, no-one could say what would happen. There were no longer one or two big Powers who could control the destinies. In relation to peace, therefore, the two very serious matters which he had in mind were, first of all, the denunciation of the Washington Treaty, and secondly, a breakdown of negotiations. If such a breakdown occurred now, it seemed to him that we should not be able to arrange a conference with Japan within the next seven to ten years, and that this would make a terrible gap in the peace structure of the world.

MR. NORMAN DAVIS said he took the question of denunciation just as seriously as did the Prime Minister. At the same time, he was not certain that either the United States or the United Kingdom had done enough to impress on Japan what a lamentable thing this denunciation was. He thought that for the moment it would be wiser to concentrate on an appeal to Japan not to denounce the Treaty rather than to attempt to carry on with technical negotiations. He felt that the moral pressure of the two greatest nations in the world would have a definite effect upon the Japanese, coupled with the great desire of both these countries for peace. He had gathered an impression that if Mr. Matsudaira and even, perhaps, Admiral Yamamoto, could do what they thought was best in the interests of their own country, matters might be different. The question was whether it would really help the peace by trying to make a settlement with people who were bound hand and foot as regards the scope of their negotiations.

THE PRIME MINISTER said he was anxious to come to an understanding in regard to the question of any further negotiations. It was obviously not possible to get agreement now, nor was that the intention: rather had these conversations been held with a view to exploration, and in an attempt to find common ground, which could be extended to include France and Italy.

SIR JOHN SIMON, in answer to a question from Mr. Norman Davis, said he felt that, in a way, the problem was worse for us than for the United States. He would like to express the situation as a choice of risks. As he had already said, we were not being surprised by Japan's attitude to terminate the Washington Treaty. This was a very grave step which we had already emphasized, but it was not so grave a step as if the Treaty was actually about to be terminated. He would describe the two risks as follows:— Mr. Norman Davis was impressed with the feeling that if we shewed ourselves willing to continue conversations with the Japanese in view of the step they proposed to take, then there was a risk of condoning this step. He could quite see the force of this argument; but what was the other risk with which this must be contrasted? Surely it would be a far worse thing to make further conversations impossible and to shut the door for ever on any hope of agreement. He acknowledged that he was extremely frightened as to what might happen in the press all over the world if this should occur. It would be bad enough in countries with a free press, such as the United States and the United Kingdom, but in Japan, who controlled her press, there was no knowing what might happen. It seemed to him that there might be tremendous jubilation and ebullition of feeling. This was, of course, a matter of judgment, but he would be very unwilling to take this second risk, which he felt was the bigger of the two, until every possible alternative had been explored.

THE PRIME MINISTER agreed that that was generally his fear.

MR. NORMAN DAVIS said that the most determined efforts had been made during the last six weeks to try to find something which would save the situation. Did the United Kingdom Government really believe that there was any hope of reaching even an understanding?

SIR BOLTON EYRES MONSELL said he had a feeling that though Japan might denounce the Treaty, she had really got very little out of the conversations. There was no agreement in respect of her proposal for a common upper limit, and it seemed to him that Admiral Yamamoto was perhaps more anxious for accommodation now than he had been in the past.

THE PRIME MINISTER, while admitting that hopes could not be placed very high, was not satisfied that the situation was yet quite hopeless. He did not believe that we had yet got all that was possible from Admiral Yamamoto.

MR. NORMAN DAVIS agreed that if Admiral Yamamoto had the necessary authority and influence there might be possibilities in the situation. As a result of conversations he had formed the impression that Admiral Yamamoto would not even have been sent to this country unless it had been quite certain that he would maintain a rigid attitude. At the same time, as a result of the talks, he did think that Admiral Yamamoto had seen things in rather a different light, and that if he could go home it might be possible for him to bring his country round. It would be a good test for the Japanese, if they really wanted an agreement, to postpone denunciation of the Washington Treaty. Mr. Matsudaira had told both the United Kingdom and the United States Delegations that he was anxious to continue the conversations, and he thought that both the United Kingdom and the United States should tell Mr. Matsudaira that they would be glad to do so, and hoped that no action would be taken by the Japanese to prevent this, but that if they denounced the Washington Treaty, it would be taken as tantamount to a termination also of the conversations. He thought it could be put to the Japanese that if they wanted to keep the conversations going, then they must hold up their denunciation action, because, if once this had taken place, they would be destroying the whole basis on which the conversations had been initiated. He did not see why their decision to denounce the Treaty should be so irrevocable that they could not arrange to postpone the announcement pending the result of the conversations.

THE PRIME MINISTER reminded Mr. Norman Davis that the denunciation could not take effect for two years, and that therefore there was still an opportunity of negotiation.

SIR BOLTON EYRES MONSELL also pointed out that by the terms of the Washington Treaty the parties concerned would be bound to meet within a year of denunciation by any one of the Signatories.

SIR JOHN SIMON thought that it would be a pity to deal too tragically with the announcement that Japan proposed to terminate the Treaty. It seemed to him rather to correspond to the act of a man who had taken the lease of a house for a certain period and who, at the end of this period, had given notice to end the lease because he desired to discuss a variation of the terms. Japan was rather like a business man who had an agreement which he now wished to revise. He had accordingly given notice which could not operate for two years, but which would free his hands for negotiation. That was obviously Japan's view, and he thought it would be a mistake in consequence to take the matter too seriously at the present moment.

MR. NORMAN DAVIS said he felt that it was not possible to force Japan into an agreement, nor did anyone wish to do so, but if she really wanted agreement, then the Japanese Government ought to postpone denunciation and arrange to speed up the negotiations.

THE PRIME MINISTER reminded Mr. Norman Davis that the Japanese had a military Government at present, but that there was a strong civil element which was not in sympathy with its actions and aims. Mr. Matsudaira had estimated that it might take two years to get the Japanese Government into a more reasonable frame of mind. In the meantime he thought it would be very foolish for us to cut ourselves away and refuse to use any opportunity for keeping in touch with the Japanese. He thought that it might not perhaps be too difficult to get some sort of recommendation which would enable the Japanese to go home, but which would not enable them to go home saying they had achieved an enormous success. He dreaded the idea of having a sudden break now for the reasons which he had already explained.

MR. NORMAN DAVIS said he had formed the impression in the last few days that the Japanese thought that by accelerating their denunciation of the Washington Treaty they might make the negotiations easier. If this was so it might be useful to tell the Japanese that their view was misguided.

SIR JOHN SIMON said he was clear that a further interview ought to be held with the Japanese in order to see whether it might be possible to persuade them to postpone instead of to accelerate their denunciation of the Washington Treaty in the general interests. He was not yet satisfied that the position had been entirely explored with the Japanese.

THE PRIME MINISTER agreed, and said that he attached the very greatest importance to there being no misapprehensions of any kind as to our not having made the fullest attempts to get agreement.

MR. NORMAN DAVIS said that if Japan would postpone her denunciation until the 31st December, that would leave three weeks for negotiation. He suggested that Mr. Matsudaira might be informed that it was understood Japan was anxious to continue conversations, but that also it had been decided to speed up the denunciation of the Washington Treaty. It should be pointed out to him at the same time that this act of denunciation would greatly change the situation, and would be considered to be, in fact, a denunciation also of the conversations.

THE PRIME MINISTER agreed that there would be every value in seeing Mr. Matsudaira and putting to him plainly the unfortunate consequences of the act which was being contemplated by his Government.

SIR JOHN SIMON said there was another useful distinction, which was that no matter when the Japanese gave notice of their intention to terminate the Washington Treaty, the earliest date on which this could take effect would be the 31st December, 1936. The Japanese would, therefore, be losing nothing, unless they had any special domestic reason, by postponing their denunciation until the end of this year, 1934.

MR. NORMAN DAVIS said he had heard the opinion expressed that Japan's intention was not so much to get a modification of the Naval Treaty as to force us to re-open the political situation.

SIR JOHN SIMON remarked that Japan had always insisted that she did not want to confuse politics with naval matters.

MR. DOOMAN added that he thought there was a tendency now to admit that in discussing technical matters issues of policy were really involved.

THE PRIME MINISTER said that it was generally agreed, he thought, that both the United States and the United Kingdom Delegations would see Mr. Matsudaira.

(The meeting adjourned at this point).

## No. 86

### Letter from Mr. Craigie to Mr. Fletcher

### [A 9423/1938/45]

Private and Confidential                    FOREIGN OFFICE, December 4, 1934

Dear Fletcher,

I was interested in your letter to Leeper[1] of the 16th ult. and particularly in your statement that Birchall[2] had considered the tone of the 'New York Times' telegrams from London on the naval conversations to be unsatisfactory. We here have been at a loss to understand their persistently unfriendly tone, particularly as I have been informed once or twice by the American delegation that they regret these messages and have done their best to induce Selden to take a more sensible line. I enclose, for your own information, a copy of a record of a recent conversation I had with Selden.[3] Willert[4] has also spoken to him more than once.

[1] Not printed. Mr. R. W. A. Leeper was head of the News Department in the Foreign Office.                    [2] Cf. No. 572, below.
[3] Not printed.                    [4] See No. 50, note 2.

Anything you can do discreetly at your end to have instructions sent to Selden to change his tone will certainly be of value. We would not worry our heads much if we were dealing with one of the sensational newspapers, but one had expected something better from the 'New York Times'. American newspapers would have reason for criticism if the effect of our policy here had been to sow discord between the Americans and the Japanese; in point of fact, all efforts here have been directed to improving those relations, since it is felt that the only way out of our present difficulties is a tripartite understanding and such an understanding—political or purely naval—cannot be brought about until the Americans and Japanese become a little less unreasoningly suspicious of each other.

I think that the American Naval representatives here are now a little happier in their own minds as to our policy and objectives and we must hope that this frame of mind will communicate itself gradually to the American newspaper correspondents. The point to impress on the more responsible newspaper people in the United States is that on fundamentals we and the Americans here are entirely in agreement. If there has been any difference of view at all it had relation purely to questions of method and procedure.

We have found your summaries of quotations from London press despatches a most useful supplement to the invaluable daily telegrams we have been receiving from the Embassy.

I am sending a copy of this letter to Wiggin.[5]

Yours ever,

R. I. CAMPBELL

(in Mr. Craigie's absence at a meeting)

[5] Mr. A. F. H. Wiggin was First Secretary in H.M. Embassy at Washington.

### No. 87

*Sir R. Clive (Tokyo) to Sir J. Simon (Received December 6, 12.10 p.m.)*
*No. 341 Telegraphic [A 9705/1938/45]*

TOKYO, *December 6, 1934, 7 p.m.*

My telegram No. 328.[1]

French Ambassador tells me that idea prevails in Paris as it appears also to have done in Rome that intention underlying Japan's invitation to the two Governments to join in abrogation of Washington Treaty was to form bloc against Great Britain and America.

My French colleague considers this to be false interpretation of Japanese action and I agree with him.

[1] See No. 83, note 1.

## No. 88

*Record by Vice-Admiral Little of a conversation with Vice-Admiral Yamamoto on December 6, 1934*[1]

*N.C.(J) 7th Meeting [A 9713/1938/45]*

Mr. Craigie and I visited the Japanese Embassy this afternoon and had a frank discussion for about two hours on the naval question with the Ambassador and Vice-Admiral Yamamoto.

At the end of one hour the Ambassador withdrew on account of another engagement.

In order not to confuse, or to make this report longer than necessary, I only propose to record any new proposals which the Vice-Admiral had to make.

As a preliminary, the Ambassador pointed out to us the Japanese desire for a considerable reduction in the global tonnage of our respective Navies, and we replied that the British plan also provided for a global reduction by our qualitative proposals and elimination of the submarine in spite of the fact that our quantitative proposals in the cruiser category showed an increase.

*Capital Ships.* It became clear towards the end of our conversation that the Vice-Admiral had in mind a common upper limit of 15 for capital ships, this being the minimum which we considered necessary. He considered that whereas Great Britain should scrap ship for ship on completion of new ships, Japan would be enabled to retain her old ships and by this means she would, as new ships were completed, approach the number of 15.

The Vice-Admiral thought that this might conceivably be accomplished within say 12 years as this entailed building only six ships during that period to add to their present number of nine. He realised, however, that such a proposal would not be acceptable to us and that was why he had proposed limiting the programmes to the first six years, as at the end of that period the departure from the present relative capital ship strengths would not be so apparent. He had suggested, therefore, that we should lay down six ships between 1937 and 1942 inclusive, and Japan four.

The probable position at the end of 1942 would be as follows:—

|  | New Ships completed. | Old Ships retained. | Total. | Ships still building. |
|---|---|---|---|---|
| United Kingdom | 2 | 13 | 15 | 4 |
| Japan | 2 | 9 | 11 | 2 |

The Vice-Admiral also suggested that either Navy should be allowed to retain battleships demilitarised for training purposes and hinted that Japan might require two of these.

*Aircraft Carriers.* The Vice-Admiral pressed us very much to know whether our qualitative proposal for 22,000 tons and quantitative of 110,000 tons

[1] Mr. Craigie and the Japanese Ambassador were also present.

147

was the lowest to which we could reduce. I pointed out that this question had been very carefully considered from every aspect and that the Naval Staff could not recommend any further reduction.

The Vice-Admiral expressed the view that the Japanese Navy considered 20,000 tons to be a maximum qualitative limit for aircraft carriers. He did not think, however, that it would be impossible to secure agreement at our figure.

*8-inch Gun Cruisers.* Vice-Admiral Yamamoto asked whether we thought it would be practicable to get the Americans to reduce their number of 8-inch gun cruisers to sixteen by persuading them to mount 6-inch guns on the last two 8-inch cruisers laid down in America. I think we persuaded him that such a proposal coming at the present time could not possibly find acceptance, and that the only chance of getting America to agree to a cessation of building in this category depended very much on allowing her to retain her present superiority; the numbers being:—

United States 18
Great Britain 15
Japan 12

The Japanese agreed with us that eventually they would like to see this type eliminated.

*6-inch Gun Cruisers.* The Vice-Admiral agreed with our qualitative limit of 7,000 tons and said that he thought they might like to see this limit even further reduced. He stated that Japan would only require to build three cruisers every two years, that is to lay down about nine ships during the six year period under consideration. The total tonnage in this category for Japan to be 130,000 tons.

*Destroyers.* Japan would require to lay down 10,000 tons of destroyers a year or 60,000 tons for the period. The total tonnage of destroyers to be 120,000 tons.

Vice-Admiral Yamamoto expressed the view that Japan would like to see the 6-inch gun cruiser and destroyer categories combined in one.

*Submarines.* The Vice-Admiral stated that although he had mentioned the figure of 120,000 tons for the submarine category he thought that Japan might be induced to accept a figure somewhat below 100,000 tons. He stated that Japan would require freedom to lay down 9,000 tons of submarines a year for the six year period.

Vice-Admiral Yamamoto stated that although he would like to see the qualitative agreement included with the building programmes and not in the treaty, he did not think this presented an insuperable difficulty. We stressed the importance of putting the qualitative agreement into the treaty.

I then had a further discussion with the Vice-Admiral in order to try and discover his objections to a qualitative limitation in the absence of any limit in numbers, and endeavoured to explain that Japan would have considerable freedom to build special types under the qualitative limits which we might propose, but that it was necessary to set a lower limit in the battleship category in order to prevent the cruiser limit becoming meaningless.

Vice-Admiral Yamamoto said that the special types Japan might require to build might conceivably be cruisers of about 13,000 tons in reply to American building and this was why they did not want to be bound qualitatively. (I had mentioned 13,000 tons by way of illustration.)

We tried to impress him with the seriousness of the absence of any qualitative limit.

It was made quite clear that we were throughout speaking merely on our own authority.

A table[2] is appended showing how the building programme might work out during the first six years.[3]

[2] Not reproduced.

[3] Sir R. Vansittart minuted as follows: 'The Japanese submarine proposition seems utterly fantastic. How comes it that in N.C.M.(35)37 [not printed] the Admiralty can even contemplate 80,000 tons. R.V.' Lord Stanhope, Parliamentary Under-Secretary of State for Foreign Affairs, added: 'Admiralty I believe consider submarines less of a danger than formerly, at any rate as regards battle fleets, owing to the development of protective measures in recent years. S.'

## No. 89

*Sir R. Clive (Tokyo) to Sir J. Simon (Received December 8, 11.30 p.m.)*
*No. 346 Telegraphic [A 9824/1938/45]*

TOKYO, *December 8, 1934, 11.37 p.m.*

Naval Conversations.

I had talk with Minister for Foreign Affairs after dinner last night. I said it seemed that unyielding attitude of Japan might result in conversations breaking off with little prospect of success for next year's conference. Although I was speaking without instructions I felt you must be very disappointed at Japanese reaction (? to reasonable)[1] British compromise proposal. He said that in view of intransigeant [*sic*] attitude of navy and present internal position in Japan it had been impossible to allow any discretion to Japanese delegates. That did not however imply that Japan would maintain the same attitude next year. Great pressure had been put on him to denounce Washington Naval Treaty before conversations began. He was postponing doing so as long as possible. I said it seemed important to prevent Americans leaving with impression that Japan was utterly unreasonable. He agreed and said that Japan was most anxious that conference should be held next year and agreement reached but it was impossible for Japanese delegates to be more forthcoming *at present*.[2] Once treaty was denounced and ratios eliminated, navy would be more reasonable. He hoped you would realise his difficulties.

[1] The text was here uncertain.

[2] In a minute of December 10 referring to this sentence Mr. Craigie wrote that this statement 'is important and is an additional argument in favour of an adjournment *before* Japan denounces the Washington Treaty'. Sir R. Vansittart minuted: 'I agree. Proceed as proposed. But this reads rather like "Jam tomorrow". R.V. Dec. 11.'

## No. 90

### Sir J. Simon to Sir R. Clive (Tokyo)
### No. 206 Telegraphic [A 9862/1938/45]

Secret                    FOREIGN OFFICE, *December 11, 1934, 12.55 p.m.*

In a conversation with Japanese Ambassador on the 6th December I said that each of the parties to the naval discussions had their own public opinions to consider, and that the Americans had made it clear that should the Japanese denunciation of the Washington Treaty occur during present conversations it might be difficult for them to continue to participate.[1] His Majesty's Government could only regret equally deeply the Japanese Government's decision, and in view of the gravity of the issues involved they would be very sorry to see the present conversations terminate abruptly as a result of such a step. I was unable to judge the effect on Japanese domestic politics of deferring denunciation until the 31st December, but I felt sure it would be very helpful if the Japanese Government could delay notification at least until that date.

The Ambassador replied that he appreciated the difficulty, and promised to inform his Government at once of our view. Owing to the domestic situation there was no chance, he felt, of his Government waiting longer than the 31st instant. He agreed that an abrupt termination of the discussions would be most unfortunate, particularly if there were any hope of agreement.

The Japanese Embassy informed us on the 8th December that the question of denunciation would come before the Privy Council on the 19th December, and that the formalities in connexion with notification would cause a delay of four or five days more at least. No reply has, however, been received as to whether notification will be postponed until the 31st.

[1] See No. 85.

## No. 91

### Letter from Mr. Craigie to Mr. Fletcher
### [A 9788/1938/45]

FOREIGN OFFICE, *December 11, 1934*

Dear Fletcher,

You will have noticed that Norman Davis made a speech in London on the 6th December[1] which may have tended to give the impression that the United States alone favour reductions in naval armaments.

In order that this impression might be corrected representatives of the Press were reminded orally on the 8th December that we also stand for reductions. It was pointed out to them that for many years this country has

[1] The reference is to Mr. Norman Davis's speech at a luncheon given on December 6 by the Association of American Correspondents in London to the members of the United States delegation to the preliminary naval conversations; see *The Times*, December 7, p. 8.

been opposed to extreme sizes in the most important types of ships, such as capital ships, aircraft carriers and cruisers and has offered at Geneva, and is prepared now to accept, reductions in the limit sizes of vessels in these categories of as much as 30%.[2] These reductions, though they have not been accepted by all Powers, have received the agreement of the majority of the principal naval Powers.

You may find occasion to make use of this information.

R. L. Craigie

[2] Cf. Volume III, Appendix VI, and N.C.M. (35) 1.

## No. 92

*Sir R. Clive (Tokyo) to Sir J. Simon (Received December 12, 11.30 a.m.)*
*No. 348 Telegraphic [A 9934/1938/45]*

TOKYO, December 12, 1934, 6.10 p.m.

Committee of Privy Council unanimously decided to recommend abrogation of Washington treaty to plenary session on December 19th.

Press reports that Prime Minister, Minister for Foreign Affairs and Minister of Marine replied as follows to questions by committee.

Question. Why have the Government decided to terminate treaty?

Answer. International relations in the Pacific have much changed since the war. Radius of action of battleships, submarines and aircraft carriers has greatly increased and naval technique has enormously developed. Consequently Government can no longer recommend maintenance of Washington treaty and desire conclusion of new treaty.

Question. Will not termination of treaty affect international relations?

Answer. Foreign powers are already aware of Japanese Government's decision and any suspicions will be calmed by diplomatic means. Termination of treaty has no connexion with naval conversations.

Question. If no new treaty emerges will there not be building race between powers?

Answer. Japanese Government have no intention to start building race and wish to continue negotiations at preliminary naval conversations and at the conference next year. Japanese Government will maintain adequate armaments for defence but not for offence and are convinced that with submarines and other vessels they can hold their own. Building competition is a groundless fear.

Question. Will agreement about fortifications in the Pacific be affected by the termination of treaty?

Answer. Japanese Government earnestly hope this will remain in force but navy is prepared for whatever happens.

## No. 93

*Sir R. Clive (Tokyo) to Sir J. Simon (Received December 13, 9.30 a.m.)*

*No. 349 Telegraphic [A 9969/1938/45]*

TOKYO, *December 13, 1934, 10.14 a.m.*

Minister for Foreign Affairs told me last night that notice of termination of treaty will be given in Washington probably on December 22nd but that he hoped Japanese delegates will be able to submit a 'concrete plan' in London on December 15th which may be helpful. I understood him to say that plan would include British proposal for declaration in advance of building programme. He was to discuss the matter with the Minister of Marine today.

His Excellency assured me that press report of replies to questions put by Privy Council was substantially accurate (see my immediately preceding telegram).[1]

[1] No. 92. In a minute of December 14 Mr. Craigie wrote: 'I feel that, with the Americans in their present frame of mind, it will be quite fatal if the Japanese produce a "concrete plan" next Saturday . . . As there was no time to be lost I went to see Mr. Matsudaira late yesterday evening and informed him of my personal opinion that the production at this stage of a "concrete plan", which would have to be published owing to leakages, would almost certainly have the effect of destroying the work we have been doing here in the last fortnight.' Mr. Craigie thought that it would be best for the Japanese Government to say that they would 'carefully consider the suggestions put forward but would be unable to return any definite reply before the adjournment'. Mr. Matsudaira shared this view and 'did not believe that Tokyo had any intention of putting forward a definite plan at this stage'. Later Mr. Matsudaira informed Mr. Craigie that he had duly telegraphed to Tokyo on the previous night 'in the above sense'.

## No. 94

*Sir J. Simon to Sir R. Clive (Tokyo)*

*No. 208 Telegraphic [A 10101/1938/45]*

*Immediate. Confidential*     FOREIGN OFFICE, *December 13, 1934, 9.45 p.m.*

My telegram No. 206 Secret[1] (of December 11th) and your telegram No. 349[2] (of December 13th).

We understand that the United States delegation would be unlikely to agree to continue to participate in the naval conversations in London after the denunciation of the Washington Treaty by Japan has actually been communicated to their government. They feel that denunciation must necessarily terminate the first phase of the discussions which have taken place under the terms of the London Naval Treaty whereas any further discussions would in their view take place under the Washington Treaty. While His Majesty's Government regret no less keenly than do the United States government the decision of the Japanese government to terminate the Washington Treaty, they are nevertheless anxious that contact should not be broken as long as there is any hope of avoiding the evils of competitive naval

[1] No. 90.          [2] No. 93.

construction which may follow upon the termination of the existing Naval Treaties. In fact they feel that, if an adjournment is to take place, it would be preferable from a political standpoint that it should take place before rather than after denunciation. They are furthermore anxious that, even if it is decided to arrange before Christmas an adjournment of two or three months, informal talks should, if necessary, proceed until the end of this month.

We are unable to appreciate what advantage Japan can expect to derive from denouncing the Treaty before the 31st instant, seeing that the Treaty cannot in any case come to an end before December 31st, 1936.

Unless you see objection, please speak frankly and most confidentially to Minister for Foreign Affairs in the above sense and report his answer as quickly as possible.

For your own information I may say that Mr. Matsudaira has been consulted privately and sees no objection to your taking this step.

## No. 95

*Notes of a meeting between representatives of the United Kingdom, the United States of America, and Japan on December 19, 1934, at 3.50 p.m.*[1]

*N.C. (J.D.) 1st Meeting*

Present: *United Kingdom*: Mr. J. Ramsay MacDonald, Sir J. Simon, Sir B. M. Eyres Monsell, Admiral Sir A. Ernle Chatfield, Sir Warren Fisher, Vice-Admiral C. J. C. Little, Mr. R. L. Craigie, Wing Commander E. J. Hodsoll, Commander A. W. Clarke.

*United States*: Mr. Norman Davis, Admiral W. H. Standley, Mr. R. Atherton, Mr. E. H. Dooman, Commander R. Schuirmann, Lt.-Commander Duncan, Mr. N. H. Field, Mr. S. Reber.

*Japan*: Mr. H. E. T. Matsudaira, Vice-Admiral I. Yamamoto, Mr. S. Kato, Captain Iwashita, Mr. Mizota (interpreter).

THE PRIME MINISTER expressed his pleasure at being able to take the Chair at this meeting between the representatives of the United Kingdom, the United States of America and Japan. He said he understood that a draft communiqué for issue to the press had been circulated to those present.[2] In this communiqué an adjournment of these preliminary conversations was announced, and when the time had arrived for these talks to be resumed the invitation would be initiated by the United Kingdom.

MR. NORMAN DAVIS and MR. MATSUDAIRA said that they raised no objections to the form in which the communiqué had been drafted.

SIR JOHN SIMON then raised the question of the time at which this communiqué should be handed to the press.

Arrangements were made so that the communiqué could not appear in the United Kingdom press until Thursday morning, December 20th. It

[1] This meeting was held in the Prime Minister's Room at the House of Commons.
[2] Reproduced in *The Times*, December 20, p. 12.

was left to the representatives of the United States of America and Japan to make their own mutual arrangements.

MR. MATSUDAIRA drew attention to an error on the first page of the communiqué—*Rear*-Admiral Yamamoto should read *Vice*-Admiral Yamamoto.

THE PRIME MINISTER took the opportunity of congratulating the Vice-Admiral on his promotion.

He then said that what remained for him to do was to wish all a pleasant Christmas and a prosperous New Year. He regretted that the conversations had extended so far as to prevent the American Delegation from returning to their own country in time for Christmas. He then said how very seriously impressed he was by the importance of the work that these delegations had commenced. There had been no work on international problems in which he had been engaged which would have more consequential results than this problem which the parties had been examining. The United Kingdom, he said, was going to do everything that was possible to make the continuation of peace a certainty. Great Britain could not yield on essentials, and he asked the representatives not to assume that it was only a matter of pressure or time for the United Kingdom to give way. It was most necessary that the United Kingdom should look after her self-defence: at the same time the United Kingdom representatives were quite able to put themselves in the position of the United States of America and Japan, and they appreciated that they had requirements of self-defence as well. What was therefore necessary was a negotiation which would find a way out consistent with our respective honour and security. He was certain that all parties would feel the same. Our desire was for peace in the Pacific, and co-operation in the Pacific. Collective security would achieve this, and it could be found if all parties made up their minds to this. This adjournment was only a temporary suspension. He hoped that the representatives would keep in touch with the United Kingdom and let the British Government know how their Governments felt on the subject. On the other part, the United Kingdom would keep America and Japan fully informed in turn. Trouble always arose through the existence of hidden corners. He hoped that there would be none between the parties, and that light would shine into the darkest corner.

MR. MATSUDAIRA expressed his appreciation of what the Prime Minister had said, and agreed with his sentiments and hopes. The Japanese Delegation were quite ready to co-operate and find a common basis for agreement. He hoped that the time would come very soon when it would be possible to resume negotiations.

MR. NORMAN DAVIS said how much he appreciated the spirit of the Prime Minister's remarks. The American Delegation felt as he did. Nothing was more vital to peace and progress than that the three great Naval powers should work together in a friendly spirit. If all parties agreed to co-operate in promoting peace and collective security it would facilitate the achievement of an agreement on naval questions. He also wished to thank his hosts for all their guidance and helpful efforts in preparing the ground on which the parties might usefully meet again.

THE PRIME MINISTER thanked the American and Japanese Delegations for their remarks, and the meeting concluded.

## No. 96

*Sir J. Simon to Sir R. Lindsay (Washington)*
*Nos. 304 and 305 Telegraphic [A 10223/1938/45]*

FOREIGN OFFICE, *December 20, 1934, 9.30 p.m.*

The Preliminary Naval Conversations were adjourned on the 19th December in an amicable atmosphere after a meeting at which representatives of the three Powers concerned were present.[1]

It was agreed that conversations had reached a stage where there should be an adjournment in order that the delegates might resume personal contact with their governments. The governments concerned will keep in close touch with each other, and if and when the situation so develops as to justify a subsequent meeting, His Majesty's Government in the United Kingdom will take the appropriate steps to arrange a further meeting.

The United States representatives are starting home on the 29th December.

It is anticipated that the Japanese will defer denunciation of the Washington Treaty until the end of the month but the exact date is unknown.

Please report fully effect on United States Government and on public opinion when notice of termination is actually given to the United States Government.

[1] See No. 95.

## No. 97

*Sir R. Clive (Tokyo) to Sir J. Simon (Received December 28, 9.30 a.m.)*
*No. 367 Telegraphic [A 10401/1938/45]*

*Confidential*                                TOKYO, *December 28, 1934, 10 a.m.*

Naval Attaché has received invitation to visit Kure[1] with assistant Navy Attaché in February on board newly modernized battleship 'Fuso'.

In conveying this invitation Naval Secretary at Ministry of Marine said that not only Naval authorities but the whole Japanese people were grateful to Great Britain for her understanding of Japanese point of view during naval conversations. He added that Japan definitely wants new treaty and relies on Great Britain to help her to obtain one which will be satisfactory to the Japanese people.

[1] Japanese naval base and commercial port.

## No. 98

*Record of a meeting between United Kingdom representatives and Vice-Admiral Yamamoto on December 28, 1934, at 4 p.m.*[1]

*N.C.(J) 10th Meeting [A 51/22/45]*

Present: *United Kingdom*: Admiral Sir Ernle Chatfield, Mr. R. L. Craigie, Captain E. L. S. King (Director, Plans Division, Admiralty).
  *Japan*: Vice-Admiral Yamamoto.

ADMIRAL YAMAMOTO said that he had now received further instructions from his Government concerning the British compromise proposal.[2] He regretted the answer was not favourable. His Government felt bound to maintain their original plan regarding the fundamental principle of equality of status including a Common Upper Limit, and a considerable reduction in the numbers of what they regarded as 'offensive' types of vessels. On the question of concrete figures his instructions were not clear, but he thought his Government considered the maximum upper limits proposed were far too high, and they had in mind, he thought, something as follows:—

*Capital Ships.* 6 to 8, though if other Powers could be got to agree they would be still willing to abolish them.

*Aircraft Carriers.* The Japanese Government would still prefer their abolition, but if this was not possible, the figure they had in mind was 3.

*8" Cruisers.* 8.

*6" Cruisers, Destroyers and Submarines.* In these categories he thought his Government favoured a global tonnage of about 350,000 tons, though for the maximum limits in each of these categories he gave the following figures:—

| | |
|---|---|
| 6" Cruisers | 200,000 tons. |
| Destroyers | 150,000 ,, |
| Submarines | 100,000 ,, |

In reply to a question, Admiral Yamamoto said he thought the intention was that Powers who possessed figures in excess of those mentioned should gradually scrap down to these figures in the course of a few years.

2. ADMIRAL CHATFIELD said he felt the answer of the Japanese Government was disappointing. He supposed that the Japanese Government felt that those figures would give them security, but they certainly would not give the British Empire security. We had always supported the principle of equality of security, and for the British Empire, which was spread all over the world, those figures would not meet our requirements.

3. MR. CRAIGIE suggested that the Japanese Government did not sufficiently take into account the requirements of other Powers. As Admiral Yamamoto knew, we had to look at the European situation, and to the changes which were occurring not only in the matter of naval strengths but also in political relationships. We ourselves had already made large reductions in our naval forces, but the tendency of several European Powers had, on the contrary, been to increase their naval strengths in recent years.

---

[1] This meeting was held at the Admiralty.     [2] Cf. No. 67.

Furthermore, no agreement on land and air forces was yet in sight at Geneva, and even if such agreement were eventually to be achieved, it was doubtful whether any reduction would be secured. In these circumstances it was not practical politics to expect us to make further reductions in our naval strength. We had tried very hard during the recent conversations to put ourselves in the place of Japan and to take account of her special difficulties: it was now the turn of the Japanese Government to take some account of our special requirements and difficulties.

4. ADMIRAL CHATFIELD said he was sure that His Majesty's Government could not possibly consider figures such as those that had been indicated by Admiral Yamamoto, and he asked whether the Japanese Government had finally turned down the idea of negotiating on the basis of a 'programme of construction', such as had been proposed by ourselves. He again urged Admiral Yamamoto to put before his Government the benefit that a settlement on these lines would have. He pointed out that, following the denouncement of the Washington Treaty, the ratio would have been abolished and the Japanese would be negotiating with their hands free.

5. ADMIRAL YAMAMOTO replied that he himself sincerely wished for agreement; he felt that the proposal for 'programmes of construction' over a term of years might still form a basis for agreement. He thought it would be best if he returned to Japan to explain this proposal to his Government more fully, and he would do his best to secure agreement. He did not think that his present instructions could be regarded as final.

6. MR. CRAIGIE pointed out that progress had been made with the United States and that they had not rejected the idea of an agreement on programmes, such as we had had under discussion. He felt that the attitude of the Japanese Government, as now disclosed, might have a most unfortunate reaction on the Americans. He was going to see Mr. Norman Davis, and he felt he would have to say that the Japanese answer was disappointing, but he suggested he might add that Japan had not rejected, though she had not accepted, the plan for exchange of programmes; that possibly the Japanese Government had not properly understood the proposal, and that Admiral Yamamoto might go back to explain it to them more thoroughly.

7. ADMIRAL CHATFIELD pointed out that it was very important to get the Americans to agree not to make any announcement that would increase Admiral Yamamoto's difficulties, and he enquired whether Admiral Yamamoto had given the figures mentioned to Admiral Standley.

8. ADMIRAL YAMAMOTO said that he had indicated to Admiral Standley the attitude of the Japanese Government in general terms, and he had mentioned the figures by way of illustration but not in such a concrete form.

9. MR. CRAIGIE pointed out to Admiral Yamamoto that the European Powers would be anxious to know the outcome of the present conversations, and we should have to resume conversations with them. Time was getting short and we might find it necessary to discuss with them the idea of limitation by an exchange of programmes, but the Japanese Government must not think for a moment that we should be doing this in order to exert pressure at

Tokio. We had been at pains to prove to Japan that there was no question of any common front against her, and further discussions with other Powers would be conducted in the same spirit.

10. ADMIRAL YAMAMOTO said he quite understood, and he was grateful for the attitude that the British had taken up in this matter.

11. MR. CRAIGIE pointed out that there was not much time if some agreement was to be concluded next year, and he felt that it would be very difficult to resume contact if once it was broken off. With this Admiral Yamamoto agreed, and asked when we would be ready to resume conversations if his Government agreed to accept the 'programmes of construction' as a basis for negotiations.

12. ADMIRAL CHATFIELD said we should be ready at any time, but he felt there might be difficulty with the United States of America.

13. MR. CRAIGIE said that, speaking quite personally, he should not regard the presence of special American representatives (apart from the staff of the United States Embassy) as essential to a resumption of the conversations. It might be that when Admiral Yamamoto had been able to explain matters to his Government, a position would be reached which, in Admiral Yamamoto's opinion, offered a prospect of resuming our conversations with some hope of success. We should have, of course, to inform the United States Government but he did not think we should refuse to continue discussions with Japan even if the United States Government felt unable to join in at the moment. When the time came for a resumption, the matter could no doubt be amicably arranged with the Americans. He suggested that the initiative should lie with Admiral Yamamoto, and that he should say when, in his opinion, the conversations could be usefully resumed.

14. ADMIRAL YAMAMOTO expressed his general concurrence with this procedure, and suggested that Mr. Craigie should discuss this point with Mr. Matsudaira on the following day.

No. 99

Record by Mr. Craigie of a conversation with Mr. Matsudaira<br>on December 29, 1934[1]

[A 33/22/45]

FOREIGN OFFICE, December 29, 1934

The Japanese Ambassador called to-day and said that he had been instructed to communicate to me, as representing the Secretary of State for this purpose,[2] a copy of the Note[3] which is being addressed to the United States Government by the Japanese Ambassador at Washington notifying Japan's decision to terminate the Washington Naval Treaty. The Ambassa-

---

[1] This record was circulated by direction of Sir J. Simon: it was numbered N.C.M. (35) 41.

[2] Sir John and Lady Simon were on holiday on the Riviera. They returned to London on January 7, 1935.

[3] Not here printed: for the text see *F.R.U.S.*, *op. cit.*, p. 416.

dor stated that this communication was made only as a matter of courtesy because, according to the terms of the Treaty, it would be for the United States Government to make the formal announcement to the other signatory powers of the Treaty.

Mr. Matsudaira handed to me at the same time a copy of a Note Verbale[4] which Mr. Saito will leave with the State Department explaining the grounds on which the Japanese Government have decided to take this step. The third paper which Mr. Matsudaira left with me was a copy of a statement which is being made to-day in Tokyo by the Foreign Office spokesman.[5]

I thanked His Excellency for his courtesy in communicating these documents so promptly, but made no further comment. (I had at an earlier interview informed His Excellency privately, that I thought His Majesty's Government might wish, in reply to this communication, to place on record their regret that the Japanese Government should have felt it necessary to take this grave step at this particular moment, although they of course fully recognised Japan's right to do so).

R. L. CRAIGIE

[4] See *ibid.*, pp. 416–18.          [5] See *ibid.*, pp. 418–19.

## No. 100

*Continuation of record by Mr. Craigie of a conversation with Mr. Matsudaira on December 29, 1934*[1]

[*A 77/22/45*]

Secret                                    FOREIGN OFFICE, *December 29, 1934*

After disposing of the question of the denunciation, Mr. Matsudaira referred to yesterday's interview between Admiral Chatfield and Admiral Yamamoto[2] and said that he could tell me quite privately that the Japanese Government's instructions had not been very clear. He thought, however, that it was the desire of the Japanese Government to continue discussions on the basis of the programme idea. What was quite clear, however, was that the Japanese Government had very strongly objected to the high levels in each category of ships which may be maintained if the tentative figures we had been discussing were agreed upon. He said that it was a fundamental part of the Japanese Government's proposal that there should be progressive reductions in the sizes of fleets, whereas the British proposals represented an actual increase in certain categories.

Admiral Yamamoto had now definitely decided to return to Tokyo, leaving early next month, and he would do his best to explain at Tokyo the extent of our needs, the scope of our responsibilities, and the troubled position in Europe with which we now have to deal. This was all perfectly clear in his mind, and he would make good use of the arguments we had put forward. Nevertheless, both Mr. Matsudaira and Admiral Yamamoto felt that if they had to inform Tokyo that the figures we had put forward represented our

[1] See No. 99.                    [2] See No. 98.

last word and that we would not be prepared to reduce them by a ship or a ton, Admiral Yamamoto's task would be an impossible one. While recognising Great Britain's needs, Japan could not but note the reaction of the British figures on naval construction in the United States, and it seemed to Mr. Matsudaira to be essential that there should be some flexibility in the British proposals for the maximum upper limit if an agreement were to be negotiated.

I told Mr. Matsudaira that, so far as the number of units was concerned, I saw no hope of a reduction in our figures for the maximum limit, which represented also our minimum limit. Furthermore, these figures had been put forward as a basis for an international agreement; if no agreement were possible and competition in building started, I felt sure that the tonnage figures which would be reached in the various categories would be higher still.

As regards the size of ships, we were, of course, prepared to make very big reductions if other Powers would agree.

As regards the tentative construction figures, put forward by us in recent conversations, I did not think that the Admiralty considered these as necessarily fixed or final, particularly as we still had to have further discussions with the European Powers, but it would give a wrong impression if I told the Ambassador that there was a likelihood of any considerable change in the rate of construction during the six years for which figures had been given.

Mr. Matsudaira said that, nevertheless, he hoped that we would consider this point very carefully before Admiral Yamamoto left and would give him any help we could in his difficult task. I said that we hoped to prepare a memorandum giving the reasons for the minimum tonnages which were required in various categories and he said that this would be most useful.

R. L. CRAIGIE

## No. 101

*Record by Mr. Craigie of a conversation with Mr. N. Davis*

[*A 76/22/45*]

*Secret*                                      FOREIGN OFFICE, *December 29, 1934*

After the meeting with Admiral Yamamoto yesterday afternoon,[1] I called on Mr. Norman Davis to tell him of the latest position. Mr. Atherton was also present. I was careful that my account should not err on the side of pessimism, but I said that it was clear that the Japanese Government were still insisting on reductions in our naval strength which it would be quite impossible for His Majesty's Government to accept. I added that this was a phase through which we were bound to pass, but the important thing was that the Japanese Government had not rejected the idea of a programme arrangement, and I believed that eventually it would prove possible to reach an understanding on the basis we had been discussing. I appealed to Mr.

[1] See No. 98.

Norman Davis to do his best to see that Mr. Matsudaira and Admiral Yamamoto, who had shown great courage and vision, should be given a fair chance to explain these plans to their Government, and he replied that it was certainly his intention to do what he could in this direction.

Mr. Norman Davis replied that the United States Government would certainly desire that everything should be done to facilitate the course of future discussions with the Japanese through the diplomatic channel so long as His Majesty's Government felt that these communications could profitably be continued, although American official circles were less sanguine than we appeared to be as to a possible successful outcome of the discussions. The point which both Mr. Norman Davis and Mr. Atherton particularly insisted on was that there should be no more informal discussions with Admiral Yamamoto after the Americans sailed if we wished to keep the American press in a reasonable frame of mind: to the United States Government it mattered not at all if such talks continued since they would be kept informed, but public opinion in the United States would undoubtedly construe the continuance of talks with Admiral Yamamoto as something detrimental to American interests. Would it not be possible to inform the press that, as inferred in the Three Power communiqué of December 19th,[2] any further intergovernmental communications on this subject would henceforth pass through the ordinary diplomatic channel? It would be for us to determine exactly what that channel should be and, if Admiral Yamamoto remained in this country, it was obvious that he would advise the Ambassador on technical subjects; but the important thing was that any discussions in London should henceforth be between Mr. Matsudaira and the Secretary of State or his representative.

As it was necessary to rush a decision at once as to what was to be said to the journalists, I agreed that an announcement in this sense should be made, provided Mr. Matsudaira saw no objection.[3]

R. L. CRAIGIE

[2] See No. 95, note 2.

[3] *Note in original*: 'Mr. Matsudaira and Admiral Yamamoto having readily agreed, an announcement in this sense was made by the News Department today.'

## No. 102

*Sir R. Lindsay (Washington) to Sir J. Simon (Received December 31, 9 a.m.)*
*No. 412 Telegraphic [A 10418/1938/45]*

WASHINGTON, *December 30, 1934, 9.55 p.m.*

After delivering note yesterday announcing denunciation of Naval Treaty[1] Japanese Ambassador made statement expressing sincere hope that there would be substitute accord embodying Japanese proposals. He emphasized that in proposing total abolition of capital ships and aircraft carriers Japan was ready to go down to half her present naval strength. However her claim for parity was necessary pre-requisite to such real reduction. It was not

[1] No. 99, note 3.

desired to attain common upper limit overnight but each Power must have right to build up to it as necessity of situation dictates. Three great Naval powers had enough difficult work on hand without contemplating possibility of war. Accord on reasonable basis should therefore be attainable within next two years. But even if no accord were reached he was not anxious over consequences and there was no logical reason for Japan and America to compete over armaments. It was gratifying that Japanese and American Governments were endeavouring to stop Jingoes from making irresponsible and inflammatory utterances.

Secretary of State has also issued statement[2] expressing regret at denunciation but admitting that any nation has right not to renew a Treaty and that any movement towards disarmament if it is to be successful must rest on agreements voluntarily entered into. While each nation naturally desires to be on basis of absolute equality in matter of national security experience teaches that conditions of peace or measures of disarmament cannot be promoted by doctrine that all nations regardless of their varying defensive needs shall have equality of armaments. Existing treaties have involved no invasion of sovereign rights and have provided that armaments of participating nations be established by voluntary undertaking on proportionate basis. Treaty has still two years to run and American Government is ready to enter upon negotiations whenever it appears that there is prospect of arrival at mutually satisfactory conclusion which would give further effect to American desire that nations of world shall not be burdened by avoidable or extravagant expenditures on armament. It is still among fundamental objectives of American foreign policy to prompt [promote] peace through disarmament and co-operative effort along certain defined lines.

Press also publishes statement made by Foreign Minister in Tokyo.[3]

[2] See *F.R.U.S. 1934*, vol. i, pp. 420–1.   [3] Cf. *The Times*, December 31, p. 14.

## No. 103

### Sir R. Vansittart to Sir J. Simon (Monte Carlo)
### Unnumbered Telegraphic [A 33/22/45]

FOREIGN OFFICE, *January 1, 1935, 6.15 p.m.*

As it would be unwise from the point of view of the effect on public opinion in this country, the United States and Japan that H.M. Government should appear to be taking too lightly the denunciation by Japan of the Washington Treaty, it is suggested that a politely worded note should be sent to the Japanese Ambassador here pointing out that the decision of the Japanese Government has been received in this country with sincere regret. The note would add that, as H.M. Government would regard the failure to negotiate a new arrangement as a confession of despair, they note with the greatest satisfaction the assurance conveyed to the U.S. Government that the Japanese Government will actively collaborate with the other Powers in a determined endeavour to ensure a future settlement.

The note would subsequently be published provided that the Japanese Ambassador saw no objection.

Mr. Craigie has informed the Japanese Ambassador that such a note might be addressed to him and His Excellency seemed to consider this a perfectly natural step. It is not, however, proposed that any note should be sent unless the U.S. Government, as the convening Power, also address one on these lines to the Japanese Government. Sir R. Lindsay is being instructed to inform us at once if the U.S. Gov[t]. do so act.[1]

It is understood that Mr. Craigie has already discussed this matter with you provisionally in anticipation of denunciation. Now that it has actually taken place, would you let us know as early as possible whether you approve of the action suggested?

[1] These instructions were given in Foreign Office telegram No. 1 to Sir R. Lindsay of January 1, 1935, despatched at 7.30 p.m.

## No. 104

*Sir R. Lindsay (Washington) to Sir R. Vansittart*
*(Received January 4, 9.30 a.m.)*
*No. 1 Telegraphic [A 105/22/45]*

WASHINGTON, *January 3, 1935, 10.30 p.m.*

Your telegram No. 1.[1]

In addition to Secretary of State's statement summarized in my telegram No. 412[2] a purely formal note was addressed to Japanese Ambassador acknowledging his communication and stating that other signatories will be notified.[3] Under Secretary of State informed me today it has now been decided to address no further note to Japanese Ambassador.[4]

[1] No. 103, note 1.
[2] No. 102.                                                   [3] Cf. *F.R.U.S. 1934*, vol. i, p. 423.
[4] In a minute of January 4 Mr. Craigie wrote: 'The initiative in such action should more properly come from the United States as the convening Power of the Washington Conference, and for His Majesty's Government to take the lead would be for them to assume a rôle which should properly be played by the United States.' It was accordingly decided that a note on the lines set out in No. 103 should not be delivered.

## No. 105

*Sir R. Lindsay (Washington) to Sir J. Simon (Received January 11, 9.30 a.m.)*
*No. 6 Telegraphic [A 343/22/45]*

WASHINGTON, *January 10, 1935, 8.45 p.m.*

Press state that Mr. Norman Davis, after discussions at State Department, has disclosed 'British Naval counter-proposal' and expressed belief that it will be accepted by the three Powers concerned within a year.

Counter-proposal, Mr. Davis explains, provides that the Powers, while not binding themselves to any fixed ratios (all reference to which will in future be abandoned) should in fact limit their construction to limits imposed by Washington Treaty, agreeing under an 'escape clause' not to exceed those limits without affording due notice. Secretary of State is reported to have induced Mr. Davis to give publicity to above disclosure and forecast, rather against the latter's will.

Mr. Davis is said simultaneously to have emphasised that Great Britain stood as firmly against Japanese pretensions in London as did the United States of America.

## No. 106

*Minute by Mr. Craigie*

*[A 478/22/45]*

FOREIGN OFFICE, *January 11, 1935*

Shortly after the American naval delegation left London last summer, we communicated to the U.S. Embassy unofficially a memorandum explaining as lucidly and forcibly as possible the grounds on which we were unable to make further reductions in our naval strength and were indeed obliged to make a certain increase in our cruiser strength.[1] We afterwards learned from the Americans that this document was most useful and proved, in fact, to be the principal means of converting the American Navy Department to the view that our demand for 70 cruisers was in all the circumstances a reasonable one.

It occurred to me that we might repeat the same process with the Japanese, and hand Admiral Yamamoto, before he leaves, a memorandum which would, *mutatis mutandis*, give a summary of the British case, in the hope that this may be of assistance to Admiral Yamamoto in bringing his Government to a better understanding of our needs. The annexed draft memorandum[2] has accordingly been prepared in consultation between the Naval Staff and myself.

If this document is approved, I would propose to hand it first to Mr. Matsudaira and ask him to state frankly whether, in point of form or presentation, he would like to suggest any amendments, since our whole purpose in preparing the memorandum was to be of assistance to Admiral Yamamoto. I would make it clear that this was not to be regarded in any sense as a diplomatic communication but merely as a summing up of the arguments which have been used in the course of our discussions. It is important that we should be able to deny that any written communication has been addressed to the Japanese Government.

We have reason to believe that Admiral Yamamoto may be leaving on the 15th instant,[3] but we understand from the Japanese Embassy that no decision has yet been taken, and we surmise that the Admiral may be waiting for this

---

[1] No. 2.  [2] Not printed; cf. enclosure in No. 110 below.
[3] A marginal note here read: 'We have since heard that the Admiral will not leave until later in the month. R.L.C.'

memorandum which we told him we would prepare for him.[4] I would suggest that a copy of the memorandum should be sent to the Secretary of State by bag to-night[5] and perhaps the Private Secretary would let us know by telephone whether or not the Secretary of State concurs.[6] A copy of the memorandum, with a copy of this minute, should, I think, be sent simultaneously to the Prime Minister.[7]

Sir Warren Fisher concurs in the memorandum, which contains several of his amendments.

As soon as the memorandum has been handed to Mr. Matsudaira I suggest that it should be circulated to the Ministerial Committee.[8]

[4] See No. 100.
[5] Sir J. Simon had left London for Geneva on January 10 to attend the opening meeting of the 84th session of the Council of the League of Nations.
[6] Sir J. Simon returned from Geneva in time to minute his approval of the memorandum on January 12. He suggested that the covering note but not the memorandum itself should be marked 'secret', with a view to possible future publication.
[7] Mr. MacDonald concurred in the memorandum on January 12 subject to the concurrence of Sir J. Simon and to an amendment in paragraph 10.
[8] See No. 110 below.

## No. 107

### Sir R. Vansittart to Sir R. Lindsay (Washington)
### No. 6 Telegraphic [A 343/22/45]

Immediate                                FOREIGN OFFICE, *January 12, 1935, 5.10 p.m.*

Your telegram No. 6.[1]

It is difficult to believe that Mr. Norman Davis, without previous consultation with His Majesty's Government, could have disclosed 'British naval counter-proposal', particularly as it was understood when he left that nature of tentative suggestions which have been under discussion here would be kept strictly confidential. In particular, alleged statement that under this proposal the Powers 'should in fact limit their construction to limits imposed by Washington Treaty' is unfortunate and may, indeed, be calamitous at this stage, for it may well sterilise in advance any tendency to compromise, which report of Japanese representatives in recent discussions might conceivably recommend. It has already produced a very uncompromising counter-statement by Japanese Foreign Office spokesman.[2] It must be obvious that premature publicity of this kind is bound to prejudice such chances as there may be of ultimate acceptance by the Japanese Government of a solution on the lines of the scheme recently under discussion.

[1] No. 105.
[2] *The Times* of January 12 contained a report from its correspondent in Tokyo dated January 11 of a statement by the Japanese Foreign Office spokesman, who 'defined naval parity as actual equality of armaments with the United States. He implicitly repudiated the idea that parity could somehow be conceded in theory and withheld in practice, at least as between Japan and America. Great Britain was not mentioned.' Elaborating this viewpoint, the spokesman said that Mr. Davis's statement 'simply meant denial in fact of parity in armaments'.

I trust that Mr. Norman Davis may have been misreported. It seems indeed hard to believe that the State Department should have pressed him into such an indiscretion. It is however important that we should be informed at once what he did say to the press on this subject, in order that we may be able to decide what line to take with our own press. Meanwhile, we propose to confine ourselves to saying that we are unable to confirm accuracy of the statements attributed to Mr. Norman Davis in regard to nature of tentative suggestions which have been under discussion in London.

Please speak to State Department in above sense, and again remind them of the tacit understanding between representatives in London that no information should be given to press in regard to nature of solution we have been considering.

## No. 108

*Sir R. Lindsay (Washington) to Sir J. Simon (Received January 15, 9.30 a.m.)*
*No. 11 Telegraphic [A 455/22/45]*

*Confidential*                                    WASHINGTON, *January 14, 1935, 11.15 p.m.*

1. Under Secretary of State today gave me unofficially confidential copies of notes exchanged with French Ambassador about denunciation of Naval Treaty.[1]

2. French Note is dated 2nd January and includes the following statements—

(a) recalls French declaration of August 17th, 1923 made on ratification of treaty;

(b) French Parliament when considering ratification indicated intention that treaty should terminate in 1936;

(c) Past year has shown what difficulties arise out of system of quantitative limitation;

(d) French Government would not in any case have been able to agree to its continuation;

(e) Position of Powers not represented at Washington in 1922 would have to be taken into account in a settlement of naval questions and a new treaty should not be limited to the five Powers;

(f) New treaty will have to maintain and perhaps make more strict principle of qualitative limitations.

3. United States Government reply dated January 12th says that statement reproduced in (d) above is a source of surprise and disappointment. United States Government has indicated its regret and its views in Secretary of State's statement of December 29th[2] and in Mr. Norman Davis' speech of December 6th.[3]

4. When French Ambassador presented Note Under Secretary of State expressed regret that French Government should thus appear to be identify-

[1] See *F.R.U.S. 1934*, vol. i, pp. 421–3, 426.          [2] Cf. No. 102, note 2.
[3] Cf. No. 91, note 1.

ing itself to some extent with Japanese attitude. French Ambassador had replied that his Government had only German re-armament in mind.

5. Under Secretary of State told me it was not intended to publish these Notes.

## No. 109

*Sir R. Lindsay (Washington) to Sir J. Simon (Received January 15, 9.30 a.m.)*
*No. 13 Telegraphic [A 451/22/45]*

WASHINGTON, *January 14, 1935, 11.15 p.m.*

Your telegram No. 6.[1]

I saw Under Secretary of State this morning and as instructed spoke strongly about Mr. Norman Davis' disclosure of British naval suggestion and I asked to be told exactly what he had said. He replied that substance of this suggestion had already appeared in the press (which is true as regards press telegrams from London) and that some papers had misrepresented language used. He then sent for shorthand transcription of what Mr. Norman Davis had said and read to me long extracts (but not all). What he read was innocuous and in general terms and conveyed no real information.

My telegram No. 6 was mainly based on report of a press conference given by a very reliable Washington correspondent and I surmise what really happened was that Mr. Norman Davis and Secretary of State attended the conference together without having agreed beforehand exactly what they would say and that Secretary of State who was less familiar with all the circumstances precipitated Mr. Norman Davis into an indiscretion.

I pointed out that revelation of suggestion coming thus from an official source must greatly increase difficulty of its acceptance by Japan. Under Secretary of State agreed and admitted that the response from Tokyo had been strong and unfavourable. He said that he would do what was possible to induce the press to make little of British suggestions.

[1] No. 107.

## No. 110

*Letter from Mr. Craigie[1] to Commander A. W. Clarke*
*[A 478/22/45]*

*Secret*　　　　　　　　　　　　　　　FOREIGN OFFICE, *January 16, 1935*

Dear Clarke,

The enclosed memorandum has been handed this morning to the Counsellor of the Japanese Embassy, for communication to Admiral Yamamoto. It has been approved by the Prime Minister, the Secretary of State and the

[1] Mr. Craigie (cf. No. 1, note 1) had been promoted to be an Assistant Under Secretary of State in the Foreign Office on January 15, 1935.

First Lord, but I think it should also be circulated to the Ministerial Naval Committee. Would you be good enough to do this 'by direction of the Secretary of State for Foreign Affairs and the First Lord of the Admiralty'? The covering note should, I think, state that it is understood between the Japanese Embassy and the Foreign Office that the memorandum will not be regarded as a communication from Government to Government but merely as a note which it is hoped may be useful to Admiral Yamamoto personally in the discussions which he will have with his Government on his return to Japan.[2]

Yours sincerely,

R. L. CRAIGIE

ENCLOSURE IN No. 110

*Notes on the minimum British Naval Strength necessary for Security*

*January 15, 1935*

At the final meeting of the three delegations on the 19th December, 1934,[3] the Prime Minister urged the representatives of Japan and the United States of America to realise that Great Britain was basing herself on essentials and asked them, therefore, not to assume that it was only a matter of pressure or time for the United Kingdom to change. The figures that have been communicated to the Japanese and the United States of America representatives are, in fact, not maxima up to which the United Kingdom desires to be able to build, but minima below which the British Empire cannot feel a sense of security.

2. As stated in the Japanese fundamental claim[4] 'To possess the measure of armaments necessary for national safety is a right to which all nations are equally entitled' and 'due regard must be given to that right in order that the sense of national security of the various powers might not be impaired'. The unique situation of the British Empire lies in the fact that it is not a single unit geographically concentrated in one area of the world but consists of a number of Dominions and Colonies scattered over the whole world. Consequently, the strength of the British Navy must be calculated so as to produce a sense of national security in all the Dominions and Colonies, each of which has a right to its own safety.

3. In estimating the naval needs of the British Empire, it is accordingly necessary to take into account responsibilities in European waters and in the Atlantic, Indian and Pacific Oceans. This implies the possession of a fleet of sufficient strength to be able to dispose simultaneously in more than one area forces adequate to meet all reasonable defensive needs.

4. *Capital Ships*. When the matter of capital ship strength was considered at Washington in 1922 and again in London in 1930, it was decided that 15 capital ships represented the minimum which would give to the British

[2] The memorandum and covering note were circulated as N.C.M. (35) 42.
[3] See No. 95.                                                                     [4] See No. 37.

Empire the requisite defensive strength. Since then Germany has not only built 4 battle-cruisers of a special type but will undoubtedly insist on naval expansion qualitatively as well as quantitatively. Italy is already building 2 capital ships of 35,000 tons each; France will wish to lay down ships of the same size and is understood, in addition, to wish to increase her capital ship strength beyond the limits imposed by the Washington Naval Treaty. If these tendencies continue and if there is no international agreement on naval limitation after 1936, the probabilities are that, far from any decrease in British capital ship strength being possible, a further increase in numbers would be rendered necessary.

5. With less than 15 capital ships it would not be possible to provide reasonable security both in European waters and elsewhere. The tonnage figure in this category communicated to the Japanese representatives, however, is dependent also on the qualitative limit to be arrived at for new capital ships. The British Government have, as is well known, proposed a limit of 25,000 tons with 12″ guns, a reduction of 28 per cent. on the existing limit. Could this limit be generally agreed upon, the tonnage in the capital ship category could ultimately be correspondingly reduced.

6. *Aircraft Carriers.* The under-age tonnage of aircraft carriers that was communicated to the Japanese representatives was calculated on 5 units of the proposed maximum size of 22,000 tons each. This is the least number of units that could be accepted for the normal operations of the British Fleet. The Japanese representatives have proposed, however, that the future qualitative limit should be reduced to 20,000 tons. If there is a reasonable prospect of agreement in other categories, the British Government would be willing to consider this reduction with a corresponding reduction of the tonnage in the category.

7. Further, if it should prove possible to bring about the abolition of bombing, still greater reductions might be made in the aircraft carrier category.

8. *Cruisers.* The British Government have already announced their hope of the ultimate abolition of the 8″ gun cruiser. All such vessels, however, are comparatively modern, and it is highly improbable that foreign Powers would agree to scrap them before the end of 1942. France and Italy each have 7 of these vessels in service already, and Japan has 12, while America has 18 built and building. It is not possible, therefore, for the British Empire to reduce below the 15 ships already built.

9. In the London Naval Treaty the British Empire agreed to the low total cruiser figure of 339,000 tons, which was calculated on a basis of 50 cruisers. Even if it were possible to make a further agreement on such a basis (and reasons why it is not are given below) the tonnage figure would have to be considerably larger than 339,000 tons. The British Empire cannot replace existing small war-time cruisers by ships that would be outclassed from the start by those of other navies. From this it follows that there must be an automatic increase, even without any increase in the number of ships, from a tonnage of 339,000 tons to about 410,000 tons. This figure is

based on the general acceptance of a future qualitative limitation of 7,000 tons, and would be made up as follows:—

| | |
|---|---|
| 15 8″ Gun Cruisers . . . . . . . | . 146,800 tons |
| 10 Large 6″ Gun Cruisers . . . . . | . 95,000 ,, |
| 8 Leanders . . . . . . . . | . 57,000 ,, |
| 4 Arethusas . . . . . . . . | . 20,800 ,, |
| 13 New ships @ 7,000 tons . . . . | . 91,000 ,, |
| 50 | 410,600 ,, |

10. In the London Naval Treaty the British Empire accepted a cruiser tonnage figure based upon the tonnage of 50 cruisers for the following reasons:—

(a) Under the international conditions existing at that time, the prospect for the next six years was more unclouded than it can be said to be to-day.

(b) It was accepted subject to the Powers other than the three signatories to Part III of the London Naval Treaty agreeing to corresponding reductions. This has not occurred: on the contrary, the naval forces in Europe have greatly increased.

(c) In 1930 we were on the eve of a General Disarmament Conference from which much was hoped.

(d) In the process of a steady reconstruction of the fleet after the war, a halt had been called in cruiser building for some years, in the hope of inducing a corresponding halt in foreign building. Thus, the curve indicating the number of British under-age cruisers was at its lowest during the period of the treaty.

It is unfortunately the case that since the London Naval Treaty was concluded in 1930, a serious deterioration in the international and political outlook has occurred. Further, there are not present to-day any of the other conditions that rendered possible the acceptance in 1930 of a cruiser tonnage based on 50 ships.

11. The British 6″ gun cruiser under-age tonnage is governed by the intention of the British Government to arrive, by a programme of steady building of about 3 ships a year, at an ultimate total (including 15 8″ gun cruisers) of 70 ships, of which 10 would be over-age. Due to the necessity for building large 6″ gun cruisers, brought about by the building of such ships by the United States of America and Japan, the 243,800 tons of under-age tonnage at the end of 1942 (the figure given to the United States of America and Japanese representatives) would represent only 32 ships, making at that time with the 8″ gun cruisers a total of 47 under-age cruisers in all. A balance of over-age ships must, therefore, be retained to provide security.

12. *Destroyers.* The 150,000 tons of under-age destroyer tonnage is the same as that agreed upon in the London Naval Treaty and could only be reduced if submarines were abolished or drastically reduced in numbers.

(If submarines were abolished, 100,000 tons of destroyers would be sufficient.) As, however, an increase of submarine tonnage appears likely in certain European navies as well as in the Japanese Navy, it will be necessary to retain additional over-age destroyer tonnage.

13. *Submarines.* The British Government desires to abolish all submarines. If this cannot be achieved, however, they neither desire nor intend to increase their tonnage beyond that agreed upon in the London Naval Treaty and would consider the additional destroyer tonnage required by an increase in the submarine tonnage of others as a provision in lieu of an increase in their own submarine tonnage.

## No. 111

*Memorandum on the Present Position of Naval Conversations and Recommendations as to Future Procedure[1]*

[A 901/22/45]

*January 17, 1935*

In the draft report of the Cabinet Committee on preparations for the 1935 Naval Conference (N.C.M.(35)12, also D.C.(M)(32)121),[2] the Committee included the following recommendation:—

'We desire that the foregoing recommendations should be treated as provisional and for the purpose of the exploratory conversations with the interested Powers, and that the formulation of a final policy should be governed by the outcome of the preliminary exchange of views with the other Powers of our respective desiderata for the 1935 Conference.'

2. The conversations which have just terminated have revealed the views of the principal maritime Powers, and the present situation is as follows:—

3. The United States of America maintain their insistence on parity with the British Commonwealth fleet, but they would like parity on their own level based upon their smaller naval needs. They consider their absolute requirements to be at least 20 per cent. less than the treaty strength allowed to them under the London Naval Treaty.[3] They have, as far as their representatives in London are concerned, reacted not unfavourably to the British compromise proposal for declarations of building programmes, although they have indicated that they consider our figures unduly high in some respects; more particularly, they do not desire to build up to our requirements in numbers of capital ships or in total tonnage of cruisers. Nevertheless, they recognise the strength of the arguments put forward by the British representatives in favour of our minimum requirements, and they have hinted that, subject to agreement with and about Japan, it would be possible to reach a quantitative settlement as between the United Kingdom and the United States of America.

---

[1] This memorandum was prepared by Mr. Craigie in consultation with the Naval Staff. It embodied a certain number of amendments proposed by Sir Warren Fisher. After approval by Mr. Ramsay MacDonald, Sir Bolton Eyres Monsell, and Sir John Simon, it was circulated as N.C.M.(35)46.

[2] Of June 11, 1934; not printed.       [3] Of April 22, 1930.

4. Japan also demands parity. In her case what she primarily means is parity with the United States, of whom she has considerable doubts, if not actual fear. As in the case of the United States, so also with Japan, national prestige is a very definite factor, for, clearly, the security of neither of these two Powers requires a fleet equal to the British. Like the United States of America, however, Japan does not desire to achieve this parity upon our level, but upon her own, and she is prepared apparently to place her absolute requirements in this respect at a figure approximately 50 per cent. below the tonnage of her present fleet. Officially, she has not rejected, although she has not accepted, the British compromise proposal for declaration of building programmes, and there is some hope that, after Admiral Yamamoto's return to Japan, the Japanese Government may be induced to adopt a favourable attitude towards this proposal. It appears that their principal objection is to the level at which the British figures in the various categories will be maintained rather than to the principle of the compromise proposal.

5. We have made it clear to other Powers that the absolute requirements for ensuring the security of the British Commonwealth do not admit of reductions in any of the categories other than the great reduction that could be brought about by reducing the qualitative limits of the individual ships, against which only the United States of America stands out. Moreover, it has been pointed out that our minimum requirements for cruisers are not met by the London Naval Treaty figures, and that an increase in this category is imperative. It has been made clear that we cannot be expected to yield on essentials, and the United States representatives have been informed frankly that the level of parity must be assessed in London and not in Washington. The building programme figures which have been communicated to the United States of America and Japanese representatives are based upon these considerations.

6. So far as qualitative limitation is concerned, the conversations with the Americans and Japanese have not led to any concrete results, but we should probably not be over sanguine in hoping for agreement on the following general lines: reduction of the capital ship to 30,000 tons with a 14″ gun; reduction of aircraft carriers to 22,000 tons; numerical limitation of large cruisers and reduction in displacement of all other cruisers to 7,000 tons; other qualitative limitations to remain approximately as in the present Treaties.

7. In the conversations in the summer with the representatives of France and Italy, it was apparent that no great exception would be taken by those countries to the British figures, either quantitative or qualitative, and that their problem was to reach a satisfactory agreement as between themselves and other European Powers.

8. On the whole, it is believed that the recent conversations, particularly with the representatives of the United States of America and Japan, have secured a clear understanding of the British position, and in none of these conversations have they denied the strength of the British arguments.

(The change in the views of Admiral Standley regarding British cruiser strength is a notable example.) It is particularly satisfactory to note that close and friendly relations have been maintained with the United States and Japanese representatives throughout the conversations and that there has been every evidence of a sincere desire on all sides to reach agreement. Appreciation has been expressed in Japanese official circles of the friendly efforts of His Majesty's Government to take account of Japan's point of view.

9. The desire of the United States and Japan for a reduction in their naval strengths is a tacit admission by those Powers of the inherent security of their respective strategical positions, a contention which has always been maintained by the Naval Staff. For one reason and another, the naval strength of the British Empire has, since the war, been reduced to the point at which it now stands, i.e., below that required for security in the present altered condition of international politics. The United States of America and Japan have built up naval armaments exceeding their real needs and, wishing now to reduce the consequent unjustifiable expenditure, they are, for reasons of prestige, asking the British Empire to reduce its naval strength below what is safe.

10. Turning to the future it seems desirable that we should now inform both France and Italy, the other two signatories of the Washington Treaty, of the stage the negotiations have reached. Although proposals for agreement on building programmes have been made in the past between France and Italy without success owing to the insistence in [? on] equality, it is possible that the British building programme compromise, which purports to settle the question of prestige, may have more chance of success. It is proposed that we should take an early opportunity of ascertaining whether the Franco-Italian problem is capable of solution on these lines, maintaining as the basis of our own figures the minimum requirements hitherto stated (see N.C.M.(35)12).²

11. The prospect of France and Italy now being prepared to negotiate direct with each other on the naval problem is perhaps increased by the outcome of the political negotiations recently carried through between the two Powers.⁴ But in any event we should not be forcing their hand if we merely invite them at this stage to consider the possibility of basing future negotiations on the plan which has formed the subject of recent discussions with the Americans and Japanese. In the qualitative field, also, we could very hopefully carry a little further with the French and Italians the discussions we had with them on this subject last summer, and so lay the foundations of a treaty on qualitative limitation between all the naval Powers.

12. It is unlikely, however, that much progress can be made in further discussions with France until it is known what would be the probable demands of Germany if she is to be a party to any future convention on naval limitation. It is therefore desirable to consider when, and by what channel,

⁴ See Volume XII, enclosure in No. 335, for an account of the Franco-Italian agreements of January 7, 1935.

contact on this question can best be established with the German Government. The matter of Germany's naval claims is, of course, a part of the whole question of German rearmament and of her claim to 'Gleichberechtigung,' and this question may become the subject of renewed negotiations with Germany in the near future.[5] But, even so, it would be desirable that the question of the limitation of naval armaments should continue, as in the past, to be discussed separately from that of land and air armaments. In the case of naval armaments, a time limit to the naval discussions is set by the provisions in the Washington and London Naval Treaties which call for a naval conference this year, and we might have difficulty in completing preliminary discussions in time for a conference in the first half of this year (as we should like) if we were now to mark time until the whole question of German rearmament has been finally settled. Furthermore, the French Government themselves have recently insisted that the next naval conference must be a general conference of the naval Powers and not one between the Washington Treaty Powers only, so that it would be somewhat illogical if they were at the same time to delay such a general conference by holding up preliminary discussions with the Germans, or by making a naval understanding with Germany dependent on a complete settlement with Germany as regards armaments in general.[6]

13. Hitherto we have discussed the possible maximum tonnage of Germany's future navy (N.C. (F), 4th meeting),[7] but it is now for consideration whether we should not change this method and deal with the German naval problem by building programmes, as we are proposing for the signatories of the Washington Treaty. If we continue to discuss the possible maximum tonnage of Germany's fleet it is probable that, to satisfy her public opinion, she will formulate demands which will only aggravate the naval situation in Europe and lead to no solution. It is suggested that the more practical form of building programmes, coupled with the declaration in regard to prestige, is more likely to produce from Germany figures which can be

[5] See *ibid.*, chapters III and IV, for the Anglo-German conversations in Berlin on March 25, 1935, and preceding events.

[6] In a minute of January 20, Sir J. Simon wrote: 'The main difficulty which occurs to me about this scheme is that Germany may reply to suggestions that she should define (*query* and agree to be limited by?) her building programme, that she must first have conceded to her the right to build what she pleases and then she will be prepared to consider what voluntary limitations are possible for the next few years. She will thus raise *Gleichberechtigung* as a preliminary question. There is, however, this distinction. As regards navies, France, Italy and ourselves *are* bound by treaty limits, whereas we are not as regards armies or air-forces. There is therefore no inequality of status if parties all of whom are now limited by treaty endeavour to agree limits for the future.' On January 23 Mr. Craigie commented as follows on Sir J. Simon's minute: 'From what we know of the view of the German Ministry of Marine it is on the whole unlikely that Germany will raise the principle of *Gleichberechtigung* before she agrees to enter into conversations with us on the naval question: on the contrary we have had several hints that the German Ministry of Marine are very anxious to start these discussions with us as soon as possible.'

[7] This meeting between French and British naval experts was held at the Foreign Office on July 11, 1934.

reconciled with the programmes of France and Italy. It would, of course, be understood that, if the negotiations with Germany in regard to building programmes were to be successful, and if Germany were to become a party to any future naval treaty, the same qualitative limits would apply to the German navy as to other navies.

14. What is therefore proposed at this stage is not the opening of formal negotiations with the German Government, but the taking of soundings as to Germany's requirements for a building programme on the British basis. This would commit neither ourselves nor any other foreign Government, but would enable us to ascertain what in fact are likely to be the practical steps Germany wishes to take should she eventually participate in a general naval conference. It would be necessary, before commencing naval discussions with the German representatives, to make it clear to the German Government that this was being done without prejudice to the present validity of the naval clauses of the Treaty of Versailles, and to any general conditions which the ex-Allied Governments may wish to make in return for the application in practice of the principle regarding equality of rights laid down in the Declaration of the 11th December, 1932.[8] As regards the method of communication, it is thought that the best course would probably be for discussions to take place with the German Ambassador in London, who would, of course, be free to equip himself with any experts he might consider necessary.

15. The forthcoming visit of French Ministers to London[9] would offer a good opportunity of representing to the French Government the desirability of sounding the German Government on this question as soon as possible, and of inviting their concurrence. The idea of taking these soundings will not be a novel one to the French Government, because it was mooted during the visit to London last summer of M. Barthou and M. Piétri, and the French experts were on that occasion informed unofficially of the naval strength in the various categories for which we thought Germany might reasonably ask if she were to become a party to any new naval treaty. While the discussions on this point were not conclusive, the French representatives did not raise any strong objection to the suggestions which we put forward at that time.[10]

16. If the French Government agree to our sounding the German Government as proposed, it would be desirable similarly to consult the Italian Government before taking action at Berlin.

17. *General Conclusion.* The preparatory discussions in which we have been engaged since last summer with representatives of the other signatory States of the Washington Treaty have served the purpose for which they were designed, and give ground for hope that a basis may be found for the

[8] See Volume IV, enclosure in No. 220.

[9] For the Anglo-French conversations in London, February 1–3, 1935, see Volume XII, Nos. 397–400.

[10] The proposals in paragraphs 12–15 above were somewhat elaborated in paragraphs 3–11 of a further paper of January 25, circulated as C.P. 23 (35); cf. Volume XII, No. 372.

conclusion of a new naval treaty which will deal both with quantitative and qualitative limitation. The parity demands of the U.S.A. and Japan referred to in paragraphs 3 and 4 above constitute the fundamental difficulty. It is certain that the U.S.A. will continue her insistence on parity with us and on superiority to Japan. We cannot hope to change the American attitude, and this is an undoubted element in the reluctance of the Japanese to modify theirs. But Admiral Yamamoto, who quite recognises our special position and requirements, is expected shortly to return to Japan, where it is hoped he will succeed in persuading the Ministry of Marine to adopt a compromise of the kind we have suggested. The resumption in the spring of the discussions with the United States and Japan will depend on the degree of success which attends Admiral Yamamoto's efforts. The initiative for suggesting their resumption has, for the time being, been left to the Japanese.

The following recommendations are made as to the action which might be taken pending the resumption of the discussions with the United States and Japan:—

(a) The French Government should be asked whether they would be prepared to send representatives to London in order that we may explain to them fully the result of the conversations up to date, and make suggestions to them in regard to future procedure. It would be suggested to the French representatives that, in any future discussions they may have with the Italian Government on the naval question, the building programme compromise proposal now under consideration in Washington and Tokyo should form the basis, though we would naturally leave it to the French Government to decide when the appropriate moment had arrived to enter upon naval discussions with Italy. (It could be left to the French Government to decide whether these naval discussions should coincide with M. Laval's proposed visit or not.) The line we would propose to take in sounding the German Government on this question would also be explained to the French representatives.

(b) The Italian Government should be informed through the diplomatic channel of what passes between the French and ourselves. (It is understood that the Italian Government are in no immediate hurry to send a special mission to London to discuss the naval question.)

(c) Provided the French and Italian Governments do not raise serious objections, the German Government should be invited to commence discussions through the diplomatic channel in the manner suggested in paragraph 14 above.

(d) If the discussions with the German representatives hold out some hope of ultimate success, the Italian Government should be invited to send representatives, and a serious effort should then be made to lay the foundation for a naval limitation agreement amongst the European Powers.

It would, of course, be understood that any views or statistics put forward by the British representatives in the course of such discussions would remain subject to a satisfactory agreement being ultimately reached with the United States and Japan.

## No. 112

### Sir J. Simon to Sir R. Clive (Tokyo)
### No. 41 [A 10309/1938/45]

Secret                                   FOREIGN OFFICE, *January 25, 1935*

Sir,

As I informed Your Excellency in the fourth paragraph of my despatch No. 729 of the 21st November last,[1] I discussed on that date with the Japanese Ambassador certain questions connected with the continuance of the Four Power Treaty, with the result that His Excellency promised to refer to his Government for an answer to certain enquiries which I made during our interview.

2. Towards the end of December M. Matsudaira alluded to this matter again in the course of a conversation with Mr. Craigie. He first recapitulated his conversation with me by saying that I had put to him two points: (1) Was it the idea of the Japanese Government that the Four Power Treaty, which was now terminable at one year's notice, should be continued for a further period of, say, ten years? (2) Would the Japanese Government suggest that we should renew at the same time the assurances given to Holland and Portugal at the time of the signature of the Four Power Treaty? M. Matsudaira went on to say that the answer to question (1) was in the affirmative. As regards question (2), the Japanese Government did not think it was either necessary or desirable to renew these assurances which, in their view, remained automatically binding upon those Powers which had given them so long as the Four Power Treaty remained in force. It was therefore obvious that, if it were to be agreed between the Four Powers concerned that the Treaty should remain in force for a further term of, say, ten years (i.e. that none of them would give notice denouncing it during this period) the validity of the assurances to Holland and Portugal would simultaneously be extended for that period.

[I am, &c.,
JOHN SIMON]

[1] No. 76.

## No. 113

### Sir R. Clive (Tokyo) to Sir J. Simon (Received February 9, 9.30 a.m.)
### No. 45 Telegraphic [A 1253/22/45]

TOKYO, *February 9, 1935, 12.45 p.m.*

Press report that Minister of Marine's reply to questions in Committee of Diet February 6th that non-acceptance of[1] fortification clause Article 19 of

[1] It was suggested on the filed copy of this telegram that the words 'acceptance of' should be deleted.

Washington Treaty should be extended to include Hawaii and Singapore has created much comment.

Naval Attaché enquired yesterday as to exact sense of Minister's statement and was told that no mention was made of Hawaii and Singapore. Statement was to the effect that owing to increase in endurance and speed of naval and[2] air-craft, area included in any new non-fortification agreement would have to be extended.

> [2] It was suggested on the filed copy that this word should be deleted.

## No. 114

### Sir J. Simon to Sir G. Clerk[1] (Paris)
### No. 445 [A 1713/22/45]

Sir,                                                    FOREIGN OFFICE, February 21, 1935

I spoke to M. Corbin to-day about the recent naval negotiations, and outlined to him what I thought should be their future course.[2] I reminded him that, during the discussions in London between the Americans, the Japanese and ourselves, we had kept the French Government fully informed, so that I did not now propose to go into detail. I thought, however, the situation might be summed up as follows:—

2. During the recent discussions it had come to be generally recognised that there was no prospect of any agreement on quantitative limitation being reached on the basis of agreed ratios of naval strength; we had therefore discussed with the Americans and the Japanese the idea of issuing voluntary and unilateral declarations containing our respective programmes for the six years 1937–42. These programmes would not be contractual in form, but, in practice, it would have to be understood between the Powers concerned that there must be no departure from the figures indicated in the programmes unless notice of, say, one year had been given in advance. The American and Japanese representatives had returned to their respective countries in order to discuss with their Governments the possibility of an arrangement along these lines. Should such an arrangement prove possible so far as the United Kingdom, the United States and Japan are concerned, it was highly desirable that the forthcoming discussions between the European Powers should proceed on the same basis.

3. We were anxious to have a further talk with representatives of the French Government on this subject at an early date. We felt, however, that

> [1] H.M. Ambassador at Paris.
>
> [2] Sir J. Simon's remarks were based on a memorandum by Mr. Craigie of February 13, in the course of which he remarked that since the memorandum of January 17 (No. 111 above) the visit of the French Ministers to London had taken place and it had not been possible to mention the naval question (cf. Volume XII, Nos. 397–400); furthermore, he had received a private message from M. Massigli 'intimating that we should probably be wise not to insist on securing the formal assent of the French Government to our opening naval discussions with the Germans, as this might be a little embarrassing for the French Government, but to go ahead with our enquiries which he personally felt to be a necessary preliminary to any further European discussions'.

the first step should now be to sound the Germans as informally as possible as to what their own desiderata in the naval sphere were likely to be in the event of a general naval conference taking place. M. Barthou and M. Piétri had been informed, when they visited London last July, that we thought the moment would shortly arrive when such soundings should be taken, subject, of course, to the reservation of all rights under the Treaty of Versailles. M. Piétri had stated on that occasion that France agreed to the suggested procedure, but reserved all her rights.[3]

4. The main purpose of our enquiry of the German Government would, I said, be to ascertain Germany's probable naval requirements for a building programme during the period 1937–42. This would commit neither ourselves nor any other foreign Government, but would enable us to ascertain what, in fact, were likely to be Germany's demands should she eventually participate in a general naval conference. It would be necessary, before commencing naval discussions with the German representatives, to make it clear to the German Government that this was being done without prejudice to the present validity of the naval clauses of the Treaty of Versailles and to any agreement regarding armaments generally, which, as part of the general settlement foreshadowed by the London proposals of February 3rd, 1935,[4] may, in the case of Germany, replace the provisions of Part V of the treaty.

5. I added that we would, of course, keep the French Government fully informed throughout the course of any discussions we might have with the German Government, which we think should probably take place through the German Ambassador in London. Once the conversations with the German representatives had been concluded, we thought the next step should be further discussions between the representatives of the British and French Governments.

6. The Ambassador thanked me for my communication, which he promised to report to his Government at once.[5]

I am, &c.,

JOHN SIMON

---

[3] See Volume VI, No. 490.      [4] See Volume XII, No. 400, note 4, and Annex.
[5] In a private letter to Sir E. Drummond of March 22 Sir R. Vansittart wrote that, shortly after Sir J. Simon had seen M. Corbin, he had himself spoken to Signor Vitetti, Italian Chargé d'Affaires at London, and told him of Sir J. Simon's intention to raise the naval question with the Germans when he went to Berlin and to invite them to send representatives for discussions in London.

**No. 115**

*Sir R. Clive (Tokyo) to Sir J. Simon (Received February 28, 9.30 a.m.)*
*No. 58 Telegraphic [A 1947/22/45]*

My telegram No. 55.[1]       TOKYO, *February 28, 1935, 12.42 p.m.*
Minister for Foreign Affairs said at our interview that he hoped naval

---

[1] In this telegram of February 26, not printed, Sir R. Clive reported that during a conversation with the Japanese Minister for Foreign Affairs on the previous day Mr. Hirota

conference would meet as soon as possible—perhaps June or July. I said I supposed that if all signatories to the Treaty agreed conference could be postponed until next year. His Excellency said this would be very difficult and it was essential that conference should be held this year.

Japanese press has been saying that it is owing to impression made on Chinese by denunciation of Washington Treaty that China has been willing to enter on discussions with Japanese Government. Naval Attaché tells me in support of this view that Japanese naval officers argue that it is essential for Japan's prestige vis à vis China to be on an equality with other great naval Powers.

Repeated Saving to Peking.

had mentioned an improvement in Soviet-Japanese relations and 'said he was determined still further to improve relations with China and with U.S.S.R. before Naval Conference met this year'.

## No. 116

### Sir J. Simon to Sir R. Clive (Tokyo)
### No. 43 Telegraphic [A 1947/22/45]

FOREIGN OFFICE, *March 6, 1935, 6 p.m.*

Your telegram No. 58.[1]

You may inform Minister for Foreign Affairs orally that we fully concur in his view that Naval Conference should be held as soon as possible. His Majesty's Government feel that it is of the first importance from the point of view of world opinion that the Conference should result in a general measure of agreement and they therefore are disposed to doubt the desirability of the Conference meeting until the ground has been further prepared. From this point of view it would be very helpful to be informed whether the compromise proposal under discussion in London before Japanese Representatives left (i.e., the formal exchange of unilateral declarations of programme) would be in principle acceptable to the Japanese Government. In that case it might be possible, so far as Japan, the United States and this country are concerned, to dispense with further discussions between specially appointed delegations and to complete our preparations for a Conference by means of exchanges of view through the diplomatic channel.

Even so, however, it will—for reasons explained orally and in writing to Admiral Yamamoto—be necessary for us, before entering such a Conference between the five Powers, to have further preliminary talks with the European Powers primarily concerned in naval limitation. We hope that these consultations with the European Powers will commence shortly and we shall of course keep the Japanese Government fully informed.

[1] No. 115.

180

## No. 117

*Sir R. Clive (Tokyo) to Sir J. Simon (Received March 9, 2.30 p.m.)*
*No. 73 Telegraphic [A 2280/22/45]*

TOKYO, *March 9, 1935, 6 p.m.*

Your telegram No. 43.[1]

I made oral communication to Minister for Foreign Affairs today. His Excellency said he would at once speak to Minister of Marine. I reminded him of his remark that once Washington Treaty was out of the way he believed Navy would be more reasonable. (See my telegram No. 346 of December 8th).[2] He said he held to this view in spite of extremists.

[1] No. 116.          [2] No. 89.

## No. 118

*Memorandum by the Foreign Office and Admiralty on Questions of Naval Limitation*[1]

*[A 3205/22/45]*
*March 30, 1935*

On the 30th December, 1934, the Japanese Government informed the Government of the United States of their decision to terminate the Washington Treaty of the 6th February, 1922, for the Limitation of Naval Armaments.[2] This the Japanese Government were perfectly entitled to do under article 23 of that treaty, but, as a result of this action, there will be no naval treaty in existence after the 31st December, 1936, unless another agreement can be negotiated in the meanwhile.

2. A consequence of this step was to bring into effect paragraph 2 of article 23 of the Washington Treaty, which lays down that, 'within one year of the date on which a notice of termination by any Power has taken effect, all the Contracting Powers shall meet in conference'. Article 23 of the London Naval Treaty also contains a provision for the meeting in 1935 of a conference of the Naval Powers parties to that treaty. Thus, under both treaties, a conference must take place during the present year between representatives of the Governments of the British Commonwealth, the United States, Japan, France and Italy, unless the provisions of these treaties were to be modified with the unanimous consent of the parties.

3. It would obviously be highly undesirable that a conference of this scope and importance should be summoned without adequate preparation, and bilateral exchanges of views between the Governments concerned have

[1] This memorandum, which was circulated as N.C.M. (35) 48, was prepared in connexion with forthcoming meetings of British Commonwealth Prime Ministers during their visits to London in May 1935 for celebration of the Silver Jubilee of the accession to the throne of Their Majesties King George V and Queen Mary on May 6, 1910. Official celebrations were to be held during the week May 6–11, 1935.

[2] Cf. No. 99, note 3.

accordingly been taking place since June 1934. The resultant situation may be outlined as follows:—

4. *Quantitative Limitation.* So far as quantitative limitation is concerned (*i.e.,* the limitation of the total tonnages which each Power may retain in the various categories), one satisfactory result of the conversations was a statement by the United States Principal Naval Adviser that he did not propose to question the number of Cruisers needed for the security of the British Commonwealth[3]—a point which in the past has been a source of difficulty between the United States and ourselves. Nevertheless, the result of the preliminary talks with Japan has been to demonstrate the uselessness of any further attempt to conclude another naval treaty which establishes, or appears to establish, a definite relationship of naval strength (or 'ratio') between the parties to it. Japan's insistent demand for parity with the British Commonwealth and the United States remained unshaken during the whole period of the negotiations from the 23rd October to the 19th December. This demand took the form of a proposal for the establishment of a common upper limit which each Power would theoretically have the right to attain, though it was admitted that Japan would not necessarily seek to build up to that limit. The representatives of the United Kingdom and the United States, on the other hand, could see no valid ground for the Japanese claim to a change in the relative strengths laid down in existing treaties, and the British representatives drew attention to the far greater vulnerability of the nations of the British Commonwealth and their world-wide responsibilities, as compared with the more local responsibilities and the stronger strategical position of Japan. The Japanese claim is, in fact, one which His Majesty's Government in the United Kingdom could not admit without serious risk to the future security of the British Empire.

5. This principle of parity for which the Japanese are contending is of the same nature as that on which Italy bases her claim to parity with France, and, like the Italian claim, is bound to wreck any naval conference of the future unless some way of circumventing the difficulty can be found. His Majesty's Government in the United Kingdom accordingly reached the conclusion that the only hope of preserving some form of quantitative limitation lay in eliminating from any future treaty figures which appeared to constitute a ratio as between the various signatory Powers, and to substitute for the existing treaty engagements on this point a system under which each Power would make a voluntary and unilateral declaration of its construction programme for the years 1937–42. To take account of national susceptibilities, it was proposed that these declarations should not have the force or form of contractual obligations. Nevertheless, the construction figures appearing in the programmes would require to be concerted beforehand between the Powers, and it would further be necessary that each Power should undertake in its declaration not to modify its announced building programme without giving previous notice of at least one year to other Powers making similar declarations.

[3] Cf. No. 111, paragraph 8.

6. A proposal in this sense was made to the United States and Japanese representatives,[4] and, up to the present, the plan has been neither accepted nor rejected by either Government. When the conversations were officially adjourned on the 19th December, it was decided that the Governments which had been concerned in them should keep in close touch with each other, and that, if the situation developed so as to justify a subsequent meeting, the Government of the United Kingdom would take the appropriate steps. A copy of this communiqué will be found in Annex I.[5]

7. A private understanding was subsequently reached with the Japanese Naval Representative, Vice-Admiral Yamamoto, that he would, on his return to Tokyo, do his best to explain to his Government the scope and intention of the British compromise proposal, and would then cause his British colleagues to be informed of any progress he might make. It is this message which is awaited before any decision is taken by His Majesty's Government as to what the next step should be. It is anticipated that, if the Japanese Government accept the new proposals in principle, and, *a fortiori*, if they agree to the figures for insertion in the programmes which have been tentatively and privately discussed between the representatives in London, the United States Government for their part are likely to accept the proposals as a basis for further discussion.

8. By agreement with Vice-Admiral Yamamoto he was handed a note entitled 'Notes on the minimum British Naval Strength necessary for security' to assist him in representing the views of the United Kingdom Government in the discussions which he will have had with his own Government on his return to Japan. A copy of this note is attached as Annex II[6] to this paper; it will be seen that this note explains the minimum naval strength considered here to be required in the case of the British Commonwealth in the various categories, and the reasons which prevent a reduction below these figures. The figures themselves will be found summarised in Annex III.[7]

9. *Qualitative Limitation.* Turning to qualitative limitation (*i.e.*, limitation of the sizes of ships in the various categories and the guns which they may carry), it should be mentioned that at the beginning of the discussions in London the Japanese Government declared their desire to see the abolition of what they termed 'offensive' types, namely, capital ships, aircraft carriers and 8-inch-gun cruisers, and to increase what they called 'defensive' types, such as submarines. Neither the United Kingdom nor the United States representatives were prepared to entertain proposals for the abolition of capital ships and aircraft carriers. The British Government's views on the capital ship were expressed in their recent 'Statement relating to defence' (Command 4827),[8] in which they stated that 'The Main Fleet is the basis upon which our naval strategy rests,' and that 'in the main Fleet the capital

---

[4] Cf. Nos. 54 and 56.          [5] Not printed; cf. No. 95, note 2.

[6] This note was the same as enclosure in No. 110 and is not here reproduced.

[7] Not printed.

[8] Issued in connection with the debate in the House of Commons on March 11, 1935; see 299 *H.C. Deb.* 5 *s.*, cols. 35–162.

ship remains the essential element upon which the whole structure of our naval strategy depends.' The statement also pointed out that an adequate provision of aircraft (which are becoming more and more important to the Navy) is essential to our Fleet. For these reasons the United Kingdom representatives were unable to agree to the abolition of capital ships and aircraft carriers.

10. It was also pointed out by the United Kingdom representatives that the types termed 'offensive' by the Japanese Government were not so regarded by the United Kingdom, and that, on the other hand, His Majesty's Government in the United Kingdom consider the submarine equally offensive and have themselves proposed that this type should be abolished.

11. The Japanese representatives, while still maintaining officially the demand for the abolition of capital ships, aircraft carriers and 8-inch-gun cruisers subsequently exchanged views unofficially with the United Kingdom representatives as to what should be the qualitative limits of these types if they were to be retained. The Japanese representatives made it clear, however, that Japan was not prepared to be a party to a treaty on qualitative limitation unless simultaneous agreement could be reached on quantitative limitation. In explanation of this attitude, the Japanese representatives stated that Japan could not expect to compete either with the British Commonwealth or with the United States of America in the number of ships she might build, nor would she wish to do so. But she must reserve the right to build types of ship particularly suited to her needs if an agreement on quantitative limitation proved impossible.

12. Summarising briefly the results of the discussions on qualitative limitation, it may be said that the United States Government still stand in general for the big ship and have so far given no definite indication of their willingness to reduce below the present treaty limitations (*i.e.*, 35,000 tons, with a 16-inch gun for capital ships and 10,000 tons, with an 8-inch gun for cruisers). At the same time there is a possibility that the United States would agree to a 14-inch gun on a ship with a tonnage between 30,000 and 35,000 tons, and a certain sympathy was shown with the desire for some reduction in the size of cruisers. This country, on the other hand, while unable to reduce the numbers of vessels in the various categories, is willing to make more drastic reductions in their size. At one time it had looked as if agreement could be reached without much difficulty between the British Empire, Japan, France and Italy on the basis of the United Kingdom proposal for a 25,000-ton capital ship with a 12-inch gun (although Japan might have stood out for a 14-inch gun), but the situation has recently been complicated by Italy's decision to lay down two 35,000-ton capital ships mounting a 15-inch gun, and the subsequent decision of France to follow this example.[9] This new race in the construction of the largest type of capital ship, which has thus been started by Italy, may increase our difficulties in obtaining a reduction in the size of future capital ships. But the efforts already made to induce the Italian Government to modify their construction plans will be continued, and

9 Cf. No. 24.

it seems just possible that, if Italy can be persuaded to substitute 14-inch guns for the 15-inch guns now proposed for her two 35,000-ton ships, this may open the way for the reduction in the maximum size of the capital ship of the future from 35,000 tons with a 16-inch gun to 30,000 tons with a 14-inch gun. As stated above, we have not entirely lost hope that in the last resort the United States would agree to a 30,000-ton ship with a 14-inch gun, if agreement on these figures could be reached between the other principal naval Powers.

13. As regards aircraft carriers, His Majesty's Government have proposed that the future qualitative limit in this category should be 22,000 tons with 6·1-inch guns. The Japanese Government would like a still further reduction to a tonnage of 20,000 tons, to which proposal we were not unsympathetic.

14. So far as cruisers are concerned, the proposal of His Majesty's Government in the United Kingdom is that no further 8-inch gun cruisers should be constructed during the period of the next treaty; that 10,000-ton cruisers mounting 6-inch guns should be limited by number (to 10 for the British Empire and the United States and 6 for Japan); and that all other new cruisers should be limited in size to 7,000 tons with 6-inch guns. There seems a reasonable hope that these qualitative limits—or something nearly approaching them—may ultimately prove acceptable to the other principal naval Powers.

15. As regards destroyers, there was general agreement between the representatives of the United Kingdom, the United States and Japan for the retention of the existing naval treaty limits, namely, 1,850 tons for a leader and 1,500 tons for a destroyer, with 5·1-inch guns.

16. The Governments of the United Kingdom and the United States remain in favour of the abolition of the submarine. In view, however, of the determined opposition both of Japan and of France to the abolition of this type, the United Kingdom representatives have proposed that the maximum size and gun calibre should remain as defined in the London Naval Treaty (namely, 2,000 tons mounting a 5·1-inch gun). This proposal seems likely to be acceptable to the other principal naval Powers.

17. Under the British proposal, all these provisions in regard to qualitative (as distinct from quantitative) limits would be embodied in the treaty. This treaty would also contain many of those useful provisions in existing naval treaties regulating such matters as the non-fortification of naval bases in the Pacific, the notification of particulars of ships to be laid down, the category definitions, &c.

18. *Future Procedure.* We are now awaiting word from Tokyo as to the result of the Japanese Government's examination of the British proposals, in the light of Vice-Admiral Yamamoto's report on his return to his country. In the meantime, however, a further exchange of views will take place with certain European Powers, the first of which will probably be Germany, since France and Italy cannot be pinned down to any definite construction figures until the German requirements are known. During his recent visit to Berlin, the Secretary of State for Foreign Affairs informed Herr Hitler that

His Majesty's Government in the United Kingdom hoped that the German Government would take part in any general conference of the naval Powers which might be held in the near future.[10] With this end in view, it would be useful if informal exchanges of views could now take place in London between representatives of His Majesty's Government and of the German Government. Sir John Simon added that this proposal was made without prejudice to the validity of the existing treaty provisions and without prejudice to any agreement regarding armaments generally which might be reached as part of the general settlement foreshadowed in the London proposals of the 3rd February, 1935. Herr Hitler accepted the proposal that Anglo-German conversations on the naval question should take place in London, but no date has yet been fixed for the commencement of these talks.

19. The German Government have already intimated that they would like their future fleet to be about 35 per cent. of the British Commonwealth Naval Forces. But such a figure, if persisted in, would render quantitative limitation definitely impossible so far as the European Powers are concerned and it is hoped that, when it comes to giving a programme of her actual requirements of naval construction for the years 1937–42, Germany may prove more reasonable. Following on the conversations with the German representatives, it is proposed that further discussions should take place with representatives first of the French and then of the Italian Government.

20. Should the result of all these conversations be negative, it may be proposed in some quarters that, rather than risk an abortive meeting, the Conference should, by unanimous consent of the parties to existing treaties, be postponed until next year. This step is clearly undesirable except as a last resort, since its psychological effect must necessarily be bad, it would leave the door open to uncontrolled rearmament by Germany and to competitive building between France and Italy, and finally it would give rise to a number of practical difficulties owing to the short period which must elapse between the holding of the Conference and the lapsing of the existing naval treaties on the 31st December, 1936.

21. No decision has yet been reached as to the venue of the Conference. The idea which seems most likely to command general assent is that the first step, once the bilateral talks have terminated, should be a relatively informal meeting in London of the Powers parties to existing treaties, to be followed, if successful, by a Conference of all the Naval Powers.

22. It will be seen that the conclusion of a new treaty, laying down total tonnages in categories, is now extremely unlikely. Nevertheless, when drawing up programmes of construction for insertion in an agreement of the form now under consideration, His Majesty's Government in the United Kingdom must have in mind the ultimate figures that would be attained by the building set out in their own programme. Again, in scrutinizing the suggested programmes for foreign Powers, they must equally bear in mind the relative strengths resulting from the building thus foreshadowed. The

[10] See Volume XII, No. 651, p. 728.

strength of the British Commonwealth Naval Forces, which His Majesty's Government in the United Kingdom consider necessary for the security of the Empire, is set out in Annex III attached.[7] The figures of total tonnages are dependent on the qualitative limitations that it is hoped may be agreed upon, which are also set out in the table, and on the supposition that the relative strengths of the principal naval Powers will be maintained approximately at their present level. Should any considerable increase of strength either in the Japanese Fleet or in the fleets of European Powers result from the building undertaken in the next few years, it would be necessary to reconsider the minimum British naval strength necessary for security.

23. If as a result of the conversations it is evident that no treaty embodying quantitative limits or even building programmes is practicable, it is the view of His Majesty's Government in Great Britain that every effort should be made to obtain a treaty containing qualitative limits in the various categories. It is considered that such a limitation would be of the greatest value in preventing a race in naval armaments.

# CHAPTER III

# Questions of German rearmament and of security: proposals for Anglo-German naval conversations
## April 18–May 28, 1935

### INTRODUCTORY NOTE

CHAPTERS III to VI print documents relating to the general discussions between the European powers on questions of naval, air, and land armaments between April 18 and December 3, 1935. They thus continue the story of German rearmament and the problem of security during the period from August 1934 to the close of the Stresa Conference on April 14, 1935, which formed the main theme of Volume XII of this Series.

A number of documents relating to the initiation of Anglo-German naval discussions in March and April 1935 were printed in Volume XII, in connexion with the negotiations for a general agreement between Germany and other European powers. On March 26 Sir John Simon, in his conversations with Herr Hitler, suggested that informal conversations on the naval question between British and German representatives would be useful, with London as a suitable venue. The proposal was accepted (Volume XII, No. 651, p. 732). On April 3 Sir G. Clerk and Sir E. Drummond both suggested that any invitation to Germany to send representatives to London to discuss naval matters on the eve of the Stresa conference would have a bad effect on the French and Italian Governments (*ibid.*, Nos. 685 and 686). Acting on this advice, the Foreign Office postponed the invitation and on April 9 Baron von Neurath told Sir E. Phipps that, having accepted the British Government's invitation to naval conversations in London in principle, the German Government were now waiting for a further intimation as to the date of the conversations (*ibid.*, No. 708). Sir E. Phipps was finally instructed on April 18 to suggest the opening of talks on May 1 or at the earliest convenient subsequent date (No. 121 below).

### No. 119

*Sir J. Simon to Sir E. Phipps (Berlin)*
*No. 86 Telegraphic* [*C 3343/55/18*]

FOREIGN OFFICE, *April 18, 1935, 5.45 p.m.*

The Counsellor of the German Embassy asked on April 17th the meaning of the reference to the 'bilateral agreements which might accompany' the Air

Pact.[1] He was told that there was not yet in existence a general framework of the Air Pact. We had our ideas, which I had explained at Berlin. The Chancellor had his ideas. The French had their ideas; and the Italians and Belgians had also given us one or two ideas in the early spring. But there was no general framework or common draft as yet, and that would presumably be for the five Powers eventually to draft together. Until there was a general framework, no one could say whether any bilateral agreements would be necessary or not.

Prince Bismarck asked what the bilateral agreements would deal with, and he was told that until there was a general framework of the Air Pact it was impossible to say. He was reminded, however, of what I had told the Chancellor about the Anglo-Italian position under the Air Pact,[2] and it was mentioned that the Chancellor himself had made certain comments on this. But even in respect of this, one could not say now that a bilateral agreement would be necessary. Perhaps it would be dealt with in some clause in the agreement. Perhaps not. But all this was speculation.

Prince Bismarck then said that he had read in the press that there would be bilateral military agreements. He quoted an article in the *Daily Herald* of April 17th and asked if it was true that we and the French, or the Italians and the French, were already at work on military agreements. He was told that so far as we were concerned at any rate, this was absolutely untrue. We could not answer for what the French and Italians were doing; but we had certainly not heard that any such negotiation was in progress.[3] He was told further that the article was nothing to do with us; and our object was a five-Power agreement.

Prince Bismarck then asked if there was anything behind the Stresa communiqué. He was told that it was not our habit to conceal what we did. The communiqué told the truth of what had passed.

Prince Bismarck asked if something had not passed on this matter at Geneva. He was told that we had received no information whatever to that effect.[4]

Repeated to Paris, Rome, and Brussels.

[1] See paragraph 4 of the *Joint Resolution of the Stresa Conference* (Cmd. 4880); cf. Volume XII, No. 722, 6th meeting. Prince Bismarck was talking to Mr. Wigram, head of the Central Department of the Foreign Office, who remarked in a minute of April 17 on the draft of this telegram: 'I did not feel that it was wise to refuse to answer Prince Bismarck's enquiry as the News Dep[artmen]t—who are being heavily questioned on the bilateral agreements—are answering in this sense.'

[2] During the Anglo-German conversations at Berlin, March 25–26, 1935; see Volume XII, No. 651, 4th meeting.

[3] Cf. No. 197 below, note 2.

[4] Sir J. Simon, who returned to London from Geneva on April 18, minuted as follows: 'Mr. Wigram answered excellently. Mr. Ewer [of the *Daily Herald*] asked me at Geneva if there was "anything behind" the Air Pact reference and I answered that everything was stated in the Communiqué. J.S. 18 April.'

## No. 120

### Sir J. Simon to Sir G. Clerk (Paris)
### No. 108 Telegraphic [C 3333/55/18]

FOREIGN OFFICE, *April 18, 1935, 8 p.m.*

M. Laval[1] undertook at Stresa (see page 22 of record of conversations,[2] copy of which goes to you by tonight's bag) to communicate to the British and Italian Governments the main lines of the agreement for mutual assistance which he said the French Government were negotiating with the Soviet Government. This communication has not yet been made and as M. Laval may shortly be leaving for his visits to Moscow and Warsaw please ask him whether he is now in a position to furnish the information promised.

For your own information, we are particularly anxious to make sure that the agreement does not oblige France to attack Germany in circumstances which would bring into play our guarantee on behalf of Germany under Locarno.[3] This situation might arise if France were under this agreement obliged to go to war with Germany in circumstances not contemplated by any of the exceptions to Article 2 of the main Locarno Treaty.

[1] French Minister for Foreign Affairs.
[2] See Volume XII, No. 722, 4th meeting (p. 885).
[3] For the text of the Treaty of mutual guarantee between the United Kingdom, Belgium, France, Germany, and Italy, signed at Locarno on October 16, 1925, see *B.F.S.P.*, vol. 211, pp. 923–6.

## No. 121

### Sir J. Simon to Sir E. Phipps (Berlin)
### No. 89 Telegraphic [C 3245/206/18]

FOREIGN OFFICE, *April 18, 1935, 9.20 p.m.*

Your telegram No. 94 Saving.[1]

His Majesty's Government would be glad to open naval conversations in London on May 1st or the earliest subsequent date that would be convenient to the German Government.

In view of recent developments[2] I feel however that an invitation in the above sense if conveyed to the German Government at the present moment might meet with a refusal, which would be very unfortunate. Unless therefore you feel confident that a refusal will not be returned if you convey the invitation forthwith or can take soundings to ascertain that there is no such

[1] Volume XII, No. 708.
[2] A reference presumably to the adoption, unanimously except for the abstention of the Danish representative, by the Council of the League of Nations on April 17 of the Resolution presented by France, Italy, and the United Kingdom in connexion with the repudiation by Germany of international obligations in regard to armaments; cf. Volume XII, Nos. 731 and 732, also *League of Nations Official Journal (L/N.O.J.)*, May 1935, pp. 550–5, 556–64.

risk, it would probably be better if you deferred extending invitation for some days.[3]

[3] A marginal note on the filed copy by Mr. Hoyer Millar, Assistant Private Secretary to Sir J. Simon, read: 'The S. of S. who was consulted by telephone wanted a telegram in this sense sent to Berlin. F.R.H.M. 18.4.35.'

## No. 122

*Sir G. Clerk (Paris) to Sir J. Simon (Received April 20, 4.30 p.m.)*
*No. 78 Saving: Telegraphic [C 3328/55/18]*

PARIS, *April 19, 1935*

Your telegram No. 108.[1]

In my absence from Paris (I have been obliged to go to Nice to attend a number of Franco-British celebrations connected with Their Majesties' Jubilee)[2] Mr. Campbell saw M. Laval this evening and asked him if he was yet in a position to implement the promise which he had given at Stresa to communicate to you the main lines of the agreement which he was negotiating with M. Litvinoff.

2. M. Laval replied that there had been an eleventh-hour hitch. The Russians were making difficulties as they were not satisfied with what they were getting, and M. Litvinoff had in fact left Geneva for Moscow in a huff. In its broad lines, the French scheme was as follows:

3. The arrangement was a bilateral one for mutual assistance, to come into play in the event of a German aggression against either Russia or France. No attempt was being made to define exactly what would constitute an act of aggression. Assistance would not be automatic and neither party could be called upon to render it until there had been a reference to the League and the Covenant procedure had run its course. If the Council (other than the parties to the dispute) reached a unanimous decision the parties would conform to it. If it failed to reach a unanimous decision the parties would regain their liberty of action (paragraph 7 of article 15 of the Covenant), in which case the provision for mutual assistance would become immediately operative, subject to the further condition that France would not be called upon to go to the assistance of Russia in any case which would put her in the wrong under the Treaty of Locarno.

4. Thus France, M. Laval explained, had the double safeguard that she could not be called upon to do anything that would be in contradiction with the Covenant or that would bring her into conflict with Great Britain or Italy under the Treaty of Locarno. Russia, on the other hand, not being a party to Locarno and having no coterminous frontier with Germany such as would enable similar conditions to be established ad hoc, would have to render assistance to France in any circumstances not excluded by the Covenant. It was for that reason that the Russians were claiming that not only was the rendering of assistance not sufficiently automatic but that they were getting the worst of the bargain. M. Laval admitted that this was so, but

[1] No. 120.    [2] Cf. No. 118, note 1.

claimed that the balance was redressed by the fact that if it came to the point French assistance would be of immeasurably greater advantage to Russia than Russian assistance would be to France.

5. Negotiations were proceeding through the Soviet Ambassador in Paris and M. Laval hoped that the present difficulties (one of which was that the Soviet Government insisted that there should be no explicit reference to the Treaty of Locarno) would be overcome, and that it would soon be possible to initial an agreement on the above lines. His visit to Moscow had had, however, to be postponed, and he doubted now whether he would leave in any case until after the French municipal elections, which take place on May 6th.

6. M. Laval emphasised that in view of the difficulties raised by the Soviet Government the above information could only be regarded as provisional. On being pressed to do so he agreed to communicate the actual text of the agreement after it had been initialled and before it was made public.

## No. 123

*Prince Otto von Bismarck to Sir J. Simon (Received April 22)*

[*C 3330/55/18*]

*Translation*                    GERMAN EMBASSY, *London, April 20, 1935*

Sir,

I have the honour to make the following statement to your Excellency in the name and by direction of my Government:—

'The German Government contest the right of the Governments who framed the resolution of the 17th instant in the Council of the League of Nations[1] to constitute themselves judges regarding Germany. They perceive in the resolution of the Council of the League of Nations an attempt to discriminate anew against Germany, and therefore most emphatically reject the resolution. They reserve the right to make known at an early date their attitude to the individual questions dealt with in the resolution.'

I have, &c.,
BISMARCK[2]

[1] Cf. No. 121, note 2.

[2] In a minute of April 23 Mr. Creswell, a member of the Central Department, recorded: 'A simple acknowledgement has been sent.'

## No. 124

*Viscount Chilston[1] (Moscow) to Sir J. Simon (Received April 21, 12.30 p.m.)*

*No. 57 Telegraphic* [*C 3326/55/18*]

MOSCOW, *April 21, 1935, 12 noon*

My telegram No. 2 Saving.[2]

Nothing appears to be known about Franco-Soviet convention which is

[1] H.M. Ambassador at Moscow.

[2] Not printed. In this telegram of April 16, received April 22, Lord Chilston had summarized an article in *Izvestiya* of April 16 on the results of the Stresa conference.

reported to have been agreed on at Paris and Geneva. Even French Ambassador[3] seems to have little information as to its precise nature or at any rate is very reserved about it.

Press, while expressing great satisfaction and complacency with this success for Soviet diplomacy, can as yet give no details at all and only says the text is being drawn up and will ultimately be signed here.

Meanwhile it is understood that Laval will not come here until about a month hence if then.

It is being wondered whether any hitch has arisen.

[3] M. Charles Alphand.

## No. 125

*Sir E. Phipps (Berlin) to Sir J. Simon (Received April 22)*
*No. 102 Saving: Telegraphic [C 3351/55/18]*

BERLIN, *April 21, 1935*

Geneva telegram No. 74.[1]

German Government have hitherto believed that aim of British policy was to secure return of Germany to League and her co-operation in a general European system. In my telegram No. 150[2] I indicated that Chancellor was in a less uncompromising mood. Subsequently, in your telegram No. 1 from Stresa[3] you instructed me to make a specific enquiry regarding Eastern pact and you explained that opportunity for keeping the door open for German co-operation must on no account be missed. The German reply[4] marked a step in advance and was considered here a contribution of definite value. Consequently the Geneva resolution[5] came as an unpleasant shock to the German Government. Resulting uncertainty regarding real aims of British policy has caused misunderstanding and resentment. Chancellor's private Secretary tells me that Herr Hitler is convinced that the French proposed Geneva resolution for the express purpose of rendering German return to Geneva impossible. I replied that in that case it was important from German point of view to avoid taking any sudden and violent step.

I share your views as to difficulty of obtaining Germany's return to the League but I do not think German public opinion is likely to play decisive part. It is undoubtedly hostile and Herr Hitler will exploit this fact to the full if it suits him. But were he to decide to return he could afford to ignore the public as he did in the matter of Polish agreement.[6]

[1] Volume XII, No. 734.
[2] *Ibid.*, No. 710.
[3] *Ibid.*, No. 717.
[4] *Ibid.*, No. 715.
[5] See No. 121 in this Volume, note 2.
[6] A reference to the Declaration of Non-Aggression and Understanding between Germany and Poland signed at Berlin on January 26, 1934; for an English translation of the text see B.F.S.P., vol. 137, pp. 495–6. Cf. Volume VI, No. 219.

## No. 126

*Mr. Palairet*[1] *(Stockholm) to Sir J. Simon (Received April 26)*
*No. 116 [C 3436/55/18]*

STOCKHOLM, *April 23, 1935*

Sir,

On the resumption today after the Easter holidays by the Swedish Minister for Foreign Affairs of his weekly receptions, I paid His Excellency a visit and asked him whether he could enlighten me as to the attitude of the Swedish Government towards the recent resolution of the League of Nations.[2] The Swedish press, I observed, seemed to be divided on the subject, but had been for the most part critical of the League's action.

2. Herr Sandler was as cautious and reticent as usual. The Swedish Government had not, he said, been called upon to take any side in this question. The Danish representative on the Council[3] had (as he had himself just declared) spoken only on behalf of Denmark, and indeed there had been no opportunity for the Scandinavian countries to confer as to the attitude to be adopted towards the resolution. Sweden's main interest was, he said, to see the League strengthened as an instrument of peace, and I gathered from Herr Sandler's language, cautious though it was, that he did not consider the recent resolution calculated to lead in that direction or to assist Germany's return to Geneva. It might, he thought, have been differently worded so as to give less offence; and there were passages in it, such as those referring to the prevention of future treaty violations, which seemed to him to require elucidation.

3. He concluded our conversation by observing that Germany had destroyed the basis of the existing situation and that the important thing now was to find a new basis. I had the impression that he regarded the resolution as useless recrimination, though he did not commit himself to so strong a phrase and was careful to point out, what is undoubtedly true, that several Swedish newspapers are coming round to the view that a public reproof to Germany was justified by the facts.

4. I am sending copies of this despatch to His Majesty's Ministers at Oslo and Copenhagen.

I have, &c.,
MICHAEL PALAIRET

[1] H.M. Minister at Stockholm.    [2] See No. 121, note 2.
[3] Dr. Munch; cf. *ibid.*

*Memorandum by Sir R. Vansittart on the German Air Programme*[1]

*[C 3228/55/18]*

FOREIGN OFFICE, *April 24, 1935*

I have read the Air Ministry's memorandum C.P. 85 (35)[2] of the 15th April, and feel bound to differ from it on four fundamental points.

(1) The Air Ministry reassert (paragraph 20) that Germany will not be ready for war before 1942. This is getting near the recently discarded assumption of ten years' immunity from any major war. The Foreign Office cannot concur in such a speculation, which is shared by no one else in Europe. I have recently had opportunities of discussing this question with the representatives of a number of Powers at Geneva. The French General Staff put the date as early as the spring of 1936. This may be considered as over-anxiety. Other Powers put it at some point in 1937.[3] I met nobody who dared to put it later than early in 1938. To postpone the date by another full four years is surely to make a wish father to a comfortable thought. The rate at which Germany is now moving makes any such venture into the realms of prophecy a most unreliable and dangerous flight, especially as previous assumptions of this nature are already in course of being falsified.

(2) The Air Ministry assume (paragraph 6) that Germany is aiming at a total first-line strength of 1,512 aircraft. This is admittedly a conjectural figure. There are already persistent reports that Germany means to build up a strength of 1,800 and even 2,000 first-line machines. Indeed, whether or not the Air Ministry 'seriously regard the figure of 2,091 as Germany's present goal,' the fact remains that this is the figure which was given by

---

[1] The notes on which this memorandum was based were prepared in the Central Department of the Foreign Office, mainly by Mr. Creswell, on April 16.

[2] Cf. Volume XII, No. 713, note 2. This memorandum, considered by the Cabinet on April 17, put forward proposals by the Chief of the Air Staff for 'large additions to the present approved expansion scheme of the Royal Air Force' in order to meet Germany's air expansion, and 'outlined the measures which must be authorised in the present financial year if the proposed programme was approved in principle'. While supporting these proposals as fully justified, Lord Londonderry, Secretary of State for Air, said that he would be content 'provided he could obtain Cabinet authority for the steps immediately necessary to the inauguration of the programme of further expansion' for these steps to be examined and reported upon by the Ministerial Committee on Disarmament 'before a decision was reached upon the precise details of the Programme of Expansion'. The Cabinet referred the memorandum to the Ministerial Committee on Defence Requirements, which was due to meet on Monday, April 29.

A note of April 24 by Sir J. Simon, submitting Sir R. Vansittart's memorandum to this committee, read: 'The Memorandum of the Secretary of State for Air was written and circulated when Sir Robert Vansittart and I were at Geneva. The annexed comments by the Permanent Under Secretary have been prepared for the consideration of the Ministerial Disarmament Committee. J.S.'

[3] *Note in original*: 'In paragraph 8 the Air Ministry say that "Germany hopes to complete the programme in the early part of 1937". This statement is based on Intelligence Reports, according to which 1937 is the *latest* date on which the programme will be complete: the same sources consider that the date may well be considerably anticipated.'

Herr Hitler in Berlin for the French air forces at the same moment as he categorically claimed parity with France in the air. This is a statement too explicit to be dismissed.[4]

(3) A further conjecture follows in the Air Ministry memorandum (paragraph 23): that Germany will, from April 1937, remain at the figure of 1,512, and conveniently give us time to reduce the arrears into which we are already falling. Germany will most assuredly do nothing of the kind, and Sir E. Phipps (Berlin telegram No. 161)[5] has now reported the possibility of an acceleration of the existing programme, and even of its expansion. If we base our programme on so facile a conjecture we shall never overtake the arrears and, far from fulfilling the Lord President's pledge,[6] shall in all probability see the German lead widen. Once allow the Germans over a period of years to grow used to a long lead in the air, and they will hang on to it, as we did to our naval lead. To reckon otherwise is to gamble without justification on a change of human nature in general and German character in particular.

(4) The Air Ministry write (paragraph 9) that 'if Herr Hitler's statement is to be accepted at its face value, we have already fallen behind Germany, and as things stand we shall, by April 1937, possess but half her number of first-line aircraft.' This conclusion is only avoided by the disquieting premise that Herr Hitler does not know his own figures, to which the German Air Ministry have since given explicit precision to our Air Attaché.[7] It is surely more normal to believe that we are not omniscient in regard to a country where accurate data are notoriously and increasingly hard to come by.

Thus, even under the new programme proposed by the Air Ministry, Germany will have an approximate superiority of 2 to 1 over our own home-stationed regular first-line till 1937, and, by even a slight expansion of the programme to which the Air Ministry believe Germany to be working, will be able to continue this superiority long after 1937 and perhaps indefinitely.

It is, moreover, pertinent to point out that until we do catch Germany up there is no real possibility of a limitation of air armaments in Western Europe, and that an inadequate programme on our part will encourage Germany to further efforts as surely as an immediate and adequate acceleration would discourage her.

It would be appropriate here to emphasise the alarming capacity of Germany's factory output noted in paragraph 8 of the Air Ministry memorandum which may make it necessary for our aircraft industry to be re-organised; but I understand that this will form the subject of a separate paper by the Air Ministry.

There is a further most important aspect of this matter, which is of prime

---

[4] Cf. Volume XII, No. 704, note 2.  [5] *Ibid.*, No. 730.

[6] A reference presumably to Mr. Baldwin's statement in the House of Commons on March 8, 1934, that any Government of this country 'will see to it that in air strength and air power this country shall no longer be in a position inferior to any country within striking distance of our shores'. See 286 *H.C. Deb.* 5 *s.*, col. 2078; cf. 295 *ibid.*, col. 883 (November 28, 1934).  [7] See Volume XII, No. 687.

importance to the Foreign Office. Air policy, in its broadest aspects, cannot now be divorced from foreign policy. In recent years we have been heavily handicapped by our loss of material weight. This is a view which has been uncomfortably and repeatedly confirmed from many foreign sources. To impose upon us inferiority till 1939 will confirm it still further. Apart from the visibly growing German menace, any continued inferiority in the air will weaken our influence throughout Europe, where we are already considered to need more support than we can give, and the difficulty of conducting an independent and effective foreign policy will increase if this general estimate of us is allowed to continue. We should surely wish to avoid too great dependence on the defensive assistance of any other Power. I have often heard it said that we should never be exposed to a war in Europe without French assistance. Is that really so, and, even if it is, what guarantee have we that the French Air Force will be efficient? At the moment less than 400 out of their 1,400 first-line machines are supposed to be really fit for extended war service. It must also be remembered that at present France is undertaking commitments in Eastern Europe and in regard to Austria. These might well in an emergency reduce her capacity for assistance. Moreover, our policy is to exercise a moderating and stabilising influence; and if we are insufficiently independent, foreign pressure and the sense of our own weakness in darkening circumstances may restrict our liberty in that direction, and even influence for the worse the line which our foreign policy should take.

When the Lord President of the Council made his speech on the 8th March, 1934[8] it was permissible to hope that the handicap era would speedily be put an end to. Parity was promised, and no one has ever before suggested either to the Foreign Office or to the public that we must wait four years, and even then run the risk of not attaining so simple and vital a requisite. And these four years may well be the most crucial in the history of Europe; indeed, they will probably decide its fate. If a clear foreign policy is adequately backed, there need be no fear of the future. There is much to fear if this is not the case; and it cannot, I submit, be the case on these dates and figures.

I earnestly trust, therefore, that the independent policy of this country may be ensured by the promised parity, without the interposition of a delay which may render it unattainable, and thereby entail incalculable consequences, not only to ourselves, but to the world.[9]

R. V.

[8] Cf. note 6 above.

[9] There is some discussion of this Foreign Office reply to the Air Ministry's estimates in The Eden Memoirs, Facing the Dictators (London, 1962), pp. 185–6, where it is remarked that 'the Führer's claim was certainly false, for we now know that, in March 1935, his total number of operational aeroplanes, as the Air Ministry stated in their memorandum of April 1935, was probably rather over one thousand, whereas Great Britain's was more than twice as great'. He did not believe that Herr Hitler was in error about the facts. 'More probably he was lying to impress us.' Lord Londonderry defended the Air Ministry's views in Wings of Destiny (London, 1943), pp. 125–32.

## No. 128

*Sir J. Simon to Sir E. Phipps (Berlin)*

*No. 94 Telegraphic [A 3771/22/45]*

FOREIGN OFFICE, *April 25, 1935, 6.15 p.m.*

Your telegram No. 103 Saving[1] of April 23.

In view of difficulty of obtaining accommodation in London during Jubilee week,[2] we feel it preferable that opening of conversations should be postponed till week following. Please inform Minister for Foreign Affairs.[3]

[1] In this telegram, not printed, Sir E. Phipps reported that he had conveyed the suggestion in No. 121 relating to a date for Anglo-German naval conversations to Herr von Bülow, Secretary of State in the German Ministry of Foreign Affairs, on April 23. Herr von Bülow had replied that as May 1 was a German national holiday the experts could not leave until some date after that.

[2] Cf. No. 118, note 1.

[3] Baron K. von Neurath.


## No. 129

*Sir E. Phipps (Berlin) to Sir J. Simon (Received April 26, 9.30 a.m.)*

*No. 165 Telegraphic [C 3446/206/18]*

BERLIN, *April 25, 1935, 8.25 p.m.*

My telegram No. 97 Saving.[1]

Admiral Raeder[2] sent his liaison officer to Naval Attaché[3] this afternoon to deny a report in the 'Daily Telegraph' of April 25th that Germany was building large submarines. Orders had however just been given for construction of 12 250-ton submarines.

Naval Attaché protested vigorously that he had been assured on April 12th that no submarines were included in 1935 programme. Liaison officer replied that this was regretted but that Naval Attaché had been informed of Germany's intention to build submarines in future and that decision to start construction at once had only been reached after latter's departure for London.

Naval Attaché had earlier in the day been received by Admiral Raeder and delivered Chief of Naval Staff's verbal message[4] for which Admiral Raeder expressed thanks.

Please repeat to Admiralty.

[1] For this telegram of April 12 relating to the German naval building programme for 1935, see Volume XII, No. 716.

[2] Chief of German Naval Command in the Reichwehr Ministry.

[3] Captain G. C. Muirhead-Gould.

[4] For this message from Admiral of the Fleet, Sir Ernle Chatfield, see No. 138 below, enclosure 2.

## No. 130

### Sir G. Clerk (Paris) to Sir J. Simon (Received April 26)
### No. 80 Saving: Telegraphic [C 3429/55/18]

PARIS, *April 25, 1935*

My telegram No. 78 Saving.[1]
Franco-Soviet negotiations remain at a standstill, but it is expected that they will be resumed within the next few days. French Government are standing firm, but will probably agree to some slight modification of form if pressed by the Soviets for face-saving purposes.

[1] No. 122.

## No. 131

### Sir G. Clerk (Paris) to Sir J. Simon (Received April 26)
### No. 81 Saving: Telegraphic [C 3430/55/18]

PARIS, *April 25, 1935*

Having learnt that His Majesty's Government have acknowledged receipt of German note[1] French government propose shortly to follow suit.

[1] Cf. No. 123, note 2.

## No. 132

### Sir E. Phipps (Berlin) to Sir J. Simon (Received April 26, 10 a.m.)
### No. 106 Saving: Telegraphic [C 3438/55/18]

BERLIN, *April 25, 1935*

Herr Hitler is expected to return here to-day from Munich, where he has been discussing the Geneva resolution with Herr von Ribbentrop[1] and other experts.

So far as I can gather he has either come to no definite decision or is keeping his own counsel. After his first outburst[2] he became serious again on hearing of the defection of Poland and the sudden recall of Litvinoff[3] to Moscow—incidents which seem to him to indicate such a serious change in Franco-Polish relations as to place him in a quandary.

In the meantime the legal expert at the Ministry for Foreign Affairs is drafting a reply to the Geneva resolution.

Monsieur Beck's, 'volte-face', like the League vote itself, has I hear, given a certain amount of malicious pleasure (*Schadenfreude*) at the Ministry for Foreign Affairs. Warsaw has demonstrated its unreliability, while Geneva has demonstrated its reliability—the former as a friend and the latter

[1] The Reich Chancellor's Commissioner for Disarmament Questions. For the Geneva resolution of April 17, see No. 121, note 2.
[2] See No. 123; cf. Volume XII, No. 731.
[3] M. Litvinov was the U.S.S.R. representative on the Council of the League of Nations.
[4] M. Beck was the Polish Minister for Foreign Affairs.

as an enemy of Germany. The Ministry feel that Hitler must now admit that there was some justification for the Rapallo[4] policy, the anti-Polish policy and the policy of joining the League, if only to prevent a common front against Germany.

Hitler is said to console himself with the reflection that the Polish pact, for which he alone was responsible, served its main purpose of warding off intervention during the critical period. He is also said to have remarked that in any case there was no place for sentiment in foreign policy and that a violent gesture such as General Göring[5] and others suggested would serve no useful purpose.[6]

[4] See *B.F.S.P.*, vol. 118, pp. 586–7, for the text of the treaty between Germany and Russia signed at Rapallo on April 16, 1922.                                                    [5] Reich Air Minister.

[6] In minutes on this telegram Mr. Creswell and Mr. Sargent both took the view that the French would be unwise to throw themselves unreservedly into the arms of Russia. 'A Franco-Russian alliance would be bound in present circumstances to check any further Polish inclination to return to the French fold and would drive her back on Germany. If M. Laval is well-advised he will try and carry on negotiations *pari passu* with both Poland and Russia. O. G. Sargent. April 22, 1935.'

### No. 133

*Mr. Ronald[1] (Oslo) to Sir J. Simon (Received April 27, 8.30 a.m.)*
*No. 13 Saving: Telegraphic* [*C 3474/55/18*]

OSLO, *April 25, 1935*

My despatch No. 165[2] of 23rd April.

Hearing last night that the Norwegian Cabinet had approved the action of their Foreign Minister in stating publicly that he associated himself with the line taken by Dr. Munch at Geneva, I decided to ask Professor Koht to be kind enough to furnish me with some particulars for communication to you showing a little more explicitly than did the interview with the 'Berlingske Tidende' what his views really were.

2. His Excellency received me this morning. I said that I found it a little difficult to understand precisely what Dr. Munch's motives had been. I gathered that he had objected to the resolution on two grounds.

(*a*) it was not the function of the Council to pass judgment in such a matter
(*b*) it was unwise to mention Germany by name, as this could only further exacerbate the temper of that country, which was already running high, and make her return to the League still more difficult.

[1] Mr. N. B. Ronald was First Secretary in H.M. Legation at Oslo.

[2] In this despatch, not printed, Mr. Ronald quoted the words attributed to Dr. Koht, the Norwegian Minister for Foreign Affairs, in the Danish newspaper, *Berlingske Tidende*, towards the end of the previous week, concerning the line taken by the Danish representative, Dr. Munch, at Geneva on April 17 when he abstained from voting on the draft resolution (cf. No. 121, note 2). Dr. Koht was reported to have said: 'I can say that I entirely agree with the Danish point of view: it has afforded me great pleasure. I think that from the point of view of the future of our countries it is the best attitude to adopt. I authorise you to say that Norway stands behind Denmark in the attitude taken up by her representative at Geneva.'

3. The League, I submitted, could only function by a reign of law, i.e. respect for contracts and international obligations. Here was a manifest breach of contract: (if Germany could make out some case in equity, the proper place and time to do this was during the negotiations contemplated by the London communiqué[3]). The least the League could do was to formulate some sort of condemnation of such a breach. The resolution, and still more your speech at the Council, made it perfectly clear that condemnation of this particular breach was not the main object of the resolution which aimed at condemning breaches of contract in general. Germany's action was indeed the occasion more than the subject matter of the resolution. The second part of the resolution and the fourth paragraph of your speech also made it obvious that the passing of the resolution was not to be regarded as calling off or impeding the conversations contemplated by the London communiqué. Finally, as regards the return of Germany to the League, surely if a state threatened to leave the League without due justification, there must be no question of tempting her back with cajolery and bribes? If Germany wanted rights, she must remember that rights connote obligations and, if she were to make a practice of unilateral repudiation of obligations, she must not be surprised if other people hesitated to confer on her the rights corresponding with those obligations.

4. Professor Koht replied that he agreed with Dr. Munch in thinking that it was not the function of the Council to pass judgment in such a matter; it was rather for the Permanent Court at The Hague. He thought he recalled a discussion about 10 years ago of a somewhat similar case in the Council, in which Lord Cecil had at first argued for consideration by the Council, but had eventually agreed that that body had no *locus standi* in that particular matter. His Excellency unfortunately could not give me chapter and verse and we did not pursue the point further.[4]

5. Professor Koht also agreed with Dr. Munch in thinking that it was injudicious to mention Germany by name in a resolution, the object of which was to reaffirm the general sanctity of treaties. He feared that anything calculated to keep Germany away from Geneva was likely to promote the system of alliances (he mentioned the Franco-Soviet discussions now in progress) which could only spell the end of the League. Norway and Denmark were intensely interested in the maintenance and strengthening

---

[3] A reference to the communiqué issued on February 3, 1935, at the close of the Anglo-French Conversations in London, February 1–3; see Cmd. 4798 of 1935. Cf. Volume XII, No. 400, note 4, and Annex.

[4] The reference appears to be to a discussion on procedure in regard to Article 17 of the Memel Convention at the 17th meeting of the Council of the League of Nations on September 28, 1925; see *L/N.O.J.*, October 1925, p. 1398. Viscount Cecil had then recalled that, under the Memel Convention, certain infractions of that Convention had to go to the Permanent Court of International Justice. In a later letter to Mr. Ronald of June 5, 1935, Mr. Strang said: 'As a matter of fact the two cases are not at all on all fours, since the Memel Convention provides explicitly (Art. 17) for reference to the P.C.I.J. . . . while there is of course no equivalent stipulation in the Versailles Treaty; and you might remind Prof. Koht of this if an opportunity offers.'

of the League. They feared that the proceedings of last week were likely not to strengthen but to weaken the League in the eyes of all practical minded people. Although legally and logically the resolution and its terms were easily defensible and even understandable, he questioned whether considerations of practical commonsense ought not to have been allowed to prevail rather than those of law and logic. It was in fine not the principle of the resolution he and Mr. Munch queried; it was its manner and its opportuneness of which they had such serious doubts.

6. There had, he concluded, been breaches of contract by great Powers in the past which the League had overlooked without passing resolutions of this sort; Corfu, Manchuria, Minorities in Poland, for instance. I reminded His Excellency that the Corfu incident[5] happened a long time ago, that the Assembly resolution about Manchuria[6] was really just as stiffly worded as the Council's of last week and that, when Colonel Beck threatened to denounce the Polish Minorities Treaty, he had been sharply told that he just could not do it.[7] There was, I ventured to submit, no analogy between these cases and that discussed last week at Geneva.[8]

Copies by post to Stockholm and Copenhagen.

[5] On August 31, 1923, the Greek island of Corfu had been bombarded and occupied by Italian troops. For subsequent discussions of the Italo-Greek dispute at the League of Nations, see *L/N.O.J.*, *S.S. No. 23*, *Records of the Fifth Assembly*, Annex 2, pp. 256–62.

[6] For the adoption, on February 24, 1933, by the Assembly of the League of Nations of the Report of the Committee of Nineteen which declared that sovereignty over Manchuria belonged to China, see *L/N.O.J.*, *S.S. No. 112*, pp. 22–3, 56 ff. Cf. Volume XI, Chapter II.

[7] See *L/N.O.J.*, *S.S. No. 125*, *Records of the Fifteenth Ordinary Session of the Assembly*, September 1934, pp. 42 ff.

[8] Mr. Ronald's language in this interview was approved in Foreign Office telegram No. 107 of May 4, 1935, to Oslo.

## No. 134

### *Minute by Sir R. Vansittart*[1]

### *[C 4411/55/18]*

FOREIGN OFFICE, *April 25, 1935*

While I was at Geneva[2] I had conversations both with M. Benes[3] and with M. Léger[4] on the subject of the Eastern Pact, and of the suggested German text for a multi-lateral non-aggression pact.[5] I said that I thought it would be a great mistake to let this remain ignored, particularly now that Germany

[1] In this minute Sir R. Vansittart comments on a memorandum (not printed) by Mr. Sargent of April 24 which asked whether any further action by the Stresa Powers was 'necessary in order to give effect to the Stresa Resolution of April 14th [see Volume XII, No. 722, note 44] and the Council Resolution of April 17th [see No. 121 above, note 2] either by approaching Germany at once and direct, or after and as a result of further negotiations between themselves?'

[2] Sir R. Vansittart had accompanied Sir J. Simon to Geneva from Stresa for the 85th (Extraordinary) session of the Council of the League of Nations held from April 15 to 17, 1935.                                        [3] Czechoslovak Minister for Foreign Affairs.

[4] Secretary-General of the French Ministry of Foreign Affairs.

[5] See Volume XII, No. 651, Annex to Third Meeting.

had declared that she would still maintain her offer, even if others were to conclude pacts of mutual assistance.[6] To do so, I said, would provide Germany with a grievance which would have some effect in this country, namely, that she made an offer and that nobody had taken the trouble to carry the matter further. I added that I was well aware that the text itself was subject in their eyes to considerable criticism, but that while we might criticise we should negotiate, and not ignore or reject it out of hand.

M. Benes replied that he was fully of this opinion and indeed had intended to express the same opinion to me. The German offer was an unsatisfactory one, but was a great deal better than nothing. I said that I intended to speak to M. Léger in the same sense as I had spoken to him, and that since his views coincided with mine I hoped he would speak in the same sense to M. Léger.

We both did so, and M. Léger informed us both separately that he needed no convincing on this point, and that he entirely shared our views.

Although the Eastern Pact is not strictly our business, I think we might now remind the French privately of what passed at Geneva, and ask what steps they have taken, or are contemplating taking, in this direction.

This I think disposes of the point raised in Mr. Sargent's memorandum concerning the Eastern Pact. As to the Central European agreement, no further action is necessary on our part.

In regard to the Air Pact I should be rather inclined to defer taking action as suggested by Mr. Sargent, i.e., calling a meeting of the jurists of the three Powers, until the French and Italians approach us in the matter, as they almost certainly will do.[7] My reason for suggesting this course is that it will give us a little more time for seeing whether Germany really means business in regard to the Eastern and Central European Pacts, and further whether we can really hope for solid progress in the direction of an Air Pact between all five Powers.

In regard to armaments I think the answer is simple. There seems no scope for negotiations at present as regards military effectives, and the French and Italians both made it quite clear that in these circumstances they would be very 'naive' (to use their own words) to consider any reduction of the small and dwindling lead that they now possess in heavy war material. As regards aeronautical armaments, I have already expressed my views on this point to the Ministerial Committee on Disarmament,[8] and I do not think we have any hope of approaching this problem satisfactorily until

[6] See *ibid.*, No. 715.

[7] Mr. Sargent had pointed out that the Stresa Resolution recommended that the three Powers should continue actively the study of the question of the air pact 'with a view to the drafting of a pact between the five Powers mentioned in the London communiqué and of any bilateral agreements which might accompany it'. This appeared 'to require a meeting of the jurists of the three Powers in order, not to work out an agreed text for presentation to Germany, but, to quote the Secretary of State's words at Stresa, "to find out the terms in which the Pact would be expressed"'. He suggested that France and Italy should be sounded as to a meeting of the jurists of the three governments without further delay.

[8] See No. 127.

we have made it clear not only in word but in deed that we intend to give full effect to our declared policy of maintaining aerial parity with Germany.

The foregoing are my views on the points raised by Mr. Sargent. I concur of course in thinking that the final answer to them must depend on whether Germany is about to slam the door on all further negotiations, as Mr. Sargent puts it. I trust this will not be the case, but in any event we shall soon know.[9]                                                                                         R. V.

[9] Sir R. Vansittart's minute was initialled by Sir J. Simon, Mr. Eden, and Lord Stanhope.

## No. 135

*Minute by Sir W. Malkin*

[*C 4234/55/18*]

FOREIGN OFFICE, *April 25, 1935*

1. I am not aware of any previous discussion of this particular point,[1] but in my opinion the position is as follows.

The effect of Articles 42 and 43 of Versailles is to establish not a neutralised zone but a demilitarised zone; their object is to ensure not that in time of war no fighting shall take place in the zone, but that in time of peace the zone shall not be used by Germany for the purpose of preparations for an attack upon France or Belgium. Once war has broken out, the restrictions on Germany resulting from these two articles lose their *raison d'être*. In the event, therefore, of France going to war with Germany in virtue of her guarantee to a third Power (i.e. in circumstances where no violation of Article 2 of Locarno is involved) and marching into the demilitarised zone, I do not think that Germany would violate Article 43 by sending troops into the demilitarised zone to resist the French attack or (in the event of the French troops having penetrated beyond the zone and then being driven back into it) by following the French troops into the zone. Were this not so, the effect of Article 43 would be, in the event of war, to make the zone a sort of Alsatia for French troops in which they could not be attacked without Germany thereby violating the article in question and bringing our Locarno guarantee into operation against her. It seems to me that this is a quite impossible result, and that the article would not be interpreted in that way. It may be worth while noting that if Article 43 is interpreted as forbidding the entry of armed forces into the zone in the event of war between France and Germany, the terms of the article would, if literally interpreted, be applicable to the

[1] In a memorandum (not printed) of April 23, Mr. Sargent had asked some questions as to the situation which would arise if France, in fulfilment of her Locarno Treaties with Poland or Czechoslovakia, or of obligations under her forthcoming pact with the Soviet Union, had to invade the demilitarized zone. '. . . if Germany were to resist the French invasion by sending troops into the Demilitarized Zone, could France claim that Germany had violated Articles 42 and 43 of the Treaty of Versailles, and that therefore Great Britain must intervene in the war in virtue of Article 4 of the Treaty of Locarno on the side of France? Or would it be held that Germany's right of legitimate defence (i.e. subhead 1 of Article 2) overrode her undertakings regarding the Demilitarized Zone?'

entry of French troops into the zone, and this supports the view that the article was not intended to be applicable to movements of troops in the event of a war between France and Germany.

In my opinion, therefore, France could not claim, in the circumstances postulated, that Germany had violated Article 43, and that our Locarno guarantee came into operation. If France wished to maintain the contrary view, she would, under Article 4 of Locarno, have to convince the Council that it was right, and we could bar a decision by the Council to that effect. If she claimed that the case came under paragraph 3 of that article, then the decision would rest with us.

I do not think that the provision about Germany's right of legitimate defence (Article 2 (1)) would be applicable, because that right is defined as resistance to a violation of France's undertaking not to attack or invade Germany, and in the circumstances postulated France would not have violated that undertaking.

2. (*a*).[2] I agree.

(*b*) and (*c*).[3] These two cases only differ as regards the seriousness of the German violations of the demilitarised zone provisions. The point is really covered by my memorandum of January 9th, 1934 (C 247/247/18) of which a copy is attached.[4] In Sir Cecil Hurst's[5] view, as there explained, the Council[6] ought not to find that a breach of Articles 42 and 43 had been committed except in a case where the breach was so grave as to justify immediate military action to repress it. On the alternative view suggested in that memorandum, the Council might find a breach of those articles without taking a decision permitting military action, and in that event our assistance to France might take the form of participating in means of pressure not involving the employment of force. The French proposals for dealing, by means of financial and economic measures, with threats of war resulting from the repudiation of treaty obligations[7] (which, under the recent Council resolution, are to be studied by a committee)[8] suggest that they have measures

[2] In his memorandum Mr. Sargent had written: '2. (*a*) If Germany violated the Demilitarized Rhineland as the first step of an attack on France or Belgium, the issue would be clear and our armed intervention under Locarno would not be in dispute (paragraph 3 of Article 4).'

[3] Mr. Sargent had called attention to two situations: (*b*) 'if Germany denounced unilaterally Articles 42 and 43 of the Treaty of Versailles and placed troops in the Demilitarized Zone without in any way threatening to attack or invade France or Belgium', and (*c*) if 'Germany were to try to undermine the demilitarization of the Rhineland by a series of small, unimportant, and unavowed violations' and 'France (or Belgium) accused Germany of these violations before the Council.'

[4] Not printed.

[5] Sir Cecil Hurst, Legal Adviser in the Foreign Office, 1918–29, had been a Judge of the Permanent Court of International Justice at The Hague since 1929.

[6] i.e. the Council of the League of Nations.

[7] For the French memorandum of April 6, handed to the British delegation at Stresa on April 13, on economic measures with the object of restraining German rearmament, see Volume XII, No. 723.

[8] A reference to the Resolution of April 17; cf. *ibid.*, No. 732; see also No. 121 above, note 2.

of this sort in mind in connexion with violations of the demilitarised zone provisions, and I think indeed that M. Laval mentioned the zone expressly in this connexion in the course of the Stresa conversations.[9]

H. W. M.

[9] Sir W. Malkin's paper was minuted as follows by Mr. Sargent, Sir R. Vansittart, and Sir J. Simon. 'Sir W. Malkin has effectively disposed of the danger I had foreseen in 1. As regards (b) and (c) in 2, the danger here too is got rid of if we can adopt Sir W. Malkin's thesis that the Council has to take two separate decisions, one on the question of fact and the other on the nature of the action to be taken. I would suggest that we should definitely adopt this thesis and not hesitate to state it if the French raise the question with us. O. G. Sargent. April 25th, 1935.' 'I agree. I had always assumed that we should take this line ... R.V. April 26.' 'This paper will be of great value in the next discussion about the working of Locarno—which I find a most *difficult* topic to explain in simple language. J.S. May 28.'

No. 136

*Record by Mr. Troutbeck[1] of a conversation with Signor Fracassi*

[A 3802/22/45]

FOREIGN OFFICE, *April 25, 1935*

Signor Fracassi, the First Secretary of the Italian Embassy, called this morning to enquire about naval conversations with Germany. He asked if the Secretary of State had mentioned the matter in his conversations in Berlin with Herr Hitler. I informed him briefly that the Secretary of State had expressed to Herr Hitler the hope that the German Government would participate in any general conference on the limitation of naval armaments and that they would send delegates to London to discuss naval matters. I added that the Secretary of State had reserved the position under the Versailles Treaty. I also stated that a specific invitation had since been made to the German Government to open informal conversations in London,[2] but that no reply had as yet been received.

J. M. T.

[1] A member of the American Department of the Foreign Office.    [2] See No. 121.

No. 137

*Sir J. Simon to Sir R. Lindsay (Washington)*

*No. 332* [A 3755/22/45]

FOREIGN OFFICE, *April 25, 1935*

Sir,

On the 5th of April last, the Counsellor of the United States Embassy called on Mr. Craigie at the Foreign Office and explained that he had heard from Soviet Russian sources that, during the visit of the Lord Privy Seal to Moscow,[1] an invitation had been addressed to the Soviet Government to send representatives to England for discussions on the Naval Question.[2] Mr. Atherton asked whether there was any truth in this report.

[1] Mr. Eden had visited Moscow on March 28 and 29; see Volume XII, No. 673.
[2] Cf. *F.R.U.S. 1935*, vol. i, p. 43.

2. Mr. Craigie replied that he had seen no telegraphic report to that effect, but he had not yet seen Mr. Eden's written report, and it was, of course, possible that the subject of naval limitation had cropped up in the conversations. It had been Mr. Eden's intention, if the Russians were to raise the question and to suggest naval conversations with His Majesty's Government in the United Kingdom, to reply that they would, naturally, be very pleased to have discussions with the representatives of the Soviet Government and with representatives of other naval Powers at the appropriate moment, but that no date for such conversations could be suggested until the talks with the German Government, which had already been suggested, had taken place.[3]

3. Mr. Atherton enquired whether His Majesty's Government had considered the possible effect on the Japanese Government of embarking on naval discussions with the U.S.S.R. Mr. Craigie replied that His Majesty's Government had not lost sight of this, and that it was for this reason that they did not propose to take the initiative in raising the question with the Russians, and would adopt a non-committal attitude if it were raised by the latter. Nevertheless, it had been felt here that it would be a great mistake to allow the Russians to gain the impression that His Majesty's Government were holding them at arms length in this matter, and as Germany's naval strength would almost certainly be based to some extent on the strength of the Soviet Union, it was obvious that the time must eventually come when His Majesty's Government would have to ascertain Soviet intentions.[4]

4. Mr. Craigie then informed Mr. Atherton that the present plan of His Majesty's Government was to re-open talks with the French and Italians once the proposed conversations with the Germans had terminated. Mr. Craigie expressed the view that when the conversations with the French and Italians took place a determined effort should be made to induce the Italians to agree to mount 14″ guns on their new capital ships, instead of the 15″ guns now projected. If His Majesty's Government were unsuccessful in persuading the Italians on this point, it was possible that the 15″ gun would become a maximum calibre for the capital ship of the future, despite the readiness of

[3] See Volume XII, Nos. 655 and 659.
[4] In a minute of April 10 Mr Craigie asked for further information as to the conversation between Mr. Eden and M. Litvinov about the naval conference on the last day of Mr. Eden's visit. Mr. R. M. A. Hankey, Private Secretary to Mr. Eden, replied in a minute of April 11: 'Mr. Eden says that he told Mr. Litvinov that there would be a naval conference and that when there was he hoped the Soviet Government would take part. We had already held conversations with a number of Powers and further conversations would take place before the Conference took place. In due course we hoped that similar conversations might be held with Soviet representatives, but it was quite impossible to say at present when that would be. Mr. Litvinov was evidently grateful for this intimation and agreed with Mr. Eden that the conversation should be kept strictly confidential. Mr. Eden knows that Mr. Litvinov was later asked by the Chinese Minister whether Soviet naval representatives had been invited to London and that Mr. Litvinov returned a negative reply. In the circumstances, Mr. Eden suggests that it is unnecessary to say more to Mr. Atherton. If later we want to say more to them we should, he thinks, tell M. Maisky [Soviet Ambassador at London] that we intend to do so.'

all other Powers to reduce to 14″ guns, and the extent of the additional financial burden which such a decision must place on all the naval Powers of the world requiring capital ships could well be imagined. This was a matter in which the attitude of the United States Government was of special importance. His Majesty's Government had understood that there was some hope that the United States Government might agree to a 14″ gun, but apparently they still reserve their official decision on the point. Would it be too much to ask that before the conversations with the French and Italians were begun, His Majesty's Government should be authorised to say that they had every reason to believe that the United States Government would agree to a 14″ gun if other countries were found to be ready to accept this maximum calibre? Mr. Craigie thought that if His Majesty's Government could do this, it would have a considerable effect on the ultimate decision as to the maximum calibre of the guns to be placed on the new French and Italian capital ships.

5. Mr. Atherton promised to enquire of his Government accordingly.

I am, &c.,<br>
(for the Secretary of State)<br>
J. M. Troutbeck

### No. 138

*Sir E. Phipps (Berlin) to Sir J. Simon (Received April 26)*<br>
*No. 394 [A 3810/22/45]*

BERLIN, *April 25, 1935*

His Majesty's Ambassador at Berlin presents his compliments to H.M. Secretary of State for Foreign Affairs and has the honour to transmit to him the under-mentioned document.

| *Name and Date* | *Subject* |
| --- | --- |
| Memo. by Naval Attaché, Berlin (G. 46/35) of 25th April. | German Naval Mission |

Enclosure 1 in No. 138

*German Naval Mission*

Admiral Raeder, Chef der Marineleitung, received me this morning in a most friendly manner. I read him the attached message from the 1st Sea Lord,[1] and explained very carefully that it was purely a private and personal message and had no official character whatever. Its intention was merely to give Admiral Raeder some idea of the course the conversations might be expected to follow, so that Admiral Raeder would be able to instruct his Mission accordingly.

Printed as enclosure 2 below.

2. Admiral Raeder asked me to thank the 1st Sea Lord for his kindness, and to say that he much appreciated the advance information as to the course the conversations were likely to take. He said that unfortunately the situation had altered since Germany had accepted the invitation to send a Mission to London, and he was now waiting for the Chancellor to return to Berlin, when he would decide whether the Mission was to go and when. He, himself, hoped that it would be sent. He would let me know about this immediately a decision was reached.

3. He said that I already knew the names of the two Officers who would be sent,[2] and he would also like Captain Wassner[3] to join the Mission in London.

G. C. Muirhead-Gould

Enclosure 2 in No. 138

*Aide-Mémoire of a Statement made by the Naval Attaché to Admiral Raeder, Chef der Marineleitung on April 25, 1935*

The 1st Sea Lord of the Admiralty has instructed me to give you a personal message from him, as from one Naval Officer to another. The message is in no way official, but as you have, in the past, been so kind as to keep us informed in advance of Germany's attitude towards naval disarmament, and recently of Germany's building programme for 1935, the 1st Sea Lord wishes to reciprocate by sending you advance information about the naval conversations which, it is hoped, will take place shortly between Great Britain and Germany.

In the first place, the 1st Sea Lord wishes to extend a sincere welcome to the German Naval Officers you may select to form the mission.

Secondly, he wishes you to know that the discussions will be of a general nature. It is hoped that it will be found possible for Germany and Great Britain to reach agreement on the subject of qualitative limitation of naval armaments. (Great Britain's views on this limitation were made public in 1932.)[4]

Thirdly, it is hoped that Germany will be prepared to put forward a general outline of her minimum naval requirements up to 1942 in the form of a building programme, it being understood that this programme would not necessarily be considered binding. This procedure is being adopted with all the Naval Powers, and it is hoped that it will give more chance of general agreement than any system of ratios or percentages.

G. C. Muirhead-Gould

[2] Rear Admiral Schuster and Commander Kiderlen. This information had been received in a note of April 13 from H.M. Naval Attaché at Berlin, copy enclosed in a letter of April 16 to the Foreign Office from the Berlin Chancery.

[3] German Naval Attaché at London.

[4] See Mr. Baldwin's statement in the House of Commons on July 7, 1932; 268 *H.C. Deb.* 5 *s.*, cols. 624–9 and Volume III, Appendix VI; cf. No. 91.

## No. 139

### Sir J. Simon to Sir G. Clerk (Paris)
### No. 109 Telegraphic [C 3328/55/18]

FOREIGN OFFICE, *April 26, 1935, 6.5 p.m.*

Your telegram No. 78 Saving.[1]

Our Locarno obligations give us a very real and direct interest in the terms of the proposed Franco-Soviet agreement. While we are glad to see that M. Laval is alive to the consideration mentioned in the last paragraph of my telegram No. 108,[2] we feel that as he is apparently not ready to show us the agreement before it has been initialled, and as it is possible that he may be forced to yield to pressure by M. Litvinov, it would be wise to let him know frankly at this stage the exact nature of our preoccupation, i.e. that France should not be induced to subscribe to any agreement which might oblige her to go to war with Germany in circumstances not permitted by Article 2 of the Treaty of Locarno lest Germany should ask for an assurance that if France were to attack Germany in such circumstances His Majesty's Government would go to Germany's assistance in accordance with their Locarno obligations.

I shall be glad therefore if you will see M. Laval immediately and explain this point to him though he no doubt shares our preoccupations on this subject.

[1] No. 122.          [2] No. 120.

## No. 140

### Sir E. Ovey[1] (Brussels) to Sir J. Simon (Received April 26, 8.30 a.m.)
### No. 36 Saving: Telegraphic [C 3428/55/18]

BRUSSELS, *April 26, 1935*

Your telegram No. 8 Saving.[2]

Secretary General of Belgian Ministry of Foreign Affairs being absent for some days I sent Mr. MacKillop[3] to make the desired communication through Chef de Cabinet, who fully understood and will inform Prime Minister and Secretary General.

[1] H.M. Ambassador at Brussels.

[2] In this telegram of April 18, not printed, Sir E. Ovey was instructed, in reply to an enquiry by the Belgian Minister for Foreign Affairs concerning the 'bilateral agreements which might accompany' the projected Air Pact mentioned in paragraph 4 of the Stresa Communiqué, to hold similar language to that described in No. 119.

[3] Acting Counsellor of H.M. Embassy.

## No. 141

*Sir G. Clerk (Paris) to Sir J. Simon (Received April 27)*
*No. 85 Saving: Telegraphic [C 3475/55/18]*

PARIS, *April 26, 1935*

The Prime Minister's article in the 'News Letter'[1] is widely reproduced in the French press today. It has created a deep impression in responsible circles here and it is the subject of a remarkable leading article by Ormesson[2] in 'Figaro'. The opinion is unanimously expressed that these views coming from Mr. MacDonald with his unimpeachable record for fairness towards Germany, should have great weight in Berlin.

2. Copy of 'Figaro' article follows by despatch.[3]

[1] Mr. Ramsay MacDonald's article in the current issue of *News Letter* was entitled 'Peace, Germany, and Stresa', and was reprinted in *The Times* of April 26, pp. 16 and 18.
[2] Count Vladimir d'Ormesson was a distinguished publicist and writer of special press articles on international relations.
[3] Not printed.

## No. 142

*Sir E. Phipps (Berlin) to Sir J. Simon (Received April 27, 11 a.m.)*
*No. 108 Saving: Telegraphic [C 3493/206/18]*

*Immediate*                                          BERLIN, *April 26, 1935*
My telegram No. 165.[1]

Naval Attaché was informed at Marineleitung this morning that order for construction of submarines had been given after his interview with Liaison Officer on April 12th. Liaison Officer explained that orders for submarines were given in three parts.

Part 1 was order to prepare designs and estimates. This order was given 'some months ago'.

Part 2 was order to manufacture machinery, instruments, torpedoes, tubes, etc. This order was given about Christmas.

Part 3 was order to construct hull and assemble the component parts. This order had not been given on April 12th at which time Liaison Officer maintains that his statement that no submarines were being ordered was true. The order was given by the Chancellor to Admiral Raeder. It was a *political* order not a naval one. Liaison Officer could not or would not state exact day on which order was given.

As a result of extensive preparations which had been made the first submarines would probably be delivered within six months.

[1] No. 129.

## No. 143

*Sir E. Phipps (Berlin) to Sir J. Simon (Received April 27, 11 a.m.)*
*No. 109 Saving: Telegraphic [C 3491/55/18]*

*Immediate*                                               BERLIN, *April 26, 1935*

My telegram No. 166.[1]

Naval Attaché was informed today at Marineleitung that Prime Minister's article had caused considerable stir in Ministry of Defence and that telephone to Chancellor in Bavaria had been kept busy.

[1] In this telegram of April 26, not printed, Sir E. Phipps said that the German press 'reproduces with great prominence Mr. MacDonald's article [see No. 141] . . . I am informed that instructions were given to keep the comment mild'.

## No. 144

*Sir E. Phipps (Berlin) to Sir J. Simon (Received April 27)*
*No. 110 Saving: Telegraphic [A 4071/22/45]*

BERLIN, *April 26, 1935*

Your telegram No. 94[1] of 25th April.

Herr von Bülow asked me to call this afternoon and read to me the following message which had been dictated by Herr Hitler in Munich over the telephone to his secretary in Berlin:—

'The German government thanks His Majesty's Government for the invitation to send a delegation to London at the beginning of May for the discussions on naval questions which were agreed upon at the time of the visit of the British Ministers in Berlin, and of the value of which the German government is convinced. The German government intends to make a declaration of foreign policy in the second week of May, in reply to the resolution of the Council of the League of Nations of 17th April,[2] and therefore begs His Majesty's Government to postpone the naval conversations until this declaration has been made. The German government —assuming the agreement of His Majesty's Government—will then have the honour to propose a new date for these conversations.'

[1] No. 128.                    [2] Cf. No. 121, note 2.

## No. 145

*Sir G. Clerk (Paris) to Sir J. Simon (Received April 27, 7.50 p.m.)*
*No. 80 Telegraphic [C 3494/55/18]*

PARIS, *April 27, 1935, 6.25 p.m.*

Your telegram No. 109.[1]

As Monsieur (? Laval)[2] was unavailable and in view of urgency of your

[1] No. 139.                    [2] The text was here uncertain.

communication since Franco-Soviet negotiations are being actively pursued I saw Monsieur Léger this morning.

2. I explained the nature of your preoccupations and said that whilst you were confident that Monsieur Laval fully shared them you thought it wise in view of pressure which was doubtless being brought on him during the present hitch to let him know frankly the dangers you saw ahead.

3. Monsieur Léger said that you might rest fully reassured. French Government had made it an absolute condition that Franco-Soviet agreement must be subordinated not only to the working of Covenant[3] but also to that of Locarno Treaty. That was indeed the reason for the present hitch but French Government were absolutely resolved on the subject. Their intention was to have it specifically stated either in the Treaty itself or in a general declaration accompanying it that all its provisions were subordinated to operation of Locarno Treaty. This was considered to be a better method of bringing it into conformity with Locarno Treaty than to attempt to define each case in advance. Their determination to secure this was prompted not only by their natural sentiments towards Great Britain and Italy but also by further consideration that there was great danger lest Germany if afforded a pretext might denounce Locarno Treaty itself. Such a pretext whether tenable or not might be furnished by some change in the situation such as would be constituted by an undertaking by France to come to the immediate and automatic assistance of Soviets in case of sudden unprovoked attack. The Soviets had tried hard to secure such a provision but French Government had refused. The latter were so impressed by importance of not affording Germany any excuse for denouncing Locarno Treaty (thereby involving for France loss of British guarantee) that they were determined to take every precaution.

4. Monsieur Léger said that Monsieur Laval and Monsieur Litvinov had reached agreement at Geneva on a satisfactory draft. When, however, this had been submitted to Moscow it had been disapproved and an attempt was now being made there to reopen the whole question. An entirely new draft had just been sent to Soviet Ambassador and would be discussed this afternoon. This draft, however, in Monsieur Léger's opinion, was tendencious and obscure and could not be accepted. Either the Soviets must agree to French requirements or negotiations must be suspended. He was inclined to think the Soviets would give way and agreement would eventually be reached, possibly early next week.

I asked Monsieur Léger to what he attributed this sudden stiffening on the part of Soviet Government. He said that apart from oriental methods of bargaining there was a slight Soviet-German flirtation in progress at the moment as proved by the recent Soviet-German economic agreement[4] which was extremely advantageous to Moscow and was undoubtedly

[3] Of the League of Nations.
[4] For the agreements signed at Berlin on April 9, 1935, by Dr. Schacht, Reich Minister of Economics, and M. Kandelaki, Trade Delegate of the Soviet Union, see *D.G.F.P.*, Series C, vol. iv, Nos. 20 and 21.

somewhat of a gesture by Berlin. After all, except for Herr Hitler (and even he might change his mind) the Reichswehr, Wilhelmstrasse and industrial interests in Germany all favoured rapprochement with Soviet Russia.

I reminded Monsieur Léger of Monsieur Laval's promise to furnish you with a copy of the agreement as soon as it was initialled. Monsieur Léger said that at the present stage owing to the Soviet attitude there was no text which it would be of any use to show.

## No. 146

*Sir G. Clerk (Paris) to Sir J. Simon (Received April 29)*
*No. 86 Saving: Telegraphic [C 3495/55/18]*

PARIS, *April 27, 1935*

M. Laval, as mayor of Aubervilliers, was invited by the local Communist section in connexion with the municipal election campaign to explain at a public meeting his attitude towards the present Franco-Soviet negotiations.

2. M. Laval declined the invitation but has issued a poster in reply in which he states that he has been violently attacked by representatives of the Third International for his share in the negotiations but that he has no intention of disclosing diplomatic documents in order to defend himself. After describing his work for peace at Geneva, Rome, London and Stresa, M. Laval proceeds: 'As regards the Franco-Russian pact, if it were to be such as the French Communists desire, it would risk bringing the country into war and I would absolutely refuse to sign it. The pact I am considering in conjunction with the Soviet Government, has as its object to stop war, not to provoke it. It is a pact which must be part of the necessary organisation of collective security in Europe but which must not be directed against any one country.'

## No. 147

*Sir E. Phipps (Berlin) to Sir J. Simon (Received April 29, 7.15 p.m.)*
*No. 168 Telegraphic [C 3515/55/18]*

BERLIN, *April 29, 1935, 6.28 p.m.*

My telegram 106 Saving.[1]

Chancellor's doctor dissuaded him from coming to Berlin as arranged and is even trying to prevent him from speaking at May day celebrations owing to state of his throat.

I hear on excellent authority that Herr Hitler aggravated his throat trouble by shouting at Baron von Neurath for the best part of three hours after Geneva proceedings.[2]

[1] No. 132.     [2] Cf. No. 157 below, last paragraph.

# No. 148

### Letter from Mr. Gurney[1] (Copenhagen) to Mr. Collier[2]
### [C 3729/55/18]

COPENHAGEN, *April 29, 1935*

My dear Laurence

I went to see Munch this afternoon, being his first weekly reception day after his return from Geneva, with a view to ascertaining whether he had anything to tell me about the attitude he had adopted there. I found that he had not much to add to what I have already reported in my despatch No. 78[3] of the 23rd April. He told me that he had explained to Sir John Simon that, whilst he was quite ready to support the greater part of the French resolution in regard to German re-armament, he took exception to the sections condemning Germany's action, as he thought that this was a question which should be dealt with rather by The Hague Court than by the Council of the League. As he said at the time, he hoped the action taken by the other Powers would achieve the object they had in view, but it was clear that he very much doubted it.

I told him that I had seen that the Norwegian Minister for Foreign Affairs had approved his attitude[4] and I asked whether the Swedish Minister for Foreign Affairs had also supported him. He told me that M. Sandler had not so far expressed himself very clearly on the subject. He had been away and had not had time to study the question. He had, however, to make a statement in Parliament one of these days.

I observed that in any case his action had been welcomed by Germany. He replied 'rather too much so' and it is evident that he is rather embarrassed by their reaction. As he told me, Denmark is most anxious to keep out of any disputes between the Great Powers and evidently the last thing he wishes is to be identified in any way with the German point of view.

At the same time he told me he thought the Powers were going the wrong way to work as regards Germany. The Germans regarded themselves as martyrs and the more the Powers criticised them the more they would rally round Hitler. He did not say, however, what alternative policy could be adopted. Finally he inveighed against the growth of armaments. Naval armaments did no harm, he said with a smile, but when land armaments increased too much, the machine was inclined to take charge as happened in Germany and Russia in 1914.

Yours ever

HUGH GURNEY

P.S. May 1, 1935. I see in today's newspapers that Sandler yesterday made a statement approving the attitude adopted by Munch at Geneva.

---

[1] H.M. Minister at Copenhagen.

[2] Head of the Northern Department of the Foreign Office.

[3] This despatch, not printed, was mainly a summary of comments in the Danish press on Dr. Munch's speech at Geneva on April 17 (cf. No. 121, note 2).

[4] Cf. No. 133.

Etatsraad Andersen[5] told me this morning that the King had been a little doubtful when he first heard what Munch had done, but that he had subsequently agreed with Andersen that it was the soundest line for him to take in the circumstances.

[5] Etatsraad H. N. Andersen (born 1852) was President of the Danish East Asiatic Company and was reported to 'play to some extent the rôle of "elder statesman" '.

## No. 149

*Sir G. Clerk (Paris) to Sir J. Simon (Received April 30, 8.50 p.m.)*
*No. 81 Telegraphic [C 3527/55/18]*

PARIS, *April 30, 1935, 6.45 p.m.*

My telegram No. 80.[1]

Having heard that Franco-Soviet negotiations would be completed this morning, I went to see Monsieur Laval this afternoon. He said that he had had a further long discussion with Soviet Ambassador in the morning as a result of which a text had been agreed between them. This text was now being telegraphed to Moscow and he hoped to receive concurrence of the Soviet Government tomorrow morning. As soon as their concurrence was received, he would give me a copy of the documents, which will consist of a Treaty and a protocol, the latter being the more important of the two. As Monsieur Léger said on Saturday,[2] main difficulty had arisen from the determination of the French Government to subordinate Franco-Soviet Agreement to the working of the Covenant and the Locarno Treaty, and Monsieur Laval was confident that he had succeeded in securing this. His one preoccupation was not to give Germany a pretext to denounce Locarno Treaty.[3]

As at present arranged Monsieur Laval expects to leave for Moscow next week.

[1] No. 145.
[2] April 27.
[3] An undated note by Mr. Ramsay MacDonald on the filed copy of this telegram reads: 'Surely we shd have been consulted about this before final stage. Suppose we cannot agree to Locarno provisions and Germany does denounce. We shd make it clear that we reserve our attitude. J.R.M.' In the course of a minute dated May 1 Mr. Sargent wrote: 'Once Germany ceases to value the British guarantee she has no further use for Locarno: it merely constitutes a hindrance by preventing her from ridding herself of the demilitarisation of the Rhineland. . . . In these circumstances I do not think we ought to exclude the possibility of Hitler denouncing the Treaty of Locarno and the demilitarisation of the Rhineland in return for the Franco-Russian alliance. O. G. Sargent.' Sir J. Simon thought this 'a very shrewd comment' and asked on May 5 for 'a collection to be made of the declarations made by Germany about Locarno'. These were embodied in a memorandum by Mr. Perowne dated May 21, not printed. From this it appeared that Herr Hitler had only once 'made a *public* declaration that he intends to respect the Locarno Treaty'. This was in a speech in the Reichstag on January 30, 1934. He had, however, made more than one *private* declaration that he intended to observe this Treaty. Cf. *D.G.F.P.*, Series C, vol. iv, No. 72.

## No. 150

*Sir E. Phipps (Berlin) to Sir J. Simon (Received May 1, 11.30 a.m.)*
*No. 111 Saving: Telegraphic [C 3544/206/18]*

*Immediate*                                                    BERLIN, *April 30, 1935*

Admiral Raeder summoned Naval Attaché to-day to make a statement on the publication in England of the German submarine programme.[1]

He said that the communication made to the Naval Attaché regarding the twelve submarines[2] was not a government communication, as stated by you in Parliament,[3] but one for the confidential information of the Admiralty. It had been made because of the desire of the Naval Attaché to be kept continually in touch with German naval shipbuilding.

The Chancellor had said during your visit that Germany would also take all the necessary steps for defence at sea.[4] The communication to the Naval Attaché was an outcome of this statement. Moreover it was intended to clear the air for the forthcoming naval conversations. As a result of publication it had had the opposite effect.

Admiral Raeder requested that his statement should not be published in the press, but should be reported to you.

Full record of the Naval Attaché's conversations at the Marine Leitung go by to-morrow's bag.[5]

Please inform Admiralty.

[1] See *The Times*, April 29, p. 14. This telegram was apparently drafted on April 29.
[2] See No. 129.                          [3] See 301 *H.C. Deb.* 5 s., col. 33 (April 29).
[4] See Volume XII, No. 651, p. 730.                          [5] See No. 154 below.

## No. 151

*Note from Sir R. Vansittart to M. Maisky*
*[C 3554/55/18]*

FOREIGN OFFICE, *April 30, 1935*

My dear Ambassador,

You will remember asking me the other day a question regarding the obligations of the United Kingdom under the Treaty of Locarno.[1] Your question, I believe, was as follows:—

In the event of Germany attacking Soviet Russia, and of France going to the assistance of Soviet Russia and attacking Germany, what would His Majesty's Government in the United Kingdom feel it their duty to do under the Locarno Treaty?

The answer to your question is that France has undertaken in the Locarno Treaty not to attack Germany except in certain specified circumstances. If

[1] M. Maisky put his question to Sir R. Vansittart on April 26. When the lines of a reply were suggested by Mr. Sargent (on April 27) and Sir W. Malkin (on April 29), Sir R. Vansittart commented, on April 29: 'I agree that this may help the French. Please draft a letter to M. Maisky today (he wanted the reply in writing).'

France attacks Germany in any other circumstances, Great Britain is bound under the Locarno Treaty to come to the assistance of Germany.

We should, in fact, be bound under the Locarno Treaty to come to the assistance of Germany if France attacked her under circumstances not falling within one of the exceptions to article 2 of that treaty, which, for this purpose, are (1) action in pursuance of article 16 of the League Covenant; (2) action as the result of a decision of the Assembly or the Council of the League; (3) action in pursuance of article 15, paragraph 7, of the League Covenant, provided that such action is directed against a State which was the first to attack.

Yours sincerely,
R. VANSITTART

## No. 152

*Mr. Charles[1] (Moscow) to Sir J. Simon (Received May 1, 5.30 p.m.)*
*No. 60 Telegraphic [C 3579/55/18]*

MOSCOW, *May 1, 1935, 4.30 p.m.*

My telegram No. 57.[2]

French Ambassador believes that negotiations for Franco-Soviet conventions are being satisfactorily concluded in Paris and that M. Laval will arrive in Moscow about May 10th. M. Alphand states that negotiations were held up at one moment when on refusal of French Government to guarantee Baltic States Soviet Government refused to guarantee Belgium. He declares that there never has been any question of 'automatic' assistance on the part of the French who insist on previous reference to League Council in every case.

Repeated to Paris.

[1] Acting Counsellor, H.M. Embassy at Moscow.　　　[2] No. 124.

## No. 153

*Sir E. Phipps (Berlin) to Sir J. Simon (Received May 1, 8.30 p.m.)*
*No. 171 Telegraphic: by telephone [C 3552/55/18]*

*Most Immediate*　　　　　　　　　　　　　　　BERLIN, *May 1, 1935*

Your telegram No. 96[1] and my despatch No. 413[2] of May 1st.

Minister for Foreign Affairs only returned to Berlin today so I asked him on the telephone for his views on this article in general and passage quoted by you in particular. His Excellency replied that he had himself only seen article this morning in the press. He had not in any way inspired it but

[1] This telegram of even date, despatched at 4.45 p.m., asked for Sir E. Phipps's comments, in time for the House of Commons debate of May 2, on the German semi-official diplomatic commentary of April 30 (see note 2, below), and especially on the portion summarized in *The Times* of May 1, p. 16, the last paragraph of which was quoted in telegram No. 96.

[2] This despatch transmitted the text of the article entitled 'Rearmament or Understanding' published in the *Deutsche Diplomatisch-Politische Korrespondenz* of April 30.

passage quoted was generally speaking in accordance with the views of the German government that is to say that the latter had always been and still were ready, as provided in Article 16 of the Covenant, to combine in taking action against an aggressor but were unwilling to enter into undertakings to do so by an Eastern or a Central European Pact.

This view does not in my opinion indicate any real change on the part of German government. Nevertheless tone of the German press since outburst in Great Britain and United States caused by publication of German submarine building plans[3] has undoubtedly become more conciliatory. The reaction in America particularly has aroused considerable misgivings in German Ministry of Foreign Affairs whose function it is to issue sedatives on such occasions.

[3] Cf. No. 150, notes 1 and 3.

<h2 style="text-align:center">No. 154</h2>

Sir E. Phipps (Berlin) to Sir J. Simon (Received May 2)<br>No. 414 [C 3557/206/18]

*Immediate*                                                          BERLIN, *May 1, 1935*

Sir,

With reference to my telegram No. 111 Saving,[1] I have the honour to transmit to you, herewith, a copy of two records by the Naval Attaché of conversations at the Marine Leitung regarding the publication of the German submarine building programme.

2. The press publishes telegrams from London describing the importance attached in England to this latest development. The French and Italian press are also said to express pleasure that England should at last be waking up to the danger of German rearmament. There is, however, no editorial comment.

I have &c.,<br>ERIC PHIPPS

ENCLOSURE 1 IN NO. 154

Captain Muirhead-Gould to Sir E. Phipps

No. 4/35

*The Ambassador*                                                    BERLIN, *April 29, 1935*

The Liaison Officer from the Marineleitung called upon me at 11.00 today.[2] He said that Admiral Raeder was 'unangenehm überrascht' that information about the German submarine plans, which had been given to me privately and in strict confidence, should have been published in full in the English press.[3] Had the German Government wished to disclose this information they would obviously have published it in the German press,

[1] No. 150.

[2] For the official German report of this interview see *D.G.F.P.*, Series C, vol. iv, No. 58; see also *ibid.*, Nos. 51 and 52.                                          [3] See No. 150, note 1.

219

and it was very disconcerting and unpleasant that it should have been made public in the English press first. He would be glad to have an explanation of how such an unfortunate disclosure should have been made.

2. I replied that I took strong objection to the suggestion that I had been guilty of any breach of confidence. The information about the submarines had been given to me on Thursday (25th April) afternoon in the form that Admiral Raeder wished to deny a report in the 'Daily Telegraph'[4] that Germany was building large submarines when in fact orders for 12 small ones had only just been given. I was not told that the information was being given in confidence. It was my duty to report this information to the Ambassador and to the Admiralty, and I had done so.[5] I notified the Liaison Officer to this effect on Friday, 26th April.

3. The Liaison Officer replied that the information about the German building programme for 1935 had been given me in confidence on 12th April,[6] and that Admiral Raeder had naturally expected that the new information about submarines, which was now part of the general programme, would also have been treated as confidential by me.

4. I replied that while I regretted the misunderstanding my conscience was absolutely clear. The information had been given me on a separate occasion and in a different manner to the information about the building programme, and it was undoubtedly my duty to report it at once. The decision to make it public in London was nothing whatever to do with me: that was purely a political decision. I had given no information to anyone in Berlin except to the Ambassador himself. I certainly had not even discussed the matter with any newspaper correspondents.

5. Subsequent, however, to the release of the information by the Foreign Office to the Press, I had been bombarded by the Berlin Press Correspondents for confirmation or denial of the reports. I had, so far, succeeded in putting them off, but at least 4 correspondents were coming to see me in the course of the afternoon and I strongly urged that Admiral Raeder should give me permission to give them the full outline of the building programme, including the submarines. In this way, and in this way only, could the exaggerated reports which were appearing, and to which Admiral Raeder took exception, be stopped.

6. I went on to point out that more frankness on the part of the Marineleitung in the first place (i.e. at my interview on 12th April) would have avoided all this unpleasantness and suspicion. Admiral Raeder had often told me that the Chancellor had always insisted that the Marineleitung were not to put forward plans for building which might cause apprehension in England, and he must really not blame me if the announcement that Germany had given orders for submarine construction to commence had caused alarm in England, especially as he had assured me, through the Liaison Officer, that no submarines were included in the 1935 programme.

7. The Liaison Officer said that privately he thought that it was a pity that the Chancellor had not announced his intention of building submarines

[4] Of April 25.          [5] See No. 129.          [6] See Volume XII, No. 716.

and generally increasing the Navy on 16th March, at the same time as he announced the increase in the Army.[7] I agreed.

8. The Liaison Officer said that he quite understood my explanation, and thought that Admiral Raeder would be satisfied with it. I replied that I hoped so too, but that once again I wished to make it quite clear that while regretting the misunderstanding I had nothing to apologise for, and that my conscience was quite clear. I hoped he would see Admiral Raeder as soon as possible and urge very strongly that I should be authorised to give the information to the Press.

9. During the afternoon the Liaison Officer rang me up and said that he had been unable to obtain permission to make any statement whatever, and he begged me not to disclose any information which had been given me to the Press Correspondents. He hoped that permission to make a statement on the Naval Building Programme might be given tomorrow or the day after. I pointed out again that this refusal of information would only lead to further exaggerated reports in tomorrow's papers, but he said the decision was not his, but that it was a political matter.

10. I accordingly made the following telephonic announcement to 5 Press Correspondents, and sent a copy of it to the Marineleitung:—

'The Naval Attaché regrets that he has not yet been able to obtain the permission of the German authorities either to deny or confirm the reports which have appeared in the English press concerning German submarine construction. He will communicate with you as soon as such permission is received.'

G. C. Muirhead-Gould

### Enclosure 2 in No. 154

#### Captain Muirhead-Gould to Sir E. Phipps

*The Ambassador*                                                     BERLIN, *April 30, 1935*

I was summoned to the Marineleitung by Admiral Raeder at 12.30 p.m. today to receive a statement on the situation which has arisen as a result of the publication of the German submarine programme.

I was subsequently supplied with an aide mémoire of Admiral Raeder's statement, of which the attached is a translation.[8]

In the covering letter from the Marineleitung it is stated: 'The Head of the Marineleitung requests that this statement should not be published in the Press. He would, however, be pleased if paragraphs 1 and 3 could also be brought to the notice of the Foreign Office as well as to the notice of the Foreign Secretary, Sir John Simon.'

G. C. Muirhead-Gould

[7] See *ibid.*, No. 570.
[8] Printed as enclosure 3 below. See also *D.G.F.P.*, *op. cit.*, No. 59.

*Aide mémoire of a Statement made by the Head of the Marineleitung to the Naval Attaché on 30th April, 1935*

1. The communication in question was not a Government communication, as stated by Sir John Simon in Parliament, but one of our *confidential* communications to the Naval Attaché and intended for the *Admiralty*.

The reason for these communications was the desire of the Naval Attaché to be kept continually in touch with our shipbuilding. We have always notified such building after the decision to lay down a ship, in some cases even before the keel has been laid. (2 cruisers 1935, 12 destroyers 1935).

2. This also accounts for information being supplied in driblets, about which individual officers of the Admiralty have expressed surprise (according to Captain Wassner, German N[aval]. A[ttaché]. in London) and which is said to have given rise to suspicion. But there is indeed very little delay when particulars of the budget passed at the end of March 1935 are announced in April (Cruisers, Destroyers). Even England does not lay down all ships at once. In addition, the Head of the Navy must in every case obtain the permission of the political authorities for each communication.

3. The Chancellor said at the time of the Berlin conversations that we would also take all necessary steps which were necessary for our defence at sea. The communication in question was therefore in accordance with this statement.

4. The object of the communication was to clear the atmosphere for the Naval Conference. It has only resulted in creating a lack of confidence as a result of the English press campaign.

## No. 155

*Sir E. Phipps (Berlin) to Sir J. Simon (Received May 2, 3.5 p.m.)*
*No. 175 Telegraphic [C 3598/55/18]*

BERLIN, *May 2, 1935, 2.7 p.m.*

My telegram No. 102 Saving.[1]

General von Reichenau and other senior officers of the army have in the course of farewell conversations with Military Attaché[2] strongly expressed their resentment against England's apparent change of attitude. During the Berlin conversations Herr Hitler, they say, placed his cards on the table. His frank statement of Germany's intentions regarding rearmament provoked no strong criticism on the part of British Delegation. Now, however, when practical steps were being taken to put into effect plans which had been revealed to His Majesty's Government there was a wild outburst in England for which it was difficult to account. It seemed that His Majesty's Government were abandoning their previously declared policy and were swinging towards that of encirclement of Germany.

[1] No. 125.
[2] Colonel Thorne was to be succeeded as Military Attaché by Colonel F. E. Hotblack on May 13.

General von Reichenau said that in Government circles resentment was so great that it was no easy matter to dissuade responsible men from preferring war to peace as the solution of their difficulties.

## No. 156

*Sir G. Clerk (Paris) to Sir J. Simon (Received May 2, 8 p.m.)*
*No. 82 Telegraphic: by telephone [C 3599/55/18]*

PARIS, May 2, 1935

My telegram No. 87 Saving.[1]
Franco-Soviet agreement was signed at 7 p.m. this evening.[2]
Text was communicated to me just in time to send by bag tonight.

[1] This telegram of May 1 is not preserved in Foreign Office archives. According to the docket it referred to No. 145 and said that the Foreign Ministry expected the Franco-Soviet pact to be initialled about 9.30 p.m. on May 1 and that a copy of the text had been promised as soon as it was initialled.

[2] The Treaty of Mutual Assistance between France and the U.S.S.R., with Protocol of Signature, was signed in Paris by M. Laval and M. Potemkine, Soviet Ambassador at Paris. The French text is printed in *B.F.S.P.*, vol. 139, pp. 474–7.

## No. 157

*Sir E. Phipps (Berlin) to Sir J. Simon (Received May 3)*
*No. 112 Saving: Telegraphic [C 3621/55/18]*

*Immediate*                                        BERLIN, *May 2, 1935*

I had a long and friendly conversation with Baron von Neurath this afternoon. It was our first meeting since Stresa. He opened by asking what had happened in regard to submarine affair and I explained to him the awkward position in which Naval Attaché had been placed by being kept in the dark on that subject and bad impression that this had created in London.[1] His Excellency said he was very glad to learn true facts of the case and greatly deplored behaviour of German naval authorities who should naturally have included submarines in original list of contemplated ship construction handed to Captain Gould on April 12th. He would explain matter to Chancellor who for his part had been annoyed at Air[2] Attaché's publication of German programme in British press, the reason for which however now seemed clear.

I proceeded to speak with utmost frankness to Baron von Neurath giving him a brief account of successive unpleasant surprises sprung upon us by Germany since my arrival here[3] viz: departure from the League, announcement of a large air force followed by that of an enormous conscript army, and then the submarine affair, all these unpleasant surprises announced just before beginning of friendly discussions. I then referred to your visit[4]

[1] See No. 154.
[2] It was suggested on the filed copy that this word should have read 'Naval'.
[3] i.e. since August 1933.
[4] For a record of the Anglo-German conversations at Berlin, March 25–26, see Volume XII, No. 651.

undertaken despite the Chancellor's postponement and announcement of a military air force and of conscription. I knew certain circles in France had been alarmed at what Germany might have to offer you and Mr. Eden. These alarms had proved only too groundless for far from offering you anything the German Government had merely repeated its negative attitude regarding Eastern and Danubian pacts or a limitation of armaments on any reasonable basis and had in addition put forward demands for a relatively very big fleet and for colonies. The disappointment you had expressed was therefore only natural.

Baron von Neurath did not deny my facts but merely expressed regret that Germany had nothing to offer and could only claim what . . .[5] considered to be her due. He was not a naval expert but thought 35 per cent of our fleet a reasonable figure as Germany must be able to keep the Baltic open. I remarked that what rendered any limitation of armaments hopeless was continued German insistence on reference to astronomical figures in Russian air force and army. No-one could possibly believe that Russia in her present state of blue funk and with her deplorable means of communication contemplated attacking anybody. If discussions could be resumed leaving Russia out of account there might still be a good chance of agreement. This Baron von Neurath did not entirely rule out but Chancellor will probably prove recalcitrant. His Excellency again urged that negotiations proceed at once over air pact the conclusion of which would do so much to pacify a distracted and frightened Europe. I pointed out that it would be essential to reach some parallel agreement regarding numbers in this branch and to this His Excellency did not demur.

Baron von Neurath said he had had five most agitated hours with Chancellor after Geneva resolution[6] and had at length persuaded him not to take any sudden decision. That resolution, after his helpful reply to question put to him from Stresa[7] had been a great blow to him. It is now arranged that Herr Hitler will make a declaration in the Reichstag in foreign policy on May 15th. He had wished to do this on May 8th but Baron von Neurath had persuaded him to postpone it until after Silver Jubilee celebrations.[8] I said I trusted this did not mean that declaration was going to be a very disagreeable one but His Excellency reassured me on this point.

[5] The text was here uncertain. The insertion of 'she' was suggested on the filed copy.
[6] Of April 17; cf. No. 147.          [7] See Volume XII, Nos. 715 and 717.
[8] May 6–11; cf. No. 118, note 1.

### No. 158

*Sir E. Phipps (Berlin) to Sir J. Simon (Received May 3, 10 a.m.)*
*No. 113 Saving: Telegraphic [C 3622/55/18]*

*Immediate*                                                   BERLIN, *May 2, 1935*
My immediately preceding telegram Saving.[1]
Minister for Foreign Affairs told me that just before me, he had received

[1] No. 157.

a visit from General Von Fritsch[2] who said that, to prove present state of panic in France, French had actually now got 14 divisions massed on the German frontier. This was sheer madness since Germany did not dream of attacking France.

Discussing possibility of still concluding convention for limitation of armaments Minister for Foreign Affairs said that Germany now only had 20 divisions altogether and even they were not all fully armed. Figure of 36 was a maximum, only to be reached in 2 or 3 years. In reply to a question His Excellency said that German Government would reduce that maximum pro rata if other Powers reduced their present figures. I again objected to Russia being always dragged in and Minister for Foreign Affairs replied that armies of France and Italy alone were sufficiently formidable.

[2] Chief of German Army Command.

## No. 159

### Sir J. Simon to Mr. Charles (Moscow)
### No. 227 [C 3523/55/18]

FOREIGN OFFICE, *May 2, 1935*

Sir,

The Soviet Ambassador enquired of Sir R. Vansittart on April 26th[1] what would be the attitude of this country if negotiations for an Eastern Pact on the lines now contemplated by Russia and France were to be pushed forward and concluded. Sir R. Vansittart replied that no text had been shown to His Majesty's Government and that there were points in which the Government might be more than interested if they were likely to affect the Locarno obligations of this country. Generally speaking, however, Sir R. Vansittart thought that, subject to the above-mentioned considerations, M. Maisky need anticipate no criticism or obstruction from either the Government or the press of the United Kingdom, provided always that such a Pact or such pacts were concluded within the framework of the League. The somewhat grudging German reply received at Stresa in regard to the Eastern Pact had obviously facilitated matters in some measure. But, Sir R. Vansittart added, as he had already said to MM. Benes and Léger at Geneva,[2] it would be very unwise not to pursue negotiations simultaneously with Germany on the basis of the German draft, unsatisfactory though that draft might be in its present form.

2. M. Maisky did not appear to dissent from the point of view expressed by Sir R. Vansittart.

[I am &c.,
(for the Secretary of State)]
C. W. BAXTER

[1] Cf. No. 151.        [2] Cf. No. 134.

## No. 160

### Sir R. Clive (Tokyo) to Sir J. Simon (Received May 3, 9.30 a.m.)
#### No. 130 Telegraphic [A 4086/22/45]

TOKYO, *May 3, 1935, 10.45 a.m.*

In conversation with Naval Attaché Minister of Marine's secretary stated, that in view of complications which have arisen due to Germany's demand for naval expansion, navy department sees no hope of naval conference taking place this year since it will be necessary for European countries to arrive at a naval agreement before Japanese government could take part in a conference.

He stressed the unwillingness of Japanese government to take part in the conference at which any other nation except original signatories of the Washington Treaty is represented.

## No. 161

### Sir E. Phipps (Berlin) to Sir J. Simon (Received May 3, 1.21 p.m.)
#### No. 177 Telegraphic: by telephone [C 3629/55/18]

*Immediate*                                           BERLIN, *May 3, 1935*

General Goering asked me to call on him this morning. He is greatly perturbed by a report showing that Reuters correspondent misunderstood an essential passage of his speech at yesterday's press luncheon. He had been quoted as saying that in case any two powers made an air pact together German air force would act against them. This he entirely denies.

Full translation of speech of which German text was given me by General Goering will reach you by air mail tomorrow morning.[1]

[1] Received on May 4 as enclosure in Berlin despatch No. 423 of May 3. The text published in *The Times*, May 3, p. 16, corresponded with that in the enclosure.

## No. 162

### Sir E. Phipps (Berlin) to Sir J. Simon (Received May 3, 2.50 p.m.)
#### No. 178 Telegraphic [C 3636/55/18]

*Confidential*                                     BERLIN, *May 3, 1935, 2 p.m.*

My immediately preceding telegram.[1]

What especially infuriated General Goering was that a German journalist overheard correspondent of Havas Agency saying to another French journalist that Reuters correspondent had misunderstood speech but that it was a good thing in view of debate that evening in the House of Commons.[2]

General Goering vowed to me that never never again would he be the guest of the foreign press.

[1] No. 161.          [2] See 301 *H.C. Deb.* 5 *s.*, cols. 569 ff.

## No. 163

*Sir E. Phipps (Berlin) to Sir J. Simon (Received May 4, 11.45 a.m.)*
*No. 114 Saving: Telegraphic [C 3654/55/18]*

BERLIN, *May 3, 1935*

My telegram No. 177.[1]

I then had a long and friendly conversation with General Göring, who expressed satisfaction at the Prime Minister's speech in the House of Commons yesterday,[2] remarking that there seemed to be nothing in it with which he could not agree. General Göring then assured me, as he has done before, that any idea of a war between Great Britain and Germany struck him as being worthy of a madman. Nobody in Germany in their wildest dreams contemplated attacking Great Britain. I replied that I entirely agreed with this but we felt in England that peace was one indivisible whole and that if it were broken in any part of Europe, at any rate by a Great Power, all the other European Powers would inevitably be dragged in whether they wished it or not.

I then referred to the constant fears expressed by Germans regarding the Russian danger, which seemed to us in England practically non-existent, firstly because Russia had no interest in attacking, or wish to attack, Germany, and secondly because of her lack of communications and general inefficiency. General Göring promptly replied: 'The air'. He said that the élite of the Russian nation were in the air force, which he assessed, at a conservative estimate, at between 3,000 and 4,000 aircraft, only counting the latest and most efficient machines.

I pointed out how impossible it would be to conclude a western air pact if we had continually to take Russia into account. General Göring replied that, if, by the conclusion of an air pact, he could be certain that Great Britain, for instance, would be at his side in the event of a Russian attack, he would be content with a far smaller air force. In fact he even mentioned 1,000 first-line machines as being perhaps sufficient in such an event.

[1] No. 161.          [2] See No. 162, note 2.

## No. 164

*Sir E. Phipps (Berlin) to Sir J. Simon (Received May 4, 11.45 a.m.)*
*No. 117 Saving: Telegraphic [C 3655/55/18]*

BERLIN, *May 3, 1935*

Yesterday's debate in the House of Commons[1] is very fully reported in the press and has been favourably received.

Under heading 'Hopeful British demonstration', *Angriff* publishes a friendly telegram from their London correspondent, who, however, warns his readers that British Government may once again fail to hold steadfast to their policy. He attributes mild tone of Government spokesmen to

[1] See No. 162, note 2.

influence of Dominion Premiers[2] and to the disapproval with which the Geneva Resolution[3] was received in the United States of America.[4]

A discordant note is struck by the *Börsen Zeitung* which professes anxiety at your Locarno declaration.[5] What if France engineers a dispute in which Germany is obliged by circumstances to take action against Russia? Summary of this article follows.[6]

[2] The Prime Ministers of all the Dominions, except the Irish Free State, were in London for celebrations in connexion with the Silver Jubilee; see No. 118, note 1.

[3] Of April 17; see No. 121, note 2.        [4] Cf. *F.R.U.S. 1935*, vol. i, pp. 265-9.

[5] In the course of his reply to Sir H. Samuel's question as to whether the 'automatic responsibilities' of the United Kingdom would be extended or affected by the conclusion of a Franco-Russian agreement, Sir J. Simon said that if 'Germany attacks Russia and in view of a Franco-Russian treaty of mutual assistance France goes to the assistance of Russia by attacking Germany, the Locarno Treaty does not put this country in those circumstances under any obligation to go to the assistance of Germany'. See 301 *H.C. Deb.* 5 s., cols. 681-2.        [6] In Berlin despatch No. 424 of May 4, not printed.

## No. 165

### Sir J. Simon to Sir E. Phipps (Berlin)
### No. 454 [C 3653/55/18]

FOREIGN OFFICE, *May 3, 1935*

Sir,

Herr von Hoesch spent an hour with me this morning.[1] I called his attention to the striking demonstration in yesterday's debate[2] of a complete unity of view. The Opposition Parties were in complete agreement with the Government as to the action we had to take in view of Germany's recent announcements, culminating in the large developments of her Air Force. Germany would labour under a grievous mistake if she supposed that in such circumstances the reluctance felt in this country to increased expenditure on armaments would have any influence on our united action. The Ambassador acknowledged that he had been greatly impressed with this aspect of the matter and said he was so reporting to his Government. He attempted to argue that there was nothing novel or surprising in Germany's recent announcements—for example, after France had rejected the proposal made to Mr. Eden in Berlin a year ago of agreement on the basis of 300,000 men for the German army,[3] he (the Ambassador) had freely informed those who asked what Germany would do, that Germany would, he was sure, now proceed to provide herself with what she thought necessary. Herr von Hoesch further suggested that the statement made to me by Herr Hitler on the 26th March that Germany needed a navy which was 35 per cent of the British Navy[4] was in itself an intimation that Germany meant to have

[1] A slightly shorter account of this conversation was sent to Sir E. Phipps in Foreign Office telegram No. 98, despatched at 3.35 p.m. on May 4. Herr von Hoesch's report of the meeting is printed in *D.G.F.P.*, Series C, vol. iv, No. 66.

[2] See 301 *H.C. Deb.* 5 s., cols. 569 ff.        [3] See Volume VI, No. 395.

[4] See Volume XII, No. 651, pp. 731-2.

submarines, and that there was therefore nothing fresh in the statement made since. I said that I could not agree on this point, for our naval attaché had been given information last month which clearly implied the contrary, and the statement subsequently made had been challenged by us with reference to these previous assurances.[5] Herr von Hoesch went on to draw a distinction between the previous preparation of parts of submarines and the assembling of the parts in order that Germany might have actual submarines hereafter. I said that I noted the distinction which he had made, and asked whether I was to understand him to assert that at the present moment Germany had no submarines in actual existence. The Ambassador hastily explained that he was only giving me his personal impressions, and I then observed that no doubt it would be possible for him to find out and inform me on the subject with full authority.

2. The Ambassador showed himself disposed to enter into a long defence of the recent actions of Germany, and even to complain that, after my interviews with Herr Hitler when the Chancellor had been so frank, there should now be such strong feeling expressed on the subject. I replied that it would surely be much better for Germany to face the actual fact that her recent declarations and proceedings had profoundly disturbed public confidence all over Europe. If we spent our time in arguing whether this was justified or what excuses Germany could put forward, we should not reach agreement. If our common object was peace in the future, the important thing was to realise the fact that recent German action had produced widespread mistrust of her intentions. The Ambassador agreed that this result had, in fact, followed, and I urged that he should report this also to his Government as his impression from the Debate.

3. He told me that the Chancellor intended to make a declaration on German foreign policy to the Reichstag on May 15th. I called his particular attention to passages in the speeches of the Prime Minister and myself (Hansard, *Parliamentary Debates* of May 2nd, bottom of column 572 and top of column 688) in which Germany was invited to come forward to show her readiness to help to restore international confidence. We should await Herr Hitler's declaration with special interest to see what he had to say on this topic.

4. Herr von Hoesch made special reference to the passage in the Prime Minister's speech (column 571) which urged that Germany herself would take immediate steps to promote, in more concrete shape, the idea formulated by Herr Hitler of a multilateral non-aggression pact with the countries of Eastern Europe. What did this suggestion imply? I said that we felt it was not enough for Herr Hitler to say in general terms, as he did to me in Berlin, that Germany was prepared to do this, or even to add, as Baron von Neurath did when we communicated from Stresa, that Germany's intention remained even though a Franco-Russian pact of mutual assistance was added.[6] Why should not Germany formulate her offer with the definite mention of parties and a definite form of assurance and declare that this was the form of document which she was ready to sign along with other

[5] See Nos. 129, 142, 154, and 157.     [6] See Volume XII, No. 715.

parties she named? The Ambassador expressed the view that it would be difficult for Germany to take the initiative, but promised to report my suggestion to his Government. I pointed out that by positive and concrete action of this sort Germany would do a great deal more to show that she was contributing something to security than by merely putting herself on record in vague phrases.

5. The Ambassador also made a special enquiry as to the meaning in the Stresa communiqué of the reference to 'bilateral agreements which might accompany' the proposed Air Pact. I reminded him that Prince Bismarck had already addressed the same enquiry to us, and I repeated the explanation in my telegram to you No. 86[7] of April 18th. The Ambassador deplored the postponement of the negotiation of the Air Pact, and said that France was enthusiastically for it until she found that Germany also liked it; thereupon France lost interest in it. I disputed this version and pointed to the language of the Stresa Communiqué as showing the contrary. What we should like would be to see the framework of an air pact put together and the negotiation carried out as far as possible between the five Powers concerned. We had had certain suggestions from France, Italy, and Belgium, and would be glad to have any proposals which Germany wished to make as to the form of the pact. As to bilateral agreements, none such had been discussed except as to the special relations of Britain and Italy in the Air Pact, though it was quite true that the question might arise where other bilateral agreements of any sort would be needed in view of the fact that the Air Pact provided for instantaneous action. That, however, was for the future and was one of the things which might have to be considered if we all got down to the work of drafting the pact together. The Ambassador expressed the strong view that it was in fact impossible for A to have a bilateral agreement with B as to the way in which obligations would be fulfilled against C and at the same time to have an agreement with C as to how reciprocal obligations would be fulfilled against B.

I am, &c.,
JOHN SIMON

[7] No. 119.

## No. 166

*Sir E. Phipps (Berlin) to Sir J. Simon (Received May 5, 12 noon)*
*No. 115 Saving: Telegraphic [C 3657/55/18]*

BERLIN, *May 4, 1935*

My immediately preceding telegram Saving.[1]

General Göring, to explain and illustrate his fear of Russia in the air, told me that he knew from German secret sources that there were at present 27 aerodromes in Czechoslovakia at the disposal of the Russian air force for action against Germany. He could supply me with names of these aerodromes.

General Göring referred also to Franco-Russian pact just concluded[2]

[1] No. 163.          [2] See No. 156.

and expressed considerable anxiety at a clause which he declared it contained, to the effect that if the Council of the League could not reach a quick decision or if it were not unanimous France and Russia would act at once against any presumed aggression. He asked how in view of Germany's position between these two Powers and in the absence of a western air pact we could ask her to weaken herself in the air.

## No. 167

*Sir E. Phipps (Berlin) to Sir J. Simon (Received May 4,[1] 12 noon)*
*No. 116 Saving: Telegraphic [C 3658/55/18]*

BERLIN, *May 4, 1935*

My immediately preceding telegram Saving.[2]

General Goering referred to remarks exchanged between himself and Mr. Eden about Locarno (see my telegram No. 88 Saving[3] of March 28th). He said, in reply to a question Mr. Eden had informed him that if France decided to attack Germany Great Britain would use all her influence to prevent such attack but would not actually fight on Germany's side. I replied that I knew Mr. Eden had made some jesting remark on this subject across a lady at dinner but he had not ever meant this remark to be taken seriously. Moreover I pointed out that Great Britain and Italy had quite recently at Stresa reaffirmed their solemn obligations under the Treaty of Locarno.

My impression is that I was able to convince General Goering.

[1] Possibly in error for 'May 5', as in No. 166.  [2] No. 166.
[3] Volume XII, No. 661; cf. *ibid.*, No. 667.

## No. 168

*Sir E. Phipps (Berlin) to Sir J. Simon (Received May 6)*
*No. 119 Saving: Telegraphic [A 4128/22/45]*

BERLIN, *May 4, 1935*

Naval Attaché was informed at the Marine Leitung yesterday that naval circles appreciated tone of government speeches in House of Commons debate[1] and were glad that naval mission would still be welcomed in London.

[1] On May 2; cf. No. 162, note 2.

## No. 169

*Letter from Vice-Admiral Little to Mr. Craigie*
*[A 4333/22/45]*

ADMIRALTY, *May 4, 1935*

Dear Craigie,

I am very glad to hear that you are about to return to the Foreign Office,[1]

[1] Mr. Craigie was apparently on sick leave. A minute of April 29 by Mr. Troutbeck read: 'Mr. Craigie is unfortunately still not very fit and does not expect to be back till tomorrow week . . .'

as we are badly in need of your co-operation in our endeavour to get ahead as far as is possible with the question of the replacement of the Naval Treaties.

I have been looking at recent N.C.M. papers[2] and everything is now undoubtedly in order for us to sound the Germans and find out, at first hand, what their real intentions are in regard to German Naval development. In this connection the C.N.S.,[3] through the medium of our Attaché in Berlin, has told Admiral Raeder that we should like to discuss qualitative limitation and then consider building programmes for the period up to 1942, and that we think no progress could be made along the lines of a ratio between the German Naval strength and that of ours or France.[4] I very much hope, therefore, that in spite of Hitler's forthcoming statement we shall be able to get the German delegation over and start the ball rolling once more.

Should we be fortunate enough to obtain German ideas in regard to qualitative limitation and their programme intentions I think we are agreed that we should, without loss of time, convey these proposals immediately to the French and Italians and ask for renewed conversations with each of these at an early date to ascertain their reactions.

I suppose it is quite possible that in view of recent developments in Europe we may find a different atmosphere existing as between France and Italy. We shall be able to see whether France still adheres to her present policy of maintaining a Naval strength equal to the united strength of Germany and Italy.

These are questions which we have got to re-explore and should we, as a result, find ourselves in possession of French and Italian building programmes it will then be the time for the Government to decide whether, under all the circumstances, it will be desirable for the British Empire to be tied to a building programme.

There seems little doubt that the figures produced by France, Italy and Germany will be larger than we have hitherto contemplated. It seems to me that we shall have then reached a point when a decision as to whether quantitative limitation in the future is a practical question, must be taken.

As you know, as things have progressed during the past twelve months we have, all of us, including I think the Foreign Office, become sceptical in regard to quantitative limitation. Supposing, for a moment, that our worst fears are realised it will then be time to grasp at the last straw, namely qualitative limitation.

You are well aware of the great importance which the Admiralty attach to this form of limitation as preventing a race in armaments and we are still sanguine in the Admiralty that a world wide treaty embodying qualitative limitation is a practical proposition.

I think that one good point which will arise as a result of the conversations, which I hope we are shortly to have with Germany, France and Italy, will

2 i.e. papers of the Ministerial Naval Committee.
3 Chief of Naval Staff: Admiral Sir Ernle Chatfield, First Sea Lord.
4 See enclosure 2 in No. 138.

be to show that the four principal maritime countries of Europe are agreed in regard to qualitative limitation. This should be a valuable weapon [? with which] to approach the Americans and Japanese, of which I believe the former will be the easier to convert to our ideas. But whereas you know that the Americans will agree to qualitative limitation at their figure, our present information goes to show that the Japanese will want a free hand, in the absence of Naval Treaties, in order to develop 'special types'.

I think I am right in saying that the Admiralty would go a long way in compromising on the qualitative limitation of the several categories in preference to having no qualitative limitation at all, as this last state of affairs would greatly add to the difficulties of maintaining our Naval security.

Yours ever,<br>C. J. C. LITTLE

**No. 170**

*Sir E. Phipps (Berlin) to Sir J. Simon (Received May 5, 10 a.m.)*

*No. 180 Telegraphic [C 3660/55/18]*

Secret                                       BERLIN, *May 5, 1935, 12.15 a.m.*

Belgian Minister who has just returned from Brussels tells me that he found the people there in a state of panic regarding possibility of imminent German attack. He had a long interview with the Minister of Defence and Chief of Staff who are both convinced of possibility of German attack within next few weeks by means of an extended Schlieffen plan[1] through South Holland and Northern Belgium thus turning French and Belgian fortified system. It would be carried out on lines indicated in a recent series of articles in French 'Revue Hebdomadaire', with lightning rapidity by practically entire Reichswehr leaving S.A. and the S.S. formations to act as a screen on other German frontiers. Belgian military authorities maintain that Dutch are very alarmed and also French (see my telegram No. 113 Saving[2] May 2nd). They were annoyed with Count Kerchove because he refused to share their fears and declared that he had no reason to believe that Germany would be demented enough to embark on such a mad venture anyhow until her army were completely expanded in say, two or three years time. Minister of Defence maintained that Germany was now far stronger than her opponents and that effect of surprise would be annihilating. Moreover German economic position would be far less favourable later. It is probable that Belgian class due to be liberated at the end of May will be kept with the colours until October.

Reasons given for the above panic-stricken views are the following:—

    1. Two new bridges have just been completed over the Rhine near Wesel whose sole utility can be military.

---

[1] The operational plan associated with the name of General von Schlieffen, Chief of German General Staff, 1891–1905, for outflanking French fortifications by an attack through the Low Countries.          [2] No. 158.

2. Numerous strategical roads leading to Dutch frontier have been constructed.
3. Reichswehr officers in plain clothes have been arrested in Holland, spying on roads etc.
4. Drilling is proceeding in German labour camps with view to formation of reserve of officers.
5. Hidden ammunition dumps exist and block houses have been built in the demilitarized zone.
6. Many Reichswehr are in demilitarized zone disguised as S.A. (this point is not actually guaranteed by Belgians).
7. Unusual activity exists in district between Aix-la-Chapelle and Wesel.

Count Kerchove also saw Belgian Prime Minister and of course officials at the Ministry of Foreign Affairs who do not share in the same degree fears of the military authorities. He agrees with French Ambassador and me in thinking these fears absurdly exaggerated. He does not wish to be quoted at Brussels or elsewhere.

My Military Attaché's comments on above are following:—

None of the rank and file of German infantry has more than five months' service and no collective training higher than company training has begun. Training and equipment of artillery are even more backward. German army has seldom been so un-ready for war.

Repeated to Brussels.

## No. 171

*Sir E. Drummond*[1] *(Rome) to Sir J. Simon (Received May 5, 9.30 a.m.)*
*No. 278 Telegraphic [C 3664/55/18]*

ROME, *May 5, 1935, 1 a.m.*

My telegrams Nos. 276[2] and 277.[3]

It is difficult to tell what the Italian Government have in mind when inspiring these articles. Of course Signor Mussolini has become violently anti-German and he may possibly think that a press campaign criticising policy of His Majesty's Government is best method of fortifying common front against Germany. Italian Government hold that the German Government will only yield when faced with firmness and superior force and that any moderation towards Germany is thought in Berlin to be due to weakness and only leads to further excesses and demands.

I propose to see Signor Suvich[4] as soon as he returns from Venice and ask him what writers have in mind when they refer to action and sanctions.[5]

[1] H.M. Ambassador at Rome.
[2] In this telegram of May 3, received at 9.30 a.m. on May 4, Sir E. Drummond summarized Italian press comments on Mr. MacDonald's speech and the House of Commons debate of May 2.
[3] In this telegram of May 4, received at 10 a.m. on May 5, Sir E. Drummond reported further press comments, which he described as 'severe and certainly inspired'.
[4] Italian Under Secretary of State for Foreign Affairs.
[5] e.g. Dr. Gayda, the editor, was reported to have commented as follows in the *Giornale*

*d'Italia*: 'Question now was whether certain sanctions were to be applied and whether England would share in applying them as is understood to be her pledge. . . . The Prime Minister's speech caused perplexity for it did not seem to fit in with the pledges of Stresa which were not confined to use of words but implied acts. It was to be hoped that its vagueness was due to wish to leave hands freer for action.'

## No. 172

*Sir E. Ovey (Brussels) to Sir E. Phipps (Berlin)*
*No. 1[1] Telegraphic [C 3667/55/18]*

BRUSSELS, *May 6, 1935*

Your telegram No. 180 to Foreign Office.[2]

No sign of panic in evidence here. Complementary telegrams will be sent tomorrow by bag to the Foreign Office by Saving.[3]

Repeated to Foreign Office.

[1] Repeated to the Foreign Office at 4 p.m. on May 6 as Brussels telegram No. 24, received at 9.30 a.m. on May 7.
[2] No. 170.                                                   [3] See below No. 175.

## No. 173

*Sir E. Phipps (Berlin) to Sir J. Simon (Received May 7, 3.20 p.m.)*
*No. 182 Telegraphic [C 3700/55/18]*

BERLIN, *May 7, 1935, 1.30 p.m.*

French Ambassador tells me he obtained from a journalist copy of instructions issued to German press by Ministry of Foreign Affairs on May 4th to attack with great abandon Franco-Russian Pact.[1] Stress was to be laid on the fact that there was a secret military convention attached to it, that a French loan of 5 milliards of francs to Russia was imminent for construction of railways and roads etc., that pact ran counter to Article 16 of the covenant, and that a secret arrangement existed between Russia and Czechoslovakia for placing aerodromes of the latter at the disposal of the former. Press was also told to attack your interpretation of Locarno in the House of Commons debate[2] and to point out that no attack of France on Germany under the new pact could absolve Great Britain from coming to the latter's assistance.

M. François-Poncet went to see Baron von Neurath on May 5th and remonstrated on the attitude of German press (which he thinks was inspired by the Chancellor himself). He pointed out the folly of (? combining)[3] in a secret military convention which M. Laval has always done his best to avoid, he denied any loan intention or knowledge of any aviation agreement between Russia and Czechoslovakia and asked why Germany could not declare that she would accept the invitation to join the pact in which case it would be apparent to all that it was not directed against her. Baron von Neurath replied that German government could not be expected to take the initiative in view of feeling aroused here by conclusion of pact. He added

[1] See No. 156.            [2] On May 2; see No. 164, note 5.
[3] The text was here uncertain.

235

that he knew Russia had enquired of Roumania whether latter would in certain eventualities permit Soviet troops to cross through Bessarabia.

French Ambassador is disheartened at tone of German press and tells me he cannot now contemplate suggesting to M. Laval, as he had thought of doing, that he (M. Laval) should stop in Berlin on his way back from Moscow to see Hitler. If conditions had been more favourable M. François-Poncet believes M. Laval would have been ready to do this.

## No. 174

*Sir J. Simon to Sir G. Clerk (Paris) and Sir E. Drummond (Rome)*
*No. 111[1] Telegraphic [C 3265/55/18]*

FOREIGN OFFICE, *May 7, 1935, 6.30 p.m.*

We have been considering the best means of giving effect to that part of the Stresa Resolution which states that the Governments of France, Italy and the United Kingdom are agreed to continue actively the study of the question of the Air Pact for Western Europe, with a view to the drafting of the Pact between the five Powers mentioned in the London Communiqué and of any bilateral agreements which might accompany it.[2]

We would suggest for the consideration of the French/Italian Government that advantage should be taken of the presence at Geneva, on the occasion of the forthcoming session of the League Council,[3] of the jurists of the three Stresa Powers to meet privately and unobtrusively to discuss the two drafts of the proposed Air Pact which have already been put forward[4] and any other suggestions as to the drafting of the Pact which any of those Powers may wish to bring up for consideration. We would suggest that it would be desirable that the Belgian jurist also should be associated with his French, Italian and United Kingdom colleagues in these informal consultations. It is not proposed that these talks should be carried to the point of word for word agreement on a text. If it were found that a common scheme was emerging it might be well at that point to try for a meeting of all the Locarno Powers (see my statement on page 26 of Stresa record).[5] It would be understood of course that the jurists would consider only the form which a multilateral Pact might take: the French proposal for bilateral air agreements, which raises political and military issues, would not be discussed by the jurists.

Please ascertain urgently what view the French/Italian Government takes of the above-mentioned suggestions.

We should be glad also of the comments of the Government to which you are accredited on the following tentative suggestion. It was of course originally

[1] No. 111 to Paris, No. 273 to Rome.    [2] See paragraph 4 in Cmd. 4880.
[3] The 86th session of the Council of the League of Nations was to open at Geneva on May 20.
[4] For the French Government's draft see Volume XII, Annex to No. 517, and for Her Majesty's Government's draft see *ibid.*, No. 722, Annex I to 7th meeting at Stresa Conference.    [5] See *ibid.*, No. 722, pp. 889–90.

the intention that the Air Pact should be concluded only as part of a general settlement, as outlined in the Anglo-French Declaration of February 3rd. In view however of the rapidly growing strength of Germany in the air, the French & Italian governments may care to consider whether there would be any advantage to them in proceeding with the negotiation of the Air Pact by itself, on condition that agreement should be reached concurrently between the four above-mentioned Powers and Germany as to the limitation of their respective air strengths.

Repeated to Berlin No. 99 and Brussels No. 37 for information.

## No. 175

*Sir E. Ovey (Brussels) to Sir J. Simon (Received May 8, 9.45 a.m.)*
*No. 41 Saving: Telegraphic [C 3703/55/18]*

BRUSSELS, *May 7, 1935*

My telegram No. 39 Saving.[1]

General Cumont, Chief of the General Staff, whom Military Attaché saw today, admitted to 'an ever-present anxiety' regarding threat from the North, but saw no reason to apprehend an immediate invasion.

[1] In this telegram of May 6, received May 8 (not printed), Sir E. Ovey reported that he 'sat next to Minister of War for two and a half hours on Thursday last [May 2]. Our purely informal talk ranged over nearly every subject connected with our common interests. Minister never made slightest suggestion of any personal fear of imminent invasion.'

## No. 176

*Sir E. Phipps (Berlin) to Sir J. Simon (Received May 8)*
*No. 120 Saving: Telegraphic [C 3743/55/18]*

BERLIN, *May 7, 1935*

My telegram No. 117 Saving[1] last paragraph.

Press comment on the House of Commons debate and on the Franco-Russian agreement continues to show anxiety regarding Great Britain's interpretation of her Locarno obligations.[2] It is generally felt that Germany is already branded in England with the mark of the aggressor, and that whilst Great Britain in certain eventualities might intervene in favour of France, there is no practical possibility of her doing so in favour of Germany in any circumstances. Your statement in the House is declared to have been so vague as to justify Germany's worst suspicions.[3]

[1] No. 164.　　　　　　　　　　　　　　　　　　[2] Cf. No. 164, note 5.
[3] In a minute of May 9 on this telegram Mr. Wigram remarked that the 'discussions at Locarno in 1925 (which I have looked up) show clearly how, at the request of the German Delegation and with their assent, a direct reference to the Franco-Czechoslovak and the Franco-Polish guarantee treaties was omitted. They show also how instead—and again with the full approval of the German Delegation—in Article 2 of the Treaty the German, Belgian and French undertakings not to "attack or invade each other or resort to war against each other" and therefore the British and Italian guarantees of those undertakings,

The 'Frankfurter Zeitung', in a typical leader, says: 'The unfortunate vagueness of the British foreign minister compels us to demand of him confirmation that England now as before remains obliged to assist Germany, if (whether in the case of a conflict with Russia or on any other ground) the Reich found itself attacked by France. In other words: we are entitled to know whether the British Government has finally decided to come down on the other side of the fence in every case or whether it remains true to the spirit of the Locarno Treaty'.

If impression gains ground that Locarno is only operative in so far as it compels Germany to respect demilitarised zone or (from German point of view) worse still that it is merely a camouflaged Anglo-French entente German government will be strongly tempted gradually to ignore it.

were not to apply in the event of "action in pursuance of Article 15 paragraph 7 of the Covenant of the League of Nations provided that in this last event the action is directed against the State which was the first to attack". This situation is—I understand we are agreed here—safeguarded by the terms of the Franco-Russian agreement as the Secretary of State has in fact stated in the House.' He suggested that no further action was called for. Sir R. Vansittart and Sir J. Simon had already come to this conclusion on May 8.

## No. 177

### Sir J. Simon to Sir R. Clive (Tokyo)
### No. 239 [C 3705/55/18]

FOREIGN OFFICE, *May 7, 1935*

Sir,

Mr. Matsudaira called this afternoon and handed to me a message to His Majesty's Government from the Japanese Government conveying their most sincere congratulations on the occasion of the King's Jubilee and their best wishes for the long continuance of His Majesty's reign. I thanked the Ambassador on behalf of His Majesty's Government and undertook to transmit the message to the King.

2. Mr. Matsudaira then asked some questions about the European situation. First, he enquired whether it was true that in connexion with the Eastern European Pact the suggestion had been made in Moscow that this should be extended to cover in some way Russia's interest in the Far East. I said that I did not understand how a scheme like the Eastern European Pact, which was in the nature of a mutual assurance between its signatories, could be extended in this way. Next, Mr. Matsudaira referred to the resolution passed at the recent meeting at Geneva,[1] and made the comment that I had resisted M. Litvinov's suggestion that the enquiry as to sanctions might have an extension beyond Europe. I explained that the resolution set up a committee to consider the possibility of some form of sanctions against the unilateral repudiation of treaties, and that the view had been generally taken that this committee would be constituted primarily with reference to European problems; M. Litvinov had observed that of course further

[1] A reference to the Resolution passed on April 17; cf. No. 121, note 2.

enquiries in other directions might be taken in the future. Mr. Matsudaira then asked about the proposal to confer with German representatives on naval matters and enquired whether it was the fact that the German visit for this purpose was postponed and might be cancelled. I said that it was true that the date first contemplated had been postponed, but I had no reason to think the meeting would not take place; the probable date was about the end of the month. The Ambassador asked whether this meant that His Majesty's Government admitted that Germany was entitled to have naval forces over and above those provided for in the Treaty of Versailles. I explained that this was not the position at all. The meeting would be for the purpose of a preliminary discussion with a view to ascertaining what might be the agreed provision to be made if in the future a new naval agreement came into existence. It did not involve any admission about the present treaty. Lastly, Mr. Matsudaira asked as to the present European situation—did we take the view that it was very dangerous? I replied that such a phrase would be an exaggeration; I would rather say that the situation was one which gave ground for real anxiety. The ground for agreement had been very well prepared in the London Declaration of the 3rd February, and prospects were further improved by the German response to this declaration. But it was undoubtedly true that the sudden announcements by Germany of her decision to rearm in various directions had disturbed the peace of mind of Europe. I directed the Ambassador's attention to the debate in the House of Commons last Thursday[2] and the statements then made by the Prime Minister and myself, and pointed out that while this country would certainly not permit itself to occupy a position where its strength would become inferior to others, we were at the same time determined to keep the way open for promoting European agreement. The next step was likely to be the statement of German foreign policy which we were told would be made by Herr Hitler on about May 15th.

I am, &c.,<br>JOHN SIMON

[2] May 2; see No. 162, note 2.

## No. 178

### Sir J. Simon to Sir E. Phipps (Berlin)
No. 100 Telegraphic [C 3658/55/18]

FOREIGN OFFICE, *May 8, 1935, 1 p.m.*

Your telegram No. 116 Saving.[1]

Following from Mr. Eden.

I made no such remark as General Goering attributes to me. As already explained conversation was confined on my part to single observation reported in Moscow telegram No. 47.[2] It is impossible not to resent what appears to be a persistent attempt by General Goering wilfully to distort

[1] No. 167.          [2] Volume XII, No. 667.

my words and to give a political significance to a conversation which had none. These tactics have all the appearance of a political manoeuvre.

If General Goering is really anxious to know my views he has only to consult my public speeches.

You will no doubt make any use of the above which you consider desirable.

## No. 179

*Sir J. Simon to Sir E. Phipps (Berlin)*
*No. 101 Telegraphic [C 3621/55/18]*

FOREIGN OFFICE, *May 8, 1935, 7 p.m.*

Your telegram No. 112 Saving.[1]

I approve your language to Baron von Neurath: your remarks were most opportune.

As regards Air Pact it was no doubt quite clear to His Excellency that you made no suggestion that it could be concluded without a general settlement even if it were accompanied by an agreement for the limitation of air forces. As you will have seen from my telegram to Paris No. 111[2] we are indeed at present considering possible advantages of such a result: but we have of course no idea how French and Italian Governments will respond to the suggestion.

[1] No. 157.          [2] No. 174.

## No. 180

*Sir G. Clerk (Paris) to Sir J. Simon (Received May 9, 3 p.m.)*
*No. 84 Telegraphic [C 3768/55/18]*

PARIS, *May 9, 1935, 1.35 p.m.*

Your telegram No. 111.[1]

Monsieur Laval, to whom I made this morning communication as instructed, authorised me to inform you that he accepted your first suggestion (paragraph 2 of your telegram).

2. As regards enquiry contained in paragraph 4 of your telegram he remarked that suggestion of course would be abandoning principle of indivisability [*sic*] of programme sketched in London declaration of February 3rd, to which French Government had attached great importance. After a little coaxing he agreed that question was one which should seriously be considered. This could only be done in full consultation with his colleagues on his return from Moscow.[2]

3. I had the impression that M. Laval though saying nothing explicitly to justify it, might himself not be averse from the idea, but that he anticipated resistance on the part of his colleagues and also from Little Entente who cling to indivisability of the London declaration.

[1] No. 174.
[2] M. Laval was leaving that day for Moscow, visiting Warsaw on the way.

*Sir E. Phipps (Berlin) to Sir J. Simon (Received May 9, 6.40 p.m.)*
*No. 183 Telegraphic [C 3771/55/18]*

*Immediate. Very confidential*                    BERLIN, *May 9, 1935, 5.30 p.m.*

My telegram No. 182,[1] last paragraph.

French Ambassador tells me that he will accompany Monsieur Laval from Berlin to Frankfurt on Oder tomorrow morning and then return here. He will find out from Monsieur Laval whether it would be desirable or even possible, from internal French political point of view, for him to stop here in order to see Hitler on his return from Moscow. French Ambassador feels however that in this case the invitation would have to come from the German side.

I have told my French colleague that, supposing that Monsieur Laval favours a short visit here on his way home, I should be ready to convey a purely personal hint to the Chancellor or to Baron von Neurath to the effect that I had reason to believe that Monsieur Laval would break his journey here if asked to do so by the German Government. Such action on my part need not in any way compromise His Majesty's Government but might facilitate a possibly useful meeting. Pending Monsieur Laval's decision it is of course essential that no inkling of this possibility should be made public. This is all the more desirable because French Ambassador feels almost certain that Monsieur Laval will prefer to come to Berlin later, and after signature of a Danubian Pact.[2]

Repeated to Paris.

[1] No. 173.
[2] Foreign Office telegram No. 103 to Berlin of May 10 said that Sir E. Phipps' proposed action was approved.

## No. 182

*Sir E. Drummond (Rome) to Sir J. Simon (Received May 9, 9.30 p.m.)*
*No. 286 Telegraphic [C 3781/55/18]*

ROME, *May 9, 1935, 6.15 p.m.*

Your telegram No. 273.[1]

I handed to Signor Suvich yesterday evening aide mémoire embodying these suggestions and at the same time asked for an early interview with the head of the government.

In the course of subsequent conversation Signor Suvich showed some doubt as to whether proposed meeting of Jurists would be useful since the points raised by proposed Air Pact were mainly political. I replied that Jurists might perform useful work in co-ordinating the two schemes already submitted. Our main discussion, however, turned on tentative suggestion contained in last paragraph of your telegram under reply as to which Signor

[1] No. 174.

Suvich took the line that action suggested would amount to recognition and condonation of the fact that Germany had constituted an air force in violation of the treaty. While admitting logic of his position I argued in favour of realism. It emerged that he did not consider that it was necessary that agreements on all subjects mentioned in the London declaration[2] should be reached simultaneously. For instance he hoped that Germany would attend the Rome Conference and sign Danube Pact[3] and this signature ought not to wait on agreement on all other questions.

Nevertheless in regard to the Air Pacts Signor Suvich held that right method was to proceed by bilateral aerial conventions viz. one between France and Great Britain and one between France and Italy. These should be concluded solely for defensive purposes and Germany informed that owing to her action we had found it impossible to include her in any such arrangement for the time being but that if she gave evidence of a change of spirit she might either enter the bilateral arrangements or else the three Powers, abandoning these, might negotiate a multilateral agreement including Germany. Faced by combination of the three Powers to preserve peace Germany would probably in his view yield and come in. If given the idea that the Powers were running after her she would only increase her demands.

I said that these proposals differed from those now under consideration. Up to now idea under discussion had been a special application of the Locarno engagements in regard to the air forces. His Majesty's Government then declared they were determined to stand fully by their Locarno engagements but suggestions he had outlined were of a different character. Ultimately Signor Suvich agreed that whole question resolved itself into the best psychological method of treating Germany.

Signor Suvich added at the end of our conversation that Herr von Bülow had declared that Germany would not now make any fresh proposals on any point herself and that the initiative must come from the other three Powers.

Repeated to Berlin.

[2] Of February 3, 1935.
[3] Cf. paragraph 3 of the Joint Resolution of the Conference of Stresa (Cmd. 4880).

## No. 183

*Sir J. Simon to Sir G. Clerk (Paris)*

*No. 113 Telegraphic [C 3613/55/18]*

FOREIGN OFFICE, *May 9, 1935, 10 p.m.*

Your despatches Nos. 684 and 693.[1]

In view of M. Laval's offer to provide any explanations of the Franco-Soviet treaty which may be required, please ask him for information on (1)

[1] These two despatches transmitted, respectively, copies of the text of the Franco-Soviet Mutual Assistance Agreement (cf. No. 156) and the text of the joint Franco-Soviet communiqué issued to the press on the morning of May 3 (see *The Times*, May 4, p. 13).

the effect of the last sentence of Section 1 of the Protocol of Signature reading 'it is also understood that the undertakings of assistance embodied in this treaty refer only to the case of an aggression against either of the contracting parties' own territory:' and (2) section 4 of the Protocol the effect of which seems to be to confine the obligations of the parties to the case where Germany is the State which attacks one of them.

## No. 184

*Sir E. Drummond (Rome) to Sir J. Simon (Received May 10, 4 p.m.)*
*No. 289 Telegraphic [C 3806/55/18]*

ROME, *May 10, 1935, 2.5 p.m.*

My telegram No. 286.[1]
I think it very probable that Italian Government will consult the French Government before returning any definite reply to our suggestions. Visit of Signor Mussolini to Florence to meet Austrian Chancellor[2] affords useful pretext for postponing my interview with the former.
Repeated to Paris and Berlin.

[1] No. 182.
[2] This meeting with Dr. von Schuschnigg took place on May 11; cf. *The Times*, May 13, p. 15.

## No. 185

*Sir J. Simon to Sir R. Clive (Tokyo)*
*No. 81 Telegraphic [A 4086/22/45]*

FOREIGN OFFICE, *May 10, 1935, 6.30 p.m.*

Your telegram No. 130.[1]
Japanese Ministry of Marine appear to be under some misapprehension as to the position. We still believe that there should be a meeting of the five treaty Powers before any general naval conference takes place and the convening of the larger conference must of course depend on the success of the smaller one. But before this country can enter a five-Power conference they must know what demands are likely to be put forward by European countries not represented at earlier conferences, and the same consideration applies to France and Italy.

We see no reason why our conversations with the European Powers should not be concluded this summer and, unless the result of these talks is entirely negative, we still hope that the five-Power meeting may take place in the autumn. To postpone until a later date the conference which is due to take place this year under both the Washington and London Naval Treaties would be open to obvious objections of a psychological and technical order and we have hitherto understood that the Japanese Government shared this view. In any event, we hope that the Japanese Government will not delay

[1] No. 160.

their consideration of the proposals which emerged from the recent conversations with the Japanese representatives in London pending the conclusion of the talks between the European Powers, as to which the Japanese Government will of course be kept fully informed.

The above should be explained orally both to the Ministry of Foreign Affairs and the Ministry of Marine if you think they are in any doubt as to the actual position.

## No. 186

*Sir E. Phipps (Berlin) to Sir J. Simon (Received May 11, 9.50 a.m.)*
*No. 184 Telegraphic [C 3834/55/18]*

BERLIN, *May 10, 1935, 8.23 p.m.*

My telegram No. 183.[1]
French Ambassador found Monsieur Laval optimistic and in good spirits. He hopes that, unless Germans do something incredibly stupid within the next three months, Germany will by then have joined us all in some reasonable collective system.

Monsieur Laval is genuinely anxious to come to Berlin but feels his visit now would be premature.

He wishes to await Herr Hitler's speech (which I hear will be on May 17th that being the anniversary of his peace declaration in 1933)[2] and also possible conclusion of Danubian Pact before coming. His visit must be most carefully prepared so as to avoid any possibility of failure. He declares that all German interpretations of Franco-Russian pact are completely erroneous and that there is no danger whatever of its leading to any conflict with Locarno or League obligations.

Repeated to Paris.

[1] No. 181.    [2] The speech was finally made on May 21.

## No. 187

*Sir G. Clerk (Paris) to Sir J. Simon (Received May 11)*
*No. 93 Saving: Telegraphic [C 3815/55/18]*

PARIS, *May 10, 1935*

Your telegram No. 113.[1]
In absence of Monsieur Laval and Monsieur Léger who left for Moscow last night, I saw Monsieur Bargeton.[2]

2. As regards (i), the effect of last sentence of Section I of Protocol is to limit action to case of aggression on actual soil of either party. Monsieur Bargeton explained that the Soviets had sought to get France to agree that German invasion of Baltic States with a view to attack on Russia should bring treaty into operation but French Government had refused.

[1] No. 183.    [2] Political Director of the French Ministry of Foreign Affairs.

3. In answer to enquiry as to whether expression 'own territory' included colonies, Monsieur Bargeton said that the point had never been raised.

4. As regards (ii), effect of Section IV of Protocol was in fact to confine obligations of parties to cases where Germany is aggressor. Monsieur Bargeton pointed out that the object of the French negotiators had been to limit the scope of the treaty to that of the proposed Eastern Pact and to the proposed accompanying Franco-Soviet-German treaty of assistance as described in the first sentence of Section IV. France had never contemplated herself undertaking obligations of mutual assistance except towards the Soviets and Germany. As Germany had declined to join, France could only proceed to engage herself with the Soviets alone, but as indicated in Sections III and IV the door was open for Germany to conclude similar agreements.

## No. 188

*Sir J. Simon to Sir E. Phipps (Berlin)*
*No. 478 [C 3827/55/18]*

FOREIGN OFFICE, *May 10, 1935*

Sir,

The German Ambassador asked to see me to-day and dealt with certain matters mentioned in our previous conversation reported in my despatch No. 454[1] of May 3rd. He reminded me that he had then been unable to tell me officially whether Germany already had submarines or whether, as he believed, the assembling of parts already prepared had still to take place. He was now able to inform me officially that as yet Germany had launched no submarines. She expected to launch the first one (which he described as a small one) in June though this would then only be the hull and not the completed vessel.

2. With reference to the matter referred to in paragraph 4 of my previous despatch and to the suggestion that Germany should formulate her offer of a multilateral non-aggression pact for Eastern Europe in definite terms, Herr von Hoesch said that it was particularly difficult for Germany to do this after the Franco-Russian arrangement had been made and announced.[2] He pointed out that the Franco-Russian Pact, although expressed in general terms to provide for mutual assistance whatever might be the identity of a third Power attacking either of the parties, was shown by the attached protocol to be directed against Germany alone. The protocol stated that the main pact was intended only to have the operation envisaged in the scheme of last year and the generality of the phrasing in the main document was therefore 'hypocritical' and designed merely to produce the impression that it was not a military alliance against Germany. Herr von Hoesch went on to say that the German Government were now closely studying the Locarno Treaty to see whether it and the new Franco-Russian agreement were really consistent with one another. His personal view was that they

[1] No. 165.       [2] Cf. No. 183, note 1.

245

were not; there was a great effort made to fit the Franco-Russian agreement into the language of the Covenant; but all this, in his view, was artificial and unreal and concealed the real character of the arrangement. I said that I could not agree with this view: while I realised that Germany did not like the Franco-Russian arrangement, it seemed to me to have no effect at all upon the provisions of the Locarno Treaty. The Ambassador repeated that his Government were making a close study of the subject and had not yet arrived at a conclusion.

3. As regards the air pact, the Ambassador reminded me that I had said that we should be glad to have before us any proposals which Germany wishes to make as to the form of such a pact (see paragraph 5 of my above-quoted despatch). Germany, he said, was warmly in favour of the idea but was not yet able to formulate proposals though she might be prepared to do so later on. He said that the history of the air pact was a tragedy. When first mentioned in the London Declaration,[3] it was presented both to the British public and to the French public as a proposal which it was intended to carry into effect without delay, and both in the United Kingdom and in France the suggestion was warmly received. As soon, however, as the French Government learned that the German Government were also in favour of it the idea lost all attraction to the French Government. I repeated (what I said before) that I could not accept this view of the matter and that if, as I hoped, Germany wished to promote the negotiation of the terms of such a pact, we should be glad to have an indication of her ideas as to the shape which it should assume.

4. Herr von Hoesch told me in the course of the interview that it was now settled that Herr Hitler would make his declaration on German foreign policy on May 17th.[4] I pointed out that we had arranged for a discussion on air defence to take place in the week following.

I am, &c.,<br>JOHN SIMON

[3] Of February 3, 1935.          [4] Cf. No. 186, note 2.

## No. 189

*Letter from Mr. Craigie to Sir E. Phipps (Berlin)*

*[A 4438/22/45]*

FOREIGN OFFICE, May 10, 1935

My dear Phipps,

At St. Paul's yesterday[1] I had a few moments' conversation with the German Ambassador on the naval question—perhaps not a very appropriate topic for the occasion. He said that Ribbentrop would head the Delegation and he seemed to regard it as certain that he and the naval experts would be coming over to London shortly after Hitler had made his pronouncement on German foreign policy. The German Government were not, he said, sending

[1] The reference is presumably to the Thanksgiving Service at St. Paul's Cathedral on Monday, May 6, 1935, on the occasion of the Jubilee of King George V and Queen Mary.

anybody of ministerial rank because they thought it best that the conversations should take place between experts and he imagined that Ribbentrop would be my opposite number. I said that the conversations with other Powers had been conducted on our side by Ministers, the more technical aspects being discussed between experts, but that, having been away from the Foreign Office, I did not know what the arrangements would be on the present occasion. I added that I hoped very much that Herr Hitler was not proposing to say anything on the naval question which would make the conversations more difficult—what might sound perfectly natural in Germany might produce an unfavourable effect over here. To my mind the best thing was to get on with these naval talks without making any further public pronunciamentos, which usually had the effect of quite unnecessarily narrowing the scope of the subsequent confidential conversations. Herr von Hoesch appeared to agree and said that he did not believe that on the naval question anything would be said by Herr Hitler which would prejudice the talks.

2. What I am particularly hoping is that Herr Hitler will not find it necessary to revert publicly to his claim to a 35 per cent ratio. As a result of our conversations with other Powers, we believe that there is no chance whatsoever of a further agreement being concluded about quantitative naval limitation on the basis of ratios, which imply the allocation of a permanent relative naval strength to each Power. It is precisely the emphasis placed in earlier naval treaties on the system of ratios which is now causing us so much difficulty. When we have been able to explain in detail to the German representatives what has passed in our conversations with other Powers, I believe they will agree that the only hope of future agreement lies in some form of limitation by agreed declarations of programme such as we propose, complete with qualitative limitation. It would be a great pity if Herr Hitler, before he learnt of our proposals in detail, were publicly to take up a position which would impair the flexibility of the forthcoming talks.

3. We do not know whether you would think it wise or practicable to hint in the right quarter that it would be better to leave in abeyance this question of a German claim to a specific ratio until the German Government have learnt what are our proposals. But I thought I should let you know the above in order that you may decide whether any action can usefully be taken at your end.

4. As regards the question of representation, we would be quite ready to fall in with what we now understand to be the German view, namely, that the conversations should be conducted, at all events in the early stages, between naval experts and advisers, since the first business of the meeting will be to discuss what has passed in the earlier naval conversations and to exchange views on technical and procedural matters. In that event our representatives would be Vice-Admiral C. J. C. Little, Captain V. H. Danckwerts, R.N.[2] and myself. We understand from the Admiralty that the German representatives will probably be Herr von Ribbentrop, Herr Korth,

[2] Assistant Director of Plans Division, Admiralty.

247

Rear-Admiral Schuster and Commander Kiderlin [Kiderlen], with the possible addition of Captain Wassner (see enclosure in your despatch No. 394[3] of April 25th last). We assume that the Herr Korth mentioned is the private secretary to Herr von Bülow, but the Embassy will no doubt be reporting in due course the exact constitution of the German mission and anything that can be ascertained about the careers and probable attitudes of its members.

I send you the above in amplification of our telegram No. 102 of the 10th May.[4]                                                                      R. L. C.[5]

[3] No. 138.                                              [4] Not printed.
[5] The formal ending of this letter is missing on the filed copy.

## No. 190

### Letter from Mr. Atherton to Mr. Craigie

*[A 4531/22/45]*

*Private*                    UNITED STATES EMBASSY, LONDON, *May 10, 1935*

My dear Leslie:

Referring to our conversation of the other day,[1] I am jotting down for your information the substance of what I told you as to Washington's willingness to consider reduction of gun calibres on battleships to 14 inches.[2] I believe my Government's willingness has always been set forth as conditional, not only upon agreement of all naval Powers, but also upon a general naval settlement to be negotiated acceptable to the United States. While at this time the American Government cannot commit itself in favor of gun calibres on battleships on the basis of a general settlement satisfactory to all parties, I believe Washington hopes to be able ultimately to agree to such a reduction, and that, with such an end in mind, the American Government would view with sympathy the British Government's effort to induce the French and Italian Governments to abandon or suspend construction of guns exceeding 14 inch calibre.

As I pointed out, I give you this information without prejudice to the American position regarding a reduction of the size of capital ships, to which my Government continues its opposition. On the other hand, I trust it is realized that the 16 inch gun is better suited to American needs and a limitation to 14 inches represents a substantial sacrifice, to be made only with corresponding concessions on the part of other Governments in the interests of a general understanding. In other words, the American Government is unable, therefore, to treat the question of gun calibres on battleships as an isolated issue.

As I explained to you the other day, this is more or less a private word between ourselves to answer an inquiry you addressed privately and orally to me not long ago.[3]

Yours sincerely,

RAY ATHERTON

[1] No further record of this conversation has been traced in Foreign Office archives.
[2] Cf. *F.R.U.S. 1935*, vol. i, pp. 53–54.                      [3] See No. 137.

## No. 191

*Sir E. Phipps (Berlin) to Sir J. Simon (Received May 11, 2 p.m.)*
*No. 185 Telegraphic [C 3842/55/18]*

BERLIN, *May 11, 1935, 12.15 p.m.*

Rome telegram No. 286.[1]

Signor Suvich seems to be a very bad doctor for the fever-stricken patient. I should perhaps favour his suggested treatment if it could lead to curing or even to killing the latter. In fact it would only cause the thermometer to burst in our faces. It is regrettable [*sic*] a continuation of the 'outlawing' of German . . .[2] recently advocated by Signor Suvich. I hope it may be possible to convince Signor Mussolini that other remedies must be tried first.

The French doctor I am glad to say is far more sensible for Monsieur Laval told the French Ambassador in the train yesterday that he felt negotiation of an air pact (? *between*)[3] *the Locarno Powers*[4] would be the best way to get Germany back into the collective security ring again.

Repeated to Rome.

[1] No. 182.
[2] The text was here uncertain. A printed text read: 'of Germany recently.'
[3] The text was here uncertain.
[4] The words in italics were underlined on the filed copy.

## No. 192

*Sir E. Drummond (Rome) to Sir J. Simon (Received May 11, 5 p.m.)*
*No. 293 Telegraphic [C 3841/55/18]*

ROME, *May 11, 1935, 2.30 p.m.*

My telegram No. 286.[1]

Signor Suvich gave me a message from Signor Mussolini yesterday evening as the latter is leaving for Florence today to the effect that he agrees to meeting of jurists at Geneva in accordance with your proposal but without prejudice to political aspects of the whole question. On these he will consider your various suggestions and discuss them with me after his return. This tends to confirm the views expressed in my telegram No. 289[2] regarding the Italian consultation with France.[3]

Repeated to Berlin and Paris.

[1] No. 182.   [2] No. 184.
[3] Departmental agreement was reached in the Foreign Office on May 14 that the Belgian Government should be invited to be represented at the meeting of jurists at Geneva, and that telegrams should be sent informing the French and Italian Governments of this step. On May 15 Sir J. Simon minuted that an announcement of the forthcoming meeting 'would be calculated to provoke German suspicions and might colour the line of Hitler's speech next Tuesday [May 21]'. After consultation with Sir J. Simon, Sir R. Vansittart gave instructions that the relevant telegrams should not be sent until May 21, 'so that the jurists will not be in Geneva till just after Hitler has made his speech'.

## No. 193

*Sir H. Kennard[1] (Warsaw) to Sir J. Simon (Received May 12, 3.20 p.m.)*
*No. 33 Telegraphic [C 3844/55/18]*

WARSAW, *May 12, 1935, 12.5 p.m.*

I was received to-day[2] by Monsieur Laval who told me that he was very satisfied with the results of his visit here.[3] He had he hoped dissipated any suspicions Polish Government may have entertained regarding the scope of the French pact with Soviet Government or any effect it might have on other obligations of French Government.

He had proposed Polish participation in a multilateral pact of non-aggression and consultation in which he hoped Germany might also join. Monsieur Beck had accepted proposal in principle and no details as to other signatories, etc. had been discussed. Monsieur Beck had also expressed agreement with proposed course of action regarding Central European pact and had only alluded briefly to position of Hungary.

The French Ambassador tells me that delicate question of passage of Soviet forces across Polish territory in the event of war with Germany has not been raised during the visit.

Monsieur Laval leaves for Moscow to-morrow morning.[4]

Repeated to Paris, Berlin and Moscow.

[1] H.M. Ambassador at Warsaw.
[2] i.e. May 11.
[3] Cf. No. 180, note 2. See also No. 195 below and *D.G.F.P.*, Series C, vol. iv, No. 88.
[4] Fairly detailed notes on M. Laval's three conversations with M. Beck are given in Comte Jean Szembek's *Journal 1933–1939* (Paris, 1952), pp. 70–77.

## No. 194

*Sir E. Drummond (Rome) to Sir J. Simon (Received May 14, 9.30 a.m.)*
*No. 296 Telegraphic [C 3875/55/18]*

ROME, *May 13, 1935, 9.20 p.m.*

Berlin telegram No. 185.[1]

Apart from other considerations I believe Italian doctor in present circumstances thinks he is following method prescribed by his French colleague and that should he find that latter advocates a different treatment for the patient he will follow suit without too much difficulty.

Italians now normally consult French over any major European proposals involving Germany and since we are held here at present to be over-tender towards the latter French advocacy for a reasonable policy is likely to be more effective than our own.

Repeated to Berlin.

[1] No. 191.

## No. 195

*Sir H. Kennard (Warsaw) to Sir J. Simon (Received May 14, 9 a.m.)*
*No. 36 Telegraphic [C 3876/55/18]*

WARSAW, *May 13, 1935, 9.36 p.m.*

Minister for Foreign Affairs informed me today that he was pleased with result of Monsieur Laval's visit which had greatly contributed to clearing up any misunderstanding which may have existed, more especially as regards effect of Franco-Soviet pact on Polish alliance and on Poland's pacts with Germany and Russia. Monsieur Beck was vaguer than Monsieur Laval regarding a multilateral pact of non-aggression but said he was prepared to study any proposals in this direction without prejudice in view of assurances which he had received from Monsieur Laval on other points.

Both Minister for Foreign Affairs and French Ambassador are under the impression that Soviet Government may now come to some air agreement with Czechoslovakia and that Roumania, while she would be loth to agree to passage of Soviet troops across Roumanian territory, might accept some arrangement for passage of Russian aircraft.

I should perhaps mention that Monsieur Laval in his conversation with me[1] suggested that Franco-Soviet pact might finally be merged into a multilateral pact though he did not explain how mutual assistance difficulty was to be overcome.

Repeated to Paris, Moscow and Berlin.

[1] See No. 193.

## No. 196

*Sir E. Phipps (Berlin) to Sir J. Simon (Received May 14, 3.15 p.m.)*
*No. 125 Saving: Telegraphic [A 4439/22/45]*

*Immediate*                                                              BERLIN, *May 13, 1935*

Your telegram No. 102.[1]

As Chancellor is more likely to take advice on technical aspect of conversations from Marine Leitung than from Ministry of Foreign Affairs I asked Naval Attaché to take first suitable opportunity of making informal intimation in the sense desired.

He did so this morning during a friendly conversation in the course of which he communicated names of British representatives. His remarks were well received and the German officer appeared to take the point. The latter said that he expected that Chancellor would only talk of German naval claims in a general way. Herr Hitler however was preparing his own speech and it seemed unlikely that Marine Leitung would have much to say to it.

I should deprecate taking any further action. This might annoy the Chancellor and result in his claiming the larger of the two percentages that he mentioned to you, viz. parity with France.

[1] Not printed; cf. No. 189, last paragraph.

## No. 197

### Sir E. Drummond (Rome) to Sir J. Simon (Received May 16)
#### No. 37 Saving: Telegraphic [C 3977/55/18]

ROME, *May 13, 1935*

Paris telegram No. 85[1] to Foreign Office.

Visit of General Denain has coincided with the visit of the First Squadron of the French Navy to Naples, and Admiral Mouget was received by Signor Mussolini on May 12th one hour previous to the visit of the French Minister for Air. It follows that a considerable display is being made of Franco–Italian co-operation so far as the fighting services are concerned.[2]

In response to an enquiry the French Embassy here confirmed Sir George Clerk's report to the effect that General Denain would not be authorised to sign any document connected with the Air Pact. Indeed, the Embassy stated that such conversations as he had had with his Italian colleague were entirely preliminary and only sought to provide the bases for any Air Pact which might be elaborated in the future.

On the other hand, it seems that considerable progress has been made with the non-political side of the negotiations, and I understand that some kind of commercial air convention may be signed tonight.

Repeated to Paris.

[1] In this telegram of May 9, not printed, Sir G. Clerk reported that he had asked M. Laval what was the exact significance of the visit of the French Air Minister, General Denain, to Italy, and suggested that 'if the intention were to negotiate a bilateral air pact this might be a little premature'. M. Laval said that he shared this view. General Denain would 'discuss ways and means' but 'was not authorised to sign a document of any kind'.

[2] In a secret session of the French Senate in March 1940 M. Laval referred to Franco-Italian military agreements for cooperation against Germany, concluded in May and June 1935 and constituting 'a veritable military alliance'. The agreements were apparently never ratified and the texts have not been published, but it appears that an essential French condition was Italian collaboration with Yugoslavia. Cf. *Il Processo Roatta* (Rome, 1945), pp. 30–31, 200–1, and *Documents Diplomatiques Français 1932–1939*, 2e série, vol. i (Paris, 1963), No. 82.

In a minute of August 12, 1935, Mr. Gallop, a member of the Southern Department of the Foreign Office, recorded that the War Office thought that a so-called 'sandwich plan' between Italy and France had 'crystallized' at some time between January and June 1935. This was alleged to be an arrangement by which, 'in the event of a definite military invasion of Austria by Germany, both Italian and Yugoslav forces shall march into Austria separated by a division or two of French troops who will thus form the butter in the sandwich and prevent friction'.


## No. 198

### Mr. Gurney (Copenhagen) to Sir J. Simon (Received May 21)
#### No. 103 [C 4437/55/18]

COPENHAGEN, *May 13, 1935*

Sir,

The *Dagens Nyheder* printed on the 12th instant a report from Aabenraa to the effect that Germany was breaking her treaty obligations in regard to a demilitarised zone to the south of the Danish frontier. Great military works were, it was reported, being constructed. The naval station at Kiel and the aviation station at Holtenau were being placed in a strong defensive and offensive position. The defensive works along the Kiel Fjord which had been dismantled in 1920 were being reconstructed more strongly than before, and Schleswig-Holstein was being more and more militarised. The barracks at Schleswig had been enlarged and a large new barracks was being built at Flensburg, where the naval station at Mørwig had been recently enormously extended.

2. In the course of an audience which I had with the King this morning in order to thank His Majesty for attending the thanksgiving service held at the English church here on Jubilee day, and to present the officer commanding H.M.S. *Frobisher*, His Majesty mentioned this report to me in connexion with a visit which he proposes to pay in his yacht next week to Danish Slesvig, pointing out that this German activity represented a breach of treaty obligations. As today is Dr. Munch's weekly reception day I thought it well to call upon him with a view to ascertaining whether he had any official confirmation of the report. He told me that he had received no such confirmation and that he thought it exaggerated. He had no doubt, however, that the Germans were doing a great deal in those parts, mentioning incidentally the Island of Sylt, where considerable works are reported to have been carried out, particularly in connexion with aviation. The Danish Government had, however, no ground for protest, since the provisions governing the demilitarisation of the area in question were contained in the Treaty of Versailles, and it was therefore a matter for consideration by the signatories of that treaty.

3. Dr. Munch made no mention of Denmark's right to bring the question to the notice of the League of Nations under the Covenant, and I did not pursue the matter further. It seems, to say the least, unlikely that Denmark will raise the question in that form, or even take any initiative in bringing it to the notice of the signatories of the Treaty of Versailles; nor do I think that public opinion in Denmark, as a whole, is likely to be aroused.

4. I should in this connexion mention again that it is intended to hold the military manoeuvres this year in South Jutland; but this decision was taken last year, and has no connexion with recent events.

5. I mentioned to Dr. Munch, while discussing these German activities, that, according to the Press, the Prime Minister had stated in the Rigsdag that Danish disarmament was no longer possible, and that rearmament might have to be discussed by general agreement between the parties. Dr. Munch told me that a committee was considering the question of increased armaments. The Government, he said, were envisaging the construction of additional torpedo boats and the increase of the forces available for the protection of the frontier, with a view, as he put it, to preventing kidnapping. They had, he said, no fear of a raid under present conditions as the central Government in Germany were strong enough to hold their

people in check, although there was no knowing how long such a state of things might continue.

I am sending a copy of this despatch to His Majesty's Ambassador at Berlin.

I have, &c.,
HUGH GURNEY

## No. 199

*Mr. Charles (Moscow) to Sir J. Simon (Received May 14, 2.30 p.m.)*
*No. 66 Telegraphic [C 3901/55/18]*

MOSCOW, *May 14, 1935, 2.10 p.m.*

Warsaw telegram No. 36.[1]

M. Laval confirmed to me last night cordiality of his reception in Poland and expressed surprise that Soviet press has described visit as a failure. He said it was very possible that he would attend Marshal Pilsudski's funeral in person.[2] His visit to Moscow was purely one of courtesy but he said that he intended to discuss among other questions that of multilateral Pact and he hoped that the door would be left wide open for Germany.

Radek in today's Izvestia publishes a long and ungracious article on Pilsudski emphasising opportunist character of his early socialism, his blind hatred of Russia (both Tsarist and Soviet) and his hopes of expansion towards the East. Article concludes with appeal to Polish people to bury with the Marshal their distrust of the Soviet Union.

Repeated to Berlin, Paris and Warsaw.

[1] No. 195.
[2] Marshal Pilsudski had died on May 12. M. Laval represented the French Government at the state funeral in Warsaw on May 17 and at the funeral service in Cracow the following day.

## No. 200

*Sir E. Drummond (Rome) to Sir J. Simon (Received May 16)*
*No. 564 [C 3978/55/18]*

ROME, *May 14, 1935*

Sir,

With reference to my telegram No. 37 Saving[1] of yesterday's date, I have the honour to inform you that I enquired of my French colleague whether he could give me any account of the visit to Rome of the French Minister of Air.

2. Comte de Chambrun replied that General Denain had come to Rome with the fixed idea of signing some agreement and yesterday he had been able to negotiate a commercial convention on the lines described in the communiqué which had been issued to-day. (I enclose copies of this com-

[1] No. 197.

muniqué which is considerably fuller than is usual on such occasions).[2] The Ambassador went on to explain that the lines from Tripoli to Tunis, from Marseilles to Beyrout, from Paris to Turin, Venice and further, and from Lyons to Turin, were agreed to in principle as soon as the necessary money was forthcoming. His Excellency attached considerable importance to the Paris, Turin, Venice, Trieste route because it would give France an opportunity of penetration into Central Europe without passing through certain other countries which in time of crisis, might not be favourable.

3. As regards the Air Pact conversations, Comte de Chambrun informed me that he had insisted strongly that nothing should be done which would run counter to the Stresa agreements. All that had happened was that there had been personal conversations between General Denain and General Valle, the Italian Under-Secretary of State for Air, as to what help Italy and France might, in case of war, be prepared to offer each other. But he emphasised the fact that these were purely personal conversations and nothing had been signed and no agreement had been reached which committed the two Governments.

4. I have sent a copy of this despatch to His Majesty's Ambassador at Paris.

I have, &c.,

Eric Drummond

[2] Not printed. The communiqué reported, in particular, the signature in Rome at 7 p.m. on May 13 of an 'Italo–French convention regarding the establishment of lines of aerial navigation', which 'confirms the policy of commercial *entente* followed by the two Governments and especially provides for close co-operation between the French and Italian companies of aerial navigation'. Cf. *The Times*, May 14, p. 15.

## No. 201

*Mr. Charles (Moscow) to Sir J. Simon (Received May 15, 3 p.m.)*
*No. 67 Telegraphic [C 3922/55/18]*

MOSCOW, <i>May 15, 1935, 1.57 p.m.</i>

Monsieur Léger informs me that Monsieur Laval is highly satisfied with result of discussions here so far. He said that as soon as M. Laval gets back to Paris French and Soviet Governments will take the initiative with German Government and enquire whether Herr Hitler is now prepared to carry out his Stresa pronouncement and negotiate a multilateral pact of non-aggression. He was hopeful of success and if Germany signed he anticipated no difficulty with Poland. After that Baltic countries would also join. He said Soviet-Czech pact was as good as signed and followed closely the lines of Franco-Soviet instrument.

Monsieur Léger stated that he knew nothing of any negotiations between Soviet Government and Czech or Roumanian Governments[1] whereby Soviet Union would send aeroplanes into Czechoslovakia via Roumania

[1] Cf. No. 173.

in case of need. Such agreement was not necessary. He added however that it might be possible that military authorities would keep in touch with one another.

Repeated to Berlin, Paris, Warsaw and Prague.

## No. 202

*Sir E. Phipps (Berlin) to Sir J. Simon (Received May 16, 10.15 a.m.)*
*No. 128 Saving: Telegraphic [C 3946/55/18]*

*Confidential*                                                     BERLIN, *May 15, 1935*

Herr von Papen and Herr von Ribbentrop called on me successively yesterday afternoon.

Herr von Papen bewailed his fate at Vienna, filled with good intentions towards Austria as he was, but unable, owing to Austrian unhelpfulness, to carry them out. He does not believe that Germany will be able to sign a Danubian pact in the form that will be suggested by France and Italy. He declares the proposal to allow the Austrian government itself to decide what constitutes 'non-interference' to be quite unacceptable. He says that the only States willing to sign a mutual assistance pact with Austria are Italy and Czechoslovakia and that the Austrian government would not dare to sign with two such partners only, for fear of being swept out of existence.

Herr von Papen then deplored the Franco-Russian pact and tried, without much success, to convince me of his genuine fear of Russia. He declared that Great Britain's part in world affairs was of vital importance and would probably be decisive. He seems anxious about the growth of anti-Catholicism in Germany amongst the extremists, despite recent assurances given to him by the Führer.

Herr von Ribbentrop called, soon after Herr von Papen's departure, to deliver the message contained in my telegram No. 127 Saving[1] of yesterday regarding the postponement of the Chancellor's Reichstag declaration. We then had some conversation on current affairs.

Herr von Ribbentrop also referred to the importance of Great Britain's attitude towards the big questions at issue and to the influence she could bring to bear on others 'less reasonable than herself'.

He sought to justify what I described as Germany's recent bombshells by declaring them to be merely quite natural steps away from the hated and impossible Treaty of Versailles. (His language recalled rather ominously that used by the 'Börsen Zeitung' yesterday when it advocated the tearing up of the whole Treaty—see my telegram No. 126 Saving[2] of yesterday).

[1] In this telegram, not printed, Sir E. Phipps reported that Herr von Ribbentrop had informed him 'that owing to the death of Marshal Pilsudski [cf. No. 199, note 2], Herr Hitler's declaration in the Reichstag will only be made on Tuesday, 21st May . . . the Chancellor will be represented at the Marshal's funeral by General Göring who is President of the Reichstag'.

[2] Not printed: it referred to a leading article in the *Berliner Börsen Zeitung* on the 'Pact Evil'.

He expressed the opinion, which I contested, that the Franco-Soviet pact rendered Locarno valueless from the German point of view.

I used practically the same arguments to both my successive visitors. I reproached Germany for not taking advantage of the presence at the Quai d'Orsay of so reasonable and well-disposed a man as Monsieur Laval. Germany, far from facilitating his already difficult task of a Franco-German 'rapprochement', had gone out of her way to render his task impossible. Despite all this, however, I knew from my French colleague that Monsieur Laval was still hopeful and desirous of bringing about more friendly relations between the two countries and of inducing Germany to take her proper place in the ring of collective security. I reminded them of Monsieur Laval's lengthy, and seemingly successful, efforts to render the Franco-Soviet pact as anodyne as possible. I pointed out that its conclusion in its present form should be regarded as the natural sequel to the reply given to our enquiry from Stresa, and that the next step might reasonably be the expansion of this pact into a multilateral one of non-aggression and consultation.

I also reminded both Herr von Papen and Herr von Ribbentrop of the public appeals lately addressed to Herr Hitler by yourself, the Prime Minister and Lord Stanhope to make proposals of a constructive and con-crete nature.[3] The world in general, and Great Britain in particular, awaited his speech with deep interest, not to say anxiety.

Herr von Papen promised that he would convey my remarks to the Chan-cellor, whom he is to see more than once during the next few days. It is at first always a relief to talk to Herr von Papen after months of intercourse with such as Göring whose mentality is of the schoolboy-gangster order. But agreeable, civilised and man of the world though he be, insincerity oozes from Herr von Papen like soapy water from a sodden sponge.

As for Herr von Ribbentrop, few things depress me more than a conversa-tion with him on subjects other than the weather. He emits a woolly feeling of resistance without consistence, and imposes an unfair strain on the temper. He is lunching with us on May 16th and may perhaps bring me something back from his master. From what he said, however, and from his manner I fear we must not nurture many hopes in regard to Herr Hitler's declaration on May 21st.

[3] A reference presumably to speeches in the House of Commons on May 2 and in the House of Lords on May 7; see 301 *H.C. Deb.* 5 *s.*, cols. 571 and 688; and 96 *H.L. Deb.*, 5 *s.*, col. 818.

## No. 203

*Sir E. Phipps (Berlin) to Sir J. Simon (Received May 16)*
*No. 129 Saving: Telegraphic [C 3953/55/18]*

BERLIN, *May 15, 1935*

My telegram No. 128 Saving[1] of today.
Herr von Ribbentrop used to me language regarding air pact very similar

[1] No. 202.

to that of German Ambassador described in your despatch No. 454.[2] He also deplored postponement of negotiation of that pact. Not knowing yet final result of suggestion made to French and Italian Governments in your telegram No. 111[3] to Paris I pointed out that air pact was only one of five questions mentioned in London communiqué of February 3rd. I added however that on this point also the Chancellor might make useful proposals in his coming declaration by stating, for instance, numbers to which he would be willing to limit German air force and by making suggestions as to form of pact.

[2] No. 165.     [3] No. 174.

## No. 204

*Sir E. Phipps (Berlin) to Sir J. Simon (Received May 16)*
*No. 472 [C 3943/55/18]*

BERLIN, *May 15, 1935*

Sir,

I have the honour to transmit to you, herewith, in original a very interesting despatch addressed to me on 11th May by Colonel Thorne, the retiring Military Attaché to this Embassy,[1] summarising the gist of two conversations which he had with General von Reichenau whilst introducing his successor to the Reichswehr Ministry.

2. I would draw your particular attention to the following points:

(*a*) In paragraph 2 General von Reichenau is reported as advocating a transfer of populations in the east of Europe as a means of reconciling a policy of expansion towards Russia with the Chancellor's declarations that Germany does not wish to annex territory populated by another race.

(*b*) In paragraph 3 General von Reichenau is reported as making the suggestion which has found an echo in certain English circles that the best policy His Majesty's Government could pursue would be to admit Germany's hegemony on the continent and to give her a free hand in Europe in return for German non-interference in the rest of the world. This is a view which is widely held in Germany to-day.

(*c*) In paragraph 4 General von Reichenau is stated to have referred to the possibility of Germany being one day obliged, in order to break the hostile ring around her, to compose her quarrel with Russia.

(*d*) In paragraph 5 Colonel Thorne describes his discussion of the question of a reduction in the number of divisions proposed for the new German army, and you will notice that, while considering it unlikely that the German Government would agree to reduce the number of these divisions, General von Reichenau suggested that they might be prepared to discuss the strength of each division.

(*e*) In the same paragraph Colonel Thorne explains the desire of the

[1] This enclosure is not printed. Cf. No. 155, note 2.

258

German Government to arrange the future territorial organisation of Germany into 'Gaue' on a military basis.

(*f*) In paragraph 6 Colonel Thorne reproduces General von Reichenau's account of the dispute between the Reichswehr and the Labour Service regarding the term of service in the Labour Corps.

(*g*) In paragraph 9 Colonel Thorne describes General von Reichenau's views on the future organisation of the German Cabinet—views which seem to give some confirmation to the suggestion that the Chancellor will, sooner or later, himself assume direct responsibility for the conduct of foreign affairs, leaving a Staatssekretär in nominal charge of the Ministry for Foreign Affairs.

3. I desire to take this opportunity of placing on record my warmest appreciation of Colonel Thorne's services as Military Attaché to this Embassy. He has been able to establish quite unusually good relations with Germans of every class, and the information he has collected with excellent judgment on political as well as military matters has been of the greatest assistance to me. I view his departure with the utmost regret.

I have, &c.,
ERIC PHIPPS

## No. 205

*Sir E. Drummond (Rome) to Sir J. Simon (Received May 16, 9.30 a.m.)*
*No. 312 Telegraphic [C 3945/55/18]*

ROME, *May 16, 1935, 12.35 a.m.*

Your telegram No. 273[1] and my telegrams Nos. 286[2] and 293.[3]

I saw Signor Mussolini this evening and reminded him that both Italian and French Governments had agreed to meeting of jurists in accordance with your proposal. We had further suggested that if discussion showed probability of agreement it might be wise to convene meeting of all the Locarno Powers. His Excellency said he concurred; it was necessary that Germany should be kept informed and should at a given point be invited to participate in discussion.

I then passed to the subject matter of last paragraph of your telegram under reference pointing out (*a*) that declaration of February 3rd mentions air pact as a part of general settlement and (*b*) that there might be difficulty of principle owing to fact that by conclusion of such a pact we should give recognition and perhaps legitimisation to German Air Force. His Excellency affirmed that it would be wise to endeavour to conclude an air pact as soon as practicable provided that we could secure what he declared to be the main object namely a reasonable and proportionate limitation of air strengths. To wait until all questions mentioned in declaration of February 3rd were settled meant long delay. Danubian pact for instance could not be made dependent on successful issue of all other negotiations. As to question of

---

[1] No. 174.   [2] No. 182.   [3] No. 192.

principle he considered it would be foolish to shut our eyes to fact that German Air Force existed. He added however that he thought we might find the French difficult over possibility of divorcing air pact from other negotiations.

To question of His Excellency whether I was discussing in anyway bilateral pacts I replied no, that these raised political questions and I was not authorised to discuss them. Signor Mussolini stated that during French Minister for Air's visit[4] he had taken great care not to commit himself with regard to such pacts since according to Stresa agreement these were to be consequential on general pact between all the Locarno Powers.

Repeated to Berlin and Paris.

4 Cf. Nos. 197 and 200.

No. 206

*Mr. Charles (Moscow) to Sir J. Simon (Received May 16, 5.45 p.m.)*
*Nos. 68 and 69 Telegraphic* [C 3959/55/18]

MOSCOW, *May 16, 1935, 4.21 p.m.*

My telegram No. 67.[1]

Monsieur Laval left for Poland to attend ceremonies in connexion with Marshal Pilsudski's funeral at Warsaw and Cracow[2] last night, well satisfied with his reception in the Soviet capital. He had long and spontaneous ovations at the opera on arrival and on leaving when he stood in front of the box shaking hands with Monsieur Litvinov.

Visit has probably had effect of cementing understanding between the two countries. Communiqué issued to the Press last night[3] speaks of the beneficial influence on general European situation of Franco-Soviet co-operation and emphasizes undiminished importance of immediately giving effect to Eastern Regional Pact of non-aggression, consultation, and refusal to aid aggressor, embracing States sincerely devoted to the cause of peace.

Following paragraph of communiqué seems to me of special importance: Precisely in the interests of preserving peace, these nations are obliged, above all, in no way to weaken their means of national defence. In this respect, Stalin in particular expressed full understanding and approval of the policy of national defence carried out by France with the object of maintaining her armed forces on the level corresponding to the needs of her security.

Monsieur Laval explained to me before departure that clause was intended entirely for French home consumption, i.e. to keep Communists quiet. This acknowledgment of Stalin's influence in French internal affairs did not seem to worry him.

I understand Monsieur Laval during his conversation with Stalin discussed

---

<sup>1</sup> No. 201.     <sup>2</sup> Cf. No. 199, note 2.
<sup>3</sup> See *The Times*, May 16, p. 16. Cf. *Soviet Documents on Foreign Policy*, edited by J. Degras, vol. iii (London, 1953), pp. 131–2.

question of Russian debt, of Soviet propaganda and religious liberty, but I do not know the result of discussions.

Considering results of the visit as a whole, French Minister for Foreign Affairs while not giving away too much has restrained in some degree Soviet provocatively abusive policy towards Germany and Poland.

Germany will be put to the test and will be asked to discuss conclusion of Multilateral Pact of non-aggression and consultation as indicated in my telegram No. 67.[1] Soviet Government on their part have Treaty of Mutual Assistance[4] which even if it does not go as far as they wish, gives them large measure of moral assurance which they intend to reinforce by similar treaties with other Powers.

Repeated to Paris.

[4] See No. 156.

## No. 207

*Mr. Charles (Moscow) to Sir J. Simon (Received May 16, 6 p.m.)*
*No. 70 Telegraphic [C 3960/55/18]*

MOSCOW, *May 16, 1935, 4.40 p.m.*

My telegram No. 68.[1]

Soviet press emphasises that the whole atmosphere of visit was one of exceptional cordiality and this was indeed the case. The visit it is asserted was much more than a mere act of formal courtesy on conclusion of treaty and the treaty itself, so far from being a final act in the regulation of Franco-Soviet relations is a starting point in their development. Izvestia emphasises determination of both sides to continue the struggle for Eastern pact and incidentally confirms impression to be derived from communiqué that the Soviet government have abandoned the idea of the general assistance provision in such a pact. Passage in communiqué regarding upkeep of national defence is interpreted as warning to 'adventurist imperialist elements' that the Powers striving for peace do not intend to rely exclusively on mere agreements; task of keeping national defence on a level corresponding to present security needs will impose heavy burden on both nations but reduction of forces at present stage would be folly.

Towards the end of Izvestia article following further reference is made to passage regarding national defence: 'task of the *public* in both countries is to support the policy of both governments, a policy of peace and defence. The Soviet public will fulfil its obligations without hesitation. Our contact with representatives not only of the French government but also of the French press of all shades of opinion permits us to hope that the prejudices which have hitherto prevented certain sections of French public opinion from grasping the immense importance of Franco-Soviet rapprochement will in a large measure be removed.' The foregoing passage seems of special interest in view of Monsieur Laval's remark to me.[2]

[1] No. 206.        [2] See *ibid.*

## No. 208

*Sir E. Phipps (Berlin) to Sir J. Simon (Received May 16, 7 p.m.)*
*No. 187 Telegraphic [C 3985/55/18]*

BERLIN, *May 16, 1935, 4.50 p.m.*

Belgian Minister tells me that he had a conversation yesterday at the Ministry of Foreign Affairs with Dr. Gaus, the legal adviser, who has drafted an important part of Chancellor's declaration and Herr Köpke head of Western Department. They both seriously object to following points in Franco-Russian protocol attached to agreement[1] declaring them to impair notably the force of Locarno Treaty.

(*a*) Chief objection is to the words at the end of the second sentence of paragraph 1 stating that if Council[2] for some reason does not make any recommendation or does not reach a unanimous vote the obligation of assistance will nevertheless apply. They declared that Germany could never . . .[3] that by a simple decision of France for instance it should be laid down who was the aggressor.

(*b*) Their second objection is to the whole of second sentence in paragraph 4 of protocol[4] which they consider shows that agreement is not a general one and is only directed against Germany.

When Belgian Minister urged desirability of Germany joining the pact both Dr. Gaus and Herr Köpke declared that she would never join any pact with Russia. They declared that Germany was firmly decided to leave the League in October and impression they conveyed, and this is important for hitherto they have on the whole been in favour of Germany belonging to League, was that Germany would never return.

My Belgian colleague thinks that German government will probably ask for explanations on above points from Locarno Powers. This may be done in the course of Chancellor's declaration or soon afterwards.

It seems that the two German officials again referred with anxiety to your statement in the House of Commons on May 2nd.[5]

Repeated to Paris, Rome and Brussels.

[1] Cf. No. 156, note 2.     [2] Of the League of Nations.
[3] The text was here uncertain: 'admit' is suggested on the filed copy.
[4] Cf. Nos. 183 and 187.     [5] Cf. No. 164, note 5.

## No. 209

*Sir R. Clive (Tokyo) to Sir J. Simon (Received May 17, 9.30 a.m.)*
*No. 142 Telegraphic [A 4499/22/45]*

TOKYO, *May 17, 1935, 12.55 p.m.*

Your telegram No. 81.[1]

Naval Attaché made oral communication today in sense of your telegram to Vice Minister of Marine.

[1] No. 185.

With reference to penultimate sentence Vice Minister stated categorically that Japanese government had no further proposals to make and unless other countries would accept Japanese original proposals (presumably parity and common upper limit) it seemed useless to have the conference.

He added that Minister of Marine had so informed Minister for Foreign Affairs who would doubtless inform me when next I saw him.

## No. 210

*Memorandum by Mr. Wigram on the possible inclusion of Holland in the proposed Air Convention*[1]

[C 4286/55/18]

FOREIGN OFFICE, *May 17, 1935*

At the 269th Meeting of the C.I.D.[2] held on April 16th, 1935, Lord Stanhope proposed that the Chiefs of Staff should be asked to consider the question of the possible inclusion of Holland in the proposed Air Convention. He reminded the Committee that in 1918 the possibility of Holland joining the Allies had been considered and the British General Staff had been opposed to it. The Prime Minister pointed out that at Stresa the participants in the proposed Air Convention had been definitely limited to the five Locarno Powers. The relevant passage of the Stresa Resolution[3] reads:—

'The representatives of the three Governments agree to continue actively the study of the proposed Air Pact for Western Europe with a view to the drafting of a Pact between the five Powers mentioned in the London Communiqué.'

When Lord Stanhope stated that the Netherlands Government were pressing for a reply to their soundings on this matter, the Prime Minister said that the answer must obviously be to refer to the decisions taken at Stresa.

The Prime Minister's decision on this point indicates a possible answer to the Netherlands Government should they raise this matter again; but the fact remains that it has not yet been given any detailed consideration whatever from the point of view of its reaction on British interests. It seems only right that such consideration should be given. This involves a reference to and consideration by the Chiefs of Staff and Committee of Imperial Defence.[4]

A memorandum on the position is annexed.

[1] This memorandum and annex were evidently considered at a meeting in Sir R. Vansittart's room on May 17. Lord Stanhope was present. A minute by Mr. Wigram of that date remarks: 'It may eventually be decided that it would be undesirable for internal political reasons or even for reasons of foreign policy to pursue this question: but it does seem essential to give it adequate consideration from the point of view of our national interests. This has not yet been done in any way whatever.'

[2] Committee of Imperial Defence.

[3] See No. 134, note 7.

[4] See No. 245 below.

FOREIGN OFFICE, *May 17, 1935*

*Memorandum summarising the developments as regards the possible inclusion of Holland in the Air Convention.*

1. We learned from Sir H. Montgomery[5] on February 5th[6] that the Dutch Foreign Minister had asked him 'what the intention was as regards other countries, particularly of course Holland, in the case of the air pact coming into actual operation?' Was it intended that the adherence of such Powers should not be precluded? What was envisaged if an attack via the air over Holland took place? In his despatch No. 67[7] of February 7th, Sir H. Montgomery further reported that the 'Het Vaderland', a paper of some importance, had stated that if invited, it would be the duty and the national interest of Holland to adhere to the air pact.

2. The Dutch Minister made an enquiry of Mr. Eden on the subject on February 8th,[8] and on February 9th the Belgian Ambassador mentioned the matter to Sir R. Vansittart.[9] He said that the Belgian Government had evidence that the Germans had plans of invading Holland in the event of war; and seemed to be anxious that if the Dutch approached us in the matter, they should not be rebuffed. Both Mr. Eden and Sir R. Vansittart stated that the initiative in this matter must come from the Netherlands Government (i.e. presumably that the latter should formally enquire whether Holland could participate in the Air Convention or some similar arrangement).

3. On February 11th, the Netherlands Minister for Foreign Affairs informed Sir H. Montgomery (see the latter's private letter of February 12th)[10] that speaking personally he did not see how the Netherlands could stand out of the proposed air arrangement if invited to come into it. It was generally presumed that sudden aggressive air action by Germany was the danger. Supposing Germany took such action against France, and the British air force, under the terms of the 'Air Locarno', attacked Germany in France's defence, the British might well fly over Holland in order to do so. In that case the Dutch, if not a party to the arrangement, would be bound to defend their neutrality against us—a situation which would obviously be repugnant to them.

4. On February 15th Jonkheer de Graeff, speaking in the first chamber of the States General at The Hague, said 'the question whether the Netherlands should also join this possible Convention is for the time being not a question for the Government. We have not been invited, which stands to reason because the new Pact has been proposed as an extension of the existing Locarno Pact. And it is not possible at present to say whether we shall be invited or whether other Powers will be enabled in general to accede. Still less is it possible to say at present what our attitude will then have to be.'

[5] Sir H. Montgomery was H.M. Minister at The Hague.   [6] See Volume XII, No. 418.
[7] Not printed.   [8] See Volume XII, No. 459.
[9] See *ibid.* Baron Cartier's conversation with Sir R. Vansittart is there reported to have taken place on February 8.   [10] Not printed.

5. On February 23rd (see Brussels tel. No. 8)[11] the Netherlands Foreign Minister raised with the Belgian Minister at The Hague the difficulty of the situation which might arise should Holland, not being a party to the Air Pact, suffer violation of her territory by a Power acting under the Air Pact against a Power which had been guilty of the first unprovoked aggression. He also spoke of the possibility of the establishment of a system of 'territorial air', i.e. vertical territorial limit to Dutch neutrality, above which passage by air would be free. Sir E. Ovey reported that the Belgian Government would like to hear the view of His Majesty's Government on this point. This was communicated to him in Foreign Office telegram to Brussels No. 18[12] of March 2nd.

6. It will be seen that the question of Dutch participation in the Convention is very definitely raised. Do we or do we not want it? If we want it the right course seems to be, after consultation with the other Powers concerned, to find out privately whether if invited to accede to the Convention, Holland will do so. If the answer were in the affirmative, the formal invitation could be issued.

7. But before taking a step of this kind, the advantages and disadvantages of Dutch participation from the point of view of our own interests would require consideration by the Foreign Office, the Service Departments and the Committee of Imperial Defence.

8. Further it would be necessary to consider whether Holland could be a party to the Air Agreement without at the same time becoming a party to the original Locarno Treaty. On this point a minute by Sir W. Malkin setting out the legal position[13] is annexed to this memorandum. It will be noted that Sir W. Malkin points out that if Holland were a party to the air convention without being a party to the Locarno Treaty, a situation might arise in which Germany would invade Holland for the purpose of attacking France or Belgium without using the air weapon against any of the three countries. From the practical point of view and under the conditions of modern warfare, such a position seems so unlikely to arise as to enable it to be discounted. If this view is shared, it is suggested that it would not, from our point of view, be strictly necessary that if Holland became a party to the Air Convention, she should also become a party to the Locarno Treaty.

9. On the other hand we know that for some time past—indeed ever since October 1933[14]—Germany has indicated her readiness to conclude non-aggression pacts with her neighbours, presumably including Holland. It would be for consideration whether advantage should not be taken of this offer (should it be decided that Holland should be invited to accede to the Air Pact) to complete the security afforded by the Air Pact in respect of Holland by a general guarantee of the integrity of the Netherlands on the lines of the Locarno Treaty.

[11] Volume XII, No. 500.      [12] *Ibid.*, No. 522.      [13] Not printed.
[14] i.e. since Herr Hitler's announcement of the German Government's decision to leave the League of Nations and withdraw from the Disarmament Conference; cf. Volume V, Nos. 452 and 454.

# No. 211

## Memorandum by Mr. Craigie

### [A 4963/22/45]

FOREIGN OFFICE, *May 17, 1935*

Please see the Secretary of State's enquiry below.[1]

The proposals which it is suggested that we should put forward to the German naval representatives are the same as those that we have already made to the United States and Japan, namely:

(1) Negotiation of a general international convention which would deal with qualitative limitation, non-fortification of island possessions in the Pacific, notification of the characteristics of new vessels and of the dates on which they are laid down, preparation of merchant ships in time of war [? peace] for conversion to warlike purposes and other minor provisions contained in the Washington Naval Treaty.

(2) Elimination from any future naval treaty of any figures which constitute, or might have the appearance of constituting, a ratio of naval strength between the signatory Powers.

(3) Negotiation of an understanding between the naval Powers in regard to the form and substance of declarations to be issued by each Power indicating its programme of construction during the years 1937–1942. (In the case of Germany it will be necessary also to know with precision what she proposes to lay down in the years 1935–1936.) These declarations would have no contractual force, but it would be agreed between the parties issuing them that the building programmes would be adhered to unless one year's notice of any change had been given in advance by one or other of the Powers issuing a declaration.

(4) Negotiation of a protocol formally recognising the equality of national status of each signatory of the new treaty, irrespectively of the size of its navy.

As a matter of procedure it is suggested that we should first tackle qualitative limitation, as to which there is not likely to be much divergence of view between the Germans and ourselves. When we come to quantitative limitation it is not suggested that we should put forward any figures for German construction ourselves but should first hear what the Germans have to say. We should, of course, be prepared to communicate to the Germans our own tentative construction figures in exchange for a similar communication of their figures from the German representatives.

If the Germans agree to negotiate on the basis of construction figures rather than of ratios, their proposals may involve either (*a*) a slow and gradual increase in their present figure so as to obtain their ultimate objective, whatever that may be, in, say, twelve to fifteen years; or (*b*) a rapid reconstruction of their fleet so as to secure their full objective by, say, 1942; or

[1] Referring to the expression, 'our proposals in detail' at the end of paragraph 2 of No. 189, Sir J. Simon had asked: 'As a matter of information what *are* "our proposals in detail" referred to on p. 3 as far as Germany is concerned? J.S.'

(c) some variant between these two extremes. On the whole, (b) is unlikely because of the difficulty of adequately training personnel in so short a time.

If we find the Germans in a reasonable frame of mind we shall presumably try to convince them of the advantages, from their own point of view, of 'hastening slowly' in this matter. If we find them quite unreasonable and determined that their new construction shall follow a steep upward curve, then we should have to warn them that their attitude can only render impossible any further quantitative limitation of naval armaments.

If in the future there is to be a free field of competition for all, the Germans will find it more difficult to catch up with competing nations in naval armaments than in land or air armaments and they have therefore, to my mind, a definite interest in promoting the conclusion of a naval limitation agreement which leaves them scope for a gradual increase in their present naval strength. This and the fact that the Germans do not apparently wish definitely to alienate this country at present are the only levers which we can use with them.

Until we know what the German demands are to be it is hardly feasible to suggest detailed limits for future German naval construction or to say what is the maximum German construction which France and Italy are likely to agree to without any modification of their present tentative programmes. It is clear that our own original tentative figure of a German fleet of 178,000 tons[2] is now completely out of date—but this was never more than a counsel of perfection. When I saw him in Paris recently M. Piétri, in speaking to me of the German navy of the future, said that we could only try to induce the Germans to be as reasonable as possible. Answering his own question as to what figure we must propose for Germany's navy, M. Piétri said 'Mon Dieu, le plus bas possible . . .' He seemed to feel that we should be lucky to set a limit to the German navy while Germany was still in the mood for limitation.[3]

R. L. CRAIGIE

[2] This was the figure discussed at a meeting of British and French naval experts at the Foreign Office on July 11, 1934; cf. Volume VI, No. 490, note 3.

[3] In a minute of May 25 Sir J. Simon asked: 'Do we *reject* 35% or accept it or sidetrack it? That is the main point for public and parliamentary purposes.' Mr. Craigie replied: 'The answer is that we attempt to sidetrack it in favour of our own proposal for declarations of building programmes, which, if adopted, would obviate the necessity of agreeing upon any particular ratio between the two fleets. R.L.C. 27/5.'

## No. 212

*Sir E. Phipps (Berlin) to Sir J. Simon (Received May 20)*
*No. 479 [C 4030/55/18]*

BERLIN, *May 18, 1935*

Sir,

I have the honour to report that General Göring made a somewhat aggressive speech at Freiburg on May 10th.

2. According to the version of the speech given in the *Basler Nachrichten*,

General Göring began by the usual reference to the victory of National-Socialism and the rebirth of Germany. The Leader, he continued, was responsible alone to God for the future of the nation. He had not hesitated to withdraw Germany from the trickery of Geneva or to decree German rearmament. The old Parliamentary system would have died of fright at the prospect of these steps. 'What', he continued, 'was the opinion held before about your State? "Frontier State" it was called, which in the case of emergency must naturally be given up at once. That was once upon a time. To-day we declare that in Germany we no longer recognise any frontier States. The Leader has declared that we maintain peace. But if they do not grant us peace, if Germany is attacked, then our resistance begins one centimetre behind the German frontier. I repeat what I have already declared to the foreign press: we have taken the most important step for peace; we have rearmed. Nothing threatens peace more than for a great people to seek to live powerless in the midst of highly armed States. We desire no war, but if one is forced upon us we cannot stop it. Whether one or ten nations attack us we shall do our duty. We cannot do more. Germany faced the whole world for four years and the world did not defeat her. Why do they to-day make pacts? Why are they madly arming? It is still fear of Germany. I do not know if foreign nations understand what a gigantic testimonial they are giving to Germany's heroic struggle in the war. Nevertheless, they are attacking us in the foreign press in the most shameless way. I do not understand how any man can reconcile it with his intelligence to write such idiotic and such crassly stupid lies. Indeed, men who continue to write what is to-day written in a portion of the foreign press and in the small country on our frontier can have no head; they must have a screw loose somewhere. I should like to give the nations one thing to think about. We shall not continue to allow German honour to be so smirched. And if these nations do not think themselves able to put a brake on their press, then certain nations, particularly those who live entirely on the tourist trade, must not think that we shall continue to bring our good money to them. There are other decent nations whose landscapes are just as beautiful; above all, there is one country in which life is most beautiful, and that is our own country.'

3. General Göring concluded his speech by a reference to the Church conflict. He claimed that National-Socialism, by destroying communism, had saved the Church. Hitherto, the Government had respected the cloth, but if things went on as they were now doing, there would have to be a change of policy.

General Göring's speech was very shortly summarised in the German press and in the official version issued by the 'D.N.B.'[1] The passage relating to the defence of the frontier, which is regarded in some quarters as a covert threat to abolish the demilitarised zone, as well as the attack on Switzerland, were totally suppressed.

I have, &c.,<br>ERIC PHIPPS

[1] Deutsches Nachrichten Bureau.

## No. 213

### Sir J. Simon to Sir R. Clive (Tokyo)
### No. 71 Telegraphic [A 4499/22/45]

FOREIGN OFFICE, *May 20, 1935, 4.30 p.m.*

Your telegram No. 142.[1]

If in fact this represents the view of the Japanese Government, it would be better, pending our forthcoming discussions with foreign Powers, not to provoke any official pronouncement in this sense. In the circumstances you will probably prefer to avoid taking the initiative in discussing this question further with the Minister for Foreign Affairs at the present time.

[1] No. 209.


## No. 214

### Sir E. Phipps (Berlin) to Sir J. Simon (Received May 20, 8.10 p.m.)
### No. 190 Telegraphic [C 4056/55/18]

*Confidential*                                       BERLIN, *May 20, 1935, 6.45 p.m.*

I learn from a trustworthy source that the Laval-Goering interview at Cracow[1] was inconclusive though protracted. General Goering complained bitterly of French policy of encirclement and the conclusion of pacts which were merely disguised alliances of the pre-war type. It would be easier for France to come to a direct understanding with Germany than French Government imagined. To reach an agreement with Germany was just as easy as with Russia.

Monsieur Laval insisted that France was merely aiming at collective security pacts which would always be open to Germany. He argued that Germany had come to an agreement with Poland in spite of existing difficulties. Why could she not equally come into a pact with Russia? General Goering explained that public opinion regarded Poland and Russia with very different eyes. Russia symbolised communism whereas Poland symbolised nationalism which Germany understood and admired.

Monsieur Laval thinks that it was a mistake on Herr Hitler's part to entrust General Goering with this conversation as it will only make it more difficult for him (Laval) to visit Berlin and see Herr Hitler himself.

My . . .[2] stated very confidentially that though the atmosphere was a little better during his second visit to Warsaw[3] Monsieur Laval made no progress whatever but this must not be allowed to leak out. He feared that Polish problem would prove very refractory. In Moscow on the other hand everything went swimmingly for them. Stalin readily undertook to

[1] This interview took place on May 18. Cf. No. 202, note 1, and No. 199, note 2. See also *D.G.F.P.*, Series C, vol. iv, No. 98 and No. 129 (pp. 247–8).

[2] The text was here uncertain.

[3] For M. Laval's first visit to Warsaw, May 10–12, see Nos. 193 and 195.

co-operate with French Government in keeping communism out of the French army and schools.

Repeated to Geneva.

## No. 215

*Sir E. Phipps (Berlin) to Sir J. Simon (Received May 21)*
*No. 132 Saving: Telegraphic [C 4071/55/18]*

BERLIN, *May 20, 1935*

Baron Stengel of Bavarian State Chancery informed His Majesty's Consul-General, Munich,[1] on May 12th that he was convinced that German Government intended to garrison the demilitarised zone with army or S.S., probably the latter.

He and other more conservative elements regarded prospect with misgiving.

Meanwhile, press and individuals continue to maintain that Russo-French pact renders Locarno valueless (see my telegram No. 128 Saving[2] of May 15th, paragraph 6). Despite this however I cannot share fears expressed by Mr. Gainer's informant for I do not believe army would sanction violation of zone at present.

[1] Mr. D. St. Clair Gainer.          [2] No. 202.

## No. 216

*Sir J. Simon to Sir E. Ovey (Brussels)*
*No. 42 Telegraphic [C 3841/55/18]*

FOREIGN OFFICE, *May 21, 1935, 4 p.m.*

My telegram No. 37,[1] Paris telegram No. 84[2] and Rome telegram No. 293.[3]

The French and Italian Governments having now accepted our suggestion for a meeting of Jurists to consider the drafting of an Air Pact, you should ask the Belgian Government whether they also desire to be represented. In doing so you should impress upon them the necessity of avoiding any publicity since it is important that Germany should not be led to think that the ex-Allies are combining to present her with a text to be signed as it stands. This is of course in no way the case (see particularly paragraph 2 of my telegram No. 37).

Repeated to Paris No. 125,[4] Berlin No. 105 and Rome No. 291.[4]

[1] See No. 174.          [2] No. 180.          [3] No. 192.

[4] In Foreign Office telegram No. 126 of 4.15 p.m. of May 21 to Paris Sir G. Clerk was instructed to inform the French Government of the above invitation to the Belgian Government and to suggest that 'if they see fit, they should let the Belgian Government know that they agree'. A similarly worded telegram, *mutatis mutandis*, was sent at the same time to Sir E. Drummond (No. 292 to Rome).

Sir G. Clarke replied, in telegram No. 94 of 1.35 p.m. of May 22, that 'French Government are sending instructions to Brussels in the desired sense', and Sir E. Drummond, in telegram No. 320 of 9.45 p.m. of May 22, said that 'Italian Government do not anticipate any difficulty in taking suggested action in Brussels'.

## No. 217

*Sir G. Clerk (Paris) to Sir J. Simon (Received May 22, 8.30 a.m.)*
*No. 101 Saving: Telegraphic [C 4076/55/18]*

Confidential                                                    PARIS, *May 21, 1935*

I was able to see Minister for Foreign Affairs, who leaves for Geneva tonight, for a few minutes this afternoon. He told me that his conversation with General Goering[1] was carefully engineered by the latter, helped to some extent by the Poles, and it was impossible for him to avoid it. On balance he was convinced that it had been to the good.

2. Conversation was entirely on general lines and Goering was emphatic in his assurances of Germany's desire for peace. The one concrete suggestion was that Germany and France should come to a direct agreement. Monsieur Laval had replied that he would accept this, always provided that Germany made similar pacts with the other Powers. That condition was indispensable. It was agreed that the conversation should be considered as strictly private and confidential, that both sides would do their best to avoid polemics in their national press, and General Goering expressed the hope that after some months there could take place an interview between the Chancellor and Monsieur Laval.

3. Minister for Foreign Affairs said he was only going to communicate his account of the conversation to the President of the Council and the President of the Republic and he begged that it might be treated as entirely confidential.

4. Minister for Foreign Affairs took the opportunity to explain to General Goering what he thought were the misinterpretations put upon the Franco-Soviet Agreement by the jurists in Berlin and he hoped that in that direction he had cleared the air.

[1] Cf. No. 214.

## No. 218

*Sir E. Phipps (Berlin) to Sir J. Simon (Received May 24)*
*No. 484 [C 4161/55/18]*

BERLIN, *May 21, 1935*

His Majesty's Ambassador at Berlin presents his compliments to H.M. Secretary of State for Foreign Affairs, and has the honour to transmit to him the under-mentioned document.

| *Name and Date* | *Subject* |
| --- | --- |
| No. 53 from Consul-General, Munich, of 29th April. | Aviation – Germany. |

Mr. Gainer (*Munich*) to Sir E. Phipps (*Berlin*)

No. 53

MUNICH, *April 29, 1935*

Sir,

I have the honour to report that I learn from a well informed source that orders have been given largely to increase the present output of aeroplanes and that the factories building both machines and engines are all working overtime. Difficulty is being experienced however in obtaining payment from the Reichs Government for aeroplanes already delivered as the factories were in many cases not willing to wait for several months for their money and either had no reserves or if they had were unwilling to draw upon them. A case in point is that [? of] the M.A.N.,[1] who indeed possess over one million marks in cash in the Bayerische Vereinsbank at Munich but who were unwilling to utilize this. The Reichs Government advised the M.A.N. to take out mortgages upon their property which would be guaranteed by the Government and in this way the company would avoid drawing upon their reserves, while the Government could stave off immediate payment of their debt.

2. Other factories have been requested to increase their plant for manufacturing bombs, fuses, etc. and when some objected to sinking capital in plant 'which had to be destroyed in 1920' and which might have to be destroyed again, the Government replied that they would not object to paying—in time—from 15 to 20% more and would not scrutinize the accounts too closely.

I have, &c.,

D. ST. CLAIR GAINER

[1] Maschinenfabrik Augsburg Nürnberg.

## No. 219

Sir E. Phipps (*Berlin*) to Sir J. Simon (*Received May 22, 11.40 a.m.*)

No. 201 Telegraphic: by telephone [C 4102/55/18]

*Immediate*                                          BERLIN, *May 22, 1935*

My immediately preceding telegram.[1]

D.N.B. announces that with reference to paragraph 8 of the defence law (Point 6 in my telegram)[2] the Chancellor has issued the following decree:

'The period of active compulsory service in the three branches of the defence forces shall be fixed in each case at one year.'

[1] In this telegram, not printed, the text of a new Reich Defence Law which had become effective on May 21 was summarized; cf. *D.G.F.P.*, Series C, vol. iv, pp. 178–9.

[2] This section read: '(6) The Chancellor fixes the length of active military service. Normally conscripts will be called upon to serve for one year during their 20th year. Voluntary enlistment may be made earlier.'

## No. 220

*Sir E. Phipps (Berlin) to Sir J. Simon (Received May 22, 1.55 p.m.)*
*No. 203 Telegraphic: by telephone* [C 4104/55/18]

*Most immediate*                                        BERLIN, *May 22, 1935*

Following from Air Attaché to Air Minister.

I had long interview with General Goering this morning.[1] He said that when speaking of parity last night he meant parity of aircraft and personnel.[2] All formations are however not yet located in their ultimate stations but in many cases are still at schools. He emphasised that there is no question of bluff as the formations are ready for immediate embodiment. Since March the strength of 1st line has been increasing towards ultimate goal namely parity with France which Goering hopes may be reached this year. Approximately 2,000 is regarded as France's first line figure. I warned General Goering of immense importance of this statement which might be repeated in House of Commons this afternoon. He has no objection. Goering reiterated that if France reduces her figure or if we do not build up to it Germany will reduce hers. Goering added in confidence that he is prepared to give full details of German Air Force to me if a German Air Force Attaché with same privileges as me is allowed in London and if details are for Air Ministry's confidential information and not for public announcement in House of Commons. This would mean privileged situation for British Air Attaché in Berlin.

[1] For a fuller account of this interview see No. 234 below.
[2] The reference is uncertain. No relevant statement by General Göring on May 21 has been found. The reference may have been to Herr Hitler's declaration during his speech to the Reichstag that evening (cf. No. 222 below) of the German Government's intention to limit 'German air armaments to parity with the individual Great Powers of the West'.

## No. 221

*Sir E. Phipps (Berlin) to Sir J. Simon (Received May 22, 1.55 p.m.)*
*No. 204 Telegraphic: by telephone* [C 4104/55/18]

*Most immediate*                                        BERLIN, *May 22, 1935*

It is important that you and Mr. Baldwin should see before debate today[1] text of telephone message just sent by Air Attaché to Air Ministry.[2]

[1] For this debate on Defence Policy see 302 *H.C. Deb.* 5 *s.*, cols. 359–82.
[2] See No. 220.

## No. 222

*Sir E. Phipps (Berlin) to Sir J. Simon (Received May 22, 3.10 p.m.)*

*No. 202 Telegraphic [C 4121/55/18]*

BERLIN, *May 22, 1935, 2 p.m.*

The Chancellor's speech[1] has created an excellent impression on this country. As usual he has been able to diagnose the attitude of the people and appeal to their sentiments. Thus his profession of his peaceful intentions is as well received as his remarks on the League, his defence of Germany's re-armament and his slashing attacks on Lithuania and Bolshevism.

[1] This was delivered by Herr Hitler before a special session of the Reichstag on May 21. An English translation and the German text of the speech were transmitted to the Foreign Office in Berlin despatch No. 500 of May 22, received May 23 (C 4117/55/18).

On May 25 the German Ambassador transmitted the German text and an English translation to Sir J. Simon. A 'final and approved translation', of 33 pages, was produced in the Foreign Office Library and 12 copies were sent to the Library of the House of Lords and to the House of Commons Library on May 31 (see 302 *H.C. Deb.* 5 *s.*, col. 744). Copies were also sent to H.M. Missions abroad. (See C 4415/55/18). Extracts from the authorized English translation of parts of the speech dealing with foreign policy, including the '13 points' (cf. No. 227 below), are printed in N. H. Baynes, *The Speeches of Adolf Hitler, April 1922–August 1939*, vol. ii (London, 1942), pp. 1218–47; see also *The Times*, May 22, pp. 16 and 17, and *D.G.F.P.*, Series C, vol. iv, pp. 171–8.

## No. 223

*Mr. Patteson[1] (Geneva) to Sir J. Simon (Received May 22, 8.30 p.m.)*

*No. 80 L.N. Telegraphic [C 4125/55/18]*

GENEVA, *May 22, 1935, 7 p.m.*

Monsieur Laval arrived this morning and I[2] had a preliminary short conversation with him before the Council and before Sir Eric Drummond's telegram No. 317[3] had been received. He seemed well satisfied with Herr Hitler's speech which he remarked might well have been worse and said that there were some useful statements in it of which note must be taken.

Generally Monsieur Laval was comparatively optimistic about European situation though he remarked of his visit to Warsaw that though the Poles were very pleasant to him he [? it] was clear that they had moved far into the German orbit. There was no doubt of the reality of Polish hostility to Soviet Russia.

Our main conversation however was of Italian-Ethiopian situation about which Monsieur Laval like all of us here is becoming steadily more perturbed. On this subject he said Signor Mussolini appeared to be mad. He assured me most earnestly that at no time during the Rome conversations[4]

[1] H.M. Consul at Geneva.　　　　　　　　　　　　　　　　　[2] i.e. Mr. Eden.
[3] In this telegram of May 22 Sir E. Drummond reported a conversation with Signor Mussolini on the Italo-Ethiopian dispute. Documents on this subject will be printed in Volume XIV.　　　　　　　　　[4] Of January 1935; cf. Volume XII, No. 335.

did France give Italy any encouragement whatever to military adventure in Abyssinia. On the contrary when discussing economic arrangement which had been embodied in Rome agreement he had himself said half in jest half in warning to Signor Mussolini 'Your hands are strong. Be careful their efforts in Abyssinia are confined to economic objectives'. Monsieur Laval was fully alive to the impossible position in which our two Governments will be placed as members of the League in the event of Signor Mussolini persisting in this Abyssinian adventure. We have agreed to keep in continuous consultation and to act together.

Repeated to Rome, Addis Ababa and Paris.

## No. 224

*Sir G. Clerk (Paris) to Sir J. Simon (Received May 23, 12.59 p.m.)*
*No. 95 Telegraphic: by telephone* [*C 4139/55/18*]

PARIS, *May 23, 1935*

In the absence of any official pronouncement in reference to Herr Hitler's speech, French press has adopted a somewhat guarded line. Yesterday's morning papers confined themselves for the most part to extensive summaries.

More comment appeared last night and this morning, the general line being still one of reserve with a tendency to represent the speech as containing nothing new such as would constitute a serious contribution towards collective security.

Attention naturally concentrates on Herr Hitler's 13 points.[1] The references to Germany's continued respect for the territorial clauses of the treaty, for Locarno and the demilitarized zone are noted with considerable satisfaction. On the other hand, his offer to conclude non-aggression pacts with his neighbours but without provision for mutual assistance is held to have a very limited practical value. Finally, his insistence on the figures chosen by himself for the German army and navy is considered to render impossible any international reduction of armaments. None the less the German attitude towards the maintenance of Locarno, the conclusion of an air pact and the sanctity of the territorial settlement is held to have brought about a certain detente, and the view is expressed that provided always the solidarity of the Powers demonstrated at Stresa is maintained, it should be possible to turn this to good account.

In some quarters the speech is regarded as a further manoeuvre to detach Great Britain from France and some uneasiness is expressed on this account.

[1] See *The Times*, May 22, p. 16.

## No. 225

*Sir E. Drummond (Rome) to Sir J. Simon (Received May 23, 4 p.m.)*
*No. 322 Telegraphic [C 4141/55/18]*

ROME, *May 23, 1935, 1 p.m.*

First comments of Italian press on Hitler's speech are cautious but on the whole favourable. Declarations regarding Austria are received with reserve. Everywhere importance of passage regarding demilitarised zone is emphasised.

Details by Saving telegram.[1]

[1] Rome telegram No. 44 Saving of May 23 is not printed.

## No. 226

*Sir J. Simon to Mr. Patteson (Geneva)*
*No. 87 L.N. Telegraphic [C 4143/55/18]*

FOREIGN OFFICE, *May 23, 1935, 8.30 p.m.*

Following for Lord Privy Seal.

Report published here states that M. Laval intends shortly to make some public reply to that part of Herr Hitler's speech which asks for 'an authentic interpretation of the reactions of the Franco-Russian military alliance on the Treaty obligations of the individual parties to the Locarno Pact'.

It seems essential that any public reply to this enquiry should be given not by France alone but jointly by France and the other parties to Locarno, at any rate by Italy and the United Kingdom as the guarantor Powers. We hope therefore that you will be able to induce M. Laval to refrain from any public utterance on this subject until he has concerted at least with us and with the Italians on the terms of the statement to be made. Sir R. Vansittart has already spoken in this sense to M. Corbin.

Repeated to Paris, Berlin, Rome and Brussels.

## No. 227

*Sir J. Simon to Sir E. Phipps (Berlin)*
*No. 109 Telegraphic [C 4143/55/18]*

FOREIGN OFFICE, *May 23, 1935, 11 p.m.*

Your despatch No. 500.[1]

There are a number of statements (set out below) in the second part of Herr Hitler's speech (in which the attitude of the German Government is defined) on which it would be useful to have further elucidation. If you feel able to make the necessary enquiries, (which you will have to explain are not necessarily exhaustive) I leave it to your discretion how best to do so.

[1] Cf. No. 222, note 1.

You will of course take care not to present them as though the only reaction of His Majesty's Government to the Chancellor's speech was to be critical. Thus you will probably think it well to open the subject by dwelling on Mr. Baldwin's welcome of the speech[2] and by explaining that it is because we see in it prospects of useful negotiation that we think it well to clear up possible ambiguities.

(1) What further conditions have to be fulfilled in order that 'a truly juridical equality of all the parties' may make possible the return of Germany to the League of Nations (point (1)[3])? Herr Hitler states that 'this equality of rights must be extended to all functions and all rights to possessions in international life'; but what is the precise meaning of this phrase?

(2) We understand the German Government's undertaking (point (2)) 'unconditionally to respect the other Articles (of the Treaty)[4] regarding international relations, including the territorial provisions' to cover all the Articles of the Treaty which are still in force except the armament clauses of Part V, from which the German Government states that it has 'freed itself' and which are the points 'which discriminate morally and practically against the German nation'. This may only refer to the war-guilt clause, but for your own information we fear that the German Government may be trying to keep open the questions of the demilitarized zone or mandates or International Rivers, or even Austria, by the reference to 'moral and practical discrimination'.

(3) We should like to know what action Herr Hitler now proposes to take in order to give effect to his offer to conclude non-aggression pacts, which Baron von Neurath told us during the Stresa Conference the German Government would be ready to conclude in a multilateral pact.[5] Is he prepared to open negotiations immediately with the various Governments concerned? (See in this connection paragraph 4 of my despatch No. 454[6] and paragraph 2 of my despatch No. 478[7] recording two interviews with German Ambassador on this subject.)

(4) In declaring its readiness (point (8)) to limit the German air arm to a degree of parity with the other individual Western Great Powers, what concrete scheme have the German Government in mind? Can you clear up one further point in this connection, the apparent inconsistency between the statement to us in Berlin by Herr Hitler to effect that Germany wanted parity with French metropolitan first-line strength plus French first-line strength in North Africa, and the figure of 2,000 machines given to Air Attaché by General Goering?[8] Are we to understand that German Government claim French first-line strength in France and North Africa to be 2,000 machines?[9]

---

[2] See 302 *H.C. Deb.* 5 *s.*, cols. 359–60, 373.

[3] The reference here, and below, is to the 13 points made by Herr Hitler; cf. No. 222, note 1, and *The Times*, May 22, p. 16.

[4] Of Versailles, 1919.                                              [5] See Volume XII, No. 715.

[6] No. 165.                          [7] No. 188.                          [8] See No. 220.

[9] The last two sentences of this paragraph were telephoned to Berlin (telegram No. 112) and telegraphed to Geneva, Paris and Rome on May 24 as a substitute for the original

(5) The German Government state (point (8)) that they have 'made known the extent of the construction of the new German army' and that 'under no circumstances will they depart from this'. These statements seem to be inconsistent with the sentence which follows almost immediately that the German Government 'are prepared at any time to limit their armaments to any extent which is equally adopted by the other States'. Can you clear up this apparent discrepancy?

(6) In fact, we believe that all that is publicly known about 'the extent of the construction of the new German army' is that it will consist of 36 divisions. Herr Hitler indeed told us in Berlin that the maximum strength of these divisions would be 550,000 men; but the Chief of the German Army Command recently suggested to Colonel Thorne that the strength might vary between 330,000 and 660,000 men.[10] Is therefore the number of effectives, as apart from the 'construction' of the army still a matter for negotiation?

Repeated to Geneva, Paris, Rome.

second sentence of the paragraph which had read: 'For example, how do they propose to deal with the problem of the misuse of civil aviation as a supplementary force?' The amendment was made at the request of Lord Londonderry.

[10] This suggestion had been reported in the enclosure, not printed, in No. 204. Colonel Thorne reported therein the following statement by General von Reichenau: 'The figure of a total strength of 550,000 given by the Reichskanzler to Sir John Simon was not intended as an exact number, but simply as illustration; the total might be as low as 330,000 or as high as 660,000.'

## No. 228

### Sir J. Simon to Sir E. Phipps (Berlin)
### No. 111 Telegraphic [A 4679/22/45]

*Important*                                            FOREIGN OFFICE, *May 23, 1935, 11.15 p.m.*

Your telegram No. 125 Saving.[1]

Now that Herr Hitler has delivered his speech[2] we are anxious to push on with the naval conversations as soon as possible. Apart from the conversations with the German representatives, there are a number of conversations with other Powers which have still to be held in order to prepare the way for a naval conference. Since that conference should, under existing treaties, take place this year, there is little time to be lost. Please therefore enquire of Minister for Foreign Affairs what is the earliest date at which it would be convenient for the German representatives to proceed to London.

[1] No. 196.                     [2] See No. 222.

## No. 229

### Sir J. Simon to Sir G. Clerk (Paris)
### No. 128 Telegraphic [C 4104/55/18]

FOREIGN OFFICE, *May 23, 1935, 11.40 p.m.*

1. Now that Herr Hitler has stated in terms that he sets a limit on the German Air Force at the level of that of France,[1] it is very important for us to know figure at which French put their peace establishment first line strength.

(1) in France itself and North Africa.

(2) the world over; and also whether any increase is in contemplation.

2. *Confidential, and for your own information.* Shortly after Berlin visit, German Government (who had indicated in Berlin that their aim was parity with French first line strength in France and North Africa)[2] gave French first-line strength 'including colonies' as 2,091 machines.[3] We have now received information which suggests that latter is in fact figure at which Germans are aiming:[4] but we regard it as an exaggeration of the French strength.

3. Can Air Attaché obtain in confidence information mentioned in paragraph 1 above from French Air Ministry?

[1] Cf. No. 227, paragraph (4).     [2] See Volume XII, No. 651, p. 738.
[3] This was the figure shown on the map given to Sir E. Phipps by Baron von Neurath on April 4; see *ibid.*, No. 692 and No. 704, note 2.     [4] Cf. No. 220.

## No. 230

### Sir E. Phipps (Berlin) to Sir J. Simon (Received May 24, 10.13 a.m.)
### No. 135 Saving: Telegraphic [A 4661/22/45]

BERLIN, *May 23, 1935*

I cannot help feeling a certain relief that Herr Hitler has now bound himself definitely (point 8)[1] to a navy limited to 35 per cent of our's. He had mentioned this figure to too many people and it had been quoted too often in the Press and elsewhere for it to be in the least likely that he would capitulate in this respect. Moreover you will remember that Herr Hitler told you and Mr. Eden on the morning of March 26th that he 'did not see any heavenly or earthly authority who could force Germany to recognize the superiority of the French or Italian fleets'.[2] He has now publicly recognised that the German fleet will be 15 per cent below the total tonnage of the French fleet, so I think that not only we but the French and Italians should feel thankful for small mercies, and that we should not miss opportunities in the naval sphere, like we have done on land and in the air, owing to French shortsightedness. It would therefore be advisable for His Majesty's Government to place on official record their acceptance of the Chancellor's offer.

[1] In his speech on May 21; cf. No. 227, note 3.
[2] See Volume XII, No. 651, p. 732.

## No. 231

*Sir G. Clerk (Paris) to Sir J. Simon (Received May 24)*
*No. 102 Saving: Telegraphic [C 4152/55/18]*

PARIS, *May 23, 1935*

In conversation this morning M. Léger gave the following account of the Moscow and Warsaw visits.[1]

*Warsaw.* Colonel Beck, impressed presumably with the necessity of not antagonising the opposition leaders in the event of Marshal Pilsudski's early demise, had been in a much more tractable frame of mind. M. Laval and M. Léger had been at pains to explain the implications of the Franco-Soviet Pact and to show that there was no justification for the Polish apprehensions. They had pointed out that the obligations assumed by France under the Pact were less than those devolving upon her under the Franco-Polish Alliance,[2] and that, far from the Pact impairing the value of the Alliance, it was actually to Poland's advantage. If Russia attacked Poland, France remained obliged to go to Poland's assistance, while in general the existence of the Pact diminished the likelihood of a war between Germany and Russia, the fear of which being fought on Polish soil had from the first been Poland's main objection. M. Léger thought that he and M. Laval had finally succeeded in calming all apprehensions; indeed Colonel Beck had virtually admitted as much.

As regards the Eastern Pact, Poland was still holding aloof. There was no doubt in his mind, M. Léger said, that although Colonel Beck could not say so, he was influenced by the considerations (a) that he thought (erroneously in M. Léger's view) that Lithuania was getting into such difficulties that if left alone she would soon be in the mood to come to terms with Poland, and (b) that Poland was anxious to keep a free hand vis-à-vis Czechoslovakia with whom, M. Léger thought, she wished at all costs to avoid signing a pact of non-aggression. It was, however, obviously more difficult for Poland to maintain her objections now that Germany had declared her willingness to participate provided all obligations of mutual assistance were eliminated.[3] Colonel Beck had consequently given a grudging approval of principle whilst stipulating (a) that the Pact should not run counter to Poland's existing engagements, and (b) that Poland should have a voice in the negotiations. The latter stipulation, M. Léger thought, was made not only from considerations of prestige, but in order to enable Poland to create difficulties over the inclusion of Czechoslovakia.

*Moscow.* The discussions, M. Léger said, had gone very smoothly and had given rise to no difficulties whatever. M. Laval and he had had no trouble in disposing of a tendency to drop the negotiation of an Eastern Pact as being liable to undermine the importance of the Franco-Soviet Pact. In the

---

[1] Cf. Nos. 193, 199, 201, 206, and 207.
[2] For the Franco-Polish treaties of 1921 and 1925 see *B.F.S.P.*, vol. 118, p. 342, and vol. 122, p. 287, note 1.  [3] See Volume XII, Nos. 715 and 719.

end the Soviet representatives had themselves submitted a text which in addition to provisions for non-aggression and for the withholding of help to an aggressor contained also a definition of aggression.[4] M. Léger here remarked, parenthetically, that the last mentioned point would present no particular difficulty for France as Great Britain, who had always objected to definitions of aggression, would not be a party to the Pact. In general the draft required considerable modifications of form. On their side the French representatives had urged that it would be well to adhere strictly to the form of the German offer, as communicated to Sir E. Phipps by Baron von Neurath during the Stresa conference.[5] They were also inclined to think that in view of German feelings towards Russia it might be better psychologically, for the first move towards Germany to be made by France alone. These and other matters of procedure were being discussed at present between the French and Soviet representatives in Geneva.

During the Moscow visit the Soviet representatives had also made no bones about the Franco-Soviet Pact being unaccompanied by any military arrangement. They had agreed that the Pact being one for the preservation of peace, it would be a mistake to imbue it with any military flavour, and that anything that was necessary in the way of the exchange of military information could be performed by the Military Attachés or through other exchanges between the General Staffs.

The Soviet representatives had also shown themselves favourably disposed towards the proposed Danubian Pact, and had urged that the regional arrangements at present in view should eventually be completed by another, to cover South-Eastern Europe, in which Turkey might participate. In general, M. Léger remarked, the visit had strengthened the evidence that Turkey was very much in the pocket of the U.S.S.R. which had assumed towards her the role of protector and patron. Indeed, M. Léger thought, the road to Angora now lay through Moscow.

Copy sent to Geneva.

[4] In a letter of May 27 to Sir G. Clerk, Mr. Wigram wrote: 'We should be very much interested to be allowed to see the Russian text if it were possible for you to get a copy for us.' In reply, on June 1 (C 4515/55/18), Mr. Wigram was told that the Embassy had been unable to obtain a copy. M. Léger had said that 'it was not a final document and might undergo modification in Moscow before being despatched to Berlin'. It was decided in the Foreign Office not to pursue the matter.

[5] See Volume XII, No. 715; cf. ibid., No. 722, 1st Meeting.

## No. 232

*Sir G. Clerk (Paris) to Sir J. Simon (Received May 24)*

*No. 104 Saving: Telegraphic [C 4153/55/18]*

PARIS, *May 23, 1935*

M. Léger was unwilling this morning to pronounce any opinion on Herr Hitler's speech as he had not had time to analyse it carefully.

It is unlikely in any case that in M. Laval's absence he would fully disclose to what extent he considers the speech offers a fresh basis for discussion. Copy sent to Geneva by bag.

## No. 233

### Mr. Palairet (Stockholm) to Sir J. Simon (Received May 24)
#### No. 8 Saving: Telegraphic [C 4203/55/18]

STOCKHOLM, *May 23, 1935*

Herr Hitler's speech has met with a cool reception from the Swedish press in general, which shows decided scepticism regarding his good faith. Conservative newspapers are however impressed by his utterances which they consider promising.

## No. 234

### Sir E. Phipps (Berlin) to Sir J. Simon (Received May 24)
#### No. 505 [C 4174/55/18]

BERLIN, *May 23, 1935*

His Majesty's Ambassador at Berlin presents his compliments to His Majesty's Secretary of State for Foreign Affairs, and has the honour to transmit to him a record by the Air Attaché of an interview with General Göring concerning the German Air Force.[1]

### ENCLOSURE IN No. 234

#### Group Captain F. P. Don to Sir E. Phipps

BERLIN, *May 22, 1935*

Sir,

I have the honour to report that I was requested to visit General Göring this morning for an interview. This was undoubtedly the outcome of a conversation which I had with the Liaison Officer at the Reichsluftfahrtministerium the day before yesterday, at which I urged the importance of my being given some further details regarding the German Air Force, in view particularly of the coming debate on Defence in the House of Commons. I had emphasised how unsatisfactory it was that Germany's profession of parity with Great Britain last March[2] had been followed by nothing more than the bare statement that approximately 800–850 first-line aircraft existed in Germany at that time.[3] Were these aircraft incorporated in fully formed units? Were the pilots trained and serving with their squadrons? and so on. I had formed the opinion that the Chancellor's original statement to Sir John Simon, and, in particular, General Göring's later announcement at the Press Luncheon,[4] were to a certain extent 'bluff'.

[1] For a brief summary of this interview see No. 220 above.
[2] See Volume XII, No. 651, p. 739.    [3] Cf. *ibid.*, No. 704.    [4] See No. 161.

The Liaison Officer told me that my questions must be referred to higher authority; later I received a message that General Göring had ruled that no answers to my questions were to be given until after the Chancellor's speech to the Reichstag, last night, and that the matter in any case would have to be referred to the Chancellor himself. It has therefore been unavoidable that the subsequent interview with General Göring this morning has taken place only a few hours before the debate in the House of Commons, with the consequence inconvenience of last-minute information.

General Göring's attitude was very friendly and he said that he knew I would wish him to speak with complete frankness. He explained to me the system which he had found necessary in order to create and rapidly expand an Air Force—a system entirely different to that prevailing in an established Air Force, where the combatant units are filled up by pilots trained at comparatively few flying schools. In Germany the system had been to give an instructor as few pupils as possible in order to achieve rapid tuition; a large proportion of these pupils, when trained, themselves immediately become instructors. At the same time, however, trained personnel are allotted to combatant squadrons even though in a great many cases the entire squadrons may remain temporarily at the (so-called) schools, where formation flying and other military training is taught. The aircraft for the combatant units are in existence, either in use or stored. He especially emphasised that each officer belongs to a Combatant Unit which exists at a School if not at its ultimate station, and that in the event of war, by cutting down the number of flying schools and bringing out of store the first-line aircraft not in use, the combatant Air Force could be instantly mobilized. He was unwilling to give me any figures as to the number of units formed at ultimate stations, but I gathered that within a few weeks or months many more aerodromes would be occupied.

General Göring was evidently determined to convince me that he had not been bluffing, and I did not make the obvious comment that a high standard of 'military' flying and technical training as apart from the purely elementary flying instruction could scarcely be expected to have kept pace with such rapid expansion.

He proceeded to inform me that, in pursuance of their intention to reach parity with France's first-line strength (to which he gives the exaggerated figure of 2,000), the strength of the German Air Force has already considerably exceeded the parity figure indicated by the Chancellor to Sir John Simon last March. At this stage I warned him (as I had already warned the Liaison Officer) that whatever he told me might perhaps be quoted this afternoon in the House of Commons. He fully understood this. I asked him when parity with France will be reached; he hesitated; I said: 'This year?' He answered: 'I hope so.' I said that I presumed he realized what an exceedingly serious statement he had just made to me, remembering the fact that my Government may think fit to announce it this afternoon in the House of Commons. He agreed, and repeated his statement with great deliberation regarding the expansion and the ultimate aim of parity with France.

He then added with great emphasis that if France reduces her first-line aircraft strength, and if we do not build up to that figure, Germany will most willingly reduce her expansion programme accordingly. He repeated this statement more than once during our interview.

I remarked that I feared such general statements regarding Germany's expansion would only increase the anxiety in Europe if the policy of secrecy is continued as regards actual formations, types of aircraft, and all such information which enables an Air Staff to assess the strength of a foreign air power. I urged the desirability of publicity such as we have. This brought him to the question of reciprocal air force information, and he referred to some notes which he had prepared. He stated that he would be glad to give privileged information to the British Air Attaché on three conditions:—

(i) that a German Air Force Air Attaché should be accredited to the German Embassy in London.

(ii) that the German Air Attaché should enjoy the same privileges as I do.

(iii) that it should be strictly understood that the information which the British Air Attaché sends home shall be for the Air Ministry and not for publication nor for the House of Commons.

He had a lot to say about this latter point; he cited the announcement in England of Germany's 12 small submarines[5] as information which should not have been made public. I said that I was confident that if and when the political aspects of Germany's rearmament are fully cleared up, there is not the slightest reason to believe that the established practice regarding reciprocal information would be departed from in the case of information from Germany. But I contended that the instance of the 12 submarines was entirely another matter, which was essentially political, and cut straight across the terms of a Treaty. It would have been contrary to our traditional practice if the members of the House of Commons had been left in ignorance of such an event, which was to some extent on the same footing as Germany's earlier announcement of an Air Force:[6] this had been made public, and General Göring had raised no objection. He seemed entirely unconvinced and is evidently determined to keep a great deal secret from those powers which, as he said, have made a ring round Germany. During our interview he made the usual references to Germany's position as a result of the pact between France, Russia and Czecho Slovakia; to Germany's wish to conclude an Air Pact; to his intense wish to be on friendly relations with England, with whom there must never again be war; 'only a lunatic could think of it'; to his admiration of the British Air Force, and to certain small points in connection with the Richthofen Geschwader,[7] on which I shall report separately to the Air Ministry. I also gained the distinct impression from some remarks he made that his aim is to reach parity in aircraft and personnel with France's first line without simultaneously building up the appropriate large reserves of aircraft, but to rely on factory output being so great when

[5] Cf. Nos. 150 and 154.                                   [6] Cf. Volume XII, No. 562.

[7] A squadron of the German air force named after the First World War fighter ace, Freiherr von Richthofen.

that aim is reached that wastage could be made good direct from the factories. No doubt this would be only a temporary expedient to enable extremely rapid first-line expansion, and would be followed by a proper reserve subsequently when factory output is slowed down to avoid over-production in peace time. This however is largely conjecture on my part, though I thought I detected an indication of it.

Before leaving him I expressed my regret that he had not at least given me some figures as to the number of Bombing aircraft which Germany possesses now and will possess later—information of a kind which we in England publish in the Air Force List.

He then for the first time spoke with some heat, and said that I can have no details so long as every German aeroplane is spoken of in Parliament as a 'flying devil'. 'I hate Parliaments.' This ended an interview which lasted about $1\frac{1}{2}$ hours.

I would submit to your Excellency the following points which appear to emerge from this interview:—

1. The German Government has to some extent been bluffing; but there is evidently a system of 'concealed' units at so-called schools, which are nominally ready for transfer 'en bloc', as the aerodromes become ready. The system is probably developing rapidly.

2. The boasted first-line aircraft and pilots probably do exist, though not by any means all are yet at their ultimate stations.

3. The proficiency of the flying instructors cannot be very high, if many of them have only themselves just finished their training.

4. The standard of 'military' and technical training cannot yet be either universally high or very far advanced, as we understand it. But the rate of progress is probably remarkable.

5. Subject to the limitations on efficiency imposed by 1 to 4 above, Germany's first-line strength has already probably exceeded parity with Great Britain; but

6. It is quite likely that high factory output is at present to some extent taking the place of the big reserve which an Air Force normally requires.

7. So-called parity with France this year is the boasted aim.

8. Germany is exaggerating France's first-line strength.

9. The only hope of checking this ambitious programme is that France should reduce her first-line strength.

10. Secrecy has again tightened up as a result of recent political events.

11. The only hope of breaking down this secrecy is the recognition of Germany's Air Force and the appointment of a German Air Force officer as Air Attaché in London.

I should add that the conclusions I have enumerated are naturally liable to such modification as the Air Ministry, with its wider knowledge of the subject, may make.[8]

I have, &c.,

F. P. DON

[8] Minutes commenting on this document were written by Mr. Creswell, Mr. Wigram,

Sir R. Vansittart, and Sir J. Simon. Mr. Creswell remarked on May 24: 'It is not an encouraging picture, and the German Air Force will be a useful instrument for "Machtpolitik" in 1936.' Mr. Wigram wrote, also on May 24, that 'the position in the summer of 1936 will be one which this country has not before admitted ... some of us in this office were well aware last year and as early as June (when the Air Ministry and Mr. Baldwin—on Air Ministry advice—said there was no danger) of the risks that were arising'. (See 93 *H.L. Deb.* 5 s., cols. 228–9 and 292 *H.C. Deb.* 5 s., cols. 2331–2). Sir R. Vansittart minuted on May 28: 'The situation in 1936 will be an extremely dangerous one. . . . For those who attach importance to an independent foreign policy, this tale of rejected advice is a chapter not easily forgotten.' He asked Sir J. Simon whether 'this figure of 2,000 is now being taken seriously? It is the second time that we have been given it. I understand that the Air Ministry are now inclined to doubt whether the *French* have as many machines as they claim.'

Sir J. Simon on June 3 deprecated 'an "I told you so" attitude'. He questioned Mr. Creswell's statement 'that we are taking a "big risk"—this seems to imply that there is some larger programme which we could execute if we chose and which we have lightheartedly rejected. That is not my understanding of the position, though I most strongly hold that the organisation of our production (which Lord Weir has been invited to undertake) is the only way to safety. Apart from that, I understand it is the view of Sir Philip Cunliffe-Lister's Committee that we cannot produce machines faster than the present programme contemplates.' (This Air Parity sub-committee of the Ministerial Committee on Defence Requirements had been set up at the end of April 1935 to recommend steps to implement the policy of parity with any country within striking distance of Great Britain, stated by Mr. Baldwin in the House of Commons; see 286 *H.C. Deb.* 5 s., col. 2078 and 295 *ibid.*, col. 883.) Sir J. Simon believed that the French 'have an unhappy habit of exaggerating their strength' and were 'going to be hoist with their own exaggerations', and that it was 'no reason at all for assuming that Germany will not rapidly build up to 2,000 machines to say that the French exaggerated their own figures. . . .'

## No. 235

### Sir J. Simon to Mr. Patteson (Geneva)
### No. 91 L.N. Telegraphic [C 4143/55/18]

FOREIGN OFFICE, *May 24, 1935, 12.45 a.m.*

Following for the Lord Privy Seal.

1. Herr Hitler's declaration[1] that Germany is ready to discuss and agree to an air pact supplementary to the Locarno Pact combined with his declaration of willingness to negotiate agreed limitations of air strength has attracted much attention here not only in the press but in the Parliamentary debates yesterday.[2] We enquired of the French and Italian Governments a fortnight ago whether, in view of the rapidly growing strength of Germany in the air, they would not favour proceeding with the negotiation of the air pact forthwith accompanied by agreed limitation of respective air strengths (my telegram to Paris No. 111[3] of May 7th). His Majesty's Government feel that in view of the circumstances now disclosed and the fact that German air strength is rapidly growing, there would be a real advantage in pushing this negotiation forward. We realise that this could of course only be done with the full co-operation of the other Powers concerned and we should like you to speak to M. Laval on the subject immediately.

[1] In his speech on May 21.    [2] See 302 *H.C. Deb.* 5 s., cols. 359–482.    [3] No. 174.

2. Paris telegram No. 84[4] of May 9th reported that M. Laval promised to discuss with his colleagues on his return from Moscow question of possibility of proceeding with the negotiation and conclusion of an Air Pact independently of a general settlement, but accompanied by an air limitation agreement between the Five Powers. Rome telegram No. 312[5] shows that Signor Mussolini is favourable to this procedure; and in his speech of May 21st Herr Hitler states that 'German Government are ready to agree to an Air Convention supplementary to the Locarno Pact and to discuss it' and that 'German Government's limitation of the German air arm to a degree of parity with the other individual Western Great Powers makes possible at any time the fixing of a maximum which Germany then undertakes to observe.'

3. I am being pressed in the House of Commons almost daily to declare our attitude on this matter: and we may at any moment be approached officially by German Government. Moreover, a Foreign Office debate is likely very shortly. In these circumstances it seems essential to define without delay the attitude of the three Stresa Powers. We should be most grateful if you would ask M. Laval if he is now able to tell you view of French Government and we should be glad to know as soon as possible whether his view coincides with that of Signor Mussolini.

Repeated to Paris, Berlin and Rome.

[4] No. 180.          [5] No. 205.

## No. 236

*Sir J. Simon to Sir E. Phipps (Berlin)*
*No. 112 Telegraphic: by telephone [C 4143/55/18]*

*Immediate*                          FOREIGN OFFICE, *May 24, 1935, 12.50 p.m.*

My telegram No. 109.[1]

It might also be useful if you were to ask German Government with reference to my conversations with German Ambassador on May 3 and 10 (my despatches Nos. 454[2] and 478[3]) whether in view of Herr Hitler's indication of his readiness to discuss and agree an air pact, they now feel able to give us a preliminary outline of their views on the shape which the pact should assume.

Repeated to Paris, Geneva and Rome.

[1] No. 227.          [2] No. 165.          [3] No. 188.

## No. 237

*Mr. Charles (Moscow) to Sir J. Simon (Received May 24, 2.10 p.m.)*
*No. 75 Telegraphic [C 4205/55/18]*

MOSCOW, *May 24, 1935, 1 p.m.*

Hitler's speech has produced effect in Soviet Union which was to be expected. Criticism, however, is concentrated rather less on anti-Bolshevik part of the speech than on 'Feuhrer's' [*sic*] comments on collective peace, disarmament, etc. Press refuses to believe in Germany's good faith and supports wholeheartedly language used by die-hard press in France and England in regard to the speech.

Germany, according to 'Pravda' is not yet ready for war and is trying to win over certain circles in Great Britain and Japan as well as to strengthen her position in Hungary, Finnland [*sic*], Poland and elsewhere. Radek points out in 'Izvestia' that although Hitler professed to distrust multilateral agreements on principle and rejects all serious proposals for security in Eastern Europe, he is willing to abide by Locarno and to negotiate Western Air Pact since these will give him a freer hand for eastward aggression.

Fuller summary by Saving telegram.[1]

Repeated to Berlin.

[1] Moscow telegram No. 4 Saving of May 24, received May 27, is not printed.

## No. 238

### Mr. Charles (Moscow) to Sir J. Simon (Received May 24, 2 p.m.)
### No. 76 Telegraphic [C 4206/55/18]

MOSCOW, *May 24, 1935, 1 p.m.*

First reaction of Soviet press to Mr. Baldwin's speech in House of Commons on May 22nd[1] is one of disappointment. Speech declares 'Pravda' has undoubtedly encouraged those elements in England who favour an agreement with fascist Germany. Mr. Baldwin has taken ostensible pacific assurances of German Chancellor as seriously as though he believed in them. Why therefore have His Majesty's Government embarked on so extensive an air programme? Their action is obviously dictated by German menace and it must be assumed that while not really believing in Herr Hitler's professions of a desire for peace His Majesty's Government intend to make a further effort to obtain advantages for Great Britain by means of separate negotiations with Germany. Such a manoeuvre is fraught with risk for its authors.

[1] See 302 *H.C. Deb.* 5 *s.*, cols. 359–73.

## No. 239

### Sir H. Kennard (Warsaw) to Sir J. Simon (Received May 24, 5.30 p.m.)
### No. 41 Telegraphic [C 4204/55/18]

WARSAW, *May 24, 1935, 4 p.m.*

Minister for Foreign Affairs considers that Herr Hitler's speech renders it impossible[1] to take up negotiations again in certain directions and that it should produce a certain detente. He is naturally pleased with Chancellor's declaration that he will be prepared to prolong pact with Poland and he

[1] It was suggested on the filed copy that this word should read 'possible'.

informs me in his conversation with General Goering last week[2] they reciprocally confirmed that death of Marshal Pilsudski would cause no change in the attitudes of their respective governments.

I asked His Excellency if there was any truth in the rumour that the Soviets were about to approach the Polish government regarding a non-aggression pact and he told me that he had heard nothing on the subject from Moscow and thought it more likely that Soviets would leave the initiative to France. He intended to make enquiries in Prague as to the interpretation of Czechoslovak-Soviet pact[3] which appears to him somewhat obscure in certain points.

Repeated to Berlin.

[2] Cf. *D.G.F.P.*, Series C, vol. iv, No. 98.
[3] For the text of the Treaty of Mutual Assistance signed at Prague on May 16, 1935, by representatives of the Czechoslovak and U.S.S.R. Governments, see *B.F.S.P.*, vol. 139, pp. 943–6.

## No. 240

*Sir E. Phipps (Berlin) to Sir J. Simon (Received May 24, 7.50 p.m.)*
*No. 207 Telegraphic [C 4201/55/18]*

BERLIN, *May 24, 1935, 6.25 p.m.*

I learn privately that Herr Hitler's speech is regarded in Ministry of Foreign Affairs and in German Government circles as well as in military circles as marking a decisive stage in European history. It is held to be Germany's maximum offer. There is no doubt that reaction throughout Germany has been extremely favourable and that Herr Hitler has put into words what 95 per cent of people think. Therefore whatever the response to his overtures may be it is held that he can count on overwhelming support at home.

The speech which is a composite work though mainly product of Ministry of Foreign Affairs, is not expected by Herr von Bülow and pessimists in Ministry to produce much favourable effect abroad. They hold that if Herr Hitler were to offer to go to Paris tomorrow to sign Treaty of Versailles voluntarily and put his name to a cart-load of security pacts the result would be nil. The French would merely reply that this was a manoeuvre to separate France from her friends.

Herr Hitler himself takes a fatalist view. He feels that for good or evil he has shot his bolt. He is not interested in hearing the reactions of the outer world for at least a week to come. This he thinks is the minimum time required by governments and foreign opinion to form a definite judgment. Mr. Baldwin's reply[1] was, he remarked, very sensible but that was only to be expected. The line taken by Paris and Geneva might be very different.

[1] Cf. No. 227, note 2.

# No. 241

*Sir E. Phipps (Berlin) to Sir J. Simon (Received May 25, 9.30 a.m.)*
*No. 210 Telegraphic [C 4220/55/18]*

Secret                                    BERLIN, *May 24, 1935, 9.36 p.m.*

I learn from an authoritative source that Reichswehr ministry were greatly taken aback by passage in Herr Hitler's speech offering the abolishment of heavy tanks and aggressive weapons as well as reductions of calibre. This suggestion came originally from Ministry of Foreign Affairs and was resisted by Generals.

Herr Hitler kept his own counsel but finally came down on the side of Ministry of Foreign Affairs greatly to their surprise.

# No. 242

*Sir E. Phipps (Berlin) to Sir J. Simon (Received May 25, 9.30 a.m.)*
*No. 208 Telegraphic [C 4222/55/18]*

BERLIN, *May 24, 1935, 9.39 p.m.*

Your telegrams Nos. 109[1] and 112.[2]

After suitable opening and reference to Mr. Baldwin's speech which German Government much appreciate I put desired questions to His Excellency. I did not leave anything in writing but he took notes and will reply fully as soon as possible.

Meanwhile Baron von Neurath gave me the following *provisional* replies to certain points:—

(Point 2 of Speech). There are certain further minor alterations that German Government desire, such as international rivers and some restrictions connected with navigation in the Kiel Canal, etc.

Regarding non-aggression Pacts in a joint Pact it seems that Russians and French have informed German Government that they themselves are about to make proposals which Germans therefore await on this subject.

(Point 8). German Government have prepared preliminary outline of shape which Air Pact should assume and will supply this at an early date.

As to limitation of effectives Baron von Neurath reiterated remarks made to me on May 2nd (see paragraph 9, my despatch No. 422, and my telegram No. 113 Saving).[3] He said, however, that Russia would of course also have to reduce her effectives pro rata as Western Powers reduced theirs. Otherwise some form of special security Pact would have to be concluded between Western Powers and Germany. His Excellency feels that any agreement on effectives will be very difficult to reach as at Geneva agreement showed

---

[1] No. 227.                                               [2] No. 236.

[3] Berlin despatch No. 422, received May 8, is not printed. It gave a slightly fuller account of Sir E. Phipps' conversation with Baron von Neurath on May 2 reported in Nos. 157 and 158 above. Paragraph 9 was almost identical with the last paragraph in Berlin telegram No. 113 Saving (No. 158).

itself to be impossible in this respect. In regard to armaments, however, agreements should be much easier to reach.

Baron von Neurath thinks General Göring's figure of 2,000 machines for French metropolitan first line strength plus French first line strength in North Africa was only a very rough one. When Air Pact negotiations begin it will be necessary to go more thoroughly into complicated question of figures. French Ambassador informed Baron von Neurath before leaving for Paris on May 22nd that M. Laval agreed to pursue Air Pact negotiations in advance of other subjects mentioned in London declaration.

Repeated to Geneva, Paris and Rome.

## No. 243

*Sir G. Clerk (Paris) to Sir J. Simon (Received May 25, 9.30 a.m.)*
*No. 96 Telegraphic [C 4221/55/18]*

Confidential                                      PARIS, *May 24, 1935, 11.5 p.m.*

Your telegram 128.[1]

Air Attaché obtained the following confidential information from French Air Ministry this afternoon:—

Peace establishment of first line strength: (*a*) in France and North Africa: 1,528 machines. This figure includes autonomous naval air force.

(*b*) in Levant and overseas: 176 machines.

Naval Attaché has obtained following figures in respect of aircraft under orders of Ministry of Marine:—

Naval co-operation aircraft embarked, 73 machines: shore-based, 163 machines.

Figure for total French aircraft the world over would thus be 1,940 machines.

Air Ministry state that they do not contemplate any increase. Ministry of Marine contemplate a small increase of from 10 to 20 only in machines under their control to be completed by 1940.

Repeated to Geneva and Berlin.

[1] No. 229.

## No. 244

*Sir E. Phipps (Berlin) to Sir J. Simon (Received May 25, 11.30 a.m.)*
*No. 138 Saving: Telegraphic [C 4224/55/18]*

BERLIN, *May 24, 1935*

My immediately preceding telegram.[1]

There is no tendency in the press to criticise British air rearmament or to regard it as directed against Germany.

[1] Not printed. It summarized the comments in the *Deutsche Diplomatisch-politische Korrespondenz* on foreign press reactions to Herr Hitler's speech on May 21.

The 'D.A.Z.'[2] actually welcomes it on the ground that once England, France and Germany have air parity, an air limitation agreement will be easier of achievement.

[2] *Deutsche Allgemeine Zeitung.*

## No. 245

*Note from Sir R. Vansittart to Sir M. Hankey*

[*C 4286/55/18*]

*Immediate* FOREIGN OFFICE, *May 24, 1935*

I enclose a memorandum on the possible inclusion of Holland in the proposed Air Convention.

The Secretary of State would be very glad if this matter could be considered by the Committee of Imperial Defence and the Chiefs of Staff with a view to obtaining an opinion as to whether or not the inclusion of Holland would represent any new security for this country.

It seems essential to give consideration to this aspect of the question, whether or not the proposal is eventually to be pursued.

R. V.

ENCLOSURE IN No. 245

FOREIGN OFFICE, *May 21, 1935*

On a number of occasions during February last, unofficial approaches were made by the Netherlands Foreign Minister to our Minister at The Hague and also in London, for the purpose of ascertaining the intentions of the Powers respecting the participation of Holland in the proposed Air Pact. An account of these approaches is given in the annex to this memorandum.[1] For convenience of reference there is also annexed the draft of the proposed pact which has been prepared in the Foreign Office[2] as an indication of the lines which we would work on in any negotiations. Certain comments by the Air Ministry on this draft are also attached.[3]

2. Quite apart from the political aspect of the question thus raised by the Netherlands Government—which will have to be considered separately—it is essential that this question should be studied from the technical and strategic point of view. It is accordingly suggested that the C.I.D. and the Chiefs of Staff should examine it from this angle with a view to ascertaining what, if any, new security or other advantage might be expected to accrue to the United Kingdom from the participation of the Netherlands in the proposed Air Pact. Once consideration has been given to this aspect of the question the matter would then be ready for examination from other points of view.

[1] According to a marginal note on the draft of this memorandum the annex contained paragraphs 1–5 of the Annex to No. 210.

[2] Not annexed to filed copy of memorandum: cf. Appendix II in this Volume, note 4 and Annex IV. [3] These comments of May 7 are not printed.

292

## No. 246

### Letter from Mr. Law[1] to Mr. Sargent
[*C 4226/55/18*]

Extract *May 24, 1935*

My dear Moley,

*Germany*: The reception accorded in the City [of London] to Herr Hitler's speech has so far been rather mixed. The majority of persons with whom I have spoken consider that it shows the pacific intentions of Germany. These people may be divided into two groups; those who feel that Germany has made an important offer which should immediately be seized upon by H.M. Government, and those who maintain that Hitler has said nothing new and has only underlined the obvious fact that Germany would not be so foolish as to attack any member of the unanimously hostile European group. Besides these, there is a minority composed of persons who give a closer attention to foreign affairs than the generality of bankers. This minority finds its suspicions of Germany's ultimate intentions in no way diminished by the speech and they fear that Germany, by presuming too much upon the pacific sentiments of Europe and England in particular, might risk some aggressive action (Austria or Memel) which would inevitably produce war. This smaller group also entertain grave fears as to the future when the financial and economic effects of re-armament leaves Germany in a dilemma, the horns of which are inflation coupled by revolution or war. I have heard no one suggest that our aerial re-armament should be curtailed. Finally, it must always be remembered that the City as a whole is anti-French—that for some obscure psychological reason anti-French sentiment always tends to become pro-German.

From what I have heard it appears to me that the calming effect of Hitler's pronouncement was due as much to the skilful way it was dished up in this country as to its actual content. Everyone read the 13 points which I understand formed the subject matter on which the newspapers wrote their leaders. Comparatively few people troubled to read the smaller print containing the summary of the speech itself. The 13 points were so skilfully directed to placate British opinion that a rumour was even current that they had been composed in collaboration with our own Foreign Office! Even now, as far as I am aware, the full text of the speech has not been published in this country.[2]

Since writing my last letter to you, I have had additional confirmation of the extent to which the German Government pays for its purchases by promises, some discountable and therefore inflationary, others undiscountable

---

[1] Mr. Nigel Walter Law entered the British Diplomatic Service in 1913 and was appointed a First Secretary in February 1921. He was unemployed by the Foreign Office after October 1, 1922. He corresponded with Mr. Orme Sargent from time to time about German affairs. Only the above extract from his letter of May 24 has been filed.

[2] Cf. No. 222, note 1.

and therefore constituting a tax in kind on industry. In order to keep the market clear for Government issues and to ensure funds for the financing of Government bonds or Government guaranteed bills, no new issue has been allowed on the German Stock Exchange for the last two years. Even the shares of old companies which have been reconstructed are not allowed to be quoted there.

The reign of terror still goes on. Spies are everywhere and people are denounced and disappear mysteriously as before. The picture painted by Germans of the internal condition of the country and the activities of the Gestapo, makes it indistinguishable from similar accounts of Soviet Russia. Industry is very active and unemployment diminishes. The former is caused by Government orders and the latter is enforced by Nazi commissioners who insist on individual wages being reduced and the balance of the wage fund used in taking on additional workers. How long this can last no one can tell, but a nation working under such an abnormal strain must be in an hysterical state.

It is curious to find that of Hitler's colleagues Goering is the most popular. Even those opposed to the present regime say that he is a man having like appetites with ourselves, while the others are fanatics or crooks or worse.

I heard a true story of Ribbentrop. A few years ago he was 'down and out' and appealed for assistance to a wealthy Jew. The Jew lent him money and put him on his feet again. Now Ribbentrop is not only violently anti-Semitic and will not speak to this Jew, but he has not even repaid the money he owes.

Yrs ever,
NIGEL

### No. 247

*Mr. Patteson (Geneva) to Sir J. Simon (Received May 25, 4.20 p.m.)*
*No. 89 L.N. Telegraphic [C 4230/55/18]*

GENEVA, *May 25, 1935, 3.36 p.m.*

Following from Mr. Eden.

I much regret that owing to pressure of work here yesterday I had no opportunity of acting on your telegram No. 87[1] before Monsieur Laval's departure.

Repeated to Paris.

[1] No. 226.

### No. 248

*Sir E. Phipps (Berlin) to Sir J. Simon (Received May 26, 1.30 p.m.)*
*No. 211 Telegraphic [A 4748/22/45]*

BERLIN, *May 26, 1935, 12 noon*

Your telegram No. 111.[1]

Herr von Ribbentrop proposes to go to London with two naval experts

[1] No. 228.

in time to begin naval discussions on the morning of Tuesday June 4th, it
that be convenient to His Majesty's Government.

I urged earlier date but he said he must be here during the coming week
in order to discuss matters with the Chancellor.

## No. 249

*Sir J. Simon to Sir G. Clerk (Paris)*
*No. 133 Telegraphic [C 4230/55/18]*

FOREIGN OFFICE, *May 27, 1935, 3 p.m.*

Geneva telegram No. 89.[1]
Will you now please speak to M. Laval in sense of my telegram No. 87
to Geneva.[2]

[1] No. 247.    [2] No. 226.

## No. 250

*Sir J. Simon to Sir G. Clerk (Paris)*
*No. 134 Telegraphic: by telephone [C 4229/55/18]*

FOREIGN OFFICE, *May 27, 1935, 3.35 p.m.*

Geneva telegram No. 88.[1] Please communicate with M. Laval at once in
sense of my telegram No. 91 to Geneva.[2]

[1] In this telegram of May 25, not printed, Mr. Eden had referred to No. 235 and said
that his impression, after a conversation with M. Laval on May 24, was that M. Laval 'will
make no objection to action by us provided his position in connexion with the legalising of
German air re-armament can be safeguarded'. M. Laval had said that he would 'be glad to
give us a considered reply' if H.M. Ambassador would approach him on the matter as soon
as he returned to Paris.    [2] No. 235.

## No. 251

*Sir J. Simon to Sir E. Phipps (Berlin)*
*No. 115 Telegraphic [A 4748/22/45]*

FOREIGN OFFICE, *May 27, 1935, 7 p.m.*

Your telegram No. 211.[1]
June 4th will be convenient date for opening discussions.

Are we correct in assuming that only other members of the mission
besides Herr von Ribbentrop will be Admiral Schuster and Commander
Kiderlen (see enclosure in Chancery letter of April 16)?[2]

[1] No. 248.    [2] Cf. No. 138, note 2.

## No. 252

*Sir E. Phipps (Berlin) to Sir J. Simon (Received May 28, 10.50 a.m.)*
*No. 214 Telegraphic: by telephone [A 4780/22/45]*

Immediate                                                          BERLIN, *May 28, 1935*

Your telegram No. 115.[1]

German Naval Attaché in London will also take part in the conversations. Herr von Ribbentrop tells me he receives continual enquiries from the press about his mission, and he suggests therefore that a short announcement should appear in the English and German press tomorrow morning stating that these conversations will begin in London on the morning of the 4th June.

Do you agree?[2]

[1] No. 251.
[2] For the text of the agreed communiqué see *The Times*, May 29, p. 14.

## No. 253

*Sir G. Clerk (Paris) to Sir J. Simon (Received May 28, 4.40 p.m.)*
*No. 98 Telegraphic: by telephone [C 4303/55/18]*

Important                                                          PARIS, *May 28, 1935*

Your telegram No. 87 to Geneva.[1]

Monsieur Laval welcomed idea of agreement between France, Italy and ourselves on the nature of reply to Herr Hitler's request for interpretation of effect of Franco-Russian agreement on Locarno.[2] He gave instructions in my presence for French view to be drafted at once and he said that he would let me have it this evening or tomorrow morning. This he hoped would give you time to consider it and make any observations that you might wish to.

Repeated to Rome, Berlin and Brussels.

[1] No. 226; cf. No. 249.
[2] For the text of the German Government's memorandum of May 25 on this subject see *D.G.F.P.*, Series C, vol. iv, No. 107. Cf. *ibid.*, No. 106, note 12.

## No. 254

*Sir G. Clerk (Paris) to Sir J. Simon (Received May 28, 4.55 p.m.)*
*No. 99 Telegraphic: by telephone [C 4304/55/18]*

Important                                                          PARIS, *May 28, 1935*

Your telegram No. 91 to Geneva.[1]

Minister for Foreign Affairs confirmed his acceptance of discussion between jurists[2] and added that he himself was generally in favour of pursuing negotiations for an air pact and that President of Council shared

[1] No. 235; cf. No. 250.          [2] See No. 180.

this view in principle. On the other hand, the internal political situation in France at the moment was such (he said Government was up in the air) that he had not, and could not for the moment, put question to the rest of his ministerial colleagues.[3] He therefore asked that His Majesty's Government would not press him for an immediate answer.

2. He also warned me, when he gave his considered reply, there were various 'service' objections which he could not lightly brush aside. As an instance, from French point of view, his military authorities had pointed out that, once His Majesty's Government had obtained an air agreement, British public opinion would care much less about the limitation of land effectives and armaments, which still remained a vital preoccupation for France. Minister of Foreign Affairs also said that he would have to consider position of other neighbours of Germany, who derived no direct increase of security from an air agreement between the Locarno Powers, while they saw Germany's flagrant infraction of Treaty of Versailles condoned. None the less, in principle Monsieur Laval is certainly in favour of pursuing negotiations.

3. I said to Minister for Foreign Affairs that I was confident that His Majesty's Government would appreciate situation of French Government and would not desire to make difficulties for them at this juncture but what were you to say if questioned in the House? He quite saw the difficulty and suggested that it might be possible for you to say in general terms that question of possibilities opened up by Chancellor's speech was forming the subject of urgent consideration between the other Governments principally concerned.

[3] See No. 270 below, note 2.

# No. 255

*Sir E. Phipps (Berlin) to Sir J. Simon (Received May 28, 7.15 p.m.)*
*No. 215 Telegraphic [C 4302/55/18]*

*Confidential*                                                    BERLIN, *May 28, 1935, 6.15 p.m.*

I hear from an absolutely reliable source that Herr Hitler's speech has re-kindled Monsieur Laval's desire to come to Berlin (see my telegram No. 184).[1]

Quai d'Orsay however oppose this idea on the ground that it would be too soon after the Russian 'rapprochement'. Nevertheless Monsieur Laval is determined to come here if possible before the end of June unless some crisis in France prevents him.

[1] No. 186.

## No. 256

*Sir E. Phipps (Berlin) to Sir J. Simon (Received May 28, 7.40 p.m.)*
*No. 216 Telegraphic [C 4314/55/18]*

BERLIN, *May 28, 1935, 6.22 p.m.*

My telegram No. 208[1] of May 24th, paragraph 4.

I learn from French Embassy that they have no knowledge of any such proposals as German Government claim to expect. It might be worth clearing this point up in Paris.

Repeated to Paris.

[1] No. 242.

## No. 257

*Sir E. Phipps (Berlin) to Sir J. Simon (Received May 28, 9.15 p.m.)*
*No. 217 Telegraphic [C 4315/55/18]*

BERLIN, *May 28, 1935, 7.35 p.m.*

My telegrams Nos. 208[1] and 216.[2]

I now hear announcement of these proposals was made rather vaguely by Monsieur Laval to General Goering at Cracow[3] and quite definitely before Chancellor's speech, by Soviet Ambassador to Baron von Neurath under instructions from Litvinov. After Chancellor's violent attack on Russia Litvinov decided not to make proposals but it seems that Monsieur Laval, inspired by Titulescu,[4] is urging him to do so nevertheless.

Repeated to Paris and Moscow.

[1] No. 242.    [2] No. 256.    [3] Cf. No. 214.
[4] M. Titulescu was Rumanian Foreign Minister.

## No. 258

*Sir E. Phipps (Berlin) to Sir J. Simon (Received May 29, 11.55 a.m.)*
*No. 140 Saving: Telegraphic [C 4332/55/18]*

BERLIN, *May 28, 1935*

Tonight's 'Deutsche Diplomatisch-politische Korrespondenz' comments favourably on Mr. Baldwin's Albert Hall speech,[1] the tone of which is welcome as *abandoning recrimination over the past history of disarmament*[2] and looking only to the future.

Mr. Baldwin, the article states, defends the English armaments policy on the ground of England's absolute security requirements. His argument will

[1] Mr. Baldwin addressed a mass meeting at the Albert Hall, London, on May 27 on the eve of the annual conference of Conservative women's organisations; see *The Times*, May 28, p. 16.

[2] The previous eight words are underlined on the filed copy and an undated minute by Sir R. Vansittart reads: 'This wd be too easy if the Germans were allowed to get away entirely with their misrepresentation of the past. No-one wants to recriminate but it is difficult to leave the last word to distortion, indeed to falsehood.'

certainly be universally approved and can be given a general application in that country where the right of every nation to look to its own security has never been denied. A proper national armaments policy may also have an excellent effect beyond its immediate purpose, inasmuch as it gives the country concerned a feeling of calm solidity and removes the inferiority complex which creates nervousness and is only a disturbing element in international relations. It must, however, of course be understood that sane measures for self-defence must not be allowed to degenerate into a hysterical and unlimited accumulation of the most dangerous weapons of aggression.

Mr. Baldwin has been at pains to emphasise the damaging effects of a future war and the necessity of collective agreements which shall complete the national security policy. That the task is difficult he does not deny, but his remarks regarding the good relations which have been established with France after centuries of war constitute an exhortation to make every effort to follow this example. In doing so he is echoing the words of the German Chancellor, who for long has been following a policy of reconciliation with France, a policy which found expression in his last appeal to the European nations. There is no doubt that after the elimination of all territorial differences between Germany and France there is no reason why the relations between the two countries should be other than those between England and France, as depicted by Mr. Baldwin.

# CHAPTER IV

# German Government's proposal for an Air Pact: Anglo-German Naval Agreement

# May 29–June 20, 1935

## No. 259

*Sir J. Simon to Sir G. Clerk (Paris)*

*No. 135 Telegraphic [C 4336/55/18]*

*Important*                           FOREIGN OFFICE, *May 29, 1935, 11 p.m.*

The German Ambassador has handed to me a draft prepared by the German Government containing their proposals for an Air Pact between the Locarno Powers[1] and states that the French, Italian and Belgian Governments are being informed of this action. He added that if His Majesty's Government wish to supply the other Locarno Powers with copies of the German draft the German Government raise no objection, but in that event they would stipulate that we should supply the German Government with any draft proposals emanating from any of the other Locarno Powers.

2. I have objected to this procedure and have insisted that the best course would be for the German Government themselves to supply their document to the other Powers direct. The German Ambassador is reporting what I have said to his Government, but he observed that the French draft[2] had never been communicated to the German Government. We have never communicated our draft[3] to them.

3. Please tell M. Laval that I am convinced that the best course will be to have an exchange of drafts, so that each of us shall be in a position to consider the suggestions made. I understand that the jurists at Geneva have been working on the various suggestions before them[4] and our representative is returning tonight to report on the result. We have a Debate on Friday[5] morning in the House of Commons on Foreign Affairs when I am going to be pressed to say what are the efforts which have been made to promote agreement over an Air Pact and cognate matters. There is no need to decide whether or not the Air Pact could find its place only in a General Settlement involving other matters, for, in any event, the terms of a pact have to be

---

[1] For a fuller account by Sir J. Simon of his interviews with Herr von Hoesch on May 28 and 29 see No. 263 below. The draft of the Air Pact handed to him by the Ambassador is printed as an Annex to that document.       [2] See Volume XII, Annex to No. 517.

[3] See *ibid.*, No. 722, Annex I to 7th Meeting at the Stresa Conference.

[4] A marginal note on the filed copy here read: 'Sir W. Malkin telephones that no agreed draft has emerged.'       [5] May 31.

discussed and negotiated as a special operation, just as it is contemplated that the terms of the Central European Pact will be separately discussed and negotiated at Rome. What I should like to be able to say on Friday is that the Air Pact is engaging the earnest attention of us all; that various States have produced drafts; and that we have reached the stage when suggestions can be exchanged with a view to considering the future course of negotiations. Please press M. Laval to agree that I should use language to this effect. Nothing less will suffice to meet the Parliamentary position here. By such language I should completely avoid any declaration on the question of a separate agreement of the Air Pact apart from a General Settlement and should show that ourselves and the French are working in the closest contact.

4. In the meantime I am making no use of the German document and have not discussed it as we are of course determined to promote the scheme in full and equal co-operation with all parties concerned and we wish to emphasise the fact that the whole proposal springs from the joint Anglo-French declaration.[6]

Repeated to Berlin and Rome.

[6] Of February 3, 1935.

## No. 260

*Sir E. Phipps (Berlin) to Sir J. Simon (Received May 30)*

*No. 142 Saving: Telegraphic [A 4848/22/45]*

BERLIN, *May 29, 1935*

There is not much comment in the press on the announcement of the forthcoming naval conversations.[1]

The 'Börsen Zeitung', 'Lokal Anzeiger' and 'Berliner Tageblatt' all recall the Chancellor's speech[2] and repeat that Germany readily recognises England's right to superiority at sea and has no desire to engage in a naval armaments race.

The 'Börsen Zeitung' adds that Herr Hitler's declaration is a guarantee to England that the negotiations will be carried out on the German side in a truly friendly spirit. It must be expected that London will equally show the necessary understanding of the moderate German demands which are vital to Germany and do not conflict with British interests.

[1] Cf. No. 252.     [2] Of May 21; cf. No. 222.

## No. 261

*Record by Mr. Hankey of a conversation with M. Bargeton on May 25*

*[C 4355/55/18]*

FOREIGN OFFICE, *May 29, 1935*

I had a conversation with M. Bargeton, the Directeur Politique of the Quai d'Orsay, in the train from Geneva on Saturday[1] night. I told the

[1] May 25.

substance of the conversation orally to Mr. Peake[2] in Paris the next morning, but in view of Berlin telegram No. 216[3] it seems worth recording.

M. Bargeton told me that the French were determined to negotiate on the basis of such parts of Hitler's thirteen points as appeared useful and to endeavour thereby to reach some satisfactory understanding with Germany on the security and armaments problem. They would shortly be making representations to the Germans, but the present intention was that the forthcoming negotiations should not take the form of exchanges of written notes. They would be as informal as possible ('tout à fait officieuses').

I said I presumed that the French Government would be keeping us informed of the tenor of their remarks. It would be a pity if the close understanding which now existed between us should not be maintained.

M. Bargeton said 'Well, if you wish it, yes', but he went on to say that it was of the utmost importance that there should be no premature disclosures whatever. Premature publicity had done a terrible amount of harm recently and they regarded this point as vital. (I agreed—somewhat pointedly).

I told M. Bargeton that we had ourselves recently made enquiries in Berlin about the meaning of some parts of Hitler's speech. Baron von Neurath in reply had given us to understand that the Germans were expecting proposals to be made by the French Government regarding security in Eastern Europe.[4] Could he give me any idea of what the French had in mind?

M. Bargeton said that the French had not at present any definite proposals in mind. They did, however, intend to make use of the point in Hitler's speech (point 6) regarding pacts of non-aggression and security. But he emphasised at length the French insistence on some *multilateral* covering agreement for Eastern Europe in order to ensure that if the peace were broken it should not be a matter which only two parties to a bilateral treaty could discuss, but a matter of common interest to all the nations in that part of Europe.

R. M. A. HANKEY

[2] A First Secretary in H.M. Embassy at Paris.    [3] No. 256.    [4] See No. 242.

## No. 262

*Mr. Strang's notes on remarks made to him by M. Massigli at Geneva on May 29, 1935*[1]

[W 4822/1209/98]

. . .[2]

*Limitation of Air Armaments*

3. It must not be assumed that France could agree to include the North

[1] These notes were enclosed in a letter of May 31 from Mr. Strang, Adviser on League of Nations Affairs, who was then in Paris, to Mr. Peterson, Head of the League of Nations Department of the Foreign Office.

[2] Paragraphs 1 and 2 contained notes relating to the Italo-Ethiopian dispute and are not here printed; cf. No. 223, note 2.

African forces in the computation of French first-line strength for purposes of parity with Germany.

4. Any air limitation agreement must be accompanied by effective measures of supervision on the spot and by guarantees of execution. A further indispensable condition for such an agreement would be control[3] over the manufacture of aircraft both civil and military.

5. There was good reason to believe that the German air force was being organised not primarily as a long-distance bombing force (as generally supposed), but in large measure as air artillery for the support of infantry and tank operations. This would be in keeping with Hitler's oft repeated suggestion that bombardment from the air should be prohibited except in the battle zone. It was conceivable that the French frontier fortifications might be vulnerable to this form of attack.

[3] This word was queried in a marginal note which read: '? contrôle i.e. supervision'.

## No. 263

### Sir J. Simon to Sir E. Phipps (Berlin)
### No. 571 [C 4336/55/18]

Sir,                                                    FOREIGN OFFICE, *May 29, 1935*

Herr von Hoesch saw me yesterday afternoon and again this morning, as there was not time at our first interview for all he wished to say.[1] He handed me two documents, translations of which are annexed to this despatch.[2]

I. The first is a draft prepared by the German Government embodying their suggestions as to the form of an Air Pact between the Locarno Powers. The Ambassador reminded me that about a fortnight ago (see paragraph 3 of my despatch No. 478[3] of May 10th) I had enquired of him whether the German Government had attempted to formulate their ideas of a Locarno Air Pact, with the principle of which they had already expressed their concurrence, and had said that we should be glad to learn more definitely what were the views of the German Government on the subject. He also referred to the recent speeches of the Prime Minister and Mr. Baldwin in this connexion.[4] Herr von Hoesch said that his Government had waited until after Chancellor Hitler had made his speech,[5] but he was now able to hand me the text. In regard to Article I, the Ambassador recalled the statement I had made some time ago in the House of Commons that the withdrawal of Germany from the League would not automatically bring the Treaty of Locarno to an end.[6] This he said was also the German view, but since the

[1] For Sir J. Simon's telegram of May 29 to Sir G. Clerk (Paris) concerning the part of these interviews relating to the proposed Air Pact, see No. 259.

[2] The first document is printed as an Annex below. The second, the German Government's memorandum of May 25 on the relation between the Franco-Soviet Pact of May 2 and the Treaty of Locarno, is not here printed; cf. No. 253, note 2.

[3] No. 188.                                  [4] See 302 *H.C. Deb.* 5 *s.*, cols. 360–1 (May 22).
[5] On May 21.                               [6] See 281 *H.C. Deb.* 5 *s.*, col. 62 (November 7, 1933).

Treaty of Locarno contemplated in certain events a meeting of the Council Germany proposed the provision contained in Article I to meet the difficulty which might arise if Germany ceased, after next October, to be a member of the League. The Ambassador also called special attention to Article IV of the draft and repeated the observation he had previously made to me that it seemed to him impossible that bilateral agreements could be made in advance between A and B for meeting an attack by C and at the same time be made between A and C to meet an attack by B. On the other hand, the mutuality of Locarno was essential to its working.

The German Government, he said, were informing the other Locarno Powers that they were putting this draft in our hands—the Ambassador sought to justify this procedure by saying that they regarded His Majesty's Government as the promoters of the plan and moreover it was we who had expressed a wish to learn the German view. If His Majesty's Government wished to supply the other Locarno Powers with copies, the German Government raised no objection, but in that event they would stipulate that they should be supplied by the other Powers with any draft proposals emanating from them. I intimated that I saw difficulties in this procedure, as this would appear to imply that we were the recipients of some special confidences, whereas the best course would be for the German Government themselves to supply their document to the other Powers also. The sooner we exchanged ideas all round, the better. Herr von Hoesch replied that the German Government had reason to believe that the French had prepared a draft and had sent it to us, but they had never offered it to the German Government. I said that our object, and I understood the object of the German Government, was to promote the settlement of an air pact, together with air limitation and the outlawing of indiscriminate bombing, and for these purposes I was satisfied that the best course was for the German proposal to be put before all the Powers concerned; and the Ambassador, without changing his ground, said that he would report this to his Government.

II. The second document[7] handed to me by Herr von Hoesch is a memorandum on the relation of the Treaty signed on May 2nd between France and the Soviet Union to the Treaty of Locarno. The Ambassador said that the German Government considered that the provisions of the Franco-Soviet Agreement were not in harmony with the Locarno Treaty. Article II of the latter defined the three exceptional cases in which attack or invasion over the Franco-German frontier did not conflict with the main provision of that article. These were:—

(a) action in self-defence;
(b) action in pursuance of Article 16 of the Covenant;
(c) action in pursuance of Article 15, paragraph 7, of the Covenant.

The inconsistency alleged in the Franco-Soviet Treaty arose in reference to case (b) above, for the Protocol to the Franco-Soviet Treaty not only bound the two parties to act together to obtain from the Council agreed recom-

[7] See note 2 above.

mendations under Article 16 of the Pact, but went on to provide that, if the Council made no recommendation or could not reach unanimity, the obligation of mutual assistance would none the less apply. His Excellency called particular attention to the last sentence of the German memorandum which he pointed out was not framed as a protest but expressed the wish to learn the views of the other Locarno Powers on the point set out above. I said that the memorandum, which dealt with a complicated matter in an elaborate way, must of course be studied, and that in the meantime I had no observations to make except that it would receive careful attention.

I am, &c.,<br>JOHN SIMON

## ANNEX TO No. 263

*Draft Air Pact, prepared by the German Government, between the Western European Powers, with the object of reaffirming the Locarno Treaties and for the avoidance of Air Attack*

The Chancellor of the German Reich, His Majesty the King of the Belgians, the President of the French Republic, His Majesty the King of Great Britain, Ireland and the British Dominions beyond the Seas, Emperor of India, His Majesty the King of Italy,

Convinced that it is of the highest importance for the maintenance of peace in Europe still further to assure the full validity of the Treaties of Locarno which they have signed,

Animated with the desire of strengthening the guarantees for their respective countries which resulted from these Treaties in order to prevent the especial dangers of sudden air attack,

Have determined to conclude a treaty with these objects and have appointed as their plenipotentiaries:—

Who, having communicated their full powers, found in good and due form, have agreed as follows:—

### ARTICLE I.

The High Contracting Parties reaffirm the full validity of the Treaties of Locarno which they have signed.

If, in consequence of the Declaration addressed by the German Government to the Secretary-General of the League of Nations on the 19th October, 1933, Germany leaves the League of Nations in accordance with Article I, paragraph 3, of the Covenant, the other High Contracting Parties will use their influence to obtain that Germany may be able to take part, as a Power with equal rights, in the deliberations and resolutions of the Council in all cases in which the Council of the League is seized in accordance with the provisions of the Treaty of Locarno with the application of those provisions.

### ARTICLE II.

If one of the High Contracting Parties is the object of an attack by the air forces of another High Contracting Party, without having provoked that attack, the remaining High Contracting Parties will immediately come to the assistance of the Party attacked with all the air forces at their disposal.

## ARTICLE III.

The obligation provided for in Article II to render assistance comes into force for each of the High Contracting Parties as soon as that Party has been able to establish the fact of the attack. It will then act in concert with the Party attacked in carrying out the measures of assistance.

## ARTICLE IV.

In order not to impair confidence in the equal application of Articles II and III above, none of the High Contracting Parties will conclude in advance special arrangements with another High Contracting Party for carrying out the obligation provided for in these two Articles.

## ARTICLE V.

This treaty shall continue in operation as long as the Locarno Treaties signed by the High Contracting Parties remains in force.

## No. 264

### Sir G. Clerk (Paris) to Sir J. Simon (Received May 30)
### No. 784 [C 4334/55/18]

*Urgent*                                                                    PARIS, *May 29, 1935*

Sir,

With reference to my telegram No. 98[1] of May 28th, I have the honour to transmit to you herewith copies of the promised memorandum giving the views of the French Government in regard to the effects of the recent Franco-Soviet agreement on the Treaty of Locarno.

2. In delivering this document the Ministry for Foreign Affairs intimated that it will not necessarily be word for word the reply to the enquiry which they understand will shortly be addressed to them through the German Ambassador in Paris. If the enquiry contains points which are not covered in the memorandum the reply will of course have to be expanded accordingly. It was in response to your request[2] to be made acquainted with the interpretation of the French Government in advance of the debate in the House of Commons on Friday next[3] that M. Laval had had this document hastily prepared.

I have, &c.,
GEORGE R. CLERK

[1] No. 253.
[2] A marginal note by Mr. Wigram here read: 'There was no such request; though we warned Sir G. Clerk that there was going to be a debate. R.F.W.' Cf. Nos. 226 and 249.
[3] May 31.

*Memorandum giving views of French Government respecting effects of Franco-Soviet Agreement on the Treaty of Locarno*

*le 29 mai, 1935*

Dans la négociation du Traité franco-soviétique d'Assistance mutuelle, le Gouvernement français a apporté le plus grand soin à éviter toute contradiction entre cet Acte et les Accords de Locarno dont il est signataire. Il estime avoir à cet égard satisfait en tous points à une condition qu'il jugeait essentielle à la conclusion de ce traité.

Les cas dans lesquels la France, en vertu du Traité franco-soviétique, pourrait être tenue de prêter assistance à l'U.R.S.S. contre l'Allemagne, rentrent tous dans les cas visés par le Traité général de Locarno, c'est-à-dire dans les cas où, aux termes de l'article 2, paragraphe 2, numéros 2 et 3, dudit traité, il est expressément stipulé que l'engagement réciproque pris par la France et l'Allemagne de ne pas recourir à la guerre ne s'applique pas:

Action en application de l'article 16 du Pacte de la Société des Nations;

Action en raison d'une décision prise par l'Assemblée ou par le Conseil de la Société des Nations;

Ou en application de l'article 15, alinéa 7, du Pacte de la Société des Nations, pourvu que dans ce dernier cas cette action soit dirigée contre un État qui, le premier, s'est livré à une attaque.

Le Traité franco-soviétique n'est pas seulement agencé de manière à éviter que la France n'y assume des obligations en contradiction avec les obligations découlant pour elle des Accords de Locarno. Par une précaution supplémentaire d'ordre général, le protocole de signature, qui, devant être compris dans l'échange des ratifications, a la même force que le traité lui-même, énonce l'intention commune des deux Gouvernements de ne contredire en rien les engagements précédemment assumés envers des États tiers par la France et par l'U.R.S.S.

Les précisions complémentaires contenues dans ce Protocole ont nettement déterminé le champ d'application dudit Traité par rapport aux engagements antérieurs.

Le premier paragraphe précise que l'obligation d'assistance en application de l'article 16 consisterait seulement dans l'obligation de se conformer immédiatement aux recommandations du Conseil de la Société des Nations aussitôt qu'elles auront été énoncées en vertu de cet article.

Dans le cas où le Conseil ne parviendrait pas à énoncer de recommandation ou n'arriverait pas à un vote unanime, les Gouvernements signataires ont encore tenu à préciser les conditions dans lesquelles ils pourraient se prêter assistance. En ce cas, pour bien assurer la stricte conformité du Traité franco-sociétique avec le Traité de Locarno, le 2$^{ème}$ paragraphe du protocole —qui s'applique d'ailleurs au cas de l'article 15 comme à celui de l'article 16 —précise que les dispositions du nouveau traité 'ne pourront pas recevoir une application qui, étant incompatible avec des obligations conventionnelles assumées par une Partie Contractante, exposerait celle-ci à des sanctions de

307

caractère international.' Cette précision se réfère au traité général de Locarno. Il en résulte que si, dans l'application et contre toute attente, une obligation découlant du traité franco-soviétique apparaissait comme étant en contradiction avec une obligation découlant pour la France du traité de Locarno, le traité de Locarno devrait prévaloir. Ainsi, dans le cas envisagé, pour pouvoir prêter légitimement son assistance à l'U.R.S.S. contre l'Allemagne, il ne suffirait pas que le Gouvernement français eût satisfait à toutes ses obligations résultant du Pacte de la Société des Nations, il lui faudrait encore être assuré de la conformité de ses conclusions avec celles des États garants du Traité de Locarno.

## No. 265

*Sir G. Clerk (Paris) to Sir J. Simon (Received May 30, 9.30 a.m.)*
*No. 100 Telegraphic [C 4341/55/18]*

PARIS, *May 30, 1935, 2.40 a.m.*

My telegram No. 102 Saving.[1]

Position as regards Eastern Pact as given by Monsieur Léger is as follows:

On further reflection French Government recently decided that as France will not be a party to the Pact they would have no locus standi to join Soviet Government in making approach to Germany. It was therefore agreed with Monsieur Litvinov at Geneva that Soviet Government would undertake this duty whilst French Government would make a separate communication in Berlin in support of the Soviet move. This the French Government consider themselves entitled to do as one of the parties to London declaration[2] and as the Government of a Power which on account of guarantee which it has undertaken to give would have been directly concerned had pact materialized in the form in which it was originally proposed.

The Soviet communication will take the form of a proposal for the conclusion of a multilateral pact embodying obligations which the German Government are known to be ready to assume, namely non-aggression, the withholding of assistance to an aggressor, consultation in the event of a disturbance or threatened disturbance of peace, and an undertaking to settle disputes by peaceful means with addition as stated in my telegram under reference of a definition of aggression. The French communication will take note of declaration made by German Government of their readiness to join a multilateral pact embodying the four above-mentioned obligations and will express opinion that it constitutes a basis for negotiation.

Note has been ready for some days and its despatch has only been delayed in deference to a request by Monsieur Litvinov that it should not be sent until he had returned to Moscow and had had time to deliver his own communication in Berlin.

French representative in Geneva suggested certain modifications of form in Soviet communication but Monsieur Litvinov was unwilling to adopt

[1] No. 231.     [2] Of February 3, 1935.

them and stated that they could be discussed later with any modifications that might be suggested by German Government.

Repeated to Berlin and Moscow.

## No. 266

*Sir G. Clerk (Paris) to Sir J. Simon (Received May 30, 9.30 a.m.)*
*No. 101 Telegraphic [C 4354/55/18]*

*Confidential*                                                    PARIS, *May 30, 1935, 2.50 a.m.*

When I saw Minister for Foreign Affairs yesterday he said that what was satisfactory in Herr Hitler's speech should be followed up, what was discutable should be discussed, and what was bad should be refuted.

In conversation this evening Monsieur Léger on the other hand expressed his personal view that Herr Hitler's speech contained little that could be described as satisfactory for France. He mentioned in particular the absence of any offer as regards land armaments (compare my telegram No. 99)[1] except that of eliminating heavy offensive weapons which were precisely those which Germany did not yet possess. He admitted there were promising elements but he clearly considered them to be overshadowed by those which are unsatisfactory. Speaking . . .[2] and confidentially he said that Minister for Foreign Affairs had been considering expediency of making some public pronouncement stating that he would welcome those passages of the speech which offer some hope of progress. Monsieur Léger was, however, discouraging him from doing so on the ground that he could not allude to the promising element and remain silent on those [? passages] which could not be passed over such, for instance, as the statement that German rearmament had been brought about by failure of allied Powers to implement their obligations under the Treaty of Versailles. If he alluded to the unsatisfactory element there would be danger of starting a polemical discussion such as Monsieur Poincaré had delighted in and which had rendered reconciliation impossible.

I doubt if Monsieur Léger would have expressed himself so much less forthcomingly than his chief unless he was fairly sure that his view would be accepted. It therefore looks as though the probabilities are that French Government will remain silent and will be content to wait upon the efforts which you are making to arrive at a definite estimate of possibilities opened up by the speech after clearing up its ambiguities.

[1] No. 254.         [2] The text was here uncertain.

## No. 267

*Sir E. Phipps (Berlin) to Sir J. Simon (Received May 30, 2.45 p.m.)*
*No. 218 Telegraphic [C 4370/55/18]*

BERLIN, *May 30, 1935, 1.23 p.m.*

My telegram No. 208.[1]

I met Herr von Bülow last night at dinner and asked him when we might

[1] No. 242.

expect replies to our questions. He said that it was not yet certian whether Baron von Neurath will meet the Chancellor tomorrow in the South or await latter's arrival in Berlin to discuss these questions. In any case it is hoped to give us the reply by June 1st at the latest.

## No. 268

### Sir G. Clerk (Paris) to Sir J. Simon (Received May 30, 2.55 p.m.)
#### No. 102 Telegraphic: by telephone [C 4371/55/18]

*Immediate*                                                           PARIS, *May 30, 1935*

Your telegram No. 135.[1]

Minister for Foreign Affairs though completely occupied by political crisis[2] managed to give me five minutes this morning. I read to him substance of your telegram emphasising especially what you wished to say in the House of Commons tomorrow. He raised no objection to any point and indeed said that at first sight his inclination was to assent to your request. He would, however, like to think it over a little and he asked me to write a message to which he promised a reply by this evening. I have accordingly sent over a paraphrase of your telegram to the Quai d'Orsai.

2. M. Laval telephoned to M. Léger while I was with him and told him very briefly the purpose of my visit adding that he appreciated your reply to German Ambassador's suggestion that His Majesty's Government should communicate German draft to the other Locarno Powers and that he himself saw at first sight no objection to the statement you wished to make in the House tomorrow. M. Léger evidently entered some caveat to which M. Laval replied 'No, no, we must let London épuiser everything that Berlin has to put forward'.

[1] No. 259.
[2] After a financial crisis which led to the defeat of M. Flandin's government on the night of May 30–31, M. Bouisson formed a new Cabinet, M. Laval remaining at the Foreign Office. M. Bouisson's Cabinet was in turn overthrown on June 4, after which M. Laval himself became President of the Council, while continuing as Minister for Foreign Affairs. He received a vote of confidence in the Chamber and closed the session on June 28.

## No. 269

### Sir G. Clerk (Paris) to Sir J. Simon (Received May 30, 7.3 p.m.)
#### No. 103 Telegraphic: by telephone [C 4374/55/18]

*Immediate*                                                           PARIS, *May 30, 1935*

My telegram No. 102.[1]

Monsieur Léger has just informed me that French Government have no objection to your using language in the House of Commons tomorrow as indicated in paragraph 3 of your telegram No. 135,[2] it being understood that further question as to whether or not Air Pact can be isolated from

[1] No. 268.            [2] No. 259.

general settlement is reserved without prejudice since French Government have not yet been able to take a decision.

## No. 270

*Sir E. Drummond (Rome) to Sir J. Simon (Received June 1)*
*No. 46 Saving: Telegraphic [C 4431/55/18]*

ROME, *May 30, 1935*

I communicated to Signor Suvich this evening the substance of Foreign Office telegram No. 135 to Sir George Clerk.[1]

Signor Suvich said that Herr von Hassell[2] had been to see him yesterday and had told him that the German Government had communicated draft proposals regarding the Air Pact to London. He understood from what I had said that the Italian Government would, in due course, receive those proposals either from the German Government or from us. He agreed that, on the whole, it seemed preferable that the German Government should make the communication themselves, but he did not seem to attach much importance to the point. He said that Herr von Hassell had given him a short outline of the German proposals which were very simple, but no provision was made therein, he believed, for any limitation of air forces. I replied that as far as we were concerned, I thought that His Majesty's Government attached the very greatest importance to such a provision and, in fact, they had made the whole Air Pact arrangement dependent on a simultaneous arrangement as regards the strength of the various air forces. Though Signor Suvich did not definitely say so, I think he felt too that this was the right line to take.

[1] No. 259.    [2] German Ambassador at Rome.

## No. 271

*Letter from Commander Schwerdt (Admiralty) to Mr. Craigie*
*[C 4372/206/18]*

LONDON, *May 30, 1935*

Dear Mr. Craigie,

With reference to my telephone message,[1] I enclose herewith copies of Naval Attaché's report and his private letter to Admiral Dickens[2] as well as the comments thereon.

Yours sincerely,
R. SCHWERDT

ENCLOSURE 1 IN NO. 271

*Reference Sheet G/66/35*    BERLIN, *May 28, 1935*

*German Navy—New Construction*

The following is a translation of a letter I received on the afternoon of 25th May from the Marineleitung. The letter was marked 'Urgent'.

[1] No record of this message has been traced in Foreign Office archives.
[2] Director of Naval Intelligence, Admiralty.

'Dear Captain Muirhead-Gould,

As a result of a conversation which your Ambassador had early in May with the Minister for Foreign Affairs, Herr von Neurath,[3] and which was referred to recently by Admiral Raeder in a conversation with your Ambassador,[4] I would like to draw your attention to the following:—

In your Aide Mémoire of 7th January, 1935, you requested that a notification should be sent to you when a ship is ordered.[5] Admiral Raeder consequently decided that we would notify you, for the confidential information of your Admiralty, of the laying down of new ships. In accordance with this policy we notified you on the 7th February, 12th and 25th April, 1935, of the ships laid down up to that date.

A notification of the shipbuilding programme for the financial year 1935 has not—as is apparently erroneously assumed—been made; nor was it intended.

Yours etc.,
(Sd) BÜRKNER.'[6]

2. As this last paragraph was very startling I called at the Marineleitung today and discussed this letter with the Liaison Officer. He told me that at lunch recently Admiral Raeder had been in conversation with the British Ambassador, and had formed the impression that the Ambassador understood that the Naval Building Programme communicated to me on 12th April[7] was definite and final. This was not the case: it was purely provisional and subject to revision at any time. I expressed surprise, and said that I had certainly informed the Ambassador and the Admiralty that I assumed that the programme communicated to me was final. If it were not so it was hardly worth communicating at all. I added that I hoped the Naval Mission would not keep such unpleasant surprises up their sleeves.

3. I have come to the conclusion that this letter was sent to me in order that the Admiralty should not be under the impression, when the German Naval Mission arrives in London, that the building programme notified to me on 12th April was anything more than a provisional one, which—although possibly accurate at the time—had since been amended by the addition of 18 submarines and is presumably to be further amended since the Chancellor's official declaration of Germany's claim to 35 per cent of the British strength.

In view of the reference to the 12th April in the last sentence of paragraph 2 of the Marineleitung's letter, I have also come to the conclusion that the ships mentioned in my R/S G. 42/35 dated 12.4.35[8] have in fact already been laid down.

4. The Liaison Officer further surprised me by saying that it was very difficult to draw up a building programme some years in advance, and asked

---

[3] Presumably a reference to the conversation reported in No. 157 above.
[4] See paragraph 2 below.
[5] A marginal note by Mr. Wigram here read: 'This document is not in F.O. or apparently in Adm[iralt]y. I have told Berlin Chancery to send it at once. R.F.W.'
[6] Senior Officer on the Staff of the Chief of the German Naval Command.
[7] See Volume XII, No. 716.          [8] Not traced in Foreign Office archives.

me what we expected the Mission to produce. In explanation I drew up
an outline programme for the German Navy up to 1942, assuming that
Germany would voluntarily take 7 years to reach her 35 per cent of our
present strength (a quite unjustifiable assumption, of course). This appeared
to interest the Liaison Officer very much indeed and he took a copy of it for
Admiral Raeder's information.

5. I am giving a lunch party on Thursday, 30th May, in honour of
Admiral Schuster, member of the Naval Mission.

G. C. MUIRHEAD-GOULD

ENCLOSURE 2 IN No. 271

*Letter from Captain Muirhead-Gould to Rear-Admiral Dickens*

*Copy*                                                                 *May 29, 1935*

I am afraid my R.S. G 66/35 of 28th May[9] will cause you further annoyance. It has made me so angry that I feel inclined to tell the Marine Leitung
that they had better, in future, make all their communications to me in
writing.

I have not the very slightest doubt that the L[iaison] O[fficer] did, in fact,
on the 12th April announce to me the 1935 Naval Building programme. In
all such conversations of obvious importance I insist on the principal items
being repeated in English, even if I have fully understood them in German.
I did not fail to do this on this occasion. If further proof were needed I
would add that I have constantly referred to the 1935 Building Programme
in subsequent conversations with the L.O. and other Officers, especially
when I was protesting about the submarine announcement, and asked the
L.O. in the presence of the A.N.A.[10] in my own Office why he had not told
me about the S/Ms when he had given me the 1935 Building Programme:
this evoked no denial whatever.

I have no doubt that what has happened is that someone realised that the
Naval Mission were going over to London with a very moderate programme
for this year: so moderate in fact that it would give them no bargaining
power. It was felt that they would be obliged to make concessions, and it
was therefore decided to arm them with a bigger programme than had been
announced, so that they could make nice generous gestures in deleting ships
from the programme which they never actually intended to build.

It must have appeared rather a problem as to how to produce this second
programme, and the rather clumsy method of putting the blame on me, or
attributing the whole thing to a misunderstanding, has been adopted.

I do not think it is worth while taking the matter up with them. I shall
be even more careful in future in my dealings with them, and shall get every
important statement confirmed in writing.

I am giving the Naval members lunch on Thursday, but not Ribbentrop,
as he had a large lunch party last week to which he invited all sorts of Senior
and Junior Officers to meet the British Ambassador and the Mission, but

---

[9] i.e. enclosure 1 above.          [10] Assistant Naval Attaché.

left me out (I was delighted as I was going out sailing). But even the L.O. in the M[arine] L[eitung] asked me why I had not been invited!

Sorry to drop this new bombshell on you at so late a moment.

G. M.-G.

ENCLOSURE 3 IN NO. 271

*Note by Admiral Dickens*

German Navy: New Construction

As will be seen from the enclosed despatch,[11] the Naval Attaché, Berlin, has suddenly been informed

(*a*) That the naval building programme (see N.I.D. 600/35 and N.I.D. 0236/35 attached)[12] hitherto communicated to him 'was purely provisional, and subject to revision at any time.'

*Note*:—This building programme announced:—

(1) Recommencement of work on 'Ersatz Elsass' and 'Ersatz Hannover'.
(2) The ordering of 2 new cruisers.
(3) The construction of 12 destroyers in addition to the 4 already building.
(4) The construction of 10 minesweepers.
(5) The construction of 12 submarines.

(*b*) That it has since been amended to include the construction of 12 additional submarines, thus making 24 in all.[13]

2. I also enclose a private letter from the Naval Attaché, Berlin,[14] in which he states he has no doubt that this action has been taken in order to give the Naval Delegation, about to visit London, something more with which to bargain.

3. The announcement that more than 12 submarines are to be built does not come as any surprise; a report, received from secret sources, having been circulated in N.I.D. 0236/35 attached.[12]

As regards other additions to the present programme, nothing is known at present, though it is possible that more than two cruisers (in addition to 'Nurnberg', building) might be laid down.

4. The Naval Attaché's report emphasises the danger of accepting as either accurate or final any statements made by the German Admiralty.

5. Copies of these papers have been sent to Craigie.

D.N.I.

[11] Enclosure 2 above.          [12] Not attached to filed copy.

[13] A marginal note on the filed copy by Mr. Wigram here read: 'This is wrong and the Admy. admit it. R.W.'          [14] Enclosure 1 above.

## No. 272

*Sir E. Phipps (Berlin) to Sir J. Simon (Received May 31, 3 p.m.)*
*No. 220 Telegraphic [C 4407/21/18]*

BERLIN, *May 31, 1935, 2 p.m.*

My telegram No. 141 (Saving).[1]

I received trustworthy confirmation, and even expansion of Italian Ambassador's conviction that Germany would press for her Colonial demands as a condition for return to the League.

It seems that Chancellor has been persuaded by Schacht,[2] Ribbentrop and Company to adopt this course.

Germany will, I learn, insist upon *all* her former Colonial possessions being returned to her.

These are dragons' teeth sown by Lords Rothermere,[3] Lothian[4] and Allen[5] despite all my efforts (see my telegram No. 272 Saving of December 16th).[6] The above should be treated as strictly confidential.

[1] In this telegram of May 29, not printed, Sir E. Phipps reported a conversation with the Italian Ambassador during which Signor Cerruti had expressed his conviction 'that Germany will demand to be actually placed in possession of certain colonies or mandates before consenting to return to the League'.
[2] Acting Reich Minister of Economic Affairs.
[3] Chief proprietor of the *Daily Mail, Daily Mirror*, etc.; cf. Volume XII, No. 294.
[4] See *ibid.*, No. 391.        [5] See *ibid.*, No. 362, note 3.        [6] *Ibid.*, No. 294.

## No. 273

*Sir E. Phipps (Berlin) to Sir J. Simon (Received May 31, 7.30 p.m.)*
*No. 222 Telegraphic: by telephone [C 4409/55/18]*

*Immediate*                                                    BERLIN, *May 31, 1935*

My telegram No. 208[1] of May 24th.

Following is the substance of the replies made by the German Government to our enquiries. They were given to me at 5.30 this afternoon by Herr Buelow on telephonic instructions from Baron von Neurath from Munich, where he has been in consultation with the Chancellor. They are only a verbal communication taken down by me.

Begins.

'The Chancellor gave in his speech in a most free manner the guiding principles of German foreign policy and concluded with thirteen points which give the standpoint of the German Government to the actual problems of the day. Everything which Germany can say at the moment to these problems is thus as clearly and distinctly laid down as it possibly can be at the time. None of the other Governments concerned in these problems at the moment have as yet proclaimed their intentions as exhaustively. The German Government cannot see how they can now make their standpoint

[1] No. 242.

any more precise by means of definitions. No Government will be in the position finally to lay down beforehand what their attitude will be in future in all concrete problems and thus pledge themselves to other Powers unilaterally while the latter reserve complete freedom of action for themselves.

(1) League: A return of Germany to Geneva cannot be considered until Germany's international status in comparison to the international status of the other Great Powers no longer in any way implies a differentiation to her disadvantage. The differentiation at present existing could not of course be removed by the purely formal separation of the Covenant from the Treaty.

(2) The Chancellor's statement under point 2 of the speech is to the effect that the German Government have not disassociated themselves from certain articles of the Treaty by means of an arbitrary decision, but they were compelled to adopt those measures which they did as a result of the conduct of the other Powers, which constituted a breach of the Treaty, and that these measures were limited to those provisions of the Treaty which were affected by the conduct of the other Powers, i.e. all those parts of the Treaty of Versailles concerning the military status of Germany, excepting the provisions regarding the demilitarized zone, which were mentioned in point 3 of the speech. The measures which the German Government have now adopted do not extend to other provisions of the Treaty of Versailles.[2] As regards those other provisions, however, as stated in the Chancellor's speech, the possibility of a revision by means of peaceful understanding must be kept open so far as such a revision may appear necessary in the course of further developments.

(3) Eastern pact. The German Government have recently received from the French and Russian Ambassadors notice of proposals, but have not yet received those proposals.

(4) Regarding the question of the French numbers of first line aeroplanes, it is difficult to give a definite answer in the absence of General Goering and General Milch,[3] and the figures before the German Air Ministry do not quite tally, but it is thought that the 2,000 aeroplanes refer to French first line aircraft in France and North Africa, *including naval aeroplanes*.

(5) Reduction of armaments. The Chancellor's statement under point 8 was based on the fact that after the whole course of the disarmament negotiations there is no prospect whatever of a general reduction of armament, including that of effectives. In order therefore to remain within the bounds of the possible, the German suggestions are limited to possibilities of so-called qualitative limitations of armaments.'

[2] A marginal comment on the filed copy here read: 'Not even the War Guilt Clause!' Cf. No. 278 below, note 8.

[3] State Secretary at the Reich Air Ministry.

## No. 274

*Sir E. Phipps (Berlin) to Sir J. Simon (Received May 31, 7.40 p.m.)*
*No. 223 Telegraphic: by telephone* [C 4414/55/18]

Immediate                                                    BERLIN, *May 31, 1935*

My immediately preceding telegram.[1]

In reply to questions which I put to Herr von Buelow with a view to clarifying the message telephoned from Munich I gathered the following:—

(1) The German Government cannot at the present stage supply us with any list of their demands as to the conditions under which they would return to the League. It is more important that the *spirit* of the League should be changed than that purely material points should be altered though these of course will also be necessary.

Herr von Buelow referring to the 'spirit' of the League quoted the fact that the French clients invariably voted for France regardless of the question of right and wrong. When for instance had Czechoslovakia ever voted against France? I pointed out how vague all this was and how difficult it would be to define a change of 'spirit'.

(2) Herr von Buelow confirmed what I have already reported namely that the German Government would be prepared to reduce the figure of 550,000 for the effectives of their army if other Powers were to make similar reductions in their figures existing on March 16th. German Government however are highly sceptical as to the possibility of any such agreement; hence their preference for 'qualitative' disarmament.

In regard to Air Pact Herr von Buelow said that the German Government have no preference as to whether the limitation of numbers should be included in that instrument or whether it should be embodied in a separate document.[2]

[1] No. 273.
[2] In Foreign Office telegram No. 143 to Paris of June 12 (No. 320 to Rome) Sir G. Clerk and Sir E. Drummond were instructed to make 'an oral communication' to the French and Italian Ministers for Foreign Affairs of the questions which Sir E. Phipps had been instructed to put to the German Government (see No. 227) and of the German Government's replies reported in Berlin telegrams Nos. 222 and 223 (Nos. 273 and 274) omitting the paragraph of 'telegram No. 223 beginning "Herr von Bülow referring to the spirit" and ending "how difficult it would be to define a change of spirit" and final paragraph'.

## No. 275

*Memorandum by the Marquess of Londonderry*[1]
*C.P. 116(35)* [C 4447/55/18]

AIR MINISTRY, *May 31, 1935*

1. In both public and confidential statements recently Herr Hitler has expressed his willingness to limit the size of Germany's Air Forces to parity

[1] A copy of this memorandum was received in the Foreign Office on June 3.

with the other Western European Powers. In the recent speech in Berlin on the 21st May, 1935, Herr Hitler has said:—

'The German Government is prepared at any time to limit its armaments to any extent which is equally adopted by the other States. The German Government has already voluntarily made known certain limitations of its intentions. In this way it has done its best to show its goodwill to avoid an unrestrained world armaments race. Its limitation of the German air arm to a degree of parity with the other individual western Great Powers makes possible at any time the fixing of a maximum, which Germany will then undertake to regard as binding.'

During the Anglo-German Conversations in Berlin on the 25th and 26th March, 1935, Herr Hitler is reported (C.P. 69 (35), on page 27), to have said:—[2]

'If Britain would bring her air strength for the United Kingdom up to the French strength, i.e., to parity with France, then it would be that parity which Germany would demand. If Britain persuaded France to come down to the British level, the German Government would be delighted because they would have to spend less on their air force. But even if Britain did not consider herself threatened by France, and preferred to have a smaller force than France, Germany could not help it because of the necessity of protecting herself.'

2. On the latter occasion Herr Hitler defined the basis on which he would calculate the French strength as follows:—

'The parity which he demanded was parity with the force in Metropolitan France plus that in North Africa.'

It is apparent, therefore, that in the absence of any agreement between ourselves and the French as to limitation, Hitler intends to build up to his own estimate of French strength, which General Göring has informed our air attaché is of the order of 2,000 first-line aircraft, a strength which he hopes to attain this year (see telegram No. 203 from Berlin, dated 22nd May, 1935).[3]

3. The French, according to information with which they supplied us only a few days ago,[4] now claim that their actual strength in France and North Africa, excluding some 230 naval aircraft, is 1,528 first-line aircraft. This number is substantially higher than the figure of 1,404 first-line aircraft (including 135 naval aircraft) which was obtained from them confidentially earlier this year, and which was quoted by the Chief of the Air Staff in the memorandum attached to C.P. 85 (35).[5]

4. The Air Ministry has now received information through the Air Attaché in Paris[6] that this increase is no more than a prospective one and that the reason for it is French uneasiness. Colonel Duvernoy, the Liaison Officer

[2] See Volume XII, No. 651, p. 738.                                                [3] No. 220.
[4] See No. 243.                                                                              [5] Cf. No. 127.
[6] A copy of this report by the British Air Attaché in Paris was received in the Foreign Office on May 30 as enclosure in Paris despatch No. 785 of May 29.

in the French Air Ministry, has informed him that the Germans take the French figure as 2,500 and at the same time are claiming parity in the air. It is therefore necessary for the French to make a very considerable effort to increase their air forces. So far from having 2,500 first-line aircraft (he said), the French at the present time have actually less than 1,000, not all of which are modern in type and performance. It might easily take two years for the French to reach their new figure. *If some limitation could be agreed by Germany, and if they could rely on the sincerity of such an undertaking, the French would be only too glad not to have to build up to that number.*

5. It seems, therefore, that unless immediate action is taken, which will result at least in a modification of the German estimate of French strength, we must inevitably be faced with an attempt by France to increase her Metropolitan Air Force up to the German figure of 2,000, which in turn will entail a corresponding further increase by Germany and so on, *ad infinitum*.[7] Indeed, the figures just given to us by the French seem to indicate the first move in this game, since they bear little relation to figures previously given to us.

6. As I think my colleagues are aware, I have long held the view that an agreed limitation in armaments could only be reached by direct negotiation between the Germans and ourselves. In the course of the Berlin Conversations Herr Hitler has announced his basis for parity quite plainly and unconditionally. On the other hand, General Göring, in the course of a conversation with Sir E. Phipps on the 3rd May (telegram No. 114, Saving, from Berlin),[8] said that if he could be certain that Britain would be at his side in the event of a Russian attack, he would be content with a far smaller air force, and mentioned the figure of 1,000 first-line aircraft. It appears, therefore, that in fact Herr Hitler's demand for parity with France depends in some degree upon the situation *vis-à-vis* Russia. The conclusion of the recent Franco-Russian Agreement can only have the effect of hardening German determination to accept nothing less than that parity with France which Herr Hitler has already demanded.

7. It would seem only too obvious that all the circumstances conspire to form a vicious circle, which if allowed to continue must inevitably prevent any agreement on stabilisation and limitation, unless bold action is taken by us at this juncture. All hope of reaching an understanding must depend on the destruction of this vicious circle, and the first step would appear to be to make use of the conversations that are already taking place between Sir E. Phipps and Herr Hitler with regard to the latter's recent speech, to convince the Germans that they are overestimating the present French strength and that the figure for agreement should be in the region of 1,500 first-line aircraft.

8. Concurrently with this, we must persuade the French to agree, in view of our own considerable expansion, to a parity level on the same basis. Ultimately it will be inevitable that similar discussions will have to be

[7] An unsigned marginal note on the filed copy here read: 'Why, if Germany is sincere about parity?'            [8] No. 163.

initiated with the Russians, in order to obtain from them some statement of their strength and policy.

9. If, on the other hand, no such steps are taken, it will not be long before we shall have to consider a still further increase in our own metropolitan first-line strength beyond the figure of 1,500 now projected.

10. Herr Ribbentrop, who is Herr Hitler's confidential adviser upon matters connected with the Disarmament Conference, is, I understand, to visit London in the near future in connection with the projected naval talks. This seems to me to provide an opportunity for arranging a three-cornered conference with a French representative on the subject of the limitation of air armaments, and I suggest that our Ambassadors in Paris and Berlin should be instructed to sound their respective Governments as to the acceptability of an invitation to discussions of this kind in London. Hitherto discussions with Germany have followed discussions with the French, and Germany has resented this by representing that she has always been presented with an agreement between England and France which she is invited to accept or to reject. It would be, I think, a very favourable point in favour of the move I am suggesting that in this case Germany should be represented from the very initiation of the discussion.

L.

## No. 276

*Sir E. Phipps (Berlin) to Sir J. Simon (Received June 1, 12.26 p.m.)*
*No. 227 Telegraphic: by telephone [A 4898/22/45]*

BERLIN, June 1, 1935

My telegram No. 211.[1]
Present arrangements are that Mission leaves Berlin by air at noon on Sunday June 2nd. Whether these arrangements will be kept is uncertain as some members of the Mission have gone to Bavaria to see the Chancellor. Exact time of arrival will therefore best be got from the German Embassy.

Herr H. Thorner and Dr. E. Kordt will also accompany Herr von Ribbentrop[2] as adjutant and Private Secretary.

[1] No. 248.
[2] Herr von Ribbentrop was appointed Ambassador on Special Mission on June 1, 1935. He arrived in London on June 2.

## No. 277

*Sir E. Phipps (Berlin) to Sir J. Simon (Received June 1, 3 p.m.)*
*No. 226 Telegraphic [C 4433/55/18]*

BERLIN, June 1, 1935, 1.11 p.m.

My telegram No. 217.[1]
Soviet Ambassador confirmed to me this morning that his government had not yet instructed him to make these proposals to German government

[1] No. 257.

owing to Chancellor's violent attack on Russia.[2] I pointed out that this attack should be considered rather for internal than for external use.

His Excellency enquired whether it was intended to separate Air Pact negotiations from the points of London Communiqué.[3] I replied that that was not our intention and that it would be highly desirable for parallel negotiations to proceed over East[ern] Pact.

Unless pressure be brought to bear on Moscow I doubt whether necessary instructions will be sent to my Soviet colleague.

Repeated to Paris and Moscow.

[2] A reference to Herr Hitler's attack on Bolshevism in his speech of May 21.

[3] Of February 3, 1935.

## No. 278

*Memorandum*[1] *on Herr Hitler's speech of May 21 in light of Berlin telegrams Nos. 208, 220, 222, and 223*[2]

[C 4414/55/18]

FOREIGN OFFICE, *June 1, 1935*

We must now apparently suppose that this is all the information we are going to get as to the meaning of the vaguer passages in Herr Hitler's speech, except as the result of actual negotiation.

As the historical passage in the speech (which is used to justify the claim that the ex-Allies have broken the Treaty by their failure to disarm and that by so doing they have justified Germany's rearmament) has been dealt with in a detailed memorandum separately submitted[3] we may now deal with the Thirteen Points,—what Hitler calls 'the precise definition of the actual problems' and 'the definition of the attitude of the German Government thereon'.

*Point 1* contains (*a*) the rejection of the Geneva resolution of March 17th[4] on the plea that the other Powers had themselves unilaterally violated the Treaty of Versailles in failing to disarm. This is a serious accusation; on a separate paper have been urged the weighty reasons for which it seems essential to reject it in public.[3]

(*b*) The statement that Germany cannot return to the League of Nations 'before the conditions for a real legal equality of all participants have been

[1] A note on the file records that this memorandum was 'submitted with Berlin telegram No. 222 [No. 273]'. [2] See Nos. 242, 272, 273, and 274.

[3] The reference was to a memorandum of May 30 by Mr. Wigram, not printed. Sir R. Vansittart minuted the memorandum as follows: 'Herr Hitler's last speech abounded in false history. This memorandum was composed to demonstrate this. We should certainly not let the Germans get away with these distortions and misrepresentations. On the other hand it is undesirable for a Cabinet Minister to start a controversy just now; and merely to give this to one newspaper will not be sufficient. I therefore suggest that we shd give this to Sir Austen Chamberlain for him to use as he thinks fit on some occasion in the near future. The truth shd certainly be shown. R. V. June 15.' Sir S. Hoare, who had succeeded Sir J. Simon as Secretary of State for Foreign Affairs on June 7 (see No. 304 below, note 10) added: 'I agree. Let us give it to Sir A. C. I should like to read it at leisure at the weekend. S. H. 15/6.' [4] This should have read 'April 17th'; cf. Volume XII, No. 732.

created. For this purpose German Government consider it necessary to make a clear line of demarcation between the Treaty of Versailles. . . . and the League of Nations which must be built up on the estimation of all its members as being of equal value and possessing equal rights. This equality of rights must extend to all the functions and all rights of property in international "life" '. These sentences are very vague, but telegram No. 222 only tells us that 'the return of Germany to Geneva cannot be considered until Germany's international status in comparison to that of the other great Powers no longer in any way implies differentiation to her disadvantage.[5] The differentiation at present existing could not of course be removed by the purely formal separation of Covenant from Treaty'. Telegram No. 223 contains an even vaguer statement from Herr von Bülow that the German Government 'cannot at present supply us with any list of their demands as to the conditions under which they would return to the League. It is more important that the spirit of the League should be changed'; and this apparently means *inter alia* that Czechoslovakia is to sever her connexion with France!

We could scarcely have a more discouraging statement than this; the further explanations which we have been given regarding Point 2 in the speech (see below) contain certain indications as to what Herr von Bülow calls the 'purely material points' which will have to be altered as well as the 'spirit of the League' before Germany can return.

In *Point 2* Herr Hitler said that the German renunciation of the disarmament clauses of the Treaty of Versailles 'as a result of the one-sided burden laid upon Germany contrary to the Treaty' (i.e., the Allied failure to disarm) applies only 'to the points mentioned which discriminate morally and practically against the German nation'. Berlin telegram No. 222 explains that this renunciation applies to 'all those parts of the Treaty of Versailles concerning the military status of Germany excepting the provisions regarding the demilitarised zone', i.e., paragraphs 1 and 3 of Article 180, which provide that:—

'All fortified works, etc., situated in German territory to the west of a line drawn fifty kilometres to the east of the Rhine shall be disarmed and dismantled. . . .[6] The construction of any new fortification whatever its nature and importance is forbidden in the zone referred to above.'

This statement apparently means that the whole of Part V except the two paragraphs of Article 180 above mentioned disappears; thus Germany will refortify her southern and eastern frontiers, despite paragraph 4 of Article 180, which reads:—

'The system of fortified works on the southern and eastern frontiers of Germany shall be maintained in its existing state.'

Further, Articles 195 and 196 disappear; these Articles forbid the existence

[5] A marginal note by Mr. Sargent here reads: 'Although asked to define his requirements, Hitler is careful to avoid mentioning Colonies, as he did during the Berlin visit. This is noteworthy in view of Berlin tel. No. 220. O.G.S.'    [6] Punctuation as on filed copy.

of any fortifications on the Baltic coast of Germany between the Danish frontier and the Corridor, and the refortification of the North Sea coast and of East Prussia. Article 115, which demilitarised Heligoland, is *not* included in Part V of the Treaty.

It seems essential that the Admiralty should be asked at once whether any vital British interest is affected by the disappearance of these two Articles. A letter to the Admiralty is being submitted separately.[7]

Herr Hitler's speech continues 'that the German Government will unconditionally respect the remaining Articles (of Versailles) regarding international relations including the territorial provisions and will only carry out by means of peaceable understanding such revisions as will be inevitable in the course of time'.

Telegram No. 222 tells us, however, even more specifically than the speech that 'as regards the other provisions of the Treaty the possibility of a revision by means of peaceable understanding must be kept open so far as such a revision may appear necessary in the course of further developments'.[8] This phrase is of importance when compared with the definition of the conditions of the return to the League quoted above; and we may suppose that 'revision by means of peaceable understanding' is to apply to all the provisions of the Treaty—whatever they may be—which will require alteration so that Germany may have full equality of rights which is the essential preliminary of her return to the League.

We know from Berlin telegram No. 208 that those points are likely to include at least the International Rivers clauses of Part XII of the Treaty and the clause relating to transit through the Kiel Canal. Memoranda on these two points are being urgently prepared so that we may know precisely what British interests are safeguarded by these clauses of the Treaty.

As regards mandates, we have received a clear warning in Berlin telegram No. 220[9] that 'before Germany's return to the League she will insist not merely (as was thought at one time) that her right to hold mandates must be recognised' but 'upon *all* her former Colonial possessions being returned to her'. There is also of course the question of the demilitarized zone and probably Austria.

All this certainly deserves great consideration, but even though Herr Hitler may say that this will only be done 'by means of peaceable understanding', note must be taken of the vast strength particularly in the air which she will have achieved before the end of this year.

[7] On June 11 a letter, not printed, was sent to the Admiralty from the Foreign Office on this question.

[8] A marginal note by Mr. Sargent here reads: 'It is surprising that Hitler neither in his speech nor in his present explanations makes any reference to the War Guilt clause as being one of the points in the Treaty "which discriminates *morally* against the German nation". O.G.S.'

[9] No. 272. A marginal note by Mr. Sargent here reads: 'It may be a clear warning but it does not emanate from the German Govt and Hitler in his present explanations remains entirely silent on the question of Colonies and Mandates in spite of the opening we had given him for raising it. O.G.S.'

*Point 3* of Herr Hitler's speech deals with the Locarno Treaty and the Demilitarised Zone. That matter is being dealt with separately in connexion with the recent German communication;[10] but we may note that Berlin telegram No. 222 specially excepts [*sic*] 'the (Treaty) provisions regarding the Demilitarised Zone' from the articles which Germany has disavowed by her own action: if therefore it is to disappear as a condition of Germany's return to Geneva, that must be 'peaceable understanding'.

*Point 4* of the speech deals with Germany's readiness 'to take part in a system of collective co-operation to secure peace in Europe', provided allowance is made 'for the possibility of the revision of Treaties. . . .[6] Suppression of any necessary changes is only too liable to result in an explosion in the future'. We decided not to question Herr Hitler on what he meant by his 'system of collective co-operation', and it is clear from the replies now received that it would have been useless to do so. This 'system' must presumably be taken to refer to the bilateral non-aggression pacts and the air pact; there does not seem to be anything else.

The reference to 'an explosion in the future' is very striking when read in connexion with his remarks about change 'by means of peac[e]able understandings', helped in fact by a display of tremendous force on the part of Germany.

*Point 5* of the speech is of no immediate interest other than the obvious reference which it contains to the impracticability of the simultaneity of the London Declaration of February 3rd.

*Point 6* refers to the non-aggression pacts, in respect of which a Franco-Russian initiative is expected. This is confirmed by Berlin telegram No. 222; and we are in communication with Paris on the subject. No further comment is necessary.

*Point 7* is the air pact, which is being dealt with separately.[11]

*Point 8* raises (*a*) the German air strength and air limitation. Our enquiry has not cleared up the figure at which the German Government put the French first-line strength in France and North Africa and therefore the figure at which they are aiming. But this matter is being raised in a memorandum which Lord Londonderry is circulating to the Cabinet.[12]

(*b*) The effectives of the German army. Berlin telegram No. 222 shows that the German Government do not believe in the possibility of quanti[ta]tive reduction although Berlin telegram No. 223 reports Herr von Bülow's statement that 'German Government would be prepared to reduce the 550,000 figure if other powers were to make similar reductions in their figures existing on March 16th'. This is rather a queer statement, for on March 16th, though the French two-year service law was passed it had not naturally been carried into effect; but we must presumably suppose that the Germans are not now asking for 550,000 men only on condition that the French maintain one-year service.

(*c*) The navy is being dealt with separately.[13]

---

[10] Cf. No. 253, note 2.    [11] See, e.g., No. 263.
[12] No. 275.    [13] See, e.g., No. 282 below.

We did not ask for any explanation on the remaining points; but for convenience they are summarised below.

In *point 9*, comes the suggestion for the prohibition of the throwing of inflammable gas or explosive bombs outside the real fighting zone as a preliminary to a more general limitation of bombing etc.; and this is followed in *point 10* by a declaration of readiness to abolish 'first of all the heaviest artillery and secondly the heaviest tanks'; and in *point 11*, of readiness to agree 'to any limitation of the size of guns, battleships, cruisers and torpedo boats', and 'to agree to the limitation of the tonnage of submarines', and 'for their complete abolition in the event of an international agreement to this effect', and to agree 'to any international limitation of arms or abolition of arms'.

*Points 12 and 13* are concerned with non-intervention (i.e. in Austria), and it is stated that 'the German Government are ready at any time to agree to an international arrangement which effectively puts an end to all interference from outside or[14] other States', but 'such a regulation must be internationally effective, and must benefit all States', (this is a new condition), and 'it appears necessary to define the term interference ac[c]urately and internationally'. The reference to Austria in Part II of the speech is supplemented in Part I by the statement that 'Germany has neither the intention nor the will to intervene in the internal affairs of Austria or to annex Austria or to conclude an "Anschlus[s]".' Is this latter statement qualified by the remark that 'the German people and the German Government have a natural desire that the right of self-determination should be granted not only to foreign peoples, but also to the German people everywhere'? Is there a further qualification to the effect that Herr Hitler does not believe that 'the out and out German nationalist people in Europe can be denationalised at a time like this when the principle of nationality is so robust'?

[14] In the 'approved translation' (see No. 222, note 1) this passage read: 'which will effectively prevent and render impossible all attempts to interfere from outside in the affairs of other States.'

## No. 279

*Letter from the Marquess of Londonderry to Sir J. Simon*
[*C 4533/55/18*]

Secret                                    AIR MINISTRY, *June 1, 1935*

My dear Secretary of State,

I want to bring to your notice a discrepancy which exists between the figures of the French first-line aircraft as quoted in telegram No. 96[1] dated 24th May, 1935, from Paris and the last official French figures given to the Air Ministry by the French Air Attaché in London on the 15th February, 1935, which we have used as the basis of all our calculations lately.

[1] No. 243.

Summarised, the difference between these figures is as follows:—

| | New figures (Telegram No. 96 of 24.5.35). | Previous figures (Obtained officially from the French). | Difference |
|---|---|---|---|
| 1. In France & N. Africa (includes Autonomous Naval Air Force). | 1528 | 1269 | +259 |
| 2. Levant and Colonies. | 176 | 150 | + 26 |
| 3. Naval Co-operation (embarked). | 73 | 74 | − 1 |
| 4. Naval Co-operation (shore-based). | 163 | 108 | + 55 |
| Totals | 1940 | 1601 | +339 |

I should perhaps mention that the Naval co-operation figures were not included in the French Air Attaché's statement of the 15th February, 1935, but have been calculated on the best data available.

As you know, our only source of information regarding the French is through diplomatic channels: this we have found to be extremely inconsistent. De[s]pite the fact that the French have invariably told us that they have no intention of increasing their first-line strength, a number of new tactical units have been added since they first declared their total strength in 1930, but up to the present no increase has been admitted in the total. As a consequence of these manipulations no combination of figures within the grand total supplied by them has ever been the same twice.

You will doubtless have seen the report of the conversation between our Air Attaché in Paris and Colonel Duvernoy of the French Air Ministry,[2] which sheds a good deal of light on the figures supplied on 24th May. It seems clear that the strengths claimed are no more than prospective and that they have been deliberately pitched high on account of the apparent German intention to outbuild them.

I think you can take it that the figure for Metropolitan France and North Africa which we have previously given to you (1404) is still a very fair approximation of the present position.

I am sending a copy of this letter to the Prime Minister.[3]

[2] Cf. No. 275, paragraph 4.

[3] A minute by Mr. Creswell reads: 'Air Ministry have since heard once more from the French—and the result is that even this new list of figures is inaccurate. Ld. Londonderry's main point however still remains true; the programme now announced by the French is no more than a prospective one for the future. The present figures are very different, and very probably far below even those in the second column within. M. J. Creswell. 6/vi.'

## No. 280

*Sir J. Simon to Sir E. Phipps (Berlin)*
*No. 119 Telegraphic [C 4405/206/18]*

FOREIGN OFFICE, *June 3, 1935, 9.5 p.m.*

Following for Naval Attaché
From D[irector of] N[aval] I[ntelligence]

Your RS. G. 66/35 of 28th May.[1] Make it perfectly clear that the seven year programme you sketched out is merely illustrative and is not based on any views held by Admiralty of which you are unaware. For your own information Admiralty will press for a considerably longer period. Policy you must adopt now is to say nothing further in connection with disarmament talks as situation changes continually and it is impossible for you to keep in step with developments. Ends.

[1] Enclosure 1 in No. 271.

## No. 281

*Memorandum on the degree of secrecy to be maintained during the Anglo-German naval conversations*[1]

*[A 5223/22/45]*

FOREIGN OFFICE, *June 3, 1935*

The Secretary of State asked me to record the following for your consideration and views.

When Herr von Ribbentrop saw Sir John at 4 o'clock this afternoon he said that in his view the discussions which are about to commence should be kept secret from other governments. The Secretary of State said that naturally no course should be followed as regards this matter which was not mutually agreed, to which Herr von Ribbentrop at once interposed 'Then you agree in principle with what I have suggested?' The Secretary of State refused, however, to be taken as committing himself even in principle and said that it was a matter which would require consideration. After all, he added, general agreement has to be reached sometime and you can only hope to get agreement if everybody knows what the position is.

From what Sir John said to me I gathered that he is, to say the least of it, doubtful whether such secrecy *vis-à-vis* other governments should be a *sine quâ non* of the discussions, though, of course, where in the course of the discussions confidence is specially requested it will be observed. The Secretary of State is rather inclined at first sight to suspect in Herr von Ribbentrop's suggestion a manoeuvre the effects of which would be somewhat like that of Herr von Hoesch's recent suggestion that it was for us, and not for the Germans to communicate to the other interested Powers the German draft

[1] This memorandum, prepared by Mr. P. Mason, Assistant Private Secretary to Sir J. Simon, was addressed to Mr. Craigie.

of an air pact:[2] in other words, an attempt to represent these conversations as a specific Anglo-German push rather to the exclusion of other countries.

[2] Cf. No. 259.

## No. 282

### Note on Agenda for Anglo-German Naval Discussions[1]
### [A 5099/22/45]

June 3, 1935

It is proposed that we should make an introductory statement in general terms in regard to such matters as procedure, the results of the recent conversations with other Powers and our own proposals for future naval limitation. Thereafter it is proposed to go into the matter in more detail, taking first qualitative limitation, as to which there is not likely to be much divergence of view between the Germans and ourselves.

When we come to the question of quantitative limitation it will be necessary to place the German representatives in possession of some facts in regard to the future strength of the British Empire Fleet. They may ask for something more up-to-date than the London Naval Treaty figures in order to compute their 35 per cent.[2] In this case it is proposed to give them the strength of the minimum British Empire Fleet necessary for security, see Annex 3 of N.C.M. (35) 48,[3] with the exception that for capital ships and cruisers, numbers only would be given because tonnages depend on the qualitative limits finally decided upon (see Annex 4 to this paper). In this connection it is desirable to talk to the Germans, especially as regards capital ships, in terms of numbers rather than tonnages, so as to avoid, if possible, their building a larger number of smaller capital ships which would be unwelcome to us.

As a further request the German representatives may ask for our proposed building programme in exchange for theirs, in which case it is proposed to give the tentative programme which was handed to the United States and Japanese representatives, and which is subject to amendment when we know the requirements of the European Powers (see Annex 4).

With reference to the British building programme handed to the Pacific Naval Powers, the Admiralty wish to point out that, quite possibly, we may be faced with a German building programme in the capital ship category which may necessitate a more rapid replacement of the British Battle Fleet than has been visualised in the above programme.

The Germans at present have three *Deutschlands*, a type of capital ship which, although small, cannot be opposed by existing cruisers. We believe

[1] This note was circulated by direction of the Secretary of State for Foreign Affairs and the First Lord of the Admiralty: it was numbered N.C.M.(35)42.

[2] *Note in original*: 'It should be realised that if the German Government calculated their 35 per cent tonnage category by category, and not on total tonnage, their capital ships quota will be equal to that allowed to France by Washington Treaty.'

[3] See No. 118.

that, in addition, they have on the stocks two further enlarged *Deutschlands* of 20,000 tons or over. A 35 per cent. ratio of the British tonnage in the capital ship category based on a qualitative limit of 25,000 tons will permit of the Germans laying down two further capital ships of the maximum size.

When the programme under consideration is completed, we shall be faced with the German Battle Fleet of seven ships, of which four may be of the most powerful type allowed, and, in addition, the Japanese may have completed four new capital ships (if they are content with the programme suggested by Admiral Yamamoto). This is a total of eight new large capital ships plus three *Deutschlands*, against which the British tentative programme will only produce six. It will be seen therefore that under these conditions it may be essential for the Admiralty to recommend a more rapid increase in the replacement of the British Battle Fleet, in order to ensure that *in new ships* the British Fleet does not fall behind the capital ship strength of Japan and Germany combined.

If the Germans agree to negotiate on the basis of construction figures rather than of ratios, their proposals may involve either (*a*) a slow and gradual increase in their present figure so as to obtain their ultimate objective, whatever that may be, in, say, twelve to fifteen years; or (*b*) a rapid reconstruction of their fleet so as to secure their full objective by, say, 1942; or (*c*) some variant between these two extremes. On the whole, (*b*) is unlikely because of the difficulty of adequately training personnel in so short a time.

If we find the Germans in a reasonable frame of mind we shall try to convince them of the advantages, from their own point of view, of 'hastening slowly' in this matter (see Annex 2 below). If we find them unreasonable and determined that their new construction shall follow a steep upward curve, then we should have to warn them that their attitude will, in our opinion, render impossible any further quantitative limitation of naval armaments.

If in the future there is to be a free field of competition for all, the Germans will find it more difficult to catch up with competing nations in naval armaments than in land or air armaments and they have therefore, to our mind, a definite interest in promoting the conclusion of a naval limitation agreement which leaves them scope for a gradual increase in their present naval strength. This, and the fact that the Germans do not apparently wish definitely to alienate this country at present, are the best levers which we can use with them.

Until we know what the German demands are to be it is hardly feasible to suggest detailed limits for future German naval construction or to say what is the maximum German construction which France and Italy are likely to agree to without any modification of their present tentative programmes, which have not yet been communicated to us. It is clear that our own original tentative figure of a German fleet of 178,000 tons[4] is now completely out of date.

Presumably Herr Hitler will insist on his 35 per cent., which would eventually give him a fleet of some 430,000 tons. It would be unwise to make

[4] Cf. No. 211, note 2.

a frontal attack on this declared objective and preferable to concentrate on persuading the Germans to moderate the rate at which they will seek to achieve this new objective. Much may happen in, say, eight years.

Attached below will be found the agenda for the meetings with the German Representatives (an expurgated version of which will be handed to them at the first meeting), together with two confidential annexes showing the line which it is proposed should be taken by the British Representatives (*a*) in explaining our own proposals and (*b*) in answering the German proposals for a 35 per cent. fleet.

### AGENDA FOR NAVAL DISCUSSIONS WITH REPRESENTATIVES OF THE GERMAN GOVERNMENT

*Procedure at Meetings.*

1. Suggestion that proceedings should be as informal as possible. Each side will presumably keep its own notes of what passes, but propose that we should only attempt an agreed record of any conclusions that may be reached from time to time. Suggestion that we should first outline the general position as we see it and give results of recent conversations with other Powers, and that German representatives should ask questions as we go along. No communiqué to be issued to the press, but agreement should be reached after each meeting as to what is to be said to the press (the minimum possible).

2. Explanation of the necessity of holding a Five-Power Conference under the terms of the Treaties of Washington[5] and London.[6] Suggestions for holding a later general Conference (N.C.M. (35) 48, paragraphs 1–3). Importance which we attach to preventing a renewal of unrestricted naval competition.

3. Outline of the results so far reached in conversations with the United States of America, Japan, France and Italy, and of the deductions to be drawn therefrom (N.C.M. (35) 48, paragraph 4 and paragraphs 9–11).

4. Explanation of the building programmes proposal now under consideration, and of the general structure of our proposals for the further limitation of naval armament. (See Annex 1.)

5. Bearing of proposals in paragraph 4 on German proposal for a ratio of 35 per cent. of the British fleet. (See Annex 2.)

6. Qualitative limitation. Its importance and suitability for universal application. Qualitative limits proposed by the British Government (Annex 3) and the attitude of other Powers thereto (N.C.M. (35) 48, paragraphs 9–17). What are the German views? Discuss under the following headings:—

(*a*) Capital ships. (The present position as regards building.)
(*b*) Aircraft carriers.
(*c*) Cruisers.
(*d*) Destroyers.
(*e*) Submarines.

[5] Of February 6, 1922.    [6] Of April 22, 1930.

*Quantitative Limitation.*

7. Suggestion that future negotiations should be on the basis of the British proposals for declarations of programme, to take the place of the former system of ratios. What, on this basis, would be German programme of construction up to 1942? (In exchange, we must be prepared to hand in our own tentative figures (Annex 4).)

8. Mutual notification of all information relating to laying down and characteristics of new ships.

9. Other minor provisions:—

(*a*) Preparation of merchant ships in time of peace for conversion to warlike purposes. (Washington Treaty, Article XIV.)

(*b*) Prohibition of the use of vessels of war building for other Powers. (Washington Treaty, Article XVII.)

(*c*) Prohibition of transfer of vessels of war from one Power to another. (Washington Treaty, Article XVIII.)

(*d*) Definitions of category limits and age limits and standard tonnage. (See British Draft Disarmament Convention,[7] [Section II] Chapter 2, Annex I.)

ANNEX 1 TO No. 282

### Summary of British Proposals

Proposals which it is suggested should be put forward to the German naval representatives:—

1. Negotiation of a general international convention which would deal with qualitative limitation, notification of the characteristics of new vessels and of the dates on which they are laid down, preparation of merchant ships in time of war [peace] for conversion to warlike purposes and other minor provisions contained in the Washington Naval Treaty.

2. Elimination from any future naval treaty of any figures which constitute, or might have the appearance of constituting, a ratio of naval strength between the signatory Powers.

3. Negotiation of an understanding between the naval Powers in regard to the form and substance of declarations to be issued by each Power indicating its programme of construction during the years 1937–42. (In the case of Germany it will be necessary also to know with precision what she proposes to lay down in the years 1935–36.) These declarations would not be in treaty form, but it would be agreed between the parties issuing them that the building programmes would be adhered to unless one year's notice of any change had been given in advance by one or other of the Powers issuing a declaration.

4. Insertion in the Treaty of a provision formally recognising the equality of national status of each signatory of the new treaty, irrespective of the size of its navy.

[7] Of March 16, 1933.

*Confidential*

*Comments on Herr Hitler's proposal for a German Fleet limited to 35 per cent. of the British Fleet*

The opportunity might first be taken to state that we know that Herr Hitler's recognition of the special need of the British Empire to possess a relatively strong fleet has been very much appreciated by His Majesty's Government. As regards, however, the actual proposal for a 35 per cent. ratio, it will be seen that, in our considered judgment, no progress is likely to be made in these negotiations if we attempt to lay down a definite relationship of strength between the various navies. We hope, therefore, that the German Representatives will see their way to negotiate with us on the new basis of the declaration of programmes of construction rather than on the basis of a ratio. There is one general comment we should, however, like to make on this question of a 35 per cent. ratio. Put forward in its present form, we believe that the German plan is likely to lead to an acceleration of French, Russian and Italian building, which in turn might influence American and Japanese building, with the result that all Powers would be worse off financially without Germany having in fact attained the ratio she demands. Everything seems to us, therefore, to depend on the rate of German construction during the next few years, i.e., the rate at which she decides to achieve a given objective. If the upward curve of construction is to be steep, the political reaction in other continental countries is bound to be bad and the effects prejudicial—if not fatal—to hopes of future limitation. If, on the other hand, the upward curve is to be gradual and steady, it may well be possible to bring about international agreement over the period we have in view without any sacrifice of Germany's wish for a reasonable increase in the size of her present fleet. The question is not so much whether 35 per cent. of the British fleet is a reasonable percentage—on this there may be different opinions—but whether, supposing Germany desires to co-operate in bringing about a limitation agreement, she would be wise to progress too precipitately from her present figure of 10 per cent. of the British fleet to a figure of 35 per cent.

ANNEX 3 TO NO. 282

*Table showing British Proposals for Qualitative Limits*

| Class of Ship | Maximum Individual Tonnage. Tons. | Maximum Calibre of Largest Gun. | Remarks. |
|---|---|---|---|
| Capital ship | 25,000 | 12-in. | |
| Aircraft Carrier | 22,000 | 6·1-in. | |
| Cruisers Category (a) | 10,000 | 8-in. | No further construction of this type. |
| Cruisers Category (b) | 7,000 | 6·1-in. | |
| Destroyers | 1,850 | 5·1-in. | } Not more than a certain percentage |
| | 1,500 | 5·1-in. | } of vessels to be of the larger type. |
| Submarines | 2,000 | 5·1-in. | Failing abolition or agreement of 250 tons as maximum size. |

The underage British Commonwealth fleet, to which, subject to the Building programmes of foreign Powers, it is intended to build is:—

| | |
|---|---|
| Capital Ships | 15 ships |
| Cruisers | 60 ships |
| Aircraft Carriers | 110,000 tons |
| Destroyers | 150,000 tons |
| Submarines | 40,000 tons |

The following tentative British building programme was communicated to the United States of America and Japan in the autumn of 1934 during the preliminary negotiations preparatory to the 1935 Conference. This programme is based on the naval situation in the Pacific Ocean and may require modification when the programmes of European Powers are known.

Tonnage to be laid down between the 1st January, 1937, and the 31st December, 1942:—

| | |
|---|---|
| Capital Ships | 6 ships |
| Aircraft Carriers | 44,000 tons |
| Cruisers | 18 ships |
| Destroyers | 37,500 tons |
| Submarines | 17,500 tons |

On completion of the ships in this programme by 1943–45, the British underage fleet will be:—

| | |
|---|---|
| Capital Ships | 15 ships[8] |
| Aircraft Carriers | 111,500 tons |
| Cruisers | 53 ships |
| Destroyers | 150,000 tons |
| Submarines | 40,740 tons |

[8] *Note in original*: 'Including 6 ships overage.'

## No. 283

*Memorandum by Mr. Creswell on Limitation of Air Force Strengths*

[*C 4659/55/18*]

FOREIGN OFFICE, *June 3, 1935*

Convertible civil aircraft, and disparities in industrial capacity, are difficulties which are likely to confuse any negotiations which may be undertaken to limit the strength of air forces. It may be useful to consider them before the issue of limitation really comes to the fore. They were mentioned in the House of Commons on May 31st by Mr. Winston Churchill, who said:—[1]

'When you have first-line air strength which may be limited by agreement, and when you have to consider the relations of that first-line air strength and the manufacturing capacity on the one hand, and a vast

[1] See 302 *H.C. Deb.* 5 *s.*, col. 1491.

civil aviation on the other hand, it is clear that the task of reaching an agreed limitation of air armaments will be attended with almost super-human difficulties in the present state and circumstances of the world.'

2. If there is some prospect of negotiating a limited parity of first-line strengths between the four principal Locarno Powers, there is probably none whatever of arriving at an agreement which will cover such imponderabilia as the manufacturing capacity and the war potential of the aircraft industries of the different countries, and very little prospect of limiting the number of convertible civil aircraft in the possession of each. The existence therefore of these factors, which may in themselves constitute the criterion of real air parity or disparity will probably only influence the issue by making those countries which are relatively weak in these respects less inclined to accept a limitation of first-line strengths alone, and by introducing complication into the work of supervision. (Supervision will be complicated by the existence of a civil air fleet of great offensive potentialities, and by the varying sizes of reserves, which themselves depend upon disparities in manufacturing capacity).

3. Disinclination to accept a first-line limitation is not a question which can be examined here, except in so far as to say that for the reason given above the country which would be least disinclined to accept first-line limitation should be Germany, while for other reasons (since she is without any limitation at all rapidly outbuilding the other powers) she may be expected to be more and not less opposed to such an agreement than the other powers. This question, also, falsifies the hypothesis on which this memorandum is based, which is that such a first-line limitation is possible.

4. *Civil Aviation.* The importance of civil aviation will obviously become proportionately less as the number of the first-line force increases. The existence of 200 machines immediately-convertible to bombers will be very important when the first-line is limited to 500 machines; it will be less im-portant with a first-line of 1,000, and almost negligible in a force of 2,000. At present the probability seems to be that a figure of not less than 1,500 machines will be the first-line parity, and if the optimism of the Air Ministry is justified in setting the number of German immediately-convertible machines at 200, this may not appear to present much of a problem.

But even if the still greater optimism of the Air Ministry in assuming that this number of machines is not at present increasing, is also justified, it seems likely that as soon as a first-line limitation has been achieved and the German Air Force has reached that figure, Germany will forthwith equip her whole civil airline fleet (at present some 600 machines) with machines of an immediately-convertible type; they will thus increase their powers of aggression (for such machines would be all medium or heavy bombers and none of them defensive fighters) by 80 per cent (assuming the German Air Force to consist of bombers and other aircraft in equal proportions which is believed at present to be the case). If it is borne in mind that these machines can be converted for bomb-carrying in as little as two hours, it will be seen that this force can be sent off in attack very shortly after the machines of the regular air force. They could in fact, if an offensive were decided upon at midnight, and even if no conversion had taken place beforehand, reach London by dawn (at most times of the year). This force therefore does present a very considerable problem.

6. It would be most undesirable to try to limit the number of machines which a country might have for entirely legitimate civilian uses, merely because they might be misused in war time; nor is it practicable to restrict the degree of 'convertibility'. It appears that there are only two useful ways of attacking this problem.

(a) by insisting on each country declaring the number of machines in regular use on air lines, and if possible introducing a system of 'auto-limitation' on this basis.

(b) by each country seeing to it that its own air line machines are sufficiently numerous and efficient to represent an equal force to that of the country whose aggression is feared. It is improbable that this would degenerate into a mere race in outbuilding owing to the obvious necessities of civil air transport.

7. There can be little doubt that Germany is using militarily more efficient machines on her air-lines than are we or the French, (she uses extremely efficient heavy and medium bombers on the Luft Hansa notably a Junker and a Hinkel [sic] type) but we have several civil types which would make satisfactory medium bombers, though no doubt below the necessary standard in their defensive qualities. (There are certain Airspeed, Avro and De Havilland types which appear suitable, and the latter two are actually being put into experimental use in the Royal Air Force for coastal reconnaissance). It would surely not be difficult or expensive to perfect a form of fitment for bomb-stowage for these standard civil types which could be rapidly fitted.

8. *Manufacturing Capacity.* Although this is the final criterion of air power in time of war, in time of peace it is really only one aspect of the question of reserves; for it is evident that a country which can put its industry on a war basis in two months will need only half as many reserve aircraft as a country which takes four months to get war production in full swing. It is likely that any attempt to bring in the question of reserves into an air limitation agreement of which supervision forms an important part will lead to great difficulties; our own Air Ministry for example may be expected to resist such a proposal.

9. It is suggested that, since reserves and industrial capacity form in this way part of one question and since it is very difficult to devise some method of limiting or controlling the latter, which would in any case be undesirable, it would also be more logical to leave the size of reserves completely outside a limitation agreement. This would facilitate the acceptance of supervision, which would only be necessary for organised squadrons (including auxiliaries) and for civil machines engaged on regular services (as suggested above). And this would not necessarily mean that the whole agreement would become a hollow sham, for each country would have the strong incentive of

economy as well as that of military advantage in organising its industry on lines of quick expansion, rather than to amass a large reserve of constantly obsolescent types of aircraft.[2]

[2] In a minute of June 8, addressed to Sir S. Hoare (cf. No. 304 below, note 10), Sir R. Vansittart wrote as follows: 'I hope you will give your serious consideration to this paper. Mr. Creswell has greatly distinguished himself during his time in the F.O. by his papers on aviation, and is himself a very competent aviator.

'I have always maintained that we must limit at a high figure or we shall certainly be swindled. This paper bears out that view. In the existing spirit in Germany we shall almost certainly be swindled anyhow, but that will matter less if, besides limiting at a high figure, we fulfil the second requisite of close relations with the powers that are not dangerous. When the incontestable spirit now prevailing in Germany abates, we may be able to reconsider this view; not a day before. Till then we must call a spade a spade, and regard limitation very largely in the light of a requisite for internal consumption. We must never assume that the ice bears before we are quite sure.

'As to the question of civil aviation, the Air Ministry are off again playing ostrich and maintaining simply that it doesn't count. Our own press & the French will never allow us to get away with that, & they will be right. So I hope we shan't try. I think, however, that we may expect the Air Ministry to govern its hitherto ungovernable, and invariably erroneous, optimism more successfully in the hands of Sir Philip Cunliffe-Lister [cf. *ibid.*]. There will most certainly have to be some provision on this head, if we are to escape the charge of fooling the public—though the real answer is to develop our own civil aviation and to use easily convertible types like the Germans. R.V. June 8.'

Sir S. Hoare, who had been Secretary of State for Air, October 1922–January 1924 and November 1924–June 1929, remarked: 'British civil aviation policy has always run counter to the idea that we should consider military needs in designing civil machines. I should myself be sorry to see this policy—that I myself laid down when I formed the Imperial Airways Co.—changed. I believe that it is far better *and cheaper* to build military machines and to organize them in squadrons than to rely on unorganized hybrid civil machines for military raids. S.H. 14/6.'

## No. 284

*Sir E. Phipps (Berlin) to Sir J. Simon (Received June 4, 11.30 a.m.)*
*No. 229 Telegraphic: by telephone [C 4468/206/18]*

BERLIN, *June 4, 1935*

In a short leader on the Naval conversations, to-day's Volkischer Beobachter quotes passages from the Chancellor's Reichstag speech[1] to the effect that Germany recognises British superiority at sea and does not propose ever to increase the demands which she is now putting forward. It is clear, the article continues, that only Herr Hitler can decide what size the German fleet is to be and how it is to be employed in order to ensure the necessary defence of Germany's 1500 kilometre coast line. There has been a tendency in the Foreign press recently to discuss the effect of the German demands on the strength of the British fleet and how the German Navy is to be employed. These discussions are superfluous and may even be an attempt to prejudice the forthcoming negotiations.

[1] On May 21.

## No. 285

*Sir E. Phipps (Berlin) to Sir J. Simon (Received June 4, 8.15 p.m.)*
*No. 230 Telegraphic [C 4484/206/18]*

BERLIN, *June 4, 1935, 7.8 p.m.*

Your telegram No. 119.[1]
Following for Director of Naval Intelligence from Naval Attaché.

I made it perfectly clear at interview that programme outlined was entirely unofficial and only illustrative of how a programme could be made out in order to show that it was not so difficult as liaison officer seemed to imagine. I also made it clear that both periods of years and numbers of ships were entirely imaginary. I will repeat this at Marineleitung at once. Regret I should have given you impression that a definite programme had been suggested.

[1] No. 280.

## No. 286

*Sir G. Clerk (Paris) to Sir J. Simon (Received June 5, 8.30 a.m.)*
*No. 111 Saving: Telegraphic [C 4485/55/18]*

PARIS, *June 4, 1935*

My despatch No. 784.[1]
On enquiry at the Ministry for Foreign Affairs today, I was informed that the French reply to the German enquiry regarding the effects of the Franco-Soviet agreement on the Treaty of Locarno was practically complete and that it would be communicated to us in sufficient time in advance of its delivery at Berlin to enable you to express your views.

[1] No. 264.

## No. 287

*Sir G. Clerk (Paris) to Sir J. Simon (Received June 5, 8.30 a.m.)*
*No. 112 Saving: Telegraphic [C 4480/55/18]*

PARIS, *June 4, 1935*

My telegram No. 102,[1] paragraph 2.
The Ministry for Foreign Affairs informed me today that they had still not received from the German government the text of the German draft for the air pact.

[1] No. 268.

## No. 288

*Sir G. Clerk (Paris) to Sir J. Simon (Received June 5, 8.30 a.m.)*
*No. 113 Saving: Telegraphic [C 4481/55/18]*

PARIS, *June 4, 1935*

My telegram No. 100[1] and Sir E. Phipps' telegram No. 226.[2]

Ministry for Foreign Affairs informed me today, in regard to the Eastern Pact negotiations, that the Soviet government had been so incensed by Herr Hitler's speech that they were no longer willing to make the first move in approaching Berlin, but wished the French government to do so.

2. The Ministry have since communicated to me the text of a note[3] which was handed to the German Ambassador yesterday in reply to Baron von Neurath's note of April 12th indicating the conditions which the German government regarded as a basis for an Eastern Pact.[4] The French note, text of which goes by bag,[5] states that the French government also regard these conditions (subject to certain points being cleared up) as constituting a basis for agreement and invites the German government to indicate what they consider to be the best means of proceeding with the question.

[1] No. 265.  [2] No. 277.
[3] For an English translation of this French note of June 3, see *D.G.F.P.*, Series C, vol. iv, No. 127; cf. *ibid.*, No. 129.  [4] Cf. Volume XII, Nos. 715 and 719.
[5] Received on June 5 as enclosure in Paris despatch No. 813, not printed.

## No. 289

*Notes of the first meeting between representatives of the United Kingdom and Germany, June 4, 1935, at 10 a.m.*[1]

Present: *United Kingdom*: Sir J. Simon, Mr. R. L. Craigie, Vice-Admiral C. J. C. Little, Captain V. H. Danckwerts, Mr. P. H. Gore-Booth.
*Germany*: Herr von Ribbentrop, Rear-Admiral K. G. Schuster, Captain E. Wassner, Korvetten Kapitan H. Kiderlen, Dr. Kordt (Secretary), Dr. Schmidt (Interpreter).
*Secretary*: Commander J. Hughes-Hallett (Admiralty).[2]

Opening the meeting, SIR JOHN SIMON said he was glad to have this opportunity of meeting the German naval representatives and of wishing them every success in the discussions in which they were about to engage. Apart from one commercial mission,[3] this was the first occasion for many years on which an official German mission had come to England and it was

[1] The meeting was held at the Foreign Office. These notes were compiled by the British representatives and circulated as N.C.(G) 1st Mtg. *Most Secret*. For the record made by the German representatives see *D.G.F.P.*, Series C, vol. iv, pp. 253–62.
[2] Commander Hughes-Hallett also acted as secretary at the four following Anglo-German meetings on June 4, 5, 6, and 7 (see Nos. 290, 304, 311, and 318 below); at the remaining meetings the secretary was Commander A. W. Clarke.
[3] In November 1924 a German delegation had taken part in discussions in London which resulted in the signing, on December 2, of an Anglo-German Commercial Treaty; for the text see *B.F.S.P.*, vol. 119, pp. 369 ff.

therefore all the more important that they should make a good beginning and be able to say at the end that the talks had really served the purpose for which they had been designed. That these conversations would start with a friendly feeling prevailing on both sides was guaranteed by the cordial references to the British Nation and to the special needs of the British Empire for an adequate naval strength which had been made in the Reich Chancellor's speech of the 21st May.[4] These references to British naval needs, to the desire for friendly relations between the two countries and to Germany's intention not to embark on any naval rivalry, had been greatly appreciated, not only by His Majesty's Government, but in general by public opinion in Great Britain. Sir John Simon felt that if the discussions were conducted in this spirit there would be every hope of a successful issue.

He noted further that Herr Hitler, in his speech, had stated that the German navy would be limited to 35 per cent of the British navy and that this would be Germany's final and lasting demand. British experience of naval discussions, which had been a somewhat prolonged and difficult one, had led to the belief that little further progress could be expected in the quantitative limitation of naval armaments if they were to continue the attempt to establish definite proportions or relationships between the various navies. The reasons which had led to this conclusion would be explained to the German delegates in detail by the British representatives and also some suggestions for circumventing what was a very real and serious difficulty. He felt sure that the German representatives would give careful and sympathetic consideration to any suggestions which might be made on this particular point.

Judging by their experience in the conversations which had taken place with representatives of other naval Powers, progress was more likely to be rapid in this very technical and complicated subject if these talks were conducted in the first instance between experts on the two sides. The first thing they had to do was to exchange fully and frankly their information on this subject and their views as to the future. At the same time, he and his colleagues would, of course, watch the progress of the conversations very carefully and Ministers would be available for consultation should any questions arise in the course of these discussions between experts which rendered such consultation desirable. In the meantime, Sir John Simon wished the delegates every success in the task which lay before them.

On behalf of the German Government, HERR VON RIBBENTROP thanked the British Government for their invitation to the Naval Conversations, and also Sir John Simon in particular for his kind words. The German representatives reciprocated his feelings. He said that speaking on behalf of his Naval colleagues, he was sure they were glad of the opportunity, after so many years, of again meeting distinguished British Naval Officers.

The German Government believed that these meetings would help to further the common aim of both their Governments, which was to prevent a naval armaments race.

[4] Cf. No. 222.

But in order to create the conditions for success, he felt it right, before entering into any discussion, to make these observations:—

(1) In his speech, Herr Hitler had said that the German Government denounced the Treaty of Versailles because of the discrimination, unlimited in time, which it had imposed. By this action, Germany had re-established her equality.

(2) The necessity of protecting German maritime interests on the one hand, and the recognition of the British maritime position on the other, had led to the acceptance of a 35 per cent ratio of Naval strength to Great Britain. But this had only been accepted because in their minds Great Britain was excluded for ever as a possible enemy. The declaration of the Naval ratio was therefore of great historical importance.

(3) The German Delegation attached very great importance to the success of these conversations, and could only enter them if the British would recognise the 35 per cent ratio as fixed and unalterable. Would the British Delegation please confirm this?

The advantages of an agreement could not be over-estimated. It would exclude the harmful effects of Naval competition, while at the same time securing Great Britain's special position, and fulfilling Germany's requirements for defence. The possession of Colonies by Germany would not alter the ratio.

Herr Hitler had reached certain conclusions years ago; they were twofold:—

(1) The recurrence of war between Great Britain and Germany must be avoided.

(2) Ultimately only by a common attitude towards European problems by Great Britain and Germany could the settlement of those problems be brought about.

If the nucleus of common European interests could once be found, there would follow co-operation to secure the peace of the world, and the security of our culture.

In conclusion, Herr von Ribbentrop said they would find many points of agreement, and these Naval conversations might well constitute progress in the general problem of a European settlement.

SIR JOHN SIMON thanked Herr von Ribbentrop for his statement, and said that at the moment he only wished to make this reflection: there were two things that ought not to be lost sight of:—

(1) We were trying now to prepare the ground for *all round* Naval agreement.

(2) The 35 per cent declaration was a statement of a ratio. It said nothing about quantity, and in these discussions both relative and absolute strength must be considered. The British Empire has absolute needs, and therefore we have to consider actual figures as well as relative.

These two things were very important.

HERR VON RIBBENTROP referred again to the basis which was necessary for any discussions. The conversations would not be possible unless agreement on 35 per cent ratio was accepted. This was not a demand, but a final decision, not liable to alteration. It was therefore necessary for the German Delegation to be quite clear on this point, before they could proceed with the conversations. He had said this in his opening statement, and he was repeating it again now.

With regard to Sir John Simon's reference to the difficulties of ratios, he understood that these might exist, but he thought it must be possible to find a basis in agreed ratios as had been done in the past. Unless they were clear on the basis of the 35 per cent ratio, he saw no hope for success. Once this principle had been established, it would be easy to find a way of meeting any British wishes that might be put forward, and he repeated that he was sure that many points of agreement would be found.

SIR JOHN SIMON said he was afraid he would have to leave the meeting now, as he had an engagement with the Prime Minister. He was not prepared to enter into a general discussion of the ratio question at this stage. It had only been arranged that he should open the meeting, and he regretted that he must withdraw to keep his engagement. He would leave Mr. Craigie to continue the discussion on his behalf. He hoped therefore that Herr von Ribbentrop would excuse him.

(Sir John Simon then left the meeting).

HERR VON RIBBENTROP said he understood Sir John Simon's engagement. Sir John Simon had also pointed out that it was not possible to make agreements at this stage, but rather that such agreements should come at the end. But for the German Delegation the 35 per cent basis was 'unmoveable', and he again repeated that a preliminary agreement on it was essential. He appealed to Mr. Craigie to clear up this point.

MR. CRAIGIE said that the suggestion that the conversations could not proceed until an agreement in principle had been reached was new to the British, and had not been foreseen. There was no precedent, in the conversations that had taken place with other countries, for a condition of this kind being laid down prior to the continuation of the discussions. In fact, the whole purpose of the talks was to preserve perfect freedom on both sides. He thought it best to continue to preserve that freedom of manoeuvre, and to concentrate on an exchange of views, making clear at the same time the views of other Powers.

It was hoped that the present talks would lead to a general agreement, and they should not risk doing something now that might retard the conclusion of a general agreement by upsetting the other Naval Powers.

On the matter of the 35 per cent ratio, if he asked now not to be pressed on the matter it was because he was convinced that no further agreement between the Powers was possible on the basis of ratios. An agreed ratio between two countries would affect all other countries. The difficulty of negotiating on a basis of ratios was insurmountable.

The difference between the German and the British points of view was really one of method, but it went to the root of the matter. We were not asking Germany to limit herself to any particular ratio. (With all countries we have asked that ratios should not be obtruded). If they had a final objective in mind, let each country keep it to themselves. The German Delegation would not wish to prejudice the chances of agreement with other Powers, and he therefore urged them to leave the question of a ratio in abeyance for the time being. These were intended to be talks between experts, and if they were to be frank, it was better that they should be unrestricted. If, after the discussions, the German delegation still wished to lay down a condition it could take the form of a precedent to further formal negotiations. The British Delegation would like first to tell the German Delegation of their experience with other countries, but if it was still desired to revert to the ratio problem, Ministers would be available to consider it.

Mr. Craigie concluded by begging Herr von Ribbentrop to consider these observations very carefully, because Sir John Simon was convinced that to begin by an effort to reach agreement on ratios might prove a false step, likely to make a subsequent general agreement very difficult.

HERR VON RIBBENTROP said that he felt the British Government and the British Delegation's view of the situation was different from that of the German Government and the German Delegation. He could only repeat his opening declaration that the decision of the 35 per cent ratio was the result of most careful consideration, and he was disappointed that the British Government did not understand the necessity for accepting it as a basis.

He asked the British to note the importance of a sovereign power voluntarily limiting its strength to a certain percentage of another Power. But Herr Hitler was a very consistent man, and thought in long historical periods, as a result of which he had fixed this ratio.

He referred to Sir John Simon's observation that conditions should come at the end and not at the beginning, but he wished to make it clear that the Germans had come with the desire to reach a long-term Naval agreement, and to adjust vital interests. The Germans had assumed the 35 per cent ratio was an accepted decision and felt that adjustment could only proceed if this ratio was taken as a basis. He referred to the fact that German military equality was re-established, and that this must be recognised.

He felt that 35 per cent was a good ratio from the point of view of Great Britain, and he hoped that we should see its advantages, because its acceptance was essential to frank discussions. He again reiterated the unshakable [*sic*] nature of the decision on the ratio. Owing to the Versailles restrictions, which had now been repudiated, the German position was very different from that of other countries. Before she could negotiate, she must first establish a basis for equal negotiations, and therefore 35 per cent was not a bargaining point, but was about to be given practical reality. Their task was to say how this could be done, without causing undue disturbance. As a free country, Germany had wished to open the way for agreement and for confidential discussion by accepting this low percentage.

Herr von Ribbentrop therefore asked again what was Great Britain's attitude to the voluntary German invitation to the 35 per cent ratio. He reiterated Germany's determination to give effect to it in practice. If the British Delegation wished to explain their position, he would be glad to listen, but he could not enter into a discussion on the substance of these matters until the principle of a ratio had been accepted. He asked whether the British Delegation would like to consult their Government.

(At this stage the substance of Herr von Ribbentrop's opening statement was handed to the British Delegation as a document, and has been circulated as Annex I to N.C.M. (35) 50.)[5]

MR. CRAIGIE suggested that the Press should not be informed that a document had been handed to the British Delegation. A demand for publication would certainly follow, and this might prejudice the further negotiations.

HERR VON RIBBENTROP, after repeating his desire for free and friendly talks, said he had two proposals of procedure to make:—

(i) With regard to the Press he agreed that nothing should be said of the document, and further that the only communications to be made to the Press should be agreed upon between each side. His experience with the Press in the past had not been happy, and that was why he wished to avoid separate statements being made to them.

(ii) He asked that the British should agree that these talks are bilateral and confidential, and that therefore no communication to third countries should be made, except as might be agreed upon between the two Delegations.

MR. CRAIGIE fully agreed with Herr von Ribbentrop on the subject of the Press, but warned him that the Press would probably make all sorts of unauthorised statements, and he therefore asked for co-operation and mutual trust.

Mr. Craigie said that Herr von Ribbentrop's second point raised a question of some difficulty. In previous discussions it had been understood that a general idea of the course of the discussions should be communicated to other Powers, unless special points had been made in confidence. Undue secrecy would arouse undue suspicion. He therefore suggested that the rule should be that the general substance of the conversations and of any conclusions reached should be communicated to the other Powers at the appropriate moment, but that there should be prior agreement between the two sides as to the actual form and substance of such communications. If any information were given by either side in confidence, that confidence would naturally be respected. His proposal really amounted only to a change of emphasis on, rather than to an amendment of, Herr von Ribbentrop's proposal.

HERR VON RIBBENTROP agreed in principle with Mr. Craigie's proposal, but desired to amend it by saying that the Powers should be informed after the conclusion of the talks, and that they should then receive a guarded communication.

[5] See No. 305 below.

MR. CRAIGIE concurred, with the reservation that if in the course of the conversations it was agreed by both sides that a communication to other Powers should be made, this could be done.

In agreeing to this, HERR VON RIBBENTROP added that the German Government was often blamed in the Press for things for which it was not responsible. He said the Germans did not want to give the impression of great secrecy, but they considered the talks were confidential, and the publication of any details which were liable to misinterpretation should be avoided.

ADMIRAL LITTLE referred to the question of the 35 per cent ratio and said he would speak quite frankly. The Admiralty considered that Herr Hitler's statement was a generous one and had approached the whole subject on that basis, but they had not discussed it with the Cabinet. They were, therefore, taken by surprise at the request for a decision on this point. In the Admiralty's opinion it was unnecessary either to accept or to reject it.

The British Admiralty were as anxious as the German Admiralty to secure limitation at as low a level as possible. But they had found it very difficult to get general agreement on ratios for naval armaments, and at the present moment they were of opinion that it would prove impossible. Agreement by ratios had only once been accomplished, at Washington, and now France and Japan were dissatisfied. The British Government believed that they had found a middle way, which would be explained if the conversations continued.

The British Admiralty thought also that there were forms of limitation which were of great, and perhaps of equal, value as limitation by quantities, but had nothing to do with ratios. If, therefore, the German Delegation were to insist upon an answer to the question of ratio, and if a decision was refused, the two Delegations would be denied the opportunity of finding much other common ground which would help to avoid rivalry, give security, and pave the way to a general agreement.

The problem of equality of status had been raised by other countries besides Germany, and the British Government's 'middle way' would solve this difficulty.

MR. CRAIGIE said that Herr von Ribbentrop had expressed disappointment at the British reaction to Herr Hitler's speech, and at Great Britain not having accepted the proposed ratio at once. The sentiments expressed in Herr Hitler's speech in regard to our Navy had been warmly received in this country, but if the ratio were not accepted at once it was because we believed, from past experience, that to accept it might increase the difficulties of both nations in promoting international agreement.

Herr von Ribbentrop had stated that the ratio was not a proposal but a final decision. Surely therefore, it was not necessary for the British Government specifically to accept it. The mere fact that after hearing the decision, we still desired discussions to continue should be a sufficient answer.

There was one other point: with the other Powers it had always been understood that the objective was not to secure bilateral agreements but to find out whether there was a sufficient prospect of an ultimate *common* agreement to form the basis for a general conference. It would be fatal if a conference once convened were to fail. Therefore, apart from all else, it would be contrary to the method adopted in all previous talks if we started the conversations by an agreement on the ratio between our particular countries.

He was quite ready to adjourn the conversations and to consult higher authority. But at the moment he could see no way out of the difficulty if the German Representatives pressed this point. It was inherent in our proposals (which the German Delegation had not yet heard) that no ratio should be stated. In Mr. Craigie's personal view one of the main causes of dissatisfaction with existing treaties was the fact that the ratio principle had been given such clear and emphatic expression in the Washington Treaty.

He appealed to Herr von Ribbentrop to consider very carefully before pressing us further on this point. He asked him to look at the matter from an international rather than from an Anglo-German point of view. In saying so again, he did not wish to imply that no international agreement was possible on the basis that this ratio might not become an accomplished fact, but merely that if we start by laying it down, we shall prejudice the chances of international agreement.

HERR VON RIBBENTROP repeated that his communication with regard to the 35 per cent ratio was a final decision of the German Government. He noted with satisfaction that Herr Hitler's statement of the ratio had been warmly received in Great Britain.

All the other Powers had built up their Naval requirements, and Germany too was determined to have a navy in conformity with her requirements. She would therefore build up to 35 per cent of the British Navy, no more and no less.

He would like to ask for a formal appreciation by the British Government of Herr Hitler's acceptance of the 35 per cent ratio. This was important, and it was necessary to friendly discussions.

Herr Hitler's great wish was for close confidence between the two navies, and Herr von Ribbentrop reiterated his desire for a formal statement by Great Britain that the declaration limiting the ratio to 35 per cent would rule out future competition between the two Powers.

Referring to Admiral Little's remarks, he said that the Washington Agreement represented a real measure of disarmament. The ratio system could not therefore be so bad as was made out. He still felt that the British attitude to the 35 per cent declaration must be defined more clearly. At the same time he would be glad to listen to any points the British Delegation might wish to lay before them. But Herr Hitler's decision on the ratio must be placed on a higher plane than the discussion of points of detail, and must be regarded as an historic declaration.

ADMIRAL SCHUSTER said that the German Delegation did not insist that the ratio must be agreed upon now for incorporation in a future Treaty. The German Delegation wished the British Delegation to ensure that they would eventually get that percentage, because the German Government could not participate in any conference in which this minimum ratio was not safeguarded. Consequently, the British attitude must be made known.

345

MR. CRAIGIE said he hoped the German Delegation would find after consideration that the British statements had already gone a long way in their direction. The question of ratio could be submitted to higher authority, but it could not be answered by that afternoon. If the conversations were adjourned until the answer was obtained, the effect on the press would be most unfavourable. He therefore suggested that, while this more important question was under consideration, the Delegation should meet again in the afternoon for the British representatives to give an historical outline of the course of the negotiations with other Powers. Meanwhile Ministers would have time to consider the other question.

After a discussion it was agreed that an historical survey should be made in the afternoon, while the ratio question was under consideration elsewhere.

ADMIRAL LITTLE said he thought that Admiral Schuster held the same views as his own. Each country would have its own ideas of the standard of naval strength required for its security and conduct its conversations in the light of that standard. If at the end no agreement was reached, then the position would have to be reconsidered, and it might be necessary to give and take.

HERR VON RIBBENTROP said he feared that there was still misunderstanding between the two Delegations. It would be entirely wrong if the British Government thought that in any future negotiations the 35 per cent ratio could be a matter of 'give and take'.

No bargaining on this point could be accepted. In no case did Herr Hitler, after making a serious decision, change his mind one inch.

It was not so much a matter of a 35 per cent ratio as such, as the feeling that this declaration was not to be considered as a matter for bargaining. He asked the British Government to avail itself of this historic declaration, which would prove of benefit to all. Herr Hitler's offer had been made in the desire to establish closer relations, but it was essential that the British Government should make a reply to it.

It was agreed to inform the Press that the Naval Conversations had opened, with general observations from both sides.

It was agreed to meet again at 4 o'clock.

### No. 290

*Notes of the second meeting between representatives of the United Kingdom and Germany, June 4, 1935, at 4 p.m.*[1]

Present: *United Kingdom*: Mr. R. L. Craigie, Vice-Admiral C. J. C. Little, Captain V. H. Danckwerts.
    *Germany*: Herr von Ribbentrop, Rear-Admiral K. G. Schuster, Captain E. Wassner, Korvetten Kapitan H. Kiderlen, Dr. Kordt, Dr. Schmidt.

HERR VON RIBBENTROP proposed that on account of the invitations the

[1] The meeting was held at the Foreign Office. These notes were circulated as N.C.(G) 2nd Mtg. *Most Secret*. The corresponding record by the German representatives is printed in *D.G.F.P.*, *op. cit.*, pp. 262–5.

German Delegation had received, there should only be one meeting each day from 11 o'clock to 1 o'clock. This would also give time to the Delegation to consider their respective points of view in the afternoon.

MR. CRAIGIE agreed, but suggested 10.30 would be a more suitable time to begin, and this was agreed to.

MR. CRAIGIE said that before opening the British statement there was one question which had occurred to him. Herr Hitler's declaration of the 35 per cent ratio was a decision which was not to be altered. Supposing that certain third Powers increased their strength, but that Great Britain decided not to follow suit by increasing hers, were we to assume that the German strength would still remain at 35 per cent? Would it remain at 35 per cent whatever happened?

HERR VON RIBBENTROP said he would first like to ask another question. 'Does Mr. Craigie, or rather, would it not be His Majesty's Government's policy, that British Naval strength would always be maintained at a certain proportion of that of the other Naval Powers?'

ADMIRAL LITTLE asked if he might take a concrete case. Herr Hitler referring to his 35 per cent ratio had said that the German Fleet would then still be 15 per cent below the French Fleet. That is to say, Herr Hitler had assumed the French Fleet was about 50 per cent of the British. Suppose now that the French Government, on learning that the 35 per cent ratio had been decided upon by the German Government, decided to increase the French ratio to say 70 per cent of the British Fleet—if that occurred, would Germany still be content with 35 per cent of British strength?

HERR VON RIBBENTROP said that as a matter of principle, Herr Hitler held the view that the 100–35 ratio between Great Britain and Germany should be established permanently, and should not be altered. At present the French total tonnage was 50 per cent of the British—therefore Germany was to be 15 per cent below. But Herr Hitler's speech need not be interpreted as accepting permanently an inferiority as compared with the French Navy. If France increased her Navy, such an increase would not be understood by Germany, it would have no reason. On the other hand, no counter-action would necessarily follow from the German side, but this was a point on which Herr von Ribbentrop hoped for an eventual agreement on common action between Great Britain and Germany should France make so unnecessary and senseless an increase.

ADMIRAL LITTLE said that that was quite clear, and it brought them to the difficulties of ratios. France had a ratio at the moment of 33 per cent of the British battle-fleet, which was agreed upon at Washington. The Washington Treaty had been repudiated, and therefore in fact no fixed ratio between the British and French fleets existed, although it happened by chance to be about 2 : 1. Thus, if we were now to fix a ratio with Germany we might be faced with an unexpected ratio with France (say 60 per cent) and one of our two countries might be satisfied and the other country might not. Hence, it was probable that a wish would be expressed by one country to change the ratio. This had always been the difficulty. He therefore understood that

Germany would not wish to change her ratio whatever France did, even if for economic reasons Great Britain decided not to raise her fleet in proportion to any possible increase by France.

Herr von Ribbentrop confirmed that Admiral Little had described the position correctly. At the same time, he asked the British Delegation not to forget the effect of the Franco-Russian Alliance,[2] an alliance which was much regretted by Herr Hitler, who deplored the introduction of Asiatic influences in Europe. But despite this, Herr Hitler's decision to fix a 35 per cent ratio, regardless of French or Russian actions, showed his earnest desire for a settlement.

Admiral Little said he appreciated this very much.

Mr. Craigie said this was a most important point which the British Delegation would have to make clear in their report to their Government.

Herr von Ribbentrop added that Herr Hitler had accepted the 35 per cent ratio because he anticipated that on many points the two countries would be found to have common interests, and he hoped for British support of the German point of view against Powers who might desire useless increases at future Conferences.

Mr. Craigie said it was difficult to look into the future. In many respects the British and German points of view were likely to be similar. This was the reason that he regretted the pressure that was being put upon the British Delegation over the ratio question, which was a point where agreement was not so easy.

Enough had been said to show the intimate relation that this question would have on the policies of other countries. Hence, it would probably be necessary to consult other Powers before a decision could be given. He would like to ask Herr von Ribbentrop whether he had any objections to such consultations. At the same time, he would regret the necessity. It would be better to complete the rest of the useful work (which he felt sure was possible) first, and not begin with the point which was likely to cause difficulty with other Powers. But if Herr von Ribbentrop thought that a further declaration was essential, Great Britain might have to discuss the matter with other Powers, because so far we had always refused to enter into bilateral agreements, this having been the understanding on which all previous conversations had taken place. He would not press for an answer now.

Herr von Ribbentrop said that the point was too important to defer, and he would therefore like to answer now. He had nothing to add to his observations with regard to the unalterable decision on the 35 per cent ratio. He shared the regrets of Mr. Craigie that there was a prospect of Great Britain having to consult other Powers. He foresaw great difficulties arising if this was done.

This was a matter of vital importance to the two sovereign Powers. Why therefore could they not arrange it in a sovereign way, and then communicate to other Powers the results of their agreements? On the other hand, in the long run it was much the same thing if you consulted first and made your

[2] See No. 156.

348

agreement afterwards, or if you agreed first and then had your consultations.

Herr von Ribbentrop feared, however, that if Great Britain consulted other Powers, an opportunity which might never occur again would be lost through other influences coming in from outside.

MR. CRAIGIE referred first to the question of consultation at the beginning or at the end of the conversations. At their end we might possibly have reached agreement and yet have avoided the specific question of ratios, in which case we could present our agreements in a more favourable light to other Powers. The alternative would be a rather bald statement that acceptance of the 35 per cent ratio had been found necessary to the continuance of any conversations at all. In his opinion, there was all the difference in the world between the two methods. He felt, however, that agreement somewhat on the lines proposed in the morning by Admiral Schuster,[3] would be possible. Referring to the question of sovereign rights, he noted the perplexity of the German Delegation as to why two countries could not settle this matter between themselves. What would have happened, he asked, if bilateral agreements had been reached in previous conversations? They would inevitably have forced some countries to stand out; yet agreement must include all Powers. A bald decision to agree upon a 35 per cent ratio between the British and the German navies might have a catastrophic effect on other Powers.

HERR VON RIBBENTROP said he regretted he was unable to follow the suggestions made by Mr. Craigie, and he feared that the observation made by Admiral Schuster in the morning must have been misunderstood. Admiral Schuster had said that after agreement had been reached on all the points now raised, then *at a future conference* we might find other ways of expressing the ratio.

ADMIRAL SCHUSTER intervening, said that the important thing was that the final effect of a 35 per cent ratio should be recognised now, and that how this should be expressed at an International Conference was another matter.

HERR VON RIBBENTROP continuing said that much the most important thing was the question of principle: if Mr. Craigie was asking the German Delegation to revise the position which they had defined that morning, he felt he could not have made that position clear. The 35 per cent ratio was no point for bargaining; it constituted a great historic sacrifice made for the mutual benefit of the two Nations.

They were now concerned with an Anglo-German problem vital to each country; difficulties and inconveniences with other countries must not be allowed to interfere. A form of agreement could doubtless be found which would avoid other countries drawing false conclusions, but even if they did draw false conclusions, it would not affect the German point of view.

He repeated that he feared consultation with other Powers would cause a great opportunity to be missed, an opportunity which was dependent on the unreserved acceptance by Great Britain of the 35 per cent ratio.

[3] See No. 289, p. 338.

MR. CRAIGIE thanked the German Delegation for the clear statement of their position. He asked for time to refer the matter for consideration by the British Government. He proposed that the British Delegation should proceed to explain their proposals, and it was agreed to defer this till the next day.

ADMIRAL SCHUSTER said he wished to make it clear that the German Government and the German Delegation were not asking them for a guarantee of results at some future conference. When such a conference took place, Germany would herself ask for what she wanted, and would herself defend her demands. Alternatively, Germany would not go to the conference at all.

The British Delegation had declared they would not be bound by ratios. The German Delegation felt that although this was the case, it should still be possible to get a reply from the British Government of their attitude towards the relative strength between the two Navies. 'In other words, does Great Britain admit in practice that a 35 per cent ratio should exist between the two Navies or not?' He considered it should be possible to reply to that question within the framework of the present Conference.

ADMIRAL LITTLE said they could not give an answer now as there had been no consultation yet with Ministers on this subject. He wished to make it clear, however, that *the British favour ratios as a system*, but have been forced by experience to abandon them. It was not the British Government which had set the Washington Treaty aside, a Treaty with which they had been very satisfied.

It was agreed, after discussion, to inform the Press that the conversations had continued, and had remained very general in character.

## No. 291

### Sir J. Simon to Sir G. Clerk (Paris)
#### No. 1089 [C 4453/304/18]

FOREIGN OFFICE, *June 4, 1935*

Sir,

With reference to your despatch No. 785[1] of the 29th May regarding the question of the appointment of a German Air Attaché in Paris, I have to inform Your Excellency that consideration has also been given here to the question of the appointment of a German Air Attaché in London.

2. Early this year the German Ambassador asked that his Military Attaché should be given all the functions, rights and facilities of an Air Attaché. It was decided at the time that as a constituted German air force was not officially supposed to exist, it was not possible to agree that there should be the equivalent of a German Air Attaché in London. The German

---

[1] In the report enclosed in this despatch (see No. 275, note 6) the British Air Attaché in Paris said that the official view of the French Air Ministry towards the appointment of a German Air Attaché at Paris seemed 'to be that they would be glad to agree, provided such an Air Attaché did not wear uniform, as that would constitute a tacit recognition of a German Military Air Force'.

Ambassador was therefore told that his Military Attaché could not be given 'all the functions, rights and facilities of an Air Attaché,' but that, if the Military Attaché applied to the Air Ministry for facilities on those matters of aviation which he considered to fall within his sphere of duty, he could in practice obtain all the satisfaction he required.

3. The German Government can readily obtain information in this country as to what goes on in the air, whether or not they have an Air Attaché, as so much is open and unconcealed. But in Germany it is much more difficult for the British Air Attaché to obtain information; and by not receiving a German Air Attaché here a pretext is given to the German Government to maintain that they can refuse the British Air Attaché information on grounds of reciprocity because they have no Air Attaché in London. The British Air Attaché in Berlin, moreover, has recently received hints that the German authorities may avail themselves of this pretext.

4. In these circumstances, and in view of the fact pointed out in the enclosure to your despatch No. 785 that the official view of the French Air Ministry seems to be that they would be glad to receive a German Air Attaché in Paris, it is proposed shortly to inform the German Ambassador here that His Majesty's Government will raise no objection to the appointment of an Air Attaché in London.[2]

5. I should be glad if you would at once, orally and informally, so inform the French Minister for Foreign Affairs.

6. A copy of this despatch is being sent to His Majesty's Ambassador at Rome,[3] who will be instructed also so to inform the Italian Government; though, as you are aware, there has in fact been a German Air Attaché in Rome for some time past.

7. For your own confidential information, we shall not make any condition (such as that which the French Air Ministry appear to have in mind) that the German Air Attaché shall not wear uniform.

I am, &c.,
JOHN SIMON

[2] Colonel R. Wenninger assumed duties as Air Attaché at the German Embassy in London on October 1, 1935.    [3] In Foreign Office despatch No. 670 of June 4.

## No. 292

*Sir E. Phipps (Berlin) to Sir J. Simon (Received June 7)*
*No. 534 [C 4588/55/18]*

BERLIN, *June 4, 1935*

Sir,

With reference to my telegram No. 200[1] of 22nd May, I have the honour to transmit to you, herewith, a translation of the Defence Law of May 21st, 1935, and of two decrees of the Chancellor fixing the duration of military service and transferring certain rights to the Ministers of War and the Interior.[2]

[1] Cf. No. 219, note 1.    [2] These enclosures are not printed.

2. The principal feature of the Defence Law is its elasticity. The Minister of War is given discretion to modify the terms of the Law in almost every particular and notably to extend the period of service at will. I would also draw your attention to Article 12 which lays down that the ordinary civilian authorities shall be responsible for recruiting in the demilitarised zone, whereas in the rest of Germany this task is entrusted to special military offices established for the purpose.

I have, &c.,
ERIC PHIPPS

## No. 293

*Letter from Sir E. Phipps (Berlin) to Mr. Sargent (Received June 7)*
[*C 4591/55/18*]

BERLIN, *June 4, 1935*

My dear Sargent,

My Italian colleague[1] tells me that Bülow declared to him a couple of days ago that the Germans, in calculating our first-line military aircraft, would have to take into account our first-line machines in Egypt and India.

Bülow, as you know, generally out-Herods Herod, and this is no exception to his rule, for Hitler told us on the morning of March 26th that if Britain would bring her air strength '*for the United Kingdom* up to the French strength, then it would be that parity that Germany would demand'.[2]

Ribbentrop shortly afterwards declared that 'Germany did not care how many aeroplanes there were in England'.[3]

Yours ever,
ERIC PHIPPS

[1] Signor Vittorio Cerruti.   [2] Cf. No. 275.
[3] In the course of a minute of June 16 Sir R. Vansittart remarked: 'Their demands are always going up, or else they leave themselves a loophole for going up. We may well hope that this demand will not materialise, for it wd be in flagrant conflict with past professions.'

## No. 294

*Letter from Chancery (Rome) to Central Department (Received June 6)*
[*C 4541/55/18*]

ROME, *June 4, 1935*

Dear Department,

Last night at a large reception given by the Ambassador the Head of the European Department of the Ministry of Foreign Affairs, Quaroni, had a conversation with a member of the staff regarding the Air Pact negotiations and the situation generally. In his view His Majesty's Government were making rather a mistake in stressing the advantage which England would derive from the proposed Air Pact. (He had just been reading the 'Times' of June 1st reporting the previous day's debate.)[1] He held that the strength of His Majesty's Government had, in the past, largely resided in

[1] See 302 *H.C. Deb.* 5 *s.*, cols. 1423–1510.

the fact that she herself never derived any advantage from the commitments she took. The proposed Air Pact, therefore, marked an important turning point in British history. If we stressed this advantage, surely it was not unlikely that the French would take note of the fact, and would try to strike a harder bargain with us when the effectives stage of any all-round settlement was reached—when he considered that the real struggle would start. In other words, though he didn't say so, the French might try to blackmail us, withholding their full co-operation in the Air Pact until we gave in to them on the effectives.

He enquired whether we had yet received an answer from the French on the point about priority being given to the Air Pact,[2] but when he was told that, so far as the Embassy knew, that reply had not yet been received, he stated that he knew what that reply would be, viz. no objection in principle but reserves formulated over the entry into force of the actual agreement. His tone seemed to imply that he was quite certain that that would be the answer.

You have probably received by now the French reply, but in any case we report the conversation for what it may be worth.

Yours ever,<br>ROME CHANCERY

[2] Cf. Nos. 235 and 250.

## No. 295

### Sir J. Simon to Mr. Campbell (Paris)
*No. 136 Telegraphic: by telephone* [C 4524/55/18]

*Immediate*                    FOREIGN OFFICE, *June 5, 1935, 5 p.m.*

Message from Paris correspondent in today's 'Times'[1] states that M. Laval yesterday gave to German Ambassador[2] sense of French note respecting effect on Locarno of Franco-Russian Treaty.

Is this correct? We asked in my telegram No. 87 to Geneva[3] that reply to German Government on this subject should be concerted between French and Italian Governments and ourselves: and Paris telegram No. 98[4]—and again Paris telegram No. 111 Saving[5]—report M. Laval as being in agreement with this.

[1] See *The Times*, June 5, p. 15.   [2] Herr R. Köster.   [3] No. 226.
[4] No. 253.                                                   [5] No. 286.

## No. 296

### Sir J. Simon to Mr. Campbell (Paris)
*No. 137 Telegraphic: by telephone* [C 4524/55/18]

*Immediate*                    FOREIGN OFFICE, *June 5, 1935, 5 p.m.*

We are disturbed by report in today's 'Times' from its Paris correspondent[1] that M. Laval has committed himself to Soviet Ambassador to resist

[1] See *The Times*, June 5, p. 15.

any attempt to separate conclusion of air pact and air limitation agreement from that of general settlement.

We cannot believe that this report is correct; for on May 28th (Paris telegram No. 99)[2] M. Laval asked that, pending settlement of internal crisis, His Majesty's Government should not press him for a decision on this question. That was reason for nature of my reference to question in House of Commons on May 31st (see my telegram No. 135)[3] with which M. Laval agreed (see Paris telegram No. 103)[4] adding that it was 'Understood that question whether or not Air Pact can be isolated from general settlement is reserved without prejudice'.

We should like you to clear up the position at once.

[2] No. 254.      [3] No. 259.      [4] No. 269.

## No. 297

### Sir J. Simon to Sir E. Phipps (Berlin)

#### No. 121 Telegraphic [C 4433/55/18]

FOREIGN OFFICE, *June 5, 1935, 7 p.m.*

Your telegram No. 226[1] seems to report you as informing the Soviet Ambassador that it was not our intention to separate the Air Pact negotiations from those of the other points mentioned in the London communiqué. Although it was originally assumed that all the different schemes outlined in the Anglo-French Declaration of February 3rd, including the Air Pact, were to form part of the general settlement and to be concluded simultaneously, you will have seen from my telegrams to Paris No. 111[2] and to Geneva No. 91[3], Geneva telegram No. 88[4] and Paris telegram No. 99,[5] that I have now raised with the French Government the question whether in the altered circumstances the Air Pact and proposed Air Limitation agreement might not be concluded independently of the so-called 'general settlement'. As the question is still open, and the French Government have not yet committed themselves on the subject, you should as far as possible avoid discussing this aspect of the question with your Soviet colleague.

It is true that in the debate in the House of Commons on the 31st ultimo[6] I warned the House that the Air Pact might be regarded as part of the general scheme outlined in the Anglo-French Declaration of last February, and pointed out that notwithstanding this fact there was no reason why we should not actively press on with its negotiation, leaving to a later stage the question of how it is to be fitted into a more general settlement. I made these remarks in order to meet the wish of M. Laval (see Paris telegram No. 103)[7] that the question of isolating the Air Pact from the General Settlement should be reserved, since the French Government had not yet been able to take a decision. My remarks ought not however to be read to mean that His Majesty's Government have now abandoned the idea of separating the Air Pact from the 'General Settlement'.

[1] No. 277.      [2] No. 174.      [3] No. 235.      [4] See No. 250, note 1.
[5] No. 254.      [6] Cf. No. 294, note 1.      [7] No. 269.

## No. 298

*Mr. Charles (Moscow) to Sir J. Simon (Received June 5, 7.3 p.m.)*
*No. 78 Telegraphic [C 4540/55/18]*

MOSCOW, *June 5, 1935, 7 p.m.*

German memorandum on Franco-Soviet Treaty[1] according to Pravda proves that Germany is definitely trying to create a situation which would prevent France and U.S.S.R. from assisting each other in accordance with Treaty. M. Litvinov told me yesterday that he put the worst possible construction on everything Herr Hitler said in his speech on May 21st as well as on everything he has done subsequently. He pointed out that Germany has gone back on her offer to participate in Eastern Multilateral Pact of non-aggression,[2] that she was sowing dissension in South Eastern Europe and doing utmost to break up any move for collective peace. Taken in conjunction with recent articles in Polish newspaper 'Czas' advocating that Poland should definitely throw in her lot with Germany, Herr Hitler's actions proved that Germany was preparing for eventual war.

I asked M. Litvinov whether Polish Ambassador whose visit had preceded mine had said anything on the subject of articles and I gathered from his reply that the Ambassador had merely given it as his personal opinion that articles were not written by Prince Radziwill,[3] and that they were not official views of the Polish Government.

M. Litvinov finally informed me that Germany was abetting the Italian plans in Abyssinia and that he had just learned from the Soviet Ambassador at Rome that Herr Hitler had even made some direct proposition to Signor Mussolini with a view to involving Italy so as to have free hand herself in Europe.

Counsellor of the Polish Embassy told me this morning that Polish Ambassador had informed M. Litvinov at an interview yesterday that the views expressed by 'Czas' were not those of the Polish Government and had called his attention to denial published by official Government organ 'Gazetta Polska'.

Repeated to Berlin.

[1] Presumably a reference to the German Government's memorandum of May 25; cf. No. 263, note 2 and section II.
[2] An unsigned marginal note on the filed copy here read: 'The French don't think so yet.'      [3] President of the Foreign Affairs Committee of the Polish Diet.

## No. 299

*Mr. Campbell (Paris) to Sir J. Simon (Received June 5, 7.30 p.m.)*
*No. 114 Telegraphic: by telephone [C 4525/55/18]*

PARIS, *June 5, 1935*

Your telegram No. 136.[1]
I have confirmed that position remains as stated in Sir G. Clerk's telegram

[1] No. 295.

No. 111 Saving[2] of yesterday, and that French answer to German note will not be despatched until you have had time to express your views on it.

If Monsieur Laval, who is of course quite unapproachable, did in fact mention the matter to the German Ambassador it can only have been in quite general terms. Text of reply is actually not yet quite complete.

[2] No. 286.

## No. 300

*Mr. Campbell (Paris) to Sir J. Simon (Received June 5, 7.30 p.m.)*
*No. 115 Telegraphic: by telephone* [C 4526/55/18]

PARIS, *June 5, 1935*

Your telegram No. 137.[1]

I regret that owing to crisis I cannot give categorical answer to your questions until Monsieur Léger has been able to get into touch with Monsieur Laval.

I think it improbable that Monsieur Laval has committed himself or even indeed that he has yet definitely made up his mind.

[1] No. 296.

## No. 301

*Sir J. Simon to Sir G. Clerk (Paris)*
*No. 199 Saving:*[1] *Telegraphic* [C 4439/55/18]

FOREIGN OFFICE, *June 5, 1935, 7.30 p.m.*

My telegram to Geneva No. 87[2] repeated to you.

We presume that German memorandum on effect of Franco-Soviet Treaty on obligations of the signatories of the Locarno Treaty which was communicated to us on May 29,[3] has now been communicated also to the Government to which you are accredited. According to German Ambassador here, last sentence of this memorandum expresses the desire of the German Government to learn the views of the other Locarno Powers on the points set out in the memorandum. His Majesty's Government regard it as important that the terms of the reply to the German memorandum to be sent by the four Locarno Governments should be concerted between them and should, if possible, be on similar lines.

His Majesty's Government trust that Government to which you are accredited will agree that this should be done.

His Majesty's Government are preparing a draft memorandum replying to German memorandum. Text of this draft memorandum will be sent to you by air mail as soon as possible for communication to Government to

[1] This telegram was also addressed to Rome (No. 307) and Brussels (No. 49).
[2] No. 226.
[3] Cf. No. 298, note 1.

356

which you are accredited to serve as a basis for eventual joint reply to the German observations.[4]

Repeated to Berlin & Moscow.

[4] Foreign Office telegram No. 138 to Paris (No. 309 to Rome, No. 51 to Brussels), despatched at 10 p.m. on June 6, referred to the above telegram and read: 'Please cancel last paragraph'.

## No. 302

*Sir J. Simon to Sir G. Clerk (Paris)*

*No. 200 Saving: Telegraphic* [C 4439/55/18]

FOREIGN OFFICE, *June 5, 1935, 7.30 p.m.*

My telegram No. 199 Saving[1] was drafted before receipt of your telegram No. 111 Saving.[2]

We still consider it important that four Locarno Powers should concert together as to their answer to German enquiry and should if possible address in each case a reply on similar lines to German Government. I trust therefore that French Government will not present their reply to German Government without giving His Majesty's Government and the other Locarno Powers time to study it with this object in view.

Repeated to Rome No. 308 and Brussels No. 50.

[1] No. 301.
[2] No. 286. For a note on the problem of 'time-lags' in the receipt and despatch of telegrams see Volume II, Editorial Note on p. vi.

## No. 303

*Record by Sir W. Malkin of a conversation with the German Ambassador*

[C 4537/55/18]

FOREIGN OFFICE, *June 5, 1935*

The German Ambassador came to see me this afternoon with the object, as he explained, of repeating and developing the explanations which he had given to the Secretary of State on May 28th–29th of the objections which his Government felt to the Franco-Soviet Treaty. In point of fact, his explanations did not really go beyond what he had said to the Secretary of State, as recorded in paragraph 2 of the Secretary of State's despatch to Berlin, No. 571[1] of May 29th, and the Memorandum which he had handed to the Secretary of State on that occasion. Apparently the German Government have no objection to the reference to Article 17[2] in the second paragraph of Article 3 of the Franco-Soviet Treaty, and this point may be worth noting. Their objections are really based entirely on the second sentence of paragraph 1 of the Protocole de Signature. He explained that, in Dr. Gaus's[3] opinion, this provision, under which the obligation to come to the assistance

[1] No. 263.        [2] Of the Covenant of the League of Nations.
[3] Director of the Legal Department of the German Foreign Ministry.

of the attacked party is to apply even though the Council has not made any recommendation under Article 16,[2] is inconsistent with that Article. This confirms what I had already heard at Geneva, that Dr. Gaus's view is that military action can only be taken under Article 16 in pursuance of a recommendation by the Council. I am sure that this view is wrong, and I think that such would be the general view.

The Ambassador endeavoured to explain why his Government did not regard any doubt which might exist on this point as being resolved by paragraph 2 of the Protocole de Signature, but I did not find his explanation any more convincing than that given in the penultimate paragraph of the German Memorandum. He did, however, indicate a possibility, which he said had not been mentioned in that Memorandum because to do so would have suggested bad faith on the part of the other Signatories of Locarno, which was that they and the French might agree in the circumstances postulated to put a construction upon the provisions of that Treaty which would not be in accordance with its intentions and thus deprive Germany of the right to assistance which ought to result from a French violation of Article 2.

The Ambassador did not press me for any observations on what he had said, but as he had told me what Dr. Gaus's view was, I took the opportunity of saying that I had carefully studied the Franco-Soviet Treaty when we had received the text and had come to the conclusion that there was nothing in it which was inconsistent with either the Covenant or Locarno. (Incidentally, the same view was expressed to me at Geneva by my Belgian colleague.)

The only remark made by the Ambassador which may be of some importance came at the end of our interview. He asked himself what was going to happen next; he presumed that the French, and possibly the other Locarno Governments, would endeavour to persuade the German Government that their view was wrong and that there was nothing objectionable from that point of view in the Franco-Russian Treaty. He did not think, however, that his Government were likely to be convinced. Nor did he think that a reference of the point to the Permanent Court of International Justice or to some other arbitral tribunal would be a satisfactory method of procedure. He then invited my particular attention to the last sentence of the German Memorandum[4] and intimated, though without expressing any official opinion, that a statement to the effect of that sentence by the other Locarno Powers would probably remove his Government's preoccupations. If this is really so, the idea may be worth considering, for the sentence in question is really a truism and I cannot at present see what objection there would be to saying that we agree with it. It may be material to bear in mind in this connexion that if France were to come to the assistance of Russia in the circumstances postulated (i.e., where France contended that she was

[4] This read, in translation: 'They [the German Government] hope that all the Signatory Powers will agree with them in recognizing that the provisions of the Treaty of Locarno cannot legally be modified or defined by the fact that a Treaty has been concluded with a third party by one of the signatories.'

acting under Article 16 and Germany contended that she was not entitled to do so under that Article), the question would be whether France had violated the undertaking in Article 2 of Locarno, and it would then be for Germany to bring this question before the Council under Article 4, paragraph (1), and for the Council to decide the point under paragraph (2).

When leaving, the Ambassador referred to the German draft Air Pact which he had handed to the Secretary of State[5] and asked if I had seen it. I told him that I had, but that as I had only recently returned from Geneva, I had not yet been able to give full consideration to it. He did not pursue the point (at which I was rather relieved).[6]

H.W.M.

[5] See Annex to No. 263.
[6] On Mr. Wigram's suggestion Sir W. Malkin on June 6 also discussed the Franco-Soviet treaty with the Polish Chargé d'Affaires. His record of a 'somewhat desultory discussion' included the following passage. 'He told me that his Government had received from the German Government a copy of the memorandum which the latter had addressed to the Locarno Powers (this is not uninteresting), and that they would be much interested to know the views of those Powers upon it. I told him that those views would, of course, be expressed in the replies which they made to the German memorandum, but that I had considered the Franco-Soviet Treaty when its text was received, and that my personal view was that there was nothing in it which was inconsistent either with the Covenant or Locarno.'

## No. 304

*Notes of the third meeting between representatives of the United Kingdom and Germany, June 5, 1935, at 11 a.m.*[1]

Present: *United Kingdom*: Mr. R. L. Craigie, Vice-Admiral C. J. C. Little, Captain V. H. Danckwerts.
  *Germany*: Herr von Ribbentrop, Rear-Admiral K. G. Schuster, Captain E. Wassner, Korvetten Kapitan H. Kiderlen, Dr. Kordt, Dr. Schmidt.

MR. CRAIGIE said that there was not much under the present heading[2] on which we need inform the German Delegation, who were doubtless familiar with the terms of the existing naval treaties. Under Article 23 of the London Naval Treaty it was provided that a conference should take place between the five Naval Powers unless a general naval conference had reached a prior agreement, rendering the five-Power conference unnecessary. Such hopes not having been realised it would be obligatory to hold a five-Power conference unless the Powers concerned decided otherwise.

Article 23 of the Washington Treaty provided that in the event of the denunciation of that Treaty by one Power, there should be a conference within one year. Japan had denounced the Treaty on the 31st December, 1934.[3] Therefore there must be a conference this year.

[1] The meeting was held at the Admiralty. These notes were circulated as N.C.(G) 3rd Mtg. *Most Secret*.
[2] A reference presumably to item 2 of the Agenda in No. 282; cf. item 3 of the Agenda in *D.G.F.P.*, Series C, vol. iv, No. 132.  [3] Cf. No. 99.

The position really was as follows:

The ideal would be to have a general conference as soon as possible because a conference between the five Powers alone could lead to nothing final. On the other hand the British Government were impressed with the need to avoid calling a conference till the ground had been prepared; it would be the worst possible thing to call a conference that would end in a complete fiasco.

The difficulty of calling a small conference first was that the Powers left out would ask for an extension of the conference. On the other hand once it had been extended beyond the five Powers, they would be committed to a general conference. Then again the Japanese Government had declared their refusal to enter into anything save a five-Power conference.

As a compromise the British Government had suggested that there should be no formal conference between the five Powers, but that if the bilateral talks offered a prospect of agreement they should develop into a five-Power meeting—not a five-Power conference. If the prospects arising from the five-Power meeting were good, that in turn should give place to a general conference.

There was also the question of the date and place of the conference. As yet there were no definite ideas as to when or where the conference should take place. It was the British hope that the preliminary meeting and the general conference should be held next Autumn. Otherwise we should be faced with the necessity of postponing a conference provided for by Treaty; this would be a confession of failure and would have a bad psychological effect on public opinion.

As to the place, there were no definite ideas yet, but most of the Powers were anxious not to have it in their own capitals. Suggestions had been made for holding it in a smaller capital, such as The Hague, but the objection was that if the inviting Government did not share the responsibility for success, then there would be no driving force behind the conference. A suggestion had also been made that the conference should be held in London. No decision had yet been reached but His Majesty's Government would probably agree if this was the general wish.

The British Government felt that it was of great importance that the existing Treaties should not be allowed to lapse without a strenuous effort being made to check the danger of unlimited competition. The British delegation felt sure that the German representatives would agree with them in this respect, and would bear in mind the bad psychological and the bad financial results that might otherwise ensue.

HERR VON RIBBENTROP had no observations to make.

MR. CRAIGIE stated that his object was to give a general picture only;[4] Admiral Little would supplement this later with technical detail.

The British delegation had had bi-lateral conversations with the French and the Italians in the Summer of 1934 and with the Americans and Japanese in the Autumn. He would take first the question of qualitative limitation.

---

[4] Cf. items 3 and 4 of the Agenda in No. 282 which corresponded to item 4 in *D.G.F.P.*, *op. cit.*

So far as the French, the Italians and the Japanese were concerned the British delegation saw no great divergence of view on qualitative limits, with the important exception that the Japanese were disinclined to accept qualitative limitation unless quantitative limitation was secured as well, but the British believed that with these three Powers they could get a rough agreement on capital ships and cruisers. Mr. Craigie gave some approximate figures by way of example making it clear that they were purely tentative.

With the United States there was the difficulty that they still desired the larger types of ships and guns. They wanted capital ships of 35,000 tons and 16-inch guns. But he was justified in saying that if a general agreement could be concluded the United States might compromise on 14-inch guns.

Similarly the United States would like to keep the present large cruisers but the British had not lost hope of compromise.

He must make one addition to what he had said on the capital ship question. It was complicated by the Italian decision to build two 35,000 ton ships, as the French apparently intended to follow suit.

Great Britain remained in favour of the abolition of submarines, and he was glad to learn that Herr Hitler held the same view. But there was no doubt that France and Japan would refuse to agree to abolition, failing which the British Government would wish to see submarine tonnage reduced to as low a figure as possible.

Turning to the question of quantitative limitation, Mr. Craigie said that the case of France and Italy provided a good example of the ratio difficulty. For reasons of prestige the Italians refused to accept anything less than parity with France but at the same time they said that they would not necessarily build up to parity. But the French refused to accept the Italian claim to parity.

He personally had been engaged from 1930 to 1933 in continued efforts to secure agreement between the French and the Italian points of view, but he had failed.[5] Now the same problem had arisen again and the British delegation were convinced that any solution on a ratio basis was out of the question.

Turning to the position between the United States, Japan and ourselves, Mr. Craigie said that up till the previous autumn the Franco-Italian disagreement had been the only difficulty over ratios. Last autumn, however, Japan had claimed that a common upper limit of naval strength should exist between all Powers. That is to say all Powers should have the right to build up to the limit though not necessarily doing so. The Japanese also proposed the abolition of 'offensive' types in which they classed capital ships, aircraft carriers and 8-inch cruisers.

These bi-lateral negotiations, which took place concurrently with the United States and Japanese representatives, had continued for three months,[6]

[5] For documents relating to negotiations since April 1930 to facilitate a Franco-Italian naval agreement, see Volume I, Chapter V; Volume II, Chapter VI; Volume IV, Appendix III; cf. No. 7 above, note 3.　　　　　　　　　　　　　　　　　[6] See Chapter II.

and while some progress had been made they had ended with no clear views on the solution of the problem, though it had soon been realised that no ratio system would be acceptable. Neither the United States nor the British Government were prepared to accept a common upper limit. The special needs of the British Empire had been explained to the Japanese and the British representatives had put forward the 'British compromise proposal' which was roughly as follows:

From any future treaty all reference to a ratio should be completely eliminated; no figures of relative strength should be inserted. The treaty would mainly deal with qualitative limitation, reciprocal notification of building programmes, and certain minor matters. In addition the British had proposed to insert a clause recognising the equality of national status of all signatories irrespective of the size of their navies.

So far as quantitative limitation was concerned the British Government thought that the only possible method would be a declaration of building programmes over a period of years. 1937 to 1942 inclusive, had actually been proposed. These declarations should not be in treaty form, they would merely amount to a frank declaration of intentions and would contain no statement of the ultimate naval strength which it was intended to attain. Subject to one year's notice it would always be open to the Powers to modify their programmes.

In practice this would not be very different from the existing schemes of limitation, which contained an escalator clause. Great Britain believed that these building programmes would be adhered to and would at the same time solve the difficulty of national prestige.

Up to date this proposal had neither been accepted nor rejected by the United States or the Japanese Governments.

Actually, and in great confidence, the British delegation had examined with the Japanese delegation how these programmes would work out, and the results of this examination had been fairly promising. If the Japanese Government could agree in principle to this method, Great Britain believed that it would work out very well in practice.

HERR VON RIBBENTROP asked what were the other items on which Admiral Little intended to speak.

MR. CRAIGIE said that Admiral Little would speak on points 6, 7, 8 and 9 of the British Agenda.[7]

HERR VON RIBBENTROP thanked the British Delegation for the explanation they had given of the present general position *vis-à-vis* other countries.

At the same time he wished to remind the British Delegation of the conversations which had taken place the preceding day.[8] He had agreed that the German Delegation should listen to a British statement. He now felt that the exploratory stage had come to a certain conclusion. Could the British Delegation tell the German Delegation, that day or the next day, their reply to the question he had put yesterday? Namely: could they give

[7] See No. 282 and *D.G.F.P.*, *op. cit.*
[8] See Nos. 289 and 290.

a clear and formal *recognition* of the *decision* taken by Herr Hitler in laying down a 35 to 100 ratio between the two countries?

He used the word 'recognition' with deliberation. It was not a matter of agreement between the two countries but of recognition of the decision that had been taken by Herr Hitler. Herr von Ribbentrop's end was to avoid misunderstandings, hence he would like confirmation of the British Government's attitude at this stage.

The German Delegation would like to return to Germany by Whitsuntide.[9] Could, therefore, the British Delegation give a reply either that day or the next day, after which they could all enter into useful discussions on points of detail?

MR. CRAIGIE said that at this point he would like to repeat that the request for some form of recognition had taken the British Delegation unawares. When Herr Hitler's declaration had been made, it had been welcomed in England as a constructive proposal of the highest importance, and the British had assumed that the conversations would be on the basis that that was Germany's decision, and that they would have to see what arrangements should be made accordingly.

But the idea of first declaring our formal recognition was a new one. It was therefore difficult to give an answer immediately; it was particularly difficult for the British Government to decide quickly at a moment when changes were impending and the political situation was a little confused.[10]

Nevertheless the British Delegation would do their best to get a reply by the next day; they could not promise; Admiral Little thought it most unlikely, but Mr. Craigie could not say. Anyhow, the British Delegation would do their best, but Ministers might wish to have a day or two to reflect on such an important matter.

On the question of Whitsuntide, the British Delegation realised it was a complication, but they felt it would be most unfortunate to have an adjournment when the matter was actually under consideration by His Majesty's Government. It was only right and courteous that His Majesty's Government should be given sufficient time.

On the day before, the British Delegation had proposed continuing the conversations on technical points, owing to the risk of Press comments if they were to be stopped at this stage. He therefore felt that Admiral Little's technical points should be explained at a meeting on the following day, (if necessary at a meeting of the Committee only, not of the full Delegations). There was much that it might be useful for the German Delegation to learn, and he proposed that a meeting should be as late as possible, say, 5.0 p.m.,

---

[9] Whit Sunday was June 9, 1935.

[10] A reconstruction of the National Government took place two days later, on June 7. Mr. Stanley Baldwin succeeded Mr. Ramsay Macdonald as Prime Minister and Sir John Simon, who became Minister for Home Affairs, was succeeded as Minister for Foreign Affairs by Sir Samuel Hoare. Mr. Anthony Eden became Minister without portfolio with special responsibility for League of Nations Affairs. Sir P. Cunliffe-Lister succeeded Lord Londonderry as Secretary of State for Air.

in order to give the greatest chance of obtaining an answer to Herr von Ribbentrop's question.

The British Delegation therefore proposed that they should try to keep the conversations going until a reply could be given, and that if there must be an adjournment over Whitsuntide it should be for as short a time as possible. The matter was too important for holidays to play a part, although he fully appreciated the German Delegation's position.

HERR VON RIBBENTROP said he did not want to press unduly for an early reply and he would be willing to give the British Government time to come to their decision. At the same time he again expressed disappointment that Herr Hitler's historic decision should have caused a delay, but in view of the impending changes in His Majesty's Government he would of course wish to allow for ample time.

He would agree to a meeting being held tomorrow in order to avoid difficulties with the Press, at which Admiral Little should expound the details of the British position. But he was not in favour of a Sub-Committee meeting and would prefer a plenary meeting of the whole commission.

For reasons which he had explained privately to Mr. Craigie the evening before,[11] he thought it would be good for as early a reply as possible to be made. He hoped for an agreement in principle before Whitsuntide, so that after Whitsuntide there would be time for clearing up points of detail. The German Delegation would return to London for 3 or 4 days after Whitsuntide for this purpose.

If, however, there was no reply before Whitsuntide difficulties would arise, as arrangements would have to be made in Germany which might entail a delay of some weeks. He, therefore, hoped for an early reply and would greatly regret it if a delay of some weeks were to arise as might very well occur. It was in the interests of both Delegations to avoid a delay, particularly in view of the impending conference. Finally, he expressed a hope that at the conference the Delegations would be 100 per cent in agreement.

[11] No record of this conversation has been traced in Foreign Office archives.

## No. 305

*Anglo-German Naval Discussions: Report by the British Representatives*[1]

[A 5100/22/45]

June 5, 1935

1. In the course of the meetings held yesterday[2] and to-day[3] the German naval representatives made it clear that, before proceeding with further naval discussions, they would like to know whether His Majesty's Government would be prepared 'to give a clear and formal recognition of the decision taken by the German Government laying down a relationship between the British and German fleets in the proportion of 100 per cent to 35 per cent'.

[1] This report was circulated as N.C.M. (35) 50.     [2] Nos. 289 and 290.
[3] No. 304.

The German representatives explained that the German Government would regard this ratio, if accepted by His Majesty's Government, as 'final and permanent' and that the subsequent possession of colonies would not modify it.

2. In the course of the discussions the German representatives gave the following important clarifications of their proposal:

(*a*) Once agreement had been reached between Great Britain and Germany on a ratio of 35 per cent, the German Government would adhere to this limitation independently of the construction of third Powers. As an example it was stated that if, for instance, France should decide to increase the proportionate strength of the French navy to the British navy and His Majesty's Government were to decide not to respond to this by increasing British construction, Germany would likewise adhere to a level of 35 per cent of the British fleet.

(*b*) At the same time the German representatives stated that they assumed that, in the event of France deciding to make any considerable increase in her naval strength, the British Government would do their best to deter her from taking this course.

(*c*) The German Government would not insist on the incorporation of this ratio in any future international treaty provided that the alternative method eventually adopted for the future limitation of naval armaments gave Germany full guarantees that this relationship between the British and German fleets would be maintained.

(*d*) The German Government believe in the system of limitation by categories and they are prepared in principle to calculate the 35 per cent ratio on the tonnage in the separate categories, any variation from this ratio in a particular category being dependent upon the arrangements to this end that may be arrived at in a future general treaty of naval limitation. Should no international treaty be concluded or should the question of limitation by categories not be dealt with in a future international treaty, the question of the calculation of the 35 per cent ratio in the categories would be a matter for discussion between the German and British Governments.

3. The text of the German declaration on this point, of which the relevant passages will be found in paragraph 2, sub-sections 2 and 3, is attached as Annex I.[4]

4. The German representatives fully recognised that, owing to the present domestic situation here, the answer of His Majesty's Government might be slightly delayed. They pointed out, however, that there had been a certain disappointment in Germany that His Majesty's Government had not felt able to accept more promptly what the German Government regarded as an offer of the highest historical importance, under which a sovereign State voluntarily agreed in advance to accept a permanent naval inferiority of 65 per cent as compared with the British Fleet and for this reason it was important that the answer should be delayed as little as possible. It would be

---

[4] Not printed. The gist of the 'relevant passages' referred to is given in No. 289, sub-sections (2) and (3) of Herr von Ribbentrop's first speech (p. 340 above).

particularly appreciated if the answer could be returned before Whitsuntide. An extract from the British record, giving the text of Herr von Ribbentrop's observations on this point at to-day's meeting, is attached as Annex II.[5]

(The foregoing paragraphs have been submitted to the German representatives who agree that they correctly represent the view of the German Government).

5. The British representatives fully explained to the German representatives the difficulties in the way of the course they suggested, pointing out in particular that, even were His Majesty's Government prepared to accept such a relationship in so far as the British Navy was concerned, there remained the question of the repercussions on the other naval Powers, with whom there was a tacit understanding that, in advance of any international conference, there should be no bilateral agreements during the present conversations. The fact that the whole essence of the British proposal was to do away with the element of ratio and to substitute voluntary declarations of programme was also stressed. Despite these arguments the German representatives declared that it was essential for them to learn at the outset whether His Majesty's Government were or were not in a position to proceed on this basis.

6. The British representatives have since had time to consider this proposal carefully and they are definitely of the opinion that, in our own interest, we should accept this offer of Herr Hitler's while it is still open. They are confident that, if we now refuse to accept the offer for the purposes of these discussions, Herr Hitler will withdraw the offer and Germany will seek to build up to a higher level than 35 per cent. A Naval Staff memorandum dealing with the strategical aspects of the question is attached as Annex III.[6]

7. It is true there may be a certain element of bluff in these proceedings, but it is felt at the same time that, in view of Herr Hitler's action in regard to land armaments, it would be a mistake to believe that such an offer on the part of Germany will remain indefinitely open in the absence of a British acceptance of it. Having regard to past history and to Germany's known capacity to become at will a serious naval rival of this country, it is felt that we may have cause to regret it if we fail to take this chance of arresting German naval development at the level stated.

8. Even, however, if His Majesty's Government, for their part, were prepared to accept this offer, they have to consider the repercussions on other European Powers and also whether such acceptance would not be a breach of the tacit understanding which has governed our discussions with those Powers, namely that there should be no bilateral agreements between any of the Washington Naval Powers in advance of any general naval conference.

9. This German offer is of such outstanding importance that it would be a mistake to withhold acceptance merely on the ground that other Powers might feel some temporary annoyance at our action. It is, however, both

[5] The extract attached as Annex II was Herr von Ribbentrop's last speech in No. 304 (p. 364 above).
[6] Printed as Annex to this document.

desirable and necessary that we should give the Governments of those Powers with whom we have had previous naval conversations an opportunity to express their view on the point before we give a formal answer to the Germans. It is therefore proposed that we should as soon as possible address an oral communication to the United States, Japanese, French, and Italian Governments in the following general sense:

10. After informing them of the nature of the German offer, we should state that we consider that it is a contribution of great importance to the cause of future naval limitation and also furnishes an important assurance for the future security of this and other countries. We should emphasise points (*a*) and (*c*) mentioned in paragraph 2 above and say that we intend accordingly to recognise this decision of the German Government as the basis of our future discussions between the British and German naval representatives in London. Before, however, giving our formal reply to the German representatives we should be glad to learn whether the Governments concerned desire to furnish any observations, and in view of the urgency of the matter we trust that we may receive their observations in the course of the next few days.

11. It is believed that if the German representatives could be informed confidentially either on Thursday or Friday[7] that it was our intention to make the above communication to the other interested Powers they would be content and the discussions could proceed on a satisfactory basis. There is, in fact, every reason to believe that, once this difficulty is out of the way, there is a good prospect of the British and German representatives finding themselves in agreement on all other points.

12. It may be thought that His Majesty's Government are being asked to take too hurried a decision and that the matter should wait over until after Whitsuntide. The German representatives quite anticipate that such course may be necessary but at the same time they would regret the necessity because of the misunderstanding which it would create. In the view of the British representatives it would be unfortunate both from a political and psychological standpoint if the German representatives returned to Germany for Whitsuntide under the impression that His Majesty's Government are still hesitating as to whether or not the German proposal can be accepted. It is obvious of course that the effect of an acceptance of the German offer will decrease in proportion to the length of time that His Majesty's Government take to consider it and this is particularly the case in view of the confident expectation of the German Government that the acceptance of His Majesty's Government would have been forthcoming very shortly after the offer was made publicly in Herr Hitler's speech of 21st May.[8]

[7] i.e. on June 6 or 7.

[8] Sir J. Simon and Sir Bolton Eyres Monsell made reports to the Cabinet on June 5 as to the results of the meetings of the naval conversations on the previous day. The Cabinet agreed (*a*) that the British negotiators, before the conversations adjourned for Whitsuntide, should try and find out exactly what was meant by the German proposal for a 35 per cent ratio; and (*b*) that the results of the conversations should be reported to the ministers who had been dealing with the 1935 naval conference, who would give any instructions to the

*Naval Staff Memorandum on the German Proposal for a*
*35 per cent Naval Ratio*

The significance of the construction by Germany of a fleet of 35 per cent of our own must be considered in relation to the general strategical situation that has to be faced.

2. This was recently described by the Chiefs of Staff in their Annual Review for 1935, in the following terms:—

(a) 'The ability of the One-Power Standard to satisfy our strategical needs is dependent upon a sufficient margin between the strength of the one power on which the standard is calculated and the strength of the next strongest naval power. The existing margin is only sufficient on the supposition that France will not be our enemy in Europe and that we are not without allies.'

(b) 'That we should be called upon to fight Germany and Japan simultaneously without allies is a state of affairs to the prevention of which our diplomacy would naturally be directed. With France as our ally the naval situation in Europe would wear a different complexion and the main British fleet would be available to defend our Empire in the East.'

(c) 'Although His Majesty's Government in the United Kingdom would never, we presume, confide the *entire* protection of this country and its vital sea communications to a foreign navy in the absence of our Main Fleet, yet if France were our ally, her naval forces could undertake part of this responsibility. A British capital ship cruiser and destroyer strength in home waters equal to that of Germany is probably the least that we could accept.'

(d) 'It would be important to have sufficient warning to enable us to bring forward our capital ships undergoing large repairs before we were called upon simultaneously to face Germany in European waters and send our Main Fleet to the Far East. Subject to this proviso, and except for the shortage of cruisers, we should, in the next 3 or 4 years, be able to provide naval security in an alliance with France against Germany, while at the same time defending ourselves against Japanese aggression.'

3. At the present time Japan's total naval strength by tonnage is about 64 per cent of ours, and Germany's is less than 11 per cent. In the vital

delegates that might be required. The British representatives accordingly reported to the Ministerial Naval Committee in the terms of the above report (N.C.M.(35)50). The Committee authorized Sir J. Simon 'to intimate to the German representatives the acceptance of the proposal' to lay down for the future a relationship between the German fleet and the British fleet in the proportion of 35–100. Following a reminiscence by Vice-Admiral Hughes Hallett, Messrs K. Middlemas and J. Barnes in *Baldwin* (London, 1969, pp. 827–8) suggest that the effective decision was taken at an informal discussion between the senior British Cabinet ministers on June 5 in the Cabinet Room, after a luncheon given by Mr. MacDonald for the British and German delegations.

matter of capital ships, the percentages are 57 per cent and 15 per cent, so that at the moment the margin is ample. If, when Germany has reached a strength of 35 per cent of our own, as is her announced intention, Japan's relative strength remains the same as at present, we should, *on a purely tonnage basis*, have a margin sufficient to fulfil the requirements set out in paragraph 2(*c*).

4. Since our strategical requirements must take account of both Germany and Japan it is evidently to our advantage that the naval forces of each or either of them should

(*a*) Be limited.

(*b*) Be limited at as low a figure as it is possible to secure.

5. The statements of Herr Hitler, as amplified by the German representatives in the current conversations, make it clear that there is no prospect whatever of Germany coming to agreement on any question, including the extremely important one of qualitative limitation, except on the 35 per cent basis.

The German representatives have made it clear also that they are prepared to preserve this strength relative to British strength whatever France or any other country may do.

6. We have also received the impression that the German Government genuinely consider that they have made a generous and self-sacrificing decision, and that if the opportunity to close with the offer is lost it is improbable that they will stop short at the 35 per cent level in building up their fleet.

7. Our information leads us to suppose that the German resources are amply sufficient to enable them to complete the whole of the tonnage necessary to bring them up to this level by the year 1943, and that they have made arrangements for manning the fleet as it is constructed.

8. The foregoing represents the ultimate position, stated in general terms. There are, however, other aspects of the matter which necessitate more detailed examination. As stated in the body of this report, the German representatives have declared that Germany intends to calculate her tonnage in principle by categories.

9. In the first place the capital ship modernisation programme that has been undertaken by Japan has already made us relatively weak in modern or modernised ships. Until the middle of the year 1939 we shall, except for a short period, have only 11 ships available for service and quite apart from the German battle-fleet, we shall have no margin in modernised ships over Japan alone.

10. From this point of view it is important that every endeavour should be made to slow down the rate of increase of the German fleet.

11. Germany at present possesses three ships of the *Deutschland* Class, a type of capital ship, which, although small, cannot be opposed ship for ship by existing cruisers. In addition, Germany is building two further ships which it is believed will be improved and enlarged *Deutschland* Class of 20,000 tons or over.

12. A 35 per cent ratio of the British tonnage in the capital ship category would permit Germany to lay down two further capital ships of the maximum size.

13. Thus, when the programme under consideration is completed, we shall be faced with a German Battlefleet of seven ships, of which four may be of the most powerful type allowed. During this same period Japan may have completed four new capital ships (assuming they are content with the programme suggested unofficially by Admiral Yamamoto).

14. Against this total of eight new large capital ships plus three *Deutschland* Class, the tentative British programme will only produce six ships. In these circumstances it may be essential for the Naval Staff to recommend a more rapid replacement of the British battle fleet, in order to ensure that in *new ships* the British Fleet does not fall behind the capital ship strength of Japan and Germany combined.

15. This is a position which cannot be avoided by refusing to recognise the German decision and indeed such a refusal is more likely to lead to an acceleration of the German programme with consequent disadvantage to ourselves. Amelioration of the position can only be brought about by persuading the Germans to increase their navy at a moderate rate. This they are unlikely to agree to do if we do not accord them the recognition for which they are asking.

16. With regard to other categories of ships, on a basis of 50 cruisers the situation would be unsatisfactory. When, however, we have 70 cruisers, and supposing the German ratio to be calculated with respect to our under-age tonnage only, the position can be accepted. Our present contemplated rate of increase is sufficient to balance the probable rate of German building.

17. In regard to destroyers, if the German calculation is based on our under-age destroyer tonnage, the situation would be satisfactory.

18. In regard to Submarines, it was inevitable that failing general agreement for the abolition of this type, Germany would ultimately acquire a right to build them. Although the German representatives have stated their intention to calculate their tonnage category by category in principle, yet they have made it clear that if other Powers are granted in a future Treaty or retain in fact the right to have parity with the British Empire in the Submarine category, Germany will expect a similar right, although she will not necessarily build up to this level.

Should Germany exercise her power to build up to parity with ourselves in submarines, she could produce a formidable force of some 50 to 60 submarines (allowing for the fact that her first 12 are to be 250 tons each). This is a situation which must arouse some misgiving, but it is quite apparent from the attitude of the German representatives that it is a question of *Gleichberechtigung* which is really exercising their minds, and not the desire to acquire a large Submarine fleet. In the present mood of Germany, it seems probable that the surest way to persuade them to be moderate in their actual performance is to grant them every consideration in theory. In fact, they are more likely to build up to Submarine parity if we object to their theoretical right to do so, than if we agree that they have a moral justification.

Apart from this psychological aspect of the question, the only other way to ensure a reasonable limitation of German submarine building is to keep our own tonnage as low as possible.

It is in any event satisfactory to know the limit beyond which the Germans do not intend to proceed. Under these circumstances, it is considered that the situation is acceptable.

19. The German decision to preserve a 35 per cent ratio *vis-à-vis* the British Fleet limits the German Navy to 70 per cent of that of France assuming that France maintains her present ratio of naval strength with us which is about 50 per cent. In the opinion of the Naval Staff, France will be wise to accept the proposal and in informing the French Government as also in any subsequent naval discussions, it must be our aim to endeavour to persuade them to avoid any consequential increase of the French Fleet, as such an increase might call for similar action on our part in the event of the political situation changing.

20. *Conclusions.*

(*a*) On general strategical grounds a 35 per cent ratio of our naval strength for Germany is acceptable.

(*b*) The increase of the German Fleet makes it essential to preserve our Washington Treaty ratio *vis-à-vis* Japan.

(*c*) A more rapid replacement of the British battle Fleet than is visualised in the tentative British programme, may be necessary in order to ensure that in *new ships* the British Fleet does not fall behind the capital ship strength of Japan and Germany combined.

(*d*) Our present contemplated rate of increase in cruiser strength is sufficient to balance the probable rate of German building in this category.

(*e*) In other categories there are no particular comments.

(*f*) From the point of view of general limitation of naval armament it would be greatly to our advantage to recognise the decision of the German Government lest the demand should be increased.

## No. 306

*Letter from Central Department to Chancery (Paris)*

[*C 4152/55/18*]

FOREIGN OFFICE, June 5, 1935

Dear Chancery,

In para 2 of telegram No. 102 Saving of the 23rd May,[1] Monsieur Léger is reported as saying that 'if Russia attacked Poland, France remained obliged to go to Poland's assistance'.

[1] No. 231.

We enclose copy of a minute written in the Department[2] on the obligations of France towards Poland in the event of any attack on Poland by the U.S.S.R.

We suppose that Léger's statement is based on Article 3 of the Franco-Polish Agreement of 1921;[3] but it is noteworthy that in 1925 M. Briand twice told Sir A. Chamberlain that 'contrary to what had sometimes been alleged, France had undertaken no obligation to defend Poland against Russia.'[4]

We should be grateful if you could clear up this point for us by enquiring unofficially at the Quai d'Orsay, with reference to the above statement by Monsieur Léger, what precisely *are* the obligations of France to Poland in the event of an attack on Poland by Russia.

Yours ever<br>CENTRAL DEPT.

[2] This minute of May 29 by Mr. Lawford of the Central Department is not printed.
[3] Signed at Paris on February 19, 1921; see *B.F.S.P.*, vol. 118, p. 342.
[4] In Foreign Office despatch No. 2128 of June 19, 1925, to Paris Mr. A. Chamberlain, at that time Secretary of State for Foreign Affairs, informed Mr. Phipps, acting Chargé d'Affaires at Paris, that M. Briand had told him 'categorically during our recent meeting at Geneva that, contrary to what has sometimes been alleged, France had undertaken no obligation to defend Poland against Russia'. In a memorandum of October 14, 1925, from Locarno, Mr. Chamberlain recorded: 'In the course of the conversation which I had with Monsieur Briand yesterday morning, he repeated to me the statement he had made to me in Geneva, that France was under no obligation to go to the assistance of Poland in case of war with Russia. . . .'

## No. 307

*Letter from the Air Ministry to the Foreign Office (Received June 6)*

*[C 4545/55/18]*

Secret                                                                        AIR MINISTRY, *June 5, 1935*

Sir,

I am commanded by the Air Council to refer to recent demi-official correspondence (C. 3265/55/18)[1] in regard to the detailed proposals for the organisation of assistance under the Draft Air Pact, as produced by the French representatives at Stresa[2] and to forward for consideration the enclosed copy of Memorandum[1] which has been prepared by the Air Staff on this subject.

2. It will be observed that the opinions expressed in the Memorandum (see in particular paragraph 15) suggest that the ability of Air Forces to come to the assistance, under the Pact, of a Power which was in danger of aggression would not be predominantly dependent on previous bi-lateral agreements specifying in detail the form and method of such assistance. This may be a point of some importance in view of the political difficulties (to which the Secretary of State for Foreign Affairs drew attention at Stresa—

[1] Not printed.
[2] See Volume XII, No. 722, pp. 869–70, 888–9, 901–4.

see page 25 of Notes of Conversation³) involved in supplementing the Pact by bi-lateral agreements. On the one hand, an Anglo-French bi-lateral agreement, in supplement of a General Pact, would have the appearance of discriminating against other Powers also parties to the Pact. On the other hand it is difficult to contemplate that Great Britain (for example) should concurrently enter into separate bi-lateral agreements, one to concert measures of co-operation with France against the risk of German aggression, and another to concert measures of co-operation with Germany against the risk of French aggression.

I am, &c.,

J. M. SPEIGHT

³ See *ibid.*, p. 903.

## No. 308

*Letter from Sir E. Phipps (Berlin) to Mr. Sargent (Received June 7)*
[*C 4596/55/18*]

BERLIN, *June 5, 1935*

My dear Sargent,

My despatch No. 534 of June 4th.¹

We learn in strict confidence from the French Embassy, who are particularly anxious that their press should not get hold of it, that they hope to reach a *modus vivendi* with the Germans about recruiting in the demilitarised zone. In the German conscription law of 21st May, 1935, Article 12 lays down that persons liable to compulsory military service in the demilitarised zone 'shall be called up through the local civil authorities'. The Reichswehr Ministry were evidently beset by conscientious scruples and though they issued the conscription law without any previous parley with the French, they lost no time in sounding the French Embassy here as to possible reactions in view of the Locarno and Versailles stipulations. Laval, it seems, is not at all inclined to make mountains out of molehills. He realises that the Rhineland will be conscripted 'voluntarily' if necessary, and with his approval, the French here have suggested to the Germans that details of methods of recruiting to be adopted in the Rhineland shall be communicated to the French Military Attaché here confidentially. The Germans have unofficially declared their readiness to take account of any reasonable French objections. The French hope that the recruits will not be mustered within the forbidden zone, otherwise press attacks are sure to follow.

According to the French Counsellor, who is for the moment in charge, the French Embassy have been seriously considering whether they ought to recommend that a protest should be addressed to the German Government, on the ground that Article 12 of the Defence Law provides 'facilities for mobilisation' in the demilitarised zone. He asked a member of my staff for his opinion on this point. The reply was to the effect that it appeared difficult to conscript men in the zone without creating 'facilities for mobilisation'.

¹ No. 292.

Even if the recruiting offices were located outside the zone (and this would be highly inconvenient), it might be argued that the postmen who delivered the calling up notices and the railways which conveyed the men to their garrisons were affording such facilities.[2] The Germans had established a special régime for the zone and a mere formal protest would do no good, but would merely strengthen the hands of those soldiers who on administrative grounds objected to the perpetuation of the demilitarised zone.

Yours ever,

ERIC PHIPPS

P.S. The French counsellor has just rung up to say that he has made an unofficial communication at the Wilhelmstrasse to the following effect: the French Government have noted the provision in the Law providing for the recruiting of men in the demilitarised zone and are subjecting this provision to close examination. They reserve the right to revert to the matter in a subsequent communication.

E.P.

[2] In a letter to Sir E. Phipps of June 22 (C 4588/55/18), Mr. Wigram pointed out that the relevant article, No. 43, of the Treaty of Versailles prohibited 'all permanent works of mobilization', which appeared in the French text as 'facilités matérielles'. The tentative conclusion of the Foreign Office was that this expression referred to 'buildings or equipment or something of the kind' and that if 'no such buildings or equipment were collected in the zones, there would be no breach of this part of the article of the Treaty'.

## No. 309

*Sir E. Phipps (Berlin) to Sir J. Simon (Received June 6, 2.50 p.m.)*

*No. 231 Telegraphic [C 4549/55/18]*

BERLIN, *June 6, 1935, 1.23 p.m.*

Your telegram No. 121.[1]

Soviet Ambassador asked me point blank whether it was our intention to separate Air Pact from other points of the London Communiqué. As the question is still open I thought it best to reply in the negative especially as His Excellency has displayed great suspicion in the matter in conversation with the French Ambassador and myself.

Repeated to Paris and Moscow.

[1] No. 297.

## No. 310

*Sir J. Simon to Mr. Campbell (Paris)*

*No. 139 Telegraphic [C 4537/55/18]*

FOREIGN OFFICE, *June 6, 1935, 10.30 p.m.*

Your telegrams Nos. 111[1] and 114[2].

We presume that French government will be communicating their draft reply to German note to Italian and Belgian governments.

Repeated to Rome No. 313 and Brussels No. 52.

[1] No. 286.        [2] No. 299.

## No. 311

*Notes of the fourth meeting between representatives of the United Kingdom and Germany, June 6, 1935, at 5 p.m.*[1]

Present: *United Kingdom*: Sir J. Simon, Sir Bolton M. Eyres Monsell, Mr. R. L. Craigie, Vice-Admiral C. J. C. Little, Captain V. H. Danckwerts.

*Germany*: Herr von Ribbentrop, Rear-Admiral K. G. Schuster, Dr. Schmidt: *for the latter part of the meeting only*, Captain E. Wassner, Korvetten Kapitan H. Kiderlen, Dr. Kordt.

SIR JOHN SIMON opened the meeting by saying that he was very glad to be the bearer of a message from His Majesty's Government to the German Representatives in answer to the question they had put to His Majesty's Government at the first meeting.[2] He said that they had considered very carefully Herr Hitler's proposal for a relationship between the British and German fleets in the proportion of 100 : 35, a relationship which he proposed should be final and permanent. They fully recognised the historic importance of this decision, in virtue of which a sovereign State voluntarily agreed in advance to accept a permanent Naval inferiority of 65 per cent as compared with the British Fleet, and he was glad to be able to inform the German representatives that His Majesty's Government intended to recognise the Reich Chancellor's decision as the basis of future Naval discussions between the British and German Governments, and to agree to a permanent relationship between the two fleets in the proportion of 35 for the German Fleet and 100 for the British Fleet.

But before making a formal agreement with Germany in this sense we were obliged to inform the other Governments with whom we had had conversations that we intended to do so, and to give them an opportunity to offer any observations they might desire to make.

His Majesty's Government had also noted the declaration of the German Representatives that the German Government believed in the system of limitation by categories, and were prepared in principle to calculate the 35 per cent ratio on the tonnage in the separate categories. As this question of the calculation of the tonnage by categories was one of importance, and in order to prevent any possible misunderstanding, they had suggested, purely for the sake of clarification, certain amendments in the paragraph on this subject which was drafted on Wednesday evening[3] at the German Embassy by the German and British Representatives (see paragraph 2(*d*) of Paper No. N.C.M. (35) 50).[4]

A revised draft was then handed to Herr von Ribbentrop (Appendix I).

---

[1] The meeting was held at the Admiralty. These notes were circulated as N.C.(G) 4th Mtg. *Most Secret*. For the German representatives' record see *D.G.F.P.*, Series C, vol. iv, No. 141.

[2] See No. 289.

[3] June 5; see *D.G.F.P.*, *op. cit.*, No. 137. Two earlier informal meetings on that day are recorded *ibid.*, Nos. 135 and 136.                    [4] No. 305.

Sir John Simon said that it would be seen that the amendments we proposed were underlined.

He then read the revised draft.

Continuing, he said that he was very glad to be the vehicle of this message from the British Government to the German Government, and pointed out that a short adjournment of some kind would now be involved so that the British Government might communicate to the other Powers the intentions of His Majesty's Government. Would the German Delegation perhaps suggest how long an adjournment they thought suitable.

HERR VON RIBBENTROP thanked Sir John Simon for his explanation. He was pleased to hear that the British Government fully recognised the historical decision of the German Chancellor; also that they were ready to accept the relative proportion between the two Fleets of 100 : 35 as lasting.

Personally, he shared Sir John Simon's satisfaction in having been able to co-operate in reaching a conclusion of possibly world historical significance, the fruits of which the coming generation of both peoples would enjoy.

As regards a communication by the British Government to the other Naval Powers that the British Government intended to recognise the decision of the German Government to fix a relative strength of 100 : 35 as between the two Fleets, it was not clear to him whether the communication to these foreign Governments would be so worded as to convey a tacit admission of their right to demur or whether they were being informed merely in the process of international courtesy of a lasting decision which had been reached by the British Government. Herr von Ribbentrop begged of Sir John Simon to clear this point up since, as he had intimated the day before, delays and difficulties were to be feared if the other Powers were allowed to interfere. If, as he understood, the decision of the British Government was final, and if the foreign Governments were merely being informed of this decision as a matter of international courtesy, then only a short postponement of the negotiations would be involved. It was his opinion that there should not be too long a delay in resumption of the conversations, and he suggested for consideration the completion and signature of the final and formal text of the agreement, so far effected, shortly after Whitsuntide, and also a commencement of the practical work which would lead to a closer understanding between the two countries.

As regards the text just handed to him by Sir John Simon, it was desirable that it should be examined by the experts after translation, and it appeared to him that it would be useful if conversations between the respective technical experts regarding the actual text took place at the conclusion of the present meeting.

In conclusion, Herr von Ribbentrop repeated the hope that this agreement which had come about through the great foresight of the German Chancellor and which was the outcome of his earnest and heart-felt wishes to establish firmly a friendship between Great Britain and Germany would, in the future, prove to be a blessing to both people. He was happy to have taken part in such an historical decision.

SIR JOHN SIMON said that he was glad to hear that the German Representatives felt entirely at one with us in recognising the very great importance of what had passed.

As regards the question as to the implications of the language used by himself concerning the information to foreign Governments, he could reply in a sense satisfactory to the German Representatives that our language meant that we had *decided*. It was more than international courtesy which made it necessary for us to communicate with foreign Governments. It had always been understood and implied between the British Government and those with whom we have had naval conversations that one Power would not make any agreement with another Power without first informing the remaining Powers. This we should do both for courtesy and for fairness, and in any event in view of these commitments we must inform other Governments of our decision.

It was agreed that the experts should examine the language of the revised draft handed to Herr von Ribbentrop by Sir John Simon.

As regards future meetings, SIR JOHN SIMON agreed that we did not want to delay. It was unfortunate that France at the moment had not established her new Government. Subject to that, it was agreed to resume shortly after Whitsuntide. In conclusion, he repeated that we might feel on both sides of the table that we could congratulate ourselves that our two Nations should have been able to make this great contribution to the limitation of armaments, the promotion of the peace of the world, and the confirmation of the friendship between our two peoples.

After discussion, it was agreed that we should make no communication either here or in Berlin to the Press as to the point we had reached in the discussions. It was pointed out by Sir John Simon that it was extremely important that we should officially inform the other Governments before anything at all appeared in the Press, and we therefore proposed to send off these communications immediately.

HERR VON RIBBENTROP agreed, but pointed out that we may have to face the question of a leakage. It was therefore agreed that the two States should communicate with each other should this occur, and make a common statement, and that in any event when the appropriate moment comes a common communiqué should be issued.

At this point Sir John Simon and Sir Bolton Eyres Monsell withdrew from the meeting, and Captain Wassner, Korvetten Kapitan Kiderlen, Dr. Kordt and Commander Hughes-Hallett entered.

The discussion proceeded upon paragraph (*d*) of the 'revised draft reply', handed by Sir John Simon to Herr von Ribbentrop.

ADMIRAL SCHUSTER said that Sir John Simon had explained to Herr von Ribbentrop that paragraph (*d*) had been amended for the sole purpose of clarification. But it seemed to the German Delegation that the amended wording had a somewhat different meaning from that of the original draft which had been drawn up the evening before at the German Embassy.[5]

5 See *D.G.F.P.*, *op. cit.*, No. 137, enclosure 1.

He said that paragraph (*d*) could be divided into two parts, and that he only wished now to refer to the first part, that is, down to the end of the underlined sentence to the words 'corresponding reduction in others'. This part dealt with the case where a quantitative agreement on a ratio system had been negotiated between all Powers at a general Conference. Part II dealt with the case where there was only a bilateral agreement between Great Britain and Germany.

To illustrate his question he would take a concrete case. Supposing the two countries had agreed upon parity in the Destroyer or in the submarine category, was he to understand that that could only be done at the expense of tonnage in other categories, and, secondly, did this apply to all parties to the Treaty or to Germany only? By the words 'any variation' was he to infer that the transfer could be made by Germany under any general Treaty in the same way as by any other Power?

ADMIRAL LITTLE said that the answer to the first question was 'Yes'. That was what he understood.

MR. CRAIGIE said that any Convention containing a provision for a transfer must assume that the transfer is made within the total global tonnage. This had always been the basis of transfer arrangements with other countries, and Great Britain could not agree to a transfer clause under any other conditions.

HERR VON RIBBENTROP said he understood that the 35 per cent ratio was to be taken on a category basis, and that when they had been drafting clause (*d*) he had asked whether this included the possibility of Germany attaining parity in submarines outside the 35 per cent ratio.

ADMIRAL LITTLE replied that the additional submarine tonnage would have to be reckoned as part of the total tonnage, in the same way as was now done by other countries.

CAPTAIN DANCKWERTS pointed out that in the London Naval Treaty[6] total tonnages and not ratios had been fixed, so that the equality that had been agreed upon in Submarines had been provided at the expense of compensation in a somewhat different form.

ADMIRAL SCHUSTER asked whether he was to understand that the underlined sentence in the first part of paragraph (*d*) applied to all countries.

ADMIRAL LITTLE replied that the answer was 'Yes', provided other countries were in an agreement at all. But he gathered that Germany was now proposing to 'peg' (this word was translated to Herr von Ribbentrop who concurred with it) her global tonnage on that of Great Britain in any case. That would fix the German total tonnage at 35 per cent of the British tonnage, and any special arrangement in one category would have to be made at the expense of the other categories.

ADMIRAL SCHUSTER said that the first part of paragraph (*d*) was now all right so far as the German Delegation were concerned, and he had no further questions to add.

Turning to the second part of paragraph (*d*), he said that the following words occurred: 'Any proposal to *vary* the 35 per cent . . .' He asked where

6 Of April 1930.

did 'vary' begin; was he to assume that at the outset there should be no transfer at all?

HERR VON RIBBENTROP said he felt he might as well explain what was at the back of the German Representatives' minds. They would like to have a fairly large transfer. They were thinking in particular of one thing; they had made a severe sacrifice so far as France was concerned and they had to reckon with the Franco-Russian alliance. There was a possibility of France raising her tonnage in some categories to an alarmingly high level, and the German Delegation desired some arrangement within a transfer clause to meet that danger.

ADMIRAL LITTLE said that the British Representatives had tried to cover that contingency by the words 'in the light of the Naval situation at the time'. The British Government visualised that the German Government might come to them and say 'France is alarming us by her increased building, say, of Submarines—We should like to increase our Destroyers'. That was what was meant by the words 'in the light of the Naval situation'.

ADMIRAL SCHUSTER said he was afraid that when translated into German the words of this clause might be construed as making their right to transfer dependent on their first getting permission from Great Britain.

HERR VON RIBBENTROP added that the German Government would like to have a rather larger transfer right than was usual in Treaties of this kind, for although in practice they would only act in agreement with Great Britain, the Treaty would otherwise appear to be rather one-sided.

He suggested that an automatic right to transfer up to 20 per cent would meet their case.

MR. CRAIGIE said it would be difficult at this stage to agree upon a definite percentage of transfer. It was not appropriate to discuss exact figures at this stage. He suggested that the underlined words under discussion should be replaced by the following: '. . . the manner and degree in which the German Government will have the right to vary the 35 per cent ratio in one or more categories. . . .'

HERR VON RIBBENTROP asked whether they might not add: '. . . it being understood there would be some transfer allowed in all categories, the exact amount to be decided later'.

ADMIRAL LITTLE said that the idea of a general transfer was new to the British Delegation. Great Britain had always opposed transfer *into* the Capital Ship and Submarine categories, but not *out* of them.

MR. CRAIGIE said that the British Delegation recognised that there would have to be a transfer in this case, but he considered it should be defined later when they had had time to go into the matter further.

After further discussion ADMIRAL LITTLE pointed out that at present the German Navy was considerably less than 35 per cent of the British Navy in all categories. Germany, he said, was building up her Navy now. The Naval Conference must take place, if ever, within the next year or two, by which time Germany would still be well below the 35 per cent level. There would be time then for the German Government to propose variations in the percentage of categories which might appear necessary to them in the light of other nations' building programmes.

The German Delegation expressed general satisfaction with this explanation, and paragraph (*d*) was then amended as previously proposed by Mr. Craigie. (See Appendix II).[7]

MR. CRAIGIE said he thought both Delegations understood each other's general position, and that they would try to put the agreement more clearly when the drafting stage was reached after Whitsuntide. He did not think that they were very far apart.

HERR VON RIBBENTROP said it had occurred to him to ask whether it was necessary for the *details* of any agreement they might reach to be communicated to other powers. It might be simpler to keep them as a private document.

MR. CRAIGIE said the point was whether Great Britain could do that, particularly in view of her obligations under the League of Nations. She was a member of the League of Nations. He pointed out that the transfer question only arose should there be no general treaty. Furthermore, it would be obviously undesirable to make now a concession on the transfer question to Germany which Great Britain would not care to include in a General Treaty.

It was agreed to leave further discussion of the matter till the following day.

## APPENDIX I TO NO. 311

(*d*) The German Government believe in the system of limitation by categories and they are prepared in principle to calculate the 35 per cent ratio on the tonnage in the separate categories, any variation of this ratio in a particular category being dependent upon the arrangements to this end that may be arrived at in a future general Treaty of naval limitation. Such arrangements would, it is understood, include the provision that any increase in one category would be compensated for by a corresponding reduction in others. Should no International Treaty be concluded, or should the question of limitation by categories not be dealt with in a future International Treaty, any proposal by the German Government to vary the 35 per cent ratio in one or more categories would be a matter for discussion between the German and British Governments in the light of the Naval situation then existing.

---

[7] Not printed. It was identical with Appendix I except for the following agreed amendments: (i) a division into two parts, the last section being a separate paragraph; (ii) the substitution of the words 'the manner and degree in which the German Government will have the right to vary the 35 per cent ratio in one or more categories' for the words underlined in Appendix I (lines 2 and 3 from the end).

## No. 312

*Sir E. Drummond (Rome) to Sir J. Simon (Received June 11)*
*No. 674 [C 4628/55/18]*

ROME, *June 6, 1935*

Sir,

I have the honour to inform you that the German Ambassador,[1] during a conversation which I had with him today, remarked that in his view the speech of Herr Hitler (May 21st) had considerably cleared the air and had made a favourable impression. I said that I thought this was so taking it as a whole, but that one of the troubles was that many people considered that Herr Hitler was not, in reality, completely master of the situation and that he might not be able to carry out, in full, his own intentions.

2. The Ambassador replied that this was a complete mistake. The position of Herr Hitler was very strong. In the country itself he commanded even more support than Signor Mussolini did in Italy. He was also on the best of terms with the Generals and with the Army, and they were extremely loyal to him. This combination was quite irresistible and no one could do anything against it. Germany must have peace in order to consolidate her internal position. It had taken Fascism eight years to establish itself fully in Italy; Germany hoped to be able to accomplish a similar task in less time, but five or six years would certainly be necessary.

3. There still remained the question of what he called culture and 'world outlook'. There was the problem of the Jewish, Catholic, Protestant and what might perhaps be called the non-Christian outlooks in Germany. It would take a considerable time before this complex of questions could be settled and one of the reasons why many people in Germany were so anxious for an early settlement of international difficulties was that they wanted the Führer to be free to devote the greater part of his attention to solving these difficulties.

4. I have sent a copy of this despatch to His Majesty's Ambassador at Berlin.

I have, &c.,
ERIC DRUMMOND

[1] Herr Ulrich von Hassell.

## No. 313

*Sir E. Drummond (Rome) to Sir J. Simon (Received June 11)*
*No. 675 [C 4629/55/18]*

ROME, *June 6, 1935*

Sir,

I have the honour to report that the German Ambassador, who called upon me today, told me that his Government had presented to His Majesty's Government their proposals with regard to the Air Convention.[1] I said that

[1] Cf. No. 263.

I was aware of this and that I understood that they had also authorised His Majesty's Government to communicate those proposals to the other Locarno Powers, but that we had thought it better that the German Government themselves should make that communication.

2. Herr von Hassell did not continue the conversation on this subject, but remarked that the German Government had also communicated to all the Locarno Powers their criticisms of the Soviet-French Pact and the proposed Eastern Pact.[2] These were based not only on the spirit but also on the letter of the Soviet-French Agreement. On my saying to him that I did not understand how objection could be taken to the letter of the Soviet-French Pact as being inconsistent with Locarno, he read me extracts of an interview which the German Ambassador in Paris had had with M. Léger. The case assumed was that the Council of the League had under consideration an alleged act of aggression by Germany against Russia. M. Léger had stated that even if the Council of the League failed to reach a unanimous report and the French Government was therefore enabled to take such action as it thought fit for the maintenance of right and justice (paragraph 7, Article 15 of the Covenant), the French Government would not take military action against Germany without consulting and obtaining the concurrence of Great Britain and Italy. The French Government were not prepared to embody such a provision in any protocol but they were, I understood, prepared to give an undertaking to this effect.

3. The German Ambassador in Paris had of course telegraphed this to Berlin and the reply had been that M. Léger had entirely missed the point. The German Government had the fullest confidence in the loyalty and disinterestedness of Great Britain, but they held that a military attack on Germany by France as a result of an alleged attack by Germany on Russia, there being no unanimous decision of the Council, was contrary to the provisions of the Locarno Treaty and the fact that England and Italy concurred in such an attack did not affect the legal position. Germany could not agree that France should decide whether or not an aggression had taken place and Locarno limited her grounds for any attack on Germany. The argument was somewhat involved and couched in legal German, but I think I have reproduced it more or less accurately.

4. I replied that personally I was not much impressed by the argument. After all the Covenant of the League prevailed even over Locarno and it was quite certain that the provisions of Locarno were never intended to interfere with the rights given to every Power by the Covenant. Under the Covenant it might well become necessary for the individual members of the League to decide whether or not an act of aggression had taken place. The Ambassador remarked that he did not envy Great Britain and Italy being faced with a responsibility such as that which the French Government wished to entrust to them. To this I answered that even in the case of Locarno the guarantor Powers might be called upon to consider whether or not a breach had taken place. Responsibilities of such a kind could not therefore be avoided.

[2] See *D.G.F.P.*, Series C, vol. iv, No. 107.

5. The Ambassador then observed that a practical difficulty arose, namely that as France and Russia were members of the Council they could at any time ensure that there should be no unanimity in the Council. I understood him to mean that if for instance Russia attacked Germany and the question came before the League, France and Russia could prevent the Council from passing a unanimous report, in which case France would have her hands free and could act under paragraph 7 of Article 15 of the Covenant. I said to the Ambassador that it seemed to me that it was a very simple remedy for such a state of affairs and reminded him that Germany was equally still a member of the Council. The Ambassador said that what troubled the German Government particularly was that it was clear that the Franco-Soviet Treaty had been drawn up as against Germany. This was even more the case in regard to the Soviet–Czechoslovak Pact.[3] It was the first time since the war that a document of this character had been signed. I replied that as I understood it the Pact was open for German adherence. Herr von Hassel[l] brushed this argument aside by saying that everybody knew that Germany was not prepared to sign any treaties of mutual assistance.

6. I have sent a copy of this despatch to His Majesty's Ambassadors at Paris and Berlin.

I have, &c.,
Eric Drummond

³ See No. 239, note 3. Cf. *D.G.F.P.*, Series C, vol. iv, No. 105.

## No. 314

*Sir E. Ovey (Brussels) to Sir J. Simon (Received June 7, 2.35 p.m.)*
*No. 34 Telegraphic [C 4597/55/18]*

BRUSSELS, *June 7, 1935, 1.3 p.m.*

Your telegram No. 49.[1]

The Belgian government entirely agree as to the importance of reply being concerted between the four interested Powers. They are ready to proceed to the necessary exchange of views and ask to be told what procedure His Majesty's Government consider most appropriate.

Text[2] by bag tonight.

Repeated to Paris and Rome.

¹ See No. 301.
² The text of M. van Zeeland's letter of June 7 to Sir E. Ovey, not printed, was received in the Foreign Office on June 8 as enclosure in Brussels despatch No. 340 of June 7.

## No. 315

### Sir J. Simon to Sir R. Lindsay (Washington)[1]
#### No. 155 Telegraphic [A 5129/22/45]

Secret                                          FOREIGN OFFICE, *June 7, 1935, 2.45 p.m.*

The following oral and very confidential communication has been made to-day to the Counsellor of the United States Embassy:[2]—

'1. At the outset of the Anglo-German naval conversations the German Government announced their decision to build in the future a fleet which would be in the proportion of 35 for the German fleet to 100 for the British fleet.

'2. The German Government would also be prepared to agree—

(*a*) That this should be a permanent relationship between the two fleets, i.e., that the strength of the German fleet should never exceed 35 per cent of the British fleet.

(*b*) That they would adhere to this limitation in all circumstances, e.g., it would not be affected by the construction of third Powers.

(*c*) That this ratio need not be incorporated in any future international treaty provided that the alternative method eventually adopted for the future limitation of naval armaments were to give Germany full guarantees that this relationship between the British and German fleets will be maintained.

(*d*) That the ratio should, in principle, be calculated on the basis of the tonnage in the separate categories (i.e. not merely on the 'global' tonnage).

'Before, however, giving an undertaking in the sense of paragraph 2 above, they asked whether His Majesty's Government were prepared to accept this arrangement.

'The German offer has been carefully considered by His Majesty's Government, who have reached the conclusion that it should be accepted. They regard it as a contribution of great importance to the cause of future naval limitation, and consider that it furnishes an important assurance for the future security of this and other countries. Before, however, giving their formal reply to the German representatives, His Majesty's Government would be glad to learn whether the United States Government desire to offer any observations.

'In view of the urgency of the matter, they trust that they may receive any such observations in the course of the next few days.'

The Counsellor of the United States Embassy[2] was requested to impress on his Government that this communication should until further notice be regarded as secret.

The above is sent for your information and guidance.

[1] A similarly worded telegram, *mutatis mutandis,* was sent to His Majesty's Representatives at Paris (No. 140), Rome (No. 315) and Tokyo (No. 99).

[2] Also of the French, Italian, and Japanese Embassies.

## No. 316

*Sir G. Clerk (Paris) to Sir J. Simon (Received June 7, 8.15 p.m.)*
*No. 123 Telegraphic [C 4601/55/18]*

PARIS, *June 7, 1935, 6.30 p.m.*

Your telegram No. 139.[1]

The French government will also communicate their draft reply to the German note to the Italian and Belgian governments.

It is hoped that the draft may be approved this evening in time to send to you tonight but it has not yet been possible to obtain Monsieur Laval's final approval.[2]

Repeated to Rome and Brussels.

[1] No. 310.      [2] Cf. No. 268, note 2.

## No. 317

*Sir J. Simon to Sir E. Phipps (Berlin)*
*No. 125 Telegraphic [A 5233/22/45]*

*Secret*                        FOREIGN OFFICE, *June 7, 1935, 8 p.m.*

My telegram to Paris No. 140 of June 7.[1]

It is considered very undesirable that any communication in regard to this arrangement should be made to the press until after the meetings are resumed on June 14th. If, however, any serious leakage occurs, it may be necessary to issue a communiqué which it is proposed should be in the following terms:—[2]

'His Majesty's Government in the United Kingdom and the German Government have agreed that, after the Whitsuntide adjournment, the Anglo-German naval conversations will proceed on the basis of a relationship between the German and British Fleets in the proportion of 35 : 100.'

It has been further agreed that, even in the event of leakage, this communiqué should only be issued after prior agreement between the two Governments.

Herr von Ribbentrop suggests that, if the necessity for a communiqué arises, you should first communicate with him. He leaves for Berlin by air tomorrow. The conversations will be resumed on June 14.

Repeated to Washington (No. 158); Rome (No. 316), Tokyo (No. 100), Paris (No. 205 Saving).

[1] Cf. No. 315, note 1.
[2] See No. 318 below for the drafting of this communiqué.

# No. 318

*Notes on the fifth meeting between representatives of the United Kingdom and Germany, June 7, 1935, at 3.15 p.m.*[1]

Present: *United Kingdom*: Mr. R. L. Craigie, Vice-Admiral C. J. C. Little, Captain V. H. Danckwerts.

*Germany*: Herr von Ribbentrop, Rear-Admiral K. G. Schuster, Captain E. Wassner, Korvetten Kapitan H. Kiderlen, Dr. Kordt, Dr. Schmidt.

ADMIRAL LITTLE said that on the transfer question Admiral Schuster had kindly come to see him at 12 o'clock that day. They had discussed a new proposal that the following sentence should be added to the end of paragraph (*d*) of the 'revised draft reply' referred to in the report of the fourth meeting (Appendix I to N.C. (G) 4th Meeting)[2]

'It is also understood that the present requirements should be settled in the discussions now in hand.'

Admiral Little asked whether they could take this as agreed.

The German Representatives confirmed that they agreed to this proposal. The final form of paragraph (*d*) is attached as Appendix III to this record.[3]

MR. CRAIGIE referring to the question of an agreed Press Statement said that he considered the draft which had been suggested by the German Delegation on the preceding evening would meet the case very well. He proceeded to read the draft. (Appendix I.)[4]

HERR VON RIBBENTROP concurred in the Statement, and agreed that it should be issued that evening for publication in the following morning's papers.

MR. CRAIGIE said that the next question was what they were to say to the Press should a leakage occur.

HERR SCHMIDT then read a proposed communiqué which had been drafted by the German Delegation for issue in the event of a leakage, and he handed a written translation of it to Mr. Craigie.[5]

MR. CRAIGIE said that they would have to add something about the other Powers having been consulted, and also they would have to put the whole matter less definitely. He asked whether the German Delegation would object to an amended draft which should avoid all reference to formal agreement until after Whitsuntide. The British Government were anxious to avoid an announcement of definite agreement until then.

HERR VON RIBBENTROP said that the necessity for issuing some such statement might arise on Sunday,[6] from that moment there might be deliberate

---

[1] The meeting was held at the Admiralty. These notes were circulated as N.C.(G) 5th Mtg., *Most Secret*.     [2] No. 311.

[3] Printed as Appendix below.     [4] Not printed. See *The Times*, June 8, p. 13.

[5] No copy of this draft has been traced in Foreign Office archives.

[6] June 9, Whit Sunday.

misinterpretations of the position. He considered that if a further communiqué had to be issued at all, it should be as precise as possible. On the other hand, it was most unlikely that the necessity would arise before Whitsuntide.

MR. CRAIGIE reminded Herr von Ribbentrop that as Sir John Simon had stated the day before, the British Government were not prepared to make a formal agreement until the Delegations met again on the 14th June. The delay was purely a question of courtesy to other Powers. The German Delegation must take into account the difficulties of the British Government in this respect. The British Government had met them in every way, and he therefore asked Herr von Ribbentrop to take account of the fact that the British Government had held previous conversations with other Powers.

Mr. Craigie added that he must reserve his opinion of the exact form of words and he suggested he might call on Herr von Ribbentrop later. He proposed, therefore, to prepare a modification of the German draft, and he would bring it to Herr von Ribbentrop that evening.

HERR VON RIBBENTROP agreed with this proposal.

MR. CRAIGIE added that should a leakage occur during the coming week, the two Governments should issue a communiqué in the form least likely to cause disturbance among the other Powers. Later on the British Government would be prepared to publish as formal and as definite an announcement as the German Delegation wished.

(Mr. Craigie then withdrew, explaining that he had received an urgent call to speak to the French Embassy. The question of the Press was raised again on Mr. Craigie's return to the meeting half an hour later.)

MR. CRAIGIE handed a proposed re-draft of the communiqué (Appendix II)[7] to the German Delegation. It was, he said, a statement of fact, absolutely correct, though it did not go quite so far as they had actually gone.

HERR VON RIBBENTROP supposed that the reason for the amendment was that the British Government did not wish to publish anything until a draft agreement was ready.

MR. CRAIGIE replied that that was not the case. They merely wished to give the other Governments a chance of making their observations. The British Government had already informed the Powers of their decision, and, furthermore, that no formal answer would be given to the German Government until the negotiations were resumed.

HERR VON RIBBENTROP asked what was the reason for the delay.

MR. CRAIGIE said that it was a matter of courtesy pure and simple.

HERR VON RIBBENTROP said he presumed that the amended communiqué (Appendix II) would be published in the event of the Press making some fantastic comment on the situation.

MR. CRAIGIE replied that that was so, but that publication would be by agreement, and that the British Government hoped to avoid it.

HERR VON RIBBENTROP said he agreed with the revised draft (Appendix II).

[7] Not printed. The text in this Appendix was identical with that transmitted to Berlin in No. 317.

He hoped the necessity of publishing the communiqué would not arise, but if in the opinion of one of their Governments it did arise, would the British Government instruct their Ambassador in Berlin to communicate directly with Herr von Ribbentrop. Alternatively, would the British Foreign Office inform the German Naval Attaché—Captain Wassner.

Replying to a further question, Herr von Ribbentrop said that he preferred a formal communiqué to the Press rather than the issue of identic statements.

Resuming the general discussion, ADMIRAL LITTLE said he would first deal with the question of qualitative limitation. From the British point of view, qualitative limitation was at least as important as quantitative limitation. There were two ways in which an armament race could be started and conducted, (a) by building more ships, and (b) by building larger ships. The armament races of the past had usually been caused by the building by one nation of a ship that would outclass those of her rivals—the principle of going one better.

The greatest accomplishment, in the British view, of the Washington Treaty were [sic] the qualitative limitations it imposed.

Unless there had been a qualitative limit for capital ships, for instance, the only limit to their size and expense would have been the natural geographical limitations of harbours and channels. There would certainly have been battleships of 50,000 or 60,000 tons by now.

Not only would great financial savings to all countries result from the universal adoption of agreed qualitative limits but, in addition, the interests of peace and tranquillity would be served by the elimination of *surprise* and the spirit of unlimited competition.

The qualitative limits that had been proposed by the British Government were set out in Sheet 'A', (attached)[8] which Admiral Little then handed to the German representatives.

(a) *Capital Ships.* The British Government had proposed a limit of 25,000 tons with 12″ guns. This size had been reached after careful consideration. A battleship must be the final arbiter in Naval warfare, and must have nothing to fear from lesser classes of ship. The next category was the 10,000 ton 8″ cruiser, and the British Admiralty thought that the 25,000 ton 12″ ship was the smallest Battleship which could deal effectively with 8″ cruisers. The attitude of other Powers to this proposal was as follows:—

The United States Government still stood in general for the big ship, and had, so far, given no definite indication of their willingness to reduce below the Washington Treaty limitations (i.e. 35,000 tons with 16″ guns). At the same time they had some hope that the United States of America would agree to a 14″ gun on a tonnage of between 30,000 and 35,000 tons if this were to be universally agreed upon, and if it were to form part of a general arrangement for limitation, satisfactory to the United States of America.

The Japanese representatives had officially put forward a proposal for the abolition of capital ships, but had since exchanged views unofficially with

[8] Not printed.

388

the United Kingdom representatives as to what should be the qualitative limit if this type were to be retained. They were unwilling to come as low as 12" guns and preferred a limit of 28,000 to 30,000 tons with 14" guns.

The French representatives had made no difficulty about agreeing to the British proposal of 25,000 tons with 12" guns in the future, though they now intended, as they had announced, to build two ships to match the Italian 2–35,000 ton capital ships that were now building.

The Italian representatives were prepared to agree to any qualitative limits to which other powers would agree in the future. At the same time, they were building 2–35,000 tons ships in which, it was understood, they intended to mount 15" guns.

To sum up, the British Government were not without hope that a general agreement between the Washington Treaty Powers could be reached on a capital ship qualitative limitation of 30,000 tons with 14" guns.

(b) *Aircraft Carriers*. The British Government had proposed a limit of 22,000 tons with 6·1" guns, and would be prepared to reduce the size of the gun even further to 5·1" if such a proposal were generally acceptable.

The United States of America seemed to be of the opinion that the size of the gun should remain 6·1".

The Japanese representatives had been in favour of reducing the tonnage limit to 20,000 tons, and had been informed that Great Britain was prepared to give consideration to such a proposal in the event of a general arrangement being reached.

No other countries had raised any objection to the limits proposed by the British Government.

(c) *Cruisers*. The British Government would like to see no further cruisers of 10,000 tons, armed with 8" guns, constructed, since they were of the opinion that ships of this size are larger than is necessary for the duties which a cruiser has to perform.

The United States of America had so far given no definite indication of their willingness to reduce cruiser qualitative limitations. On the other hand, they were apparently satisfied that they themselves did not require to build more of this type at present.

The Japanese representatives had made an official proposal for the abolition of 8" gun cruisers.

Subject to discussion, both the French and Italian representatives had given some indication that they would agree to the cessation of 8" gun cruiser building.

As a result of the building of cruisers of 8,500 to 10,000 tons, armed with 6" guns by Japan and the United States of America, the British Government had reluctantly undertaken the building of corresponding ships of about 9,000 tons. It was their view that these large 6" gun cruisers were uneconomical and should be limited in number in the same way as 8" cruisers. The British Government would like to see the size of cruisers reduced to as low a figure as possible. In deciding what this should be they considered that a cruiser should be strong enough in all respects to destroy any armed merchant ship. In conformity with that idea they proposed a limit of 7,000 tons and 6·1″ guns. There seemed a reasonable hope that these qualitative limits, or something nearly approaching them, might ultimately prove acceptable to the five Washington Treaty Powers.

Recent French cruisers had been designed on a tonnage of 7,600 tons.

(*d*) *Destroyers*. As regards destroyers, there had been general agreement between the representatives of the United Kingdom, United States of America and Japan for the retention of the existing London Naval Treaty limits, namely, 1850 tons for a Leader and 1500 tons for a destroyer with 5·1″ guns, supplemented by the proposal that not more than a certain percentage of vessels in this category should be of the larger type.

France and Italy remained at present wedded to the proposition that 6″ gun cruisers and destroyers should be contained in the same category, to be designated 'Light Surface Vessels'. In that case a destroyer category limitation would not be applicable, as the cruiser limit would fix the maximum.

(*e*) *Submarines*. The Governments of the United Kingdom and the United States of America remained in favour of the abolition of submarines. The British Government were particularly pleased to see that the Reich Chancellor had taken the same view. The United Kingdom had also proposed that, if submarines could not be abolished, they should be limited to a tonnage of 250 tons. In fixing this size they were guided by the fact that a submarine of this size could not be used (broadly speaking) for offensive purposes in ocean warfare. In view, however, of the determined opposition of both Japan and France to the abolition of submarines or reduction to so small a size the United Kingdom was prepared to retain the maximum size and gun limits as defined in the London Naval Treaty (2,000 tons with 5·1″ guns). That proposal seemed likely to be acceptable to the other principal Powers.

ADMIRAL LITTLE said that he would now make some remarks on the subject of quantitative limitation.

Mr. Craigie had already outlined the British proposal for declarations of building programmes to take the place of the former system of total tonnage limitation. The British programme of construction was, of course, limited by the London Naval Treaty up to and including the year 1936 and, therefore, the British proposal had been for declarations of building programmes by the other Powers so limited, for the years 1937–42 inclusive.

The programmes the two countries were undertaking now, i.e. up till the end of 1936, would, he presumed, be exchanged during the present conversations.

In a passage in his recent speech, Herr Hitler had said:—

'The British Empire has an overwhelming vital necessity and therewith the right to a dominating perfection of the British world Empire at sea.'[9]

[9] In the 'final and approved translation' of Herr Hitler's speech (see No. 222, note 1) the corresponding passage read: 'The German Government voluntarily recognise the supreme vital importance, and thus the justification, for a dominating protection of the British world Empire at sea'.

This had been greatly appreciated by the British Government who felt they had great absolute and relative needs in comparison with other powers.

The ultimate intentions of the British Government were shewn on 'Sheet B'[10] which Admiral Little then handed to the German Delegation. He suggested that it might assist them in preparing a statement of the German intentions.

He might perhaps point out that the British Admiralty always desired to avoid panic building, as this, from a purely Naval point of view, was most inconvenient. The British method was to maintain steady programmes of replacement building, so that any increase in the size of the fleet was spread out over a long period, thus ensuring the greatest efficiency and steady employment in the dockyards and the least fluctuation in the number of men required to man the fleet.

In fixing their programme Admiral Little suggested that the German Government should adopt a deliberate rate of building, the advantages of which he was sure they would appreciate from a Naval point of view, and which would also have great advantages from a political point of view.

Admiral Little added that he thought it would help both the Delegations to arrive at agreed building programmes (which he hoped they would do after the Whitsuntide recess) if the German Delegation could bring back a statement similar to 'Sheet B', showing the German Government's final intention as to their absolute strength. If both the Delegations knew what the final intentions of their Governments were, they would find it much easier to agree on building programmes.

(Mr. Craigie re-entered the meeting at this point).

ADMIRAL SCHUSTER said he wished to thank Admiral Little for his statement. The German Delegation would examine the position, and would be ready to enter into the constructive phase of their negotiations after the recess.

MR. CRAIGIE asked whether he could assume that the German Delegation would bring back with them proposals for a building programme.

ADMIRAL SCHUSTER said that they would certainly propose to do this to Berlin, and he hoped to be in a position to make the desired communication on the return of the German Delegation.

MR. CRAIGIE said that, before they adjourned, he would like to say how much the British Delegation had appreciated the friendly atmosphere in which their conversations had been conducted, and the complete frankness shewn by each side. On neither side had any bargaining been attempted, and the British initial hesitation in regard to the ratio question had been on a question of method only and was due to their desire to avoid unnecessarily hurting the susceptibilities of other Powers. But there had been no bargaining, and he hoped that there would be none after Whitsuntide. In that event the two Delegations would soon reach agreement.

Speaking on behalf of the German Delegation, HERR VON RIBBENTROP

---

[10] Not printed. This reproduced the first paragraph of Annex 4 to No. 282 listing the under-age British Commonwealth fleet to which, subject to the building programmes of foreign Powers, it was intended to build.

thanked Mr. Craigie very much for his remarks, and reciprocated his wishes as to the atmosphere that should prevail after the Whitsuntide recess. He wished particularly to thank Mr. Craigie for his understanding of the German point of view. Finally, Herr von Ribbentrop hoped that the basis they had established for their future negotiations would also prove the basis for better relations between their two countries, and that the agreement just reached would prove to be only a beginning.

### APPENDIX TO No. 318
#### Final form of paragraph (d).

(d) The German Government believe in the system of limitation by categories, and they are prepared in principle to calculate the 35 per cent ratio on the tonnage in the separate categories, any variation of this ratio in a particular category being dependent upon the arrangements to this end that may be arrived at in a future general Treaty on Naval limitation. Such arrangements would, it is understood, include the provision that any increase in one category would be compensated for by a corresponding reduction in others.

Should no International Treaty be concluded, or should the question of limitation by categories not be dealt with in a future International Treaty, the manner and degree in which the German Government will have the right to vary the 35 per cent ratio in one or more categories would be a matter for discussion between the German and British Governments, in the light of the Naval situation then existing.

It is also understood that the present requirements will be settled in the discussion now in hand.

### No. 319

#### Letter from Mr. Craigie to Sir G. Clerk (Paris)
#### [A 5372/22/45]

FOREIGN OFFICE, *June 7, 1935*

My dear Clerk,

Our telegram No. 140[1] of today.

In making the communication to Cambon I gave explanations in rather greater detail than is shown in the telegram and, as Cambon has now a pretty good knowledge of this question, I think he fully understood the position. At the end of the conversation I handed him an Aide Mémoire in the terms of the telegram but emphasised that it was not to be regarded as a written communication.

This afternoon the French Ambassador called to see me,[2] and I have just time before the bag closes, to write to inform you briefly what happened. Corbin expressed his surprise that the German Government, which had so far been so insistent on having a régime of equality of rights with everybody should now be prepared to accept a ratio system which apparently would apply to Germany alone. I said that the same thought had occurred to us, but that I explained it by my belief that possibly the full implication of the

---

[1] Cf. No. 315, note 1.    [2] Cf. No. 318, p. 386.

proposal had only dawned on the Germans after the very exhaustive discussions which had occurred here. I also thought that, when Herr Hitler originally made his offer, he was under the impression that any future naval treaty would be based on ratios of naval strength, like the Washington Treaty. We believe we have convinced the German Representatives that there is not the slightest hope of such a treaty being concluded in the future.

The Ambassador then enquired as to the meaning of paragraph 2 (c).[3] I said that this was intended to provide for the case—in our opinion the only likely eventuality—in which there is no international treaty on the basis of ratios. In that case, the method of quantitative limitation will presumably be by unilateral declaration of programmes, and the Germans had received the assurance that, so far as we are concerned, the construction shown in the British and German programmes will not be incompatible with the attainment of a ratio of 35 : 100.

The Ambassador then said that he had understood that the acceptance of a 35 per cent ratio was unacceptable so far as we were concerned. I said I did not think we had ever made any statement to that effect, but that naturally we should have preferred a much lower ratio and we are far from welcoming the idea of a 35 per cent ratio. But the situation was that Germany had definitely decided to build a Fleet 35 per cent of the British Fleet and we had reached the conclusion, after exhaustive enquiries that no amount of argument would dissuade her from this course. Better, therefore, to stop Germany at this point while she is still in the mood for limitation.

As regards France, I drew attention to the great importance of paragraph 2 (b).[3] I said that the French Fleet at the moment was rather more than 50 per cent of the British Fleet. If, however, we took the figure of 50 per cent as the normal French figure, then this meant that France could rely on a permanent superiority of 30 per cent over the German Fleet. If France had to consider the difficult problem of the Italian and the German Fleet, we had to face the even more difficult problem of the possible division of our Fleet between Europe and the Pacific. So that really it was a question of agreeing to something inconvenient lest worse befall!

Corbin seemed to be reasonably satisfied with the explanations, and I gather that he will place the matter before his Government in as favourable a light as possible. I said that there was no reason for the French Government to commit themselves in any way at the present time should they not wish to do so. The best course was to wait and see what the German programme of construction up to 1942 would, in practice, amount to. If, as I believed, our acceptance of this German proposal would lead to a certain retardation of the reconstruction of the German Fleet, then it might well happen that France's new construction would not, for the present at all events, be affected by the proposed ratio. This is anyhow our sincere hope.

I am sending a copy of this letter to Phipps.

Yours ever<br>R. L. C.

[3] In No. 315.

## No. 320

*Sir G. Clerk (Paris) to Sir S. Hoare*[1] *(Received June 11)*

*No. 120 Saving: Telegraphic* [*C 4627/55/18*]

PARIS, *June 8, 1935*

Mr. Campbell's telegram No. 115.[2]

M. Léger stated yesterday that there was no foundation whatever for the belief that M. Laval had committed himself in any way to the Soviet Ambassador.

In the course of some further informal conversation on this subject he said he thought it would be a mistake to press M. Laval to declare his hand at this stage. Public opinion was not yet ripe for the separation of the air pact from the other elements of the London declaration: the Service departments had one and all expressed themselves in favour of maintaining its indivisibility. If, therefore, you were to insist on an immediate answer to your question it would have to be an unfavourable one.

On the other hand M. Laval had agreed to the French experts collaborating in the preparatory work. This process must inevitably take some time. Who could say whether, by the time it was complete, public opinion would not have advanced or other circumstances have arisen to persuade the country that it would do well to avail itself of the advantages offered by an air pact without waiting upon other more problematical agreements?

M. Léger's diagnosis of M. Laval's present position in this matter is undoubtedly correct and it seems to me that there is much to be said for the method which he advocates. Though I cannot guarantee that opinion here will come round there is at least a chance that it will, whereas at present the answer, if we insist on receiving it, must be negative.

I will of course continue to press M. Laval as strongly as possible, but it is important that you should realise how the wind blows at present here.

[1] Cf. No. 304, note 10.      [2] No. 300.

## No. 321

*Sir S. Hoare to Sir E. Phipps (Berlin)*

*No. 127 Telegraphic* [*A 5233/22/45*]

*Immediate*

FOREIGN OFFICE, *June 10, 1935*

My telegram No. 125.[1]

Morning Post this morning contains statement that in spite of secrecy maintained on both sides there is reason to believe that German claim to navy equivalent to 35 per cent of Great Britain's has been accepted in principle by British negotiators. Please inform Herr Ribbentrop that we shall for the present reply to press enquiries that the matter of a 35 per cent ratio was of course discussed but no statement can be made. If however adoption

[1] No. 317.

of this line with press does not succeed in eliminating further speculation, we think it may be desirable to issue communiqué in terms agreed morning June 11th.[2] We will communicate with you by telephone before doing so.

[2] The reference presumably was to the communiqué agreed on June 7 (see No. 318) and transmitted to Berlin in No. 317.

## No. 322

*Mr. Charles (Moscow) to Sir S. Hoare (Received June 11, 9.50 p.m.)*
*No. 80 Telegraphic [C 4660/55/18]*

MOSCOW, *June 11, 1935, 9.15 p.m.*

Following is continuation of my immediately preceding telegram.[1]

Czech Foreign Minister informed me he had agreed with Monsieur Litvinov on importance of continuing efforts to secure German agreement to an Eastern Pact of non-aggression and consultation and that he was firmly of the opinion that war in Eastern Europe would most certainly involve Western Powers. Monsieur Benes said to me that Monsieur Litvinov was anxious lest conclusion of a Western Air agreement would make Great Britain lose interest in other points in declaration of February 3rd. He had tried to quieten Monsieur Litvinov's fears in this direction as well as his misgivings over change in British Cabinet which he feared might indicate a change of policy vis-à-vis this country.

Monsieur Benes told me Soviet Union were anxious to push on Danubian Pact and hoped for his assistance with the Little Entente. I suggested that Hungary might be a difficulty and he remarked that Hungary would certainly not be allowed to re-arm unless she entered the pact. He said Italian ambitions in Abyssinia and their probable repercussions on the situation in Europe had been discussed; Signor Mussolini's activities were being watched by Soviet Union with grave anxiety and he himself had not failed to warn Italians of the danger to themselves, to the League, and to the situation in general.

[1] In this telegram of June 11, not printed, Mr. Charles referred to M. Benes's visit to Moscow, June 8–11, and summarized the official communiqué; see *Soviet Documents on Foreign Policy*, edited by J. Degras, vol. iii, pp. 135–6.

## No. 323

*Letter from Mr. Harvey[1] (Paris) to Central Department (Received June 13)*
*[C 4671/55/18]*

PARIS, *June 11, 1935*

Dear Department,

On receipt of your letter of the 5th June,[2] we took an opportunity of enquiring at the Quai d'Orsay what exactly were the obligations of France

[1] Mr. O. C. Harvey was First Secretary in H.M. Embassy at Paris.
[2] No. 306.

to Poland in the event of an attack on Poland by Russia under the Treaty of 1921, the wording of which was somewhat obscure. We were told without hesitation that it involved an obligation to defend Poland against Russia as much as against any other Power which attacked her, although no country was specifically mentioned in the Treaty. Article 3 was quoted as implying this definite obligation and it was observed that the Treaty having been concluded shortly after the Bolshevik invasion of Poland, it obviously contemplated the possibility of further attacks from Russia.

Yours ever<br>OLIVER HARVEY

No. 324

Sir E. Phipps (Berlin) to Sir S. Hoare (Received June 13, 10.30 a.m.)<br>No. 150 Saving: Telegraphic [C 4672/55/18]

BERLIN, June 12, 1935

The 'Deutsche Diplomatisch-Politische Korrespondenz' comments favourably on Mr. Baldwin's two speeches after the reorganization of the Cabinet.[1]

The programme thus officially announced is regarded as indicating no basic change in British policy, but rather as an emphasis of continuity. Mr. Baldwin, the commentary states, had made it clear that England stood by her traditional duty of preserving the peace of Europe. The inclusion in the Cabinet of two Ministers concerned in Foreign Affairs[2] was intended to assist the British Government in the successful realization of this task.

Mr. Baldwin's declaration that England's efforts to achieve national security would be coupled with the promotion of disarmament and collective security is welcomed, provided that he is contemplating a gradual and not a hurried process. Germany's aims were in no way opposed to those of Mr. Baldwin. England would achieve the desired results most quickly if those elements which favoured positive attempts to bring about equal security for all won the day against those other elements who, by means of the creation of dangerous schemes, which would inevitably be rejected, hoped to be able to point out the 'responsible disturber of the peace'.

The establishment of a kind of League of Nations Ministry did not, the commentary continues, indicate any change in English policy, which has always been inclined towards Geneva. Apart from this, the purely superficial relations of any State with Geneva were nowadays regarded as the touchstone of its peaceful or warlike temperament. Mr. Baldwin had shown that England did not agree with this naive or even malicious view when, on the day after Herr Hitler's speech, he had, in the House of Commons, deplored the weakness and imperfection of the League.[3] It would thus be consequen-

---

[1] The references were to Mr. Baldwin's speech on June 8 at a meeting in support of the National Government held in the grounds of Himley Hall in Worcestershire and to his broadcast speech on the same day; see *The Times*, June 10, pp. 10–11.

[2] Sir S. Hoare and Mr. A. Eden; see No. 304, note 10.

[3] See 302 *H.C. Deb.* 5 s., cols. 359–73.

tial and valuable if the creation of Mr. Eden's special office were governed, not by the idea of immediately providing the incomplete existing form of a basically sound idea with increased powers, but rather by the determination to give to an institution, which in the past often worked on the theory of following the line of least resistance, a real meaning and an unimpeachable effectiveness by means of an accretion of moral strength. In any case, however, the commentary concludes, it should be possible to renounce unproductive methods which could only be aimed at inducing others to give to an institution in need of reform more confidence than one was prepared to give to it oneself.

## No. 325

### Minute by Mr. Craigie
### [A 5269/22/45]

FOREIGN OFFICE, *June 12, 1935*

The Counsellor of the American Embassy called today and made an oral communication in the sense of the accompanying *aide mémoire*.

I said that I felt sure that His Majesty's Government would greatly appreciate this prompt and satisfactory response from the Government of the United States, which would help to promote the conclusion of a future international agreement.

R. L. CRAIGIE

ENCLOSURE IN No. 325

EMBASSY OF THE UNITED STATES, LONDON, *June 12, 1935*

### Aide-Mémoire

The American Government wishes to express its appreciation for the detailed information regarding the pending preliminary Anglo-German naval conversations as set forth in the British *aide-mémoire* of June 7.[1] It has noted with particular satisfaction (*a*) that Germany accepts the principle of limiting tonnage by categories, and (*b*) that Germany is prepared to regard a ratio between the British and German fleets if once agreed to as final, irrespective of future construction by third powers. While the American Government desires to cooperate fully with Great Britain in seeking a solution of all phases of the naval question, it feels that inasmuch as American interests in the size of the fleets of the Continental powers is necessarily less immediate than that of Great Britain the differential between the British and German fleets is primarily one for British decision.

The American Government is sincerely hopeful that the results of these preliminary conversations may lead to a common viewpoint among the leading European naval powers as to a mutually acceptable proportional standard for their fleets and that this in turn will contribute to a general

[1] See No. 315.

agreement between the principal naval powers for a further limitation and reduction of naval armaments in line with the principles of the Washington and London treaties.[2]

[2] Cf. F.R.U.S. 1935, vol. i, pp. 164–5.

## No. 326

### Minute by Mr. Craigie of a conversation with Captain Wassner
### [A 5305/22/45]

FOREIGN OFFICE, June 12, 1935

Captain Wassner, the German Naval Attaché, called on me this afternoon with a message from Herr von Ribbentrop, who thought that, in view of the widespread leakages and speculation in the press, it would be as well to issue our proposed communiqué.[1] After communicating with the News Department I said that we thought that the communiqué would now be of little use, since it would merely confirm the existence of an agreement which was already assumed by the press; that it would not give the information which the press now want, i.e. details of how such an agreement in principle would be applied, and that a better method would be for me to see the representatives of the more responsible newspapers and to communicate to them in confidence the information already given to the representatives of other Powers.[2]

Captain Wassner, after communicating with Herr von Ribbentrop by telephone, has now given me the following reply:

(1) Herr von Ribbentrop agrees that in the circumstances the agreed communiqué should not be issued at present. The German press will neither discuss this question of an Anglo-German naval agreement nor will it quote expressions of opinion from the foreign press.

(2) Herr von Ribbentrop has no objection to my seeing members of the British press and indicating to them confidentially the information already communicated to the representatives of the Washington Powers, in order that we may give our press a 'lead' as to the line to take.

(3) Herr von Ribbentrop has been suddenly summoned again to Herr Hitler at Munich and this will delay his departure. He asks that the meeting on Friday[3] should accordingly be postponed from the morning until the afternoon. He is anxious to call and see the Secretary of State as soon as possible after his arrival in London, which he expects to be on Friday morning.[4]

R. L. C.

[1] Cf. Nos. 317 and 318.    [2] Cf. No. 315.
[3] June 14.

[4] It appears from a note on the file that Sir S. Hoare agreed to see Herr von Ribbentrop at 10.15 a.m. on Friday, June 14. No record of this interview has been found in the Foreign Office archives.

## No. 327

### Sir E. Phipps (Berlin) to Sir S. Hoare (Received June 13)
### No. 563 [C 4684/55/18]

BERLIN, June 12, 1935

Sir,

Despite Herr Hitler's White-Paper hoarseness and the successive announcements of the existence of a German military Air Force and Germany's return to universal conscription, the postponed visit of Sir John Simon and Mr. Eden to Berlin finally took place as arranged.[1]

2. The visit was probably necessary from the point of view of British public opinion, which began to wonder why British visits to Rome and Paris, together with constant meetings at Geneva, should not be followed up by a heart to heart talk between responsible British and German statesmen. Our public opinion was perhaps right, and the visit certainly produced a good psychological effect. It removed from Germany any excuse for maintaining her attitude of hurt feelings, which, combined with raucous Teutonic cries, table-bangings and treaty-breakings, was truly hard to bear. Indeed my chief fear was lest the visit should produce too good an effect, with all the danger of subsequent violent reaction. At first the Chancellor did in fact attach exaggerated hopes to its eventual results. He had never encountered before two such civilised and courteous adversaries as Sir John Simon and Mr. Eden. Their mere presence in Berlin after the pettish White Paper postponement was a lesson in manners. But it was only some time after their departure that he realised that listening to his claims did not necessarily imply the granting of them.

3. And then, after a couple of weeks or so, came Stresa[2] and the long hoped for and altogether desirable Anglo-Franco-Italian front. This constituted the high-water mark in the affairs of the Powers whose hope it is to contain Germany. But, as a result of Ethiopian tension, these refreshing waters soon receded, and now we can only regretfully look up at the distant white line.

4. It is curious that, whereas the blame pronounced at Stresa by the three Great Powers was salutary and caused the Germans furiously to think, that pronounced a few days later at Geneva[3] merely caused them furiously to vociferate. Stresa made Hitler scratch his head, Geneva made him lose it, and Germany as a whole followed suit. This attitude is illogical, it is regrettable, but it is a fact. It can perhaps partly be explained by German hatred and contempt for the League. Blame from three strong adversaries, of whom two at least have shown a reasonable understanding for the German case, is one thing. Blame from the institution containing Bolsheviks, Czechs, and Latvians, not to mention other racially impure weaklings, is quite another, and was unbearable for the fair Nordic man, and seemed, moreover, in his blue eyes, to be the height of hypocrisy. Baron von Neurath told me in confidence that Herr Hitler, directly he heard of the Geneva resolution, had

[1] On March 25–26, 1935; see Volume XII, No. 651.     [2] See ibid., No. 722.
[3] A reference to the League Council Resolution of April 17, 1935; see ibid., No. 732.

summoned him by telephone to Munich and had raved at him for five hours without, I hear, stopping to eat or drink. General Göring and Dr. Goebbels urged the Chancellor to double the Air Force at the earliest possible moment. Baron von Neurath and Father Time, working together, finally took the edge off all this sound and fury, and then, after some beneficial delay, came the Chancellor's speech[4] which now confronts us.

5. Herr Hitler's thirteen points raise questions of high policy which are naturally outside my competence. I think it my duty, however, as an observer on the spot, to make a few remarks on one aspect of the matter.

6. I have just sent over to your Department a list of instances when Herr Hitler broke faith in the past. The list is by no means exhaustive, but I trust that I shall not be required to expand it and that, even as it stands, it may not weigh too heavily in any final decision. By rummaging Herr Hitler's actions or writings in a past of greater freedom[5] and less responsibility, we can doubtless find events and tendencies alike disquieting. To conclude therefrom that no faith can be attached to his signature in the future would condemn us to a policy of sterility.

7. His Majesty's Government may decide that it is now undesirable to conclude any convention with this country; they may prefer to maintain their liberty of action. If, however, they feel that advantage should be taken of the presence of M. Laval at the head of the French Government and of his notorious desire to come to some reasonable understanding with Germany, I earnestly hope that they will not allow themselves to be deterred by the mere contemplation of Herr Hitler's past misdeeds or breaches of faith. After all, he now leads nearly 70 millions of industrious, efficient and courageous, not to say pugnacious, people. He is, like most men, an amalgam, and he may, like many men, have evolved since the old, somewhat gangster-like days at Munich. His signature, once given, will bind his people as no other could. It need not bind Great Britain to any state of undue weakness: it need not blind her to the undoubted dangers lying ahead. And if the worst befall, and Hitler decide to break his freely-given, solemn pledge, surely our battle-ground would be all the firmer for having put him to the test?

I have, &c.,
ERIC PHIPPS

---

[4] On May 21, 1935.

[5] On the filed copy the first five lines of paragraph 6 have been crossed out and the following substituted: '6. It would be easy to produce a list of instances when Herr Hitler broke faith in the past. By rummaging Herr Hitler's actions or writings in his past of greater freedom.' The amended version was used in the Confidential Print copy of the despatch. A communication of July 3 from the Central Department of the Foreign Office to the Embassy at Berlin read: 'The alteration has been made with the Ambassador's approval and at his request.'

## No. 328

### Sir S. Hoare to Sir R. Clive (Tokyo)
### No. 105 Telegraphic [A 5446/22/45]

FOREIGN OFFICE, *June 13, 1935, 6 p.m.*

My telegram No. 99.[1]

The Japanese Ambassador called to-day and communicated the reply of the Japanese Government which was to the following effect. Begins:

The Japanese Government have no objection to the proposal relating to the ratio between the British and German naval strength as set forth in the Aide-Memoire of the 7th June, provided that this does not prejudice or affect in any way the fundamental policy of the Japanese Government in regard to naval disarmament expounded at the preliminary naval talks in London.

Repeated to Berlin, Paris, Rome, and Washington.

[1] See No. 315, note 1.

## No. 329

### Minute by Mr. Craigie
### [A 5414/22/45]

FOREIGN OFFICE, *June 13, 1935*

The two points mentioned in this letter[1] were discussed at a meeting with the Secretary of State this afternoon, at which Sir Robert Vansittart, Mr. Beckett[2] and I were present. As regards the form of the agreement, the Secretary of State was impressed with the argument that to conclude a definite binding treaty with Germany at this stage might create the maximum of irritation in other countries likely to be affected, especially France, Italy and Russia, and would also make it more difficult to meet the argument that we were condoning or confirming Germany's breach of the Treaty of Versailles. It was therefore decided that we should in the first instance propose to Herr von Ribbentrop, when he raises the point, that our agreement should for the moment only be in the form of an exchange of agreed declarations at the final meeting. Should the German representatives wish it, we could also agree that these declarations would be initialled. If, however, the German representatives press very strongly for the conclusion of a formal treaty at this stage and we are unable to move them by our arguments in favour of the course we prefer, then it will be necessary to adjourn the discussion of this point in order that the matter might be submitted to the Ministerial Naval Committee.

[1] The reference is to a letter of June 13 from Admiral Chatfield to Sir R. Vansittart saying that the Admiralty favoured a naval agreement with Germany being made as binding as possible 'so as to leave no loophole for a subsequent withdrawal of Germany', and, on the other hand, could see no advantage 'from a naval point of view in having discussions with Russia at the present time'.

[2] Second Legal Adviser in the Foreign Office.

As regards the second point, it was agreed that after the termination of the German talks we should endeavour to arrange immediate conversations with the French and Italians. If the result of these conversations were to leave some hope of our being able to reach a quantitative naval agreement, then would be the time to approach Russia. In the meantime, however, it was desirable to inform the Soviet Government of the position so far reached and to explain to them the order which was proposed for the suggested conversations.

I attach a draft telegram to Moscow.[3]

R. L. C.

[3] Cf. No. 346 below.

## No. 330

### Memorandum on Air Pact and Limitation of Air Strength[1]
### [C 4903/55/18]*

FOREIGN OFFICE, *June 13, 1935*

(A) HISTORY OF THE QUESTION[2]

(B) FUTURE PROCEDURE

1. The first step is to *ascertain whether the French will agree to the negotiation (and conclusion)*[3] *of an air pact and air limitation agreement independently of that of the general settlement*, or at least to their negotiation independently of that settlement, leaving over the question of conclusion until the negotiation is com-

---

[1] The first draft of this memorandum was compiled by Mr. Sargent and Mr. Wigram following the Cabinet meeting on June 5, at which the Secretary of State for Air had commented on the French air figures. The British Air Attaché in Paris had, he said, been informed 'that the Germans were taking the French figure as 2,500 and claiming parity, whereas the French had actually less than 1,000, not all of which were modern in type and performance' (cf. No. 275). He accordingly suggested that 'the first step should be to convince the Germans that they were over-estimating the present French strength and that the figure for agreement should be in the region of 1,500 first-line aircraft', and that a tripartite conference for this purpose might be arranged with a French representative during the Anglo-German naval talks. The Cabinet had agreed at this meeting that the Air question 'should be taken up as a separate question and should no longer be considered to be necessarily linked up with a general settlement', and that 'the Secretary of State for Foreign Affairs should consider this decision with a view to early action'. The final text of the memorandum, as here printed from Confidential Print, differed in a few respects from the original draft: the more important changes are noted in footnotes below.

[2] This Section, not printed, outlined the early stages, from February 3 to June 1, 1935, in the proposed negotiations of an air pact, an air limitation agreement, and an agreement on the prohibition of indiscriminate bombing. It contained extracts from the following documents printed in this Series:—in Volume XII, Annex to No. 400, Nos. 517, 651, and 722; in Volume XIII, Nos. 174, 180, 205, 254, Annex I to No. 263, and No. 274. References were also made to Sir W. Malkin's report of June 1, 1935, printed as Appendix II in this Volume, and to debates in the House of Commons on May 2 and May 31, 1935 (301 *H.C. Deb.* 5 s., col. 576, and 302 *ibid.*, cols. 1447–54, 1504–10).

[3] These two words were not in parenthesis in the draft.

plete.[4] At this stage it will probably be much wiser to press the French only on *negotiation*. If we try to force the question of *conclusion* now we may well wreck everything. A draft telegram to Paris is separately submitted.[5]

One can imagine several possible answers to our enquiry. The French may say that nothing can be negotiated, and still less concluded, independently of the general settlement; or that an air pact, but not a limitation agreement, can be negotiated independently; or that both can be negotiated, but not concluded, independently.[6] It is idle to expect that they can agree to independent negotiation *and conclusion*.[7] This aspect of the problem is dealt with in greater detail in Annex IV.[8]

2. Once the French point of view is definite—and we must hope that it will be one which we can accept—we must *ascertain that Germany will agree to the negotiation*. It is improbable that there will be any difficulty about Italy and Belgium. We cannot consult Germany at least until we know the French reply, as the understanding between us at present is that the air pact will not be negotiated independently of the general settlement.

3. When there is general agreement to the principle of the negotiation of the Air Pact and limitation agreement, we shall have to *obtain the agreement of the Five Powers to the bases on which it is to proceed*. This would seem to necessitate decisions on the part of His Majesty's Government on the following points:—

*General.*

(*a*) Is there to be one instrument embodying air pact, limitation agreement and prohibition of indiscriminate bombing, or are there to be separate instruments?

*As regards Air Pact.*

(*b*) Which of the proposed signatories are to give guarantees and which are to receive them? (see paragraph 3 of Sir W. Malkin's memorandum).[9]

(*c*) What are the circumstances in which the guarantees will operate? (see paragraphs 5 and 6 of Sir W. Malkin's memorandum).

(*d*) Are the guarantees to apply to territory only or to fleets and mercantile marines on the high seas? (see paragraph 7 of Sir W. Malkin's memorandum).

(*e*) Are Powers, other than the Five Powers, in any way to be approached in connexion with the pact? (see paragraph 9 of Sir W. Malkin's memorandum and article 3 of the French draft).[10]

[4] In the draft, the next sentence here read: 'We ought without delay to press the French for a decision on this point which at present holds up all further progress' and a marginal comment by Sir R. Vansittart read: 'It will be much wiser to press them only on *negotiation*. Please do not let us raise the question of *conclusion* at this stage. We may well wreck everything. R.V.' The next three sentences in the final text—'At this stage . . . submitted'—were not in the draft.

[5] Not traced in Foreign Office archives. Cf. No. 331 below, paragraph 2.

[6] In the draft this sentence continued: '; or that both can be negotiated and concluded independently.'       [7] This sentence was not in the draft.

[8] The filed copy of this Annex, printed below as an Appendix to No. 330, appears to be the modified text mentioned by Mr. Sargent in his note on Sir R. Vansittart's minute of June 11, see note 16 below.       [9] See note 2 above.       [10] Volume XII, No. 517.

(*f*) Is the pact to be supplemented by bilateral military agreements? (see paragraph 2 of Sir W. Malkin's memorandum, and article 4 of the French draft and article 4 of the German draft).[11]

*As regards Limitation Agreement.*

(*g*) To what category or categories of air power and strength is limitation to apply?

(*h*) As one of these categories, is it accepted that limitation shall be on a basis of parity in the first line strength of military aircraft? If so, shall that strength be the French first-line strength in metropolitan France and North Africa, as proposed by Germany? or shall it be expressed as a definite figure, and, if so, what?

(*i*) If limitation is to apply to any category or categories of air power and strength other than first-line strength in military aircraft what are to be the bases of calculation?

(*j*) Is there to be supervision?

*As regards Prohibition of indiscriminate Bombing.*

(*k*) Is there to be any mention of the prohibition of bombing of certain areas other than as contained in the preamble to the British draft?

4. *It would be for consideration by what method these bases of negotiation should be settled by the Five Governments.*

(*a*) Should it be through the diplomatic channel? or (*b*) should it be by a Five Power Conference? or (*c*) should it be (as suggested in Lord Londonderry's paper[12] C.P. 116 (35)) by a discussion between British, French and German representatives whose recommendations would be submitted later to Italy and Belgium?[13] The latter course would seem to be a dangerous one.[14]

5. When the bases of the negotiation have been settled by the Five Governments, the way would be clear—

(*a*) *for the preparation of a common draft of the air pact* (including the reference to the restriction of bombing), and

(*b*) *for the preparation of the heads of the air limitation agreement.*

6.[15] It is submitted that the drafts of the air pact, which are already in existence, cannot be further used at present. The British and French drafts have really been superseded by the report of the Malkin Committee (Annex I);[16] but it would be inadvisable to communicate that report to the Germans, who do not know of its existence. On the other hand, it would not be helpful to communicate the German draft (Annex II) to the French, as it raises at least one contentious issue, that of the bilateral agreements.

[11] See Annex to No. 263.  [12] No. 275.
[13] A marginal note by Sir R. Vansittart on the draft here read: 'This, I think, is the worst way. R.V.'
[14] This sentence was not in the draft.  [15] This paragraph was not in the draft.
[16] See note 2 above.

We should concentrate now on obtaining agreement between the Five Governments on the bases of the negotiation (see B (3) above).[17]

FOREIGN OFFICE, *June 13, 1935*

### The French Position

The French have a good deal of leeway to make up before they are ready for a discussion with Germany. It is true that they agreed to the Secretary of State saying in the House of Commons on the 31st May that 'we have reached the stage when suggestions can be exchanged with a view to considering the future course of the negotiations', but in doing so M. Laval stipulated clearly that the French Government reserve without prejudice their attitude to the further question as to whether the Air Pact can be negotiated apart from the other subjects mentioned in the London communiqué.

In fact, the present position of the French Government is that, (*a*) as regards the Air Pact proper, they still adhere to the Stresa resolution; and (*b*) as regards air limitation, they hold that there can be no legalisation of Germany's armaments generally except as part of the 'general settlement' outlined in the February declaration.

When pressed to reconsider their position, the French may either:—

(1) Insist that there can be no separation of either the Air Pact or Air Limitation for the 'general settlement', and that so long as the prospects of a general settlement remain so uncertain they would refuse even to start negotiations for either an Air Pact or Air Limitation. If they took this line, the French would probably revert to the proposal they made at Stresa, namely, that we should at once proceed to a series of bilateral air pacts, from which Germany would be omitted, while providing for her subsequent admission if she so desired.

---

[17] In a minute of June 11, after giving instructions for the memorandum to be sent to the Secretary of State, Sir R. Vansittart wrote: 'I do not think that the tactics recommended in Annex IV [see note 8 above] will deliver the goods . . . [A marginal note by Mr. Sargent read: 'Annex IV has now been modified.'] Let us rather get him [M. Laval] and all the Locarno powers involved as deeply as possible in *negotiation*, before we actually begin to talk of conclusion. It is anyhow going to be a long job, and may well take longer than the now simplified remains of an Eastern Pact. (In view (*a*) of Signor Mussolini's initial response about the Air Pact, and (*b*) the reports of Italo-German negotiation in regard to Austria, we can omit for the present the contemplated Danubian pact from our calculations of simultaneity, as provided in the London agreement of Feb. 3.) Meanwhile therefore—that is while we are *negotiating* the Air Pact—let us put all the pressure we can on everyone concerned to go forward with the now easy Eastern Pact. (It may not be easy, but it ought to be.) The two *may* come to the boil simultaneously, and then we shall have no difficulty. Even if there *is* difficulty, we shall have gone so far that it may be easier then to press for passing from negotiation to conclusion. Whereas if we put all our weight on the latter right away, the ice will probably not bear, and we shall have compromised everything from the start by taking a risk that might not have been necessary. . . .' A note on the file states that the matter was discussed by Sir Samuel Hoare, Mr. Eden, Sir P. Sassoon (Under Secretary of State for Air), Sir R. Vansittart and others on June 17.

(2) While maintaining the indivisibility of the 'general settlement', the French might agree to the negotiation, as distinct from the conclusion, of an Air Pact (by accepting the Stresa resolution they may be said to have practically acquiesced in this course), while at the same time refusing even to negotiate an air limitation agreement, on the ground that Germany's air armaments and their legalisation can only be dealt with as part of the 'general settlement' as regards all Germany's armaments.

(3) The French might agree to the negotiation, but not the conclusion, of both the Air Pact and the Air Limitation Agreement.

(4) France might agree to the immediate negotiation and conclusion of both the Air Pact and the Air Limitation Agreement.

Course (1) would be entirely unsatisfactory and would mean the abandonment of the whole scheme of both air pact and air limitation, for we know already that there is no prospect whatsoever within a calculable period of achieving in present circumstances the totality of the 'general settlement' contemplated in February.

If the French insist on the letter of the 'general settlement' as stated in the February declaration, then, of course, courses (2) and (3) would be merely an academic exercise with no real prospects of practical achievement. But since February the situation has so changed that it is to be hoped that the French may have modified their idea of what they consider to be a 'general settlement'.

In February the 'general settlement' required three contributions from Germany:—

(*a*) The conclusion of pacts, freely negotiated between all the interested parties, and ensuring mutual assistance in Eastern Europe.

(*b*) The system foreshadowed in the Rome *procès-verbal* for Central Europe.

(*c*) Agreements regarding armaments generally.

(*d*) Return of Germany to the League.

As regards (*a*), Germany, while refusing flatly to negotiate mutual guarantee pacts in the East, has now offered to negotiate non-aggression pacts, and France has accepted this offer. Does this mean that she has abandoned the demand for mutual guarantee pacts?

As regards (*b*), it is Italy who is primarily interested in obtaining Germany's co-operation in a Central European settlement, including more particularly the conclusion of a non-interference pact in respect of Austria. As, however, Mussolini has agreed to the separate conclusion of the Air Pact and Air Limitation Agreement without insisting upon the simultaneous conclusion of a Central European settlement, it is to be hoped that the French will not be more exacting than the Italians in this respect. The present prospects of a Central European settlement are, of course, extremely doubtful.

As regards (*c*), here the French may very well take the line that they cannot agree to legalising both Germany's naval and air armaments, unless they obtain at the same time some satisfaction as regards Germany's land armaments, more particularly a reduction in Germany's military effectives at present fixed at 550,000. The recent conversations between Sir E. Phipps and Herr von Neurath show that the prospects of such a reduction being negotiated are extremely slight, and that all the Germans are prepared to offer is the abolition of certain heavy war material, which does not particularly appeal to the French, since it would be French material which would have to be destroyed.

As regards (d), Hitler's recent speech shows that he has no wish or intention to return to the League in present circumstances.

Seeing how greatly the European situation has changed since the 'general settlement' was defined in the February Declaration, one might be inclined at first sight to ask the French straight away what they now mean by a 'general settlement'. But it would probably be unwise to try and pin the French down at this juncture. If the French insist upon making the 'general settlement' a pre-condition of any air negotiations, we will no doubt have to ask them sooner or later what they mean by the expression, but we will probably obtain better results if we carry out this process of questioning gradually and piecemeal as occasion offers.

Of course, none of these difficulties will arise if the French agree at once to course (4), *i.e.* to the immediate negotiation and conclusion of both the Air Pact and Air Limitation Agreement; and one's first inclination would be to ask the French point blank to agree to a complete separation of the air question from the rest of the 'general settlement', but it is clear that if we took this line now we should get a flat negative reply (see Paris telegram No. 120, Saving).[18] It would probably be better tactics, therefore, to get the French and the other Locarno Powers all well immersed in negotiations, and endeavour in the course of these negotiations gradually to eliminate the other elements of the 'general settlement' which are obviously unobtainable.

It is possible that M. Laval, if the matter rested entirely with him, would not prove himself unreasonable or obstructive. The real opponent with whom we have to deal in this matter is Litvinov, who will fight hard to preserve the principle of simultaneity in all its aspects, and may be expected to bring considerable pressure to bear on the French Government. He will too, in this matter, be strongly supported by the Little *Entente*.

The reasons why he may be presumed not to wish a Western Air Pact to materialise may be summarised as follows:—

(a) He is afraid that once Great Britain is satisfied as regards her own security she will lose interest in the rest of the 'general settlement'.

(b) He is afraid that once France reaches a direct agreement with Germany, even if only limited to the air, she will no longer attach as much value as she does at present to Russian co-operation and assistance. It is thus to Russia's interest to keep alive the jealousies and fears of Western Europe.

(c) Anything that decreases the possibility of Germany breaking out in the West increases *ipso facto* the chances of her breaking out in the East.

[18] No. 320.

## No. 331

### Sir S. Hoare to Sir G. Clerk (Paris)
### No. 1160 [C 4746/55/18]

FOREIGN OFFICE, *June 13, 1935*

Sir,

I received the French Ambassador this morning. As I had noticed some ill-informed paragraphs in the French press in connexion with my appointment, I thought it well to disabuse his mind of the idea that the change of Government implied a change of policy. His Majesty's Government were set upon peace and were determined to follow the line of advance that seemed most likely to achieve their objective. So far as new friendships were concerned, we were anxious for them wherever we could make them, but we had no intention of sacrificing old friends on the chance of making new ones.

2. These remarks seemed to reassure M. Corbin. We then proceeded to discuss the possibilities of the Air Pact. His Excellency repeated to me what I imagine we had known for sometime, namely that the French Government and the French public were nervous of the conclusion of an Air Pact if it were isolated from the other main issues of peace, particularly the question of the restriction of land armaments and the question of the Eastern Pact. I told him that we were anxious to see some concrete result achieved without delay and that I greatly feared that if it was impossible to separate one problem from the rest we might repeat the experiences of the Disarmament Conference and end by achieving nothing at all. He by no means excluded the possibility of dealing with the Air Pact separately provided that we made it clear that when once the Pact was concluded Great Britain did not dissociate herself from the other parts of the problem. He also seemed inclined to think that the best method of approach was through discussions between the jurists and technicians. He did not seem to exclude the possibility of including the Germans in these discussions provided that the Germans treated the other parties concerned with frankness and gave them their draft for discussion.

3. I then raised with the Ambassador the question of the naval discussions with Herr von Ribbentrop and told him that on no account did we wish to appear to be making a separate treaty behind the backs of the other naval powers, least of all at a time when there had been proceeding a Cabinet crisis in Paris. His Excellency told me that he was not anxious as to what had happened and that although the French Cabinet had not yet considered the question he had no reason to suppose that they would disapprove of what we were doing.

[I am, &c.,
(for the Secretary of State)]
J. V. PEROWNE

## No. 332

*Sir E. Drummond (Rome) to Sir S. Hoare (Received June 17)*
*No. 52 Saving: Telegraphic [C 4744/55/18]*

ROME, *June 14, 1935*

I had a short conversation with Signor Suvich last night in the course of which we dealt with the following points:—

(1) *Questions put by His Majesty's Government to the German Government in order to elucidate certain points in Herr Hitler's speech.* (Your telegram No. 320).[1]

I communicated orally to His Excellency these questions and the replies of the German Government. Signor Suvich expressed his gratitude for this information.

(2) *Danubian Conference.*

I asked Signor Suvich if he could tell me anything about the present position in regard to this Conference. He said that the Italian Government were still waiting for an answer from Paris. They had found that the French Government was practically immobilised for the time being on all questions of foreign policy. The Italian Ambassador reported that though he could always see Monsieur Léger and Monsieur Bargeton, he had, up to now, not been able to obtain an interview with Monsieur Laval.

(3) *Appointment of German Air Attaché in London.* (Your despatch No. 670).[2]

I informed His Excellency of the decision of His Majesty's Government in this matter. I explained to him that we thought it necessary to have a British Air Attaché in Berlin in order to follow aid [air] developments there and the only way of obtaining this was by having a similar officer in London. Signor Suvich remarked that a German Air Attaché had been accredited to Rome for some time past.

(4) *Air Pact.*

Signor Suvich told me that the Italian Government had not yet received from the German Government their proposals in regard to the Air Pact. They were, therefore, still in ignorance of what these proposals were.

The subject of Abyssinia was not mentioned during this interview.

[1] See No. 274, note 2.      [2] See No. 291, note 2.

## No. 333

*Sir E. Phipps (Berlin) to Sir S. Hoare (Received June 21)*
*No. 570 [C 4867/55/18]*

BERLIN, *June 14, 1935*

His Majesty's Ambassador at Berlin presents his compliments to H.M. Secretary of State for Foreign Affairs, and has the honour to transmit to him the under-mentioned document.

| *Name and Date* | *Subject* |
|---|---|
| Minute by Military Attaché, dated 14th June. | German Army. |

BERLIN, *June 14, 1935*

*The Ambassador,*

A.M.A.[1] met General von Reichenau today. The latter asked if I had received the answers to my recent questions and said they were trying to pursue that policy of particular openness towards us which he had promised Colonel Thorne.[2] When relatively complete openness will be possible depends somewhat on the recent naval negotiations. He did not care particularly as to details, but it would be a great thing if they could achieve a 'treaty' (meaning perhaps written agreement), the first outside the framework of Versailles. He could not give us information in advance of the German army's own general knowledge, and some degree of stability must be attained first e.g. while regiments were still wearing obsolete numbers, he could not announce to us their new ones. He thought in October or November it would be possible to be really open.

Speaking of the report he had just been reading by the last German officer to be attached to the British Army, who returned some days ago, he said he was greatly impressed by the excellent reception given him both in official and social life and he thought the mutual attachments of army officers had been a great success.[3]

F. E. H[OTBLACK]

[1] Major R. A. Hay was the British Assistant Military Attaché at Berlin.

[2] Cf. No. 155, note 2.

[3] For the attachment for six weeks, in the spring of 1935, of three British officers to the German army and of three German officers to units of the British army in the United Kingdom, see 301 *H.C. Deb.* 5 *s.*, col. 553.

## No. 334

*Sir E. Drummond (Rome) to Sir S. Hoare (Received June 15, 3.10 p.m.)*
*No. 346 Telegraphic [C 4724/55/18]*

ROME, *June 15, 1935, 1.10 p.m.*

Your telegram No. 307.[1]

Italian government inform me that they have received German memorandum on effects of Franco-Soviet treaty on obligations of signatories of Treaty of Locarno, and have also received a copy from French government of the latter's draft reply to this memorandum.

Both documents are now being studied by Italian government who state that they are fully in agreement with His Majesty's Government in holding that reply of the four Locarno Powers should be previously concerted between them in order that it may so far as possible be in analogous terms. Italian government promise to let us know as soon as possible their views.

Repeated to Paris and Brussels.

[1] See No. 301, note 1.

## No. 335

*Sir G. Clerk (Paris) to Sir S. Hoare (Received June 17)*

*No. 123 Saving: Telegraphic* [*C 4725/55/18*]

PARIS, *June 15, 1935*

Your telegram No. 143.[1]

M. Laval, who has been continuously absorbed during the week by internal affairs, has now gone to Clermont-Ferrand to attend the funeral of a colleague who succumbed on Thursday[2] to heart-failure during a Cabinet Council. In the meantime an oral communication in accordance with your instructions was made this morning to the Secretary-General of the Ministry for Foreign Affairs who will doubtless have passed it on to M. Laval by the time I see him, as I hope to do, on Monday.

2. In the course of an exchange of views which ensued on a quite informal basis M. Léger unburdened his heart with great frankness. He made no secret of the fact that he regards the Stresa front as having been torn to ribbons by Herr Hitler's last speech[3] and by the Abyssinian imbroglio, and that he views with the utmost anxiety the turn which the European situation is taking.

3. He could only deplore, he said, that the British public saw in the Chancellor's words the promise of better things. He, himself, had searched the speech in vain for evidence of real sincerity; the more closely he scrutinised it, the more it appeared to him in the light of the cleverest attempt yet made to drive a wedge between Great Britain and France. The communication which he had just received did nothing to mitigate that opinion, inasmuch as the answers returned to Sir Eric Phipps' enquiries could hardly be said to clarify the ambiguities of the speech. The German purpose was clearly to lure the British public to seek a limitation of those arms (aerial and naval) which it felt insti[n]ctively to be its principal menace, whilst offering no hope of a limitation of the land arm, which was the principal menace for France, on any reasonable basis. If that design succeeded, not only would it annihilate what hope remained of reaching a limitation of land armaments and effectives but the French public would inevitably feel that it had been sacrificed on the altar of British egoism.

4. M. Laval, M. Léger continued, ardently desirous as he was of promoting a settlement with Germany, and despite a natural optimism, was much discouraged. Among other things, he was disagreeably impressed by the absence of any response to the note, delivered in Berlin, some ten days ago,[4] in which the French Government had accepted the German proposals for a multi-lateral Eastern pact as offering a basis of negotiation. There, at least, was a matter in which immediate progress could be registered if the German Government were sincere, and the delay in making even some provisional reply seemed to indicate a lack of good faith. It was difficult to avoid the conclusion that Germany was at her old game of sowing dissension among

---

[1] See No. 274, note 2.  [2] June 13.
[3] Of May 21.  [4] Cf. No. 288.

the Western Powers; indeed there was positive evidence that she was turning the Abyssinian affair to her advantage in the hope of weakening Signor Mussolini's resistance to her designs in Austria.

5. For M. Léger's further observations on the Abyssinian question please see my telegram No. 124 Saving[5] and for those on the naval question see my telegram No. 125 Saving,[6] both of today.

[5] Not here printed.          [6] No. 336 below.

## No. 336

### *Sir G. Clerk (Paris) to Sir S. Hoare (Received June 17)*
### *No. 125 Saving: Telegraphic [A 5328/22/45]*

PARIS, *June 15, 1935*

My telegram No. 123 Saving.[1]

M. Léger foreshadowed this morning that the reply of the French Government to the enquiry addressed to them through the French Embassy in London (see Sir John Simon's telegram No. 140)[2] would be unfavourable. He himself was going to spend the afternoon in a final consultation with the naval authorities after which the terms of the reply would be submitted for M. Laval's approval, probably on Monday.[3]

2. On being pressed for rather more detail, M. Léger said that, though he was not yet in a position to go into figures, he believed the naval staff had calculated that owing to her responsibilities in the Mediterranean and elsewhere the German proposal would leave France in a position of dangerous inferiority in the English Channel. On wider grounds it was inacceptable as violating the thesis of the inseparability of the three arms which the French had upheld at Geneva since the early days of the disarmament conference. (See also in this connexion my telegram under reference.)

3. M. Léger seemed unwilling to say any more. Even that, he stated, was merely a forecast and must not be taken as official.

4. The press is beginning to take notice of this question, the general line being to reproach us with seeking to settle those problems which more nearly concern us without troubling ourselves over those which vitally affect our friends.

[1] No. 335.          [2] See No. 315, note 1.          [3] June 17.

# No. 337

*Notes of the sixth meeting between representatives of the United Kingdom and Germany, June 15, 1935, at 12.30 p.m.*[1]

Present: *United Kingdom*: Mr. R. L. Craigie, Vice-Admiral C. J. C. Little, Captain V. H. Danckwerts.

*Germany*: Herr von Ribbentrop, Rear-Admiral K. G. Schuster, Captain E. Wassner, Korvetten Kapitan H. Kiderlen, Dr. Kordt, Dr. Schmidt.

MR. CRAIGIE opened the discussion by referring to the draft of the Agreement to be made between the two parties (see Annex). He distributed copies of the draft, and suggested that it should be examined with a view to discussing here and now any differences of opinion. He emphasized that he was not asking the German Delegation to agree finally to the draft at this meeting. He made one reservation in submitting the draft, and that was that it had not yet been submitted to the British Legal Advisers. Any comments the Legal Advisers might have to make would not, of course, alter the substance of the Agreement. In any case he would let the German Delegation know at once if any changes were proposed by these Advisers.

Mr. Craigie then referred to paragraph (*a*), and suggested the substitution of the expression 'friendly agreement' for the expression 'loyal, etc.'.

HERR VON RIBBENTROP agreed to this change.

MR. CRAIGIE then referred to paragraph (*b*). This, he said, had been carefully drafted with the purpose of not giving offence to any other Powers when the Agreement was finally published.

HERR VON RIBBENTROP said that before expressing a final opinion on this paragraph he would like to refer back to the private discussions which had taken place yesterday.[2] He suggested that it had there been agreed that the general formula should be achieved through the exchange of notes, and that this formula should be followed up by a detailed statement which, he thought, might take the form of a confidential protocol.

MR. CRAIGIE demurred to the suggestion of a secret protocol. He thought that the statement as to details should be contained in an agreed official record of the proceedings. This might take the form of a record of Question and Answer, and he hoped this idea might meet the German views.

HERR VON RIBBENTROP concurred in this arrangement, and thought it might prove sufficient. He emphasized that it would be necessary for the record to be agreed.

MR. CRAIGIE returned to the suggestion of a secret understanding, and explained that there would be determined opposition to such a proceeding. He wondered whether it would not be sufficient to have something which, while not publicly issued, would yet be in such a form that it could be communicated to a third party if necessary.

[1] The meeting was held at the Admiralty. These notes were circulated as N.C.(G) 6th Mtg. *Most Secret.*　　　　　　　　　　　　[2] Cf. No. 326, note 4.

413

HERR VON RIBBENTROP agreed, and said he would call this an 'interpretation' of the general formula. He then caused to be read out a German draft[3] of such an interpretation.

MR. CRAIGIE said that this draft did not appear to him to be satisfactory. He felt that we should not have anything in an agreement between the two parties which could not be communicated to other Governments. He suggested that paragraph (b) went a long way towards meeting the German proposals, and perhaps this could be followed up by a Question and Answer. A German statement might be recorded as follows:—

> 'It is understood by the German Delegation that in the past it has been the policy of the British Government to discourage exceptional building by other Naval Powers. May we therefore assume that independently of the present agreement the British Government will still continue to follow their past policy?'

To this, in the record, the reply of the British Delegation could be 'Yes'.

Mr. Craigie felt that such a statement of fact would be one to which no other Power could object. It was very necessary to give Germany full satisfaction without running the risk of giving offence elsewhere.

HERR VON RIBBENTROP said he would like time to consider this suggestion, though his first impression was that such a formula would prove acceptable. The whole matter must be clearly understood, and the point made in paragraph (b) was a very important one to Germany. Although he agreed that it was desirable to avoid any form of secret agreement, he still felt that a statement must be recorded in some way. He felt that such a statement as had been under discussion would be merely emphasizing and underlining the British policy towards limitations in Naval armaments, and therefore it should be possible to draft a protocol covering this matter which could not give offence to others.

MR. CRAIGIE observed that this was mainly a political question, and he suggested that it would be best further discussed between himself and Herr von Ribbentrop.

It was agreed that the matter should be pursued on the following Monday[4] morning.

MR. CRAIGIE informed the German Delegation that he had not yet, in fact, even the authority to put forward the proposal for the confidential record which he had suggested, but he felt that such would be agreeable to the British Government. The interpretation, he thought, could take the form at the final meeting of an agreed 'procès verbal' which would be initialled by the parties concerned.

HERR VON RIBBENTROP agreed that this would be a possible means, and suggested that consideration should be given to the proposal during the week-end, and that he should discuss it personally further with Mr. Craigie on Monday, the 17th June, at 10 a.m.

MR. CRAIGIE then turned to paragraph (c). He said this remained un-

---

[3] Not traced in Foreign Office archives.     [4] June 17. See No. 348 below, note 3.

changed from the previous version which the German Delegation had seen, and he suggested that any discussion of it should be left for the moment.

As regards paragraph (*d*) he suggested that the words 'it is understood' in line 8 should be deleted, and that the words 'it is agreed' should be substituted for the words 'being understood' in line 10.

HERR VON RIBBENTROP said that at first sight he could see no objections to these changes, and would give them consideration.

MR. CRAIGIE then read out a new draft of the final sub-paragraph of paragraph (*d*).

HERR VON RIBBENTROP said this raised a point of principle. Germany had accepted the ratio of 35 per cent. permanently and as a lasting solution. It was, however, necessary for Germany to be able to use fully that 35 per cent. In a previous discussion it had been repeatedly stated that there had been cases where, under the ratio agreements of the Washington and London Naval Treaties, certain Powers had found themselves in a position in which they were unable to make use of the full tonnages allotted to them. Germany did not wish to be faced with a similar position. To-day there was uncertainty as to the future with regard to the tonnages to be permitted to the various Naval Powers, and consequently there was uncertainty as to the balances that might remain in various categories. In one category Germany might find herself with some tonnage remaining which she could not use, and in taking tonnage from another category to complete the first she might, in turn, dislocate the allotment of tonnage in the second category. This was a matter of the greatest importance to the German Navy in view of its small-ness, and he asked the British Delegation to help in the finding of a solution which would permit Germany to make full use of the tonnage permitted to her.[5]

MR. CRAIGIE said he had hoped the draft in the final sub-paragraph of (*d*) would have achieved the end desired by Herr von Ribbentrop. He pointed out that if the agreement allowed of the possibility of substantial changes, then it would be going back on Herr Hitler's declaration. He felt that what-ever faults the British nation had, it was generally agreed that they were a fair-minded people. There was no difficulty in meeting the German require-ments if it was only a question of fitting in a few extra tons. On the other hand, one might take the extreme case of the German Delegation coming along and saying that they found they had a thousand tons left over in one category which they were unable to use, and therefore they might then ask for permission to add a very considerable tonnage to these thousand tons so that a complete ship, possibly of capital-ship size, could be added to their Fleet. The difficulty at the moment was that the British Delegation were working in the dark as to what the German building programme was to be, and it was for this reason that it was a pity that the German Delegation could not have seen their way to producing at this stage their proposed building programme. However, this, it appeared, had been impossible, and he only

[5] A secret German Staff memorandum on this point is printed in *D.G.F.P.*, Series C, vol. vi, No. 148.

asked that the German Delegation should not put forward a draft text which substantially upset Herr Hitler's declaration.

HERR VON RIBBENTROP repeated the German view that the non-utilisation of any tonnage would be very serious to them in view of the smallness of their Navy. He suggested that he should have time to study the draft paragraph referred to, and also put forward the proposal that the word 'slight' in line 4 of this paragraph should be deleted; such a deletion would go a long way to meet the German view. He wondered whether again in this case it would be possible to put in here in the agreement a general formula and to specify this formula in more detail in a protocol which might take the form of an agreement to a limit beyond which no readjustment could go. He emphasized that Germany had no intention of increasing beyond the 35 per cent. agreed to. Any such readjustment would be merely advance payment on tonnage, which would have to be reimbursed at some future date. Arrangements would be made that there would be automatic adjustment in the long-run and consequently that the 35 per cent. would not ultimately be exceeded.

REAR-ADMIRAL SCHUSTER suggested that the British Delegation could be prepared to accept the deletion of the word 'slight' because of the last sentence of all of the paragraph in question.

MR. CRAIGIE proposed a compromise. He suggested that the word 'slight' on line 4 should be omitted, and that the words 'or permanent' should be added after the word 'substantial' in line 10.

HERR VON RIBBENTROP agreed to consider this proposal.

VICE-ADMIRAL LITTLE then referred to the two-line penultimate subparagraph of paragraph (d). He questioned whether, in view of the further explanations in the last sub-paragraph, this sentence was any longer necessary.

REAR-ADMIRAL SCHUSTER said that this sentence was, in their view, complementary to the sub-paragraphs on either side of it. The preceding paragraph dealt with the situation which would arise if there were no general treaty agreement in the future as regards categories. The following sub-paragraph dealt with the situation that might arise in future. The sentence referred to was an attempt to deal with the considerations that would arise during the present discussions, and the German Delegation were anxious that the agreement should be in such a form that they would be in a position to consider variations in the present situation.

CAPTAIN DANCKWERTS suggested a re-phrasing of this sentence as follows, and that it should run on as part of the previous sub-paragraph:—

'As regards the present situation, this matter will be discussed in the discussions now in hand.'

MR. CRAIGIE proposed that both parties should give this further consideration before Monday. He then said he would like to point out to the German Delegation that up to the present the conversations had employed the terms 'British' and 'German' Fleets. If, however, now it was proposed to put their agreement into a form of an exchange of notes which would be published, it would be necessary to substitute some other term for the expression 'British Fleet'. He referred to the relationship between Great Britain and the Dominions, and he said he supposed that Germany did not contemplate a 35 per cent. ratio based on the United Kingdom Fleet alone, but intended that ratio to be based on the combined strength of the United Kingdom and Dominion Navies. The term that would probably be suggested would be 'the naval strength of the Members of the British Commonwealth of Nations'.

HERR VON RIBBENTROP said he understood the point and expressed agreement. The German Government were not prepared to base the ratio on the tonnages of the United Kingdom only.

MR. CRAIGIE said that he proposed to inform the press that a further meeting had taken place between the experts, and it was hoped that on Monday, 17th June, there would be a more formal meeting, and that subsequently it would be possible to issue a communiqué.

HERR VON RIBBENTROP said that the German Delegation would inform the press on the same lines. Finally he suggested that it should be agreed to hold only one meeting a day in future.

This was agreed to, and it was provisionally arranged that the next meeting of the Delegations should take place at 4 p.m. on Monday, 17th June, 1935.

ANNEX TO No. 337

*Copy of draft Agreement discussed at the Meeting*

I have much pleasure in notifying to Your Excellency the formal acceptance by His Majesty's Government of the proposal of the German Government that the future strength of the German Navy in relation to the strength of the British Navy should be in the proportion of 35 : 100. They regard it as a contribution of the greatest importance to the cause of future Naval limitation and consider that it furnishes a valuable assurance for the security of this and other countries. His Majesty's Government further agree with the explanations which were furnished by the German Representatives in the course of the discussions as to the method of application of this principle. These explanations may be summarised as follows:—

(*a*) This is to be a permanent relationship between the two Fleets, i.e. the strength of the German Fleet shall never exceed 35% of the British Fleet, the 35% being calculated on the British Treaty-Tonnages or, if such Treaty-Tonnages should not exist in future, on the actual tonnages of the British Fleet. Furthermore within this strength Germany shall have the right to possess a submarine tonnage of 100% of the British submarine tonnage.

Germany would, however, be prepared to build until further notice not more than 45% of the British submarine tonnage. Should a situation arise which would make it necessary for Germany to avail herself of the right to a percentage exceeding the above mentioned 45% this would be the subject of a loyal and friendly understanding between the German and British Governments.

(*b*) Germany will adhere to this limitation in all circumstances, e.g. it will not be affected by the construction of third powers.

Should the general equilibrium of naval armaments, judged by the experience of the past, be violently upset by any abnormal and exceptional construction, the German Government reserve the right to invite His Majesty's Government to examine the new situation which will thus have been created. His Majesty's Government in the United Kingdom have taken note of this reservation and recognise this right.

(*c*) The German Government will not insist on the incorporation of this ratio in any future international treaty, provided that the alternative method eventually adopted for the future limitation of naval armaments gives Germany full guarantee that this relationship between the British and German Fleets will be maintained.

(*d*) The German Government believe in the system of limitation by categories, and they are prepared in principle to calculate the 35% ratio on the tonnage in the separate categories, any variation of this ratio in a particular category being dependent upon the arrangements to this end that may be arrived at in a future general treaty on naval limitation. Such arrangements would, it is understood, include the provision that any increase in one category would be compensated for by a corresponding reduction in others. It being understood that if other powers should have a single category for cruisers and destroyers Germany should have the same right.

Should no international treaty be concluded, or should the question of limitation by categories not be dealt with in a future international treaty, the manner and degree in which the German Government will have the right to vary the 35% ratio in one or more categories would be a matter for discussion between the German and British Governments, in the light of the naval situation then existing.

It is understood that the present requirements will be settled in the discussion now in hand.

Since it is manifestly impossible that the 35% calculation should give tonnage figures in each category exactly divisible by the maximum individual tonnage permitted for ships in that category, slight adjustments may be made by agreement between the German Government and His Majesty's Government so that Germany shall not be debarred from utilising her tonnage to the full. This procedure shall not result in any substantial departure from the relation between the German and British Fleets of 35 to 100.

## No. 338

*Sir G. Clerk (Paris) to Sir J. Simon (Received June 17)*
*No. 127 Saving: Telegraphic [A 5329/22/45]*

PARIS, *June 16, 1935*

My telegram No. 125 Saving.[1]

The Anglo-German naval conversations are being closely followed in the French press. Whilst official circles have carefully refrained from any public expression of views, opinion in the press and in general is much disconcerted at the opening of the negotiations at all at the present moment but still more at the apparent readiness of His Majesty's Government to accept unchallenged the proposed German percentage of ships. The view is expressed that a further blow has been struck at Part V of the Treaty since the negotiations are tantamount to official recognition of the new German Navy. Exception is also taken to the way in which it is believed an agreement in principle has been reached in London before consultation with the other Powers concerned.

2. Among those who admit that the above views are unreasonable and realise the necessity of now negotiating with Germany and even the advantage of acceptance of the present German offer, the fear is openly expressed that Great Britain, having protected herself as regards the seas, will be even less interested in the question of land armaments and that France will be left alone to face exaggerated German claims for effectives and guns etc. This fear is similar to that aroused by the idea of proceeding with the negotiations for the conclusion of an Air Pact accompanied by air limitation without waiting for a general settlement of all questions including security (Eastern and Central European Pacts) and agreement regarding all arms.

3. Certain papers (e.g. Sauerwein in 'Paris Soir', Fernand de Brinon in 'Information' and also 'République') take the line that Great Britain has created a precedent by reaching a direct agreement with Germany which France would now do well to follow.

[1] No. 336.

## No. 339

*Sir S. Hoare to Sir G. Clerk (Paris)*
*No. 148 Telegraphic: by telephone [A 5416/22/45]*

FOREIGN OFFICE, *June 17, 1935, 5.50 p.m.*

I have just seen M. Corbin and have emphasized to him the two reasons that make it essential for us to confirm without delay the Naval Agreement with the Germans, the reasons being, firstly, the fact that the Chief of the Naval Staff and the British Naval experts are convinced that on the Naval merits of the case the Agreement is advantageous not only to ourselves but also to the French and Italian Governments. In this connection the Admiralty are anxious to enter into conversations with the French Naval experts as soon as possible. They are convinced that in these conversations they will be able to show to the French experts that many of their anxieties are without foundation and that the Agreement contains substantial advantages for France. The second reason that I emphasized is the state of British public opinion. If we did not make the Agreement or even if we delayed making it, British public opinion being almost unanimously in favour of it, will react violently against France with the result that Anglo-French relations will be very gravely damaged. In this connection I assured M. Corbin that the Agreement meant no change in British policy and that I had emphasized this fact over and over again to Herr Ribbentrop. There emerged from this conversation and a previous discussion that I had had with the Prime Minister, Mr. Eden and Sir R. Vansittart the proposition that Mr. Eden should come to Paris as soon as possible and explain our position to M. Laval. He would at the same time take the opportunity of discussing with M. Laval the best procedure for approaching the discussion of the Air Pact and it may be also would deal with the question of Ethiopia. M. Corbin liked this idea and undertook to mention it unofficially to Paris. The Prime Minister, Mr. Eden and I attach great importance to this visit taking place and taking place without delay if possible Thursday or Friday of this week.[1] We realise that M. Laval's time is fully occupied but we do not contemplate that the visit need involve him in any unduly long discussion.

[1] i.e. June 20 or 21.

## No. 340

*Sir S. Hoare to Sir E. Drummond (Rome)*
*No. 328 Telegraphic [A 5387/22/45]*

FOREIGN OFFICE, *June 17, 1935, 7.45 p.m.*

My telegram No. 315.[1]

Italian Counsellor communicated on the 15th June a reply in the following terms.

'The Italian Government have the honour to refer to the British memorandum of the 7th June. They recall the repeated communications and declarations in which are set forth their own views on the general aspects of the problem of the limitation of armaments and, in particular, of naval armaments, which communications and declarations were made in the course of or in connexion with the Washington Conference, the Naval Conference of London, 1930, and the General Disarmament Conference.

'As regards the ratio which should be established between the German fleet and the British fleet, the ratios adopted by the Treaty of Washington having been established in relation to the general situation then existing, it does not appear to the Italian Government to be possible, in appreciating the problem, to leave out of account the situation which has been developing since that time. It might, therefore, be difficult to express an opinion on the

[1] See No. 315, note 1.

relation to be established between the British and German fleets independently of the consideration of the position of the various fleets and the repercussions which this has, or might have, on the ratios of these fleets one to another. In the opinion of the Italian Government the problem of German naval armaments should, therefore, be examined in relation to the general problem of the armaments of the individual States.

'The Italian Government are prepared to participate in the conversations which may take place on the subject, and are anxious to contribute as effectively as possible towards a satisfactory understanding on this important problem.'

Repeated to Paris (No. 150) and Tokyo (No. 111).

## No. 341

### Sir S. Hoare to Sir G. Clerk (Paris)
*No. 149 Telegraphic [C 4632/55/18]*

FOREIGN OFFICE, *June 17, 1935, 10 p.m.*

Your despatch No. 832.[1]

His Majesty's Government agree with the views expressed in the French draft memorandum and do not desire themselves to suggest any additions or amendments.

It appears to His Majesty's Government that since Belgium, Great Britain and Italy are not parties to the Franco-Soviet Treaty, it is not for them to interpret its terms. In these circumstances His Majesty's Government would suggest, subject to the consideration of any views to be expressed by the Belgian and Italian Governments and of any additions or corrections to the French draft which may be suggested by these Governments, that it would be sufficient if the replies of the three Locarno Powers to the German memorandum were to take the form of a statement that they agree, so far as they themselves are concerned, with the views expressed in the French memorandum regarding the Franco-Soviet Pact, and that they likewise agree with the view of the French and German Governments that the provisions of the Locarno Treaty cannot legally be modified or defined by the fact that a treaty has been concluded with a third party by one of the signatories. Lastly, it is proposed to state in the British reply that under the Treaty of Locarno the United Kingdom, as one of the guarantors of that Treaty, has the right and duty of deciding when and whether the circumstances are such as to call its guarantee into operation, that this right and duty cannot be affected or altered by the act of another signatory of the Treaty.

Please inform French Government accordingly.[2]

Repeated to Berlin, Brussels, Moscow and Rome.

[1] This despatch of June 10, not printed, contained the French Government's draft reply to the German memorandum of May 25 (cf. No. 263, note 2, and No. 264, enclosure) relating to the effects of the Franco-Soviet Agreement of May 2 on the Treaty of Locarno.

[2] In Foreign Office telegrams No. 327 to Rome and No. 57 to Brussels Sir E. Drummond and Sir E. Ovey were instructed to make a similar communication to the governments to which they were accredited.

## No. 342

*Sir G. Clerk (Paris) to Sir S. Hoare (Received June 18)*
*No. 129 Saving: Telegraphic [C 4755/55/18]*

PARIS, *June 17, 1935*

My despatch No. 832.[1]

Minister for Foreign Affairs would be grateful for early observations on draft French answer to German enquiries about Franco-Soviet Treaty. He does not want, when complaining of German delay in replying about Eastern Pact (my telegram No. 123 Saving,[2] paragraph 4), to be met with a 'tu quoque'.

[1] See No. 341, note 1.                    [2] No. 335.

## No. 343

*Sir G. Clerk (Paris) to Sir S. Hoare (Received June 18)*
*No. 131 Saving: Telegraphic [C 4768/55/18]*

PARIS, *June 17, 1935*

My telegrams Nos. 123,[1] 124[2] and 125 Saving.[3]

I saw Minister for Foreign Affairs this morning, but interview did not advance matters very far.

German explanations of Chancellor's speech (your telegram No. 143).[4]

Monsieur Léger had apparently had no opportunity to inform Minister for Foreign Affairs of oral communication made to him (Monsieur Léger) on Saturday[5] and Monsieur Laval preferred to keep his own observations until he had had time to study the question more deeply. He did say, as Monsieur Léger had done on Saturday, that he was unfavourably impressed by complete lack of response of German Government to French acceptance of German proposals for a multi-lateral Eastern pact as basis of negotiation. . . .[6]

Naval Disarmament. Minister for Foreign Affairs said that considered reply, which was being prepared in co-operation with naval authorities, would he hoped be ready tomorrow. Meanwhile all he would say was that, while he did not quarrel with the 'fond' of the proposed proportion of 35 for German fleet and 100 for British fleet, and still less with His Majesty's Government for catching the German ball as it bounced, he did regret that His Majesty's Government seemed prepared to accept the offer as an arrangement quite separate from the general question. Not much appeared to him left of the London Declaration of February 6th [? 3rd].

I said, again uttering a purely personal opinion, that if His Majesty's Government had rejected the German offer, British public opinion would have condemned them severely. The one thing to do was not to let Germany

[1] No. 335.                    [2] Not here printed; cf. *ibid.*, paragraph 5.
[3] No. 336.          [4] See No. 274, note 2.          [5] June 15; see No. 335.
[6] The section of the telegram here omitted dealt with the Italo-Ethiopian dispute: it will be printed in Volume XIV.

drive a wedge between France and ourselves. I was confident that my Government was as determined as ever to work in close collaboration with France and that it would have been folly not to have taken up German offer at once, and that though form of that offer obliged us to answer it individually, the very fact that before returning a formal reply to Germans we had referred to our friends was proof of our faithfulness to common cause. The important thing was to try to prevent, or anyhow damp down, Anglo-French press polemics. Monsieur Laval said this was what he was consistently endeavouring to do, but he was clearly moved from his usual serenity.

## No. 344

*Sir E. Phipps (Berlin) to Sir S. Hoare (Received June 21)*
*No. 574 [C 4869/55/18]*

BERLIN, *June 17, 1935*

His Majesty's Ambassador presents his compliments to H.M. Secretary of State for Foreign Affairs and has the honour to transmit to him the undermentioned document.

| *Name and Date* | *Subject* |
| --- | --- |
| From: Air Attaché, Berlin | Invitation to British Air Attaché to visit |
| 15th June, 1935 | certain German aircraft factories, schools, etc. |

### ENCLOSURE IN No. 344

*Group Captain F. P. Don to Sir E. Phipps*

BERLIN, *June 15, 1935*

*The Ambassador*

The first signs of a relaxation of the policy of secrecy regarding Germany's Air Force have taken place by an official offer from the Reichsluftfahrtministerium that I should visit four schools, a seaplane station and three important aircraft factories within the next two or three weeks. I am informed that these are all privileged visits for the British Air Attaché only, with the exception of the seaplane station (at Holtenau) to which the Air Attachés of France, Italy and Finland will also be invited during the Kiel Regatta week. My instructions will permit me to take advantage of this offer and I hope it will lead to other facilities.

F. P. DON

## No. 345

*Sir G. Clerk (Paris) to Sir S. Hoare (Received June 18, 3.45 a.m.)*
*No. 126 Telegraphic: by telephone [A 5408/22/45]*

PARIS, *June 18, 1935*

Within ten minutes of receipt of Mr. Craigie's telephone message[1] and

[1] No record of this telephone message has been traced in Foreign Office archives.

before your telegram No. 148[2] had been decyphered Monsieur Laval telephoned to me himself and asked me to come to the Quai d'Orsay to receive document containing observations of French Government on communication made to Monsieur Cambon (your telegram No. 140)[3] regarding the Naval conversations with Germany. I told Monsieur Laval that I would prefer to wait until I could give him the substance of a telegram which was in the process of being decyphered for I had reason to hope that it would lead him to modify the views which I surmised were contained in the document he wished to hand to me. He replied that that note was an answer to communication made to Monsieur Cambon, that it had only been delayed on account of his inability to give his mind to it until today, that it was essential from his point of view that it should be delivered before agreement with Germany was concluded and that if message which I was to deliver to him called for any further observations on his side he would make them in due course.

As I could not shake him from this attitude and as he persisted in asking me to call on him immediately I had no alternative but to comply. On arrival[4] I begged him not to hand me document until I had said what I had to say to him. I then spoke in the sense of Mr. Craigie's message and developed in their broad sense the arguments contained, as I found subsequently, in your telegram above referred to. Monsieur Laval said, as he said this morning (my telegram No. 131 Saving)[5] that he would not go into technical aspect; that was for experts. What concerned him, as he had already told me, was *conclusion* of an arrangement on Naval armaments independently of any limitation of land and air armaments. I here pointed out to him that His Majesty's Government had always taken view that Naval armaments must be treated on a somewhat different footing from land and air armaments inasmuch as the former were already the subject of a treaty which by its terms was due to come up for renewal or revision next year. But this argument did not seem to carry much weight with him. I concluded by emphasizing what I had said this morning as to the position of His Majesty's Government vis-à-vis British public opinion begging Monsieur Laval to try to put himself in their shoes and observing that if no agreement had been reached today experience had taught us that the German claim tomorrow would have become fifty per cent instead of thirty-five per cent. Monsieur Laval replied that in all his dealings with His Majesty's Government he had always tried to see every question from their angle as well as from his own. But he also had his public opinion and he had no alternative but to deliver document[6] which he then handed to me and which I was compelled to receive. It was clear to me from the first that his mind was made up and that nothing I could have said would have altered it. I told him that what has happened is that Monsieur Corbin telephoned the communication which you made to him today[7] and Monsieur Laval then hastily put the finishing touches to the

[2] No. 339.
[3] See No. 315, note 1.
[4] This interview took place on June 17.
[5] No. 343 of June 17.
[6] Cf. No. 352 below.
[7] See No. 339.

document which he had told me this morning would not be ready until tomorrow.[8]

I intend to see Monsieur Laval again tomorrow[9] in order to find out how he views proposal that Mr. Eden should visit Paris during the course of the week. I was unaware of it when I saw him this evening.

[8] See No. 343.     [9] i.e. on June 18.

## No. 346

*Sir S. Hoare to Viscount Chilston (Moscow)*

*No. 80 Telegraphic [A 5439/22/45]*

FOREIGN OFFICE, *June 18, 1935, 5.30 p.m.*

In view of the interest which the Soviet Government must necessarily take in the naval discussions now proceeding with representatives of the German Government you should make to M. Litvinov an oral communication in the following terms, leaving with him an aide-mémoire if you think it desirable:—

1. At the outset of the conversations the German Government announced their decision to build in the future a fleet which would be in the proportion of 35 for the German fleet to 100 for the British fleet.

2. The German Government would also be prepared to agree:

(a) That this should be a permanent relationship between the two fleets, i.e., that the strength of the German fleet should never exceed 35% of the British fleet;

(b) that they would adhere to this limitation in all circumstances, e.g. it would not be affected by the construction of third powers;

(c) that this ratio need not be incorporated in any future international treaty provided that the alternative method eventually adopted for the future limitation of naval armaments were to give Germany full guarantees that this relationship between the British and German fleets will be maintained;

(d) that the ratio should, in principle, be calculated on the basis of the tonnage in the separate categories (i.e., not merely on the 'global' tonnage).

Before, however, giving an undertaking in the sense of paragraph 2 above, they asked whether His Majesty's Government were prepared to accept this arrangement.

The German offer has been carefully considered by His Majesty's Government, who have reached the conclusion that it should be accepted. They regard it as a contribution of great importance to the cause of future naval limitation and consider that it furnishes an important assurance for the future security of this and other countries.

It is expected that the conversations with representatives of the German Government will continue for some days longer, after which it is suggested that conversations should be undertaken with the French and Italian Governments. If, as a result of all these conversations, there is still some hope of an agreement on quantitative limitation being reached between the naval Powers, His Majesty's Government would greatly appreciate the opportunity for discussion with representatives of the Soviet Government on this question.

The object of these various conversations is to prepare the way for an agreement between all the naval Powers to take the place of the Washington and London naval treaties.

If however it should prove impossible to find the basis for an agreement on quantitative limitation, it is still the earnest hope of His Majesty's Government that an international convention may be concluded dealing with qualitative limitation.

You may also assure the Soviet Government that we will endeavour to keep them generally informed of the progress of events.

No. 347

Sir S. Hoare to Sir G. Clerk (Paris)[1]

No. 152 Telegraphic [A 5415/22/45]

FOREIGN OFFICE, June 18, 1935, 6.30 p.m.

My telegram No. 140.[2]

An agreement was reached to-day between His Majesty's Government in the United Kingdom and the German Government accepting the ratio of 35 to 100 as between the German and British fleets substantially on the conditions mentioned in my telegram under reference.

Text is being communicated to the French Ambassador here.[3]

[1] A similarly worded telegram, referring to No. 315 above, was sent on the same day to Rome (No. 329), Tokyo (No. 112), Washington (No. 173), Berlin (No. 135), and, referring to No. 346 above, to Moscow (No. 81).　　　　　　　　　　　　　　　　[2] No. 315.

[3] Alternatively, the Italian, Japanese, United States, and Soviet Ambassador. This last sentence was not included in telegram No. 135 to Berlin. For the text of the agreement see No. 348 below and *B.F.S.P.*, vol. 139, pp. 182–5.

No. 348

Notes of the seventh meeting between representatives of the United Kingdom and Germany, June 18, 1935, at 11 a.m.[1]

[A 5729/22/45]

Present: *United Kingdom*: Sir Samuel Hoare, Sir Bolton M. Eyres Monsell, Mr. R. L. Craigie, Vice-Admiral C. J. C. Little, Captain V. H. Danckwerts, Mr. R. C. Cox.

*Germany*: Herr von Ribbentrop, Rear-Admiral K. G. Schuster, Captain E. Wassner, Korvetten Kapitan H. Kiderlen, Dr. Kordt, Dr. Schmidt.

SIR SAMUEL HOARE opened the proceedings by saying how very glad he

[1] The meeting was held at the Foreign Office. These Notes were circulated as N.C.(G) 7th Mtg. A note on the circulated record stated that they were 'Agreed to by both delega-

was to be here to-day to meet the naval members of the German Delegation and also to conclude with them an agreement which would, he believed, not only serve the interests of their two countries but also be an important factor in facilitating the conclusion of a general agreement for the limitation of naval armament. The proposal of the Chancellor of the Reich had been recognised by His Majesty's Government and by public opinion in this country as an event of historic importance which should have a beneficial influence on the future relations of their two countries. But the significance of what the two parties were about to do to-day would be even greater if the two Governments regarded it also as a stepping stone on the road towards a general international treaty designed to avert that most serious of all evils—unlimited competition in the construction of naval armaments. There would, he thought, be a great responsibility on both Governments to see that this agreement was used by their two countries in no selfish spirit but was, on the contrary, made the occasion to ease the problems and difficulties facing the various naval Powers. If applied in this spirit, he believed that the work they were doing here to-day would prove of permanent benefit not merely to Germany and the members of the British Commonwealth of Nations, but also to mankind as a whole.

Herr von Ribbentrop thanked the British Foreign Secretary very much for the words which he had just addressed to the German Delegation, and he said he associated himself in the name of his Delegation fully and completely with those remarks. He also said he was glad and proud that he was able to-day on behalf of his Government to conclude this Anglo-German Naval Agreement which had been made possible by the generous and far-sighted outlook of the Chancellor of the German Reich, and by the understanding attitude of His Majesty's Government. He believed that, through this agreement, after years of negotiations and Conferences, the first practical step had been taken towards a limitation of armaments and the pacification of Europe in general. The German Government would be happy if further steps along this road should follow. The Naval Agreement which they had prepared regulated once and for all, with wise judgment, the naval questions as between Great Britain and Germany. Any naval rivalry was thus rendered impossible for ever. Thus began a new chapter in the history of their countries, and the foundation was laid for a future friendship of the two great countries. He said he knew he was representing the views of the Chancellor of the German Reich and the whole German people in expressing the wish that the 18th of June, 1935, may prove for future generations of Englishmen and Germans an historic date which has brought nothing but happiness and blessings to both countries.

Herr von Ribbentrop then said that he had two more questions to put forward in connection with the Agreement. Firstly, it is the understanding of the German Government that it has in the past been the general policy of the United Kingdom to endeavour to deter other naval Powers from embarking

tions and initialled on their behalf by Herr von Ribbentrop and Mr. Craigie'. Cf. *D.G.F.P.*, Series C, vol. iv, pp. 319–26.

on abnormal or exceptional construction of a kind calculated to upset the general equilibrium of naval strength. When such endeavours have failed, it has been the consistent policy of the United Kingdom to increase her naval strength when her vital interests have been threatened by increased construction by other Powers. May the German Government assume that, quite independently of the present agreement, the United Kingdom is likely to follow a similar policy in future?

SIR SAMUEL HOARE said that this was a question which he could unhesitatingly answer in the affirmative.

HERR VON RIBBENTROP then asked whether the German Delegation could assume that, as regards the present situation, the questions dealt with in subparagraph (d)[2] will be settled in the discussion now in hand.

SIR BOLTON EYRES MONSELL replied 'Yes, in accordance with the principles contained in sub-paragraph (d).'

He then said that the British Delegation were handing the German Delegation the Note defining the Agreement that has been reached, although it is an unusual procedure to sign a Naval Agreement until the details had been examined. The British Delegation did so in full confidence that the German Delegation would now bring forward their proposals regarding the strength and building programme of the German Navy. On the part of the British Delegation, they had no intention of making any stipulations or proposals that might be surprising or embarrassing to the German Delegation or the German Government, and they confidently anticipated that the German Delegation would approach the further discussions in a similar spirit.

HERR VON RIBBENTROP in reply said the German Delegation were of opinion that now agreement on the matter of principle had been concluded, there should be no obstacle in the way of open and frank discussions on the details. On their side, these discussions would be conducted in a spirit of loyal and friendly exchange of opinions between two nations who were friends. He hoped that if any surprises were forthcoming in the future discussions they would prove to be agreeable ones.

SIR SAMUEL HOARE then asked Herr von Ribbentrop whether he would agree to take the Note and the reply by the German Delegation as read.

HERR VON RIBBENTROP said he concurred in this proposal as both parties were already fully aware of the contents of the Notes.[3]

The Notes were then signed and exchanged between Sir Samuel Hoare and Herr von Ribbentrop.

[2] Of Sir S. Hoare's note of June 18 to Herr von Ribbentrop; see Annex below.

[3] Informal meetings of members of the British and German delegations had been held at the Carlton Hotel, London, on Monday, June 17, at 10 a.m., and again at 6.30 p.m. the same day (N.C.(G)6A and 6B Mtgs.). At the former meeting Mr. Craigie and Captain Danckwerts were present, and at the latter, Vice-Admiral Little, Mr. Craigie, and Captain Danckwerts. At these meetings the text of the Notes to be exchanged between the delegations was discussed in detail and modified to meet the views of both parties. The final views arrived at were contained in the text printed in the Annex below. A record by the German representatives of the second meeting on June 17 is printed in *D.G.F.P.*, Series C, vol. iv, No. 154.

(A copy of the British Note and the German reply is attached to this record as an Annex.)

SIR SAMUEL HOARE said that the British Government were proposing to publish these Notes in the morning Press the next day, Wednesday, the 19th June. Meanwhile, a White Paper would be prepared to inform the House of Commons of what had taken place.[4] He inquired whether the German Delegation would be willing to make similar arrangements to withhold the issue of these Notes until a time which would prevent any earlier publication than in the next day's Press.

HERR VON RIBBENTROP acquiesced in this arrangement, and it was agreed that the text of the Notes should not be released before 6 p.m. that night.

SIR SAMUEL HOARE explained that the British Delegation contemplated handing copies of the Notes that afternoon to the Representatives in London of the four other Powers, who were signatories of the Washington Treaty, and he hoped that this procedure was agreeable to the German Delegation.

HERR VON RIBBENTROP said he was quite agreeable, and that they on their part would take no steps to communicate the Notes to those Powers. He then enquired what should be told to the Press that day with regard to the morning's Meeting.

MR. CRAIGIE suggested that the Press should be informed that agreement had been reached at that morning's Meeting, and that the text of this Agreement would be issued late that evening for publication in the next day's papers.[5]

HERR VON RIBBENTROP signified that he would speak in the same sense to the Press. It was then agreed to adjourn until 4 p.m. that afternoon, when a further Meeting would take place at the Admiralty.[6]

This record has been read and found correct:—

J. v. R.
R. L. C.

[4] Cmd. 4930. *Exchange of Notes between His Majesty's Government in the United Kingdom and the German Government regarding the Limitation of Naval Armaments, London, June 18, 1935.*

[5] See *The Times*, June 19, p. 14.

[6] Four further meetings of the British and German representatives were held, on June 18 at 4 p.m., on June 19 at 10.30 a.m., on June 20 at 10.30 a.m., and on June 22 at 9 p.m., all at the Admiralty; there was also an 'informal' meeting at the Carlton Hotel at 6.15 p.m. on June 21. The essential purpose of these meetings was to reach agreement on the building programmes of the two powers. The points on which the two parties found no divergence of view were set out in a paper entitled, *Anglo-German Naval Conversations, 1935. Summary of Discussions between the British and German Naval Representatives,* initialled as correct on behalf of their respective delegations by Vice-Admiral Little and Rear-Admiral Schuster on June 23. Extracts from this summary are contained in Appendix I to No. 461 below: the full text is printed in *D.G.F.P.*, *op. cit.*, pp. 339–44. It was included, as Annex I, in the minutes of the meeting held on June 22. Annex II was headed *Anglo-German Naval Conversations, 1935. Points for future discussion.* Paragraph I of this Annex read: 'The following questions were discussed and proposals made for their solution by the British Delegation, which the German Admiralty will consider.' The remaining paragraphs of this Annex were identical with paragraphs 19 to 24 as printed in *D.G.F.P.*, *op. cit.*, pp. 344–6, and are not reproduced here.

*Note from the Secretary of State for Foreign Affairs to Herr von Ribbentrop*

FOREIGN OFFICE, *June 18, 1935*

Your Excellency,

During the last few days the representatives of the German Government and His Majesty's Government in the United Kingdom have been engaged in conversations, the primary purpose of which has been to prepare the way for the holding of a general conference on the subject of the limitation of naval armaments. I have now much pleasure in notifying your Excellency of the formal acceptance by His Majesty's Government in the United Kingdom of the proposal of the German Government discussed at those conversations that the future strength of the German Navy in relation to the aggregate naval strength of the Members of the British Commonwealth of Nations should be in the proportion of 35 : 100. His Majesty's Government in the United Kingdom regard this proposal as a contribution of the greatest importance to the cause of future naval limitation. They further believe that the agreement which they have now reached with the German Government, and which they regard as a permanent and definite agreement as from to-day between the two Governments, will facilitate the conclusion of a general agreement on these subjects of naval limitation between all the naval Powers of the world.

2. His Majesty's Government in the United Kingdom also agree with the explanations which were furnished by the German representatives in the course of the recent discussions in London as to the method of application of this principle. These explanations may be summarised as follows:—

(*a*) The ratio 35 : 100 is to be a permanent relationship, i.e., the total tonnage of the German fleet shall never exceed a percentage of 35 of the aggregate tonnage of the naval forces, as defined by treaty, of the Members of the British Commonwealth of Nations, or, if there should in future be no treaty limitations of this tonnage, a percentage of 35 of the aggregate of the actual tonnages of the Members of the British Commonwealth of Nations.

(*b*) If any future general treaty of naval limitation should not adopt the method of limitation by agreed ratios between the fleets of different Powers, the German Government will not insist on the incorporation of the ratio mentioned in the preceding sub-paragraph in such future general treaty, provided that the method therein adopted for the future limitation of naval armaments is such as to give Germany full guarantees that this ratio can be maintained.

(*c*) Germany will adhere to the ratio 35 : 100 in all circumstances, e.g., the ratio will not be affected by the construction of other Powers. If the general equilibrium of naval armaments, as normally maintained in the past, should be violently upset by any abnormal and exceptional construction by other Powers, the German Government reserve the right to invite His Majesty's Government in the United Kingdom to examine the new situation thus created.

(*d*) The German Government favour, in the matter of limitation of naval armaments, that system which divides naval vessels into categories, fixing the maximum tonnage and/or armament for vessels in each category, and allocates the tonnage to be allowed to each Power by categories of vessels. Consequently, in principle, and subject to (*f*) below, the German Government are prepared to apply the 35 per cent. ratio to the tonnage of each category of vessel to be maintained, and to make any variation of this ratio in a particular category or categories dependent on the arrangements to this end that may be arrived at in a future general treaty on naval limitation, such arrangements being based on the principle that any increase in one category would be compensated for by a corresponding reduction in others. If no general treaty on naval limitation should be concluded, or if the future general treaty should not contain provisions creating limitation by categories, the manner and degree in which the German Government will have the right to vary the 35 per cent. ratio in one or more categories will be a matter for settlement by agreement between the German Government and His Majesty's Government in the United Kingdom, in the light of the naval situation then existing.

(*e*) If, and for so long as, other important naval Powers retain a single category for cruisers and destroyers, Germany shall enjoy the right to have a single category for these two classes of vessels, although she would prefer to see these classes in two categories.

(*f*) In the matter of submarines, however, Germany, while not exceeding the ratio of 35 : 100 in respect of total tonnage, shall have the right to possess a submarine tonnage equal to the total submarine tonnage possessed by the Members of the British Commonwealth of Nations. The German Government, however, undertake that, except in the circumstances indicated in the immediately following sentence, Germany's submarine tonnage shall not exceed 45 per cent. of the total of that possessed by the Members of the British Commonwealth of Nations. The German Government reserve the right, in the event of a situation arising which, in their opinion, makes it necessary for Germany to avail herself of her right to a percentage of submarine tonnage exceeding the 45 per cent. above mentioned, to give notice to this effect to His Majesty's Government in the United Kingdom, and agree that the matter shall be the subject of friendly discussion before the German Government exercise that right.

(*g*) Since it is highly improbable that the calculation of the 35 per cent. ratio should give for each category of vessels tonnage figures exactly divisible by the maximum individual tonnage permitted for ships in that category, it may be necessary that adjustments should be made in order that Germany shall not be debarred from utilising her tonnage to the full. It has consequently been agreed that the German Government and His Majesty's Government in the United Kingdom will settle by common accord what adjustments are necessary for this purpose, and it is understood that this procedure shall not result in any substantial or permanent departure from the ratio 35 : 100 in respect of total strengths.

3. With reference to sub-paragraph (c) of the explanations set out above, I have the honour to inform you that His Majesty's Government in the United Kingdom have taken note of the reservation and recognise the right therein set out, on the understanding that the 35 : 100 ratio will be maintained in default of agreement to the contrary between the two Governments.

4. I have the honour to request your Excellency to inform me that the German Government agree that the proposal of the German Government has been correctly set out in the preceding paragraphs of this note.

I have, &c.,

SAMUEL HOARE

*Translation of Note from Herr von Ribbentrop to the Secretary of State*

LONDON, *June 18, 1935*

Your Excellency,

I have the honour to acknowledge the receipt of your Excellency's note of to-day's date, in which you were so good as to communicate to me on behalf of His Majesty's Government in the United Kingdom the following:—

(Here follows a German translation of paragraphs 1 to 3 of the text of the British note.)

I have the honour to confirm to your Excellency that the proposal of the German Government is correctly set forth in the foregoing note, and I note with pleasure that His Majesty's Government in the United Kingdom accept this proposal.

The German Government, for their part, are also of the opinion that the agreement at which they have now arrived with His Majesty's Government in the United Kingdom, and which they regard as a permanent and definite agreement with effect from to-day between the two Governments, will facilitate the conclusion of a general agreement on this question between all the naval Powers of the world.

I have, &c.,

JOACHIM VON RIBBENTROP

**No. 349**

*Sir E. Drummond (Rome) to Sir S. Hoare (Received June 20)*

*No. 724 [C 4829/55/18]*

ROME, *June 18, 1935*

Sir,

With reference to my telegram No. 346,[1] I have the honour to transmit to you herewith copies in translation of a semi-official letter, with enclosures, which reached me yesterday evening from Signor Suvich on the subject of the effects of the Franco-Soviet Treaty on the obligations of the signatories of the Treaty of Locarno. It will be seen that the Italian Government agree

[1] No. 334.

432

on the whole with the thesis of the French Government in this matter as expressed in the latter's draft reply to the German memorandum, of which, as you are aware, a copy was communicated to the Italian Government.

2. I have since received your telegram No. 327[2] instructing me to make known to the Italian Government the views of His Majesty's Government on the French draft and the procedure His Majesty's Government now envisage. As the views held by the Italian Government seem generally in harmony with those of His Majesty's Government, I am at once making the communication to the Italian Government as set out in your telegram to Paris No. 149.[3]

3. I have sent copies of this despatch to His Majesty's Ambassadors at Paris and Brussels.

I have, &c.,
ERIC DRUMMOND

ENCLOSURE IN No. 349

*Signor Suvich to Sir E. Drummond*

*Translation*          MINISTRY FOR FOREIGN AFFAIRS, ROME, *June 17, 1935*

My dear Ambassador,

Following upon my letter of the 14th June,[4] I send you an aide-mémoire and relative annex[5] on the subject of the Royal Government's point of view on the German Memorandum regarding the Franco-Soviet Treaty and on the draft reply of the French Government to this Memorandum. I confirm that the Royal Government is in agreement with the proposal that the text of the replies to be sent by the other signatory Powers should be drawn up in analogous terms. In this connexion I draw your attention to the Italian aide-mémoire which has been sent to the French Government. If the point of view of His Britannic Majesty's Government is in accord with that set out by the Royal Government in this aide-mémoire, the replies from the other Powers signatories of the Locarno Treaty might be drafted in the sense of the arguments indicated in the above-mentioned aide-mémoire.

Accept, &c.,
SUVICH

² See No. 341, note 2.                    ³ No. 341.
⁴ Not traced in Foreign Office archives.   ⁵ These two enclosures are not printed.

## No. 350

*Letter from Sir E. Phipps (Berlin) to Mr. Sargent*
[*C 4925/55/18*]

BERLIN, *June 18, 1935*

My dear Sargent,

My letter of June 5th.[1]

The French Chargé d'Affaires came to see me yesterday and gave me

¹ No. 308.

a copy of the inclosed *aide-mémoire*, which he had just handed to Bülow 'à titre officieux'.[2]

Bülow promised a written reply shortly, but meanwhile answered the questions put to the German Government in a satisfactory manner. That is to say (1) the recruiting offices in the demilitarised zone will only serve for the census and recruiting of men domiciled in the zone and who are to be incorporated afterwards in their units in the rest of Germany: (2) these recruiting offices will not have any other functions, and (3) no other organism will have such functions in the zone.

Yours ever,
ERIC PHIPPS

P.S. The French are particularly anxious this should not get into the Press, so don't allow leaks, please!

E. P.

[2] In this *aide mémoire*, not printed, the French Government reserved its position with regard to the application to the demilitarized zone of the German law of May 21, 1935, and 'des ordonnances ultérieures instituant, sur l'ensemble du Territoire du Reich, des bureaux chargés du recrutement de l'armée de conscription organisée en vertu de la Loi du 16 mars'.

**No. 351**

*Sir E. Phipps (Berlin) to Sir S. Hoare (Received June 19, 11.50 a.m.)*
*No. 233 Telegraphic: by telephone [A 5454/22/45]*

BERLIN, *June 19, 1935*

Berlin press enthusiastically welcomes Anglo-German Naval agreement. The following are the chief points made:

(1) The agreement is the first freely negotiated armaments agreement.

(2) It is a practical recognition of Germany's equality of rights.

(3) It excludes the possibility of Naval rival[r]y between England and Germany and thereby constitutes the first real step towards a general limitation of armaments and an example which will, it is hoped, be followed in other spheres.

(4) It constitu[t]es a definite recognition by Germany of the British Commonwealth position and needs as a Naval World Power and a renunciation by Germany of the ill judged policy of competition with England and therefore opens a new chapter in the relations between the two countries.

(5) The corollary is that British should likewise recognise Germany's essential interests as a continental Power.

(6) The agreement is a triumphant vindication of Herr Hitler's diplomatic methods and recognition of his sincerity. It shows that when there is a real will for understanding even the most difficult political problems can be solved.

## No. 352

### Sir S. Hoare to Sir E. Drummond (Rome)
#### No. 330¹ Telegraphic [A 5399/22/45]

FOREIGN OFFICE, *June 19, 1935, 1.20 p.m.*

My telegram No. 140 to Paris.²

The French reply which was received yesterday was substantially as follows. Begins:

The French Government feel obliged to point out that the repercussions of this agreement would not be limited to naval armaments of Great Britain and Germany. They wished therefore to make certain reservations:—

(1) It was the French view, derived from the London and Stresa conversations and the subsequent events at Geneva, that none of the Powers whose solidarity was confirmed at these meetings would be in a position to enter into an agreement with Germany on its own which would involve revision of the Versailles Treaty. The fear was expressed lest the conclusion of partial agreements of this kind might not involve the successive granting of all the German demands in the different spheres of armament.

(2) The terms of the proposed agreement envisaged a quadrupling of German naval strength. Since France has to take into account, among other things, the size of the German fleet, this increase will involve a considerable increase in French global tonnage. This may mean that the future tonnage of the French fleet may materially exceed its present relation to the tonnage of the British fleet. It is added that a more precise determination of this point is dependent on the German rate of construction.

(3) The possibility of Germany concentrating her fleet in the North Sea or the Baltic cannot leave the other littoral States indifferent, especially as the German Government have refused to subscribe to any mutual assistance agreement with the Soviet Union, and in view of the fact that there is some doubt as to whether they are prepared even to take part in a simple non-aggression pact in Eastern Europe. The possibility of the Soviet Union in their turn increasing their fleet must therefore be borne in mind.

The French Government ask whether, in the opinion of His Majesty's Government, the principle laid down in the agreement, that the proportion fixed between the German and British fleets will not be affected by the construction programmes of third Powers, covers the points raised under heading (3).

¹ Identic telegrams were sent on the same day to Washington (No. 174), Tokyo (No. 113), and Berlin (No. 136).
² No. 315.

## No. 353

*Sir G. Clerk (Paris) to Sir S. Hoare (Received June 19, 2.35 p.m.)*
*No. 127 Telegraphic: by telephone [A 5465/22/45]*

Immediate                                                       PARIS, *June 19, 1935*

Following for Sir R. Vansittart. Strictly private and confidential.

Although too late to modify terms of French memorandum I thought it well none the less to speak here in the sense of your private and confidential telegram of June 17th.[1] I therefore called yesterday evening on M. Laval and Mr. Campbell on M. Léger.

2. While they were both touched by personal character of your message it would be idle to pretend that on merits of the question we succeeded in making much impression. In their eyes the situation is that one of parties to the Treaty of Versailles, by concluding a separate agreement with Germany on naval clauses, has placed the other parties in a position of having to adapt their building programme to an arrangement in the negotiation of which they had no voice, and has prejudiced prospect of reaching an acceptable solution of armament problem as a whole. It is precisely the same, they claim, as if France, without reference to other parties had made a separate arrangement with Germany agreeing to a German Air Force based on a percentage of that of France.[2]

3. But their objections go deeper than that. The whole value in their eyes of declaration of London[3] was that it treated problem of security as a whole and precluded any party, so long as there was no evidence of German good faith, from feeling it had been left in the lurch. When General Goering at Crácow meeting[4] suggested that a Franco-German agreement would enable French and German armies to unite in dominating Europe,[5] M. Laval replied that he would always be ready to conclude with Germany any arrangement which she would conclude with, and which would be acceptable to, her other neighbours, but that he would never conclude any separate arrangement which diminished rather than increased their sense of security. M. Laval (a man whose instinct is to reach agreement whenever and wherever he can get it) having only been brought round with some difficulty to collective policy of the Quai d'Orsay, is naturally prone to take exaggeratedly tragic view and he plainly feels he has been let down. He had, moreover, a rough time in the Cabinet yesterday (especially at the hands of M. Herriot)[6]

---

[1] Not traced in Foreign Office archives. A note in the file by Mr. Norton, Sir R. Vansittart's private secretary, reads: 'I think it would be better not to enter Sir R. V.'s tel. even Green [a security classification]. C.J.N. 7/9/35.'

[2] A marginal note on the filed copy here reads: 'Why not? R.L.C[raigie]—(provided our hands remain free).'

[3] Of February 3, 1935.                    [4] On May 18, 1935; cf. Nos. 214 and 217.

[5] A marginal note on the filed copy, presumably by Mr. Craigie, read: 'There is no question in our agreement of British and German navies "dominating Europe".'

[6] M. Herriot, leader of the Socialist Radical party, was a Minister without Portfolio in M. Laval's cabinet formed on June 7, 1935.

and is looking forward to a similar fate when he meets the Foreign Affairs Commissions where there is considerable indignation and a tendency to hold that it is impossible to co-operate with Great Britain.

4. While both M. Laval and M. Léger made no attempt to conceal their feelings, neither showed any tendency to recriminate but rather a desire to make the best of what they consider a bad job.

5. Both M. Laval and M. Léger are delighted that Mr. Eden is coming here.[7]

[7] Cf. No. 345, last paragraph.

## No. 354

### Sir S. Hoare to Sir E. Phipps (Berlin)
#### No. 137 Telegraphic [C 4827/55/18]

FOREIGN OFFICE, *June 19, 1935, 5.15 p.m.*

Your telegram No. 226.[1]

Opportunity was taken of farewell interview with Herr von Ribbentrop on June 18th to remind him that the German reply was still outstanding to the French official note of June 3 regarding proposed multilateral non aggression Pact.[2] Herr von Ribbentrop promised to look into the matter on his return to Berlin and to try to expedite matters.

Repeated to Paris, Moscow and Warsaw.

[1] No. 277.          [2] See No. 288, note 3.

## No. 355

### Sir G. Clerk (Paris) to Sir S. Hoare (Received June 20)
#### No. 133 Saving: Telegraphic [A 5460/22/45]

PARIS, *June 19, 1935*

The Anglo-German naval agreement remains the principal topic of the press this morning. Comment, whether from the Right or the Left, is almost without exception hostile both to the principle and to the matter of the agreement.

2. It is generally held, though more in sorrow than in anger, that its conclusion, which has developed out of an exchange of views between technical experts and which amounts to an abrogation of the naval clauses of the Treaty of Versailles, has dealt a serious blow to the common front of Stresa, and is directly contrary to the undertakings entered into by the Franco-British declaration of February 3rd. However stoutly Great Britain may declare that this is not the case, the fact remains that a rude blow has been dealt at all international understanding. In the second place criticism is directed to the technical side of the agreement and in particular to the provisions relating to the construction of submarines by Germany.

3. Some writers recall that many times France has rejected overtures for

437

a separate agreement with Germany on the ground that her engagements with her friends precluded her from embracing such a policy.

4. 'Temps', in leading article, professes to understand England being tempted to make the experiment of a separate agreement with Germany which definitely recognises her naval superiority, but holds that she must not be surprised if other countries see the agreement in a very different light and consider it to be an actual encouragement to a naval armaments race. It will be interesting, the article concludes, to learn from Mr. Eden how the British Government reconcile the new method, which it has just inaugurated, with the theory, to which it has always professed its fidelity, that the interdependence of armaments and the connection between the problem of the limitation of national forces and the problem of security constitute a solid basis for a wide policy of European co-operation.

## No. 356

*Memorandum by Sir R. Vansittart on an interview with Herr von Ribbentrop*
*[C 4952/55/18]*

FOREIGN OFFICE, *June 19, 1935*

Herr von Ribbentrop came to see me to-day and I congratulated him on the conclusion of the naval agreement, which, I said, was his first exploit as Ambassador at large.

After some discourse on the part of Herr von Ribbentrop as to his views on the future of Europe, he proceeded to say that he trusted the next step would now be the speedy conclusion of an air agreement.

I replied that we also were anxious for the conclusion of such an agreement, but that it would be a matter in which all the Locarno Powers would be involved and in which they would all have to act in unison. It was therefore in the power of Germany now to make (and at as early a date as possible) a considerable contribution to this unison. I was referring, I said, explicitly to the Eastern Pact. Herr von Ribbentrop, I said, would no doubt have noticed that the reception of the naval agreement in France had not been a favourable one. That was to be expected, and I felt confident that with the passage of a little time this impression might well change into a better appreciation of the general advantages inherent in the agreement. These advantages, I said again, I for one very fully appreciated and endorsed. The reaction in the French press however must be noted, and the necessary lesson drawn from it. It was being intimated in France that we had been occupying ourselves only with the things that particularly interested us, to the exclusion of subjects that interested others more. It was obvious that were the French Government to proceed with an air pact without the necessary progress having been made in regard to the Eastern Pact, they would be exposed to the same charge from Russia and the Little Entente. I felt sure that in their present mood they would be very reluctant to expose themselves to it. The remedy however was a very simple one, and it lay in the hands of Germany.

Germany had refused to contemplate any sort of mutual assistance in Eastern Europe, and that was now well understood and accepted. At the time, however, of the British visit to Berlin, the German Government had stated that it would be prepared to negotiate on a basis of non-aggression and consultation, and had, indeed, handed to Sir John Simon a project to this effect.[1] After the lapse of some time the French, as we now knew, had informed the German Government on the 3rd June,[2] that they were prepared to take this as a basis of discussion. An Eastern Pact was now, therefore, open to the German Government on their own terms, and there could surely now no longer be the slightest reason for not proceeding with it.

Herr von Ribbentrop replied that the German Government already had a series of treaty arrangements with the Russian Government, and that Herr Hitler himself had renewed the latest of them.[3] He therefore did not see the necessity for any addition to this complex.

I replied that I was well aware of the existing treaties and of Herr Hitler's renewal, and, therefore, for the very reason stated by Herr von Ribbentrop himself, I thought that there was no reason any longer for not proceeding with the Eastern Pact in its now simplified draft form. The very fact that the German Government thought that it added little to the existing situation must be an argument against recalcitrance on their part. On the other hand, if goodwill were shown in the making of this advance from their own basis, an excellent impression would be produced, and I felt convinced that we should all find the negotiation of an air pact would thereby be facilitated at no real additional cost to the German Government.

Herr von Ribbentrop replied that progress in this direction would be difficult because of the strained relations between Germany and Russia and the fundamental divergences of their two systems. Nobody in Germany felt disposed to embrace Soviet Russia.

I replied that there was no question in anybody's mind of embraces or affections, which on either side might conceivably be held to be unnatural. That was not the point. What really mattered was that Germany, by taking the action I now proposed, would be disarming her critics, and they were many, particularly in Eastern Europe where, as he was well aware, Germany's ultimate intentions were matters of deep suspicion.

Herr von Ribbentrop repudiated any hostile intention on the part of Germany towards Russia. I replied that I took full note of what he said. None the less those suspicions existed and it was in the power of Germany to take a very small and easy step forward which would largely discount them.

Herr von Ribbentrop assured me that when he returned to Berlin he would take the matter up with Herr Hitler and would bear in mind in so doing the observations that I had made to him.

[1] See Volume XII, No. 651, Annex I to Third Meeting.
[2] See No. 288, note 3.
[3] In 1933 the German Government had ratified the Protocol of June 24, 1931, prolonging the German-Soviet Treaty of Friendship of 1926 and the Conciliation Convention of 1929; cf. No. 437 below, paragraph 3.

I repeated as we parted, after renewing my congratulations, that I thought that this next step would be particularly welcome if the delay in replying to the French communication of June 3rd was not unduly prolonged.

I think it might be well to inform the French and Russian Governments of the substance of this interview.

Herr von Ribbentrop, in a word, appeared somewhat embarrassed on this topic but by no means unwilling to listen to reason.

R. V.

### Note by Sir Samuel Hoare

The three interviews that I have had with Herr von Ribbentrop were all on similar lines. With me he went somewhat further in promising to investigate the delay in answering the French note of June 3.

S. H. 22/6

## No. 357

### Sir S. Hoare to Sir G. Clerk (Paris)
### No. 1184 [A 5484/22/45]

FOREIGN OFFICE, *June 19, 1935*

Sir,

The French Ambassador called upon Sir Robert Vansittart to-day and expressed concern over the Anglo-German naval agreement. He briefly recapitulated the views of the French Government, which are of course well known to you.

2. Sir Robert said in reply that he sincerely hoped the French Government would not take a tragic or indeed an unreasonable view of the agreement. It was surely clear that no Government in this country could have rejected the unilateral offer of Germany without incurring the disfavour of public opinion, weakening its internal position and therefore its prospects. It was no longer possible to stand on a purely legalistic basis, and it was mere common sense to seize the opportunity to tie the Germans down to a maximum level before they raised their demands to unreasonable and disquieting heights.

3. It might, of course, be argued that it was in Germany's mind to attempt to drive a wedge between ourselves and France. His Majesty's Government, however, had no intention of allowing this to be done, and indeed felt that Anglo-French relations would have suffered far more if an apparently advantageous settlement were in sight and France could have been represented as having prevented it. That would have been to play entirely into the hands of German propagandists. Moreover, on any long view, the agreement was of great value to France as well, in view of the German admission that they would base their percentage figures on ours irrespective of anything but abnormal increases on the part of any other Power.

4. The agreement did not for one moment imply that the Stresa front had been broken, although there was a danger to it on another question, i.e., that of Abyssinia. The imminence of this latter problem made it all the more

necessary for us to see that no unnecessary damage was done to the Anglo-French link by avoidable misinterpretation of an unavoidable development.

5. Sir Robert added that we had reason to believe that naval circles in Germany were by no means pleased at Herr Hitler's offer, and that, had the latter been rejected the influence of those in Germany who were thinking in terms of a higher percentage would undoubtedly have been increased, with the result that France would have been faced with the necessity for a far greater financial effort to keep pace with German naval construction.

6. Sir Robert said that he was very glad that the French Government had agreed to Mr. Eden's visit,[1] which would be a very useful means of showing solidarity between this country and France, and he ended by emphasising the desirability of taking every possible step to ensure that the French press should not give vent to an outburst of anger such as would injure Anglo-French relations.

I am, &c.,

SAMUEL HOARE

[1] Mr. Eden arrived in Paris on the evening of June 20, left for Rome on June 23, and visited Paris again on June 27 on his return to London on the same day.

## No. 358

*Sir S. Hoare to Sir G. Clerk (Paris)*

*No. 154 Telegraphic* [C 4888/55/18]

FOREIGN OFFICE, *June 20, 1935, 5.45 p.m.*

Following for Strang[1] from Wigram.

Vansittart approves the memorandum on air pact and limitation agreement.[2] With regard to last paragraph[3] he says that the French must be humoured and not rushed and that this must be the key to our tactics for some time to come.

[1] Mr. Strang, Adviser on League of Nations Affairs, was in Paris in connexion with the forthcoming Anglo-French conversations.

[2] The reference was to a 'Memorandum on the Air Pact and Limitation of Air Strength for the guidance of Mr. Eden in Paris', compiled by the Foreign Office and Air Ministry, and dated June 20. The substance of it was the same as No. 364 below.

[3] This dealt with the question of supervision and read: 'Mr. Eden can therefore give no detailed information as to our views on this matter: but if the French raise it and show signs of intending to insist on limitation and supervision of other categories of air strength such as civil aircraft, manufacturing capacity, etc. and of being likely to ask for an agreement on guarantees of execution, Mr. Eden could discourage them strongly and point out that demands of this kind will almost certainly result in a complete breakdown of the negotiations. He could emphasise the very great importance which the British Government and British public opinion attach to the success of these negotiations.'

# Reactions to Anglo-German Naval Agreement: further discussions on proposed Eastern and Air Pacts

## June 20–July 31, 1935

### No. 359

*Viscount Chilston (Moscow) to Sir S. Hoare (Received June 21, 9 a.m.)*
*No. 85 Telegraphic [A 5538/22/45]*

MOSCOW, *June 20, 1935, 8.38 p.m.*

I was received this afternoon by Monsieur Litvinov to whom I read communication contained in your telegram No. 80[1] regarding Anglo-German Naval Agreement. After thanking me for this Monsieur Litvinov remarked more sorrowfully than cynically 'Herr Hitler has now[2] a great diplomatic victory'. He added that this agreement having been made separately in spite of the London declaration and in spite of Stresa, implied the end of Anglo-French co-operation (which I of course denied). Monsieur Litvinov said that Germany would now hasten to build as quickly as possible up to the limit which afterwards she would no longer observe.

[1] No. 346.    [2] Possibly in error for 'won'.

### No. 360

*Sir E. Phipps (Berlin) to Sir S. Hoare (Received June 21, 10.25 a.m.)*
*No. 157 Saving: Telegraphic [C 4849/55/18]*

BERLIN, *June 20, 1935*

I hear from a trustworthy source that the Ministry of Foreign Affairs are genuinely looking forward to the conclusion of an Air Pact, after the successful naval agreement. Hitler supported them against the German Admiralty who wished at the last moment considerably to increase their demands. The Ministry of Foreign Affairs hope to be able to persuade His Majesty's Government that the Franco-Russian Agreement is incompatible with Locarno.

They were not to be drawn on the subject of Austria but they did not hide their glee at the Abyssinian imbroglio.

On the subject of colonies, they declared that Germany's requirements were not territorial so much as economic. Germany needed certain mineral ores, and her eventual colonial demands would in general be governed by her requirements in raw materials. In this connexion they stated that Hitler was opposed in principle to putting forward his demands in driblets. He preferred to state his minimum[1] requirements at once so that the other Powers would get only one shock. This had been his policy in the case of Germany's Army, Navy and Air Force requirements.

From another excellent source I learn that the Germans are trying to frighten the French in Paris by pointing to the rapid conclusion of our naval agreement and by asserting that we are ready to come to terms with Germany alone equally quickly in the air.

[1] It was suggested on the filed copy that this word should read 'maximum'.

## No. 361

### Sir E. Phipps (Berlin) to Sir S. Hoare (Received June 21)
### No. 591 [C 4878/55/18]

BERLIN, *June 20, 1935*

Sir,

I have the honour to transmit to you, herewith, a record of a conversation between the Military Attaché to this Embassy and a pre-war German General Staff Officer who now enjoys an influential position in the Nazi Party.

2. I would draw your attention to item 3 of this record in which Colonel Hotblack summarises the view which his informant expressed regarding the difficulty which Germany would have, as a result of her central strategic position on the continent, in agreeing to a pact which contained provision for the definition of the aggressor.

I have, &c.,
ERIC PHIPPS

ENCLOSURE IN No. 361

*Colonel Hotblack to Sir E. Phipps*

BERLIN, *June 17, 1935*

The Ambassador,

*German views on the beginning of war*

1. *Position of Informant.* The following notes are from conversations with a pre-war German general staff officer. He is no longer in the army, and has for many years been an ardent Nazi. His knowledge of the past is good, and although we do not consider that he is in a position to know the plans of the present general staff, he received a contemporary military training with many officers now holding important positions.

The attitude which he, in general, adopted during the long conversations was that of a man who knew both the Army and the Party from inside and who wished to present both in a favourable light.

The subsequent two paragraphs arose out of a question as to whether the pre-war (Schlieffen) Plan had not involved undue risks in that it depended

443

upon getting rapidly through the fortress of Liège and on finding the bridges and tunnels incompletely destroyed.

2. *Pre-War Plan.* He stated that as the result of the work of agents and of reconnaissances by officers the conditions at Liège were known very accurately. The German general staff possessed exact information as to the time it would take to put the whole of the fortress into its full state of defence on mobilization.

The essential part of the German plan was that the fortress should be over-run before the garrison was ready.

He did not think that any arrangements had been made to buy Belgians whose duty it was to destroy tunnels, &c. The German general staff relied upon speed and surprise; they also had hopes of friction between the Flemish and Walloon troops concerned in the defence.

He stated that as far as he was concerned there had been three particularly anxious periods:

(*a*) Plans for an alternative mobilization on either front had proved to be too complicated, with the vast masses of troops involved, and had been abandoned some time before the war.

There only remained the plan for the major concentration on the west.

Grave anxiety had been caused by the fear that France would at first remain neutral and the German terms demanding the 'neutralization' of the French fortresses had been designed to bring France into the war.

(*b*) The troops who had been hurried against Liège had not fought so well as German troops subsequently fought elsewhere and the whole plan was nearly wrecked. Ludendorff's[1] well-known exploit of advancing between the forts into the town had done much to relieve the situation but even that had not immediately cleared the way.

(*c*) During the delay at Liège it was thought that it would be necessary to advance through Holland. No adequate supply of maps of Holland had been printed though the copperplates were available.

3. *Post-War Plans.* Our informant insisted on more than one occasion that Germany's central position was unlike that of other Great Powers and that in the future as in the past, it would be essential for Germany, when she has to fight again, to fall upon one enemy by speed and surprise whilst holding the other front with few troops.

He said that France had tried, through the League of Nations, to entangle Germany into commitments which would hamper Germany, since they were designed to take an unreasonable view of what was aggression and to pile up sanctions against the aggressor; by her geographical position Germany would be obliged to be the 'aggressor'. He said that it had been impossible to make Stresemann[2] realize the disadvantages of such entanglements. He added that, fortunately, the present Government understood the situation.

[1] At the time Major General Erich Ludendorff was a senior intelligence officer attached to the invading forces.     [2] German Minister for Foreign Affairs, 1923–9.

4. *Germany a Soldier Nation.* Our informant said that he now realized that France was not as strong, militarily, as had been supposed. He thought that all French establishments (as far as they depended upon voluntary service such as extensions of service beyond the compulsory period) were very much under strength.

He considered that the French population was not now anxious to serve in the forces, whereas everyone in Germany wanted to serve and the vacancies for volunteers had all been filled at once.

5. *Economic Position.* He agreed that Germany's rearmament must be costing a great deal. He said that at some future date Germany would have to return to a normal currency. He thought, however, that the situation would continue to be satisfactory as long as:—

(*a*) The people trusted the mark and did not panic.

(*b*) The people did not save, but put all the extra money into circulation forthwith.

He thought that this was working well in Germany, though it would be impossible in France.

6. *Relationship between Army and Party.* He stated that there was some friction and jealousy between the Army and Party. He hoped that a display of tact and understanding on both sides would cure whatever small troubles there might be at present. He considered that this good understanding would be of great importance to the future of Germany.[3]

ELLIOT HOTBLACK

[3] This report led to extensive minuting in the Foreign Office, in the course of which Mr. Wigram wrote on June 26, 'the worst part is that the more they think the Western Powers are committed to Russia, the more likely they are to fall on the Western Powers first, i.e. a new Schlieffen plan'. Mr. Sargent wrote on June 27: 'So long as Hitler lives I don't think there is any possibility of co-operation between Nazi Germany and Bolshevik Russia, much as the German soldiers may wish for it. . . . The penalty of France allying herself again with Russia will be to attract Germany's first fire on to herself as in 1914. Germany's attack would, of course, be a[n] 'act of defence' in such a case and not of aggression. This raises a question of vital importance to this country which I do not think has been sufficiently studied or reflected upon.' Sir R. Vansittart on June 30 gave instructions for Colonel Hotblack's paper to be put 'on my file of evidences of eventual German aggression'. He also gave instructions for the drafting of a private letter to Sir Warren Fisher concerning the possible financing of German rearmament by the City of London (see No. 412 below).

**No. 362**

*Sir G. Clerk (Paris) to Sir S. Hoare (Received June 21, 7.30 p.m.)*

*Nos. 128 and 129 Telegraphic: by telephone* [C 4901/55/18]

*Immediate*                                               PARIS, *June 21, 1935*

Following from Mr. Eden.

The conversations today[1] with Monsieur Laval and Monsieur Piétri in the afternoon were distinctly difficult. Monsieur Laval was clearly troubled. He

[1] See No. 363 below.

had come straight from a Cabinet meeting where [he] had had a rough passage from his colleagues and where he had been accused of sending us a note[2] on Anglo-German naval conversations which was much too mild in tone. Monsieur Herriot in particular, he assured me, had been furious. Altogether Monsieur Laval was less buoyant than I have ever known him.

Today's conversations have left me with the following definite impressions. The Anglo-German naval agreement is regarded here as having struck a blow at communiqué of February 3rd. Nothing that we can say will modify that judgment. None the less Monsieur Laval is himself not unduly disposed to cry over spilt milk. He is however determined to preserve what is left in the can of February 3rd.

The French Government are prepared to continue naval conversations with us to pave the way for the naval conference. After much pressure however the best I could secure was that our joint experts might meet in about six weeks' time, but no definite announcement to that effect can be made now. A meeting earlier than that, Monsieur Laval argued, would imply acquiescence in Anglo-German naval arrangement, and this was quite out of the question. He hoped that the meeting with the Italian naval experts would be subsequent to that with the French.

The French Government maintain that they will not agree to piece-meal conclusion of agreements upon portions of communiqué of February 3rd. I am convinced that they consequently will not conclude an agreement for an air pact and for limitation unless as part of a general settlement which will cover an eastern pact of non-aggression (mutual assistance being dropped as unattainable), the Danubian pact and land armaments.

If above understanding is accepted, French Government are willing to agree to opening of negotiations for an air pact and for limitation at once provided it is in any case understood that pact will be reinforced by bilateral agreements to be concluded between any two of the parties who so desire. One of those bilateral pacts would have to be between United Kingdom and France.

I fear it will be impossible to secure agreement with the French Government for negotiation of an air pact and limitation upon any other terms, and my present judgment is that it will be better to work upon this basis than to allow all negotiations to come to a standstill. We have agreed to adjourn conversations until midday tomorrow, when I am lunching with Monsieur Laval, by which time I should be grateful if I may be given some material to enable me to reply to him.

If you consider it impossible to come to any definite conclusion on this matter at once, I might perhaps tell Monsieur Laval that I hope to be in a position to take up this discussion again on my way back from Rome, when in any event I shall have to see him to report on outcome of discussions there.

[2] See No. 352.

## No. 363

### Sir G. Clerk (Paris) to Sir S. Hoare (Received June 22)
### No. 880 [C 4902/55/18]

PARIS, *June 21, 1935*

His Majesty's representative at Paris presents his compliments to the Secretary of State for Foreign Affairs, and has the honour to transmit to him a record of conversations between British and French representatives at the French Ministry for Foreign Affairs on the 21st June, 1935.

### ENCLOSURE IN No. 363
*Record of Anglo-French Conversation held at the Quai d'Orsay on June 21 at 11.30 a.m.*

#### FIRST MEETING

Present: *Great Britain*: Mr. Anthony Eden, Minister for League of Nations Affairs; Sir George Clerk, His Majesty's Ambassador in Paris; Mr. Campbell, His Majesty's Minister in Paris; Mr. Strang, Foreign Office; Mr. Hankey, Foreign Office.

*France*: M. Pierre Laval, President of the Council; M. Alexis Léger, Secretary-General of the Ministry for Foreign Affairs; M. René Massigli, Ministry for Foreign Affairs.

#### Anglo-German Naval Agreement

M. LAVAL opened the discussion by observing that the Anglo-German Naval Agreement[1] had caused great difficulties for the French Government. French public opinion was thoroughly aroused, and the recent French Note[2] was not generally regarded as sufficiently strong. Great Britain was bound by the Treaty of Versailles as well as France, and a deplorable impression had been created by the fact that there was no mention of it in the Agreement.

MR. EDEN admitted that from the strictly juridical point of view this position might be strong. From a practical point of view, however, no British Government could have done otherwise.

M. LAVAL went on to elaborate the juridical point of view. Not only was the Agreement an infringement of the Treaty of Versailles. It was also contrary to the undertaking contained in the communiqué of February 3rd that the various parts of the security and armaments problem were to be treated as an indivisible whole. Moreover, at Stresa we had, if he was not mistaken, told the French that we should not accept the German claim of 35 per cent. of the British fleet. The united front of Stresa was equally broken in pieces.

M. Laval observed that in what he had said he had been more moderate than either the French Government or French public opinion. He quite understood that His Majesty's Government might say that they could have followed no other course in dealing with the naval question, as otherwise the same thing would have happened to the navy as had happened since last

---

[1] See No. 348.     [2] See No. 352.

447

year in regard to land and air armaments. The truth was that the French Government placed themselves on a legal basis, whereas His Majesty's Government placed themselves on a basis of fact. Even so, he did not think that His Majesty's Government had made a good bargain.

There was, however, a further point in his case. The London communiqué had laid down a programme for the replacement of the disarmament clauses of Part V of the Treaty of Versailles as part of a general settlement. His Majesty's Government had now departed from the procedure agreed upon in the London communiqué.

But, as he had said, he did not think the step His Majesty's Government had taken was, on its merits, a good one. Why should not other Powers now deal separately with Germany? France might have done so. She had not done so and would not do so. France would always inform Great Britain of the course of any negotiations which she undertook and consult Great Britain before coming to a conclusion. It was the German policy to deal separately with each subject and with each party concerned.

He wished to make peace with Germany, but on the condition that Germany would make peace with everybody else. He was afraid that His Majesty's Government's action would tend to encourage Germany not to make peace with everybody. Was there not a risk that, while the West was being secured, the East would be laid open to German attack?

Mr. Eden said that he wished first to assure M. Laval that the change of Government in England[3] did not mean any change in policy. He had been asked by Sir Samuel Hoare to emphasise this to M. Laval.

So far as naval agreement was concerned, it was important to get the matter into proper perspective. The German Government had, during the Berlin conversations, made their offer to limit the German fleet to 35 per cent. of the British fleet, and since the Stresa Conference Herr Hitler had reaffirmed this offer in his speech.[4] At the meeting with the German naval experts it had been the intention of His Majesty's Government to conduct preliminary conversations only. They had, however, been faced by a refusal on the part of the German representatives to pursue conversations unless a definite answer could be given as regards the 35 per cent. offer.

This offer was one which no Government in the United Kingdom could possibly have refused, more particularly in the light of the experience of the past year as regards the increase in German claims in respect of land and air armaments. An increase in the German claim as regards naval armaments would be more serious than, for example, an increase in German claims as regards air armaments. It was bad enough to have to double the air force; it would be still worse to have to double the fleet in these days of budgetary difficulties. The expense would be very much greater.

He appreciated that Germany might be attempting to drive a wedge between Great Britain and France, but he did not believe it was possible to drive such a wedge. If, however, His Majesty's Government had refused the German offer in order to meet French criticism, the outcry in England

[3] On June 7, cf. No. 304, note 10.     [4] On May 21.

against France would certainly have been such as to drive a wedge between England and France.

In spite of all this, His Majesty's Government would not have accepted the German offer if they had not been convinced that acceptance was in the interest of France as well as of Great Britain. France retained complete liberty of action. In support of this statement, Mr. Eden drew attention to paragraph 2 (c) and paragraph 3 of Sir Samuel Hoare's note to Herr von Ribbentrop of June 18.[5]

Mr. Eden thought it might be useful to look at the figures. He thought at the outset the German Government had made a slight miscalculation. During the Berlin conversations, Herr Hitler had spoken to the British Ministers about a German claim for 35 per cent. of the British fleet or parity with France. He apparently thought that these figures were identical. This was not so, as the French fleet was 50 per cent. of the British fleet. The present German proposal, therefore, did not give Germany parity with France. On the contrary, it gave France a 30 per cent.[6] superiority over Germany, even if France did not increase the present tonnage of her fleet. This was worth comparing with a German superiority of 30 per cent. over France before the war.

As regards the future, he wished to say that the British experts were convinced that they could persuade the French experts that the Anglo-German Naval Agreement was in the interests of France, and His Majesty's Government hoped that the French Government would at an early date send experts to London to pursue conversations on the naval question.

His Majesty's Government hoped to receive this week from the German delegation the German programme of construction.[7] They would be glad if the French experts could bring with them their own tentative programme of construction based on the assumption of a reasonably slow German programme of construction up to the 35 per cent. limit.

There was one further point. Supposing that, as a result of the Anglo-German arrangement, France were to increase her fleet in her own national defence, His Majesty's Government would examine the influence of the French increase upon their own naval strength. They might not think it necessary to increase the British fleet; in that event there would be no further increase by Germany; if, on the other hand, they should think an increase necessary, then Germany would also increase up to a proportion of 35 per cent. The utmost Germany could do would be to invoke the saving clause contained in paragraph 2 (c) of Sir Samuel Hoare's note, on the assumption, of course, that the French construction violently upset the existing equilibrium.

M. LAVAL said that this would mean that His Majesty's Government had liberty to revise their agreement with Germany if they thought that the French increase was so great as to upset the existing equilibrium.

[5] See Annex to No. 348.
[6] On another copy of this Record '43 per cent' is here suggested.
[7] Cf. No. 348, note 6.

He assumed, however, that it was Russia and not France whom the German Government had in mind.

M. MASSIGLI pointed out that under the Anglo-German arrangement Germany would have parity with France in respect of capital ships, as under the Washington Treaty France had 35 per cent. of the British fleet in capital ships.

MR. EDEN observed that this meant that the French superiority over Germany would be proportionately higher in the other categories of vessels.

M. MASSIGLI agreed that this was so as regards lighter vessels and submarines.

M. LAVAL said that he could not contemplate sending experts to London at this moment, for public opinion in France would not understand it. It would be better to wait.

MR. EDEN observed that one of the difficulties at the earlier Anglo-French naval conversations was that the German plans were not known. Now they were known, and this in itself would make further Anglo-French conversations desirable.

His Majesty's Government had good reason to believe that the 35 per cent. offer was made by Hitler himself and that the German naval authorities disliked it. He believed that during the Whitsun adjournment pressure had been brought upon Hitler by the naval authorities, who would have been only too glad of any pretext for securing the withdrawal of the offer.

M. LAVAL said that this might be an argument for Mr. Eden, but it was not one for himself. It was quite clear that the German Government was delighted with the London naval arrangement.

He felt it necessary to say that he had not changed his mind since February 3rd. If he agreed at this moment to send naval experts to London, this would mean that Germany had succeeded in detaching the naval question from the general settlement. He could not allow himself to become involved in such a procedure. He had other things to bear in mind, such as German intentions in Austria and as regards the Eastern Pact.

He had been as conciliatory as possible. He had taken as the basis for the Eastern Pact the communication made by Baron von Neurath to Sir John Simon during the Stresa Conference.[8] It was because he had not yet sent a reply to Berlin on the subject of the Franco-Soviet Pact that the German Government were delaying their reply to the French note of June 3rd on the subject of the Eastern Pact.[9] He had already had an expression of views from His Majesty's Government about the Franco-Soviet Pact, and was grateful for it. As soon as he had a reply from Rome he would send an answer to Berlin.

He would then wait to see what Germany would do. There was some hope that the German Government would be willing to do something. They had seemed to change their mind several times during the last few months, but he had some hope that their disposition was now more favourable to a multilateral pact of non-aggression and consultation.

[8] See Volume XII, No. 715.      [9] See No. 288, note 3.

If he now allowed himself to become involved in naval discussions, he would have given encouragement to the German desire to take one subject at a time.

If he might express his own personal view, he would say that he complained more of the form and method of the Anglo-German agreement than of its substance. He was more disturbed by what he might call the apparent relaxation of collaboration than by the concessions His Majesty's Government had made to Germany. He, like us, thought that an arrangement with Germany was necessary, but he disagreed with us about methods.

MR. EDEN observed that the real object of the proposed naval conversations was to prepare the way for the Naval Conference later in the year.

M. LAVAL repeated that the matters for discussion formed a single whole and that it was a mistake to treat the various matters separately with Germany. But he would be only too glad to discuss with Germany the whole of the matters comprised in the general settlement. If he now sent naval experts to London, Germany would profit by it to break up the general scheme.

MR. EDEN observed that if the French refused to send experts now, it would be generally assumed that there were serious differences of opinion between the two Governments.

M. LAVAL said that he thought that a form of words could be discovered to avoid this difficulty. The trouble was that His Majesty's Government had placed Germany in a better moral position than France, and that they were encouraging the German attitude of resistance.

MR. EDEN observed that Sir Samuel Hoare had asked Herr von Ribbentrop in London to press the German Government to send a reply to the French note of June 3rd about the Eastern Pact.[10]

He repeated that what the experts would come to London to talk about would not be merely, or even principally, the Anglo-German Agreement, but matters preparatory for the forthcoming Naval Conference.

M. LAVAL said that the French Government had to pay even greater attention to their public opinion than did His Majesty's Government. He had never seen the French press so unbridled as at present, and he himself had done nothing to egg them on.

He thought it would be better for His Majesty's Government not to ask for French experts to be sent to London at present. This did not mean that Anglo-French talks would not take place later; they would indeed be indispensable. But Germany must first reply about the Eastern Pact.

If His Majesty's Government now dealt with air armaments as they had dealt with the Navy, they would be in a fair way to give Germany all she wanted. Germany would then ask for the colonies.

MR. EDEN said he wanted to avoid any appearance of an Anglo-French breach. If the French experts did not come to London it would be said that the two Governments had fallen out.

M. MASSIGLI did not think the matter was so urgent. His Majesty's

[10] See No. 354.

Government could certainly not be afraid that the French Government would build against them.

Mr. EDEN said that the Naval Conference would have to open this year. His Majesty's Government did not wish to talk to the Italian Government until after they had talked to the French Government. That was one reason why it was desirable to open fresh conversations as early as possible.

Would it perhaps be possible for British experts to come to Paris?

M. LAVAL said that perhaps this might be better, but in any case it could not be settled now, otherwise the French press would be in a state of excitement.

Mr. EDEN at this point quoted a passage from the reply which was to be given to a question in the House of Commons, showing that His Majesty's Government regarded negotiations on naval questions as being in a different category from negotiations on other arms.[11]

M. LAVAL said that the sending of naval experts to London now was a very delicate matter in view of the state of French opinion. The Naval Conference was not until the end of the year. He thought the normal time for the meeting of experts would have been in the autumn.

Mr. EDEN pointed out that the experts had already met once.[12] We must on no account let it look as if on account of the Anglo-German agreement there was a rift between Great Britain and France. In reply to a suggestion by M. Laval he said that it would hardly be possible to continue expert discussions in London without hearing the French views as to their naval programme. His impression was that we should not want to discuss programmes with the Italian experts before we had seen the French.

M. LÉGER said that the naval agreement had made it much harder for the French to obtain understandings on air and land armaments. Part V of the Treaty of Versailles was now sacrificed, and the French would not be able to bargain it against security.

Mr. EDEN said that if we had merely said 'no' to the German offer it would surely not have made it any easier to obtain agreement in those fields. Did M. Léger really think that Part V was now worth anything as a bargaining counter? Surely not. He failed to see why we were better off if no agreement was reached in any field. In reply to a suggestion by M. Massigli that we might have made our agreement conditional on the conclusion of agreements in other fields, he pointed out that we might in that case not have got the agreement after all. Supposing the French had made an agreement on, say, air armaments with Germany, inviting Germany to a percentage of the French figure and leaving us liberty, we should have been delighted.

M. LAVAL said, so would he.

In reply to a question by M. Laval, Mr. EDEN said that nothing had been done about an air agreement in the discussions with Herr von Ribbentrop in London, though the matter had been mentioned in general terms.

[11] See 303 *H.C. Deb.* 5 *s.*, col. 707 (June 21, 1935).
[12] In July 1934; cf. Volume VI, No. 490, note 3.

M. LAVAL said he quite understood Great Britain's position. The Naval Agreement was now concluded. So be it. Nevertheless, he could not send experts to London now because it would give the appearance of acquiescence. He did not object to the ratio of 35 per cent. It was a matter of form. He could not acquiesce in the matter of the agreement by sending experts to London now. It would have a disastrous effect on French public opinion, which would not understand and in Berlin there would be enthusiasm because the French hand had been forced.

MR. EDEN questioned this. He did not think the Germans would have any cause for enthusiasm at the sight of Anglo-French collaboration. On the contrary, if the experts did not come, everyone would ask why not and the appearance would be created that the French were annoyed with us.

After some further discussion, M. LAVAL agreed that they might say that they had mentioned the question of experts coming to London to discuss at some future date the question of naval programmes in preparation for the naval conference at the end of the year.

### Air Pact

The discussion then turned to the question of air agreements.

MR. EDEN asked whether the French Government were favourable to the opening of negotiations between the five Locarno Powers regarding an air pact and an air limitation agreement.

M. LAVAL said that the question must be kept in step with the negotiation of an agreement on land armaments.

MR. EDEN asked M. Laval what he was going to do about land armaments. Was he going to start negotiating with the Germans?

M. LÉGER said that there was one essential point. Were we in agreement with the principle of concluding bi-lateral pacts for the application of an air pact?

MR. EDEN said agreement must be reached on an air pact first and then, if necessary, measures for the application of it might be considered, between all parties to it.

M. LAVAL said that, if His Majesty's Government would not accept such bi-lateral pacts, then the air pact was of no advantage to France.

If Germany were given the air pact, then she must accept the other conditions in the London communiqué. If the air pact were to be made without bi-lateral agreements, Great Britain would no longer be interested and France would be left alone to deal with Germany's claim as regards land armaments. He emphasised that since Hitler's speech the Germans had passed the law of military organisation.[13] Including the period of labour service, the period of military service in Germany was now effectively two years. Moreover, the men could be recalled to the colours without special measures of mobilisation being taken. In fact, the period of service was now almost indefinite. No other Western European Power had got such effectives. Moreover, France depended for man-power upon communications

[13] Cf. Nos. 219 and 292.

with her colonies, and now these were endangered by the Anglo-German Naval Agreement. France, therefore, needed the help of His Majesty's Government to get an agreement on land armaments.

Mr. Eden said that on no account must M. Laval suppose that His Majesty's Government were not interested in an agreement on land armaments.

M. Laval said that the essential point was somehow to get Germany to moderate her demands and to come back into the fold of general discussion.

M. Léger asked whether the United Kingdom Government proposed the separate conclusion of the air pact, or would it be subject to agreements being reached on other subjects?

Mr. Eden said His Majesty's Government wanted to begin the negotiation of an air pact. The Rome Conference was to meet to begin negotiation of the Central European Agreement.[14] He must draw attention to the difference between 'conclusion' and 'negotiation'.

(At this point the meeting adjourned for lunch.)

## Second Meeting

The meeting was resumed after lunch, M. Piétri, the French Minister of Marine, also being present.

### Anglo-German Naval Agreement: Air Pact

M. Laval said that France would not abuse the liberty left to her by the Anglo-German Naval Agreement. Great Britain might be right in principle; it was the method to which he took exception.

Mr. Eden said that what His Majesty's Government could not admit was that an agreement for naval limitation should go by default in the same way as agreements for air and land limitation appeared to have done.

M. Piétri said he quite understood.

M. Laval said that many people in France agreed with the principle of an agreement with Germany. There would be elections in France next May, but they would not make any difference to French policy. But there was a minimum requirement, and it was this: any air agreement must be accompanied by bi-lateral agreements, and its entry into force must be dependent upon agreements of some kind on the other subjects mentioned in the London communiqué, i.e., an agreement on Austria, a security agreement for Eastern Europe (he emphasised that he was prepared to do without a mutual assistance clause), an agreement on land armaments, and Germany's return to the League of Nations. On this understanding, he would see Herr von Ribbentrop at any time, and would do his best to reach agreement.

Mr. Eden said that the idea of His Majesty's Government had been to discuss with the other Powers concerned certain preliminary questions which must be settled before there could be any effective negotiation of an air pact.

[14] This conference, at which Great Britain was to have been represented by an observer (cf. 301 H.C. Deb. 5 s., col. 571) was not held.

He would have liked to leave those questions with M. Laval, and also send them to the other Powers concerned.

M. LAVAL said that for the moment he was mainly concerned with the other questions he had already enumerated mentioned in the London communiqué of February 3rd. He was anxious to get away from the atmosphere of notes and to discover what Germany would do about all of them. He could not allow the air to be dealt with separately. This would land him in the greatest difficulties with the Little Entente and with Russia, and indeed also with Italy.

MR. EDEN reminded M. Laval that the German Government was asking His Majesty's Government to make progress with the Air Pact, and pointed out that it was essential that people in England should not say that His Majesty's Government could not make progress with the problem of air armaments because of the attitude of the French Government.

M. LAVAL agreed, but said that His Majesty's Government might endeavour to keep British public opinion straight, and urge Germany to make proper efforts with the other subjects outstanding. Subject to this, he was ready for any discussions with Germany, even though they might run counter to all the principles which had guided French diplomacy since the war, as exemplified by the policy of M. Barthou.

MR. EDEN said was he then to understand that they were, for example, to make progress with the Austrian pact at Rome, but not proceed with the negotiation of the air pact?

M. LAVAL said 'no'. There was no time to waste. The air pact should be studied at once between the five Powers concerned, but its realisation must be subject to arrangements on the other questions. He was not asking us to give any new undertaking; it was merely the communiqué of February 3rd he was asking for—or what remained of it. He was prepared to work together with His Majesty's Government now to get an air pact, to collaborate with them for a pact about Austria, to co-operate with Germany for an agreement in Eastern Europe, and to work generally for an agreement on land armaments. But these subjects were all interdependent.

MR. EDEN asked what procedure M. Laval envisaged for land armaments.

M. LÉGER interposed to say that they would have the best chance of getting an agreement on that subject by refusing to make prior agreements on other subjects.

MR. EDEN, summarising, said that he understood that the French Government were ready for His Majesty's Government to negotiate on air questions with all the Powers concerned, provided that the Germans were persuaded to proceed with the other subjects.

In conclusion he hoped the French would come for naval discussions in London before they started any fresh naval construction.

M. LAVAL agreed, and added that there might be expert conversations on naval questions, say, early in August.

MR. EDEN urged July.

Agreement was reached as to the line to be taken by M. Laval and Mr. Eden with the press. No communiqué was issued.

The conversations were then adjourned in order that His Majesty's Government might be consulted on the points that had arisen.[15]

[15] The substance of this Anglo-French conversation is given in The Earl of Avon, *Facing the Dictators*, pp. 230–1.

## No. 364

*Memorandum by the Secretary of State for Foreign Affairs and the Secretary of State for Air on the proposed Air Pact and Air Limitation Agreement*[1]

*C.P.129 (35) [C 4907/55/18]*

*June 21, 1935*

The Cabinet have asked us to circulate for their consideration a joint memorandum on the Air Pact and Air Limitation Agreement.

2. A review of the position made as the result of the Cabinet decision of the 5th June that the 'Air Pact and Air Limitation should be taken up as a separate question and no longer linked up with a general settlement'[2] showed that, while the Italian and German Governments were unlikely to make any objection, the French Government were still withholding their consent to such a procedure.

3. In these circumstances we felt that the first step must be a determined effort on the part of His Majesty's Government to secure the French agreement at least to the immediate opening of *negotiations* between the five Locarno Powers on both the Air Pact and an Air Limitation Agreement, leaving aside for the present the difficult question of the conditions in which such pact and agreement should be ultimately concluded. It was decided for this purpose to take advantage of a visit which Mr. Eden was about to make to Paris in connection with the naval negotiations; and to ask him to try to clear up the point. It was further decided that if the French Government agreed to the opening of negotiations, Mr. Eden should (i) give them a list of some questions on which it seemed to us that the five Powers must, preferably through the diplomatic channel, define their views and, if possible, reach agreement before work could usefully be begun upon a common draft either of the Air Pact or of the Limitation Agreement, and (ii) inform them that we should now seek the formal agreement also of the Belgian, German and Italian Governments to the opening of the negotiations through the diplomatic channel in the first instance, and—provided those Governments agree—ask them, as well as the French Government, for their views on the list of questions.

4. These questions seem to us to be as follows:—

*General.*

(a) Is there to be one instrument embodying Air Pact, Limitation Agree-

[1] This memorandum was considered by the Cabinet on June 26, 1935.
[2] Cf. No. 330, note 1.

ment and prohibition of indiscriminate bombing, or are there to be separate instruments?

*Air Pact.*

(*b*) Which of the proposed signatories are to give guarantees, and which are to receive them?

(*c*) What are the circumstances in which the guarantees will operate?

(*d*) Are the guarantees to apply to territory only or to fleets and mercantile marines on the high seas?

(*e*) Are Powers other than the five Powers in any way to be approached in connection with the Pact?

(*f*) Is the Pact to be supplemented by bilateral agreements?

*Limitation Agreement.*

(*g*) To what category or categories of air power and strength is limitation to apply?

(*h*) Is it accepted that limitation shall be on a basis of parity in each category? And if any of the parties is not to enjoy parity, what is to be the relation of its strength to that of the other parties?

(*i*) What is to be included in the term 'Metropolitan first-line strength'?

(N.B.—It will be observed that the foregoing questions do not include that of supervision, but for this see paragraph 6 below.)

5. The following are our recommendations to the Cabinet as to the view which we consider His Majesty's Government should take on these questions:—

*Question (a).*—There should be two separate instruments embodying respectively the Air Pact and the Agreement on Limitation of Air Strengths. It would not be desirable to embody in the Air Pact, which should be an agreement of a permanent nature, an agreement relating to air strengths, which may at a later date be subject to revision and even reduction, and which may one day fall under the authority of the Permanent Disarmament Commission.

It would be desirable that the two agreements should enter into force simultaneously. We regard both the pact and limitation as very desirable; but of the two, we consider limitation the more important. If the conclusion of an air pact in advance of a limitation agreement precluded or prejudiced the conclusion of a limitation agreement, we think this would be a strong and indeed conclusive reason for deferring the conclusion of the pact. If, however, as we have reason to believe, in the case of France at any rate, the existence of an air pact would facilitate agreement on limitation, there would be no objection to concluding the air pact in advance of the limitation agreement. If, in the course of the negotiations, it were found that the conclusion of an air pact were possible, but that the conclusion of a limitation agreement were either impossible or indefinitely postponed, then we are clearly of opinion that we ought to go for the conclusion of the air pact, in order that we may get one positive objective at any rate in our negotiations.

We do not abandon hope of the conclusion at a later date of a separate instrument to lay down the rules of aerial warfare. But apart from the fact that the record of past attempts to arrive at international agreement in this matter is not encouraging, it is hardly one which could be dealt with by the five Powers independently of other countries. The negotiation of such an instrument will in any case involve long discussions. In these circumstances we recommend that for the time being our efforts in this matter should be confined to the reference[3] made to it in the preamble to the British draft of the Air Pact.

*Question (b)*.—This question can only be finally elucidated by each State indicating the guarantees which it is disposed to give and those which it desires to receive. It is certainly not the intention that every signatory of the Air Pact should guarantee every other signatory against air attack by any other signatory.

As far as the United Kingdom is concerned, we recommend that—

  (i) we should only guarantee France and Belgium against Germany, and Germany against France and Belgium;

 (ii) we should require for ourselves a guarantee from France and Belgium against Germany, and from Germany against France and Belgium;

(iii) we should admit a guarantee of Germany by France and Belgium against us, and a guarantee of France and Belgium by Germany against us;

(iv) we should give no guarantee to Italy, and we should not require a guarantee from her; we should not guarantee any Power against her or agree that she should guarantee any Power against us.

*Question (c)*.—The question of the circumstances in which the guarantees should operate was discussed, in relation to the position as between Germany and Belgium and Germany and France, at the recent secret meeting of the British, Belgian, French and Italian jurists at Geneva.[4] As the result of this discussion it appears that the substantial question which will arise is likely to be whether the guarantees are to operate where there has been an air attack in violation of Article 2 of the Treaty of Locarno (see Annex),[5] or whether, in addition, it should be necessary that this violation should constitute an act of 'unprovoked aggression'.

In view of the fact that the case in contemplation is really an instance of that provided for in Article 4 (3) of Locarno (see Annex)[5] in which the element of unprovoked aggression appears, we recommend that we should endeavour to secure the insertion of the provision respecting 'unprovoked aggression'. If strong resistance is encountered on this point from the French or some other Power, the matter could be reconsidered.

It will be realized that in any event we must retain the right to decide whether the circumstances in which the guarantee is to operate have arisen; the present question is as to how these circumstances are to be defined in the Pact. Once this point has been settled in regard to the position as between

---

[3] *Note in the original*: 'This reads as follows: "Anxious in particular to safeguard the civil populations of their countries against the danger of indiscriminate attacks from the air, which they recognise to be contrary to the Law of Nations." '

[4] Cf. No. 254 and Appendix II at the end of this volume.       [5] Not printed.

Germany and Belgium and Germany and France, a similar solution could be adopted as regards the other guarantees to be given under the Pact.

*Question* (*d*).—In our opinion a deliberate air attack against the ships of any of the parties to the Pact could only be an act of war; and it is for this reason that we recommend that the Air Pact (though confined to Europe) should cover such a case of unprovoked aggression outside as well as inside territorial waters. Otherwise we should be deprived of the assistance of the other parties to the Pact in such an eventuality.

We think the better course to be not to provide for this eventuality in specific terms, but to employ a general expression which would cover the case of a deliberate air attack upon ships (or aircraft) outside territorial waters.

*Question* (*e*).—The Power whom we and, it is understood, also the French have in mind in connection with this question is Holland.

Our information is that Holland would not necessarily be averse from participation if invited; and, though we do not know that the French actually contemplate inviting Holland to be a party to the Pact, we understand that they have given thought to the possibility of asking Holland not to hinder or even in certain circumstances assist (as by allowing flying over their territory) operations undertaken in pursuance of the Air Pact.

The strategic advantages and disadvantages of Dutch participation in the Pact are discussed in the Chiefs of Staff report of the 20th June (C.O.S. 381).[5] In the time at our disposal we have not been able to give adequate consideration to this report; and we would propose to circulate our views on it to the Cabinet at a later date.

*Question* (*f*).—Bilateral agreements might be of three kinds:—

(1) Bilateral military agreements between two of the parties for the application of the Pact, i.e., operational plans, administrative arrangements, &c.; and the French have already communicated skeleton drafts of such an agreement.

We do not consider that the effective value of the Air Pact as a deterrent against aggression is dependent upon the conclusion of bi-lateral agreements for its application, though a bi-lateral agreement between ourselves and France in the matter, for example, of an allocation of aerodromes in Northern France, would be of material assistance to attacks by our bombing squadrons on Germany. As between Belgium and this country, such an agreement might also be useful for the assistance which it would give us of the Belgian warning service. On the other hand, if we conclude a bi-lateral agreement with France only, it would have the appearance of discriminating against Germany, while it is difficult to contemplate that we should concurrently enter into separate bi-lateral agreements, one of co-operation with France against Germany and another of co-operation with Germany against France. The German Government have already taken up position against bi-lateral military agreements.

We recommend that, for the time being, and if further pressed by the French Government on this point, we should maintain that we must first secure at least an agreed draft of the Pact. The question whether any machinery for rendering it effective is necessary or desirable can be considered subsequently.

(2) Bi-lateral agreements in which certain Powers, viz., Italy and the United Kingdom, would, *vis-à-vis* of one another, contract out of the general guarantee given under the Pact. At this stage it is impossible to say whether any agreement on this point supplementary to the general instrument will be required or will be possible.

(3) Bi-lateral agreements under which any two Powers would give to one another pending the entry into force of the general Pact, the guarantees which will be subsequently provided by it. The French Government actually asked us for such a bilateral agreement at the time of the London meeting, and such agreements are provided for in the French draft.

If such a proposal is repeated, we do not think such an agreement possible at the present stage, though the situation might change if the general negotiation became impossible owing either to German or French obstruction. As a matter of fact, the agreement to conclude such an arrangement would diminish the pressure which we can bring to bear on France and Germany in the matter of the general air pact and of air limitation.

*Question (g).*—We recommend that limitation should be applied to the following categories of aircraft:—

(i) Numbers of first line military aircraft (including shore-based naval aircraft) maintained in commission in combatant units for the operation of which pilots are available without measures of mobilisation.

(ii) Numbers of military aircraft additional to those in category (i) which may be held for reserves, training or any other purposes.

Category (i) will include the forces which are maintained in a condition of more or less immediate readiness as regards equipment and personnel, for active operations, and would therefore provide the best practical index of the initial striking capacity of an air force. It covers broadly the same meaning as the term 'rifle strength' as applied to standing armies. This category would cover only military aircraft in combatant units, and would not include military aircraft held in units maintained exclusively for training or other non-combatant purposes. It is, however, necessary that these aircraft (as also the numbers of military aircraft held as reserves) should also be limited, as otherwise training establishments might be so organised as to render nugatory the limitation imposed.

Category (ii) therefore includes the numbers of military aircraft which may be held for reserves, training or any other purpose. The maximum number permissible under category (ii) would probably have to be negotiated on the basis of a uniform ratio to numbers allowed under category (i).

We also recommend a limitation on the number of *military pilots*. The record of Geneva discussions shows the extreme complexity of any proposal for the limitation of effectives; but the absence of any provision for that purpose would be widely criticised and might work definitely to the advantage of Germany as compared with France or Great Britain by reason of the amenability of the German people to militarization.

*Questions (h) and (i)*—

We recommend that the air forces of Great Britain, France, Germany and Italy should be on a basis of metropolitan parity in each of the categories of limitation, and that the Belgian Government should be asked to formulate its own proposals for a percentage of strength to that of the four Great Powers. The principle of parity as between those Powers was the basis of the British Draft Convention in 1933[6] and affords the best starting point for negotiations. Metropolitan parity as a basis of limitation would be in general accord with recent Ministerial declarations of policy. If confined to the above-mentioned categories it would not in itself provide true equality of air strength; but the essence of an agreement which has any hope of acceptance is simplicity, and for that reason it is necessary to disregard, for the present purpose, such factors as relative vulnerability, manufacturing capacity, potentialities for rapid expansion, &c., and to take our own measures to see that we are not outstripped by other Powers in such matters.

On this basis of limitation the aircraft in overseas squadrons would not be included in the parity figure, and we recommend that aircraft provided for operation from aircraft carriers and other ships of war should also be excluded from the agreement. The five Powers, however, should be asked mutually to agree that aircraft held for this latter purpose should be limited in proportion to the number of ships of war respectively maintained by them and fitted for the operation of aircraft.

On these assumptions the limitation would cover for Great Britain all first line aircraft in the United Kingdom, and for Germany all first line aircraft in that country. As regards France, it is to be remembered that Herr Hitler in the Berlin conversations declared that he would accept nothing short of parity with French metropolitan air forces, including those stationed in North Africa. His point of view was not altogether unreasonable in view of the fact that squadrons held in North Africa can be moved by air at short notice to French metropolitan territory. On the other hand, it is obvious that the French would object strongly to including their North African air forces on the same basis as those stationed in France itself, and there is indeed no evidence that France is yet prepared to accept parity of metropolitan air forces as between Germany and herself even if those in North Africa were excluded. On this point it will be essential to obtain the French views.

Until those views are obtained it is hardly practical to discuss any actual figures for the basis of limitation. The present actual first line strength of French air forces at home and in North Africa as estimated by the Air Ministry could not be put higher than 1,500 aircraft, but until some discussions with the French have taken place, it is hardly possible again to take this aspect of the matter any further. It will be remembered that information has been received that Germany intends to build to a first line strength of 2,000 aircraft, which is apparently her estimate of the present French strength.[7]

[6] See Cmd. 4279 of 1933. Cf. Volume IV, Appendix IV.
[7] Cf. No. 234.

6. There remains the question of *supervision*. The methods hitherto evolved have all postulated the existence of a central international supervisory organ. The British Draft Convention of March 1933 proposed to entrust the task of supervision of the execution of the convention to the Permanent Disarmament Commission, giving it the power to conduct local investigations in certain circumstances. In December 1933 a Committee of the Disarmament Conference elaborated this proposal, largely at the instigation of the French Government, into a system of permanent and automatic supervision with periodical local inspections to be conducted by regional committees of the Permanent Disarmament Commission. His Majesty's Government are not committed to acceptance of this particular system, but they are committed by their memorandum of the 29 January, 1934,[8] 'if general agreement is reached on all other (disarmament) issues to agree to the application of a system of permanent and automatic supervision to come into force with the obligations of the Convention.'

The draft proposals put forward by the United States Government in November 1934 for the control of Arms Manufacture and Trade provided for permanent and automatic supervision with a restricted and fairly anodyne system of local inspections.[9] His Majesty's Government have decided not to accept such a system of supervision in connection with a restricted convention of this kind and have put forward a simpler system of documentary supervision at Geneva. They have, however, reiterated their willingness to accept permanent and automatic supervision with local inspections as part of a general limitation convention.

It may be confidently expected that the French will make their concurrence in an Air Limitation agreement conditional upon the inclusion of provisions for permanent and automatic supervision with local inspections. Moreover, the German Chancellor, during the Berlin conversations with Sir John Simon and Mr. Eden, said that he was ready to accept the principle of permanent and automatic supervision in connection with an arms limitation agreement.[10]

But the present aim is a limitation agreement confined to air armaments and to five Powers, and we recommend that an attempt should be made to come to some arrangement whereby a modified form of supervision should be exercised in connection with an Air Limitation Agreement pending the constitution of an international supervisory organ which would eventually assume the task of watching over the execution of the agreement. This modified form of supervision might be as follows:—

(i) The observance of the measures of air limitation now proposed should be vouched for by full and regular exchange of information between the five Powers in regard to the distribution, organisation and establishments (both in material and in personnel) of their respective air

[8] See Cmd. 4498 of 1934; cf. Volume VI, Nos. 206 and 232.
[9] See *Conference for the Reduction and Limitation of Armaments, Conference Documents*, Volume iii, No. 167; cf. *F.R.U.S. 1934*, vol. i, pp. 187, 191–204.
[10] See Volume XII, No. 651, p. 737.

forces. It may be observed that we have already published extensive information on these subjects and it should not be difficult to arrive at a uniform basis for exchange of information between the five Powers.

(ii) Each of the five Powers should undertake to afford full facilities for investigations by the Air Attachés (or other officers) of the other parties to the Pact in order to satisfy themselves on the above points.

*Summary.*

7. While reserving the necessary latitude for our negotiators, the general procedure which we recommend that the Cabinet should approve is as follows:—

(1) Provided the French Government agree to the opening of negotiations between the five Locarno Powers on both the Air Pact and an Air Limitation Agreement, we should at once seek the formal agreement also of the Belgian, German and Italian Governments to the opening of negotiations and ask them as well as the French Government for their views on the list of questions contained in paragraph 4 above.

(2) The view of His Majesty's Government on these questions should be as follows:—

(a) The Air Pact and the Agreement on Limitation of Air Strengths should be embodied in separate agreements which should if possible enter into force simultaneously; and any attempt to go beyond the reference in the preamble to the British draft of the Air Pact to indiscriminate bombing should be reserved to a later date.

(b) Belgium, France and Germany should be the only countries which should give us, receive from us and give against us guarantees under the Air Pact.

(c) We should endeavour to secure that the guarantees under the Air Pact will operate where there has been an air attack in violation of Article 2 of the Treaty of Locarno, provided that this violation constitutes 'unprovoked aggression'; if this proves impossible the matter could be reconsidered, though we could not cede the right ourselves to decide whether the circumstances in which the guarantee operates have arisen.

(d) The Air Pact should cover unprovoked aggression outside as well as inside territorial waters.

(e) The question of the possible inclusion of other Powers (notably Holland) in the Pact is reserved for further consideration.

(f) If we are urged to supplement the Pact by bi-lateral agreements of a technical nature, we must maintain that we must first secure at least an agreed draft of the Pact; the necessity for machinery for rendering it effective can be considered subsequently; we should refuse to agree to conclude with any Power a bi-lateral agreement to bring into force, pending the conclusion of the general Pact, the guarantees to be provided by it.

(g) Limitation of aircraft should primarily be applied to numbers of aircraft in commission in combatant units, with a correlative limitation (i) on numbers of military aircraft in reserve or held for training or other purposes, and (ii) on numbers of military pilots.

(h) and (i) The area in which limitation would operate should be the metropolitan territories of the United Kingdom, Belgium, France, Germany and Italy, it being for further consideration whether the North African territories of France and Italy should be regarded as part of the metropolitan territories of these countries; aircraft provided for operation from ships of war should be separately limited by regard to the size of the fleets of the Contracting Powers.

(3) Pending the constitution of an international supervisory organ, we should attempt to secure the agreement of the five Powers to a modified form of supervision comprising full and regular exchange of information in regard to the distribution, organisation and establishments of the respective air forces, and an undertaking to afford full facilities for investigations by the Air Attachés of the parties to the Pact to satisfy themselves on these points.

S. H[OARE]

P. C[UNLIFFE]-L[ISTER]

## No. 365

### Sir S. Hoare to Sir G. Clerk (Paris)
No. 156 Telegraphic [C 4901/55/18]

*Most Immediate*　　　　　　　　FOREIGN OFFICE, *June 22, 1935, 11.35 a.m.*

Following for Mr. Eden,

I have received your telegrams Nos. 128 and 129.[1]

I am very glad to know that the French Government are prepared to initiate a negotiation on Air Pact and air limitation on certain conditions flowing from the London Communiqué of February 3rd.

The reason why I cannot give you definite reply today is that the Prime Minister (and incidentally also Sir R. Vansittart) are away in the country.

[1] No. 362.

## No. 366

### Sir S. Hoare to Sir G. Clerk (Paris)
No. 157 Telegraphic: by telephone [C 4908/55/18]

FOREIGN OFFICE, *June 22, 1935, 12 noon*

*Most Immediate*　　*Personal and Private*

[Following for Mr. Eden.]

For your own information.

You know position with Cabinet and you also know you can rely on me to attempt to persuade Cabinet to meet French susceptibilities in every possible way.

I am assuming that both French conditions are conditions on which French will negotiate and not conditions which they are asking us ourselves finally to accept now.

So far as procedure here is concerned I would prefer to deal with question at regular Wednesday Cabinet[1] rather than seem to rush matters before we know Mussolini's views.[2] From my point of view therefore it would be helpful if you found means of postponing your arrival in Paris on your journey home[3] until after Wednesday's Cabinet. I must however be guided by your advice in matters of this kind.

[1] i.e. on June 26.
[2] This presumably referred to Signor Mussolini's views concerning the Anglo-German naval agreement and the proposed air pact. Mr. Eden however had also been instructed to put to Signor Mussolini a plan for a settlement of the Ethiopian question including the cession to Ethiopia of the port of Zeila. Documents relating to these Ethiopian discussions will be printed in Volume XIV. [3] Cf. No. 357, note 1.

## No. 367

*Sir E. Phipps (Berlin) to Sir S. Hoare (Received June 22, 4.10 p.m.)*
*No. 235 Telegraphic [C 4911/55/18]*

BERLIN, *June 22, 1935, 2.27 p.m.*

Rome telegram No. 52 Saving.[1]

I learn informally that German government do not contemplate communication of their proposals for air pact to the French and Italian governments. They consider that, as His Majesty's Government are in possession of the views of the other governments concerned, the next step lies with them.

While the German government attach importance to conclusion of pact, they do not wish to press matters, realising that to do so might be embarrassing and thus more of a hindrance than a help to the object in view.

[1] No. 332.

## No. 368

*Sir G. Clerk (Paris) to Sir S. Hoare (Received June 22, 7.40 p.m.)*
*No. 130 Telegraphic: by telephone [C 4912/55/18]*

*Immediate*                                            PARIS, *June 22, 1935*

Following from Mr. Eden.

I had an hour's conversation alone with M. Laval this morning previous to a luncheon which he gave in honour of His Majesty's Minister before his departure for Belgrade.[1] M. Laval began by expressing his most sincere gratitude for personal letter[2] which he had received from you and which had clearly greatly pleased him. I told M. Laval that I had communicated to His

[1] Mr. R. H. Campbell had been appointed H.M. Minister at Belgrade as from August 10, 1935.
[2] Not traced in Foreign Office archives.

Majesty's Government[3] my appreciation of the previous day's conversations in the following terms:—

The French government were willing to proceed with negotiation of an air pact and limitation on two conditions

(1) That the pact was buttressed by a bilateral arrangement which might be between several Powers but must be between France and Great Britain;

(2) That the pact should not become operative until agreement had also been reached upon other subjects mentioned in communiqué of February 3rd. M. Laval replied that this was a true statement of the position of the French government and I informed him that I hoped to be in a position to talk over with him the reply of His Majesty's Government on my way back from Rome.

In the meanwhile there were one or two personal observations on the situation which I wished to make. His Majesty's Government attached importance, as did the French Government, to all matters in the communiqué of February 3rd. My own anxiety was lest after weeks of negotiation we should find ourselves unable to make progress on one of these items, for example the Danubian pact, in respect of which the situation was clearly complex. If at the end of that period the coming into operation of the air pact was to be held up for what might appear an indefinite period our public opinion would certainly become restive. Moreover if it was true, and I thought it was, that the German government attach value to the negotiation of an air pact was there not a danger that with the rapid increase of the German air force this might prove a waning asset. It was for these and other reasons that we attached the utmost importance to making rapid progress with the air pact and limitation. M. Laval said that he quite understood our position but that it was not necessary now to visualise the position which might arise if progress upon one item of the London communiqué were unduly delayed. What was essential was that Germany should make some positive contribution in Europe. If negotiation of the Eastern pact of non aggression (he himself had now yielded on mutual assistance which had been included in London communiqué) could be rapidly advanced this would much facilitate his task. He hoped that His Majesty's Government would give him all the support they could with the German government to this end.

The conversation this morning was definitely less difficult than that of yesterday and at its close M. Laval and I agreed to the terms in which he should report to the press the results of the last two days.[4]

I admit that delay in sending the French experts for the Naval conversations is disappointing and I will take up this subject again with M. Laval on my return. In the meanwhile it would I am sure be wiser not to press the French government on this subject through their Embassy in London.

French insistence on bilateral pacts as a supplement to the air pact is due to their conviction that only thus can pact itself be made fully operative and only thus therefore can they obtain a quid pro quo for the new commitment which they are undertaking towards us.

[3] See No. 362.
[4] See *The Times*, June 24, p. 14.

## No. 369

*Memorandum communicated to the French Embassy, June 22, 1935*[1]

[*A 5573/22/45*]

FOREIGN OFFICE, *June 22, 1935*

The memorandum communicated to the Foreign Office on the 18th instant, giving the preliminary views of the French Government on the recently concluded naval agreement with Germany,[2] has received the careful consideration of His Majesty's Government in the United Kingdom. It is their hope to enter upon conversations with representatives of the French Government at an early date, at which this and other matters relating to the complex question of the limitation of naval armaments can be more suitably discussed than through the exchange of written communications. They will be happy during the proposed discussions to give to the French Government a full and detailed explanation of the reasons for their acceptance of the Reich Chancellor's proposal and of the implications of the agreement thus reached, and in the meantime they would propose to offer only a few general observations on the French Government's memorandum.

2. For the reasons given below, His Majesty's Government in the United Kingdom do not consider that the conclusion of this agreement can be regarded as contrary to the principle of co-operation embodied in the London Communiqué of February 3rd and the Stresa Resolution, to which they remain firmly attached. There has been no question of conferring upon Germany an authority to do something she would not otherwise have done. On the contrary, the purpose of this step has been to circumscribe, by agreement with Germany, the ultimate consequences of a unilateral decision to which Germany had already begun to give effect. It was essentially a case in which prompt action was required and His Majesty's Government are convinced that in the long run the action they have taken will be found to constitute a real contribution to European, and especially French, security.

3. His Majesty's Government have never agreed that the progress of the naval discussions necessitated by the impending expiration of the London and Washington Treaties should be held up, or a possibly favourable outcome deliberately deferred, pending the conclusion of international agreements in regard to land and air armaments. It is their desire to press on with all three branches of this necessarily interconnected subject and, should agreement be reached between all the interested Powers as regards naval armaments, they would regard this as an encouragement to redouble their efforts to assist in bringing about general agreement as regards land and air armaments. But they would consider it an error to make progress in the one branch necessarily dependent on simultaneous progress in the other two. The fact that the limitation of naval armaments has during the last thirteen years been governed by international treaties, to the great benefit of the maritime nations

[1] A note on the file records that this memorandum 'was handed to M. Cambon on the 22nd June and a copy sent to Paris by air mail on the same day'.

[2] See No. 352.

467

concerned, is, in the view of His Majesty's Government, an added reason why the negotiations on this subject should continue in the future, as they have been in the past, to be carried on between the principal naval Powers as occasion arises.

4. The effects of this agreement, to which the French memorandum refers, appear in almost every case to flow not from the agreement itself, under which Germany voluntarily undertakes to fix a definite limitation to the future size of her fleet, but from Germany's decision, to effect forthwith a considerable expansion in the strength of the German fleet. It is desirable to distinguish carefully between these two elements in the situation, and it is difficult to see in what way France's naval position would have been better if the expansion of the German fleet had been left without limitation than it will be under a limitation conferring upon France a permanent and substantial margin of strength over the level of strength voluntarily accepted by Germany.

5. The French memorandum rightly draws attention to the importance of the question of the rate at which Germany will seek to reach the new level of 35 per cent. of the fleets of the members of the British Commonwealth of Nations. His Majesty's Government agree as to the importance of this point, and it is one of those on which His Majesty's Government feel that conversations with representatives of the French Government would be desirable at an early date.

6. As regards the question put in paragraph 3 of the French note, the French Government will observe from sub-paragraph 2 (c) of the exchange of notes,[3] the text of which has since been communicated to them, that the agreement on a ratio of 35 per cent. remains unaffected by the naval construction of the U.S.S.R. as by the naval construction of other third Powers, on the assumption, of course, that the U.S.S.R. do not contemplate construction of so abnormal and exceptional a character as to necessitate an appeal by Germany in virtue of the concluding sentence in that sub-paragraph.

7. His Majesty's Government trust that the above preliminary observations will serve to allay some of the misgivings with which the French Government appear to have learnt of the conclusion of this agreement. His Majesty's Government remain firmly attached to the policy of close and friendly collaboration with France and Italy along the lines laid down in the Stresa Resolution, and they believe that the step they have now taken will, in the long run, be found to facilitate such collaboration in the future.

[3] See No. 348.

## No. 370

*Record by Mr. Butler[1] of Mr. Baldwin's conversation with
Herr von Ribbentrop on June 20[2]*

[*C 4953/55/18*]

Secret                                                                    *June 22, 1935*

The Prime Minister saw Herr von Ribbentrop for rather over half an hour on Thursday[3] morning, and later in the day I asked Mr. Baldwin whether any points of interest had been discussed. The Prime Minister said that he had already given the Foreign Secretary an account of what had passed. He had told Herr von Ribbentrop that he was very pleased with the Naval Agreement which he hoped would become part of a general one. He was now concerned that the air, in which he had always been interested, should be dealt with, and he wanted the Air Pact with limitation of air armaments proceeded with as speedily as possible. Mr. Baldwin had never believed that the air arm could win a war, but it was particularly dangerous in that it could be used at almost a moment's notice.

Mr. Baldwin then spoke to Herr von Ribbentrop of some of the principles of British foreign policy, and the effect of aircraft upon them.

In the old days when we concerned ourselves mainly with the sea, we regarded the countries immediately confronting us across the Channel as of vital interest. Therefore when the integrity of Belgium was broken in 1914 we had inevitably been brought to war. A similar contingency in the future must inevitably have a similar result.

Aircraft had in fact increased our anxiety about the countries across the Channel; we were now bound to consider countries within striking distance of us by air, and for obvious geographical reasons and mutual interest we and France were bound to keep on close and friendly terms. The above had been the meaning of his reference to the Rhine being now our frontier.[4]

These were some general views of British policy which Mr. Baldwin wanted to make clear to Herr von Ribbentrop; for anything more detailed he would refer him and the German Government to the Foreign Secretary. No mention was made of the League of Nations nor of the problems of Eastern Europe.

N. M. B.

[1] Mr. N. M. Butler, a First Secretary in the Foreign Office, was Second Private Secretary to the Prime Minister.

[2] Two copies of this record were sent to the Foreign Office on June 22. In his covering note Mr. Butler said it was 'a record of what the Prime Minister told me about his talk with Ribbentrop. Mr. Baldwin has read it and approved it'. A copy was sent to Sir E. Phipps on June 22.

[3] June 20.

[4] See 292 *H.C. Deb.* 5 *s.*, col. 2339 (July 30, 1934).

## No. 371

*Sir G. Clerk (Paris) to Sir S. Hoare (Received June 24)*
*No. 135 Saving: Telegraphic [C 4924/55/18]*

PARIS, *June 23, 1935*

The French press today is noticeably calmer on the subject of the Anglo-German naval agreement. Mr. Eden's visit has brought about what one paper describes as a very definite psychological détente. Whilst there are still mutterings over the manner in which the agreement was signed and much ink is still spilt over the alleged breach of the declarations of London and Stresa the tendency now is to concentrate on the necessity of avoiding further unilateral action in future. The papers express no criticism of the technical aspects of the agreement.

The view of the French Government that the conclusion of an Air Pact by the Locarno Powers must be dependent on a general settlement including the Eastern and Central Pacts and agreement regarding land armaments is strongly upheld. On the whole, however, there is considerable restraint as to the subject matter of the conversations and judgment is evidently being suspended pending their resumption next Thursday.[1]

[1] June 27.

## No. 372

*Sir E. Phipps (Berlin) to Sir S. Hoare (Received June 25, 4.30 p.m.)*
*No. 160 Saving: Telegraphic [C 4955/55/18]*

BERLIN, *June 24, 1935*

The French Ambassador has returned here from a month's leave, during which he had several long conversations with M. Laval, with whom he is on very friendly terms.

M. François-Poncet tells me that M. Laval is still determined to pursue his efforts throughout the summer towards reaching a better understanding with Germany, but within a system of collective security. M. Laval would not be allowed by French public or parliamentary opinion to conclude any kind of separate arrangement with Herr Hitler, nor, indeed, would M. Laval himself dream of attempting this. He feels, however, that he must make the most of the French parliamentary recess to push on his negotiations as far as possible before the Chamber of Deputies meets again about the middle of October, when anything may happen.

M. Laval, it seems, has some hope that Germany will eventually consent to join the East[ern] Pact on the lines suggested in the question put to her from Stresa. He feels, however, that it is essential to show all possible consideration for Soviet susceptibilities in replying to the German memorandum on the relations between the Franco-Soviet pact and the Treaty of Locarno.

Incidentally, M. François-Poncet tells me in confidence that he does not believe that it will be possible to avoid a devaluation of the franc, although M. Laval intends to do his utmost to reach his goal by deflationary methods in the first instance.

## No. 373

*Sir E. Phipps (Berlin) to Sir S. Hoare (Received June 25)*
*No. 161 Saving: Telegraphic [C 4956/55/18]*

BERLIN, *June 24, 1935*

I called today upon the Minister for Foreign Affairs and upon Herr von Bülow to take leave of them before proceeding tonight to England.[1] From my conversations with them I gathered as follows—

(1) Eastern Pact.

Baron von Neurath told me that the German Government could not answer the French note of 3rd June[2] before receiving the replies of the Locarno Powers to the German memorandum regarding the effects of the Franco-Soviet Pact on the Treaty of Locarno.[3] His Excellency remarked that it was impossible to exaggerate the importance of those replies. Any indication that the full force of Locarno had been in the slightest degree impaired by that Pact would not only prevent Germany from contemplating a possible adherence to an Eastern Pact of Non-Aggression, but would oblige her to reconsider her own position in regard to Locarno. I enquired whether, if those replies were satisfactory, Baron von Neurath could hold out good hopes for the Eastern Pact, and he replied in the affirmative. He indicated, however, that it would be necessary for Lithuania to mend her ways, and not to allow herself to be egged on, as at present, against Germany by Russia. He objects strongly to the numerous Memelland naturalisations of Lithuanian citizens, carried out lately with a view to the elections in September. He also urges that Czechoslovakia should not proceed any further with her flirtation with Russia, whereby Germany risks encirclement. His Excellency said that he had had a talk recently with the Estonian Minister for Foreign Affairs, who had expressed the readiness of Estonia to enter into a multilateral non-aggression pact, provided Germany and Poland were parties, in view of the protection it would afford her against *Russian* aggression.

Baron von Neurath admitted that the Chancellor's speech[4] had not made very pleasant reading for the Russians, but it had merely indicated the difference in 'Weltanschauung' that existed between Germany and Russia, it did not in any way imply the intention of the former to attack the latter, and it should not be taken too tragically.

Herr von Bülow, always more outspoken than his master, told me when I saw him later on, that he would keep the French note of June 3rd in his

[1] Sir E. Phipps was on leave of absence, June 24–September 11. During this period Mr. Newton, Minister at Berlin (since March 1, 1935) was in charge of H.M. Embassy.
[2] See No. 288, note 3.          [3] See No. 263, note 2.
[4] Of May 21.

drawer until the replies of the Locarno Powers were received. If those replies were satisfactory it might be possible to begin considering the numerous technical difficulties in the way of an Eastern Pact, and how it could be brought into harmony with the already existing, vast net-work of pacts converging on Moscow, Berlin and Warsaw, respectively.

(2) Air Pact.

Baron von Neurath said that the German Government did not contemplate giving their draft[5] to the other Locarno Powers, with whom they had had no detailed conversations on this subject. The German Representatives in the capitals concerned, however, possessed copies of the German draft, and could answer any questions that might be put to them.

Herr von Bülow explained that the Germans were not particularly enamoured of their own draft, which had been drawn up when it had been suggested that the Air Pact, the limitation of air-forces, and the prohibition of bombing behind the lines should all be in separate instruments. The idea now seemed to be to include them in one only. The German Government had no particular preference, except that they would deprecate holding up the Air Pact itself if the technical difficulties of the other questions should prove to necessitate really inordinate delay.

(3) Danube Pact.

Baron von Neurath similarly remarked that this was a sleeping dog that he preferred to let lie. Both he and Herr von Bülow think that Signor Mussolini himself feels that the difficulties in connection with this pact are at present practically insuperable and that it is postponed 'sine die'.

(4) Limitation of Armaments and effectives on land.

Baron von Neurath repeated the oft-stated readiness of the German Government to abstain from mounting to the 'plafond' announced on March 16th,[6] viz 36 divisions of 550,000 men, provided the other Powers make corresponding reductions in the effectives they had on that date. Again, however, he expressed scepticism as to the possibility of reaching such an agreement and against [*sic*] he remarked that it would be preferable, anyhow as a first step, to aim at a qualitative limitation by abandoning the heaviest tanks, guns, etc.

(5) Return of Germany to the League.

As neither Baron von Neurath nor Herr von Bülow referred to this, I felt that in my turn I had better let this particular dog lie. In any case he sleeps at the end of a long and muddy lane, and when he wakes will presumably open his mouth very wide indeed for Colonies and other dainty morsels. Until we see clearly what Italy's intentions are in regard to Geneva it would seem better to avoid this subject.

Baron von Neurath and Herr von Bülow admitted satisfaction at the conclusion of the Anglo-German Naval Agreement. This would, however, presumably have been greater and more spontaneous had not Herr von Ribbentrop been the fortunate signatory on the German side chosen by Providence and the Führer.

[5] See No. 263, Annex.  [6] See Volume XII, No. 570.

## No. 374

*Memorandum by Sir S. Hoare on the proposed Air Pact and Air Limitation Agreement*

### C.P. *132* (*35*) [*C 5046/55/18*]

FOREIGN OFFICE, *June 24, 1935*

MR. EDEN has asked the French Government whether they would agree to enter into negotiations with the other Locarno Powers in respect of the proposed Air Pact and Air Limitation Agreement.

The two telegrams from Paris now attached[1] show the result of this enquiry. The telegram which I sent him in reply to the first of these telegrams is also attached.[2]

Considering how unfavourable was the moment when the enquiry had to be put, the answer must be considered as satisfactory. The two conditions which the French Government have attached to their consent to negotiate were almost inevitable.

I would suggest, therefore, that Mr. Eden should be authorised to take note of the fact that the French Government have made these conditions, and then proceed to discuss with them the procedure to be adopted for initiating negotiations for the Air Pact and Air Limitation. As to methods of practical procedure in regard to the other elements in the London declaration, His Majesty's Government propose to keep an open mind until the situation has further developed and the prospects of general agreement can be more clearly estimated than at present.

Also it is important that the French Government should agree not to lay down these two conditions at the outset to the German Government, for to do so would probably render the initiation of all negotiations impossible. Since, however, it is to be foreseen that the French Government will be unable to maintain this attitude *vis-à-vis* of their press and public, it would be sufficient if the French Government were to confine themselves to intimating that they expect progress on other subjects to be simultaneous.

As regards procedure, I feel that the time is not ripe for any meeting either of statesmen or of technicians. The various questions set forth in C.P. 129 (35)[3] ought, in my opinion, first of all to be discussed and settled in principle through the diplomatic channel. But this raises the further question, by whom these discussions are to be initiated and directed. Should Great Britain, France and Italy make a joint approach to the German Government and invite their views on the various questions at issue; or should His Majesty's Government offer to circularise all the Locarno Powers and to act as the clearing house for the exchanges of views which it is hoped thus to provoke? There is a great deal to be said for this latter course, and I would recommend that Mr. Eden should be authorised to press for it.

Lastly, there is the question as to what line Mr. Eden should take when the French Government enquire, as they doubtless will, what His Majesty's

---

[1] i.e. Nos. 362 and 368.    [2] i.e. No. 365.    [3] No. 364.

Government propose to do in order to help forward concurrent negotiations on the other three problems which the French Government wish to see settled, i.e., multilateral non-aggression pact in the East, Danubian pact and limitation of land armaments. In regard to the Eastern Pact, the reply is simple. We have only to refer to the interviews which I and Sir R. Vansittart had with Herr von Ribbentrop (Annex 4)[4] and to say that we shall, of course, pursue this pressure. In return, M. Laval should be told that we count on him to see that there will be no obstruction or delay from the Russian or Polish side in any negotiations there may be for the proposed multilateral pact. (The Soviet Government must not be allowed to think that it is in their power to prevent an Air Agreement between the Western Powers merely by blocking progress in the non-aggression negotiations in the East.)

In regard to the Danubian Pact, we should say that here also we shall continue to help to our utmost; but that success in this matter must turn largely on the attitude of the Little Entente. As the French Ambassador has been already informed, the conditions so far imposed by the Little Entente on the meeting of the Rome Conference are so unreasonable as effectively to prevent either the meeting or the fruition of the Conference.

As regards limitation of land armaments, it rests with France herself whether there is to be any possible basis on which to negotiate with Germany.

To sum up the future course of His Majesty's Government.

In regard to the Eastern Pact, there is no longer any valid reason why a scheme reduced to such relative simplicity should not now be speedily furthered and completed on the terms originally proposed by Germany, which the French Government have now accepted as a basis of discussion. Indeed, the technical difficulties in this matter are considerably less than in the case of the Air Pact. Adherence to the London communiqué will therefore entail no sacrifice on the part of His Majesty's Government. Indeed, it has always been fairly clear, and is now completely clear, that no air pacts will be otherwise obtainable.

In regard to the Danubian Pact, we must be guided by developments. Progress here will be slower than in the case of the Eastern Pact. If the project matures abreast of the Air Pact, our course will be easy. If it does not, we must so conduct ourselves that the last word lies with Signor Mussolini, not with the French; for Signor Mussolini has already shown a strong practical disposition to conclude an air pact aside from other considerations. In any case, therefore, so far as we are concerned, if we wish for practical progress in the Air Pacts, we must at present not allow the French to suppose that we are in any way aiming at a divorce between these two subjects.

As to the limitation of land armaments, it is highly probable that the psychological moment has been missed, and that the settlement, which has evaded us for three and a half years, will continue to prove unattainable. Our eventual tactics, in such an event, would be to put to the French Government that we should all be foolish to allow the three other pacts, then either ready or nearly ready, to fail for lack of the fourth. In this attitude we should have

---

[4] The reference was to Sir R. Vansittart's memorandum of June 19, printed as No. 356.

the support of Italy and Belgium, and probably of a considerable number of other countries. It is necessary in this respect to look ahead; but here also, for the present, it would be a costly mistake in tactics to adopt any attitude which might be construed as a definite departure from the London declaration.

S.H.

## No. 375

*Memorandum on the Report by the Chiefs of Staff's Sub-Committee on the possible inclusion of Holland in the Air Pact*[1]

*[C 4906/55/18]*

FOREIGN OFFICE, *June 24, 1935*

The real conclusion of the report of the Chiefs of Staff[2] is that what we should aim at is the effective neutrality of Holland.

2. Dutch participation in the Air Pact, as the Chiefs of Staff point out, would finally dispose of this possibility; and for the reasons given by the Chiefs of Staff it does not seem possible to argue that the strategic advantages of Dutch participation in the Pact are such as to outweigh this disadvantage.

3. In these circumstances it remains to consider how best the effective neutrality of Holland may be maintained.

4. The Chiefs of Staff put forward for consideration the possibility of inviting Germany to agree that the neutrality of Holland should be mutually guaranteed by the Powers signatories of the Air Pact.

5. The objections to the adoption of this suggestion seem to be overwhelming. First, it seems most improbable that Holland would listen to a suggestion of this kind which would run counter to the assertion of her national independence of which she has always been so jealous. Secondly, the suggestion would not seem feasible in view of the reaction upon it of the insistence of the Dutch possessions in the Far East. Thirdly, its adoption would be in complete conflict with Holland's membership of the League of Nations. Lastly, it would be open to all, and indeed more than all, the objections to Dutch participation in the Air Pact for it would imply a new and serious paper commitment for the United Kingdom without giving us any title to bring pressure upon Holland to keep her defences up to date.

6. There seem to be two other possible ways of increasing the chances of the maintenance of Dutch neutrality. The first would be by taking up again the offer of Herr Hitler made in 1933, and on various occasions since, to conclude with Germany's neighbours bilateral pacts of non-aggression. The

---

[1] In a minute of July 10 addressed to Sir S. Hoare, Sir R. Vansittart wrote: 'I submit this Departmental memorandum to you, but, as you know, I do not agree with its conclusion because I do not agree with the premise that it would be possible to preserve Dutch neutrality in the event of another European war. The Chiefs of Staff consider that Dutch neutrality is of less interest to Germany than formerly, and in my view the violation by Germany of that neutrality by air, and even by land, seeing the importance of turning the new French and Belgian fortifications, is a practical certainty. If this be admitted, the Chiefs of Staff would have to give us a more explicit opinion than they have in the present paper.'

[2] Cf. No. 364, paragraph 5, question (*e*).

German Government could be asked whether they were still ready to conclude a bilateral non-aggression treaty with Holland. This would re-inforce the general guarantee given by Germany under the Kellogg Pact; and a special reason for it would exist in the approaching final withdrawal of Germany from the League of Nations. The question would, of course, remain whether or not Holland would be willing to accept such a bilateral non-aggression treaty. In any case it would be useless to expect her to take the initiative in the matter.

7. The other possible method of re-inforcing the likelihood of Dutch neutrality would be by a unilateral declaration on our part (of a kind that was considered in the Foreign Office at the beginning of this year) that we regarded the integrity and independence of Holland as vital to our own security. Such a declaration might be thought to be the logical development of Mr. Baldwin's declaration of the summer of 1934 that our frontier lies on the Rhine. It is possible there might even be a combination of the two methods during the negotiations for the Air Pact.

8. It will be remembered that in the paper C.P. 6 (35)[3] submitted to the Cabinet on January 9th by Sir John Simon regarding the material for the impending discussions with the French Ministers, one of the proposals submitted to the Cabinet was a declaration by His Majesty's Government to the effect that Great Britain should consider any attempt to interfere with the independence or integrity of Belgium, and possibly of Holland, as dangerous to her peace and security. The Cabinet, at their meeting on January 14th, considered this proposal and decided that the British negotiators should be authorised, if they found it necessary or desirable, to make a declaration to the effect that Great Britain would consider any attempt to interfere with the independence or integrity of Belgium as dangerous to her peace and security. The question of including Holland was not to be raised by British Ministers in the conversations[4] in question.

As a matter of fact the question of His Majesty's Government making such a declaration was not raised in the conversations, and the subject has remained dormant since. In the light of the present developments it would seem desirable that it should be reconsidered, not merely in the form of a declaration applying to Belgium solely, but to Belgium and Holland, i.e. the Low Countries as a whole. The reason why the Cabinet on January 14th decided that the proposed declaration should not apply to Holland was that they feared that Holland, a country with a very independent attitude, might resent or repudiate any such declaration. Since then, however, the interest displayed by the Dutch Government in the proposed Air Pact[5] shows that they are beginning to fear the German danger, and it is probable therefore that they will not resent, as they might have done at an earlier date, any measures taken by His Majesty's Government for their security.

9. *In conclusion* it is recommended (*a*) that in view of the nature of the

---

[3] Cf. Volume XII, No. 359, note 2, and No. 366.

[4] i.e. the Anglo-French conversations in London, February 1–3.

[5] See, e.g., Volume XII, Nos. 418, 459, and 544.

report of the Chiefs of Staff question (e)[6] 'are Powers other than the five Powers in any way to be approached in connection with the Air Pact?' should now be erased from the list of questions which we propose to put to the other parties to the negotiations for the Air Pact; and that Mr. Eden should be so informed before his return to Paris; (b) that the possibility of the re-inforcement of Dutch neutrality by means of the conclusion of a bilateral pact of non-aggression between Holland and Germany in connexion, possibly, with a unilateral declaration by His Majesty's Government of the vital importance to the United Kingdom of Dutch and Belgian integrity and independence, should be kept open for consideration during the Air Pact negotiations.

[6] Cf. note 2 above.

## No. 376

*Sir S. Hoare to Sir G. Clerk (Paris)*
*No. 1209 [C 4952/55/18]*

FOREIGN OFFICE, *June 25, 1935*

Sir,
With reference to my telegram No. 137 to Berlin[1] of the 19th June, I transmit to your Excellency herein copies of a memorandum by Sir Robert Vansittart[2] regarding an interview with Herr von Ribbentrop respecting the Eastern Pact. I have myself spoken to Herr von Ribbentrop on this matter on three separate occasions.

2. You are authorised to inform the French Government of the general nature of the representation made to Herr von Ribbentrop in this matter.

3. A similar despatch has been addressed to His Majesty's Ambassador at Moscow.[3]

I am, &c.,
SAMUEL HOARE

[1] No. 354.　　[2] No. 356.　　[3] Foreign Office despatch No. 318 of June 25 to Moscow.

## No. 377

*Sir E. Drummond (Rome) to Sir S. Hoare (Received June 27)*
*No. 751 [C 5020/55/18]*

ROME, *June 25, 1935*

His Majesty's Representative at Rome presents his compliments to the Secretary of State for Foreign Affairs, and has the honour to transmit herewith copy of the under-mentioned paper.

| *Name and Date* | *Subject* |
| --- | --- |
| Record of Anglo-Italian Conversation, held at the Palazzo Venezia on 24th June, 1935, at 10 a.m. | Anglo-German Naval Agreement. Air pact: Programme of London Communiqué. |

*Record of Anglo-Italian Conversation, held at the Palazzo Venezia on Monday, June 24, 1935, at 10 a.m.*[1]

Present: *Great Britain*: Mr. Eden, Minister for League of Nations Affairs; Sir Eric Drummond, His Majesty's Ambassador at Rome; Mr. Strang, Foreign Office.

    *Italy*: His Excellency the Head of the Government; His Excellency Baron Aloisi, 'Chef du Cabinet'; His Excellency Signor Suvich, Under-Secretary of State for Foreign Affairs.

### Anglo-German Naval Agreement

Mr. Eden said he wished first to assure Signor Mussolini that the change of Government in England did not mean any change in policy.

As regards the Naval Agreement, he recalled that the German Government had, during the Berlin Conversations, made their offer to limit the German Fleet to 35 per cent. of the British Fleet, and that since the Stresa Conference Herr Hitler had reaffirmed his offer in his speech. At the meeting with the German naval experts in London, it had been the intention of His Majesty's Government to conduct preliminary conversations only. They had, however, been faced by a refusal on the part of the German representatives to pursue conversations unless a definite answer could be given as regards the 35 per cent. offer.

The British representatives had then put the question whether the 35 per cent. would be calculated upon British naval strength alone, or whether it would be affected by the naval programmes of other Powers. The German representatives had replied that the German figure of 35 per cent. of the British tonnage would be a permanent relationship and would not be affected by the programmes of other countries except in the event of such programmes violently upsetting the existing equilibrium. Signor Mussolini would see from the terms of the Anglo-German arrangement that even in the event of violent disturbance of the equilibrium, Germany would only have the right to invite His Majesty's Government to examine the new situation, and that no variation of the existing ratio of 35 : 100 could be made without the consent of His Majesty's Government.

Such a reply on the part of the German representatives had been unexpected, and the offer of 35 per cent. was one which no Government in the United Kingdom could possibly have refused. His Majesty's Government and the British public still remembered the great increases in German claims as regards land and air armaments since Herr Hitler's moderate offer of 1934 had been refused. His Majesty's Government could not afford to allow the same increases to take place as regards naval armaments.

In any event, His Majesty's Government would not have accepted the

---

[1] A summarized account of this meeting was received in the Foreign Office at 9.30 a.m. on June 25 in Mr. Eden's telegram No. 361 from Rome, not printed.

German offer if they had not been convinced that acceptance was in the interests of France and Italy, as well as of Great Britain.

Supposing that Italy had now 45 per cent. of the tonnage of the British Fleet, the fixing of the German tonnage at 35 per cent. of the British would give Italy a permanent superiority over Germany of 20 per cent.

Supposing that, as a result of the Anglo-German arrangement, Italy were to increase her fleet, His Majesty's Government would naturally examine the influence of the Italian increase upon their own naval strength. They might not think it necessary to increase the British Fleet; in that event there would be no further increase by Germany. If, on the other hand, they should think an increase necessary, then Germany would also be free to increase, but only up to a proportion of 35 per cent.

Finally, His Majesty's Government had good reason to think that the German offer was made by Herr Hitler himself and that the German naval authorities disliked it. Mr. Eden believed that during the Whitsun adjournment pressure had been brought upon Herr Hitler by the naval authorities who would have been only too glad of any pretext for securing the withdrawal or modification of the offer.

SIGNOR MUSSOLINI said that the Anglo-German Naval Agreement was now a *fait accompli*. His Majesty's Government had concluded it in their own interest because they felt that they could not do otherwise. His own opinion was that if Great Britain had acted without giving France and Italy the impression that she had taken the decision without consulting them (as distinct from informing them) she could have reached the same objective.[2]

As regards the substance of the question, how did His Majesty's Government intend to fit the new agreement into the proposed new naval treaty?

MR. EDEN said that His Majesty's Government would like the Italian Government to send naval experts to London to carry on further naval discussions. He thought it right to say that the French were unable, in view of the state of their public opinion, to agree to send experts to London at once, but he hoped that both French and Italian experts would be sent at a reasonable date. This could perhaps be arranged through the diplomatic channel.

SIGNOR MUSSOLINI enquired whether the Anglo-German arrangement was a permanent basis from which the proposed new naval negotiations would start.

MR. EDEN said that the ratio of 35 : 100 was to be a permanent one, with the possible exception which he had already mentioned. In one category only Germany would have the right to more than 35 per cent. namely, submarines. But this would mean that she would have less than 35 per cent. in some other category or categories, as her percentage of the total British tonnage was not to exceed 35 per cent.

SIGNOR MUSSOLINI said that as regards the past, there was no need to recriminate. What the Governments had to do was to think about the future.

[2] In Rome telegram No. 361 Mr. Eden said: 'I gave Signor Mussolini an explanation of the agreement and of reasons for its conclusion similar to that given to M. Laval. Signor Mussolini showed no very great concern or interest in the question . . .'

The naval arm was the most important of the three for Great Britain, then the air arm and then the land. For Italy, on the other hand, the order was first land, then air, then the sea. What world opinion was anxious to know was whether there was any likelihood of a bilateral air agreement being negotiated in the same way as the naval agreement.

### AIR PACT: PROGRAMME OF LONDON COMMUNIQUÉ

MR. EDEN said that His Majesty's Government wished to make progress with all the subjects mentioned in the London Communiqué of February 3rd. They did not disinterest themselves in any of these subjects. He had asked M. Laval whether it would not be possible to push on with the negotiation of a Five-Power Agreement for an Air Pact and air limitation.

M. Laval had expressed willingness, on two conditions: these were—firstly, that the Five-Power Air Pact should be supplemented by bilateral agreements, one of which must be an Anglo-French agreement; secondly, that nothing should be signed without settling, at the same time, all the other matters dealt with in the Communiqué of February 3rd.

SIGNOR MUSSOLINI enquired whether Mr. Eden had accepted these two conditions.

MR. EDEN said that he had reported to London and hoped to be in a position to reply to M. Laval on his way back.

He saw one difficulty. If, for example, an Air Pact and a Central European Pact were ready for signature, but the negotiation of an Eastern Pact was held up, were they to hold up the two former until the latter was ready?

SIGNOR MUSSOLINI said that he thought it was essential to establish an order of importance as between the various parts of the Communiqué. In his own view the order ought to be: (1) Air Pact, (2) Central European Pact, (3) Eastern Pact. In his view the Eastern Pact had lost its importance since the conclusion of the Franco-Soviet and Czechoslovak-Soviet agreements. It could not, of course, be omitted from the list.

Although the German naval specialists might not approve of the Anglo-German Naval Agreement, this agreement was a great political success for Germany, and it was possible that she might in consequence increase her pressure upon Austria. Her pressure was, in fact, already increasing in newspapers and on the wireless. He hoped that British opinion would realise that if Germany had 90 million inhabitants, she would be difficult to contain. Germany at Vienna would mean Germany at Prague. Czechoslovakia was surrounded by Germans. No one could stop a German march to the Eastern Mediterranean, and they would arrive at the Bosphorus. There were 200 German experts in Turkey, and in spite of the Soviet–Turkish alliance German influence was strong.

Difficulties had arisen in regard to the Conference for the Central European Pact, but these difficulties would be met. If the conference could not be well prepared, it would be better not to hold it at all. If the conference received a check, there would be confusion in Central and South-Eastern

Europe. Great Britain had therefore a direct interest in the convocation and conclusion of a conference.

MR. EDEN agreed that the various subjects might usefully be graded in order of importance. His Majesty's Government were ready to help to promote agreement on all of them.

SIR E. DRUMMOND observed that the French Government were unwilling that an agreement should be signed on any subject prior to an agreement on land armaments. He thought it would be most difficult to hold up agreements in this way.

SIGNOR MUSSOLINI wondered what action it was possible to take regarding land armaments. Germany was already constituting the effectives she required and there was no way of stopping her.

MR. EDEN said the French view was that as Germany wanted an Air Pact she ought to be made to pay a price for it, and part of that price ought to be an agreement about land armaments. He himself was inclined to think that the Air Pact was a waning asset from this point of view, and that the more the German Air Force grew, the less Germany would need the Pact.

SIGNOR MUSSOLINI thought that it was true that Germany wanted an Air Pact upon a high level of limitation. Her chief reason for wanting the Pact was her difficult position from the point of view of anti-air defence. Her population and industrial areas were concentrated in vulnerable positions. If any price were to be asked from Germany in return for the Air Pact, emphasis ought to be laid first upon the Central European Pact, and in the second place upon the Eastern Pact. France might perhaps agree to bargain the Air Pact against a Central European Pact, leaving the Eastern Pact and land armaments for a later stage.

Like Great Britain, Italy had no direct interest in the Eastern Pact, but would be glad if it could be concluded. Her attitude was one of benevolent indifference. The Central European Pact was, however, of primary interest to Italy. Italy was not herself threatened; she had a line of defence upon the Alps. But Germany would take the line of least resistance and dominate Central and South-Eastern Europe.

It was necessary to prevent the absorption of Austria either from without or from within. The Austrian Chancellor had stated in Florence[3] that the Austrian situation was improving from the internal point of view, both politically and economically.

Signor Mussolini enquired whether the possible contents of an Air Pact had been considered during the conversation with M. Laval.

MR. EDEN said that he had intended to leave with M. Laval a list of questions for consideration by the five Powers concerned, but that he had thought[? it] wiser to wait until he could himself answer M. Laval's questions. His list would, of course, be communicated to the Italian Government at the same time. What Mr. Eden wished to avoid was to give a formal undertaking that His Majesty's Government would not conclude any agreement whatever

[3] Dr. von Schuschnigg had visited Italy, May 9–15, 1935, and had a conversation with Signor Mussolini at Florence on May 11.

on any of the points in the London Communiqué unless some agreement upon effectives had been previously reached.

Sir E. Drummond thought that His Majesty's Government could not give any such undertaking.

Signor Mussolini said that the French would object that the Communiqué of February 3rd was indivisible.

Would Germany agree to accept a position of inferiority in the air or would she want parity?

Mr. Eden replied that Germany wanted parity with France.

Signor Suvich asked whether it was parity with France or with the most highly armed Air Power in Europe.

Mr. Eden said that for the moment it was parity with the air forces of France, including those in North Africa. Germany was ready to agree to parity as between the four Great Western Powers. The figure of 2,000 first-line aeroplanes had been mentioned, but it was to be hoped that the figure would not be so high.

What he would like to do would be to arrange with M. Laval that all the Powers concerned should work hard together on all points of the London Communiqué and then see what could be done as regards the conclusion of agreements. His Majesty's Government were ready to help with the Eastern Pact and the Central European Pact.

Signor Mussolini asked what ideas M. Laval had about land armaments.

Mr. Eden replied that he had twice put this question to M. Laval, but had received no clear reply. His impression was that the French Government still hoped to secure an agreement about effectives in return for an Air Pact.

Signor Suvich thought it would be well to establish a balance between those parts of the programme which were favourable to Germany and those parts which were not.

Signor Mussolini repeated that the various parts of the programme had not the same value for Great Britain, France and Italy. The Eastern Pact, for example, was less important than the Central European Pact. It should be included in the programme of negotiations, but not made a *sine qua non*. There were signs that the French Government were coming to attach more importance to the Central European Pact and less to the Eastern Pact.

If the Italian memorandum of January 1934[4] had been accepted the present situation would not have arisen. The French note of the 17th April, 1934,[5] lay at the root of the present situation.

Mr. Eden observed that it was precisely the recollection of that note which had made the conclusion of the Anglo-German Naval arrangement inevitable.

Signor Mussolini said that in order to achieve results it would be necessary to decide upon the order of importance of the various agreements which would be asked of Germany in return for the Air Pact.

Sir E. Drummond thought it would be difficult for M. Laval to choose

[4] See No. 3 in Cmd. 4512 of 1934; cf. Volume VI, No. 161, enclosure.
[5] See *ibid.*, No. 395.

between the Central European and the Eastern Pacts, especially in public. The Soviet Government still held strongly to the Eastern Pact.

SIGNOR MUSSOLINI said that he did not suggest that the order of importance should be proclaimed in public, but that it should be borne in mind particularly as a method of work. His view was that the programme of February 3rd was indivisible, but that some parts of it were more important than others and that the conclusion of some of them could wait. It would be a mistake to assert or undertake that all parts of the programme should be concluded at the same time.

MR. EDEN said that the difficulties about the Central European Pact were not all of German making.

SIGNOR MUSSOLINI observed that the Germans were still causing difficulty. They still asked for a definition of non-interference and their general attitude was unhelpful. Germany would be invited to the Rome Conference and would probably not refuse. The German Government had been kept informed of developments but had shown no enthusiasm. They also refused to admit the conclusion of mutual assistance pacts within the framework of the Central European Pact. Their attitude to the Eastern Pact differed from their attitude to the Central European Pact.

SIR E. DRUMMOND wondered whether they could refuse to admit the conclusion of the mutual assistance agreements outside the Central European Pact.

SIGNOR MUSSOLINI stated that his impression was that Germany would refuse to admit this also if the agreements in question were for the purposes of the Central European Pact.

SIR E. DRUMMOND said that he did not think, once the Central European Pact was in force, that Germany could object to a mutual assistance agreement between, say, Italy and Austria.

SIGNOR SUVICH said that he thought that the conclusion of the Franco-Soviet Pact had made the German attitude to the Eastern Pact less favourable and that they were endeavouring to go back on the concession made at the time of the Stresa Conference.

MR. EDEN said that M. Laval was hoping for progress on the Eastern Pact as soon as he had sent a reply to Berlin about the relation between the Franco-Soviet Pact and the Locarno Treaties. As soon as he had received Italian assent he would send the reply to Berlin.

SIGNOR SUVICH said that the Italian Government had agreed to the terms of the French reply to Germany.

### ANGLO-GERMAN NAVAL AGREEMENT

MR. EDEN added that the basis upon which His Majesty's Government were at present proceeding was programmes of construction rather than percentages of tonnage. It was hoped to get from the German representatives in London during the present week an outline of the German programme of construction. Germany would not, of course, reach her maximum of 35 per cent. of British tonnage for some years to come.

SIGNOR MUSSOLINI asked whether anything had been said in London about the calibre of guns or about supervision.

MR. EDEN said he thought that full information would be given to the Italian Naval experts when they came to London.

(The meeting then adjourned).[6]

[6] Minutes of the afternoon meeting concerning the Ethiopian problem will be printed in Volume XIV. Cf. No. 366, note 2.

## No. 378

*Sir S. Hoare to Mr. Newton (Berlin)*

*No. 22 Saving: Telegraphic* [*C 4849/55/18*]

FOREIGN OFFICE, *June 26, 1935, 2 p.m.*

Your telegram No. 157 Saving,[1] last para.

You should take any opportunity which may present itself to make it clear to those concerned that there never has been any question of our coming to terms with Germany alone in the matter of air limitation. As for the Air Pact it is obviously a matter which requires the combined cooperation of the Five Locarno Powers. If you think fit, you can add what we have repeatedly impressed on Herr von Ribbentrop—that Germany herself is in a position, by bringing about an Eastern Pact, to make an important preliminary contribution to a rapid conclusion of the desired agreement as regards the air.

Copied to Paris.

[1] No. 360.

## No. 379

*Sir S. Hoare to Sir G. Clerk (Paris)*

*No. 213 Saving: Telegraphic* [*C 5018/55/18*]

*Immediate*                    FOREIGN OFFICE, *June 26, 1935*

The Cabinet considered this morning your telegrams Nos. 128, 129 and 130[1] of June 21st and 22nd regarding the Air Pact and Limitation of Air Strengths.

It was explained to the Cabinet that the French Government are willing to proceed with the negotiation of an Air Pact and of an Air Limitation Agreement on two conditions:—

(*a*) that the Air Pact is completed by bilateral military agreements which might be between several pairs of Powers but must include one between France and the United Kingdom, and

(*b*) that the Air Pact and Limitation Agreement should not become operative until agreement had also been reached on the other subjects mentioned in the communiqué of February 3rd, viz. Eastern Pact, Danubian Pact and limitation of land armaments.

[1] Nos. 362 and 368.

The Cabinet decided to authorise you to take note of the fact that these are the conditions on which the French Government will participate in the negotiations. But they asked me to emphasize to you the two following points:—

(1) They are most anxious that you should be careful not to say or agree to anything which could subsequently be quoted as committing us, even by implication, to having accepted the French view that all these agreements must be *concluded* simultaneously. This does not mean that the London declaration does not still hold the field for us; and we still intend to try with the French Government to obtain a simultaneous settlement of all these questions. To more than that we cannot commit ourselves. Nor were we committed to more by the London declaration. As proof of our intention to continue to work on the lines of the London declaration, you can, if you think it useful, again mention the strong representations which I and Sir R. Vansittart have made to Herr von Ribbentrop in regard to the Eastern Pact (see my tel. No. 137 to Berlin and my despatch No. 1209 to Paris).[2]

(2) The Cabinet are somewhat uneasy as regards the bilateral agreements. While they agreed that we should be prepared to discuss such agreements simultaneously with the Air Pact there was a feeling that we may be getting into a dangerous position if we embark on them. In any event now that we know the French view as regards completing the Pact by these agreements, it will be unnecessary for you to pursue the question with the French Government at the moment. It will however be essential that you should urge upon M. Laval the great importance of no statement about bilateral agreements being made or allowed to leak out at this stage. In this connection you should tell M. Laval for his own confidential information that in the draft of the Air Pact which the German Government have communicated to us admittedly only as a first draft (and on which no action is being taken by us)[3] they have inserted a clause which seems to prohibit the conclusion of bilateral agreements between any two of the parties. If then the French condition about these agreements becomes known now, the effect may well be to drive the Germans out of the negotiation altogether.

The question of the opening of the negotiations being, we hope, settled in this manner the Cabinet would be grateful if you would give M. Laval the list of questions on which we think it will be necessary that the Five Powers should define their views preferably through the diplomatic channel in advance of any general meeting or attempt to prepare a common draft. This list is contained in my immediately following telegram.[4] We hope and indeed expect to receive the French Government's view of the answers to these questions with very little delay.

If M. Laval asks whether we intend also to communicate with Italy and Belgium and with Germany, you can tell him that we are approaching the French Government first; but that naturally we shall find it necessary to approach the other three Powers also at a very early date.

[2] Nos. 354 and 376.　　　[3] See No. 259.　　　[4] No. 380.

# No. 380

## Sir S. Hoare to Sir G. Clerk (Paris)
### No. 214 Saving: Telegraphic [C 5018/55/18]

*Immediate*                                         FOREIGN OFFICE, *June 26, 1935*

Following is list of questions referred to in my immediately preceding telegram[1]:—

(a) Is there to be one instrument embodying Air Pact, Limitation Agreement and prohibition of indiscriminate bombing, or are there to be separate instruments?

(b) Which of the proposed signatories to the Air Pact are to give guarantees, and which are to receive them?

(c) What are the circumstances in which the guarantees in the Air Pact will operate?

(d) Are Powers other than the five Powers in any way to be approached in connection with the Air Pact?

(e) Is the Air Pact to be supplemented by bilateral agreements?

(f) To what category or categories of air power and strength is limitation to apply?

(g) Is it accepted that limitation shall be on a basis of parity in each category? And if any of the parties is not to enjoy parity, what is to be the relation of its strength to that of the other parties?

(h) What is to be included in the term 'Metropolitan first-line strength'?

You will note that the above questions do not mention supervision; if M. Laval raises the point there will be no objection to your saying that that matter too will require consideration.

[1] No. 379.

# No. 381

## Sir E. Ovey (Brussels) to Sir S. Hoare (Received June 27, 1.30 p.m.)
### No. 41 Telegraphic [C 5026/55/18]

BRUSSELS, *June 27, 1935, 10.27 a.m.*

Your telegram No. 57.[1]

Belgian Government agree that it is not for Great Britain, Italy and Belgium, who are not parties to Franco-Soviet treaty, to interpret its terms, and in general with whole of proposed reply to Germany, except the last point which they think it would be well to make more precise in following more closely the text of article 4 of Locarno treaty.

They propose following alternative wording:

'As regards more specially the assistance to be rendered to a state in virtue of Article 4 of Treaty of Locarno, every signatory has under that article, subject to findings and recommendations of Council of the League of Nations

[1] See No. 341, note 2.

the right and duty of deciding if and when the conditions foreseen for grant of assistance have been realised. This right and duty remain intact and cannot be modified.'

Text[2] by bag.

Repeated to Berlin, Moscow, Paris and Rome.

[2] Received on June 29 as enclosure in Brussels despatch No. 380 of June 27, not printed.

## No. 382

*Sir E. Ovey (Brussels) to Sir S. Hoare (Received June 27, 2.15 p.m.)*
*No. 42 Telegraphic [C 5027/55/18]*

BRUSSELS, *June 27, 1935, 12.24 p.m.*

My immediately preceding telegram.[1]

Baron Van Zuylen, Assistant Political Director of Ministry of Foreign Affairs, in returning text of Belgian reply, referred to his conversations at Foreign Office in 1933 (see Sir J. Simon's despatch No. 584 of December 22nd, 1933)[2] and said that Belgian Government in framing proposed modification of British draft had been anxious to maintain their point of view that there must be previous 'accord' between the *guaranteeing and guaranteed* Power before the former came to the assistance of the latter. It was true that the divergence of views on this point still continued, but Belgian Government did not wish the point of view opposed to their own to succeed by default.

Belgian Government would be very grateful to know when His Majesty's Government propose to return reply to German Government and what its exact text will be.

[1] No. 381.
[2] Not printed. An account of Baron van Zuylen's conversation at the Foreign Office with Mr. Sargent on December 15, 1933, is printed in *Documents Diplomatiques Belges 1920-1940*, vol. iii (1964), pp. 270-4.

## No. 383

*Sir G. Clerk (Paris) to Sir S. Hoare (Received June 27)*
*No. 141 Saving: Telegraphic [C 5031/55/18]*

PARIS, *June 27, 1935*

Following from Mr. Eden:—

I had a conversation of two hours with Monsieur Laval this morning.[1] I began by giving him some account of my conversations with Signor Mussolini at Rome on the subject of Abyssinia. . . .[2]

We then had a difficult conversation upon Anglo-French relations. Monsieur Laval maintained that while he had no objection to the Eastern Pact coming into force in advance of the other items of February 3rd, he could not agree that an air pact should come into force unless an agreement on land

[1] Cf. No. 357, note 1, for Mr. Eden's return to Paris.
[2] The omitted three paragraphs will be printed in Volume XIV.

armaments should come into force at the same time. Monsieur Laval complained that His Majesty's Government were not saying now what they had said on February 3rd. I argued that France stood to gain as much as His Majesty's Government from the conclusion of an air pact which limited the German air force. In reply Monsieur Laval contended that this would certainly not be so unless the air pact were reinforced by bilateral pacts.

I am bringing home with me tonight full record[3] of this conversation. Although it will appear from this record that hard things were said, in fact, while the points of view were often opposed, the atmosphere was at all times friendly.

I am convinced that it will be impossible to persuade the French to agree to get to work on an air pact and limitation unless we agree that such a pact shall be buttressed by bilateral pacts and shall not be concluded without them. If we could consent to this it is just possible that the French would be willing to enter upon and even conclude negotiations for an air pact and limitation without the further condition that these agreements should not come into force until agreement had been reached on land armaments.

Monsieur Laval's position here is undoubtedly very difficult. He has gone to the furthest lengths he can, even to the extent of endangering his position, in order to meet us. Unless we can give him some satisfaction on one or other of the heads I have mentioned, further progress would not seem possible.

Naval armaments were not discussed but there is a strong impression here that the French Embassy were told in London that the French government need not formulate their views about the Anglo-German agreement until Germany's programme of construction was made known. Now it seems, so they contend, that they cannot even be told of the rate at which Germany is breaking the Treaty of Versailles until they submit their own perfectly legitimate programme.

Copy Rome by air mail June 29th.

[3] See No. 384.

## No. 384

*Record of Anglo-French Conversation held at the Quai d'Orsay on Thursday, June 27, at 11.30 a.m.*[1]

*[C 5032/55/18]*★

Present: *Great Britain*: Mr. Eden, Minister for League of Nations Affairs; Mr. Strang, Foreign Office.

*France*: M. Pierre Laval, President of the Council; M. Alexis Léger, Secretary-General of the Ministry for Foreign Affairs.

ACCOUNT OF MR. EDEN'S CONVERSATIONS WITH SIGNOR MUSSOLINI
*Europe*

MR. EDEN said that, quite briefly, Signor Mussolini's views were as follows.

[1] Cf. No. 383.

No part of the London programme ought to be dealt with bilaterally. The London programme was in principle indivisible, though the various parts of it were not of the same urgency or importance. Signor Mussolini's own order of importance was: (1) Air Pact, (2) Central European Pact, (3) Eastern Pact, (4) land armaments.

M. LAVAL interposed to say that at the meeting of the Foreign Affairs Committee of the Senate on the previous day great importance had been attached to the question of land armaments.

MR. EDEN said that Signor Mussolini's idea was that the three Governments might agree among themselves as to the order of importance of the various parts of the programme, though he did not suggest that it was necessary to make any public statement in regard to their views on this subject.

*Abyssinia . . .*[2]

## PROGRAMME OF LONDON COMMUNIQUÉ[3]

M. LAVAL asked whether Mr. Eden had had any reply from London to the points which he had put to His Majesty's Government when he was last in Paris.

MR. EDEN replied that he had explained to His Majesty's Government[4] that the French Government were willing to proceed with the negotiations for an Air Pact and for an air limitation agreement on the two conditions which M. Laval had stated to him. His Majesty's Government were ready to take note of the fact that these were the conditions on which the French Government would participate in the negotiations.

His Majesty's Government were ready and anxious to work on all the subjects mentioned in the London communiqué, but not to agree in [*sic*] terms that none of the matters enumerated in the communiqué should, in any circumstances, be put on foot before all the other matters were ready. It might well be that in the future, say in a few weeks' time, the French Government themselves might wish to get on with the conclusion of one of these matters.

M. LAVAL said that he was ready that His Majesty's Government should refrain from making an express public statement to this effect, but he expected them to remain faithful to the spirit of the London communiqué and the Stresa resolution.

MR. EDEN said that supposing the Air Pact and the Eastern Pact were ready to be brought into force, did M. Laval want an undertaking that they would not come into force until an agreement on land armaments could come into force?

M. LAVAL said that he had no objection to the Eastern Pact coming into force in advance of the others. But he could not agree that an Air Pact should come into force unless an agreement on land armaments could also come into force at the same time.

[2] The omitted section will be printed in Volume XIV.
[3] Of February 3, 1935.                                                    [4] See Nos. 362 and 368.

M. Laval said that he had read to the Foreign Affairs Commission of the Senate an account of his conversation with General Göring.[5] The commission had realised from this account that Herr Hitler's speech had been affected by what had passed between himself and General Göring. M. Laval had, in fact, been applauded by the commission, a thing which rarely happened. This showed that he had parliamentary and public support for a policy of agreement with Germany. But the condition of such a policy was that there should not be perpetual concessions and nibbling away of the position in such a way that the final objective would not be reached. It was important that the whole programme should be discussed, including land armaments.

MR. EDEN asked how it was proposed to deal with the question of land armaments.

M. LAVAL thought that a procedure could be found, outside Geneva if necessary. It ought not to take long to agree upon the proportions to be allotted to each country, whether in the land or in the air. In the air Germany wanted parity with France and Great Britain. She wished to include in the French forces those stationed in North Africa, which could not of course be used against Germany. But did Germany also claim to include those stationed in Indo-China?

MR. EDEN said he did not so understand the position.

M. LAVAL said that if Germany really sincerely desired the organisation of peace, and if she felt that France was moved by the same sincerity, these matters ought to be of secondary importance.

MR. EDEN said that it would be difficult for His Majesty's Government to undertake not to put on foot any of the matters dealt with in the London communiqué unless the question of land armaments was settled at the same time. An agreement on land armaments would take a long time to reach. That had been the experience of recent years. At present what Germany wanted was an Air Pact, but with every passing month she would want it less, as her air force grew in strength. The German desire for an Air Pact was a wasting asset.

M. LAVAL could not understand how His Majesty's Government had changed their mind so soon. What they were saying now was not what they said on the 3rd February.

MR. EDEN said that His Majesty's Government had not changed their view.

M. LAVAL said that France's chief interest was land armaments.

MR. EDEN said that surely they were interested in the air also. Would not France gain by the establishment of parity with Germany? Could not Germany outbuild France?

M. LÉGER said that the only effect, so far as France was concerned, would be that there would be much greater difficulty in reaching a settlement about land armaments.

M. LAVAL thought that, for financial reasons, Germany could not go on

[5] On May 18, 1935.

490

much longer rearming.  She could not pay her Ambassadors more than 50 per cent. of their salaries.

If Great Britain and France held firm together and let Germany see that they wanted to make peace, Germany would make an agreement.

Mr. Eden then explained what had passed between Sir R. Vansittart and Herr von Ribbentrop in regard to the Eastern Pact (Foreign Office despatch to Paris, No. 1209 of the 25th June, 1935).[6]  Herr von Ribbentrop had pressed for the conclusion of the Air Agreement, and the reply had been that progress should be made with the Eastern Pact.

M. Laval said that if Herr von Ribbentrop came to Paris he would say the same thing to him.

Mr. Eden said he understood that M. Laval's view was that if Germany asked for the conclusion of an Air Pact, the reply he wished His Majesty's Government to make would be that no such pact would be concluded unless Germany was in agreement with France about land armaments.  He doubted whether such an attitude would really be in the best interests of France.  The result would probably be that there would be no Air Pact.

M. Laval did not agree.  If His Majesty's Government and the French Government could adopt this line, he would do his very utmost to reach an agreement with Germany.  The attempt to secure a universal disarmament convention had rendered the problem insoluble.

Mr. Eden said that His Majesty's Government had no intention of letting go the agreement of the 3rd February.

M. Léger said that the land problem was nine-tenths of the whole problem for France.  An agreement on land armaments was necessary in the interests of European peace and co-operation.

M. Laval wondered whether the time had not come for Herr von Ribbentrop to visit Paris.

The trouble was that if Germany obtained the Air Pact without agreeing to anything else, she would have obtained all she wanted in the West and would be free to attack in the East.

M. Léger asked whether Mr. Eden could say anything about the conclusion of bilateral pacts within the framework of the Air Pact.

Mr. Eden said that His Majesty's Government did not refuse to contemplate the possibility of such bilateral pacts, but they could not undertake to regard their conclusion as a *sine qua non*.

M. Léger said that this presumably meant that neither did they undertake not to conclude an Air Pact without bilateral pacts.

Mr. Eden said that he did not think his Majesty's Government would wish to give such an undertaking.

M. Léger observed that without bilateral pacts, the Air Pact would be of no use to France.  The value of the Air Pact was the provision for immediate assistance which France did not enjoy under Locarno.  In return for this France was prepared to give Great Britain a guarantee which she did not give in the Locarno Treaty.  But an undertaking for immediate assistance

[6] No. 376; see also No. 356.

would be of no avail unless mechanism was provided in advance for the rendering of immediate assistance. This was why bilateral pacts were indispensable.

MR. EDEN said it was important that the French attitude about bilateral pacts should not be allowed to leak out at this stage. In the German draft for an Air Pact there was a clause which seemed to prohibit the conclusion of bilateral agreements between any two of the parties. If the French contention about these agreements became known, the effect might be to drive the Germans out of the negotiations altogether.

M. LÉGER thought that this meant that the Germans did not wish to have any mechanism of application. They did not wish the Air Pact to be effective.

MR. EDEN said that if this was so he did not understand why Germany should want an Air Pact at all.

It seemed to him that the best thing would be to start negotiations at once for the Air Pact itself and think about bilateral pacts of application later.

M. LAVAL said that these bilateral arrangements could, of course, be made with Germany also.

M. Laval said that he would be ready to agree to enter upon negotiations for an Air Pact if His Majesty's Government were ready to agree now that bilateral pacts were essential. He was prepared, of course, that this should remain secret, and should not be stated to the Germans for the present.

MR. EDEN said that he was not in a position to assent to this proposal, but that he was prepared to report it to his colleagues.

M. LAVAL said that the Anglo-German Naval Agreement would start an armaments race. Japan would certainly increase her fleet and Great Britain would follow, and Germany would have the right to follow Great Britain. The result would be that other countries would build, and an agreement made for purposes of limitation would lead to an armaments race.

MR. EDEN said that in the absence of an Anglo-German Agreement, Germany could have gone on to build without limitation.

M. LAVAL said that he was convinced that Germany would not have built. Great Britain was too much impressed by Germany. Great Britain had shown weakness after weakness, and the result would be that Germany would have superiority everywhere. This was what His Majesty's Government's policy would lead to.

MR. EDEN said he could not accept this argumentation. Summing up, he said that he understood M. Laval's position to be that there should be no Air Pact unless there were at the same time an agreement about land armaments; and no Air Pact unless it were agreed, as between France and Great Britain, that the Air Pact should be completed by bilateral arrangements.

M. LAVAL said that if there were close collaboration between France and Great Britain, Germany would be brought to an understanding of her duty of collaboration. Germany counted on Great Britain now to help her to get what she wanted. He himself was quite ready to show Germany that France desired an agreement with her.

Mr. EDEN said that supposing His Majesty's Government were to agree to M. Laval's condition as to bilateral pacts, was it still in the French interest to make a condition as regards land armaments? He thought emphatically not.

M. LAVAL said that if it were agreed that there were to be bilateral arrangements within the framework of the Air Pact, the question of the condition as regards land armaments could be discussed, but it would be in any event essential that land armaments should be discussed.

As regards supervision, M. Laval himself did not believe it could be completely effective, but some system of supervision was essential, if only as some check and for the sake of appearances.

Mr. EDEN said that it had been His Majesty's Government's intention to communicate to the French Government a number of questions relating to the Air Pact and air limitation, but he thought that, in view of the present situation, this would be premature. It would be better to wait until matters were further advanced.

M. LÉGER said that Signor Mussolini's insistence on the Central European Pact was interesting. The three Governments had different ideas as to the relative importance of the various matters in question. Great Britain wanted a naval and air agreement. France wanted a land agreement. Italy wanted a Central European Pact.

Mr. EDEN repeated that he thought that a good air agreement would be useful to France.

M. LÉGER agreed that this would be so if the Air Pact were accompanied by provisions for air limitation. But this in its turn would render the conclusion of a land agreement more difficult.

M. LAVAL asked whether Great Britain could agree to parity with the French metropolitan forces. If so, it would be difficult for Germany to ask for more than Great Britain did.

Mr. EDEN said that the German Government were quite aware that the French air force did not disturb Great Britain.

Mr. Eden added that what he had said did not mean that the London declaration did not still hold the field in the view of His Majesty's Government. His Majesty's Government still intended to try with the French Government to obtain a simultaneous statement of all the questions concerned.

M. LAVAL and M. LÉGER said that this did not comfort them. On the contrary. It was no more than an expression of goodwill. In effect it meant that His Majesty's Government were not ready to abide strictly by the London communiqué.

It was agreed that M. Laval should speak to the press in the terms of the annexed statement.

(The meeting then adjourned.)

STATEMENT MADE TO THE PRESS BY M. LAVAL WITH MR. EDEN'S CONSENT[7]

On his return from Rome Mr. Eden gave me an account of the conversations which he had just had with Signor Mussolini.

[7] Cf. *The Times*, June 28, p. 16.

Keeping within the framework of the communiqué of the 3rd February we concentrated on finding the best line of negotiation to bring about a rapid solution of the problems raised therein. We shall continue to examine by the diplomatic channel those questions which the shortness of our conversations made it impossible to deal with exhaustively.

We are both equally anxious to co-ordinate the action of our respective Governments with a view to the fulfilment of the programme of the 3rd February.

Mr. Eden communicated to me the substance of his conversations on the Italo-Ethiopian dispute.

## No. 385

*Sir G. Clerk (Paris) to Sir S. Hoare (Received June 29)*
*No. 142 Saving: Telegraphic [C 5053/55/18]*

PARIS, *June 28, 1935*

Since Mr. Eden's second conversation with M. Laval[1] French press has adopted a much calmer attitude in the belief that as the result of the frank exchange of views which has taken place the two Governments will be able to agree upon a mutually satisfactory course of action. M. Laval's declaration to the press is well received but emphasis is laid on the necessity for very early agreement being reached in regard to procedure.

[1] See No. 384.

## No. 386

*Sir G. Clerk (Paris) to Sir S. Hoare (Received July 2)*
*No. 144 Saving: Telegraphic [C 5104/55/18]*

PARIS, *July 1, 1935*

The Prime Minister's reference on Saturday to the Naval Agreement and his reaffirmation of the Stresa policy is prominently reported in the French press.[1]

Whilst, however, Mr. Baldwin's words are noted with the respect which his speeches always receive here, the press still find it difficult to reconcile the Anglo-German agreement with the policy of co-operation adopted in London and Stresa.

At the same time there is considerable and not on the whole unfavourable discussion of the possibility of a Laval–Ribbentrop meeting which has been started by Monsieur Laval's statement before the Foreign Affairs Commission of the Senate (see my despatch No. 905 of June 27th)[2] and the consequent comments of the German press. The idea appears to be gaining ground

[1] Mr. Baldwin was speaking at an open-air demonstration at Bramham Park, Yorkshire, organized by the National Union of Conservative and Unionist Associations on Saturday, June 29: see *The Times*, July 1, pp. 10 and 16.

[2] Not printed.

slowly that such direct discussion might be useful especially after the example of the Anglo-German conversations. On the other hand, it would be unwise to exaggerate the strength of the movement in view of the great weight of latent scepticism apart from the active opposition of important elements in the cabinet itself.

## No. 387

*Record by Mr. Collier*[1] *of a conversation with the Soviet Ambassador*
[*C 5112/55/18*]

FOREIGN OFFICE, *July 1, 1935*

On June 28th, at the reception given by the Emir Saud,[2] I was 'button-holed' by the Soviet Ambassador, who expressed to me, with even more than his usual freedom, his anxiety at recent developments in the policy of H.M. Government.

After making the now familiar comments on the Anglo-German Naval Agreement and the manner in which it was negotiated, M. Maisky pressed me to say whether H.M. Government intended to pursue the same tactics over the proposed Air Convention. If there was such an intention, he said—and he had indications to that effect from various sources—the conclusion would be drawn everywhere that this country was as much in the German orbit as Poland, the Germans would have no further inducement to conclude an Eastern Pact, and the prospects of peace in Eastern Europe would be gravely imperilled.

I replied that I did not know the Cabinet's intentions about the Air Convention (—a statement which, luckily for me, I could then truthfully make, as I had not yet seen the latest papers on that subject—); and I added that, as far as I could see, there was no great need to worry about our intentions in that matter, since the proposal there was not for a bilateral agreement but for a multilateral pact between the Western Powers, so that nothing could be done without the consent of the French Government, at least,—for, if they refused to push on with the Air Convention in advance of the other items on the Stresa programme, nothing of the sort could take place. In any case, moreover, it now seemed likely that the Eastern Pact in its modified form of a pact of non-aggression could be concluded quite as soon as any Air Convention, provided only that the Memel question were got out of the way—and there I thought his Government might be able to help by using their undoubted influence with the Lithuanian Government to make the latter see reason.

M. Maisky did not deny this; but he still seemed uneasy lest H.M. Government should be pressing the French Government to negotiate an Air Convention in advance of anything else, and he ended the conversation by remarking that, as he had often been told in the Foreign Office that the

[1] Mr. L. Collier was Head of the Northern Department of the Foreign Office.

[2] The Crown Prince of Saudi Arabia, the Emir Saud, Viceroy of Nejd, had arrived in London on June 17 for a private visit: for the first two weeks he was a guest of His Majesty's Government.

further improvement of Anglo-Soviet relations depended not merely upon protestations of goodwill but also upon positive deeds or at least avoidance of action contrary to British interests, he would like to point out that, on that analogy, it was equally desirable that H.M. Government should avoid action contrary to Soviet interests.

I derived the impression from the whole conversation that the Soviet Government had intimated to M. Maisky that he must keep a close watch on developments here and try to find out what H.M. Government really meant by their recent apparent change of policy—as to which they were still uncertain, though of course suspicious.

L. COLLIER

## No. 388

*Letter from Mr. Craigie to Sir G. Clerk (Paris)*

*[A 5925/22/45]*

*Confidential*                                        FOREIGN OFFICE, *July 1, 1935*

Dear Clerk,

You probably saw the letter which the Secretary of State wrote to Eden on the 26th instant[1] on the question of communicating to the French confidential information supplied to us by the Germans during the recent naval discussions. I enclose a copy of M. Corbin's letter to Vansittart[2] which formed the enclosure in the Secretary of State's letter. It was thought that the best way to deal with this matter would be to have a talk between M. Corbin, M. Cambon, Vansittart and myself and this took place on the 28th instant.

Taking M. Corbin's letter as our text we first pointed out to him that the only 'decisions' which had been taken in the course of these discussions were those contained in the Exchange of Notes[3] and on this matter we were prepared to give the ambassador forthwith the fullest information on any point on which he might require elucidation. In the discussions with the Germans on programmes, etc., there had been no question of any 'decisions' but merely of an exchange of information on exactly the same basis as the exchanges of information which had previously taken place with other Powers.

[1] Not printed.

[2] In this letter of June 25 M. Corbin wrote: 'Le Président du Conseil me rappelle que c'est à la prière du Foreign Office lui-même que le Gouvernement Français avait sursis à tout jugement définitif concernant l'accord anglo-allemand, jusqu'à communication du programme naval allemand. Dans cette attente il a répondu en se contentant d'énoncer des réserves et de poser des questions. Il lui paraît incompréhensible aujourd'hui que le Gouvernement britannique refuse de renseigner *confidentiellement* le Gouvernement français sur la portée des décisions prises à Londres sans accord avec nous et qui entraînent révision des clauses navales de la partie V du traité de Versailles . . .' An undated minute on this letter by Sir R. Vansittart reads: 'This must be entered and dealt with *urgently*. It has the makings of a very ugly question. R.V.'

[3] Of July 18, 1935; see No. 348.

We also drew attention to the paragraph in M. Corbin's letter in which M. Laval is stated to be wondering whether there is not some new German demand that His Majesty's Government should obtain general recognition of the principle of the 35 per cent ratio. We assured M. Corbin that there was no such demand and that the idea had never entered our heads.

Before leaving the question of the Exchange of Notes we asked whether there were any points on which the Embassy desired elucidation. M. Corbin replied that in the aide-mémoire communicated to the French Embassy on June 7th[4] nothing had been said about the proposed granting to Germany of parity in submarines nor had we said anything about the provision which subsequently appeared in paragraph 2 (c) that, in certain circumstances, Germany would have the right to invite us to re-examine the situation.

We replied as follows:

The aide-mémoire of June 7th represented exactly the situation which obtained on that date. We had always been nervous of letting the Germans go back to Berlin because we had good grounds for believing that Herr Hitler had overruled the German Naval Staff (who had strongly objected to the 35 per cent offer) and we feared that, if the delegation returned, they would come back to London with fresh demands. Nevertheless, it was felt so important to give the French Government at least a week in which to consider the decision of His Majesty's Government, before the matter was pushed further, that it was decided to take this risk and to adjourn the conversations over Whitsuntide. After the holiday the Germans did, as we had anticipated, return with considerably increased demands, a number of which we resisted, but two of which we accepted at the last moment, i.e. shortly before the Exchange of Notes took place. In neither case, however, did the amendment appear to us to modify the essential basis of the Agreement. As qualified by paragraph 3 of the Exchange of Notes, Germany had no right to modify the 35 per cent ratio except with our assent—and it was perfectly obvious that, even should no such clause exist, it would always be open to the British and German Government[s] to modify the Agreement at any time by common assent. As regards parity in submarines, this was a concession we should have preferred not to make but, in effect, it did not greatly change the situation. In practice, the clause meant that Germany would, without the necessity of further consultation with us, have the right to make a 10 per cent transfer into the submarine category—and, as transfer provisions go, 10 per cent was by no means high (cf. Treaty of London, Draft Disarmament Convention, etc.). Actually, the programme we had been discussing with the Germans up to 1942 was on the basis of a 35 per cent ratio in submarines and it was unlikely that, if Great Britain retained her existing strength in submarines, Germany would wish even to go as high as the 45 per cent limit. There were, however, two other cases to be considered: (a) the case in which Great Britain might reduce her existing submarine strength of 52,700 tons: this might be embarrassing for Germany, who had certain absolute or minimum

4 See No. 319 and No. 315, note 1.

requirements so far as her submarine strength was concerned; and (*b*) the case in which a parity figure for submarines might be provided in a future naval treaty, on the analogy of the parity figure in the London Naval Treaty. In that case Germany would, in accordance with her claim to *Gleichberechtigung*, be entitled to the theoretical right to parity in this type of ship. The point was mainly a theoretical one and we thought that we had been singularly successful in binding Germany down in categories even to the extent we had, seeing that the original 35 per cent offer was on the basis of global tonnage only.

Having thus dealt with questions arising out of the Exchange of Notes we then turned to the problem of communicating to the French Government the information in regard to programmes communicated confidentially to us by the German representatives.

I first of all repeated what I had said to M. Cambon on June 22nd last,[5] since it appeared to have been misreported. I had said:

(*a*) We thought it would be a mistake to communicate information to the French Embassy piecemeal—in reply to questions on individual points—since this method could only give the French Government a distorted picture. It was for this reason that we were most anxious that French experts, with a full knowledge of the technical points at issue, should come over at once in order that we might give them a full survey of the position as we saw it.

(*b*) The Germans had only given us a general outline of their intentions (not yet complete) on condition (i) that we reciprocated and (ii) that if we passed it on to other Powers it would only be done on a similar reciprocal basis. It had seemed to us so important to extract all this information from the Germans, which would be of equal value to the French, that we had agreed to these conditions. I had therefore said that we hoped that the French representatives, when they came, would be prepared to give us some similar general and non-binding indication of their future intentions.

The above could not by any stretch of the imagination be construed as a refusal to supply the French Government confidentially with information (cf. M. Corbin's letter).

As regards the future, we informed M. Corbin that the position was that the Germans had gone home to think about certain questions we had put to them and, until we had their replies, we were not in a position even to give a general outline of Germany's intentions. We hoped, however, to have this information in the course of the next day or two.

If the French Government still felt that it was impossible for them to send naval representatives at once then we suggested the difficulty might be got over in the following way:

(*a*) Our representatives had already during the conversations urged on the German representatives that the German Government should communicate as soon as possible to the French Naval Attaché at Berlin particulars of the ships already laid down outside the Versailles Treaty limit. This the German

[5] No earlier record of this conversation has been traced in Foreign Office archives: cf. No. 369, note 1.

representatives had said they would recommend to their Government and we had again pressed the German Government to adopt this course.

(*b*) As regards future construction, we thought it might be possible to arrange to communicate to the Ambassador and to the Naval Attaché the general outline of Germany's intentions (as communicated to us) as soon as it was complete, provided that we could first come to a 'gentleman's agreement' that the French Government would, within a fortnight or three weeks, give us a similar general and non-binding outline of France's intentions in the matter of new construction up to 1942.

(*c*) This information, together with the information we would give about our own programme, would give the French Government material for a reply, which we hoped would be delivered to us by sending over French representatives for discussions in London. In any case we considered that these matters were not suitable for treatment by means of the exchange of written communications. As Ministers would be dispersing for the holidays at the end of July, we thought that such conversations should begin at the latest in the middle of July.

I have given you this long and rather technical record of our conversation of last Friday[6] because the Quai d'Orsay are evidently trying to work up a further grievance against us on this matter and may raise the question with you. I think you will agree that the solution we have suggested is a very fair one and I cannot think of any reasonable ground on which the French could refuse it. But then I quite realise that, when the French are angry, pure reasonableness is not their strong suit.

Yours ever,<br>
R. L. Craigie

[6] June 28.

## No. 389

*Memorandum by Sir S. Hoare on the Air Pact and Air Limitation Agreement*<br>
*C.P.135(35) [C 5301/55/18][1]*

FOREIGN OFFICE, July 2, 1935

1. The Cabinet will recollect that at their meeting on the 26th June they agreed that the Minister for League of Nations Affairs should be authorised to conduct his conversations in Paris with the French Foreign Minister regarding the Air Pact and an Air Limitation Agreement on the following basis. Without tying the hands of His Majesty's Government on either point, Mr. Eden could take note of the two conditions on which he had previously reported that the French Government would participate in the negotiations:—[2]

(*a*) That the Air Pact was completed by bilateral military arrangements which might be between several pairs of Powers, but must include one between France and the United Kingdom, and

[1] Only the printed copy of this memorandum as circulated to the Cabinet is preserved in Foreign Office archives.  [2] See Nos. 362, 363, and 379.

(b) That the Air Pact and Limitation Agreement could not become operative until agreement had also been reached on the other subjects mentioned in the declaration of the 3rd February, viz., Eastern Pact, Danubian Pact and limitation of land armaments.

2. On the first point—accompaniment of the Air Pact by a bilateral military arrangement at least between France and the United Kingdom—Mr. Eden's report[3] shows that M. Laval was very stiff. He indicated that without a bilateral arrangement the Air Pact would be of little use to the French Government. M. Laval said that for France the value of the Air Pact was the provision for immediate assistance which she did not enjoy under Locarno. An undertaking for immediate assistance would be of no avail unless mechanism was provided in advance for its rendering. That was why a bilateral military arrangement was indispensable. It was in return for an advantage of this kind, which France did not enjoy under the Locarno Treaty, that she was prepared to give the United Kingdom a guarantee which she did not give in the Locarno Treaty.

3. There can at the moment be no question of committing this country to anything in the nature of a separate military alliance with France. Such a commitment would be in direct contradiction to the spirit of reciprocity towards France and Germany which underlies the proposal for the Air Pact just as much as the Locarno Treaty. On the other hand, objection need not necessarily be taken to the proposal for providing between this country and France what in practice will only be the technical machinery necessary for rendering the Air Pact effective, on condition that similar machinery is provided between ourselves and Germany.

4. The Cabinet is accordingly asked to approve the following reply to M. Laval's request about the accompaniment of the Air Pact by bilateral military arrangements. His Majesty's Government would not merely take note of the French Government's requirement that the Air Pact shall be accompanied by a bilateral military arrangement at least between the United Kingdom and France; but would be prepared to agree to the accompaniment of the Air Pact by a bilateral arrangement containing such technical provisions as might be agreed to be necessary for rendering it effective as between this country and France. This would be on the understanding that His Majesty's Government will propose a similar agreement between the United Kingdom and Germany, and naturally between the United Kingdom and Belgium.

In return the French Government will be asked not to object to the immediate initiation of discussions between all the Locarno Powers, with a view to the negotiation (as distinct from the conclusion) of an Air Pact and Air Limitation Agreement.

(N.B. If and when this communication is made to the French Government, it will be important that they should not be led to believe that we have in any way agreed to the technical provisions which they have suggested as suitable for inclusion in the arrangement.)

[3] See No. 384.

5. As regards the second condition, Mr. Eden reports that M. Laval seemed on the whole less uncompromising than at the previous interview. In appearance he continued to insist on the conclusion of a general settlement including the Eastern Pact, the Danubian Pact and more especially limitation of land armaments as a condition of the entry into force of the Air Pact and an Air Limitation Agreement. On the other hand, Mr. Eden had the impression that if we could agree now to the accompaniment of the Air Pact by a bilateral arrangement at least between this country and France, it was just possible that the French Government would be willing not only to enter upon negotiations for an Air Pact and air limitation, but even to conclude them without the further condition that the agreements on these subjects should not come into force until agreement had been reached on land armaments, though they would, of course, at present give no such undertaking.

6. In these circumstances it is not considered necessary to pursue this second point further with the French Government for the moment; though they will be again assured that it is still the wish of His Majesty's Government to see the conclusion of the General Settlement as outlined in the London Declaration, and, in order the better to work for its attainment, they hold that, as far as possible, negotiations with regard to the different elements in that General Settlement should be initiated and carried on simultaneously.[4]

S.H.

[4] The memorandum was considered by the Cabinet on July 3. Its conclusions were embodied in a telegram to Sir G. Clerk of July 6: see No. 398 below.

## No. 390

*Sir W. Selby*[1] *(Vienna) to Sir S. Hoare (Received July 6)*
*No. 32 Saving: Telegraphic [C 5241/55/18]*

VIENNA, July 3, 1935

Minister for Foreign Affairs[2] informed Mr. Mack[3] today that he entirely agreed with the view of French and Italian governments that air pact and Danubian and Eastern pacts should all be dealt with together. He feared that if air pact were negotiated separately Germany would have no incentive to participate in the others; and Danubian pact was of vital importance for Europe. Minister for Foreign Affairs thought that Rome conference[4] might meet at the end of August or beginning of September. But early agreement between Paris and London was an essential preliminary. He had instructed Austrian Minister in London to make enquiries and keep him informed of developments.

[1] H.M. Minister in Vienna.
[2] Baron von Berger-Waldenegg.
[3] First Secretary in H.M. Legation at Vienna.
[4] Cf. No. 363, note 14.

## No. 391

### Sir S. Hoare to Sir E. Ovey (Brussels)[1]
### No. 65 Telegraphic [C 5027/55/18]

FOREIGN OFFICE, *July 4, 1935, 5 p.m.*

Your telegrams Nos. 41 and 42.[2]

2. His Majesty's Government have now considered text of French note as handed to German Chargé d'Affaires in Paris on June 25th.[3] They assume that copy has also been communicated to Government to which you are accredited.

3. His Majesty's Government consider it important that replies of the other Locarno Powers to German memorandum should be despatched as soon as possible. They therefore intend to make communication at an early date to German Ambassador here on lines indicated in my telegram to Paris No. 149[4] last sentence of which [is] being amended to read 'under the Treaty of Locarno, the United Kingdom, as one of the guarantors of that treaty, has the right and duty of deciding, *subject to the findings and recommendations of the Council of the League of Nations*,[5] when and whether etc.'. Words underlined have been inserted to meet suggestions made in your telegram No. 41.[6]

4. His Majesty's Government trust that the Government to which you are accredited will despatch a similar reply to the German memorandum.

[1] A similarly worded telegram, No. 352 to Rome, was sent at the same time to Sir E. Drummond.

[2] Nos. 381 and 382. The corresponding reference in telegram No. 352 to Rome was 'Your despatch No. 724', i.e. No. 349 above.

[3] For the text of this note see *D.G.F.P.*, Series C, vol. iv, No. 170. A copy of the note was received in the Foreign Office on June 27 as enclosure in Paris despatch No. 898 of June 26, not printed. The differences between the final text and the draft (see No. 341, note 1) were not considered such as to alter His Majesty's Government's original intention to inform the German Government of their agreement (see No. 341) with the views expressed by the French Government. [4] No. 341.

[5] The words in italics were underlined on the filed copy of this telegram.

[6] In telegram No. 352 to Rome this reference read: 'Brussels telegram No. 41 repeated to you.'

## No. 392

### Sir S. Hoare to Mr. Newton (Berlin)
### No. 721 [C 5149/55/18]

FOREIGN OFFICE, *July 4, 1935*

Sir,

The German Ambassador asked to see the Minister for League of Nations Affairs on July 1st in order to enquire if he could give him any information as to the outcome of his visits to Paris and to Rome. Mr. Eden told the Ambassador that there was little that he could add to the statement which he had just made in the House of Commons that afternoon.[1] He had sought to

[1] See 303 *H.C. Deb.* 5 *s.*, cols. 1520–2.

reassure M. Laval as to the Anglo-German Naval Agreement, and had explained to him that useful as His Majesty's Government thought this instrument for the United Kingdom and for Germany, they would, in fact, never have agreed to it had they not also been convinced that it was in the interest of Europe as a whole. He thought that M. Laval was inclined to accept this view, and that the French Government took exception more to the manner than to the matter of the agreement.

2. The Ambassador then asked Mr. Eden how he visualised future negotiations. Mr. Eden said that the conclusion of the Anglo-German Naval Agreement made it more than ever necessary for His Majesty's Government to make it clear that they were intent upon making progress with all parts of the London communiqué of February 3rd. The German Government could make a contribution by furthering to the best of their ability the speedy conclusion of the Eastern Pact.

3. The Ambassador replied that he appreciated this and that he was himself greatly troubled about the Eastern Pact, and he did not know what the Chancellor's final decision would be. Mr. Eden must appreciate that the position had been profoundly modified by the Franco-Soviet Treaty. The Ambassador begged him closely to examine that document. According to Article 2 the Treaty professed to refer to an unprovoked aggression 'on the part of any European State'. On the other hand, if Mr. Eden would carefully read Article 4 of the Protocol of Signature he would find there a qualification which, however obscurely expressed, showed that the real purpose of the Treaty was directed against Germany. The second sentence of Article 4 of the Protocol of Signature ran as follows: 'Although circumstances have not hitherto permitted the conclusion of these agreements, which the two parties still look upon as desirable, it remains a fact, nevertheless, that the undertakings set forth in the Franco-Soviet Treaty should be understood to come into play only within the limits contemplated in the tripartite agreement previously projected.' The tripartite agreement which was referred to in this sentence was the agreement in the previous abortive Barthou negotiations,[2] by which France could go to Russia's aid in the east, and Russia could go to France's aid in the west, in the event of a German aggression bringing into force either the Locarno Pact or the Eastern Pact.

4. Mr. Eden replied that this paragraph might, for all he knew, bear the construction which the Ambassador put upon it, but even if it did, he could not see that this fundamentally altered the situation, since Germany had no intention of contemplating an aggression against either France or Russia. A treaty of mutual assistance which would only come into force in the event of such an aggression could hardly be so sinister an instrument. The Ambassador said that it was of course true that Germany contemplated no aggression against anyone. On the other hand, to sign a non-aggression pact at this stage would be to imply some measure of approval of this Franco-Soviet Treaty, and indeed that was the one reason why France and Russia desired this non-aggression pact, and they were alone in desiring it.

[2] See Volume VI, Nos. 487 and 488.

5. Mr. Eden said that he sincerely hoped that whatever the view of the German Government of this Franco-Soviet Treaty, they would on no account go back on the position they had taken up in reply to the questions addressed to them by Sir John Simon from Stresa.[3]   If the German Government were now to say that they could not conclude a pact of non-aggression in the East on account of the Franco-Soviet Treaty, this would produce the worst of impressions here.  The Ambassador was, he felt sure, fully aware of the state of public opinion in this country, and the refusal of Germany at this time to take part in a pact of non-aggression, whatever the motives might be for such a refusal, would be very badly received.  This was the more true since His Majesty's Government were most anxious to make rapid progress with the Air Pact, and they realised that such progress must be dependent to a considerable extent upon the results achieved in respect of the Eastern Pact and other matters mentioned in the London communiqué of February 3rd.

6. The Ambassador asked what Mr. Eden meant by the other matters referred to in the communiqué, and Mr. Eden mentioned the Eastern Pact, the Danube Pact and the agreement on land armaments.  The Ambassador said that so far as concerned the Eastern Pact, he quite saw that it might be possible to come to some arrangement with reference to such a pact, though he did not at all know what the attitude of the Chancellor in respect to it might be.  As to the Danubian Pact, no pact existed, and he did not see how any progress could be recorded in respect of this matter for a considerable time to come.  Mr. Eden then asked the Ambassador whether the German Government had any views about land armaments, since His Majesty's Government were interested in this problem also.  For instance, did the German Government contemplate making any approach to the French Government in this matter?  The Ambassador replied that he did not think that any such move was in contemplation.  It was useless to discuss land armaments unless heavy war material were included in such discussion, and the French Government had shown no disposition to do this.  Mr. Eden reminded the Ambassador that effectives were an important part of land armaments, and asked if the German Government had no proposals to make about this category which might facilitate agreement.  The Ambassador replied that he did not think that the figure of thirty-six divisions was one which the German Government would be willing to negotiate.  They were, however, very anxious to make progress with the Air Pact.  If that question depended upon the United Kingdom and Germany alone, the Air Pact could be signed tomorrow.  Mr. Eden replied that he did not think the issue was quite as simple as that, and that in any event Herr von Hoesch knew as well as he that progress depended upon co-operation of others, which in turn depended upon real progress being made with all the items in the London communiqué of February 3rd, and more particularly with the Eastern Pact. The Ambassador thanked Mr. Eden for the exposition of the situation as he saw it, and undertook to report to his Government the view which he

[3] See Volume XII, Nos. 715 and 717.

expressed about the Eastern Pact. He gave the impression that he himself shared this view.

7. Before leaving Herr von Hoesch asked what were the prospects of a settlement of the dispute between Italy and Abyssinia. Mr. Eden gave him, in reply, an outline of the statement which had been made in the House.[4] The Ambassador remarked that he thought it was generous on the part of His Majesty's Government to offer compensation in the shape of British territory to Abyssinia.

I am, &c.,
SAMUEL HOARE[5]

[4] See 303 *H.C. Deb. op. cit.*, cols. 1521–2.
[5] For Herr von Hoesch's report of this conversation see *D.G.F.P.*, Series C, vol. iv, No. 189.

## No. 393

*Viscount Chilston (Moscow) to Sir S. Hoare (Received July 19)*
*No. 295 [C 5521/55/18]*

MOSCOW, *July 4, 1935*

Sir,

In accordance with the authorisation given in your despatch No. 318[1] of the 25th June, I have informed M. Litvinov, orally, of the general nature of the representations which you and Sir R. Vansittart made to Herr von Ribbentrop as to the desirability of the German Government taking a step towards negotiating an Eastern Pact.

2. M. Litvinov thanked me for this information, but made no remark upon it except to say that perhaps one reason for the German delay in replying to the French note on the subject was that they had waited for Colonel Beck's arrival in Berlin.[2]

3. M. Litvinov then asked me if His Majesty's Government were now negotiating for a bilateral air pact with Germany, to which question I replied in the negative.

I have, &c.,
CHILSTON

[1] See No. 376, note 3.
[2] The Polish Minister for Foreign Affairs visited Berlin, July 3–4. Cf. *D.G.F.P.*, Series C, vol. iv, No. 190.

## No. 394

*Mr. MacKillop[1] (Brussels) to Sir S. Hoare (Received July 5, 6.15 p.m.)*
*No. 45 Telegraphic [C 5229/55/18]*

BRUSSELS, *July 5, 1935, 4.46 p.m.*

Your telegram No. 65.[2]

I saw Political Director at Ministry of Foreign Affairs this morning who informed me Belgian Government greatly appreciated this modification of

[1] First Secretary in H.M. Embassy at Brussels.          [2] No. 391.

our original draft and would make a communication to German Government in the sense of their note of June 26th (see Sir E. Ovey's despatch No. 380).[3] Since, however, German Government had made no distinct and separate approach to them but had merely communicated copy of memorandum addressed to other Locarno signatories, Belgian Government had not yet decided whether to reply orally or in writing, and for the same reason they thought it would be unsuitable for their observations to precede reply of His Majesty's Government. They would therefore be grateful to learn date on which latter is sent and will make their own communication a day or two later.

Repeated to Berlin, Moscow, Paris and Rome.

[3] Cf. No. 381, note 2.

## No. 395

*Sir E. Drummond (Rome) to Sir S. Hoare (Received July 6, 9.30 a.m.)*
*No. 374 Telegraphic [C 5234/55/18]*

ROME, *July 5, 1935, 9.40 p.m.*

Signor Suvich informed me this afternoon that the Italian Government will shortly send a reply to German Government which will certainly follow the same lines as our own although wording will not necessarily be identic.[1]

Repeated to Paris, Berlin, Brussels and Moscow.

[1] Cf. No. 391.

## No. 396

*Minute by Sir R. Vansittart*[1]
*[C 5178/55/18]*

FOREIGN OFFICE, *July 5, 1935*

In the Defence Requirements Committee at the beginning of 1934 I urged upon the Chiefs of Staff that they were not asking enough in the Air. 1935 has borne me out. And I am confident that I shall also be right in my repeated predictions that Germany will be ready for trouble before 1939.

The other main point is our confident taking for granted that we shall always have allies. I have often pointed out that this is probably but not necessarily so. It depends on ourselves; and I am bound to say that H.M.G. have done nothing of late years to warrant the certainty of that assumption. At the present moment they are in fact alienating both France and Italy, while France and Italy have drawn visibly and increasingly together since December 1934. If H.M.G. are not very careful this policy is going to end by

[1] This minute was written in connexion with a memorandum, not printed, reviewing German war preparations and the state of British defence programmes, prepared by Mr. Wigram and Mr. Creswell 'for the information of the Secretary of State and Mr. Eden' at the following week's meetings of the Sub-Committee on Defence Policy and Requirements and of the Committee of Imperial Defence.

landing us in complete isolation at the moment of our greatest weakness. (There is not an item in the whole range of these papers where we are not perilously behind the galloping times; and there are some, such as coast defence, where our position is frankly hopeless.)

I confess, and must record, that this situation causes me, and I think all of us, the gravest anxiety. We have let National Defence run down in the name of various virtues, but really because we wanted the money for other purposes. Of late we have procrastinated in the name of the Disarmament Conference, both before and after its meeting. This w[oul]d perhaps have been dangerous in any case. It becomes far more dangerous if we are to alienate all our prospective friends and allies as well, those in fact who have felt themselves hitherto in the same boat. This alienation has, of late years, been largely influenced by the desire to placate Germany. In reason that is well. But beyond reason—and it goes beyond reason in some quarters, including Ministerial quarters—the pursuit of a jack-o'-lantern will land us irretrievably in a bog. I do not feel at all sure that, in the quarters cited, it is realised what has been the general trend of our policy, and how it tends to be intensified to a point where all other ends but the German end tend to be overlooked.

R. V.

## No. 397

### *Note from Sir S. Hoare to Herr von Hoesch*
### [*C 5027/55/18*]

FOREIGN OFFICE, July 5, 1935

Your Excellency,

I have the honour to refer to the memorandum which Your Excellency was so good as to hand to my predecessor on May 29th,[1] and in which were set forth various considerations regarding the manner in which the Treaty of Locarno was, in the view of the German Government, affected by the terms of the Franco-Soviet Pact of May 2nd. Since then His Majesty's Government in the United Kingdom have had cognisance of the Note which the French Government communicated to the German Government on June 25th[2] in reply to the same memorandum.

2. His Majesty's Government are in entire agreement with the views expressed and the arguments used by the French Government in this Note, and after further consideration of the points made by the German Government they are satisfied that there is nothing in the Franco-Soviet Treaty which either conflicts with the Locarno Treaty or modifies its operation in any way. They likewise agree with the French and German Governments in holding that the provisions of the Locarno Treaty cannot legally be modified or defined by the fact that a treaty has been concluded with a third party by one of the signatories.

3. I would also observe in this connexion that, under the Treaty of Locarno, the United Kingdom, as one of the guarantors of that treaty, has

<hr>

[1] See No. 263.    [2] See No. 391, note 3.

the right and duty of deciding, subject to the findings and the recommendations of the Council of the League of Nations, when and whether the circumstances are such as to call its guarantee into operation, and that this right and duty cannot be affected or altered by the act of another signatory to the treaty.

4. I venture to express the hope that, after examining the views thus set forth in the French Note of June 25th and in this present communication, the German Government will recognise that the rights and duties of the signatories of the Treaty of Locarno, including those of Germany, have in no way been prejudiced or modified by the conclusion of the Franco-Soviet Treaty.[3]

I have, &c.,
SAMUEL HOARE

[3] As soon as this Note had been presented to the German Ambassador the text was telegraphed to Brussels (No. 67), Rome (No. 355), Paris (No. 217 Saving), Moscow (No. 89), and Berlin (No. 147).

## No. 398

*Sir S. Hoare to Sir G. Clerk (Paris)*
*No. 171 Telegraphic: by telephone [C 5302/55/18]*

*Immediate*                                    FOREIGN OFFICE, *July 6, 1935, 1 p.m.*

His Majesty's Government have carefully considered the views expressed by M. Laval to Mr. Eden on the 27th June[1] regarding the conditions on which the French Government would agree to the immediate negotiation between the Locarno Powers of an Air Pact and air limitation agreement. Provided that the French Government are ready to agree to the immediate initiation of discussions between all the Locarno Powers with a view to the negotiation, as distinct from the conclusion, of an Air Pact and air limitation agreement, His Majesty's Government are prepared to accept in principle bilateral arrangements for making effective a general Air Pact, one of these bilateral arrangements being between Great Britain and France, and other bilateral arrangements being open to any of the signatories that desired them. His Majesty's Government are prepared at once to use their influence with the German Government to bring the Germans into the discussions upon this line.

2. If the French Government agree to this, you should ask them to give no publicity whatever to the proposed procedure, until we have had time to explain matters to the German Government and to secure their agreement also. The draft German proposal[2] —on which, as you are aware, no action has been taken—contains a clause according to which bilateral arrangements should be excluded. I naturally hope that there will be no undue insistence on this objection, and that it will be possible for us to remove it speedily, and we would therefore propose to approach the German Government as soon

[1] See Nos. 383 and 384.                    [2] See Annex to No. 263.

as we have the French assent to the course described above. But it would be deplorable if, owing to premature disclosure or distortion to the effect that France and England had concluded a separate agreement, the German objection were increased to the point of obstinacy.

3. For your own information Sir E. Phipps informed me a few days ago that, if we proceeded on these lines, he thought the German Government would agree.

4. Lastly, you should avoid any discussion with M. Laval as to the actual contents of the proposed bilateral technical arrangement, while at the same time making it clear that in accepting the principle of a bilateral arrangement between Great Britain and France, His Majesty's Government must not be considered to have accepted in any way the schemes which have been communicated to us unofficially by the French on two separate occasions.

5. For your own information you should know that these schemes contain various provisions which it would be impossible for us to accept, and which the French Government themselves may well not desire on closer acquaintance. We will of course have to make this fact clear to the French in due course, but we wish if possible to avoid having to do so at the present stage lest the French should fasten on a discussion of such technical details as a reason for delaying the initiation of the general negotiations for the Air Pact itself.

6. You may at the same time assure the French Government that His Majesty's Government will continue to exercise all their endeavours to ensure progress on all points included in the London Communiqué. And you can in this connexion point to the action already twice taken in regard to the Eastern Pact during Herr von Ribbentrop's visit to London.[3] I am, moreover, impressing on all the representatives of the Powers concerned the necessity of adopting a reasonable and constructive attitude, which will facilitate the early meeting of the Danubian Conference.[4]

[3] See No. 356.
[4] Sir G. Clerk handed to M. Laval on July 8 an *aide-mémoire* based on the instructions in this telegram. A copy, not printed, was received in the Foreign Office on July 11.

## No. 399

*Mr. Newton (Berlin) to Sir S. Hoare (Received July 6, 6 p.m.)*
*No. 241 Telegraphic [C 5238/55/18]*

BERLIN, *July 6, 1935, 4.20 p.m.*

Your telegram No. 67 to Brussels.[1]

I have just asked the Secretary of State how matters stand here in regard to the Eastern Pact and whether the German Government are satisfied by French reply to the fears expressed by Germany as to the effect of Franco-Soviet pact on the Treaty of Locarno. Herr von Bülow informed me that while satisfactory in other respects French reply in regard to article 16 of the

See No. 397, note 3.

Covenant only confirmed German fears. He regretted therefore that reply of His Majesty's Government expressed agreement with French note but was glad to learn of the other British views expressed. He did not know yet whether the German Government would try to continue discussion or would merely record their disagreement with the French view.

He was very discouraging over prospects of the Eastern Pact. Germany—as also Poland—was quite satisfied with existing agreements and feared that their force could only be weakened by conclusion of a new multi-lateral engagement. He did not see why Germany should accept and still less why she should actually take the lead in drafting proposals which would bring her no advantage and in fact some disadvantage. I pointed out one advantage was a general one of European appeasement, that Baron von Neurath had furnished Sir John Simon with a note of what Germany was prepared to do[2] and that during Stresa conference Germany had stated she was willing to enter into a pact of non-aggression even if pacts of mutual assistance were separately concluded.[3] He retorted that Germany had not then expected conclusion of such a pact as that between France and the Soviet Government which was specifically directed against her.

Herr von Bülow did not however intimate that Germany would necessarily refuse to proceed with an Eastern Pact but indicated that, if she did so, it would only be if made worth her while. I do not moreover gather in his view conclusion of an air pact would be regarded as quid pro quo.

[2] See Volume XII, No. 651 (p. 739).          [3] See *ibid.*, No. 715.

## No. 400

*Sir G. Clerk (Paris) to Sir S. Hoare (Received July 6, 6.15 p.m.)*
*No. 134 Telegraphic: by telephone [C 5240/55/18]*

*Confidential Immediate*                                         PARIS, *July 6, 1935*

Your telegrams Nos. 171,[1] 172,[2] and 173.[3]

Decyphering was finished at 3.45 p.m., I saw President of the Council at 3.55 and he left to catch his train at 4.10. It was thus impossible to do more than convey conditional offer about air pact and to put question as to your proposing at Rome a meeting of France, Italy and Great Britain under articles 1 and 3 of 1906 agreement.[4] I also emphasised with all the force I could (*a*) that there should be no publicity about proposed air pact procedure until German agreement had been secured and (*b*) the importance of the time factor in the Abyssinian question. I further made it clear that acceptance of principle of bilateral arrangement between Great Britain and France did not mean acceptance of the French schemes.

[1] No. 398.

[2] This telegram of July 6 dealt with matters connected with the Ethiopian question and is not here printed.

[3] In this telegram of 2 p.m. on July 6 Sir G. Clerk was instructed to broach the subject of an air pact with M. Laval before alluding to the Ethiopian question.

[4] This proposition was in Foreign Office telegram No. 172; see note 2 above.

The reaction of Monsieur Laval to both points was not unfavourable but he said that obviously it was impossible to give an answer there and then or until he had consulted his colleagues.

Moreover as regards Abyssinia, he would need to communicate with the French Ambassador at Rome.[5] He was returning from the country on Monday,[6] there was a Council of Ministers on Tuesday and he hoped to let me have a definite answer on Wednesday.

Monsieur Léger has also left for the country but I hope to get into touch with him over the week-end.

[5] Comte de Chambrun.      [6] July 8.

No. 401

Mr. Newton (Berlin) to Sir S. Hoare (Received July 8)<br>
No. 166 Saving: Telegraphic [C 5257/55/18]

BERLIN, July 6, 1935

Your Savingram No. 22.[1]

I took the opportunity today of mentioning to the Secretary of State that I had some reason to think that communication of German air pact proposals to His Majesty's Government alone had given rise to apprehension that Germany might contemplate separate air limitation agreement with Great Britain. I said that there was no such intention on the part of His Majesty's Government and I presumed that there was equally no such intention on Germany's part, seeing that she wished for equality not only with Great Britain but also with France. Herr von Bülow said my presumption was quite correct and that in fact Germany was not interested in air limitation so much as in an air pact.

[1] No. 378.

No. 402

Sir G. Clerk (Paris) to Sir S. Hoare (Received July 9)<br>
No. 957 [C 5280/55/18]

PARIS, July 6, 1935

His Majesty's Representative at Paris presents his compliments to the Secretary of State for Foreign Affairs and has the honour to transmit to him the under-mentioned document.

| Name and Date | Subject |
| --- | --- |
| From: Air Attaché<br>5th July 1935. | French air programme:<br>Question of parity with Germany:<br>Control of aircraft production. |

511

*Group Captain R. M. Field to Sir G. Clerk (Paris)*

Secret                                                          PARIS, *July 5, 1935*

Sir:

I have the honour to report that I called yesterday at the French Air Ministry, where I was informed that the programme establishing a plan for 1500 First-Line aircraft of the Armée de l'Air (including the 'Aviation Autonome Maritime'), in France and North Africa, has been abandoned, and the previous plan for a total of 1010 First-Line aircraft has been reverted to.

I was also informed that the Air Ministry would be prepared to accept parity in the Air with Germany, more particularly as it is recognised that Germany can probably outbuild France if they wish to do so.

My informant also stated that from a military point of view, the French Air Ministry considered that control by means of inspectors attached to each factory capable of producing aircraft or parts of aircraft, would constitute a satisfactory form of guarantee in regard to limitations: that the French were prepared to accept the presence of such foreign inspectors in their factories, but that it seemed more than doubtful if other powers would agree to this.

I have, &c.,
R. M. FIELD

## No. 403

*Letter from Mr. Craigie to Sir W. Selby (Vienna)*

[*A 5777/22/45*]

FOREIGN OFFICE, *July 6, 1935*

My dear Walford,

I can see from your letter of the 24th June to Sargent[1] that you are both concerned about the conclusion of the recent Anglo-German Naval Agreement and worried about its effect on Austrian public opinion.

You will, I hope, shortly be receiving a despatch which will provide you with a certain number of arguments which may help you in rebutting any criticisms that may be directed against this Agreement. From the Austrian point of view, I imagine their main concern is that it might be held to represent a change in the orientation of British foreign policy. This is not, of course, the case, since we think that the Agreement will in future be found to be even more valuable to our friends, the French and the Italians, than it is to ourselves. Already there are signs that the technical advantages of the Agreement are being recognised both in Paris and in Rome but, nevertheless, if we had asked France's permission to accept, this would undoubtedly have been withheld for political and other rather short-sighted reasons. The real answer to any criticism from the Austrians is that the Government were not prepared, so far as naval limitation is concerned, to embark on the game of

---

[1] Not printed.

political huckstering which has resulted, in so far as land and air armaments are concerned, in the Germans working for a peace-time army of 550,000 men and apparently intending to claim an air force of some 2,000 front-line machines. The Agreement represents a purely practical step without any political *arrière pensée*. Without in any way abandoning our attitude regarding the unilateral repudiation of the Treaty of Versailles as set forth in the Geneva resolution,[2] we have taken at least one essential preparatory step in order to render possible that 'general settlement' of outstanding problems which was outlined in the London Communiqué of February 3rd and recommended in the Geneva Resolution itself.

R. L. Craigie[3]

[2] Of April 17, 1935; cf. Volume XII, No. 732.
[3] The formal ending of this letter is missing on the filed copy.

## No. 404

### *Sir S. Hoare to Mr. Aveling*[1] *(Warsaw)*
### *No. 278* [*C 5001/55/18*]

FOREIGN OFFICE, July 8, 1935

Sir,

The Polish Ambassador, at his request, called on me on the 25th June. Count Raczynski, who seemed somewhat apologetic about the visit, said that about the time of the Stresa Conference M. Beck had raised the question of the appropriate procedure to be adopted for substituting new international agreements for those parts of the Treaty of Versailles, including Part V, which might need immediately or in the future to be changed. He stated that Marshal Pilsudski had been obsessed with the need for settling the action that ought to be taken in this connexion.

2. I told the Ambassador that I had had no time to consider the question but that I should, of course, welcome the views upon it of the Polish Government. I said, however, that it seemed to me much more urgent to deal with the more practical questions of disarmament and the Eastern Pact. Whilst His Majesty's Government were anxious to get on with disarmament, particularly air disarmament, as soon as possible, negotiations were almost certain to be held up unless an Eastern pact of non-aggression could be negotiated. As Poland was as greatly interested in the question of disarmament as the United Kingdom, would it not be possible for the Polish Government to make some advance with the Eastern Pact?

3. The Ambassador replied that the Polish Government had now no objection, in principle, to the new version of a multilateral pact of non-aggression and that M. Beck had already said as much. It was, however, necessary for them to reserve the difficult question of Lithuania. Count Raczynski seemed to think that if this question could be settled both Germany and Poland would fall into line.

[1] First Secretary in H.M. Embassy at Warsaw.

# No. 405

## Note on the Demilitarised Zone[1]
### [C 5454/55/18]

FOREIGN OFFICE, *July 9, 1935*

*German Attitude.*

On February 3rd in an interview with the French Ambassador and Sir Eric Phipps, at which a copy of the Anglo-French communiqué was handed to him, Herr Hitler stated that France had shown no gratitude for his renunciation of Alsace Lorraine and the acceptance of the demilitarised zone but always asked for further sacrifices from Germany. 'If this continued, Germany would be obliged finally to declare that that zone must be abolished or at least made reciprocal. He indicated that in any case German acceptance of the zone was not going to be eternal.'[2] He conveyed the impression that German acquiescence in the existence of the demilitarised zone would only last so long as the German Army was in the process of expansion and not a day longer.

During the Berlin conversations[3] Herr Hitler maintained the attitude which he had previously reaffirmed on several occasions that he regarded himself as bound by the Treaty of Locarno. Sir Eric Phipps observed that it was difficult to reconcile these various declarations with the language used by Herr Hitler on February 3rd.

More recently, however, the attitude of the German Government has been more moderate, and on March 19th our Military Attaché was categorically 'informed by the Reichswehrministerium that the German Government had decided to make no (military) changes in the demilitarised zone which might be considered to alter the Treaty status'.[4]

Evidence, however, has been collecting that Germany would not be averse to re-militarise in the Rhineland if there were any indication that the other signatories of Locarno did not intend to honour their obligations (see attached memorandum by Mr. Perowne).[5]

Herr Hitler stated in his speech on May 21st that 'the German Government . . .[6] will painstakingly observe any treaty which it voluntarily signs even if it was concluded before its accession to power. It will, in particular, therefore observe and fulfil all obligations arising out [of] the Locarno Pact so long as the other parties to the Treaty for their part are also willing to stand by this Pact. The German Government regards the respecting of the demilitarised zone as an exceedingly difficult contribution for a sovereign State to make to the appeasement of Europe. It feels, however, obliged to point

---

[1] A note on the file records that 'this note was prepared for Mr. Wigram's recent draft memo. on Germany'; cf. No. 396, note 1.

[2] See Volume XII, No. 408.

[3] On March 25–26, 1935; see *ibid.*, No. 651.    [4] See *ibid.*, No. 615.

[5] Not attached to filed copy of note. The reference appears to have been to Mr. Perowne's memorandum of May 21; cf. No. 149, note 3.

[6] Punctuation as in original quotation.

to the fact that the continued increase of troops on the other side cannot in any way be regarded as supplementing these endeavours'.

*Infringements.*

The Germans have been careful hitherto to avoid any open infringements of the demilitarised zone clauses. Military possibilities in the Rhineland have certainly not been neglected, but the Landespolizei (police quartered in barracks) and S.S. formations have been used for the purpose. We have various indications from secret sources that certain defensive works have been constructed, and there has certainly been great activity in training police, S.S. and other National Socialist forces.

Sir Eric Phipps reported (despatch No. 341[7] of April 6th) that 'the Army Command objects to the demilitarised zone not only on obvious strategic grounds but also because the population is losing military feeling, a fact which is proved by their difficulty in obtaining the proper quota of recruits from this area'.

In general, the attitude of the German military authorities seems to have been to prepare the area as far as possible for defence, for which purpose the open use of Reichsheer resources is not necessary, and to strengthen their strategical position in this way.

Considerable precautions have been taken to ensure that the recruiting, in accordance with the recent Defence Law,[8] of conscripted persons in the Rhineland should be carried out without violating the Demilitarisation Clauses. The French Embassy in Berlin have recently been negotiating with the Germans on this subject,[9] and a written reply to the French Chargé is now outstanding and was promised by Herr von Bülow, who gave assurances which seemed to amount to a satisfactory outcome of the question.

[7] Volume XII, No. 700.  [8] Of May 21, 1935; cf. No. 292.
[9] Cf. No. 308; see also *D.G.F.P.*, Series C, vol. iv, No. 163.

## No. 406

*Memorandum by Sir R. Vansittart*

[*C 5355/55/18*]

FOREIGN OFFICE, *July 9, 1935*

The German Ambassador came to see me this afternoon and informed me that the French Ambassador in Berlin had asked the German Government to communicate to him the German draft for an Air Pact.

The German Government, Herr von Hoesch said, did not feel at present disposed to do so, as they did not think this might be the quickest method of achieving progress. His Government considered that the best method of procedure would be if we would circulate in one document the texts of all the proposals that had been made—French, British and German. The German Government thought that the British Government was the most suitable one to undertake this step. I promised to consult the Secretary of State on the matter.

The Ambassador then went on to enquire what I thought the prospects of progress were in regard to an Air Pact. I replied to him much on the same lines as I had spoken to Herr von Ribbentrop.[1] The Ambassador's objections were much the same. He added, however, with considerable emphasis, that the French and the Russians had concluded an alliance against Germany and that the Germans were now being asked to condone and regularise this action by concluding a general eastern pact of non-aggression.

I told him that I did not think he was accurately or fairly describing the Franco-Russian Agreement, and I deprecated any exaggeration of its effects. The German Government and the Ambassador himself, I observed, had often and, I did not doubt, truthfully asserted that they had no intention of attacking either France or Russia, and there was not in that case much reality in the agreement. In any case we must look at the situation as practical men, and I felt sure that no real progress would be made with the Air Agreement, which we both desired, unless we were prepared to work for progress on a wider front as well.

The Ambassador was most reasonable and amiable, but he said he felt it likely that his Government would see considerable difficulty in making any forward move in regard to the Eastern Pact.

R. V.

[1] See No. 356.

## No. 407

*Sir S. Hoare to Sir R. Lindsay (Washington)*
*No. 604 [A 6077/22/45]*

FOREIGN OFFICE, *July 9, 1935*

Sir,

The American Ambassador discussed with me this morning the future arrangements for further naval discussions. He is leaving for the United States at the end of the month and is then to have conversations on the subject with the President and the Secretary of State. After recounting to me in detail the events that led up to the last discussions and describing to me the point that was now reached, he drew the conclusions, firstly, that publicity, by his own admission due to the American press, had done great harm, secondly, that if there is to be a Conference, the Conference must be only summoned to confirm arrangements that have already been made between the Powers, and, thirdly, that there would be great advantage in the American Government being closely and constantly informed as to the course of the conversations that we are having with the various European Powers.

2. I told him that I had not had time to put myself in possession of the details of the question, that I would convey to the Admiralty and my own advisers the views that he had expressed and that I should hope to give him

some further information before he leaves for America at the end of the month.[1]

I am, &c.,

SAMUEL HOARE

[1] For Mr. Bingham's report of this conversation see *F.R.U.S. 1935*, vol. i, pp. 76–7. In Foreign Office despatch No. 628 of July 16 Sir S. Hoare informed Sir R. Lindsay that, during a conversation that day with Mr. Bingham, the United States Ambassador had 'insisted once again upon the need for the closest possible liaison' between the British and United States Governments and said he was prepared to wait for an answer to the questions raised at the meeting on July 9 until he saw Sir S. Hoare again before his departure for America. See No. 438 below.

## No. 408

*Mr. Newton (Berlin) to Sir S. Hoare (Received July 11)*

*No. 678 [C 5333/55/18]*

BERLIN, *July 9, 1935*

Sir,

In my telegram No. 241[1] of the 6th July I had the honour to summarise an explanation of the German attitude towards the Franco-Soviet Pact and the Eastern Pact given to me by the Secretary of State.

2. In the course of our conversation Herr von Bülow also mentioned that Germany had to be on her guard against French attempts to secure the right to decide unilaterally the circumstances which would justify action against Germany. Such attempts had been made more than once, but had never been admitted by the League of Nations and were not admitted in the Treaty of Locarno. He thought that we might not have been so ready to agree with the French views had we been in the position of Germany, against whom the Franco-Soviet Pact was specifically directed. It was no answer for France to suggest that Germany could accede to the Pact herself, since it was already known that Germany in fact could not accede. In the circumstances such an intimation was rather the admission of a bad conscience.

3. Herr von Bülow's objections to the Franco-Soviet Pact may be genuine, but the subsequent coupling of it with the Eastern Pact would seem to be an afterthought. Herr Dieckhoff[2] informed me some days ago that, when the possible effect of the Franco-Soviet Pact on the Treaty of Locarno was first considered, it was by no means certain that the German Government would take any action in the matter, and I gathered that the utmost at first contemplated was some statement putting on record the German point of view. Moreover the coupling of the two questions seems quite inconsistent with the reply to the enquiry made by His Majesty's Government during the Stresa Conference.[3] To a charge of such inconsistency Herr von Bülow himself seemed indifferent, while no doubt the German Government were very

[1] No. 399.
[2] Herr Dieckhoff was Director of Department III in the German Ministry of Foreign Affairs.      [3] See Volume XII, Nos. 715 and 717.

517

disappointed with the result of the concession made to the Stresa Powers. Even if it were possible, however, to convict them of an attempt to go back on what they said, they could doubtless find plenty of other excuses for delaying indefinitely their adhesion to an Eastern Pact. Herr von Bülow, for example, reiterated in his conversation with me the technical difficulties mentioned in Sir E. Phipps's telegram No. 161, Saving,[4] of the 24th June. He evidently thinks that Germany should in any case refuse to take the initiative in drafting the pact and thus leave herself free to object to drafts prepared by others. It is moreover a question who is to prepare such a draft. Herr von Bülow said he was uncertain whether France would be a party to an Eastern Pact of non-aggression. From another source I have heard it suggested that Germany may enquire whether the Pact is to be regional or general. If regional, France could presumably not take the lead in drafting a pact; if general, Germany might insist that both France and Great Britain should participate. Nevertheless, in spite of all the difficulties indicated, Herr von Bülow's remarks did not contain any refusal of an Eastern Pact: in fact, by asking what advantage there was in it for Germany, he implied that she might enter into one if it were made worth her while.

4. Germany herself, as Herr von Bülow remarked to me, is not a party to the Stresa programme, so why should she go out of her way to promote the aims of other Powers. If something is wanted from her, something must be given in return. He did not respond to a question that the facilitation of an Air Pact would be such a return. Nevertheless no secret is made of the fact that Germany would welcome an Air Pact. If therefore its advantages are thought to be greater for Germany than for France there seems no reason why its conclusion should not be accepted as a *quid pro quo*. To make it acceptable, however, some definite assurance might be required, and not a mere hint that once Germany has committed herself to an Eastern Pact other Powers will be more ready to consider an Air Pact. Although Herr von Bülow may now be unresponsive to the bait of an Air Pact and cynical in regard to Germany's reply to the enquiry made from Stresa, perhaps Herr Hitler himself might then show a better appreciation of Germany's good name and a greater desire to contribute to the pacification of Europe.

5. In conclusion, I would like to draw attention to the fundamental change which has taken place in Germany's bargaining position since it has become apparent that her open decision to rearm will not be effectively challenged. Hitherto it might be thought that Germany would pay a price for the right to rearm and that this price might be a contribution to French security. The boot is now on the other leg; the longer the limitation of arms is postponed, the stronger Germany becomes relative to France, so that delay is to Germany's advantage. The greater the complications put in the way of arms limitation by an Eastern Pact and a Danube Pact, &c., the greater the delay and the better for Germany. In time, of course, Germany's economic extravagances may come home to roost and exercise a chastening political effect. But the Bankruptcy Court is not yet casting any shadows on political and

4 No. 373.

military fields whereas France is thought to be in much more imminent danger of suffering from internal political and financial complications.

I have, &c.,<br>B. C. NEWTON

## No. 409

Sir G. Clerk (Paris) to Sir S. Hoare (Received July 11, 1 a.m.)<br>No. 136 Telegraphic: by telephone [C 5324/55/18]

PARIS, July 10, 1935

My immediately preceding telegram[1] and your telegram No. 171.[2]

Monsieur Laval then turned to the question of the air pact. He began by saying that he would send a written answer but that I could inform you straight away that he noted with satisfaction the acceptance by His Majesty's Government in principle of bilateral arrangements, and then broke off and gave me the text of Memorandum on our offer which had been prepared for him in the Quai d'Orsay.

2. The Memorandum, text[3] of which will be sent by air mail tomorrow morning, recalls that Monsieur Laval, in his last interview with Mr. Eden,[4] made an immediate negotiation for an air pact dependent on two indispensable conditions:

(a) An undertaking to respect effectively the interdependence of the different points of the programme set forth in London communiqué of February last.

(b) An undertaking not to conclude any operative air pact unless completed by bilateral agreements. On the other hand Monsieur Laval had admitted that these two indispensable conditions need not necessarily be formulated as such from beginning of negotiations, provided it was clearly understood between Great Britain and France that they remained so in reality.

3. In aide-mémoire of July 8th (a précis of relevant parts of your telegram No. 171 which Monsieur Laval had asked me to give him to refresh his memory of what I had said to him on July 6th[5]) His Majesty's Government accepts in principle bilateral agreements and in particular a bilateral arrangement between France and Great Britain. Thus on this point the French request is met.

4. His Majesty's Government however expressed the hope that for the moment strict secrecy will be observed in order that they may have time to secure assent of German Government to this solution. Thus an Anglo-German negotiation may be started at once. Therein lies a risk, but it seems difficult to refuse British request provided it is clearly understood that general

---

[1] Not here printed.      [2] No. 398.

[3] Received in the Foreign Office on July 11 as enclosure in Paris despatch No. 993; not printed.

[4] See Nos. 383 and 384.      [5] See No. 398, note 4 and No. 400.

negotiations will only begin when His Majesty's Government, having secured the assent of German Government to the French view, will find themselves able to adhere absolutely to the principle of bilateral agreements.

5. Memorandum then points out that our acceptance of principle does not imply acceptance of details of French schemes, a reservation which is natural, and against which the Quai d'Orsay cannot protest but the hope is expressed that greater part of French suggestions will be retained.

6. As regards other points in communiqué of February 3rd, the memorandum notes that His Majesty's Government affirm their readiness to use their influence to ensure progress on negotiations as a whole. Again his Majesty's Government claim that intention is to negotiate, as distinct from concluding, air pact and admit that the negotiation of an air pact is not separate from an air limitation agreement. Moreover they reaffirm their interest in the conclusion of Eastern and Danubian Pacts.

7. On the other hand no mention is expressly made of territorial armaments. In this respect it is the more necessary to recall original Quai d'Orsay point of view that Ministry of War has expressly linked its assent to negotiation of an air pact to that of an agreement in regard to territorial armaments. It is thus important that there should be joint representation upon this point.

8. I presume that in due course we shall receive a formal note on these lines and I would only observe that I reminded Monsieur Laval that purpose of our demand for secrecy and of our intention to approach German Government forthwith was in order to induce Berlin to waive the objections which we knew were held there to bilateral agreements. The Quai d'Orsay fears of an Anglo-German negotiation therefore seemed to me exaggerated. I also reminded Monsieur Laval that you had expressly assured French Government that His Majesty's Government would continue to exercise all their endeavours to ensure progress on *all* points included in London communiqué and I surmised that reason for special reference to Eastern and Danubian pacts was because, on those two points, you had already made, or were about to make definite efforts to secure progress.

## No. 410

### Report by Captain Muirhead-Gould[1]
### B. 5/35 [A 6432/22/45]

BERLIN, *July 11, 1935*

*Anglo-German Naval Agreement—Views on*

During my recent visits to Latvia and Lithuania I had many opportunities of discussing the Anglo-German Naval Agreement with officers and politicians of these Nations.

2. In Latvia, both in Libau and Riga, I found a general feeling of uneasiness at the possible results of the agreement, but at the same time a disposition

[1] A copy of this report by H.M. Naval Attaché at Berlin was transmitted to the Foreign Office by Sir E. Phipps on July 15, received July 19.

to look at the agreement from the British point of view, and to admit the value of the agreement as a basis or starting point for future naval limitation.

3. In Lithuania, however, the opposition to the agreement was uncompromising and universal. I was told 'that England had broken the Treaty of Versailles every bit as much as Germany, and in thus permitting Germany (and even encouraging her) to become Mistress of the Baltic England had delivered the unfortunate Baltic States to the mercy of an implacable foe'.

4. The following notes are based on the substance of various conversations, and do not necessarily represent my own views:—

(*a*) At Geneva and at Stresa England, France and Italy presented a united front to Germany, which, had it been allowed to develop, would inevitably have forced Germany to come to terms on land, on sea, and in the air, since those three Powers would have had the unanimous support of the Little Entente, Poland and the Baltic States. As a result of England's sudden reversal of policy and secession from Geneva and Stresa, Germany would now feel that she had convinced England of her growing power, and of England's need of Germany as an ally. Germany would now naturally assume an even more uncompromising attitude, and everyone of her neighbours must expect new demands. Lithuania in particular, was in a dangerous position.

(*b*) It was doubtful whether Russia would so readily accept Germany as Mistress of the Baltic, and though in recent years Russia had done little in the way of big-ship construction, she had built a number of destroyers and submarines, and it must now be expected that Russia would make a determined effort to keep abreast [of] Germany in small-craft strength. It was not too much to say that a race in naval armaments would take place between Russia and Germany, and this would cause the political relations between these countries to deteriorate still further. The possibilities of war between Russia and Germany could no longer be excluded.

(*c*) A war between Russia and Germany would be bound to drag in at least all the Baltic States, if not all Europe. Russia's first thought would be to overrun Estonia so as to seize Reval and the Islands, while Germany would at once occupy Lithuania, partly from sound strategical reasons, and partly from a desire for revenge. Latvia would become the actual battleground. Germany would have to make use of the Corridor, and so would probably make considerable sacrifices elsewhere to get Poland to take part on Germany's side. In view of Poland's antipathy to Lithuania this might not prove very difficult. What then would be the attitude of France and Italy and on which side would England fight?

(*d*) It seemed to be the general opinion in the Baltic States that England had lost her Naval Superiority in the North Sea, and that a German Fleet 35% of the strength of the British Fleet, would, in fact, be considerably superior to the British Fleet in home waters. At the same time England dared not weaken her forces in the Mediterranean, since she had now offended both France and Italy, nor dared she weaken her Far Eastern Fleet, since Japan was only waiting for an opportunity to adopt a dominating policy in those waters, and any weakening of the British Fleet there might result in the loss of Hong Kong.

(e) Nobody believed that Great Britain or France or the League would be able to stop Italy making war on Abyssinia in September. And nobody believed that Italy realised what she had taken on. A campaign at least as severe and prolonged as the Spanish and French operations in Morocco was everywhere expected.

(f) But once this war started the League of Nations, already dead, must quickly be buried for the sake of decency. And on what would Great Britain's policy then depend? She would no longer be able to look to France for friendship. Italy would be resentful of Great Britain's attempted interference in Abyssinia, and Russia hated Great Britain as the most dangerous foe of Communism. Germany would be England's only friend in Europe![2]

G. C. MUIRHEAD-GOULD

[2] In an undated minute on the filed copy Mr. Craigie commented: 'One wd. think from this Lithuanian stuff that, had it not been for the agreement, Germany wd. have built nothing!'

## No. 411

*Admiralty to Foreign Office (Received July 13)*

[*C 5401/55/18*]

Secret                                                                              ADMIRALTY, *July 12, 1935*

Sir,

I have laid before my Lords Commissioners of the Admiralty your letter of the 11th June,[1] asking for the views of the Admiralty on the question whether vital British interests would be affected by a disregard by Germany—

(1) Of Articles 195 and 196 of the Treaty of Versailles, forbidding the existence of fortifications on the Baltic coast and the refortification of the North Sea Coasts and of East Prussia, &c.; and

(2) Of Article 115 forbidding the re-establishment of fortifications, &c., on the Islands of Heligoland and Dune.

2. My Lords assume that the circumstances in which we might become involved in war with Germany are most probably those arising out of our commitments under the Locarno Treaty, and the Air Pact, if the latter is concluded. It is, and presumably will continue to be, no part of our policy to enter into commitments in respect of Eastern European affairs.

3. On this assumption, My Lords consider that the only British interest which will be directly affected in the event of war by the situation in the Baltic will be the security of our trade in that area. This trade is not vital; alternative sources of supply for the commodities obtained from the Baltic countries can be found. In general, the additional security which would be afforded to German Naval Bases by the removal of the restrictions in Article

[1] Not printed.

522

195 would increase the effectiveness of the German naval forces and tend to limit our operations. Much the same considerations apply to Article 196, which forbids the increase of existing fortifications or the construction of new fortifications within 50 kilometres of the German coast or on German Islands off that coast.

4. The general conclusions which My Lords have reached regarding the effect of the removal of the restrictions in both articles are as follows:—

(a) The possibility of protecting our trade in the Baltic will not be determined by the existence or otherwise of gun defences in the area covered by the articles.

(b) The possibility of our undertaking offensive operations in the Baltic would be circumscribed, since such operations could only be undertaken with an increased risk of loss that we might be unable to accept, or these operations would have to be limited in their scope.

(c) The strategical situation would be altered to our disadvantage, but it cannot be said that any vital British interest would be directly affected.

5. At the same time, My Lords desire me to point out that while, in their opinion, no vital British interests would be affected by the removal of the restrictions, their retention is advantageous to us in that it greatly facilitates the task of penetrating and operating in the Baltic. With fortifications, the entry of large ships into the Baltic would be difficult, and moreover, if Germany were to take action in the direction of re-establishing or strengthening her fortifications, it could only be with the intention of closing the entrance to the Baltic or, at any rate, of controlling it.

6. As regards Article 115, the refortification of Heligoland and the reconstruction of the Harbour Works would have the effect of extending and strengthening Germany's defensive position in the Bight. Heligoland is not, however, sufficiently far in advance of the important German Naval Bases in that area to facilitate to any material extent offensive operations against ourselves. My Lords consider, therefore, that although it would be strategically to our advantage that Heligoland should remain undefended, its fortification cannot be said to constitute a threat to our security. Nevertheless, the Secretary of State may consider that any action of the German Government in the direction of removing the restrictions, so far as it arises from the intention of re-establishing the fortifications and works and is not merely due to the wish to attain equality of status, is hardly consistent with the desire to reach, and remain on, the friendliest terms with this country. Such action clearly would not be viewed in this country with any favour.

7. Copies of this letter have been sent to the War Office and Air Ministry.

I am, &c.,

J. S. Barnes[2]

[2] A Principal Assistant Secretary in the Admiralty.

## No. 412

### Letter from Sir R. Vansittart to Sir W. Fisher[1]

[C 4878/55/18]

FOREIGN OFFICE, *July 15, 1935*

My dear Warren,

Consideration of the problem of the financing of German rearmament has led me to wonder whether in a few months' time, when public opinion has become accustomed to Germany's rearmament as something reasonable and natural, we may not see the German Government start a campaign in the City in order to prepare the way for a new loan to Germany: this loan would no doubt ostensibly have the object of enabling her to put her financial house in order and to revive her import trade, but in reality would be nothing more than the financing of her expenditure on armaments, which is now being met by short-term borrowing in the domestic market.

I do not of course know how probable such an eventuality is; on this no doubt the Treasury are in a better position to decide than we are in the Foreign Office and I should be glad to have your views. Meanwhile you may perhaps think it worth while to mention this possibility to the Governor of the Bank in order that he may be on his guard against any German advance of this sort. Indeed I personally feel clear that you sh[oul]d do so.

Yours ever,

R. VANSITTART

[1] Cf. No. 361, note 3.

## No. 413

### Note on Interim Report of the Sub-Committee of the Committee of Imperial Defence on Defence Policy and Requirements[1]

[C 5539/55/18]

FOREIGN OFFICE, *July 16, 1935*

The only point which concerns the Foreign Office in this report, whose object is to provide air defence not only against France as hitherto arranged but against attack from Germany and the Low Countries, is that of the date of completion of the preparations.

The original proposal provided for the completion of stage 1 by 1940 and stage 3 by *1950*. The Home Defence Sub-Committee (see page 3 of HDC 16 M)[2] agreed with the opinion expressed by the Brooke-Popham Sub-Committee[3] that '*the air defence of Great Britain cannot be considered as providing*

[1] This Interim Report (D.P.R. 7), not printed, was circulated as C.P. 144 (35) for consideration by the Cabinet at their meeting on July 18. A minute on the file by Mr. Wigram states that this Note had been asked for by Sir S. Hoare.

[2] The reference is to a memorandum of April 11, 1935, of the Home Defence Committee of the Committee of Imperial Defence.

[3] This Sub-Committee had been formed on August 2, 1934, to 'prepare a plan for the reorientation of the defensive system of the Air Defence of Great Britain in the light of

*an adequate security until this third stage is completed'*. The Home Defence Committee proposed two schemes for acceleration, one (called Scheme (A)) which would provide for the completion of stages 1 and 2 by 1940 and that of stage 3 by 1942, and another (called Scheme (B)) which would complete stages 1 and 2 by 1943 and stage 3 by 1946. The Chiefs of Staff expressed their preference for Scheme (A) and hold the view that this scheme 'is the only one which, from the air defence point of view, can be considered satisfactory'.

The Sub-Committee on Defence Policy, in the Interim Report now before the Cabinet, reaches the conclusion that *certain parts only of stage 1* of the original proposal should be completed by 1940, certain other parts being reserved for further discussion; this recommendation is subject to the further consideration now being given (presumably by the Sub-Committee itself) to the rate at which the stages of the whole original proposal should be completed.

It is relevant to point out that this conclusion not only fails to provide for work being done in accordance with either of the two schemes for acceleration, but does not, apparently, even represent a beginning of the work being undertaken on the scale of the original unaccelerated proposal. The differences from the original proposal are, however, slight.[4]

Germany's rearmament in the air and the consequent possibilities of attack from her direction'. The Chairman, Air Chief Marshal Sir Robert Brooke-Popham, was Air Officer Commanding-in-Chief Air Defence of Great Britain.

[4] Minutes on the above Note include the following by Mr. Orme Sargent and Sir R. Vansittart. 'It is certainly discouraging when one realises that this three months' progress through this maze of committees and sub-committees has been backward instead of forward. O. G. Sargent. July 17th, 1935.' 'I agree with Mr. Sargent. We have for years laboured under the burden of these endless committees and sub-committees which spend nothing but time. The results are nearly always astonishingly futile, particularly in this matter of Air Defence. Our view is a short and simple one. Anything that fails to provide security by *1938* is inadequate and blind. Even Scheme A, therefore, is not what our situation and the situation of Europe require. And now apparently we do not seem to be getting even Scheme A after all this talking and writing. We may well pay dearly for these futilities. R. V. July 17.' At its next meeting the Defence Requirements Committee accepted the advice of the Foreign Office that January 1, 1939, was now reckoned to be 'the latest date which could reasonably be assumed for the purpose of our own security, and it could not be guaranteed that Germany would remain quiescent until then . . .'

## No. 414

*Letter from Sir W. Selby (Vienna) to Mr. Craigie (Received July 26)*

[*A 6590/22/45*]

VIENNA, *July 16, 1935*

My dear Craigie,

Very many thanks for your letter.[1] Of course I appreciated the reasons for the signature of the agreement, but it shook the position here badly for a moment owing in particular to the French and Italian reaction, and as I now

[1] No. 403.

have some acquaintance with how to deal with such developments I considered that the best plan was to keep my counsel, refrain from all discussion, and allow the little storm of apprehension to calm down. In the state of nervous tension which unfortunately prevails in this capital, argument at such moments only makes matters worse. For a few days the agreement was regarded as a stupendous German success, and this view was held at the Ballhaus Platz[2] although expressed in more guarded terms than outside.

Now I am glad to say I think the temporary impression has passed, and so far as we are concerned all has been forgotten in Austrian pleasure at the explicit pronouncement of the Secretary of State in the House as regards Austria.[3] It has been interpreted on all hands as: no further separate agreement with Germany of any kind without the interests of Austria also being cared for, and I think we can leave matters at that.

In the meantime many thanks for your letter and the arguments, which incidentally I should have used had I in any way been pressed.

Yours ever,<br>
W. SELBY

² i.e. in Austrian Government circles.   ³ See 304 *H.C. Deb.* 5 *s.*, col. 5.

## No. 415

*Memorandum by the Foreign Office and Admiralty on the future course of naval negotiations*[1]

*[A 6525/22/45]*

*Secret*                                          FOREIGN OFFICE, *July 18, 1935*

There are four good reasons why a naval conference—between the five principal naval Powers at least—should be held this year. The first is that both the Washington and the London Naval Treaties provide for the holding of such a conference and that a postponement until next year by the formal and unanimous assent of the five signatory Powers would not only produce a bad psychological impression, but would be generally regarded as a confession of failure. The second reason is that our own Admiralty—and presumably also the naval authorities of other Powers—should know not later than the end of this year what are to be the sizes of the ships (with the maximum gun calibres) to be constructed in the various categories from 1937 onwards. Otherwise it is impossible to make the necessary technical preparations in time or to frame the financial estimates with any degree of accuracy. No capital ship, for instance, can be laid down early in 1937 unless provision is

¹ After receiving the approval of Sir S. Hoare and other members of the Ministerial Naval Committee this paper was printed as N.C.M. (35) 58, with a covering note of August 1 saying that 'the action proposed therein has now received the concurrence of the members of the Committee'. Mr. MacDonald had communicated his views on July 24 and minuted the memorandum as follows:— 'I favour attempt. We may be in a fix however unless we get something out of the Conference. In any event, do not lay ourselves open to the accusation that we, having been asked, failed to call the Conference. If we think no good can come out of it, get the others to refuse. Nothing will justify our doing nothing. J.R.M.'

made in the 1936 Naval Estimates. The third reason is that in all Admiralties the personnel dealing with these problems of naval limitation changes at relatively short intervals, with the result that the advantages derived from the personal contacts and understandings established during the last year of negotiation are liable to be lost and the whole work of consultation may have to be recommenced *ab initio*. The fourth reason is that, if the Conference is postponed until 1936, the political disturbance in this country caused by the approach of the General Election may seriously interfere with the preparatory work as well as with the Conference itself.

There remain five months in the present year, of which August is usually of little use for purposes of negotiation. The Japanese Government will require notice of at least two months, so that, if the Conference is to be held in November, the invitations would require to be issued in September. Taking into account inevitable postponements, it would be wise to fix some time in October as our first date for a Conference. Time for further preparatory work is therefore very limited.

The conclusion of the Anglo-German naval agreement has profoundly modified the situation as it existed before the opening of the Anglo-German conversations. On the quantitative side we have now two fixed points on which to base future naval relationships—parity with the United States and a 35 per cent. ratio with Germany. On the other hand, France appears— temporarily, at all events—to be less disposed than she was to co-operate with us in promoting an international agreement for quantitative limitation. Valuable time has already been lost owing to the disinclination of the French Government to send experts to London for the purpose of examining the situation with us and exchanging programmes. Italy in present circumstances is likely to follow France's lead in this matter of naval limitation.

Without under-estimating the importance of quantitative limitation, which prevents the race in numbers of units and looms so large in the public eye, it is felt that the elimination of competition in the evolution of sizes and types of gun calibres is a matter of even more urgent importance. This question was dealt with in a Memorandum by the Chief of the Naval Staff circulated in N.C.(M)(35)23,[2] in which he stated his view that 'it is of outstanding importance to the British Commonwealth to have the sizes of ships fixed as low as possible, but almost any limit is better than none.' In view, therefore, of the delay caused by French hesitations, a change of tactics appears desirable and the following proposal is put forward for consideration:—

(1) Communicate to the French and Italian Governments a paper showing—

(a) The qualitative limits which we understand would be acceptable to the European countries so far consulted (United Kingdom, France, Italy and Germany); and

(b) The lowest qualitative limits which we think are likely to secure general acceptance (including, that is, the requirements of the United States and Japan).

[2] This memorandum of October 30, 1934, is not here printed.

527

(c) Explain to the French and Italian Governments that, without abandoning in any way their search for some form of quantitative limitation likely to secure general assent, His Majesty's Government feel that it is of even more urgent importance to lay the basis of an agreement on qualitative limitation. Point out that qualitative limitation is immediately effective in limiting naval armaments and checking future expenditure, whereas quantitative limitation, by its nature, takes a period of years to come to fruition and that from a technical point of view the conclusion of a quantitative agreement is, therefore, less immediately urgent. Ask whether they agree, and whether the list of qualitative limitations acceptable to the European Powers correctly represents the views of the French and Italian Governments. Say that, if there is a sufficient measure of agreement on qualitative limitation to make general agreement possible, we think a conference of the Washington Powers should meet in October to reach agreement on this branch of the subject and, if possible, on some form of quantitative limitation also.

(2) Make a similar communication, *mutatis mutandis*, to the German and Soviet Governments.

(3) Inform the United States and Japanese Governments of the communication we are addressing to the European Governments and of our view that a Conference of the Washington Powers should, if possible, meet in October. Ask the United States Government, orally and very confidentially, whether they would be prepared to come into a general agreement regulating qualitative limitation only, should it prove impossible to secure any form of agreement on quantitative limitation. We could assure the United States Government that the absence of any general quantitative agreement would not in any way impair our acceptance of the principle of parity as between the navies of the British Commonwealth and the United States. (It is unnecessary and undesirable to make a similar confidential enquiry of the Japanese Government for the moment, because we know they are opposed to the idea of an agreement limited to qualitative limitation. But it remains to be seen whether they would adhere to this attitude in the face of a general agreement in the opposite sense among the remaining Powers.)

(4) It will, of course, be necessary to keep the Dominions and India fully informed as to the procedure we propose and the steps we are taking by way of approach to foreign Governments. The Washington Treaty was signed by representatives of Canada, the Commonwealth of Australia, New Zealand, the Union of South Africa and India, and the London Naval Treaty by representatives of the same Dominions and of India, and of the Irish Free State, and it follows that the Dominions should be invited to be represented at the proposed naval conference.

The difficulty in respect of a single quota for the Members of the Commonwealth as a whole, or, alternatively, separate quotas for each Member, has still to be solved, but this point does not seem to affect the immediate steps we have in view, and in so far as qualitative limitation, which is the principal subject for immediate discussion with foreign Powers, is concerned, the point does not arise. Nevertheless, it will probably be desirable to have further discussion on the question of Dominion quotas before any Conference meets, so as to reach prior agreement with the Dominions on this question.

(5) If the replies received are sufficiently encouraging, it would be for His Majesty's Government to consider whether they would summon in London a conference of the five Washington Powers (to be expanded afterwards into a general Conference of the naval Powers), the primary purpose of which would be to secure international agreement on the qualitative limitation of naval armaments. A second purpose would be to consider the British plan for quantitative limitation by means of unilateral declarations in regard to future constructions, and any quantitative plans which other countries may wish to put forward. By placing the emphasis on the qualitative side of the question, we could diminish the risk of the conference being regarded as a failure should no agreement be reached on quantitative limitation.

It will be seen that action in the sense of paragraphs (1)–(3) above would not commit His Majesty's Government either to summon a Conference or to decide on the venue for a Conference. The final decision of His Majesty's Government on this matter could only be reached when the results of the action under paragraphs (1)–(3) had been analysed and considered. But it is to be hoped that action as proposed in paragraphs (1)–(3) may be authorised as soon as possible in order that the short time still available for the summoning of a Conference this year may be fully utilised.

## No. 416

### Sir S. Hoare to Sir G. Clerk (Paris)
### No. 1344 [C 5418/55/18]

FOREIGN OFFICE, *July 18, 1935*

Sir,

You will recollect that during Mr. Eden's visit to Paris on June 21st, M. Massigli gave to Mr. Strang, privately and unofficially, a memorandum on land armaments.[1] This memorandum had apparently been prepared for M. Laval's use during his conversations with Mr. Eden and clearly could not be regarded as in any sense an official document.

2. On the other hand, this document and the references to the question of land armaments made by M. Laval to Mr. Eden have led to the position of this question being reviewed here, and a memorandum has been prepared, of which copies are enclosed.

3. I should be glad if you would find an opportunity of speaking to M. Laval in a friendly and unofficial manner in the sense particularly of paragraphs 11 and 13 of this memorandum. You should impress upon him the desirability of the French Government, if indeed they attach importance to

---

[1] For the gist of this memorandum, see paragraph 12 of the enclosure below.

land armaments, coming down to realities and making to Germany some offer, both as regards effectives and heavy material, which there is some chance of her accepting. Possibly as, for reasons which I quite understand, M. Laval is occupied with many other questions at the moment, it would be useful if your representations to him could be duplicated by a conversation between a member of the Embassy staff and the Secretary-General or the competent official in the Ministry for Foreign Affairs.

I am, &c.,<br>SAMUEL HOARE

ENCLOSURE* IN No. 416

FOREIGN OFFICE, July 15, 1935

Memorandum on limitation of French and German land armaments

On the 29th January, 1934, we circulated to the Powers a disarmament proposal[2] which provided (1) for parity in effectives as between France, Germany and Italy at a figure somewhere between 200,000 and 300,000 men stationed in the home country (though we expressed a preference for 200,000 men, which was the figure mentioned in the United Kingdom Draft Disarmament Convention, rather than 300,000, which was the figure claimed by Germany), and for short-term service of twelve months; and (2) for limitation of tanks to 16 tons (Germany to be allowed tanks up to 6 tons), and the limitation of mobile land guns to 155 mm.

2. In February 1934 Mr. Eden obtained a counter-offer from Germany.[3] This was reduced to the form of an agreed memorandum on the 16th April, 1934.[4] By it the German Government accepted our January proposals for land armaments, but demanded an air force. It was, however, understood by this that the German Government maintained their claim for 300,000 men.

3. On the 10th April, 1934,[5] we asked the French Government what guarantees of execution of a Disarmament Convention they would require as the condition of their acceptance of our January proposals as modified by the German counter-proposals.

4. On the 17th April, 1934,[6] the French Government stated that Germany's attitude as exemplified by the publication of her military and air estimates for the years 1934–35 rendered it impossible to continue negotiations.

5. Although Germany continued steadily to rearm there were no further developments of importance in the matter of land armaments until March 1935, when (on the 15th March) the French Chamber passed the so-called Two-Year Military Service Bill. This Bill was subsequently also passed by the Senate. Prior to its passage the total strength of the French army, including native and colonial troops in France and overseas, was 545,000 officers and men; of these only some 350,000 were serving in France. Owing

<hr>

[2] See Cmd. 4498 of 1934; cf. Volume VI, Nos. 206 and 232.
[3] Cf. *ibid.*, Nos. 303, 305, and 306.
[4] No. 6 in Cmd. 4559; cf. Volume VI, No. 402.
[5] See No. 7 in Cmd. 4559; cf. Volume VI, No. 385.
[6] See No. 8 in Cmd. 4559; cf. Volume VI, No. 395.

to the approach of the so-called 'lean years', 1936–40, the total number of men serving in France (including those in the native overseas expeditionary force) would have fallen in 1936 to about 280,000, and still further in 1937–38, and the object of the Bill passed by the Chamber was to prevent this reduction in strength.

6. On the 16th March, 1935, Herr Hitler used the announcement of the passage of this Bill to publish a military decree[7] disavowing the military clauses of the Treaty of Versailles, reintroducing conscription in Germany and fixing the peace establishment of the German army at 36 divisions, with the strength, it was understood, of 550,000 men. During the Berlin visit of the 25th and the 26th March Herr Hitler told Sir John Simon that this strength was roughly equivalent to the strength of the French military forces in Metropolitan France and North Africa, which he estimated at 500,000 men.[8] A subsequent War Office letter, dated the 4th April,[9] stated that the French effectives in France for 1935 were 350,000 men and in North Africa 123,500, a total of 473,500. The General Staff believe that this figure will be increased to about 540,000 when the new law of two years' compulsory service becomes fully effective towards the end of 1936.

7. In his speech of the 21st May, 1935, Herr Hitler stated that 'the German Government have made known the size of the new German army. Under no circumstances will they depart from this.' Enquiries made subsequently in Berlin (Berlin telegrams Nos. 222 and 223 of the 31st May)[10] showed that the German Government did not believe in the possibility of any general limitation of land effectives, and hence of any reduction in the size of the German army, though Herr von Bülow stated 'that the German Government would be prepared to reduce the 550,000 figure if other Powers were to make similar reductions in their figures existing on the 16th March.'

The exact meaning of this statement has never been cleared up. Did, therefore, Herr von Bülow mean that the German figure of 550,000 men could only be reduced if the French reduced from their one-year service, or would he be content to reduce if the French reduced from their two-year service? As Herr Hitler partly based his justification for the increase of the German army on the reintroduction of two-years' service in France, it seems possible that the German Government might, at present, be willing to reduce their proposed establishment below 550,000, provided France reverted to one-year's service. (It must be emphasised that any agreement will have to be come to shortly; once the German Army has been fully expanded to a peace strength of 550,000 it will be very difficult to induce the German Government to reduce. In any case it is not believed that the Germans will reduce the number of divisions in the new army.)

It is not considered that the German Government will suggest any reduction in French effectives below the figures maintained by France under the one-year's service. It does, however, seem certain that Germany will now never be content with parity in effectives with France. Germany will claim

---

[7] Cf. Volume XII, No. 570.  [8] See *ibid.*, No. 651, p. 735.
[9] Not printed.  [10] Nos. 273 and 274.

that she is always exposed to the dangers of a war on at least two fronts, whereas France is only likely to have to fight on one front. At the same time, in view of the disparity in population Germany will no doubt demand a larger army on the basis of equality.

8. In his speech of the 21st May Herr Hitler added 'that the German Government are ready to agree to any limitation leading to the abolition of the heaviest weapons . . . such as the heaviest artillery and the heaviest tanks'. (N.B.—The French warned us in a memorandum[11] communicated on the eve of the Berlin visit that they could not consider a limitation of material while Germany maintained the figure fixed for her army on the 16th March. Such a limitation, they said, would merely redound to the further disadvantage of France, whose existing superiority in material (i.e., heavy guns and spare tanks) would thereby be destroyed.)

9. The question of land armaments was next raised during Mr. Eden's visit to Paris on the 21st June and again on the 27th June.[12] M. Laval said on the 21st June that 'if the Air Pact were to be made, France would be left alone to deal with Germany's claim as regards land armaments,' and 'France needed the help of His Majesty's Government to get an agreement on land armaments.' During the second conversation on the 27th June, M. Laval said 'that he could not agree that an Air Pact should come into force unless an agreement on land armaments could come into force at the same time'; he added that 'France's chief interest was land armaments' and that if an air agreement was concluded, 'there would be much greater difficulty in reaching a settlement about land armaments' . . .[13] 'the land problem was nine-tenths of the whole problem for France. Agreement on land armaments was necessary in the interests of European peace and co-operation'. He thus made the conclusion of an Air Pact (and by this expression he clearly included the proposed Air Limitation Agreement) conditional on the simultaneous conclusion of an agreement for the limitation of land armaments. Subsequently he slightly modified this condition by saying that 'if it were agreed that there were to be bilateral arrangements within the framework of the Air Pact, the question of the condition as regards land armaments could be discussed, but it would be, in any event, essential that land armaments should be discussed.' In telegram No. 141, Saving, from Paris,[14] of the 27th June, Mr. Eden reported his impression that if we could consent to bilateral pacts 'it is just possible that the French would be willing to enter on, and even conclude, negotiations for an air pact and limitation, without the further condition that these agreements should not come into force until agreements had been reached on land armaments.' But a memorandum on the Air Pact handed to Sir G. Clerk on the 10th July[15] states that it is necessary to recall 'that the War Minister has expressly conditioned his assent to the negotiation of an Air Pact to that of an agreement on land armaments.'

10. In response to the demand that the conclusion of an Air Pact must be

[11] See Volume XII, No. 696, pp. 832–3.
[13] Punctuation as in the original quotation.
[15] See No. 409.

[12] See Nos. 363 and 384.
[14] No. 383.

conditional on the simultaneous conclusion of an agreement for the limitation of land armaments, Mr. Eden twice asked M. Laval during the Paris visits what he was going to 'do about land armaments.' 'Was he going to start negotiating with the Germans, and what procedure he envisaged for land armaments?' On the first occasion M. Léger interposed with a question on some other subject and on the second M. Léger interposed again to say: 'They would have the best chance of getting an agreement on land armaments by refusing to make prior agreements on other subjects.'

11. All that we know, therefore, is that the French Government have abandoned the *non possumus* attitude adopted in their note of the 17th April, 1934, and are now once more, though somewhat belatedly, prepared to negotiate an agreement on land armaments. But they have given us no indication whatsoever of the basis on which they would like to negotiate, nor what procedure they would like to follow for the purpose of these negotiations.

12. The only information which the French Government have given us as to their views on these points is contained in a memorandum on the land armaments question, which was communicated privately and unofficially during Mr. Eden's first visit to Paris on the 21st June. In this memorandum[16] it is claimed—what is presumably the truth—that Germany was seeking 'a situation of military preponderance'; that Germany would only reduce her claims if the other Powers would reduce their existing effectives; and that 'only the firm and united action of the Powers could prevail upon Germany to reduce her claims. Was it indeed possible that Britain, by the concessions which she freely made in the naval question, had deprived France of an essential trump in the negotiations?' Further, the Anglo-German Naval Agreement had resulted in endangering the communications between France and North Africa; and now France could take no account of her North African troops in any discussion of parity with Germany. Lastly, the French memorandum of the 21st June reiterated the French view stated to us before the Berlin visit, that France could not agree to the German proposal for qualitative limitation of heavy guns and tanks, in that it would imply the destruction of the existing French superiority in that material. The French memorandum also contained a suggestion that a limitation agreement might be reached as regards 'programmes of manufacture.'

13. The following comments may be made on this situation:—

(a) It has for some time been more than questionable—if, indeed, there is any doubt at all on the subject—whether Germany is prepared to pay anything for the recognition of her right to rearm in defiance of Part V of the Treaty of Versailles. In his speech of the 21st May Herr Hitler definitely stated that he had taken that right to himself; and his contention was that it was not taken in defiance of Part V, as the ex-Allied Powers themselves had broken that Part of the Treaty and therefore destroyed it. Further, Germany has already announced the strength of her peace-time army, viz., 36 divisions, the rough equivalent of

[16] Not printed.

550,000 men; and the War Office believe that this army will be fully manned and equipped during the first quarter of 1937. Lastly, it is pertinent to recall that, though the ex-Allied Powers were 'solid' in their disapproval of all three kinds of German re-armament through the year 1934, that in no way prevented Germany from rapid expansion in all three spheres. It is perhaps worth noting that the danger of the situation is aggravated by the fact that the French Government are still thinking in terms of German 'claims' to land armaments, whereas in fact the German Government have passed from the stage of 'claims' to the execution of a definite programme. It is to be expected that the German Government will only modify their programme if other Powers also reduce their land armaments.

(b) We do not admit the French contention that the Naval Agreement has endangered the French communications with North Africa; and that that would consequently be a reason in itself why France could not now agree to count in the North African troops in any calculation of parity with Germany. This question is argued in a memorandum of the 12th July[17] on the various criticisms brought against the Naval Agreement. Beyond that this question of the inclusion of the North African troops in any Franco-German parity arrangement is clearly one, in the first instance, for the French themselves.

(c) The French attempt—if, indeed, it is an attempt—to bargain qualitative limitation of big tanks, guns, &c., against a reduction in German effectives, seems to be an almost hopeless quest. Although France may have superiority for the moment, the German superior manufacturing capacity must also inevitably wipe out this superiority in the end. So far as we are concerned it would be to our advantage to obtain this qualitative limitation; and we believe that it would be to the advantage of France as such limitation would enhance the value of the French frontier defence. Qualitative limitation, of course, raises the question of supervision. But, as in the case of our proposals respecting air limitation, we can, for the moment, leave the French to open the discussion of this question.

(d) We dislike the French proposal to attempt limitation by means of 'manufacturing programmes' or advance detailed publicity for the armaments orders placed by each Government, showing everything except production costs. We consider it far too complicated and as likely to give rise to endless discussion.

14. It seems desirable to make to the French Government some friendly and unofficial statement in the sense of the statements suggested in paragraphs 11 and 13 above; and to urge them—if indeed they attach importance to limitation of land armaments—to come down to realities and to make to Germany some offer both as regards effectives and heavy material which

---

[17] This was the date of a draft memorandum prepared by Mr. Craigie. For the final text, dated July 17, see No. 419 below, enclosure.

there is some chance of her accepting. It seems difficult to suppose (though it would be too discouraging to say this to the French at the moment) that—unless the French are prepared to make an effort, the maintenance of which is likely to prove beyond their capacity—they can, in such an offer, avoid the recognition of some kind of German superiority. But even under such conditions, the General Staff take the view that agreement would have a certain value. Thus, in a report of the 25th June, they state:—

'It is considered that any agreed limitation of the peace establishment and equipment of the German army would be of great importance in reducing the offensive value of the forces which Germany would have available at the outbreak of war. Nevertheless, in connexion with any such limitation agreement, it must be borne in mind that the proved efficiency of German plans for industrial mobilisation will allow Germany to disarm to the level of less favoured nations, and still to remain potentially the stronger; while no system of inspection can be devised to discover and check this source of power.'

### No. 417

*Letter from Captain Danckwerts (Admiralty) to Mr. Gore-Booth*
*[A 6479/22/45]*

LONDON, *July 18, 1935*

Dear Gore-Booth,[1]

There is no doubt that if the German submarine was actually put in commission on the 29th June that fact would not be consistent with the impression that we might reasonably expect to be produced by the information we were given earlier in the year. On the other hand, the question is largely dependent upon the exact meaning of the terms employed, none of which have any strict definition.

2. Thus, the 'Morning Post' says, 'Put in commission on June 29th'. In our Navy that would mean the ship was complete and had passed her trials; in this instance it probably means nothing of the sort, but simply that a Commanding Officer and advance party had joined the ship to carry out trials.

3. Again, in the light of the explanations of the peculiar method by which these submarines were ordered that were given to our Naval Attaché by the German Admiralty it is difficult to say just what is meant by 'orders had just been given for the construction of 12–250 ton submarines'. It is quite apparent from the information given on the 26th April that the manufacture of all the parts of these submarines had begun about Christmas 1934.

[1] In a letter to Captain Danckwerts of July 17 Mr. Gore-Booth had called attention to a cutting from the *Morning Post* of July 9, from which it appeared that the first of the German 250-ton submarines had been put into commission on June 29. He asked 'whether the fact that a submarine was ready at such an early date was consistent with the information about German submarine building given to us earlier in the year'. Cf. No. 142.

535

4. In the view of our constructors, if the submarine was constructed by assembling numbered parts and units, six months would be quick work since the space is confined and the number of men that could work on board simultaneously would be strictly limited.

5. It is probable, therefore, that the assembly of the parts of the first submarine did begin before the 12th April if that submarine was in a state to go to sea on the 29th June.[2]

Yours sincerely,

V. H. DANCKWERTS

[2] A minute to this letter reads: '25/7. It is pretty clear that the Germans were lying even when they tried to explain away their previous gaffe. M. J. Creswell.'

## No. 418

*Letter from Mr. Newton (Berlin) to Sir R. Vansittart (Received July 19)*

[*C 5811/55/18*]

BERLIN, *July 18, 1935*

Dear Vansittart

The Italian Ambassador, Cerruti, whom I met at dinner last night, has been told by Bülow that although the Chancellor proposes to leave the Secretary of State's recent appeal[1] unanswered, Hoesch will call on him to express the disappointment felt with the speech in general and in particular with the fact that it seems to ignore Hitler's own speech and his Thirteen Points.[2]

It is not clear, however, why greater importance should be attached to the Chancellor's general, and, as it were, 'multilateral' declaration of May 21st than to his previous declarations to Sir John Simon during his visit to Berlin and during the Conference at Stresa, which were not only bilateral, i.e. the form considered by Hitler to have the most force, but multilateral seeing that a public declaration and explanation of Germany's readiness to enter into an Eastern Pact was also made at the time of the Stresa Conference. Of the two, one would think that the former declaration must come before the latter, not only in point of time but in the degree to which it is binding. The value to be

[1] In his speech to the House of Commons on July 11 surveying the whole field of foreign policy, Sir S. Hoare said with regard to the Anglo-German naval agreement that he wished to make an appeal to Herr Hitler. 'We have, thereby, as we hope, taken a step forward on the road to reconciliation. But reconciliation, like peace, is one and manifold; and all roads lead to many capitals. Let him therefore take the next necessary step forward, and help on the negotiation of the Eastern and Danubian Pacts, thereby giving a great impulse to the conclusion of an Air Pact, which I know that he desires.' See 304 *H.C. Deb.* 5 *s.*, cols. 515–16.

[2] Minutes by Sir R. Vansittart and Sir S. Hoare relating to this point read: 'If Herr von Hoesch makes any such call in any such terms, he should have a somewhat caustic reply, for which Mr. Newton's letter furnishes good material. Such an expression of disappointment wd indeed be rather impertinent. There is no reason for taking Hitler's sometimes nebulous expressions as a Bible compared with the concrete proposals of other people. R.V. July 19.' 'I entirely agree . . . S.H. 21/7.'

536

attached to the speech must therefore surely be affected by the extent to which it is found possible to give practical effect to previous declarations. Moreover in his point 4 Hitler himself says 'The German Government is ready at any time to take part in a system of collective co-operation for the securing of peace in Europe'. The suggestion that the Franco-Soviet Agreement has created a new situation seems disingenuous because, as the Germans well knew at the time, it was precisely in contemplation of such an agreement that the enquiry from Stresa[3] was made.

No doubt to Germans the idea that Germany should be invited to make a special contribution goes against the grain, especially as they consider they have already made important contributions in the renunciation of Alsace-Lorraine, the promise to respect the demilitarised zone (specially mentioned in point 3), and in the acceptance of a navy only 35% of ours. On the other hand it seemed to me that in describing what was asked of Germany as a new contribution, the Secretary of State was being very polite and generous, as he was offering to give Germany extra credit for a contribution which was not really new, seeing that we were only asking her to act in accordance with declarations made some time ago.

I fear, however, that whatever may be done to drag the German mule to the water of the Eastern Pact, to make it drink will be very difficult, so that except from the point of view of putting Germany in the wrong and establishing a kind of claim, I doubt whether there is much to be gained by rubbing in her default.

I have also heard that in pursuance of a personal suggestion let fall by François-Poncet, Köster may shortly ask the French Government whether an Eastern Pact could replace the Franco-Soviet Agreement. I understand from François-Poncet that his suggestion was based on the vague language of paragraph 4 of the Protocol to the Agreement. Neither he nor Bülow, who had mentioned it to me previously, seemed optimistic of its leading to any useful result. Bülow thought that in any case the Soviet Government would object to such a solution.

Perhaps the interview with the German Ambassador will have taken place before this letter reaches you, but I take the opportunity of sending it by this bag in case it should still be of any use.

Yours ever<br>BASIL C. NEWTON

[3] See Volume XII, No. 717.


### No. 419

*Sir S. Hoare to Sir G. Clerk (Paris)*

*No. 1356 [A 6441/22/45]*

FOREIGN OFFICE, July 19, 1935

Sir,

I transmit to you herewith copies of a memorandum containing answers to the criticisms directed from the juridical and political point of view against the conclusion of the Anglo-German Naval Agreement.

2. My impression is that the agitation in France against this Agreement has now considerably diminished, and I certainly wish to do nothing to revive it.

3. On the other hand, the answers to certain of these criticisms have a bearing on matters now under discussion or about to be discussed, notably the air pact and air limitation, future negotiations leading up to the naval conference and the limitation of land armaments.

4. In these circumstances it seems to me to be very desirable that the French Government—and indeed informed French opinion—should be aware of the view taken here of the criticisms directed against the Agreement. I should therefore welcome any steps which you could take to secure this: and I should even have no objection were it possible for you or a member of His Majesty's Embassy to show a copy of the enclosed memorandum privately and confidentially to someone in authority at the Ministry of Foreign Affairs. The memorandum would in no sense be a communication to the French: and the purpose of showing it to them would simply be to let them know in a friendly way how we feel on the points dealt with.

5. For your own information I may say that His Majesty's Government would regard with some anxiety any attempt by the French Government to hold up further progress in naval limitation as a means of pressure on His Majesty's Government in connexion with the limitation of land armaments or, indeed, a French decision to embark on such an increase in [her] fleet as would render a general naval agreement impossible. There is at the moment a prospect of making real progress towards a general limitation of naval armaments if France will co-operate, but if the present opportunity is missed as a result of non-co-operation by France, the impression created on British public opinion is bound to be adverse.

I am, &c.,
SAMUEL HOARE

ENCLOSURE* IN No. 419

*Answers to criticisms directed from the Political and Juridical point of view against the conclusion of the Anglo-German Naval Agreement*

FOREIGN OFFICE, *July 17, 1935*

I. *Criticism:—*

(i) *That His Majesty's Government have committed a breach of the Treaty of Versailles;*

(ii) *That His Majesty's Government have condoned a breach by Germany of the Treaty of Versailles.*

(i) Where, as in the Treaty of Versailles, a treaty is concluded between one State on the one hand and a number of States on the other, the position is that the one party, Germany, contracts a series of similar obligations towards each of the other parties to the treaty severally. Each of the other parties, if it should wish to do so, has a legal right (apart from any specific undertakings to the contrary), by a separate agreement with Germany to waive its rights in any particular under the treaty. If it does so, it affects only its own rights and the provisions of the treaty remain in full legal force as regards the other parties thereto. Therefore, though Germany has to obtain the assent of all the other parties in one way or another before she is released from any particular obligation under the Treaty of Versailles, there is no reason as a matter of law why this cannot be done piecemeal by separate agreements with the other parties individually, and, if this course is followed, any of the other parties who concludes such an agreement commits no breach of the treaty but is merely doing what it is entitled to do. The recent agreement with Germany has the effect of a waiver, so far as the United Kingdom is concerned, of any obligations incumbent on Germany under Part V of the Treaty of Versailles in the matter of naval armament, provided that German armaments are kept within the limits of the new agreement. The rights of France and other parties to the Treaty of Versailles to claim that the Versailles limits must be observed are legally unaffected; and His Majesty's Government have committed no breach of the treaty.

(ii) The German Government have declared that they no longer consider themselves bound by Part V of the Treaty of Versailles. The latest pronouncement to this effect was contained in Herr Hitler's speech of the 21st May last, the relevant extract from which will be found in Annex A.[1] The principal other parties to that treaty, His Majesty's Government included, taking the view that legally there was nothing to justify the German claim that conditions had come into existence rendering Part V no longer binding, protested against this decision, declared that it was a breach of the treaty and that nothing had happened to prevent the application of the usual principle that Germany could only obtain her release from Part V by agreement with all the other parties thereto. The other parties placed all this on record, but the German Government proceeded to act in accordance with their decision, and it was clear that the other parties were not going to take any action to enforce their view of the legal position upon Germany. The present bilateral Agreement with Germany is based upon the admitted *de facto* situation and constitutes an attempt to limit the consequences thereof. It contains no admission that the *de facto* situation was a legal one, though to the extent that the new Agreement is fulfilled it removes for the future the right of His Majesty's Government to protest against that situation further as regards naval armaments. The countries who complain of this 'condonation' in fact still contemplate and desire agreements with Germany under which Germany will have the right to armaments in excess of those of Part V. From this point of view what would be the difference between such agreements and the action taken by His Majesty's Government, except that these agreements are intended to have more parties thereto? But this does not alter the fact that, if His Majesty's Government's action in arriving at an agreement involved condonation, then these other agreements would involve it also. The

[1] Not printed.

procedure of acting together or separately is irrelevant to the 'condonation' point.

II. *Criticism:—*

*That His Majesty's Government have not acted in accordance with the London Communiqué of February 3 and under the Stresa Resolution.*

The relevant passages from these two documents are quoted in Annexes C[1] and D.[1] Throughout the discussions which led up to the drafting of these two documents no reference was ever made to the particular position of naval disarmament. In the absence of any such reference it is impossible to say that any of the parties concerned adopted any definite line in the matter. But in the absence of any contrary statement by the other parties, His Majesty's Government are entitled to argue that they have always maintained that naval armaments are in a separate category from land and air armaments, having been regulated by international treaties since 1922, and that therefore when subscribing to the London and Stresa Declarations they assumed that the limitation of naval armaments would be negotiated separately from the other elements constituting the proposed General Settlement. The possibility that these separate negotiations might result in the conclusion of a direct Anglo-German Agreement was, it is true, not contemplated before the Anglo-German naval talks took place, but in so far as we can argue that this Anglo-German Agreement is in effect a contribution towards the General Settlement and not prejudicial to it, the French Government have no reason to object to it on that score. This argument involves the practical appreciation of existing circumstances rather than the legal interpretation of texts. Viewed in this light it is reasonable to maintain that the Anglo-German Agreement is an essential prelude to the conclusion of a general naval settlement, since Germany had (1) already definitely decided to increase the size of her fleet; (2) was already giving practical effect to that decision; and (3) was not prepared to enter upon any negotiations for an international settlement until the basis of her future naval relationship to this country had been finally established.

If there is to be any future general limitation of naval armaments, it can only be on the basis of one or both of the following systems:—

Qualitative limitation, i.e., limitation of the sizes of ships in each category and the armament which they may carry; and

Quantitative limitation, i.e., on the basis of an exchange of declarations of programme (a settlement on the basis of agreed ratios being now definitely out of the question).

The placing of a limit on the expansion of the German navy cannot be held to prejudice the chances of an ultimate general agreement on the basis of either of these systems of limitation. Were it not for the Agreement, there is reason to believe that the first naval objective of Germany would have been not 35 per cent. of the British fleet, but parity with France. Such a claim, if made, would have rendered yet more difficult the conclusion of that 'general settlement' to which the London Communiqué referred.

In this connexion it is perhaps worth while contrasting the attitude adopted by the French Government towards their own bilateral agreement with the Soviet Government, and our bilateral agreement with Germany. When His Majesty's Government conclude a bilateral agreement with Germany, as their contribution towards those 'agreements regarding armaments generally' recommended in the London Declaration, it is a cause of criticism. But when the French Government conclude a mutual guarantee treaty with the Soviet Government, as their contribution towards the 'conclusion of pacts freely negotiated between all the interested parties in Eastern Europe,' it is regarded as a matter for congratulation. It is to be observed, also, that when the French Government decided, not merely to negotiate but to bring their Russian Treaty into force in advance not only of the General Settlement, but of the so-called Eastern Pact to be concluded between all the parties concerned, they did so without requesting or awaiting the consent of His Majesty's Government.

III. *The criticism that we gave the French Government no chance to influence our view and that the summary of the Agreement handed to them on June 7[2] was inadequate.*

The German representatives intimated that this was an offer which was made to this country and to this country only, and that, as it was made independently of the construction of third Powers, they saw serious objection to the prior consultation with such Powers before His Majesty's Government gave their answer. Furthermore, we had good reason to believe that, in making his offer, Herr Hitler had overruled the German Ministry of Marine, which, if we had hesitated to accept it, would have been favourably placed for securing an amendment of the German proposal in the sense desired by the German navy.

We gave the French Government ten days in which to express an opinion, leaving them in no doubt that this was a matter on which our own minds were already made up. In doing so we ran the risk of letting the Germans proceed to Germany and return—as they did—with an offer less satisfactory from our point of view than the original offer. The real answer to this charge is that the acceptance of this German offer was a matter of vital interest to this country; that on the juridical side it did not constitute a breach of the Treaty of Versailles by this country; that it did not directly concern the naval construction of France nor prejudice the chances of an ultimate general settlement; and that no British Government could have taken the risk of losing the agreement simply on the ground that it might conflict with a French interpretation of the Declaration of the 3rd February.

The French Government are also disposed to complain that the aide-mémoire which was communicated to them on the 7th June was not an adequate summary of the Agreement which afterwards contained the clause about parity in submarines (paragraph 2 (*f*)) and the clauses about Germany's right to draw attention to any abnormal and exceptional construction by other Powers (paragraphs 2 (*c*) and 3). The reason for this is that these

[2] See No. 319.

clauses were only inserted at the last moment as the result of representations by the German representatives on their return from Berlin after Whitsuntide. In actual fact, neither point has the significance which the French Government at first appeared disposed to attach to it. The aide-mémoire of the 7th June contained an exact representation of the position as it stood at that date. These points have since been explained to the French Ambassador.[3]

IV. *Criticism:*—

(a) *That, by concluding the Naval Agreement with Germany, we have deprived France of a trump card in connexion with the negotiations on land and air.*

(b) *That by endangering France's communications with North Africa we have made it impossible for France to take account of her North African troops in any discussion of military parity with Germany.*

(1) We cannot admit that the Naval Agreement has taken a trump out of the French hand for securing land limitation. It has for some time been more than questionable—if indeed there is any doubt at all on the subject—whether Germany is prepared to pay anything for the recognition of her right to rearm in defiance of Part V of the Treaty of Versailles. In his speech of the 21st May Herr Hitler definitely stated that he had taken that right to himself; and his contention was that it was not taken in defiance of Part V, as the ex-Allied Powers themselves had broken that part of the treaty and therefore destroyed it. Further, Germany has already announced the strength of her peace-time army, viz., thirty-six divisions, the rough equivalent of 550,000 men. Lastly, it is pertinent to recall that, though the ex-Allied Powers were 'solid' in their disapproval of all three kinds of German rearmament through the year 1934, this in no way prevented Germany from rapid expansion in all three spheres.

(2) It is further necessary to contest the French contention that the Naval Agreement has endangered the French communications with North Africa; and that that would consequently be a reason in itself why France could not now agree to count in the North African troops in any calculation of parity with Germany. As a matter of fact, what the Naval Agreement has done is, without restricting the French freedom of action, to limit the expansion of the German fleet, and to enable France to maintain a permanent naval superiority over Germany which must be at least 43 per cent. if France preserves her present level of naval strength *vis-à-vis* the British Commonwealth.

V. *The criticism that His Majesty's Government have not acted in accordance with the spirit of Anglo-French co-operation.*

Acceptance of the principle of co-operation does not mean that one party gives any special rights of control over its actions to the other party, but that both parties recognise that the actions of each shall in every case be the subject of consultation between them and shall be directed towards the common objective which both have in view. If such co-operation is to be

[3] See No. 388.

wholehearted and fruitful, it must not be used for the purpose of preventing one of the parties from taking action which it considers essential to its own vital interests. In the present case the French Government have ignored our naval interests, which to us are vital, and have shown a wish to refuse us the latitude necessary to secure them. Such an attitude on their part is, in our view, entirely contrary to the whole spirit of that co-operation to which we are both pledged, and gives us strong ground for complaint. In a word, Anglo-French co-operation must on both sides be supple and dynamic; it must be constructive and not obstructive.

VI. *The criticism that His Majesty's Government have withheld from the French Government information with regard to the German building programmes.*

The German construction programme may be divided into two parts. The first is their 1934–5 programme, most of which has already been laid down. This was published in Berlin on the 9th July (largely at our instigation). It consists of—

2 capital ships of 26,000 tons each, with 11-inch guns.
2 cruisers of 10,000 tons each, with 8-inch guns.
16 destroyers of 1,625 tons each, with 5-inch guns.
20 submarines of 250 tons.
6 submarines of 500 tons.
2 submarines of 750 tons.

Of the above, the two capital ships, the two 8-inch gun cruisers, sixteen destroyers and twelve of the submarines had already been laid down before the conclusion of the Anglo-German Naval Agreement. This fact had been conveyed to our naval attaché at Berlin before the naval conversations commenced. The information as regards the size of the ships and their guns was communicated to our representatives during the conversations, and, at our suggestion, it was communicated direct to the French, Italian, United States and Japanese Governments in advance of publication.

The second part of what is known as the German building programme relates to the construction to be undertaken by Germany up to the year 1942 (the year originally suggested by this country as that up to which building programmes should be exchanged in any future agreement). This part of the programme was communicated to us on two conditions: (1) that we should communicate our own programme to Germany on a reciprocal basis; and (2) that we should only communicate this programme to other foreign Powers on a reciprocal basis, i.e., in return for the building programmes of those Powers up to and including 1942. This part of the German programme, like our own and other programmes of all other nations, must for the time being of course remain confidential, for premature publication of advance programmes could only serve to increase the difficulty of arriving at an ultimate international agreement on this subject.

We have informed the French Government[3] that we are ready and anxious to communicate to them all the information communicated confidentially to us if they will undertake, within a reasonably short time, to communicate to us, for transmission to the German Government (or else to communicate direct to the German Government), the particulars of the French building programme up to the end of 1942. We have not so far received from the French Government a reply to this suggestion.

It will be seen from the above that one important result of the Anglo-German Agreement is that, in the matter of naval armaments, Germany is now prepared to depart from the policy of secrecy which, in connexion with armaments generally, has done so much to cause uneasiness throughout the world. Furthermore, so far as naval armaments are concerned, Germany is prepared from now on to exchange on a reciprocal basis with the other naval Powers particulars in regard to the date of laying down and characteristics of future warships, even in advance of the conclusion of a general naval treaty. It may confidently be asserted that this satisfactory result could never have been achieved without the prior conclusion of the Anglo-German Agreement.

VII. *The suggestion that His Majesty's Government would raise strong objection if other Powers were to conclude similar arrangements with Germany (e.g., in regard to land and air armaments) as that which we have just concluded in regard to naval armaments.*

The answer is that, far from objecting, we should regard the conclusion of such separate agreements as a great step in the direction of peace and appeasement, provided that our own liberty of action remained unimpaired (just as the liberty of action of other foreign Powers remains unimpaired under the Anglo-German Agreement), and provided that the purpose of the agreement was to facilitate that 'general settlement' referred to in the London communiqué of the 3rd February.

VIII. *The criticism that, in concluding this agreement with Germany, His Majesty's Government have acted purely from interested motives in contradiction to the spirit of the League of Nations.*

This criticism is to some extent answered in the reply to Point VII, but it can be added that the step which has been taken was an essential preliminary to the general limitation of naval armaments and, had it not been taken by His Majesty's Government, all foreign Powers must have suffered from the race in naval armaments which would have resulted. As it is, other foreign Powers whose naval construction is not directly affected by the agreement know the limits of German naval expansion and can regulate their programmes accordingly. If France remains at her present level (approximately 50 per cent. of the tonnage of our navy), she will still retain a permanent superiority in tonnage over Germany of 43 per cent. (as compared with an inferiority of about 30 per cent. before the war).

One of the primary purposes of the League of Nations is to limit and, if possible, reduce world armaments, and the League cannot suffer if, as a result of this agreement, which we regard as a useful contribution to a general settlement between all the naval Powers, the threatened race in naval armaments can be prevented.

## No. 420

*Sir S. Hoare to Sir G. Clerk (Paris)*

*No. 222 Saving: Telegraphic* [*C 5327/55/18*]

FOREIGN OFFICE, *July 22, 1935, 5.5 p.m.*

*Air Pact*

You should see M. Laval and say that you understand from your interview with him on July 10th (your telegram No. 136)[1] and the memorandum which he gave you on that date (your despatch No. 993)[2] that he accepts the position of His Majesty's Government in this matter; that is to say, that His Majesty's Government are prepared to accept in principle bilateral arrangements for making effective a general Air Pact, one of these bilateral arrangements being between the United Kingdom and France and other bilateral arrangements being open to any of the other signatories desiring them; and that His Majesty's Government are prepared at once to use their influence with the German Government to bring the Germans into the discussion upon this line. His Majesty's Government cannot go beyond that.

2. On the understanding that M. Laval accepts this we propose to ask the German Government to agree (1) to the principle of the accompaniment of the Air Pact by such arrangements between any two parties as those two parties may judge necessary to render it effective; and (2) to the opening of the general negotiations on that basis. I should like you also to obtain confirmation that if the German Government agree to this the French Government will themselves agree to the opening of the general negotiations.

3. Pending a definite answer by the French Government to these two enquiries you should resist any attempt which may be made to engage you in discussion on the other points raised in the French memorandum.

4. But you should see to it that M. Laval realises that our consent to the principle of bilateral arrangements is not absolute but is dependent not only upon these arrangements making the general Air Pact effective, but also, on that Pact maturing, which in its turn implies general agreement between the parties.

5. For your own information and guidance, we could not commit ourselves on the hypothetical point raised in paragraph 3 of the French memorandum, to the effect that general negotiations should only begin when His Majesty's Government, having obtained German assent to the French thesis, are in a position to adhere without restriction to the principle of bilateral arrangements. The words 'without restriction' might easily lead to subsequent misunderstandings. For instance we must be careful not to give away our liberty to work for an Air Limitation Agreement alone if the Air Pact were to suffer shipwreck on the rocks of the bilateral arrangements. We

---

[1] No. 409.      [2] See *ibid.*, note 3

could not possibly agree that there must be no Air Limitation Agreement without bilateral arrangements.

6. While still unwilling to enter into a discussion of the French schemes for an Anglo-French bilateral arrangement—see paragraph 5 of my telegram No. 171[3]—I do not wish to cause subsequent misunderstanding by acquiescing tacitly in the hope expressed in the French memorandum of July 10th to the effect that we will be prepared to accept the larger part of these schemes. You should therefore make it clear to M. Laval that the very fact that these bilateral arrangements may be mutually entered upon by any two parties to the Pact, will make it necessary to limit the scope of any one arrangement and, to a certain extent, to preserve a balance between the provisions which each may contain.

7. If you find M. Laval still inclined to make difficulties or to delay progress you should point to the favourable reception given by the British public to those references in my speech of July 11th[4] regarding Anglo-French friendship, and you should impress upon him the importance of keeping this sentiment alive by showing that Anglo-French co-operation, to which both our Governments are pledged, is capable of producing prompt and constructive results. It would be deplorable if, after all the efforts which His Majesty's Government have been making to promote progress as regards the Eastern and Danubian problems, the French Government were now to show themselves obstructive when it comes to making progress with the equally urgent Western problem.

8. As regards the reference to land armaments in the last paragraph of the French memorandum of July 10th, please see my despatch No. 1344.[5] You may think it desirable to put to M. Laval the questions indicated in that despatch at the same time as you discuss the Air Pact with him.

[3] No. 398.          [4] See 304 *H.C. Deb.* 5 *s.*, cols. 509–24.
[5] No. 416.

## No. 421

*Record by Sir R. Vansittart of a conversation with M. Corbin*

*[A 6691/22/45]*

FOREIGN OFFICE, *July 23, 1935*

The French Ambassador came to see me this morning on instructions from his Government in connection with the naval question.

He said that M. Laval had now had more time to reflect on this matter and other questions of foreign policy, and that he was not indisposed towards a gentlemen's agreement such as we had suggested to him.[1] M. Corbin said, however, that there was still an aftermath of disquiet in France as the result of the Anglo-German Naval Agreement, and this disquiet had been very largely augmented when the details of German construction had become known. M. Corbin said that his Government thought it certain that the

[1] On June 28; see No. 388.

German Government would double-bank their efforts in naval construction and would reach their proportion of 35 per cent. long before 1942.

I replied that our experts were of opinion that the German Government would be unable to accomplish this and that even with a maximum of effort they could hardly reach 35 per cent. of our fleet much before that date.

The Ambassador went on to say that in any case there remained the question of qualitative limitation, which seemed to his Government no nearer to solution owing to the persistent divergencies between the United States and Japan. This made it exceedingly difficult for the French Government to formulate their own programme. His Government thought nevertheless that we should communicate the German programme to them.

I replied that this seemed really impossible except on condition of reciprocity. It was only on that condition that we had extracted their programme from the German Government, and we had agreed to the condition of reciprocity because, after all, as I had already explained to M. Corbin at our last interview on the subject,[1] it seemed better to obtain this interesting and important information on such terms rather than to go without it altogether. It was really not open to us, having accepted the condition, to whip round after we had got the information and to say that we did not intend to observe the condition. M. Corbin interpolated that this was rather a German method. I replied that it was not ours.

After this brief excursion we resumed the course of our conversation, and the French Ambassador then made the suggestion which he had been authorised to put forward. M. Laval, he said, had remembered a possibility suggested by Mr. Eden,[2] to the effect that a delegate of the British Admiralty might go to Paris for the necessary consultation. M. Corbin said, speaking personally, that he very much hoped this suggestion might be adopted. He thought that it would be helpful because it would break the ice and set discussions in motion again. Even if we found that there was still difficulty in drawing up the French programme, it would be a first step in the resumption of discussions, which could only have good effect.[3]

R.V.

[2] On June 21; cf. No. 363.

[3] Minutes on this record by Sir S. Hoare, Mr. Eden, and Sir R. Vansittart read as follows. 'I agree S.H. 23/7.' 'I agree, but of course the Admiralty representative could not tell the French Ministry of Marine the German programme except, I suppose, on the strict basis of reciprocity. I never gave M. Laval any encouragement to think that he could. It is desirable that French Govt should not think this a way round reciprocity. A.E. July 24.' 'I agree. There is no way round reciprocity. I expect the Admiralty are already quite clear on this. But we can re-emphasise the point in recommending the present proposal to them. R.V. July 24.'

# No. 422

*Record by Mr. Sargent of a conversation with the Belgian Chargé d'Affaires at London*[1]

[*C 5686/55/18*]

FOREIGN OFFICE, July 23, 1935

The Belgian Chargé d'Affaires told me to-day that when in Brussels last week he had learnt in the Belgian Foreign Office that they were somewhat surprised at the news they had received from their Embassy in Paris in regard to the latest developments in the matter of the Air Pact. M. Léger had told the Belgian Embassy that Mr. Eden, on the occasion of his recent visit to Paris, had agreed (1) that the Air Pact ought to be accompanied by bilateral agreements between the various parties; and (2) that the entry into force of the Air Pact was to be adjourned until the conclusion of all the other items in the general settlement set forth in the February Declaration.

I explained to M. Silvercruys that we had necessarily taken note of these two conditions, on which the French Government had insisted, and being realists, we were prepared, if the French Government would agree to the starting of negotiations between the five Locarno Powers, to do our best to meet the French desire for bilateral agreements 'in order to make the Air Pact effective', and to use our influence to help on the negotiation of the Eastern and Danubian Pacts. Owing to M. Laval's preoccupation with internal affairs it had not been possible recently to make much progress in these discussions, but it was to be hoped that now that M. Laval had published his decrees[2] an early understanding would be reached. But H.M. Government had not, and did not intend to define their future attitude towards what must needs be purely hypothetical circumstances: they were merely dealing with the problem of procedure in the light of present conditions, and their immediate objective was the initiation of negotiations with the Five Powers.

M. Silvercruys went on to say that the Belgian Government had been considering the question of the Air Pact in the light of the jurists' report,[3] and had been struck more particularly by the three following considerations:—

(1) They felt that in order to avoid any conflict between the Air Pact and the Treaty of Locarno it would be desirable, when formulating the conditions in which the Air Pact guarantees would operate, to reproduce as far as possible textually the wording of paragraph 3 of Article 4 of the Treaty of Locarno.

(2) They hoped that in the matter of supervision it would be possible to adopt the scheme set forth in the British draft disarmament convention, and

[1] M. Silvercruys.

[2] On July 17 the French Government had promulgated 29 economic decrees dealing with the national economy and reduction of the cost of living; cf. *The Times*, July 18, p. 16.

[3] For this report of May 28, 1935, see Annex I to Appendix II in this volume.

that this might be further supplemented by some system for controlling the manufacture of and trade in aeronautical material.

(3) As regards bombing, the Belgian Government felt most strongly that nothing would satisfy them short of an unconditional prohibition of bombing between the five signatories. Hitler's offer of prohibition of bombing outside the battle zone[4] would be completely inadequate from the Belgian point of view, since it would be impossible in the case of a war to divide Belgian territory into battle zone and non-battle zone. For the same reason they were not satisfied with the proposal made by Sir John Simon in his speech on the 31st May[5] for the prohibition of 'indiscriminate bombing'.

I explained to M. Silvercruys that these were all questions which no doubt would figure in the agenda of the Five-Power discussions, whenever they took place. We too would want to raise various points which had occurred to us, but we considered it premature to start any such discussion between one or other of the interested Powers, and must reserve all these matters until it had been definitely decided to start the negotiations between all Five Powers.

O. G. SARGENT

[4] In his speech on May 21.          [5] See 302 *H.C. Deb.* 5 s., cols. 1452–3.

No. 423

*Sir S. Hoare to Mr. Newton (Berlin)*

*No. 801* [C 5355/55/18]

FOREIGN OFFICE, *July 23, 1935*

Sir,

In my despatch No. 768[1] of the 15th July I informed you of an interview which Sir R. Vansittart had with the German Ambassador on July 9th,[2] in which His Excellency suggested, on the instructions of his Government, that His Majesty's Government should circulate in one document the texts of the various drafts of the Air Pact, i.e., those of the British, French and German Governments.

2. I propose as soon as they have all agreed to the opening of negotiations about the Air Pact to circulate to the Belgian, French, German and Italian Governments a paper raising a number of questions on the subject; and when there is general agreement on the answers to these questions it will be possible to proceed with the preparation of a common draft. In these circumstances I feel that it would be waste of time and only lead to confusion to circulate the three existing drafts.

3. My views on this matter have been brought to the notice of the French and German Embassies here.

I am, &c.,
SAMUEL HOARE

[1] Not printed.          [2] See No. 406.

## No. 424

*Sir S. Hoare to Mr. Newton (Berlin)*

*No. 807 [C 5592/55/18]*

FOREIGN OFFICE, *July 23, 1935*

Sir,

The German Ambassador called upon me at my request this afternoon. Questions had already been asked in the House of Commons as to whether the Chancellor had made any answer to the appeal that I made to him in the Foreign Office debate of July 11th,[1] and rumours had been current in Berlin that the German Government were inclined themselves to make a complaint that I had failed sufficiently to consider the German position. This being so, it seemed best for me to raise at once the questions at issue with the Ambassador.

2. I started by saying that I had greatly hoped for a response to my request that the Chancellor would facilitate the conclusion of an Eastern Pact, and that I was the more disappointed by the absence of any response from the fact that Herr von Ribbentrop had more than once given me the impression that the German Government were likely to reply at once to the French note of June 3rd, and that in his view there seemed to be no insuperable objection in the way of the conclusion of the Pact. The Ambassador made the obvious German case in reply, the conclusion of the Franco-Russian alliance, the uselessness of the Pact, the fact that a conclusion of the Pact would condone the Franco-Russian Alliance. I replied that all these factors were present when Herr von Ribbentrop and I were discussing the future. In any case, as a practical man, I had come to the conclusion that the Air Pact that both the British and German Governments desire was unattainable if there was no simultaneous progress along the line of the Eastern Pact. If the Eastern Pact was as useless as the Germans claim, why should they allow it to stand in the way of an Air Agreement that they really wanted? The Ambassador took the line in reply that, in addition to the German objections there were the Polish objections and that these had been brought out in the recent conversation between M. Beck and the Chancellor in Berlin.[2]

3. I purposely kept the Eastern Pact in the forefront, though I had mentioned the Danubian Pact in connection with it. The Ambassador proceeded to make some observations about the Danubian Pact, in the course of which he told me that Signor Mussolini had recently informed the German Government that, having made his initiative for the pact and having found great difficulties in the way of concluding it, he was at the moment prepared to take no further action in the matter. As to the Danubian Pact, the obstacle, in the Ambassador's view, was the definition of non-interference. I did not make any lengthy argument about the Danubian Pact, particularly in view of Signor Mussolini's alleged attitude towards it. I continued rather to insist

[1] Cf. No. 418, note 1.
[2] On July 3, 1935; see *D.G.F.P.*, Series C, vol. iv, No. 190.

upon the Eastern Pact. Why, asked the Ambassador, did I insist so much upon it? Why had I failed in my speech to deal with many of the other questions that had been prominent in the Chancellor's speech? At this point he produced a copy of the Chancellor's speech and read me out a series of paragraphs from it. I told him that it was unnecessary to read the speech to me, as I had myself read it the night before the debate in the House of Commons. My speech was not intended in any way to be an answer to the Chancellor's speech. The answer had already been given to it by Mr. Baldwin and Sir John Simon in the debate that immediately followed it. My speech had been directed to one object and to one object alone, namely, to stir waters that were becoming hopelessly stagnant and to regain liberty of movement in a field that was becoming completely blocked with insuperable obstacles. Surely the Chancellor wanted movement as much as I did. Indeed, the desire for movement seemed to me to be the very spirit of his speech. Would he not see that if there was to be movement with the Air Pact, there must be movement along these other lines and particularly along the line of the Eastern Pact?

4. The Ambassador seemed relieved with the description that I gave him of the object of my speech and assured me that he would convey my observations in detail at once to Berlin. Before leaving, he repeated a statement that he had made at the beginning of the interview, namely, that the German Government had not closed the door upon the Eastern Pact, and that whilst there were serious difficulties in the way of its conclusion no decision had been reached against it.[3]

I am, &c.,
SAMUEL HOARE

[3] See *D.G.F.P.*, *op. cit.*, No. 221, for Herr von Hoesch's report on this conversation.

## No. 425

*Sir R. Lindsay (Washington) to Sir S. Hoare (Received August 2)*
*No. 850 [A 6845/22/45]*

WASHINGTON, *July 24, 1935*

Sir,

I have the honour to report that the announcement of the abandonment of naval ratios, which was made in the House of Commons by the First Lord of the Admiralty on the 22nd instant,[1] has not really come as a surprise to this country. No official pronouncement on the subject has been made by the Administration, but the State Department has let it be known that they were neither astonished or dismayed by the First Lord's remarks. The Department has also intimated that an effort will now be made to find a practical solution of the naval problem on the lines of equality of security for all nations.

[1] See 304 *H.C. Deb.* 5 *s.*, cols. 153–89.

2. Editorial comment in the Eastern papers is absolutely calm, although the fear is expressed in some quarters that the abandonment of ratios may result in a naval race. The *New York Times* says that the announcement came as no surprise. On the other hand, the plans for the future, as outlined by the First Lord, are a good illustration of the circles and mazes into which disputants about naval strength are always led when they begin to match ship with ship and offset one naval problem with another. The fact remains that Great Britain has resolved to build up her fleet speedily, just as she has greatly to enlarge her air force, all in the name of national defense.

3. The *New York Tribune* is also not surprised at the announcement. It expresses the fear that naval limitation in any form is likely to be difficult to achieve, but notes with relief that there is no longer the sense of jealous rivalry between the British and American navies which existed prior to the Washington Conference.

4. The *Baltimore Sun* remarks that it seems that the clearing away of the remaining debris of the Washington and London naval treaties is complete. 'No doubt it is the part of realism to recognize a fait accompli for what it is'. The paper expresses the opinion that London is striving to retain a key position in any future bargaining, no doubt in the hope of preventing a ruinously expensive, uncontrolled race: but the First Lord's scheme is not likely to effect limitation. What really is ended is not the ratio system but the limitation in various categories that was fixed in connection with a particular application of that system. It is pretty evident that a new period of competition in building is at hand.

5. The *Washington Post*'s leading article is entitled 'Preparing for War'. It says that the British Government has merely recognized the hopelessness of trying to negotiate a new naval agreement on the basis of ratios. Great Britain has frankly recognized existing conditions and is now trying to be conciliatory. There is nothing sacred about the principle of naval ratios and fair limitations by other means would be just as effective. The only trouble is that the abandonment of ratios leaves everything in a muddle from which no escape is apparent. There is a drift towards more naval construction as a means of offsetting the failure of disarmament negotiations.

6. The *Philadelphia Inquirer* admits that the First Lord's suggestions are possibly as good as any other in the circumstances, but declares that they offer little in the way of security. They virtually clear the track for naval expansion at will.

I have, &c.,
R. C. Lindsay

## No. 426

*Report by Captain Danckwerts of an interview with Captain Anderson on July 25, 1935*[1]

*[A 6603/22/45]*

ADMIRALTY, *July 25, 1935*

Captain Anderson came to enquire whether the First Lord's speech on the 22nd July, in which he referred to the abandonment of the idea of ratios,[2] was intended to indicate that the British Government have any fresh proposals or whether the building programme arrangement, as outlined in the conversations of November and December 1934,[3] still held the field.

2. I explained to him that no new proposals were under consideration and pointed out that the First Lord's remarks constituted almost the first official statement made in the House of Commons as to the abandonment of the ratio system and the substitution of an alternative method of quantitative limitation.

3. To make the matter quite clear I described again precisely the building programme proposal as it was put forward to the Japanese and American Delegations at the end of last year, and informed the Attaché that it was first described to Mr. Norman Davis on the 6th November, 1934.[4]

4. Captain Anderson then asked a few more general questions on the future prospects of naval limitation for the 1935 Conference. I told him that I understood the Secretary of State for Foreign Affairs was going to see Mr. Bingham again before the latter returned to America on leave, and would probably hand him an aide mémoire, but, speaking for myself, I said that the Admiralty hoped that a Conference of the Washington Powers will meet towards the end of this year and that the Admiralty regarded it as of the highest importance to reach a fresh agreement on qualitative limitations before the end of this year to take the place of those at present in existence, so that Naval Powers should be able to make the necessary preparations for their building programme in 1937 and later years. I also pointed out that this, in our opinion, was a problem of immediate urgency, whereas agreement on a new quantitative arrangement, whether by building programmes or any other method, was a matter which could continue to be discussed during 1936 if necessary, since it had little immediate effect on the building programmes to be laid down in 1937. Captain Anderson appeared to agree with these ideas.

5. In response to his further enquiries I also told him that we had not, as yet, succeeded in arranging further meetings with the French and Italians, but that we hoped to do so very shortly.

6. Captain Anderson also hinted that the U.S.A. rather expected us to communicate to them all the information we might have received from the

---

[1] Copy received in the Foreign Office from the Admiralty on July 26. Captain Anderson was the United States Naval Attaché at London. For his account of the interview see *F.R.U.S. 1935*, vol. i, pp. 81–2.  　　　　　　　　　　　　　　　　　　[2] Cf. No. 425.
[3] See Chapter II.  　　　　　　　　　　　　　　　　　[4] Cf. *F.R.U.S. 1934*, vol. i, pp. 325–6.

Germans as to their future intentions. I explained to him that the German building programmes subsequent to that already announced in the press were probably somewhat tentative, even if they had been worked out at all as yet, since they depended in part on the type of building undertaken by France and in part on the capability of the German dockyards to undertake more work than they already have in hand. I also told him that we had not finally completed the examination of the exact application of the 35% ratio.

7. Captain Anderson remarked that he regarded the Vinson Bill[5] as being the most authoritative statement of the U.S.A.'s future intentions that could be produced.

[5] This Bill (H.R. 6604) had been approved on March 27, 1934 (48 Stat. 503). It authorized naval construction up to the full strength permitted by the naval treaties of Washington (1922) and of London (1930). Cf. *F.R.U.S. 1935*, vol. i, p. 83. Mr. Vinson was chairman of the Naval Affairs Committee of the United States House of Representatives.

## No. 427

*Mr. Aveling (Warsaw) to Sir S. Hoare (Received August 2)*
*No. 290 [C 5786/55/18]*

WARSAW, *July 25, 1935*

Sir,

Having occasion to see the Minister for Foreign Affairs yesterday for the purpose of exchanging ratifications of the Anglo-Polish Commercial Treaty,[1] I took the opportunity to enquire of him whether he could give me some account of his recent visit to Berlin[2] and of the conversations which he had had with Herr Hitler. M. Beck said that he was glad to have the opportunity to do so as he was anxious that you should be kept informed of what had taken place in Berlin, particularly having regard to the frank and full manner in which Mr. Eden had spoken to him of his journeys to Berlin and Moscow in March last.[3] He added that he had given a short account of his Berlin visit to the Polish Ambassador in London, and he presumed that either you or Mr. Eden would already have received the substance of this report from Count Raczynski.

2. M. Beck, as is his wont, proceeded to talk at great length, but at the end of some three-quarters of an hour's conversation he had contrived to impart little if any more information than had Count Szembek[4] in the short interview I had with him on July 16th, the gist of which I reported in my telegram No. 17, Saving.[5] Indeed the bulk of M. Beck's loquacity consisted in the reiteration of banalities such as characterised the officially inspired comments on the visit which appeared in the Government press. His visit was, he explained, mainly one of courtesy and it was never intended that

[1] This treaty, signed on February 27, 1935, provided for tariff reductions on a large number of British goods exported to Poland.
[2] Cf. No. 393, note 2.
[3] See Volume XII, No. 689.
[4] Polish Under-Secretary of State for Foreign Affairs.
[5] Of July 17, not printed.

any negotiations should be entered into. Poland, no less than Germany, was anxious to bear witness to the beneficial results that had flowed from the Polish-German Declaration of January 1934,[6] and the official visit had, he thought, served the useful purpose of demonstrating the importance which both sides attached to the greatly improved relations which now existed between the two countries.

3. M. Beck said that he thought that probably the most useful result of the visit was the fact that it had enabled him to make the acquaintance of Herr Hitler and to study his psychology. His impression of him was obviously a very favourable one, and he was particularly struck by the total absence of any bitterness in his comments on the policies of other countries with which he was known to disagree. This was especially the case when he was speaking of France, with whom Herr Hitler said he desired to see close and friendly relations established. Throughout the entire conversations he had found no trace of bellicosity in the Chancellor, and though he admitted that he might have formed an entirely erroneous impression he felt convinced that Herr Hitler was genuinely anxious to see war abolished in Europe.

4. On the subject of the Eastern Pact M. Beck confirmed what Count Szembek had already told me, namely, that such willingness as Germany might have at one time displayed to subscribe to a multilateral pact of consultation and non-aggression had given way to a desire to hold aloof from any engagements of that nature, the conclusions of the Soviet pacts with France and Czechoslovakia[7] having created grave misgivings in the mind of the Führer. The Soviet-Czechoslovak Pact Herr Hitler regarded as the more dangerous of the two since it was not an agreement between equals and could only result in Czechoslovakia tending to become a mere instrument of Soviet policy in Central Europe. M. Beck added that he thought it improbable that Germany would subscribe to the Eastern Pact and that in any case he doubted whether she would take any steps in the matter for the time being.

5. The subject of the Eastern Pact being under discussion, I took the occasion to tell M. Beck that in a recent conversation which you, Sir, had had with the Polish Ambassador in London you had stressed the importance of Poland making some advance in the matter. (Please see your despatch No. 278 of the 8th July.)[8] Could he tell me, I enquired, what were the Polish Government's intentions in regard to the Pact? M. Beck replied that he had already made his position clear to M. Laval during the latter's visit to Warsaw in May,[9] when he had stated that he accepted the revised Eastern Pact in principle. That, His Excellency added, was still the position of the Polish Government. M. Beck showed no inclination to pursue the subject, and as I am convinced that he will make no further advance, unless and until the German Government indicate their readiness to participate in the Pact, it did not seem to me that any useful purpose would be served by pressing the matter. In the course of a conversation which I subsequently had with the

[6] Cf. No. 125, note 6.
[7] On May 2 and May 16, 1935, respectively; cf. No. 156 and No. 239, note 3.
[8] No. 404.          [9] Cf. No. 231.

French Ambassador,[10] the latter told me that since he had taken up his appointment in May he had had no instructions from his Government to broach the subject of the Eastern Pact with the Polish Government. M. Laval was satisfied with the assurance which he had received from M. Beck and he, the Ambassador, entirely shared my view that, if further progress was to be made with the project, pressure must be concentrated on Berlin, since so long as Germany declined to participate there was little likelihood of Poland being prepared to go beyond the present stage of acceptance of the Pact in principle. Indeed M. Noel rather feared that if M. Beck were pressed too much at the present juncture he might even go back on the assurance he had already given.

6. Reverting to the subject of France, M. Beck said that he had given Herr Hitler clearly to understand that, whilst he was anxious to do everything in his power to foster good relations with Germany, the Polish-French alliance must remain inviolable; this was a cardinal point of Polish foreign policy. Herr Hitler, he continued, appeared to appreciate this fact as he showed no disposition to question it.

7. As to the possibility of Germany returning to the League of Nations, M. Beck said that he had nowhere found any enthusiasm for such a course, nor did he think there was any likelihood of her re-considering her attitude in the near future.

8. Whilst the discussions with Herr Hitler had covered a very wide field, there was, he said, little of particular interest to record. In the matter of the Polish-Danzig dispute,[11] arising out of the Free State's currency restrictions, both he and the Chancellor were in accord in desiring to localise the issue with the object of preventing it from becoming a subject of contention between Warsaw and Berlin.

9. The conversation then turned to the subject of the Italo-Abyssinian dispute, a question which M. Beck said did not directly concern Poland. He realised, however, that the issue was fraught with danger for the League of Nations and trusted that some solution could be found. He would not himself attend the forthcoming meeting of the League Council called to consider the question but he would, of course, be in contact with the Polish representative at Geneva and would give him whatever instructions the situation seemed to call for.

10. I am sending copies of this despatch to His Majesty's representatives at Paris and Berlin.

I have, &c.,
A. F. AVELING

[10] M. Léon Noel had succeeded M. Laroche as French Ambassador at Warsaw on May 29, 1935.
[11] Cf. *D.G.F.P.*, Series C, vol. iv, p. 407, note 8.

## No. 428

### Letter from Sir G. Clerk (Paris) to Sir R. Vansittart
### [A 6742/22/45]

Private and Personal                                      PARIS, *July 25, 1935*

My dear Van,

In Foreign Office despatch No. 1356 of July 19[1] there is one paragraph which I entirely endorse. It is the second paragraph, which says that 'my impression is that the agitation in France against this (the Anglo-German Naval) agreement has now considerably diminished, and I certainly wish to do nothing to revive it'. That puts the situation in a nutshell and describes the attitude which, with your permission, I should like to adopt.

The next paragraph very rightly points out that certain of these criticisms have a bearing on matters now under discussion or about to be discussed, such as the air pact and air limitation, and negotiations for the naval conference and the limitation of land armaments. What I feel is that the time to answer the criticisms of the Anglo-German naval agreement is as and when the different points crop up during such discussions. If I now entertain the French Government and French opinion with our view of the criticisms, and still more if I show Léger, or whoever it may be at the Quai d'Orsay, the memorandum enclosed in the despatch, it will merely give time for counter answers to be worked out and open the way to a wide polemic discussion which cannot do anybody any particular good.

The French 'ont fait leur deuil' of the naval agreement, and in my humble opinion the wisest course is to let it rest at that. Our answers to the criticisms will come with all the more force if they are made during the actual discussions than if the French have had time to consider and meet them beforehand.[2]

Yours ever,
G. R. C.

[1] No. 419.

[2] Replying in a private letter to Sir G. Clerk of July 29, Sir R. Vansittart said that he quite agreed 'that we should not be wise gratuitously to revive controversy on this subject, and that the time to answer criticisms will be as different points crop up during the forthcoming discussions'.

## No. 429

### Sir S. Hoare to Sir R. Lindsay (Washington)
### No. 210 Telegraphic [A 6632/22/45]

FOREIGN OFFICE, *July 26, 1935, 9 p.m.*

It appears from press reports from Washington[1] that there may be some misunderstanding in the United States of the First Lord of the Admiralty's speech of the 22nd July on naval limitation, especially in regard to the passage in which he explained that it has been found necessary to abandon

[1] Cf. No. 425.

the system of ratios, and that we have gone in for a system of programme declarations instead. You are authorised therefore to assure the United States Government that the First Lord merely said in Parliament what the United Kingdom representatives said to the United States delegation last autumn and what has been repeated several times since. No change of policy is envisaged.

I am informing the United States Ambassador orally in the same sense, and a further statement will be made in the House of Lords on Monday.[2]

[2] July 29.

## No. 430

### *Record by Mr. Eden of a conversation with the Polish Ambassador*
### [*C 5813/55/18*]

FOREIGN OFFICE, *July 26, 1935*

The Polish Ambassador asked to see me this afternoon when he enquired as to whether His Majesty's Government had any information about the forthcoming meeting of the Council with reference to the Italo-Abyssinian dispute. I told Count Raczynski that we anticipated that the Council would meet on Wednesday 31st July, but that we were not yet clear as to whether there would be general agreement as to the scope of the subject with which it was to deal. We had made it clear for our part that it seemed to us difficult, in view of the present state of relations between Italy and Abyssinia, and of the Abyssinian application, to limit the scope of the Council to the Walwal incident.[1] The Ambassador agreed and remarked that from what he knew of Geneva he thought that the Council would be expected to have a public discussion unless some arrangement could be arrived at whereby a promise of real progress could be shown in the course of the next few weeks.

The Ambassador went on to deplore the attitude of the Italian Government. He said that since he had been in London he had been enabled to understand more clearly the objectives of British policy. He was sure that our endeavours, both in respect of the Anglo-German Naval Agreement, the Air Pact and the general European situation, were upon the right lines. He had the impression that if we had been allowed to pursue them there might have been in the autumn a real détente in Europe. Whether this would have lasted or not, he could not tell, but even a détente for a few months might have had vital consequences for the future of Europe. Unfortunately this Italian-Abyssinian dispute had intervened and darkened the whole European horizon. Now he saw no possibility of any détente, and it was difficult indeed to foretell the consequences of Signor Mussolini's mistaken policy for Europe and for the League.

Having referred to the League the Ambassador reminded me that Poland came up for re-election to a semi-permanent seat on the Council at the

[1] See Volume XIV.

Assembly of this year. M. Beck had asked him to come and see me and to say how grateful the Polish Govt. would be if His Majesty's Government could support Poland's candidature. Count Raczynski added that from information he had gleaned when last at Geneva, he thought that there would be no great difficulty in Poland's re-election. I replied that as the Ambassador knew, it was our tradition not to give any promises in advance as to how we should vote. I would, however, look into the matter and would give to the Polish representative at Geneva when the Council met such answer as might be possible. The Ambassador said that he perfectly understood the situation and would be grateful if we would follow this procedure.

A. E.

## No. 431

*Sir G. Clerk (Paris) to Sir S. Hoare (Received July 29)*

*No. 1076 [C 5700/55/18]*

Confidential                                                   PARIS, *July 26, 1935*

Sir,

When, in accordance with the instructions in your despatch No. 1344[1] of July 18th, I opened the question of land armaments in the course of my interview with M. Laval to-day, he said that though he was aware of what I was going to say to him he was not in a position to discuss the matter. He was referring it to the 'Haut-Comité militaire,' and would take it up with me when he had received their advisory opinion.

2. I am therefore unable to give you as yet any authoritative report of the views of the French Government, but the following summary of the observations made by M. Léger, to whom I had instructed His Majesty's Minister to speak, as suggested in your despatch under reference may be of interest as showing the probable nature of the French reply.

3. When Mr. Campbell had given a brief account of the past history of the question and had gone on to speak in the sense of paragraphs 11–13 of your despatch,[2] M. Léger observed that, like the French Government, His Majesty's Government appeared to have reached the conclusion that there was little or no hope of reducing the German programme as published in the decree of March 16th. On what basis, then, did His Majesty's Government suggest that the French Government should now approach Germany? France could hardly make an offer that would set the French seal on a German programme which, when completed, would give Germany an overwhelming preponderance if France remained at her present level. The French Government could not go to their public and announce that they had *come to an agreement* with Germany which, whilst acquiescing in the German programme, would involve a considerable increase in the French forces and entail a corresponding sacrifice on the part of the French people. If the conditions requisite for a more reasonable settlement remained absent and

---

[1] No. 416.

[2] This word was amended to 'memorandum' on the filed copy, i.e. enclosure in No. 416.

Germany continued to carry out her programme, France, ill though she could afford it, would have no alternative but to make the effort required to keep her abreast of Germany. That in fact was what the French Government were proposing to do, and the General Staff were already at work on a two-year programme.[3]

4. When Mr. Campbell remarked that that would lead to an inevitable race in which France in the long run must always be beaten, M. Léger retorted: 'In the long run, yes, but not necessarily in the short run; there may well be a limit imposed by financial and even social factors on Germany's present power of expansion.' There were only two things, he continued, which might bring Germany to reason. The first was that she should realise that France intended to spare no effort to keep ahead, or at least abreast, of her (Mr. Baldwin's declaration that Great Britain would never allow Germany to outdistance her in the air[4] had, in M. Léger's opinion, had a most salutary effect so far as the air arm was concerned); the second was that the Powers should unite in showing greater resolution than they had hitherto shown in resisting German rearmament on the present scale. Though Mr. Campbell questioned the force of both these arguments, M. Léger stuck to his guns. Neither of the above conditions, he went on, was present to-day; the second need not be discussed, whilst as regards the first, it was clear that the German Government were banking on the present apparent weakness of France. Not only did they centre their hopes on the exchanges which were taking place between ex-combatants, but they thought they had in M. Laval a man who was ready for peace at almost any price. It was true, M. Léger said, speaking privately and confidentially, that M. Laval was a man who had no passions save that of a deeply-rooted love of peace. He had that passion in the way that an animal had its instincts; it was at once his strength and his weakness. At the same time, he had an infinite fund of horse sense, and his heart would never over-rule his head. He was not therefore the man to make terms with Germany which sanctioned her military superiority over France.

5. There was much talk, M. Léger concluded, of a visit to Paris by Herr von Ribbentrop. The facts were that he would be discouraged from coming unless and until he could do so with some proposal which France could reasonably and honourably accept.

6. The above are merely M. Léger's personal views and do not necessarily represent those of M. Laval, but I have thought it well to report them as indicating the direction in which M. Léger's very considerable influence will be cast.

I have, &c.,

GEORGE R. CLERK[5]

---

[3] In a minute on this despatch (see note 5 below) Mr. Wigram commented that 'a two-year programme' was 'presumably a programme based on two-year service'.

[4] See 295 *H.C. Deb.* 5 *s.*, col. 883 (November 28, 1934).

[5] Minutes were written on this despatch by Mr. Wigram, Sir R. Vansittart, and Sir S. Hoare. Mr. Wigram wrote (July 29): 'This has the appearance of a very unsatisfactory

interview. As a matter of fact the Embassy were in possession of sufficient information . . . to have carried the discussion further; and it is a pity that they did not do so. It will have to be done eventually . . .' Sir R. Vansittart on July 30 agreed 'that the Paris Embassy shd return to the charge, and charge hard. Things cannot be left as they are in this despatch; for that is a confession of stagnation and bankruptcy in regard to land armaments. . . . On the other hand, I do not agree with Mr. Wigram that we can go in for Air Limitation without the French. If the basis of such an idea is partly that the Govt will wish to do so for electoral purposes, let me say at once that the Naval Agreement was by no means an unqualified success with the press and in wider circles . . .' Sir S. Hoare wrote: 'I agree with Sir R. Vansittart that any kind of separate Air Agreement with Germany is in present circumstances out of the question. This being so, it is essential to make a big offensive on the French. The Embassy should be told to make our points and to stick to them. Could not also the military attaché be mobilized to talk to the French soldiers. I am sure that we must concentrate on all these peace questions between now and the autumn, whilst M. Laval has a breathing space from the Chamber. S.H. 5/7.'

## No. 432

### Letter from Mr. Fletcher (New York) to Mr. Leeper
### [A 6896/22/45]

NEW YORK, *July 26, 1935*

Dear Leeper,

I have not sent you a detailed report on the London despatches concerning the Anglo-German naval treaty. The correspondents appear to have reflected the British and Continental press. It seemed likely that the storm would be allowed to subside before any further explanation could usefully be offered by London. The extreme annoyance of the French, and the jubilation of the Germans have thus been well publicised throughout the country. So has the apparent inconsistency of this change in British policy.

So far as we are concerned the only line to be followed, I take it, is the belief of H.M. Government that the agreement will facilitate the eventual conclusion of a more general agreement between the naval powers of the world.

In the meantime the announcement has been made that the system of naval ratios has been abandoned by Great Britain, and the reasons for this have been set forth in the despatches from your side of the water.

The despatches describing the Anglo-German agreement were most prominently displayed and those announcing our decision on naval ratios also received front page prominence.

It can be taken for granted in fact that any British steps in regard to naval matters will invariably enjoy much greater and sometimes more sensational publicity in the American press than they would in the British press.

Yours ever,
ANGUS FLETCHER

## No. 433

*Sir G. Clerk (Paris) to Sir S. Hoare (Received July 27, 9.30 a.m.)*
*No. 150 Telegraphic [C 5690/55/18]*

PARIS, *July 27, 1935, 12.46 a.m.*

Your telegram No. 222 Saving.[1]

I saw Monsieur Laval today[2] and carried out your instructions leaving him in no doubt over the several points on which you desired that there should be no room for misunderstanding.

I was unable to induce him to give a final answer until I had obtained from you an interpretation of the words 'His Majesty's Government cannot go beyond that' which occurred at the end of paragraph 1 of your telegram. Monsieur Laval suggested that they meant that if result of your conversation with German Government was to show that they did not accept principle of an air pact accompanied by bilateral agreements, apart from whether they wished to conclude any such bilateral agreement themselves, the proposal put to Germany would fall to the ground and (? the problem)[3] would be reconsidered in its entirety by French and British Governments.

Though your words seem to me to bear such interpretation I fear that Monsieur Laval will require an assurance of this kind before giving you a categorical reply. In other words he does not want to commit himself to participating in negotiations for an air pact unless he is certain in advance that it will be supplemented so far as France is concerned by a bilateral agreement with United Kingdom. He maintains that without it the air pact would have no interest for France—rather the contrary—as she would be adding nothing to Locarno to her own advantage but undertaking a new and heavy commitment.

You will appreciate that assurance desired by Monsieur Laval would bind you to no more than a reconsideration with him of the whole question. If you can see your way to give it I feel sure from what he said that he will approve of your going ahead on lines of paragraph 2 of your telegram.

[1] No. 420.　　　　　　　　　　　[2] i.e. July 26, the day on which this telegram was drafted.
[3] The text was here uncertain.

## No. 434

*Sir R. Lindsay (Washington) to Sir S. Hoare (Received July 28, 9.30 a.m.)*
*No. 187 Telegraphic [A 6666/22/45]*

WASHINGTON, *July 27, 1935, 8.25 p.m.*

Your telegram No. 210.[1]

Assurance has been conveyed.

United States government fully understand position and as far as they are concerned see no need for any further public statement.

[1] No. 429.

## No. 435

*Sir S. Hoare to Sir G. Clerk (Paris)*

*No. 189 Telegraphic* [*C 5690/55/18*]

FOREIGN OFFICE, *July 27, 1935, 9 p.m.*

Your telegram No. 150.[1]

As a matter of fact the words 'H.M. Government cannot go beyond that' were intended by me only to apply to the views contained in paragraph 1 and 4 of my telegram No. 222 Saving.[2]

2. But, of course, if the result of our representations to the German Government is to show that they do not accept the principle of an Air Pact accompanied by bilateral agreements, apart from whether they wish to conclude any such bilateral agreement themselves, a completely new situation will arise. Both we and the French Government will then be entirely uncommitted and we shall each of us have to reconsider the situation in its entirety.

3. Please so inform M. Laval immediately, and in these circumstances I hope that he will agree to my approaching the German Government on the understanding outlined in paragraph 2 of my telegram No. 222 Saving.

4. It would be very convenient if possible to have his reply by July 29th in order that I may at once open the question with the German Ambassador here.

[1] No. 433.        [2] No. 420.

## No. 436

*Sir G. Clerk (Paris) to Sir S. Hoare (Received July 30)*

*No. 167 Saving: Telegraphic* [*C 5708/55/18*]

PARIS, *July 29, 1935*

Your telegram No. 189.[1]

I saw M. Laval this evening and gave him your explanation.

He expressed himself as satisfied and after a little persuasion (he is clearly not very enthusiastic) agreed to your opening the conversation with the German Government whenever you wish on the proposed basis.

He reminded me of the other stipulation already made,[2] namely that the French Government are unable to agree to the air pact being concluded (as distinct from negotiated) in advance of the conclusion of agreements on the other matters ennumerated [*sic*] in the declaration of February 3rd.

[1] No. 435.        [2] See Nos. 362 and 363.

## No. 437

### Sir S. Hoare to Mr. Newton (Berlin)
### No. 826 [C 5592/55/18]

FOREIGN OFFICE, *July 29, 1935*

Sir,

In continuation of my interview with the German Ambassador on July 23rd (my despatch No. 807 of July 23rd)[1] a further conversation on the subject of the Eastern Pact took place at the Foreign Office on July 25th, this time with the Acting Counsellor of the German Embassy.[2]

2. The attention of Baron Marschall von Bieberstein was drawn to Baron von Neurath's communication to Sir Eric Phipps of April 13th (Berlin telegram No. 153[3] of the 13th April) in which it is stated that 'the German Government was ready to give its consent to a collective security pact if it were based on mutual and general obligations of non-aggression and arrangements for arbitration, if in the case of a breach of the peace a consultative procedure were provided for, and on the understanding that the German Government would be ready to adhere to general measures for withholding support from such an aggressor.' It was pointed out to Baron Marschall that Baron von Neurath's communication added that 'just as the German Government is unable to join any pact which contains military engagements as an essential element of its contents, so can arrangements of this sort which lie outside this pact not deter the German Government on its side from concluding pacts of non-aggression on the basis set out above.' Baron Marschall's attention was specially drawn to the fact that with regard to such military alliances there was in Baron von Neurath's statement of April 13th no qualification whatever either as regards the present or the future. Baron Marschall was further reminded of the statement in the sixth of the thirteen points in Herr Hitler's speech of May 21st to the effect that 'the German Government are ready in principle to conclude pacts of non-aggression with their various neighbouring States.'

3. Baron Marschall was then informed that our understanding is that the neighbouring States are Russia, Latvia, Estonia, Lithuania, Poland and Czechoslovakia. All these States were covered by the general obligation of non-aggression assumed by Germany in the Kellogg Pact and in the case of Russia there were also the Berlin Treaty of 1926[4] and the Conciliation Treaty of 1929,[5] the protocol renewing which was signed in 1931 and ratified by Germany in 1933. These, with the Kellogg Pact, seemed to cover much the same ground as a bilateral non-aggression pact. Therefore, as regards Russia at least, the German Government were not being asked to do anything new, but that did not mean that the confirmation of what, in practice, already

---

[1] No. 424.
[2] This conversation, conducted by Mr. Wigram, is referred to in *D.G.F.P.*, Series C, vol. iv, No. 236. It is there reported as having taken place on July 26.
[3] See Volume XII, No. 719, note 2.     [4] See *B.F.S.P.*, vol. 125, pp. 738–41.
[5] See *ibid.*, vol. 130, pp. 758–60, and vol. 134, pp. 848–9.

largely existed would not at this time have an important psychological and calming effect. It was pointed out that the Air Pact, which a helpful attitude on the part of Germany in the matter of the Eastern Pact would certainly assist both us and Germany to secure, was in itself in many respects a duplication of the Locarno Treaty, but that did not mean that it was useless; there was also the psychological and tranquillising effect which it would have to consider.

4. Baron Marschall was told that we understood that both Latvia and Estonia would welcome bilateral non-aggression arrangements with Germany, if Germany could see her way to offer such arrangements to them; and, after all, those two States already enjoyed *vis-à-vis* Germany the benefit of the Kellogg Pact.

5. His Majesty's Government had taken note of the German view that Lithuania must put herself in order as regards the Memel Statute before Germany could make any arrangements with her. Between Germany and Poland there was already a non-aggression and arbitration treaty. We understood that Germany had offered Czechoslovakia such a treaty in 1933 (see Prague telegram No. 11 of the 10th November, 1933).[6]

6. In conclusion, Baron Marschall was told that what had been said to him on this matter represented the manner in which the position was interpreted in the Foreign Office. We wished to have confirmation from the German Government that that interpretation was correct.

7. I request that you will take an early opportunity of using at the Ministry for Foreign Affairs the same language as that recorded above and in my despatch No. 807 of the 23rd July. You should report the result by telegraph.

I am, &c.,
SAMUEL HOARE

[6] Not printed. Cf. *D.G.F.P.*, Series C, vol. ii, No. 68.

## No. 438

### *Sir S. Hoare to Sir R. Lindsay (Washington)*
### *No. 678 [A 6690/22/45]*

FOREIGN OFFICE, *July 29, 1935*

Sir,

The American Ambassador came to see me this morning before his departure for the United States. I had promised to give him some information for which he had asked concerning the probable course of the naval negotiations.[1] I attach a copy of the memorandum[2] that I handed to him in this connexion. Having read the memorandum he asked me whether it was our intention that Germany should take part in the Naval Conference. I replied that our present view was that the Conference would, in the first

[1] See No. 407.
[2] The text of this memorandum, dated July 23, 1935, is printed in *F.R.U.S. 1935*, vol. i, pp. 84–5 and is not reproduced here.

instance, be a conference of the Washington Powers, and that probably out of it would emerge a second chapter or a new conference, in which both Germany and Russia would take part. He also raised the question as to whether we could not give his Government the details of the German programme up to 1942, on the ground that as the American programme had already been published to the world[3] there would in effect be reciprocity between Germany and the United States. I told him that my first impression of such a course was that it would make difficulties with the French and Italian Governments.

2. He also asked that the United States Embassy in London should be kept as closely as possible informed of the course of any future discussions. When I alluded to the close relations that existed between Mr. Atherton and the Foreign Office, the Ambassador seemed to suggest that the liaison had been weakened during the Anglo-German discussions. I told the Ambassador that I would look further into the points that he had raised, but that our general desire was that the liaison between Mr. Atherton and the Department should remain unimpaired. . . .[4]

I am, &c.,

SAMUEL HOARE

[3] A reference to the Vinson Bill; cf. No. 426, note 5.
[4] The last two paragraphs dealt with the Italo-Ethiopian dispute and are here omitted.

## No. 439

*Letter from Sir R. Vansittart to Admiral Sir E. Chatfield*
*[A 6691/22/45]*

Secret                                    FOREIGN OFFICE, *July 29, 1935*

My dear Chatfield,

You will probably already have heard that the French Ambassador approached us recently with the suggestion that a delegate from the Admiralty should go to Paris shortly in order to break the ice which has formed since the Anglo-German Naval Agreement and to set in motion the preliminary discussions on naval limitation. A copy of my minute of the conversation[1] is enclosed.

2. We agree with M. Corbin that the visit, as a first step in the resumption of discussions, could only have a good effect. On the other hand, we feel that there are two points which should be made quite clear to the French from the start. In the first place, we are no more prepared now than we have been to date to give the French Ministry of Marine the German programme except on the strict basis of reciprocity, nor did the Minister for League of Nations Affairs give M. Laval any encouragement to think that the Admiralty representative would be authorised to depart from this principle. The French must not suppose that the course which they suggest is a way round reciprocity; there is, in fact, no way round.

[1] See No. 421.

3. Secondly, it must be made clear that the visit to Paris by an Admiralty representative will not replace the preliminary conversations proper which, it is intended, will take place in London like the preliminary talks with the other Powers. We think that any divergence from this rule, besides being undesirable in itself, would only land us in difficulties with other Powers.

4. If you agree with the above, I would propose so to inform M. Corbin myself and to say that the Admiralty representative will go to Paris on this understanding.

5. Would you let us know whether you agree with the proposed course of action? If you do agree perhaps you would suggest at the same time the name of a suitable officer for the mission.[2]

6. Incidentally, if the mission takes place we shall have to consider whether the proposed communication to the French Government on qualitative limitation shall be made before, after or during it.[3]

[2] A marginal note on the filed copy by Mr. Craigie here read: 'We should have said that it would be preferable that the officer should not be of too high a rank (i.e. not flag rank). But I presume you have said this privately.' Mr. Gore-Booth added: 'Yes. P.H.G-B. 31/7.'

[3] Admiral Chatfield wrote on July 31 to say that he was in general agreement with Sir R. Vansittart's letter, and that Captain Danckwerts would be the officer nominated.

### No. 440

*Mr. Newton (Berlin) to Sir S. Hoare (Received July 30, 6.45 p.m.)*
*No. 246[1] Telegraphic: by telephone [C 5730/55/18]*

BERLIN, *July 30, 1935*

Your despatch No. 807.[2]

I learn from Secretary of State this morning that German Ambassador in Paris had a long conversation with M. Laval on July 27th following one some days previously with M. Léger as regards Eastern Pact.[3] Without going into details about the Pact itself M. Laval explained at some length why its conclusion would help him for reasons of internal politics. Either he or M. Léger seem to have given some encouragement, although in language which was not very precise, to an idea originated by French Ambassador here that Eastern Pact might supersede Franco-Soviet agreement—see penultimate paragraph of my letter to Sir R. Vansittart of July 18th.[4] M. Laval mentioned that in any case this agreement would lapse after 5 years. Herr von Bülow here observed to me that French Government wished to water down the Franco-Soviet Agreement. According to Soviet Embassy in Berlin whom he had consulted when the French Ambassador first made his suggestion, an Eastern Pact could not, in Soviet view, supersede Franco-Soviet Agreement.

M. Laval then intimated to Herr von Köster that although Eastern Pact was an objective it was not urgent and French Government might be equally or even more content with satisfaction in some other field mentioning either

[1] This telegram was originally numbered 'No. 174 Saving.'  [2] No. 424.
[3] See *D.G.F.P.*, Series C, vol. iv, Nos. 220 and 231; cf. *ibid.*, No. 235.  [4] No. 418.

Danubian Pact or, to Herr von Bülow's surprise, an arms agreement. As regards the latter Herr von Bülow said that he did not know yet what M. Laval had precisely in mind but he had referred expressly to Chancellor's speech of May 21st. In reply to my enquiry as to German attitude in particular in regard to limitation of effectives Herr von Bülow did not go beyond that speech. He said Germany would welcome qualitative limitation and feared that prospect of any agreement about effectives was slight having regard to abortive result of negotiations over the last ten years. His impression was moreover that M. Laval's particular aim was to secure relief for French budget.

M. Laval stated very clearly that France would no longer expect Germany to return to the League of Nations as part of a general settlement. Herr von Bülow here drew my attention to omission in your speech of July 11th to[5] this part of declaration of February 3rd. I told him I was sure that Germany's return was still greatly desired and assumed you had merely refrained from mentioning this point as you thought it useless to do so at this juncture.

M. Laval had intimated that he might be free to begin serious negotiations in about 3 weeks. Herr von Bülow however was uncertain whether members of German Government and experts concerned would have returned from holidays and be ready to negotiate much before latter part of September.[6]

From previous conversation with M. Léger German Ambassador understood that France would not be a party to an Eastern Pact but proposed to guarantee it. This was a proposal which suggested reversion to M. Barthou's original ideas and would be inacceptable to Germany. Much however was obscure in Ambassador's report of this conversation.

[5] See 304 H.C. Deb. 5 s., cols. 509–24. The text here should, presumably, have read: 'to omission in your speech of July 11th of any reference to . . .'.

[6] In a letter to Baron von Neurath of July 30, Herr von Bülow said that 'our vague and evasive attitude is making us suspect and is reuniting the Stresa front'. Baron von Neurath replied on August 7 that owing to the Abyssinian developments there was 'marked disunity in the Stresa front'. Herr von Bülow was instructed 'calmly to declare (and to instruct the Missions accordingly) that no German views can be expected before October'. See D.G.F.P., op. cit., Nos. 234 and 252.

## No. 441

*Record by Mr. Wigram of two conversations with Herr von Hoesch*
[C 5795/55/18]

FOREIGN OFFICE, *July 30, 1935*

I have had yesterday afternoon and this morning two conversations with the German Ambassador about the Eastern Pact.[1]

At the first conversation I repeated to the Ambassador what I had said to the Acting Counsellor of the Embassy on July 25[2] that we considered the position of the German Government in the matter of the Eastern Pact to

[1] For Herr von Hoesch's account of these interviews see D.G.F.P., Series C, vol. iv, No. 236.        [2] See No. 437.

be defined by the pronouncement of April 13 (Berlin tel. 153)[3] in which Baron von Neurath had stated to Sir E. Phipps in writing that Germany would consent to a collective security pact of non-aggression which would not include mutual assistance arrangements itself but which would be unaffected by the conclusion of mutual assistance arrangements concluded outside it. We further considered that Baron von Neurath's statement had been completed by the relevant passage in the Chancellor's speech of May 21 in which the latter had declared the readiness of the German Government to conclude bilateral pacts of non-aggression with the various neighbouring states.

The Ambassador replied that we were under a misapprehension. The declaration given on April 13 no longer held owing to the Franco-Russian Alliance of May 2. The field was now held by the Chancellor's speech of May 21; and the only thing offered was bilateral non-aggression pacts with Germany's neighbours; and that meant 'neighbours', i.e. states adjacent to Germany, i.e. in the East, Lithuania, Poland and Czechoslovakia.

I said that this was very surprising to me. Germany had given us (i.e. to the British Ambassador in Berlin) a promise and an undertaking on April 13 which contained no reservation and no qualification. It was to give a collective security pact of non-aggression even if mutual assistance arrangements were concluded outside the pact. I then showed the Ambassador Berlin telegram No. 153[3] and I pointed particularly to the words 'as it has no aggressive intentions the German Government does not feel affected by real *offensive* agreements either . . .[4]. Just as it is, therefore, unable to join any pact which contains such military engagements as an essential element of its existence, so can agreements of this sort which lie outside this pact, not deter the German Government on its side from concluding pacts of non-aggression on the basis set out above. Such was the sense of the German Government's reply to the British Ambassador's enquiry'.

This morning Herr von Hoesch has pointed out to me that the word 'offensive' is wrong and should read 'defensive'. He shewed me the German original and the 'Times' message of the same date; and declared that there had been a mistake in transmission. This is unfortunate; but, as I told the Ambassador, it does not really affect the issue.

Our position, I repeated to him this morning after consulting Sir R. Vansittart, is that we consider the German Government bound by the pronouncement of April 13 supplemented by the relevant passage in the speech of May 21.

The Ambassador repeated that he must also make clear the position of the German Government which is that the offer of April 13 has lapsed as a result of the Franco-Russian Alliance of May 2 against Germany. I said that we did not consider it an offensive alliance but a mutual assistance agreement in accordance with the principles of the League; and we made our view clear in our note to the German Government of July 5th.[5] Herr von Hoesch said that neither we nor the French Government had ever been able to contradict

[3] See Volume XII, No. 719, note 2.　　　[4] Punctuation as in original quotation.
[5] No. 397.

the German Government's view that the Franco-Russian Treaty was directed solely against Germany. He claimed that the French Ambassador in Berlin had himself admitted it. Further the German Govt. claimed that it was not in accordance with the spirit of the Covenant or of its stipulations. He continued that the German offer was now limited to that made in the Chancellor's speech of May 21, i.e. bilateral pacts of non-aggression with neighbours, i.e. with Lithuania (under reserve of Memel), Poland and Czechoslovakia. He said that he did not know that the German Government would actually refuse to conclude also bilateral pacts of non-aggression with Latvia and Estonia if they were asked; but he could give no indication about Russia.

He repeated that this was the point of view of the German Government; though he added that no definite decision against the Eastern Pact had yet been taken.

I said that the position on the two sides seemed now to have been clearly stated; and that I would report accordingly.[6]

R. F. W.

[6] A minute of July 30 by Sir R. Vansittart on this document included the following comment: 'This [is] a complete breach of faith, and a very serious one. (It cannot be honestly argued that the Franco-Soviet Pact has caused the undertaking to lapse. We have already rebutted that argument, and the Germans have never yet come into the open with it.) This breach of faith is serious, because it will hold up all progress in effect, if persevered with.' He added: 'The only lever we shall eventually have will be publicity. There will be plenty when we tell the French and Russians—as we must—apart from what we do (and will do) with the Press here, if there is no other way.'

## No. 442

*Sir R. Lindsay (Washington) to Sir S. Hoare (Received August 12)*
*No. 863 [A 7073/22/45]*

WASHINGTON, *July 30, 1935*

Sir:

I have the honour to refer to the statement made in the House of Commons on July 22nd by the First Lord of the Admiralty about naval limitation,[1] and to report that on the evening of the 25th I met Mr. Norman Davis at a dinner, who told me that the State Department had been somewhat taken aback by the statement. I said that I was sorry to hear this, as it seemed to me that the First Lord had said nothing new in substance, and that he had merely depicted a state of affairs which had obviously prevailed for a good many months. Mr. Davis admitted this quite fully, but he said that the Department would nevertheless have been glad if it had been possible to forewarn it of the impending statement. It had no objection to the substance of the First Lord's speech, and would probably have raised no objection to any proposal made beforehand that a speech in these terms should be made; but as a matter of fact the American press had at first fancied that a sensational new policy was being started and had prepared to write it up. The State Department had

[1] Cf. No. 425, note 1.     [2] No. 425.

a good deal of difficulty in quieting them down. I expressed gratitude at the success which had attended the Department's efforts in this direction; and on this I reported to you in my despatch No. 850[2] of July 24th.

2. I did not gather from Mr. Davis's language that the State Department felt at all deeply on the subject. From his tone rather than from the actual language he used I should infer that when an important statement on naval policy is to be made, anxious as the Department undoubtedly is to cooperate closely with His Majesty's Government, it likes to be at least warned beforehand and of course to be consulted if the circumstances require consultation. This attitude is the more natural as American newspaper reporters are excitable and ignorant, and liable, as they were in the present case, to give a wrong twist to events unless they are carefully guided.

3. Your telegram No. 210,[3] referring to the impression created in the State Department by the First Lord's speech, and informing me that a further statement would be made in the House of Lords, reached Washington when I had left town for three days. Mr. Broadmead, First Secretary of the Embassy, conveyed the substance of your telegram immediately to Mr. Dunn, Head of the Western European Department, who admitted at once that there had been no misunderstanding in the State Department, and referred Mr. Broadmead to the conversation which I had had with Mr. Davis, at which he himself had been present. As reported in my telegram No. 187[4] of July 27th, Mr. Dunn said that so far as the United States Government were concerned, there was no real need for any further statement at all.

I have, &c.,<br>R. C. LINDSAY

[3] No. 429.      [4] No. 434.

**No. 443**

*Sir R. Clive (Tokyo) to Sir S. Hoare (Received July 31, 1.10 p.m.)*
*No. 204 Telegraphic [A 6788/22/45]*

TOKYO, *July 31, 1935, 5.43 p.m.*

Naval disarmament.

Vice Minister for Foreign Affairs asked whether I had any news. I said nothing but what I had read in the press about the speech by First Lord of the Admiralty[1] and his remarks about ratios. I had noted this had been welcomed by Japanese press. I believed that His Majesty's Government wished for conference but only if success was assured in advance. I asked if Japanese navy authorities still held to their extreme views. He said Admiral Kanji Kato was due to retire in November and that a more accommodating view might then prevail. I asked if they would then consider British suggestion of declaring their building programme in advance. He could not say but favoured bilateral conversations. He believed this was the only way of reaching understanding. I said it seemed to me essential that Japanese should drop insistence on parity with America which led nowhere. He was

[1] Cf. No. 425, note 1.

disposed to agree and said that some way round must be found as Japanese navy considered their defensive requirements as great or greater than America.[2]

[2] This telegram was repeated to Washington as Foreign Office telegram No. 216 of August 2.

## No. 444

### Sir S. Hoare to Sir G. Clerk (Paris)
### No. 194 Telegraphic [C 5730/55/18]

FOREIGN OFFICE, *July 31, 1935, 6.30 p.m.*

Mr. Newton's telegram No. 174 Saving[1] of July 30th.

Please ascertain whether Herr von Bülow's remarks accurately represent sense of what M. Laval and M. Léger have told German Ambassador in Paris.

Is it correct that French Government no longer regard Eastern Pact proposal as either urgent or of the first importance, and that they have indicated that supersession of Franco-Russian agreement by Eastern Pact might be explored? It seems difficult to credit either of these statements. On the other hand we should clearly know exactly how the matter now stands in the view of the French Government, seeing that we have recently on several occasions pressed the German Government to realise the necessity of including an Eastern Pact in a general settlement.

What exactly was said as regards Arms Agreement and limitation of land armaments? And is it correct that French Government no longer intend to press for German return to the League?

[1] The reference was to No. 440.

## No. 445

### Letter from Mr. Newton (Berlin) to Mr. Wigram (Received August 3)
### [C 5812/55/18]

BERLIN, *July 31, 1935*

My dear Wigram,

In the course of my conversation with Bülow on the 30th July,[1] I asked if he could tell me what was the Chancellor's attitude to the Secretary of State's appeal[2] and whether any reply was in prospect. Bülow replied that he could not say what the Chancellor's intentions were as regards an answer, but 'speaking between you and me' I should not be surprised if he ignored it, an anticipation which I have heard he expressed also some days ago to a colleague.[3]

On my pointing out that the Secretary of State was only asking the Chancellor to do something which he had already promised to Sir John Simon first

[1] See No. 440.     [2] See No. 418, note 1.     [3] See No. 418.

in Berlin and then again at Stresa, Bülow retorted with some heat that it had never then been expected that a Franco-Russian alliance would be concluded against Germany, followed by a Russo-Czech alliance, or that there would be such offensive proceedings at Geneva. He therefore considered that there was no obligation to carry out the offer made in previous circumstances. Germany might of course conclude an Eastern pact but felt perfectly free to do as she liked in the matter. Evidently the Germans made their concession to us at Stresa in the hope that it would blunt, if not turn aside, the point of the Franco-Soviet agreement which was in prospect, and that in any case it would avert such condemnation as was expressed at Geneva.[4] They feel therefore that they have not had their *quid pro quo*.

Bülow also said: 'Who in any case really wants the Eastern pact?'—by which presumably he meant who of the proposed participants really want it. He added that the Baltic States do not really want a pact of non-aggression; what they want is one of mutual assistance. They have, however, already been told that, although Germany might intervene in the event of aggression, she is not prepared to undertake any treaty obligation to do so.

As all this was in the nature of an aside in a conversation which I had only sought for the purpose of keeping in touch, I do not want to give these remarks more importance than they perhaps deserve by reporting them officially. In any case I could not in fairness report what was said 'speaking between you and me'. I think however that these details may be of interest and give you further help in understanding his attitude.

Yours ever,
BASIL C. NEWTON

P.S. The Belgian Minister who gets hold of a good deal of information—some good, some less so—tells me that certain officials in the Ministry for Foreign Affairs are inclined to recommend that, if Germany is pressed over the Eastern pact, she should propose a regional pact of non-aggression in the East to be supplemented by a general Consultative pact to which France at any rate, and probably also England, would be expected to adhere.

B. C. N. 1/8

---

[4] A reference to the Resolution of the League of Nations Council of April 17, 1935; see Volume XII, No. 732.

## CHAPTER VI

# Abortive discussions on proposed Eastern and Air Pacts: preparations for the Naval Conference

## August 1–December 3, 1935

### No. 446

*Sir G. Clerk (Paris) to Sir S. Hoare (Received August 2, 9.30 a.m.)*
*No. 155 Telegraphic [C 5771/55/18]*

PARIS, *August 1, 1935, 11.15 p.m.*

Your telegram No. 194.[1]

Head of European Department who is temporarily in charge of Ministry of Foreign Affairs was totally unable to deal with your questions. Though I had not expected a full answer,[2] I thought he might be able to give some indication that would have been useful as a pointer.

2. Monsieur Charveriat could in effect do no more than say that he considered all the remarks attributed to Monsieur Laval to be inherently improbable, and some of them fantastic. I (? would not)[3] myself however accept his opinion without some reserve. Monsieur Laval speaks very freely and informally to the German Ambassador, often, probably, with the object more than anything else of feeling his way. I suspect that he does not intend all his remarks to be passed on to Berlin nor always care himself to disclose them even to his own officials.

[1] No. 444.
[2] Foreign Office telegram No. 97 of 5.30 p.m. on August 1 to Mr. Strang, at Geneva, referred to Nos. 440 and 444 and repeated the following telephone message received that afternoon from Mr. Campbell: 'H.M. Ambassador, Paris, feels doubtful if, in absence of M. Laval and M. Léger at Geneva, it will be possible to obtain any information on this matter at Ministry of Foreign Affairs.' Mr. Strang was requested, if he had an opportunity, 'to make enquiries of French Delegation'. The 87th (Extraordinary) Session of the Council of the League of Nations was being held at Geneva from July 31 to August 3, 1935: Mr. Eden represented the United Kingdom. [3] The text was here uncertain.

### No. 447

*Sir S. Hoare to Mr. Newton (Berlin)*
*No. 832 [C 5708/55/18]*

FOREIGN OFFICE, *August 1, 1935*

Sir,

I asked the German Ambassador to call upon me this morning for the purpose of discussing the position of the Air Pact. I began by repeating to him what I had often said before as to the necessity of beginning the Eastern Pact negotiations if we were to have any chance of starting upon the Air Pact. The Ambassador made his usual answer about the Eastern Pact. He added, however, that he was glad to be able to make to me a verbal communication from his Government as to the position of the Locarno Powers under the Franco-Russian Treaty. He then read to me the communication that I attach as an appendix.

2. I thanked him for the communication and told him that I assumed that it meant that the German Government did not henceforth intend to regard the Franco-Russian Treaty as an obstacle in the way of an Eastern Pact. He did not dissent from this assumption though he stated that his Government still maintained their juridical position and would have to argue it in future negotiations. As to the negotiations for the pact, he repeated to me the statement which he had made in his interview with me of July 23rd (see my despatch No. 807 of that date)[1] that his Government had come to no decision.

3. As I was anxious to discuss the Air negotiations, I brought to an end as soon as I was able the conversation about the Eastern Pact, telling Herr von Hoesch that I was purposely not dealing with it in detail as Mr. Wigram had fully explained to him my position on the subject two days ago (see Foreign Office telegram No. 150 to Berlin).[2]

4. As to the Air negotiations, I explained to him the present position, namely, that the French Government would not embark upon them until it was accepted that bilateral agreements should form part of a general Pact. The Ambassador started by attempting to make this an issue of principle between the German and French Governments. I asked him whether it was really a question of principle at all, and whether the question did not really depend upon the scope and character of the contemplated Agreements. I then outlined to him our conception of the Agreements and made it quite clear that we were only contemplating arrangements that were incidental to the general Pact, that were necessary to it for making it effective, and that would be open to all five powers. This interpretation seemed somewhat to disarm him. More than once, however, he declared that the suggestion even of these Agreements showed the duplicity of French policy. With one hand the French were ready to give Locarno guarantees, with the other hand they were anxious to withdraw them from Germany by bi-lateral agreements. I repeated to him as strong[ly] and definitely as I could that the Agreements that we contemplated were based upon the spirit and principles of Locarno. They would not interfere with the Locarno equilibrium and they would not be used to the disadvantage of any of the Locarno powers. That was our conception of the Agreements. Such Agreements were regarded as both safe and useful and the German Government could rely upon us in the negotiations to maintain this position. This being so, it seemed to me entirely safe for the German Government to enter the negotiations on these lines.

5. The Ambassador said that he would convey at once to his Government the views that I had expressed. He added that so far as the place and method

<hr>

[1] No. 424.    [2] No. 449 below.

of the discussions were concerned, assuming that the discussions could begin, he agreed with our proposals that London should be the clearing-house and that the discussions should, in the first instance, proceed through the diplomatic channels.

I am, &c.,

SAMUEL HOARE

APPENDIX TO NO. 447

The German Government are now in possession of the answer of the four Locarno Powers. They welcome the declarations of the four Governments with regard to the importance of the Locarno Pact, and they state in accordance with them that the provisions of the Rhine Pact of Locarno cannot legally be modified or defined by the fact that a treaty has been concluded with a third party by one of the signatories.

They take notice with satisfaction of the declaration of the two guaranteeing Powers that the rights and duties of these Powers cannot be prejudiced or altered by the act of another signatory of the Treaty.

The German Government can however not agree with the juridical point of view exposed in the French Memorandum and endorsed by the other three Governments. They do not think, however, that any useful purpose would be served by the continuation of an exchange of juridical memoranda and hold the opinion that there will be sufficient opportunity for the necessary further discussions in the framework of the other pending negotiations.

## No. 448

### Sir S. Hoare to Mr. Newton (Berlin)

*No. 151 Telegraphic: by telephone* [*C 5792/55/18*]

FOREIGN OFFICE, *August 2, 1935, 1.25 p.m.*

Following is extract from my speech in Debate yesterday:[1]

'With regard to the question of an Eastern Pact, the honourable Gentleman will remember the answer that I gave yesterday.[2] I repeat it. I regard the conclusion of an Eastern Pact as one of the cardinal factors in the field of European progress. It is quite clear to me that, unless an advance can be made on the lines of an Eastern Pact, there will be great difficulty in making satisfactory progress with the Air Pact and certain of the other measures for the pacification and reconciliation of Europe. The honourable Gentleman can rest assured that I shall go on pressing that view upon the German Government and upon other Governments in Europe. I myself see no reason why, in the present position, an Eastern Pact should not be concluded, and I am quite sure that, if an Eastern Pact were concluded, it would be regarded as a measure of reconciliation in Central and Eastern

[1] See 304 *H.C. Deb.* 5 *s.*, cols. 2962–3.

[2] On July 31, in reply to a question from Mr Cocks, Member of Parliament for Broxtowe, Sir S. Hoare said that since his speech in the House on July 11 (cf. No. 418, note 1) he had on several occasions reverted to the matter of an Eastern pact of non-aggression with the German Government. 'I have, however, up to the present received no definite reply.' See *ibid.*, col. 2632.

Europe, and would greatly help on the conclusion of an Air Pact such as is desired, not only by ourselves, but by the German Government as well. I can assure the House that, in these matters of disarmament and these Pacts of security and reconciliation, I shall go on trying. It is not an easy task, but I shall go on trying, and if I fail, just as in the event of my failing in our peace-making efforts at Geneva, it will not be for want of any desire, and it will not be for want of making attempts, night and day, during the time that I hold this responsibility.'[3]

[3] This telegram was repeated on August 3 to Paris (No. 199) and Moscow (No. 101).

## No. 449

### Sir S. Hoare to Mr. Newton (Berlin)
No. 150 Telegraphic: by telephone [C 5795/55/18]

Important             FOREIGN OFFICE, August 2, 1935, 2.30 p.m.

My despatches Nos. 807[1] and 826.[2]

From two conversations with the German Ambassador on July 29 and 30[3] it transpires that His Excellency is under the impression that the German Government consider that as a consequence of the Franco-Russian Treaty of May 2 the undertaking given to Sir E. Phipps by Baron von Neurath on April 13 regarding the Eastern Pact[4] has lapsed; and that the German Government's commitment in the matter is now limited to the observations contained in the Chancellor's speech of May 21.

This means that instead of a 'collective security pact' of non-aggression, all the German Government promise are separate bilateral pacts of non-aggression: further it seems that whether there is to be a collective security pact or separate bilateral pacts, the neighbours who the German Government intend shall benefit are limited to States with territory contiguous to Germany, i.e. Lithuania (under reserve presumably of a Memel settlement), Poland and Czechoslovakia.

If the German Ambassador has correctly represented the intentions of his Government, this of course is a most discouraging situation, the creation of which by the German Government we have every right to deplore. It seems likely in fact to bring all progress to a standstill.

We have naturally considered and still consider that in Baron von Neurath's written communication to Sir E. Phipps of April 13th[3] we hold a binding undertaking from the German Government to conclude a collective security pact of non-aggression, whether or not mutual assistance arrangements are concluded outside it. That undertaking was given without any reserve or qualification whatever and we are entitled to expect the German Government to adhere to it.

But that will obviously not be enough if the German Government are now going to give to 'neighbouring States' the narrow interpretation of States bordering upon Germany. With that interpretation there can surely be no

[1] No. 424.      [2] No. 437.      [3] See No. 441.      [4] See Volume XII, No. 719.

hope of the French Government being satisfied; and the result will therefore be, as I have warned both Herr von Ribbentrop and Herr von Hoesch, that the prospects of the Air Pact, to which we, and we have hitherto understood the German Government also, attach such great importance, may well vanish. I earnestly hope therefore that the German Government will agree to include in a collective pact of non-aggression not only Lithuania (subject to a settlement of the Memel difficulty), Poland and Czechoslovakia, but also Latvia, Estonia and Russia. In regard to the German position *vis-à-vis* of all these States useful arguments are contained in my despatch No. 826.[2]

It will be remembered that on June 3 the French Government intimated that they would be prepared to accept the German draft as a basis of discussion, and asked the German Government to inform them as soon as possible of their views as to the most practical method of procedure.[5]

You should see the Minister for Foreign Affairs and speak to him on the above lines in as friendly a manner as possible. You should also give him the substance of your remarks in an *aide mémoire* and ask that this may be shewn to the Chancellor, whose personal attention His Majesty's Government feel entitled to call to the matter in view of the emphasis which, in his speech of May 21st, he laid on the importance of a peaceful settlement in Europe. You should recall also that in that speech Herr Hitler not only referred to the 'big aim' which the German Government had in view, but stated his opinion that such an aim could only be achieved step by step. This view exactly coincides with that of His Majesty's Government and I restated it in the House of Commons yesterday afternoon.[6] In these circumstances I earnestly trust that as one step towards the accomplishment of the big aim of European reconcilliation [*sic*], Herr Hitler will be prepared to proceed with a collective non-aggression pact with the six Eastern States on the lines of the German draft communicated to Sir John Simon in Berlin.[7] You should make it clear that we shall expect an answer on this matter.

I am taking steps to ascertain whether Herr von Koester has correctly reported M. Laval's views, (see your telegram No. 174 Saving).[8] But at first sight there appears to be some inconsistency between paragraph 1 and paragraph 2 of your telegram.[9]

[5] See No. 288.  [6] See No. 448.
[7] See Volume XII, No. 651, Annex to Third Meeting.
[8] The reference was to No. 440.
[9] This telegram, No. 150, was repeated to Moscow (No. 98), Warsaw (No. 40), and Paris (No. 234 Saving).

## No. 450

*Mr. Newton (Berlin) to Sir S. Hoare (Received August 2, 10.40 p.m.)*
*No. 247 Telegraphic [C 5819/55/18]*

BERLIN, *August 2, 1935, 9.15 p.m.*

Your telegram No. 150.[1]
Although the Chancellor's speech specifies bilateral pacts with individual

[1] No. 449.

States original draft referred to in undertaking of April 13th offered an Eastern Pact to be concluded by 'the Powers interested in the Eastern European questions'.

I do not understand from your telegram that the German Ambassador has sought to limit scope of that offer, his point being that offer itself has lapsed. I doubt therefore whether it is politic to suggest that even if they can be held to their original offer they are fortunate [*sic*][2] to interpret it so narrowly that it will not be enough.

Unless you see objection I propose therefore to use your argument in my communication in such a way as to avoid such suggestion.

I also propose to incorporate much of penultimate paragraph of your telegram in aide mémoire itself so as to ensure that it reaches Chancellor with undiminished force. References to his own speech will I hope carry special weight with him.

[2] Another copy of this telegram here read: 'are trying to interpret it.'

## No. 451

*Mr. Newton (Berlin) to Sir S. Hoare (Received August 2, 10.40 p.m.)*
*Unnumbered Telegraphic [C 5819/55/18]*

BERLIN, *August 2, 1935, 9.15 p.m.*

Following for Sir R. Vansittart:
Your telegram No. 150[1] and my telegram No. 247.[2]

As I understand matter is not of special urgency I will apply tomorrow for interview on Monday[3] to give time for any reply to my telegram No. 247. I understand Minister for Foreign Affairs is in Wurtemburg and doubt whether he or Herr von Buelow would appreciate diplomatic visit to him there. I will therefore ask to see the Secretary of State in the absence of the Minister for Foreign Affairs.[4]

[1] No. 449.  [2] No. 450.  [3] August 5.
[4] A minute by Sir R. Vansittart reads: 'He need not have hurried. I have already telegraphed asking for explanation of his last telegram. R.V.' Cf. No. 453 below.

## No. 452

*Sir S. Hoare to Sir R. Clive (Tokyo)*
*No. 154 Telegraphic [A 6788/22/45]*

FOREIGN OFFICE, *August 2, 1935, 9.30 p.m.*

Your telegram No. 204.[1]
Your language to Vice-Minister for Foreign Affairs is approved.

If, at the cost of criticism from certain circles here, we have suggested a system of quantitative limitation by programmes to take the place of the ratio system, this has been primarily to ease the way for Japan and not

[1] No. 443.

because we ourselves would prefer another system. An international agreement on programmes covering a short period of years would give time for the controversy over ratios to die down. If in addition this breathing space were to be used to improve political relations where improvement is required, the whole question of naval relationships between Japan, the United States and the British Empire should enter upon a new and pleasanter phase. On the other hand, the present attitude of the Japanese naval authorities in claiming parity with the United States at Japan's level will not only lead nowhere but will tend to promote a general increase in naval construction which it is Japan's purpose to avoid.

I note with interest what the Vice-Minister said about Admiral Kato's impending retirement. We are disposed to think that a Conference of the five Washington Powers should meet as early as possible in the autumn, but further instructions will be sent to you on this point when our conversations with the Governments of European Powers have proceeded a little further.

Meantime you may use the above confidentially in all conversations with the Japanese authorities as and when you think fit.[2]

[2] This telegram was repeated to Washington as Foreign Office telegram No. 217 of August 2.

## No. 453

*Sir S. Hoare to Mr. Newton (Berlin)*
*No. 154 Telegraphic [C 5819/55/18]*

FOREIGN OFFICE, *August 3, 1935, 11 p.m.*

Your telegram No. 247.[1]

I am of course disposed to be guided by what you think most tactful and effective course. Before, however, coming to a decision I should be glad of a little fuller explanation of paragraphs 1 and 2 of your telegram. It seems to me that very wide expression, which you quote, rather re-emphasizes than otherwise the present tendency toward narrowing—if the German Ambassador's attitude correctly reflects that of his Government.

[1] No. 450.

## No. 454

*Mr. Newton (Berlin) to Sir S. Hoare (Received August 4, 2 p.m.)*
*No. 250 Telegraphic: by telephone [C 5822/55/18]*

BERLIN, *August 4, 1935*

From your telegram No. 150[1] I have understood that German Ambassador maintains that in consequence of Franco-Russian Treaty Germany no longer considers herself bound by obligations resulting from undertaking of April 13th and written offer handed by Baron von Neurath to Sir J. Simon during his visit to Berlin. Such an attitude on the part of the German

[1] No. 449.

Ambassador is in accordance with Herr von Buelow's attitude as I have reported.

I have not understood from your telegram or from anything said to me here that even if German Government do accept the above obligations they would still try to restrict their scope to States bordering on Germany. If therefore this issue has not been raised it seems to me a pity to raise it at this juncture as would be done by sentence in fourth paragraph of your telegram beginning 'but that will obviously not be enough'.

If the German Government are determined to be obstructive they may catch at any straw. If and when point has to be dealt with however it ought to be comparatively easy to refute seeing that Baron von Neurath's offer related quite obviously to Russia and has as its preamble 'in the opinion of the German Government the Powers interested in Eastern European questions might'. If we raise this question unnecessarily it will only give them the opportunity to go off on subsidiary points. It seems to me therefore that we ought to concentrate in the first place on holding them to obligations in Baron von Neurath's draft as confirmed in undertaking of April 13th.

Unless I hear otherwise I propose therefore to interpret this part of your telegram in my verbal and written communication by words to the following effect 'if German Government fail to adhere to above-mentioned obligations and proceed now to restrict themselves to what was said in Chancellor's speech of May 21st, *giving moreover to phrase neighbouring States the narrow interpretation States contiguous with Germany* there seems no prospect that any advance can be made['].

I am seeing Herr von Buelow Monday[2] at 11.30.[3]

[2] August 5.

[3] Foreign Office telegram No. 155 telephoned to Mr. Newton at 8.45 p.m. on August 4, read as follows: 'Your telegram No. 250. Following from Sir R. Vansittart. I agree.'

## No. 455

*Mr. Newton (Berlin) to Sir S. Hoare (Received August 5, 6.35 p.m.)*
*No. 251 Telegraphic: by telephone [C 5823/55/18]*

BERLIN, *August 5, 1935*

Your telegram No. 150[1] and your telegram 155[2] and my telegram 247[3] and my telegram 250.[4]

I have this morning August 5th made communication accordingly to Secretary of State in the absence of Minister for Foreign Affairs. I started by an allusion to your speech in the House of Commons on August 1st and quoted your words 'I regard conclusion of an Eastern Pact as one of the cardinal factors in the field of European progress'. I observed that this question had been discussed quite recently three times with German Ambassador in London and that I had also reported my two conversations with him. The communication which I was going to deliver was therefore made with the full knowledge of information obtained at these various interviews.

[1] No. 449.   [2] See No. 454, note 3.   [3] No. 450.   [4] No. 454.

Before entering upon it I wished however to say that apart from history of Eastern Pact and points with which I would deal more specifically later on there was a general and as I much hoped he would agree an overriding consideration which I would like to emphasise. That was, that conclusion of a pact on lines proposed to Sir John Simon during his visit to Berlin, would in firm conviction of His Majesty's Government be an invaluable means of improving atmosphere in Europe at this time. Its conclusion would be hailed as a sign that something positive was at last being achieved to tranquillise feeling and remove anxieties and fears. These anxieties and fears might be unreasonable: there might also be technical and other difficulties in the way of a pact. However that might be, His Majesty's Government felt most strongly that its conclusion would be more than worth while because result would be a profound sense of relief and encouragement which would be felt throughout Europe and beyond Europe. His Majesty's Government believe that it lay within Chancellor's power to produce this feeling of relief and encouragement: in his speech Chancellor spoke of his desire for tranquillity and peace and His Majesty's Government could not but believe that in such a case he would be willing to use the power which he possessed.

Before passing to my subsequent remarks I made it clear that my intentions and indeed my instructions were to speak in as friendly a way as possible.

This introduction, although in substance only a recapitulation, seemed to me desirable as I feared that Herr von Buelow might otherwise be less receptive to the first part of my subsequent communication with its insistence on the undertaking of April 13th.

I then spoke on lines of your telegram No. 150 and in conclusion handed an aide-mémoire to Secretary of State. I asked him to submit to Minister for Foreign Affairs and to Chancellor—I hoped very much with his own recommendation—the communication which I had made. I trusted that we should receive an early and what was more important a favourable reply. I took the opportunity of handing to him at the same time extract from speech contained in your telegram 151[5] omitting the last two sentences. Copies of aide-mémoire[6] are being sent by air mail tonight.

Herr von Buelow said that he thought he would be able to arrange for my communication to reach Minister for Foreign Affairs in south Germany tomorrow and he believed that Baron von Neurath might have an opportunity to discuss it with the Chancellor in the course of the week. The Chancellor's plans were however not very definite so that he could not be sure when a reply would be possible.

I am reporting some further comments by Herr von Buelow separately by Saving telegram.[7]

Repeated to Moscow and Warsaw.

[5] No. 448.
[6] Received on August 6 as enclosure in Berlin despatch No. 769, not printed. The text of the aide-mémoire is printed in *D.G.F.P.*, Series C, vol. iv, pp. 536–8.
[7] See No. 456 below.

*Mr. Newton (Berlin) to Sir S. Hoare (Received August 6, 11 a.m.)*
*No. 174 Saving: Telegraphic* [C 5839/55/18]

BERLIN, *August 5, 1935*

My telegram No. 251.[1]

The Secretary of State said that he himself had little to add to what he had told me in our two previous conversations. He dissented from our view as to efficacy of such measures for improving the atmosphere. From German experience of dealing with French Government he feared that so soon as Germany had done what was wanted in regard to the Eastern Pact, the French Government would say that they attached no particular importance to such a concession but now wanted something else. I suggested that quite apart from the French Government, and even if in the German view the conclusion of an Eastern Pact would not be of much use, there was at any rate no particular German objection to it, while in our view its conclusion would serve a most valuable purpose. He replied that there was a considerable German objection because it would inevitably weaken the existing arrangements with which Germany was quite satisfied.

German Government had however, he admitted, been considering Eastern Pact question purely in relation to Franco-Russian Treaty. Their communication of April 13th had been made in other circumstances and as at the time no particular notice had been taken of it, the German Government had no longer taken it into account. He felt moreover that the two matters were on an altogether different scale of importance. In agreeing to the Pacts of Mutual Assistance the German Government had never contemplated a military alliance which discriminated solely against themselves, as Franco-Russian treaty did specifically by virtue of paragraph IV of the Protocol.[2] Herr von Bülow also observed that he still did not know whether or no[t] the French intended to guarantee an Eastern Pact although he understood that they would not be an actual party to one. I suggested that however the foregoing might be, there seemed no reason why Germany should not take the lead and obtain credit for an Eastern Pact on lines acceptable to herself namely those proposed by Herr von Neurath to Sir J. Simon during his visit to Berlin. Even if Franco-Russian Treaty were as bad as he thought how would the Eastern Pact make it worse? Surely if the Pact affected the Treaty at all it might weaken it and thus make it better for Germany. That, said Herr von Bülow was what the German Government wanted to ascertain but so far without success.

Our interview was of a most friendly character and Herr von Bülow listened attentively to all I had to say but I am not optimistic that he has been much moved from his previous attitude.[3]

Repeated to Moscow and Warsaw by post.

[1] No. 455.          [2] See No. 156, note 2.
[3] In Foreign Office telegram No. 202 of August 6 to Paris Sir G. Clerk was instructed to inform the French Ministry of Foreign Affairs 'generally of the sense of the representations

recently made to the German Ambassador and now to the German Government about the Eastern pact', reference was made to Nos. 424, 437, and 449. Viscount Chilston was similarly authorised to inform the Soviet Ministry of Foreign Affairs, in Foreign Office telegram No. 105 of August 16 to Moscow.

## No. 457

### Sir S. Hoare to Sir G. Clerk (Paris)
#### No. 203 Telegraphic [A 6951/22/45]

FOREIGN OFFICE, *August 6, 1935, 6.15 p.m.*

My telegram No. 201.[1]
We are inclined to think that it would be better if no statement were to be made to the press about Capt. Danckwerts's visit. If however the French wish for a statement to be made, we suggest if you see no objection that it should be to the effect that the visit was purely informal and that it was made in order that certain technical points might be discussed and explained.

[1] This telegram of August 5 stated that Captain Danckwerts (cf. No. 439, note 3) would arrive in Paris by air at 3.30 p.m. on August 6 and return the following evening.

## No. 458

### Letter from Mr. Wigram to Mr. Grant Watson[1] (Helsingfors)
#### [C 5567/55/18]

FOREIGN OFFICE, *August 6, 1935*

Dear Grant Watson,
Your letter of the 18th July to Collier[2] about the possible inclusion of Finland in the Eastern Pact.
It will be seen from Sperling's despatch No. 232 of the 15th August 1934[3] that Finland was included in the original French draft of the 27th June 1934[4] principally out of politeness. But as the Finns have since that date made it fairly clear that they do not want to join the pact there wd. not seem to be much likelihood of their being approached again by the French or the Russians.
If however you shd. be asked to support a French or Soviet invitation to the Finnish Govt. to join the Eastern Pact, you shd. refer to us for instructions before taking any action.

Yours sincerely,
R. F. WIGRAM

[1] H.M. Minister at Helsingfors since June 1935. Only the approved draft of this letter is preserved in the Foreign Office archives.
[2] Mr. L. Collier was head of the Northern Department of the Foreign Office. This letter is not printed.
[3] Not printed. Mr. Sperling was at that time H.M. Minister at Helsingfors.
[4] See Volume VI, No. 492.

# No. 459

*Sir G. Clerk (Paris) to Sir S. Hoare (Received August 7, 9.45 p.m.)*

*No. 158 Telegraphic [C 5860/55/18]*

PARIS, *August 7, 1935, 7.15 p.m.*

Your telegram No. 194.[1]

Conversation between German Ambassador at Paris and President of Council on 27th July was a long and informal talk, which incidentally, my German colleague said he would not report to his Government, designed to help Herr Köster to clear his own mind as to what line of approach offered the most hopeful prospect for future relations of France and Germany. Monsieur Laval told German Ambassador that he was profoundly and sincerely anxious to promote a détente between France and Germany and all he asked was that if France came to agreement with Germany, Germany would come to agreement with other countries. He (Monsieur Laval) cared little for procedure, but very much for '*fond*'. He regretted that Germany had never answered the French note about the Eastern Pact,[2] which after all was based on Herr von Neurath's own proposals. Herr Köster replied with a long statement of German objections to Franco-Soviet agreement. Monsieur Laval answered if what Germany feared was Russian aggression, all she had to do was to make a declaration of non-aggression against Russia and she could have her mind at rest during the five years which was the term of agreement. Monsieur Laval continued that if Germany did not want to discuss Eastern Pact at once he was quite ready to begin by discussing any of the other points of the London communiqué of 3rd February, for instance, land armaments, only it must be quite understood that Eastern Pact and the other points must all be examined in due time and included in any final settlement. In fact, said Monsieur Laval, he took towards Herr Köster just the same attitude as he had taken to me on the question of the Air Pact.

As for the League of Nations, to the best of Monsieur Laval's recollection, that institution was never mentioned.

Repeated to Berlin.

[1] No. 444.     [2] Of June 3, 1935; cf. No. 288, note 3.

# No. 460

*Sir S. Hoare to Sir G. Clerk (Paris)*

*No. 1460 [A 6954/22/45]*

*Confidential*                          FOREIGN OFFICE, *August 7, 1935*

Sir,

As Your Excellency will have ascertained from the semi-official letter sent by this Department on the 3rd August last to a member of your staff,[1]

[1] The reference is to a letter of August 3 sent by Mr. Broad to Mr. Harvey, First Secretary in H.M. Embassy at Paris, telling him that he had handed to the Marquis de Castellane, a Second Secretary in the French Embassy at London, on that day a memorandum of the

a memorandum has been handed to the French Embassy in London in which it is suggested to the French Government that it is of urgent importance to lay the basis of agreement for the qualitative limitation of naval armaments. A copy of the memorandum is enclosed.

2. It has been felt that, as time was short in view of the fact that a conference must be convened before the end of 1935 and as the French Government were still disinclined to send experts to London for preliminary discussions, the problem should be attacked from a fresh angle; and as the moment is approaching when all the naval Powers will have to determine their construction programmes for 1937, the first year when the present treaty limitations will no longer apply, it was held to be most urgent that some agreement for the elimination of competition in gun-calibres and sizes and types of ships should be reached. It was decided therefore that a memorandum containing certain figures of qualitative limitation should be submitted in the first place to the French Government, the figures being those which the European countries so far consulted in this matter seem likely to find acceptable. As explained in the preceding paragraph, the French Government have now been furnished with these figures and asked whether they are, in fact, acceptable as far as France is concerned.

3. An identical memorandum, *mutatis mutandis*, has been handed to the Counsellor of the Italian Embassy[2] and it is proposed that a similar memorandum should be communicated in due course to the German and Soviet Embassies in London in order that the observations of these Governments may be obtained. Copies will also be furnished to the United States and Japanese Governments for their information.

4. Should a sufficiently encouraging response be received from the interested Governments, His Majesty's Government would consider the summoning of a conference of Washington Powers to meet in October of this year, the primary purpose of which would be to secure international agreement on the qualitative limitation of naval armaments. A secondary purpose would be to consider the British plan for quantitative limitation by means of unilateral declarations in regard to future construction and any quantitative plans which other countries may wish to put forward.

5. While this memorandum on qualitative limitation was in course of preparation, the French Ambassador called on Sir R. Vansittart and a copy of the latter's record of the conversation is enclosed.[3] It will be observed that the suggestion was discussed that a visit should be paid to Paris by a representative of the Admiralty and might serve to break the ice and set the naval discussions in motion again. This visit was in due course arranged, but it was made clear (i) that His Majesty's Government are no more prepared now than they have been previously to give the French Ministry of Marine the German programme except on the strict basis of reciprocity, and (ii) that

naval discussions and that Captain Danckwerts was expected to arrive in Paris the following week.

[2] Mr. Broad handed a copy of the memorandum to Signor Vitetti on August 6.
[3] Not here reproduced: see No. 421.

the visit of the Admiralty representative will not replace the preliminary conversations with the French which it is intended will take place in London like the preliminary talks with other Powers.

6. I am sending a copy of this despatch to His Majesty's Ambassadors at Washington (No. 714), Rome (No. 904), Tokyo (No. 436), Moscow (No. 422) and Berlin (No. 864).

I am, &c.,

SAMUEL HOARE

ENCLOSURE IN NO. 460

*Memorandum*

FOREIGN OFFICE, *August 2, 1935*[4]

His Majesty's Government in the United Kingdom have been considering carefully the results of the bilateral conversations, regarding the limitation of naval armaments, that have taken place during 1934 and 1935. These conversations were intended to prepare the way for a preliminary conference in accordance with treaty requirements during the year 1935, as a result of which it is hoped to hold a general conference of all naval Powers with a view to reaching agreement on general naval limitations for the future.

2. The exploratory conversations have been delayed by external events and the process of exploration is taking longer than was originally anticipated. It is now clear, however, that the system of limitation by total tonnages in categories that was pursued in the Washington and London Naval Treaties will not again meet with general acceptance. The alternative proposal for achieving some form of quantitative naval limitation, viz., the issue by the various naval Powers of unilateral declarations in regard to their building programme intentions over a number of years, has not yet been subjected to full and detailed discussion between all the principal naval Powers, and considerable time must elapse before it becomes clear whether this system will prove satisfactory.

3. It is clear that all the principal naval Powers will require to undertake the construction of capital ships and cruisers in the year 1937 and later years. The Washington and London Naval Treaties both come to an end on the 31st December, 1936. Unless, therefore, agreement can be reached before that date on fresh qualitative limits to replace those which lapse with the treaties, there will be no limitation at all on the sizes and gun-calibres of the ships to be built in 1937 and later years. This is a situation which cannot be regarded with equanimity by any of the principal naval Powers, and agreement on new qualitative limits is therefore urgently required. Moreover, agreement on qualitative limits is of more immediate importance than agreement on quantitative limits, since the former will have immediate effect on the limitation of armaments and financial commitments by its

---

[4] The copy of this memorandum circulated as N.C.M.(35)61 was dated July 30. Apart from a few minor differences in layout and capitalization the copies were identical.

application to all the ships to be laid down after the 31st December, 1936, whereas the latter, by its nature, becomes effective only over a period of years and may have little effect on the construction programmes to be laid down in the year 1937.

4. As a result of the conversations held during the past eighteen months, His Majesty's Government in the United Kingdom believe that the lowest qualitative limits likely to be acceptable to the European countries so far consulted (United Kingdom, France, Italy and Germany) are as follows:—

|  | Tons. | Guns. |
|---|---|---|
| Capital ships ... ... ... ... ... | 25,000 | 12-inch |
| Aircraft carriers ... ... ... ... ... | 22,000 | 6·1-inch |
| Category A cruisers ... ... ... ... | 10,000 | 8-inch |
| Category B cruisers and light-surface vessels ... | 7,600 | 6·1-inch |
| Submarines ... ... ... ... ... | 2,000 | 5·1-inch |

NOTE.—It is hoped that agreement could be reached that no more Category A cruisers should be laid down in the future.

5. His Majesty's Government in the United Kingdom, however, cannot accept qualitative limits which, though they might be agreeable to all European Powers, are not acceptable also to the United States of America and Japan, and it would be their endeavour to obtain the agreement of the United States of America and Japan to figures as near as possible to those mentioned in the previous paragraph.

6. Without abandoning in any way their search for some form of quantitative limitation likely to secure general assent, His Majesty's Government feel that it is of far more urgent importance to lay the basis of agreement on *qualitative limitation.* They desire to know, therefore, whether the French Government agree with this view and whether the list of qualitative limits acceptable to the European Powers correctly represents the view of the French Government.

7. If a sufficient measure of European agreement on qualitative limitation exists, His Majesty's Government will put forward this European view to the United States of America and Japan with a view to a conference of the Washington Powers in October 1935, so as to reach an agreement at least on this branch of the subject and so regulate the size of warships to be built after the 31st December, 1936. Although this should, in the view of His Majesty's Government, be the principal purpose of the proposed conference, the occasion should also be taken to make further progress with the negotiation of an arrangement for the quantitative limitation of naval armaments on the lines suggested in paragraph 2 above.

8. In addition, it would be desirable to reach agreement as to the reciprocal notification of information relating to the laying down and characteristics of new ships (Washington Treaty, Chapter II, Part 3, Section I (*b*), and London Naval Treaty, article 10); the definitions of categories and standard tonnage (Washington Treaty, Chapter II, Part 4, and London Naval Treaty, articles 3 and 6); the preparation of merchant ships in time of peace for

conversion to warlike purposes (Washington Treaty, article 14); the prohibition of the use for war of warships building for other Powers (Washington Treaty, article 17); and the prohibition of the transfer of vessels of war from one Power to another (Washington Treaty, article 18).

## No. 461

*Record of Anglo-French naval discussions held in Paris, August 6 and 7, 1935*[1]

[*A 7062/22/45*]

PRESENT: *British:* Captain Danckwerts, R.N. (Admiralty); Captain Hammill, R.N., Naval Attaché, Paris.
  *French:* Rear-Admiral Abrial, 2ème Sous-Chef d'Etat major; Rear-Admiral Decoux.

*N.C.(F.) 6th Mtg.*[2]

The first meeting took place in the French Ministry of Marine at 5.30 p.m. on Tuesday, 6th August.

ADMIRAL ABRIAL, opening the meeting, said that he only had two things to say. The first was that Germany had laid down a great deal of tonnage in the first year of her programme, more than 100,000 tons and, if they continued to build at this rate, they would very soon reach their limit of about 400,000 tons. This situation caused France great anxiety. Secondly, he wished to say that he understood perfectly that Captain Danckwerts was not free to communicate to the French representatives the German building programme in 1936 and later years and he wished to assure Captain Danckwerts that he would not press him for any such information.

CAPTAIN DANCKWERTS, in the general discussion which followed, made it clear that his principal object in this visit was to outline in a preliminary manner questions which would be discussed in London, say, in September, if the French Ministry of Marine would be willing to send representatives to London for that purpose. The general views of the British Government were outlined in the memorandum which had been handed to the French Government through their London Embassy,[3] and this memorandum might perhaps serve as a form of agenda.

REAR-ADMIRAL DECOUX asked whether the memorandum had been handed to any other Power besides France.

CAPTAIN DANCKWERTS replied, no, but that it would be handed to Italy this week and in reply to a question he stated that it had not yet been communicated to Japan. There was some misunderstanding on this point, as apparently the French Embassy in London had informed Paris that the memorandum had been handed to Japan.

---

[1] This record, made by Captain Danckwerts, was circulated by direction of the First Lord of the Admiralty.

[2] Exploratory Anglo-French naval conversations, recorded as N.C.(F.) 1st to 5th Mtgs., had been held in London, July 9–12, 1934. Cf. Volume VI, Nos. 489 and 490.

[3] See No. 460.

The French officers were in general agreement with the thesis of the British memorandum that it is a matter of urgency and importance to reach some kind of qualitative agreement during the course of the current year, but as regards the building programme suggestion they felt that it would be very difficult to discuss programmes now or to discuss any arrangement of programmes over such a long period of years as 1937–1942 as suggested in the British memorandum.

ADMIRAL ABRIAL made it clear that not only did he foresee great technical and parliamentary difficulties in producing any French programme for any such long period of years, but that actually France has not any clear idea at present of what her programmes would be likely to be so long ahead and certainly is unable to make any exact suggestions until she knows much more about how the German building progresses.

In response to a question from Captain Danckwerts as to whether there were any portions of the Anglo-German Agreement as set out in Sir Samuel Hoare's note[4] which were obscure and might perhaps be cleared up, the French representatives stated that their only difficulty was with paragraph 2(c). The French view is that it is absurd to talk in this Agreement about violently upsetting the general equilibrium of naval armaments since Germany has already done this very thing by beginning to build a fleet of great size at great speed.

CAPTAIN DANCKWERTS was unable to give any very exact interpretation of the phrase 'abnormal and exceptional construction by other Powers' but pointed out that Germany certainly has Russia in mind in this connection and stressed the importance of paragraph 3 wherein Germany agrees to maintain the 35% ratio even in the circumstances set forth in paragraph 2(c).

A rough agenda was then agreed upon and the meeting was adjourned until the following morning.

*Meeting in the Ministry of Marine at 10 a.m. on Wednesday, August 7*

PRESENT: as above.

*N.C. (F.) 7th Mtg.*

CAPTAIN DANCKWERTS began by explaining that he did not expect to receive any definite replies from the French representatives that day on the points about to be discussed but that he hoped that they would form the subject of discussions to be undertaken in London in September at which the French representatives might be ready to deal definitely with the questions at issue. As each point was dealt with Captain Danckwerts conveyed the information of the German views contained in Appendix I attached.[5]

---

[4] Of June 18, 1935; see Annex to No. 348.

[5] The following comment appears in another account of this meeting: 'During the visit to Paris, which only lasted one day, Captain Danckwerts gave the French Naval Staff the information on the attached sheets [as in Appendix 1] about German views on qualitative limitations, the exchange of information, the minor provisions of the Washington

*Qualitative Limitation in general.* France agrees in principle as to the necessity and desirability for qualitative limits but, since the new German fleet has started and if its progress in the future is at the same rate, they might desire to compensate for the *quantity* of German construction by superior *quality* of French construction. It was pointed out that this applied to both sides and that surely it would be better to limit Germany qualitatively rather than to indulge in some sort of a race in the size and power of individual ships.

*Capital Ships.* The information in Appendix I was amplified by the statement that Germany would certainly stipulate that before adhering to future qualitative limits as low as those suggested she would desire to build one or more ships of the maximum size now being built by other Powers and it was suggested that, if France could see her way to build ships less than the present maximum tonnage in spite of the fact that Italy was building two such ships, it might be of advantage to all parties concerned.

ADMIRAL ABRIAL pointed out, however, that the first French ship was actually under construction although not yet laid down and that, in his view, it was quite impossible that France should reduce the size of either of her first two ships. The 'Dunkerque' and 'Strasbourg' had been France's effort to lead other Powers to build smaller ships and this effort had proved vain since Italy had ignored it. As regards the limits proposed Admiral Abrial said that French investigations showed that 25,000 tons for a ship with 12″ guns was '*très juste*' and that France would prefer to make the tonnage perhaps 2,000 or 3,000 tons greater.

CAPTAIN DANCKWERTS informed them of the general position as regards the United States of America and Japan and explained that we want to be able to tell the United States of America that European Powers will agree to ships with 12″ guns but that there was no great hope that the United States of America would do the same.

In confidence, ADMIRAL ABRIAL stated that the guns of the 'France' would be 15″.

Finally, CAPTAIN DANCKWERTS asked whether in September the French Naval Staff would give a considered answer as to the possibility of building one or both of their ships to a smaller size than 35,000 tons in spite of Italy's two ships.

*Aircraft carriers.* France sees no difficulty in the limits proposed.

CAPTAIN DANCKWERTS informed the French representatives that Japan would like to reduce the limit to 20,000 tons and that we had told her that, if agreement is reached on other matters, we are prepared to consider it.

*Cruisers A.* ADMIRAL ABRIAL said that the trouble about cessation of building of this type was that the early ships built were far inferior to the latest ones. He stated that the early French 10,000 tons cruisers had no

Treaty, and definitions, these being matters the French views on which had been conveyed to the German representatives during the London discussions. The principle of reciprocity was thus observed. No other information of German intentions or programmes was given to the French representatives on this occasion . . .' Cf. No. 348, note 6.

protection and were not comparable to their latest ships, and would, he was sure, be no match for the new German ships. He suggested as a possibility that the German 'compensation' for not building the last three ships might be to transfer into this category the three Deutschlands and to re-arm them with 8″ guns. Finally, he said that, if Germany built five A class cruisers, the existing French seven would not be enough. If, on the other hand, Germany stopped short with only two A class cruisers, France's present number would probably be sufficient. If Germany goes beyond two, France may have to make some stipulations.

*Cruisers B.* CAPTAIN DANCKWERTS explained the difficulty in this class introduced by the building of large 6″ gun cruisers by Japan, the United States of America and subsequently Great Britain and stated that we proposed to try to stabilise this situation on the basis of ten for Great Britain and the United States of America and six for Japan. He also pointed out the difficulty that was being introduced into the cruiser position by the fact that the United States of America were exercising their right to build the sixteenth, seventeenth and eighteenth 8″ gun cruisers and that Japan would probably not be content to remain with only twelve.

*Destroyers.* CAPTAIN DANCKWERTS stated that the United Kingdom would not be prepared to agree to destroyer qualitative limits unless all other Powers did so and ADMIRAL ABRIAL confirmed that France's position was to keep cruisers B and destroyers together in one category termed light surface vessels. In reply to the question whether the United Kingdom would accept one light surface vessel category Captain Danckwerts repeated that, although the United Kingdom would prefer to divide the category, yet they were not prepared to do so unless all other Powers agreed. It was also pointed out that, in the absence of any quantitative arrangement, there was no very great object in dividing destroyers from cruisers B.

A discussion then took place on the possibility of introducing a gap between cruisers and capital ships for the purpose of making the cruiser qualitative limits work in the absence of any quantitative agreement. The French representatives were fully in agreement that the best solution would be to have a gap in which no building should take place but also agreed that the great difficulty about such a solution would be to obtain the agreement of the smaller naval Powers. They undertook, however, to consider the matter carefully and make any suggestions that struck them for a solution of the problem. In this discussion all parties agreed that a qualitative agreement only without any quantitative arrangement would be far better than no agreement and that it would be better to include cruiser qualitative limits in such an agreement even if it were not possible to arrange for a gap or other device to make the cruiser limits fully effective.

*Submarines.* ADMIRAL ABRIAL said that it was quite clear that abolition was not a feasible proposition and that France was not the only country that held this view. He stated that possibly 1500 tons would be a sufficient limit for France but had no objection to keeping the existing limit of 2000 tons. He also said that in the matter of submarines France feels she might like an 'escalator' clause in case Germany builds too fast or builds submarines too big but, after further questioning, agreed that the clause would not provide that France should build more submarines but that she should build more of some other type to compensate for the German submarines.

*Exchange of Information.* CAPTAIN DANCKWERTS amplified the information in Appendix I by stating that the British Admiralty were even now engaged in discussing with the German Admiralty whether they should not begin to exchange information henceforth without waiting for the conclusion of a general agreement, and pointed out that the German Government are prepared to enter into conversations to this end with any other Power.

ADMIRAL ABRIAL appeared to agree that it might be a good thing for France to approach Germany on this matter. He agreed that the exchange of information would be of value but appeared to have some doubts concerning Germany's good faith.

ADMIRAL DECOUX asked what guarantee had we that German information was accurate.

A discussion took place on the French proposals made at Geneva for 'préavis' and CAPTAIN DANCKWERTS pointed out that on examination the Admiralty found many difficulties both parliamentary, constitutional and technical.

The French representatives agreed that the problem was full of difficulties but felt that an extension of the principle of exchange of information in some form of 'préavis' was probably the only advance we could make in the direction of quantitative limitation.

*Submarine Warfare.* The French representatives stated that France agrees with the rules of Part 4 of the London Naval Treaty but that they are really matters of general international law and probably not suitable for inclusion in an agreement for the limitation of naval armaments.

*Minor provisions of the Washington Treaty.* No difficulties were raised about these provisions and it was agreed that they should be included in any future agreement.

*Definitions.* No difficulties were raised about definitions and the French representatives were interested to learn of the German objection to apply so long a term of life as 20 years to the Deutschland class.

The meeting was then adjourned until 3.30 p.m.

*N.C.(F.) 8th Mtg.*

On resumption CAPTAIN DANCKWERTS explained in detail the British proposal for the building programme arrangement and the reasons which led to its formulation.

ADMIRAL ABRIAL stressed again the French objection to fixing any programme for so many years ahead and gave it as his opinion that, if such an arrangement is discussed, each country is likely to draw up the maximum programmes it thinks it may possibly require and then subsequently to build up to the maximum instead of keeping to the minimum. In his view, finance was by far the best limiting factor in naval armaments and no quantitative agreement would be likely to produce any better results. On the contrary such agreement would be apt to increase construction in naval armaments. He felt that a qualitative agreement accompanied by provisions for the exchange of information, with possibly some form of 'préavis' and with the minor provisions mentioned above, was as much as we should expect to get out of the forthcoming negotiations.

In this agreement ADMIRAL DECOUX suggested that there ought to be included an arrangement for a gap between capital ship and cruiser categories.

CAPTAIN DANCKWERTS explained the difficulty of getting Japanese representatives to attend any conference on this basis alone and that it was for this reason that the United Kingdom felt it essential to continue to search for some form of quantitative limitation. Finally, Captain Danckwerts said that it might be of assistance to the French representatives to consider their own proposed building programmes in relation to hypothetical German programmes so that, when they came into possession of the actual German programme, they would be able to state definitely its reaction on French building. For this purpose he suggested that they might consider the possibility that Germany would build one or two or three more capital ships after those already notified in the period up till 1942. Similarly they might build one or two or three more 8″ gun cruisers in the same period. The French representatives undertook to consider what reaction these possible programmes would have on the French building.

*Agenda for September.* CAPTAIN DANCKWERTS finally suggested that the following questions might be discussed in September if the French Ministry of Marine were inclined to send representatives to London for that purpose:—

(a) French views on the procedure for preparing for the 1935 Conference as set out in the British memorandum;

(b) French views as to the building programme arrangement suggested, or any modification of it which France thought might be more suitable;

(c) French figures of their building programmes in the future for as far ahead as they were prepared to calculate, if possible up to 1942;

(d) confirmation of the French views on qualitative limitation, exchange of information, and the minor provisions of the Washington Treaty.

Both M. PIÉTRI, who had received Captain Danckwerts in the morning, and ADMIRAL DURAND VIEL, the chief of the French Naval Staff, were agreeable to the suggestion that French representatives should go to London about the middle of September to resume these discussions, but they stated that there were political reactions and they could not definitely undertake to make the visit until they had consulted the Quai d'Orsay.

ADMIRAL ABRIAL undertook that, if possible, a written French reply to the British memorandum and the proposal for further conversations should be made about the first week in September.[6]

[6] The appendix below consists of extracts from Annex I, entitled 'Summary of discussions between the British and German naval representatives', to the minutes of the meeting on June 22, 1935, between British and German representatives; see No. 348, note 6.

*Qualitative Limitations.* The German Delegation supports the aim of the United Kingdom to reach qualitative limitation in any future agreement.

Germany will be ready to accept any limitation of types, for instance reduction of displacements and reduction of gun calibre, as well as any abolition of types, e.g. the abolition of Cruisers A and Submarines, if such regulations applied, and were at the same time carried through, by all other naval Powers. Germany would particularly welcome any such measures as a further step towards the limitation of naval armaments.

*Capital Ships.* Germany supports the British proposal for the limitation of capital ships to 25,000 tons with 12″ guns, and would be prepared to accept an even lower limit, if general agreement could be obtained on it.

*Aircraft Carriers.* Germany supports the British proposal for limitation to 22,000 tons, and would like to see an even smaller type agreed to.

*Cruisers A.* Germany is in agreement with the desirability of avoiding future construction of these ships by general agreement if possible, subject to later arrangements to compensate for the disadvantage that the prohibition of future construction might involve for Germany.

*Cruisers B.* Germany is satisfied with the limit proposed, viz., 7,000 tons.

*Destroyers.* Germany, in so far as her experience goes at present, agrees that an 1850 ton upper limit is sufficient. In principle, she would like to have a percentage distribution between the flotilla leader and the smaller destroyer (under 1500 tons), but owing to the number of vessels of the larger size constructed by other powers and the small German total tonnage, she is not able to accept this in practice at present.

The German Delegation also agree that the name 'Flotilla Leader' is misleading and serves little purpose, and that the entire category might well be called 'Destroyers'.

*Submarines.* Germany supports the British Government's desire for the complete abolition of submarines, and if it could be achieved would be prepared to scrap the submarines they might have built or be building at the time.

Germany is also prepared, in the absence of abolition, to agree to any maximum tonnage limit for submarines that may be generally agreed upon.

*Submarine Warfare.* Germany is prepared to adhere to the rules regarding submarine warfare as set out in Part IV of the London Naval Treaty, and to accept them for herself irrespective of whether they are adhered to by all other powers.

*Exchange of Information.* The German Delegation agrees that Germany is prepared to participate in all agreements regarding the exchange of information concerning the building of new ships, such as those set out in Article 10 of the London Naval Treaty, and paragraph (b), Section I, Part 3, Chapter II of the Washington Treaty, provided they are similarly and fully applied to all other Powers. Should there be no general international agreement, Germany and the United Kingdom would be prepared to observe the confidential bilateral exchange of information between themselves. Further, the German Government are prepared to enter into conversations with other Powers concerning the possibility of exchanging this information on a strictly reciprocal basis henceforth, pending the conclusion of a general agreement.

*Minor Provisions of the Washington Treaty.* The German Delegation state that Germany would agree to the inclusion of the provisions of Article XIV, XVII and XVIII of the Washington Treaty, provided they apply equally to all parties.

*Definitions.* The German Government agree to the definitions of categories, standard displacement and age limits given in Annex I to Chapter 2 of Section II of the British Draft Disarmament Convention,⁷ provided they apply to all countries, except that they claim a shorter term of life than 20 years as applied to the *Deutschland* class of ships.

⁷ Of March 1933; cf. No. 364, note 6.

## No. 462

### Letter from Sir R. Lindsay (*Washington*) to Mr. Craigie
#### (*Received August 23*)
#### [*A 7416/22/45*]

WASHINGTON, *August 7, 1935*

Dear Craigie:

Norman Davis dined with me yesterday and asked me to tell you, when next I see you, that he hoped you would get on well in your naval conversations with European states, and that you would make your progress as rapid as possible. He also hoped very much that, if you succeeded in this and were proceeding to the next stage of something like a general conference, an effort would be made to have some previous coordination of plans with the United States. He thought it likely that he himself might have to go over to Geneva some time this autumn (query in October) for the Arms business,¹ in which case he could easily slip over to London for informal discussion which he felt sure would be valuable. He said also that in some previous discussion with you about a prospective resumption of the Conference, he had differed from you in that he had wished that Conference to be formal and official from the first.² He was now rather inclined to depart from that view, and perhaps to prefer that it might start as a resumption of the previous conversations, and then perhaps develop into the full conference if circumstances warranted.

I expect to be sailing for home this day week and shall hope to see you in due course.

Yours sincerely,
R. C. LINDSAY

¹ The question of a convention for the control of manufacture of, and trade in, arms was to be discussed by the Conference for the Reduction and Limitation of Armaments; cf. *F.R.U.S. 1935*, vol. i, pp. 57–62.　　² Cf. No. 101.

## No. 463

### Sir S. Hoare to Mr. Newton (*Berlin*)
#### No. 159 Telegraphic [*C 5839/55/18*]

FOREIGN OFFICE, *August 9, 1935, 5.30 p.m.*

Your telegram No. 174 Saving.¹

There are of course pertinent answers to the observations of Herr von

¹ No. 456.

Bülow reported in paragraphs 1 and 2 of your telegram. Some of them you may have made to him yourself; but I give them to you now in case you find either the need or the occasion to revert to this matter in conversation at the Ministry for Foreign Affairs.

1. Herr von Bülow dissents from our view as to the efficacy of such measures as the Eastern Pact for improving the atmosphere; but if it was generally believed in Europe that Germany intended to honour the obligations which she has already declared herself ready to assume in a collective pact of non-aggression in Eastern Europe, or indeed in an Air Pact, it seems to us very difficult to believe that the general situation would not be greatly tranquillized.

2. Herr von Bülow stated that as soon as Germany had done what was wanted in regard to the Eastern Pact the French Government would say that they wanted something else, and that they attached no importance to this concession. As a matter of fact, whilst we are pressing the German Government about the Eastern Pact we are also doing all we can in Paris to ensure that unreasonable demands are not made in respect of the other elements of the general settlement.

3. Herr von Bülow's contention that the Eastern Pact would inevitably weaken existing arrangements seems to us very feeble. The Eastern Pact could, if necessary, take note of and recall existing arrangements which (except in the case of Poland) are admittedly incomplete.

4. We have already pointed out,[2] with reference to the German claim that the communication of April 13th was made prior to the Franco-Russian Treaty, that in fact it contained no qualification or reserve whatsoever on this point. If the German Government wanted to qualify the promise given us on April 13th they had every opportunity of doing so at the time; but they did no such thing. On the contrary the German Government said definitely that they had no objection to other Powers concluding mutual assistance arrangements.

5. The claim that 'no particular notice' was taken at the time of the German communication of April 13th is very specious. The Stresa communiqué[3] contained a statement that '*the information which the three Powers have received* has confirmed their view that the negotiations should be pursued for the development which is desired in security in Eastern Europe'. Then there was an interval necessitated first by the excitement in Germany about the Geneva Resolution[4] which rendered unwise at the time any new communication about the Eastern Pact, and secondly by our desire to hear what the Chancellor would say on this subject in his speech of May 21st. Immediately afterwards came the French note of June 3rd[5] proposing negotiations on the basis of the promise of April 13th.

[2] See No. 449.
[3] Of April 14, 1935; see Cmd. 4880. Cf. Volume XII, No. 722, p. 911.
[4] Of April 17; cf. *ibid.*, No. 732.          [5] Cf. No. 288, note 3.

## No. 464

### Sir S. Hoare to Mr. Newton (Berlin)
### No. 160 Telegraphic [C 5860/55/18]

FOREIGN OFFICE, *August 9, 1935, 5.45 p.m.*

Paris telegram No. 158.[1]

It might be well, if you see no strong objection, to let Herr von Bülow know that our information is that the French Government have in no way abandoned their view that an Eastern Pact is an essential part of any general settlement (see in this connection the opening sentence of paragraph 2 of your telegram No. 246).[2]

[1] No. 459.    [2] No. 440.

## No. 465

### Record by Mr. Broad of his conversations with Mr. Atherton and Mr. Fujii[1] on August 9
### [A 7125/22/45]

FOREIGN OFFICE, *August 9, 1935*

It was arranged for me to see Mr. Atherton and Mr. Fujii this afternoon in order to hand them copies of the memorandum on qualitative disarmament.[2]

Mr. Atherton was somewhat upset (*a*) that we had not handed him this memorandum on the same day as we had handed it to the French, and (*b*) that we had not told him in advance of Captain Danckwerts' impending visit to Paris.[3] I reminded Mr. Atherton, however, that Mr. Craigie had told Mr. Bingham on the 5th August[4] that Captain Danckwerts would probably soon be going to Paris, and I went on to explain that this visit had been arranged in a hurry since the Admiralty were anxious that Captain Danckwerts should take the opportunity (which is unlikely to recur for him for some time) of taking some leave this month. The whole purpose of his visit to Paris (which was only for one day) had been, I explained, to enable him to resume contact with the French Admiralty, and to break the ice with a view to the resumption of preliminary informal discussions. When we knew that Captain Danckwerts was to visit Paris within a few days, it obviously became necessary for us to communicate the memorandum to the French immediately in order to avoid misunderstandings. Mr. Atherton went on to say that it was unfortunate that the first intimation that the Americans should get about this visit was through the press. I reminded him again of Mr. Craigie's conversation with Mr. Bingham, and emphasised that we had said nothing to the press (because Captain Danckwerts' visit

[1] Counsellor of the Japanese Embassy at London.

[2] See enclosure in No. 460. Cf. *F.R.U.S. 1935*, vol. i, pp. 87–90.

[3] A marginal note by Sir R. Vansittart here reads: 'Why should we? R.V.'

[4] No record of this conversation has been traced in Foreign Office archives. Mr. Craigie had since resumed his leave of absence.

was of so informal a nature) and that therefore it could not be said that we had informed the press before informing the United States Government.

I then handed Mr. Atherton a copy of the memorandum, which he read through. He expressed the opinion that the memorandum would cause an unfortunate impression in the U.S.—particularly our reference to the maximum tonnage of capital ships, in view of the nature of the U.S. construction programme. I referred Mr. Atherton to the first sentence of paragraph 5 of the memorandum in which it was emphasised that we 'cannot accept qualitative limits which, though they might be agreeable to all European Powers, are not acceptable also to the U.S.A. and Japan'. I emphasised that the memorandum simply represented the method which we thought best for getting a move on for preparations for the forthcoming conference. (I think, and Captain Danckwerts agrees, that it is rather unreasonable of the Americans to expect us invariably to let them know in advance whenever we say anything at all to the French).[5]

Shortly after Mr. Atherton's call I saw Mr. Fujii, with whom the discussion followed on similar lines. I added, on the strength of the minute by Mr. Craigie on the attached copy of Tokio telegram No. 204,[6] that we understood from what the Japanese Vice Minister for Foreign Affairs had told Sir R. Clive that the Japanese Government favoured bilateral conversations. As regards this, I said that we were ready for bilateral talks at any time convenient to them but, on the other hand, time was now getting rather short. Mr. Fujii's attention, however, was almost all the time directed to the memorandum alone and therefore if we are to be certain that the point in Mr. Craigie's minute is made, it might be as well to send a short telegram to Sir R. Clive, as I am not at all sure that Mr. Fujii will report what I said about bilateral conversations.

A draft to inform H.M. Representatives at Washington and Tokyo is attached—if approved I will add a paragraph in the draft to Tokyo on the particular point mentioned in the above paragraph.[7]

P. BROAD

P.S. In order to avoid misunderstandings, it might be advisable for us to let the French and Italians know without delay now that we have given copies of this memorandum to the Americans and to the Japanese for their information. Eventually the Germans and Russians are also, I understand, to be given copies,[8] but I take it that we need not hurry in their case.

A draft telegram to Berlin, explaining Captain Danckwerts' visit to Paris, is being submitted on a separate paper.[9]

P.B.

---

[5] A marginal note by Sir R. Vansittart here reads: 'It is more than unreasonable. It is intolerable. R.V.'

[6] No. 443.    [7] See No. 466 below for the telegrams as despatched on August 12.

[8] For the arrangements made to inform the German Government of the memorandum, see No. 467 below, note 2. The Counsellor of the Soviet Embassy at London, Mr. Cahan, was given details of the memorandum on August 19.

[9] See No. 467 below for the telegram as despatched.

## No. 466

*Sir S. Hoare to Sir R. Lindsay (Washington) and Sir R. Clive (Tokyo)*
No. 227[1] Telegraphic [A 7125/22/45]

FOREIGN OFFICE, *August 12, 1935, 5.35 p.m.*

At the suggestion of the French Government, Captain Danckwerts of the Admiralty paid a visit, on the 6th August to Paris to set in motion again the discussions on Naval matters which had been in abeyance since the conclusion of the Anglo-German Agreement. It was made clear to the French that the visit was only for the purpose stated, and was on no account intended to replace the further preliminary discussions, which it is hoped will take place in London in September.

The nature of the visit was explained to the United States/Japanese Counsellor who was also handed, for the information of his Government, a copy of a memorandum on qualitative limitation which has been communicated to the French and Italian Governments.[2] A copy of the memorandum is being sent to you by bag. It was explained to the United States/Japanese Counsellor that the communication of this memorandum to the French and Italian Governments was in no sense intended as a means of forming a front against, or bringing pressure on the United States/Japanese Government. The procedure adopted was simply regarded by His Majesty's Government as the best method of clearing the way for agreement, at least on the qualitative side of naval limitation.

With[3] reference to your telegram No. 204[4] Japanese Counsellor was told that we understood from what Japanese Vice-Minister for Foreign Affairs told you that the Japanese Government favoured bilateral conversations; he was assured that we were ready for bilateral talks at any time convenient to the Japanese Government, but it was pointed out also that time was now getting rather short.

[1] No. 227 to Washington, No. 159 to Tokyo.
[2] See No. 460, enclosure.
[3] This last paragraph was sent to Tokyo only. It was referred to in Foreign Office telegram No. 163 to Tokyo of 10 p.m. on August 16 which read: 'You will no doubt take an opportunity of repeating to Vice Minister for Foreign Affairs what was said to the Counsellor here about bilateral conversations.'                                [4] No. 443.

## No. 467

*Sir S. Hoare to Sir E. Phipps (Berlin)*
No. 161 Telegraphic [A 7134/22/45]

FOREIGN OFFICE, *August 12, 1935, 5.45 p.m.*

My despatch No. 864.[1] As reports of Captain Danckwerts' visit to Paris for one day have appeared in the press, you may tell the German Govern-

[1] See No. 460, paragraph 6.

ment that the only purpose of the visit was to have informal discussions with a view to arranging for further preliminary conversations with the French at a later date.[2]

You should add that as the French did not communicate any projected construction programme, to Captain Danckwerts, no details of the proposed German programme were given to the French, the French were only given the German views on qualitative limits, exchange of information and the minor provisions of the Washington Treaty. These are matters on which the French views were communicated by us to the German representatives when the latter were in London.[3]

[2] Arrangements had been made on Saturday, August 10, for Captain Danckwerts to communicate orally to Captain Wassner, on his return to London from Berlin the following week, the gist of Appendix 1 to No. 460. In a minute of August 9, Mr. Gore-Booth explained that this procedure was being followed as 'Herr von Ribbentrop specially asked that all information touching on the Anglo-German Naval Agreement should be conveyed to the German Government via the Admiralty, and Captain Wassner, and we agreed'. Cf. No. 488 below, note 2.

[3] In June 1935.

## No. 468

### Sir S. Hoare to Mr. Aveling (Warsaw)
### No. 319 [C 5786/55/18]

FOREIGN OFFICE, *August 12, 1935*

Sir,

The Polish Chargé d'Affaires called here on August 7th to enquire what was the present position with regard to negotiations for an Eastern Pact.

2. M. Orlowski was informed that H.M. Government had recently renewed with energy their representations to the German Government on this matter (see my telegram No. 150[1] of the 2nd August to Berlin, and Mr. Newton's telegram No. 251[2] of the 5th August).

3. H.M. Government, it was explained, did not feel that they were demanding very great sacrifices from anyone. They considered that the conclusion of an Eastern Pact would ease the situation, and they attached importance to its conclusion because other Powers did so and also because they regarded progress in the negotiations for an Eastern Pact as essential to progress in other directions.

4. M. Orlowski was also informed that H.M. Government were at the moment concentrating their efforts on Berlin and that if they succeeded in these efforts they would certainly expect no difficulties to be made in other quarters.

I am, &c.,
(for the Secretary of State)
C. W. BAXTER

[1] No. 449.    [2] No. 455.

## No. 469

*Letter from Mr. Newton (Berlin) to Mr. Sargent (Received August 19)*
[*C 6059/55/18*]

BERLIN, *August 12, 1935*

My dear Sergo,

It is always useful to have extra material for arguing one's point of view, so I appreciated Foreign Office telegram No. 159[1] of August 9th.

In case, however, there is any misapprehension as to my own attitude and action despite my telegrams, I would observe that, while Germany's honour is a delicate matter, point 1 was a consideration which I went out of my way specially to emphasise—see my telegram No. 251.[2] Point 2 is of course a common German complaint which is, I am inclined to think, not altogether without justification. I remember at the time of the reparations moratorium proposed by Hoover[3] we tried to make things easier for the French by pressing the Germans to desist from laying down one of the few ships to which they were entitled under Versailles. Despite great efforts by ourselves and the Americans we were in this unsuccessful, and a little later on, if my recollection is not at fault, the French intimated that a concession on these lines would in any case not have been of much use to them. Similarly the French pressed very hard for the replacement of long-term service by short-term service in the German army,[4] but when the Germans showed readiness to meet this request the French were no nearer being satisfied. I am glad therefore to be able to assure the Germans that His Majesty's Government are doing everything they can to ensure that the French Government will be reasonable. It would of course help to convince them if I could definitely say that in return for a concession in the Eastern Pact the French would in fact make a concession in regard to the Air Pact or in any other field.

Point 4 was emphasised by me first verbally and then in writing in the course of my communication.

Point 5. My telegrams were already rather lengthy but perhaps I ought to have added to my telegram No. 174 [Saving][5] that I pointed out to Bülow that so far from no particular notice having been taken of the German reply[6] to our enquiry from Stresa, it had been received with great satisfaction as was well known from the prominence given to the matter in the press. Moreover I could not admit that in a matter of such importance and in comparison with the procedure of other governments, the delay in the French reply was excessive. In any case it in no way invalidated the German offer.

Point 3. Not only is this particular contention weak but I took Bülow's remarks generally to be merely a kind of marking time. I did not read to

[1] No. 463.           [2] No. 455.

[3] For President Hoover's scheme of June 1931 for one year's suspension of all inter-governmental claims and obligations see Volume II, Chapter II.

[4] Under Article 174 of the Treaty of Versailles the period for enlistment for non-commissioned officers and privates had been fixed as 'twelve consecutive years'.

[5] No. 456.           [6] Of April 13, 1935.

him my aide-mémoire, but spoke slowly and emphatically following closely its lines. I did not produce the aide-mémoire until I had finished my verbal communication which, with the introduction mentioned in my telegram No. 251,[2] must have lasted twenty minutes or more. Although Bülow presumably felt he must say something and must reserve his position, I could hardly expect him, and in fact did not wish him then and there, to give me a considered reply. I had made it clear that the matter must be referred to Herr von Neurath and the Chancellor.

From various references made to me by other officials it is clear that the Ministry has been considerably impressed by my communication but expect that the Chancellor will continue to delay.

Any obscurities in the French attitude or alleged differences in their attitude and ours will no doubt be used in the cause of obstruction. If therefore this particular method can be circumvented, so much the better.

Yours ever<br>BASIL C. NEWTON

## No. 470

*Mr. Newton (Berlin) to Sir S. Hoare (Received August 14, 2.30 p.m.)*
*No. 181 Saving: Telegraphic* [*C 5983/55/18*]

BERLIN, August 13, 1935

My telegram No. 251.[1]

I asked Herr Pruefer who has been in charge of British affairs at Ministry of Foreign Affairs in the absence of Herr Dieckhoff whether I might expect early reply to my representations. He said it was expected that Chancellor would be visiting Herr von Neurath during this week when decision as to reply might be taken. He also told me that Herr von Bülow had written privately to German Ambassador in Paris in order to ascertain more closely the French attitude.

Repeated to Moscow, Paris and Warsaw.

[1] No. 455.

## No. 471

*Mr. Newton (Berlin) to Sir S. Hoare (Received August 14, 2 p.m.)*
*No. 182 Saving: Telegraphic* [*C 5984/55/18*]

BERLIN, August 14, 1935

My immediately preceding telegram Saving.[1]

From Herr Pruefer's attitude I gathered that he did not really expect reply would be more than provisional. He evidently doubted whether in such matter Chancellor would be willing to take a final decision until after the holiday period and Nuremberg party rally (September 10th to September 16th).

[1] No. 470.

I should not be surprised if allegation that French attitude is obscure or different from ours were not made pretext for further delay.

Speaking quite informally and unofficially Herr Pruefer asked whether I thought His Majesty's Government would be willing to join Eastern Pact. I said I thought not. What His Majesty's Government were pressing for was a pact with the six States specified in accordance with Germany's own offer which had also been accepted as a basis by the French Government.

Repeated to Moscow, Paris and Warsaw Saving.

## No. 472

### Note from M. Corbin to Sir S. Hoare (Received August 15)

### [A 7170/22/45]

AMBASSADE DE FRANCE, LONDRES, le 14 août 1935

L'ambassadeur de France a l'honneur de remettre ci-joint à Son Excellence le Principal Secrétaire d'État de Sa Majesté britannique aux Affaires Étrangères la réponse du Gouvernement français au Mémorandum[1] du Gouvernement de Sa Majesté britannique en date du 2 août 1935 sur la question navale.

M. Corbin saisit, &c.

ENCLOSURE IN No. 472

#### Memorandum from the French Government[2]

Le Gouvernement de la République a pris connaissance avec le plus vif intérêt du Mémorandum en date du 2 août 1935, dans lequel le Gouvernement de Sa Majesté a bien voulu exposer sur quelles bases, à la suite des conversations relatives aux armements navals qui ont eu lieu en 1934 et 1935, il envisage la possibilité d'un règlement de la question navale.

2. Le Gouvernement de la République est heureux de constater son plein accord avec le Gouvernement de Sa Majesté pour considérer que l'objet essentiel de ce règlement doit être de déterminer les limites qualitatives à respecter dans l'avenir par les constructions des diverses Puissances navales. Sur les chiffres précis mis en avant à cet égard au paragraphe 4 du Mémorandum du Gouvernement de Sa Majesté — et sans dissimuler qu'ils correspondent sensiblement à sa propre conception desdites limitations — le Gouvernement de la République estime, toutefois, difficile de se prononcer tant que ne seront pas élucidées certaines données essentielles du problème; en particulier la nature des constructions par lesquelles le Reich donnerait suite au récent arrangement naval anglo-allemand, ainsi que les limites qualitatives que seraient disposées à accepter les Puissances visées au paragraphe 5 du Mémorandum.

[1] See No. 460, enclosure.

[2] An English translation of this memorandum is printed in *F.R.U.S. 1935*, vol. i, pp. 95–6.

3. Quant aux questions d'ordre quantitatif, le Gouvernement de Sa Majesté souligne avec juste raison quelles difficultés et quelle lenteur comporte leur règlement sur la base envisagée au paragraphe 2 de son Mémorandum. De l'avis du Gouvernement de la République, ces obstacles seront d'autant plus aisément surmontés que l'on s'en tiendra à des déclarations de constructions portant sur une très courte période.

4. Dans cet ordre d'idées et parmi les divers points visés au paragraphe 8 du Mémorandum du Gouvernement de Sa Majesté — dont aucun n'offre de difficultés en ce qui le concerne — le Gouvernement de la République retient pour l'avenir la suggestion d'un échange réciproque d'informations concernant les constructions navales à entreprendre; il voudrait souligner qu'un accord à ce sujet prendrait une valeur accrue si les notifications de mises sur cale étaient complétées par des préavis. Par là, en effet, le problème si délicat des limitations quantitatives pourrait sans doute être engagé dans la voie d'un règlement progressif; il trouverait une solution d'attente permettant de compléter de suite le règlement qui doit, de toute façon, intervenir d'abord dans le domaine qualitatif.

5. Telles sont les observations qu'appellent, de la part du Gouvernement de la République, les vues que le Gouvernement de Sa Majesté a bien voulu lui communiquer quant à la solution d'un problème qui intéresse à un si haut degré la paix du monde, et à laquelle l'approche de l'échéance des traités navals en vigueur donne un caractère de particulière urgence. Il croit devoir les porter sans retard à la connaissance du Gouvernement de Sa Majesté.

## No. 473

### Sir S. Hoare to Sir G. Clerk (Paris)
### No. 1524 [C 5700/55/18]

FOREIGN OFFICE, *August 16, 1935*

Sir,

In my despatch No. 1344[1] of July 18th, respecting the limitation of land armaments, I asked Your Excellency to impress upon M. Laval the desirability of the French Government coming down to realities and making to Germany an offer, both as regards effectives and heavy material, which there was some chance of her accepting. My reason was that the French Government had indicated on a number of occasions that they were averse to the settlement of the air question (Air Pact and air limitation) unless accompanied by a settlement of land armaments, and that they were against any limitation of heavy material without some limitation of effectives.

2. In your despatch No. 1076[2] of July 26th you reported M. Laval's statement to you that he was referring the question of land armaments to the 'Haut-Comité militaire' and would take it up with you when he had received the advisory opinion of the Committee. You also reported, as showing the

[1] No. 416.    [2] No. 431; cf. Sir S. Hoare's comments in *ibid.*, note 5.

probable nature of the eventual French reply, certain observations made to His Majesty's Minister by M. Léger. Those observations were to the effect that His Majesty's Government, like the French Government, seemed to have reached the conclusion that as regards effectives there was little or no hope of reducing the German programme as published in the Decree of March 16th; that the French Government could not come to an agreement with Germany on a basis which, while acquiescing in that programme, would involve a considerable increase in the French forces; that in these circumstances France had no alternative but to make the effort required to keep her abreast of Germany, presumably on the basis of two years' service (a 'two-year programme' M. Léger apparently called it); and that it was useless for Herr von Ribbentrop to come to Paris unless he could bring with him some proposal which France could reasonably and honourably accept.

3. M. Léger's observations are most disappointing. Were we to accept a final answer on these lines it would apparently mean that a settlement of the question of effectives was for the time being impossible; and that, therefore, on the basis of previous French statements, there can be no limitation of heavy material and—still more important—no settlement of the air question (although in this case the ingredients for a settlement are available, provided that the present opportunity is seized in time).

4. Although His Majesty's Government are naturally interested in the limitation of heavy material, I propose, for the purpose of the present despatch, to confine myself to considering the effect which M. Léger's *non possumus* attitude, if confirmed by the French Government, would have on the prospects of the Locarno Powers being able to conclude between themselves an Air Pact and an Air Limitation Agreement.

5. Basing themselves on the principle of simultaneity laid down in the Anglo-French Declaration of February 3rd, the French Government have already stipulated that such an Air Pact and Air Limitation Agreement, even if negotiated, shall only enter into force concurrently with agreements regarding the other subjects mentioned in the declaration of February 3rd.[3] It is true that His Majesty's Government have accepted this stipulation in principle, and the efforts which they have been making to further the negotiation of the Eastern Pact and the Danubian settlement are proof of their sincerity and goodwill. But, not unnaturally, His Majesty's Government have throughout assumed that in making this stipulation the French Government had in mind only such questions figuring in the February declaration as were in present circumstances susceptible of international agreement and settlement. In the case of the Eastern Pact and the Danubian problem it is permissible to hope that such agreement and settlement is possible. But if we are now to be told by the French Government at one and the same time, first, that an agreement regarding land armaments and more particularly effectives is beyond the possibility of achievement, and, secondly, that its achievement is nevertheless a condition without which they will not consent to the conclusion of an Air Pact or Air Limitation Agreement, then it is

[3] See No. 363.

obvious that we are faced with an entirely new and unexpected situation—a situation where the French Government, by setting up an impossible condition, would in effect have imposed a definite veto on the settlement of the air problem on the lines hitherto contemplated by the two Governments. His Majesty's Government cannot imagine that this can ever have been or is now the intention of the French Government, and I shall therefore continue to assume, notwithstanding M. Léger's analysis of the present situation, that, since the French Government have themselves demanded an agreement on land armaments as part of the so-called 'general settlement', they must have some positive plan in view as to how to achieve such an agreement in present circumstances.

6. If therefore the French Government wish to claim that no settlement of the question of heavy material, and still more no settlement of the air question, are possible without a settlement of the effectives question, then His Majesty's Government feel that they are entitled to ask that the French Government should now, without further delay, give some clear and practical indication of the kind of composite settlement which they have in mind when they thus link up the land and air problems. His Majesty's Government cannot believe that after the long period which has elapsed since the March Decree and the Chancellor's speech of May 21st the French Government are still without any ideas of their own on the subject.

7. M. Léger stated in his conversation with Mr. Campbell that France had no alternative but to make the effort required to keep her abreast of Germany, apparently on the basis of two years' service. It will be useful to examine further the implications of this statement. We must assume on the one hand that the German peace establishment of 36 Divisions is fixed and unalterable and that the total number to be incorporated in those divisions—550,000 men—is only susceptible of reduction in the eventuality, now clearly most improbable, of other Powers reducing from their present strengths. On the other hand we are led to understand that the present law will probably give France by the end of 1936 a peace establishment (in Metropolitan France and North Africa) of 540,000 men; and that a two-year service law fully applied might at the end of the 'lean years' in 1940 give a peace establishment of 600,000 men in France alone.

8. In the face of these facts and estimates do the French Government see any prospect in the more or less immediate future of some limitation or stabilisation of strengths as between France and Germany on the basis of the 36 Divisions and some French strength resulting from a form of two-year service?

9. If the French Government consider that some such arrangement is possible, and if they still insist that there can be no settlement of the other questions without a settlement of this question, then His Majesty's Government consider that they ought to approach the German Government without delay on the subject. If, on the other hand, they consider that there is nothing to be done as regards effectives on the basis of this suggestion or on any other basis, it will be necessary to point out to them that in these

circumstances it will be neither fair, nor logical, nor practical to hold up the proposed Air Pact and Air Limitation Agreement because the avowedly insoluble problem of reaching agreement as regards land armaments cannot be achieved simultaneously.

10. Incidentally, His Majesty's Government are very definitely of the opinion that every delay will add to the difficulty of the French in coming to any sort of agreement either on effectives or armaments. As Germany progresses with her rearmament programme she will be ever less inclined to discuss any limitations. In heavy material France may have a superiority over Germany for the moment; but this is bound to disappear in a short period. Any agreement on this matter is surely of advantage to France as enhancing the value of her frontier fortifications.

11. Respecting the Eastern Pact His Majesty's Government are ready to help the French Government, and help them very energetically; and here you should emphasise the numerous communications recently made to the German Government in this matter (see my despatches No. 807[4] of the 23rd July, No. 826[5] of the 29th July and No. 832[6] of the 1st August to Berlin, and my telegram No. 150[7] to Berlin, and Berlin telegrams No. 251[8] and No. 174, Saving,[9] of the 5th August). As regards the Danubian Pact His Majesty's Government have already shown their anxiety to help. At the moment they understand that negotiations on the matter are actually in progress between France, Italy and certain other Powers; but His Majesty's Government remain perfectly ready to consider any means by which, in M. Laval's view, their influence could be further exercised.

12. In the matter of land armaments also His Majesty's Government are willing to lend their good offices should the French Government desire them, but in that event it is, as stated above, essential that the French Government should now, without further delay, work out and explain to us the kind of settlement which they will accept. If they have no such proposal to make they will only alienate opinion in this country by continuing to make a settlement in the air conditional on a settlement on land, for by doing so they will inevitably give the impression of intentionally obstructing the efforts of His Majesty's Government to deal in practical fashion with the problem which has been created by the uncontrolled rearmament of Germany in the air, and in which the British public is so acutely interested. It cannot possibly be in the interests of the French Government that such an impression should be created. Moreover, the French Government are surely no less affected than His Majesty's Government by this aeronautical problem; in which case one would suppose that they would be particularly anxious for their own sake not to repeat as regards air armaments the purely negative policy followed in the spring of last year in the matter of land armaments.[10]

[4] No. 424.                    [5] No. 437.                    [6] No. 447.
[7] No. 449.                    [8] No. 455.                    [9] No. 456.
[10] A reference to the French Government's note of April 17, 1934; cf. Volume VI, No. 395, enclosure.

13. These are the general lines on which I should be grateful if you would speak, and speak with emphasis, to the Minister for Foreign Affairs. You should support your representations and reinforce your pressure in this matter by such further arguments as may seem appropriate to you. You should make clear the different points set out in this despatch, hold to them and combat any counter-arguments which may be used.

14. I think that it would also be useful that the Military Attaché should see and speak with some of the high officers on the French General Staff on this matter and himself endeavour to ascertain what policy they have in mind.

15. In general I feel that we must concentrate on all these unsettled questions in the weeks that remain before the reassembly of the Chambers; and I rely upon Your Excellency to handle them with energy and firmness.

I am, &c.,
SAMUEL HOARE

## No. 474

*Letter from Mr. Atherton to Mr. Broad*
[*A 7286/22/45*]

EMBASSY OF THE UNITED STATES OF AMERICA, LONDON, *August 17, 1935*

My dear Broad:

On August 9th you were good enough to give me, for the information of my Government, a copy of a memorandum dealing with the general subject of limitation of naval armaments,[1] which you told me had been handed the week preceding to the French and Italian representatives in London. At that time you indicated that, in the absence of Mr. Craigie on holiday, there was no one at the Foreign Office prepared to discuss the memorandum, although you were under instructions to point out certain passages of particular interest to my Government.

The text of the memorandum which you handed me on that occasion was duly communicated to my Government, and I have since received instructions to convey certain observations thereon to the appropriate authorities of His Majesty's Government. As it happens that I shall be seeing Mr. Craigie on Tuesday next,[2] I shall at that time invite his attention and discuss with him those observations of my Government to which I refer. I am enclosing an aide-mémoire[3] outlining those observations of the United States Government on the memorandum you handed me on August 9th, which I shall discuss with Mr. Craigie on Tuesday.

Yours sincerely,
RAY ATHERTON

[1] Cf. No. 465.
[2] August 20. Cf. No. 483 below.
[3] The aide-mémoire was based on instructions sent to Mr. Atherton by the United States Secretary of State on August 14; see *F.R.U.S. 1935*, vol. i, pp. 91–2.

LONDON, *August 17, 1935*

*Aide-Mémoire*

In the view of the American Government, in the British memorandum to the French and Italian Governments, copy of which was handed to the American Chargé d'Affaires on August 9th, there are proposals with regard to tonnage and gun calibres of future construction which are contrary to American views as they have been set forth many times. Furthermore, it would seem that these proposals are not in accord with the explanation given by British representatives of the British 'middle course' proposal advanced last year in that such proposal was to include: first, measures of qualitative limitation, but such were not to be devised in an effort to change existing types, but were rather to prevent competition in new types; and, second, programmes for future construction which would have as one of their objects the maintenance of present ratios as closely as possible.

The American Government understood that this 'middle course' proposal was to be studied by both the American and Japanese Governments and that the British Government would keep in touch with the two other Governments to determine whether such proposal offered substantial hope of agreement, and that the British Government would arrange in the light thereof for the calling of a further meeting.

The British Government is now, however, upon its own initiative, without prior discussion with the American Government, evidently proceeding in an endeavor to reach 'a sufficient measure of European agreement' so that it can put forward 'as a European view' proposals which, from previous and repeated expressions of the American viewpoint, it was believed the British Government must have realized embody such a wide divergence from existing Treaty types as to make them unacceptable to the American Government.

In the circumstances, while the American Government wishes to be as co-operative as possible and shares the desire of the British Government to reach agreement on general naval limitation, the American Government feels that little hope of achieving these ends is offered by a conference so long as the positions of the two major participants are still so far apart.

As a preliminary to any such meeting, the American Government feels that it is of primary importance that the two Powers possessing the largest fleets should reach more nearly a community of views than now exists. The American Government had anticipated that during the process of exploration and before the British Government would embark upon a definite programme of proposals which include major questions of fleet construction they would have made a further attempt to reconcile such differences as are now shown to exist. While, in view of the denunciation of the Washington Treaty which was then impending, no attempt was made to reach agreement on technical questions between the United States and Great Britain during last year's preliminary conversations, it was in the opinion of the American

Government brought out at that time that the definite possibility existed of reconciling the technical views of the two Navies. In the circumstances the American Government has had in mind suggesting the desirability of an informal exchange of views, without publicity,—say between the Naval Attaché to the American Embassy in London and officials of the Admiralty—on the respective positions of the two Governments, in an attempt to clear up divergencies with respect to future building, qualitative limitations, and disposal of over-age tonnage. Should such a suggestion commend itself to the British Government, this Embassy is prepared to seek the necessary instructions to undertake such an informal exchange of views at the earliest convenient date.

## No. 475

*Sir G. Clerk (Paris) to Sir S. Hoare (Received August 20)*
*No. 193 Saving: Telegraphic [C 6077/55/18]*

PARIS, *August 19, 1935*

Following from Mr. Eden.

M. Laval asked me to come and see him this morning before leaving Paris . . .[1]

6. We then spoke of the European situation generally. M. Laval was anxious to make progress with all the items mentioned in the London communiqué of February 3rd. If it were possible at this time to begin a negotiation with Germany, it might to some extent distract opinion from this troublesome dispute between Italy and Abyssinia. I replied that we were only too anxious to make progress and would help in any way that we could. Had M. Laval any ideas as to how to make progress in negotiations about land armaments, for instance, with Germany, since he had told me that while he was willing to go ahead with negotiations of the various items in the London communiqué, he wished them to be concluded together? M. Laval was vague in his answer and it is clear that he has no clear-cut ideas as to how to proceed with these negotiations. He maintained that political agreements with a country such as Germany were in truth more valuable than technical arms agreements. It was easy enough to work an arms agreement between two countries who trust each other, such as Great Britain and France, but even with supervision, he was himself sceptical of the value of arms agreement with Germany. He was, however, going to turn the whole matter over in his mind once again. He is certainly anxious himself to produce a political détente with Germany if he can. I insisted that time was the essence of the matter. In the air, for instance, Germany's expansion was rapid, and delay would not make agreement easier. M. Laval said he understood that we were at last increasing our air force. He was glad of it. He feared that the general state of our national defences was very weak.

[1] The first five paragraphs of this telegram dealt with the Italo-Ethiopian question and will be printed in Volume XIV. Mr. Eden had been in Paris since August 13 for discussions relating to that question and was returning to London on August 19.

Was it not true that our army strength had been allowed to fall very low, and were we sure this was wise? Perhaps if we had been a little stronger, Signor Mussolini might have been more amenable. At any rate, in the present state of the world, he felt himself bound to do what he could to maintain the strength of France, and he proposed in the next few months further to increase the credits for national defence.

7. At the conclusion of the conversation we returned to the consideration of the 4th September at Geneva.[2] M. Laval speaking with an earnestness unusual with him, assured me that he had no intention of turning his back upon the League or upon the policy which we were pursuing in respect of the League. At the same time, he knew that I understood the reality of his own difficulties in relation to an Italy with whom he had recently concluded a Treaty,[3] and he begged me to take account of them in any advice which I might give to my colleagues.

---

[2] The first meeting of the 88th session of the Council of the League of Nations was to be held at Geneva on September 4: the main subject for discussion was to be the Italo-Ethiopian dispute.　　　　　　　　　　　　　　　　　　[3] i.e. of January 7, 1935.

## No. 476

### Sir S. Hoare to Mr. Aveling (Warsaw)
### No. 324 [A 7130/22/45]

FOREIGN OFFICE, *August 19, 1935*

Sir,

On the 2nd of this month, the Polish Chargé d'Affaires called at the Foreign Office to make certain enquiries about the Anglo-German Naval Agreement and British naval policy in general. Captain Danckwerts, Assistant Director of Plans at the Admiralty, was present at the interview.

2. M. Orlowski began by explaining that Poland had become interested in the naval question since the conclusion of the Anglo-German Agreement, whereupon Captain Danckwerts suggested that it might be more correct to say that the interest had begun since Germany began to build a navy. M. Orlowski appeared to accept this correction.

3. He then drew attention to the passage in the speech of the First Lord of the Admiralty on the 22nd July, a copy of the text of which is enclosed,[1] in which allusion is made to the abandonment of the ratio principle in respect of future naval agreements. M. Orlowski was handed a copy of the reply of the Lord Privy Seal to Lord Cecil in the House of Lords on the 29th July, a copy of the text of which is also enclosed,[2] which gives a fuller explanation of what the First Lord had outlined; and in reply to an objection that the system of unilateral declarations of programme proposed by His Majesty's Government in the United Kingdom was merely the ratio system in disguise, Captain Danckwerts explained that, on the contrary, it was essentially

---

[1] Not here reproduced: see 304 *H.C. Deb.* 5 s., cols. 1538–9.
[2] Not here reproduced: see 98 *H.L. Deb.* 5 s., cols. 880–1.

different, in that while the ratio system only granted, e.g. to Japan, the right to a navy three-fifths of the strength of the British navy, the essential premise of the programme system was that equality of rights was explicitly granted to every nation. The declarations of programme would be voluntary and unilateral, but naturally these programmes would have to be concerted before-hand if any agreement was to be reached.

4. M. Orlowski said that his interest in this matter was largely political, and he was particularly anxious for information about the position of Germany and the Soviet Union; if a conference were held would these two countries participate? Captain Danckwerts answered that a conference for the Washington Powers was provided for in the Washington Treaty, at which conference Germany and the U.S.S.R. would obviously not be represented. On the other hand, it would ultimately be necessary for the programme system and qualitative limitation to be universalised, and in this universalisation all the naval Powers would be interested.

5. In response to further enquiries about the forthcoming conference, Captain Danckwerts explained that, speaking personally and as a naval officer, he would say that the most important thing was to secure qualitative limitation as soon as possible, in order that there might be qualitative limits in existence when, on the 1st January 1937, all countries became free of the present treaty limitations. On the other hand a big navy could not be built up in a year, and there was less hurry therefore to reach agreement on programmes. As for the venue of the conference, this had not yet been decided.

6. M. Orlowski mentioned that the initiative for his enquiry had rested on an inaccurate report in Poland about the views of His Majesty's Government on the abolition of submarines. On this point Captain Danckwerts explained that His Majesty's Government and the German Government were in favour of the abolition of submarines, and would probably bring the matter up again at any future conference, although there was not much hope of success as France was still wedded to the submarine. M. Orlowski said that Germany might have been in favour of the abolition of the submarine knowing that the idea would not be acceptable to France; Captain Danckwerts suggested that it might, on the other hand, be because Germany, with her previous experience of submarines, had decided that they were not worth the expense and trouble which they caused.

I am, &c.,
(for the Secretary of State)
A. HOLMAN[3]

---

[3] Mr. A. Holman, previously First Secretary in H.M. Embassy, Peking, had recently been transferred to the American Department of the Foreign Office.

## No. 477

### Letter from Mr. Holman to the Marquis de Castellane[1]
[A 7170/22/45]

FOREIGN OFFICE, *August 19, 1935*

Dear Castellane,

You were so good as to communicate to the Foreign Office a few days ago a memorandum from your Embassy dated August 14th,[2] containing the views of the French Government on the proposals of His Majesty's Government as set out in their memorandum of July 30th[3] on the subject the limitation of Naval armaments.

In this connection I shall be grateful if you can inform me at your early convenience

(*a*) Whether the French Government would be disposed to send delegates to London in the middle of September to take part in preliminary naval conversations, and

(*b*) Whether the French Government have any objection to His Majesty's Government communicating copies of the French memorandum of August 14th to the Washington Treaty powers, and keeping the German and Soviet Governments generally informed of the substance thereof.

Further I presume that you do not object to the Press being acquainted with the fact that the reply of the French Government has now been received.[4]

A. HOLMAN

[1] Cf. No. 460, note 1.       [2] See No. 472.       [3] Cf. No. 460, note 4.
[4] The formal ending of this letter is missing on the filed copy.

In his reply of August 20 the Marquis de Castellane said that Mr. Holman's first question had been referred to the French Government and that the answer to the second question, as telephoned from Paris, was as follows: '*a*) The French Memorandum of August 14th has been communicated to the Italian, American and Japanese Governments. The Soviet Government is being informed of its substance. *b*) We would object to any communication to the German Government who makes none to us on the subject. *c*) The French Government do not think it desirable at this early stage to give any particulars to the Press.'

## No. 478

### Viscount Chilston (*Moscow*) to Sir S. Hoare (*Received August 20, 1.50 p.m.*)
No. 115 Telegraphic [C 6091/55/18]

MOSCOW, *August 20, 1935, 1.55 p.m.*

Your telegram No. 105.[1]

In conversation to-day with acting People's Commissary for Foreign Affairs I informed him of further steps which you had taken in urging German Government to make progress towards conclusion of a collective pact of security in the East in accordance with undertaking which they had given in their note of April 13th last; and I told him I presumed that Soviet policy was still desirous of such outcome.

[1] See No. 456, note 3.

Monsieur Krestinski said that he was very appreciative of the action taken by His Majesty's Government and that policy of Soviet Government had undergone no change. They were still waiting to know what was the reply of German Government to French Government's note to Germany in this matter.[2]

[2] Cf. No. 288.

## No. 479

*Sir S. Hoare to Sir G. Clerk (Paris)*

*No. 248 Saving: Telegraphic [C 6059/55/18]*

FOREIGN OFFICE, *August 21, 1935, 7 p.m.*

My telegram No. 202[1] of August 6. Eastern Pact.

You should explain to the French Government that no reply has yet been received to communication made to German Government on August 5 by Mr. Newton[2], and enquire whether French Government think the present moment suitable for pressing German Government for a reply.

Before taking such action I should like to make sure that the French are still working on the lines of the 'general settlement'.

You may if you think it necessary show the Quai d'Orsay the text of the Aide Mémoire handed by Mr. Newton to the German Government on August 5th.[2]

[1] See No. 456, note 3.     [2] See No. 455.

## No. 480

*Mr. Newton (Berlin) to Sir S. Hoare (Received August 22, 9.15 p.m.)*

*No. 259 Telegraphic [C 6148/55/18]*

BERLIN, *August 22, 1935, 7.45 p.m.*

My telegrams Nos. 181[1] and 182 Saving.[2]

I reminded Herr von Bülow on August 22nd that I was still without a reply to my communication of August 5th regarding the Eastern Pact.[3]

He said that meeting between the Chancellor and Minister for Foreign Affairs had not yet taken place. In any case however the Chancellor had intimated that he could not define his attitude in a question of such intricacy until after the holidays when he could conveniently consult other members of the Government and experts. For such discussions the earliest probable date would be shortly after the party congress at Nuremberg ending September 16th. The German Ambassadors had been authorized to make communication to this effect in London and Paris. When I expressed surprise and disappointment Herr von Bülow could only explain that holiday season was by tradition much more completely observed in Germany than in England. Obviously however the Chancellor is not prepared at present to say yes and does not want to come out with no or commit himself at this critical juncture in international affairs.

[1] No. 470.     [2] No. 471.     [3] See No. 455.

Herr von Bülow also said that he had not yet received an answer to private letter in which he had asked German Ambassador in Paris to clear up obscurities in French attitude. Delay might be due to absence of Monsieur Léger.

## No. 481

*Letter from Mr. Holman to the Marquis de Castellane*[1]

*[A 7377/22/45]*

FOREIGN OFFICE, *August 22, 1935*

Dear Castellane

You will have noticed that in spite of the confidential nature of the memorandum on Qualitative Limitation of Naval Armaments which was communicated to the French and Italian Governments for their observations and to the United States and Japanese Governments for their information,[2] reports bearing on its contents have appeared in the United Kingdom press.[3]

I need hardly say that we made no announcement ourselves which could possibly have caused these reports to appear. When however they did appear, we took the line in answer to enquiries that we for our part were anxious to go ahead as fast as possible with the preparatory measures which would lead up to the holding of the Naval Conference proper. We had accordingly communicated in writing to the Governments of the signatory powers of the Washington Treaty, our views as to the next steps that should be taken in view of the short time left if the Conference is to take place in accordance with the terms of the Treaty. These views were briefly that the further necessary bilateral conversations: e.g. with French and Italian representatives should be held as soon as possible. It was explained that we had not, as reported in some press messages, called a conference for October 4.[4] No further description of the contents of the communication was furnished to the newspapers, nothing was given to them in writing.

We suggest for your consideration that if any enquiries are addressed to you by the press, you should take roughly the same line.

Yours sincerely

A. HOLMAN

[1] An identic letter was sent at the same time to Signor Vitetti at the Italian Embassy.

[2] See Nos. 460 and 466.

[3] See e.g., *The Times*, August 16, p. 10, and August 17, p. 10, and *The Evening News*, August 15.

[4] In a minute in this file Mr. Holman wrote: 'I will see the Jap[anese] Counsellor, give him a copy of the memo. and take him to task about Press leakages in Tokio. 20.8.35.' The memorandum referred to summarized the line taken with the British press: it embodied the substance of the second paragraph of Mr. Holman's letter above. A copy was given to the Japanese Counsellor on August 22.

## No. 482

### Sir S. Hoare to Mr. MacKillop (Brussels)
### No. 495 [C 6093/55/18]

FOREIGN OFFICE, *August 22, 1935*

Sir,

With reference to my despatch No. 454[1] of the 29th ultimo, I transmit to you herewith copy of a memorandum setting forth the observations and suggestions of the Belgian Government on the subject of the proposed Air Pact,[2] which was communicated to this Department by the Counsellor of the Belgian Embassy on August 19th.

2. According to M. Silvercruys a copy of this memorandum has been communicated also to the French Government by the Belgian Embassy in Paris.

I am, &c.,
SAMUEL HOARE

[1] This despatch forwarded to Brussels a copy of the record of conversation between Mr. Sargent and M. Silvercruys on July 23; see No. 422.

[2] This memorandum, not printed, set out in more detail the considerations summarized in No. 422.

## No. 483

### Record by Mr. Holman of a conversation with Mr. Atherton on August 23
### [A 7442/22/45]

FOREIGN OFFICE, *August 23, 1935*

In accordance with the instructions contained in Mr. Craigie's letter of August 20th I saw Mr. Atherton at the Foreign Office this afternoon and took the opportunity of communicating to him the draft memorandum which Mr. Craigie had prepared as His Majesty's Government's reply to the American memorandum of August 17th.[1] I explained to Mr. Atherton that this was purely a personal draft which might later be considerably modified, but that I would in any case like him to read it and furnish me with any observations or criticisms which he might have to make. After perusal Mr.

[1] Mr. Craigie was on holiday in Sussex. He had spoken to Mr. Atherton on the long distance telephone on August 17 and invited him to lunch on Tuesday, August 20. Mr. Atherton's account of the ensuing conversation is printed in *F.R.U.S. 1935*, vol. i, pp. 97–8. In his letter to Mr. Holman on the same day Mr. Craigie asked him to show the draft reply to the U.S. aide-mémoire of August 17 (No. 474, enclosure) 'privately and confidentially to Ray Atherton. . . I am anxious to heal this trouble with the Americans as soon as possible, but I nevertheless think that we must take quite firmly the line that Washington has misunderstood what we are about'. He wrote later in the same letter: 'Atherton was here today and I had quite a satisfactory talk with him. He is always helpful (that's why I want to consult him about the draft), but my impression is that the rather acrid tone of the U.S. aide-mémoire is due to Norman Davis rocking the boat the other end. I hope neither the F.O. nor the Admty. will take this more seriously than I do.' For the final version of Mr. Craigie's draft see No. 498 below.

Atherton stated that he had no remarks to make thereon except that the final sentence of the draft[2] might be omitted. He felt that any communication regarding these conversations to the other Powers concerned might well be left over until the eve of those conversations, when he would apply to the State Department for the necessary instructions.

I remarked that, after myself reading the American memorandum of August 17th, I had gained the impression that its acrid tone might be due to the fact that the American Government disliked having a European point of view on qualitative disarmament held like a pistol at their head. He agreed. What the American Government had taken exception to was the suggestion that European proposals rather than *desiderata* had been envisaged. If the American Government had European proposals submitted to them it might place them in an embarrassing position, seeing that as far as battleships were concerned they could not reduce the tonnage limitation very much below 35,000 tons owing to the fact that they had to take into serious consideration the cruising radius of their capital ships, particularly between America and the Philippines. In reply to my question as to whether there had been any publication of the American building programme over the period 1937–1942, as had been suggested by the American Ambassador to the Secretary of State in his conversation of July 29th,[3] he said that all that had appeared was the Vinson Bill.

Before leaving he expressed the hope that we would say nothing to the press regarding the receipt of the American memorandum, as he did not intend to do so himself.

A. HOLMAN

[2] This sentence read: 'The United States Government will no doubt agree that the fact of these conversations being held should, at the appropriate moment, be communicated confidentially to the Governments of the other Powers parties to the Treaty of Washington.' It was subsequently deleted.　　　　　　　　　　　　　　　　　　　[3] See No. 438.

## No. 484

*Letter from Mr. Baxter to Wing-Commander Medhurst (Air Ministry)*
[*C 6036/55/18*]

*Confidential*　　　　　　　　　　　　　　　　　FOREIGN OFFICE, *August 23, 1935*

Dear Medhurst,

Don has no doubt sent you a copy of his report (A 8/2)[1] of August 14th about his relations with the German Air Ministry and the progress of the German air force, and in any case you may have been able to discuss it with him now that he has gone on leave. But in accordance with our usual practice, I am sending you an extra copy of the report and covering despatch[1] herewith.

We shall be glad to receive in due course your observations on the information now supplied by the German authorities. We understand from

[1] Not printed. A copy was received in the Foreign Office on August 16 as enclosure in Berlin despatch No. 800 of August 15.

Don's report that the German 'lists' will permit you to estimate more accurately than hitherto the probable total of German first line aircraft in October 1936; and we shall be interested to hear whether, in the light of the fuller information now available, you adhere to the view expressed in para. 10 of the Air Staff memo of June 14 last,[2] namely that while Germany may possess a total of 2,000 military aircraft and pilots by the end of 1935 she will probably not be able to attain a greater *first line strength* (i.e. including equipment, personnel and maintenance up to the British standard) than about 1,500 by April 1937.

Yours sincerely,
C. W. BAXTER

[2] Not printed.

## No. 485

*Sir S. Hoare to Sir R. Clive (Tokyo)*
*No. 171 Telegraphic [A 7493/22/45]*

FOREIGN OFFICE, *August 26, 1935, 10 p.m.*

My telegram No. 164.[1]

Japanese Counsellor communicated to Foreign Office to-day memorandum[2] containing views of Japanese Government on proposals set out in His Majesty's Government's memorandum of July 30th regarding limitation of naval armaments. Views of Japanese Government are:

(*a*) That they are unable to accept any agreement on naval limitation except on a basis of qualitative *and* quantitative limits and

(*b*) That they cannot agree to a system of unilateral declaration of building programmes, which is so at variance with their claim to a system of a 'common upper limit'.

[1] This telegram of August 16 referred to No. 466 and contained a summary of the enclosure in No. 460.
[2] The text of this memorandum, as amended at the request of the Japanese Government on August 30, is printed in *F.R.U.S. 1935*, vol. i, p. 102.

## No. 486

*Sir S. Hoare to Mr. Newton (Berlin)*
*No. 27 Saving: Telegraphic [C 6181/55/18]*

FOREIGN OFFICE, *August 26, 1935*

Your telegram No. 259.[1]

German Chargé d'Affaires called on August 23, on instructions from his Government, to say that they would be unable to answer your *aide mémoire* of August 5 until the beginning of October. The reasons given for the delay were that the German Government could not at present devote to this complicated question the requisite care and attention, owing in the first place

[1] No. 480.

to the holiday season, secondly to the Party Congress at Nuremberg in September, and thirdly to the need for clearing up some doubtful points arising out of the conversation between M. Laval and the German Ambassador in Paris.[2]

Prince Bismarck was informed that His Majesty's Government would much regret this postponement. It was pointed out to him that we and the French Government had not been awaiting the German answer only since August 5; we had been waiting ever since June 3, the date of the French note to Germany,[3] which was long before the holiday season.

Prince Bismarck was not clear whether his Government's decision not to reply till the beginning of October applied equally to my enquiry of August 1 regarding the completion of the Air Pact by means of technical bilateral agreements.[4] He promised to enquire of Berlin.

[2] Cf. *D.G.F.P., op. cit.*, Nos. 231, 235.　　　[3] See No. 288, note 3.　　　[4] See No. 447.

## No. 487

*Sir G. Clerk (Paris) to Sir S. Hoare (Received August 28, 11.15 a.m.)*
*No. 202 Saving: Telegraphic [C 6195/55/18]*

PARIS, *August 27, 1935*

Your telegram No. 252 Saving.[1]

When informing Monsieur Laval of the attitude of Germany as regards the Eastern Pact, I took the occasion to press him to get on with land armaments, speaking, in the few minutes at my disposal, in the sense of your despatch No. 1524[2] of the 16th instant. Monsieur Laval said that he would stir up the Haut Comité Militaire and let me know what progress had been made.

Monsieur Léger is away on holiday but will be back in a day or two and I will then go into the question more fully with him and Monsieur Laval.

[1] This telegram of August 26 referred to No. 479, and said that in view of the German Government's announcement recorded in No. 486 'there can now be no question of our addressing a formal reminder to them. You should inform French Government of the position'.　　　　　　　　　　　　　　　　　　　　　　[2] No. 473.

## No. 488

*Letter from Mr. Holman to Captain Phillips[1]*
*[A 7574/22/45]*

FOREIGN OFFICE, *August 30, 1935*

Dear Phillips,

We have been giving careful consideration to the question of the channel of communication for naval information between the German Government and ourselves with special reference to paragraphs 8 and 9 of Captain

[1] Captain T. S. V. Phillips had succeeded Captain King as Director of Plans Division of the Naval Staff in the Admiralty.

Danckwerts' record of his two meetings with the German Naval Attaché on the 31st July and the 12th August (N.C.(G)13th and 14th Meetings).[2]

We note that the procedure suggested is only to be regarded as a temporary expedient. It will be recalled however that, when Craigie agreed to Herr von Ribbentrop's suggestion that Captain Wassner should be the channel of communication for matters arising immediately out of the Anglo-German conversations,[3] he also stipulated that Captain Wassner should convey to the Foreign Office any information which was not purely technical. We think that this general principle should be adhered to, and that, if Captain Wassner has any important communication to make, he should make it at the Foreign Office, though there would, of course, be no objection at all to an Admiralty representative being present. For instance, the reply as regards Annex II to N.C.M.(35)56[4] had better be made through the Foreign Office since, although the details are purely technical, the implications and possible repercussions of the subject dealt with are highly political.

We are also strongly of the opinion that, if the German Naval Attaché continues to be the channel of information on naval matters, a very clear and definite assurance should be obtained from him that the German Ambassador (or Chargé d'Affaires) is aware that these conversations are going on and approves the procedure whereby, on the German side, they are carried on by Captain Wassner under direct instructions from the German Admiralty.

Yours sincerely,<br>A. Holman

[2] Not printed. Paragraphs 8 and 9 read as follows:— '8. As regards the channel of communication, Captain Wassner stated that the German Admiralty would much prefer to exchange this information with us, at least so far as concerns the information from Germany, through the German Naval Attaché in London. They pointed out that the information they proposed to give is still secret, since they have not as yet given it to anyone else and therefore would prefer to limit, as far as possible, the channels through which it passes. 9. I told Captain Wassner that we could scarcely arrange to exchange information with Germany through channels different from those adopted for every other Power, but that as a temporary expedient since this arrangement refers only to the period before the conclusion of a general agreement, I would suggest to the Foreign Office that we might adopt the procedure proposed by the German Admiralty and exchange information in both directions through the German Naval Attaché in London.'

[3] Cf. No. 490 below.

[4] The reference was to an undated British memorandum explaining the 'points left for future discussion after the Anglo-German naval conversations'. It was handed to the German Naval Attaché on July 4, and was circulated as Annex II to the undated third report of the British representatives on 'the course of the Anglo-German Naval Conversations since the conclusion of the Anglo-German Agreement of 18th June, 1935' (N.C.M. (35) 56). The text is printed in *D.G.F.P.*, *op. cit.*, No. 193.

## No. 489

### Letter from Squadron-Leader O'Neill (Air Ministry) to Mr. Baxter
[C 6321/55/18]

*Confidential*                                                    LONDON, *September 3, 1935*

My dear Baxter,

Thank you for your letter C 6036/55/18 of the 23rd August.[1] We have already received the documents enclosed. These, together with the Air Attaché's reports upon his recent visit to various German Training Schools, confirm our opinion that the statements made by General Goering last June, regarding the strength of the German Air Force had little relation to actual fact.

The list of Air Force Stations, the map of Air Force Areas and the Organization of the German Air Ministry provide a valuable check, and some additions to the information already in our possession.

The accompanying remarks, although too vague and incomplete to allow us to form any definite conclusions, tend to confirm the information upon which the Air Staff based their estimates of Germany's rate of air re-armament. Our views expressed in the Air Staff Memorandum of June 14th last, remain, therefore, the same.

Yours sincerely
H. W. O'NEILL

P.S. I am replying for Medhurst who is on leave.

[1] No. 484.

## No. 490

### Record by Mr. Holman of his conversation with the German Naval Attaché on September 4
[A 7775/22/45]

FOREIGN OFFICE, *September 4, 1935*

I saw Captain Wassner, Naval Attaché at the German Embassy, this morning with a view to discussing with him methods of procedure for communication of information between the German Embassy and His Majesty's Government in the matter of naval questions.[1] I said that, as he knew, Mr. Craigie had agreed to his being the channel of communication, but had emphasised the fact that any communications, unless they were of a purely technical nature, should be made direct to the Foreign Office. I explained to Captain Wassner that much of the information which he would probably be furnishing to us would, although technical in appearance, be of a highly political nature and that in those circumstances we had agreed with the Admiralty that he should communicate with the Foreign Office direct. I added that, of course, there would be no objection to a representative of

[1] Cf. No. 488.

our Admiralty being present at any conversations. Captain Wassner fully agreed and promised to work on those lines.

I then explained to the German Naval Attaché that, although we were very pleased that he should act as the channel of communication with us on naval matters, we felt that we should like to be assured that such procedure had the full support and approval of his Ambassador. Captain Wassner replied that he kept his Ambassador fully informed of all communications which he made to us and that the Ambassador, who was naturally not an expert on naval questions, fully concurred in the present procedure.

Before the close of the conversation I communicated to Captain Wassner, who is leaving on a holiday for ten days on Monday,[2] the substance of the Japanese memorandum communicated to us on August 26th on the matter of the limitation of naval armaments.[3]

A. HOLMAN

[2] September 9.          [3] Cf. No. 485.

## No. 491

*Memorandum communicated by the Italian Embassy on September 4, 1935*
*[A 7833/22/45]*

*Translation*                 ITALIAN EMBASSY, LONDON

The Italian Government have examined with the greatest care the memorandum in which the British Government, after the conversations which they have had on the subject of naval armaments, set forth on what bases in their opinion an agreement could be reached.[1]

1. In the opinion of the British Government it is necessary, in the first instance, to move in the direction of qualitative agreements intended to take the place of those contained in the existing treaties, for which purpose the essential aim of the coming conference should be, precisely, the conclusion of new qualitative agreements.

As the British Government are aware, the Italian Government have always in the past supported the principle of the limitation of global tonnage. Nevertheless, with the view of rendering possible new agreements between all the greater naval Powers, the Italian Government are prepared to adhere to the principle of qualitative limitation.

2. As regards the limits of tonnage and armament for the different categories of ships suggested by the British Government in paragraph 4 of the memorandum, as possible bases of agreement, these in principle coincide with the views of the Italian Government. On this point, however, the Italian Government must at once point out that their definite support can only be accorded if the figures of qualitative limitation proposed are accepted by all the principal Naval Powers.

3. As regards the possibility of a quantitative limitation of naval armaments as well, in the opinion of the Italian Government the only practical

[1] See No. 460, enclosure.

possibility which appears to exist to-day is the communication by the various Powers concerned of their annual programmes in good time.

4. As regards the questions mentioned in paragraph 8 of the British memorandum, the Italian Government declare themselves in favour in principle of their being considered at the coming conference with a view to an eventual general agreement in the matter.

## No. 492

### Letter[1] from Sir G. Clerk (Paris) to Sir S. Hoare
### [C 6525/55/18]

*Confidential*                                          PARIS, *September 7, 1935*

My dear Sir Samuel,

You will remember that about three weeks ago you instructed me to press the question of limitations of Land Armaments with Laval and suggested that my Military Attaché might also take the matter up with the French military authorities.[2] For various reasons, chiefly Abyssinia and the fact that internal legislation has taken up all Laval's time, while Léger has been having a holiday, I have had no real opportunity of tackling the question, though I did try to spur Laval on at my interview of August 27th.[3] As I reported to you, he then said that he would find out what the Haut Comité Militaire, to whom he had referred the matter when I first broached it, were doing about it.

As all this was not advancing matters much, I told Heywood to see what he could get out of the French Generals direct. The result of his conversations is the two enclosed despatches, especially No. 17.[4] I am sending them to Van[sittart] and suggesting to him that they should have no distribution until you have had a chance to [*sic*] talking to Laval yourself. I would venture to ask you, in any talk you may have with Laval, not to give Gamelin[5] and Petitbon[6] away to their Prime Minister. I imagine that the reply which Laval would in due course have given me would have been more or less on the lines indicated by the Generals, but if he realises that we have had it from the latter in advance, we may lose a valuable source of information.

In view of the French attitude, might I suggest that, supposing that attitude is reflected in anything Laval may say to you, a possible line to take is to say to him that, such being the situation as regards Land Armaments, would it not be better to leave the question alone for the present and perhaps let it die a natural death and to go on with the other points of the London Communiqué, for His Majesty's Government are going to be more and more hardly pressed by British public opinion for the conclusion of an Air Pact,

---

[1] This letter and its enclosures were given to Sir S. Hoare in Paris on his way to Geneva, see No. 496 below. Copies were sent to the Foreign Office on September 8.

[2] See No. 473.                                          [3] See No. 487.

[4] Despatch No. 17 from H.M. Military Attaché is printed as an enclosure below; despatch No. 18 dealt with the Italo-Ethiopian question and is not here printed.

[5] Chief of the French General Staff.              [6] See enclosure below, paragraph 1.

and it will be impossible for them to hold up the negotiations for such an agreement indefinitely, or indeed for more than a short time longer.

Yours very sincerely<br>GEORGE R. CLERK

ENCLOSURE IN No. 492

*Colonel Heywood to Sir G. Clerk*

No. 17

Secret                                    PARIS, *September 5, 1935*

Sir:

1. With reference to F.O. Despatch No. 1524[7] of the 16th August and to my Memorandum No. 794[8] of 30th August, I have the honour to report that in accordance with Your Excellency's instructions I was able to discuss the question of the possible limitation of land and air armaments in the course of a conversation with General Gamelin yesterday evening. I subsequently had a second conversation with Commandant Petitbon, who holds the same position on General Gamelin's staff as that held by Colonel de Lattre on General Weygand's,[9] and is in charge of the Operations and Plans Section of General Gamelin's personal staff.

*Conversation with General Gamelin*

2. In the course of this conversation General Gamelin stated that, in his opinion, an agreement for the limitation of land armaments offered no appreciable military advantage to France and, in fact, might be a source of disadvantages. To start with, he could have no confidence in German undertakings, then:

(*a*) *As regards effectives*: in war these depended on the size of the population of the countries concerned; in peace, with the régime at present in existence in Germany, effectives were impossible to control. For even if the Germans observed a given figure as regards the Reichswehr, their system of pre-military training, of labour camps and intensive reserve training, would render such an agreement quite illusory. Germany therefore would always have a definite advantage over France as regards effectives.

(*b*) *As regards material*: he did not admit that material could be divided into the two categories of offensive and defensive material; practically all land material could be employed for both purposes; there could be no question of limiting *light* material.

I urged on him that surely the limitation of *heavy* material would increase the value of the frontier fortifications.

To this he replied that this was true only to a certain extent; that it was a two-edged weapon and would reduce the offensive value of the French

---

[7] No. 473.                          [8] Not traced in Foreign Office archives.
[9] General Weygand was Vice-President of the French Supreme War Council and Inspector-General of the Army.

army and might completely nullify it if the Germans built a similar system of fortifications to tackle which guns of at least 155 mm. or 220 mm. calibre would be required. We could not expect the French to destroy their existing heavy materials? I replied that any agreed limitation might possibly be made to apply only to material not yet in existence.

3. I went on to inform General Gamelin that public opinion in England, and the British Government itself, were very anxious to conclude some sort of an air pact and air limitation agreement; that, however, in accordance with the Anglo-French declaration made last February the conclusion of such a pact and agreement had been made dependent on the conclusion of other agreements, amongst which was the conclusion of an agreement regarding the limitation of land armaments; that if, as I gathered from what he had just told me, no great value was attached by France to a limitation of land armaments, and, in consequence, no progress was made with this question, the conclusion of an air agreement might be held up indefinitely, and we should thus reach an impasse. Would not a possible way out of this be to dissociate the conclusion of an agreement regarding land armaments from that of the other agreements contemplated?

4. He admitted that a very unfortunate and difficult situation might be created, but that it was a political question and no longer a military one; but he added that if the political leaders of France considered that there were certain political advantages to be gained by the conclusion of an agreement regarding land armaments, he would, of course, agree; he had already told his Government that, in his opinion, the only two points on which any effective limitation could be achieved were the limitation of the output of factories and the limitation of budgetary credits.

5. As regards an air pact or air limitation agreement, he held the same view as General Weygand that they would have a certain value, mainly from the moral point of view, but that their observance would be difficult to control.

6. In conclusion, General Gamelin said that there were definite advantages in the conclusion of a naval agreement, because its observance could be controlled—ships could not be secreted away for any length of time but had to come out into the open. He attached a certain value to air agreements, although control of their observance would be more difficult, whilst he saw very few advantages in the conclusion of an agreement affecting the limitation of land armaments, mainly owing to the fact that effective control was practically impossible and the definite disadvantages such an agreement might have for the French army.

7. The only possible advantages were political, the greatest of which was to have the signature of the British Government to an agreement, whilst, from his own point of view as Commander-in-Chief, another disadvantage would be that an agreement regarding the limitation of land armaments might create such a false sense of security that public opinion in France might insist on the reduction of military expenditure to a dangerous degree.

Although their fortified system was now practically completed, the programme for the rearmament of the French army and the replacement of obsolete material would not be completed for another two or three years. The advent of a new government might well mean such a reduction in credits as seriously to hamper him in his task of renovating the French army in order to make it a really effective instrument of modern warfare.

### Conversation with Commandant Petitbon

8. With Commandant Petitbon I had a longer and more detailed conversation of which the salient features are contained in the following paragraphs.

9. He laid great emphasis on the point that whereas public opinion in England seemed to be prepared to trust Germany's promises and signature, French public opinion was profoundly mistrustful of Germany's word; they had repeatedly had cause to regret having trusted German signatures in the past; therefore to them the only real value of any agreement with Germany was the value which they attached to the signatures of their co-signatories; for instance, they attached implicit trust and the greatest value to the signature of Great Britain; they considered, however, that much less reliance could be placed on the signatures of Italy and Russia. These countries were ruled by Dictators who were apt to blow hot and cold and to change under the necessity of keeping their régime alive. The tragedy of Dictators like Mussolini and Hitler was that they had to keep their people constantly in a state of fever heat.

10. Apart from the great difficulty of control of any agreement for the limitation of land armaments, such an agreement would also have the great disadvantage of reducing the offensive value of the French army. The Germans had at last realised the strength of the French fortified system, and that the French army had regained an offensive value which was on the increase. Their eyes were therefore turned away from the west to the east; they had given up all thought, for the moment, of attacking France but were concentrating on the questions of Austria and Czechoslovakia. French information showed that Germany in her armoured fighting vehicle programme was going essentially for speed and therefore light armour. They could not be intended for action in the west and could only be intended for action in the east. The main deterrent to German action against Czechoslovakia and Austria was the knowledge that such action might result in a French offensive against Germany. A diminution in the offensive value of the French army would greatly reduce the value of that army in the eyes of the weaker powers of Europe who looked to France to assist them against German encroachments, and might easily give rise to the suspicion amongst the Little Entente powers that France would be incapable of fulfilling her engagements should the occasion arise. The limitation of land armaments was therefore a distinct advantage to Germany rather than to France.

11. I pointed out that if there were no limitation of land armaments, it would only be a question of time before the German army became stronger

than the French army, both in effectives and material, in view of Germany's larger population and greater industrial capacity.

12. He replied that it might be quite a long time before this occurred; the financial and economic situation in Germany was so bad that they had the greatest difficulty in securing the necessary raw materials for their armaments. All their information showed that, the German army having reached a certain stage (25 to 28 divisions, including 3 cavalry divisions), had not during the last few months increased beyond that stage.

13. They had had a very interesting item of information from secret sources, to the effect that the speech made by Schacht[10] recently, which had generally been considered to be an attack on Hitler, was the result of an all-night meeting between Hitler, Goering, Goebbels, Blomberg and Schacht; the move had been designed to lift the veil a little on the economic situation of Germany in order to impress upon the nation the necessity for further sacrifices and to extract the last few remaining gold marks out of them for the purchase of the raw materials which Blomberg found it more and more difficult to procure. The fact that Schacht had not been disavowed by Hitler seemed to confirm this account.

14. As regards an air pact, the French did not much like the idea of a pact on the lines of the pact originally proposed by us, for this reason: one of the suggestions made was that each of the signatories should communicate to the others complete information regarding their organization enabling them to take joint action against the third party. While the French were quite prepared to give all the necessary information to the English, who were ex-allies and whom they could trust, they were not prepared to give to Germany detailed information regarding their aerodromes, auxiliary landing grounds and anti-aircraft defence system, to enable the latter to attack England.

15. I said that I quite saw his point but that these proposals had been made as a basis for discussion and that the difficulty he mentioned could surely be got round; he must own that there was a definite moral and financial interest for all of us in the limitation of air armaments.

16. He agreed that an air limitation agreement would have a good effect on public opinion and would enable certain budgetary economies to be made, but he was afraid that it might turn out to be very deceptive owing mainly to the different mentality and political systems in force in Great Britain, France and Germany; it was certain that the two former countries would observe a limitation agreement and, owing to their democratic system of government, its observance could be controlled, every penny spent on our air forces had to be voted by Parliament and accounted for in the annual budgets. In Germany it was quite impossible to control military and air expenditure. The rearmament of Germany had been financed by extra budgetary credits the publication of which was strictly forbidden, and the French Secret Service had been unable to ascertain how much money

[10] A reference presumably to the speech made by Dr. Schacht, Acting Reich Minister of Economic Affairs and President of the Reichsbank, at the opening of the East German Fair at Königsberg on August 18, 1935; see *The Times*, August 19, p. 10.

Germany had spent or was spending on rearmament and on her fighting services.

17. Limitation agreements would have the great disadvantage of lulling public opinion into a false sense of security and making it far more difficult for the responsible heads to keep the national defence services up to the necessary degree of efficiency.

*Conclusion*

18. The main impressions which I have derived from these two conversations are:

(1) The profound mistrust of Germany which still exists in the minds of General Gamelin and his staff.

(2) As regards an agreement for the limitation of land armaments, the French General Staff believe that:

(*a*) From the military point of view:
  (i) whilst such an agreement would be strictly observed by themselves, it would not be respected by Germany;
  (ii) the impossibility of effective control would render such an agreement illusory;
  (iii) it might reduce the offensive power of the French army;
  (iv) it would therefore be to the advantage of Germany and to the disadvantage of the French army.

(*b*) From a political point of view:
  (i) it would have the disadvantage of reducing the value of the French army to the Little Entente powers;
  (ii) but it would have the advantage of securing the English signature to an agreement.

(3) If, however, the French government consider an agreement regarding the limitation of land armaments desirable, General Gamelin is prepared to agree to an arrangement which would bear mainly on the control of the output of factories and limitation of budgets.

(4) As regards the Air Pact and Limitation Agreements:

(*a*) the French General Staff dislike the idea of an air pact which would give to Germany too intimate a knowledge of French organization;

(*b*) but they see advantages in the conclusion of such agreements from the financial and moral point of view, influenced, however, by the belief that the agreements would not be observed by Germany and the fear that they would create a false sense of security among their own people.

(5) Finally I was very struck by the fact that almost for the first time since I have held the appointment of Military Attaché in France,[11] the possibility of the French army taking definite offensive action against Germany, has been mentioned to me; hitherto, the action of the French army has been considered almost solely in relation to the defence of the country. The

[11] i.e. since May 1932.

increase in the German army and the growing ability of Germany to undertake offensive action in the East, appear to have impressed on the French General Staff the necessity for the French army to have offensive power and may create a situation in which it would be deemed necessary for the French army to take offensive action. The feeling of confidence created by the completion of the frontier fortified system, the economies in manpower obtained from this system and the friendship with Italy, the intensive re-armament programme which is being put through, and the possibilities of improved training afforded by the longer period of military service now in force—are gradually enabling the leaders of the French army to create a force with considerable offensive power with which the French General Staff consider that they could successfully undertake an offensive action should the occasion arise.

I have, &c.,

T. G. G. Heywood

## No. 493

### Letter from Mr. Sargent to Sir H. Montgomery (The Hague)[1]
### [C 5925/55/18]

FOREIGN OFFICE, September 9, 1935

You may like to know that the Netherlands Minister, during his first (introductory) interview with the Secy of State last July, made it quite clear that, in his view, Germany, in case of a war in the west, would violate the neutrality of Holland: in fact M. van Swinderen even made the proposal that the Netherlands should enter the Air Pact.

The S. of S. did not think that the Minister's suggestion was put forward in a sufficiently definite way for future action to be based upon it, and no record of the interview was therefore made and sent to you in the ordinary way at the time. But of course M. van Swinderen's remarks afford a peg on which to hang a further enquiry if the occasion shd arise.

The incident seems to mark yet another step in the evolution of Dutch opinion away from its old views of strict neutrality which you have reported in recent letters and despatches.[2]

[1] Only the approved draft of this letter, initialled 'J. V. P[erowne] 7/ix', has been preserved in Foreign Office archives.

[2] Replying to Mr. Perowne on September 14 (C 6604/55/18), Sir H. Montgomery agreed that 'van Swinderen's suggestion was not sufficiently definite to make it necessary or desirable to pursue the matter with him, at present at any rate'. He suggested, however, that if it was accepted that Germany would in any case violate the neutrality of Holland in the case of a war in the West the balance of advantage was 'in favour of having the Dutch in any pact that may eventually be arrived at' as this would furnish 'a lever to persuade them to set their house in order'. Mr. Perowne wrote on September 25 (C 6604/55/18) that for the moment the Italo-Ethiopian difficulties were holding up progress and Sir S. Hoare was also awaiting the opinion of the Chiefs of Staff on the strategical aspects of the subject.

## No. 494

### Sir E. Phipps (Berlin) to Sir S. Hoare (Geneva)[1]
#### No. 38 Telegraphic [C 6483/55/18]

BERLIN, *September 13, 1935*

My telegram No. 33.[2]

Reserved attitude of German press towards your speech[3] continues but stress is laid in certain newspapers on favourable impression made in German political circles by language you employed regarding possible revision of treaties and desirability of removing causes for future wars. Every word you said in this respect should be considered and remembered.

Repeated to Foreign Office.

[1] Repeated to the Foreign Office at 12.42 p.m. on September 13 as Berlin telegram No. 273, received at 1.40 p.m. on the same day.

[2] This telegram, addressed to Sir S. Hoare at Geneva, is not printed: it referred to the Ethiopian question.

[3] The reference is to Sir S. Hoare's speech on September 11 to the Assembly of the League of Nations; see *L/N.O.J. S.S. No. 138*, pp. 43–6. The text was also printed in *The Times*, September 12, p. 7.


## No. 495

### Sir S. Hoare to Sir R. Clive (Tokyo)
#### No. 181 Telegraphic [A 7988/22/45]

FOREIGN OFFICE, *September 13, 1935, 4.35 p.m.*

According to the 'Sunday Times' of August 18th the following statement is alleged to have been made to the press by a spokesman of the Japanese Ministry of Marine:

'After December 31st there can no longer be any question of the convocation of the conference provided for by the Washington Treaty but only of an entirely new conference which we will only accept if our principles of naval disarmament are previously admitted; otherwise we prefer to remain without a treaty.'

Seeing that the Japanese principle of the 'common upper limit' is unacceptable, the implication of the above statement appears to be that we are unlikely to get Japan into a further naval limitation conference unless such a conference is summoned this year under the terms of the Washington Treaty. I shall be glad of your considered opinion as to whether the Japanese Government are, in fact, likely to adopt such an attitude.

## No. 496

*Mr. Edmond[1] (Geneva) to Foreign Office (Received September 16)*
*No. 89 L.N. [C 6516/55/18]*

GENEVA, *September 13, 1935*

The United Kingdom Delegate to the League of Nations presents his compliments and has the honour to transmit copies of the undermentioned document, of which copies have been sent to Paris and Rome.

| *Name and Date* | *Subject* |
|---|---|
| Record of Anglo-French conversation, Sept. 11 (Part II)[2] | Programme of London communiqué[3] |

ENCLOSURE IN NO. 496

*Record of Anglo-French Conversation held at the Hôtel des Bergues, Geneva, at 5.30 p.m. on Wednesday, September 11, 1935*

PRESENT: *United Kingdom*: Sir Samuel Hoare, Secretary of State for Foreign Affairs; Mr. Eden, Minister for League of Nations Affairs; Mr. Strang, Foreign Office.

*France*: M. Pierre Laval, President of the Council and Minister for Foreign Affairs; M. Alexis Léger, Secretary-General of the Ministry for Foreign Affairs; M. René Massigli, Ministry for Foreign Affairs. (Continuation.)[2]

*Programme of the London Communiqué.*

SIR SAMUEL HOARE said he would now pass from Abyssinia to other questions. It was clear that if war broke out, disarmament and cognate questions would be of no immediate urgency, but he would give M. Laval his views on the assumption that these questions would shortly be dealt with.

M. Laval would have noticed that in his speeches in the House of Commons Sir Samuel Hoare had insisted on his desire to make progress on all these questions as quickly as possible. In the several interviews he had had with the German Ambassador he could not have spoken more strongly on the urgency of making progress on the Eastern and Danubian Pacts. Unless progress was soon made, public opinion would become restive. Moreover, Germany would be likely to proceed with her unrestricted rearmament. He had insisted in his conversations both with Herr von Ribbentrop and the German Ambassador that he could not contemplate the isolation of one

---

[1] Mr. C. A. Edmond had succeeded Mr. Patteson as H.M. Consul at Geneva on June 16, 1935.

[2] The Anglo-French conversations began on Tuesday, September 10, at 11 a.m. There were further sessions on the same day at 7 p.m., and on September 11 at 5.30 p.m. The record printed here is of the second half of the last conversation. The other sessions were concerned with the Ethiopian question. The record of these will be printed in Volume XIV.

[3] Of February 3, 1935.

subject—as, for example, the Air Pact—from the others. At the same time, if agreement on all subjects were held up, the position would be serious.

He would like to ask M. Laval two questions. The first was: did the French Government think that any progress could be made on land disarmament? The second was: did the French Government wish for an Air Pact and did it still wish for an Eastern and Danubian Pact as strongly as before? He put these questions for information only; there was no ulterior motive behind them.

M. LAVAL replied that France still remained attached to the London programme. He regretted that His Majesty's Government had, contrary to their undertaking, made a separate agreement with Germany on naval matters. He did not, however, wish to recriminate. As he had explained to Mr. Eden, if it were understood that an attempt were to be made to realise all the points in the programme, he had no objection to examining one of them singly, namely, the Air Pact. His Majesty's Government had undertaken to ask the German Government whether they were ready to make bilateral agreements. Had this enquiry been put, and what answer had been received?

Land armaments were of capital importance to France, much as air armaments were to Great Britain. He had not, however, imposed the condition that the examination of land armaments should take first place, but had agreed that a beginning might be made with the Air Pact, provided that it was intended to reach agreement on all the others.

In regard to land armaments, he had his own opinion, which was perhaps somewhat unorthodox. He did not believe in supervision. Supervision would not be much use unless it were applied in circumstances of political security. If Germany became a party to the Eastern and Danubian Pacts and the Air Pact, arms limitation would be more likely to be respected than if an attempt were made to proceed to measures of limitation in the absence of other political agreements. With every day that passed, the German claims became greater. At one time they had claimed only 300,000 men, and on this occasion the French Government had sent a magnificent note, i.e., the note of April 17th, 1934. This was his own Government's doing and he would say no more about it. Germany now claimed a much higher figure for effectives. But on the other hand, they seemed to wish for qualitative and quantitative limitation of material. The Ministry of War would examine this proposal with great care, but they did not look on it with favour.

His views on reconciliation with Germany had never changed. There would be no peace in Europe until a Franco-German rapprochement was achieved. In the years that had passed since the war, France had spent her time making peace with her friends. Was it not now time to make peace with her enemies?

In his conversation with General Goering at Warsaw, the latter had repeated that Germany wanted bilateral agreements. This was the reason for her dislike of the Eastern and Danubian Pacts. Germany was apparently prepared to make any kind of agreement with France and had no territorial claims against France. He had replied to General Goering that France could not make any agreement with Germany unless Germany made agreements with other Powers. It was clear to him that the system of collective security was not favoured by Germany, because Germany had ulterior motives in respect of Austria, Czechoslovakia and Lithuania. General Goering had complained that the Franco-Soviet Agreement was directed against Germany. This was not so. It fell within the framework of the Covenant and was in conformity with Locarno. General Goering had not been convinced; nor had he seemed to be satisfied when M. Laval had said that France was prepared to give Germany the same guarantees as she had given to Russia.

M. Laval was quite willing that His Majesty's Government should pursue the policy of appeasement with Germany and the French Government were quite ready to collaborate. Germany was only too ready to profit by any misunderstanding between France and Great Britain.

Sir Samuel Hoare agreed that no useful purpose would be served by raking up the past. He would have been quite ready to argue with M. Laval about the Anglo-German Naval Agreement—as also about the French note of April 17th—but he would now confine himself to the future. He would like another approach to be made to Germany, if for no other purpose than to test Germany's sincerity. He would like to make a new offensive at Berlin all along the line, in order to see whether it were possible to make progress or not with the various Pacts and with the question of armaments.

As regards land armaments, France had of course a greater right to speak than Great Britain. He quite understood France's anxieties. What he wished to know was whether the French Government thought that progress in this field was impossible. If so, would it not be wise to begin negotiations about air armaments? If the French Government thought progress on land armaments impossible, he was the last person to press them to do the impossible.

M. Laval replied that he thought it would be possible to start negotiations as regards air armaments and not impossible to do something about land armaments. Sir Samuel Hoare's speech that morning[4] ought to facilitate his task.

France would never attack Germany; she was essentially pacific even though she was perhaps the strongest military power. It might be possible now to examine in rather better conditions the problems outlined in the London Communiqué. He thought His Majesty's Government were wise to maintain their resolution to proceed to rearm. Germany would only respect Great Britain and France in so far as she realised that there would be serious danger if she troubled the peace.

Sir Samuel Hoare said he would be glad if M. Laval could let him know in the near future his views as to the possibility of making progress on land armaments.

M. Laval replied that he had already had a study made and would give Sir Samuel Hoare some information. The Ministry of War had little

4 Cf. No. 494, note 3.

confidence in an agreement with Germany. They trusted in arms rather than in words, and perhaps they were not wrong. He would, however, give Sir Samuel Hoare an indication of what France might find it possible to do in the matter of land armaments.

Sir Samuel Hoare said that he put the question for the following reason: if it were found impossible for the moment to proceed with land armaments, ought they not, as realists, to accept the fact for the time being and concentrate on other matters?

Mr. Eden said that the last thing Great Britain wanted to do was to make France any weaker.

Sir Samuel Hoare added that if no progress were possible on land armaments, and if progress were, on the other hand, possible on air armaments, M. Laval need have no anxiety, so long as Sir Samuel Hoare had influence with His Majesty's Government, that His Majesty's Government would disinterest themselves in land armaments or the Danubian and Eastern Pacts, having once obtained the agreement in the air which they wanted.

As regards air armaments, he had seen the German Ambassador at the end of July,[5] and had told him that in connexion with any air pact His Majesty's Government would regard themselves as free to make bilateral agreements, provided that (1) these agreements were part of the general pact; and (2) that they were open to all parties to the pact. The German Ambassador put certain arguments against this idea, but promised a definite answer. No answer had yet been received owing to the holidays, but he would press for one on the German Ambassador's return.

Sir Samuel Hoare added that what he would like would be for Great Britain and France to approach Germany at the earliest opportunity in similar terms and press for answers to all the questions which had been put at Berlin.

He would like to put a further question to M. Laval. Did the French Government think that they stood to gain by an air pact or not? His Majesty's Government certainly thought that an air pact would be an advantage. Even though Germany might not strictly carry out the limitation provisions, this might not perhaps very much matter. It was easier to identify aircraft than effectives. If there were an agreement on numbers this in itself would afford some check on construction. How much did the French Government want an air pact?

M. Laval said that both he and the French Air Ministry wanted an air pact. If there was no limitation, Germany, with her powers of industrial expansion, would be able to build aeroplanes in large quantities, the number of which would be limited only by finance.

Sir Samuel Hoare recalled that he had been for seven years Secretary of State for Air,[6] and said that, in his own view limitation was very important. Limitation would make it more difficult for Germany to deliver a sudden and overwhelming offensive. If hostilities lasted a long time Germany

[5] See No. 437.     [6] 1922–29.

would, of course, be able to develop a very extensive manufacture of aircraft. But limitation would have an influence during the first few weeks of a war, and it was to this first few weeks that Germany attached great importance.

M. MASSIGLI recalled that both the French and British Governments had received a memorandum from the Belgian Government in regard to the air pact[7] in which mention was made of the control of civil aviation. The French Government were in agreement with the Belgian Government on this point. What was the view of His Majesty's Government?

SIR SAMUEL HOARE replied that the control of civil aviation raised very difficult problems. He was very anxious that there should be some limitation of military aircraft, even though it might not be found possible to institute a control of civil aviation. If the limitation of military aircraft was at a relatively high figure, civil machines would not be a very serious military danger. It was only if military aircraft were restricted at a low figure that civil aircraft would become a menace.

The best thing would be to start with the limitation of military aircraft and confine the control of civil aviation to publicity. Then if it became clear that civil aviation was, in fact, a danger, it could perhaps be dealt with subsequently.

He was glad to hear that M. Laval was interested in the air pact and air limitation. It was desirable that both the French and British Governments should take a suitable opportunity of approaching the German Government in similar terms on this subject. But it was doubtful whether this could be done so long as the Abyssinian affair occupied the stage.

M. LAVAL said that the survey they had just made had been very useful. He agreed that as soon as the general situation allowed, it would be well to develop diplomatic activity in the organisation of collective security so as to be able to proceed with an examination of the various questions at issue with Germany. He hoped that Signor Mussolini's action would not pass certain limits and that the efforts of the French and British Governments would not be hindered. His Majesty's Government seemed to prefer Geneva to Paris as the place for conversations. However that might be, conversations must be continued on all the elements in the London programme. Dictators must not be allowed to assume the direction of foreign affairs. If Great Britain were as resolute as France for the organisation of peace this was already half-way to success.

SIR SAMUEL HOARE agreed. He was anxious that none of the matters at issue should be allowed to sleep, and that the two Governments should not merely work together, but produce results.

(The meeting then adjourned.)

7 See No. 482.

## No. 497

*Sir R. Clive (Tokyo) to Sir S. Hoare (Received September 16, 12 noon)*
*No. 246 Telegraphic [A 8011/22/45]*

TOKYO, *September 16, 1935, 6 p.m.*

Your telegram No. 181.[1]

I asked Naval Attaché to take the opportunity of visit to Navy Department to condole about recent accident to Japanese cruiser[2] to say that he had seen report in 'Sunday Times' as indicated in your telegram.

He was told that this statement had no authority as there is no spokesman of the Navy Department.

It would appear however that statement does in fact represent the views of Navy Department and Naval Attaché reports substance of views expressed to him by Secretary of Minister of Marine as follows 'your Foreign Office was told at preliminary conference that Japanese navy considers qualitative and quantitative limitation are so intermixed that it is no use discussing one without the other. Japanese navy will not discuss any quantitative limitation except a common upper limit and *would not* enter a conference which is only to discuss qualitative limitation'.

I cannot avoid the impression which Naval Attaché shares that Navy Department neither want conference nor a new treaty.

I do not propose to raise the matter with Minister for Foreign Affairs without instructions.

[1] No. 495.
[2] Fire had broken out in the Japanese cruiser 'Ashigara' during target practice on September 14 resulting in casualties, see *The Times*, September 16, p. 11.

## No. 498

*Sir S. Hoare to Mr. Osborne (Washington)*
*No. 856 [A 8031/22/45]*

FOREIGN OFFICE, *September 17, 1935*

Sir,

On August 17th Mr. Atherton, Counsellor of the United States Embassy, personally communicated to the Foreign Office a memorandum,[1] copy of which is enclosed herein, setting forth his observations on the proposals contained in the memorandum of His Majesty's Government in the United Kingdom of the 2nd August in regard to the general question of limitation of naval armaments (see my despatch No. 714 of the 8th August).[2] Mr. Atherton explained that, as the memorandum of His Majesty's Government had been transmitted to the United States Embassy for purposes of information only, and therefore called for no reply, his communication should not in any way be interpreted as an official reply from the United States Government.

[1] See No. 474, enclosure.      [2] See No. 460.

2. Mr. Atherton was invited to call at the Foreign Office on September 12th and was handed a reply to his communication of August 17th, copy of which is also enclosed herein.[3] It was explained to him by Mr. Craigie that this reply should be regarded in the same way as the United States memorandum of August 17th, namely, as a record of a verbal and unofficial communication. As, however, the United States Government appeared to labour under certain misapprehensions, it was felt that the reply should assume some written form, however unofficial. Mr. Atherton fully agreed. Mr. Craigie added that the tone of the United States communication had not given entire satisfaction and that it might have been better if the United States Government, instead of mistrusting the motives and intentions of His Majesty's Government, had first enquired whether there had, in fact, been any departure from the procedure agreed upon last autumn.

3. Mr. Atherton stated that he had not yet received instructions from his Government as to the line which he and the United States Naval Attaché should adopt in the proposed conversations, but that he hoped to receive them in the course of the next ten days. As an illustration of the kind of questions which it might be necessary to discuss, Mr. Craigie mentioned the following:—

(a) Supposing that at any conference which might be summoned all the Powers were able to reach agreement on certain qualitative limitations and on other minor matters covered by the Washington and London Treaties but were quite unable to reach agreement on quantitative questions, would the United States Government be prepared to come into a Treaty dealing only with the points on which agreement could be reached?

(b) Supposing that agreement on qualitative limitation were to be reached between all Powers but that Japan, while giving assurances that it was not her intention to upset the agreement in practice, declared her inability to sign an international agreement containing qualitative provisions only, would the United States Government be likely nevertheless to sign such an agreement with a suitable 'let out' clause?

4. Mr. Craigie said that he did not wish to imply that His Majesty's Government had yet reached any decision on these points. It seemed to him,

[3] Printed as enclosure below. This was the final version of the draft by Mr. Craigie mentioned in No. 483, note 1. After being read by Mr. Atherton on August 20 it was circulated. The Admiralty approved the draft with the omission of Mr. Craigie's original final paragraph (*ibid.*, note 2). Sir Warren Fisher suggested certain amendments. Mr. Craigie made the following comments on the final version of the draft on September 10: Mr. Atherton had stated that his own aide-mémoire of August 17 'should not be regarded as a written communication but only as a record of what he had wished to state orally. If I had not been away on leave he would not have left any written document. Strictly speaking, therefore, there is no need to make a written reply, but, since the American aide-mémoire is in existence and since it betrays several misapprehensions, I think it is important that there should also be a written record of our reply. It is perhaps unnecessary, however, to study the phraseology of these two documents as carefully as if they were to be regarded as official communications.'

however, that there would have to be some understanding between the Powers in regard to them before any Government would take the responsibility of issuing invitations to a conference.

5. Mr. Atherton replied that he believed that, if His Majesty's Government were to issue an invitation to the United States Government to take part in a conference, the purpose of which would be to salvage as much as possible from the Washington and London Treaties, the answer would be in the affirmative. From this it might be inferred that, if it were found impossible to secure agreement on qualitative limitation, an attempt should nevertheless be made to conclude a treaty on all points on which agreement was possible. As regards actual figures for qualitative limitation, Mr. Atherton believed that the only serious divergence between the two Governments was in the matter of the size of the capital ship. If His Majesty's Government intended to insist at the conference on a 25,000 ton ship and the United States Government on a 35,000 ton ship, then it would be better that no conference should be held. If, on the other hand, the divergence could be brought within very narrow limits the whole position would be changed. Mr. Craigie concurred in this view, adding that it would similarly be desirable to reach a close approximation of views in regard to the size of the cruiser.

6. As regards quantitative limitation, Mr. Craigie said that he thought it would be helpful if during the forthcoming conversations Mr. Atherton were able to communicate to His Majesty's Government a tentative and hypothetical United States construction programme on the lines of that communicated to them last autumn. The situation was constantly changing, but, as the Governments concerned must clearly make an effort at any future conference to reach agreement on quantitative as well as qualitative limitation, it would be desirable to ensure beforehand that there would be no serious divergence of views on this question between the United States of America and the United Kingdom.

7. On the question of informing other interested Powers about the holding of the proposed conversations, Mr. Atherton was at first inclined to argue that nothing should be said until it became clear that the conversations were likely to produce some tangible and useful result. Otherwise it might be alleged that the conversations had merely displayed the existence of serious divergences of view between the Governments of the United States and the United Kingdom. Mr. Craigie said that he felt it essential that at least the Japanese representative here should be informed, though this could be done casually in order to avoid creating the impression in the Japanese mind that the conversations had more importance than was in fact the case. Mr. Atherton finally agreed that no harm would be done if the Japanese Chargé d'Affaires were to be informed in this manner.

8. Mr. Atherton took note of these points and promised to let Mr. Craigie know as soon as he was ready to start conversations.

I am, &c.,
SAMUEL HOARE

*Aide-mémoire replying to Mr. Atherton's memorandum of August 17*

*Confidential*                              FOREIGN OFFICE, *September 12, 1935*

The aide-mémoire communicated by the United States Embassy to the Foreign Office on the 17th August on the subject of the recent discussions on naval limitation appears to betray a certain misapprehension of the real purpose of the memorandum of the 30th July which was addressed to the French and Italian Governments. It is desirable that this misapprehension should be cleared up without delay.

When the conversations between representatives of the Governments of the United States, Japan and the United Kingdom ended in December last, it was understood on all sides that the next step would be for the United Kingdom to enter upon conversations with certain of the European Powers. Conversations were accordingly arranged with representatives of the German Government, but up to the present it has not proved possible to institute any further bilateral discussions with the French and Italian Governments. As an alternative method of procedure His Majesty's Government in the United Kingdom have set forth in the form of a memorandum what they had understood, from the earlier conversations held in 1934, to be the desiderata of the French and Italian Governments so far as qualitative limitation was concerned, and they enquired of those Governments whether the limits mentioned did, in fact, correspond with their views. The objective of His Majesty's Government has been, not to make to the United States or the Japanese Government anything in the nature of joint European proposals, but simply to ascertain, by the only method remaining open to them, the definite views of the French and Italian Governments on these points. Once the facts had been ascertained and the views of the French and Italian Governments as to the holding of a conference had been made known, it had been the intention of His Majesty's Government to communicate these facts to the Governments of the United States and Japan and to invite an expression of their views before attempting to reach a final opinion as to whether a conference could usefully be held this autumn. Thus His Majesty's Government had in any case contemplated the holding of further Anglo-American conversations on the lines suggested in the United States Embassy's memorandum before anything in the nature of 'proposals' for submission to a conference of the Washington Powers could be drawn up.

It is doubtless a misconception of the intentions of His Majesty's Government on this point of procedure which led the United States Government to state in their memorandum that His Majesty's Government are endeavouring to put forward 'as a European view' proposals which His Majesty's Government must have known to be unacceptable to the Government of the United States. His Majesty's Government have made no such endeavour, and their proceedings throughout have been strictly in accord with the understanding reached with the representatives of the United States and Japanese Governments before they left London.

In this connexion it is observed that the United States aide-mémoire, when speaking of the qualitative provisions of the British 'middle course', states that these 'were not to be devised in an effort to change existing types, but were rather to prevent competition in new types'. To avoid misunderstanding it should be made clear that the British proposals have always visualised the taking of measures not only to prevent competition in new types, but also to secure some reduction in the maximum displacement of ships and the calibre of guns as one means of diminishing the burden of naval armaments in the world at large. Although they are aware of the preference of the United States Government for a larger ship and a larger gun than those favoured by His Majesty's Government, they have hoped that the Government of the United States would be prepared to contemplate some appreciable reduction in the Washington limits. They have always believed that, when the United States Government are prepared to indicate definitely to His Majesty's Government what are their minimum views in the field of qualitative limitation, no great difficulty should be experienced in reaching a friendly understanding on the point.

Furthermore, the Government of the United States will readily recognise that the countries of the British Commonwealth of Nations have to take into account both European problems and world problems. Obviously, if the other European countries were prepared to agree to a lower limitation, there would be a general advantage if such qualitative limits were acceptable to the Oceanic Powers, as against the alternative of setting the pace all round in the matter of size.

His Majesty's Government had concluded from previous conversations—and they still hope—that there is no considerable divergence of view between the two Governments on this question. They feel with the United States Government the desirability of establishing as close an approximation of views as possible in this sphere, and for this reason they agree with the United States Government that an informal exchange of view would be a helpful course. Such conversations would most naturally take place through the ordinary diplomatic channel between a representative of the United States Embassy and of the Foreign Office, it being, of course, understood that the Naval Attaché of the United States Embassy and a representative of the British Admiralty would also be present. If this procedure is agreeable to the Government of the United States, it is suggested that the proposed exchange of views should take place as early as possible in the present month.

## No. 499

*Letter from Chancery (Berlin) to American Department, Foreign Office*
[*A 8087/22/45*]

BERLIN, *September 17, 1935*

Dear Department,
    In your letter A 7786/22/45[1] of the 5th September you asked for the
Not printed.

Naval Attaché's observations on some correspondence with the Admiralty about German submarine building.

The enclosed minute gives Muirhead-Gould's views on this subject.

Yours ever,

CHANCERY

ENCLOSURE IN NO. 499

*Minute by Captain Muirhead-Gould*

BERLIN, *September 14, 1935*

I am surprised at the F.O. being so concerned over Germany's morality. I should have thought by now that the F.O. would have realised that the German official never tells the truth except when it suits his purpose, and that he considers that his duty to his country entitles him to tell any story which he thinks will be believed.

It is humiliating to me to know that the German Marineleitung have so low an opinion of my intelligence and professional ability that they believe they can stuff me up with such fairy stories as the building of a submarine in 2 months.

I can only confirm the statements contained in F.O. letter of 17th July.[2] I have no doubt whatever that the construction of the submarine which was commissioned ('in Dienst gestellt') on 29th June had actually been started before April last.

Possibly the building yards were told last year that they could commence construction in secret, but that the 'official order' would not be placed until later. This would have enabled Captain Bürkner (the Liaison Officer), each time I asked him whether submarines were being built, to reply with teutonic truthfulness that 'No orders have yet been placed'.

I may add that on various occasions prior to the conclusion of the Naval Agreement Admiral Raeder himself assured me, with regard to the size of future German warships, that:—

1. The battleships would not exceed 25,000 tons,
2. The cruisers would not exceed 7,500 tons,
3. The destroyers would not exceed 1,300 tons, and
4. The submarines would not exceed 500 tons.

I no longer believe anything I am told by the Marineleitung unless I can obtain corroboration.

G. C. MUIRHEAD-GOULD

[2] A reference presumably to a letter of this date from Mr. Gore-Booth to Captain Danckwerts recapitulating the information about German submarine building given to His Majesty's Government earlier in the year (see Volume XII, No. 716, and Volume XIII, Nos. 129, 142, 150, and 154) and querying whether information could be consistent with the report that the first German 250-ton submarine had been put into commission on June 29. Mr. Gore-Booth wrote: 'If the first submarine was put into commission on the 29th June, it can only have taken just over two months to build. The shortness of the time may be accounted for by the explanation given to the Naval Attaché on the 26th April [see No. 142]. . . . Even so, the Naval Attaché added in his account that the first submarine would probably be delivered within *six* months, counting from April.'

## No. 500

*Sir E. Phipps (Berlin) to Sir S. Hoare (Received September 19)*
*No. 201 Saving: Telegraphic [C 6556/55/18]*

*Very confidential*                                    BERLIN, *September 18, 1935*

The following may be taken as an authentic account of Hitler's reactions in the Abyssinian affair.[1]

He is at no pains to conceal his 'Schadenfreude'. Indeed 'Schadenfreude' is felt throughout official circles more and more as the plot develops. But this is tempered with extreme caution and Hitler's instructions are that neutrality and reserve are to be shown in the press and in diplomatic conversations. Though his sympathies are with his brother dictator on the merits of the case he has never forgiven Mussolini for his sabre-rattling on the Brenner last year in connexion with the Dollfuss murder[2] which compelled him (Hitler) to climb down. The reference in his last Reichstag speech (see my despatch No. 904 of September 16th)[3] to the international press treating German friendship as an object at the disposal of every statesman who feels a need to reach out his hand for it was meant as a snub to the Duce in reply to Signor Gayda's[4] hints that Abyssinia might bring about an Italo-German 'rapprochement'.

Before leaving for Nuremberg Hitler discussed the situation briefly and remarked in conclusion that Germany had nothing to lose and probably something to gain from a quarrel in which three of the participants (the League, France and Italy) were Germany's enemies, while the fourth (England) was a doubtful neutral. The quarrel could only end in an armed clash or the permanent estrangement of two if not more of the quartet. Furthermore it was a welcome diversion during this stage of 'German reconstruction' (of the air force and army). As for sanctions the Chancellor thought that Germany might profit materially by the occasion if Geneva adopted economic measures. The question should be studied attentively.

He was a little mystified by the attitudes of the participants, as reported by his diplomatic missions. Paris and Geneva, it seems, reported that the attempt to mobilise the League against Italy was merely a general rehearsal in case the League should ever be called upon to deal with Germany as an aggressor. London, on the other hand, reports cynically that the British attitude is prompted by internal electoral considerations, and by the intention to open an early campaign for rearmament. Rome reports that Mussolini is at the mercy of circumstances over which he has no control. His plans have been elaborated to a point whence he cannot withdraw and his boats may

---

[1] This document is included in this volume because of its general background interest: the main body of documents about the Italo-Ethiopian crisis at this period will be printed in Volume XIV.

[2] Cf. Volume VI, No. 533.

[3] Not printed. This despatch had transmitted a translation of Herr Hitler's speech to the Reichstag at Nuremberg on September 15.

[4] Editor of the Italian newspaper, *Giornale d'Italia*.

be considered as burnt (see moreover my telegram No. 71 of February 23rd).[5] He cannot retire gracefully like a parliamentary government. Defeat in his case means disgrace. Ever since the cessation of Italian emigration to North and South America his thoughts have been turned to Abyssinia as an outlet for his ever growing population, and the intervention of the League so late in the day came as an unpleasant surprise.

The Chancellor is somewhat embarrassed by visits from Austrian Nazis of Italian nationality as well as Nazis from the Austrian Tyrol with wild-cat schemes and demands for financial help, which he has no intention of granting.

To resume, Hitler is chuckling (and arming) on his fence, where he means to stay as long as possible. In the event of an Anglo-Italian conflict he will only come down, armed to the teeth, at the time he considers the most favourable for Germany, and the price of his friendship or even of his neutrality will be a heavy one.

[5] This telegram relating to the Italo-Ethiopian dispute will be printed in Volume XIV.

## No. 501

*Sir S. Hoare to Sir G. Clerk (Paris)*
*No. 1711 [A 8071/22/45]*

FOREIGN OFFICE, *September 18, 1935*

Sir,

The French Ambassador called on Mr. Craigie on September 11th, in order to put certain questions to him in regard to plans for the Limitation of Naval Armaments. M. Corbin first enquired whether the invitation recently conveyed to the French Government to send naval representatives to London[1] should be regarded as official. Mr. Craigie replied in the affirmative, adding that, if there were to be a conference this year, little time remained for preparation, and that His Majesty's Government in the United Kingdom were anxious, before going into such a conference, to secure the closest possible approximation of views with the French Government.

2. M. Corbin next asked whether the proposed conference or meeting was to be regarded as preliminary to a general European naval conference. Mr. Craigie replied that this was certainly the view of His Majesty's Government. If the Five-Power Conference showed signs of coming to an agreement, His Majesty's Government would doubtless desire to expand it at once into a general conference. If, on the other hand, there seemed no prospect of agreement at the Five-Power Conference, then it would obviously be useless to think of a general conference.

3. M. Corbin enquired whether, in the opinion of His Majesty's Government, there seemed any likelihood of a successful issue to such a preliminary conference, having regard in particular to the attitude of Japan. Mr. Craigie expressed the view that an agreement on qualitative limitation was possible,

[1] See No. 477.

although there seemed little chance at present on the quantitative side. The best hope of making Japan realise the advantages of an agreement on qualitative limitation lay in bringing her into an international conference of Powers already favourable in principle to such an agreement. If, at such a conference, everyone, including Japan herself, found themselves in favour of certain qualitative limitations, it seemed on the whole unlikely that Japan would seek to wreck that agreement merely because the conference found it impossible to go as far as Japan might wish in the matter of quantitative limitation. In the last resort, Japan might not prove too uncompromising on this point.

4. M. Corbin then raised the question of the probable Italian attitude. He observed that the Italian reply[2] to the memorandum of His Majesty's Government of the 2nd August had been quite correct, but he wondered whether Italy, when it came to the point, would send representatives to a conference here in the present circumstances. Mr. Craigie pointed out that this must, of course, depend on developments in regard to the Abbyssinian question in the next few weeks. The feeling of His Majesty's Government, however, at present, was that if there were no radical change in the next few weeks in the situation as far as Italy was concerned, and if a convening of a conference were in other respects held to be desirable, the issue of invitations should probably not be deferred on account of the Abyssinian crisis. If Italy refused to attend, then the conference could not take place, but the responsibility for this eventuality would rest on the Italian Government, not on His Majesty's Government.

5. The French Ambassador admitted that the opposition in France to the Anglo-German Naval Agreement on political grounds had now died down. He said, however, that there were still doubts in regard to its technical efficacy. In particular, it was believed in France that Germany would violate the Agreement as soon as it suited her. Mr. Craigie gave his reasons for holding the contrary view, and said that on the technical side discussions between French and British representatives would be particularly useful, if the former were in a position to promise to communicate, on a reciprocal basis, tentative and hypothetical figures of future construction.

6. Mr. Craigie proceeded to inform the French Ambassador that, while there were certain obvious advantages in deferring further action in the matter of Naval Limitation pending future developments in regard to the Abyssinian question, there were also reasons which militated against further avoidable delay. In the first place, there had been indications in the press that, while Japan would come to a naval conference if summoned this year, in accordance with the provisions of the Washington and London Naval Treaties, she would only attend a conference thereafter on her own conditions, first amongst which stood the general adoption of the principle of the 'common upper limit'.[3] If this really represented the view of the Japanese Government, it meant that the only hope of getting Japan into a naval conference would be to convene that conference before the end of the present

[2] See No. 491.          [3] See No. 497.

year. Secondly, there was the difficulty that many Powers would be laying down new capital ships early in 1937, so that a final decision on the ultimate size of gun calibre of these ships could not be postponed any longer. If, therefore, it were decided to defer discussions on qualitative limitation until next year, the Powers concerned might then find that the 'pass had been sold', irrevocable decisions having meanwhile been taken by certain Powers. The net result in the future would probably be a greatly enhanced cost of naval construction all round.

7. M. Corbin said that he would now furnish his Government with a full report on the position, and would communicate their reply as soon as possible.

I am, &c.,

SAMUEL HOARE

## No. 502

*Sir E. Phipps (Berlin) to Sir S. Hoare (Received September 21, 2.5 p.m.)*
*No. 282 Telegraphic [C 6631/55/18]*

BERLIN, *September 21, 1935, 1.10 p.m.*

My (? telegram) 201 Saving.[1]

I hear from a good source that development of Anglo-Italian dispute is causing genuine consternation at the Wilhelmstrasse. The 'Schadenfreude' of last week is giving way to fear that conflict will extend to Europe generally. In that event Germany would be caught in the midst of her military re-organisation. There is now danger of Communist class[2] in Europe.

From another good source I hear that Chancellor is afraid that a blow to Fascism would adversely affect his own position.

[1] No. 500.
[2] In a printed copy of this telegram this passage read: 'There is also danger of Communist chaos.'

## No. 503

*Sir S. Hoare to Sir G. Clerk (Paris)*
*No. 1737 [C 6516/55/18]*

FOREIGN OFFICE, *September 24, 1935*

Sir,

I transmit to Y.E. herewith the record of a conversation which took place between M. Laval and myself at Geneva on September 11th regarding the programme of the London Communiqué.[1]

2. It will be noted that M. Laval promised on this occasion to give me 'an indication of what France might find it possible to do in the matter of land armaments'. I am still awaiting details of the views of the French Government on this point though it seems clear from your confidential and

[1] No. 496, enclosure.

unofficial letter of September 7[2] that the prospect of any considerable advance being made in this field is remote. If, however, the French Government decide that some arrangement with Germany regarding land armaments is still possible, they should, as pointed out in paragraphs 9 and 12 of my despatch No. 1524[3] of August 16 approach the German Government without delay on the subject; and if they desire assistance from His Majesty's Government they should at once work out and explain to the latter the kind of settlement which they will accept.

I am, &c.,

(for the Secretary of State)

C. W. BAXTER

[2] No. 492.    [3] No. 473.

## No. 504

*Letter from Mr. Baxter to Mr. Strang (Geneva)*

[*C 6516/55/18*]

FOREIGN OFFICE, *September 25, 1935*

Dear Strang,

Please see your despatch No. 89[1] of September 13th recording a conversation between the Secretary of State and M. Laval on the subject of the programme of the London Communiqué. I attach a print copy for convenience of reference.

Sargent, who is now on leave, has written to me suggesting that certain phrases used by the Secretary of State regarding the Air Pact (page 3 of the enclosed print)[2] are not quite clear, and as they deal with points of considerable importance, he thinks that you should be consulted with regard to what exactly was said.

The three points which he mentions are the following:

(a) Did the Secretary of State stipulate merely that bilateral pacts should be part of the general Pact? This would open the door to practically anything. The relevant phrase, as used with the German Ambassador,[3] was: 'We were only contemplating arrangements that were incidental to the general Pact, *that were necessary to it for making it effective*'.[4]

(b) We presume that, when the Secretary of State and M. Laval discussed the advantages and disadvantages of an 'Air Pact' they had in view the Air Pact *plus*[4] the Air Limitation Agreement. Are we right in supposing that the merits of the Air Pact proper (apart from the Air Limitation Agreement) were not discussed on this occasion?

(c) The Secretary of State seems almost to contradict himself when he says first that it might not much matter if Germany did not strictly carry out the limitation provisions, and then subsequently that in his view limitation was very important. We wonder, therefore, whether

<hr>

[1] No. 496.         [2] i.e. page 635.         [3] See No. 447.

[4] The words in italics were underlined on the filed copy of the letter.

the Secretary of State is not more likely to have said that it might not much matter if there was no system of strict supervision to ensure the observance by Germany of the limitation provisions.

Yours sincerely,<br>C. W. BAXTER

## No. 505

*Sir E. Phipps (Berlin) to Sir S. Hoare (Received September 27)*
*No. 952 [C 6728/55/18]*

BERLIN, September 26, 1935

Sir,

I have the honour to inform you that the Military Attaché to this Embassy has received from the Ministry of War a confidential statement of the strength which the German army will have attained on the 1st November next.

2. This shows a total of 29 divisions:

24 Infantry divisions.
3 Armoured divisions.
2 Cavalry divisions.

Extra troops amount to approximately one more division.

3. The S.S. division and the Regiment Herrmann [*sic*] Göring are not included; these are both believed to be the subject of discussions between the Army and the Party. Herr Himmler and General Göring are both interested in military matters and wish to maintain their small but select private armies. They may also have personal political reasons.

4. The statement is in general agreement with Colonel Hotblack's information and is, he believes, correct. It contains no information on further developments or on the number of trained reserves.

I have, &c.,<br>ERIC PHIPPS

## No. 506

*Letter from Sir E. Phipps (Berlin) to Mr. Sargent*
*[C 6741/55/18]*

*Confidential*                                           BERLIN, *September 26, 1935*

My dear Sargent,

Your letter C 4588/55/18[1] of the 22nd June about the demilitarised zone.

Hotblack informs me that in his presence a general staff officer who works under General Blomberg recently told the American Military Attaché that the General Staff considered that the Rhineland Demilitarised Zone was a grave disadvantage for a sovereign state. He added that Germany had no

[1] No. 308, note 2.

intention of changing this condition as long as there was any prospect of understanding and friendship with England. He said that they realised that this friendship was not easy of achievement but that great value was placed upon it. Everyone, he added, now realized that nothing that Germany could do or say could bring about an understanding with France.

Yours ever,<br>ERIC PHIPPS

No. 507

*Draft Record of a Meeting held in the Foreign Office on Friday, September 27, at 10.30 a.m.*[1]

[A 8361/22/45]

*Present*: Mr. R. L. Craigie, CB., CMG., Assistant Under-Secretary of State, Foreign Office.
Captain V. H. Danckwerts, R.N., Admiralty.
Mr. Ray Atherton, Counsellor of the U.S. Embassy in London.
Captain Anderson, U.S. Naval Attaché.

Mr. Craigie recalled that the present meeting was being held at the request of the U.S. Embassy and suggested, therefore, that they should open the proceedings. At the suggestion of Mr. Atherton Mr. Craigie then read the following documents aloud so that it might be certain there was no misunderstanding or difference of view as to their meaning:—

N.C. (M) (35) 61 – Memorandum communicated to the French Embassy on August 3rd.[2]

N.C. (M) (35) 66, Annex II – Aide Mémoire left at the Foreign Office by Mr. Atherton on August 17th.[3]

N.C. (M) (35) 66, Annex I – Aide Mémoire communicated to the U.S. Embassy on September 12th.[4]

2. Mr. Atherton then confirmed that, as far as procedure was concerned and the proposals of the British Government for advancing the prospects of the 1935 Conference his difficulties as expressed in his Aide Mémoire had been removed as explained by the subsequent British Aide Mémoire. He said that, for the U.S.A., the Japanese denunciation of the Washington Treaty[5] had removed the whole basis of the Naval Limitation Treaties. The position of the U.S. Government before this occurred had been made clear to us last year, viz., that they understood entirely our desire for an increase in cruiser tonnage but that they hoped to proceed on the basis of the existing treaties and to secure a 30% cut all round. To-day their general standpoint was that they wished to salvage everything possible in the Washington Treaty. The

[1] This draft record, received in the Foreign Office from the Admiralty, was approved by Mr. Craigie in a minute of September 30. For the account of the meeting transmitted to the United States Secretary of State by Mr. Bingham, see *F.R.U.S. 1935*, vol. i, pp. 116–18.
[2] No. 460, enclosure.
[3] No. 474, enclosure.
[4] No. 498, enclosure.
[5] See No. 102.

U.S. Government was therefore ready to pursue qualitative limitation together with such measure of quantitative limitation as was now possible in the manner set out in the British Memorandum, but he made it plain that they did this without any enthusiasm. Further, they were ready to meet the British desires by making what they regarded as a very substantial contribution by agreeing to a reduction in the maximum gun calibre of the capital ships.

3. The discussion then turned to the capital ship question and was mainly conducted on behalf of the U.S.A. representatives by Captain Anderson. Captain Anderson asked whether we would agree to the proposition which represented the view of the U.S.A. that the existing qualitative limits were better than nothing if their continuation could be secured. Captain Danckwerts agreed but stressed the point that the British Government stood for reduction on the existing qualitative limits if possible. Captain Anderson then stated that the U.S.A. were ready to agree to a 14″ gun for capital ships in the future, provided that general agreement on this point could be secured and that it was recorded in an agreement which should not be in other respects contrary to the U.S.A. views. He then stated that if a reduction in tonnage from 35,000 was to be made in the future it would be only a small reduction and threw out the suggestion, which he said was on his own behalf, might it not be possible instead of fixing a tonnage limit to fix a limit to the maximum number of guns they might have mounted in one ship? Captain Danckwerts stated that such a proposal had been considered by the Admiralty and rejected at the time of the Washington Conference. Some discussion then ensued to elucidate in what manner the proposal would affect the situation, and Captain Anderson made it clear that his idea had been put forward in conjunction with quantitative limitation of capital ships and in his view would permit Great Britain to build a greater number of capital ships on a smaller tonnage perhaps than those of the U.S.A. being guarded by the knowledge of the maximum offensive power that could be put into her ships by the U.S.A. On the whole, he agreed that without quantitative limitation the proposal had no particular advantage over a tonnage limitation.

4. He made it clear that the U.S. Navy Board were very reluctant to state any figure less than 35,000 tons for the capital ship of the future. Captain Danckwerts then reminded him that Admiral Standley last year had tentatively suggested that the first one or two ships should be built up to 35,000 tons, and that as a result of experience in designing these they might be able to reduce the size of subsequent ships. Captain Anderson appeared to receive this suggestion with enthusiasm and said that was still their view, and discussion ensued as to what form such a proposal could take. Captain Anderson was of the opinion that they would like to state no tonnage for the ships after the first two but to undertake, say, to reduce the tonnage of subsequent ships as far as could be done in the light of the experience gained. Captain Danckwerts then outlined the situation of European capital ships building and asked whether that situation would not affect the U.S.A. point of view, and pointed out that if no subsequent figure could be stated until

after experience, it might perhaps be a matter of five years during which the European Powers might very well go on building ships of the maximum size as they were now doing and thus that size would get perpetuated. Captain Anderson said that the U.S.A. could not be indifferent to the capital ship building of European Powers, and suggested that we should take away for consideration the idea that the first two capital ships, say, to be built should be limited only by the Washington Treaty limits and that subsequent ships should be limited to the 14″ gun and such tonnage as might be agreed upon, though he thought the Navy Board would be unwilling to state any tonnage less than 35,000 tons. The possibility was also mentioned of stating no reduction in tonnage for the future 14″ gun capital ship but instead limiting the number of guns to be mounted to, say, 12. Captain Anderson stated that he thought the U.S. Navy Board would rather maintain the existing limits for the two ships than limit them to 15″ guns supposing that to be the gun being mounted by European Powers because the U.S.A. already has experience of the 16″ guns and the 14″ gun but none at all of the 15″ gun.

5. The discussion was then directed to the possibility of having a lower limit to capital ships as well as an upper limit so as to produce a gap between cruisers and capital ships, thus making the cruiser qualitative limitation effective in the absence of any quantitative limitation. Captain Anderson was reminded that this matter had been discussed by Admiral Standley last year. He was only able to say that the Navy Board view would probably be much the same as Admiral Standley's view[6] that some such expedient was desirable if it could be arranged, but had no views on the size of the lower limit for capital ships.

6. The Qualitative limit of aircraft carriers was then touched on, and Captain Anderson said that the British proposal of 22,000 tons with 6·1″ guns would, he thought, form a good basis for discussion at the Conference and would meet with no opposition from the U.S.A.

7. The meeting was then adjourned, and it was decided that all parties should think over the discussion that had taken place regarding capital ships, and it was understood that Captain Anderson would get into touch with the Navy Board on the subject.

[6] See No. 75.

## No. 508

*Sir S. Hoare to Sir H. Kennard (Warsaw)*

*No. 373 [C 6555/55/18]*

FOREIGN OFFICE, *September 27, 1935*

Sir,

The Polish Minister for Foreign Affairs called on me at Geneva on the 13th September. After some discussion had taken place on the subject of the Italo-Abyssinian dispute, I enquired what were Colonel Beck's views regarding the Eastern Pact. I explained that I had already stated in the

House of Commons the attitude of His Majesty's Government towards the pact.[1] They were not so much concerned with the exact terms of the pact, but were impressed with the important evidence which its conclusion would offer of a general *détente* between the various European nations, and in particular of a *détente* between France and Germany.

2. Colonel Beck said that, speaking personally, he himself had never been optimistic with regard to the prospects of the Eastern Pact. As I knew, he had been in Berlin not long ago and had had a long talk with Herr Hitler.[2] He had definitely derived the impression that no direct feeling of hostility to France existed in Berlin. But it was always necessary to take account of what he would call the psychology of a country. He mentioned this because Germany was a country which was at present peculiarly swayed by psychological influences, and these took the form of a definite antagonism to Russia. It was against Russia rather than against France that Germany's face was set, and Colonel Beck must frankly state that the conclusion of the Franco-Russian Pact,[3] and perhaps even more of the Russo-Czechoslovak Agreement,[4] had seriously prejudiced the success of an Eastern Pact. Colonel Beck had warned M. Laval some months ago at Geneva that the conclusion of a Franco-Russian Pact would be likely to have this effect.

3. I replied that I quite saw Colonel Beck's point, but could not help feeling that the formula for an Eastern Pact had now been reduced to a point which ought to minimise Germany's dislike of it on the ground of her dislike of Russia. For instance, there was now no question of Germany and Russia having in certain eventualities to furnish what I might call a common army, a point which had been so distasteful to Germany. I must again point out, however, how important the conclusion of an Eastern Pact would be as a sign of a tendency towards European appeasement.

4. Colonel Beck said once again that he was not hopeful of the prospect of an Eastern Pact. It was the origins of the pact which were wrong. I would no doubt recollect that its origin had lain in the desire of Russia to have some form of agreement destined to contain Germany.[5] The scope of the pact had, of course, been very considerably widened in the course of M. Barthou's visit to London in July 1934.[6] But the Germans could not get the taste of the original form out of their mouth. For Poland the problem presented special difficulties, as the pact might, in certain circumstances, involve her coming to the help of either her eastern or her western neighbour against the other neighbour. The problem for Poland was therefore as much geographical as it was political, and it could hardly be expected that the idea of an Eastern Pact would find popularity in Poland. Colonel Beck repeated that, while not hopeful as to the prospects of an Eastern Pact, he was more optimistic about direct Franco-German relations.

I am, &c.,

Samuel Hoare

[1] On July 11; see 304 *H.C. Deb.* 5 *s.*, cols. 514–15.  [2] Cf. No. 393, note 2.
[3] On May 2, 1935; cf. No. 156.  [4] On May 16, 1935; cf. No. 239, note 3.
[5] Cf. Volume VI, e.g., Nos. 450 and 465.  [6] Cf. *ibid.*, Nos. 487–9.

## No. 509

*Letter from Mr. Strang (Geneva) to Mr. Baxter*

[C 6780/55/18]

GENEVA, *September 27, 1935*

My dear Baxter,

Your letter of the 25th September, 1935.[1]

I am pretty sure that my record of the interview between the Secretary of State and Monsieur Laval on September 11th accurately reproduces what passed. The Secretary of State spoke very slowly, and I was able to check over my notes while Massigli was interpreting. The Secretary of State revised the record before it was sent home in final form. The record was not communicated to the French Delegation.

Now as to your three points:

(a) The record reproduces what was actually said, but I do not think there was any misunderstanding between the Secretary of State and Monsieur Laval as to the nature of the proposed bi-lateral Pacts.

(b) I think the record makes it clear in a number of places that what was talked about was an Air pact, plus an Air limitation agreement. The Air pact proper (apart from the Air limitation agreement) was not discussed.

(c) I do not think that there is necessarily any contradiction. In the Secretary of State's view, the importance of limitation is that it will make it difficult for Germany to deliver a sudden and overwhelming offensive, with unexpectedly large forces of aircraft. Gross violations of the agreement would be easily noticed. Failure by Germany to carry out the strict letter of the agreement would be of less importance. Minor violations of the agreement would not be so dangerous.

This seems to me to be a consistent argument, and the suggestion made in the last paragraph of your letter would follow logically from it, though it was not—so far as I can remember—expressed.

Yours ever

W. STRANG

[1] No. 504.


## No. 510

*Sir S. Hoare to Sir R. Clive (Tokyo)*

*No. 190 Telegraphic* [A 8397/22/45]

FOREIGN OFFICE, *October 1, 1935, 9.30 p.m.*

Japanese Chargé d'Affaires was invited to call at the Foreign Office on September 27th to discuss naval limitation. He was reminded that French and Italian Governments had in their replies to His Majesty's Government's memorandum of July 30th expressed themselves in favour of qualitative limitation.[1] It was then explained that, like His Majesty's Government, both United States Government and German Government would prefer agreement regulating qualitative limitation only to no agreement at all. Mr. Fujii was warned that Japanese Government's contention that qualitative limitation was unacceptable without quantitative limitation might block last possible approach to any form of naval limitation and he was asked how this could serve Japan's own interests. As His Majesty's Government were anxious to decide on possibility of naval conference this year, it was proposed to Chargé d'Affaires that conversations might take place between Foreign Office and Japanese Embassy to find some compromise between Japanese claim to common upper limit and United States desire to continue ratio system. As regards form of quantitative limitation, it was suggested that, if other Powers were unable to accept the British proposal for a six years' agreement, construction declaration might cover some shorter period, say two years. In this way Japanese condition in regard to any future agreement applying to both qualitative and quantitative limitation might still be met. Chargé d'Affaires was requested to inform his Government that an informal discussion had already taken place between Foreign Office and United States Embassy along the same lines[2] and that further talks would probably take place through the same channel.

Mr. Fujii replied that Japanese Ministry of Marine desired reduction in all categories of ships by most heavily armed Powers and felt that justice of United States claim to superiority could never be understood in Japan. He was informed that in present unsettled political situation no British Government could contemplate further reductions in British Navy.

Mr. Fujii gave no hint that Ministry of Marine would modify their attitude, but welcomed proposal that Anglo-Japanese conversations should be conducted here through diplomatic channel and the further personal suggestion made to him that bilateral conversations might be allowed to develop into an Ambassadors' conference and so avoid the necessity of sending large delegations from overseas.

[1] See Nos. 472 and 491.     [2] See No. 507.

## No. 511

*Draft Record of a Meeting held in the Foreign Office on Tuesday, October 1, 1935, at 10.30 a.m.*[1]

*[A 8471/22/45]*

*Present*: Mr. R. L. Craigie, Captain V. H. Danckwerts, Mr. Ray Atherton, Captain Anderson.

The meeting proceeded to discuss those questions that had not already been dealt with in the previous meeting on the 27th September.[2]

[1] This draft record, received in the Foreign Office from the Admiralty, was approved by Mr. Craigie in a minute of October 3. Cf. *F.R.U.S. 1935*, vol. i, pp. 120–2.
[2] No. 507.

2. *Cruisers.* At Mr. Atherton's request, Mr. Craigie outlined the British proposals already made to the U.S.A. Delegation on the subject of cruiser limitation. Captain Anderson then made it clear that the U.S.A. are opposed to the proposal to reduce the qualitative limits of cruisers, either as to tonnage or gun calibre, below those of the Washington Treaty. He then raised the question of the *Hawkins* class, and said that it had much bearing on the U.S.A. attitude towards the proposition not to build any more 8″ gun cruisers.

3. Captain Danckwerts said that, speaking without instructions, he felt quite sure that the British Government would willingly agree that the *Hawkins* class should not continue to exist as Category A. cruisers after 31/12/36, if this would in any way facilitate agreement by the U.S.A. Government not to build more 8″ gun cruisers. He mentioned that one of the *Hawkins* class was now being used as a cadet training ship and that we should probably desire to retain her for such services in the future and perhaps more than one ship, but for that purpose we would be quite willing to remove the 7·5″ guns and replace them by 6″ guns.

4. Captain Anderson said that he regarded this statement as very re-assuring. The U.S.A. had been afraid that Great Britain would propose to retain the *Hawkins* class as Category A. cruisers. He would certainly transmit to his Government, as a tentative proposition, the assurance that the *Hawkins* class would not be retained as Category A. cruisers in the future.

5. Mr. Craigie outlined the difficulties that would be caused by the U.S. refusal to agree that no more 8″ gun cruisers should be built. He pointed out that such a standpoint would have to be conceded to all other countries, and that it would probably result in further 8″ gun cruiser building by Japan, by Germany and by other European countries; in fact it would lead to a general cruiser building competition again.

6. Captain Danckwerts pointed out that the British proposals were really divisible into two steps. Firstly, the reduction in the gun calibre from 8″ to 6″ and, secondly, the reduction in the tonnage from 10,000 to 7,600. Even if the tonnage reduction could not be secured it would be a great advance to achieve reduction in gun calibre.

7. Captain Anderson said that he would report the conversation of course, but that he held out little hope that the U.S.A. Government would alter their attitude. Finally, he made it clear that there might perhaps be some difference in the mind of the U.S.A. between the proposition that no more 8″ gun cruisers should ever be built and the proposition that no more should be built until the existing ones required replacement. Captain Danckwerts said that the latter proposition though not as attractive as the former would still be a great advance.

8. *Destroyers.* The British position as regards qualitative and quantitative requirements was outlined by Mr. Craigie. It was made clear in the discussion that there was no practical hope of obtaining French agreement to separate the destroyer category from the cruiser category and that, therefore, the discussion of these qualitative limits and a percentage distribution

between destroyers and destroyer leaders were academic questions. The possibility was mentioned of perhaps getting French agreement to make a differentiation between the two categories in a short term arrangement for limitation of building though this was not really very hopeful. Captain Anderson indicated that the U.S.A. position as regards qualitative limits for destroyers coincided with that of the United Kingdom.

9. *Submarines.* Captain Danckwerts outlined the British attitude to this question, and it appeared that the U.S.A. attitude was identical.

10. Captain Anderson said that he had no instructions as regards the questions mentioned in paragraph 8 of N.C. (M) (35) 61,[3] viz., notification of information, definitions, Washington Treaty Articles XIV, XVII and XVIII. It seemed, however, that they were all covered by the general U.S.A. decision that they desired to salvage as much as possible of the Washington Treaty. In the discussion on notification of information the French idea of 'Pré-Avis' and the difficulties inherent in it were described.

11. Mention was made of Article XIX of the Washington Treaty, the status quo in the Pacific. It was suggested that this was not altogether suitable for inclusion in a multilateral treaty since it only affected three Powers, but that it was probably a question which should be taken up with Japan. Mr. Atherton's personal impression was that the U.S.A. would like to re-enact this Article in some form.

12. Part IV of the London Naval Treaty was also discussed—the rules for submarine warfare. Mr. Craigie pointed out that this part of the London Naval Treaty did not lapse as between the three signatories, U.S.A., Japan and the British Commonwealth, but that it seemed to us more suitable to extend it to other Powers by means of a protocol rather than to attempt to include it in a future naval limitation treaty.

13. The meeting then adjourned until such time as Mr. Atherton should indicate that they had received further instructions from Washington.[4]

[3] See enclosure in No. 460.

[4] Commenting on these Anglo-American discussions, Mr. Craigie minuted on October 2: 'On the whole, the arrangement proposed is not unsatisfactory, because we must now in any case build 2 more maximum sized capital ships because the silly Italian building is provoking building of two outsize ships apiece by France and Germany—armed with 15″ guns.'

## No. 512

*Sir R. Clive (Tokyo) to Sir S. Hoare (Received October 4, 2.20 p.m.)*
*No. 258 Telegraphic [A 8506/22/45]*

TOKYO, *October 4, 1935, 7 p.m.*

Your telegram No. 190.[1]

Japanese press have published much misleading information on the subject of recent conversation with Japanese Chargé d'Affaires and today's

No. 510.

656

leading paper stated that Cabinet had decided on reply to latest British proposals and this would be categorically no.

As I felt that Chargé d'Affaires might not have correctly reported whole conversation, I saw Vice-Minister for Foreign Affairs today, and showed him your telegram. He was extremely interested and read several times sentence beginning 'in this way Japanese condition' down to 'there must still'[2] and asked exactly what it meant with reference to preceding sentence. I said I took it to mean that as His Majesty's Government would rather have an agreement on qualitative limitation than none at all, reduction from six years to[3] period for declaration of building construction had been suggested as a concession to Japanese, that it was hoped that at a conference Japanese Government would agree to discuss qualitative limitation and that in the course of period of two years for which next declaration would be made, way might be found for a general agreement on quantitative limitation also. I pointed out that persistence in common upper limit proposal could only result in rendering general agreement impossible and odium would fall on Japan. His Majesty's Government wished to avoid this.

He was also very interested in last paragraph and said neither of these points had been made clear in Chargé d'Affaires' telegram. He asked me for a copy as there would be Cabinet meeting tomorrow and I am sending him one tonight.

[2] A marginal note here suggests that this last quotation should read 'still be met'.
[3] A marginal note here suggests the substitution of 'as' in place of 'to'.

## No. 513

*Sir S. Hoare to Mr. Osborne (Washington)*
*No. 280 Telegraphic [A 8587/22/45]*

FOREIGN OFFICE, *October 7, 1935, 2.40 p.m.*

The Counsellor of the United States Embassy called on October 4th and, under instructions from his Government, made the following oral communication.

The Japanese Ambassador at Washington had recently called at the State Department and enquired of the Secretary of State:

(1) What was the American attitude towards the suggestion that a naval conference should be held this year?
(2) What was the American attitude towards the proposal for an agreement regulating qualitative limitation only?

The Secretary of State's answer was to the following effect:

As regards question (1), the United States Government concurred in the desirability that a naval conference should be held before the end of this year. They recognised the difficulty of concluding a treaty along the lines of previous treaties, but they considered it very important that limitation of naval armaments should not be allowed to terminate completely, with the result that the whole armament question would again be thrown open. They hoped that a solution could now be found for those elements of the problem on which agreement could be reached and so avoid an unrestricted naval race. At least this would make it possible to tide over the situation for a period in the hope that the matter might be taken up later in more favourable conditions.

In reply to question (2), the United States Government stated that in their view both qualitative and quantitative limitation should be continued. As, however, the difficulties which had arisen related to quantitative rather than to qualitative limitation, it should not be difficult to work out some mutually satisfactory arrangement for continuing the existing types of ships, subject to such modifications and reductions as might be found desirable and mutually agreeable.

The Japanese Ambassador was informed that His Majesty's Government were being told of the sense of the reply returned to the Japanese Government. Repeated to Tokyo.

## No. 514

### *Sir S. Hoare to Sir R. Clive (Tokyo)*
### *No. 198 Telegraphic [A 8506/22/45]*

FOREIGN OFFICE, *October 7, 1935, 7.35 p.m.*

Your telegram No. 258.[1]

Your action approved.

You should, however, explain to Japanese Government that suggestion of reducing period for which construction declarations would be made was a purely personal and tentative one and should not be regarded as an official proposal of His Majesty's Government.

[1] No. 512.

## No. 515

### *Sir R. Clive (Tokyo) to Sir S. Hoare (Received October 8, 9.30 a.m.)*
### *No. 263 Telegraphic [A 8558/22/45]*

*Important*                                        TOKYO, *October 8, 1935, 1.28 p.m.*

Your telegram No. 198.[1]

I submit with all respect that it would only give rise to misunderstanding on the part of Japanese Government if I sent explanation as instructed.

I understand that serious struggle is going on between Japanese Government and naval extremists in regard to reply to be sent and if I sent explanation which latter would interpret as withdrawal of proposal for reduced period I fear, and Naval Attaché agrees, we could only expect no for an answer.

Japanese reply is expected to be sent about the end of this week.

[1] No. 514.

## No. 516

*Sir S. Hoare to Sir E. Drummond (Rome)*

*No. 501 Telegraphic [A 8608/22/45]*

FOREIGN OFFICE, *October 9, 1935, 8.25 p.m.*

My despatch No. 1021.[1]

In course of conversation with Sir Robert Vansittart on October 5th, Italian Ambassador stated that Italian Government would be prepared to send naval experts to London for preliminary conversations in connexion with the forthcoming naval conference. Signor Grandi later confirmed statement in writing.

Matter will be further discussed tomorrow with Signor Vitetti, who will be informed of the present position of the negotiations.

[1] This despatch of September 10 forwarded to Rome a copy of the Italian memorandum of September 4: see No. 491.


## No. 517

*Sir R. Clive (Tokyo) to Sir S. Hoare (Received October 10, 9.30 a.m.)*

*No. 266 Telegraphic [A 8633/22/45]*

*Confidential*                                    TOKYO, *October 10, 1935, 11.20 a.m.*

Your telegram No. 202.[1]

Following for Mr. Craigie.

Nothing is settled about Matsudaira's return.

He is away from Tokyo at present but his wife told me a few days ago that he might return without her. Meanwhile, I know he has done his best to clear up Japanese misunderstanding of British policy—and with some success so far as Japanese Foreign Office is concerned. The latter are trying to induce navy diehards to agree to conciliatory answer but as Vice Minister for Foreign Affairs told me privately 'young officers' are being exceedingly difficult and reply may be delayed till next week.

[1] This Foreign Office telegram of October 8 referred to M. Matsudaira's promise to do what he could while in Japan 'to promote agreement between Japan and ourselves on the naval question'. Sir R. Clive was asked to keep in touch with him and to 'ascertain discreetly what his present plans are'.


## No. 518

*Sir E. Phipps (Berlin) to Sir S. Hoare (Received October 11)*

*No. 228 Saving: Telegraphic [C 6983/55/18]*

BERLIN, *October 10, 1935*

General von Blomberg lunched with us on October 8th and I had some conversation with him afterwards.

He said that what Mussolini felt especially bitterly was the fact that all

Communist and extreme Socialist elements throughout the world were banded against him; this made it peculiarly difficult for him to extricate himself from his present position. General von Blomberg deplored this anti-Fascist wave, although he remarked that the mobilisation on the Brenner[1] had been a childish and quite unnecessary proceeding. He added that Mussolini complained that he had not been sufficiently warned regarding the real feelings of H.M. Government or of the British public.

I replied that public opinion in Great Britain was unanimous in condemning the attack on Abyssinia, but the reason was, apart from the extreme left, anti-aggressor and anti-war, not anti-Fascism. As for insufficient warning, Mussolini had been solemnly and repeatedly warned from February onwards both in London and in Rome.

General von Blomberg thinks that Italy has undertaken a task beyond her powers, and that the very large number of troops that she has thrown into East Africa may prove fatal for her, owing to the possibility of terrible and widespread epidemics amongst them. He remarked, however, that Mussolini's real excuse was the vital need for expansion, and that applied to Germany as well as to Italy. If Germany were not allowed to expand the 'kettle would some day burst'. He recalled your words at Geneva regarding raw material,[2] but said that was not enough. Germany must have Colonies again. I reminded my guest how little raw material Germany had drawn from her colonies before the war, and how few colonists, apart from officials, she had sent there. The reply of the Minister for War was that Germany had not been sufficiently long in possession of those colonies to be able to develop them to the full; it was, moreover, intolerable for her to be considered unworthy to possess them now.

General von Blomberg repeated, as he usually does when we meet, that the Chancellor's one wish is to cultivate friendly relations with Great Britain. Moreover, I would remember that that was what he advocated in 'Mein Kampf'. I agreed, but, pointing to the French Ambassador, who was in earnest conversation in another room with Herr von Ribbentrop, I observed that the French never forgot the violent hatred of France contained in that work. General von Blomberg replied that 'Mein Kampf' was written in 1923, in very different circumstances to the present; but new editions appeared, I observed, and its sale continued. The reply was that Herr Hitler could not alter it by a series of postscripts or sequels. He therefore allowed its sale to continue, as showing his innermost thoughts at the time. His present thoughts would shortly appear in a volume containing a selection of his recent speeches, and these were full of genuine offers of reconciliation with France, but they had hitherto fallen on deaf ears. The last French note

[1] In July 1934; cf. Volume VI, No. 533.

[2] In his speech at Geneva on September 11 (cf. No. 494, note 3) Sir S. Hoare said *inter alia* with regard to the problem of raw materials: 'The Government that I represent will, I know, be prepared to take its share in any collective attempt to deal, in a fair and effective way, with a problem that is certainly troubling many people at present and may trouble them even more in future.'

to Great Britain,[3] for instance, was not agreeable reading for Germany, as it was so evidently directed against that Power.

You will notice how convenient, and indeed soothing, a text-book 'Mein Kampf' has become; its bellicosity and fanaticism faded away with the autumn roses of 1923, and only such sweet reason as it may have expounded is to remain to us as a joy for ever.

Meanwhile, as I heard afterwards from the French Ambassador, he and Herr von Ribbentrop were reproaching one another for the German–Polish Agreement of 1934 and the Franco-Soviet Pact of 1935 respectively. Herr von Ribbentrop told Monsieur François-Poncet that the French should never have allied themselves to a Communist and Asiatic Power, to which my French colleague replied that Russia had evolved since Peter the Great, she was as much European as Asiatic, and the French pact with her was merely the reply to the unfortunate German–Polish Agreement, which, concluded in an atmosphere of undue secrecy, had sown suspicion and distrust throughout Europe.

[3] A reference presumably to the French Government's note of October 5, 1935, communicated by M. Corbin on that day. It was printed in *The Times* of October 8, p. 13.

## No. 519

*Record of a Meeting held in the Foreign Office on Thursday, October 10, 1935*[1]

*[A 8850/22/45]*

*Present*: Mr. R. L. Craigie, Captain V. H. Danckwerts, Mr. Ray Atherton, Captain Anderson.

Mr. Craigie said that we had been thinking over our conversation with the U.S.A. representatives on the 27th September[2] when we had talked about the possible effect, on the size of future capital ships to be built by the U.S.A. and ourselves, of the present building being undertaken by the European countries. It had on that occasion been suggested as a possibility that the U.S.A. might desire to build her first two ships to the present maximum limitations. Our own fear was that such an action might very well lead to the perpetuation of these limits instead of their reduction. The Admiralty, therefore, had formed the opinion that we should be prepared to limit the guns of our first two as well as all later ships to 14" as it was understood the American Government were also prepared to do. Mr. Craigie made it clear that this was not a Government decision but that the Admiralty having reached this conclusion he thought it important to convey it to the U.S.A. representatives as early as possible.

2. As a result of further conversation, Mr. Atherton asked whether he correctly represented the situation in the following terms.

First, that the British Admiralty were prepared to put 14" guns in their

[1] Cf. *F.R.U.S. 1935*, vol. i, pp. 123–5.     [2] See No. 507.

first two ships, provided the U.S.A., Japan and Great Britain agreed on this calibre; second, that they were prepared to adopt the 14″ gun for all later ships, provided that France and Italy, as well as the U.S.A. and Japan, were prepared to make a similar agreement; third, that from now on the British Government might try to induce France and Germany not to put a larger gun than 14″ into the ships they had now projected.

3. Mr. Craigie confirmed that this was so and added that the third proposition made it extremely important that we should keep the communication we had made to the U.S.A. absolutely confidential.

4. Captain Anderson reverted to the discussion which had taken place on the previous occasion as to the possibility of adopting a limitation of the number of guns in a capital ship. He said the proposal had been made by himself with a view to assisting the United Kingdom point of view, and on that occasion Captain Danckwerts had given his personal view that the proposal was not one we would be likely to adopt. Captain Anderson wished to know whether, supposing the limit was placed at some lower figure than the 12 previously suggested, say 9 guns, would that alter our view. Captain Danckwerts again made it clear that the matter had not been discussed by the Naval Staff but that his personal view still was that it was not a proposal that would assist us. Captain Anderson indicated that he did not think the Navy Board had any desire to pursue the proposal.

## No. 520

### *Sir S. Hoare to Mr. Osborne (Washington)*
### *No. 932 [A 8599/22/45]*

FOREIGN OFFICE, *October 10, 1935*

Sir,

It will be recollected that, in conversation with Mr. Atherton, Counsellor of the United States Embassy, on September 12th, personal enquiries were made as to whether, in the event of it proving impossible to induce the Japanese Government to sign any naval treaty dealing with qualitative limitation at the present time, the United States Government would be likely to favour the conclusion of a general agreement on qualitative limitation even without Japan, on the understanding that the Japanese would undertake, in the form of a 'gentleman's agreement,' not to construct vessels of a type likely to upset the general agreement. A full record of this conversation was contained in my despatch No. 856 of September 17th.[1]

2. On October 4th Mr. Atherton called at the Foreign Office and stated privately and confidentially that he was able to confirm his understanding of the United States point of view, namely, that it would be desirable for the United Kingdom and the United States to reach a naval agreement which, if possible, would also include France and Italy, but with the necessary clause of elasticity. He considered that it would be advisable in the circumstances

[1] No. 498.

662

that such an agreement should be in effect a continuation of existing naval treaties with such modifications as the circumstances might require and that, for the reasons set out in my above-mentioned despatch, it should be left open for Japanese adherence at any time.

3. In view of the fact that both the Washington and London Naval Treaties provided for the summoning of a conference before the end of the year, Mr. Atherton understood that his Government 'believed it to be desirable that His Majesty's Government should arrange such a meeting to satisfy this requirement, if in any way possible, preferably in consultation with the United States Government in advance.' He felt that since the initiative rested in British hands and since it was not desirable to hold two meetings, it would seem preferable that His Majesty's Government, should they decide to summon such a conference, should cover the provisions of both Treaties.

4. Mr. Atherton was thanked for his message, which he was informed would be of great assistance to His Majesty's Government in deciding on the best course of action.

I am, &c.,

SAMUEL HOARE

## No. 521

*Sir S. Hoare to Sir R. Clive (Tokyo)*

*No. 203 Telegraphic [A 8756/22/45]*

FOREIGN OFFICE, *October 11, 1935, 10 p.m.*

Your telegram No. 263.[1]

'Times' of October 10th contained a telegram from its correspondent in Tokyo[2] stating that the public had learned for the first time that a substantial reduction in the period to be covered by proposed declaration of naval construction had been suggested. Foreign Minister had, after reporting recent conversation with you, brought the suggested alteration to the Cabinet's notice. Message added that delay in replying suggested that Japanese Foreign Office was endeavouring to avoid a blank refusal which might saddle Japan with responsibility for breakdown of the negotiations.

In view of the above Japanese Chargé d'Affaires was asked to call yesterday and his attention was drawn to the unfortunate publicity which had been given to the private conversation of September 27th.[3] Mr. Fujii was asked to use his influence to prevent similar leakages with reference to future conversations on this subject.

In subsequent conversation it was pointed out to Chargé d'Affaires that press message seemed to indicate that Japanese Government thought it necessary to send a definite reply to the suggestion made in regard to period of validity. This was not the case, since the suggestion had been merely put forward in order that the Japanese Government might reflect on it and

---

[1] No. 515.          [2] See *The Times*, October 10, p. 14.          [3] No. 510.

possibly discuss it with us later, together with any other proposals that might be made for facilitating general agreement. It was important that the Japanese Government should realise that, if a conference were called by His Majesty's Government, it would be for the purpose of carrying out the relevant provisions of the Washington and London Naval Treaties. It was not suggested that this or any other plan should be the basis of discussion at such a conference and each Government would be free to make any proposal it wished.

Mr. Fujii was further informed that the main purpose of the conversation of September 27th was to suggest that Mr. Fujii should be authorised to enter into discussions with us through the diplomatic channel, similar to the talks which are taking place with the American Embassy and will probably shortly take place with the French and Italian Embassies. The purpose of these talks, as of the earlier talks, was to prepare the way for a conference in accordance with the provisions of existing treaties.

You will see from the above that the suggestion made on September 27th has not been withdrawn, though we would deprecate any hasty decision by the Japanese Government. For your own information I may add that we would prefer that the Japanese Government should not return an answer on this point pending a decision in regard to the summoning of a naval conference.

## No. 522

*Memorandum by the Foreign Office and Admiralty on the course of the Naval Negotiations*[1]

*[A 8758/22/45]*

*October 11, 1935*

In a joint Foreign Office and Admiralty memorandum, dated the 18th July, 1935,[2] which was subsequently approved by the members of the Ministerial Committee, an outline was given of the procedure to be followed in the ensuing international discussions on the naval question. In this paper it was pointed out that, without under-estimating the importance of quantitative limitation, it was felt that the elimination of competition in the evolution of sizes of ships and gun calibres was a matter of even more urgent importance. It was proposed that, in view of the delay caused by French hesitation to enter into discussions with us, we should make a written communication to both the French and Italian Governments making definite proposals for future procedure, as indicated in paper N.C.M. (35) 58.[2]

2. This action was duly taken. Before making further recommendations for future procedure, it may be useful to give a summary of the terms of the memorandum communicated to the French and Italian Governments and of the subsequent oral and written communications which have passed on the subject with those Governments and with the Governments of the United States and Japan.

---

[1] This memorandum was circulated as N.C.M. (35) 72.

[2] No. 415.

# I. *Developments since the joint Foreign Office and Admiralty Memorandum of July 18, 1935*

. . .[3]

## II. *Present Position*

19. The situation resulting from these various exchanges and from the earlier conversations may now be summarised as follows:—

### (a) *Qualitative Limitation.*

20. The United States, French, Italian and German Governments are all prepared, *faute de mieux*, to become parties to an international agreement dealing with qualitative limitation only. The concurrence of the United States is, however, dependent on the acceptance of their proposals for heavier tonnage in the case of capital ships and cruisers than we consider necessary or desirable. The Japanese Government, on the other hand, while regarding it as of importance 'to reach agreement on general naval limitation comprising both qualitative and quantitative limits, are unable to agree to consider only qualitative limits apart from quantitative limits.'[4]

21. Assuming that it were possible to reach some compromise on this subject with Japan, the limits at which it seems possible that an international agreement on qualitative limitation might be attained are the following:—

*Capital Ships.*—35,000 tons with a 14-inch gun (instead of a 16-inch gun as under the Washington Treaty). This is the lowest limit to which the United States Government are at present prepared to agree, although their representatives have suggested the possibility that, with the experience gained in the construction of the first two new capital ships, the United States Government might be prepared to agree to a reduction of from 1,000 to 2,000 tons in the displacement of future ships.

Assuming that all the principal naval Powers, including Japan but excluding the United States, were prepared to agree to a 30,000-ton capital ship with a 14-inch gun, it has been tentatively suggested by the United States representatives that the United States of America should be left free to build capital ships up to 35,000 tons, on the understanding that the total capital ship tonnage of the United States should not exceed the total capital ship tonnage of the British Empire. Such a proposal implies the prior conclusion of a quantitative agreement laying down a definite ratio of naval strength as between the United States, Japan and the British Empire, and of this there is, at the moment, no hope whatever. But, apart from this, there are technical objections to the proposal, of which the following may be mentioned: The balance of tonnage allowed to the individual units to be built by the United States of America would permit the construction of ships superior in some or all of the important qualities other than gun calibre. Thus, they

---

[3] Paragraphs 3 to 18, here omitted, contained a chronological summary of developments relating to international discussions on the naval question between July 18 and October 7. For these developments see documents from file A 22/45 for this period printed above.

[4] A quotation from the Japanese Government's memorandum of July 26, 1935, see No. 485, note 2.

might have a greater number of guns, greater speed, greater air or anti-aircraft armament and, most important of all, greater protection against above-water and under-water attack. A limitation of the number of guns to 12, as suggested by the United States Embassy, would not equalise the position, because it would still be impossible to put an equal number of guns into the smaller ship without accepting inferiority in some other quality. Even if the number of ships could be limited, the advantage would rest with the United States of America in possessing a battlefleet of individually more powerful vessels. Since, in the ultimate resort, sea power rests upon the fighting strength of the battlefleet, this situation would be far removed from parity.

In the absence of any quantitative agreement, it is desirable to negotiate if possible a minimum limit to the size of any capital ship that may be constructed and the calibre of its guns, so as to produce a gap between the capital ship and the cruiser and make the cruiser qualitative limitation effective. France and U.S.A. are known to agree with this proposition, but the views of Italy and Japan on it are quite unknown.

*Aircraft Carriers.*—20,000 to 22,000 tons with a 6·1-inch gun.

*Cruisers.*—Construction of cruisers during the period of the agreement to be limited to cruisers not exceeding 10,000 tons with a 6·1-inch gun. (The effort to limit the number of large 6-inch gun cruisers has not been actually abandoned, but the attitude of the United States is not favourable to the proposal, and the Japanese Government are also unlikely to agree.)

*Destroyers.*—1,850 tons with a 5·1-inch gun (as in the London Naval Treaty), provided that agreement can be reached with the European Powers for making a division in the future between cruisers and destroyers. Since the prospects of such agreement are slight and it is undesirable that this country should continue to be at a disadvantage in this respect *vis-à-vis* of the other European Powers, it seems probable that there will be in the future a single category for cruisers and destroyers.

*Submarines.*—Retention of the London Naval Treaty limits, namely, 2,000 tons displacement with a 5·1-inch gun.

22. While it is obvious that the limits mentioned above are in some respects in excess of what we should like, the Admiralty and Foreign Office feel that, both from a technical and political point of view, it would be better to get agreement even on these relatively high limits than to see the naval Powers relapse into competition in the evolution of new and possibly even larger types of ships—a competition which has proved so costly in the past. The Admiralty, indeed, consider that from the point of view of reducing expense, the attainment of an agreement on qualitative limitation is even more important and urgent than on quantitative limitation. (See paper N.C.M. (35) 58, paragraph 4.)[2]

(*b*) *Quantitative Limitation.*

23. The position may be summarised as follows:—

While the United States tend to be insistent on their qualitative views, they have moved on the quantitative side a considerable distance from the attitude which they have consistently followed since the Geneva Naval Conference of 1927. For instance, they have recognised our need for a larger number of cruisers, and are not likely to put pressure on us about numbers, though they will maintain parity. The U.S. Government are also less insistent than they were on building cruisers with 8-inch guns, and they are prepared to reduce the calibre of gun for the capital ship from 16-inch to 14-inch.

24. With the exception of the United States and Germany no Power has accepted, as a basis of discussion, the British proposal for an agreement based on the making by each Power of a voluntary declaration limiting the new construction which it proposes to undertake over a period of, say, six years. Japan objects on the ground that the effect of this programme is to perpetuate the existing ratio in fact if not in name. France and Italy consider that the difficulties in the way of any such quantitative limitation are almost insuperable, and that it will be necessary for the Powers to content themselves with giving advance notice of their programmes of construction (i.e., the system of the 'préavis'). While therefore it may still be desirable, as a matter of tactics, that His Majesty's Government should submit to any naval conference that may be held a definite proposal for the regulation of future construction on the above basis, it is now most unlikely that the plan will secure general acceptance, at all events for so long a period as six years. As an alternative, the French system of the 'préavis' merits consideration. The difference between the French system and the British system is that, while under the first each Power would notify to the others, as far ahead as possible, the actual programme of construction, complete with all details, which it intends to put in hand in any given financial year, the British system provides that each Power should declare that, during a given period, its new construction in each category would not *exceed a certain maximum*. The main difficulty about the French system is that it would, unless the period of notice were to be quite short, appear to encroach on parliamentary prerogatives. For instance, in the case of this country, it would obviously be impossible to make to a foreign Government a notification in regard to the intention of His Majesty's Government to embark on a definite programme of construction before parliamentary sanction for that programme had been obtained. The British proposal of giving a maximum tonnage figure in each category is, however, free from this objection, seeing that Parliament would always be in the position to reduce the figure of actual construction below the maximum figure so communicated, and generally to modify the details of the programme for any given year within that maximum figure. A compromise with the French view has been tentatively and unofficially suggested by the Foreign Office to the Japanese Chargé d'Affaires[5] on the basis of reducing the period to be covered by the declarations of construction from six to, say, two years. This would be accompanied by a proposal limiting

---

[5] See No. 510.

the period of the 'préavis' to, say, six months (i.e., the normal interval between the passage of our naval estimates through Parliament and the laying down of the ships so authorised).

25. It must be remembered that the original Admiralty proposal for a treaty regulating quantitative limits for ten years has already been reduced to six. (See N.C.M. 35 (1) Part II.)[6] The Admiralty dislike a two-year agreement. The objection to a short-term agreement of this kind is that it would necessitate the holding of a further conference on quantitative limitation shortly, and the future strength of fleets would remain as uncertain as with no quantitative treaty at all. The British programmes for these two years are likely to be so large as to be not only misleading as to our genuine intentions, but to make the arrangement valueless for the purpose of limiting or reducing construction by any other Power. It is true a two years' agreement would have its uses if it enabled us to overcome Japan's objection to the conclusion of a qualitative treaty, and if Japan were to agree that the qualitative arrangement would be for a longer duration than the quantitative one. Although the choice before us, so far as quantitative limitation is concerned, may be either a short-term agreement of this character or no quantitative agreement at all, the Admiralty consider that a two years' quantitative agreement is definitely undesirable. The Foreign Office, while agreeing that a longer agreement would be far preferable, consider that the shorter agreement, if obtainable, may on this occasion serve a definite purpose. Many competent observers forecast that during the next two years moderating influences are likely to make themselves increasingly felt in the conduct of Japan's foreign policy, with the result that the Cabinet would be in a position to exercise better control over the extremists at the Japanese Ministry of Marine. (This assumes, of course, that war does not, in the meantime, break out in Europe.) If, however, at the end of that period, Japan is still disinclined to enter into a long-term agreement on a reasonable basis, it will be time enough to consider whether the effort to preserve the limitation of naval armaments should be definitely abandoned.

26. The present position of France and Italy is that they are not agreeable to any quantitative limitation, though they are in favour of a system of advance notice ('préavis').[7]

(c) *Other Provisions of the Treaty.*

27. The other provisions upon which it is hoped to reach agreement are the exchange of information, and the minor provisions of the Washington Treaty contained in Articles XIV, XVII and XVIII, dealing with preparations for the installation of armaments in merchant ships, the use of vessels of war under construction by other Powers, and the sale of vessels of war from one Contracting Power to another. The attitude of Japan towards the exchange of information is doubtful, but no difficulty is anticipated in reaching agreement with all Powers on the other points.

[6] This memorandum of March 23, 1934, is not here printed.
[7] See Nos. 472 and 491.

### III. *Possible Courses open to His Majesty's Government*

28. The relevant provisions of the Washington and London Naval Treaties dealing with the summoning of a new conference are as follows:—

Article XXIII, paragraph 2, of the Washington Naval Treaty:—

'Within one year of the date on which a notice of termination by any Power has taken effect, all the Contracting Powers shall meet in conference.'

(Japan's notice of termination took effect on the 29th December, 1934.)

Article 23, paragraph 2, of the London Naval Treaty:—

'Unless the High Contracting Parties should agree otherwise by reason of a more general agreement limiting naval armaments, to which they all become parties, they shall meet in conference in 1935 to frame a new treaty to replace and to carry out the purposes of the present Treaty, it being understood that none of the provisions of the present Treaty shall prejudice the attitude of any of the High Contracting Parties at the conference agreed to.'

29. Under each of the above provisions the summoning of a conference is mandatory, although the responsibility for taking the initiative does not rest with any one Power. In all the preparatory discussions His Majesty's Government have taken the initiative and, should they now decide that the results of the preparatory conversations do not justify their taking the further step of summoning a conference, it is desirable that the other Washington Powers should be so informed at the earliest possible moment. Otherwise, they may lay themselves open to the criticism that, having taken the initiative hitherto but failed to summon a conference, they have blocked the path of any other Power which might in other circumstances have been ready to summon a conference.

30. If a conference is summoned by His Majesty's Government, what are the chances of a successful outcome?

31. So far as the United States, France, Italy and this country are concerned, there seems every reason to believe that agreement could be reached on the qualitative limits set forth in section II (*a*) of this memorandum, on exchanges of advance information in regard to building intentions and on other minor provisions of the Washington and London Naval Treaties. (We also have the assurance of the German Government that they, too, would agree on all these points.) It is the definite opinion of the Admiralty that an agreement on these lines, if it could be made universal, would be of the greatest possible value in avoiding a race in new types and sizes of ships and in keeping down expense. From the political point of view also such an agreement would be of considerable value, particularly if the public were gradually prepared beforehand for the dropping of the quantitative form of limitation.

32. The question of the success or failure of a conference therefore depends on the attitude of Japan towards our proposals and on the extent to which

the other Washington Powers are prepared to continue qualitative limitation between themselves, irrespective of Japan's attitude.

33. Japan may—

(a) Remain completely uncompromising and refuse any sort of co-operation.

(b) Refuse to sign any treaty, but enter into a 'gentleman's agreement' that no Power will, without giving notice to the contrary, build types of ships which would fall outside the limits mutually agreed upon.

(c) Sign a qualitative treaty provided that a short-term quantitative arrangement (i.e., something less than the six years' arrangement which she rejects) can be reached simultaneously.

Course (b) above is on the whole the most probable, but, in estimating the chances of success, we must take all these possibilities into account.

34. The Admiralty view is that the conference should be called as already laid down in the previous treaties, and they do not consider that if it should prove a failure on account of the attitude of Japan, any odium would be cast on His Majesty's Government. The Admiralty also recommend that course (b) above should be accepted unless, better still, Japan falls in with the views of the other Powers when faced with their united front at the conference table.

35. The view of the Foreign Office is as follows: If, relying on the arrangement outlined in paragraph 36 below, His Majesty's Government would be prepared to enter into an agreement with the other naval Powers irrespective of the course which Japan may choose, a not unimportant result from the conference is assured in advance. If, on the other hand, His Majesty's Government were to decide that, should Japan adopt course (a), they must, on that account, refuse to be bound by a qualitative treaty with the other Washington Powers, then the risk of failure is considerable. It is true that the responsibility for that failure could be squarely placed on the shoulders of Japan, but it is inevitable that criticism should also be directed against the Government which had taken the initiative in summoning a conference, and His Majesty's Government may in that event deem it wiser not to take the risk.

36. It should be observed that, as stated in paragraph 16 of this memorandum, the United States Government would be ready to conclude a treaty with the other Washington Powers whichever course Japan were to follow.[8] Although the point has not yet been put to the French and Italian Governments, it may be assumed that they would conform their attitude in this matter to that taken up by the United Kingdom and the United States. It should also be remembered in this connexion that much greater elasticity could be retained under a qualitative than under a quantitative treaty. Thus, the proposed qualitative treaty could be drafted in such a way that any signatory Power would have the right to depart from the limits laid down in the treaty should any non-signatory Power construct a vessel falling outside

[8] See No. 520.

those limits. Liberation from treaty limits would thus be automatic and would depend solely on the fact of an 'irregular' construction by a non-signatory Power. There need be none of the difficulty associated with the invocation of an 'escalator' clause, as in the case of a quantitative treaty.

37. A decision on the points raised in the paragraphs 32–36 above seems to be essential before it is possible to estimate with any degree of accuracy the chances of success or failure of the proposed conference.

38. The courses open to His Majesty's Government may now be summarised as follows:—

(1) To inform the other signatory Powers that, having regard to the absence of any satisfactory basis of agreement between the Powers with which this country has been in consultation, His Majesty's Government propose to take no further initiative in this matter.

(2) To propose the postponement of the conference until next year.

(3) To summon a formal conference in the knowledge that the United States will insist on her maximum qualitative demands, but in the hope that Japan, once in conference, may find it easier to participate in such measure of agreement in other matters as the other four Powers may find possible. (If such an invitation is to be despatched, this should be done not later than the middle of October, since the Japanese Government always require at least two months' notice for the necessary preparations and the long journey to Europe.)

(4) To carry on the present diplomatic discussions with the representatives of the four Powers to a point at which it would be possible to summon, before the end of the present year, a Meeting of Ambassadors in London which could put the finishing touches to any agreement that might be in sight.

(5) To combine courses (3) and (4) as follows: Notify the Washington Powers at once that, unless any one of them raises serious objection, it is the intention of His Majesty's Government to issue invitations to a Conference at which the various countries could be represented by their Ambassadors, assisted by naval experts. It is suggested that at such a conference this country could appropriately be represented by the Secretary of State for Foreign Affairs and the First Lord of the Admiralty. The conference could be summoned to meet on, say, the 1st December, in London, to carry out the purposes of Article XXIII of the Washington Treaty and Article 23 of the London Naval Treaty.

39. Course (1) is a counsel of despair. If once it were followed, it would become more than ever difficult at some future time to gather together again the strings of this complex problem and to find a basis of agreement even on qualitative limitation. Such progress as has been achieved and such clarification of the varying attitudes as has been made in the past two years of preparation would be sacrificed.

40. Course (2), while superficially attractive, is open to two serious

objections. As things stand, the other signatories of the Washington Treaty are bound to attend a conference if summoned by one of the signatories during the present year, but indications are that Japan might be unwilling to do so next year except on her own terms. The second difficulty is that, owing to the necessity of getting out the designs of warships many months ahead of the date when the keel is laid down, the various Governments must, like His Majesty's Government, be on the eve of taking decisions in regard to future qualitative limits which may prove irrevocable (see also N.C.M. (35) 58, paragraph 1). Thus, from the qualitative point of view, a conference next year would probably prove much less useful than one held before the end of the present year. It would, however, always be possible to propose a postponement of the conference should the negotiations proposed under course (5) prove abortive.

41. In all the circumstances it is felt that course (5) offers the best prospects of success. Since the result we can hope for is relatively limited (i.e., qualitative limitation plus the minor provisions of existing treaties, as a six years' programme now seems impossible), it would seem unnecessary to go to the expense, trouble and publicity of summoning a full dress conference (course (3)). If foreign Governments desire to send technical advisers to assist their Embassies, this could be done without undue publicity in the course of the bilateral talks which, in the meantime, would be continued. Similarly, the Dominions could, if they so desire, be represented by their High Commissioners in London, though this may not be considered necessary during the technical discussions.

*Summary*

42. The position under Section III of this memorandum may therefore be summarised as follows: Both the Admiralty and the Foreign Office consider that, in all the circumstances, a conference should be summoned at once, on the lines suggested under course (5), paragraph 38.

43. The Foreign Office, like the Admiralty, consider a qualitative treaty obtained on the lines of course (*b*), paragraph 33, the least objectionable alternative. The Foreign Office also suggest that, if Japan were to follow course (*a*) or course (*c*), acceptance by His Majesty's Government of a qualitative agreement with the other Washington Powers would, in the last resort, be preferable to a complete breakdown of the conference. In that case, the risk of a failure of the conference would be practically nil.

44. The Admiralty, on the other hand, consider that, if Japan were to follow course (*a*), a qualitative agreement with the other three Washington Powers would be unacceptable, but agree that if necessary (*c*), as it does not affect our naval security, could be accepted if it is considered politically expedient to do so in order to obtain a long-term five-Power qualitative treaty.

## No. 523

### Letter from Mr. Atherton to Mr. Craigie (Received October 14)
### [A 8757/22/45]

LONDON, *October 12, 1935*

My dear Leslie:

In view of the naval conversations and possible naval conference, I am informed that the Navy Department would desire to send, if agreeable to the British Government, two Assistant Naval Attachés to London, to be assigned to the office of the Naval Attaché. This would obviate the appearance of any extended mission being sent to Europe in case a conference finally developed.

May I have a word of reply?[1]

Yours sincerely,
RAY ATHERTON

[1] In his reply of October 14 Mr. Craigie said that the proposal was 'entirely agreeable to His Majesty's Government'.

## No. 524

### Sir S. Hoare to Sir G. Clerk (Paris)
### No. 1850 [A 8772/22/45]

FOREIGN OFFICE, *October 16, 1935*

Sir,

M. Cambon, Counsellor at the French Embassy, called at the Foreign Office on October 8th. He stated confidentially that, whilst the Quai d'Orsay were anxious that French naval experts should be sent over to London as soon as possible to start discussions on questions of naval limitation, the Ministry of Marine were holding back and apparently wished to impose certain conditions.

2. M. Cambon was informed that, in the view of His Majesty's Government, the best procedure for the moment would be for any conversations to be held through the diplomatic channel. It was naturally understood that the French Ambassador or other representative of the French Embassy would be supported by a technical adviser and that the Admiralty would be similarly represented. This method had produced favourable results in the recent informal Anglo-American conversations and did not, as in the case of a special mission, attract the interest of the journalists to the same extent. It was made clear that similar Anglo-French informal conversations might take place without any publicity, with the result that the hesitation of the French Ministry of Marine might in some measure be overcome.

3. M. Cambon appeared to agree and said that in that case M. Corbin would probably represent the French Embassy.

4. It was explained to M. Cambon that the following deductions had been

drawn by His Majesty's Government from the French memorandum of the 14th August:—[1]

(a) that the French Government considered it important that an effort should be made to reach an agreement at least on qualitative limitation.

(b) that, if it were decided to hold a naval conference this year under the provisions of the Washington and London Naval Treaties, the French Government would be represented.

5. M. Cambon expressed the personal view that these deductions were correct, but undertook to make further enquiries of the French Government before giving a definite answer.

I am, &c.,<br>
SAMUEL HOARE

[1] No. 472.

## No. 525

### Sir E. Phipps (Berlin) to Sir S. Hoare (Received October 18)
#### No. 239 Saving: Telegraphic [C 7105/55/18]

BERLIN, October 17, 1935

The German press is showing great sensitiveness in regard to any suggestion that Germany may one day be the aggressor. Thus for example the 'Berliner Tageblett' objects to Sir Austen Chamberlain's interview[1] and the implication that England may well be called on to come to the assistance of France against Germany. On the other hand the 'Frankfurter Zeitung' published a telegram from Rome under the title 'Italy's Bad Argument: she threatens Paris with the German peril'. The author complains that Italy is showing little gratitude for Germany's attitude of strict neutrality.

[1] A reference presumably to Sir A. Chamberlain's interview with M. Bertrand de Jouvenel as reported in the *Paris-Soir* of October 16. Extracts from the report there printed were sent to the Foreign Office in Paris despatch No. 1461 of October 16 (J 6322/1/1), not here printed. They included the following: '. . . je me rends compte que Sir Austen m'a dit en somme: Si vous ne faîtes pas aujourd'hui abstraction de votre amitié pour l'Italie, si vous ne marchez pas à fond avec nous dans l'application de sanctions, ne comptez pas trop sur nous en cas de conflit avec l'Allemagne.'

## No. 526

### Memorandum by Mr. Craigie
#### [A 8992/22/45]

FOREIGN OFFICE, October 17, 1935

I handed to Prince von Bismarck to-day the reply[1] to the German memo-

[1] Printed as Appendix below.

randum, which was communicated by Captain Wassner on August 31st,[2] in regard to the application of the Anglo-German Agreement.[3] In doing so I said that it seemed to me that this exchange of memoranda would reduce to narrow limits the points on which there might be divergence. The only point on which I was apprehensive was lest the German Admiralty, in their desire to secure 'elbow room', were to strain Article 2(g) of the Anglo-German Agreement in such a way as to seek a virtual departure from Herr Hitler's declaration that in no circumstances should Germany's naval strength exceed 35 per cent of that of the United Kingdom. I asked Prince von Bismarck to be good enough to convey a private message from me to Herr von Ribbentrop, pointing out that the unfortunate political effect in this country of any step which might be represented by the enemies of the Anglo-German Agreement here as being a virtual increase in the ratio would be altogether out of proportion to any conceivable naval gain to Germany. It was therefore essential that every effort should first be made to compensate any increase in one category arising from the existence of surplus tonnage by a corresponding decrease in another category. It was only after the possibilities of transfer had been genuinely exhausted and it was found that a surplus still remained to be dealt with, that recourse should be had to Article 2(g) and even then only for some specified period of time. I hoped therefore that Herr von Ribbentrop would watch this question from the political as distinct from the purely naval angle.

Prince von Bismarck promised to convey this message. At his request I then gave him an outline of the present position, in regard to the holding of a naval conference during the present year, in the course of which I mentioned that we now saw little hope of getting international agreement for the size of the capital ship at any figure much below 35,000 tons.

R.L.C.

APPENDIX TO No. 526

*His Majesty's Government's reply to the German Memorandum of*
*August 31, 1935*

[*A 8991/22/45*]

*Confidential*                    FOREIGN OFFICE, *October 16, 1935*

His Majesty's Government in the United Kingdom have studied with interest the communication handed to the Deputy Chief of the Naval Staff by Captain Wassner on the 31st August, 1935.[2] They appreciate the friendly nature of this reply and now desire to offer the following observations upon it.

*Paragraph (c).*

2. His Majesty's Government note the intention of the German Government to transfer tonnage out of the Cruiser B. category when expanding their submarine

---

[2] The text of this German memorandum is printed in *D.G.F.P.*, Series C, vol. iv, No. 273, and is not here reproduced. It was the German Government's reply to the British memorandum of July 4 (see No. 488, note 4).          [3] Of June 18, 1935; see No. 348.

tonnage to the level of 45% of the British tonnage. As regards the German Government's statement that they regard it as their right to effect this transfer between any categories of ships they may choose, His Majesty's Government are in agreement with this statement in so far as it applies to the transfer of tonnage into the submarine category, as in the case under consideration. They would not be disposed, however, to accept this statement as applying to the question of transfer in general, which they consider is governed by paragraph 2(d) of Sir Samuel Hoare's note.[3] The final sentence of this paragraph runs as follows:—

> 'If no general treaty on naval limitation should be concluded, or if the future general treaty should not contain provision creating limitation by categories, the manner and degree in which the German Government will have the right to vary the 35% ratio in one or more categories will be a matter for settlement by agreement between the German Government and His Majesty's Government in the United Kingdom, in the light of the naval situation then existing.'

In the opinion of His Majesty's Government, therefore, the general question of transfer into categories other than the submarine category is still a matter for future discussion and agreement between the two Governments when the position as regards future naval limitation is clearer.

3. With reference to the last sub-paragraph of paragraph (c)[4] respecting aircraft carriers, His Majesty's Government agree that an adjustment of the tonnage in the aircraft carrier category should if necessary be made in accordance with paragraph 2(d) of the Agreement.

4. As regards the reference to paragraph 2(g) in this part of the German memorandum, the views of His Majesty's Government on the application of the terms of the Agreement to particular cases are as follows. They consider that the whole agreement is governed by the original proposal of the German Government that the future *strength* of the German navy should be 35% of the aggregate naval *strength* of the Members of the British Commonwealth of Nations. In the interpretation of this general governing consideration, paragraph 2(a) states that the total tonnage of the German Fleet 'shall never *exceed* a percentage of 35 of the aggregate tonnage of the naval forces of the Members of the British Commonwealth of Nations'. Paragraph 2(d), dealing with transfer, permits the principle of transferring tonnage between categories so as to modify the strict application of the category system. Paragraph 2(g) finally admits the possibility that, provided no substantial or permanent departure from the 35% ratio results, some excess over the tonnage represented by this ratio may occasionally be agreed upon. When therefore the German Government desire to increase the tonnage in a particular category above that permitted by the 35% ratio, they should, in the view of His Majesty's Government, first have recourse to the procedure of transfer in accordance with paragraph 2(d) and only resort to the method of adjustment, described in paragraph 2(g), in respect of such small quantities of tonnage as cannot be satisfactorily dealt with by transfer. Thus, clause 2(g) should never be strained so as to contradict clause 2(a) and cause any substantial or permanent departure from the general guiding principle of the agreement.

5. His Majesty's Government are disposed to suggest that a reasonable interpretation of the provision in Clause 2(g) that adjustment should not result in any 'permanent' departure from the 35% ratio would be assured if, whenever a

[4] Of the German Government's memorandum of August 31.

temporary excess was proposed, the German Government would indicate a definite date forecasting the time at which the temporary excess would come to an end, and that this date should not be unreasonably distant.

6. As regards the interpretation of the word 'substantial' in paragraph 2(g), the matter can best be dealt with by reference to paragraph (f) of the German Memorandum. An excess of about 3% of the total tonnage as contemplated in the German memorandum must, in the view of His Majesty's Government, be regarded as a 'substantial' one. So large an increase in the capital ship category as 15,000 tons should, it is considered, be dealt with by transfer from other categories, and this appears to be recognised in the German Memorandum itself when it states that 'probably no excess in the total fleet strength will occur'.

7. As regards the particular question of making up a possible deficiency in tonnage in the capital ship category in order to provide for a third German vessel, His Majesty's Government agree that the relinquishment of a possible 24,000 tons, or even 15,000 tons, could not be regarded as being more equitable than a possible excess in that category of vessel of 10,000 tons or 15,000 tons, provided that any excess in that category is dealt with by transfer as suggested in paragraph 4 above. As an equitable basis on which to work when this question of transfer arises, the following formula is suggested:—

'At no time shall the German capital ship tonnage exceed 35% of the British capital ship tonnage by more than half the tonnage of the maximum size of the capital ship allowed to be constructed by general agreement.'

*Paragraph (d).*

8. His Majesty's Government note with satisfaction the declaration of the German Government that they are prepared, subject to certain specified conditions, to accept in principle the British proposal that the German 35% of the British category of 'permanently over-age cruiser and destroyer tonnage' should be composed exclusively of similar over-age tonnage of these classes of ships. They also note the agreement expressed in paragraph (d) (1) as to the ages at which the cruisers *Emden* to *Nürnberg* and the destroyers of the *Möwe* and *Wolf* classes should be deemed to be over-age.

9. It is noted from paragraph (d) (3) that the German Government intend to use old cruiser tonnage for destroyer tonnage and vice versa. His Majesty's Government accordingly agree with the suggestion in paragraph (d) (2) of the German memorandum that the tonnage and not the number of ships shall be decisive for calculating the 35%. They had only refrained from giving the tonnage of the permanently over-age cruisers on account of the uncertainty as to the particular vessels that would be so retained, and the variations in the tonnage caused by the changing of these ships from time to time. In view of paragraph (d) (2) of the German Memorandum, however, His Majesty's Government are prepared to state a tonnage for the permanently over-age cruisers they intend to retain. As far as can be foreseen this tonnage will, by about 1942, amount to some 42,000 tons, and in subsequent years may rise as larger cruisers pass into this particular category. For the purposes of the present discussion, therefore, it is proposed to use the figure 55,000 tons which will probably be larger than the actual tonnage to be retained in this category at any time which can now be foreseen, and thus cannot be disadvantageous to the German Government. Thus, the British permanently over-age cruiser and destroyer tonnage combined may amount to 105,000 tons, and Germany would then have the right to 35% of this tonnage, i.e. 36,760 tons.

10. In paragraph (d) (3) of their Memorandum the German Government give reasons why the 14 old destroyers and torpedo boats cannot be reckoned in this tonnage. His Majesty's Government accept the contention in the memorandum that these vessels must be scrapped in the near future and cannot therefore be retained as part of the permanently over-age tonnage.

[11.] In paragraph (d) (4) the German Government make proposals for meeting the difficulty resulting from the absence of over-age tonnage in the German Fleet. It should here be observed that the proposals to reduce the age limit of the ships built in accordance with the provisions of the Treaty of Versailles was put forward not because the proper United Kingdom authorities thought it 'absolutely impossible' to keep them in service any longer, but solely in order to assist in solving the problem of filling the permanent over-age category. His Majesty's Government agree that these vessels should not be kept up to ages of 30 for cruisers or 23 years for destroyers. They also agree in principle with the solution proposed by the German Government that, after a certain period, these vessels should be replaced in the permanently over-age category by a corresponding tonnage in newer cruisers or destroyers to be 'moved up' in their stead, irrespective of whether they have or have not already reached the prescribed age, provided that the process does not result in any excess of the tonnage in the over-age cruiser and destroyer categories over and above that to which the German Government are entitled at the time.

12. In applying this principle, however, His Majesty's Government desire to point out that the 20 years age limit proposed by the German Government for the cruisers in question is the ordinary age limit of cruisers, and that the cruisers which the United Kingdom will keep in this over-age category will for many years be vessels which, by reason of war service, cannot be made to last so long as ships more recently built. In this category His Majesty's Government will normally keep cruisers up to 24 years of age, and for many years to come ships will have to be retained to a considerably greater age. Similar observations apply to the destroyers to be placed in this category, and it may be observed that the age at which the German Government propose that their existing destroyers shall be scrapped—15 years—is one year less than the normal under-age life of modern destroyers.

13. His Majesty's Government, therefore, suggest that the 6 cruisers from the *Emden* to the *Nürnberg* should not be replaced until the age of 22 years by newer tonnage to be 'moved up' into the permanently over-age category, and that the 12 destroyers of the *Möwe* and *Wolf* classes should similarly not be replaced until the age of 16 years. They agree, also, that this special arrangement would automatically cease as soon as the over-age tonnage category is filled with cruisers and destroyers completed after 1935.

14. His Majesty's Government note the declaration of the German Government in paragraph (d) (5) that they reserve the right in principle to revoke their assent to these proposals on the occurrence of special circumstances. His Majesty's Government suggest that, since this reservation deals with a similar point to that mentioned in paragraph 2 (c) of Sir Samuel Hoare's note,[3] the German Government should in the same way agree that the new situation should be examined between the two Governments before the German Government revoke their assent to these proposals.

15. With reference to paragraph (e) of the German Memorandum, His Majesty's Government agree that, should no new treaty applicable to all the naval powers

concerned regulate the length of the life of capital ships, this question should form the subject of agreement between the German and British Governments. In this connection they would point out that, although in the Washington Treaty the life of capital ships was fixed at 20 years, the capital ship building holiday enforced by the London Naval Treaty overrode that provision of the Washington Treaty, and that since that date general agreement was reached, when discussing the Draft Disarmament Convention produced by the Preparatory Commission of the Disarmament Conference in 1930, that 26 years would be a suitable life for capital ships in the future. His Majesty's Government themselves agree with this proposal.

16. As regards the 3 vessels of the *Deutschland* class, His Majesty's Government are for their part prepared to agree that a 15 year life shall be applied to these vessels, i.e. that these vessels may be scrapped when they reach the age of 15 years and the tonnage thus released be applied to fresh capital ship building.

17. His Majesty's Government note the declaration of the German Government in paragraph (g) that, in the absence of any general agreement to build no more category A cruisers, they are unable to agree to provide the necessary amount of tonnage for the completion of capital ships by the renunciation of two Category A cruisers.[5]

[5] In a lengthy 'Answer to the U.K. Memorandum of October 16, 1935' (A 10060/22/45), dated November 23, 1935, the German Government welcomed generally 'the appreciation of their proposals by the British Government' and with regard to paragraph 2 (g) of Sir S. Hoare's note of June 18, 1935, made the following comment. 'The German Government propose as the main principle to be applied in this connexion [i.e. how far adjustment was permissible to Germany] that the total amount of the adjustments obtaining at a given date should not exceed half the displacement of the standard battleship and that the term of an adjustment should not be longer than 10 years. In making this proposal the German Government expect that this principle will not be interpreted in a narrow sense and that when necessary in the case of small excess amounts an agreement will be reached by friendly negotiations between the British and German Governments.' With regard to paragraph 13 of the British memorandum of October 16, however, the German Government felt that the six cruisers were considerably less efficient in fighting strength as compared with the 'B' class of other countries. They therefore regretted 'that they are unable to assent to this one point in the British proposal (to undertake the replacement of the cruisers only after twenty-two years). They repeat their proposal that the six cruisers in question should be replaced after twenty years by newer tonnage to be transferred to the permanently over-age category.'

### No. 527

*Draft*[1] *Record of Meeting held in Foreign Office at 10.30 a.m. on Thursday, October 17, 1935*

[*A 8892/22/45*]

*Present*: Mr. R. L. Craigie, Captain V. H. Danckwerts, Mr. Ray Atherton, Captain Anderson.

The American representatives handed in the attached Précis of Conversation (Annex I).[2] This was read through and discussed as follows.

*Paragraph 1.*

2. Mr. Craigie asked the exact meaning of the last sentence which asks

[1] Thus in heading on filed copy.
[2] Cf. *F.R.U.S. 1935*, vol. i, pp. 125–7. See note 5 below.

for a 'definite comprehensive statement' in return. It was made clear that this did not mean a public statement of any kind but merely that the U.S. Government desired to receive definite replies to the points put forward in this Précis. Their meaning would be better presented by the substitution of the word 'answer' for the word 'statement' in paragraph 1.

3. In a subsequent part of the conversation Mr. Craigie stressed the importance of maintaining the position that in these bi-lateral conversations documents were not being exchanged. It was agreed that a Précis of Conversation did not constitute a document and that it was simply a record of the oral exchange of views, and that this course should be taken as regards any British reply.

*Paragraphs 2, 3, 4 and 5 call for no comment.*

*Paragraph 6.*

4. Captain Danckwerts made it clear that the 20,000 ton figure which had been mentioned in the previous conversation was a very tentative one, and might certainly be varied as the question was developed in the future. Captain Anderson confirmed that this was the exact position of the U.S.A. in the matter.

*Paragraphs 7 and 8 call for no comment.*

*Paragraph 9.*

5. Captain Danckwerts asked what was meant by the expression 'as part of a comprehensive accord on cruisers'. In reply, Captain Anderson gave the impression that the U.S.A., like ourselves, have no desire to build any more 8″ gun cruisers (though without prejudice to the possible replacement of the existing ships when they become over-age), but that they do not wish to bind themselves to this unless the general structure of the agreement reassures them as to their decision *vis à vis* other Powers. It was understood that the 'comprehensive accord' did not necessarily include a quantitative arrangement on the lines of paragraph 10.

*Paragraph 10.*

6. Mr. Craigie again made it clear that we do not now think it possible to reach any quantitative agreement of the same kind as that of the London Naval Treaty. Thus, any discussion on matters, such as the transfer system, which are dependent upon quantitative limitation by tonnage and categories is really academic. The U.S. representatives agreed with this statement.

7. Paragraph 10 was then discussed, subject to this governing consideration. Captain Anderson and Mr. Atherton did not seem very certain as to the exact meaning of this paragraph, but in view of the last sentence they stated that in their opinion it really only envisaged a moderate proportion of transfer between Category B cruisers and destroyers, and not a proposition to give transfer into the capital ship or submarine categories.

*Paragraph 11 required no comment after the previous discussion.*[3]

[3] See No. 540 below for a later comment on this paragraph.

*Paragraph 12(a).*

8. Mr. Craigie made it clear, with reference to the second sentence of this paragraph, that the British desire to retain 50,000 tons of over-age destroyers was connected with the submarine tonnage to be retained by foreign Powers and that it could not be related to the desired cruiser increase. He said it would be very unfortunate if the American Government maintained the view expressed in this paragraph that over-age and under-age tonnage must all be counted together, although the whole matter was now, as before explained, somewhat academic. Captain Anderson suggested that perhaps if the United Kingdom were to retain over-age cruiser tonnage the U.S.A. might compensate herself by building new cruiser tonnage instead. It was explained that this would scarcely be acceptable to the British Government. In the course of the discussion the British representatives mentioned that a very much more satisfactory solution from the British point of view would be reached if over-age tonnage were altogether excluded from any future quantitative agreement, and mentioned that this suggestion had actually been made by the Japanese representatives at Geneva before the Japanese Government took up its present attitude. This proposition seemed to interest Captain Anderson considerably. The discussion of this point since it was more or less academic was then abandoned.

*Paragraph 12(b)* called for no comment.

*Paragraph 13.*

9. Considerable discussion took place concerning the suggestion contained in this paragraph for establishing a 'ratio' of say 3 : 1 between destroyer and submarine tonnage for the purpose of inducing nations to reduce the latter. Captain Danckwerts stated that the Admiralty would not like to pin themselves to a definite numerical ratio of this kind if the proposal referred to the process of negotiating figures to be inserted in the Treaty. If, however, the proposal was for a kind of yardstick transfer that should apply within treaty figures once they had been agreed to there might be less objection to a hard and fast figure, though as with all these quantitative questions, the matter was somewhat academic. Captain Anderson indicated that he thought the proposal was the latter one.

*Paragraph 14.*

10. Captain Danckwerts reminded the American representatives that Part IV of the London Naval Treaty did not terminate with the rest of the Treaty at the end of 1936, so that it was not necessary to negotiate it again as between the three Powers who had ratified the London Naval Treaty but only to extend it to other Powers by some means.

11. The remaining paragraphs called for no comment.[4]

---

[4] A further meeting of British and United States representatives was held in the afternoon of October 28, see *F.R.U.S. 1935*, vol. i, pp. 132–4. A memorandum of October 29 by the Foreign Office and Admiralty summarizing these discussions was circulated as N.C.M. (35) 78. It included the following passage:— 'The general effect of this Anglo-American Exchange of views is to reduce to very small dimensions the margin of difference

*Précis of Conversation submitted by the American representatives*

(1) As a result of the recent informal and tentative exchange of views on naval questions, Mr. Atherton and Captain Anderson presented the American Government's views in as direct terms as possible, as follows hereafter. The American Government considers it essential to present a final, unequivocal position, to which it is hoped a definite comprehensive statement may be returned.

(2) With regard to capital ships, referring to the proposition that subject to American, British or Japanese concurrence, there should be no American, British or Japanese construction whatever with guns larger than 14-inch, but that the first two capital ships could be of the present allowed individual maximum displacement: the American Government concurs, and further agrees to:

(3) the proposition that the British would urge the French and Germans to keep down to 14-inch caliber the guns of the capital ships they are now building, although it is realised it is too late to get the Italians to do this.

(4) The American Government understands if this could be accomplished there would then be only two post-Treaty capital ships in existence with guns larger than 14-inch, that is the Italian ones, but if it could not be accomplished, there would then only be two such vessels for each of the three countries, Italy, France and Germany and that:

(5) *in any event* all capital ships subsequent to the two now building or scheduled in each of the three beforenamed countries should be limited to 14-inch guns.

(6) Referring to the British proposal for a minimum displacement limit for capital ships at approximately 20,000 tons, the American Government is in general accord.

(7) Referring to the British suggestion of an age limit of 26 years for capital ships, the American Government concurs.

(8) With regard to Aircraft Carriers, the American Government perceives no objection to the proposed maximum of 22,000 tons with 6·1-inch guns.

(9) With regard to cruisers, referring to the British proposal that no more

between the Americans and ourselves. It is true that there has been no recent discussion with the Americans of figures for inclusion in a quantitative agreement, but it is most unlikely that the Conference will ever get down to a discussion of details on the quantitative side of the question. Furthermore, there would probably still be found to be certain divergences on technical points if we were to attempt to negotiate a quantitative agreement on the old basis of limitation by total tonnages in categories. But, since the prospects of concluding an agreement on such a basis are nil, the points are purely academic.

For all practical purposes, therefore, we are justified in counting on American cooperation in the forthcoming Conference.'

[5] No Annex was attached to the filed copy of No. 527. The précis of conversation submitted by the United States representatives was circulated as Annex I to N.C.M. (35) 78 (see note 4 above).

8-inch gun cruisers be built, the American Government, as part of a comprehensive accord on cruisers, might be disposed to agree not to build at the present time 8-inch cruisers except as replacements of the 18 existing ships.

(10) Referring to the British desire for an increase in 6-inch gun cruisers, the American Government's action must be contingent on acceptance of a transfer system which will permit the United States to distribute any Category 'B' cruiser tonnage in excess of present limitations among other types as needed by the United States. The American Government stresses a general solution of the cruiser problem with moderate transfer clauses because it deems such a solution more susceptible to acceptance by other nations.

(11) Referring to the British view that at the present moment, particularly with the Japanese attitude undefined, it is impracticable to discuss any quantitative limitation now, even such as building agreements, the American Government concurs with the British view as further expressed that when the time for such discussion came Britain and America would have no difficulty in coming to a satisfactory mutual agreement.

(12 a) With regard to destroyers, the American Government appreciates the desire of the British Government for 50,000 tons of over-age destroyers. Unfortunately, however, this increase if unrelated to or not included in the desired cruiser increase results in still further increase of total tonnage. In general, the American Government considers that no distinction should be made between over-age and under-age tonnage in any category and that the question should be answered by necessary category increases or in emergency by utilisation of escape clauses.

(12 b) The American Government sees the logic of the British objection to present treaty qualitative limitations of destroyers, but feels that a general method of solution may be found by limited transfer between destroyer and cruiser B categories. However, the American Government will consider any proposal the British may make to end the difficulty in which they find themselves in respect to qualitative limitations of destroyers.

(13) With regard to submarines, the American Government does not favor reduction in present characteristics of submarines and considers reduction of that category tonnage as the only feasible method of limiting submarines. It concurs generally in the British attitude as to the relationship of destroyer tonnage to submarine tonnage. The American Government suggests for consideration as a means of influencing reduction of submarine tonnage an allowance at the ratio, for example, of 3 : 1, of destroyer tonnage for purposes of defence against submarines on the part of nations who desire to reduce their allowed submarine tonnage.

(14) Referring to the London Treaty, Part 4, subject 'Submarine Warfare', the American Government concurs in the British view that the next naval agreement is not the best place for rules for submarine warfare, but that they should be in a separate protocol to which it is hoped adherence of all nations might be obtained.

(15) With regard to miscellaneous items, referring to the British Government's mention of Article 19 of the Washington Treaty and the expressed

British view that this is not a subject for discussion at this stage, the American Government concurs.

(16) Referring to the British Memorandum of August 2, paragraph 8, and the British view in connection with reciprocal notification relating to laying down new ships and the French desire expressed at Geneva for (pre-avis) earlier notification, the American Government concurs generally with the expressed British view as to constitutional and technical difficulties for more than six months notification.

(17) Referring to the other items from existing naval treaties mentioned in paragraph 8 of the British Memorandum of August 2, the American Government concurs that they form a proper basis for consideration at the Conference with continuation probable.

## No. 528

*Sir S. Hoare to Sir E. Phipps (Berlin)*
*No. 1100 [C 7125/55/18]*

FOREIGN OFFICE, *October 17, 1935*

The German Ambassador called upon me this afternoon after his return from six weeks' leave. He was particularly anxious to learn more of the recent developments at Geneva and to point the moral of French wickedness. I did my best to ignore his many aspersions upon French perfidy, and I took the opportunity of pointing out to him one of the lessons that the German Government should learn from the crisis. The British Government and the British public were showing their deep interest in the League, but in the League as the organ of resistance to unprovoked aggression from whatever quarter that unprovoked aggression might come. We had refused to accept the interpretation of the Covenant as a treaty directed against any single Power or group of Powers. Our conception of the League was the conception of an institution designed for the impartial and comprehensive maintenance of peace.

2. I went on to tell the Ambassador that I had noted two types of misstatement in the German press. Firstly, it was being assumed that our interest in the Abyssinian controversy was due to our desire to destroy the Fascist Government. No such motive was in our minds. Every country must decide for itself its own form of government, and we had no desire to intervene in what does not concern us. Secondly, the view was being expressed in certain sections of the German press that war was inevitable between Great Britain and Italy. There was not the least foundation for any such statements. We had never contemplated isolated action, and the last thing in the world that we desired was war with an old friend. There had been no talk of military sanctions and the only way that war could break out would be as the result of some mad and provocative act by Italy.

3. The Ambassador asked me some questions as to the last French note.[1]

[1] Cf. No. 518, note 3.

684

Were we going to answer it and were we likely to admit the French comments in it that had so much disturbed the German Government? I told him that there was no risk of our taking any action that would give the German Government ground for saying that the basis of Locarno had been compromised.

4. Finally, I had some talk upon the subject of Memel. I took the opportunity of telling the Ambassador that for the last three months I had been constantly pressing the Lithuanian Government to carry out in the letter and in the spirit the Memel Convention. This pressure would have been more quickly successful if the Italian Government had not time after time refused to act with the French and ourselves. Thanks to our efforts, the elections had passed off without much trouble.[2] A large German majority had been returned, and the Lithuanian Government ought now to deal with the Directorate in the spirit of the Convention. The Ambassador seemed grateful for what we had done in the matter and assured me that if the chief German grievances could be reasonably met, the German Government would be prepared to resume normal relations with Lithuania.

5. As this was the first interview that I had had with the Ambassador for some weeks I thought it best not to raise at once with him any question as to the attitude of Germany towards the Abyssinian controversy and the economic sanctions.

I am, &c.,
SAMUEL HOARE

[2] See *The Times*, September 28, p. 12, for the text of the note of September 27 sent by Great Britain, France, and Italy, the Guarantors of the Memel Statute of 1924, to the Secretary-General of the League of Nations expressing their satisfaction with the Lithuanian Government's reply to their representation concerning the elections to be held in Memel on September 29.

## No. 529

*Sir S. Hoare to Mr. Osborne (Washington)*
*No. 962 [J 6368/1/1]*

FOREIGN OFFICE, *October 17, 1935*

Sir,
The American Ambassador came to see me this morning. . . .[1]

4. Before leaving, the Ambassador spoke of the possibilities of a Naval Conference. He said that his Government were anxious for it and that, in his view, the American atmosphere was favourable. When I asked him as to what he thought about time and dates, he said that he himself intended to leave London in the middle of December and that, so far as his own convenience was concerned, he would greatly prefer that the detailed discussions did not begin until February. He was most anxious to take part in the discussions himself and would greatly prefer that the delegation should be as small as possible, the American delegates consisting only of himself

[1] The first three paragraphs of this despatch dealt with the Italo-Ethiopian question.

and Admiral Standley. I said that we must, of course, take into account the convenience of the participants but that one of the difficulties as to a postponement until so late a date was the complication of naval programmes.

I am, &c.,

SAMUEL HOARE

## No. 530

*Sir S. Hoare to H.M. Representatives at Berlin, Brussels, Paris, and Rome*

*No. 202[1] Telegraphic [C 7126/55/18]*

FOREIGN OFFICE, *October 18, 1935, 9 p.m.*

We think it possible that when Parliament meets next week the Government will be asked what effect Germany's withdrawal from the League of Nations (which now becomes definite) has on Treaty of Locarno.

2. Should such a question be put, I shall reply that, under Article 17 of the Covenant, the provisions of the Articles of the Covenant referred to in the Treaty of Locarno can become applicable to disputes where one of the parties is not a member of the League, and therefore there is a means by which all the provisions of the Treaty of Locarno can still receive their due application in the new circumstances.

3. You should so inform the Government to which you are accredited, but you should not ask for a reply to your communication.

[1] No. 202 to Berlin, No. 86 to Brussels, No. 287 to Paris, No. 537 to Rome.

## No. 531

*Sir S. Hoare to Sir E. Drummond (Rome)*

*No. 1172 [A 8837/22/45]*

FOREIGN OFFICE, *October 18, 1935*

Sir,

With reference to my telegram No. 501[1] of October 9th, I transmit to you herewith, for purposes of record, copies of the letters[2] exchanged between the Italian Ambassador in London and Sir Robert Vansittart, in which the former conveyed an assurance of the readiness of his Government to send Italian naval experts to London for preliminary conversations regarding the forthcoming Naval Conference.

2. Signor Vitetti, Counsellor of the Italian Embassy, called at the Foreign Office on October 10. He explained that the assurance given by his Government should not be regarded as a new Italian initiative but rather as a repercussion of the conversation which he had at the Foreign Office in August last in connexion with His Majesty's Government's memorandum of July 30th, on the subject of limitation of naval armaments. He was then given a brief outline of the position which had now been reached as regards the

[1] No. 516.        [2] Not printed.

various questions connected with naval limitation. He was told that it had been concluded from the Italian memorandum of September 4th last[3] that the Italian Government would be prepared to enter into a qualitative agreement even if no quantitative agreement could be achieved and that they would also be prepared to be represented at any conference that might be summoned for the purpose. Signor Vitetti said that this was also his understanding of the position but that he would make enquiries from his Government in the matter.

3. As regards the question of the Italian Government sending a naval mission to London, it was explained that although it might be very useful for representatives of the Italian and British Governments to discuss naval questions, it seemed to His Majesty's Government preferable that such discussions should for the time being be confined to the diplomatic channel with the addition of an Italian technical expert and a representative of the Admiralty. This was the method which had been tried with some success in the case of the recent informal Anglo-American conversations and it had the advantage of avoiding undue publicity. Similar procedure had already been suggested to the French and Japanese Governments.

4. Signor Vitetti expressed his personal approval of this procedure, but undertook to ascertain the views of his Government on this point as soon as possible. In conclusion he was informed that no decision had yet been taken in London as to whether or not a conference could usefully take place this year.

I am, &c.,
(for the Secretary of State)
J. M. TROUTBECK

³ No. 491.

## No. 532

*Sir S. Hoare to Sir R. Clive (Japan)*
*No. 567 [A 8846/22/45]*

FOREIGN OFFICE, *October 18, 1935*

Sir,

In my telegram No. 203[1] of October 11th I communicated to you a brief record of a meeting which took place at the Foreign Office on October 10th with the Japanese Chargé d'Affaires and Mr. Terasaki, secretary to the Japanese Embassy, on the subject of limitation of naval armaments.

2. In the course of the interview, Mr. Terasaki, who appeared better informed than Mr. Fujii, expressed the view that the Japanese Government were bound to come to a decision on the question of the reduction of the term of validity for any future quantitative agreement before deciding whether any useful purpose would be served by further Anglo-Japanese naval discussions. His Majesty's Government knew, he thought, exactly what the view of the Japanese Government was, however distasteful this might be. As this view remained unchanged, he enquired what could be the

¹ No. 521.

purpose of further discussions between representatives of the Japanese and British Governments.

3. Mr. Terasaki was informed that His Majesty's Government could hardly believe that the Japanese Government really intended to wreck all future hope of naval limitation merely for the sake of a theory which was acceptable to no other naval Power. Moreover, there had been discussions with other Powers since the naval discussions of last autumn and it was possible that information in regard to the views of other Powers might modify those of the Japanese Government. Nevertheless, His Majesty's Government had no wish to place any pressure on the Japanese Government in the matter but merely desired to ascertain whether the Japanese Government would be disposed to open discussions with His Majesty's Government on the same lines as those with other signatories of the Washington Treaty. If the Japanese Government were unwilling, there was no more to be said.

4. It was then explained to Mr. Terasaki that His Majesty's Government were at a loss to understand why the Japanese Government should have declined hitherto to discuss qualitative limitation merely on account of the difficulty of reaching a quantitative agreement. He replied with the well-worn argument about the seas round Japan being rougher than those in other parts of the world, and pointed out that this fact necessitated the evolution of special types of vessels. He was asked whether any Power had indicated that, in concluding a qualitative agreement, it would not be prepared to consider the inclusion of types specially suitable for Japanese requirements. The answer was in the negative.

5. Mr. Fujii then enquired as to any developments resulting from the recent Anglo-American informal discussions. He was told that these discussions had mainly centred on the question of the desirability or otherwise of a conference being held this year, and further that it had been ascertained that the United States Government were in favour of such a step. The *desiderata* of the various naval Powers had also been under consideration but no discussion of technical matters bearing on quantitative limitation had taken place.

I am, &c.,
SAMUEL HOARE

## No. 533

*Sir S. Hoare to Sir R. Lindsay (Washington)*

*No. 311 Telegraphic*[1] *[A 8963/22/45]*

FOREIGN OFFICE, *October 21, 1935, 11 p.m.*

An oral communication in the following general sense was made to-day to the Counsellor of the United States Embassy[2]:

His Majesty's Government in the United Kingdom have been giving

[1] A similarly worded telegram was despatched on the same day to Tokyo (No. 209), Rome (No. 546), and Paris (No. 289).

[2] Alternatively: Counsellor of the Japanese, Italian, French Embassy.

careful consideration to the results of the preliminary bilateral conversations which have been proceeding between representatives of the signatory Powers of the Washington and London Naval Treaties to prepare the way for a Naval Conference. In view of the express provisions of Article XXIII of the Washington Naval Treaty and of Article 23 of the London Naval Treaty, which lay down that those Powers must meet in conference during the present year, and in view of the fact that this country has so far taken the initiative in arranging for these bilateral discussions, His Majesty's Government are prepared to summon a Conference to meet in London on December 2nd next. The purpose of this Conference would be to secure agreement on as many aspects as possible of naval limitation with a view to the conclusion of an international treaty which would take the place of the two Naval Treaties expiring at the end of 1936. It is hoped that, once agreement is in sight between the representatives of the signatory Powers, the scope of the Conference may be extended so as to include representatives of the other naval Powers, but this will be a matter for discussion in the first instance between the representatives of the Washington and London Naval Powers. Formal invitations to the Conference will probably be despatched in the course of the present week and the present confidential communication is merely designed to give the United States Government[3] advance notice of the more formal communication to follow.

The suggestion was made that, as a matter of convenience and in order to keep the size of Delegations as small as possible, the head of each Delegation should be the Ambassador in London. In any event it is hoped that there will be authoritative naval representation from the start.

[3] Alternatively: Japanese, Italian, French Government.

## No. 534

*Sir R. Clive (Tokyo) to Sir S. Hoare (Received October 22, 1.10 p.m.)*
*No. 271 Telegraphic [A 8984/22/45]*

TOKYO, *October 22, 1935, 7.50 a.m.*

I called on Minister for Foreign Affairs today to present Mr. Wiggin[1] and Australian Trade Commissioner.

His Excellency said that he had received telegram from Japanese Chargé d'Affaires on lines of your telegram No. 209.[2] He asked if Ambassador was to be senior delegate in each case. I said that I understood this was proposed and enquired whether M. Matsudaira would return for the Conference. He said this was impossible but probably M. Sato Japanese Ambassador at Paris would be instructed to act as senior Japanese delegate. The latter had experience of Disarmament Conference and had attended London Naval Conference.

[1] Mr. A. F. H. Wiggin, previously First Secretary in H.M. Embassy at Washington, had been appointed Acting Counsellor in H.M. Embassy at Tokyo.
[2] See No. 533.

## No. 535

*Sir R. Clive (Tokyo) to Sir S. Hoare (Received October 22, 1.10 p.m.)*
*No. 272 Telegraphic [A 8976/22/45]*

TOKYO, *October 22, 1935, 7.50 p.m.*

My immediately preceding telegram.[1]

I subsequently met Matsudaira who spoke highly of Mr. Sato's competence and suitability.

He regretted intransigeant [*sic*] attitude of the Navy and saw little chance of their moderating this attitude.

[1] No. 534.

## No. 536

*Sir E. Phipps (Berlin) to Sir S. Hoare (Received October 24)*
*No. 1060 [C 7199/55/18]*

BERLIN, *October 22, 1935*

Sir,

I have the honour to inform you that the termination of the notice given by the German Government two years ago of withdrawal from the League of Nations has passed almost without comment by the German press.

2. Such comment as there is takes the line that all Germany will agree with the words of the Minister of the Interior, reported in my savingram No. 223 [233][1] of the 14th October, to the effect that 'there is not one among us who is not happy that the Führer took this decisive step two years ago'. Germany had been unable to secure recognition of her rights in Geneva. That which she had vainly begged other Powers for years to grant she had since obtained in a few months by her own efforts. The 14th October (the day on which the German Government gave notice of withdrawal from the League)[2] would therefore, like the 16th March,[3] be a proud day in German history.

I have, &c.,
ERIC PHIPPS

[1] Berlin Savingram No. 233 of October 14 reported a speech by Herr Frick, Minister of the Interior, at Saarbrücken on October 12, 1935, in which he said that Germany's withdrawal from the League would become legally effective on October 14, 1935.

[2] See Volume V, No. 454.

[3] See Volume XII, No. 570.

# No. 537

*Sir E. Phipps (Berlin) to Sir S. Hoare (Received October 23, 10.15 p.m.)*
*No. 305 Telegraphic [C 7207/55/18]*

BERLIN, *October 23, 1935, 9.41 p.m.*

Your telegram No. 202.[1]

Minister for Foreign Affairs asked me to come and speak to him this afternoon.

Baron von Neurath remarked, with reference to the note[2] which I had addressed to him on October 19th with a view to carrying out instructions in your telegram under reply, that he must make a certain reservation as to *procedure* in regard to this matter, although the German Government were quite in agreement regarding substance of the matter at issue, viz., the continued application of all provisions of the Treaty of Locarno. His Excellency added that this merely meant that the German Government did not necessarily accept the view that they, although no longer members of the League, should continue to be bound by provisions of article 17 of the Covenant.

His Excellency pointed out that the German Government had more or less indicated their point of view as to the right procedure after Germany left the League in article 1 of draft air pact which the German Ambassador handed to your predecessor on May 28th.[3]

Baron von Neurath indicated that the German Government did not mean to address any written communication to His Majesty's Government on this point, and I gathered that his reservation was really academic.

[1] No. 530.
[2] Not printed. A copy of this note was received in the Foreign Office on October 25 as enclosure in Berlin despatch No. 1066 of October 23.     [3] See Annex to No. 263.

# No. 538

*Note from Sir S. Hoare to Mr. Bingham[1]*
*[A 8984/22/45]*

FOREIGN OFFICE, *October 24, 1935*

Your Excellency,

His Majesty's Government in the United Kingdom have been giving careful consideration to the results of the preliminary bilateral conversations which have been proceeding between representatives of the signatory Powers of the Washington and London Naval Treaties to prepare the way for a naval conference.[2] In view of the express provisions of Article XXIII

[1] A similarly worded note, *mutatis mutandis*, was sent to M. Corbin, Signor Grandi, and Mr. Fujii.
[2] The Cabinet on October 23 considered the report of the Ministerial Committee on the Naval Conference, 1935, which had met to review the course of the preliminary naval negotiations of the previous three months. The Committee's recommendations included

of the Washington Naval Treaty and of the corresponding article in the London Naval Treaty, the effect of which is, in the circumstances which have occurred, that the signatory Powers must meet in conference during the present year, and in view of the fact that this country has so far taken the initiative in arranging for these bilateral discussions, His Majesty's Government are prepared to summon a conference to meet in London on December 2nd next. The purpose of this Conference would be to secure agreement on as many aspects as possible of naval limitation with a view to the conclusion of an international treaty which would take the place of the two Naval Treaties expiring at the end of 1936. It is hoped that, once agreement is in sight between the representatives of the signatory Powers, an extension of the scope of the Conference may be possible so as to include representatives of the other naval Powers.

2. I should be grateful if Your Excellency would be so good as to inform me as soon as possible whether the United States Government are prepared to be represented at the proposed Conference.

3. I have the honour at the same time to suggest that it may prove convenient to all concerned, and may serve to keep the size of each Delegation as small as possible, if Your Excellency's Government and the Governments of France, Italy and Japan were to be represented by their Ambassadors in London. It would furthermore be very desirable that there should be present at the Conference from the outset naval representatives or advisers of sufficient rank to speak authoritatively on behalf of their respective Governments.[3]

I have, &c.,
(for the Secretary of State)
R. L. CRAIGIE

the following:— (i) That the qualitative limits proposed [cf. Section II of No. 522], should be accepted if found to be the best obtainable. (ii) 'That the British proposal for an agreement limiting naval construction by means of unilateral declarations for six years should, as a matter of tactics, be brought forward by His Majesty's Government. In view, however, of the attitude of Japan, France and Italy, it will probably be impossible to reach any agreement at all on quantitative limitation. In that event it is important that the blame for this decision should be made to rest on the three Powers named and not on this country.' (iii) That any future treaty should include the provisions listed in Paragraph 27 of N.C.M. (35) 72 [No. 522], but not those relating to the non-fortification of possessions in the Pacific, which would best be left for separate treatment between the British Empire, the United States, and Japan. (iv) 'That agreement should be sought with Japan along the lines of Course (b) in paragraph 33 of Paper No. N.C.M. (35) 72. Failing this, agreement should be sought along the lines of (c), and, failing both these, resort should be made to obtaining a qualitative agreement without Japan, in which the signatory Powers would have the right to depart from the limits laid down in the Treaty should Japan construct a vessel falling outside those limits.' The Cabinet approved these recommendations and agreed that formal invitations to the conference should be sent out the same day. Invitations were sent in Foreign Office telegrams of October 24 to Washington (No. 320), Tokyo (No. 210), Rome (No. 558), and Paris (No. 294).

[3] In Foreign Office telegram No. 115 of October 25 to Moscow, Viscount Chilston was informed that the Soviet Counsellor had also been told on October 23 of the decision to summon a Naval Conference on December 2.

## No. 539

### Sir S. Hoare to Sir R. Clive (Tokyo)
#### No. 213 Telegraphic [A 9099/22/45]

FOREIGN OFFICE, *October 26, 1935, 8.40 p.m.*

The Japanese Chargé d'Affaires called at the Foreign Office on October 23 and observed that, if intention of His Majesty's Government was to propose at the Conference the conclusion of a qualitative agreement only, then a deadlock must immediately arise, since Japan was opposed to such a course. He was informed that His Majesty's Government were most desirous of securing an agreement both on quantitative and qualitative limitation and that undoubtedly any proposals which they made to the Conference would be designed to secure this result. It would, of course, be open to the Japanese Government to put forward what proposals they thought fit. As to subject of discussion and agenda, Chargé d'Affaires was informed that general purpose of Conference would be to find some means of continuing the limitation of naval armaments by international agreement after the expiry of existing Treaties. No detailed agenda had, however, yet been prepared.

## No. 540

### Record by Mr. Craigie of a conversation with Mr. Atherton
#### [A 9213/22/45]

FOREIGN OFFICE, *October 28, 1935*

I took the opportunity of a call by Mr. Atherton to say that there was a point on which I wished to speak to him quite privately and unofficially. In the attached extract from the 'précis of conversation'[1] it was stated that the United States Government concurred in the British view that, when the time for discussion came, Britain and America would have no difficulty in coming to a satisfactory mutual agreement on quantitative limitation. This was probably a reference to something I had said at an earlier meeting, which in turn had been founded on the indications given by the United States representatives last autumn that their Government appreciated the force of the British contention that an increase in British cruiser strength had now been rendered necessary. I was still of opinion that, if ever the Conference got down to questions of quantitative limitation, the Americans and ourselves would have little difficulty in agreeing, provided that there was the same disposition at Washington to take account of the peculiarly difficult position in which we were now placed and the necessity for increases above treaty figures. It was particularly important, I thought, that the United States Government should not regard the figures which had been communicated last autumn as more than tentative illustrations of the kind

[1] The reference was to paragraph 11 of the Annex to No. 527.

693

of arrangement we had in mind. We had at the time emphasised the tentative character of these figures, but sometimes Government Departments were inclined to lose sight of the reservations with which a particular figure had been put forward. Since the autumn of 1934 the general European situation had, however, deteriorated; we now knew that Germany as well as other continental European Powers would be building at an accelerated pace, while in the Mediterranean an entirely fresh strategical problem had arisen. While no decisions had been taken over here, it seemed to me that it would be the part of wisdom for the United States Government to assume that the illustrations given in the autumn of 1934 would be found to be below rather than above the mark. I made it clear, however, that I was referring only to the rate of building for replacement purposes and not to any figures the American delegation might have been given last autumn in regard to total strengths in the various categories.[2]

Mr. Atherton said he thought that the tentative character of the talks in the autumn of 1934 was fully appreciated in Washington. Nevertheless, he considered it desirable that my unofficial communication should be brought to the notice of the United States Government and he thought the best way would be to send a private telegram to Admiral Standley. This would ensure secrecy.

R. L. CRAIGIE

[2] In a minute of October 28 Mr. Craigie explained that he thought it preferable to make this point clear in a 'private talk rather than in a more official meeting. At all events it will now not be possible for the Americans to say that we had given them no hint of the possible increases before they accepted our invitation to the Conference.'

## No. 541

*Sir S. Hoare to Sir R. Clive (Tokyo)*

*No. 581 [A 9070/22/45]*

FOREIGN OFFICE, *October 29, 1935*

Sir,

The Japanese Counsellor called at the Foreign Office on the 18th October to make a verbal communication concerning the attitude of the Japanese Government on naval limitation.[1] He stated that the Japanese Government found it impossible to accept a plan for the mutual declaration of building programmes, whatever the proposed period might be, on the grounds that such a scheme would constitute in substance a continuation of the ratio system. For the same reason the Japanese Government, although in favour of the drastic limitation or abolition of capital ships, A class cruisers and aircraft carriers, were unable to accept such qualitative limitation without quantitative limitation. They were anxious, however, for further free and frank exchanges of views between the interested Powers and the speedy

[1] Mr. Craigie's record of this conversation with Mr. Fujii and the text of the communication were circulated as N.C.M. (35) 74. See also *F.R.U.S. 1935*, vol. i, pp. 128–9.

conclusion of a satisfactory naval agreement, to attain which they were prepared to do everything in their power.

The Japanese Counsellor was informed that the effect of this communication appeared to be that the Japanese Government refused to make any advance towards a compromise settlement. The Japanese attitude meant, in practice the probable abandonment of any agreement on quantitative limitation, while the refusal of the Japanese Government to accept qualitative without quantitative limitation would result in serious competition both in numbers and in the evolution of new types. It was pointed out to Mr. Fujii that, if Japan desired to build new types of ships to suit her particular requirements, there was no reason why some form of qualitative limitation should not be evolved to meet these special needs. So far, however, no explanation had been forthcoming from the Japanese Government on this point. If, therefore, further conversations were to take place, the question of the best way of satisfying Japanese needs might form the basis of discussion.

Japanese Counsellor enquired whether it was not possible for His Majesty's Government to revise their view on the Japanese plan for a common upper limit. He was informed that there was no possibility of any change of opinion on the part of His Majesty's Government. In conclusion, Mr. Fujii was requested to enquire of his Government how they could reconcile their principle of a state of non-menace and non-aggression, with which His Majesty's Government were in full agreement, with a proposal to give free scope to competition in the evolution of new types of ships.

I am, &c.,
(for the Secretary of State)
J. M. TROUTBECK

No. 542

*Letter from Mr. Craigie to Mr. Atherton*

[*A 9112/22/45*]

FOREIGN OFFICE, *October 29, 1935*

My dear Ray,

You will no doubt remember that, with the concurrence of the interested Governments, the Secretary-General of the League of Nations was invited to send an official observer to attend the meetings of the London Naval Conference in 1930 on behalf of the League without, naturally, the right of discussion or vote. We think it desirable that we should issue a similar invitation to the Secretary-General on this occasion, particularly in view of the fact that the scope of the conference may later be extended to include representatives of other Naval Powers.

Before, however, approaching the other Powers concerned in the matter, I am anxious to know whether your Government would be prepared to concur in the proposed line of action, and I should be grateful if you would

695

be kind enough to let me have a reply in the matter at your earliest convenience.[1]

Believe me, Yours sincerely,
R. L. CRAIGIE

[1] The United States Government concurred in this proposal; see *F.R.U.S. 1935*, vol. i, p. 142.

## No. 543

*Sir R. Clive (Tokyo) to Sir S. Hoare (Received October 30, 9.30 p.m.)*
*No. 279 Telegraphic [A 9166/22/45]*

TOKYO, *October 30, 1935, 3.30 p.m.*

My telegram No. 271.[1]

Minister for Foreign Affairs told me today that Mr. Sato had asked to be excused owing to his poor knowledge of English. Minister for Foreign Affairs had accordingly asked Mr. Nagai, former Ambassador to Berlin,[2] to go to London as chief delegate.

[1] No. 534.
[2] Mr. M. Nagai was Japanese Ambassador at Berlin, 1933–4.

## No. 544

*Sir S. Hoare to Sir E. Phipps (Berlin)*
*No. 1147 [C 7207/55/18]*

FOREIGN OFFICE, *October 30, 1935*

Sir,

I have received your telegram No. 305[1] of October 23rd in which you reported certain observations made by Baron von Neurath regarding the effect on the continued application of the Treaty of Locarno of the withdrawal of Germany from the League of Nations. Baron von Neurath stated that, although the German Government were in agreement regarding the substance of the matter at issue, namely the continued application of all the provisions of the Treaty of Locarno, he must make certain reservations as to procedure, since the German Government did not necessarily accept the view that Germany, who was no longer a member of the League, should continue to be bound by the provisions of Article 17 of the Covenant.

2. I am advised that Baron von Neurath's remarks may be based on misunderstanding, since it is not contended that Germany is bound by Article 17 of the Covenant as such when she ceases to be a member of the League. On the other hand, Germany continues to be bound by the Treaty of Locarno, and in order to fulfil that Treaty she is obliged to accept an invitation extended to her as a non-member State under Article 17 of the Covenant, as well as the position of a member of the League, for the purposes of a dispute covered by the provisions of the Treaty of Locarno. It appears from the reference made by Baron von Neurath in his conversation with you

[1] No. 537.

to the draft Air Pact communicated to my predecessor on May 28th last, that the German Government do, in effect, recognise this obligation and are really concerned only to secure that, when an invitation is extended to Germany under Article 17 of the Covenant, Article 4 (5) of the Covenant shall also be applied, so that she shall have, for the purposes of the dispute, the position of a member of the Council. As a matter of fact, an undertaking such as figures in Article 1 of the German draft Air Pact—that the other Powers will use their influence so that Germany may be able to take part as a Power with equal rights in the deliberations and resolutions of the Council in all cases where the Council is seized, in accordance with the provisions of the Treaty of Locarno, with the application of these provisions —is really unnecessary. For Article 17 of the Covenant provides that the non-member State shall be invited to accept the obligations of membership of the League for the purposes of the dispute and that, if such an invitation is accepted, Articles 12 to 16 inclusive shall apply. Article 4 (5) of the Covenant provides that any member of the League not represented on the Council shall be invited to send a representative to sit as a member at any meeting of the Council during the consideration of matters specially affecting the interests of that member of the League. If Article 4 (5) is applied to a non-member State also which has accepted the invitation under Article 17, then the German desiderata would appear to be fully met. It is, in my view, most improbable that the Council would, in the event of a Locarno dispute, be guided by considerations other than those developed above as regards the participation of Germany in the discussions; that is to say, the Council would, in making the conditions for Germany's participation under Article 17 (1), inevitably accord to Germany the rights of a member of the League under Article 4 (5) for the purposes of the dispute.

3. The preceding paragraphs are intended for your personal information and guidance only: there appears to be no necessity for you to pursue the matter with the German Government.

I am, &c.,
(for the Secretary of State)
R. F. WIGRAM

## No. 545

*Sir S. Hoare to Sir R. Clive (Tokyo)*
*No. 218 Telegraphic [A 9139/22/45]*

FOREIGN OFFICE, *October 31, 1935, 3.40 p.m.*

My telegram No. 210[1] of the 24th October.

Communication received from Japanese Chargé d'Affaires yesterday stating that Japanese Government accept invitation and will inform His Majesty's Government later whether the Japanese delegates will be able to arrive before the 2nd December. Names of the delegates are not given.

[1] Not printed. See No. 538, note 2, last sentence.

# No. 546

*Summary of the account of the meeting of United Kingdom and French representatives held at the Foreign Office on October 31, 1935*[1]

[*A 9314/22/45*]

PRESENT: *United Kingdom*: Mr. Craigie, Vice-Admiral James, Captain Danckwerts.

*France*: M. Cambon, Contre-Amiral Decoux, Capitaine de Vasseau Deleuze, Capitaine de Frégate du Tour.

The French Ministry of Marine's views on naval limitation were explained by Admiral Decoux as follows.

*Qualitative Limitation.*

(1) Capital ships. Admiral Decoux said that the French, while apprehensive of German re-armament, favoured qualitative limitation, and were ready to agree to a limitation of capital ship tonnage to 27,000 tons with 12-inch guns or, failing that, as a first step, to 30–32,000 tons with 13-inch guns. On the other hand, the addition[2] of two 35,000 ton ships with 15-inch guns had been authorised and this could not be altered, so that if other countries could not agree to come down to a 13-inch gun France would propose to make the limit 15 inches.

(2) Gap between capital ships and cruisers. Admiral Decoux suggested that no ships should be built between 7,600 and 10,000 tons and that there should be no guns between 6·1 inches and 11 inches. This would also prevent the construction of further Category A cruisers.

(3) Category B cruisers. The French are in agreement with the limits in size and gun calibre proposed by His Majesty's Government.

(4) Cruisers and destroyers. The French think it undesirable to distinguish between the two.

(5) Submarines. Admiral Decoux expressed the view that various nations besides France required them. The limitation figures suggested by His Majesty's Government were agreeable to the French.

*Submarine Warfare.*

The French representative stated that Part 4 of the London Treaty regulating submarine warfare was acceptable and that France would be prepared to sign a protocol embodying the provisions of that Part.

*Quantitative Limitation.*

In general Admiral Decoux was not hostile to the British proposal for unilateral declarations limiting naval construction, but felt that the Conference must decide the length of the period.

---

[1] This summary, together with a more detailed record of the meeting, was circulated as N.C.M. (35) (79).

[2] In the draft of the summary, and in the minutes, this word read 'construction'.

698

## No. 547

*Sir R. Lindsay (Washington) to Sir S. Hoare (Received November 2, 9.30 a.m.)*
*No. 352 Telegraphic [A 9218/22/45]*

WASHINGTON, *November 1, 1935, 7.46 p.m.*

Under Secretary of State today asked me to convey to you the following message about Naval Conference.

Begins. American Government would appreciate learning whether information of British Government confirms its own understanding that principal claim advanced by Japan last year continues to constitute the basic aim of that Power and is likely again to be put forward during the Conference, viz., the claim for 'a common upper limit' in such form as to amount to increase in Japanese ratio and ultimately designed to bring about parity with fleets of United States and British Empire.

When this claim was brought forward by Japanese Delegation during secret conversations, it was the view of both British and American Governments[1] that, regardless of form in which a quantitative agreement might be cast, for the sake of meeting Japanese preoccupations the two must reject unconditionally Japanese demand for parity, in whatever name and in whatever guise, and that they could not agree to a settlement which would in effect alter to the advantage of Japan relative fleet strengths resulting from Washington–London Treaties. This Government continues to adhere to this position and intends to maintain it during the forthcoming Conference. It would appreciate being informed whether it is correct in assuming that this is and will also be the position of British Government. Ends.

I shall be glad to be informed what reply should be made to this enquiry.

[1] Cf. No. 551 below, note 4.

## No. 548

*Sir E. Phipps (Berlin) to Sir S. Hoare (Received November 8)*
*No. 1116 [C 7501/55/18]*

BERLIN, *November 2, 1935*

Sir,

I have the honour to report that the Air Attaché recently asked the German Air Ministry, officially, to let him have particulars and figures of the German Air Budget for 1935/36. In reply he received a private note from the Liaison Officer in the following terms: 'I want to write you quite open and frankly, that I can't get for you the detailed figures of our Air Budget. I think you will understand that. I do not want to give you figures you will find out as wrong.'

2. The admission of the German officer that any information he might give would in fact be incorrect is a further illustration of the military secrecy practised in Germany to-day.

I have, &c.,
ERIC PHIPPS

## No. 549

*Sir G. Clerk (Paris) to Sir S. Hoare (Received November 5)*
*No. 1532 [C 7411/55/18]*

PARIS, November 4, 1935

His Majesty's Ambassador at Paris presents his compliments to the Secretary of State for Foreign Affairs, and has the honour to transmit to him the under-mentioned document.

| *Name and Date* | *Subject* |
|---|---|
| Note from Ministry for Foreign Affairs, 31st October 1935. | Germany's withdrawal from the League of Nations and its effect on the Treaty of Locarno. |

ENCLOSURE IN No. 549

PARIS, le 31 octobre 1935

Par une note en date du 19 de ce mois,[1] l'Ambassade de Sa Majesté a bien voulu faire connaître au Ministère des Affaires Étrangères la réponse que le Secrétaire d'État britannique ferait à la question qui pourrait lui être posée à la Chambre des Communes quant à l'effet du retrait de l'Allemagne de la Société des Nations sur le Traité de Locarno.

Le Ministère des Affaires Étrangères remercie l'Ambassade Britannique de son obligeante communication et a l'honneur de lui faire savoir que le Gouvernement français est pleinement d'accord sur la réponse que le Principal Secrétaire d'État se propose de faire éventuellement à une telle question.

La sortie de l'Allemagne de la Société des Nations laisse entièrement subsister les traités de Locarno.

D'autre part, le mécanisme d'application de ces traités est étroitement lié à l'institution de la Société des Nations et comporte en particulier l'intervention du Conseil.

Ces deux constatations ne sont pas contradictoires et les dispositions des traités de Locarno qui prescrivent l'intervention du Conseil de la S.D.N. restent pleinement applicables depuis que l'Allemagne a quitté la Société.

L'Allemagne serait, le cas échéant, invitée à prendre siège au Conseil et elle y siègerait sur le pied d'égalité: cette procédure serait conforme tant à l'article 17 du Pacte qu'à la pratique suivie dans les cas analogues par le Conseil de la Société des Nations; on peut en effet signaler que l'article 3 du traité de paix de Lausanne[2] ayant chargé le Conseil de fixer la frontière entre la Turquie et l'Irak, le Conseil a rempli cette mission à une époque où la

[1] Cf. No. 530.
[2] For the text of this treaty signed at Lausanne on July 24, 1923, by representatives of the British Empire, France, Italy, Japan, Greece, Roumania, and Turkey, see *B.F.S.P.*, vol. 117, pp. 543 ff. Correspondence and memoranda relating to this Treaty are printed in First Series, Volume XVIII.

Turquie n'était pas Membre de la Société des Nations et [sic] en invitant la
Turquie à siéger au Conseil.[3]

[3] See L/N.O.J., October 1924, p. 1318.

## No. 550

### Sir S. Hoare to Sir R. Clive (Tokyo)
No. 221 Telegraphic [A 9139/22/45]

FOREIGN OFFICE, November 6, 9.30 p.m.

My telegram No. 218.[1]

Japanese Delegates cannot arrive by the 2nd December. Date for meeting
of Conference has therefore been changed to 5th December.

[1] No. 545.

## No. 551

### Sir S. Hoare to Sir R. Lindsay (Washington)
No. 338 Telegraphic [A 9218/22/45]

FOREIGN OFFICE, November 6, 1935, 5.10 p.m.

Your telegram No. 352.[1]

The attitude which the Japanese Government may be expected to adopt
at the forthcoming Conference was defined in an oral communication made
by the Japanese Chargé d'Affaires to the Foreign Office on the 18th October,[2]
of which the substance was subsequently given to Mr. Atherton. The terms
of this communication are given in my immediately following telegram,[3]
the text of which should be handed to the Under-Secretary of State.

As regards the second paragraph of the United States Government's
message, you may inform them that the attitude of His Majesty's Government towards the Japanese proposals remains as indicated to the representatives of the United States Government during the conversations which took
place last year. The Japanese representatives were similarly informed of the
attitude of His Majesty's Government towards their proposals, particular
emphasis being laid on the special responsibilities devolving on this country
as a result of the deterioration in the political situation in Europe and the
increased building by many European Powers.[4]

[1] No. 547.　　　　　[2] Cf. No. 541.　　　　　[3] Not printed. See ibid., note 1.
[4] This telegram was based on a minute by Mr. Craigie of November 5 discussing the
Anglo-American consultations in June 1934. In an additional minute of the same date
(A 9338/22/45) he wrote as follows: 'Secret. In addition to the reference, contained in my
minute within to the British and American attitude towards the Japanese claim for a
"common upper limit" there was an exchange of views on this point which it was decided to
treat as secret and not to include in the circulated records. My own record of the understanding on this point runs as follows: At the first meeting on June 18th [1934] Mr. Norman
Davis suggested that both sides should undertake that in no circumstances would either
country agree to any increase in the Japanese ratio of naval strength. The Prime Minister
pointed out that it might be a mistake to lay down a hard and fast rule of this character but,

as a compromise, it was agreed that neither side would depart from its attitude of opposition to any increase in the Japanese ratio in any category without previous consultation with the other. It was agreed by both sides that it would be both risky and unnecessary to incorporate such an understanding in the official record, particularly when it was remembered that throughout the preparations for the London Naval Conference and during that Conference there was the fullest consultation between the two delegations on all points without there having been any previous written undertaking to this effect.'

## No. 552

*Summary of the account of the meetings of United Kingdom and Italian representatives held at the Foreign Office on November 6th and 7th*[1]

*[A 9578/22/45]*

PRESENT: *United Kingdom*: Mr. Craigie, Vice-Admiral [Sir W. M.] James[2] (not present on Nov. 7), Captain Danckwerts.

*Italy*: Signor Vitetti (not present on Nov. 7), Admiral Raineri-Biscia, Commander Margottini,[3] Captain Capponi.[4]

*Qualitative Limitation.*

*Capital Ships.* Admiral Biscia stated that the Italian Ministry of Marine were prepared to accept a figure lower than 35,000 tons; he suggested 28–29,000 tons. In his opinion a ship of 28,000 tons might have a 12-inch gun and a 35,000 ton ship of 15-inch gun. Although the 2 Italian 35,000 ton ships would be armed with 15″ guns, there appeared to be no objection in principle to a 14″ gun with a ship of that tonnage or even a lower tonnage. He felt that, if the United States Government built two further 35,000 ton ships and Japan and His Majesty's Government followed suit, then the Italian Government must have the right to do likewise. The present two 35,000 ton ships with 15-inch guns now building in Italy did not, in the view of the Italian Government, come into the scope of the forthcoming Conference. This matter, as well as the question of the establishment of a gap between capital ships and cruisers, would have to be referred to Rome.

*Aircraft Carriers.* Admiral Biscia raised no objection to the limitation figure proposed by His Majesty's Government.

*Cruisers.* Admiral Biscia expressed the view that if there were no reduction in the size of 10,000 ton cruisers, it might be difficult to reduce the gun calibre below 8 inches. He suggested that the maximum size of cruisers might be fixed at 8000 tons. He preferred no distinction between B cruisers and destroyers.

*Submarines.* The submarine limitation figures laid down in the London Treaty were acceptable to the Italian Government.

*Exempt Class.* Admiral Biscia proposed that the present tonnage limitation might be reduced to 500 tons.

[1] This summary, together with more detailed records of the meetings, was circulated as N.C.M. (35) 81.
[2] Vice-Admiral Sir W. M. James was Deputy Chief of the British Naval Staff.
[3] Deputy Chief of the Italian Naval Staff.     [4] Italian Naval Attaché at London.

*Quantitative Limitation.*

Admiral Biscia did not favour the proposal for declarations limiting construction over a period of six years as such a course lacked elasticity and might tend to remove any liberty of action. He preferred notifications of yearly building programmes in advance.

## No. 553

*Letter from Mr. Craigie to Mr. Stevenson[1] (Geneva)*

*[A 9444/22/45]*

FOREIGN OFFICE, *November 8, 1935*

My dear Stevenson,

Many thanks for your letter of the 31st October[2] in regard to the proposed Naval Conference in London.

You were quite right in saying that we had anticipated that the Secretary-General would, if he thought fit, pass on to the States represented at the Disarmament Conference the information given him in regard to the summoning of this Conference. The title 'Naval Conversations' is, however, inadequate, since this is to be the Conference of the naval Powers foreshadowed in Article 23 of both the Washington and London Naval Treaties.

As regards the attendance of a League observer, I should be grateful if you would assure the Secretary-General that this point had not escaped our notice. Shortly after the issue of the invitations we had already, as a matter of form, started asking the other Washington Powers whether they would see objection to this being done[3] and we hope to get off the formal invitation to the League within a few days. We very much hope that the Secretary-General will be able to send a really good man who will have some understanding of the points at issue and will be sympathetic with the objects we have in view. Colban, who was the League representative in 1930, was quite admirable.

A question that will have to be decided will be the manner in which the Conference is to be extended to the other naval Powers, should the five Washington Powers find themselves in sight of an agreement. I doubt whether the Conference would contemplate the signature of a treaty between the five Powers before the other naval Powers have been brought into consultation. In any case we shall, during the Conference, endeavour to keep in close touch with the representatives of the principal naval Powers not participating in the Conference. If we were to achieve agreement between the Washington Powers on any branch of naval limitation it would from many

[1] Mr. R. C. S. Stevenson, Assistant Adviser on League of Nations Affairs, was a member of the United Kingdom delegation to the League of Nations.

[2] In this letter Mr. Stevenson referred to a conversation with Mr. Walters, an Under-Secretary-General of the League of Nations, who had asked 'whether we intended to invite the Secretary-General to send an observer to attend the conversations, as was done in 1930'. [3] Cf. No. 542.

points of view seem proper—and would certainly be convenient—if the larger Conference could be held at Geneva.

On the other hand, experience of past Conferences leads us to believe that it might be dangerous to have an adjournment or a change of venue if agreement had been, with difficulty, achieved here on this or that branch of the subject. The probabilities are that general agreement will be more likely to be obtained if the other Powers can be carried along at once with the momentum which would have been achieved in London. Should the Washington Powers succeed in reaching agreement among themselves on this or that aspect of this problem, a possible way out would be to bring the diplomatic representatives of the other naval Powers into consultation in London at the appropriate moment and then, once a full outline of an agreement has been drawn up and, perhaps, initialled in London, to adjourn to Geneva in order to complete the preparation of the treaty and proceed to the signature under League auspices. These are questions which will have to be considered nearer the date and which we shall be happy to be able to discuss with the proposed League observer.

We should be glad if you would discuss the matter with Walters and pass on to the Secretary-General orally as much as you consider desirable of the above information. At all events you can assure Avenol that we are most anxious to avoid creating any impression that this question of naval limitation is being, in any sense, removed from the purview of the League. On the contrary, His Majesty's Government regard themselves as acting in this matter as in accordance with the general wishes of the League (which specifically approved of the naval negotiations being handled separately from other aspects of the disarmament question) and under an obligation to report back to the League as soon as agreement is in sight on any branch of this complex subject.

Yours ever,
R. L. CRAIGIE

## No. 554

*Sir S. Hoare to Sir E. Drummond (Rome)*
*No. 593 Telegraphic [A 9323/22/45]*

FOREIGN OFFICE, *November 11, 1935, 6.30 p.m.*

My telegram No. 558.[1]

Although we assume from verbal assurances given by Italian Embassy here that Italian representatives will attend forthcoming Naval Conference, no official acceptance has yet been received from the Italian Government. We have reminded Italian Embassy more than once, but without result. In view of the fact that United States, French, and Japanese Governments have all accepted, please urge Ministry of Foreign Affairs to send early reply leaving question of names of representatives open, if desired. You should at the same time enquire whether they have any objection to a League

[1] See No. 538, note 2, last sentence.

observer attending meetings of the Conference as in the case of the London Naval Conference of 1930 without power to vote or discuss. Japanese, French and United States have already concurred in this proposal.

## No. 555

*Sir E. Drummond (Rome) to Sir S. Hoare (Received November 14, 9.30 a.m.)*
*No. 716 Telegraphic [A 9593/22/45]*

ROME, *November 14, 1935, 12.30 a.m.*

Your telegram No. 593.[1]

Secretary-General of Ministry of Foreign Affairs in reply to representations on this subject was unable to give definite answers without reference to higher authority but expressed opinion that invitation would be accepted and His Majesty's Government notified to this effect through Embassy in London within the next forty-eight hours. He also stated that he did not believe that his Government would raise any objection to presence of League observer. On this point too he hoped an answer would be given within the next two days.

[1] No. 554.

## No. 556

*Record of a conversation with representatives of the Japanese Embassy held at the Foreign Office on November 14*
*[A 9751/22/45]*

*Present*: Mr. Fujii, Mr. Terasaki, Captain Fujita,[1] Mr. Craigie, Captain Danckwerts.

In opening the proceedings, MR. CRAIGIE stated that he was very pleased to have the opportunity of a frank and friendly talk with the Japanese representatives. In order to maintain good relations it was above all necessary to avoid misunderstandings. After reviewing briefly the attitude of the French and Italian Governments on naval limitation, Mr. Craigie made it clear that His Majesty's Government were anxious to secure agreement both on qualitative and quantitative limitation, but that if agreement were impossible on the quantitative side they would still hope for an agreement on qualitative limitation. As His Majesty's Government were unable to accept the Japanese principle of a common upper limit, they had made an effort to reach a compromise by proposing a system of unilateral declarations limiting naval construction. They intended to submit this proposal to the forthcoming Conference and they assumed that Japan would likewise put forward her views. An attempt would have to be made to find a solution satisfactory to all concerned. His Majesty's Government were willing to

[1] Japanese Naval Attaché at London.

listen to any suggestions. MR. FUJII at this point made enquiries as to the question of the establishment of a gap between capital ships and cruisers, and at the same time asked what had been the result of our conversations with the United States representatives in the matter of capital ships. He stated that he was without any instructions from his Government.

MR. CRAIGIE, after giving him the required information, proceeded to comment on the memorandum left by Mr. Fujii at the Foreign Office on October 18th.[2] He was unable to agree with the Japanese statement that great Powers should be the first to set an example in the matter of the limitation of armaments. He laid particular emphasis on the vulnerability of Great Britain's position, the growth of European navies during the last few years, and the low figure to which the British navy had now fallen. His Majesty's Government had gone too far and now the Japanese Government were suggesting that they should reduce still further.

MR. FUJII replied that if European Powers were really sincere in their desire to secure reduction in armaments the most heavily armed countries might first make a sacrifice. Japan desired a reduction in the strength of all naval Powers to some common basis. After mentioning the danger of Russia and China in the Far East, he referred to the position of the United States, whose naval power, although distributed between the Atlantic and the Pacific, was for all practical purposes concentrated in the Pacific.

CAPT. DANCKWERTS explained that it was not a matter for him to defend the United States position, but he wished to point out that the naval requirements of Japan and the British Commonwealth were completely different. It was impossible for His Majesty's Government to effect the concentration of the whole Fleet at any particular moment in any one area. On the other hand, the position of Japan was secure. Mr. Fujii fully appreciated these considerations.

MR. CRAIGIE then expressed the opinion that it would be a mistake to get lost in the realm of theory. The United States could, if she liked, outbuild both the United Kingdom and Japan. This would, in fact, appeal to large sections of opinion in the United States. He then enquired why the Japanese Government, as stated in their memorandum of October 18th, considered that any qualitative limitation, unaccompanied by quantitative limitation, would only prove to be a convenient means of preserving the existing relationships in naval strengths amongst Powers. The Japanese Government could build any ships which they required under a system of qualitative limitation. In any system of that kind full consideration would, of course, be taken of Japanese requirements. It appeared that the Japanese Government might be labouring under some misapprehension as to the meaning of qualitative limitation. It did not mean that only ships of a certain size in each category could be built, but that no ship exceeding the limitation figure laid down in respect of each category would be permitted.

MR. FUJII replied that without qualitative limitation Japan would be in a position to build such types of ships as she specially required, but it was

---

[2] Cf. No. 541, note 1.

706

difficult for him to explain why it was not possible to build those ships under some system of qualitative limitation.

During the conversation, Captain Fujita hinted in a vague and confused manner that Japan might require to build a capital ship of more than 35,000 tons, or possibly a small ship with a few guns of very large calibre. It is difficult to know how much importance to attach to his observations. Similarly, it was not very clear as to whether in the view of the Japanese representatives their principle of a common upper limit should apply to the United States, Japan and the United Kingdom, to the Washington Powers, or universally. Captain Fujita repeated that he had no instructions.

## No. 557

*Letter from American Department to Chancery (Washington)*

[*A 9404/22/45*]

FOREIGN OFFICE, *November 19, 1935*

Dear Chancery,

Many thanks for your letter of the 28th October[1] enquiring whether you should send daily telegrams containing press summaries during the Naval Conference, 1935.

The telegrams you sent last year during the discussions with the United States and Japan were most useful and enabled us to nip several mischievous rumours in the bud, and we shall therefore be glad if you will repeat the practice this year as you suggest.[2]

We take this opportunity of saying a word about answers to press enquiries. It will no doubt be the case that during the Naval Conference enquiries will be addressed to you concerning the progress of the negotiations, but the question is so complicated and events move so quickly that you will doubtless prefer to refrain from making public statements or answering press enquiries, and take the line that the matter is 'London news'. Of course, if there are enquiries either from United States Government sources or from outside which you think should be answered locally we will deal with the matter as promptly as possible if you will refer back by telegram.

The distribution of information will be undertaken by the News Department here and we will try to keep you generally as well informed as possible of what is going on. But as you know, it is not always possible to do this from day to day.

Yours ever,
AMERICAN DEPARTMENT

[1] Not printed.
[2] Letters were also sent to the Chanceries in Moscow, Rome, and Berlin asking for full and up-to-date information about comments in the local press on the forthcoming Naval Conference.

## No. 558

### Letter from Mr. Craigie to M. Cahan (Soviet Embassy)
### [A 9761/22/45]

FOREIGN OFFICE, *November 20, 1935*

Dear M. Cahan,

In our conversation on the 12th instant I mentioned to you the importance which we attached to keeping in close touch with the Soviet Embassy during the course of the impending Naval Conference, particularly in view of the probability that the scope of the Conference may be extended so as to include naval Powers other than those who are parties to the Washington and London Naval Treaties. I also said we would very much appreciate it if your Government could see their way to give us their preliminary views on the information which we have communicated to you from time to time in regard to the course of the preparatory discussions between the Washington Powers.

As the matters under discussion are so highly technical, it occurs to us that it might be useful to both sides if there were in London, during the course of the Conference, an expert of the Government of the U.S.S.R., who could cooperate with you in exchanging information with us and with the representatives of other Powers participating in the first stage of the Conference. To avoid the appearance that Soviet Russia was receiving any special treatment, your Government may consider it desirable that any such naval expert should be given the temporary rank of Naval Attaché, thus placing Soviet Russia in the same position as other countries which are not taking part in the Conference but which have Naval Attachés in London.

Unless your Ambassador sees objection, might I suggest that this entirely unofficial proposal should be communicated to your Government? I am writing to you rather than to our Embassy at Moscow because it is useful that all correspondence in regard to the Naval Conference should, as far as possible, pass through one channel.

Should your Government approve of this idea it would be useful if the expert were to reach London a little in advance of the opening date of the Conference (probably early in December) in order that we may have a preliminary exchange of views before the Conference opens.

Believe me, Yours sincerely,
R. L. CRAIGIE

## No. 559

### Letter from Mr. Holman to Mr. Terasaki (Japanese Embassy)[1]
### [A 9629/22/45]

FOREIGN OFFICE, *November 22, 1935*

Dear Terasaki,

I am writing to let you know that it has now been decided, with the

[1] An identic letter was also sent to M. Cambon (French Embassy), Signor Vitetti (Italian Embassy), and Mr. Reber (United States Embassy).

concurrence of the United States, French, Italian and Japanese Governments that the Naval Conference should open in London on the morning of December 6.

Yours sincerely<br>A. HOLMAN

## No. 560

### Sir R. Lindsay (Washington) to Sir S. Hoare
*(Received November 26, 9.30 a.m.)*
*No. 394 Telegraphic [A 9890/22/45]*

*Immediate*  WASHINGTON, *November 25, 1935, 7.35 p.m.*

I have had an urgent message from Mr. Norman Davis asking me to support request that opening of Naval Conference be postponed till December 9th as American Delegation cannot arrive in London till late afternoon of December 6th even if their ship is not delayed by bad weather. I hope very much that it will be possible to meet American Delegation's wishes.

I understand that he has a speech which ought to be deliv[er]ed on the opening day.[1]

[1] Foreign Office telegram No. 366 of November 28 stated that it had been arranged to postpone the opening meeting until Monday, December 9, at 10.30 a.m.

## No. 561

### Letter from Captain Wassner to Mr. Craigie
*No. 993 [A 10026/22/45]*

*Translation*  LONDON, *November 27, 1935*

Dear Mr. Craigie,

Referring to our conversation on November 9th,[1] during which you asked me three questions which I forwarded to my superiors, the answers are as follows:—

(1) Would Germany also go down to the calibre of 14″ if Great Britain goes down to this calibre?

Reply: As Mr. Craigie states, Great Britain regards the 15″ calibre to be the most suitable for capital ships. This is also true in the case of Germany.

In the event, however, that at the Conference the calibre of 14″ is laid down as the maximum calibre for battleships placed under construction after the 1st January, 1937, Germany is prepared to accept this calibre for future battleships.

(2) Would Germany, in the event of a building holiday being decided upon for 'A' cruisers, build not more than the two 'A' cruisers already notified?

[1] Captain Wassner had called at the Foreign Office 'to ascertain what had passed in connexion with the naval question since his departure for Germany some weeks earlier'.

Reply: If, as the result of the Naval Conference, a building holiday for 'A' cruisers from the 1st January 1937 is prescribed for all naval Powers, after the commencement of the holiday period no more such vessels would be laid down. The three 'A' cruisers placed on the stocks by that date would be completed.

(3) Would Germany be prepared to be represented on a Committee of the Naval Conference at Geneva?

Reply: there is no question of Germany being represented on a Committee of the Naval Conference at Geneva.

(Decision of the Führer and Chancellor of the Reich).

Yours sincerely,

E. WASSNER

## No. 562

*Sir E. Drummond (Rome) to Sir S. Hoare (Received November 29, 2 p.m.)*

*No. 769 Telegraphic [A 10072/22/45]*

*Immediate*                    ROME, *November 29, 1935, 1.50 p.m.*

Your telegram No. 626[1] and my telegram No. 757.[2]

Ministry of Foreign Affairs stated this morning that although Italian Government regarded presence of such an observer as 'inutile' nevertheless if the other parties desired one and were agreed on matter Italian Government for their part would not raise any objection.[3]

[1] This telegram of November 25 referred to No. 555, and said that the delay of the Italian Government in replying concerning the attendance of a League of Nations observer at the naval conference was 'placing us in a very embarrassing position'.

[2] Not preserved in Foreign Office archives. According to the docket this telegram referred to Foreign Office telegram No. 626 and reported that the Secretary-General of the Ministry of Foreign Affairs had promised to expedite a reply.

[3] After receipt of this telegram Mr. Craigie sent a letter of November 30 to M. Avenol expressing the hope that it would be possible for a representative of the League of Nations to attend meetings of the forthcoming naval conference as an observer. For the text of this letter, and of M. Avenol's reply of December 2 appointing M. Aghnides, Director of the Disarmament Section of the Secretariat of the League of Nations, to represent the League at the conference, see *L/N.O.J.*, December 1935, pp. 1658–9.

## No. 563

*Sir E. Drummond (Rome) to Sir S. Hoare (Received November 30, 9.30 a.m.)*

*No. 772 Telegraphic [A 10078/22/45]*

ROME, *November 30, 1935, 12.5 a.m.*

Comments on approaching Naval Conference, including messages from London and Paris are pessimistic in tone. Various obstacles are pointed out and it is emphasised that Japan, France and Italy are united in advocating principle of 'globular' tonnage and in resisting proposal to abolish submarines. Further difficulty was introduced by the appearance of a new German navy. One writer suggests that British naval policy has been affected by Franco-

Italian entente and argues that England is wrong in considering, as she evidently does, that this entente is necessarily against her interests.

Fuller summary[1] follows by post.

[1] Not printed.

## No. 564

*Mr. Wiggin (Tokyo) to Sir S. Hoare (Received November 30, 9.30 a.m.)*
*No. 312 Telegraphic [A 10091/22/45]*

TOKYO, *November 30, 1935, 10.30 a.m.*

Your despatch No. 581.[1]

Secretary of Minister of Marine remarked to Naval Attaché yesterday in connexion with press reports of His Majesty's Government's intentions, that Japanese Navy preferred no treaty to the abandonment of their plan for a common upper limit. He added that in any case six years would in their view be too short a period for duration of gentleman's agreement understood to be contemplated. Ten years would be more suitable inasmuch as building programmes had to be made out more or less to a five years plan.

[1] No. 541.

## No. 565

*Letter from Chancery (Moscow) to American Department*
*[A 10310/22/45]*

MOSCOW, *December 3, 1935*

Dear Department,

Many thanks for your letter of the 19th November[1] about the Soviet attitude towards the forthcoming Naval Conference. We will keep a sharp lookout for comments, but we may say that so far extremely little interest has been shown by the Soviet press, and there has been nothing worth reporting.

With regard to what you say about mischievous rumours and press enquiries, we should explain that no Soviet journalist would dream of making any enquiry here, on this or any other subject, since if he did he would probably spend the rest of his life in the Arctic Circle. By the same token, it is never possible here to scotch mischievous rumours by means of a *démenti*. The only thing that can be done in particularly bad cases is to protest to the People's Commissariat for Foreign Affairs, but it cannot be said that such protests have so far had much effect. A vigorous wigging for Maisky in London is probably the best course as a rule.

We mention these points as conditions here are peculiar and apt to be misunderstood.

Yours ever,
MOSCOW CHANCERY

[1] Cf. No. 557, note 2.

# CHAPTER VII

# Correspondence relating to the earlier proceedings of the London Naval Conference

## December 4, 1935–January 16, 1936

### *Introductory Note to Chapters VII and VIII*

THE first plenary session of the Conference was held at the Foreign Office on Monday, December 9, 1935, at 10.30 a.m. The second and final plenary session was held on March 25, 1936, and concluded with the signature of the 'Treaty for the Limitation of Naval Armament' of that date.

Between these dates the main work of the Conference took place in the First Committee, sixteen meetings of which were held between December 10, 1935, and March 21, 1936. This followed the proposal of Viscount Monsell, First Lord of the Admiralty (who had taken the chair at the first plenary meeting after the proceedings had been opened by the Prime Minister, Mr. Stanley Baldwin), 'that the Conference shall resolve itself into a Committee of the whole Conference, to be called the First Committee'.

Delegates of the governments of the following eleven states attended the first plenary session: the United States of America, Australia, Canada, France, Great Britain, India, the Irish Free State, Italy, Japan, New Zealand, and the Union of South Africa. M. Aghnides attended as Observer from the League of Nations Secretariat. There had been some correspondence between the Dominions Office and the Commonwealth Governments at the end of November as to the form in which limitation of the naval forces of the Members of the British Commonwealth of Nations should be expressed in any future naval treaty. The South African Government had suggested to other Members of the Commonwealth that it would strengthen the bargaining position of the United Kingdom if the Dominions Governments refrained from participating in the forthcoming conference. This view was strongly controverted by the Commonwealth of Australia, and it was pointed out by the Dominions Office that the question of separate Dominions' quotas had ceased to be a practical issue owing to Japan's rejection of quantitative limitation in the form of the earlier ratio system. The South African Government accordingly agreed to participate in the conference.[1]

After the tenth meeting of the First Committee on January 15 the Japanese delegation announced its withdrawal from the Conference on the ground that its proposal 'for a common upper limit of naval tonnage' 'cannot secure

---

[1] Correspondence on this question with the Dominions Office and a memorandum by the Dominions Office are printed in Appendix III at the end of this volume.

general support'. It was agreed that Japanese observers could continue to attend meetings of the First Committee. After this the First Committee resumed its earlier discussion of quantitative and qualitative limitation. At its meeting on January 17 it set up a Technical Sub-Committee, with Mr. Craigie as chairman, to examine questions of advance notification and exchange of information. This sub-committee held five meetings from 17 to 30 January. A second Technical Sub-Committee, on Qualitative Limitation, with the First Sea Lord, Admiral Sir Ernle Chatfield, as chairman, was then set up and held six meetings between February 3 and March 9; it also appointed a sub-committee to report on definitions and age limits of combatant vessels and this sub-committee held three meetings on February 5 and 6.

Minutes of the meetings of the plenary sessions, of the First Committee, and of the second Technical Sub-Committee, together with the reports of all the sub-committees and the text of the treaty, are printed in French and English texts in *Documents of the London Naval Conference 1935, December 1935–March 1936* (H.M.S.O., 1936, 967 pp.), and are not re-printed here.

## No. 566

*Admiralty Memorandum on the retention of Cruisers and Destroyers in excess of the London Naval Treaty tonnages*[1]

*[A 10406/22/45]*

December 4, 1935

In the attached memorandum the necessity for retaining cruiser and destroyer tonnage in excess of the London Naval Treaty figures for the British Commonwealth is examined, and the following conclusions are reached[2]:—

(i) The 4 *Hawkins* class should be rearmed with 6″ guns and retained after 31st December, 1936.

(ii) That a special proposal should be made to the U.S.A. and Japan at the London Naval Conference to enable the *Hawkins* class to be rearmed with 6″ guns and classified as sub-category (*b*) cruisers.

(iii) An explanation should be given to the U.S.A. and Japan to obtain their agreement to the retention of a small excess in British cruiser tonnage without invoking the 'Escalator' clause.

(iv) We should retain a total tonnage in the destroyer category not exceeding 190,000 tons on the 31st December, 1936.

(v) That a special proposal should be made to the U.S.A. and Japan to enable this tonnage to be retained without invoking the 'Escalator' clause.

[1] This memorandum was circulated by request of the First Lord of the Admiralty. It was numbered N.C.M. (35) 82. At their meeting on December 6 the Sub-Committee on Defence Policy and Requirements approved the proposals summarized above.

[2] See paragraphs 17 and 27 below.

(vi) We should endeavour to limit any Japanese *quid pro quo* to a corresponding retention of overage destroyers but in the last resort we should agree to the retention of some Japanese submarine tonnage instead.

## Part I—Cruisers

In Paper No. N.C.M. (35) 1,[3] a Memorandum by the Chief of the Naval Staff in preparation for the 1935 Naval Conference, it was pointed out in paragraphs 30 and 31 that the London Naval Treaty cruiser tonnage, which was based on the provision of 50 cruisers for a strictly limited period, subject to reconsideration at the end of that period and in the expectation that corresponding reductions would be made in the programmes of other Powers, would be insufficient in the future. It was stated that 70 is the minimum number of cruisers that can be accepted for our security, of which 10 may be over the age limit agreed upon for this class of vessel.

2. Paragraph 49 of the same paper reads as follows:—

It is apparent that should our future allowance of cruiser tonnage be increased at the 1935 Conference as considered necessary by the Naval Staff, we shall be, during 1936, in the position of requiring to build up our cruiser forces from the dangerously low level accepted temporarily in the London Naval Treaty, with as little delay as practicable.

It would be most undesirable that at the same time we should have to scrap existing cruisers in order to reduce to the tonnage limit of 339,000 tons prescribed for us on 31st December, 1936, in the London Naval Treaty.[4]

This would entail not only an unnecessary sacrifice of cruiser strength but possibly also an increased rate of new construction with consequent increased expenditure.

The Naval Staff consider, therefore, that it will probably be necessary to make provision for retaining that portion of cruiser tonnage over the 339,000 tons prescribed, which is considered at the time to be serviceable from the material aspect.

3. Of the cruisers that might be retained, the *Hawkins* class are the most seaworthy and have the greatest endurance; on the other hand, they are armed with 7·5″ guns and are, therefore, classed as sub-category (*a*) cruisers, and special arrangements were made in the London Naval Treaty to enable the United Kingdom to scrap them all by 31st December, 1936, although two of them will then still be under-age. This was so essential a feature in the negotiations of the London Naval Treaty that any suggestion to retain them now as sub-category (*a*) cruisers would cause the utmost disturbance to the United States of America and probably destroy any

[3] Of March 23, 1934; not printed.
[4] See article 16 of the London Naval Treaty of April 1930.

hope of getting agreement from that country and Japan not to build more 8″ gun cruisers in the future.

4. It is, therefore, the opinion of the Admiralty that the 4 ships of the *Hawkins* class, which are the most recently built of the cruisers that might be retained beyond 1936, should be re-armed with 6″ guns and retained as part of our sub-category (*b*) tonnage.

5. The number of cruisers that can usefully be retained for the purpose of building up rapidly our cruiser strength is limited by the number that can be manned by the men that will be available in the first few years after 1936. It would be uneconomical to retain and refit at great expense all the old 'C' class cruisers that are available when they could not be provided with proper crews until Vote A[5] had risen sufficiently, by which time they would be due for scrapping on replacement by new construction. It is, therefore, the Admiralty proposal to scrap 5 of the 'C' class cruisers that are now in reserve and re-arm and retain the 4 ships of the *Hawkins* class.

6. By definition the *Hawkins* class are cruisers of sub-category (*a*), i.e., 'with guns of more than 6·1″ calibre'. The London Naval Treaty, Article 16, paragraph 3, states:—

'The maximum number of cruisers of sub-category (*a*) shall be as follows . . . for the British Commonwealth of Nations 15. . . .'

(From the wording of Article 16, paragraph 1, it may be assumed that this statement refers to the date 31st December, 1936.)

7. It was the assumption of the Treaty that *Hawkins* and *Vindictive*, becoming over-age in 1935 and 1934 respectively, would be scrapped to comply with Article 16, paragraph 3. In order that *Frobisher* and *Effingham*, which ships would be under-age on 31st December, 1936, might be scrapped also, Article 20, sub-paragraph (*a*) reads:—

'The *Frobisher* and *Effingham* (United Kingdom) may be disposed of during the year 1936.'

Without this clause there might have been difficulty in disposing of *Frobisher* and *Effingham* since Annex I, Section I, lays down that 'a vessel shall not be replaced before it becomes over-age'.

8. With regard to the re-arming of *Hawkins* class with 6″ guns, there is no provision in the Treaty for converting a vessel classed in cruiser sub-category (*a*) into a vessel classed in cruiser sub-category (*b*). It will, therefore, be necessary to make a special proposal to the other Signatory Powers (United States of America and Japan) to obtain their agreement to this method of disposal of the superabundant cruisers from sub-category (*a*).

9. The tonnage position in 6″ cruisers on 31st December, 1936, assuming

---

[5] i.e. the Parliamentary Vote on the Naval Estimates relating to the numbers of naval personnel.

that the *Hawkins* class have been re-armed and 5 'C' class scrapped, will be as follows:—

| | | | | | |
|---|---|---|---|---|---|
| 4 | *Hawkins* | .. .. .. | 39,426 | tons | (assuming that there is no change in tonnage due to rearmament). |
| 3 | *Ceres* (including 2 H.A. Ships) | .. .. .. | 12,870 | ,, | |
| 5 | *Carlisle* | .. .. .. | 21,000 | ,, | |
| 8 | 'D' | .. .. .. .. | 38,800 | ,, | |
| 2 | 'B' | .. .. .. .. | 15,130 | ,, | |
| 1 | *Adelaide* | .. .. | 5,100 | ,, | |
| 8 | *Leander* (including *Sydney*) | .. | 55,940 | ,, | |
| 3 | *Arethusa* | .. .. | 15,660 | ,, | |
| 34 | Ships | .. .. .. | 203,926 | ,, | |
| add 15 | –8″ gun Ships | .. .. | 144,220 | ,, | (assuming *Cumberland* increased to 10,000 tons by modernisation). |
| *Total* 49 | Ships | .. .. .. | 348,146 | ,, | |
| | L[ondon] N[aval] T[reaty] Allowance | .. .. .. | 339,000 | ,, | |
| | | *Excess* | 9,146 | ,, | |

10. In making this calculation, advantage has been taken of the wording of Article 16, paragraph 1, which says:—

'The completed tonnage in the cruiser, destroyer and submarine categories which is not to be exceeded on the 31/12/36 is given in the following table.'

Relying on this wording the deficiency of 2,580 tons in *sub-category* (*a*) has been set off against part of the excess in *sub-category* (*b*), leaving 9,146 tons in excess of the Treaty allowance to be accounted for.

11. This excess can be arranged for in one of two ways:—

(*a*) Making use of the 'Escalator' Clause of L.N.T.

(*b*) By obtaining the agreement of the U.S.A. and Japan.

12. With regard to (*a*), Article 21 of the London Naval Treaty reads as follows:—

'If, during the term of the present Treaty, the requirements of the National security of any High Contracting Party in respect of vessels of war limited by Part III of the present Treaty are, in the opinion of that party, materially affected by new construction of any Power other than those who have joined in Part III of this Treaty, that High Contracting Party will notify the other Parties to Part III as to the increase required to be made in its own tonnages within one or more of the categories of such vessels of war, specifying particularly the proposed increases, and the reasons therefor, and shall be entitled to make such increase. Thereupon the other Parties to Part III of this Treaty shall be entitled to make a proportionate increase in the category or categories specified; and the said other Parties shall promptly advise with each other through diplomatic channels as to the situation thus presented.'

13. In order therefore to justify this departure from the cruiser figures of Part III of the London Naval Treaty, under Article 21, it would be necessary to state that the requirements of our National security are materially affected by the new construction (since 1930) of another Power, and it would be necessary to specify the reasons therefor, i.e. the Power concerned and the new construction concerned. It is considered that the only justification we could quote in this manner for an increase in our 6″ cruiser tonnage would be the construction by France of 8 ships of the *Fantasque* and *Mogador* classes. (With one exception, the other 24 small French light cruisers were laid down before or during 1930.) To quote these particular ships would be somewhat invidious and perhaps regarded as insufficient.

14. Even, however, if we were to rely upon the provisions of Article 21 of the London Naval Treaty and declare our intentions to exceed our Treaty limits by 9,146 tons, the solution would be open to attack as evading the spirit of the Treaty since it is at least an open question whether the 2,580 tons deficiency under sub-category (*a*) can legitimately be offset against an excess under sub-category (*b*) and, in any event, the tonnage calculation in paragraph 9 above has been made by omitting the tonnage of all the cruisers in the 1933 programme which normally should have been completed in 1936 but are actually not expected to complete until January, 1937. This is in accordance with the letter of the Treaty but not altogether in accordance with its spirit.

15. With regard to the alternative course proposed in paragraph 11(*b*) above, in a document communicated to Mr. Atherton for transmission to President Roosevelt on 26th July, 1934 (Paper No. N.C.M. (35) 16),[6] it was stated that Great Britain accepted a cruiser tonnage figure based on the tonnage of 50 cruisers for the following reason, among others:—

(*b*) It was accepted subject to the Powers, other than the three signatories to Part III of the London Naval Treaty, agreeing to corresponding reductions. This has not occurred; on the contrary, the naval forces in Europe have greatly increased. If the 'Escalator' clause has not been invoked this has not been because the building of other naval Powers did not justify such a step but because it was thought better to await the meeting of the 1935 Conference to explain the grounds on which the cruiser tonnages accepted by Great Britain in 1930 could no longer hold good.

[6] No. 2.

It is thought that it would be better to adopt this line of argument, and to explain to the United States of America and Japan during the forthcoming Conference the reasons for which an increase in British cruiser tonnage after 1936 is essential, and adherence to the Treaty figure on 31st December, 1936, is not possible. This would produce an altogether better feeling of frankness and sincerity than would result from invoking Article 21 of the London Naval Treaty and quoting figures that are open to argument. It would be important to choose the psychological moment for making the proposal first to the United States of America and then to Japan.

16. Japan will probably demand some *quid pro quo*. This can only take the form of retention of some tonnage that would otherwise be scrapped under the terms of the London Naval Treaty, but the tonnage she has available for the purpose is small. If it was our intention to invoke Article 21, Japan would only acquire the right to a proportionate increase in 6″ gun cruiser tonnage, i.e., 60 per cent. of 9,146 = 5,488 tons.

*Summary*

17. It is therefore proposed . . .[7]

### Part II—Destroyers

18. The destroyer position is covered by Article 16 of the London Naval Treaty.

(*a*) 'The completed tonnage in the . . .[8] destroyer . . .[8] categories which is not to be exceeded on the 31st December, 1936, is given in the following table. . .[8]

British Commonwealth 150,000 tons.

(*b*) Vessels which cause the total tonnage in any category to exceed the figures given in the foregoing table shall be disposed of gradually during the period ending on 31st December, 1936.'

19. The reason for accepting 150,000 tons of destroyers at the London Naval Conference was explained at a meeting of the United Kingdom Delegation on February 28th, 1930, by Mr. Alexander[9] as follows:—

'As regards submarines, the question had been discussed by the American delegates on the basis that the Japanese would allow their tonnage to fall by wastage to 52,700 tons by 1936, thus enabling the British and American destroyer tonnage to be fixed at 150,000 tons. He and the Prime Minister had made it clear that though the figure of 150,000 tons might be accepted for the period of the agreement, it must be understood that this figure was subject to a proper agreement with France as regards Submarines and anticipated the subsequent reduction of Japanese submarines to 40,000 tons after 1936. When that reduction took place we should still require 150,000 tons.'

---

[7] The proposals here omitted were identical with conclusions (i), (ii), and (iii) listed in the opening paragraph of this document.  [8] Punctuation as in the original.

[9] Mr. A. V. Alexander, First Lord of the Admiralty.

20. During the subsequent discussions in which endeavours were made to get France and Italy to adhere to the London Naval Treaty, our right to an increased destroyer tonnage if France did not reduce her submarine tonnage was always upheld, and in the White Paper summarising the results of these negotiations (Command 3812 of 1931) it was stated that, in order to take account of the contingency that a satisfactory solution of the submarine problem may not prove possible in 1932, the right of the members of the British Commonwealth of Nations to increase their destroyer figure under Article 21 of the London Naval Treaty is fully reserved in paragraph B(*c*) of the Bases of Agreement.

21. At the present time France has 83 submarines of total tonnage 78,118 tons. 74 of these vessels are under age. During the period of the London Naval Treaty there have been no indications of a substantial reduction in her submarine tonnage, and reports from Japan show that the latter is likely to increase her submarine strength considerably as soon as she is free to do so. Italy has 67 submarines (49,242 tons) built and a further 12 vessels (7,830 tons) building.

22. It is clear that the basis on which we limited our destroyer tonnage to 150,000 tons has not been upheld and we are justified in retaining additional tonnage. This view was set out in N.C.M. (35) 1,[10] paragraphs 64 to 67, and in N.C.M. (35) 12,[11] Draft report of the Cabinet Committee, the Committee recommended:—

'That if submarine tonnage cannot be so reduced we require 200,000 tons in the destroyer category, of which not more than 150,000 tons may be under the age of 16 years.'

23. This recommendation, of course, was made when there was a prospect of quantitative limitation in the old form. That prospect has now vanished. The majority of the over-age tonnage in question is available and in view of the present international situation it is, in the opinion of the Admiralty, essential to retain it.

24. The tonnage position that the Admiralty desire at the end of 1936 is as follows:—

|  | Flotillas. | No. of Vessels. | No. of tons. |
|---|---|---|---|
| A to H.* | | 72 | 97,710 |
| Dominions. | 1 | 9 | 10,394 |
| 4·7″ V & W. | 2 | 18 | 20,920 |
| V & W. | 5 | 45 | 51,490 |
| S. Class. | — | 10 | 9,050 |
|  | | 154 | 189,564 |

* C. Flotilla assumed as 5 C. Class, 2 *Amazon* class and 2 S. Class.

[10] See note 3 above.    [11] Of June 11, 1934; not printed.

25. As explained in paragraph 12 above, Article 21 of the London Naval Treaty is the means provided in the treaty for varying the limitations agreed to. To invoke this article as regards destroyer tonnage involves a statement that we feel menaced by a certain Power—in this case France—on account of her submarine tonnage. To make such a statement now would be politically most undesirable. It is thought, therefore, that the method suggested for increasing cruiser tonnage should be adopted for obtaining the agreement of the U.S.A. and Japan to the retention in the Commonwealth destroyer category of 40,000 tons of over-age destroyers in excess of the London Naval Treaty figure.

26. Japan will probably demand some *quid pro quo* which will presumably take the form of retention of some tonnage that would otherwise be scrapped under the terms of the London Naval Treaty. She should have plenty of over-age destroyer tonnage to enable her to retain 60% of our proposed increase. To this we could not object. In view, however, of her expressed desire to increase her submarine strength it is possible that her proposal for a *quid pro quo* may take the form of a demand to retain some or all of the 10 or 12 submarines (totalling about 11,300 tons) which become over-age in 1937 to 1939. These submarines have to be scrapped under the terms of the Treaty by the end of 1936 to keep her tonnage within the agreed limits. It is considered that such a proposal should be resisted using the argument that if we chose to exercise our right of using the 'Escalator' clause she would only be entitled to claim an increase in destroyers. In the last resort, however, it is considered that it would be better to agree to the Japanese demand to retain some submarine tonnage rather than to make use of Article 21 of the London Naval Treaty which must involve a reference to French submarine tonnage.

*Summary*

27. It is proposed, therefore. . . .[12]

[12] The proposals here omitted were identical with conclusions (iv), (v), and (vi) listed in the opening paragraph of this document.

## No. 567

### Record by Mr. Craigie of a conversation with Mr. Atherton

### [A 10448/22/45]

*Most secret*                         FOREIGN OFFICE, *December 5, 1935*

Mr. Atherton called to-day at my request and I told him that I had heard from the Secretary of State that he (Mr. Atherton) thought it highly desirable that we should have a frank talk with the American representatives before the Conference opened in order to dispel any misunderstandings that might be in the air.[1] I asked Mr. Atherton to say, for my private and personal information, what particular points he had in mind.

[1] In a note to Mr. Craigie of December 2, Sir S. Hoare wrote: 'I lunched with Mr. Atherton today as he wished to raise with me the following question about the Naval

He replied that the main preoccupation was the question of our attitude towards Japan, since mischief-makers were always at work to give the idea that our real purpose was to improve our relations with Japan at America's expense. He himself knew that there was nothing in this but he was sure that there would be great advantage, particularly during Mr. Phillips' presence in London, in making it clear to the American representatives that there was, in fact, no divergence in policy between our two delegations. He thought that the main thing was to demonstrate that our objectives were the same, even though we might not altogether agree on the method of attaining these objectives.

I said I thought that our objectives might be briefly outlined as follows:—

(1) That we should try and preserve as much as possible of the limitation embodied in existing Naval Treaties even though changes had to be made to suit altering conditions. That meant that we should like to see a treaty emerge which provided both for quantitative and qualitative limitation.

(2) Having regard to Japan's attitude on the ratio question, it seemed hopeless to secure a quantitative agreement on the old lines. We should therefore try for an agreement limiting construction over a period of years without, however, cherishing much hope of attaining it. We had told the Japanese Government on several occasions that we could see no justification for their proposal for parity with the British Empire and that we were unable to agree to it. In the course of the discussions with the American delegates in June, 1934, it had been agreed that neither side would depart from its attitude of opposition to any increase in the Japanese ratio in any category without previous consultation with the other.[2] We had not changed our view on this point, though we were as strongly as ever of the opinion that anything in the nature of an Anglo-American front against Japan would be a great mistake. It was clearly in the interests of both our delegations, as well as of the Conference itself, that there should be no misunderstandings or suspicion on this or any other point between the American and United Kingdom delegations.

(3) Should it prove impossible to secure agreement on quantitative limitation, then we should concentrate our efforts on obtaining a qualitative treaty. On this point it would be a great mistake to take any step which had the appearance of endeavouring to isolate Japan. It would be much wiser to let the Japanese ascertain, by their own processes, that general opinion would be against them if they endeavoured to block a qualitative treaty.

(4) Should it unfortunately prove impossible to secure any multilateral

Conference. In his view there is no difference between the British and American views. He thinks, however, that Norman Davis is suspicious and that Philips [i.e. Mr. William Phillips] needs persuasion. This being so, he says that it is essential for N. Davis, Philips and [Admiral William] Standley to have a quiet and if possible a confidential meeting as soon as they arrive with the First Lord, Chatfield and you. I was impressed by his view. Could you take the matter up with him and if you and the others agree, arrange the meeting. S.H. 2/12.'                                                    [2] See No. 551, note 4.

agreement on any point, it would, of course, be desirable that there should be no competition between the British and the American navies. While it seemed to me impossible for the two countries to bind themselves in any way if everyone else was to remain free, I felt sure His Majesty's Government would be glad for the most complete exchange of views between the two countries in regard to their intentions. In any case, the principle of parity would remain intact.

Mr. Atherton stated that he considered that what I had said constituted a summary of objectives with which the American delegation could agree without difficulty. He believed that, if the First Lord were able to define our objectives in much the same way as I had done, we should completely disarm any suspicions that might be in the mind of any American delegate in regard to the policy we would pursue during the Conference. He added that, once this particular question was out of the way, he believed that we should find the American delegation far more accommodating when it came to decisions on technical matters.[3]

R. L. CRAIGIE

[3] In a minute referring to the last sentence of Sir S. Hoare's note (note 1 above), Mr. Craigie wrote as follows. 'A meeting with Mr. Norman Davis, Mr. Phillips and Admiral Standley has been arranged accordingly for Sunday evening [December 8] at 6 p.m. It is not possible to have the meeting sooner because the First Lord has a long-standing arrangement which obliges him to leave London about the same time as the Americans arrive. I have also had a talk with Mr. Atherton to-day in order to arrange the lines which Sunday's interview should follow. In order to make this interview with the Americans possible (for it is bound to leak out) we have been obliged to arrange similar interviews with all the other delegations. The interview with the Japanese delegates took place this morning, the First Lord, the First Sea Lord and I being present on our side. The Japanese had no suggestions to make, except that they wished the Christmas adjournment to be as short as possible! ... R.L.C. 5th December, 1935.' A United States memorandum on the meeting of British and American delegates on December 8 is printed in *F.R.U.S. 1935*, vol. i, pp. 156–8. No record of this meeting appears to be preserved in the Foreign Office archives.

## No. 568

*Letter from Sir S. Hoare to Mr. N. Davis*

[*A 10448/22/45*]

FOREIGN OFFICE, *December 5, 1935*

I am exceedingly sorry that, for urgent reasons of health, it will not be possible for me to welcome you when you arrive or to take part in the earlier proceedings of the Naval Conference. I write you this line, however, to say that I shall be following the proceedings of the Conference with great interest and that I hope to be able to participate in the work when the Conference meets again after Christmas.

SAMUEL HOARE

[1] Similarly worded letters were sent on the same day by Sir S. Hoare to the French and Italian Ambassadors. The formal opening and ending of the letters are missing on the filed copies.

## No. 569

*Memorandum by Mr. Eden on Article XIX of the Washington Treaty*[1]

*C.P. 238 (35) [A 10659/22/45]*

*December 7, 1935*

In accordance with the decision of the Sub-Committee on Defence Policy and Requirements on the 6th December, I circulate to my colleagues herewith an appreciation of the political considerations involved in the retention or otherwise of Article 19 of the Washington Treaty.

A. E.

FOREIGN OFFICE, *December 1935*[2]

### ARTICLE XIX OF THE WASHINGTON TREATY

In their memorandum of the 27th November, 1934[3] (circulated in D.P.R. 60)[3] the Chiefs of Staff reach the conclusion that, from the strategical point of view, it would be to our advantage to be no longer bound by the provision in the Washington Treaty which maintains the *status quo* in regard to the fortification of certain insular possessions in the Pacific. They point out, however, that there are other matters outside the strategical field which will have a material bearing on the ultimate decision as to the retention or otherwise of this article in any agreement that may be reached.

It may be mentioned at the outset that the fortification of the Japanese mandated islands and the establishment of military and naval bases in them are forbidden by the terms of the mandate itself, which is of earlier date than the

[1] Cf. No. 1, note 11, and First Series, Volume XIV, Nos. 545 and 563. Article XIX read as follows:—

'The United States, the British Empire and Japan agree that the *status quo* at the time of the signing of the present Treaty, with regard to fortifications and naval bases, shall be maintained in their respective territories and possessions specified hereunder:—

1. The insular possessions which the United States now holds or may hereafter acquire in the Pacific Ocean, except (*a*) those adjacent to the coast of the United States, Alaska and the Panama Canal Zone, not including the Aleutian Islands, and (*b*) the Hawaiian Islands;

2. Hong Kong and the insular possessions which the British Empire now holds or may hereafter acquire in the Pacific Ocean, east of the meridian of 110° east longitude, except (*a*) those adjacent to the coast of Canada, (*b*) the Commonwealth of Australia and its territories, and (*c*) New Zealand;

3. The following insular territories and possessions of Japan in the Pacific Ocean, to wit: the Kurile Islands, the Bonin Islands, Amami-Oshima, the Loochoo Islands, Formosa and the Pescadores, and any insular territories or possessions in the Pacific Ocean which Japan may hereafter acquire.

The maintenance of the *status quo* under the foregoing provisions implies that no new fortifications or naval bases shall be established in the territories and possessions specified; that no measures shall be taken to increase the existing naval facilities for the repair and maintenance of naval forces, and that no increase shall be made in the coast defences of the territories and possessions above specified. This restriction, however, does not preclude such repair and replacement of worn-out weapons and equipment as is customary in naval and military establishments in time of peace.'

[2] The date was incomplete on the filed copy.        [3] Not printed.

Washington Treaty. This prohibition would not be affected by the renewal or non-renewal of article 19 of the Washington Treaty, though non-renewal followed by further fortification of Hong Kong and American bases might strengthen Japanese desire to disregard the prohibition contained in the mandate, and it would be a difficult matter to enforce compliance or to take away the mandate.

I.—*International Political Considerations.* Amongst the other matters which must be considered are political considerations arising out of our relations with Japan. The Chiefs of Staff memorandum makes it clear that what is contemplated is a 'first-class naval base'. While the Chiefs of Staff memorandum does not say that any half-measures in this matter of fortification would not greatly help our strategical position in these regions, this conclusion seems to follow from the general arguments contained in the memorandum.

What is therefore likely to be the effect on Japan if we decide to turn Hong Kong into a first-class naval base? At the worst Japan might decide that it is best to strike while we are still weak in the Pacific and the capture of Hong Kong is a relatively simple matter. Again Japan might, in her present temper, decide to seize or 'lease' certain territory for an air base on the mainland of China and so greatly increase the difficulty of defending Hong Kong against air attack. While neither of these alternatives can be regarded as likely courses for Japan to take, they should not be dismissed out of hand as impossible. Thirdly, Japan might take no offensive action of any kind, but might nevertheless regard our action in creating a first-class base at Hong Kong as something even more dangerous for Japan than our activities at Singapore and as evidence of definitely hostile intentions on our part. A change for the worse in our relations with Japan would necessarily follow. The development of Singapore as a naval base has all along been distasteful to the Japanese, whose feelings would no doubt have been stronger if the progress made had been faster. A similar development so much nearer home as Hong Kong would certainly be resented in a much more lively manner. Much the same result would follow from a less ambitious but still considerable strengthening of Hong Kong, while the countervailing benefit would be materially less.

It is not suggested that these possibilities should, in themselves, deter us from fortifying Hong Kong, because, if we are to retain our position as a Great Power in the Pacific, we must be prepared to run risks and to take all steps we think fit for the defence of our territories. Nevertheless, this political aspect of the question should be given full weight in reaching a final decision as to the retention or otherwise of the provisions of article XIX of the Washington Treaty, and this is particularly the case at a time when the preservation of good relations is considered to be an object of great importance.

II.—*Considerations of Domestic Policy.* The fact that the Washington Treaty contains a provision limiting the fortification of certain possessions in the Pacific is well known to the general public here and is regarded in many quarters as one of the most useful provisions of that Treaty. Were His

Majesty's Government either to take the lead in abandoning this provision or even to make no effort to maintain it, a certain amount of public criticism must be expected, even though our case on strategical grounds may be strong.

III.—*Use of Article XIX as a bargaining counter with the Japanese Delegates.* Such indications as we have, whether direct from the Japanese or from secret sources, do not indicate any strong Japanese desire to retain this provision of the Treaty. Indeed, there is some reason to believe, from the wording of Japanese communications to us, as subsequently illustrated by Japanese press comment, that Japan would only wish to renew this provision if the area under consideration were to be modified in a sense favourable to Japan. It also seems possible that the development of the air-arm may have contributed to a change of view on the part of the Japanese Government since 1922. While, therefore, there is force in the Chiefs of Staff contention that we should endeavour to obtain some *quid pro quo* from Japan in other directions for the retention of Article XIX, it would be unwise to set too much store on the efficacy of this bargaining counter.

*Conclusion.* If the above political considerations are held to have some weight, then our best course may perhaps be as follows:—

(1) At the appropriate moment, express readiness to prolong this provision of the Washington Treaty, subject only to such modifications as may be necessary to bring it up to date in view of the development of the requirements of air defence since 1922.

(2) If Japan demands modifications unacceptable to us, they can be rejected with the knowledge that we shall not much mind if Article XIX disappears. If Japan proves intractable, she must take the blame for the non-renewal of the Article.

(3) In any case, ascertain the views of the United States Delegation (who may have new instructions) before a definite decision is taken that it would be in our general interest, from a political as well as from a strategical point of view, to allow these dispositions of the Washington Treaty to disappear.

### No. 570

*Draft[1] Record of a meeting with Japanese delegates at the Admiralty on Saturday, December 7, 1935, at 10.30 a.m.*

[*A 10356/22/45*]

PRESENT: *United Kingdom*: Admiral Sir A. Ernle Chatfield, Sir Warren Fisher, Mr. R. L. Craigie, Captain V. H. Danckwerts.

*Japan*: Admiral O. Nagano, Mr. M. Nagai, Rear-Admiral Iwashita, Mr. T. Terasaki, Mr. Mizota (Interpreter).

The basis of the discussion was the communication handed to Mr. Craigie

[1] This draft record, received in the Foreign Office from the Admiralty, was approved by Mr. Craigie on December 8.

by the Japanese Chargé d'Affaires on the 18th October (annexed to N.C.M. (35) 74).[2] Admiral Chatfield first raised the question of the common upper limit and whether Japan intends that it should apply to all Powers in the world. Admiral Nagano made it clear that, in the Japanese view, the relative strengths of the three principal Powers (United Kingdom, U.S.A. and Japan) was the matter which caused them the most concern. They would have no objection to the inclusion of France and Italy in the common upper limit formula since they were signatories to the existing Treaties, but had given no consideration to the extension of the idea to all other Powers. Later in the conversation, when pressed, he stated that there might be no objection to the inclusion of all Powers, even Russia, in view of the fact that they had not so far built up to the same level as the highly armed Naval Powers. Asked whether Japan intended to propose at the Conference a common upper limit applying to the three Powers only, Admiral Nagano replied no, it would be in a more general form.

2. After further considerable discussion it appeared that the Japanese idea was that starting from the theoretical right of parity to all countries, variation might subsequently be made in strength in accordance with the vulnerability of each of the countries concerned. This, in the Japanese view, would result in equality between Japan and U.S.A. but not necessarily equality between Japan and the British Empire. Admiral Nagano stated that Japan had no intention of taking any steps which would impair British security.

3. The Japanese representatives were asked to explain the passage in Mr. Fujii's communication which stated:—

'Any qualitative limitation unaccompanied by quantitative limitation would only prove to be a convenient means of reserving the existing relationship in naval strength among the Powers.'

Admiral Nagano explained that the existence of large ships, some of 35,000 tons with 16″ guns, many of them having been modernized, meant that ships of this size would be in existence for many years to come as powerful factors. If, therefore, in future ships were limited to a substantially smaller size, construction of such smaller ships would not, for many years, overtake the advantage already possessed by the Powers with the larger navies. It was explained to Admiral Nagano that we had no idea of gaining any advantage over Japan and that our 25,000 tons proposal was principally made for financial reasons. We felt that any qualitative agreement was better than none, and we were prepared to consider and hoped we would be able to accept any qualitative limitations that Japan might suggest.

4. Admiral Nagano made it clear that, in the opinion of Japan, the greatest factor for security is quantitative limitation and that security was the principal Japanese consideration. As regards the reduction in size of ships, if unaccompanied by quantitative limitation they felt that it might lead to an increase in numbers of ships thus facing [*sic*] a large fleet of small ships

[2] Cf. No. 541, note 1.

instead of a small fleet of large ships. For this reason they were inclined, if no quantitative limitation was reached, to allow qualitative freedom. In the Japanese opinion, quantitative limitation without qualitative limitation is a lesser threat to security than qualitative limitation without quantitative limitation.

5. It was made clear to the Japanese representatives that the United Kingdom's effort was also directed towards obtaining quantitative limitation, but that in the United Kingdom's view if it proved impossible to obtain it then it is far better to get qualitative limitation alone than no limitation at all. Admiral Nagano reiterated that Japan's latest concern was to obtain quantitative equality, and that if she could not get it she would have to give consideration as to how to meet her disadvantageous situation most economically. When asked whether that consideration would take place during the Conference period he would only reply that we must hope that we should not reach such a situation.

6. Admiral Chatfield drew the attention of the Japanese representatives to the passage in Mr. Fujii's communication which states that:—

'If abolition of capital ships, aircraft carriers and A. class cruisers cannot be obtained, the need for a sweeping qualitative limitation of these types is still recognised.'

The Japanese representatives were very unwilling to face this question, but finally said that once quantitative limitation was obtained their ideas would become very flexible.

7. Admiral Chatfield finally summed up the discussion as follows.

8. We both want to obtain equality of security.

9. Japan wants a common upper ratio for the three principal Powers. If that is agreed, she is willing to discuss qualitative limitation, but unless satisfied quantitatively, she reserves her position.

10. The United Kingdom wants quantitative agreement if we can get it, but we feel from previous discussions that the chances are very slender. If we cannot get quantitative limitation we stand for qualitative limitation applied to all Powers. We feel that in the London Naval Treaty we agreed to a three-Power arrangement, intending that France and Italy should subsequently adhere to it; we needed the adherence of these two Powers because their navies determine the strength of the European navies, and Great Britain has great responsibilities both of her own and as a Member of the League. When France and Italy failed to adhere to the London Naval Treaty we did not exercise our right to increased construction but determined to wait for the termination of the Treaty. Now we cannot go on with a three-Power agreement leaving out the European Powers. Within those limits we want to maintain close co-operation with Japan only asking her to recognise that equality of security may not be obtainable with a common upper limit. If that is so we then want to be free to build in accordance with the feelings of our people and the demands of our security. To have no limit, either quantitative or qualitative, would in our view be a calamity.

## No. 571

*Sir R. Clive (Tokyo) to Sir S. Hoare (Received December 9, 12.5 p.m.)*

*No. 326 Telegraphic [A 10440/22/45]*

TOKYO, *December 9, 1935, 6.45 p.m.*

In statement to the press December 8th Minister of Marine stated that Japan's fundamental policy of a common upper limit is unchanged and that reasonable settlement can be achieved 'if other Naval Powers cease to press for unreasonable superiority'.

Asahi says that Japan's demands for parity in Naval tonnage and restriction of offensive types of ships are fundamentally all important. Japan is not anxious to retain article 19 of Washington treaty but has no reason to object if retention is desired by the United States. A non-aggression pact in the Far East is superfluous as Japan's disarmament policy is based on making aggression impossible.

Jiji while in general agreement with above adds that independence of Manchukuo has placed on Japan responsibility for stabilising political situation in Eastern Asia and this together with rapid progress in naval armaments has rendered Japan's naval strength compared to that of the United States insufficient.

Other editorial comment is slight but vernacular press generally shows little optimism that the conference will achieve useful results.

## No. 572

*Sir R. Lindsay (Washington) to Sir S. Hoare (Received December 10, 9.30 a.m.)*

*No. 427 Telegraphic [A 10450/22/45]*

WASHINGTON, *December 9, 1935, 8.15 p.m.*

Naval Conference.

Apart from general atmosphere of pessimism there is little of note in to-day's papers. 'New York Times' however publishes a cable sent from London by Birchall[1] in which suspicion is expressed that United Kingdom hopes to manoeuvre Conference into a contest between Japan and United States with the latter resisting Japanese claims to parity and United Kingdom sharing in any benefit that may eventually result. 'British are good at that sort of tactic.'[2]

[1] Mr. F. T. Birchall, a press correspondent for the *New York Times*.

[2] Minutes attached to this telegram included the following. 'It is discouraging that this sort of thing should be beginning already . . . Mr. Craigie will speak to Mr. Davis . . . P. H. Gore-Booth. 11/12.' 'I did so—and Mr. Birchall, when Mr. Davis spoke to him, said that, being an Englishman, he had to be careful not to send anything which might savour of pro-British propaganda! R.L.C. 14/12.'

## No. 573

### Letter from Mr. Craigie to Captain Wassner

[A 10026/22/45]

FOREIGN OFFICE, *December 9, 1935*

Dear Captain Wassner,

I am much obliged to you for your letter of the 27th ultimo (No. 993)[1] in regard to certain points arising out of our conversation of the 9th November about the forthcoming Naval Conference.

On point (1) I am quoted as stating that Great Britain regards the 15″ calibre to be the most suitable for capital ships. I had certainly not intended to convey this impression to you and I am sorry if you obtained it from anything which I said. Actually, we would be prepared to go down to a calibre as low as 12″ if we could obtain general agreement for this purpose and we would consider such a calibre perfectly suitable for capital ships. The point, however, is not of great importance since we know, unfortunately, that there is very little hope of the United States Government agreeing to a gun calibre inferior to 14″.

There is also one other point which I should perhaps mention. You record my third question as being whether Germany would be prepared to be represented on a 'Committee of the Naval Conference at Geneva'. This was not quite the suggestion. The possibility I held out was that, once a general agreement had been reached in London, it might be held desirable by some Powers to complete the formalities of signature, etc. at Geneva. Unless I hear to the contrary, however, I will take it that your answer on this point means that the German Government would not wish to be represented at Geneva even for the purely formal purpose to which I have referred.

Yours sincerely
R. L. CRAIGIE

[1] No. 561.

## No. 574

### Sir R. Clive (Tokyo) to Sir S. Hoare (Received December 10, 9.30 a.m.)

*No. 327 Telegraphic* [A 10451/22/45]

TOKYO, *December 10, 1935, 12.50 p.m.*

Reports of opening of Conference[1] are fully reported to exclusion of other news. Asaka thinks that the British views are unsatisfactory because no basic formula for reduction of armaments is indicated. United States suggestion

[1] Speeches of delegates at the plenary opening meeting of the naval conference held at the Foreign Office on December 9 at 10.30 a.m. were fully reported in the press: cf. *The Times*, December 10, p. 21. Reports on meetings of the First Committee, which began at Clarence House on December 10 at 10.30 a.m., were confined to fairly brief, agreed press statements.

for twenty per cent all round reduction is made from selfish motives because that country will have to spend large sums to achieve present treaty limits while the suggested reduction will entail great sacrifices by Japan and none by United States. All the papers express pessimism with regard to results being achieved.

**No. 575**

*Letter from Captain Wassner to Mr. Craigie*

[*A 10709/22/45*]

LONDON, *December 10, 1935*

Dear Mr. Craigie,

I thank you very much for your letter of December 9th.[1]

May I give some explanations to the two points you mentioned:

ad 1.) In Sheet A which you gave us during the Anglo-German Naval talks, the British intention for Capital Ships was given with 25,000 t[on]s and 12″ guns. You told me at the 9th November that there would be no hope to carry through this size of Capital Ships in the now sitting conference but that the size of 35,000–32,000 ts would probably be fixed. Therefore it would be necessary to suggest another caliber of guns. And then in that case the British Government are thinking a 15″ gun to be the best caliber.

This was the idea I conveyed to my Government.—

ad 2.) In my report to Berlin I made the following statements:[2]

'Reference was made to the fact that the Disarmament Commission was still in existence at Geneva and that therefore, although the Naval Conference would reach its results in London through counter-signature, since the limitation of navies forms a part of the work of the Disarmament Conference, the final and concluding proceedings could possibly take place at Geneva without any additional discussions on the subject being held there. The British themselves preferred to bring the Naval Conference completely to an end in London, but they would not be in a position to resist the desire to terminate matters in Geneva should such desire be expressed by all other parties. Even though this question is not yet acute at present, the British would be glad to know what attitude Germany would adopt in such a case.'

I thought this report to be the exact meaning of our conversation—and so I am also understanding now from your letter of 9th December.—Therefore the German Government gave their answer in full knowledge of your suggestions.

I am

Yours sincerely

E. WASSNER

---

[1] No. 573.

[2] A filed Foreign Office translation into English is here substituted for the original passage in German.

# No. 576

### Sir E. Phipps (Berlin) to Mr. Eden
### No. 296 Saving: Telegraphic [A 10493/22/45]

BERLIN, *December 11, 1935*

My despatch No. 1306 of December 10th.[1]

A number of leaders have now appeared in the provincial press, but they contain no fresh comment of note.

Telegrams from London generally take the line that the Conference is doomed to early failure. On this ground and because of the interest shown in the Italo-Abyssinian compromise proposals little prominence is given to the question.

[1] This despatch, not printed, gave summaries of lengthy articles on the naval conference in the German press.


# No. 577

### Sir R. Lindsay (Washington) to Sir S. Hoare (Received December 13, 9.30 a.m.)
### No. 435 Telegraphic [A 10538/22/45]

WASHINGTON, *December 12, 1935, 4.48 p.m.*

My telegram No. 430.[1]

Japanese demand for parity is fairly widely reported in today's papers but there has been no tendencious news or editorial comment of interest either today or yesterday.

[1] This telegram of December 10 said that there had been no comment of interest in the Eastern press on the opening of the naval conference.


# No. 578

### Sir R. Clive (Tokyo) to Sir S. Hoare (Received December 13, 9.30 a.m.)
### No. 331 Telegraphic [A 10537/22/45]

TOKYO, *December 13, 1935, 12 noon*

Naval authorities reported to take exception to British view that equality in security and in armaments can be separated. They regret that Powers are unable to accept Japan's formula of common upper limit but do not necessarily abandon hope on that account. No editorial comment.

## No. 579

*Sir R. Lindsay (Washington) to Sir S. Hoare (Received December 14, 9.30 a.m.)*
*No. 442 Telegraphic [A 10561/22/45]*

WASHINGTON, *December 13, 1935, 7.32 p.m.*

My telegram No. 435.[1]

No editorial comment.

Messages from London give prominence to the united front created by the Japanese demands, due partly to the irritation of France and Italy at their omission by Japan from the list of countries to which the common upper limit should apply. Birchall in the 'New York Times' declares that the Japanese can understand the British need for a larger navy than theirs but cannot appreciate that the United States, a self-contained entity with the advantage of the Panama Canal, have a similar need.

This idea has, however, he says, not come out in direct conversations between the United States and the Japanese delegations, which have not been extensive but has rather been gleaned from minor delegations.

[1] No. 577.

## No. 580

*Record of a meeting between representatives of the United Kingdom and Japanese delegations held at the Admiralty on Friday, December 13, 1935, at 5.30 p.m.*

*L.N.C. (35) (U.K.) 1 [A 10612/22/45]*

PRESENT: *United Kingdom*: Viscount Monsell,[1] Admiral of the Fleet Sir Ernle Chatfield, Sir Warren Fisher, Mr. R. L. Craigie, Vice-Admiral W. M. James, Captain Danckwerts.

*Japan*: Admiral O. Nagano, Mr. M. Nagai, Rear-Admiral Y. Iwashita, Mr. T. Terasaki, Mr. K. Mizota.

ADMIRAL CHATFIELD enquired how, in the Japanese common upper limit proposal,[2] differences of vulnerability could be met by adjustments between the Powers. ADMIRAL NAGANO said that a Special Committee of Experts was required to study what are the various factors of vulnerability applying to each country and the relation between these factors. He held strongly that the best plan would be for this Committee to represent only the three principal Powers, but if the other Powers insisted Japan would be prepared to agree to a Five-Power Committee. In the opinion of the Japanese Delegation this Committee should only be appointed and work after the Conference had accepted the Japanese thesis of a common upper limit. If,

[1] Sir Bolton M. Eyres Monsell, First Lord of the Admiralty, had been created a Viscount on November 20, 1935.

[2] At the fourth meeting of the First Committee on the morning of December 13 (see *L.N.C. 1935 Docs.*, pp. 357–72) Admiral Nagano had completed his statement of the view of the Japanese delegation with regard to the establishing of a common upper limit.

however, it proved absolutely impossible to obtain the agreement of all Powers to the common upper limit first, then the Japanese Delegation would agree that the common upper limit might be discussed simultaneously with studies of the Committee on vulnerability.

2. ADMIRAL CHATFIELD pressed the Japanese representatives to explain what was in their minds as to the method of adjustment to be made between the different Powers; was it to be adjustment by varying strengths or by variation of the types of ships? ADMIRAL NAGANO finally stated that this question could only be decided by an actual case, it might be by different types, or by different numbers, or by both. He suggested that the most vulnerable Power should make a statement of its own requirements, then the Committee could consider those needs.

3. ADMIRAL CHATFIELD explained that we have stressed the great vulnerability of the British Empire on account of its geographical distribution in the world. This determined our absolute requirements alone, but we have also, of course, relative requirements depending on the strengths of other Powers. It seemed to him that our absolute requirements made the acceptance of any common upper limit so difficult. ADMIRAL NAGANO, whilst reiterating that the details of the vulnerability of the British Empire required future study, admitted that Great Britain's vulnerability is very great on account of the large scattered British Empire mainly dependent on seaborne commerce. Nevertheless, the degree of adjustment was something that could not be settled without further study.

4. ADMIRAL CHATFIELD pressed the point that the British Navy cannot all be concentrated in one part of the world; thus if we had a navy equal to that of Japan we could not send a force to the Pacific equal to that of Japan since we must keep forces in Europe. ADMIRAL NAGANO said that the Japanese understood our position very well and that they did not intend that we should have the same strength of Navy as Japan. Even in the Japanese formula differences of vulnerability are recognised, and the fact that Great Britain must keep forces at home is part of the difference of vulnerability. ADMIRAL CHATFIELD pointed out that the common upper limit theory meant permanent inferiority for the British Empire in the Pacific. All we required was equality in the Pacific to give our Dominions a sense of security to which they were entitled. ADMIRAL NAGANO reiterated that differences in vulnerability will call for adjustments so that the country with the greatest vulnerability will have the largest navy. He then drew a diagram to explain the Japanese theory. The horizontal line represented the common upper limit, above this peaks shewed the 'adjustments' required by the vulnerability of Great Britain, Japan and America respectively, the peak for Great Britain being larger than that for Japan and America. He then explained that the Japanese view was that having started from the common upper limit and calculated the increase required by vulnerability a proportionate reduction should be made by each Power so that the strength of that with the greatest vulnerability, viz. Great Britain, should coincide with the common upper limit, the strength of Japan and America being less. On the

diagram as drawn Japan and America were shewn as of equal strength. It was apparent that the Japanese plan simply means substituting a fresh set of ratios for those in the Washington Treaty and, if possible, reducing the general level of naval strengths. The Japanese Delegates maintained that their plan was fairer than prolonging the ratio of the Washington Treaty because they said it gave due consideration to vulnerability, i.e. a ratio based on vulnerability. Admiral Nagano said that though we might have a stronger navy than that of Japan we must not have a very large navy under the pressure of which Japan always feels that she is curbed. Speaking frankly, he said that they had studied relative strengths with great care and were convinced that the Japanese forces were inadequate vis à vis those of Great Britain. He quoted as an example the Russo-Japanese war[3] in which practically the whole of Russia's fleet was eventually sent to the Far East.

5. ADMIRAL CHATFIELD made it clear that we had found so far no ground for any reduction in British naval strength, nor do we think that our strength is too great relative to that of Japan. Should such a plan as the Japanese be agreed upon, the adjustments we would require would depend to a large extent on the strengths of the European Powers. Nevertheless, we would be willing to enter into a discussion on vulnerability if other Powers agreed to do so.

6. The discussion then centred round the procedure to be followed at next Monday's meeting.[4] The Japanese Delegates were asked whether they contemplated proposing to set up a Committee for the examination of vulnerability. At first they demurred to this procedure until the common upper limit had been generally accepted, but subsequently said that if a deadlock were reached on that point they would be willing, perhaps, to propose a discussion on vulnerability. It was pointed out to them that other Delegations would almost certainly refuse the common upper limit and would probably refuse to discuss vulnerability. It would be better, therefore, for the Japanese Delegation to prepare their path by further bilateral conversations with the other Delegations. Finally, the Japanese Delegation asked for further time to think over the question of procedure, and it was agreed that they should communicate their decision on Monday morning. They also agreed to bear in mind, whilst reflecting on the question, the British proposal to leave on one side for the time being the discussion of the common upper limit and to turn to some fresh subject, such as the British Quantitative Proposal.

7. It was agreed that the Press might be informed that the two Delegations had met to discuss between themselves the problems at present under the consideration of the First Committee of the Conference. It was further agreed that other Delegations might be informed that the two Delegations had had a discussion of the Japanese proposal in the First Committee, including the

---

[3] 1904–5.

[4] Following the proposal of the Japanese delegation it had been agreed at the meeting of the First Committee on December 13 that the meeting on Monday, December 16, should be confined to 'Heads of Delegations with one or two advisers present'.

exploration of the meaning of 'adjustments' to the common upper limit and the application of vulnerability. Nothing was to be said to the other Delegations about the Japanese views on the relative vulnerability of Japan and other countries, or the proposal to set up a Committee to examine this subject.

## No. 581

*Sir R. Lindsay (Washington) to Sir S. Hoare (Received December 16, 9.30 a.m.)*
[*A 10563/22/45*]

WASHINGTON, *December 15, 1935, 5.10 p.m.*
My telegram No. 445.[1]
Associated Press messages today express concern at introduction of secret bilateral conversations between delegations adding that United States delegates felt there is danger of one nation being played off against another. Suggestion is made that Japanese are trying to drive a wedge between Americans and British.[2]

Only editorial comment is in the New York Tribune which points out that if Japan is bent on policy of rule or ruin in the Far East, Western Powers will be better off without a Treaty of Naval Limitations than with one which while granting Japan equality of tonnage would in fact assure Japanese supremacy in the whole Western Pacific.

[1] This telegram of December 14 summarized reports of that date in the American press.
[2] A minute relating to this paragraph read: 'Mr. Davis has been urged not to let this hare escape again. And in any case the U.S. are arranging for a talk with the Japanese at an early date. P. H. Gore Booth. 16/12.'

## No. 582

*Sir R. Clive (Tokyo) to Sir S. Hoare (Received December 16, 9.30 a.m.)*
*No. 332 Telegraphic* [*A 10559/22/45*]

TOKYO, *December 16, 1935, 1 p.m.*
The 'Asahi' in an editorial believes that the United States and His Majesty's Government mean to present common front versus Japan on quantitative limitation, this opinion being strengthened by the report that His Majesty's Government is coming near the United States on the question of size of capital ships.

## No. 583

*Record of a meeting between representatives of the United Kingdom and Japanese delegations held at the Admiralty on Monday, December 16*

L.N.C. (35) (U.K.) 2 [A 10612/22/45]

PRESENT: *United Kingdom*: Admiral of the Fleet Sir Ernle Chatfield, Vice-Admiral W. M. James, Mr. R. L. Craigie, Captain V. H. Danckwerts.

*Japan*: Admiral O. Nagano, Mr. M. Nagai, Rear-Admiral Iwashita, Mr. T. Terasaki, Mr. K. Mizota.

The meeting was summoned for the purpose of learning the decision taken by the Japanese Delegation as to their next action after the reflection of the week-end.[1] Admiral Nagano stated that the question of vulnerability requires very deep study by all of us and all Powers participating must recognise the need for that study without which a solution to the present difficulties would be very difficult. Therefore if Admiral Nagano sees that he cannot yet get agreement on the principle of the common upper limit and sees that Delegations nevertheless are ready still to consider the question, he would postpone the proposal made on Friday for the setting up of a Committee to investigate vulnerability. He then quoted what was presumably a Japanese proverb:—

'It is better to wait for the Spring before sowing the seed.'

After further discussion it was made clear that Admiral Nagano would like to continue discussion of the principle of the common upper limit in Committee.

2. Admiral Chatfield recalled that at the meeting on Friday, 13th December,[2] the Japanese Delegation had put forward what seemed to us a modification of the idea of the common upper limit. To this Admiral Nagano replied that he did not consider that he had modified his original proposal in any way and reiterated that he considered equality or the common upper limit to be the essential preliminary to attaining a state of non-menace and non-aggression, but that he was willing to consider differences of vulnerability. Admiral Chatfield said that it still seemed to him that there was a modification since the common upper limit had been converted into an upper limit and resembled a return to the principle of ratios. He suggested, however, that no deadlock had yet been reached but that the other Powers did not yet clearly understand the Japanese idea. Until they did so it would be impossible for them to come to a decision about the common upper limit.

3. Mr. Nagai intervening said that he thought there might be a misunderstanding. In the Japanese mind no idea remained of any trace of a ratio. He also stated that the British increase above the common upper limit could not be published in black and white but must somehow be allowed for by a formula to be devised by a clever lawyer. Admiral Nagano added that all Powers would have the right to build up to the common

[1] Cf. No. 580, paragraph 6.      [2] See No. 580.

upper limit; he had, however, recognised the special British position in trying to formulate a plan to give effect to it without exciting a public commotion.

4. Admiral Chatfield pointed out that though he could understand the Japanese believed in their plan, other countries did not believe in it, and the Japanese Delegation has so far failed to convince them. The other Powers expect proof and not reiterated statements. He therefore proposed that at the next meeting of the Heads of the Delegations the British Delegation should ask this question:—

'The Japanese Delegation have put forward proposals for a common upper limit which we understand to mean that all Powers have the right to build up to equality in naval strength. The Japanese Delegation have also said that they realise that there are differences of vulnerability which must be met by adjustments within the common upper limit. Will the Japanese Delegation explain further what these adjustments are to be and whether they are to allow certain Powers to exceed the limit and others to reduce below it?'

Admiral Nagano indicated his readiness to reply in Committee.

5. Mr. Craigie, answering a remark of Admiral Nagano, pointed out that we have discussed the common upper limit principle for four days and that, so far, no Power except Japan has accepted it. It is no good asking Powers to accept a principle, the consequences of which they cannot foresee. The principle, if accepted, must inevitably apply to all the other Powers outside the present conference. Each country must be able to calculate the result of the application of the principle on its own defences. Admiral Chatfield added that under present circumstances even if the other Powers agreed to the common upper limit principle they would all do so with mental reservations governing its application to their own case. Admiral Nagano asked what then was to be the course of action to ensure the smooth progress of future discussions. Admiral Chatfield replied that the British Delegation would ask their question. The Japanese should give an answer and explanation and if they thought fit make proposals for establishing a Committee to examine vulnerability. Alternatively, if it seemed an easier course after to-day's discussion, the British proposal for declarations of construction could be taken up next without reaching any final judgment on the common upper limit principle.

## No. 584

*Sir R. Clive (Tokyo) to Sir S. Hoare (Received December 17, 12.20 p.m.)*
*No. 336 Telegraphic [A 10617/22/45]*

TOKYO, *December 17, 1935, 7 p.m.*

Naval Conference.

Minister for Foreign Affairs expressed to me today great satisfaction at good understanding between British and Japanese delegations.

Each he said fully understood the point of view of the other.

If no general naval agreement resulted he considered political understanding between Great Britain, United States of America and Japan was essential.

None of these three countries believed in possibility of war between any or all of them.

He did not actually mention non-aggression pact but evidently had this in mind; see my telegram No. 172, July 3rd, 1934.[1]

1 Cf. No. 8, note 1.

## No. 585

*Record by Mr. Craigie of a conversation with Mr. Nagai on December 16, 1935*
*L.N.C. (35) (U.K.) 4 [A 10612/22/45]*

*December 17, 1935*

After yesterday's Heads of Delegations meeting,[1] I had a private talk with Mr. Nagai. I said that we expected to have a Delegation meeting with the United States Delegation to-day, and that we might be asked whether Japan had agreed that the British Commonwealth might be entitled, under the Japanese scheme, to a greater naval strength than the United States.[2] We were a little embarrassed as to what we could say in reply and I wondered what the Japanese Delegation intended to say on this point when they met the Americans to-day.

Mr. Nagai replied that in no circumstances would the Japanese Delegation even hint to the American Delegation that they might agree to a higher level of strength for the British Commonwealth than for the United States, and the Japanese Delegation regarded it as of the utmost importance that the United Kingdom Delegation should respect their confidence on this point.

I suggested that, if the American Delegation put the question to us, we might reply that the Japanese Delegation had certainly indicated that account should be taken of the variations in vulnerability of the various Naval Powers, but that we had been unable to ascertain how the variations were to be calculated or precisely between which Powers they would operate. Mr. Nagai fully concurred in this suggestion.

We then passed to a general discussion of the Japanese common upper limit proposal. I said I thought he would agree that one result of the Conference so far had been to show that a common upper limit, even were it otherwise practicable, would have to be applied equally to all the Powers represented. It was an obvious corollary that the principle if adopted, must therefore apply to all the naval Powers of the world. Thus Japan was asking us to agree that every naval Power was to have the right to build up to parity with the British Commonwealth. It was true that the Japanese Delegation had suggested that, within the common upper limit, there should be adjustments according to vulnerability. But was it not obvious that,

1 See *L.N.C. 1935 Docs.*, pp. 389–400.
2 Cf. Admiral Nagano's comments in paragraph 4 of No. 580.

difficult as it was to agree on relative naval strengths even as things stood, it would become quite impossible if, as a first step, we had agreed that every European Power would have the right to parity? It was like asking the United Kingdom to go into a negotiation with its right arm tied behind it. I did not see how any British Government could ever agree to this proposition and survive.

It therefore seemed to me that, quite apart from the fact that we felt the present distribution of naval strength to be, if anything, more favourable to Japan than to us, there was an insuperable practicable difficulty in the necessary extension of any such principle to the other Powers of the world. Moreover, the attitude of the other Powers represented at the Conference had been extremely unfavourable. While therefore we in this country were most anxious to find some way of meeting Japan's difficulty in the matter of prestige, it was, I thought, only right to tell Mr. Nagai that I personally saw no prospect whatever of Japan's proposal being adopted by the Conference in its present form. On the other hand, we were on the point of putting forward a compromise proposal which we believed would, in practice, remove all possible ground for complaint in the matter of prestige and was certainly put forward in a very friendly spirit to Japan.

Mr. Nagai did not attempt to controvert my arguments and merely asked at the end what then I thought would be the procedure. I said the United Kingdom Delegation believed that, after the United Kingdom quantitative proposal had been given careful consideration at the Conference, we might proceed to the Franco-Italian proposal of 'préavis' and thereafter to the question of qualitative limitation. All these questions were intimately connected and I doubted whether definite decisions could be reached on any one point before the whole field had been surveyed. Mr. Nagai did not dissent from this procedure, nor did he indicate that Japan would have to adopt a passive rôle when we came to consider qualitative limitation.

R. L. Craigie

## No. 586

*Draft*[1] *Record of a meeting between United Kingdom and United States representatives held at the Admiralty on Tuesday, December 17, at 11 a.m.*

L.N.C. (35) (U.K.) 3 [A 10612/22/45]

Present: *United Kingdom*: Viscount Monsell, Admiral of the Fleet Sir Ernle Chatfield, Sir Warren Fisher, Mr. R. L. Craigie, Vice-Admiral W. M. James, Captain V. H. Danckwerts.

*United States*: Mr. Norman H. Davis, Admiral W. H. Standley, Mr. Ray Atherton, Mr. Noel H. Field, Commander R. E. Schuirmann.

The First Lord was not present at the opening of the meeting, being detained elsewhere. The First Sea Lord briefly outlined the United Kingdom

[1] As on circulated copy. For Mr. N. Davis's report of this meeting see *F.R.U.S. Japan 1931–1941*, vol. i, pp. 289–90.

bilateral interviews with the Japanese.[2] The United Kingdom had gained the general impression that the Japanese have some scheme at the back of their minds for adjusting the common upper limit for some Powers either above or below the general level. The Japanese idea is not at all clear. The United Kingdom representatives had finally stated that further clarity was necessary and that we should question the Japanese Delegation as was done at the Meeting of the Heads of Delegations on Monday afternoon.[3]

2. Mr. Norman Davis then gave a general account of the meeting between the U.S.A. and Japanese Delegation[s] on the morning of Tuesday the 17th.[4] The Japanese had reiterated their statement about the removal of menace and aggression and said that public opinion demanded that they should have parity with America. The U.S.A. had repeated their argument that the Washington Treaty gave equal security and that Admiral Kato had at that time said he did not want equality with the U.S.A. An attack on Japan with the existing ratios was not a possibility. On the other hand, the U.S.A. had the Philippines and Alaska to protect, both of which were nearer to Japan than to America, and the Japanese proposal would make it impossible for the U.S.A. to defend these places if Japan attacked them. The U.S.A. representatives said that if there was anything they could do to remove Japanese suspicion of the menace from the U.S.A. they would do it, provided that thereby they did not jeopardise their whole position. Finally, they said that definitely they could not accept the common upper limit and Japan could not accept the ratios. The world position at present is very disturbed— witness the war in Abyssinia and the Japanese armies on the march in China. The U.S.A. could not understand what Japan's policy was or what it might develop into. Consequently, the political foundation of the past treaties is now defective, and we could not erect another building on this faulty foundation.

3. The First Lord entered the meeting at this point.

4. Mr. Norman Davis said that he felt that the talk about non-menace and non-aggression meant ultimately that Japan would make a proposal of some kind of non-aggression pact. Admiral Standley said that a modus vivendi of some kind would be necessary. Since parity and the common upper limit alike could not be accepted he thought we might think over some form of agreement to continue the general structure of the present treaties with modifications. A preamble would be necessary setting forth equality of national status in some form, and the quantitative limitations of the existing treaties might be replaced by something on the lines of the British Building Declaration Proposal.[5]

Later, Admiral Standley suggested that we should have an upper limit of new construction for a period of years which no country might exceed; then we should have declarations of building intentions, and we should also require an 'Escape' clause which would permit the United Kingdom and

[2] See Nos. 580, 583, and 585.
[3] See *L.N.C. 1935 Docs.*, pp. 389–400.
[4] See *F.R.U.S. Japan 1931–1941, op. cit.*, pp. 285–9.       [5] Cf. No. 8.

U.S.A. in some way to exceed their intentions if the Japanese building rendered it necessary.

5. The First Lord asked whether the U.S.A. Delegation had obtained any idea of what special and particular types of warships Japan might have in view for securing her own defensive position in the absence of agreement to the common upper limit principle. Admiral Standley said they had tried to find out this but had got nothing.

6. Turning to future procedure, the First Lord thought it would be desirable to discuss the British proposal to be made this day, the French 'Pré-avis' proposal and then qualitative limitation, all without taking any hard and fast decision on any point. It was essential to get a general view of all the proposals and the possibilities before deciding to press for agreement on particular points.

7. Mr. Norman Davis said he would very much like to have three-cornered conversations. In reply to this the difficulties with France and Italy were pointed out to him. Mr. Norman Davis also agreed that we must be very patient with the Japanese and that we should bring them up to qualitative limitation very slowly. He suggested that it was important that we should adhere to principles but that we should not speak about 'principles', instead he accepted the suggestion of Mr. Craigie that we should use the word 'methods'.

Mr. Atherton asked if there was any particular objective that we wished to reach by Friday,[6] and Admiral Chatfield said we might look at it from the point of view of how would we like things to work out so that we can start on something fresh on the 2nd January. He suggested a possible course would be, we should all spend the Recess thinking what we should do next, and that the first meeting after the Recess should be one of Heads of Delegations to decide the next step.

8. It was generally agreed that we should carry on with discussion of the British proposals and possibly, also, the French proposal of 'Pré-avis', up to the time of the Recess, and that it might be more convenient and easier for the Japanese Delegation if some portion of that discussion was adjourned over the Recess so as to avoid too much of a break.

9. Mr. Norman Davis said that we must definitely state to Japan some time before the Conference breaks up, that if Japan does anything to disturb the present relative strengths, this action will be countered by the U.S.A. and Great Britain who will outbuild her whatever she does. He also thought the time will come when we must definitely say that we will not accept the common upper limit, but admitted that this had practically been said already.

10. Admiral Chatfield asked what would be the American view if Japan agreed to the building programme idea provided that it was accompanied by acceptance of the right to parity. Mr. Norman Davis and Admiral Standley replied very definitely, 'No, we could not accept that.'

11. Mr. Craigie explained that he had on several occasions used the U.S.A. as a 'bug-bear' when talking with European representatives, saying that if

[6] December 20.

there was no qualitative limit the U.S.A. might build very big ships, and that therefore any limit was better than no limit. He wished the U.S.A. to know that he had used this argument and to back it up if necessary. Admiral Standley was understood to say that they were prepared to build 70,000 ton capital ships if necessary. Admiral Chatfield pointed out that on the same naval income Japan could do much better than we could. She has cheaper labour and no large pension bill to absorb a portion of her Estimates. Nevertheless, Admiral Standley felt confident that either the U.S.A. or United Kingdom could easily outbuild Japan. Mr. Norman Davis said that two months ago, or more, the State Department at Washington had told the Japanese Ambassador that they were prepared to accept qualitative limitation alone if no quantitative arrangement could be made in order to ensure that a building race of types should not take place.

## No. 587

*Sir R. Clive (Tokyo) to Sir S. Hoare (Received December 19, 9.30 a.m.)*
*No. 343 Telegraphic [A 10680/22/45]*

TOKYO, *December 19, 1935, 12.35 p.m.*

Press is unanimous that His Majesty's Government's proposal, for declaration of programmes, is the ratio principle in another form.

At the meeting of the naval budget committee of the Lower House, Vice-Admiral Yamamoto is reported as saying that if the Japanese demand for common upper limit is not accepted, the Conference must break up, and Japan has no intention of signing any agreement devoid of both qualitative and quantitative limitations.

Nichinichi quotes naval authorities as saying that if non-treaty conditions result, Japan will in no circumstances take the lead in naval competition and Japan has a policy of armaments prepared in accordance with her own needs.

## No. 588

*Letter from Mr. Craigie to Captain Wassner*
*[A 10709/22/45]*

FOREIGN OFFICE, *December 20, 1935*

Dear Captain Wassner,

I am sorry that, owing to pressure of work, I have not been able to reply sooner to your letter of the 10th instant[1] in which you refer to certain points arising out of our conversation of the 9th ultimo.

With reference to what you say about a British preference for a 15″ gun, I think I should make it clear that our preference is definitely for a smaller gun, if general agreement on such smaller gun can be secured. As things

[1] No. 575.

742

stand, we think that the smallest gun on which agreement is likely to be reached is the 14″ gun and failing agreement on a smaller calibre it is the adoption of this calibre of gun which the United Kingdom Delegation may be expected to urge at the Conference. It was certainly never my intention to convey to you the impression that we would prefer the 15″ gun failing the general adoption of the 12″ gun and I should be grateful if this point could be made clear to the German Ministry of Marine.

As regards the second point in your letter, I am much obliged to you for letting me know the terms in which you had reported to Berlin our conversation in regard to the question of the final formalities of any naval agreement being concluded at Geneva. I quite agree with your record of what I said on this point.

Yours sincerely,<br>R. L. CRAIGIE

## No. 589

*Sir S. Hoare to Sir R. Lindsay (Washington)*[1]

*No. 410 Telegraphic [A 10799/22/45]*

FOREIGN OFFICE, *December 21, 1935, 9 p.m.*

After the Plenary Session on the 9th of December the Naval Conference resolved itself into a Committee of the whole Conference which held one meeting each day from the 10th to the 13th December inclusive.[2] At these meetings the Japanese proposal for a common upper limit of Naval strength between countries possessing Naval forces was discussed. A number of questions were put to the Japanese Delegation, but the answers given were somewhat too general in form completely to satisfy the Committee, and, in particular, the Japanese failed to explain how their plan would make proper allowance for differences of vulnerability and responsibility as between different countries. The Japanese reply was to the effect that the chief difference in vulnerability between different Powers lay in the difference between the armed strengths of those countries.

The proposal for a common upper limit was criticised not only by the Delegations representing the United States and members of the British Commonwealth, but also by the French and Italian Delegations. Both of the latter Delegations objected to the institution of any common upper limit which might not apply to them and the French Delegation particularly urged a more practical approach to the problem.

With a view to producing an informal atmosphere more favourable to progress, a Heads of Delegations meeting was held on the 16th of December[3] at which it was agreed that further discussion of the Japanese proposal should be deferred and a period allowed for reflection on them and if desired

---

[1] Identic telegrams were sent on the same day to Tokyo (No. 256), Paris (No. 340 Saving), Rome (No. 128 Saving), Berlin (No. 49 Saving), Moscow (No. 10 Saving).

[2] For stenographic notes of these meetings see *L.N.C. 1935 Docs.*, pp. 263–388.

[3] *Ibid.*, pp. 389–400.

bilateral conversations about them. In order, however, that the Committee's time should not be wasted it was decided that the meetings should continue and that the next meeting should take up consideration of the United Kingdom proposals for quantitative limitation by voluntary and unilateral declarations regarding future naval construction.

This proposal was advanced at a full meeting on the 17th of December.[4] The reception given to the proposal made was in general favourable; the United States accepting it as a basis of discussion and the Delegates of the Commonwealth of Australia, Canada, India and New Zealand expressing general approval. At a further meeting on the 19th[5] the French and Italian Delegates both expressed the view that the scheme put forward merited careful examination though both showed a preference for a shorter period than 6 years for giving notice of intended construction. The Italian delegation were not inclined to accept the view that building plans could be concerted in advance consistently with declarations being really unilateral.[6] The Japanese delegation on the 20th December sharply criticized the U.K. plan and restated their view that a common upper limit was a basic necessity for an agreement.[7] The Conference then adjourned until the 6th January when the United Kingdom plan will be discussed further.

The atmosphere at the discussions has been friendly throughout. Particular exertions have been made by the United Kingdom Delegation to maintain continuous and friendly contact with the Japanese with whom bilateral discussions have been held on two occasions[8] and the relations between the two Delegations are satisfactory. Useful bilateral talks have also taken place between the United States and United Kingdom Delegations[9] and the United States and Japanese Delegations have also met.[10] Close touch is being maintained between the United Kingdom and Dominions Delegations, who have held two meetings together.

The United Kingdom press has not devoted very much space to the Conference but such comment as there has been is for the most part innocuous and well informed.

---

[4] *L.N.C. 1935 Docs.*, pp. 415–28.    [5] *Ibid.*, pp. 443–54.    [6] *Ibid.*, p. 482.
[7] *Ibid.*, pp. 476–79.    [8] See Nos. 580 and 583.    [9] See No. 586.
[10] See *ibid.*, note 4.

## No. 590

*Sir R. Clive (Tokyo) to Sir S. Hoare (Received January 14, 1936)*

*No. 626 [A 400/4/45]*

*Very confidential*                                                  TOKYO, *December 21, 1935*

Sir,

I was somewhat taken by surprise when the Minister for Foreign Affairs opened our conversation on December 17th by expressing his great satisfaction at the good understanding between the British and Japanese delegations to the Naval Conference in London.[1] To judge from such limited newspaper comments as there have been since the Conference opened, I was not prepared for this gratuitous appreciation from the Foreign Minister.

2. Mr. Hirota's remarks may, however, have been deliberately intended to lead up to what he then proceeded to say, namely, that if no general naval agreement resulted, a political understanding between Great Britain, the United States of America and Japan was in his opinion essential.

3. You will recollect that shortly after my arrival in this country Mr. Hirota said to me in the course of an interview on July 3rd, 1934, as recorded in my despatch No. 369[2] Confidential of July 5th (paragraphs 7 and 8) that Japan would be only too ready to conclude non-aggression pacts with America and Great Britain.

4. The same idea still lingers but the underlying motive may be different. His Excellency, when referring to the unfortunate possibility of no general naval agreement materialising, said that if there was a political understanding between the three big Powers in the Pacific, the actual size of fleets or types of ships would be matters of secondary importance. Once it was admitted that war between any of these three countries was not a problem to be considered—and he himself did not in fact consider that it was to-day a problem—we could then begin seriously to discuss naval disarmament.

5. I mentioned this conversation in strict confidence to my American colleague,[3] who came to see me yesterday on his return from leave. He said, as I expected him to say, that so far as he knew his Government had never considered any sort of political understanding as hinted at by Mr. Hirota. A collective pact might be different. I said I did not believe that a collective agreement embracing the U.S.S.R. and China was practical politics for the simple reason that the Japanese Government would never for a moment consider it. On the one hand nothing would induce the Japanese Government to tie their hands in China, on the other the Japanese military still look upon Soviet Russia as their natural enemy to fight whom is not only their ambition but their predestined duty.

6. It is perhaps worth while to reflect on the changes which have come about in the Far Eastern situation during the past eighteen months, *i.e.* since Mr. Hirota first hinted at a political understanding between Japan, Great Britain and America.

7. In the first place Japan has pursued unchecked her policy of consolidation in Manchukuo. She has purchased the Chinese Eastern Railway; she has driven out the two great foreign oil companies.

8. Secondly, by her forward policy last summer in North China and the present active support of autonomy for the provinces of Hopei and Chahar, she is relentlessly continuing what Mr. Owen Lattimore calls the 'process' begun by the conquest of Manchuria (see my despatch No. 618 of December 20th).[4]

---

[1] Cf. No. 584.    [2] Cf. No. 8, note 1.    [3] Mr. J. C. Grew.

[4] Not here printed; documents relating to Far Eastern Affairs at this time will be printed in a subsequent volume in this Series. The reference was to an article in the December 1935 issue of *Pacific Affairs* by Mr. Owen Lattimore, editor of that periodical.

9. Thirdly, she has scrapped the Washington Treaties and to all appearance fully intends to submit to no restrictive engagements regarding the development of her Navy or her policy in China.

10. Fourthly, the Philippines have now acquired limited independence and everything seems to point to an ever-increasing disinterestedness on the part of the United States in political developments in the Western Pacific.

11. Fifthly, prognostications of Japanese financial exhaustion have been belied. Her currency has remained stable, her trade has continued to develop and for the first time in several years has shewn a favourable balance (*viz*: Yen 17,000,000 for the eleven months ending November 30th).

12. During the past year we have been passing through one of those periodical waves of anti-foreign, notably anti-British, feeling in spite of the fact that the Emperor of Japan and his Court, the Foreign Minister and many distinguished Japanese desire nothing better than really good relations with Great Britain. Mr. Matsudaira, the Japanese Ambassador in London, has actually toured important centres, with the approval of Mr. Hirota, to work for a good understanding with Great Britain and to explain the British point of view.

13. I have carefully re-read Sir John Simon's despatches Nos. 624[5] and 672[6] of October 8th and 30th, 1934, but venture to submit with all respect that Mr. Hirota's latest hint should not be lightly ignored and that it is again a matter for serious consideration in the light of current events whether we stand to gain more or to lose more by coming to a political understanding with Japan. I presume that the objections would be considerably less if the Americans were prepared simultaneously to consider doing so. If any such understanding comprised a Japanese guarantee about the Philippines it might perhaps be less unpalatable to them. I trust therefore that you will approve my action in confidentially informing my United States colleague of what Mr. Hirota said.

14. From the British point of view I imagine that the antagonism which might be aroused in Canada and possibly Australia would be allayed if the United States' attitude was sympathetic.

15. On Soviet Russia such an understanding would inevitably fall like a bombshell, but to Germany, judging from the attitude of my German colleague,[7] it would be more likely to appear as a natural and perhaps not unfavourable development.

I have, &c.,

R. H. CLIVE

[5] No. 26.  [6] Not here printed; cf. No. 67 and note 4 above.
[7] Dr. H. von Dirksen.

## No. 591

*Letter from Sir R. Clive (Tokyo) to Sir V. Wellesley (Received January 14)*
*[A 401/4/45]*

Private                            TOKYO, *December 21, 1935*

My dear Victor,

The Japanese are apt to make a vital proposal in a casual and off-hand manner.

I have discussed Hirota's latest suggestion in my despatch No. 626 of to-day.[1] The interview at which it was made was quite unexpected.

A few days after my return from a short holiday I thought it well to go and have a talk with Shigemitsu.[2] We actually talked for nearly two hours. When I got up to go I apologised for staying so long. He said, 'not at all, wouldn't you like to see Mr. Hirota?' I said of course I was always at His Excellency's disposal, but I did not wish to trouble him unnecessarily. 'I'm sure he would be delighted to see you', he replied. So I went across to his room. After exchanging the usual politeness he started straight off on the Naval Conference and astounded me by expressing his gratification at the admirable understanding between the British and Japanese delegations. Press reports had led me to expect nothing of the sort, although there had been no mention of any friction.

When he came to talk of some political understanding between the Japanese and ourselves and the Americans it was not in the nature of an offer but more of a pious hope, but that I take to be merely the Japanese method. If there is no reaction from our side there is no loss of face to himself. No offer would have been turned down because none had been made.

I met Matsudaira the day before and he too spoke of the good understanding between our delegations. It is not improbable therefore that Hirota and Matsudaira had put their heads together before this 'pious hope' was expressed. I can hardly believe, however, that the Americans will even consider it, but thought it well to tell Grew at once in case anything leaked out and also in order to see his reaction. He will no doubt inform his Government.

Yours ever,
R. H. CLIVE

[1] No. 590.        [2] Japanese Vice-Minister for Foreign Affairs.

## No. 592

*Sir R. Clive (Tokyo) to Mr. Eden[1] (Received December 27, 9.30 a.m.)*
*No. 347 Telegraphic [A 10894/22/45]*

TOKYO, *December 27, 1935, 12.55 p.m.*

In press interview believed to be authentic Navy Minister stated that

[1] Mr. A. Eden had been appointed Minister for Foreign Affairs on December 22, on the resignation of Sir S. Hoare.

unless Great Britain and the United States abandoned their idea of superiority and frankly furthered real spirit of disarmament it would be extremely difficult for further discussion to result in new agreement. Great Britain and United States must either accept or reject Japan's fundamental policy of common upper limit. These were the two alternatives. Japan would merely reiterate explanations of this policy when conference reassembled but it seemed unlikely that Great Britain or United States would alter their opinion during the recess.

Asahi in probably inspired leader, after saying that there is no reason for optimism in the future of the conference, states that Great Britain and United States wish to maintain existing ratio because they are suspicious of Japan's policy in the Far East which amounts to saying that naval limitation by ratios as desired by these Powers threatens Japan's security.[2]

This want of confidence is a more serious threat to international peace than is any agreement or lack of agreement regarding naval limitation. In order to secure international peace it is essential to discover the underlying causes which make agreement impossible to achieve.

[2] A marginal note in Mr. Craigie's handwriting on the filed copy here read: 'non-sequitur.'

## No. 593

*Sir R. Clive (Tokyo) to Mr. Eden (Received December 27, 9.30 a.m.)*

*No. 349 Telegraphic [A 10893/22/45]*

TOKYO, *December 27, 1935, 1.20 p.m.*

My telegram No. 347[1] appears to show that Japanese will not budge from this attitude and never intended to. My despatch No. 626[2] amplifying and discussing the subject of my telegram No. 336[3] will only reach you about January 20th by bag. I have no doubt that Japanese Government would welcome some political understanding with us and if possible Americans which would justify reduction in their naval expenditure. I told my United States colleague at the time of what Minister for Foreign Affairs said and now venture to suggest that it might be of interest to ascertain unofficially reaction of United States Government to Minister for Foreign Affairs' idea. See also my telegram No. 346[4] in this connexion.

[1] No. 592.     [2] No. 590.     [3] No. 584.     [4] Of December 27, not printed.

## No. 594

*Minute by Mr. Craigie*

*[A 164/4/45]*

FOREIGN OFFICE, *December 29, 1935*

Mr. Holman's memorandum[1] gives a good summary of the proceedings

[1] This memorandum of December 28 is not printed. It gave a short summary of the work of the Naval Conference from December 9 to December 20. Mr. A. Holman (cf. No. 476, note 3) had been appointed Secretary-General of the Naval Conference at the first plenary session on December 9, 1935.

748

up to date. It may be useful to summarise my impressions and indicate the line we propose to take in the future.

The more satisfactory features of the discussions up to date are:

(1) The French and Italians have played up well during the debate on the Japanese proposal for a common upper limit. Resisting the temptation to fish in troubled waters, they have given the Japanese no encouragement.

(2) After a full and friendly discussion of their common upper limit proposals, the Japanese Delegation agreed readily enough to the adjournment of the discussion to some future date, thus leaving the field clear for the discussion of the British proposal for quantitative limitation. Had the Japanese wished to be completely uncompromising, they would first have forced a decision on their proposals and then, after their inevitable rejection, have refrained from playing any further useful rôle. This rock has been avoided for the moment.

(3) The Japanese Delegation have admitted that, once the principle of a common upper limit has been accepted by all the Powers represented at the Conference, 'adjustments' in naval strength will have to be made to take account of varying degrees of vulnerability (the higher relative vulnerability of the British Commonwealth having been recognised by the Japanese Delegation in *private* and *secret* conversation). But this admission has little practical value because (*a*) Japan considers her vulnerability to be at least as high as that of the U.S.A.; and (*b*) neither France nor Italy will look at any plan which re-establishes the ratio system (and this is what the Japanese talk of 'adjustments' means).

(4) Amongst the many conflicting and confusing statements made by the Japanese Delegation, the British Delegation believe they detect, as through a glass darkly, a proposal that the standard for measuring varying vulnerabilities should be 'equality of strength at the point of attack'. Such value as this admission might have was, however, largely discounted by the subsequent remarkable contention that any Power can at any given moment concentrate all its fighting ships at one given point.

Taking the discussions on the Japanese scheme as a whole, it may be said that, the more closely it is examined, the more impracticable and unacceptable it appears. When a Delegation solemnly and insistently avers that differences in vulnerability between States, due largely to geographical causes, can be to a great extent eliminated by the mere equalisation of navies, it is difficult to find any common ground for a compromise. Our hope has been that, if the Japanese are given a 'good run for their money' and have time to satisfy themselves that their proposal is acceptable to no-one, they may agree in the end to participate in the subsequent discussions on qualitative limitation and to be a party to the treaty which we hope to conclude on this subject and on all matters covered by existing treaties except quantitative limitation. But this hope may well prove illusory and what then? Is there any way in which Japan can be enabled to drop her common upper limit proposal without loss of face?

Many face-saving solutions have been investigated and rejected as being either dangerous or ineffective. There might, for instance, be a limit of construction which no Power would exceed during a certain period of years. But, to be acceptable to us, the limit would have to be sufficiently high to give us plenty of elbow-room in the event of Japan or any other Power embarking on an unexpectedly high construction programme; and to put forward a maximum limit well above anything *we* in fact expect to build would be rather a farcical proceeding. Similarly, we have for some time been considering whether any form of political understanding between the United States, Japan and ourselves would ease this naval difficulty. So far no very hopeful method of approach to a political *détente* has been discovered, but I am not sure that our earlier examination of the political aspect has been sufficiently exhaustive, and I propose shortly to submit certain further suggestions in this field. We need only, of course, fall back on such face-saving schemes if we satisfy ourselves that our plan to bring Japan into line with the other Powers on qualitative limitation is definitely doomed to failure.[2]

R. L. CRAIGIE

[2] This minute was initialled by Sir R. Vansittart on December 30, and minuted 'Seen by S. of S.' by Mr. Hoyer Millar, Assistant Private Secretary to Mr. Eden, on January 2, 1936.

## No. 595

### Letter from Mr. Wallinger[1] to Mr. Dixon[2]
### [A 630/4/45]

CAPE TOWN, December 31, 1935

My dear Dixon,

The South African press, of course, took notice of Admiral Nagano's objection to the presence of Dominion representatives at the Naval Conference.[3] Most of the papers, however, only report the incident and do not venture upon comments.

The 'Bloemfontein Friend', however, considers that the Japanese objections are not difficult to understand. It admits that constitutionally Mr. te Water[4] has every right to be present, but it suggests that it would be 'wiser on practical and realist grounds if the Union Government decided to ask him to stop away'. The writer considers that as the South African Navy is a

[1] A member of the Office of the British High Commissioner in the Union of South Africa.

[2] An Assistant Secretary in the Dominions Office. Mr. Dixon's covering letter of January 20, 1936, transmitting to the Foreign Office a copy of the above letter, has not been preserved in Foreign Office archives.

[3] At the fourth meeting of the First Committee, held on December 13, Admiral Nagano had said: 'We came with the understanding that we were attending a five-Power Conference, but if each of the Dominions is to be counted as an independent country, what will be the number of participants in the Conference?' See *L.N.C. 1935 Docs.*, pp. 366–72.

[4] High Commissioner in London for the Union of South Africa and delegate to the Naval Conference.

figment of the imagination, good sense 'should decide the High Commissioner to leave the naval problems of the world to the Naval Powers'.

Yours sincerely,

G. A. WALLINGER

## No. 596

*Mr. Eden to Sir R. Clive (Tokyo)*

*No. 3 Telegraphic [A 10895/22/45]*

*Confidential*                    FOREIGN OFFICE, *January 4, 1936, 3.5 p.m.*

Your telegram No. 349.[1]

I had gathered from your telegram No. 336[2] that Japanese Minister of Foreign Affairs favours a political understanding merely as a substitute for a naval treaty and not as a means of securing naval agreement. Pending the receipt of your despatch No. 626,[3] now on its way, I should be glad of your views by telegram on this important point.

If there is failure to secure agreement even on the qualitative limitation of naval armaments, this would be the result of the Japanese attitude, since the other Powers appear ready to recognise the importance of preventing a race in type and sizes of ships and guns and are prepared to make mutual concessions with a view to reaching general agreement. It is obvious that the failure in such circumstances of a conference to which Pacific Powers other than Japanese attach importance would be a poor foundation on which to seek to build a political understanding between those Powers and Japan. From our point of view—and we believe also from the point of view of the United States of America—the value of such a political understanding must to a great extent depend on its effectiveness in promoting a naval agreement and so obviating the risk of naval competition.

Japan's proposal for a common upper limit, based on the thesis that the equalisation of naval strengths between all Powers would in itself confer virtual equality of security on such Powers, is not only unacceptable to the countries represented at the Conference but, so far as we know, receives no support from any other naval Power. The further consideration by the Conference of the Japanese proposal has been postponed to some later date but, if the Japanese Delegation press for a decision, the plan is bound to be rejected. Furthermore, the Japanese Delegation, have so far opposed the only practicable compromise which has been suggested, namely the United Kingdom proposal for limiting construction by voluntary and unilateral declarations. The chances of any agreement on quantitative limitation are therefore very remote.

Apart from abstruse and questionable arguments of a theoretical order, the ground put forward by Japan for this rigid attitude is that, with naval strengths as they are, Japan is under the constant threat of naval aggression, more particularly from the United States. While this argument may appear to us to be somewhat far-fetched, it is fair to assume that Japan's attitude

[1] No. 593.        [2] No. 584.        [3] No. 590.

751

towards the naval question is not based purely and simply on her determination to secure a free hand in China. In the circumstances the only alternative to a breakdown of the Conference may be the conclusion of pacts which would give Japan such additional security in the political field as will compensate for the failure to secure equality in naval armaments. So far the idea of non-aggression Pacts between Japan, the United Kingdom and the United States of America has broken down owing to Japanese reluctance to include any undertaking to respect the integrity of China south of the wall. If, however, there is any chance of a Sino-Japanese non-aggression treaty, the conclusion of similar Pacts between the principal Pacific Powers would doubtless be facilitated. You will appreciate however that we should not and cannot exercise any pressure in this direction.

Pending the receipt of a reply to the question put in the first paragraph of this telegram, please regard the above appreciation of the position as being sent for your own information and for such observations upon it as you may wish to offer. In particular you should not discuss the matter with your U.S. colleague, since the first approach to the U.S. Government would require to be made through their Delegation here. I should also be glad to know whether Mr. Hirota is expecting an answer to the suggestion made in paragraph 3 of your telegram No. 336[2] or whether this is to be regarded merely as a passing observation.[4]

[4] This telegram was drafted by Mr. Craigie. The draft was extensively minuted. Mr. Craigie's minute of January 1 included these comments: '. . . our objections, and those of the United States, to the conclusion of non-aggression pacts with Japan would lose much of their force if China herself were to conclude such a pact simultaneously. I do not wish to exaggerate the practical importance of such pacts, of which there are already too many. But their psychological effect is sometimes such as to start policies moving along new and better lines and, in the present case, we have the practical incentive of seeking to prevent a breakdown of the Naval Conference. There is the further advantage that a political détente of this character would tend to enhance the credit of the civilian elements in the Japanese Cabinet at the expense of the militarists.' Mr. C. W. Orde of the Far Eastern Department feared, however, that 'Japan would find it hampering and that it would be of no particular value to her unless it meant Chinese abstention from intrigues in, and attempts to recover, Manchukuo and Inner Mongolia. And unless the Japanese army have changed their mind about a non-aggression pact with Russia, the conclusion of which they prevented a couple of years ago, they would hardly want the precedent of one with China. But if a Sino-Japanese pact were to materialise it would certainly remove any grievance the Chinese might have over a U.S.–U.K.–Japanese one. C.W. Orde. 1/1.' The draft was sent to Sir Warren Fisher and the Admiralty for comments. It was approved by Mr. Eden on January 4.

No. 597

*Mr. Eden to Sir R. Clive (Tokyo)*
*No. 4 Telegraphic [A 145/4/45]*

*Secret*                                    FOREIGN OFFICE, *January 4, 1936, 10 p.m.*

My immediately preceding telegram.[1]

The Japanese Delegation have informed us in strict secrecy that, in view of

[1] No. 596.

752

the greater vulnerability of the Members of the British Commonwealth of Nations as compared with that of other countries, their Government would be prepared to agree to some excess over the common upper limit being made in our case—but in our case only.[2] This suggestion does not of course help towards a solution because: (a) the United States would in no circumstances agree to parity with Japan or to less than parity with the British Commonwealth; (b) France and Italy, who are already strongly opposed to the Japanese proposal, would like it even less if accompanied by such an amendment; (c) we gather that the margin to be accorded to the British Commonwealth of Nations should, in the Japanese view, be well below the superiority over Japan which we at present possess and which, in our special geographical, economic and strategical position, we consider essential for our security.

[2] Cf. No. 580.

## No. 598

*Sir R. Clive (Tokyo) to Mr. Eden (Received January 6, 9.30 a.m.)*
*No. 2 Telegraphic [A 126/4/45]*

*Confidential*                                        TOKYO, *January 6, 1936, 1.40 p.m.*

Your telegram No. 3[1] paragraph 1.

In paragraph 4 of my despatch No. 626[2] I wrote as follows:—

'His Excellency when referring to unfortunate possibility of no general naval agreement materializing said that if there was a political understanding between the three big Powers in the Pacific, the actual size of the fleets or types of ships would be a matter of secondary importance. Once it was admitted that war between any of these three countries was not a problem to be considered—and he himself did not in fact consider that it was today a problem—we could then begin seriously to discuss naval disarmament.'

My own view of Japanese attitude, which is shared by Naval Attaché, is that the Navy are absolutely determined to have a free hand and will accept no compromise to their own proposal of common upper limit. Naval Attaché thinks that they do not want a Naval Treaty.

Minister for Foreign Affairs, whose policy is good relations with all countries and definitely pacifist, knowing that owing to uncompromising attitude of the Navy, Japanese, British and American views on naval limitations are quite incompatible, has reverted to the idea which he first raised with me 18 months ago of a political understanding between three Pacific Powers.[3] I doubt if he has thought out the matter in detail and he did not request me to submit his suggestion to you. It was an obvious 'ballon d'essai' but he will be intensely interested to know your reaction.

His Excellency should be under no illusion as to the views of His Majesty's Government on the subject of Japanese policy towards China. While Japanese Government will not, I feel sure, give us or the Americans any

[1] No. 596.          [2] No. 590.          [3] Cf. No. 8, note 1.

guarantee regarding China excepting possibly in regard to foreign interests they are equally determined to avoid hostilities and it seems likely that Chinese proposal for conference to discuss Sino-Japanese problems may be accepted by Japanese Government.

I believe that if United States Government attached as condition for any political agreement Japanese guarantees about the Philippines the Japanese Government would not refuse to consider this.

## No. 599

*Record by Mr. Craigie of a conversation with Mr. Nagai on January 5*
*[A 277/4/45]*

Secret                                                    FOREIGN OFFICE, *January 6, 1936*

In the course of a talk on the naval question with Mr. Nagai at my house yesterday, I expressed the purely personal opinion that we had not yet exhausted the 'political' method of finding a way round the difficulties now confronting the Conference. As Mr. Nagai doubtless knew, we had had, about a year ago, some talk with Mr. Matsudaira about the possibility of a political understanding between Japan, the United Kingdom and the United States[1] which should have the effect of assuring Japanese public opinion that no thought of aggression against Japan existed in either of the other countries, but the matter had been allowed to drop. I understood that it was the desire of the Japanese Government that no political discussions should take place in the Naval Conference itself but that they would probably not object to political talks through the diplomatic channel. Mr. Nagai confirmed this. I said that, while I was in no way speaking officially, I was wondering whether we ought not to explore this question a little further, particularly as I had seen from the newspapers that Japan and China were apparently trying to arrange an amicable settlement of their differences.

Mr. Nagai said that it was true that a serious effort was now being made to settle Japan's differences with China. He quite took the point that an amicable arrangement between China and Japan would facilitate an improvement in political relations with the United Kingdom and the United States and said that he personally was of the opinion that his Government had no aggressive design on China proper. This feeling had been confirmed when, on his way through Manchukuo, he had had a long talk with the Commander-in-Chief of the Kwantung army, who had stated that Japan's main preoccupation now was to prevent subversive activities by discontented Chinese elements along the Manchukuo-China frontier; these activities, if not suppressed, were liable to have serious repercussions in Manchukuo itself. Once this matter was settled there was no reason why relations between Japan and China should not be put on a satisfactory footing.[2]

[1] Cf. No. 67.
[2] A minute by Sir R. Vansittart read: 'Mr. Nagai overestimates our credulity in paragraph 2. R.V. Jan. 7.'

I thought it wise to give this purely personal hint to Mr. Nagai because it is undesirable that, if we start negotiations in Tokyo, the Japanese Delegation here should get the impression that we are working behind their backs. Mr. Nagai clearly thought that any discussions on political subjects should take place at Tokyo and his attitude was not discouraging. His main doubt was whether the United States would be prepared to enter into any such arrangement.[3]

R. L. C.

[3] Mr. Eden commented: 'The last sentence is probably true, and must be decisive for us. A.E. Jan. 8.'

No. 600

*Record by Mr. Craigie of a conversation with Mr. Davis on January 5*
[A 278/4/45]

Secret                                                    FOREIGN OFFICE, *January 6, 1936*

I took the opportunity of a talk with Mr. Norman Davis at my house yesterday, to ask whether he had thought any more of the possibility of some political understanding with Japan as a means of preventing Japan from completely breaking away from the present Conference. He said that he had discussed the matter with Mr. Roosevelt before leaving the United States but had found the President very doubtful about the expediency of such a course, having regard to Japan's present attitude towards China. I said that there were now indications that negotiations were on foot for a settlement of Sino-Japanese differences. It seemed to me that, if an agreement were reached between the two countries, under which China would receive certain further guarantees for her territorial integrity, the whole situation would be changed and the conclusion of a political understanding between the United States, Japan and ourselves would be facilitated. Mr. Davis agreed and thought that we should certainly consider very carefully whether anything useful could be done in the political sphere. The present feeling of the United States Delegation was, however, that the best course now would be to let the Japanese Government realise that, even should Japan leave the Conference, the discussions would continue between the other four Powers with a view to concluding a qualitative treaty between them and probably also with all the other naval Powers.[1] The Japanese Delegation seemed to think that their withdrawal now would bring the Conference to an end. I replied that, while there was something to be said for this course, it seemed to me doubtful whether we should be prepared to enter such a treaty unless Japan agreed at least to enter into a general agreement for the exchange of advance information on construction. Otherwise the position would be far from satisfactory. To take the course which he had suggested (i.e. to tell the Japanese definitely that we proposed to continue the Conference without

[1] Mr. Eden minuted this sentence as follows. 'There seems to me to be force in Mr. Davis's argument . . . A.E. Jan. 8.'

them) might tend to confirm Japan's isolationist tendencies and to render the Japanese Government more reluctant than ever to enter an agreement for the exchange of information. Mr. Norman Davis agreed that this was a point to be carefully considered.

I impressed on Mr. Davis that what I had said about a political understanding represented purely my personal views and that, if anything official were to be said on this subject, this would no doubt be done by the Secretary of State.[2]

R. L. C.

[2] See *F.R.U.S. 1936*, vol. iv, pp. 1–2, for Mr. Davis' report on this conversation.

No. 601

*Letter from Sir R. Vansittart to Sir E. Drummond (Rome)*

[*A 67/4/45*]

Secret                                              FOREIGN OFFICE, *January 6, 1936*

My dear Eric,

On receipt of your confidential letter of the 20th December[1] we promptly made investigations, to the best of our ability, into the story that the Germans have been building more naval tonnage than they are entitled to under the Anglo-German Naval Agreement. As far as we can judge there is no truth in the report. The building particulars recently communicated to us by the Germans tally with the estimates which they furnished last summer, and in general the Germans have fallen in better than we had expected with our proposals for the practical application of the Naval Agreement. You may be sure, however, that we shall continue to keep as careful a watch as we can on German construction with a view to ensuring that no infringements of the Agreement occur.

Yours ever,[2]

[1] Not printed. It referred to a statement to *The Times* correspondent in Berlin by an unnamed German that 'You have now found out that we have been building more ships than we were entitled to under our Naval Agreement with you'.

[2] Signature missing on filed copy.

No. 602

*Sir R. Clive (Tokyo) to Mr. Eden (Received January 7, 9.30 a.m.)*

*No. 5 Telegraphic* [*A 159/4/45*]

TOKYO, *January 7, 1936, 3.30 p.m.*

Following is summary of telegram published today by 'Asahi' from London correspondent; after referring to complicated situation which His Majesty's Government has to face arising from (1) Naval Conference deadlock, (2) Oil sanctions against Italy, (3) North China question, (4) United States neutrality bills, telegram states that Mr. Eden who is preparing a report on foreign policy for the Cabinet meeting on January 8th is in a dilemma between Japan's determination to demand naval parity and America's desire to achieve naval treaty excluding Japan.

Telegram continues, 'in such circumstances Mr. Eden is planning Anglo-Japanese agreement on Far Eastern question and it is reported that as means to that end he is working on the one hand for an Anglo-Soviet rapprochement by removing friction between those two countries in Persia, Turkey and other parts of the Near East, and on the other hand for an understanding with Japan on China question by moderating America's anti-Japanese attitude at Naval Conference and thereby displaying some appreciation of Japan's standpoint. Accordingly interest is being shown in attitude of our Foreign Office and Ministry of War and approaching return of Ambassador Matsudaira to London is significant.

'Attention has passed beyond Naval Conference and is being turned to strengthening of British navy and to Anglo-Japanese political negotiations in the Far East.'

## No. 603

*Sir R. Clive (Tokyo) to Mr. Eden (Received January 9, 1.15 p.m.)*
*No. 8 Telegraphic [A 279/4/45]*

*Very confidential*                                            TOKYO, *January 9, 1936, 6.40 p.m.*

My United States colleague called on me this morning and said he would like a talk to clarify his ideas about the situation in the Far East if as seemed probable Naval Conference broke down.

As regards China Chiang Kai-shek wanted to come to an understanding with Japan and would he believed welcome a non-aggression pact even if this involved de facto recognition of Manchuria. If this came about, his government, who still insisted on validity of 9 Power Treaty,[1] would have to admit that the treaty was dead.

He had been turning over the idea of political understanding between United States and Japan. He believed there was so much in common between British and American views regarding the Far East that if any way could be found to ease the tension we should do everything possible to find it. His government would never consider political agreement as substitute for naval agreement but if political understanding would make it easier for Japan to accept the principle of existing ratio they might be more ready to consider it. One difficulty was that no one in State Department could visualise the future from broader standpoint. They were tied to the letter of existing but really defunct treaties. I observed that Japanese had never liked collective treaties but had honourably adhered to bilateral treaties. He agreed. He said that the President who had always been a big navy man would never yield about necessity for American naval superiority to Japan but might

[1] Signed at Washington on February 6, 1922; No. 11 in Cmd. 1627 of 1922.

take a broader view than the State Department about some sort of understanding. Personally he considered that a serious effort should be made to improve relations and this would be easier if Japanese would make a reasonable agreement with China. His difficulty was to put this in a convincing way so that Washington would take notice. Secretary of State was mainly interested in tariffs.[2]

[2] Minutes on this telegram by Mr. Craigie, Sir V. Wellesley, Sir R. Vansittart, and Mr. Eden were as follows: 'I confess I share Mr. Grew's views on this. R.L.C. 11/1.' 'I agree: as the price of a Naval Agreement. V.W. 13/1/36.' '(But we don't seem likely to get the naval agreement). R.V. Jan. 13.' 'I don't think that we can make any further headway with this at present. I would consider a political agreement if U.S.A. would come in and as price of Naval Agreement. A.E. Jan. 13.'

## No. 604

### Sir R. Clive (Tokyo) to Mr. Eden (Received January 10)
### No. 9 Telegraphic [A 243/4/45][1]

TOKYO, January 9, 1936

My immediately preceding telegram.[2] Conversation was really a monologue in which I said very little.

In view of last paragraph of your telegram No. 3[3] I had not referred to subject with my United States colleague since I first told him what Minister for Foreign Affairs had said—see my telegram No. 349.[4]

He agreed that press telegram summarized in my telegram No. 5[5] was a typical Japanese ballon d'essai.

[1] The original copy of this telegram (A 280/4/45) has not been preserved in Foreign Office archives. The copy here printed is that circulated on January 13 (see L.N.C. (35) (U.K.) 10): the times of despatch and receipt were missing.
[2] No. 603.    [3] No. 596.    [4] No. 593.    [5] No. 602.

## No. 605

### Record of a meeting held in the Secretary of State's room at the Foreign Office on January 9, 1936, at 12.15 p.m.
### L.N.C. (35)(U.K.) 8 [A 350/4/45]

PRESENT: Mr. Anthony Eden,[1] Viscount Monsell, Earl Stanhope, Admiral of the First Fleet Sir E. Chatfield, Mr. R. L. Craigie, Vice-Admiral Sir W. M. James, Sir H. Batterbee,[2] Captain V. H. Danckwerts, Mr. A. Holman.

THE FIRST LORD explained that the present policy of the United Kingdom Delegation was to induce the Japanese to enter into a discussion on qualita-

[1] Mr. Eden's appointment as one of the delegates of the United Kingdom delegation to the Naval Conference, in succession to Sir S. Hoare, was communicated to the other delegations to the Conference in identic letters of January 6, 1936.
[2] Assistant Under-Secretary of State for Dominion Affairs.

tive limitation. In order to attain this object, it was considered necessary to review all proposals in connection with quantitative limitation and then put them into cold storage without taking any decisions. No delegation could agree to the Japanese proposal for a common upper limit, nor had the United Kingdom plan any better chance of acceptance. When the French modification of the United Kingdom plan providing for exchange of information was submitted for discussion,[3] it was thought that the Japanese had acquiesced in this procedure, but on the contrary the Japanese Delegation eventually objected on the ground that the question of exchange of information was outside the scope of quantitative limitation. Until a decision had been reached on quantitative limitation they were not prepared to discuss any other questions. The First Lord added that the U.S. Delegation considered that, once a decision had been taken on the question of the common upper limit, the Japanese would continue in the Conference. He therefore considered it necessary that the Japanese Delegation should be asked what their intentions were and whether, if the common upper limit were not accepted, they would be prepared to examine other questions. Continuation of the examination of the common upper limit would make the Conference appear ridiculous.

THE FIRST SEA LORD pointed out that the Japanese Delegation had only said that it would be difficult to discuss the question of the exchange of information without a settlement of quantitative limitation (See L.N.C. (35) 1st Committee, 9th meeting, pages 2 & 3).[4] He felt that in view of the statement made by Admiral Nagano (See L.N.C. (35) HD, 1st Meeting, page 14)[5] the Japanese Delegation, if asked whether they desired to return to the discussion of the common upper limit, would only reply in the affirmative as they were anxious to convince the Conference of the practicability of that plan.

THE SECRETARY OF STATE enquired whether it would not be possible to examine qualitative and quantitative limitation simultaneously at morning and afternoon meetings as was done at the Disarmament Conference at Geneva.

MR. CRAIGIE did not think that the Japanese would discuss anything but quantitative limitation and the common upper limit. In that case the Japanese might be asked whether they wished to go back to the discussion of the common upper limit and wanted a decision on that plan. If the decision were adverse, it would be necessary to ascertain what the Japanese intended to do next. If they replied that they could not continue in the Conference, the position would at least have been made clear.

THE SECRETARY OF STATE said that he was to see Mr. Norman Davis during the afternoon, when he would explain to him the procedure which it was proposed to adopt.

THE FIRST SEA LORD expressed the view that the Japanese Delegation

[3] At the eighth meeting of the First Committee on January 6, see *L.N.C. 1935 Docs.*, pp. 509–11.

[4] *Ibid.*, pp. 534–5.　　　　　　　　　　　　　　　[5] *Ibid.*, pp. 399–400.

had not placed before the Conference the whole of their case particularly as regards the strength of fleets. The matter had not been fully debated. The Japanese Delegation had not communicated to the Conference the confidential information which had been imparted by them to the U.K. Delegation.

THE SECRETARY OF STATE considered that it was unnecessary to talk about Conference discussions. It was desirable to restrict the meeting to questions of procedure. Was it desirable to mention to the Japanese that the Conference might continue without them?

MR. CRAIGIE said that any mention of the possibility of a Conference without Japan might have a strong effect on the Japanese attitude. It was, however, necessary to avoid offending Japanese susceptibilities, as it was still hoped to secure some form of co-operation with Japan in the matter of the exchange of information. He was of the opinion that the Italian Delegation would remain in the Conference and that the French Delegation would probably adopt the same line.

THE FIRST LORD enquired whether it would not be better to ascertain the views of these Delegations as soon as possible.

THE SECRETARY OF STATE replied that it might be better to await the result of the meeting with the Japanese Delegation. There would be no harm in the meantime in warning the Dominions as to the position.

THE FIRST SEA LORD stated that, if the stage were now reached when the Japanese wished to leave the Conference, it would be highly desirable that the whole Conference and not the United Kingdom Delegation alone pronounced themselves as opposed to the Japanese thesis.

MR. CRAIGIE proposed that the U.S. Delegation might put up a statement against the Japanese. The French would probably not be prepared to take such a step.

SIR HARRY BATTERBEE asked whether from the political aspect the Dominions should not be informed of the position by the Secretary of State or the First Lord.

THE SECRETARY OF STATE replied in the affirmative in the event of anything drastic occurring.

LORD STANHOPE made the suggestion that, if a decision on the common upper limit were now taken, the Japanese Delegation might refuse to discuss further questions but would at any rate remain in the Conference as observers.

THE FIRST SEA LORD expressed the view that, if a decision were taken by the Conference against the common upper limit, Japan would still remain in the Conference.

The meeting was adjourned at 1 p.m.

## No. 606

*Record of a meeting between United Kingdom and Japanese Delegations on January 9, 1936, at 4.30 p.m.*[1]

*[A 453/4/45]*

PRESENT: *United Kingdom*: The Secretary of State for Foreign Affairs, The First Lord of the Admiralty, The First Sea Lord, Mr. Craigie. *Japan*: Admiral Nagano, Mr. Nagai, Mr. Mizota.

The discussion may conveniently be divided under the three following heads: procedure, qualitative limitation and political.

### I. *Procedure.*

In answer to a number of questions put by Lord Monsell, ADMIRAL NAGANO defined the position of his Delegation as follows:

(a) If there were no proposals for quantitative limitation other than those now before the Conference, the Japanese Delegation would like the discussion of their common upper limit proposal to be continued as soon as possible.

(b) They would like a decision taken either for or against this proposal as soon as convenient.

If the decision were adverse, the Japanese Delegation must, on their existing instructions, leave the Conference, the only other subject they were authorised to discuss in such circumstances being Part IV of the London Naval Treaty (use of submarines against merchant ships).

MR. EDEN and LORD MONSELL thereupon drew attention to the unfortunate political effects of such a decision, adding that representatives of certain Powers had suggested that, should the Japanese Delegation leave, the Conference should nevertheless continue. Would it not be possible for the Japanese Delegates to remain at least as observers?

ADMIRAL NAGANO did not reject this suggestion but promised to ask for further instructions from his Government.

In reply to suggestions that exchange of information could not properly be considered as anything but one method of quantitative limitation, Admiral Nagano merely repeated that he was unable to discuss exchange of information pending a decision in regard to the common upper limit.

### II. *Qualitative Limitation.*

ADMIRAL CHATFIELD explained our difficulty in understanding Japan's position on qualitative limitation, seeing that the whole thesis was based on the necessity of reducing the sizes of ships in order to limit their offensive powers. How in that case could Japan possibly gain if, in the absence of a qualitative treaty, the United States were to build ships of, say, 45,000 tons.

ADMIRAL NAGANO, in reply, stated that it had been the hope of the Japanese Delegation to help the United Kingdom Delegation in its effort to secure

---

[1] This meeting was held in the Secretary of State's room at the Foreign Office. The record was circulated as L.N.C. (35)(U.K.) 11.

reduction in the size of ships had the common upper limit been adopted. In the contrary event, however, it was the view of the Japanese Government that qualitative limitation merely served to continue the existing relationship between fleets. Furthermore, the security of a country depended to a great extent on its spirit, and a failure on quantitative limitation, followed by an agreement by the Japanese Government to enter a qualitative treaty, would have the most depressing effect on public opinion in Japan. The assassination of two Japanese Prime Ministers[2] as a direct consequence of the signature of the London Naval Treaty was cited as proof of the high feeling prevailing in Japan on this subject.

### III. *Political.*

MR. EDEN emphasized the serious political consequences of Japan leaving the Conference in present circumstances. This would be deplorable at a time when we in this country were doing our best to improve relations with Japan. Mr. Eden hoped that the Japanese Delegates would impress this aspect of the question on their Government.

ADMIRAL NAGANO replied that this aspect of the question was appreciated in Japan. He paid a tribute to the friendly relations which had throughout prevailed between our two Delegations, and said Japan would never forget Great Britain's assistance at the time of her war against Russia.[3] The Japanese Government would be most anxious to avoid the ill effects of a failure of the present Conference and hoped that further improvement in our political relations would still be possible. He was sorry that the two Delegations had sometimes appeared to be at odds during the meetings of the First Committee. The Japanese Delegation fully appreciated the special position of the British Commonwealth of Nations, and they have never had any idea that we could accept equality with France and Italy. They would like to see an increase rather than a decrease in Britain's defensive power, though he emphasised the word *defensive*, since Japan believed that the *offensive strength* of all Powers should be curtailed.

Finally the following decisions were taken:

(1) It should be suggested to the other Powers that the next meeting of the Conference should be postponed until Monday[4] afternoon at 5.30 p.m., in order to give time for further consultations between Delegations and for the receipt of further instructions from Tokyo, and that the agenda for Monday's meeting should be the Japanese proposal for a common upper limit.

[2] A reference presumably to the attempt, on November 14, 1930, on the life of Mr. Hamaguchi, Prime Minister at the time of the ratification of the London Naval Treaty of 1930 (Mr. Hamaguchi died the following August) and the attack on May 15, 1932, on Mr. Inukai (see Volume X, Nos. 347–8, 357).

[3] In addition to giving moral support to Japan the Anglo-Japanese Alliance of January 30, 1902, localized the Russo-Japanese war of 1904–5 by the provision that each signatory would support the other if the other were attacked by two or more great powers.

[4] January 13.

(2) The United Kingdom Delegation would inform the other Delegations of the general sense of the discussion, it being understood that the fact that the Japanese Delegation would ask for new instructions should be regarded as strictly confidential.

## No. 607

*Sir R. Clive (Tokyo) to Mr. Eden (Received January 10, 9.30 a.m.)*
*No. 11 Telegraphic [A 301/4/45]*

TOKYO, *January 10, 1936, 11.28 a.m.*

Naval disarmament.

Hochi which is known to be in close touch with Navy Department gives the following views of naval authorities.

On breakdown of conference England will take the lead in making proposals for the future which may be as follows:

(1) to hold another conference within 12 months. Japan absolutely opposes as it would hamper new defence preparations of non-treaty period.
(2) To establish standing technical committees. Japan considers this useless citing Geneva failure.
(3) 4 Power agreement without Japan. Difficult as American consent is doubtful.

There would be no objection to postponing conference 5 years by which time Powers will regret non-acceptance of Japan's proposals.

## No. 608

*Mr. Eden to Sir R. Clive (Tokyo)*
*No. 6 Telegraphic [A 126/4/45]*

FOREIGN OFFICE, *January 10, 1936, 11 p.m.*

Your telegram No. 2.[1]

From conversation which First Lord of the Admiralty and I had yesterday with Admiral Nagano and Mr. Nagai[2] it emerged that the Japanese Delegates desire an early decision on their proposal for a common upper limit and that, should the decision be adverse, they must, on their present instructions, leave the Conference. We drew attention to the unfortunate political effects of such a course and suggested that the Delegates should remain to take part in the debates on such points as Japan desired to discuss, and should act as 'observers' when other points were under consideration.

The Japanese Delegates, who expressed their appreciation of the courteous and considerate attitude displayed throughout by the First Lord as Chairman of the First Committee, promised to telegraph for further instructions. The

---

[1] No. 598.   [2] See No. 606.

next meeting of the Committee, at which the common upper limit proposal will be again discussed, has been postponed until Monday[3] afternoon to give time for the new instructions to arrive. As regards the question of a political pact, the matter has been discussed informally with Mr. Phillips,[4] who thought that his Government would be averse to entering into any such arrangement at the present time. The most he thought they might contemplate would be some kind of consultative pact, though even this idea would require very careful consideration before any definite opinion could be given upon it. This expression of views confirms what your United States colleague stated to you in regard to the probable attitude of the State Department (see your telegram No. 8).[5]

The question now arises whether there is anything which Your Excellency can usefully do to impress on Mr. Hirota the undesirable political effects which must follow from the departure of the Japanese Delegates at this juncture. On the one hand it is important to avoid creating the impression (particularly in the press) that we are seeking to put undue pressure on the Japanese Government in this matter. On the other hand, it would be well that Mr. Hirota should be under no misapprehension in regard to the serious concern which we feel as to the consequences of such a step, not only on the future of naval limitation but also in the political sphere. If the Conference were to go on and an agreement on qualitative limitation were to be reached not only between the Powers represented at the Conference, but also with all naval Powers other than Japan, this would tend to emphasize Japan's disassociation from a work which the other naval Powers consider to be in the interest of world appeasement. Whatever happens, the political consequences must be bad and it is certainly undesirable that Mr. Hirota should be left under the impression that a political pact with the United States and with this country would be feasible as a substitute for a naval treaty. On the contrary, such difficulties as there are already to the negotiation of a pact would be greatly increased if Japan were to leave the Conference. Should you decide to have a conversation with Mr. Hirota you should state that even if the Japanese Delegates were authorised to stay on merely as observers, this would have the advantage of gaining time. While fully appreciating the Japanese objection to the idea of entering a quantitative agreement which contains any element of the ratio system, we have been quite unable to fathom the Japanese objections to entering a qualitative treaty if agreed with the rest of the world, and we still hope that, given more time, conversations on this point with the Japanese Delegates may bear fruit.

Repeated to Washington.

[3] January 13.    [4] See No. 615 below.    [5] No. 603.

## No. 609

*Record by Mr. Eden of a conversation with Mr. Davis on January 9, 1936*

[*A 402/4/45*]

FOREIGN OFFICE, *January 10, 1936*

1. Mr. Norman Davis came to see me yesterday about the position of the Naval Conference.[1] He read me a telegram from Mr. Hull which advised a procedure for the conference similar to that which the First Lord of the Admiralty and I had agreed to endeavour to further in conversation with the Japanese later in the evening.

2. I rehearsed with Mr. Davis the questions which we proposed to put to the Japanese. He warmly approved them, and seemed relieved at the course we were proposing to pursue. He said that the United States Delegation were prepared for further discussion of the common upper limit, but that they would hope that after that discussion had lasted a reasonable time a decision could be taken in the matter. I remarked that it seemed important that if and when the common upper limit were turned down an authoritative explanation should be issued by the other four delegations explaining their respective reasons why they could not agree to the common upper limit. It seemed to me desirable that our two delegations should keep in close touch in this matter, and if possible should arrange their answers together. Mr. Davis at once agreed to do this.

3. Mr. Davis went on to speak of the possibility of securing some political agreement in the Far East which would assist the progress of the Naval Conference. He said that Mr. Craigie had spoken to him about this.[2] Mr. Davis said that he was confident that it would not be possible for the United States to enter into a non-aggression pact with us and Japan. Public opinion in the United States would regard this as condoning Japanese aggression in Manchuria. He fully appreciated that our position was not quite the same since we were members of the League, but of course that did not apply in respect of the United States. A consultative pact might be a different matter, but even in respect of such a pact he did not think that the United States could sign it unless it were accepted by the other signatories of the Nine-Power Treaty.

4. Mr. Davis also spoke of the Far Eastern position generally. He was confident that the United States would not fight for China or for any part of Chinese soil, nor was it likely that they would fight to maintain their position or their present rights in China, but they would fight for the right to trade with China. This, as so often before in their history, would be the big issue for the American people.

A.E.

[1] In No. 605 it is stated that this meeting was to take place during the afternoon of January 9. Cf. *F.R.U.S. 1936*, vol. i, pp. 26–27 for Mr. Davis's account of this conversation. It is also referred to in Mr. Davis's letter of January 30, 1936, to President Roosevelt: see *Franklin D. Roosevelt and Foreign Affairs*, edited by Edgar B. Nixon (Massachusetts, 1969), vol. iii, p. 179.     [2] See *F.R.U.S. 1936*, *op. cit.*, pp. 24–25.

## No. 610

*Sir R. Clive (Tokyo) to Mr. Eden (Received January 11, 9.30 a.m.)*
*No. 12 Telegraphic [A 355/4/45]*

TOKYO, *January 11, 1936, 1.5 a.m.*[1]

Following from leader in Hochi.

We think that if England and America intend to restrain Japan by naval strength and to preserve their interests in the Far East in a spirit of opposition to Japan their calculations will be very much out.

Japanese people are not slow to understand this. If it is evident that the navies of Great Britain and the United States do not intend to be a menace to Japan she will be prepared to conclude political agreement with them with an easy mind. But if attempt is made to extract concessions by pressure of force it will be very difficult to get Japanese people to consent.

[1] Possibly in error for 1.5 p.m.; cf. No. 611 below.

## No. 611

*Sir R. Clive (Tokyo) to Mr. Eden (Received January 11, 9.30 a.m.)*
*No. 13 Telegraphic [A 366/4/45]*

TOKYO, *January 11, 1936, 1.5 p.m.*

My immediately preceding telegram.[1]

Naval Attaché was asked this morning at Ministry of Marine if he had . . .[2] He was left in no doubt that it was inspired. Secretary of Minister said that political agreement with Great Britain would suit them far better than any naval treaty. Secretary drew attention to rumours appearing in press about the possibility of another Anglo-Japanese Alliance.

[1] No. 610.
[2] The text was here uncertain: 'seen the article' was suggested on the filed copy.

## No. 612

*Sir R. Clive (Tokyo) to Mr. Eden (Received January 11, 12.25 p.m.)*
*No. 14 Telegraphic [A 378/4/45]*

*Important*　　　　　　　　　　　　　　　TOKYO, *January 11, 1936, 6.40 p.m.*

Your telegram No. 6.[1]

I saw the Minister for Foreign Affairs this afternoon and read to him, and gave him a copy of the end portion of your telegram beginning 'If the Japanese delegate were authorised'. I said that I did not want our interview reported in the press. His Majesty's Government were not seeking to put pressure on the Japanese Government but they wished the Japanese Government

[1] No. 608.

to realise the unfortunate consequences if the Japanese delegates left the conference after Monday's[2] session. He said that the matter must be referred to the Cabinet who could not meet before January 14th. I suggested the possibility of provisional instructions. He agreed and suggested that perhaps no (? vote)[3] need be taken on January 13th. Telegram had been received from Japanese delegates who highly appreciated the consideration shown by the First Lord of the Admiralty and meeting was now taking place between representatives of the Foreign Office and the Navy Department.

I then referred to the other points mentioned in your telegram but said that I was not speaking under instructions. I said that I was convinced that neither His Majesty's Government nor the United States Government could seriously consider political agreement as a substitute for a naval treaty. I told him that I had reported what he had said on December 17th[4] but if the Japanese attitude remained completely uncompromising the difficulties in the way of any possible political understanding would be almost insuperable.

His Excellency listened carefully but made no comment.

[2] January 13.     [3] The text was here uncertain.     [4] See No. 584.


## No. 613

*Sir R. Clive (Tokyo) to Mr. Eden (Received January 13, 9.30 a.m.)*
*No. 15 Telegraphic [A 379/4/45]*

TOKYO, *January 13, 1936, 11.40 a.m.*

My telegram No. 14.[1]

No reference to my interview with the Minister for Foreign Affairs on January 11th has appeared in the press but I am disposed to believe that it resulted in urgent Cabinet meeting yesterday when new instructions were decided.

Outline of instructions was telegraphed by the 'Times' correspondent.[2]

[1] No. 612.
[2] Cf. *The Times*, January 14, p. 14, and *F.R.U.S. 1936*, vol. i, pp. 31–32.


## No. 614

*Sir R. Lindsay (Washington) to Mr. Eden (Received January 14, 9.30 a.m.)*
*No. 13 Telegraphic [A 415/4/45]*

WASHINGTON, *January 13, 1936, 11.5 p.m.*

In telegrams exchanged between you and His Majesty's Ambassador Tokyo I see mention of some kind of political pact regarding Far East, to which presumably the United States' adhesion would be sought. Though my information may be imperfect I venture to offer the following comment.

First forecast I ever had of the present administration's policy towards

Japan is to be found in paragraph 13 of my telegram No. 70 of 1933.[1] In its effect Mr. Roosevelt's policy has been consistent with that forecast ever since. The United States government has never ceased to express or imply unrelenting disapproval of Japanese encroachments. It is true the present state of public opinion precludes any action but there is no reason why the administration or anyone else should assume that public opinion will remain for ever wedded to the present extreme and almost ridiculous form of isolation. If some day a departure from this attitude is to be expected it would surely be important for the United States government now to keep record clear and above all to avoid anything that could ever be construed as condonation of Japanese encroachments. This is what United States Ambassador Tokyo really refers to when from a different point of view he describes State Department as 'tied to the letter of existing but really defunct treaties'.[2]

If policy of United States government is as suggested above to bide its time and maintain diplomatic position intact, it would also naturally wish to keep its powder dry; and sure enough we find it rearming on a scale of almost unexampled extravagance.

My conclusion is that United States government would scrutinise any suggestion for a political pact in the Far East with care amounting to suspicion especially if it tended to make any political concession to Japan.

Finally I may cite the circumstances of the moment when everything is judged in the light of its electoral value. Failure of Naval Conference has long been discounted and cannot damage administration. But a political pact in the Far East would be full of potential danger at the polls.

[1] The reference should have been to Washington telegram Nos. 67 and 68 of January 30, 1933, in which Sir R. Lindsay reported a conversation with the President-elect on January 29, 1933. Paragraph 13 read: 'In regard to the Far East his view is that there is nothing to be done at present to stop Japanese government and that the question can only be solved by the ultimate inability of Japan to stand the strain any longer. His policy would be to avoid anything that would tend to relieve the strain.'

An earlier, though briefer, reference to Mr. Roosevelt's reported attitude towards Far Eastern affairs was contained in Sir R. Lindsay's despatch No. 97 from Washington of January 18, 1933; see Volume XI, No. 219.　　　　　　　　　　　[2] See No. 603.

## No. 615

### Mr. Eden to Sir R. Lindsay (Washington)
### No. 26 [A 126/4/45]

Confidential　　　　　　　　　　　　　　　　FOREIGN OFFICE, January 13, 1936

Sir,

The United States Ambassador brought Mr. Phillips to see me on the morning of the 8th of January.[1]

2. After a few preliminary remarks, in the course of which I was able to

[1] This is apparently the conversation briefly referred to in F.R.U.S. 1936, vol. i, p. 25, as taking place on January 8 'before the Conference this afternoon'.

assure Mr. Phillips personally of what the Ambassador already knew, namely, of my strong desire to do what was possible to maintain close and friendly relations with the United States, the conversation turned to the question of the Naval Conference. Mr. Phillips felt that we had now reached a very difficult stage, and wondered whether it would not be possible to devise some means of lifting the Conference out of the rut of technicalities in which it seemed to be losing momentum. I replied that it was difficult to see what other procedure could be followed at the Conference itself, but Mr. Craigie, who was present at the interview, had been explaining to me the position reached in previous discussions with the Japanese Government for some form of political pact between Japan and the United States, on the one hand, and Japan and the members of the British Commonwealth of Nations on the other.

3. The subject was new to me, and I was myself doubtful whether anything could be done on these lines at the present juncture, so I asked Mr. Craigie to explain what were the possibilities. He stated that Mr. Hirota was understood to be in favour of some such political understanding, but as a substitute and not as an aid to a naval agreement. This of course would be of no use to us. There were two possible forms for a political agreement, i.e. the non-aggression pact and the consultative pact. The difficulty as regards the first was that we could not tie our hands not to come to China's assistance in any circumstances, although this difficulty could in our case be largely overcome by reserving our obligations under the Covenant of the League. Furthermore, we could do nothing which might be taken as an encouragement to Japan to intensify her present aggressive attitude towards China. As against this might be set the recent news that the Japanese and Chinese Governments were at present negotiating a settlement of their differences; the conclusion of a Sino-Japanese pact would clearly assist the conclusion of a political pact between the other Pacific Powers.

4. If, however, it was held that a non-aggression pact should not be contemplated in present circumstances, there was, Mr. Craigie pointed out, always the possibility of a 'consultative' pact. This type of pact merely provided that the parties to the pact would agree to consult in all matters of mutual interest to each other. It meant little in practice, since the idea of consultation on subjects of mutual concern was inherent in the existence of diplomatic relations, but sometimes such a pact had a useful psychological effect. The question was whether the conclusion of some such political pact could be made to serve as a face-saving device to enable the Japanese to come into a treaty dealing with qualitative limitation.

5. Mr. Phillips stated that he did not think for a moment that his Government would consider a non-aggression pact with Japan in present circumstances. It would be different if we had reason to believe that Japan had reached the end of her course of aggression in the Far East, but unfortunately we had no such assurance, and the conclusion of such a pact in the United States might be looked upon as an invitation to Japan to adopt a yet more aggressive attitude, not only as regards China, but also as regards Soviet

Russia. There might be less objection to a consultative pact, though the idea was new to him and he was not sure what it implied. He was personally against the conclusion of pacts which did not, in fact, mean anything, but he would like to consider this matter further before giving a decided opinion. In any case, he did not think that in any such political arrangement we could leave China and Soviet Russia out of account. An idea which occurred to him, on the spur of the moment, was that the existing consultative clause in the Nine-Power Treaty might be expanded so as to include all other questions arising in the area of the Pacific.

6. I said that, clearly, we should have to proceed in this matter with great caution and that there could be no question of doing anything which would have the appearance of abandoning China to her fate.

I am, &c.,
ANTHONY EDEN

## No. 616

*Sir R. Clive (Tokyo) to Mr. Eden (Received January 14, 9.30 a.m.)*
*No. 17 Telegraphic [A 399/4/45]*

TOKYO, *January 14, 1936, 12.45 a.m.*

*Naval Conference.*

Jiji leading article considers that the present deadlock has resulted from the discussion of technical matters to the exclusion of political questions. Real disarmament can be achieved only after diplomatic negotiations have taken place and political agreement reached between Japan, Great Britain and America.

Kokumin leading article does not understand why Great Britain, in view of scattered empire and proximity of other Powers, should be satisfied with parity with the United States, which is geographically isolated. Japan, who has Russia and China as neighbours, and must be prepared to face America and Great Britain, is in much the same position as Great Britain, and ought to have parity. If the Conference breaks up, Japan will be the chief sufferer.

Nichinichi publishes the views of the Ministry of Finance to the effect that if no agreement is reached, financial consequences for this country will be unfortunate. They express the hope that armament race will be avoided.

# No. 617

*Record of a meeting between United Kingdom and United States Delegations on January 14, 1936, at 10.30 a.m.*[1]

*L.N.C.* (*35*)(*U.K.*) *13* [*A 243/4/45*]

PRESENT: *United Kingdom*: Secretary of State for Foreign Affairs, First Lord of the Admiralty, Admiral of the Fleet Sir A. Ernle Chatfield, Sir Warren Fisher, Mr. R. L. Craigie, Captain Danckwerts.

*United States*: Mr. Norman H. Davis, Mr. W. Phillips, Admiral Standley, Mr. Ray Atherton.

The First Lord recalled the meeting held with the Japanese in the Foreign Office on the 9th January,[2] as a result of which the Japanese cabled to Tokyo for further instructions.

2. A further meeting was held with the Japanese Delegates in the Admiralty at 6 p.m. on the 13th January.[3] From this it had become apparent that the further instructions received by the Japanese Delegation were that the Delegation was to withdraw from the Conference on account of failure to reach agreement on the common upper limit, but that they were anxious, before withdrawal, to discuss the rules for submarine warfare (Part IV of the London Naval Treaty).

3. The Japanese had made three proposals. The first, that they should discuss submarine warfare now before reaching disagreement on the common upper limit proposal; the second, that they should discuss and reach decisions concerning the common upper limit proposal and the United Kingdom quantitative proposal, and then adjourn the Conference for six months or more; the third, that after reaching a decision on the common upper limit proposal the present Conference should be wound up and that, if the other Powers desired, they might summon a new Conference altogether. All these proposals were refused and reasons given against their adoption. Procedure was then agreed upon with the Japanese as follows. Discussion of the common upper limit should be resumed at the next meeting; at the end of the discussion the Chairman would sum up the situation and propose adjournment and the resumption of the examination of other problems, as a result of which the Japanese would write a letter withdrawing from the Conference, which the Chairman would read as the first business at the next subsequent meeting.

4. Mr. Norman Davis then reported a conversation with Mr. Nagai on the previous evening.[4] Mr. Nagai said he was sorry to go, but that the Japanese Delegation must refuse to discuss any other subject if the common upper limit was not agreed to. He admitted that qualitative limitation would be in favour of Japan as of every other country, but, nevertheless,

---

[1] This meeting was held in the Secretary of State's room at the Foreign Office.

[2] See No. 606.

[3] No record of this meeting has been traced. For the subjects discussed, see below and *F.R.U.S. 1936*, vol. i, pp. 32–34.   [4] Cf. *F.R.U.S. 1936*, vol. i, p. 33.

they cannot discuss it now. Mr. Nagai thought it better to adjourn the Conference till September when public opinion in Japan might be improved.

5. Mr. Norman Davis also reported that the U.S.A. Ambassador in Tokyo had telegraphed that Mr. Hirota had told him that the Foreign Office had won as against the Navy and that the Japanese would stay.[5] The meeting thought that this must refer to observers and not to Delegates. Mr. Hirota had apparently suggested that Mr. Nagai might stay although Admiral Nagano would go back to Japan.

6. The First Lord then outlined some of the consequences of the Japanese withdrawal and the possibilities of carrying on with a four Power Conference.

7. Admiral Standley pointed out that, in the absence of Japan, the existing Treaties could not be modified by agreement and that, therefore, we were bound to the scrapping arrangements of the London Naval Treaty. Mr. Norman Davis developed the thesis that it was essential to turn down the common upper limit proposal very definitely. The First Sea Lord said that we must avoid receiving a letter from the Japanese Delegation that would need a rejoinder. The First Lord said that it had been agreed that we should see the letter before it was sent.

8. The draft paper on procedure was then read, and various amendments were proposed. Mr. Craigie pointed out the importance of letting the Japanese down lightly without registering a definite rejection of their proposal because that would make it harder for the Japanese to come back eventually, and the First Sea Lord suggested that it would be desirable to ask the Japanese whether they have any other quantitative proposals, so as to ensure that they could not go back to Japan and tell a story to that effect.

9. The Secretary of State for Foreign Affairs said there were two things we were trying to do. The first was to end the present position and permit the Japanese to withdraw without producing more friction than was necessary, and the second was simultaneously to make it clear to the world why the Japanese were going so that they should not be able to make capital out of their withdrawal. It was agreed that Mr. Craigie should make a redraft of the paper on procedure and circulate it.

10. Mr. Norman Davis then read the statement he proposes to make at the First Committee meeting on the common upper limit to which no objection was taken.

11. Mr. Atherton raised the question of observers. How many would there be, would they sit in at all meetings, or how would they work? It was generally agreed that the Japanese observers must attend all meetings of the First Committee. Admiral Standley, supported by Mr. Phillips proposed that they should not sit on the technical committees as there are some things that the U.S.A. will not agree to unless the Japanese are a party to them. Such things could not be discussed in the presence of the Japanese. One such question was the qualitative limits of capital ships, and Admiral Standley stated definitely that the U.S.A. would not agree to reduce the gun calibre

[5] See *F.R.U.S. 1936*, vol. i, p. 32, for Mr. Grew's telegram No. 11 of January 13 to the United States Secretary of State.

of their capital ships unless Japan was a party to the agreement. The First Sea Lord suggested that the Technical Committees should meet without observers, but that when they reached the process of drafting their report, the observers might be invited to attend.

12. Mr. Norman Davis then raised the question of the attendance of Russia, Germany and other Powers, supposing the four Power Conference reached agreement. Considerable discussion took place on this question and it was thought that there might be two stages of the Conference, or perhaps three. In the latter event, Russia and Germany would be invited to attend as soon as agreement between the four Powers was in sight, and the remaining Powers after Russia and Germany had adhered to the agreement. In the former event all Powers not now represented would be invited simultaneously. On the whole the two stage suggestion was that most favoured as it was intended to keep Russia and Germany in touch with the proceedings throughout.

13. The First Sea Lord suggested that we should seek some Gentleman's undertaking from Japan that they would give us notification before exceeding any agreed qualitative limits. Mr. Craigie gave it as his opinion, which was supported by Mr. Norman Davis and Mr. Phillips, that there were two reasons why Japan was unlikely to go beyond the terms of any Treaty agreed upon—

(1) Japan would have both naval and political interest in keeping the Treaty so that other Powers would keep it;
(2) He was convinced that Japan's real reason for refusing qualitative discussion and agreement was as a lever to bring us into the common upper limit. This lever would soon become useless.

14. He concluded, therefore, that we need not assume that Japan would try to wreck the Treaty.[6]

6 For Mr. Davis's account of this meeting see *ibid.*, pp. 33–35.


## No. 618

*Minutes of a meeting between representatives of the United Kingdom and French Delegations on January 14, 1936*[1]

L.N.C.(35)(U.K.)14 [A 243/4/45]

PRESENT: *United Kingdom*: Mr. Craigie, Captain Danckwerts, Mr. Gore-Booth.
*France*: M. Cambon, Le Contre-Amiral Decoux, Le Capitaine de Vaisseau Deleuze.

MR. CRAIGIE opened the meeting by saying that its purpose was to give him an opportunity of explaining the latest developments in connection with the Japanese leaving the Conference. At the first meeting held with

1 The time of this meeting, which was held at the Foreign Office, is not recorded.

the Japanese, the latter had explained that if the common upper limit were rejected they would have no alternative but to leave the Conference. As for the course they would have to take if it were not explicitly rejected, they would have to refer home for instructions. The Japanese had been asked whether they could secure any modifications of their instructions and the political difficulties which their withdrawal from the Conference would create had been pointed out. Evidently this statement of the position had given rise to serious consideration in Tokyo, but unfortunately the only concession which had emerged had been that the Japanese would be willing to appoint an observer in the event of their leaving the Conference on the question of the common upper limit.

As regards the manner in which the Japanese would leave the Conference they had stated that they did not want rejection by vote or by an explicit statement of rejection since such a course might make difficulties for the future. It was suggested, therefore, that it should be made clear that no delegation could accept the common upper limit; the Japanese would then write to the Chairman to the effect that, as they saw there was no support for their policy, they would attend no more meetings.

The terms of the Japanese letter were not yet known, but the United Kingdom Delegation had insisted that it must be related to tomorrow's procedure, i.e., there could be no question of letting the Japanese off easily at the meeting only to find that the Japanese were writing an offensive letter.

M. CAMBON thought that they would not be likely to do so.

The Japanese had then, Mr. Craigie continued, made two suggestions for procedure.

(1) That Part IV of the London Treaty should be dealt with next. This suggestion had been rejected on various grounds, e.g. that Part IV did not give much scope for discussion and that the Conference would not be disposed to make yet another change in its programme. In any case this matter could easily be settled through diplomatic channels.

(2) The Conference might reject the Japanese proposal and the United Kingdom proposal, and, as there were no further quantitative proposals (i.e., proposals which the Japanese regarded as quantitative) there should be an adjournment until the autumn. This suggestion had also been rejected for various reasons notably because an adjournment of the Conference meant leaving much undone, while in any case adjournments in the past had proved a bad precedent.

MR. CRAIGIE stressed the desire of the Japanese and the United Kingdom Delegations that the Japanese exit should not be dramatised and the suggested procedure was shown to the French representatives who agreed with it.

M. CAMBON then asked whether in Mr. Craigie's opinion a Four-Power Conference would have the same character as the Five-Power Conference which was concluded. He had raised this point as the Quai D'Orsay attached considerable importance to the juridical aspect of the question. He suggested that the presence of the Japanese observer might be sufficient to enable the Conference to retain its identity.

M. Cambon then asked whether Article XIX of the Washington Treaty[2] was mentioned by the Japanese among the points on which they thought that discussions should be pursued.

Mr. Craigie said that they had not mentioned it.

M. Cambon said that it was desirable to know exactly what the position of the Japanese would be if Article XIX of the Washington Treaty were reserved or completely scrapped.

Amiral Decoux interjected that it would in any case be in force until the end of 1936.

Mr. Craigie said that it was the United Kingdom view that Article XIX should be kept for later consideration to which M. Cambon rejoined that the French would be much interested in any further discussion of it, particularly if there were to be any modification of the geographical limits.

In reply to a question from M. Cambon, Mr. Craigie said that it was the view of the United Kingdom Delegation that there should be no interval in the work of the Conference due to the Japanese departure.

It had been indicated by members of the United States Delegation, Mr. Craigie went on to say, that the departure of the Japanese meant alteration in what the American Delegation would accept in the way of qualitative reduction. If this became the prevailing American view, it would be most unfortunate since it was particularly desirable to frame a convention to which Japan could ultimately adhere. Even if they did not come in, it should be a convention which would render it possible for Japan to give an agreement that she would let the other Powers know if ever she undertook construction for which the convention did not allow. There would naturally have to be an escape clause in any agreement into which Japan did not enter.

The French and United Kingdom Delegations must try to convince the United States that a change of policy in the matter of qualitative limitation would be most serious.

M. Cambon asked whether the United States had expressed their readiness to reduce the size of battleships.

Mr. Craigie said that the reduction would only mean a few thousand tons, and Amiral Decoux thought it would be a pity not to obtain that measure of reduction small though it was.

The discussion then turned to the question of the non-Washington Powers.

Mr. Craigie said that in some quarters it had been suggested that there there would have been[3] three stages: (1) the present stage, (2) the introduction of Germany and the U.S.S.R. and (3) the introduction of other naval Powers: His Majesty's Government in the United Kingdom preferred to omit stage (2).

M. Cambon said that the French Government would wish the negotiations to be carried on a considerable distance before Germany and the U.S.S.R.

[2] Cf. No. 569.

[3] Presumably this should have read: 'would have to be'; cf. No. 617, paragraph 12.

were invited to join. In any case this invitation from their point of view was not very urgent for political reasons, and because Germany's position was safeguarded by qualitative assurances and by the Anglo-German agreement.

CAPTAIN DELEUZE said that if Japan had not agreed to qualitative limitation he did not see how other Powers could be expected to do so if everything were so unstable.

MR. CRAIGIE replied that there was also an opposite point of view that, if it were desired to show Japan that she ought to come in, the agreement should be made world-wide. In this form it would be less likely to be upset than would a narrower treaty.

Further, Mr. Craigie had always understood it to be a cardinal point of French naval policy to bring the other naval powers into an agreement, and in any case the United Kingdom could not limit themselves vis-à-vis some Powers, while leaving others, particularly Germany and the Soviet Union, free.

M. CAMBON replied that the question of including other Powers was still open, Captain Deleuze said that the United States might not accept a system which would entail giving of information to all small Powers, while Amiral Decoux suggested that it might be better to try and get in Japan before getting in the other naval Powers.

MR. CRAIGIE repeated that Japan was more likely to come in if the agreement were world-wide. Such an agreement should be fairly easy to bring about, especially if the French would help with the Soviet Union, from whom the United Kingdom had had no response.

Mr. Craigie went on to explain that the course envisaged was to invite all the other naval Powers to the Conference when negotiations had gone sufficiently far and when it would be possible to say what measure of agreement there was between the Powers represented at the Conference. Germany and the Soviet Union would have been kept informed in the meantime as to the progress of the negotiations.

M. CAMBON again said that the French Government had not given instructions or expressed an opinion about the inclusion of Germany in a future treaty.

MR. CRAIGIE replied that he hoped that the French would give reasons for what appeared to be a change of policy, and reiterated that the United Kingdom could not subscribe to an agreement which did not include the other important European Powers.

## No. 619

*Minutes of a meeting between representatives of the United Kingdom and Italian Delegations on January 14, 1936*[1]

*L.N.C. (35)(U.K.) 15 [A 243/4/45]*

PRESENT: *United Kingdom*: Mr. Craigie, Captain Danckwerts, Mr. Gore-Booth.
  *Italy*: Admiral Raineri-Biscia, Signor Vitetti, Commander Margottini.

MR. CRAIGIE began the meeting by giving an explanation of the latest developments in connection with the impending Japanese departure from the Conference, similar to that recorded in the Minute[s] of the Meeting with the French representatives.[2] The proposed procedure for the meeting on the 15th January was handed round and agreed to.

ADMIRAL RAINERI-BISCIA then said that Admiral Nagano had asked the Italians to be as mild as possible in their criticism of the common upper limit. If they were, the Japanese would answer equally mildly; otherwise their reply might be less friendly.

MR. CRAIGIE said that he had not understood that Admiral Nagano would reply at all. He was against carrying mildness too far. It was obvious that the common upper limit was not acceptable, and the Japanese must be told so clearly and firmly.

ADMIRAL RAINERI-BISCIA said that from some points of view the Italians liked the Japanese proposals, e.g., they were in favour of theoretical equality for all. They did not, however, view the Japanese idea of adjustments with favour. On a question from Captain Danckwerts as to whether the Italians would be ready to continue in the Conference if the Japanese withdrew, Signor Vitetti replied that the Italian Ambassador had agreed to do so without considering it necessary to consult Rome.

MR. CRAIGIE went on to say that the United Kingdom Delegation were anxious to get ahead with constructive work. In particular the question about bringing in other Powers would shortly arise. It would be possible:

1. to bring in Germany and the U.S.S.R.
2. to bring in all other naval Powers, or
3. not to extend the Conference until the ultimate attitude of the Japanese is known.

MR. CRAIGIE explained that 3. was a French idea on which the United Kingdom Delegation were not keen, since in any case they would need to know the qualitative situation in Europe before subscribing to any agreement, and moreover world unanimity would carry more weight with the Japanese than agreement among the Four Powers only.

ADMIRAL RAINERI-BISCIA said that the French were anxious to know the programmes of Germany and the Soviet Union. To this end limitation must

---

[1] The time of this meeting, which was held at the Foreign Office, is not recorded.
[2] No. 618.

777

be discussed between the Four Powers at the Conference, and when agreement had been reached, Germany and the Soviet Union should be called in.

CAPTAIN DANCKWERTS said that that had previously been the French point of view, but that they now suggested trying to include Japan in an agreement before Germany and the U.S.S.R. He expressed considerable doubt as to whether Japan would come in at an early date.

MR. CRAIGIE said also that the plan set out by Admiral Raineri-Biscia had been the French idea in 1934, but the French now were not quite sure whether the situation had not been radically altered by the impending departure of Japan. Mr. Craigie's personal view was that any adjournment of the Conference would be most undesirable.

ADMIRAL RAINERI-BISCIA said that there was this to be said for the French hesitation namely that every unknown ship built by Japan concerned Italy and France as well as everybody else, to which CAPTAIN DANCKWERTS replied that the absence of any agreement at all which the French alternative might lead to, was even worse, in that no country would know what any other was proposing to do. In any event there would be an escape clause in any agreement in case Japan started building.

ADMIRAL RAINERI-BISCIA suggested that it was the object of the Japanese in staying as observers to keep in touch with negotiations in case Japan would eventually wish to come in.

MR. CRAIGIE agreed and said that the chief difficulty caused by the departure of the Japanese was that it made the whole question of exchange of information much more difficult. The Conference would probably have to draw up two drafts for the exchange of information:

1. a draft in the event of all Powers concurring;
2. a less comprehensive draft in case the Japanese remained out.

CAPTAIN DANCKWERTS suggested that the Japanese might agree not to build outside the figures arrived at between the other Powers, without notifying these Powers. If such a gentleman's agreement were arrived at, it might be possible, he thought, to let the Japanese have the full information given to everyone else.

THE ITALIAN DELEGATION said that they would discuss the new French view of the position of Germany and the Soviet Union with the French at an early opportunity.

SIGNOR VITETTI said that the French might be trying to exploit the Anglo-German Agreement[3] in the sense that if Germany kept to it, so much the better, and if she did not, it would embroil her with the United Kingdom to the advantage of France. For this reason the French had no interest in making a further agreement to include Germany.

[3] i.e. the Anglo-German Naval Agreement of June 18, 1935; cf. No. 348.

*Sir R. Clive (Tokyo) to Mr. Eden (Received January 15, 11.10 a.m.)*
*No. 19 Telegraphic [A 452/4/45]*

TOKYO, *January 15, 1936, 4.55 p.m.*

Asahi states that Foreign Office here notes one satisfactory result of Conference in final burial of ratio principle which can never be resurrected.

Japan's national policy of strengthening her position as stabilizing influence in the Far East does not preclude other powers and United States in particular from playing their part in ensuring Far East peace. United States inability to agree to Japan's disarmament proposals is due to suspicion of Japan's motives for which there are no grounds.

Hochi states that the naval authorities having made full preparations are not alarmed at present situation. Navy will not build under foreign pressure but will construct only those ships best fitted to ensure security. Following points are stressed. Japan has ample trained naval personnel for increased fleet while the United States lacks personnel. Japan has much surplus building capacity while the United States cannot even complete present building plan for four years.

In another article dealing with financial aspect of the withdrawal Hochi forecasts tax increases to provide for naval expansion and admits uneasiness in financial circles because Japan, although securing freedom of action, is now isolated internationally. This may lead to economic pressure by other powers.

## No. 621

*Record by Mr. Craigie of a conversation with Captain Wassner*
*[A 575/4/45]*

FOREIGN OFFICE, *January 15, 1936*

I asked Captain Wassner to call today in order to explain to him the present position of the Naval Conference. I stated that it was now quite certain that the Japanese Delegation would withdraw from the Conference, though they would probably leave an observer. Nevertheless it was the intention to proceed with the work as originally proposed, and I hoped that rapid progress would now be made, at all events as regards advance notification of programmes and qualitative limitation. It was our intention to keep Captain Wassner fully posted of developments in regard to these technical questions so that, when the time came for extending the scope of the Conference, the German Government would have received advance information on all points on which agreement seemed likely.

I then asked Captain Wassner whether we might assume that the position of the German Government remained the same as indicated to us last Spring, namely that Germany would be able to accept whatever maximum limits were agreed upon at the present Conference and would be prepared to join the Conference in company with other Naval Powers when the Conference considered that the appropriate moment had arrived.[1]

He replied that he thought this to be the case. I asked him to be good enough to inform his Government that we were acting upon this assumption, and he promised to do so.

R.L.C.

[1] Cf. the memorandum of June 23, 1935, entitled *Anglo-German Naval Conversations, 1935. Summary of discussions between the British and German Naval Representatives* (referred to in No. 348, note 6) and No. 630 below, penultimate paragraph.

No. 622

*Letter from Admiral Nagano to Viscount Monsell*[1]

[*A 183/4/45*]

JAPANESE DELEGATION, LONDON, *January 15, 1936*

My Lord,

I have the honour hereby to notify Your Lordship that as it has become sufficiently clear at to-day's session of the First Committee[2] that the basic principles embodied in our proposal for a comprehensive limitation and reduction of naval armaments cannot secure general support, our Delegation have now come to the conclusion that we can no longer usefully continue our participation in the deliberations of the present Conference.

We remain, nevertheless, firmly convinced that our proposal is one best calculated to attain an effective disarmament, and we regret to state that we cannot subscribe, for the reasons we have repeatedly set forth, to the plans of quantitative limitation submitted by the other Delegations.

I desire to assure you, on this occasion, that we most sincerely appreciate the cordial manner in which you have been good enough to conduct the Conference; at the same time, I should like to tender our deepest thanks on behalf of our Delegation, for the hearty co-operation of all the Delegations to this Conference.

I have, &c.,<br>OSAMI NAGANO

[1] This letter and Viscount Monsell's reply (No. 623), are also printed in *L.N.C. 1935 Docs.*, pp. 138–9.

[2] Stenographic notes of the tenth meeting of the First Committee, held on Wednesday, January 15, 1936, at 3 p.m., are printed *ibid.*, pp. 565–90.

No. 623

*Letter from Viscount Monsell to Admiral Nagano*

[*A 183/4/45*]

LONDON, *January 16, 1936*

Sir,

I have submitted to the First Committee of the Naval Conference at its meeting to-day[1] the letter which you addressed to me yesterday[2] stating that the Japanese Delegation had reached the conclusion that they could no longer usefully continue their participation in the deliberations of the present Conference. All the Delegations feel that the decision of the Japanese Delegation is a matter for real regret. Despite the difficulties created by this decision they have decided that the work of the Conference shall proceed.

The Committee desire me to enquire whether the Japanese Government would wish to leave behind an observer or observers who would be able to keep in touch with the work of the Conference and inform their Government of its progress.

I have, &c.,
MONSELL

[1] Stenographic notes of the eleventh meeting of the First Committee, held on January 16, at 3.30 p.m., are printed *ibid.*, pp. 619–28.  [2] No. 622.

# CHAPTER VIII

## Correspondence relating to the proceedings of the London Naval Conference after the withdrawal of the Japanese Delegation

## January 17–March 25, 1936

### No. 624

*Mr. Eden to Mr. Lloyd Thomas[1] (Paris)*

*No. 91 [A 563/4/45]*

FOREIGN OFFICE, *January 17, 1936*

Sir,

The French Ambassador asked to see me this morning, when he said he wished to speak to me about the present situation of the Naval Conference. The French Government were most anxious that everything possible should be done to keep contact with the Japanese Government, and to leave the door open for the return of that Government to the Conference at some later stage, if that were possible.

2. I replied that we had been fully alive to the importance of this aspect of the situation, and that the First Lord of the Admiralty had in fact shown the most untiring patience and had exerted himself in every way to try to keep the Japanese within the Conference. Unfortunately this had not been possible, but in response to an appeal which we had made to the Japanese representatives they were consulting their Governments as to whether they should leave observers behind. This was something gained. The Ambassador agreed, but asked whether the Japanese representatives had made their representation by an observer dependent upon the conference being convened afresh as a Four-Power Conference—the Five-Power Conference being wound up.

3. I said that I did not understand that this was the position, but that the Japanese representatives had made it clear that though they would prefer that the Conference should be reconvened, they had not made the leaving of an observer dependent on this procedure being adopted. The Ambassador continued that his Government were anxious as to the position which would be created were Germany and Russia to be asked to join the Conference as he understood was the intention of His Majesty's Government. He was anxious lest the addition of Russia would make it more difficult for Japan to return, while Germany's inclusion would raise once again French political misgivings against the Anglo-German Naval Agreement, which his Government

---

[1] H.M. Minister at Paris since August 13, 1935.

would much prefer to avoid. Furthermore, the French Government had never agreed to legalise German rearmament, and they could hardly discuss naval terms with the Germans at a conference without doing so.

4. I replied that so far as I was aware there was no intention of inviting the Germans and Russians alone, but that when agreement had been reached among the four Powers, then the other naval Powers would be invited as a whole, in order that the agreement arrived at should be world-wide, as clearly it ought to be. The attitude of the French Government as described to me by the Ambassador seemed to me to indicate a change of view on their part. I remembered very well when M. Barthou and M. Piétri were here in London and the Naval Conference had been discussed, they had both expressed their reluctance to take part in a Five-Power Conference and their preference for a world conference.[2] The Ambassador admitted this, but contended that the modifications for which the French Government now sought were in procedure rather than in principle. They fully agreed that it was desirable that the agreement should be generally accepted. Would it not, however, be better to follow a modified form of procedure? Once the Four Powers had agreed among themselves, should they not invite Japan to agree, and then whatever the nature of the Japanese answer they could invite the other naval Powers to concur through the diplomatic channel, thus avoiding so large an extension of the conference?

5. I replied that it was a matter for consideration at what stage the Japanese Government should be once more approached. It seemed to me that to ask all other Powers through the diplomatic channel might be a cumbersome procedure.

6. After further discussion the Ambassador and I agreed that he should ask to have a conversation with the First Lord of the Admiralty on the subject, since as Chairman of the Conference it was upon him that the task of guiding the conference's procedure rested. The Ambassador indicated that he would greatly welcome the opportunity of a talk with the First Lord on the matter.

I am, &c.,

ANTHONY EDEN

[2] Cf. Volume VI, Nos. 489 and 490.

### No. 625

*Mr. Eden to Sir R. Lindsay (Washington)*[1]

*No. 20 Telegraphic [A 568/4/45]*

FOREIGN OFFICE, *January 18, 1936, 6.5 p.m.*

My telegram No. 410.[2]

The First Committee resumed meetings on the 6th January[3] with a further

[1] Identic telegrams, referring to No. 589, were sent on the same day to Tokyo (No. 12), Paris (No. 10 Saving), Rome (No. 2 Saving), Berlin (No. 3 Saving), Moscow (No. 1 Saving). [2] No. 589.

[3] For stenographic notes of this eighth meeting of the First Committee, see *L.N.C. 1935 Docs.*, pp. 501–14.

discussion on the United Kingdom proposal. The French and Italian Delegations objected to the period of 6 years for advance notification envisaged in the plan, and the Italians presented a formula for the annual voluntary exchange of information as to building programmes. The United Kingdom and subsequently the French Delegation also circulated formulae for the exchange of information, the latter including a provision for consultation. It was agreed to consider all three formulae at the next meeting on the 8th January.[4]

At that meeting, however, the Japanese maintained that the exchange of information was not a matter of quantitative limitation and said that they were therefore not prepared to discuss it. Those portions of the French and Italian plans which in their view dealt directly with quantitative limitation the Japanese criticised sharply, saying that they made no provision for disarmament. The other Delegations disagreed with the Japanese view on the exchange of information, feeling that it was vital to quantitative limitation and that the discussion should continue.

As further progress appeared to be blocked, the United Kingdom delegation held a bilateral meeting with the Japanese on the 9th[5] at which the latter revealed that according to their instructions they were to press for fresh discussion of the common upper limit plan and, if the plan were not accepted, to withdraw from the Conference. The political consequences of such action were pointed out to the Japanese who were urged to consult their Government again. At a further meeting on the 13th,[6] the Japanese disclosed that their instructions to withdraw from the Conference could not be modified in the event of the common upper limit being rejected. They suggested, however, either that Part IV of the London Treaty (Restriction of Submarine Warfare) should be discussed or that after the Japanese and United Kingdom proposals had been formally put up and rejected, the Conference should adjourn until, say, the autumn when political conditions might have improved. Neither of these proposals was acceptable, Part IV giving little scope for discussion and an adjournment being considered most undesirable in principle.

The procedure eventually adopted consisted of a lengthy restatement by the Japanese on the 15th of their proposal at a First Committee meeting.[7] All the other Delegations then expressed their inability to agree to the proposal, the opposition mainly taking the line that equality of armaments would not mean equality of security in that, for instance, the length of communications to be protected by a fleet and the distance from its bases of that fleet when operating are factors of importance in reckoning its fighting strength. The Italians, however, accepted the Japanese thesis of theoretical equality for all but did not think their proposals practicable.

After this meeting, the Japanese Delegation addressed a letter[8] to the

[4] See *L.N.C. 1935 Docs.*, pp. 529–46, for notes of the ninth meeting.
[5] See No. 606.                                           [6] See No. 617, paragraphs 2 and 3.
[7] Stenographic notes of the tenth meeting of the First Committee, held on January 15, at 3 p.m., are printed in *L.N.C. 1935 Docs.*, pp. 565–90.                    [8] No. 622.

Chairman to the effect that as the Japanese proposals for quantitative limitation were unacceptable, the Delegation could not participate further in the work of the Conference. A reply[9] was agreed by the Committee to the effect that, while the Japanese withdrawal was a matter for great regret, the Conference would proceed with its work. The Japanese were invited to appoint an observer to keep in touch with the work of the Conference. The First Committee then continued the discussion of quantitative limitation and passed a resolution to the effect that the exchange of information was essential to any agreement for naval limitation, and advance notification of programmes most desirable.[10]

At a further meeting on the 17th,[11] the First Committee set up a Technical Sub-Committee with Mr. Craigie as Chairman to work out the best method for advance notification of naval construction and this Sub-Committee got to work immediately.

Almost the entire United Kingdom Press has taken the line that the withdrawal of the Japanese is both unjustifiable and a blunder. The passing on the very next day of the resolution in regard to exchange of information made a favourable impression.

[9] No. 623.
[10] See *L.N.C. 1935 Docs.*, pp. 625–8. The text of the resolution was printed in *The Times*, January 17, p. 12.    [11] See *L.N.C. 1935 Docs.*, pp. 652–4.

## No. 626

*Record by Mr. Craigie of a conversation with Mr. Nagai on January 17, 1936*

*[A 574/4/45]*

FOREIGN OFFICE, *January 18, 1936*

At Mr. Nagai's request I called to see him yesterday evening. He stated that he had just had a conversation with the First Lord of the Admiralty in regard to the Japanese acceptance of the invitation and the presence of Japanese observers at the Conference. On the first point he said that the Japanese Delegation had been somewhat taken aback at the wording of the last paragraph of the Chairman's letter[1] in which the Delegation were asked 'whether they would wish to' leave an observer. The First Lord had stated that this could be regarded as a form of invitation and Mr. Nagai then showed me the draft of a reply in which the Japanese Delegation 'accepted the invitation' of the Conference to appoint observers. In reply to his enquiry I said that I thought this was a good way of dealing with the matter and I further suggested that the Chairman, when answering the Delegation's letter, might take the occasion to state that the presence of the two observers named in the letter (namely Mr. Fujii and Admiral Iwashita) would be entirely welcome to the Conference.

Mr. Nagai thought this might help, but he then proceeded to express his concern at the statement made by the First Lord that Japanese observers

[1] No. 633.

would not be expected to be present at meetings of technical sub-Committees. Mr. Nagai had looked up the precedents and found that at the Geneva Conference of 1927[2] the French and Italian observers had sat on all the technical sub-Committees. In the circumstances could not the same procedure be adopted on the present occasion, seeing that the circumstances were very similar? I said that I doubted whether the circumstances in the two cases could be regarded as similar. In any case there was the later precedent of 1930 when the League of Nations observers had not been present at the meetings of small technical sub-Committees. He had stated that his Government wished their observers to be present at 'all important meetings'. I felt that this desire would be fully met if the observers assisted at the meeting of the Plenary Conference and at the First Committee, since each technical sub-Committee would submit full reports of its proceedings to the First Committee and these reports would be available to the Japanese observers. The decision of the Committee seemed to me to rest on the purely practical basis that these technical sub-Committees should be kept as small as possible, and for this reason it was intended that neither the League of Nations observer nor the Japanese observers should be present.

I then raised the question of Heads of Delegation[s] meetings and said that as the Japanese observers would not be delegates it would obviously not be appropriate that they should be present at any such meetings that might be held. There again the results of any such meetings must naturally be reported to the First Committee, so that the Japanese observers would in due course know of any decisions taken. Mr. Nagai fully agreed on this point, his preoccupation being primarily with the question of representation on the technical sub-Committees.

I should say that it is now touch and go whether the Japanese will leave observers at all.

R.L.C.

[2] Cf. No. 56, note 8.

No. 627

*Mr. Eden to Sir R. Lindsay (Washington)*
*No. 59 [A 608/4/45]*

FOREIGN OFFICE, *January 18, 1936*

Sir,

Mr. Norman Davis asked to see me this morning, when he spoke about the future of the Naval Conference. He remarked that now that the common upper limit proposal was dead he was very anxious to do everything possible, as, he was sure, were His Majesty's Government, to keep the Japanese Government in as close contact with the conference as was practicable.

2. He said that he understood that the Japanese delegation had indicated that, if this present conference were wound up and a new conference were opened unconnected with the Washington Treaty, they would have been

prepared to join in its work. I replied that this was not the position as I had heard the Japanese representatives explain it. It was quite true that the Japanese delegates had expressed a wish that the Five-Power Conference should be wound up,[1] but their idea had been that a Four-Power Conference should take its place. The only reason that they had given for preference for this procedure was that it would be less embarrassing for the Japanese representatives when they had to withdraw from the Conference.

3. Mr. Davis thanked me for my explanation and said that he had not understood the position in this way. In the circumstances he fully appreciated that there was nothing to be done in the direction suggested.

4. Mr. Davis then went on to speak of the possibility of some approach being made to the Japanese Government, the pretext being the official statement given out in Tokyo that the Japanese Government were most anxious to avoid a race in armaments. Would it not be possible for His Majesty's Ambassador and the United States Ambassador at Tokyo to see Mr. Hirota together, to say with what satisfaction their Governments had read this statement, to point out that the best way of realising the object stated was to reach an agreement about qualitative limitation and the exchange of information, and to say how glad His Majesty's Government in the United Kingdom and the United States Government would be if the Japanese Government would co-operate with them in that task?

5. I replied to Mr. Norman Davis that it seemed to me that, while we might consider the possibility of taking some such initiative at a later stage, the moment was not yet. When the four Powers had reached agreement as to what they wished to do about qualitative limitation and the exchange of information, there might well be something to be said for communicating the results jointly to the Japanese Government and for making to them an appeal upon the lines suggested by Mr. Davis. If, however, we did this at present, I much feared that we should receive a rebuff, and perhaps even spoil the opportunity that there might be later on.

6. Mr. Davis said that he fully appreciated this, and that he agreed that it was probably not now the moment for the intervention which he had had in mind, nor, for that matter, had he yet consulted his own Government. He might, however, have an opportunity of saying something to the First Lord of the Admiralty about it in the course of the next few days, and if it was in accordance with my wishes, he would be glad to pursue the matter further with me next week.

I am, &c.,

(for the Secretary of State)

R. L. CRAIGIE

[1] See No. 617.

## No. 628

*Sir R. Clive (Tokyo) to Mr. Eden (Received January 20, 9.30 a.m.)*
*No. 24 Telegraphic [A 570/4/45]*

Confidential                                             TOKYO, *January 20, 1936, 4.18 p.m.*

Your telegram No. 9 (*sic*).[1]
*Secret*

Minister for Foreign Affairs a few days ago invited the Belgian Ambassador to a Japanese dinner. The latter told me in confidence that His Excellency became very cheerful and speaking of Naval Conference said that Japanese idea was common upper limit of a million tons but that the Japanese had no intention of building beyond 800,000 tons.[2] After saying this His Excellency changed the subject as though he had said too much.

Naval Attaché believes that there would have been serious repercussions, possibly mutiny in the Navy, if Japanese Government had yielded at all at the Naval Conference. Yesterday thirty Lieutenant Commanders demanded to see Vice Admiral Commanding Yokosuka Naval Station. Press reports that they harangued him for 3 hours, complained of weakness of Cabinet and discussed political questions in a manner which to the English is quite unthinkable.

Young officers both Naval and Military are today the real element of danger and Japanese Government dare not ignore them.

[1] The reference was uncertain. Foreign Office telegram No. 9 of January 19 dealt with another subject. No relevant alternative suggestion was made in the Foreign Office.

[2] A minute by Mr. Craigie reads: 'There was no breath of any such proposal here. If they had put it forward, we could not have accepted it, but rejection might have been more embarrassing for us than in the case of the common-upper-limit proposal. R.L.C. 22/1.'


## No. 629

*Notes on Tokyo telegram No. 24 of January 20, 1936 [No. 628][1]*
*[A 570/4/45]*

1. By the terms of the Washington and London Naval treaties—the total tonnage permitted to be possessed on 31st December 1936 by the principal naval powers is:—

| | |
|---|---|
| British Commonwealth .. .. | 1,151,450 tons. |
| U.S.A. .. .. .. .. .. | 1,115,600 tons. |
| Japan .. .. .. .. .. | 720,120 tons. |

(Note:— In the U.S.A. total 20,000 tons of 8″ Cruisers have been included of which 10,000 tons cannot be completed till 1937 and a further 10,000 tons till 1938.)

[1] A minute on No. 628 by Mr. Gore-Booth explains that this note was supplied by Commander S. H. Paton of the Admiralty on January 22 following a request for 'figures showing exactly what the proposal wd involve'.

788

2. The estimated completed Japanese tonnage on January 1st, 1936 is 761,337 tons and 84,480 tons are estimated to be building or projected.

3. To conform to the London Naval Treaty provisions Japan will have to scrap about 88,159 tons during this year. This assumes that of the 84,480 tons now building and projected, about 42,000 tons is completed during 1936 and the remaining 42,000 tons (approximately) is uncompleted.

4. Thus Japan, whilst adhering strictly to the provisions of the London Naval Treaty, will still be able to attain a global tonnage of 800,000 tons shortly after the expiration of that treaty without any abnormal building programme.

No. 630

*Record by Mr. Craigie of a meeting at the Admiralty on January 20, 1936, between the First Lord of the Admiralty, the French Ambassador, Captain Deleuze, and Mr. Craigie*

[A 730/4/45]

The FRENCH AMBASSADOR began by saying that he had had a talk with the Secretary of State on the 17th instant in regard to the future procedure of the Naval Conference,[1] and it had been arranged that M. Corbin should come and discuss the matter with the First Lord of the Admiralty as Chairman of the First Committee of the Conference.

The French Delegation had gained the impression that it was proposed to extend the scope of the Conference at an early date in order to include other naval Powers, in particular Germany and Russia. The French Government were not in favour of this course, for a variety of reasons. In the first place, it would tend to increase Japan's feeling of isolation if, shortly after she had left the Conference, we proceeded to bring in a number of other Powers, and the French Government doubted whether this would be the best way of assuring ourselves of Japan's eventual cooperation. The inclusion of Russia in the Conference might have an especially unfortunate effect on Japan. The French Government thought that a better plan would be, once we had reached agreements between the Powers now participating in the Conference, to submit the results to Japan and only to consider the procedure to be followed thereafter when we had received Japan's reply.

Another objection which the French Government felt to extending the Conference was that the inclusion of Germany would involve the recognition by France of Germany's right to depart from the naval clauses of the Versailles Treaty and would prejudice France's position when it came to discussing the military clauses of the Treaty. France had so far not admitted Germany's right to depart in any particular from the provisions of the Versailles Treaty. It would be very embarrassing for the French Government to have to revive this question at the present moment.

The FIRST LORD observed that this seemed to indicate a change of policy on the part of the French Government, since he remembered that, at the time

[1] See No. 624.

of the visit to London of M. Barthou and M. Piétri in the summer of 1934, they had been prepared to enter a general naval conference but more reluctant to enter a five Power conference. Finally, a compromise was reached to the effect that there should be a preliminary 'meeting' between the Washington Powers which should not be regarded as a formal conference but as a preparation for a general naval conference to follow,[2] and it was on this understanding of the French Government's position that His Majesty's Government had been working ever since. In reply to M. CORBIN's observation that this was before the conclusion of the Anglo-German Naval Agreement, VISCOUNT MONSELL pointed out that this did not seem to affect the question of France's position in regard to the military clauses of the Versailles Treaty, and, furthermore, that the Anglo-German Naval Agreement dealt with quantitative limitation only whereas the international treaty we were now seeking to reach would deal with qualitative limitation and exchange of information. In reply to M. CORBIN's further objection that we must bear in mind the unpopularity in France of the Anglo-German Naval Agreement, the FIRST LORD pointed out that, from a naval point of view, the Agreement was of the greatest benefit to France and had been recognised as such by their naval authorities. This the AMBASSADOR did not deny, but maintained that, from a political point of view, the existence of the Anglo-German Naval Agreement made it more difficult for France to sit down with Germany at a Naval Conference.

MR. CRAIGIE pointed out that, as the new international treaty would deal purely with qualitative limitation, whereas the Anglo-German Naval Agreement dealt with quantitative limitation, it could be claimed by the French Government with full justice that, in entering a general qualitative treaty, they were neither confirming nor expressing any opinion upon the merits of the Anglo-German Naval Agreement. He added that the juridical position under the Treaty of Versailles was that France could agree to a modification of the naval clauses of the Treaty without weakening her juridical position in regard to the military or any other clauses of the Treaty, and she could safeguard her position by making a reservation to that effect. M. CORBIN, however, refused to be comforted by either of these suggestions.

The FIRST LORD then observed that, according to our information, there was a distinct tendency towards a *rapprochement* between Japan and Germany. In our view, nothing could be more calculated to drive Germany into the arms of Japan than to exclude her from the Naval Treaty which we hoped to conclude or even to give her the impression that there was some juridical difficulty to admitting her to the enlarged Conference which we had in mind. It was desirable that the French Government should remember that, if Germany were to go to war in respect, say, of some Eastern European question France would no doubt turn to this country for aid. But if by that time there was a close political understanding between Japan and Germany, it would be obvious that a large part of our naval forces would have to be despatched to the Far East, where we had interests more vital than those in

[2] See Volume VI, No. 490.

Eastern Europe, with the result that the amount of naval assistance from this country which could be forthcoming would necessarily be reduced. The French Government should surely ponder this point very carefully before embarking on a policy which might end in Germany sharing that exclusion from our naval discussions which Japan had imposed upon herself. M. CORBIN said he fully recognised the importance of this consideration and would report it to his Government. At the same time he did not consider that there was any real risk of a German-Japanese *rapprochement*, if only because it would involve too many risks for Germany and might, in particular, wreck Germany's policy of friendship with the United Kingdom.

The FRENCH AMBASSADOR returned evasive replies to the FIRST LORD's enquiries as to how long a period should, in the view of the French Government, elapse between the end of the present Conference and the summoning of a new Conference to include Germany. The suggestion that possibly a month might elapse in order to give the various naval Powers an opportunity to study the new proposal was brushed aside as totally inadequate.

MR. CRAIGIE pointed out that Germany had, in the course of the Anglo-German conversations of last spring, agreed to accept the lowest qualitative limits adopted by *all other naval Powers*.[3] The implication was, of course, that Germany would become a party to a general qualitative treaty only if she had been represented at the Conference of all the naval Powers in question. There was nothing in our records to indicate that Germany would blindly accept whatever decisions were taken by the present Conference of the Washington Powers. This appeared to be news both to the French Ambassador and to Captain Deleuze, the former implying that the French had been informed both by the Foreign Office and by Captain Danckwerts in Paris[4] that Germany had undertaken to accept whatever qualitative limits were agreed to by the Washington Powers. M. CORBIN also noted the First Lord's statement that, in any case, the idea of exchange of information was not discussed in detail with the Germans last spring and that it was of the utmost importance to France to know what Germany was building.

It was finally agreed that both sides should think over the arguments put forward by the other and that there might be a further discussion at some later date.

R.L.C.

3 Cf. No. 461, Appendix I.
4 A reference to Captain Danckwerts's visit to Paris in August 1935; see No. 461.

## No. 631

*Record by Captain Danckwerts of a meeting with Commander Schuirmann on Wednesday, January 22, 1936*

*L.N.C.(35)(U.K.)20 [A 243/4/45]*

At COMMANDER SCHUIRMANN's suggestion I met him to-day. His object was to discuss with me, on a purely personal and unofficial basis, any possible method of escaping from the present deadlock.

791

2. COMMANDER SCHUIRMANN was very insistent, as he has been before, that there is no possibility of persuading Congress to accept an agreement for any reduction in the cruiser qualitative limits, either in guns or tons, unless it is accompanied by what is, in the U.S.A. view, a satisfactory and comprehensive cruiser quantitative agreement.

3. He also said that the Navy Department desired to build 16″ gun battleships, and have never wanted 14″ gun ships; they only agreed to this reduction in gun calibre because they thought it would enable them to get a six year building programme, or other form of quantitative agreement, which would preserve the ratio basis.

4. He then suggested the following scheme as being, in his opinion, the farthest limits to which it would be possible to get the Navy Department to go, but he emphasized that the scheme had not been put up to the Navy Department and they might not agree to it:—

*Capital Ships.*

Qualitative limit of 35,000 tons with 16″ guns unless before the 1st January, 1937, Japan would agree to come into a qualitative limit of 35,000 tons with 14″ guns.

*Cruisers (a).*

Qualitative limit of 10,000 tons with 8″ guns.

*Cruisers (b).*

Qualitative limit of 10,000 tons with 6·1″ guns. The High Contracting Parties to agree amongst themselves not to build any cruisers (a), or any cruisers (b) in excess of some limit (say 8,000 tons) to be agreed upon, for a period of 3 years, unless Japan did, in fact, lay down any such ships herself.

5. COMMANDER SCHUIRMANN agreed that we required a 'let-out' clause to free us from qualitative limits in the event of Japan exceeding whatever limits were agreed upon: he also said that the U.S.A. required a 'let-out' clause which would permit them to build cruisers (a) or large cruisers (b) if Japan exceeded her present ratio in those types. He agreed that this could not be so expressed in any written agreement, but should be based on the formula 'If any High Contracting Party feels her security to be menaced etc.'

6. COMMANDER SCHUIRMANN asked my comments on his scheme. I said that it was very disappointing to us. I suggested that the same result as regards capital ships would be produced by putting it the other way round, viz., the calibre limit agreed upon to be 14″ unless Japan refused to come into the agreement. He said that he did not feel that they could present it to Congress in that way.

7. I also said that a limit of 3 years on large cruiser building was too short to be of real value, and would merely be postponing the evil moment that is coming to us on the 1st January, 1937, when we have to begin cruiser building without knowledge of Japan's intentions. He agreed that a longer term might be inserted and that it might be selected so as to coincide with the replacement of existing 8″ gun cruisers, i.e., 7 or 8 years.

8. Finally, he asked me for some counter proposition for consideration. I suggested the following formula:—

*Capital Ships.*

Qualitative limit of 35,000 tons with 14″ guns. If Japan or any other principal Naval Power refrained from coming into this agreement by the 1st January, 1937, we should revert to the Washington limits.

*Cruisers (a).* 10,000 tons with 8″ guns.

*Cruisers (b).* 7,500 tons with 6·1″ guns.

The High Contracting Parties to agree not to build any cruisers (*a*), or any cruisers (*b*) exceeding 7,500 tons, for a period of 8 years from the 1st January, 1937, unless Japan or some other principal Naval Power laid down or built ships exceeding that limit.

9. COMMANDER SCHUIRMANN and I agreed to report this conversation to Admirals Standley and Chatfield respectively before their conversation to-morrow (Thursday).

## No. 632

*Record of a meeting between representatives of the United Kingdom and United States on Thursday, January 23, 1936, at 12 noon[1]*

L.N.C.(*35*)(*U.K.*)*21* [*A 773/4/45*]

PRESENT: *United Kingdom*: Admiral of the Fleet Sir Ernle Chatfield, Captain Danckwerts.
　　　　*United States*: Admiral Standley, Captain Ingersoll, Commander Schuirmann, Lieutenant Ayrault.

ADMIRAL CHATFIELD opened the meeting by referring to the conversation that had taken place between Commander Schuirmann and Captain Danck-werts on the previous day.[2] He then described the cruiser situation facing the United Kingdom. He said we should have to build some twenty-five to thirty cruisers in the next five or six years. Consequently the limiting size of cruisers was very important to us, they had to be large enough to do their work and to keep the sea, but they must not be so large that the British Cruiser force would bear the appearance of being a threat to the entire world. We concluded that the best size was from 7–8,000 tons.

He then referred to the Japanese situation that would come about with the lapse of present treaties when there would be no quantitative restrictions. For this reason we desire the specific declaration that there should be no more building of Category (*a*) cruisers and no more building of Category (*b*) cruisers above a certain size. One of the difficulties was that this declaration could be represented as a quantitative limitation on Japan since it would maintain the existing ratio in the large size cruisers. We had, however,

---

[1] This meeting took place at Claridge's Hotel, London.　　　[2] See No. 631.

hope[d] that Japan would accept the situation in her own interests and refrain from beginning a cruiser construction race, and we even hoped that she might give some assurance of compliance with the limits.

To make the scheme attractive to us it was necessary that it should be for some long term of years, the longer the term the more likely it was that the arrangement would persist, since Japanese departure from the limit after such a long term would only outclass the ships that she herself had built meanwhile. We ought, therefore, to press for the provision that there should be no more building of Category (a) or large Category (b) cruisers and that a new qualitative limit of 7–8,000 tons for 6″ cruisers should be set, with the proviso that all other naval powers must be bound by the treaty or give some signed assurance.

ADMIRAL STANDLEY outlined the general American position. Qualitative limitation was unattractive unless accompanied by quantitative limitation, but for powers with large navies qualitative limitation is better than nothing at all. The overriding object of the United States Delegation was to foster a closer Anglo-American understanding, but in so doing it was all important that it should not be possible for them to be accused, on return, of having 'sold out to the British'. They had come to this country prepared to give a six year building programme. They were ready to refrain from 8″ gun cruiser building and to agree, for a period of years, not to build any more 6″ gun cruisers of 10,000 tons. Then for a period of years they would be free to match our cruiser building with their own, but they cannot make this declaration for an unlimited period.

COMMANDER SCHUIRMANN pointed out that the United States had only provided for nine 6″ gun 10,000 ton ships which was all that she could provide under the tonnage limitations of the London Naval Treaty. If the declaration was made as suggested, the United States would, in fact, be condemning herself to have only nine of these ships as against ten of the United Kingdom, since he understood that we should lay down the ninth and tenth ships of the *Southampton* Class this year.

ADMIRAL CHATFIELD pointed out that against this they had the counter-balance of eighteen 8″ gun ships against our fifteen. He would be heavily criticised in this country for agreeing to this inferiority in Category (a) cruisers. COMMANDER SCHUIRMANN suggested that the United Kingdom should build only nine of the *Southampton* Class. ADMIRAL CHATFIELD pointed out that nine cruisers at 10,000 tons for the United States corresponded to ten cruisers of 9,000 tons for the United Kingdom. A suggestion was then discussed to limit the number of these cruisers to ten for each country, but it was pointed out that this would certainly never receive the assent of Japan. COMMANDER SCHUIRMANN then suggested that the United States could build a tenth ship by making use of the 10% transfer provision of the London Naval Treaty (Article 17). He also stated his opinion that Japan would refrain from transgressing the qualitative limitation adopted for cruisers.

ADMIRAL STANDLEY then suggested that the proposal should be put up for

794

the consideration of the Navy Department, the term of years being six years. COMMANDER SCHUIRMANN suggested five years. ADMIRAL CHATFIELD insisted on six years. ADMIRAL STANDLEY suggested until the 1st July, 1942 which was the termination of the present building programme envisaged by President Roosevelt.

CAPTAIN INGERSOLL at this point enlarged on the importance of including in the Treaty some definition of age limits, although it would not have any direct connection with the undertakings of the Treaty.

The meeting then turned to the discussion of capital ships. ADMIRAL STANDLEY said the question was a matter of approach. We were agreed upon the facts, viz. that if everybody came into the Treaty the gun calibre limit should be fourteen inch, whereas if Japan or any other country was out of the Treaty the limit should be sixteen inch.

It was important to maintain the Anglo-American accord, and at the same time to be able to meet criticism in the United States. The approach that had been proposed by Commander Schuirmann would disarm American criticism, whereas to approach in a reverse manner would provoke it. ADMIRAL CHATFIELD described the United Kingdom views on the size of ships and guns and their relation to each other. He said that we did not believe 35,000 tons was big enough for a 16″ gun and certainly we could not build a fast 16″ ship on this tonnage. We, however, were faced with the problem of capital ship building in Europe. There were already seven ships building, next year there would be more. We could not afford to wait for a whole year before beginning our building in reply. It would take us a year from the time of decision before we could lay down a ship. It was necessary, therefore, for us to decide now, consequently we should probably have to lay down two ships by the 1st January, 1937 with 14″ guns. These might be regarded as anti-European ships. If, therefore, the approach was made in the manner proposed by Commander Schuirmann (L.N.C. 35)[3] we should be accused of building below a qualitative limit without any sure prospect that that limit would come down. He said that from a purely naval point of view it would not much matter whether the ultimate decision was 14″ or 16″ although with 16″ guns he would really prefer to come up to a tonnage of 40,000; but it would be a great moral advantage from a disarmament point of view to be able to get some reduction, at least until the position was upset by the action of Japan. Our suggestion for approach would put more moral pressure to bring others in. We should even hope that Japan would give the assurance required, but this could not be hoped from the American approach.

ADMIRAL STANDLEY explained that the gunnery experts of America favoured the 16″ gun as a better weapon. Therefore they could only say that they would agree to a 14″ if all other countries wanted it. CAPTAIN INGERSOLL suggested that this too should only be for a limited number of years.

ADMIRAL CHATFIELD developed the argument that since Japan only wanted to act defensively in her corner of the Pacific, she might only build slow, heavily protected battleships. Therefore it was to her advantage if the size

---

[3] The reference is presumably to No. 631.

of the gun were kept up. Therefore we ought to persuade her to adopt the smaller gun if possible.

CAPTAIN INGERSOLL said that on return the United States Delegation would be criticised for having no quantitative limitation and no reduction in tonnage and that the exchange of information gives no limitation.

Finally it was agreed that the views of both sides were clear to each other and that it would be necessary for the United States Delegation to obtain instructions from Washington and to consider in what way the debate was to be conducted when the First Committee next met. The importance of knowing the French and Italian views was also touched on.

## No. 633

*Record by Mr. Craigie of a conversation between the First Lord of the Admiralty and Mr. Nagai on January 23, 1936*

[*A 854/4/45*]

FOREIGN OFFICE, *January 23, 1936*

Mr. Nagai called to-day on the First Lord of the Admiralty to continue the discussion of certain points arising out of Japan's withdrawal from the Naval Conference. I was present at the interview.

The first point touched on was Part IV of the London Naval Treaty, relating to the treatment of merchant ships by submarines in time of war. It was arranged that any draft agreement which might be reached between the Powers remaining in the Conference should be forwarded to Japan through the diplomatic channel. Provided the form was acceptable to the Japanese Government, the agreement could then be signed by the Japanese Chargé d'Affaires in London. It was, Mr. Nagai said, desirable to devise some form which would not necessitate re-submission of the agreement to the Japanese Privy Council, a body which was apt to make difficulties on small and formal points. But, if this did not prove possible, Mr. Nagai felt sure that the agreement would, subject to criticism of details be accepted by the Privy Council, since it represented the definite policy of the Japanese Government.

The First Lord then said he wished to put to Mr. Nagai a question in regard to submarines. Had Japan remained in the Conference for the discussion of qualitative limitation, it would have been our intention to invite the views of the Japanese Delegation on the British proposal for the abolition of the submarine. As this was no longer possible, the First Lord desired to ask Mr. Nagai formally whether Japan would be prepared to agree to the abolition of this type of vessel. Mr. Nagai replied categorically that Japan was not prepared to agree to the abolition of the submarine.

Mr. Nagai then stated that there were certain articles of the Washington Naval Treaty containing provisions which Japan would be glad to see perpetuated in a future treaty between the naval Powers. These were Article XIV (preparation of merchant ships for armament in time of peace),

Article XVII (prohibition of acquiring, in time of war, vessels building for other Powers), Article XVIII (prohibition of transfer of vessels of war from one Power to another). Mr. Nagai suggested that provisions dealing with these subjects should be put in a separate treaty in order that Japan might be able to adhere to them independently of any other provisions on which the four Powers might agree. The First Lord took note of this suggestion but said that he was not sure whether we should be prepared to enter a treaty dealing with these particular points independently of the other aspects of naval limitation. If, for instance, there were to be no treaty dealing with qualitative limitation, it was possible that the United Kingdom might prefer to be able, in time of peace, to prepare her merchant ships to carry armament in time of war. However, we would certainly bear Mr. Nagai's request carefully in mind.

Article XIX of the Washington Treaty (non-fortification of naval bases in the Pacific) was then briefly touched upon. We said that this was a question which would have to be tackled sooner or later and we should be glad to know whether Mr. Nagai could inform us of the views of his Government upon it. Mr. Nagai expressed ignorance as to whether, in present circumstances, the Japanese Government would wish to prolong these provisions. He appeared, however, to concur in the First Lord's suggestion that it was desirable that the Japanese Government should take an early opportunity to let His Majesty's Government know whether or not they favoured the retention of these provisions after December 31st, 1936.

I then took the opportunity to say that I knew it was the desire of His Majesty's Government, as we believed it to be also of the Japanese Government, that Japan's unfortunate withdrawal from the Conference should not be allowed to have any political repercussions on Anglo-Japanese relations. As the conveners of the Conference, the United Kingdom Delegation had been obliged to take a prominent part in the discussion of the common upper limit proposal and this conception of naval limitation was indeed one entirely unacceptable to this country. Nevertheless, it was well known to both countries that, were it not for other countries, we could probably reach a naval understanding without much difficulty, and this fact should always be remembered by the two Governments in estimating the results of the Conference. Mr. Nagai agreed and said that, so far as he had been able to judge, there was no bitterness from Japan against Great Britain for the part which the latter had played int he Conference. Only on one point was there criticism by his Government, namely, the failure to agree to the Japanese proposal for an adjournment, in order that the Conference between the four Powers might continue under quite new auspices—i.e. unconnected with the Washington and London Naval Treaties. This would have eased the situation for the Japanese Government. I stated, in reply, that the Japanese Delegation had not made it clear at the time that they would have been satisfied with a purely formal adjournment of, say, one day, in order to mark the transition from one conference to the other. The expression used at the crucial interview between the Japanese and United Kingdom

797

Delegations[1] had been an adjournment *sine die* and that was impossible for practical reasons. In any case, it was obvious that, once we extended the Conference so as to include other naval Powers, the result of such an extended Conference must be something which would be entirely independent of the Washington and London Naval Treaties, so that there would be no question of perpetuating either the spirit or the substance of those Treaties.

Finally, Mr. Nagai undertook, on his return to Japan, to report on what had occurred here in as favourable and conciliatory a manner as possible. While promising nothing, he did not reject the suggestion that possibly, after a few months' time, the Japanese Government might be able to consider more impartially the draft of any qualitative treaty which might be presented to them.

R.L.C.

[1] A reference presumably to the meeting on January 13; see No. 617, paragraphs 2 and 3.

## No. 634

*Record by Mr. Craigie of a conversation with Admiral Decoux and Captain Deleuze on January 23, 1936*

[*A 852/4/45*]

FOREIGN OFFICE, *January 23, 1936*

After the conclusion of to-day's Sub-Committee,[1] I asked Admiral Decoux and Captain Deleuze to stay behind and have a talk with me on the subject of France's refusal to agree to the extension of the Conference so as to include Germany. I stated that my purpose was simply to clear my own mind, as I was completely mystified as to the arguments and purposes of the French Delegation in this matter.

After recounting the earlier history of this question, I asked why it was that France, who was perfectly prepared to come into a general naval conference in the summer of 1934, now said that it was impossible to do so without prejudicing her position in regard to those clauses of the Treaty of Versailles other than the naval clauses; secondly, what rôle did (*a*) the Anglo-German Naval Treaty and (*b*) Japan's departure from the Conference play in determining this new French attitude.

The answers may be summarised as follows:

When the French Ministers agreed in the summer of 1934 to the idea of a general naval conference, this was at a time when the Disarmament Conference was still sitting and it was therefore hoped that any general naval agreement reached could be fitted into a general disarmament convention. The interdependence of armaments would thus have been preserved. Now, however, that the Disarmament Conference had definitely broken down and there was no immediate hope of agreement on land armaments, the French Government were no longer prepared to enter into a naval conference with

[1] i.e. the Technical Sub-Committee on Advance Notification and Exchange of Information; cf. No. 625, penultimate paragraph.

Germany. In the present circumstances, no French Government could survive which agreed to do so, though Captain Deleuze hinted that, possibly, the situation might be easier after the coming elections.[2]

As regards the Anglo-German Naval Agreement, the French representatives maintained that we had always given them to understand, both when Captain Danckwerts was in Paris[3] and when Admiral Decoux was here in October,[4] that Germany had agreed in the course of the Anglo-German discussions last June that she would accept any qualitative limits agreed to by the five-Power Conference and it had therefore been the view of the French Government that there was no necessity whatsoever to bring Germany into the Conference. As regards Russia, we could well afford to ignore her, and the French Government could probably bring us the necessary assurance that she had no idea of building beyond the quantitative limits now in contemplation.

I said that in both conversations it had been made clear by the United Kingdom representatives that Germany would agree to the limits accepted by *all* other Powers. The implication of this was, of course, that Germany would participate in the Conference which would be necessary to secure agreement between 'all other Powers'. We had been perfectly justified in assuming, from our conversations in the summer of 1934, that the French Government would not object to such a general conference and our conversations with the Germans had rested on the assumption that such a conference would take place. I maintained that never until this moment had the French Government made it clear that they would not enter a naval conference with Germany. The French representatives were not prepared to agree on this point but they did agree that, quite irrespective of this, the fact that Germany would not be bound by the qualitative limits agreed at this conference (even if Japan had remained) was one which the French Government would have to take into consideration.

The French view as to the bearing of Japan's departure from the Conference on this particular controversy is apparently that Sir John Simon himself had stated to M. Piétri in the summer of 1934 that it was only after an understanding had been reached between the *five* Powers that we should think of summoning a general naval conference.[5] In the French view, it followed that, as there were now only four Powers left, the general conference would not be summoned. I said this seemed to me purely a debating point. The underlying idea in Sir John Simon's statement in 1934 was that it was useless to go to the expense and effort of summoning a big naval conference if it proved impossible to get agreement even between five Powers. But if we reached agreement between four Powers with the prospect of Japan coming in before the end of the year, surely this represented a sufficient body of agreement to make it worth while bringing in the other naval

---

[2] M. Laval's ministry had resigned on January 22. Two days later M. Sarraut formed a ministry in which M. Flandin was Minister for Foreign Affairs: M. Piétri retained his position as Minister of Marine. A general election was not held until April 26 and May 3.

[3] In August 1935; cf. No. 461.    [4] Cf. No. 546.    [5] Cf. Volume VI, No. 490.

Powers. The French representatives, however, stubbornly maintained that no approach should be made to the other Powers until after Japan had come in. As an alternative, Captain Deleuze suggested that we should transfer the whole question to Geneva where we could, in a short time, bring in all the Powers other than Germany and Japan and, once that had been done, make our arrangements with the two remaining Powers.

Finally, I said that this cry about the interdependence of armaments had blocked the way towards a settlement of the armaments question for the last fifteen years or so and that I did not believe that His Majesty's Government, so far as they were concerned, were prepared to allow it to block the way any longer. The problem of arms limitation was so vast that it must be tackled piecemeal if any progress were to be made at all.

So far as I could glean, this present difficulty seems to have originated in the French General Staff, who are accusing the Navy of letting them down on the armaments question vis-à-vis of [sic] Germany. The French representatives hinted that, as long as the General Staff felt like this, no French Government could face up to the question. This was not stated definitely by either Admiral Decoux or Captain Deleuze, but by putting two and two together I do not think this surmise is far wrong.

(for Mr. Craigie)
P. H. GORE-BOOTH

No. 635

*Memorandum for the German Government*[1]

[*A 383/4/45*]

FOREIGN OFFICE, *January 25, 1936*

His Majesty's Government in the United Kingdom have studied with care the communication from the German Government dated the 23rd November, 1935,[2] in reply to their Memorandum of the 16th October, 1935.[3] His Majesty's Government note with appreciation the general agreement between the two Governments on the points under discussion.

2. Whilst maintaining the views expressed in paragraph 4 of their communication of the 16th October, 1935, on the relation between 'transfer' and 'adjustment', as expressed in paragraphs 2 (*d*) and 2 (*g*) of Sir Samuel Hoare's note of 18th June, 1935,[4] His Majesty's Government take note of the explanations in Section III of the German communication, and in particular of the proposal, as the main principle to be applied, that the total amount of the adjustments obtaining at a given date should not exceed half the displacement of the standard battleship, and that the term of adjustment should

[1] This memorandum was drafted by the Admiralty and revised in the Foreign Office, after which a copy was handed to Captain Wassner on January 25.

[2] See No. 526, note 5.　　　　　　　　　　　　　　　[3] Appendix to No. 526.

[4] See Annex to No. 348.

not be longer than 10 years. His Majesty's Government consider that 10 years is a very substantial period for an adjustment which is not to be a 'permanent departure' from the ratio. Nevertheless, they are prepared to accept this period as a maximum and thus to agree to the German proposal quoted above.

3. The German Government state in their communication that they expect that the principle described above will not be interpreted in a narrow sense and that, when necessary in the case of small excess amounts, agreement will be reached by friendly negotiations between the two Governments. His Majesty's Government are in agreement with these sentiments but must point out that, in their view, it is not necessary that a departure from the general rule shall always give an excess in favour of Germany. On the contrary, if the agreement is to be interpreted in no narrow sense it may sometimes result in a temporary deficiency in favour of the British tonnage.

4. The only other point requiring further elucidation is the age at which cruisers from the 'Emden' to the 'Nurenberg' may be replaced in the permanently over-age category by tonnage not genuinely over-age. The German Government state that they are unable to assent to the United Kingdom proposal not to undertake the replacement of these cruisers until after 22 years, and repeat their proposal that the six cruisers in question should be replaced after 20 years by newer tonnage to be transferred to the permanently over-age category. The result of the German proposal would appear to be that in the years 1949 and 1950 cruisers completed in 1937 and 1938 will be moved up into the over-age category and counted as part of the German over-age tonnage corresponding to the British permanently over-age category when in fact they are only 12 years' old. Thus, for some years the German Government would obtain a virtual increase in strength beyond that contemplated by the general agreement. It is therefore proposed that, in order to smooth out the drop from four over-age cruisers in 1948 to one actual over-age cruiser in 1951 and subsequent years, the six ships in question should be finally scrapped and replaced by tonnage to be moved up at the following ages:—

| | | | | | |
|---|---|---|---|---|---|
| *Emden* | .. | .. | .. | .. | 20 years |
| *Karlsruhe* | .. | .. | .. | .. | 20 ,, |
| *Königsberg* | .. | .. | .. | .. | 21 ,, |
| *Köln* | .. | .. | .. | .. | 21 ,, |
| *Leipzig* | .. | .. | .. | .. | 22 ,, |
| *Nüremberg* | .. | .. | .. | .. | 20 ,, |

His Majesty's Government trust that the German Government will be able to accept this proposal and, in thus disposing of the last point at issue, reach with His Majesty's Government a mutually satisfactory understanding for the practical application of the Anglo-German Naval Agreement.

## No. 636

### Minute by Mr. Craigie
### [A 814/4/45]

FOREIGN OFFICE, *January 27, 1936*

The French Delegation to the Naval Conference have somewhat abruptly notified the United Kingdom Delegation that on no account will they agree to the Conference being extended so as to include Germany.[1] They say, first of all, the situation is changed as a result of Japan's departure from the Conference. Secondly, they say that when in the summer of 1934 M. Barthou and M. Piétri agreed to a world conference on naval limitation, this was subject to prior agreement between the *five* Washington Powers. Furthermore, the General Disarmament Conference was then still sitting and there was still a prospect of an agreement in regard to land and air, so that all three armaments (land, air and sea) could have been fitted into one general armaments convention. This is no longer the case so that the French reservation about the interdependence of armaments holds good and no French Government could live if the French Naval Delegation were to invalidate all the clauses of Part V of the Versailles Treaty by sitting down with Germany to discuss the modification of the Naval Clauses.

This is, briefly, the French argument. If we accept it, it means that we can never make progress in any direction—whether as regards naval armaments or air armaments—because of the unlikelihood of our ever being able to reach an international agreement on land armaments. On this ground alone it seems desirable to challenge the French thesis immediately and to urge the necessity of beginning somewhere if progress is to be made in any direction. But there is also the risk that, if the present Naval Conference ends with an agreement between the four Washington Powers only (subject to ultimate accession of other Powers) and if no provision is made for bringing in at least Germany and Russia at an early date, there is every probability that the work here will have been done in vain, and there will be a complete fiasco. The First Lord of the Admiralty holds this view very strongly and will represent it to M. Piétri while he is here.[2] He hopes very much that the Secretary of State will take an equally strong line with M. Flandin. There are, of course, other arguments (technical and political) which could be used in urging the French to abandon their attitude but, as M. Flandin presumably knows nothing about the question, it seems best at this stage to avoid details and simply to say that it is becoming impossible for His Majesty's Government to agree that all progress in the direction of limitation of armaments should be continually held up by this French cry about the

[1] Cf. Nos. 630 and 634.

[2] Cf. No. 634, note 2. M. Flandin and M. Piétri were in England in connection with the funeral on January 28 of His late Majesty King George V. For Mr. Eden's conversation with M. Flandin see No. 637 below. A record, not here printed, of Lord Monsell's conversation with M. Piétri at the Hyde Park Hotel, London, at 6.30 p.m. on January 28 was circulated as L.N.C. (35) (U.K.) 25.

interdependence of armaments. This is all the more ridiculous when it is well-known that while at one moment the French say that for them to recognise in any way the Anglo-German Naval Treaty will prejudice discussions which they may be going to have on land armaments, at another moment they indicate that they have no ideas whatever on how to make progress on land armaments.

R. L. Craigie

## No. 637

*Mr. Eden to Sir G. Clerk (Paris)*

*No. 143* [*C 573/92/62*]

FOREIGN OFFICE, January 27, 1936

Sir,

M. Flandin came to see me to-day and we had our first conversation since his appointment as French Foreign Minister.[1] He began by expressing his earnest wish that during the period of his tenure of the Foreign Office, Anglo-French relations should be improved. He would always endeavour to consult me before taking any action and he hoped that I would do the same so that in any move which we made we could show the world clearly that we were in step. . . .[2]

7. I then told M. Flandin that I wished to speak to him about the Naval Conference. He might not yet have had time to familiarise himself with the details of the position, but I wished to take this first opportunity of asking him to make a constructive contribution to help the progress of that Conference. It seemed possible that a Four-Power Agreement would shortly be reached and that it might be that the four Powers would submit their proposals to Japan and ask that country to associate herself with them. In any event it was desirable to include all naval Powers in any agreement which was finally reached. For this purpose it would be necessary to approach Germany and Russia amongst others. M. Corbin had told me that the French Government would find some difficulty in this course.[3] I much hoped however that they would not now persist in their objection. It was in the interests of France, as in our own, to bring Germany into any naval agreement which might finally be reached. Though it was true that the Anglo-German Naval Agreement limited Germany quantitatively, it was also important to France as well as to ourselves that she should come into a qualitative agreement also.

8. M. Flandin in reply reiterated the arguments which M. Corbin had previously used about the difficulty for any French Government of sitting down to a conference with Germany which legalised her naval armaments in defiance of the Treaty of Versailles, more particularly since no agreement had been reached or was in sight in respect of military or air armaments.

---

[1] Cf. No. 634, note 2.

[2] Paragraphs 2–6 which dealt with matters other than the naval conference are here omitted.        [3] See No. 624.

Upon my pressing him further, M. Flandin admitted that this was largely a question of French internal politics. He did not despair of finding some way round the difficulty—perhaps by means of the diplomatic channel. He hoped, however, that His Majesty's Government would give him time. It would really not be possible for him or for any French Foreign Minister, with the very best will in the world, to agree to meet the Germans at a Conference which would legalise German rearmament before the French elections. If, however, it was possible to hold matters up till then, we could continue to seek to find ways and means of overcoming the very real difficulty, which the French Government felt, as soon as the elections were over.

9. Finally, M. Flandin stated that he wished to approach the Chancellor of the Exchequer during his visit to this country to attempt to secure a measure of financial accommodation. He would not ask for a loan for he knew the difficulties of that, but he would like help for a few months of a character similar to that which the French Government had given His Majesty's Government during the crisis of 1931. I replied that this was of course a matter for the Chancellor of the Exchequer as to which I was in no way qualified to speak. M. Flandin said that he understood this, but he did not wish to approach Mr. Chamberlain before he had made sure that I had no political objection to this course. I assured M. Flandin that I had none and we agreed that he should speak to the Chancellor of the Exchequer on the matter later in the evening.

I am, &c.,<br>
ANTHONY EDEN

## No. 638

### Letter from Mr. Craigie to Sir R. Clive (Tokyo)

### [A 415/4/45]

FOREIGN OFFICE, *January 27, 1936*

My dear Clive,

Wellesley has passed on to me your letter of the 21st December[1] about the possibility of a political understanding between Japan, the United States and ourselves. The whole question has interested us very much; we found the appraisal of the situation given in your despatch No. 626[2] of the 21st December very valuable and we entirely agreed with the line which you have taken.

One of our chief troubles at this end has been the shortness of the time which elapsed between Mr. Hirota throwing out the suggestion of a pact and the Japanese leaving the Naval Conference. If a political pact would have helped us to achieve an acceptable Naval Treaty, Mr. Hirota's idea might well have been worth pursuing. The situation has, however, been entirely changed by the action of the Japanese, since, as we implied in our telegram No. 6[3] of the 10th January, we could not consider the possibility of concluding

---

[1] No. 591.   [2] No. 590.   [3] No. 608.

a political pact with the United States and Japan as a substitute for a Naval Treaty. Indeed it is difficult to see what benefit in the present circumstances such a pact could be to us.

Apart from this insuperable difficulty the Americans have shown fairly clearly that they are not prepared, at any rate at present, to depart from a Far Eastern Policy of extreme rigidity. They are, we gather, unlikely to consider a non-ag[g]ression pact at all, and even if we limited ourselves to the idea of an agreement extending the consultation clause of the Nine-Power Treaty, they would apparently only be willing to give such an idea serious thought if the proposed agreement were designed to include not only Japan and ourselves but also the other parties to the Nine-Power Treaty.

The idea may arise again later, particularly if and when the Naval Powers, other than Japan, arrive at some kind of agreement on qualitative limitation and the exchange of information and are then anxious to bring Japan into this agreement. We shall be grateful, therefore, if you will continue to watch the situation carefully and report any developments that may occur.[4]

Yours ever,<br>R. L. Craigie

[4] In the course of a minute of January 18 Mr. Craigie, while agreeing that 'for the moment at all events, there can be no point in pursuing the idea of a political pact with Japan', added that the 'danger of a policy of complete inactivity lies in the present tendency to a rapprochement between Japan and Germany—if rumour speaks true this is already more than a tendency. If on top of Japan's withdrawal, we allow ourselves to be influenced by the present French demand that no attempt should be made to bring Germany into this Conference at all and only into some later Conference at some indefinite date in the future, we shall be almost inviting those two powers to come to an understanding . . .' Mr. Orde wrote on January 20: 'I agree; though as regards a Japanese rapprochement with Germany I am inclined to think that a political agreement with Japan would have no particular effect in discouraging it. Japan I think will remain anxious for it as a weapon against Russia whether or not she has a political understanding with us. But the French move to exclude Germany from the Naval Conference, if successful, would seem likely to encourage Germany to pursue agreement with Japan.' These minutes were approved by Sir R. Vansittart on January 20 and were subsequently seen by Mr. Eden.

No. 639

Sir R. Clive (Tokyo) to Mr. Eden (Received January 31, 9.30 a.m.)<br>No. 37 Telegraphic [A 900/4/45]

TOKYO, January 31, 1936, 12.50 p.m.

Naval Conference.

In obviously inspired article in two leading papers conclusion is reached with regard to new British qualitative proposals that despite British efforts there seems no hope of arriving at an agreement in [?on] qualitative restrictions as America will never join in unless Japan also participates.

## No. 640

*Letter from Sir E. Drummond (Rome) to Sir R. Vansittart (Received February 6)*
*[A 1088/4/45]*

ROME, *January 31, 1936*

My dear Van,

I had a long conversation with Sugimura[1] on various points the other day and he told me one thing which may be of some interest.

When the decision as to Japan abandoning the Treaty of Washington unless she could get a new treaty on her own terms, came before the Japanese Privy Council,[2] which, Sugimura said, consists of some twenty of the most eminent people and is presided over by the Emperor, one of the members—I think the Minister for Foreign Affairs, or it may have been Viscount Ishii[3] —turned to the Admiral, who was representing the Navy's case, and said to him, 'If your policy is adopted, will you give us an assurance it does not mean a race in naval armaments?' The Admiral had replied, 'I can give you that assurance'.

I understand that the object of the question was to commit the Admiralty definitely on this point in front of the Emperor, and if any race did take place, the Admiralty would have to bear the responsibility and become considerably discredited.

If this information is new to you please regard it as confidential, as it does not come to Sugimura from his Foreign Office, but from an ancient chief who is a member of the Japanese Privy Council.

Yours ever,
ERIC DRUMMOND

[1] Japanese Ambassador at Rome.　　　[2] Cf. No. 92.
[3] A Privy Councillor since 1929.

## No. 641

*Mr. Eden to Sir R. Lindsay (Washington)[1]*
*No. 35 Telegraphic [A 961/4/45]*

FOREIGN OFFICE, *February 1, 1936, 7 p.m.*

My telegram No. 20.[2]

On the 31st January the Sub-Committee on Advance Notification and the Exchange of Information presented to the First Committee a report covering the text of provisions for a treaty.[3] The principal provisions are substantially as follows:

The High Contracting Parties will inform each other confidentially in the first four months of each year of their building and acquisition programmes as far as concerns naval vessels over 100 tons.

[1] Identic telegrams, referring to No. 625, were sent on the same day to Tokyo (No. 17), Paris (No. 24 Saving), Rome (No. 5 Saving), Berlin (No. 5 Saving), Moscow (No. 2 Saving).
[2] No. 625.　　　　　　　　　　　　　　[3] See *L.N.C. 1935 Docs.*, pp. 154–61.

Four months before any vessel is laid down, detailed information as to its characteristics will be communicated by the Power laying it down to the other Contracting Powers.

Provision is also made for the notification of important alterations in ships.

The draft was adopted by the First Committee.[4]

The First Committee held on the 29th January[5] a general discussion on qualitative limitation and on the 31st referred this question, together with allied questions such as definitions, age of ships, etc., to a second Technical Sub-Committee, on which the First Sea Lord will be the chief United Kingdom representative.

The Japanese observers[6] were present for the first time on the 29th January and were welcomed by the Chairman on behalf of all the Delegations.

[4] See *ibid.*, pp. 703–16.    [5] See *ibid.*, pp. 673–86.
[6] Mr. Fujii and Captain Fujita.

## No. 642

*Sir E. Phipps (Berlin) to Mr. Eden (Received February 6)*
*No. 152 [A 1095/4/45]*

BERLIN, *February 4, 1936*

Sir,

I have the honour to transmit to you, herewith, a copy of a minute by the Naval Attaché to this Embassy recording a conversation with the Head of the Navy on the 1st February.

2. Admiral Raeder was evidently misinformed regarding developments at the Naval Conference but his remarks may none the less be of interest to you.

I have, &c.,
ERIC PHIPPS

ENCLOSURE IN No. 642

*Captain Muirhead-Gould to Sir E. Phipps*

BERLIN, *February 3, 1936*

I left your card at the Marineleitung on Saturday 1st February and thanked Admiral Raeder for having sent Admiral Witzell to represent him at the Memorial Service for His late Majesty at the British Church on 28th January, and for having sent Admiral Albrecht to London for the funeral.

Admiral Raeder said he could assure me that he himself and the whole German Navy really joined the British Navy in mourning for their King who had throughout his life been so closely associated with the Navy. King George was a man for whom everyone in the German Navy had a sincere admiration.

2. Admiral Raeder then asked me to sit down and referred at once to the Naval Conference. He said he was glad to have news of an agreement, at

which I expressed surprise as I had heard nothing about it, except a brief reference on the wireless to agreement being reached on exchange of programmes. Admiral Raeder said that he had a summary of the news telegraphed to him every morning early, and that his information was that agreement had also been reached in regard to qualitative limitation at any rate as regards capital ships and their guns. He understood that capital ships would be limited to 35,000 tons and 38 cm guns. He asked me what Power was responsible for making the tonnage so high, and supposed that it was America with her passion for having the largest of everything: or possibly France who had to have something bigger than Germany had. He thought it was [a] great pity that France should still look upon the German Navy with suspicion. Was not Germany's gesture in voluntarily basing her Naval strength at a small percentage of the Naval strength of Great Britain sufficient proof that the German Navy was for defensive purposes only? He had hoped that everyone, even France, would have been convinced of Germany's pacific intentions.

He very much regretted that the limits had been set so high. He would have preferred to build more ships and smaller ones, and he expected that the British Admiralty felt the same, but had had to agree in order to get any sort of agreement.

3. That brought him to another point. He had found that some English papers, particularly the Morning Post, were still from time to time publishing articles accusing Germany of breaking the Anglo-German Naval agreement by building more ships and bigger ships, particularly submarines, than were allowed to her under the Agreement. He wished once and for all to deny this categorically and to give me his personal assurance that the terms of the agreement were being closely adhered to, and that nothing was being built and that nothing would be built which was not allowed to Germany under the agreement.[1] He hoped that I was convinced that this was so.

I replied that I willingly accepted Admiral Raeder's assurances, and that if any such reports came my way I would deny them.

4. The whole of the interview was most friendly. On leaving I expressed regret that I had been unable to accept Admiral Raeder's invitation to dinner on 29th January, and hoped that in the circumstances he would later accept an invitation to dine privately with me if I could persuade you also to come. He said he would be delighted to do so, and looked forward to the opportunity of meeting you again.

5. Before leaving the Marineleitung the Liaison Officer asked me if I would like to put forward a programme of visits to the German Naval ports, and I said I would do so in the course of the next few days.

---

[1] In Berlin despatch No. 105 of January 20 Sir E. Phipps had reported Herr von Ribbentrop's assurance 'that the Anglo-German Naval Agreement was regarded by the German Government as absolutely definite and intangible'.

# No. 643

*Mr. Eden to Sir R. Lindsay (Washington)*

*No. 129 [A 1159/4/45]*

FOREIGN OFFICE, *February 7, 1936*

Sir,

Mr. Norman Davis asked to see me this evening, when he said that he wished to give me certain information which had reached him from Paris. Mr. Marriner, United States Chargé d'Affaires in that capital, had had a conversation with M. Massigli[1] in the course of which the latter had stated that there was no insuperable objection on the part of the French Government to a Naval Agreement which included Germany. The French Government considered, however, that the Germans were eager to come into some such agreement and they wished to extract a price. When asked what price, M. Massigli referred to other spheres of armaments, the air and land. To this Mr. Marriner replied that if the French Government were in fact to persist in such an attitude, they would surely be making the same mistake as they had been guilty of on many occasions in the past. By attempting too much they would be in danger of losing the limited agreement which was possible.

2. Mr. Davis added that he was communicating with Mr. Marriner agreeing with the line which he had taken and asking him to take any further opportunity of speaking in the same sense. He added that he had tried to see M. Corbin to-day for the same purpose but had been told that the French Ambassador was in Paris.

3. Mr. Davis then went on to tell me of some information which he had received from the United States Counsellor in Berlin. In the course of a conversation with a high official of the German Foreign Office, the latter had emphasised the desire of the German Government to come into a Naval Agreement. He maintained that the German Government when treated reasonably behaved reasonably, and instanced the Anglo-German Naval Agreement. In this connexion the German official had emphasised the importance of not presenting Germany alone with a *fait accompli* and asking her to concur. Such a procedure was always resented. Mr. Davis added that our own experience at the Disarmament Conference emphasised the truth of this remark. He stated that he had replied to the United States Counsellor in Berlin furnishing him with arguments to use with the German Foreign Office. These would include reminding the German Government that the Naval Conference had been summoned under treaties to which they were not parties and stating that so far as the United States Government were concerned they were confident that when an approach was made to Germany it would be made to her at the same time as to other Great Powers not represented at the Conference.

4. Mr. Davis then went on to speak of the procedure at the Conference, and appeared to consider that some such procedure as he understands the

[1] On February 4; cf. *F.R.U.S. 1936*, vol. i, p. 57.

United Kingdom Delegation contemplate, would be exactly suited for the present state of affairs (i.e., adjournment of the present Conference after agreement has been reached between the countries now represented and, as a next step, the communication of the draft of a treaty to Japan, Germany and Soviet Russia). He repeated that the United States and British Delegations could come to an agreement within a week and that the only outstanding difficulty was the attitude of France. He did not, however, despair of overcoming this.

5. Finally, Mr. Davis spoke of Anglo-American relations in general. He said that he had had an opportunity of meeting Mr. Runciman[2] at luncheon to-day and had said to him, while admitting that the matter was not in any sense directly his concern, how great a contribution he was convinced could be made to world confidence by an Anglo-American Trade Agreement. Mr. Runciman had not contested this but had added that the breakdown of the World Economic Conference[3] had resulted in economic nationalism all over the world, including the United Kingdom. Since this conversation Mr. Davis had been further reflecting upon the situation and wondered whether it would not be possible for His Majesty's Government and the United States Government jointly to consider the economic situation, not only with a view to making a treaty for their mutual benefit, but also with a view to seeing what contribution, if any, could be made by them to the world economic situation. Mr. Davis had Germany more particularly in mind in saying this. Unless some outlet could be found for Germany economically, there was bound to be trouble sooner or later. There was much talk of a Conference on Raw Materials, but this of course was not the root of the trouble. What Germany wanted was markets. He wondered, for instance, whether anything could be done in the way of giving Germany a special economic position in South-Eastern Europe. In any event, he was certain that Mr. Hull was genuinely anxious to help if he could and that some joint Anglo-American effort in this direction might have important results.

6. In answer to a question from me Mr. Davis made it quite clear that he did not consider that any such approach should be made to Germany unless it were contemplated that any concession offered to Germany should be in return for an arms agreement and Germany's return to the League. 'You cannot trust them', he added.

I am, &c.,<br>ANTHONY EDEN

[2] President of the Board of Trade.
[3] The World Economic Conference had met in London, June 12–July 27, 1933.

## No. 644

### Mr. Eden to Sir R. Lindsay (Washington)
### No. 45 Telegraphic [A 773/4/45][1]

*Confidential*  FOREIGN OFFICE, *February 11, 1936*

Question has arisen here as to the latest date in this year on which it is probable the United States Congress would be able to ratify the proposed naval treaty. Mr. Norman Davis states that, being an election year, the intention is to adjourn Congress by May 1st though he does not believe that adjournment will in fact take place before June 1st.

These dates appear to us to be exceptionally early, even for an election year, and I should be glad to know what is opinion in authoritative circles as to probable date of adjournment. If enquiries are necessary they should not be connected in any way with Naval Conference.

[1] The original text of this telegram, filed as A 1219/4/45, has not been preserved. The text printed above is that circulated as L.N.C. (35)(U.K.) 32. Times of despatch and receipt are not recorded.

## No. 645

### Sir R. Lindsay (Washington) to Mr. Eden (Received February 12)
### No. 36 Telegraphic [A 773/4/45][1]

WASHINGTON, *February 11, 1936*

Your telegram No. 45.[2]

I am afraid there are no authoritative circles worth consulting but I value Mr. Norman Davis' opinion if only because it coincides with my own. Position is that everyone without exception will desire early adjournment, Administration, because they always do desire it and Congress, because they will want to get away to their conventions in June. It should be possible to finish the business by June 1st but these plans may be upset by unforeseeable contingencies. I think that June 1st is a good date to bet on.

[1] The original text of this telegram, filed as A 1228/4/45, has not been preserved. The text printed above is that circulated as L.N.C. (35) (U.K.) 36. Times of despatch and receipt are not recorded.

[2] No. 644.

## No. 646

*Record by Mr. Craigie of a meeting held in the Secretary of State's room at the Foreign Office on February 11, 1936, at 4 p.m.*

L.N.C. (35)(U.K.) 31 [A 1342/4/45]

PRESENT: *Foreign Office*: Mr. Anthony Eden, Lord Cranborne, Sir William Malkin, Mr. Craigie, Mr. Wigram, Mr. Harvey, Mr. Gore-Booth.

*Admiralty*: Admiral of the Fleet Sir Ernle Chatfield, Captain Danckwerts.

The meeting had under consideration a Memorandum on the United States attitude, a copy of which is attached.[1] MR. EDEN said that he felt some sympathy for Mr. Davis. If the countries now in Conference actually signed a Treaty, it would be a more effective document to present to Japan than a Draft Treaty, besides which such a course of action should not give Germany any cause for grievance since she would be treated in the same way as other Powers not signatories of the Washington Treaty.

MR. CRAIGIE explained that the Germans had rather hoped that they would come into the Conference in the first place. Later they had been led to suppose that the Conference would be extended in order to admit them, a proposal which had been rendered abortive by the attitude of the French. It would create a very bad impression if we were to approach them with a third disappointment.

In reply to a question from Mr. Eden, MR. CRAIGIE said that the Germans would presumably not be debarred from suggesting alterations in the text.

MR. EDEN thought that the proposed procedure by means of a Protocol, though ingenious, was perhaps a little difficult to explain to public opinion.

SIR WILLIAM MALKIN said that a similar procedure had been adopted at Locarno. A Protocol had been signed by which the Governments concerned bound themselves to sign the Treaties without alteration on a certain date.[2] Presumably in this case the parties would bind themselves to sign say on the 1st of June. It could probably be arranged that, if Germany desired alterations, the Treaty could be in a different form with respect only to the relations between the various Powers and Germany.

ADMIRAL CHATFIELD felt, after recent conversations with the German Naval Attaché, that the German Government probably would agree through the diplomatic channel to a Four-Power agreement, and that their adhesion

[1] Printed as Annex I below.

[2] By the Final Protocol of the Locarno Conference (see Cmd. 2525 of 1925) the representatives of the German, Belgian, British, French, Italian, Polish, and Czechoslovak Governments, who had met at Locarno from October 5 to 16, 1925, gave their approval to the draft treaties and conventions framed in the course of the conference and agreed that those instruments 'hereby initialled *ne varietur*, will bear today's date [October 16, 1925], the representatives of the interested parties agreeing to meet in London on the 1st December next, to proceed during the course of a single meeting to the formality of the signature of the instruments which affect them.'

would not be made dependent on that of other Powers. Equally Germany could be asked, diplomatically, at an earlier date whether she wished to put forward any views. ADMIRAL CHATFIELD then described the procedure which might be adopted in order to clear up the difficulty of the capital ship first, and added that if this question were settled the resultant conclusion of a qualitative agreement would create an excellent impression, while public opinion would be indifferent to the matter of form.

MR. CRAIGIE thought that it might prove essential to settle the procedure question with Mr. Norman Davis first of all; otherwise United States representatives might leave the Conference.

ADMIRAL CHATFIELD said that the Admiralty could not sign a Treaty without some assurance that other Powers would come in. The case of Japan could be covered by an Escalator Clause, but this clause would, in the Admiralty view, be insufficient to cover the case of Germany.

SIR WILLIAM MALKIN suggested that there could be a clause in the Treaty to the effect that it would not be in force until Germany came in, upon which point MR. CRAIGIE observed that Italy might insist upon a similar condition to cover other Mediterranean Powers. MR. CRAIGIE went on to explain that Mr. Norman Davis's attitude was not justified on the basis of any conversations which had taken place with United States representatives. There had never been any talk on the United Kingdom side of a Four-Power Treaty. Referring to the attitude of France, MR. CRAIGIE said that the French had suggested there might be some difficulty in approaching Germany with a document containing a French signature. On the other hand they were prepared, apparently, to accept the Protocol idea and were ready for the United Kingdom to approach Germany through the diplomatic channel to obtain an assurance from the Germans that they would sign a Treaty at the right moment after the French elections. The objection to signing a Treaty straight away was that two things were required of Germany:—

(a) agreement to the terms of the Treaty, and,
(b) agreement as to the form in which it is presented to the German Government, i.e., if Germany were to be asked to sign along the dotted line, she might not sign at all.

The difficulty of giving Germany material in draft was that it might be impossible to obtain a definite German answer before the maximum limit of time which Mr. Norman Davis would be prepared to allow before signature of a Protocol. If, however, a Protocol were signed without German adhesion, it would mean that the United Kingdom would have to rely upon the Escalator Clause as a safeguard against Germany.

ADMIRAL CHATFIELD said that it ought to be possible to get Germany tied up by qualitative limitations, and in the circumstances to make another Treaty without her was undesirable.

MR. EDEN suggested that it might be possible to argue the case with Mr. Norman Davis from the German point of view. MR. CRAIGIE agreed with LORD CRANBORNE that it might take much longer to secure the adherence of the Soviet Union than that of Germany. Moreover, Germany might not give an assurance without the Soviet Union, though there was a 99% chance that Germany would come in if properly handled.

ADMIRAL CHATFIELD said that the United Kingdom were in danger of being rushed by the United States into doing without German and Soviet consent.

Further discussion led to the expression of the view that, while Germany would probably not create difficulties by linking up the naval question with others, she might be unable to give a detailed assurance before a Protocol of the kind contemplated was signed.

ADMIRAL CHATFIELD suggested that the difficulty might be explained to the Germans, and they might be asked how long they would want for perusal of a draft Treaty. He thought it would be three months, and the Protocol might last for that period.

MR. CRAIGIE said that Mr. Norman Davis wanted to sign something binding at the first possible opportunity, and MR. EDEN observed that the Protocol would in fact bind the United Kingdom to take certain steps whatever Germany might subsequently do.

ADMIRAL CHATFIELD said that the Admiralty would not wish this to happen.

MR. CRAIGIE observed that according to his information M. Piétri was making satisfactory progress in Paris in this matter, in a direction satisfactory to the United Kingdom. He could not, however, yet say what France would want and would need another week or 10 days.

ADMIRAL CHATFIELD suggested that the battleship question might be cleared up first. The French could be told that it was a case of 35,000 tons or nothing, and asked to consult their Government. Next, the Germans and the Soviet would be asked whether they could let the Conference know whether the proposals were likely to be acceptable, while after three months they might send a written assurance. After this a Protocol or a Treaty with reservations could be signed. He still did not feel that the Escalator Clause by itself was sufficient.

MR. EDEN suggested that unless it was possible to move Mr. Norman Davis from his present position, this plan might mean that neither a Treaty nor a Protocol would be signed. It was eventually agreed that the Secretary of State, the First Lord of the Admiralty and the First Sea Lord might start by seeing the French Ambassador and explaining that there was no hope at present of reducing the size of the capital ship and they could ask him to put the difficulty to his Government. After this the same United Kingdom representatives could see Mr. Norman Davis and Admiral Standley, tell them of the line which had been taken with the French, and ask Mr. Norman Davis to reconsider his decision on the point of form with a view to allowing the United Kingdom representatives time to consult Germany and the Soviet Union before committing themselves to the limitations agreed upon by the Conference.

SIR WILLIAM MALKIN asked whether, supposing a written assurance were obtained from Germany that she would become a party to the Treaty, the

Admiralty would make it a condition of signing either the Treaty or a Protocol that the Treaty should contain a provision under which it could not come into force unless Germany were a party to it.

ADMIRAL CHATFIELD thought not.

It was arranged that the Secretary of State should receive M. Corbin at 4 o'clock and Mr. Norman Davis at 5 o'clock on Wednesday, 12th February.

ANNEX I TO No. 646

*Points for discussion at a meeting in the Secretary of State's Room*

FOREIGN OFFICE, February 11, 1936

1. The Americans have definitely refused to reduce the limitations for the capital ship below 35,000 tons and a 14″ calibre gun. (The acceptance of the 14″ gun is dependent on Japan's agreeing to this gun before December 31st, 1936—otherwise the Americans insist on a 16″ gun.) While this result is somewhat disappointing, we have known for a long time (well before the present Conference opened) that it would be impossible to bring the Americans below these limits. The French and Italians, on the other hand, are taking the American attitude very much amiss and have so far refused to accept these limitations. The danger of a continuation of the present situation is that the United States Delegation may withdraw the valuable concession they have made in regard to the size of the cruiser (i.e. a holiday in construction of 10,000 ton cruisers, the maximum limit for cruisers to be 8,000 tons with a 6″ gun). The best course now would be for the Secretary of State and the First Lord to see M. Corbin and to explain that we do not think that we can induce the United States to come below 35,000 tons at this time though we might get them to agree to some formula for reconsideration at a later date. A draft formula is attached as Annex I.[3] If the French can be got round it will then be necessary to see the Italians.

2. The original plan had been to bring Germany, Russia and other naval Powers into the present Conference as soon as we were in sight of a naval agreement. This has been destroyed by the French refusal to sit at the same table as the Germans. As a compromise it has been suggested that the treaty should not be signed at the present time but should be submitted in draft form to all the other naval Powers at the end of the present Conference. It would, however, be desirable that a protocol should be signed between the Powers represented at the Conference setting forth clearly the procedure to be followed after the adjournment. A paper showing the points which might possibly be covered by such a protocol is attached as Annex II.[4] It will be seen that under this draft we would definitely undertake to sign the treaty on a certain date, independently of the action of other Powers.

It is possible that a compromise on these lines would be accepted by the French and Italians. Mr. Norman Davis, however, is very strongly opposed and considers it essential that the treaty should be signed between the Powers represented at the Conference before the adjournment. He says

---

[3] Printed as Annex II below.          [4] Printed as Annex III below.

that the United States Government have always been acting on this assumption; that any indication that a 'Four-Power' treaty will not be possible will cause the greatest disappointment and concern in Washington; that there is even the possibility of the American Delegation being withdrawn before an agreement is reached; that the American Senate and people would never understand the subtleties of the protocol proposal; and, finally, that, as Congress will adjourn early this year, there will be no time for American ratification under the suggested procedure.

Lord Stanhope and I had a long interview with Mr. Norman Davis last night[5] at which he expressed these views. We both have the impression that it is with him largely a matter of personal prestige and *amour propre*, though the difficulty of obtaining the agreement of the Senate may have some substance.

Mr. Sargent and the Central Department entirely agree with my view that it is essential that this treaty should be submitted to Germany in draft form (and not after signature) if we are to obtain Germany's agreement without too much difficulty—otherwise we may raise the old bogey of *Gleichberechtigung*.

On the whole, the best course seems to be to press for some solution on the lines of the annexed draft protocol. The Admiralty, however, are not yet convinced that it will be safe to agree to sign either the treaty or a protocol until we have at least had an assurance from Germany that she will come in. But such an assurance is unlikely to be forthcoming until Germany has had ample opportunity to study the draft treaty.

R. L. CRAIGIE

## ANNEX II TO No. 646

### Draft Formula

Each country to have the right to build two capital ships of 35,000 tons (and 14″ guns if Japan comes in before December 31st, 1936). Exchange of views to take place through the diplomatic channel in January, 1937, to see whether reduction in displacement tonnage could be arranged for future capital ships, provided that Japan has meanwhile accepted the 14″ gun.

## ANNEX III TO No. 646

### Points for inclusion in a Protocol

1) His Majesty's Government in the United Kingdom would submit the draft treaty through the diplomatic channel to the other naval Powers for their consideration and observations.

2) The Governments represented at the present Conference would undertake to sign the treaty on their behalf on June 1st (? June 15th) next, the treaty to be signed at the same time by as many Powers as have agreed up to that date to participate in it.

[5] No other record of this meeting has been traced.

3) The Governments represented at the present Conference would agree to abide by the provisions of the draft treaty in any preparations they may make during the present year for the construction of ships to be laid down after December 31st, 1936.

4) The question whether it will be necessary to hold a conference on this subject with the naval Powers not represented at the present Conference should be left open until the consultation has taken place with those Powers, as provided in paragraph 1 above.

## No. 647

*Record by Mr. Craigie of a conversation with Prince von Bismarck and Captain Wassner on February 12*

*[A 1311/4/45]*

FOREIGN OFFICE, February 12, 1936

I asked the German Chargé d'Affaires and Captain Wassner to call this morning in order to discuss certain matters connected with the naval question.

I began by saying that we were most anxious, as they knew, to keep the German Government fully informed of the progress of the Conference and that the time had now come when I thought we could supplement the information already given orally by communicating to them copies of the texts which had been agreed upon by the Sub-Committees dealing with the exchange of information and definitions.[1] These texts were not yet in their final form, as they would have to be fitted into a general treaty, but it was unlikely that any further material alterations would be made in them. In addition, I handed to Captain Wassner the document entitled 'Lowest qualitative limits on which there appears to be prospect of obtaining general agreement', which was used as a basis of discussion by the First Committee when it was dealing with qualitative limitation.[2] I explained that, as far as we could see at present, any agreement reached on qualitative limitations was likely to follow these lines. A technical committee was drafting the text of an agreement dealing with limitations in all categories excepting the capital ship, the latter category being reserved at present for further discussions between Delegations. Copies of this text I would also communicate to Captain Wassner as soon as it had been prepared. The only other provisions likely to appear in this treaty were a 'safeguarding' or 'escape' clause and clauses incorporating certain of the minor provisions of the Washington Treaty. The German Government would thus be enabled, with the texts which we were now communicating, to form a fairly accurate idea of the probable scope and terms of a future treaty. But I emphasised that these documents were being communicated privately and on our own responsibility and not in virtue of any decision of the Conference.

[1] Cf. No. 641.       [2] See <i>L.N.C. 1935 Docs.</i>, p. 679.

We were thus communicating this information to the German Government in advance of any other Government because we were particularly anxious to have their opinion on the treaty before agreement was actually reached. Judging from the Anglo-German naval conversations of last year, we believed that the proposed texts would be generally acceptable to the German Government. We sincerely hoped this would prove to be the case. We should now be grateful if Captain Wassner would study these texts at his early convenience, and either Captain Danckwerts or I would be happy to give full explanations on any point on which he might require further elucidation. Additional copies were furnished for Captain Wassner to send at once to his Government. Captain Wassner agreed to do this at once.

Having then said that agreement had not yet been reached in regard to the capital ship, I proceeded to explain the difficulties that had arisen in regard to the signature of any agreement which might be reached (possibility of one Power running out if the agreement is not actually signed at this stage; difficulty of obtaining ratification of the United States Senate, etc., etc.). I enquired whether, supposing either the treaty itself or a protocol relating to it were to be signed by all the Washington Powers except Japan and were to be then submitted for consideration to all the other naval Powers, this would create any difficulty for Germany, assuming that the treaty were in other respects acceptable to her? We ourselves had throughout been anxious to submit the treaty to Germany in draft form, but several somewhat unexpected difficulties had arisen and the matter was now the subject of close consideration. I emphasised that my enquiry was of a private and unofficial character.

Prince von Bismarck promised to transmit my enquiry to Berlin at once. Speaking for himself, he said that it had undoubtedly been the anticipation of the German Government that they would sign this treaty on a complete equality with, and at the same time as, all the other principal naval Powers. On the other hand, he appreciated the force of the argument that a precedent had been set for the signature of treaties by the Washington Powers and that Germany would be in exactly the same position as all the other naval Powers in the world. He therefore found it difficult to forecast the probable reply of his Government.

I said that, in any case, whether the agreement was merely to be left in draft form, whether there was to be the signature of the treaty, or whether there was to be the signature of a protocol as between the remaining Washington Powers, we were anxious to learn the preliminary views of the German Government on this treaty at the earliest possible moment. We fully recognised that the details would want careful and possibly lengthy study, but we thought that the main outlines of the draft treaty were now fairly clear and were, in fact, almost exactly what we had forecast in our conversations with the German Delegation last June. It should therefore be possible for the German Government to give us their preliminary observations at an early date.

Prince von Bismarck asked whether we had made a similar communication to any other Government, for example, Soviet Russia. I answered in the negative. As regards Soviet Russia, the question of advance notification must to some extent depend on Germany's attitude. If, for instance, she were to make her acceptance dependent on Russia's, this would seem to necessitate an early consultation with that Power. If, on the other hand, she would be prepared to rely on the terms of the safeguarding clause, then the discussions with Soviet Russia would be less urgent. It was obvious that if every Power made its signature dependent on the signature of one or two other Powers we might end by getting a formidable list which might prevent the treaty from ever coming into force.[3]

Prince von Bismarck enquired whether he was to understand that the difficulties made by France in regard to Germany's accession to the treaty had been removed. I said that the position was as follows: France had felt that it would not be possible for her, at the present moment, to enter a conference with Germany on this question. She recognised, however, fully, that no such treaty would be any use without Germany's participation and I believed that all that was necessary would be a certain lapse of time in order to prepare public opinion in France for what would be, after all, a change in France's traditional attitude on this question. Prince von Bismarck said that clearly Germany could not give any assurance that she would sign the treaty until she had been informed that France's objection to her signature had been removed. I agreed that there was point in this contention, at all events so far as an official and public assurance from Germany was concerned, but that I did not think that this consideration should prevent Germany from giving us the kind of private assurance in regard to her intentions, of which I had spoken earlier.

The German representatives were clearly gratified that the texts agreed upon should have been communicated to their Government in advance of any other Government.[4]

R.L.C.

[3] In a minute of February 12, Mr. Craigie wrote: 'The next point to be considered is whether we should make a similar advance notification to Soviet Russia. So far the Soviet Govt. have been at no pains to conceal their complete lack of interest in this Conference. It is true that, at our suggestion, they have agreed to appoint a Naval Attaché, but I have not heard that the officer has yet arrived. My inclination would be to do nothing about this at the moment. R.L.C. 12/2.' Lord Stanhope added: 'I should be inclined not to be in too much of a hurry about the U.S.S.R. but to await Germany's reply. S. 28/2/36.'

[4] For Prince Bismarck's report of this conversation see *D.G.F.P.*, Series C, vol. iv, No. 555.

## No. 648

*Draft[1] Record of a meeting between representatives of the United Kingdom and French Delegations on February 12, 1936, at 4.15 p.m.[2]*

### L.N.C. (35)(U.K.) 34 [A 773/4/45]

PRESENT: *United Kingdom*: Mr. Eden, Lord Monsell, Admiral of the Fleet Sir Ernle Chatfield, Mr. Craigie, Mr. Gore-Booth.

*France*: M. Corbin, Vice-Admiral Robert, M. Carde, Captain Deleuze.

LORD MONSELL opened the meeting by giving a resumé of the position in regard to the capital ship, remarking that the French Delegation took the view, with which the United Kingdom Delegation agreed, that there was no technical necessity for the 35,000 ton ship. As had already been explained, however, to the French Delegation, United Kingdom representatives had been trying for 2 years without success, to get the Americans to agree to a reduction; it had been possible to move them from the 16″ gun, but the most that could be hoped in the matter of tonnage was some small reduction after experience of new 35,000 ton ships.

This position was unsatisfactory to the French Delegation; none the less, if the matter were viewed from the political standpoint, it might be that the moment had arrived when it was essential to obtain some kind of agreement rather than risk complete failure. After all, much that was valuable had been agreed upon, including the préavis (the French Delegation's own proposal) and various qualitative limits, and too persistent an opposition to the United States thesis might mean losing these important gains.

M. CORBIN said that he understood Lord Monsell's preoccupations but was still not sure whether the capital ship question was exhausted. It was possible that the Conference had reached a critical period where the strongest views could be modified in face of even greater difficulties which might be caused by persistence in them. Was there perhaps no other solution to that proposed, especially in the light of the probable reaction of world opinion? M. Corbin drew attention also to the fact that Mr. Norman Davis had at the beginning of the conversations confidentially spoken to the French Delegation of possible reductions; now there was apparently no question of them.

ADMIRAL ROBERT said that it was clear that the United States had no adequate technical reason for their attitude on capital ships. Their immovability was only to be explained by supposing that there were political considerations behind it. There were, however, other political considerations to be reckoned with, for instance the fact that it was the duty of the Conference to seek for a positive measure of disarmament, and as quantitative disarmament had proved unobtainable this object must be pursued in the qualitative field. Both the moral and the economic effect of a measure of disarmament must be thought of.

[1] The record here printed was identical with the final text except for the omission in the heading of the word 'Draft' and the addition of 'Final Copy'.

[2] This meeting was held in the Secretary of State's room at the Foreign Office.

Admiral Robert confessed himself disappointed that the United States had been as rigid over qualitative as Japan over quantitative limitation, and he thought that at a Conference where all parties had to sacrifice something, the party which stood for a higher level of armament and greater expenditure should give way most. He suggested therefore that a compromise should be considered by which the countries not possessing new 35,000 ton vessels should each build two, and that then there should be some reduction. He thought this practicable as Admiral Standley had not shut out all ideas of a compromise.

Mr. EDEN expressed grave doubt as to whether the United States would agree to any reduction.

ADMIRAL CHATFIELD said that he had found, as Chairman of the Qualitative Sub-Committee, that when Admiral Robert suggested the reference of the capital ship discussion to a Plenary Session, the United States were not at all pleased by this prospect of publicity. At the end of the Sub-Committee meeting[3] Admiral Standley had kept on asking him to put the question 'Did any Power refuse 35,000 tons?' He had refused to do so, feeling it premature. After the meeting Admiral Standley said to him that it was useless suggesting further limitation, for even if the United States' Delegation agreed to consider it, they would never be supported by Washington. The only possible concession lay in some unforeseeable political development.

On the other hand he, the First Sea Lord, realised that it was a terrible prospect to have to go on building 35,000 ton ships for ever, and he had therefore considered the possibility of coming down to 27,000 in, say, 20 years. It was difficult to arrange this since, if there were a high limit now and a low one were to be instituted later, it would be an advantage to build ships as soon as possible. The United Kingdom would have to do this anyway and it would doubtless be thought that she was taking advantage of the provisions of such an arrangement. Again, different rates of building made this reduction by stages almost impossible.

The impossibility of a technical solution on these lines had been the reason why the political members of the Delegations had been called in at this stage.

In reply to a question from M. Corbin, ADMIRAL CHATFIELD explained that while the United Kingdom would like to see a reduction in gun calibre they thought that the technical arguments against sudden reductions were sound. There were at present too many 14″, 15″ and 16″ guns in existence to permit of an immediate reduction to 12″. Besides, the 14″ gun would, it was understood, be acceptable to Japan and the United States had also accepted it after a great struggle.

ADMIRAL ROBERT suggested that if agreement could have been reached on the 12″ gun, the United States might have built 35,000 ton ships with 12″ guns while other nations could have built smaller ships with the same calibre which would have been quite capable of tackling the United States ships.

[3] i.e. the meeting of the Technical Sub-Committee on Qualitative Limitation held on February 10 at 3.15 p.m.; see *L.N.C. 1935 Docs.*, pp. 835–49.

He recognised the difficulty of finding a formula for progressive reduction, but thought something might be done by applying such a formula to calibre only. For instance, a 15-year Treaty might provide for 14″ guns during the first five years, 13″ during the next five and 12″ for the last five. Such a formula seemed easier as applied to calibre than to tonnage—apart always from the possibility that the 12″ gun of to-morrow may be as good as the 14″ gun of to-day.

ADMIRAL CHATFIELD said that it would be extraordinarily difficult to arrange the periods under such an agreement. Suppose, for instance, Germany built two 35,000 ton ships. The British Empire could then have six. What would Japan have? It was very hard to arrange anything of this kind without quantitative limitation. It would, of course, be possible to try to obtain United States views on the principle, and for this purpose it would probably be best if all Delegations met together rather than one Delegation presenting its views in isolation.

MR. EDEN said that he felt that the Conference was approaching the psychological moment at which some agreement must be arrived at rather than nothing. Would the French Delegation agree to a meeting of the principal Delegates, political and technical, with a view to discovering the best that could be done on the capital ship question? Meanwhile the United Kingdom Delegation would try to ascertain from the Americans whether the latter would be ready to discuss provisions for a reduction of capital ship tonnage and gun calibre at a later date.

ADMIRAL ROBERT admitted that this would be something, but stressed that France could not undertake to accept 35,000 tons and 14″ for a long period. He was convinced, however, that the Americans would not change their minds on this subject.

M. CORBIN said that the present problem raised difficult political questions such as relations with the United States and public opinion on the result of the Conference, on which MR. EDEN commented that a complete breakdown was the worst thing that could happen.

M. CORBIN said that the French would like to exhaust all possibilities before admitting failure.

MR. EDEN then asked whether the French would prefer to sign a Treaty or a draft to be transformed into a Treaty and MR. CRAIGIE enquired whether, in fact, France would be ready to sign without Germany. M. CORBIN replied that the French were anxious to sign a Four-Power Treaty. The difficult question of Germany M. Piétri had in hand at present, and he was understood to be making satisfactory progress with it.

## No. 649

*Draft[1] Record of a meeting between representatives of the United Kingdom and United States Delegations on February 12, 1936, at 5.15 p.m.[2]*
### L.N.C. (35)(U.K.) 35 [A 773/4/45]

PRESENT: *United Kingdom*: Mr. Eden, Lord Monsell, Admiral of the Fleet Sir Ernle Chatfield, Mr. Craigie, Mr. Gore-Booth.
*United States*: Mr. Norman Davis, Admiral Standley, Mr. Atherton.

MR. EDEN opened the meeting by explaining the anxiety of the French about the future of capital ship construction and added that they had suggested possible future reduction in gun calibre, if not necessarily in tonnage. MR. CRAIGIE gave an account of Admiral Robert's suggestion for a diminution of gun calibre only by 1″ every five years.

MR. NORMAN DAVIS felt that the French had something in their minds, probably to do with Germany, which they had not yet explained. Their suggestion might be of some value if they would accept quantitative limitation, but, as it was, the United States could not commit themselves in advance until some degree of political stability had been reached throughout the world. He felt that it would look absurd for the United States to insist now on a 35,000 ton ship and then to say that they would be willing to reduce this size later. If they were ready to reduce later, why should they not do so now?

Discussion then turned on the possibility of finding a formula which would open the way to ultimate reduction in size.

MR. CRAIGIE said that the French, of course, wanted an undertaking that the size would actually be reduced.

LORD MONSELL suggested that there might be a clause in the Treaty to the effect that, after a certain number of years, the parties should meet and discuss the possibility of reduction, and MR. NORMAN DAVIS said that this was the most the French could expect.

ADMIRAL CHATFIELD then explained that the United Kingdom would be under the necessity of building a large number of capital ships at an early date, and added that he felt it important that the United States should realise this.

ADMIRAL STANDLEY said that, provided no Power deviated in a large measure from its present naval strength the United States building programme would remain roughly as proposed at present.

LORD MONSELL remarked that, in any case, most countries had so many old capital ships that anything in the nature of a real expansion was impossible in the near future.

The discussion turned next on the interval which would be necessary for sufficient experience to be obtained of capital ships for a meeting to discuss possible reduction to serve any useful purpose.

[1] The record here printed was identical with the final text except for the omission in the heading of the word 'Draft' and the addition of 'Final Copy'.
[2] This meeting was held in the Secretary of State's room at the Foreign Office.

ADMIRAL STANDLEY explained that the United States difficulty was that, as they had not constructed a large capital ship for a considerable time, the first one would indubitably be full of new gadgets, and it would be necessary then for the Navy Department to decide which of them could be dispensed with. For this purpose the ship must be in commission. Accordingly three years would not be time enough as the United States would not lay down a capital ship till next year.

It was felt that conversations might start in 1940. If they were held earlier it would merely mean that they would have far less chance of success, —a point which could be explained to the French.

ADMIRAL STANDLEY said that he did not estimate that United States experience of capital ship building would lead to any change in future in regard to gun calibre. In any case he could give no such assurance.

MR. EDEN felt some doubt as to whether the French would be satisfied with the procedure suggested.

MR. NORMAN DAVIS said that quite apart from the technical question, it was impossible for the United States to talk of departing from existing types now that Japan was outside any system of limitation; besides which the United States felt that without quantitative limitation there was no guarantee that qualitative limitation would make for economy. He felt it important to stress in this connection that it was the French themselves who had insisted that quantitative limitation was impossible. He had said as much to M. Corbin.

ADMIRAL STANDLEY doubted whether it was worth agreeing to anything which would somewhat disturb the navy department at home, even if it might secure French adhesion.

After some further discussion it was finally agreed that it would probably be best to begin conversations in 1940 with a view to discussing capital ships in 1941. Supposing the Treaty were to be a 10-year treaty this would in fact be a discussion at half-time.

MR. EDEN suggested a meeting of the political and technical heads of the United Kingdom, United States, French and Italian Delegations to discuss this suggestion. He then raised the question of signature and said that he understood that the United States wished to sign a Treaty immediately. The United Kingdom difficulty was that they did not wish to hand Germany a naval treaty as it were 'on a plate'.

MR. DAVIS said that it would look absurd for the four Delegations to go away without having actually done anything and Lord Monsell felt that public opinion would demand the signature of some kind of agreement.

MR. EDEN reminded the meeting, however, that Locarno, which was at once recognised as an accomplishment, was only signed as a protocol.[3] Such a procedure might be better than the immediate signature of a Four-Power Treaty as providing for simultaneous signature of the Treaty by all Powers concerned at a later date.

MR. DAVIS said that Congress would probably adjourn by 1st June and

[3] Cf. No. 646, note 2.

that a Treaty ought to be ratified by the Senate before the end of 1936 when it would come into force. On the other hand it might be possible for the President to give an undertaking that the United States would abide by the provisions as far as naval programmes were concerned until ratification took place (perhaps in January or February 1937). As the President had control over the naval estimates, this should be adequate.

The United Kingdom representatives agreed.

MR. DAVIS added that he had been told that the French were preoccupied by the fear that if they condoned the naval breach of the Versailles Treaty, the Germans might fortify the Rhineland. He himself had pointed out that the Germans were much more likely to create some such disturbance if they were *not* allowed to participate in this treaty as equals. The French had intimated to him that they did not wish for a date as early as June for the adhesion of Germany; August or September would be better.

MR. CRAIGIE thought that the problem would solve itself when the French elections were over, and LORD MONSELL said that the procedure proposed by which all countries concerned could sign together, would be acceptable if the Presidential assurance could be obtained from the United States and if Germany would give the necessary assurance before signature of the protocol.

In reply to a question from MR. CRAIGIE, MR. DAVIS said that the Senate could of course ratify the protocol but that difficulties might be raised if the Treaty were modified after ratification of the protocol. He added that he had not completely abandoned the hope that Germany would sign straight away.

It was agreed that it would be an excellent idea for the Heads of the Delegations to meet in order to discuss this difficulty and in particular MR. CRAIGIE felt that it was important to let the French know exactly what the difficulties were before the French Government took their decision.

MR. DAVIS said that it was not desirable to have too many original signatures.

ADMIRAL CHATFIELD drew attention to the reservations made by Admiral Robert at the 3rd meeting of the Qualitative Sub-Committee (L.N.C. 35 Q.L. 3rd Meeting)[4] to the effect that the acceptance of the cruiser holiday depended on the actions of another Power (Germany) and that certain other points depended on the final decision about capital ships.

LORD MONSELL then explained again, and Mr. Davis appreciated, the United Kingdom difficulty that while she was prepared that Japan should be covered by the 'escape clause' this clause was not regarded as sufficient against both Japan and Germany. An assurance from Germany was indispensable and that was a question of time.

It was decided to try to arrange the proposed meeting of the Heads of the Four Delegations for 11 o'clock on Friday, the 14th February.

LORD MONSELL, ADMIRAL CHATFIELD and MR. CRAIGIE had a further talk with the American representatives at which Mr. Craigie explained to Admiral Standley the psychological advantage of the protocol idea.

4 On February 10, 1936; see *L.N.C. 1935 Docs.*, p. 852.

Mr. Craigie also showed Mr. Davis and Mr. Atherton a memorandum[5] of his conversations with the latter on the subject of the extension of the Treaty to include Germany, and it appeared that the Americans had been acting on the assumption that Germany was bound qualitatively by the Anglo-German Agreement. For this reason and not because of anything which had been said on the United Kingdom side, they had concluded that the Treaty was to include France and Italy only.

It was pointed out to the Americans that the invitation to the Conference[6] had specifically alluded to an extension when an agreement was in sight.

[5] Presumably a reference to a Foreign Office memorandum of February 11, 1936, not printed, which summarized Mr. Craigie's conversations with Mr. Atherton on September 12 and October 4, 1935; see Nos. 498 and 520.

[6] See No. 538.

## No. 650

*Sir E. Drummond (Rome) to Mr. Eden (Received February 13, 9.30 a.m.)*
*No. 80 Telegraphic [A 1251/4/45]*

ROME, *February 13, 1936, 1.50 a.m.*

This morning Messag[g]ero publishes a leading article on Naval Conference. Article states that Japan's withdrawal from the conference will affect the situation not only in the Pacific but also in the Mediterranean and will facilitate formation of an Anglo-American anti-Japanese front.

After reviewing the attitude of the Powers represented at the conference to the principal questions at issue the article states that any agreements reached will be valueless unless they are intended to cover all Naval Powers. If Germany and Russia are called into the conference there is no reason why other Naval Powers such as Spain, Turkey, Greece and the Argentine should not [be] also; this might form later stage otherwise there would have to be safeguarding clauses. The writer thinks that in such circumstances Japan might perhaps be ready to come back.

Article concludes by saying that while expectations of reductions in naval strength have been disappointing the conference has not lost its importance; there is still hope that conference may achieve something that will help to reduce existing international tension.

# No. 651

*Memorandum on the proposed retention of certain Cruisers and Destroyers in excess of London Naval Treaty tonnages*[1]

*[A 1640/4/45]*

*February 14, 1936*

In N.C. (M) (35) 82,[2] certain proposals relating to the retention of cruisers and destroyers in excess of London Naval Treaty tonnages were put forward by the First Lord of the Admiralty. These proposals were approved by the D[efence] P[olicy and] R[equirements] Committee at their 15th Meeting on the 6th December, 1935.

2. The details of these proposals were:—

(*a*) The 4 *Hawkins* class should be rearmed with 6-inch guns and retained after the 31st December, 1936.

(*b*) A special proposal should be made to the United States of America and Japan at the London Naval Conference, 1935 to enable the *Hawkins* class to be rearmed with 6-inch guns and classified as sub-category (*b*) cruisers.

(*c*) An explanation should be given to the United States of America and Japan to obtain their agreement to the retention of a small excess in British cruiser tonnage without invoking the 'Escalator' clause.

(*d*) We should retain a total tonnage in the destroyer category, not exceeding 190,000 tons on the 31st December, 1936.

(*e*) A special proposal should be made to the United States of America and Japan to enable this tonnage to be retained without invoking the 'Escalator' clause.

(*f*) We should endeavour to limit any Japanese *quid pro quo* to a corresponding retention of over-age destroyers, but in the last resort we should agree to the retention of some Japanese submarine tonnage instead.

3. Conversations have taken place with the United States of America Delegation concerning our desire to retain the *Hawkins* class rearmed with 6-inch or smaller guns. The United States of America raised no objections to these proposals, provided that our intentions were officially notified before the treaty, which is now being negotiated, is presented to Congress, and provided that our total cruiser tonnage on the 31st December, 1936, did not exceed the total tonnage prescribed in the London Naval Treaty.

---

[1] A draft of this memorandum was sent to the Foreign Office by Captain Danckwerts on February 24, 1936, with the suggestion that it be circulated to the Ministerial Naval Committee by the authority of the First Lord of the Admiralty. After a few minor amendments it was circulated as N.C.M. (35) 85. Copies of the agreed text, without the N.C.M. reference, were sent by the Foreign Office, on February 29, to Washington (despatch No. 209), Tokyo (No. 98), Paris (No. 381), Rome (No. 242), Berlin (No. 259), Moscow (No. 119).

[2] No. 566.

4. To avoid exceeding our total cruiser tonnage it is proposed that our cruiser strength on the 31st December, 1936, should be:—

|  | | Proposed Tonnage | Tonnage permitted under the London Naval Treaty |
|---|---|---|---|
| 8-inch cruisers | .. .. | 15 = 144,220 | 146,800 |
| 6-inch cruisers | .. .. | 33 = 194,126 | 192,200 |
| Total (including 3 *Hawkins* Class) .. | .. .. | 48 = 338,346 | 339,000 |

In this arrangement it is assumed that H.M.S. *Hawkins* will be demilitarised and used as a Cadet Training Ship, so that she will not form part of our treaty tonnage.

The *Newcastle* and *Southampton* of the 1933 building programme are not included in the above total as, due to an alteration in this programme with a consequent delay in the preparation of their design, these ships were not laid down until late in the year 1934 and are not due to complete till March 1937.

6. It should be noted that our *total* cruiser tonnage is within the limit of tonnage allowed in the cruiser category, an excess of about 2,000 tons in sub-category (*b*) being counter-balanced by a corresponding deficit in the sub-category (*a*) tonnage.

7. Our intentions regarding the future of the 4 *Hawkins* class cruisers were notified to the United States of America, French, Italian and Dominion Delegations at meetings held on the 14th February, and the Japanese Naval Attaché was handed an aide-mémoire on the subject for transmission to Japan on the same date (a copy of this aide-mémoire is attached as an Annex).

8. The Japanese reactions to our proposals are not yet known. The conversion of sub-category (*a*) cruisers to sub-category (*b*) is not specifically provided for in the London Naval Treaty, and no provision exists for adding to the number of demilitarised training ships given in Part II, Annex II, Section V, but as neither of these actions infringes the *spirit* of the treaty, it may be hoped that no objections will be raised by Japan.

*Destroyers.*

9. As Japan has now left the Conference it is no longer possible to make any special proposals to her Delegation. We should have to use the diplomatic channel with the consequent delay in exchange of views. In view of the expressed wish of the United States of America that any special points affecting the provisions of the London Naval Treaty should be dealt with before the new treaty is presented to Congress, it is considered that the delay referred to above cannot be accepted. If we are to retain the necessary destroyer tonnage, therefore, it will be necessary to invoke the 'Escalator' clause (Article 21 of the London Naval Treaty). There is little objection to

this course of action as regards destroyers, as we have from the outset clearly reserved our right to exceed the figure of 150,000 tons of destroyers, if other countries did not come down to 52,700 tons of submarines. At the time of the negotiations to try and get France and Italy into the London Naval Treaty this point was made perfectly clear to France and was stated publicly in Parliament by the then First Lord on the 11th March, 1931.[3] An advantage of using the Escalator clause is that the *quid pro quo* of United States of America and Japan is limited to destroyers, which, as far as Japan is concerned, is the least objectionable form of increase. It is therefore proposed that we should at an early suitable moment notify the United States of America and Japan of our intention to invoke Article 21 of the London Naval Treaty, stating that the requirements of our national security necessitate the retention of 40,000 tons of overage destroyers over and above our prescribed total of 150,000 tons of destroyers on account of the new construction of submarines by France and other countries since 1930. Article 21 of the London Naval Treaty states that such a notification should be made through diplomatic channels.

10. It is considered that the most suitable time to make this notification would be after the conclusion of the present stage of the Conference. If notification were left too late, the United States of America and Japan might say that they had started scrapping tonnage in accordance with the Treaty which they would have kept to counterbalance our increase had they known of it, especially since, now that we have told them (though not yet officially) about our cruiser intentions, they might draw the inference that we intended to do nothing about destroyers. It is considered, therefore, that our notification should not be delayed.

*Conclusions.*

11. (*a*) To avoid the necessity of obtaining the approval of Japan to the retention of an excess in cruiser tonnage on the 31st December, 1936, it is desired to retain, as fighting ships, only three of the *Hawkins* class after that date, and to convert the fourth ship of the class to a Cadet Training Cruiser, demilitarised in accordance with Part II, Annex II, Section V (*b*) 2, of the London Naval Treaty, 1930.

(*b*) It is desired to notify the United States of America and Japan that the requirements of our national security make it necessary for us to retain an additional 40,000 tons of overage destroyers, under the provisions set forth in Article 21 of the London Naval Treaty. This notification should be made immediately after the conclusion of the present stage of the Conference.

ANNEX TO NO. 651

*Aide-Mémoire*

In order to make clear to the other signatories of Part III of the London Naval Treaty of 1930 the manner in which His Majesty's Government in the

---

[3] See 249 *H.C. Deb.* 5 *s.*, col. 1220.

United Kingdom intend to adhere to the cruiser tonnage figures laid down in that treaty, the following information is communicated:—

2. His Majesty's Government in the United Kingdom intend to take the following measures:—

(a) To remove the 7·5-in. guns from the 4 cruisers of the *Hawkins* class before the 31st December, 1936, so that the remaining tonnage of Cruisers (a) of the Members of the British Commonwealth of Nations will be 15 ships, totalling 144,220 tons (including 2 ships of the Royal Australian Navy).

(b) To re-arm 3 ships of the *Hawkins* class with guns of a calibre less than 6.1-in. and to retain these ships as part of the Cruiser (b) tonnage.

(c) To demilitarise the 4th ship of the *Hawkins* class and retain her as a training ship only. For this purpose it is intended to treat the vessel as prescribed in Annex II, Section V (b) 2, of the London Naval Treaty, 1930.

(d) To scrap 3 ships of the *Caledon* type and 2 ships of the *Ceres* type, so that the total cruiser tonnage of the Members of the British Commonwealth of Nations remaining on the 31st December, 1936, will be 338,346 tons (including 4 ships of the Royal Australian Navy and excluding the demilitarised training cruiser referred to in paragraph (c) above).

## No. 652

*Mr. Eden to Sir G. Clerk (Paris)*
*No. 278 [A 1343/4/45]*

FOREIGN OFFICE, *February 14, 1936*

Sir,

I asked the French Ambassador to come to see me this morning in order that we might have a conversation about the state of the Naval Conference.

2. I told M. Corbin that after the previous discussion between the British and French Delegations[1] I had seen the American Delegation on the subject of the 35,000 ton limitation for capital ships.[2] The result of this interview had confirmed previous interviews that it was not possible to secure United States agreement for a lower limit than 35,000 tons at the present. The Ambassador would recall that for the past two years we had been negotiating with the United States Government on this subject and we had done all in our power to secure a lower level without success. The American attitude did not come to us altogether as a surprise, and we had even warned the French Government of our belief before the Conference opened. Since then, however, the departure of the Japanese Delegation and the failure to reach agreement on quantitative limitation, for which the French Delegation had to bear a considerable share of responsibility, had further stiffened the United States attitude. For this and other reasons I did not believe that there was any chance of securing now a reduction lower than 35,000 tons. We had,

[1] See No. 648.          [2] See No. 649.

however, obtained from the United States Delegation a statement which would be embodied in the agreement that, while the Treaty should last for ten years, there should be a conference in 1940, the object of which would be, amongst other things, to ascertain whether in the light of the circumstances then prevailing and of the experience gained in the interval of the construction of the capital ship, the limits of displacement and gun calibre for the capital ship could be reduced or should be maintained. A copy of this statement is enclosed herewith.[3]

3. I hoped that the French Delegation would not lightly dismiss this concession, for I was convinced that the United States Delegation were sincere in their desire to have such an examination. We had pressed for an earlier date, but the United States representatives had replied that a shorter period would not give time for experience to show whether a lower limit than 35,000 tons was practicable. I reminded the Ambassador that a 14-inch gun calibre (as compared with the 16-inch gun calibre under the Washington Treaty) and a 35,000 ton capital ship, though this was far from representing as much reduction as we should have hoped for, was infinitely preferable to no limitation at all.

4. I then spoke of the political consequences of failure, and reminded the Ambassador of the effect on Anglo-French relations and on relations with the United States of a failure to reach an agreement at all if such a failure appeared to be due to the attitude of the French Government. The position was, in my view, really serious and the Conference had reached a phase at which it must in the next few days either reach agreement or adjourn with the admission of failure. From time to time in recent years we had gone out of our way to meet the difficulties of the French Government, and even now I understood that the French Government were asking us to give them some temporary financial accommodation.[4] This time I was asking the French Government to do something which was, I was convinced, in their own interest and which would be appreciated by His Majesty's Government as a contribution to Anglo-French accord.

5. M. Corbin replied that he fully appreciated the anxieties of His Majesty's Government in this matter, and that naturally his Government were really anxious to help. None the less he was confident they would not be satisfied with so high a level as 35,000 tons for the capital ship. This would be regarded in France as tantamount to the failure of the Conference. For what hope would there then be of Japan coming in? It was known that Japan desired a lower level for the capital ship. It was only the United States that wished for this very large figure, and apparently the United States were to get their figure without any reduction of any kind. Would not the Japanese say that when they had left the Conference all that the Powers had done was to accept the United States draft? This was hardly the way to get agreement.

[3] Enclosure 1 below.
[4] This proposal appears to have been made to the Chancellor of the Exchequer by M. Flandin during his visit to England, January 27–28. Cf. No. 637, last paragraph.

6. Moreover, though it was quite true that we had been in consultation with the United States Government on this subject for two years, the Conference had only discussed the matter for ten days and this was too short a time to justify no further attempt being made to reduce the United States figure. I had told him at our previous meeting that the United States would make no concession in the matter. Yet I had now produced a formula which was at least an improvement on the United States attitude hitherto. If we continued to press them, it might well be that results could yet be achieved. He recollected that the United States had not seemed to be quite so rigid at the beginning of the Conference. Mr. Norman Davis, speaking personally, had hinted to him at a possible reduction of the 35,000-ton limit. M. Corbin knew that the difficulties did not lie with Mr. Davis, but with the great shipping interests of the United States. None the less it was not right that the Conference should so soon agree to the highest figure put forward. In reply, I said that if the French Ambassador considered that further efforts were to be made, how did he propose that this should be done? The conference was now at a standstill and I did not see how further progress could be possible. Would the French and United States Delegations be prepared to have meetings between themselves to attempt to reach agreement? M. Corbin replied that he was perfectly willing to try this, and thought even that it might serve a useful purpose.

7. We then discussed the question of the signature of an agreement, and the method in which the problem of the accession of other Powers was to be dealt with. I handed the Ambassador a copy of the enclosed paper headed 'Points for inclusion in a Protocol',[5] which we proposed should be signed now, telling him that His Majesty's Government would, however, not be in a position to sign this until they had received an assurance as to the attitude of the German Government towards the draft treaty. M. Corbin did not like this proposal in its present form. He took particular exception to the second sentence of paragraph 2. He said that in that sentence we were asking the French Government to admit now that the German Government would sign the treaty at some future date. What would the difference be in agreeing to that and agreeing to a German signature now? I replied that we would have preferred that the German and Soviet Governments should sign now— the French Government had objected to sitting down at a table with the German Government at present.[6] We had therefore devised this formula, which would avoid that difficulty. M. Corbin rejoined that the formula, however, none the less made it clear that at a certain date the French Government and the German Government would sign a treaty which would violate the military clauses of the Treaty of Versailles.

8. After further discussion of this sentence and of paragraph 3, to which the Ambassador also took exception, we agreed that M. Corbin would return to Paris to-morrow when he would have a conversation with M. Flandin and see what he could do to meet our wishes in respect both of the limitation of tonnage and of the form of signature of the agreement.

[5] Enclosure 2 below.          [6] See Nos. 630 and 634.

9. I should be grateful if, in the light of the above conversation, you could arrange to see M. Flandin to-morrow and impress upon him the importance which His Majesty's Government attach to reaching some agreement at the Naval Conference in the very near future. The Conference is rapidly approaching, if it has not already reached, the decisive period in its existence and there is, in our view, a very real risk that, unless agreement is reached within the next few days, we may have to admit failure. I feel sure that M. Flandin will appreciate the wide political consequences of such a failure at the present time. The reactions in the United States and in this country would certainly be deplorable and I feel justified in asking the French Government to view the position which we have now reached from the wider international aspect, which should surely be of as great concern to them as it is to us.

I am, &c.,
ANTHONY EDEN

ENCLOSURE I IN No. 652

*Capital Ship Limitation*

The displacement limit for the capital ship to be maintained at 35,000 tons. The limit of the gun to be reduced to 14-inch calibre, provided that Japan accepts the limit; should Japan not accept this limit, maximum calibre to be 16-inch.

With two exceptions, the period of validity of the treaty shall be ten years (1937–46 inclusive); the exceptions to be the provisions relating to the qualitative limits of the capital ship and those relating to the 'holiday' in the construction of large cruisers, which shall be valid for six years only (1937–42 inclusive).

There shall be a conference in 1940 between the Powers parties to the treaty. The objects of this conference shall be, in particular, to decide:—

(*a*) Whether, in the light of the circumstances then prevailing and of the experience gained in the interval in the construction of the capital ship, the limits of displacement and gun calibre for the capital ship can be reduced or shall be maintained;

(*b*) Whether the holiday in construction of cruisers in excess of 8,000 tons displacement should be continued; and

(*c*) When the next conference should be held.

ENCLOSURE 2 IN No. 652

*Points for Inclusion in a Protocol*

His Majesty's Government in the United Kingdom would immediately submit the draft treaty through the diplomatic channel to the other naval Powers for their consideration and observations.

2. The Governments represented at the present Conference would undertake that their plenipotentiaries will meet in London on . . .[7] to sign

[7] Punctuation as in the original.

the treaty on their behalf, subject to any amendments which may have been agreed upon before that date. The treaty would be signed at the same time by as many other Powers as have agreed by that date to participate in it.

3. The question whether it will be necessary to hold a conference on this subject with the naval Powers not represented at the present Conference should be left open until the consultation has taken place with those Powers, as provided in paragraph 1 above.

## No. 653

### Mr. Eden to Sir R. Lindsay (Washington)
### No. 154 [A 1355/4/45]

FOREIGN OFFICE, *February 14, 1936*

Sir,

I saw Mr. Norman Davis to-day when I gave him the gist of my interview with M. Corbin on the subject of the Naval Conference this morning.[1] Mr. Davis said that he would be very glad to have a further interview with M. Corbin on the latter's return from Paris. In the meanwhile, he wished to tell me in the strictest confidence of his own conversation with M. Corbin.[2] The latter had made it clear to him that the difficulty of the French Government was not purely technical. They were anxious before agreeing to the signature of a Naval Agreement to arrive at a political understanding with His Majesty's Government, more especially in respect of the demilitarised zone. M. Corbin had been particularly nervous lest within a few days of the signature of a naval agreement Germany should violate the demilitarised zone. Such a course of events would be utterly disastrous to any French Government. In these conditions they were compelled to be very cautious.

2. Mr. Davis had replied to M. Corbin that the French Government appeared anxious to tie His Majesty's Government rigidly in order to avoid their having any latitude in the negotiations, and that he thought this attitude was mistaken. From conversations he had had, he was clear that His Majesty's Government were as alive as the French Government to the danger constituted by German rearmament, and that they fully appreciated that in the last resort France and the United Kingdom would have to act together. But there was much to be said from the French point of view in favour of a United Kingdom which was re-arming and to some extent freer in negotiation with France, which accordingly would be in a better position to come to terms with Germany. Mr. Davis had further emphasised to M. Corbin that these European problems were nothing to do with him or with the Naval Conference, and that he much hoped that the Naval Conference would not be made an instrument for bargaining in Europe. At the same time, he felt it necessary to warn me that he expected that this was the

[1] See No. 652. Mr. Davis's account of this conversation with Mr. Eden is printed in *F.R.U.S. 1936*, vol. i, pp. 59–60.
[2] Cf. *ibid.*, pp. 58–59.

line which M. Corbin would take after his interview with the French Government.

3. After some further discussion of the Naval Conference, Mr. Davis said that he much hoped that I might find it possible to visit the United States before very long. It was, he thought, a great pity that I had never met President Roosevelt in person, and he knew that the President wished for an opportunity to meet me. Would it not be possible for me to come to the United States in September and to stay with Mr. Davis, whose house was only a few miles from President Roosevelt's country residence? Meetings between the President and myself could in this way be both frequent and informal and Mr. Davis was confident that they would be of the greatest value.

4. I replied that, while I should highly value the privilege of visiting the United States and of meeting President Roosevelt, I was a little doubtful whether there might not be some difficulty in such a visit at the present time. The Presidential Elections were looming ahead, and September might therefore be an inconvenient time for such a visit. Moreover, was there not a risk that at a time when an election campaign was imminent an attempt would be made to construe a visit by myself to the United States as an attempt to entangle America in European complications? Finally, September was the month of the Assembly at Geneva, and therefore scarcely a possible month for me to leave Europe. Mr. Davis replied that October would do just as well as September and refused to admit the danger of my visit being misconstrued. At the same time he did concede that the proximity of the Presidential Elections might be a complication, though he added that President Roosevelt would not be taking a large personal part in stumping the country. Moreover, President Roosevelt had often said to him how anxious he was to have the problem of the debt finally resolved.[3] He had always maintained that, had he been able to have a conversation with Mr. Baldwin before the latter was Prime Minister, he was quite certain that the matter could have been arranged. Unfortunately, however, that had not been possible. Finally, he said that he would write to President Roosevelt on the matter and communicate with me afresh. I repeated that, while I should be glad on some occasion to meet President Roosevelt, I was doubtful whether this autumn was a possible moment. Perhaps next year would be better when the Presidential Elections would be over.

I am, &c.,

ANTHONY EDEN

[3] For correspondence on this subject during 1933 and the first half of 1934 see Volume V, Chapter IX, and Volume VI, Chapter IX. For later Anglo-American exchanges, see Cmd. 4763 of 1934, 4923 (June 1935), and 5042 (December 1935).

# No. 654

*Sir R. Clive (Tokyo) to Mr. Eden (Received March 16)*
*No. 77 [A 2190/4/45]*

TOKYO, *February 14, 1936*

His Majesty's Representative at Tokyo presents his compliments to the Secretary of State for Foreign Affairs and has the honour to transmit herewith copy of the undermentioned paper.

| *Name and Date* | *Subject* |
|---|---|
| Minute by Naval Attaché | Naval Disarmament |
| February 13, 1936 | Admiral Kobayashi's[1] views |

ENCLOSURE IN No. 654

*Minute by Captain Vivian*

H[*is*] E[*xcellency*]                                                  *February 17, 1936*

I called on Admiral Kobayashi (Supreme War Councillor) this afternoon and had a long conversation with him.

He told me that he had spent the whole morning at a War Council Meeting, and then went on to ask me if I had had any official news of the proposed qualitative proposals which may be agreed to in London.

I told him that I knew no more than had been reported in the Press.

He then went on to say that in his opinion Japan *must* come into some sort of qualitative agreement, but the only War Councillor who supported his view is Admiral Nomura, that the other four Admirals had never had any experience on the Administrative side at the Navy Department and consequently did not realise that, not only is it difficult to extract money from the Finance Ministry, but also that the experience of the past proved that there is always a delay of two or three years between the time that the Naval Staff lay down a building programme and the time when the money is available to start it.

This is not so in the United States of America or Great Britain, and consequently Japan will lag behind these countries unless she can have a programme spread over a number of years, which will be impossible if she has to build against other countries.

The Admiral said that this passion for a free hand in building is a great mistake, but he sees definite signs of a swing back to a more reasonable policy.

From the way in which he spoke I think that the Naval Supreme War Councillors had been discussing the possibility of signing the proposed Treaty in London, and that Admirals Kobayashi and Nomura had put up a stiff fight against the other four, in favour of doing so.

Admiral Kobayashi is a hot favourite for the Minister of Marine's port-

[1] A Japanese Naval Supreme War Councillor.

folio should Admiral Osumi go. He is a very moderate man, and proved himself a popular leader when Commander-in-Chief of the Combined Fleet, 1931–33.

J.G.P.V.

## No. 655

Letter from Mr. Davis to Mr. Craigie

[A 1342/4/45]

DELEGATION OF THE UNITED STATES OF AMERICA, *February 14, 1935*

Dear Craigie,

I am glad to have seen your tentative drafts, both for the protocol and for the capital ship formula.[1] I note that you have not shown the former to any other Delegation and I am likewise treating it as confidential.[2] It might also be well to consider the capital ship formula as confidential, since there are certain points contained in both drafts to which we cannot agree. Among other things I see no reason for any mention of cruisers, particularly in connection with capital ship discussions. I am having an alternate draft of a formula prepared, which I shall hope to discuss with you on Monday.[3] At the same time we can also discuss the suggested points for inclusion in the protocol.

Sincerely yours,<br>NORMAN H. DAVIS

[1] See enclosures in No. 652.

[2] A note of February 16 from Mr. Holman to Mr. Craigie reads: 'I have told Mr. Reber that we have communicated already the tentative formulae to the French and Italians. He quite understood and Mr. Davis will come and see you about a revised formula on capital ships in due course. A.H. 16.2.36.'    [3] February 17.

## No. 656

Mr. Eden to Sir E. Drummond (Rome)

No. 35 Telegraphic [A 1379/4/45]

*Important*    FOREIGN OFFICE, *February 15, 1936, 6.15 p.m.*

Naval Conference.

Agreement has now been reached on all technical points except that relating to the future size of the capital ship. As regards latter, the United States categorically refuse any reduction below 35,000 tons, whereas the French refuse to accept this limit. While sympathising with French desire to reduce limit, we have for some time realised that United States would be uncompromising on this point and consider it would be a mistake to imperil other concessions offered by the United States (reduction in calibre of gun to 14″ and holiday in construction of large cruisers) by further pressure on Americans in regard to capital ship displacement. We have told both French and Italian Delegations that we consider this limit, high as it is, infinitely preferable to no limit at all and that the agreement reached on all other matters appears to us to be of very great value. Moreover, United States will be prepared to reconsider present limit in four years' time. Italian Delegation, while giving general support to their French colleagues, appear to take a more reasonable and realistic view of the situation than the latter and desire to promote a friendly settlement.

Admiral Raineri Biscia left for Rome today on his own initiative to explain the position personally to the Italian Government. It is just possible that French Ambassador at Rome may be endeavouring to enlist Italian support of the French thesis and, if this surmise is correct, it would be desirable that you should take such corrective action as you can. You should, in any case, take an opportunity of saying that helpful attitude and constructive co-operation of Italian Delegation has been appreciated on all sides here and it is our hope that the Admiral will soon return to London, where his presence is urgently required.

## No. 657

*Sir G. Clerk (Paris) to Mr. Eden (Received February 15, 8.40 p.m.)*
*No. 79 Telegraphic: by telephone [A 1359/4/45]*

*Immediate*                                                       PARIS, *February 15, 1936*

In accordance with your instructions[1] I sought an interview with M. Flandin this morning, and begged him earnestly to do all in his power to assist you in your endeavour to prevent failure of Naval Conference. I adduced all available arguments both of a technical nature and of wider international aspect; M. Flandin listened most sympathetically, and finally said that he was in complete agreement with substance of His Majesty's Government's policy, though it would be difficult for him to follow us in certain matters of form. He was not at the moment prepared to discuss technical details, and he had not even been informed that M. Corbin intended to come over to Paris today. At the same time he shared your view that failure of Conference would be most undesirable; he would see Minister of Marine this afternoon, and, while he could definitely not commit latter, as far as it lay with him, French delegates would be instructed to facilitate an agreement as regards tonnage and other similar questions.

In fact in his opinion it was essential that we should make a treaty forthwith—the best that could be agreed upon between the four Powers—and that we should ultimately obtain adhesion of other naval Powers including Germany. In the form of the protocol, however, he saw a stumbling-block.

[1] In No. 652. In a telegram of February 18 to M. Corbin, M. Flandin stated that the British Minister at Paris, Mr. Lloyd Thomas, had presented him on February 15 with a copy of the draft protocol which Mr. Eden had given to M. Corbin on February 14 (enclosure 2 in No. 652). M. Flandin's telegram then gave instructions as to the line of conduct to be followed by the French delegation to the Naval Conference. See *Documents Diplomatiques Français, 1932–1939,* 2nd Series, vol. i, No. 198.

Until elections in France were over no representative of a French Government could put his signature to a document which implicitly bound that Government to recognise German naval re-armament. As Prime Minister in February, 1935, he was personally responsible for terms of Declaration of London,[2] which laid down the principle of interdependence of all armament negotiations. He himself agreed that consequences of a too strict adherence to this doctrine of interdependence had been unfortunate, but this was not the moment to make a change and he refused to be moved. Though Germany might not be mentioned by name in the protocol, the true significance of trend of terms would at once be seized upon and used as a stick to beat him with on the eve of the elections. He must have time. I pointed out Conference had already dragged on too long and that Americans were getting impatient but he replied that it had lasted so long that a few weeks more or less could make little difference, and that as we had yielded to Americans over question of tonnage, they must be accommodating over this question of form. When I asked him what alternative he could propose, he said that he had not had time to study the question and that his suggestion must not be considered as official. He was inclined, however, to think when four Powers had reached agreement, His Majesty's Government should be asked to communicate terms of treaty to Japanese Government and to endeavour to obtain their agreement. By the time this had been obtained French Government might be in a position to agree to a form of protocol which would cover the participation of other naval Powers. The above were his personal views and may be modified when he has discussed position with M. Corbin and M. Piétri which he intends to do this afternoon. I am to see him again tomorrow morning at 11 and he hopes then to be able to give me an official answer.

[2] Of February 3, 1935; see Volume XII, No. 400, note 4, and Annex.

## No. 658

*Sir G. Clerk (Paris) to Mr. Eden (Received February 17)*
*No. 81 Telegraphic: by post [A 1360/4/45]*

PARIS, *February 16, 1936*

My telegram No. 79.[1]

Monsieur Flandin received me this morning, but was unable to add anything to what he had told me yesterday, as up to the present Monsieur Corbin has given no sign of being in Paris. Monsieur Flandin has reason however to believe that he is in France, and in that case he will probably see him tomorrow. In the meantime Monsieur Piétri has summoned a meeting of the Naval General Staff for tomorrow afternoon. If these discussions call for a Cabinet decision, Monsieur Flandin thinks that he will be able to consult his colleagues of the Government on Tuesday,[2] and we may therefore

[1] No. 657.          [2] February 18.

expect to receive definite statement of the attitude of the French Government by Wednesday.

I regret that this delay should have occurred, but Monsieur Corbin, and not Monsieur Flandin, is responsible.

## No. 659

### Record by Mr. Craigie of a conversation with Mr. Davis

*[A 1565/4/45]*

*Very confidential*          FOREIGN OFFICE, *February 17, 1936*

I called on Mr. Norman Davis this afternoon to discuss the position reached in the naval negotiations.

As regards the proposed Protocol,[1] he thought there was no chance of France signing anything *now* which would bind her to agree to ultimate German participation in the treaty. In strict confidence he told me that the United States Embassy at Paris had learnt from a good source that France would 'stall' on this question until she had received satisfactory assurances of British support in the event of a German incursion into the demilitarised zone. A second reason for French hesitation was that, if the capital ship remained at 35,000 tons and if the United Kingdom indulged in an accelerated programme of capital ship replacement, there would be no money left for the army: and it was in British *military* support that France was most interested. Mr. Norman Davis believed that there was also a danger of Italy running out and that the only solution might be for the United States and the United Kingdom to make an agreement which would be open to accession by all other Powers. I said that, as an incentive to sweet reasonableness in France, the prospect of an Anglo-German-American naval agreement might be more compelling.

As regards capital ships, Mr. Davis said the French would agree to a 10 years' treaty, subject to a provision that any Power could propose a reduction in displacement during the years 1940 or 1941. (I expressed some incredulity as to this.) As regards cruisers, Mr. Davis said he could not accept any formula which implied that the replacement of *existing* 10,000 ton cruisers might be called in question at the end of the holiday. He said the point could best be covered by a general formula, which did not specifically mention the big cruisers. He was working on a formula which he would submit to us shortly.

Finally, I said that I thought that it was a real misfortune that the United States had not been able to come down to the 12″ gun ship, in the main because America had once had a 12″ gun which had not proved satisfactory. To my surprise, Mr. Davis, speaking very privately, said he entirely agreed, but that up to date his efforts to bring the naval authorities round to this view had failed. He believed, however, that after his return he would be able to interest the President in the possibility of future reduction in the gun

[1] See enclosure 2 in No. 652.

calibre and that, if Mr. Roosevelt were returned at the next election, the possibility of a reconsideration of the gun calibre in the course of the next few years was by no means negligible.

I suggested to Mr. Davis that America, by remaining entirely uncompromising over the capital ship displacement, would earn general opprobrium in Europe and that it should be possible to squeeze at least 1,000 tons out of the 35,000 tons without causing serious technical difficulties to American constructors. Mr. Davis replied that he had not given up hope of getting his Delegation to agree to something of the kind, but that he did not wish to raise my hopes unduly. It appeared, however, that what he had in mind was some indication in the treaty of a future reduction of 2–3,000 tons per ship rather than any reduction in the tonnage of the first ships. In any case, he felt sure that, vis-à-vis the French, the right policy was to appear completely unyielding for the present.

R. L. C.

## No. 660

*Sir E. Drummond (Rome) to Mr. Eden (Received February 19, 8.30 a.m.)*
*No. 88 Telegraphic [A 1428/4/45]*

ROME, *February 18, 1936, 8.35 p.m.*

Your telegram No. 35.[1]

I felt that to endeavour to ascertain whether or not my French colleague had received instructions on the subject might place both of us in a somewhat awkward position and that it was wiser to go direct to Signor Mussolini and make the point set forth in your telegram.

I saw His Excellency this afternoon. He had just had an interview with Admiral Biscia. I found that he entirely concurred in your view as to uselessness and indeed danger of pressing United States any further as regards size of capital ships. To do so he said would only irritate the United States and produce no result.

Signor Mussolini, Under Secretary for the Navy and Admiral Biscia are to meet tomorrow morning to discuss certain other points such as Germany and the Conference. I expect that the Admiral will be able to start back within the next two or three days.

His Excellency was somewhat scornful of extremely juridical attitude adopted by the French in all matters concerning Germany and part five of Treaty of Versailles. He referred in particular to his own memorandum about limitation of armaments[2] by which Germany's military forces would have been definitely fixed. He compared German present strength to what it would have been had something on lines of his plan been accepted.

[1] No. 656.
[2] A reference presumably to the Italian Government's memorandum of January 31, 1934, printed as No. 3 in Cmd. 4512; cf. Volume VI, No. 239.

## No. 661

*Letter from American Department to Chancery (Rome)*
[*A 1358/4/45*]

FOREIGN OFFICE, *February 20, 1936*

Dear Chancery,

We drew the attention of the Italian delegation at the Naval Conference to the second paragraph of your telegram No. 84[1] of the 15th February in which you reported the 'Messagero' as stating that this country was insisting on a maximum of 35,000 tons for battleships. The position is of course as explained in the first paragraph of our telegram No. 35[2] of the 15th February and we represented to the Italians that the 'Messagero's' statement was particularly obnoxious in that the United Kingdom have been trying for nearly two years to persuade the United States to agree to a lower limit.

Commander Margottini was most apologetic and promised to communicate with Rome immediately in order to arrange for a suitable correction to be published.

Yours ever,
A[MERICAN] DEP[ARTMEN]T

[1] Not printed.  [2] No. 656.

## No. 662

*Letter from Mr. Peake (Paris) to Mr. Holman (Received February 26)*[1]
[*A 1566/4/45*]

PARIS, *February 20, 1936*

My dear Holman,

You will no doubt recollect my telephoning to you on the evening of the 19th in regard to the answer which M. Flandin had promised to give us yesterday in reply to the representations which the Minister had made to him on Saturday and Sunday last.[2] The Ambassador had instructed me to ask for an interview with M. Flandin for yesterday, the day on which the reply was promised. Subsequently, as you will remember, I duly asked for the interview, and after some hours received the reply which I telephoned to you that if, as M. Flandin supposed, the subject about which the Ambassador particularly wished to talk to him was the Naval Conference, M. Flandin, in view of the very heavy pressure put upon him by to-day's debate in the Chamber on the Soviet Pact, thought that it would probably be better if the answer were to be given to me by M. Massigli, the Ambassador reserving himself for an interview with M. Flandin at some later date, if there were any special points in M. Massigli's reply which needed elucidation.

[1] Date of filing in the Foreign Office.
[2] i.e. February 15 and 16; cf. Nos. 657 and 658. No record of the telephone conversation on February 19 has been traced in Foreign Office archives.

As I told you in my telephone conversation to you this afternoon,[3] I saw M. Massigli this morning. The interview, which was protracted, was not a particularly pleasant one. M. Massigli was, unlike his usual self, extremely curt and dogmatic, and proved quite unamenable to argument.

He began by saying that France was perfectly ready either to sign a Four Power Treaty, or if we preferred it to initial the draft of such a treaty with a view to further discussion on the question of what Powers should eventually be asked to accede to it. On the subject of points for inclusion in a protocol (see the second enclosure to your despatch No. 278[4]) he said that the French Government were quite unable to accept your suggestions. There were nothing but disadvantages for France in accepting such a procedure. For the French Government to agree to Germany being invited to accede to this treaty would draw down upon the French Government a storm of abuse from the whole country which might well result in the Government's fall. And apart from that the condonation, which was what we were asking for, of Germany's violation of the Treaty of Versailles would merely weaken France's position in the face of the violation, which was now imminent, of the demilitarised zone.

But even apart from this, said M. Massigli, what possible value could there be to the French or to us in a German accession to such a treaty. German plans were so laid that we must expect Germany to go to war within the next two years. No treaty which dealt with naval disarmament could alter that or in any way hinder German plans. French public opinion would not tolerate the acquiescence by France in Germany's accession to a treaty which dealt with that one type of armament which could not now hinder German plans for aggression. The French Government were not unreasonable. They were like ourselves anxious to see a limitation of armaments but they felt that no such limitation would be acceptable unless it were linked in some way to air armaments. An agreement with Germany which took in air armaments would be of the highest value, especially if it were concluded soon, for whereas warships took years to build, aircraft could be constructed in a matter of months, and such an agreement might be potent in stopping the present German plans of aggression. The French Government could not agree that where Germany was concerned naval armaments could be separated from air and land armaments. To attempt to do so was merely to scratch the surface and to cause irritation without getting near the root of the problem.

As a result of argument, M. Massigli finally dropped the question of land armaments, but persisted in linking air and naval disarmament. There was considerably more of this kind of thing with which I need not worry you, since the French line of argument which M. Massigli reproduced will be thoroughly familiar to you.

I then passed to the question of qualitative limitation, upon which M. Massigli read me an impassioned telegram sent the day before yesterday to

[3] Mr. Holman's record of this conversation is not printed.
[4] No. 652.

843

the French Ambassador in Washington, and repeated to M. Corbin, instructing M. de Laboulaye to see both the Secretary of State and President Roosevelt and to make one last appeal to them to agree to a smaller limitation than 35,000 tons and 14 inches. 28,000 tons was the figure mentioned in M. Flandin's instructions.[5] I observed to M. Massigli that the reply to this appeal was a foregone conclusion. It was clear that the American Government would refuse. He must know this as well as I. What then in the face of an American refusal would be the French answer to us? M. Massigli told me that for the moment he could not say. He must wait until he received M. de Laboulaye's reply. The French answer would then be transmitted to the French delegates in London. I have, however, a feeling that even though the Americans decline the French will delay to the last moment, and then will give way.

Such then are the bleak results of my talk with M. Massigli. I have discussed them with the Ambassador who is prepared to ask for an interview with M. Flandin as soon as may be, to see whether what M. Massigli says really represents the final answer of the French Government. His Excellency thought it better, however, that you should see this letter in case there are any observations which the Foreign Office wish to make before he sees M. Flandin again.[6]

Yours ever,
CHARLES PEAKE

[5] The text of this telegram of February 17 is printed in *D.D.F., op. cit.*, No. 194.

[6] In a minute to this letter Mr. Wigram wrote as follows: 'Reference M. Massigli's remarks on the subject of land armaments, the Secy of State should perhaps know that the War Office have information that despite what M. Laval told the Secy of State on June 27th that the limitation of land armaments is 9/10ths of the whole problem for France [see No. 384], the French General Staff consider that such limitation offers no appreciable military advantage to France and might well be a disadvantage. No wonder therefore that M. Massigli indicates readiness to separate this question from the long-maintained theory of the interdependence of armaments. Our Air Staff have not yet given their opinion on the further limitation of air armaments: but it would be unwise to consider them to be very good. R.F.Wigram. 21/2.'

## No. 663

*Minute by Mr Craigie*

[*A 1566/4/45*]

FOREIGN OFFICE, *February 20, 1936*

M. Massigli's reply[1] is uncompromising and delivered, apparently, in his most 'cassant' style. It is interesting to note the difference between the Quai d'Orsay attitude and the attitude of M. Piétri, if one may judge of the latter from the recent telegram from the *Times* correspondent at Paris (which we now know was written after consultation with the Minister of Marine).[2]

[1] See No. 662.     [2] See *The Times*, February 19, p. 12.

I suggest that, before His Majesty's Government take a decision as to the course to be followed in regard to the Franco-German difficulty, we should await the reply of the German Government to the questions recently put to them and also the return of Admiral Raineri Biscia.

But meanwhile there are one or two points which should, I think, be made clear to the French at once:

(i) We are said to be asking for something which would not be of help to France. Of what use is a Naval Treaty to France or anyone else if Germany does not conform to it? It is even more in France's interest than it is in ours that German naval construction should be regulated and brought to the light of day. But the French attitude is apparently to leave us to shoulder the responsibility of persuading Germany to conform, without lifting a finger to help.

(ii) As regards the demilitarised zone, it is surely evident that to discriminate against Germany in regard to the Naval Treaty is the very way to incite her to some folly in regard to the demilitarised zone. If, on the contrary, Germany is invited like any other Power in the world, to come into the treaty and accepts, it becomes infinitely more difficult for the hot-heads in Germany, on the very morrow of such a decision, to push their country into an adventure in the demilitarised zone.

(iii) M. Massigli lays it down that no naval agreement with Germany must be agreed to without some arrangement for the reduction of Air Forces. Seeing that we are dealing solely with a naval agreement for qualitative (and not quantitative) limitation, there is no technical connexion between the two questions. From the technical point of view Germany would confer as big a benefit on the other naval Powers by coming into the treaty as they would confer on her by inviting her to participate. Furthermore, from the point of view of policy and tactics we disagree entirely with the French thesis that the two questions should be linked. It is this policy of linking subjects which have little, if any, real connexion which has been largely responsible for the repeated failures in the sphere of disarmament during the last five years and we must refuse to have anything further to do with such mistaken policies. We are as anxious as the French for an air agreement but we believe that French policy (as exemplified by the Massigli interview) would definitely put an end to all hope of progress.

(iv) We feel sure that the French Government will reconsider their attitude, after further reflection. If not, it is only fair to warn them that His Majesty's Government will have to reserve their full liberty of action in promoting an agreement with Germany, both as regards qualitative naval limitation and as regards air limitation, by the methods which seem best suited to attain these ends.

I venture to think that, if we could without delay speak firmly to the French on some such lines, we should save ourselves a deal of trouble in the long run.

R. L. C.

## No. 664

*Sir R. Lindsay (Washington) to Mr. Eden*
*(Received February 22, 9.30 a.m.)*
*No. 46 Telegraphic [A 1491/4/45]*

WASHINGTON, *February 21, 1936, 6.57 p.m.*

Press has reported representations by French Ambassador to State Department to induce the latter to agree to reduce tonnage of battleships and has suggested that refusal of United States government to agree was rather in the nature of a snub. I understand from State Department that no snub was administered. In accordance with his (? instructions)[1] Ambassador's representations were of an 'insistent' character; he suggested that without reduction of tonnage French government might think proposed treaty not worth proceeding with; and he urged that it was extremely difficult for French government to . . .[2] but that it would be easier for them to do so if they could point to this concession by United States government.

Refusal of the latter to . . .[3] these representations was based on reasons stated frequently in the past.[4]

[1] The text was here uncertain. Cf. *F.R.U.S. 1936*, vol. i, pp. 65–66.
[2] The text was here uncertain. A marginal note reads: 'admit German Gov[ernmen]t to discussions'.
[3] The text was here uncertain.      [4] Cf. *F.R.U.S., op. cit.*, pp. 66–67.

## No. 665

*Mr. Eden to Sir G. Clerk (Paris)*
*No. 340 [A 1537/4/45]*

FOREIGN OFFICE, *February 21, 1936*

Sir,

The French Ambassador came to see me this morning to report the outcome of his conversations in Paris as to the Naval Conference. He said that the French Government had considered how best they could meet our point of view about Germany, but it was not possible for them to undertake now to sign a protocol which bound them unconditionally to sign an agreement with Germany at a given date. This was in fact equivalent to signing an agreement with Germany now which violated the military clauses of the Treaty of Versailles. No French Government could do this. Furthermore, the French Government thought it unfortunate that the opportunity of this state of the negotiations at the Naval Conference was not used in order to make progress with the Air Pact also. Finally, the French Government fear that, if they agreed to sign a Naval agreement with Germany now, they might find themselves in this very unenviable position: that within a few weeks of the signature Germany might violate the demilitarized zone. This would be an untenable position for any French Government which had just signed an agreement with Germany.

2. The Ambassador went on to speak of the vital need for bringing in the other League Powers at Geneva in connexion with the Treaty so as to link the Treaty with the League, though of course he appreciated that this step would follow after agreements with Germany and Japan.

3. I replied that what the Ambassador had told me was profoundly disappointing. I did not think that any useful purpose would be served by discussing the final stages of the Treaty if this was really the French Government's last word, for I did not see how in such conditions we could ever hope that a treaty would be signed. As to the argument of the connexion of this agreement with the Air Agreement, I was as anxious as the Ambassador to make progress with an Air Pact, and I was quite prepared at any time to approach the German Government to try to re-start negotiations in connexion with an Air Pact and Air Limitation, but that had nothing whatever to do, in my view, with the signature of a Naval Agreement. It was the persistent desire of the French Government to maintain these subjects tightly linked that made it impossible for us to make progress with any of them.

4. The Ambassador interjected that he did not suggest that they should be linked. He had only suggested that he did think there was a useful opportunity for talking to Germany about air if we were talking to Germany about the Naval Conference. I replied that that was altogether another matter and it was probably true that if we did secure a Naval Agreement then the moment would be propitious for a fresh effort to secure an Air Agreement, but if we failed in the former the prospects of the latter would clearly be jeopardised. Finally, I did not see the connexion between reaching a Naval Agreement and a possible violation by Germany of the demilitarized zone. On the whole I should have thought that if Germany had signed a Naval Agreement she was all the less likely to violate the demilitarized zone a short while after.

5. The Ambassador rejoined that he was sorry that I took so gloomy a view of his communication. He felt that there might yet be ways and means of arriving at our objective. He explained that the French Government might be willing to accept the following procedure. First, a signature by the four Powers of a Naval Agreement. To this a protocol might be attached in which the Powers would say that they were of the opinion that this Agreement should be signed by other Naval Powers. The protocol might also contain a date when such signature might be expected to take place. But the French Government, to safeguard their own position, would have to put in a reservation to the effect that their signature of the larger agreement with other Powers would be dependent on the developments of the European situation.

6. I replied that it did not seem to me that this procedure could be worked, but that I was willing to discuss the matter further with the Ambassador and the First Lord of the Admiralty if such an arrangement suited him. The Ambassador at once agreed and stated that the French Government, in the search which they had made for some means of avoiding a signature which would consent to the violation of the military clauses of the Treaty of

Versailles, had worked out the procedure which he had put before me as securing the best means of obtaining this result, and he believed that we might contrive to agree upon 'les modalités'.

I am, &c.,
ANTHONY EDEN[1]

[1] This despatch was circulated as L.N.C. (35)(U.K.) 49.

## No. 666

*Draft[1] minutes of a meeting between representatives of the United Kingdom and French Delegations on February 21, 1936, at 5.15 p.m.[2]*

L.N.C. (35) (U.K.) 50 [A 1413/4/45]

PRESENT: *United Kingdom*: Mr. Eden, Lord Monsell, Admiral of the Fleet Sir Ernle Chatfield, Sir William Malkin, Mr. Gore-Booth.
*France*: M. Corbin, Vice-Admiral Robert, M. Paul-Boncour.

The meeting proceeded directly to a discussion of the suggestion for the signature of a naval agreement put forward by the French Ambassador on the morning of the 21st February (see L.N.C. (U.K.) 49, paragraph 5).[3]

M. CORBIN explained that it was the French idea that the Powers at present conferring would sign the Convention, thereby committing themselves to it, and that the signature by the other Powers would be merely an extension of the Convention.

MR. EDEN said that the United Kingdom could not agree to this procedure unless Germany accepted the Convention as binding straight away, and LORD MONSELL added in explanation that while the United Kingdom could accept the Japanese risk they could not take the combined risk of Japan and Germany, especially in view of a possible rapprochement between the two.

M. CORBIN said that he did not see why this consideration would prevent the United Kingdom from signing. They could easily make a reservation in respect of Germany. On the other hand, M. Corbin confessed that he did not particularly like the idea of such a reservation, since it would give the Germans an excessive idea of their own importance.

MR. EDEN thought that signature without reservation in respect of Germany would be dangerous for France.

ADMIRAL CHATFIELD thought that Germany might adhere to the agreement as accepted by the Conference if she were in a good humour. If, on the other hand, she felt that she was being kept at arm's length she might feel offended and would begin e.g. to build more 10,000 ton cruisers. The same might be said of the Soviet Union, which was rumoured in the newspapers to be contemplating a large number of 10,000 ton cruisers.

Turning to the suggestion that the French, to safeguard their own position

[1] The minutes here printed were identical with the final text except for the omission in the heading of the word 'Draft' and the addition of 'Final Copy'.
[2] This meeting was held in the Secretary of State's room at the Foreign Office.
[3] See No. 665.

would have to put in a reservation to the effect that their signature of the larger agreement with other Powers would be dependent on the development of the European situation, M. Corbin said that he did not see that this reservation should prevent Germany from adhering to a Treaty.

Mr. Eden replied that this might be so, but it would not change the fact that the United Kingdom, in signing the Treaty in accordance with the French plan, would be bound by something to which Germany did not, for the time being, adhere.

The possibility of initialling, instead of signing, the original text, was considered and Lord Monsell recalled that the advantage of the United Kingdom protocol proposal was that Germany, Spain, etc. would have time to make observations.

M. Corbin felt that any hint that amendments would be considered might positively invite amendments. Apart from this it was always possible to have amendments put into the Treaty by protocol, and the signature of a Treaty had the advantage that in communicating it to other Powers you were communicating a Treaty and not suggesting that it should be amended.

Lord Monsell thought that the communication of a finished Treaty might make all the difference—in an unfavourable sense—in the case of Japan.

M. Corbin considered that a formula could be found which would convey the possibility of amendment without suggesting that advantage should be taken of it.

Consideration was next given to the possibility of circulating some kind of protocol to the effect that 'if there is to be a Treaty it will be in the form agreed upon at the Conference'. M. Corbin thought that the Treaty itself ought to be initialled.

Lord Monsell speculated whether an agreement could be initialled in such a way as to make it applicable except for the amendments of other Powers. The disadvantage, of course, was that such a course might not be sufficient to satisfy Mr. Norman Davis.

M. Corbin thought that the other Powers would have the possibility of criticising the agreement whatever procedure were adopted, and Sir William Malkin observed that an invitation to other Powers to make observations did not necessarily mean that the Powers at present conferring were committed to accepting these observations.

It was explained to M. Corbin that Mr. Norman Davis would be satisfied with the Protocol procedure as suggested by the United Kingdom.

M. Corbin then returned to the question of the conditions of German acceptance and Mr. Eden reminded him that there were two aspects of the question of German signature, (i) that the presentation of a 'fait accompli' would be unacceptable to Germany and (ii) that the United Kingdom would not be ready to sign an agreement without an assurance of German adhesion.

M. Corbin said that France was prepared to sign without German adhesion and to rely upon the safeguarding clause in respect of Germany.

Lord Monsell observed that this would be very dangerous for France since she would not receive information from Germany and would thus not know what Germany was building.

M. Corbin agreed that it was advisable that Germany should join in, but insisted that a treaty was greatly to Germany's advantage. It meant in fact that all Powers would formally accept the abolition of the naval clauses of the Treaty of Versailles.

Mr. Eden did not think that Germany would be greatly impressed by such a concession, and Lord Monsell was of the opinion that if Germany was anxious to make trouble, she would not come into the Treaty but would stay outside and build unusual types of ships.

M. Corbin thought that Germany would not take this line since it would put world opinion against her, on which the United Kingdom representatives remarked that that might depend to what extent it had been the attitude of France which had led Germany to take such a line.

M. Corbin said that the French reservation was necessary since France would want to examine the political situation at the time of signature. The reservation did not touch Germany on the point of prestige.

Admiral Chatfield, after some discussion with Sir William Malkin, then suggested the following course. The Delegates to the Conference might sign a document as the result of their deliberations in which it would be stated that the Conference was agreed upon certain texts as the basis for a Treaty. This text should be put before certain other powers who should be invited to subscribe to it and to make suggestions if they wished. Later in the year the Powers now conferring would meet and decide whether the text had obtained sufficient support to enable all the Powers who would be interested to sign a Treaty together.

The meeting then digressed for a moment on the question whether there should be two stages in communications to other Powers or only one, but no conclusion was reached on this point.

M. Corbin said that the French Delegation would agree to a resolution of the kind suggested being passed by the Conference. They would agree to the text being submitted to the other Powers. They felt, however, that any invitation to the other Powers to suggest amendments might be a little dangerous.

Lord Monsell suggested that a formula might be found by which other countries could be invited to make observations without there being any guarantee that these observations should lead to the corresponding amendments.

M. Corbin agreed and observed that if the French were to make their reservations in a resolution of this kind it would be better than a reservation in a Treaty.

Mr. Eden and Lord Monsell felt that the suggested procedure was at first sight distinctly hopeful, and M. Corbin and M. Paul-Boncour[4] insisted

[4] M. Paul-Boncour was appointed Minister of State with special responsibility for League of Nations Affairs on January 24.

that it was a great advance on the previous position taken up by the French. It was agreed that Sir William Malkin should prepare a draft elaborating the proposal, and that it should be considered by the French and United Kingdom Delegations together before it was shewn to the United States representatives. In particular the French Delegation would explain the reservations which they would propose to make. It was felt, however, that a simultaneous presentation of the proposal to the Americans by the French and the United Kingdom Delegations might savour of pressure, and that it would therefore be preferable if, after the formula most likely to produce American acceptance had been found, it should be divulged to Mr. Davis by the United Kingdom Delegation.

*Capital Ships*

MR. EDEN asked Admiral Robert whether the French had taken a decision on the subject of capital ship tonnage, to which ADMIRAL ROBERT replied that they were still waiting for the United States answer to their démarche in Washington.[5] In this démarche they had drawn particular attention to the bad moral effect of keeping the capital ship tonnage at its present high level. A reduction was desirable as an indication that progress in disarmament had been made and that even more was hoped for in the future.

M. CORBIN thought that a present reduction would be infinitely preferable to the mere expression of a hope which was all that the Americans were apparently prepared to concede.

MR. EDEN thought that the United States sincerely wanted to know exactly how effective a 35,000 ton ship was and ADMIRAL CHATFIELD felt that there was quite a possibility that when the personnel of the Navy Department had changed, United States requirements as to tonnage might be changed also.

ADMIRAL ROBERT asked whether Lord Monsell, in putting forward before the Qualitative Sub-Committee a basic figure of 35,000 tons with a possible reduction of 2,000 or 3,000,[6] had not really hoped that that reduction would be achieved. LORD MONSELL agreed, with the qualification that the United States position on the matter seemed to have hardened recently.

ADMIRAL ROBERT suggested that a smaller tonnage would be more pleasing to Japan, upon which ADMIRAL CHATFIELD suggested that if Japan felt strongly on this matter she might well say so when the observations of the other Powers on the text were invited. ADMIRAL CHATFIELD also observed that in 1941 a much larger number of Powers would meet to discuss this matter than on this occasion and the pressure which would be put on the United States would be correspondingly greater.

LORD MONSELL felt that Mr. Norman Davis had really done his best in this matter, but agreed that all parties, except the United States, wished to get away from the figure '35'.

[5] Cf. No. 664.        [6] See *L.N.C. 1935 Docs.*, pp. 805–6.

## No. 667

*Sir E. Drummond (Rome) to Mr. Eden (Received February 22, 9.30 a.m.)*
*No. 105 Telegraphic [A 1490/4/45]*

ROME, *February 22, 1936, 8.20 a.m.*

At press conference this evening[1] official spokesman said that while discussions at Naval conference had hitherto been of a technical nature and Italian experts were returning to London after consulting the Italian Government in order to see whether an agreement was possible, the signature of any agreement that might be reached would be a political matter and in considering whether or not to sign the Italian Government would have to take into account the political situation of which sanctions were a part.

[1] This telegram was drafted on February 21.

## No. 668

*Draft[1] Record of a meeting of representatives of the United Kingdom Delegation on February 22, 1936, at 10.30 a.m.[2]*
*L.N.C. (35)(U.K.) 52 [A 1413/4/45]*

*Present*: Lord Monsell, Admiral of the Fleet Sir E. Chatfield, Mr. Craigie, Sir W. Malkin, Captain Danckwerts, Mr. Coxwell, Mr. Holman, Mr. Gore-Booth.

LORD MONSELL opened the proceedings by enquiring whether Mr. Norman Davis would accept the Draft Resolution (see Annex I). If the other Powers accepted, it was presumed that the United States Delegation, who had really secured all they required, would not stand out.

MR. CRAIGIE stated that he preferred the Draft Protocol[3] in some form, in view of its more binding character. Without some such instrument it was always possible that, when Delegations returned to their countries, pressure of public opinion might lead Governments to change their views. He presumed, however, that the French would not accept the Protocol. He pointed out that the views of the German Government on the Draft Treaty provisions had not yet been received. It would be difficult for Germany to come into a Treaty which had already been signed by the Four Powers. If Germany accepted the terms of the Draft Treaty and raised no difficulties about signature, it might be better from the point of view of His Majesty's Government to sign with a reservation that it would not be ratified by them until Germany had also become a party. In any case it was undesirable for His Majesty's Government to commit themselves too far until the German reply, which was expected on February 24th, had arrived.

[1] The record here printed was identical with the final text except for the omission in the heading of the word 'Draft' and the addition of 'Final Copy'.

[2] This meeting was held in the First Lord's room at the Admiralty.

[3] Cf. No. 652, enclosure 2.

ADMIRAL CHATFIELD agreed, provided that Germany made no reservations as regards Russia. If Russia built 10,000 ton cruisers, Germany would certainly not accept the cruiser holiday. France would then make reservations.

LORD MONSELL felt that all Powers would then begin making reservations, and we should become quite ridiculous.

In reply to an observation by Mr. Craigie that the signed Treaty might be submitted to other Powers, SIR W. MALKIN pointed out that, in that case, in the event of observations being made, no amendments would be possible unless a new Treaty were drawn up.

MR. CRAIGIE replied that the Treaty, if signed, would remain in force, unless the amendments suggested were acceptable to all the signatory Powers. Otherwise we might lose the whole Treaty.

ADMIRAL CHATFIELD felt that if we signed the Treaty now we should simply put up the backs of Russia, Germany and Japan and of other naval Powers. If, on the other hand, the draft Treaty was submitted as a fair basis of settlement, amendments could be made. He then hinted that, if we signed the Treaty now, we might have to make a new Treaty in July in the light of the observations of other Powers.

MR. CRAIGIE expressed himself as being in favour of falling back on the Treaty with a single reservation about Germany rather than of adopting the proposed procedure.

CAPTAIN DANCKWERTS indicated that under the procedure now proposed we should have the advantage of knowing whether Japan was coming into the Treaty. We should, in addition, have definite information on the capital ship question.

The question of the wording of paragraph 3 of Annex I was then discussed. It was felt that the term 'basis for a Treaty' was not strong enough and might only lead Powers to press for amendments. The United States in particular might feel that such a term would only be an invitation to European Powers to pull the Treaty to pieces. It was considered that other Powers should simply be asked for their observations.

MR. CRAIGIE emphasised that all naval Powers should be asked for their views at the same time. He suggested that it might be easier if countries having, for example, navies exceeding 50,000 tons were alone included in the request for observations. Only Germany, Russia and Japan really concerned us and, if agreement could be reached with them, the remaining Powers might be dealt with at Geneva.

In the light of Captain Danckwerts' observation that Spain had a larger navy than Russia, MR. CRAIGIE agreed that it might be preferable to bring in all the naval Powers in order to prevent any discontent on the part of small countries. Spain indeed might have considerable nuisance value, if she were not included.

The discussion then turned on the date of the meeting of the four Powers to discuss the signature of the Treaty, etc. It was generally thought that June would be preferable. As to procedure it was decided that, as soon as agreement had been reached on the terms of the resolution with the French, the latter should be asked to approach the United States Delegation in the matter.

The meeting drafted a revised text of the resolution (see Annex II).[4] It was thought that naval Powers referred to in paragraph 3 should include all those represented on the Naval Commission at the Geneva Disarmament Convention. The United States Delegation could be told that this was really a matter of form and that we would sign the Treaty as soon as Germany, Japan and Russia had come in.

It was decided that the revised draft should be discussed as soon as possible with the French Delegation.

### ANNEX I TO No. 668

#### Suggested Procedure

The Members of the Conference would sign a formal resolution to the following effect:—

1. The Conference has reached unanimous agreement on the main problems of qualitative limitation and exchange of information, and on certain other important matters.

2. The texts attached to the Resolution embody the agreement thus reached, and constitute, in the unanimous opinion of the Conference, a satisfactory basis for a naval treaty.

3. These texts will be immediately communicated by His Majesty's Government in the United Kingdom to the Governments of Germany, Japan, and the Union of Soviet Socialist Republics, with a request for any observations which they may wish to offer, and an expression of the hope of the Conference that the texts will commend themselves to those Governments as a satisfactory basis for a treaty in which they would be prepared to join.

4. The Conference will meet again on . . .[5] to consider the observations of the Governments mentioned above, to decide, in the light of those observations, the conditions in which the definitive Treaty can be signed, to complete the text of the Treaty, and to make the necessary arrangements for its signature.

5. During the period up to . . .[5] no Government represented at the Conference will construct or acquire any naval vessels which do not comply with the limitations prescribed in the attached texts.

[4] Not here printed: it was identical with Annex I to No. 669 below.
[5] Punctuation as in the original.

## No. 669

*Record of a meeting between representatives of the United Kingdom and French Delegations on Saturday, February 22, 1936, at 12 noon*[1]

*L.N.C. (35)(U.K.) 51 [A 1413/4/45]*

PRESENT: *United Kingdom*: Mr. Craigie, Captain Danckwerts, Mr. Holman, Sir W. Malkin.
    *France*: Captain Deleuze, M. Paul-Boncour.

MR. CRAIGIE stated that a tentative effort had now been made to put something in writing as a result of the meeting in the Secretary of State's room on the previous day.[2] He then handed to the French Delegates the revised draft (Annex I) which had been drawn up in the First Lord's room that morning (see L.N.C. (35) (U.K.) 52).[3]

M. BONCOUR, after reading the draft resolution, pointed out that it expressed the views of the whole conference. Would it be possible to insert in the resolution a French reservation in the form of a unilateral expression of opinion?

SIR W. MALKIN replied that the usual procedure in such cases was for the country requiring the reservation to make the necessary statement at the meeting and have it recorded in the minutes.

MR. CRAIGIE thought that the draft would enable the French Delegation to dispense with the necessity of making a reservation, as there was no indication in the resolution as to how or when the Treaty would be signed.

M. BONCOUR pointed out that Paragraph 3 of the draft alluded to the signature of the Treaty by other Powers which would naturally include Germany. France was ready to sign a Four Power Treaty now. If Germany were referred to in the resolution, a reservation would have to be made. Without it, France could not accept the draft.

MR. CRAIGIE explained that the draft resolution would allow France time to decide as to the signature of the Treaty. It did not bind her to sign.

M. BONCOUR observed that the draft resolution was a new idea and was different from the proposed protocol which had been discussed by the French Ambassador on the previous day.

MR. CRAIGIE agreed that the protocol was binding but that the Draft resolution was an attempt to meet the French Delegation half-way in order to get over the difficulty of Germany.

M. BONCOUR stated that France would sign the Protocol but would make a unilateral reservation.

MR. CRAIGIE quite understood that as regards the Protocol the French Delegation required a reservation. The new draft resolution which had been prepared was, however, unlike the Protocol in that it provided for a meeting between the Four Powers in June to discuss the procedure for signature etc.

M. BONCOUR regretted that his instructions in regard to a French reservation covered any document containing reference to Germany. As regards the

---

[1] This meeting was held at the Admiralty.      [2] See No. 666.      [3] No. 668.

proposed date of the meeting, was it thought likely that Japan would be ready by June? He did not think that the French reservation could be abandoned before the end of the year. He quite understood the American constitutional difficulties.

MR. CRAIGIE realised that American ratification might be left over until 1937, but had always supposed that ratification in respect of other Powers would take place before the end of the year.

M. BONCOUR believed that French ratification might be effected at the end of this year or at the beginning of 1937.

MR. CRAIGIE pointed out that this was a multilateral Treaty. Would France, for example, at the time of signature of the Treaty agree not to act in any way inconsistently with the provisions of the Treaty pending exchange of ratifications?

M. BONCOUR replied in the affirmative. In response to a question as to the probable date of ratification, he explained that this was the first time the question had been raised. Ratification depended on the solution of the signature difficulty. In itself ratification presented no problem. Everything depended on the European situation. The date of signature might be in December, but there was no question of the French signing in June. He went on to say that France was quite ready to sign a Four Power Treaty straight away without Germany as the safeguarding clause was thought to cover all contingencies as far as France was concerned.

MR. CRAIGIE pointed out that for the United Kingdom advance notification and exchange of information with Germany was of real value and that a safeguarding clause was not in itself sufficient. They could not sign a Treaty, unless Germany agreed to come in. France's political position was well understood, but it was desirable if possible to avoid the necessity of political safeguards being linked up with the present question. What His Majesty's Government hoped was that France would agree to sign without her reservation, say in September, to allow the Treaty to come into force at the end of the year. The resolution was so worded that France would not be obliged to sign with any non-Washington Treaty Power, but would simply meet to discuss conditions and date of signature.

M. BONCOUR stated that France would be prepared to come to a Four Power Conference to sign whenever required, but that June was too early a date to consider the lifting of any reservation. He suggested a meeting at the end of the year or whenever the President of the Conference thought fit.

In reply to a question as to how, in the event of the Treaty being signed now, the text in the opinion of the French Delegation would be communicated to other Powers, M. BONCOUR said that His Majesty's Government should do so on their own responsibility and engage in conversations with other Powers with a view to convening an international Conference at a later date. He admitted that the other Powers would not relish the idea of being handed a signed Treaty.

SIR W. MALKIN felt that His Majesty's Government could not communicate the text of the Treaty to other Powers without a mandate from the Conference.

M. Boncour said that the French Delegation could accept the Protocol as proposed by the United Kingdom Delegation with a French reservation, certain drafting alterations and the possible omission of Part 3. The date should be left vague, but might possibly be before the end of the year.

Mr. Craigie pointed out that His Majesty's Government having convened the Conference were naturally making every effort to secure a successful issue. If, however, the Conference failed, the French Government should not forget that they would suffer just as much as anybody else. We had prepared two proposals (the Protocol and the Resolution) which the French Delegation had been unable to accept. Perhaps the best way would now be for the French to draft a text which they could accept.

The question then arose as to what precise understanding had been reached at the meeting between the French Ambassador and the Secretary of State on the previous afternoon.

M. Boncour stated that in the view of M. Corbin, the Secretary of State had accepted the idea of a unilateral reservation by France being embodied in the resolution so as to get round the difficulties.

Mr. Craigie who had not been present at the meeting, doubted whether the Secretary of State should be understood as having *accepted* the idea of a reservation.

Sir W. Malkin, who had been present, said he had no recollection of the Secretary of State having said this; the only thing which he thought had been agreed was that an attempt should be made to put the First Sea Lord's suggestion on paper, for discussion with the French Delegation.

Mr. Craigie then asked the French Delegation whether they would be good enough to draft alternative resolutions acceptable to themselves, one containing the French reservation and the other modifying the present text so as to avoid the necessity of incorporating any reservation.

## Annex I to No. 669

### Suggested Procedure

The Members of the Conference would sign a formal resolution to the following effect:—

1. The Conference has reached agreement on the main problems of qualitative limitation, advance notification and exchange of information, and on certain other important matters.

2. The articles attached to the Resolution embody the agreement thus reached, and, in the unanimous opinion of the Conference, would constitute a satisfactory naval treaty.

3. These articles will be immediately communicated by His Majesty's Government in the United Kingdom to the Governments of (the other Naval Powers) with an expression of the hope of the Conference that the agreement thus reached will commend itself to those Governments as a satisfactory basis for a treaty in which they would be prepared to join.

4. The Conference will meet again on (June 1st) to examine the replies

of the Governments mentioned above, to consider in the light of any observations they may have offered, the conditions in which the definitive Treaty can be signed, to complete the text of the Treaty, and to make the necessary arrangements for its signature.

## No. 670

### Letter from M. Paul-Boncour to Mr. Craigie
### [A 1567/4/45]

LONDON, February 22, 1936

Cher Monsieur Craigie,

Voici, pour répondre au désir que vous avez bien voulu exprimer ce matin,[1] les amendements qui devraient être apportés aux suggestions de procédure dont vous nous avez soumis le projet, pour permettre d'aboutir à la formule commune sur les bases de laquelle les Délégations française et britannique paraissaient hier soir d'accord.

Après en avoir conféré, notamment avec l'Ambassadeur, je regrette de ne pouvoir entrer dans la seconde voie que, pour votre part, vous estimiez souhaitable ce matin et qui, si je l'ai bien comprise, consisterait à trouver une formule de résolution suffisamment vague en ce qui concerne l'accession ultérieure d'autres Puissances et en particulier du Reich, pour ne plus rendre nécessaire l'insertion d'une déclaration écrite unilatérale du Gouvernement français. Croyez, Cher Monsieur Craigie, à mes sentiments toujours bien sincèrement dévoués.

J. PAUL-BONCOUR[2]

ENCLOSURE IN No. 670

### Suggestions de Procédure

Les Membres de la Conférence souscriraient à une résolution formelle aux fins suivantes:

1°) La Conférence est parvenue à un accord sur les importants problèmes des limitations qualitatives, des préavis et échanges de renseignements, ainsi que sur certaines autres questions importantes.

2°) Les articles annexés à la résolution, enregistrent l'accord ainsi obtenu et, de l'avis unanime de la Conférence, constitueraient un Traité Naval satisfaisant.[3]

3°)[4] La Conférence exprime l'espoir que l'accord auquel elle est parvenue, pourra s'étendre aux autres Puissances Navales, et que les articles annexés

---

[1] Cf. No. 669.

[2] A minute by Mr. P. Gore-Booth of February 27 reads: 'It was decided at once that the reservation made further progress along these lines impossible.'

[3] A marginal note in M. Paul-Boncour's handwriting referring to the three preceding sentences reads: 'traduction pure et simple du projet britannique.'

[4] A marginal note by M. Paul-Boncour reads: 'alinea modifié.'

à la résolution leur paraîtront offrir une base satisfaisante pour un Traité auquel elles seraient disposées à devenir parties. Elle prend acte de l'intention manifestée par le Gouvernement de Sa Majesté dans le Royaume-Uni de communiquer immédiatement lesdits articles aux Gouvernements de . . . .[5]

4°) La Conférence prend acte des déclarations unilatérales formulées par certains membres de la Conférence.

*a*)[6] Déclaration française conçue en termes appropriés pour exprimer l'idée suivante: les articles annexés à la résolution ne pourront se substituer, en ce qui concerne l'Allemagne, aux clauses navales de la Partie V du Traité de Versailles, que dans le cas et dans la mesure où, comme le Gouvernement français, des progrès substantiels se trouveront réalisés avec la collaboration de l'Allemagne dans le cadre défini par le Communiqué de Londres du 3 Février 1935, pour le renforcement de la sécurité en Europe.

(Il sera précisé verbalement que la question de la zone démilitarisée est expressément comprise dans cette formule.)

*b*) Déclaration de la Délégation de . . . .[5]

5°)[7] La Conférence se réunira de nouveau avant la fin de l'année 1936 pour examiner les réponses des Gouvernements susmentionnés; étudier à la lumière des observations qu'ils auraient pu présenter, les conditions dans lesquelles le Traité définitif pourra être signé; compléter le texte dudit Traité et prendre les dispositions nécessaires en vue de sa signature./.

[5] Punctuation as in the original.

[6] A marginal note by M. Paul-Boncour reads: 'paragraphe nouveau.'

[7] A marginal note by M. Paul-Boncour reads: 'traduction pure et simple du texte anglais, sauf la date.'

## No. 671

*Mr. Eden to Sir R. Clive (Tokyo)*

*No. 25 Telegraphic [A 1546/4/45]*

FOREIGN OFFICE, *February 24, 1936, 3 p.m.*

Japanese Chargé d'Affaires called on the 18th February to say that the Japanese Government were now prepared to consider the renewal of Article 19 of the Washington Naval Treaty[1] provided its contents were incorporated in a separate Treaty. No modifications in substance appeared to be desired.

The Chargé d'Affaires asked for United Kingdom views on this proposal. It was stated in reply that, as the Clause had originally been agreed to in return for Japanese acceptance of the 5–5–3 ratio, it was a matter for consideration whether supposing Japan did not join in a Naval Limitation Treaty, renewal of clause was still in our interests. Failure to renew the Article would admittedly result in a regrettable increase in expenditure all round. A reply was promised in due course.

The Chargé d'Affaires was told in reply to a question that we could not

[1] See No. 569.

say what the United States view would be, but at his request we undertook to inform the United States Delegation of the Japanese communication.[2]

[2] In a minute of February 19 Mr. Craigie remarked that this was 'the first clear indication we have received that Japan would like a continuation of the provisions of Article XIX'. He recalled the decision of the Cabinet on December 11 that 'on balance, the renewal of these provisions is in our interest' although 'the American attitude is more doubtful'. He added: 'The question will now arise whether, supposing the Americans are agreeable, we should proceed with the drawing up of a draft agreement on this subject or whether we should hold this in reserve until we know what Japan's decision is likely to be about participating in a naval treaty. The latter course may mean deferring any action until the end of the present year and Article XIX of the Washington Treaty of course comes to an end on the 31st December next. For this reason and also for the reason that the signature of a three-Power treaty on this subject would be most useful in paving the way for Japan's ultimate accession to a naval treaty, I am inclined to favour the first alternative. From all the information we have, Japan is not so interested in the retention of these non-fortification provisions as to be willing to pay anything for it . . .' Mr. Eden wrote: 'I agree with Mr. Craigie's admirable minute. A.E. 21st Feb.'

## No. 672

*Draft[1] Record of a meeting held in Sir W. Malkin's room at the Foreign Office on Monday, February 24, 1936, at 12 noon*

*L.N.C. (35)(U.K.) 54 [A 1413/4/45]*

PRESENT: Mr. Sargent, Mr. Craigie, Sir W. Malkin, Mr. Wigram, Captain Danckwerts, Mr. Gore-Booth.

MR. CRAIGIE showed the meeting the suggestions for procedure which had been evolved by the French Delegation as a result of the meeting recorded in L.N.C. (35) (U.K.) 51[2] (see Annex I).[3] He also gave a brief explanation of what had happened on the 21st and 22nd February as recorded in the minutes of the various meetings (L.N.C. (35) (U.K.) 50, 51, 52).[4]

MR. SARGENT felt that the French reservation killed the whole idea underlying the proposed resolution.

MR. CRAIGIE said that the French were understood to mean that they could not sign a general treaty unless the European situation permitted and that they would not be willing in any case to meet for such a signature until the end of the year. Ratification would come much later still and this would mean, in fact, that the door would be open to the French to put pressure on the Germans for the next eighteen months.

MR. CRAIGIE felt that further progress on these lines was impossible. He was now convinced that the best procedure would be to sign a four-Power treaty with no reservation being made by any Power, provided that Germany would sign a bilateral agreement with the United Kingdom immediately

[1] The record here printed was identical with the final text except for the omission in the heading of the word 'Draft' and the addition of 'Final Copy'.
[2] No. 669.    [3] Annex I was a reproduction of No. 670.
[4] Nos. 666, 668, and 669.

after the four-Power agreement. The four-Power agreement could be sent perhaps to the Disarmament Conference, with a view to enabling such Powers as wished to make observation and to sign a general Treaty toward the end of the year. The French had stated their willingness to sign a four-Power Treaty without reservation. The Germans would complain that this procedure excluded them, to which the United Kingdom could give an assurance that they would not join any general naval treaty unless Germany signed as well.

Such a procedure would, incidentally, be justifiable on the grounds that the United Kingdom have a bilateral agreement with Germany on quantitative questions, and this Agreement would thus be rounded off by a similar qualitative agreement. Naval limitation would be controlled by a general system consisting of the Treaty which would eventually take the place of the Washington and London Treaties coupled with the Anglo-German agreements.

This plan would probably not appeal to the Quai d'Orsay: on the other hand it had been suggested by M. Piétri in his talk with the First Lord on the 28th January (L.N.C. (35) (U.K.) 25, page 9).[5] If successful, it would remove from the French the possibility of putting pressure on the Germans in this matter and would secure the position of the United Kingdom.

MR. CRAIGIE agreed that the Soviet Union would not be best pleased with another Anglo-German naval agreement. The solution for this might be to offer the Soviet Union a similar agreement.

MR. SARGENT asked whether a general agreement was necessary. MR. CRAIGIE and CAPTAIN DANCKWERTS thought that political reasons made it very desirable, especially from the point of view of France and Italy.

The question of German participation in a general conference was alluded to and MR. CRAIGIE explained that Germany had given a definite refusal to take part in a conference at Geneva. They had not refused to conclude a further bilateral agreement with the United Kingdom; they would not of course wish for this to be a permanent state of affairs, but any bilateral agreement with the United Kingdom would be concluded on the understanding that it was to be the basis of a future general agreement. MR. SARGENT mentioned the possibility of an Anglo-German-American agreement, but MR. CRAIGIE felt that the Anglo-German agreement was the logical basis of anything on the lines he had suggested and that probably an agreement simply between the United Kingdom and Germany would meet the case.

MR. SARGENT enquired whether Germany would be likely to accept.

MR. CRAIGIE said that the proposal would be tempting for the Germans in that they would no longer be alone at the mercy of the French in the event of their wishing to join a general treaty.

MR. SARGENT thought that the French would certainly desire Germany to be excluded from a general treaty.

CAPTAIN DANCKWERTS said that it was essential, before a four-Power

[5] Cf. No. 636, note 2.

Treaty was signed, that the United Kingdom should have an assurance from Germany that she would come into a similar bilateral Treaty. He felt, however, that Italy would not sign a four-Power Treaty without reservation.

MR. CRAIGIE felt that, even so, the present procedure was better in the circumstances than the proposal for a conference resolution with reservations. In particular, at present the United Kingdom Delegation were being accused of delaying matters by refusing to sign a Treaty without Germany. If the United Kingdom now expressed readiness to sign and Italy alone put in reservations, she would be in a minority.

In reply to Mr. Wigram, MR. CRAIGIE said that the time to tell the French of this plan would be, in his view, if and when the Germans agreed to it. It should be put up to the Germans as soon as possible. He said that the protocol idea had been put up to them and the difficulties explained.[6] The Germans had been asked whether previous signature by the other Powers would make a difference in their case, if they had the same status as all other non-signatory Powers and whether they could agree without the adhesion of the Soviet Union. Prince von Bismarck had observed that in any case Germany must be certain that, if she expressed readiness to come in, France would agree.

MR. SARGENT and MR. WIGRAM agreed generally with Mr. Craigie's suggestions.

SIR WILLIAM MALKIN pointed out a difficulty namely that if Germany were excluded from a general agreement and this meant, as it would, non-signature by the United Kingdom and if then Japan wished to come into the general agreement, a general agreement including the United Kingdom and Japan would be impossible.

CAPTAIN DANCKWERTS suggested that the treaty now in process of negotiation might be regarded as a continuation of the Washington Treaty and therefore, *ipso facto*, open to the signature of Japan.

MR. CRAIGIE doubted whether Japan would come in except to a general treaty.

MR. CRAIGIE then discussed with Mr. Sargent the best method of putting up the new proposal to the Germans and it was agreed that, subject to the Secretary of State's assent, it would be expedient for Mr. Craigie to see the German Ambassador. At the same time, Sir E. Phipps should be kept informed.

[6] Cf. No. 647.

## No. 673

*Draft[1] Note of an informal discussion by representatives of the United Kingdom Delegation on February 24, 1936, at 5.30 p.m.[2]*

### L.N.C. (35) (U.K.) 56 [A 1413/4/45]

After the meeting with the Italians recorded in L.N.C. (35) (U.K.) 55,[3] MR. CRAIGIE went over the difficulties of the present situation with Lord Monsell and put up the suggestion which had been discussed in a meeting at the Foreign Office on the morning of the 24th (see L.N.C. (35) (U.K.) 54).[4] MR. CRAIGIE urged that the proposal of a bilateral agreement between the United Kingdom and Germany might appeal to Germany provided that she liked the terms of the treaty. It would mean in fact that she would get into the naval limitations sphere without having to pay for it. If in present conditions she were to try to come into a general Treaty, France would insist on her paying. The proposal would solve all the difficulties except the Italian, which MR. CRAIGIE thought might disappear if Italy were isolated.

ADMIRAL CHATFIELD recalled that this suggestion had been made by M. PIÉTRI. The difficulty was that Germany might refuse or at least insist on a reservation in respect of the Soviet Union.

MR. CRAIGIE hoped that Germany would be prepared to see the Soviet Union covered by the general escape-clause which in the United Kingdom case would apply particularly to Japan. Japan would of course be given the opportunity of coming into the Treaty as a Washington Power. The Soviet Union was admittedly the main difficulty which might perhaps be solved by a bilateral Anglo-Soviet agreement.

ADMIRAL CHATFIELD said that he felt Germany had something up her sleeve. Since quantitative limitation had gone by the board, adhesion to the 35 per cent ratio would be difficult for her. The 10,000 ton cruiser holiday also might well raise difficulties both from German and Soviet sides.

The discussion turned on whether it was best to make a special case of Germany or to conclude bilateral agreements all round.

LORD MONSELL hoped that it would be possible to get something definite out of Germany, and it was generally felt that everything depended on the German attitude.

ADMIRAL CHATFIELD said that the plan was acceptable to the Admiralty provided that the Four Power Treaty was agreed first. The United Kingdom must not suddenly find itself qualitatively bound by an Anglo-German agreement while the other Powers were not bound qualitatively at all.

It was agreed that the proposals might be given a trial, and that they should be kept at the present stage exceedingly confidential. It was felt important also that Germany should be approached not along the line that the United Kingdom was afraid of possible German construction but that

---

[1] The note here printed was identical with the final text except for the omission in the heading of the word 'Draft' and the addition of 'Final Copy'.

[2] This discussion took place in the First Lord's room at the Admiralty.

[3] See No. 676 below.  [4] No. 672.

the special relation established between the United Kingdom and Germany in the Anglo-German Agreement should be completed by a qualitative agreement.[5]

[5] An outline of the recent discussions with the French and Italian delegations (see Nos. 666, 668, 669, and 676 below) was given to Mr. N. Davis by Lord Monsell and Mr. Craigie on February 24. In his note on the conversation Mr. Craigie recorded: '. . . we discussed what was to happen if the French and Italians remained adamant and refused to come into a treaty. The idea of an Anglo-American-German treaty was tentatively mooted but Mr. Norman Davis thought that, in a presidential election year, it might be difficult for the United States to go into a special treaty with Germany. A bilateral Anglo-American treaty would be another matter, though even this would, Mr. Davis thought, require careful consideration. Finally, it was suggested that if we failed to get a four-Power treaty, the best method might be for this country to proceed to conclude bilateral treaties with any country ready to do so.' For Mr. Davis's account of this conversation see *F.R.U.S. 1936*, vol. i, pp. 71–72.

## No. 674

*Record by Mr. Craigie of a conversation with Captain Wassner on February 25*
*[A 1651/4/45]*

FOREIGN OFFICE, *February 25, 1936*

I asked Captain Wassner to come to see me to-day in order to hand him confidentially the draft text of the qualitative limitations proposed by the Technical Sub-Committee for all categories of ship[s] except the capital ship (L.N.C. (35) (Q.L.) (C.) 9, Annexes II and III).[1] I then explained to him fully the position reached in our recent discussions with the other Delegations, without, however, mentioning the question of the French reservation or the idea of a possible Anglo-German treaty. Captain Wassner stated that an important meeting on this subject was taking place in Berlin to-day and he expected that a reply would be forthcoming to-morrow to the enquiries in regard to the German attitude which I had made about ten days ago.[2] I also informed Captain Wassner that I was on the point of communicating to the Soviet Embassy the same information that I had already communicated to the German Embassy, so that Russia could not have a pretext for obstruction on the ground that the Soviet Embassy had not been properly informed. Captain Wassner appeared to think that this was a good move.

R.L.C.

[1] These Annexes to a draft report of February 19 of the Technical Sub-Committee on Qualitative Limitation are not printed.
[2] See No. 647.

## No. 675

*Draft[1] Record of a meeting between representatives of the United Kingdom and French Delegations on February 25, 1936, at 12.15 p.m.[2]*

L.N.C. (35)(U.K.) 58 [A 1413/4/45]

PRESENT: *United Kingdom*: Mr. Craigie, Mr. Gore-Booth.
    *France*: M. Paul-Boncour, Captain Deleuze.

MR. CRAIGIE explained that he had asked the French representatives to come in order that he might make quite clear what the Secretary of State had understood to be agreed upon at the meeting on the 21st February.[3] Mr. Eden had understood that the proposed Resolution for the Naval Conference was to be drawn up by us and that suggestions in connection with any proposed reservation were to be put forward by the French.

M. PAUL-BONCOUR said that if what the United Kingdom Delegation had drawn up had been a Resolution, there would have been no difficulty. The document, however, had been called 'Suggestions for Procedure,'[4] and in this suggested procedure, there had been no mention of the possibility of a reservation. Such a reservation would be essential to the French, and they thought that the United Kingdom Delegates had understood this.

MR. CRAIGIE said that Germany would certainly not sign anything if the reservation remained as at present. The Germans wanted an assurance that any difficulty put in the way of their signature by the French should be removed whereas apparently the French wished to reserve their position under the Versailles Treaty.

M. PAUL-BONCOUR said that they did not wish simply to do this. They wished to act in accordance with the communiqué of the 3rd February, 1935, and to seek a solution of the armaments question which would include armaments of all kinds. They had no wish to reserve rights that had become empty, but they did not wish to revise the Versailles Treaty unless Germany gave adequate political assurances.

MR. CRAIGIE asked whether the French really thought that Germany would be ready to pay to come into a Treaty and to get French signature next to hers, to which M. PAUL-BONCOUR replied 'il faut qu'elle paye'. The French people thought that France had already paid enough. The matter was much simpler from the United Kingdom point of view; the United Kingdom had signed a bilateral agreement with Germany[5] and it was up to her to do the same again. It was impossible for France to sign anything which mentioned the submission of a Treaty to other Powers. Such an action would be a concession to Germany, of which the latter would simply take advantage.

MR. CRAIGIE asked whether it would not be *mal vu* in the Soviet Union if the United Kingdom made another bilateral agreement with Germany,

[1] The record here printed was identical with the final text except for the omission in the heading of the word 'Draft' and the addition of 'Final Copy'.

[2] This meeting was held at the Foreign Office.     [3] See No. 666.

[4] See Annex to No. 669.

[5] A reference to the Anglo-German Naval Agreement of June 18, 1935.

but M. Paul-Boncour thought that the reception accorded to it would not be worse than that given last year to the provisions of the Anglo-German Agreement. He then asked whether the United Kingdom could not communicate bilaterally with all the Powers concerned.

Mr. Craigie said that this had been thought of, and it was very possible that the Soviet Union, at any rate, would have to be consulted bilaterally.

The main difficulty was that of France and Germany, and the United Kingdom wanted help to get Germany in. In particular they envisaged a general Treaty in the future so that if a Treaty were signed more or less immediately, it should definitely be signed as the basis of a general Treaty.

M. Paul-Boncour said that as far as French opinion was concerned, it was helpful to bring in Geneva at some stage and the whole subject could be aired there.

Mr. Craigie said that the important thing from the United Kingdom point of view was that if and when there was a general Treaty, Germany must participate, and the French representatives agreed that, from the technical point of view, this was obviously so. It was important, then, that if German adhesion to a general Treaty were put off at the request of France, France must do her part in trying to seek a general settlement with Germany. Such a settlement must be sought sincerely, and not along the lines that if there were no settlement there would be no Naval Treaty for Germany.

M. Paul-Boncour said that as long as France were not asked to sign a paper committing herself to consult Germany, then no reservation would be made.

Mr. Craigie said that the United Kingdom could only proceed to a signature if she knew that Germany would sign the same or an equivalent agreement.

Captain Deleuze drew attention to an article in the 'Times'[6] to the effect that the Germans had received copies of certain texts which had been agreed upon by the Conference.

Mr. Craigie said that the United Kingdom Delegation had communicated the agreed texts on advance notification and definitions to the Germans, confidentially and on their own responsibility.[7] The Germans had also been told the difficulties in connection with procedure and signature. He could not understand what was meant by the 'Times' when it said that the Germans had had a Protocol communicated to them. All that happened was that he had explained to Prince Bismarck and Captain Wassner in general terms the United Kingdom idea of a Protocol. A reply was hoped for soon.

M. Paul-Boncour said that he wished to make an observation on this point. If bilateral negotiations went through successfully as between the United Kingdom and Germany, there would be no objection, but if there were any question, arising out of the communication of these documents to the Germans, of Germany wishing to join in the general negotiations, France would feel bound to protest.

[6] Presumably in *The Times* of February 25, p. 14.    [7] See No. 647.

Mr. Craigie said that as far as he understood there was no question of the Germans even wanting to join in the negotiations at this stage. It was simply the wish of the United Kingdom Delegation to keep them informed, and it was for this reason that they also wished to inform the Germans about the proposal for the cruiser holiday. The Soviet representatives were being similarly informed.[8]

Mr. Craigie enquired whether the French had made up their minds about capital ships, to which the French representatives replied that they had still had no answer from the Americans.

M. Paul-Boncour thought that Mr. Davis had been allowed a certain latitude. Mr. Craigie very strongly doubted this especially in the light of a conversation he had had on the previous day with Mr. Davis.[9] It was, however, very possible that the Americans would have more latitude in a few years' time. Admittedly a number of large ships would have been laid down by 1940, but there was something to be said for proceeding gradually to reductions rather than attempting large reductions all at once.

Mr. Craigie added that he wished to correct a misapprehension which he believed to exist in the minds of the French to the effect that by 1940 two-thirds of the United Kingdom capital ships would have been replaced. Actually the rebuilding programme had not as yet been decided upon, and, in any case, there were many factors which might intervene to affect it.

M. Paul-Boncour said that the French were not perturbed about the size of the United Kingdom navy; their point was simply that by 1940 there would be a large number of large ships in existence.

[8] Cf. No. 674.      [9] Cf. No. 673, note 5.

## No. 676

### Minute by Mr. Craigie

### [A 2355/4/45]

Secretary of State                    FOREIGN OFFICE, February 26, 1936

I attach a record of the proceedings of the last meeting between the United Kingdom and Italian Delegations.[1] The upshot of this is that Admiral Raineri Biscia has returned from Rome with instructions to pick as many holes as possible in the technical agreement which we now propose to conclude. This he proceeded to do, adding that the Italian Delegation had not been expecting to be faced so soon with the question of signature—which was a political and not a technical matter. They had always understood that the scope of the Conference was to be extended so as to include other Powers, so that no question of signature would probably arise till the summer. Meantime, the political situation had grown worse rather than better, and there was no indication of any appreciation by the United Kingdom of the efforts by Italy to help towards a satisfactory solution of the naval problem.

[1] This record, not printed, was circulated as L.N.C. (35) (U.K.) 55. The meeting was held in the First Lord's room at the Admiralty on February 24, at 4 p.m.

In a nutshell, Italian public opinion might be persuaded to accept a disappointing agreement if the political situation were better or they might be persuaded to accept a good agreement even in the present political circumstances, but the Italian Government could not make Italian public opinion swallow a disappointing agreement while the political situation was growing worse. He said that the political side of the question was rather beyond his sphere and agreed that this had best be discussed at a meeting at which Signor Grandi could be present. He did not, however, say definitely that Italy would not sign a treaty even if the limits at present contemplated could not be reduced.

This represents a complete change of attitude: the Italians, like the rest of us, had hitherto been disappointed at the American attitude on the capital ship question, but they had appeared quite satisfied on all other points, Just before leaving for Rome[2] Admiral Raineri Biscia had said that, if all efforts to get a reduction of the capital ship failed, he believed Italy would agree to the American limits.

The reason for all this is not far to seek, namely the possibility that an oil sanction may, in the near future, be applied.[3] Undoubtedly there is some element of blackmail in this move but there is also much common sense. We must expect that, if this country takes the lead in advocating the imposition of an oil sanction and if, *a fortiori*, an oil sanction is applied, the political tension would be such that it would be genuinely difficult for the Italian Government to sign any agreement with us, however technical its provisions. I do not suggest that this should deter us from whatever action in regard to oil is thought right on other grounds, but I feel that we must give up all hope of signing the proposed four-Power treaty now if an oil sanction is imposed as the result of United Kingdom leadership at Geneva.

As I understand you are seeing the Italian Ambassador this afternoon, I am sending this minute to you in the hope that you may have time to glance at it first.

R.L.C.

[2] On February 15; see No. 656.
[3] Developments in the Italo-Ethiopian dispute at this period will be covered in a subsequent volume in this Series.

## No. 677

*Mr. Eden to Sir G. Clerk (Paris)*
*No. 370 [A 1631/4/45]*

FOREIGN OFFICE, *February 26, 1936*

Sir,

During the course of a conversation this afternoon the French Ambassador spoke to me about the Naval Conference. He asked whether I had any information that the Italians were now going to make difficulties with regard to sanctions. I replied that I had not yet seen Signor Grandi, but that a meeting had been arranged for tomorrow. M. Corbin said that Signor

Grandi had said to him that he hardly thought Italy would be able to sign a naval agreement in present conditions, but he implied that the other three Powers might go on and sign. To this M. Corbin had rejoined that soon France would be signing alone.

2. The Ambassador then made a reference to a report which he had seen in the press that His Majesty's Government might be considering negotiating a separate agreement with Germany and thus avoiding the problem of Germany's present signature of the Treaty.[1] I replied that we were considering this matter in our desire to obtain a naval agreement, and I knew that the French Government had always hoped for a solution in this form. But I was not yet certain that we should be able to pursue this course; still less was I certain that the German Government would accept it. The Ambassador intimated that if this were the procedure finally decided upon, and if the German Government agreed, he hoped that he might be informed a short while before the matter was made public, so that he might warn his Government.[2]

I am, &c.,

ANTHONY EDEN

[1] Cf. No. 672 and No. 673, note 5.

[2] Viscount Monsell told the Cabinet at a meeting on February 26 that the Naval Conference was rapidly approaching its conclusion and that the main difficulty remaining 'was on the question of how the agreements were to be registered'. France 'found it very difficult to sign anything before their General Election in May. Italy said, in effect, that it was difficult for her to sign while sanctions were in force, though possibly this might be got over. In that event, if he could induce the Four Powers to sign an agreement without involving any promise that other Powers should sign it later, it might be possible to achieve success. The trouble was that a Four Power Agreement was of no use to us unless Germany and Japan adhered to it, more particularly owing to the danger lest they should combine to act against the Treaty. Consequently he wanted to try another method which had been rejected earlier, i.e. to get the signature of the Four Powers now and to try and obtain the signature of Germany, Russia and Japan by means of bi-lateral agreements.' It was hoped, however, later to secure a single document signed by all the Powers concerned. Mr. Eden agreed that the proposed procedure was a possible one. The Cabinet authorized them to proceed on the lines proposed.

No. 678

*Letter from Captain Wassner to Mr. Craigie*

[*A 1731/4/45*]

GERMAN EMBASSY, *February 26, 1936*

Dear Mr. Craigie,

I have the pleasure to forward to you the answer of the German Government concerning the British Memorandum of January 25th, 1936.[1]

I am

Yours sincerely,

E. WASSNER

[1] No. 635.

869

*Translation*[2]                                    BERLIN, *February 19, 1936*

The German Government have taken note of the British Government's memorandum of 25.1.1936. They observe with satisfaction that an understanding has now been reached between the two Governments on all questions under discussion and that with the assent of the German Government to the said memorandum of the British Government dated 25.1.1936, the negotiations relating to the practical application of the Anglo-German Naval Agreement have been brought to a conclusion in a friendly spirit.

The German Government adopt the following attitude in the matter of the various paragraphs of the note of 25.1.1936:—

I. As regards (2).—The German Government note that the British Government maintain their views relating to transfer and adjustment, but nevertheless agree to the proposals in the German memorandum of 23.XI.35[3] (No. III) relating to the application, term and amount of the adjustments.

II. As regards (3).—Noted.

III. As regards (4).—The German Government agree to the British Government's proposal relating to the replacement of the cruisers *Emden* to *Nürnberg*.

The cruisers *Emden* to *Nürnberg* can accordingly be scrapped at the ages given below and be substituted by tonnage moving up into the permanently over-age category:

|            |    |        |
|------------|----|--------|
| *Emden*     | 20 | years  |
| *Karlsruhe* | 20 | ,,     |
| *Königsberg* | 21 | ,,    |
| *Köln*      | 21 | ,,     |
| *Leipzig*   | 22 | ,,     |
| *Nürnberg*  | 20 | ,,     |

[2] This is the Foreign Office translation of the original German document.
[3] See No. 526, note 5.

## No. 679

*Mr. Eden to Sir E. Phipps (Berlin)*
*No. 32 Telegraphic [A 1638/4/45]*

FOREIGN OFFICE, *February 27, 1936, 7.15 p.m.*

My despatch No. 185.[1]

The German Ambassador, accompanied by Counsellor and Naval Attaché, saw members of the United Kingdom Delegation headed by the First Lord of the Admiralty and myself yesterday.[2]

[1] Of February 14, enclosing a copy of No. 647.
[2] This meeting was held in the Secretary of State's room at the Foreign Office at 5.45 p.m. on February 26.

The Ambassador said that the German Government was ready to sign later a Treaty which would be signed now by all the Washington Powers except Japan.[3] Their concurrence, however, was dependent on its being operative in the same manner for all signatory States, and on the principal maritime Powers, and especially the U.S.S.R., participating in it.

It was explained to the Ambassador that, while this attitude of the German Government was appreciated, it had now been ascertained that either of the procedures previously suggested to the German Embassy would entail an explicit French reservation in respect of Germany's accession, something which both the United Kingdom and Germany would wish to avoid. In fact, any procedure providing *at the moment* for the negotiation of a general treaty to which all naval Powers would be parties would, in the French view, inevitably call for such a reservation. The United Kingdom Delegation had, therefore, been considering yet another possible solution which they would like the German Ambassador to put up to his Government. This was that immediately after the signature of an agreement between the Washington Powers, excluding Japan, the United Kingdom and Germany should sign a bilateral agreement on qualitative limitation which should be in the same terms as the treaty signed by the Washington Powers. The following further considerations were urged:—

(1) Such an agreement would be in effect a rounding off of the Anglo-German Quantitative Agreement of 1935.

(2) The Treaty concluded between the Washington Powers would only be a prelude to a general treaty to be signed, it was to be hoped, towards the end of the year. The United Kingdom Delegation gave the assurance that the United Kingdom would not sign this general treaty if any difficulties should, when the time came, be placed in the way of German participation on a full equality with every other signatory. This procedure was not being urged on Germany for the reason (suggested by the German representatives) that Germany was not considered worthy to sign a general agreement but simply as a next step pending the negotiation of a general naval treaty, to which Germany would, of course, be a party.

(3) The United Kingdom would be ready to invite the Soviet Union to conclude a similar bilateral agreement so that the latter Power would be bound in a manner similar to Germany. Germany would thus be on an equality with all the non Washington Powers.

The Ambassador promised to consult his Government on these points but felt that the proposal might be difficult of acceptance since it appeared once more to create a special régime to be applicable to Germany only—an implication which we did not admit. On the other hand the German representatives appeared to be impressed by the fact that under a bilateral

---

[3] The German Government's views on this point had been set out in a memorandum, here printed as an Annex to this telegram, which was communicated by the German Embassy before the meeting. See *D.G.F.P.*, Series C, vol. iv, No. 585.

agreement they would only disclose their building plans to the United Kingdom and not to the other naval Powers with whom they had no Treaty.

If you think it would be helpful you should reinforce in the appropriate quarter the arguments used with the German Ambassador here. The matter has been made more difficult by the press having published a forecast of the plan before it was communicated to the Germans[4] and it was understood from the German Ambassador that, as a consequence, the first impression of the Minister for Foreign Affairs had been unfavourable. Possibly this may have been due to his belief that the proposed bilateral agreement was to be a final arrangement, whereas it is actually only envisaged by us as a step towards the general agreement which we hope to secure later in the year.

Copy of the minutes of the meeting[5] and of the memorandum communicated by the German Ambassador follow by Bag.

Annex to No. 679

*Memorandum communicated by the German Embassy*

[*A 1638/4/45*]

*Translation*                    German Embassy, *London, February 26, 1936*

The German Government have examined the draft texts communicated on the 12th February, 1936[6] viz., the 'Draft Text of a Treaty prepared by the Technical Sub-Committee on Advance Notification and Exchange of Information' with 'Supplementary Report,' 'Annex II,' which was likewise circulated, and the 'Lowest Qualitative Limits on which there appears to be Prospect of obtaining General Agreement, having regard to the Views expressed in the Course of the Bilateral Conversations which preceded the Present Conference.'

The German Government are, in principle, prepared to accede to a naval treaty valid as from the 1st January, 1937, and concluded on the basis of these texts. As regards ships laid down prior to the 31st December, 1936, the Anglo-German Naval Agreement of the 18th June, 1935, is accordingly exclusively applicable. The German Government must, however, make their concurrence in the future naval treaty dependent on its being operative in the same manner for all signatory States, and that the principal maritime Powers, and especially the U.S.S.R., participate in it.

On this condition the German Government consent that after prior agreement regarding the items still unsettled the treaty shall be adopted by the Powers taking part in the present London Naval Conference, and that afterwards Germany and the other maritime Powers shall be invited by them to accede to the treaty.

[4] Cf. No. 677, paragraph 2.
[5] Not printed. They were circulated as L.N.C. (35)(U.K.) 61. For Herr von Hoesch's report see *D.G.F.P., op. cit.*, No. 589.
[6] Cf. No. 647.

872

The German Government beg to make the following observations in regard to the details of the drafts:—

(1) The German Government agree in principle to the 'Draft Text of a Treaty prepared by the Technical Sub-Committee on Advance Notification and Exchange of Information' with 'Supplementary Report.' In doing so they assume, however, that article 3 of this draft and article 3c of the 'Supplementary Report' do not affect the validity of article 6 of the thirteenth convention of The Second Hague Conference of the 18th October, 1907, regarding the rights and duties of neutrals in the event of maritime warfare.

(2) *Annex* II, *Definition and Age Limits of Combatant Vessels:*—

No. I: *Standard Displacement.*

The text is agreed to.

### No. II: *Categories.*

The German Government agree to the definitions of categories. They would, however, observe with reference to the Anglo-German Naval Agreement the following:—

By the Anglo-German Naval Agreement, No. 2 (*a*), only the naval forces then 'defined by treaty' were limited in a quantitative sense, that is to say:—

Battleships, aircraft carriers, A cruisers, B cruisers, destroyers and submarines.

The above categories are comprised in the draft of the new naval treaty in Nos. II, 1, 2, 3 and 7. The German Government agree without reservation to the said items.

In Nos. II, 4, 5 and 6, those ships are included which correspond to the 'exempt ships' dealt with in article 8 of the London Treaty of 1930.

No quantitative limitation was contemplated as regards these ships in the Anglo-German Naval Agreement. In future, Germany is, consequently, not subject to quantitative limitation, that is, the ratio of 35 per cent. to the corresponding British vessels, in respect of these ships.

(*b*) In Nos. II, 4 and 5, of the draft of the new naval treaty the surface fighting vessels of 600 tons standard displacement and below, which are mentioned in the London Treaty of 1930 under article 8a, are not specified. This is entirely intelligible, since the four Powers which have drawn up the draft treaty under examination are not bound quantitatively, and vessels which would have fallen under article 8a of the London Treaty can be constructed by them and charged to the tonnage of the other light surface ships.

Germany, on the other hand, is the sole maritime Power to be quantitatively restricted, and that by the Anglo-German Naval Agreement. The German Government must therefore stipulate that the building possibilities which were afforded to Germany on the conclusion of the Anglo-German Naval Agreement, as regards warships, in accordance with article 8a of the London Treaty, shall be maintained for the future also.

873

## No. III: *Over-age.*

As regards (*a*), capital ships, the German Government feel obliged, on the signature of the treaty, to except [*sic*] from their concurrence No. III (*a*), over-age of capital ships. They consider an increase of the age of German battleships to twenty-six years to be unreasonable, since, in virtue of the quantitative limitation of Germany, other conditions apply to the replacement of battleships than in the case of all the other maritime Powers which are no longer bound in a quantitative sense.

The German Government therefore propose to the British Government that this point should form the subject of a special agreement between both Governments, and regard an age-limit of twenty years to be appropriate for German battleships.

(3) '*Lowest Qualitative Limits.*'—The German Government concur in the proposed qualitative limitations, although they would have preferred a smaller standard displacement for battleships.

As regards the A cruiser category the German Government are ready, as was agreed on the occasion of the Anglo-German naval conversations, to accept a building holiday for the duration of the treaty. Germany will utilise otherwise the remaining tonnage of 21,380 left to her in this category, and the nature of the transfer can form the subject of a later discussion between the two Governments.

## No. 680

*Draft*[1] *Record of a meeting between representatives of the United Kingdom and French Delegations on Thursday, February 27, 1936, at 5.30 p.m.*[2]

*L.N.C.* (*35*) (*U.K.*) *65* [*A 1787/4/45*]

PRESENT: *United Kingdom*: Mr. Eden, Lord Monsell, Mr. Craigie, Mr. Gore-Booth.

*France*: M. Corbin, Captain Deleuze.

MR. EDEN said that he had asked the French Ambassador to come to see him immediately after the meeting with the Italians (L.N.C. (35) (U.K.) 64)[3] in order to obtain French views on the position created by the Italian attitude. In particular he wondered whether the French would be ready to sign a Three Power Treaty.

M. CORBIN said that Signor Grandi had given him the hint as to the development which had just occurred and that he (M. Corbin) had talked the matter over with Mr. Norman Davis, who rather to his surprise, seemed ready to go ahead with a Three-Power Agreement. He himself would require more time to think it over, but it was essential to get the Italians to explain

---

[1] This record here printed was identical with the final text except for the omission in the heading of the word 'Draft' and the addition of 'Final Copy'.

[2] The meeting was held in the Secretary of State's room at the Foreign Office.

[3] The record of this meeting, held in the same room at 4.15 p.m., is not printed. Cf. No. 681.

that it was on political grounds that they would not sign. The French technical objections, at any rate in the case of the capital ship, were the same as those of the Italians. If, therefore, the Italians stood out for certain technical limits the French would have to do so as well.

M. CORBIN said that he had asked Mr. Norman Davis whether in addition to obtaining a Three-Power Agreement, it would be any use trying to persuade the Italians to come into a technical arrangement, signed by experts only. Such an arrangement would be helpful technically but would have no political implications.

LORD MONSELL said that the Italians would not be likely to do that. They had been asked whether they would state explicitly that they would do nothing to upset the present arrangement but they had not been willing to commit themselves.

MR. CRAIGIE had the impression that the Italians might be able to give some assurance and LORD MONSELL suggested that a private assurance might be obtainable.

M. CORBIN said that he had discussed an Italian-American bilateral agreement with Mr. Davis, but this hardly seemed a serious possibility.

MR. EDEN said that he felt strongly that the conferring Powers should carry on. After all, the Abyssinian affair was not eternal and, if an agreement were put off now, there would be nothing for the Italians to sign if at a later date they were ready for signature.

MR. CRAIGIE thought that if a Treaty were agreed between three Powers, and Germany adhered, the Italian technical difficulties might disappear.

M. CORBIN said that he would like to ask Signor Grandi whether in fact the Italian difficulties were not political.

MR. EDEN felt that it was impossible to prevent the Italians from giving whatever reasons they like for unwillingness to sign the Treaty.

M. CORBIN objected that if the Italians' reasons for not signing were technical, they would be no more willing to sign later.

MR. EDEN supposed that the technical difficulties might seem less if the political situation improved.

M. CORBIN thought that the word 'procedure' in the Italian explanation of their unwillingness to sign meant nothing.[4]

MR. CRAIGIE thought that the political situation was such that the Italians had to postpone signature. On the other hand the Italians were anxious not to say as much since, if they did, it would look like blackmail and their refusal to sign would be connected with the forthcoming meeting at Geneva on the sanctions question. It was possible of course that when it came to a

[4] The last paragraph of L.N.C. (35) (U.K.) 64 (see note 3) read: 'It was agreed that the press should be informed that Italy was not ready to sign a Treaty now owing to technical difficulties, including the 35,000 ton capital ship and the "gap" [i.e. suggested zone of no construction of either cruisers or battleships between certain tonnage limits; cf. No. 685 below], and to difficulties of procedure. The word "procedure" was chosen as adequately covering the political side of the question without explicitly mentioning the more provocative word "political".'

more official statement of view, the Italians might lay more stress on the political side.

M. Corbin said that on technical grounds the Italians either wanted the Treaty or not. When they said that they wanted delay, it meant that they wanted compensation and they should be called upon to explain their attitude.

Mr. Craigie said that the moment for signature had come upon the Italians more abruptly than they expected; they had wanted longer to think over the procedure question.

M. Corbin said that for that matter France had also expected a later date for signature.

Mr. Craigie pointed out that if nothing were signed at an early date there would never be an agreement at all. On the other hand, it was necessary that an assurance should be obtained from Italy that she would do nothing inconsistent with the Treaty. He was convinced that the Italians intended to come in later.

M. Corbin did not see how if some agreement were signed now, this would result in Italian technical difficulties disappearing.

Lord Monsell asked what harm the Italians could do if they did not come in or give any assurance.

Mr. Craigie said that they would not probably build any more capital ships. The only danger was the construction at some date of battle cruisers of, say, 17,000 tons but even these would not be ready for three or four years.

M. Corbin asked whether the Italians proposed to leave the Conference.

Mr. Craigie answered that they would stay and help work out the best agreement possible, but they had declared themselves not ready to sign it.

In reply to Captain Deleuze, Mr. Craigie explained that the technical difficulties referred to by the Italians were the 35,000 ton ships and the 'gap'. He felt, however, that if the 'gap' were accepted by everybody else it would be accepted by Italy.

Mr. Eden repeated that the work of the Conference must not be allowed to stop and M. Corbin agreed.

Lord Monsell thought that if this Conference failed it would probably be the last.

Mr. Craigie felt that if France, the United States and the British Commonwealth could go ahead technical difficulties could be got rid of.

In this connection M. Corbin said that there was still no official answer from the United States on the capital ship. He had told Mr. Norman Davis that something must be produced which would show clearly an idea of reduction.

Concluding, M. Corbin said that he would think over the whole situation most carefully and especially the idea of a Three Power Agreement.

## No. 681

### Mr. Eden to Mr. Ingram[1] (Rome)
#### No. 239 [A 1723/4/45]

FOREIGN OFFICE, *February 27, 1936*

Sir,

Signor Grandi asked to see me this evening[2] on the subject of the Naval Conference. He stated that when the two Delegations met officially round the table he would explain the technical reasons on account of which the Italian Government were not yet ready to sign a naval treaty. These were his instructions and he would of course carry them out. Before doing this, however, he wished to speak to me confidentially about the real position in which the Italian Government found itself. It was really not possible for Signor Mussolini to sign a naval agreement at this moment. The Ambassador knew that it was often imagined in democratic countries that a Dictator could do as he wished. This, however, was far from being true. A Dictator was also dependent upon his public opinion, indeed he had an election every day. In these circumstances it must be clear to me that it was not possible for Signor Mussolini to sit down at a table with the representatives of the United States, France and Great Britain and sign a treaty just now. Signor Mussolini thought, however, that it would be undesirable on many grounds to say this and he had decided that it was better to base his refusal on such technical grounds as the size of battleships and the gap in respect of cruiser construction.

2. I remarked that I was sorry to hear what Signor Grandi had reported to me. Hitherto, despite the differences between Italy and the League over the Abyssinian issue, the Italian Government had co-operated in the international sphere, more particularly had their delegation been helpful at the Naval Conference. This attitude, therefore, constituted a departure and I regretted it. Moreover, I did not quite appreciate the reason for what appeared to be a somewhat sudden change in the Italian attitude. If the reason was really political and connected with the imposition of sanctions, these had been in force for many months past and yet the Italian delegation had participated in all the labours of the Naval Conference. Signor Grandi in reply contended earnestly that the Italian Government had not, in fact, changed its attitude. He quoted from his own speech at the opening of the Conference and from the speeches of Admiral Raineri-Biscia in an attempt to prove his contention. The truth, he thought, was that the Italian Government in entering upon the Naval Conference had not anticipated that the Conference would be over so soon or that the Italo-Abyssinian conflict would take so long. The Ambassador himself hoped very much that it would still

[1] Counsellor in H.M. Embassy at Rome acting as Chargé d'Affaires during the absence of the Ambassador.

[2] Mr. Eden and Lord Monsell had a conversation with Signor Grandi immediately preceding the official meeting at 4.15 p.m.; see No. 680, note 3. Cf. *F.R.U.S. 1936*, vol. i, p. 75.

be possible for the Italian Government to sign the treaty, in fact he was confident that they would be able to, but not at present. We must allow time for the political situation to be sufficiently improved to give Signor Mussolini the necessary justification to over-ride the difficulties that his experts would make on technical grounds. Frequently in the past Signor Mussolini had overridden his advisers in matters of this character, but at the present moment this was not possible.

I am, &c.,

ANTHONY EDEN

## No. 682

*Mr. Eden to Sir E. Phipps (Berlin)*

*No. 251 [C 1257/4/18]*

FOREIGN OFFICE, *February 27, 1936*

Sir,

The German Ambassador came to see me this afternoon and stated that he wished first to speak about the Naval Conference. He said he had faithfully reported by telegram his conversation of yesterday with the First Lord and myself,[1] and had also telephoned to Baron von Neurath in the matter this morning. The Ambassador added that he was not yet, however, in a position to give us the German answer, but he felt that importance should be attached to one of the conditions which he had mentioned yesterday. The German Government would, he thought, scarcely find it possible to agree to 26 years for the age of capital ships. If this could be reduced to 20 years it would much facilitate the situation. There were two arguments which he wished to impress upon me in connexion with this German request: first, that Germany alone had accepted a quantitative limitation. Therefore, whereas other countries could build a new battleship whenever they liked and keep their old ones for 26 years, Germany would have to include her old battleships in the quota allowed to her. The second reason was that since Germany's battleships would all be virtually of the same age, it would be specially difficult for her if she could replace none of them until they were 26 years of age. This would mean that Germany would have at a given period a very old fleet indeed. The Ambassador added that he had received no instructions to make this matter a condition, but that in his own view he thought it very likely that it would be one, and therefore he begged me to assist him to meet his Government's requirements in this respect. . . .[2]

I am, &c.,

ANTHONY EDEN

[1] See No. 679.

[2] The remaining six paragraphs of this despatch, dealing with the general European situation, are here omitted.

## No. 683

*Sir E. Phipps (Berlin) to Mr. Eden (Received February 28, 6.35 p.m.)*
*No. 42 Telegraphic [A 1735/4/45]*

BERLIN, *February 28, 1936, 6.20 p.m.*

Your telegram No. 32.[1]
At present stage I feel that my intervention here would only confuse matters.

[1] No. 679.

## No. 684

*Sir G. Clerk (Paris) to Mr. Eden (Received February 29)*
*No. 96 Saving: Telegraphic [A 1736/4/45]*

PARIS, *February 28, 1936*

In the course of an interview this morning, Minister for Foreign Affairs asked me what I thought of the latest attitude taken up by the Italians as regards the Naval Conference. I said that it was difficult for me to express any opinion as I had had no official information of the very latest developments, but, basing my conclusions on purely unofficial, not even semi-official, information which had been conveyed to me, I had arrived at the impression, possibly quite erroneous, that the Italian Ambassador in London had given you to understand that the final attitude of Italy, as regards the Naval Conference, depended to a great extent on what happened at Geneva next week. Monsieur Flandin said that my Italian colleague here had been more direct. Monsieur Cerruti had been to see him, and told him, with considerable solemnity, that if the Geneva meeting resulted in an embargo on oil, Italy would leave the League of Nations and would reserve to herself full liberty to consider the diplomatic situation.

## No. 685

*Record by Mr. Craigie of a conversation with Signor Grandi*
*[A 1926/4/45]*

FOREIGN OFFICE, *February 28, 1936*

I lunched with Signor Grandi to-day and had the opportunity of some conversation on the naval question. Admiral Raineri Biscia was also present.

In reply to my enquiry as to whether Italy would be prepared to continue to participate in the technical work of the Conference, the answer was 'Yes'. The Italian Delegation would, however, have to reserve their position if the rest of the Conference were to decide on the present capital ship limits or on the insertion of a 'gap' between capital ships and cruisers.[1] Privately, Admiral Raineri Biscia intimated that, should it be impossible further to

[1] Cf. No. 680, note 4.

879

reduce capital ship limits, Italy would have no objection to those at present proposed once the political situation had been eased. The same, he thought, would apply to the 'gap', provided that the limits of the 'gap' were not placed too wide (I think he had in mind a gap of 10,000 tons to 15,000 tons).

I then asked whether it would not be possible in future to place a little more emphasis on the question of 'procedure' and a little less emphasis on the question of the capital ship difficulty, seeing that the appearance of Italian intransigeance [*sic*] on the question of the capital ship must obviously make it more difficult for France to accept the limits now under consideration. Signor Grandi saw the difficulty and said that the Italian Government would wish to do nothing to obstruct France's acceptance of the treaty. He considered, however, that it would be a mistake to emphasise the political side of the question.

Finally, I enquired whether the Italian Delegation could not give us some assurance that, in the event of the treaty being signed by three Powers, the Italian Government hoped to be able to come into the treaty as soon as the European political situation made this possible; and that, in the meantime, Italy would do nothing inconsistent with the treaty. Signor Grandi said that it was quite impossible for the Italian Delegation to go further on this point than they had already gone in the conversation with the United Kingdom Delegation on the 27th instant.[2] Signor Grandi had, in fact, only carried out two-thirds of his instructions so as to meet us as far as possible. He said it would be a mistake to try to press the Italian Government further at the moment, but both he and Admiral Raineri Biscia felt sure personally that, once the political situation were eased, we need anticipate no further difficulties from Italy. Signor Grandi summed up the situation as follows: Signor Mussolini had often overruled the Ministry of Marine in the past and would do so again in the future; the Ministry had, however, raised strong political objections with regard to the capital ship 'gap' and, in the present state of political relations, Signor Mussolini simply was not prepared to force the Italian naval authorities into line.

R.L.C.

[2] Cf. *ibid.*, note 3.


## No. 686

### *Mr. Eden to Sir R. Lindsay (Washington)*
### *No. 211 [A 1749/4/45]*

FOREIGN OFFICE, *February 28, 1936*

Sir,

Mr. Norman Davis asked to see me this evening when, after a conversation about the state of the Conference, he remarked that it might be that our two Delegations would have to face a situation where France might be unable to sign owing to Italy's refusal to do so. Mr. Davis hoped this would not arise, but suggested that we should consider our procedure against such an eventuality. Perhaps it might be possible for our two Delegations to sign a memorandum in which we would set out the terms of the Treaty and make it clear that we were prepared to sign it provided one other Power did so. This would avoid the criticism in the United States to which a purely Anglo-American agreement might be subject, namely, that it was in the nature of an alliance. It would also make it possible for Germany to sign and also any other Power which wished to do so. In any event Mr. Davis said he was most anxious that, even though our two countries were left alone, we should find some means of showing that so far as we were concerned there was a treaty which we could both sign.

2. I told Mr. Davis that if the eventuality which he contemplated were to arise, I fully agreed with him that we must carefully consider together what course we should pursue. I had not yet given any detailed consideration to this or had an opportunity to consult the First Lord about it, but my own view was that I too wished that, in any event, our two Delegations should in some way make it plain to the world that we were prepared to sign a treaty and declare also the terms of that treaty.[1]

I am, &c.,<br>ANTHONY EDEN

[1] Cf. *F.R.U.S. 1936*, vol. i, pp. 79–81.

## No. 687

*Sir R. Clive (Tokyo) to Mr. Eden (Received February 29, 10 a.m.)*
*No. 72 Telegraphic [A 1750/4/45]*

TOKYO, *February 29, 1936, 12.5 p.m.*

Your telegram No. 25.[1]

In view of Japanese initiative in making this enquiry I would invite your attention to rigorous and apparently unreasonable attitude adopted by Japanese authorities towards shipping in neighbourhood of Formosa Pescadores.[2]

[1] No. 671.

[2] A minute by Commander Maxse, of the Far Eastern Department of the Foreign Office, read: 'Presumably Sir R. Clive means that the strict measures recently taken by the Japanese authorities to prevent harmless merchant vessels approaching too closely to the coasts of Pescadores and Formosa are an indication that the Japanese are violating the terms of Article XIX of the Washington Treaty. There have been a number of these incidents, but there has been no proof that illegal fortifications are being erected . . .' Mr. Orde added: 'The Adm[iral]ty know all about the Japanese attitude to which Sir R. Clive refers. C. W. Orde 2/3.'

## No. 688

### Mr. Eden to Sir E. Phipps (Berlin)
### No. 268 [A 1758/4/45]

FOREIGN OFFICE, *February 29, 1936*

Sir,

Prince Bismarck asked to see me this morning, when he stated that he had received a reply from the German Government to our proposed procedure for the Naval Conference.[1] The German Government was in principle prepared to start negotiations with a view to concluding a bilateral Anglo-German Treaty which should be based (*a*) on the texts agreed to in the Naval Conference in London; (*b*) on those stipulations which the German Government regarded as necessary as the outcome of the working of the Anglo-German Naval Treaty signed last summer.

2. Prince Bismarck explained that the most important of these stipulations was that which was concerned with the age of battleships.

3. The German Government had made this reply in a desire to help the Conference to reach a better conclusion, but on no condition must the attitude of the German Government be interpreted as accepting the French thesis which that Government had proposed to mention in their reservation.

4. Finally, the German Government stated that the proposals to be embodied in the new Anglo-German bilateral agreement could only come into effect if similar proposals were agreed to by other Naval Powers and Russia.

5. I thanked Prince Bismarck for his message and for the assistance which the German Government were thus bringing to the work of the Naval Conference. I asked him, however, if he could explain what was meant by the last condition made by the German Government. What were the 'other naval Powers'? Did this condition mean that Germany would not sign unless Italy and Japan did so? If so, I feared this condition might be a very important one. Prince Bismarck replied that the text of his telegram said no more than 'other naval Powers' and this matter would no doubt have to be discussed if and when negotiations were opened. He thought Germany's chief preoccupation, however, was that she did not wish to sign a further agreement unless the limitation were fairly widely accepted.

I am, &c.,
ANTHONY EDEN

[1] Cf. *D.G.F.P.*, Series C, vol. iv, No. 596.

## No. 689

### Record by Mr. Craigie of a conversation with Mr. Atherton
### [A 1954/4/45]

FOREIGN OFFICE, *March 2, 1936*

Mr. Atherton called to see me to-day to have a private talk about the present situation in the naval discussions. He said that his Delegation was becoming restive,[1] that the American press were beginning to say that the Conference was losing itself in political questions in which an American Delegation had no part, and that a resolution had already been submitted to Congress urging the early return of the Delegation. In the circumstances, the Delegation felt they ought to leave London on the 12th instant. In answer to my enquiry whether, supposing the prospects were at that time hopeful, they would nevertheless leave the Conference in the air, Mr. Atherton replied smilingly that he thought that was unlikely. After mentioning the negotiations with the French on the capital ship question, Mr. Atherton said that if the French did not come into a treaty he was doubtful whether the idea of an Anglo-American treaty would appeal to the United States in present circumstances. But I gathered that no final decision had been taken on this point.

He then mentioned to me privately that there was a feeling in the naval section of the Delegation that, after securing American agreement for the cruiser 'holiday' we had not given the United States Delegation as much support on the capital ship question as they were entitled to expect. I replied that I was glad to have the opportunity to discuss this point, as I had heard other reports to this effect. In fact, however, I felt that our Delegation had gone to the extreme limit in trying to help on a solution of the capital ship question acceptable to the United States, seeing that we ourselves were so anxious for lower limits. At no time had it been indicated from our side that we could *support* the United States Delegation in holding out for the high capital ship limits. All we had said was that as these limits apparently represented their last word, we would not join with the French and Italians in bringing further pressure to bear for reduction at this time, although we still insisted strongly that provision should be made for possible reduction in three or four years' time. Far from bringing any pressure to bear on the United States Delegation in this matter, we had done our best to persuade the French and Italian Delegations to accept the 35,000 ton limit with the 14" gun and had incurred a good deal of odium for our pains. Mr. Atherton suggested that it might be a good thing if, should a suitable opportunity occur, the First Sea Lord would have a friendly talk on the subject with Admiral Standley.

R.L.C.

[1] Cf. *F.R.U.S. 1936*, vol. i, p. 74.

## No. 690

*Record by Mr. Craigie of a conversation with Signor Grandi on March 2*
[*A 2009/4/45*]

FOREIGN OFFICE, *March 2, 1936*

I had a further conversation with Signor Grandi on the naval question to-day. I said that, while the Ambassador had been careful, in his conversation with me on the 28th February,[1] not to link together the question of

[1] See No. 685.

sanctions and the question of Italy's signature of a treaty, I had an uneasy feeling at the back of my mind that the belief prevailed in Rome that our attitude on sanctions might be influenced by the new Italian decision about the Naval Conference. If so, I was sure that the Italian Government were making a serious mistake: that section of public opinion here which was most insistent on sanctions was not particularly interested in the naval treaty, which dealt with a danger only likely to arise a year or two hence; on the other hand, Italian participation in the Conference had done much to improve feeling towards Italy in this country and, by her sudden change of front, Italy was simply cutting the ground from under the feet of her friends in England.

Signor Grandi agreed with my thesis as to the probable effects of the Italian decision but said I was quite wrong in thinking that anyone in Rome hoped to influence decisions in Geneva by their attitude on the naval treaty; on the contrary, they realised that, in so far as it would have any effect on sanctions at all, that effect must be bad. The Italian Government felt, however, that if relations between the United Kingdom and Italy were now definitely to deteriorate as a result of action at Geneva, they must retain their liberty of action to build the types of ship most suitable for a small navy (not necessarily large capital ships) since they could never hope to rival the naval power of Britain. As long, however, as there remained a hope of the old friendly relations being re-established between the two countries, Italy would keep open the possibility of coming into an agreement which they recognised would be in the general interests of the world, if not necessarily to Italy's own advantage from a technical point of view.

In reply to my observation that it was difficult to understand how Italy could gain from the re-establishment of unlimited competition, Signor Grandi replied that each country must, of course, be judged [? judge] as to where its interests lay. There was a school in Italy which was strongly opposed to the building of capital ships and which considered that the construction of the two 35,000 ton Italian ships had been a capital error.

I asked for Signor Grandi's private opinion as to whether it might be worth while reviving this question of Italian signature after the meeting of the Committee of Eighteen,[2] should no decisions of outstanding importance have been taken meanwhile at Geneva. The Ambassador expressed the personal view that it would be worth while doing so in such circumstances but that of course it was impossible to speak with any assurance as the situation changed from day to day.

I also told the Ambassador of the interview which Sir Eric Drummond had had with Signor Mussolini on the 18th February (Rome telegram No. 88[3] of February 18th) in which the latter had stated that he entirely concurred in our view as to the uselessness and indeed danger of pressing the United States any further as regards the size of capital ships. We had concluded from this interview that Italy was in general agreement with us on

---

[2] i.e. the Committee appointed to organize sanctions against Italy in connexion with developments in the Italo-Ethiopian dispute.      [3] See No. 660.

this important question and the change in attitude therefore seemed all the more abrupt. Signor Grandi replied that it was precisely in the last fortnight that the political situation had grown so much worse, reports having reached Rome from a number of capitals to the effect that more severe sanctions were to be imposed at Geneva. The change of attitude was therefore due to the fear that, when the date for signature arrived, the political tension might be such that signature by Italy would be out of the question.

R. L. CRAIGIE

## No. 691

*Record by Mr. Craigie of a conversation with Herr von Hoesch on March 3*
*[A 1927/4/45]*

FOREIGN OFFICE, *March 3, 1936*

The German Ambassador having asked to see me, I called on him to-day on my way to see M. Corbin.[1] He said he wanted to clear his mind as to the present position of the negotiations. Germany was ready to conclude a bilateral treaty with the United Kingdom provided that other naval Powers and, in particular, the U.S.S.R., accepted corresponding obligations, and provided His Majesty's Government were prepared to accept the various proposals made in the German memorandum of the 26th February,[2] particularly that relating to the age of capital ships. Might he take it that on this last point there was now agreement in principle?

I said I knew that the First Lord was anxious to have a talk with the Ambassador on this question as soon as possible. We were engaged in trying to find some formula which would preserve the 26 year life as the rule for all Powers, but which would at the same time put Germany on exactly the same basis as other Powers as regards the replacement of her capital ship tonnage. We hoped to be in a position shortly to discuss this formula with the Ambassador. None of the other points raised in the German memorandum gave rise to any difficulty.

Herr von Hoesch then asked whether I thought any difficulties were likely to be raised by Soviet Russia. I said we had not yet actually invited the Soviet Government to conclude a treaty since we wanted first to be reasonably sure that Germany, France and the United States were prepared to sign treaties. I thought that the difficulty with Soviet Russia would be delay in replying to an invitation rather than objection to any of the technical provisions of the proposed treaty. It would be unfortunate if such delay on the part of Soviet Russia were to be allowed to hold up the signature of both treaties and I therefore hoped that the German Government might be able to rely, so far as Russia was concerned, on the terms of the safeguarding clause, just as we were relying on that clause to deal with any exceptional construction either by Italy or by Japan. I then handed to the Ambassador

[1] See No. 692 below.          [2] Annex to No. 679.

the United Kingdom draft of the safeguarding clauses,[3] explaining their purpose and saying that they had not yet been discussed with the other Delegations, who would no doubt have amendments to propose.

As regards the question of a reply to the German memorandum of the 26th February, I thought the best way would be to defer this until we had agreed with the Ambassador as to what its terms should be. The two memoranda could then go on record of the understanding reached by the two Governments on the points in question. Herr von Hoesch agreed that this would be the best course.

R.L.C.

[3] Not printed. For the final text see Articles 24, 25, and 26 of the Naval Treaty: *L.N.C. 1935 Docs.*, pp. 15–17.

### No. 692

*Record by Mr. Craigie of a conversation with M. Corbin on March 3*

*[A 1999/4/45]*

FOREIGN OFFICE, *March 3, 1936*

I called on M. Corbin to-day to discuss the position reached in the naval negotiations. I said that when he last discussed this question with the Secretary of State and the First Lord[1] the Italians had only just informed us that they could not for the present sign a naval treaty, so that we were only able to have at that time a tentative discussion as to future procedure. I was now able to inform the Ambassador that, after careful consideration, His Majesty's Government felt that the best course would be to proceed with an agreement with the United States, France and the Dominions, provided that an identical agreement could be concluded simultaneously or shortly afterwards with Germany. The three-Power agreement would, of course, remain open for signature by Italy and Japan as soon as those Powers felt disposed to come in. Had the French Government yet reached any conclusion on this question?

M. Corbin replied that his Government were anxious not to make difficulties for us in regard to this naval question and that they were therefore prepared, in principle, to come into a three-Power agreement, though there were certain points which would first require to be cleared up.

The first was as to the form of the agreement which we proposed to conclude with Germany. I said that the treaty with Germany would presumably be exactly the same as the form of the three-Power treaty. It was our hope that both treaties would ultimately be replaced by a general naval treaty, the date of such treaty being dependent to some extent on the elimination of the present difficulty between France and Germany. Our hope was that such a general treaty could be concluded at all events before the end of the present year. M. Corbin asked whether it was proposed to make any reference in either treaty to the proposed conclusion of a general treaty. I replied that I thought this might revive old difficulties and that the simplest way would probably be that, in the final procès-verbal of the Conference,

[1] On February 27, see No. 680.

886

note would be taken of the fact that His Majesty's Government proposed to conclude a bilateral treaty with Germany and that they would communicate the three-Power treaty to the League of Nations for distribution to the other naval Powers. Once the German difficulty had been got out of the way by the conclusion of an Anglo-German treaty, I did not personally see why any further conference designed to bring in the other naval Powers should not take place under the auspices of the League of Nations. M. Corbin appeared to find this procedure acceptable.

M. Corbin's second point related to the question of the inter-communication of information in regard to construction. He presumed that, unless provision were made to the contrary, information would only be communicated as between the three Powers, on the one hand, and as between Germany and the United Kingdom, on the other. Had not, however, the German Government offered last June to communicate information in regard to building programmes to other Powers on a reciprocal basis? I replied in the affirmative and said that, to the best of my knowledge, this offer still remained open. The information which we and the Germans were communicating to each other on this basis was that provided for in the London Naval Treaty and not the more extensive information provided for in the new draft treaty. It seemed to me that it might be a good beginning if France were prepared to come into this arrangement for the reciprocal communication of information on the basis of the London Naval Treaty, pending such time as the new treaty came into force. M. Corbin seemed to think that this might be possible, though not directly between Germany and France but using London as a post office, if His Majesty's Government would be prepared to undertake this task. He did not dissent from my statement that the German Government would be unlikely to communicate to France the more extended information for which the new treaty would provide until France was prepared to sign such a treaty with Germany. I added that this extended information would in any case not be exchanged before January 1st, 1937, and that it should be possible for the French to overcome before then their difficulty of a signature in company with Germany.

The third point raised by M. Corbin was the question of an air pact. It was the hope of the French Government that the conclusion of a naval agreement would be used as a means of inducing Germany to come into an air agreement. I said it would be fatal to make the conclusion of a naval agreement conditional on any assurance from Germany that she would be prepared either to negotiate or to conclude an air agreement. The Ambassador denied that there was any question of making 'conditions', but his Government felt that this opportunity should not be allowed to slip of exercising some pressure on Germany in the matter of air agreement (which, I understood, should, in the French view, include air limitation). M. Corbin had wished to discuss this question with the Secretary of State but, in his absence in Geneva, it was agreed that he should see Lord Stanhope tomorrow afternoon.

Finally, the Ambassador said that he hoped that agreement would shortly be reached between the French and American Delegations on the question of the capital ship; another meeting between the two Delegations was taking place to-day.² In this connexion it was important that the Italians should be persuaded not to put too much emphasis on the capital ship limits as one of the reasons for not signing the treaty. It would be better to state the real reason, which was the political situation. But, if any technical reason was necessary, then it would be better to concentrate on the 'gap'. This would make things easier for France. I said we entirely agreed and had already done what we could to urge this upon the Italian Delegation and would continue to do so.

In leaving, I said that the Ambassador's personal efforts to overcome difficulties and promote a naval agreement had been much appreciated by the United Kingdom Delegation.

R. L. CRAIGIE

² See *F.R.U.S. 1936*, vol. i, pp. 84–5.

## No. 693

*Letter from Mr. Craigie to Sir E. Phipps (Berlin)*
*[A 1731/4/45]*¹

FOREIGN OFFICE, *March 3, 1936*

My dear Phipps,

Since last summer we have been carrying on a correspondence with the German Govt., via the German N[aval] A[ttaché] here, with a view to settling the various details of the practical application of the Anglo-German Naval Agreement of the 18th June 1935.

We are glad to say that agreement has now been reached on all points. The matters under discussion were highly technical and we did not trouble you with details of this corres[ponden]ce at the time. We are, however, now having the corresp[onden]ce printed and copies will be sent to you as soon as they are made.

The Germans might have made many difficulties for us over this had they wished and there is no doubt that their attitude throughout the negotiations has been fair and broad-minded.

R.L.C.

¹ Only the approved draft of this letter has been filed.

## No. 694

*Letter from Mr. Craigie to Captain Deleuze*¹
*[A 1474/4/45]*

FOREIGN OFFICE, *March 3, 1936*

Dear Deleuze,

As arranged on the telephone, I hasten to send you two copies of the draft

¹ Similarly worded letters, with enclosures, were sent on the same day to Admiral Raineri Biscia and to Mr. Norman Davis.

articles we have prepared for a safeguarding clause, to be inserted in the proposed naval treaty.[2] You will see that the latitude given by these clauses is very wide but we have felt that, in view of the uncertainty as to which of the Powers will be coming into the proposed treaty and of the fact that the imposition of qualitative limits without quantitative limits is a relatively new experiment, it is necessary to make the safeguarding clauses as wide as possible.

Article 'A' deals with the case where a Power not a party to the treaty constructs or acquires vessels which do not comply with the limitations laid down in the treaty, or, while not departing from these limitations, substantially increases the strength of its naval armaments.

The second case is where a party is engaged in war. This case is dealt with in Article 'B', which is based on Article XXII of the Washington Treaty.[3]

The third case is where a party to the treaty, while complying with its limitations, embarks on construction which another party thinks it necessary to meet by departing either from the cruiser 'holiday' or perhaps some other qualitative limit. Article 'C' is intended to cover this case and also any other circumstances which might be held to affect adversely the naval interests of a particular Power. But you will see that it provides, in the first place, that there is to be consultation between all the parties with a view to agreement as to the necessary modifications in the treaty to meet the situation. This provision should, we think, militate against the irresponsible or unnecessary invocation of this particular clause.

We shall be glad to discuss these drafts with your Delegation as soon as you have had time to study them. As soon as we have had some preliminary bilateral talks it will no doubt be desirable for the clauses to be discussed by the First Committee.

Yours sincerely,
R. L. CRAIGIE

[2] Cf. No. 691, note 3.      [3] Of February 6, 1922.

## No. 695

*Letter from Mr. Gore-Booth to Mr. Broad[1] (Washington)*
*[A 1649/4/45]*

*Confidential*                                   FOREIGN OFFICE, *March 3, 1936*

My dear Philip,

You will be receiving by this Bag under cover of an official despatch a United Kingdom Delegation memorandum describing the proceedings of the Naval Conference up to the 21st February.[2]

Since that date things have been moving fairly fast, but more on the European than the American side. As far as the latter [*sic*] is concerned, the French have still not given up hope of getting some reduction in capital ship

[1] Second Secretary in H.M. Embassy at Washington since September 1935.
[2] This memorandum of February 21, 1936, is not printed.

tonnage limitations out of the Americans, while the latter have shown no inclination to budge from 35,000 tons. There is, however, some hope of a compromise by which the United States will express their willingness to discuss reductions four years hence in such a way as to make it appear that there is a reasonable prospect of reductions resulting from those discussions. Meanwhile the United States Delegation have given us to understand that they are feeling a little restive on account of the delays which have arisen on account of the European political situation.[3]

As it is the technical work of the Conference is practically complete and the questions awaiting solution are in fact mainly political, the principal difficulties being the refusal of the French to sign without explicit reservation any document which implies later consultation with or accession by Germany, and the declaration by the Italians that they are not ready to sign any treaty at the present juncture.

We hope that we have circumvented the French difficulty by means of a proposal, which has been accepted in principle by the Germans,[4] for a bilateral Anglo-German Qualitative Agreement to be framed in the same terms as any treaty which the Conference may work out. To the Italian difficulty we can see no solution at present; it is probable that we shall try simply to push ahead with a treaty between the British Commonwealth, the United States of America and France.

Yours ever,<br>PAUL GORE-BOOTH

³ Cf. No. 689.          ⁴ Cf. No. 691.

## No. 696

*Record by Mr. Craigie of a conversation between Lord Stanhope and M. Corbin*

*[A 2112/4/45]*

FOREIGN OFFICE, March 4, 1936

M. Corbin called to-day on Lord Stanhope. Mr. Wigram and I were present at the interview.

The Ambassador began by explaining that the French Government had decided in principle to come into a three-Power naval treaty with the United States and ourselves because they knew that His Majesty's Government attached importance to this and they wished to be as helpful as possible in the matter. At the same time there were various points which still had to be cleared up and, in particular, the French Government considered that the opportunity should not be missed of bringing Germany into an air pact.

Lord Stanhope said he thought it would be undesirable to try to link the two questions together but assured M. Corbin that we were as anxious as the French Government to conclude an air pact and were ready to take further steps in the matter at the first suitable opportunity. We felt that the conclusion of the proposed naval agreement with Germany might offer a good opportunity for the opening of negotiations for an air pact. M. Corbin said he agreed, on the understanding, of course, that the air pact would not be a bilateral one but one between the Locarno Powers.

After Mr. Wigram had, in reply to the Ambassador's enquiry, recalled the recent history of the discussions for an air pact, the Ambassador said that he agreed that there should be no open attempt to link the two questions but that it would be desirable to make the German Government feel that they were obtaining some political advantage in concluding this new naval agreement with us and that, in consequence, they should now be rather more forthcoming in pursuing negotiations for an air pact.

R.L.C.

No. 697

*Record by Mr. Craigie of a conversation with M. Cahan on March 4*

[*A 2230/4/45*]

FOREIGN OFFICE, *March 4, 1936*

I asked the Counsellor of the Soviet Embassy to call on me to-day and brought up to date the information I had previously given him in regard to the proceedings of the Naval Conference. I also handed him the text of the United Kingdom draft of the safeguarding clauses,[1] pointing out that these had not yet been discussed with the other Delegations and were therefore subject to amendment.

I then stated that it had for some time been the hope of His Majesty's Government that, if it proved possible to conclude agreements with some of the Washington Powers and with Germany, a bilateral naval treaty could also be concluded with Soviet Russia. We had now for the first time the virtual certainty that these agreements would be concluded and we felt that the moment had come when the Soviet Government would be in a position to form an opinion as to what might be achieved. Before, however, the Secretary of State or the First Lord communicated to the Soviet Ambassador a formal invitation to enter into a treaty with us, I was anxious to ascertain unofficially whether such a proposal, if made, would be acceptable to the Soviet Government.

M. Cahan said that neither he nor his Ambassador had any idea as to the probable attitude of his Government on this point, but he promised to transmit my unofficial enquiry to his Government and to let me have an answer as soon as possible.

R. L. CRAIGIE

[1] Cf. No. 691, note 3.

## No. 698

*Record by Mr. Craigie of a conversation with Mr. Davis on March 4*
[A 1991/4/45]

FOREIGN OFFICE, *March 4, 1936*

I lunched with Mr. Norman Davis to-day and we had a long talk on the naval question. Mr. Davis began by explaining to me the position reached in the discussions with the French in regard to the capital ship.[1] It was not quite correct to say that the American and French Delegations had reached agreement, since the formula which the American Delegation had put up to their Government differed in some small respects from that desired by the French Delegation and the United States Government in their turn had not yet accepted the formula submitted to them. A reply was, however, expected from the United States Government to-morrow morning, in time for the proposed meeting of the Technical Sub-Committee in the afternoon. The formula submitted to the United States Government was to the effect that the maximum limit for the capital ship should be 35,000 tons. The maximum calibre of the gun would be 14″ but if all the Washington Powers had not accepted this gun calibre by the 31st December, 1936, the maximum gun calibre would automatically remain at the Washington limit of 16″. In 1940 discussions would take place through the diplomatic channel with a view to ascertaining whether agreement might be possible to reduce these limits for the displacement of the gun calibre of the capital ship. (It will be noted that this proposal very closely resembles the formula which the United Kingdom Delegation put forward some weeks ago.)[2]

Mr. Norman Davis then spoke about the period of validity of the proposed treaty. The American Delegation were coming round to the view that six years was as long a period as it would probably be wise to attempt to cover in the present agreement—with rapid changes in technical developments it was extremely difficult to foresee what might happen as far as ten years ahead. Furthermore, the big cruiser 'holiday' would come to an end in 1942, and, while the American Delegation did not wish to insert a special provision for reconsideration of this point before then, the question would automatically come up for reconsideration if the period of validity were to be restricted to six years and provision were made for the holding of the next conference in 1941. I said that the main reason that we favoured the longer period (ten years) was to avoid the multiplication of naval conferences and the chances of recrimination which they provided. Perhaps it might be possible to provide for an initial period of validity of six years with the possibility of extension for a further term of four years, should all the parties to the treaty so agree. Mr. Norman Davis said he thought his Delegation would agree to this.

Mr. Davis then observed that the naval section of his Delegation had been much worried about the relationship between the 'holiday' in big cruiser construction and the United Kingdom programme for the expansion of

---

[1] Cf. *F.R.U.S. 1936*, vol. i, pp. 84–5.　　　　[2] See No. 632.

8,000 ton cruisers. While they recognised that, in the absence of quantitative limitation, the United Kingdom could not be expected to give any assurance as to her future programme, yet they felt they would be severely criticised when they got home if, in face of a big expansion of United Kingdom cruiser strength (beyond that at present contemplated), the United States were still unable to build the type of ship most favoured by a large section of American naval opinion—namely the 10,000 ton cruiser. Put somewhat differently, Mr. Davis' argument appeared to be that the United States was prepared to take out a certain proportion of its total cruiser tonnage in 8,000 ton cruisers but this proportion would be exhausted when they had matched a British strength of 70 cruisers; if the United States Government decided to build beyond that strength, they would wish to revert to the 10,000 ton type. It would, Mr. Davis said, help the United States Delegation very much with public opinion at home if there could be an exchange of letters on this subject between the two Delegations, and he handed me a draft of the kind of letter which he had in mind (see annex).

I replied that, under the safeguarding clauses as now drafted, I thought that the United States Government would have a case for invoking the clause for terminating the 'holiday' should the expansion of our cruiser strength go altogether beyond what had now been publicly announced,[3] and that this seemed to make any previous exchange of correspondence unnecessary. Mr. Davis replied that an escalator clause was never an easy thing to invoke and, above all, the American Government would dislike, for political reasons, to invoke it against Great Britain. He therefore thought it desirable from a political point of view, that something should be said now which might prevent a serious misunderstanding at some later date. He understood that Captain Danckwerts had, in a conversation with Commander Schuirmann, agreed that some declaration of this kind might be made, but I said my recollection was that Captain Danckwerts had emphasised the difficulty of our agreeing to a unilateral statement.

I said that I would submit Mr. Davis' proposal to the United Kingdom Delegation. I knew that they would wish to help Mr. Davis in any way they could in meeting his difficulties with Congress and that we were as anxious as he was to avoid any misunderstanding on such a point. Personally, I was inclined to think that, subject to certain changes in drafting, something of this kind might be considered[4] but that the proposal was clearly much more in the American interest than it was in ours and that I could make no committment [sic].

R.L.C.

[3] The reference was to Cmd. 5107, *Statement relating to Defence*, which was presented to Parliament on March 3, 1936. The text was printed in full in *The Times*, March 4, p. 8.

[4] At a further meeting with Mr. Davis and Admiral Standley on March 6 (L.N.C. (35) (U.K.) 84) Mr. Craigie suggested that 'it might be just as serviceable from the United States point of view, and less objectionable from that of the United Kingdom, if the United States Delegation could make some reservation in the sense proposed at, say, a meeting of the First Committee of the Conference'. The United States delegates expressed their willingness 'to think over Mr. Craigie's suggestion'.

*Draft of letter to British Government relating to cruiser holiday*

*March 4, 1936*

As a result of the discussions between the delegations of the United States and Great Britain relating to the agreement to refrain from building, for the period of the Treaty, cruisers exceeding 8,000 tons, it is the understanding of the American Delegation that its consent to the so-called 'cruiser holiday' is given upon the understanding that the British Government does not propose to depart from the cruiser building program made public in the Command Paper of March 3, 1936:[3] namely, that 'in cruisers the aim is to increase the total number to 70, of which 60 would be under age and 10 over age'. Should the British Government find it necessary to increase its cruiser building beyond this total, this would constitute a change of circumstances entitling the American Government to terminate the cruiser holiday by invoking the provisions of Article .[5]

It will be appreciated if you will be good enough to confirm this understanding.

[5] Omission in the original.

## No. 699

*Record by Mr. Craigie of a conversation with Mr. Davis on March 4*

[*A 2021/4/45*]

FOREIGN OFFICE, *March 4, 1936*

In the course of a conversation to-day, Mr. Norman Davis said that ever since the issue of the White Paper on British defence policy[1] the American journalists had been pestering the American Delegation with suggestions that this meant the end of the policy of parity with the United States. Mr. Davis had done his best to correct their perspective on this point: had pointed out that there was nothing new in the naval proposals, which had been known to the American Government for some time; and that the absence of any quantitative agreement in the future treaty did not mean that the British Government had gone back on the idea of parity. Nevertheless, Mr. Norman Davis felt that there was every advantage to both countries in preventing this issue of parity from raising its ugly head again and he believed that a very happy effect on Anglo-American relations would be produced if both countries were to make a declaration stating that there would be no question of naval competition between them and that the principle of parity would remain the basis of their naval policy. Mr. Davis then produced the text of a declaration which he had drafted in this sense (see annex) and asked my views upon it.

I observed, in reply, that the declaration contained an accurate statement of fact, provided it was understood that the principle of parity only gave the

[1] See No. 698, note 3.

United States the right to match the strength of the British fleet and not to offer any objection to the numbers of vessels which we elected to build. There was, I was sure, no inclination in any circles to go back on our agreement that the United States was entitled to construct a fleet of equal strength with ours. Politically, however, I was doubtful, at first sight, as to the expediency of such a formal and solemn declaration, since, following on the rejection of the Japanese proposal for a common upper limit, it could only exacerbate Japanese opinion and render less likely Japan's adherence to our naval treaty. This objection Mr. Davis countered by saying that no amount of honeyed words would bring Japan into the treaty; the only argument that would have weight with her realistic statesmen was that England and the United States intended to work closely together in naval matters and to allow no misunderstandings to arise between them. Japan might, in fact, read into the declaration more than it actually said, with salutary results. In any case, surely we would not allow a purely speculative argument based on Japanese reactions to stand in the way of a step which was bound to have an excellent influence on Anglo-American relations.

I said I would submit Mr. Davis' suggestion to the Secretary of State and the First Lord of the Admiralty and let him know our feeling about this in due course.[2]

R.L.C.

NOTE. Personally, I see no objection—and some advantage—in a short and less verbose statement being made to the effect that the absence of any quantitative agreement from the proposed treaty does not mean that the United Kingdom have gone back on their previous assurances that they regard the principle of parity as governing the naval relations between the two countries. I think, however, that this should be merely a statement of an obvious fact to which no special significance or publicity should be given at the present time, though it would be open to the United States Government to make use of this statement at some future date should they find themselves under attack on this subject.

R.L.C.

ANNEX TO No. 699

The Washington Naval Treaty of 1922 established parity in capital ships and aircraft carriers as between the Governments of Great Britain and the United States of America. In a joint statement of the President of the United States and the British Prime Minister on October 10, 1929,[3] it was recognized and accepted as a policy as between these two Governments that competitive building in the navies of the two respective countries should end and that the principle of parity should be extended to include their entire fleets and the results of this declaration were embodied in the London Naval Treaty of 1930. Notwithstanding the fact that it has not been possible to negotiate a general agreement among the Washington and London Treaty signatories

[2] This record and Annex were circulated as L.N.C. (35)(U.K.) 85.
[3] Cf. *The Times*, October 10, 1929, p. 14.

designed to continue the system of limitation of naval armaments by total tonnages in categories as provided for in the Washington and London Treaties, the Governments of Great Britain and the United States of America desire to preserve as between themselves the benefits of those agreements which are to terminate on December 31, 1936, and to avoid the dangers and expense attendant upon unrestricted competition in naval construction. The Governments of the United States and Great Britain accordingly declare that the conditions and circumstances which determine their respective naval requirements are such that the principle of parity as between their fleets shall continue to be the accepted naval policy of the two Governments.

## No. 700

*Letter from the Admiralty to the Foreign Office*

[*A 1929/4/45*]

*Immediate and Secret*                                      ADMIRALTY, *March 5, 1936*

Sir,

I am commanded by My Lords Commissioners of the Admiralty to state that They have had under consideration a report of an interview between Mr. Fujii and Mr. Craigie on the 18th February last on the subject of Article XIX of the Washington Treaty,[1] from which it appears that the Japanese Government are now prepared to consider the renewal of the provisions of this Article provided they are incorporated in a separate treaty.

The question of the continuance of Article XIX of the Washington Treaty was considered by the Cabinet on the 11th December last,[2] when it was decided that, on balance, the advantage appeared to lie in renewing the Article, but that we should endeavour to secure some compensation (i.e. from Japan) in exchange for its retention.

Since this decision in principle to retain the Article was taken, Their Lordships have had under review the question of the form which it is desirable that the renewed Article should take, in order to be prepared for any discussion of the Article which might arise in connection with the Conference.

In its present form, the Article provides in effect that the status quo shall be maintained in respect of two entirely dissimilar things, namely: (*a*) the fortifications and other defences of territories and possessions in the specified area and (*b*) the existing Naval facilities for the repair and maintenance of Naval Forces.

My Lords regard provision (*b*) above as the vital feature of the Article. So long as it is impossible for any of the contracting parties to base a larger Fleet upon any part of the territory included in the status quo area, the strategical requirements of the status quo are maintained intact.

On the other hand, the limitation (*a*) upon defences is in an entirely

[1] Cf. No. 671.

[2] Following the presentation of Mr. Eden's paper of December 7 on Article XIX: cf. No. 569.

different category. Since the signature of the Treaty, there has been a considerable increase in the offensive potentialities of the Air Arm; and in general it may be said that there is a progressive development in the means of attack, to counter which a corresponding improvement in the means of defence is a logical corollary. So long as the Article remains in its present form, it is impossible to make more than very moderate improvements in the defences at Hong Kong, whereas there is no corresponding check upon the offensive power of the Japanese Fleet.

My Lords therefore desire to suggest for consideration that if the Article is renewed it should apply to increased Naval facilities for the repair and maintenance of Naval forces alone, and that the restriction on improvement of defences, including Naval measures of defence such as mines and booms, should be removed. They would suggest that such a re-modelling of the Article would be in accordance with the trend of opinion in recent years which has tended to emphasise the distinction between aggressive and defensive action in war, and to stress the legitimacy of the latter. The Japanese, during the Naval negotiations, have themselves insisted that agreements for the limitation and reduction of armaments must be based on the fundamental principle of 'non aggression and non menace' (Admiral Yamamoto on 23rd October, 1934, N.C. (S) 1st Meeting.[3] Substantially repeated in L.N.C. (35) 1st Committee, 1st Meeting).[4]

The main consideration in favour of the continuance of Article XIX which was put forward by the Foreign Office in C.P. 238 (35)[5] was that the development of a 'first class naval base' at Hong Kong would adversely affect our relations with Japan. If the Article is renewed without any restriction for defences, but maintaining the status quo as regards Naval facilities, it would of course prevent any development of the existing Naval base. On the other hand it would be more difficult for the Japanese to capture Hong Kong in the period before the main British Fleet could arrive upon the scene.

My Lords suggest that the Japanese could only resist a proposal which would permit the strengthening of the defences at Hong Kong without adding to the offensive potentialities of the base if they were prepared to admit by implication that it is their intention at some time or other to attempt to capture the Colony.

Their Lordships understand that the Secretary of State for Foreign Affairs is anxious to settle the matter as soon as possible with the Japanese Government. They suggest, however, that it would be unwise to proceed without prior consultation with the United States Government, who are themselves vitally interested in the strategic position in the Pacific. Subject to the concurrence of the United States Government they feel that, in the light of Mr. Craigie's reminder to Mr. Fujii that Article XIX had been inserted in the Washington Treaty as a quid pro quo for Japan for the acceptance of the 60 per cent ratio, it would be perfectly reasonable to inform the Japanese Government that, whereas in 1922 H.M. Government were prepared to

---

[3] Cf. No. 37. The reference should have read: 'N.C. (J) 1st Meeting.'
[4] Held on December 10, 1935; see *L.N.C. 1935 Docs.*, p. 274.     [5] No. 569.

accept Article XIX as it now stands in return for the 60 per cent ratio, in view of the present attitude of the Japanese Government they are now not prepared to agree to more than a restriction on the establishment of new Naval bases and measures to increase existing Naval facilities for the repair and maintenance of Naval forces.

Copies of this letter are being sent to the War Office and Air Ministry.[6]

I am, &c.,

S. H. PHILLIPS

[6] The Admiralty letter resulted in extensive minuting in the Foreign Office. Comment included the following. 'It is too early yet to say whether Japanese policy will be much affected by the recent murders in Tokyo [see *The Times*, February 27, p. 12] but the only likely change is a quickening of tempo. Personally I like the Admiralty suggestion. It will serve to show our intention to keep our end up in China, without aggressiveness. The Japanese will not like it very much, no doubt, and we may in the end have to choose between full renewal & non-renewal, but I should rather expect the Japanese to prefer partial renewal to none. C. W. Orde 10/3.' Mr. Craigie thought that there was 'much to be said for this Admiralty proposal. It is not a satisfactory state of affairs that, in the face of Japan's growing aggressiveness, Hong Kong should remain, to all intents and purposes, unfortified. The knowledge that Hong Kong must fall to the first attack is not only bad for our own prestige in the Far East, but acts as an encouragement to Japanese imperialism.' He saw 'two objections to following the course recommended by the Admiralty, namely, that (1) His Majesty's Government may have to face a certain amount of criticism in this country if it becomes known that Japan favours the continuation of the provisions of Article XIX, whereas we are asking for changes; (2) there is always the possibility that Japan, if she were presented with a proposal on these lines, might use it as a pretext for running out of Article XIX altogether.' But he thought that 'these disadvantages are outweighed by the gain to our prestige and our defensive position in the Far East which might be expected from the adoption of this proposal . . . R.L.C. 1st April, 1936'. Sir Victor Wellesley wrote: 'On balance I think the Admiralty proposals have much to recommend them. I agree with Mr. Craigie's views. V.W. 2/4/36.' 'I agree. R. V[ansittart]. April 2.' A proposal for the renewal of Article XIX in a separate instrument with provision for bringing existing fortifications up to date was put to the United States Government on September 11, 1936, but on September 24 the British Chargé d'Affairs, Mr. V. A. L. Mallet, was told that the proposal was rejected. See *F.R.U.S. 1936*, vol. i, pp. 122–31.

## No. 701

### Sir E. Drummond (Rome) to Mr. Eden (Received March 11)
### No. 301 [A 2042/4/45]

ROME, *March 6, 1936*

Sir,

In your despatch No. 239[1] to Mr. Ingram you gave an account of a conversation which you had with Signor Grandi on February 27th on the subject of the Naval Conference.

2. The Italian Ambassador stated that the real reason why the Italian Government could not sign a naval agreement at this moment was that Signor Mussolini was not in a position to do so for reasons of internal policy.

3. While the Ambassador is of course far more qualified to judge of such

[1] No. 681.

matters than I am, I find the greatest difficulty in accepting such an explanation. I believe that Signor Mussolini could have signed a naval agreement without arousing any criticism here, had he wished to do so. In fact I am inclined to think that his refusal was in the nature of a last minute decision. When I saw him on February 18th[2] about the question of the tonnage of capital ships, he made no allusion whatever to a possible refusal to sign, and His Excellency is usually very frank in discussions of this character. Further, the official who replies on behalf of the Government to Press representatives declared that there was no connection between the naval conference and sanctions, but a day or two later—after my interview with Signor Mussolini—he stated that he has [sic] been in error and that the two questions were linked.[3]

4. My own view is that Signor Mussolini suddenly came to the conclusion that the refusal to sign the naval treaty might be a means of bringing some slight pressure to bear to induce His Majesty's Government not to extend the existing sanctions (see Mr. Ingram's telegram No. 121[4] of February 29th). In pursuance of this policy he has intimated to the French Government (see your telegram from Geneva No. 10[4] of March 4th) that if further sanctions are imposed he will not only leave the League of Nations but also denounce the agreement come to between the French and Italian military authorities whereby the frontier between Italy and France is more or less denuded of troops, an arrangement to which I understand the French general staff attach considerable importance.[5]

I have, &c.,

ERIC DRUMMOND

[2] See No. 660.
[4] Not printed. Cf. No. 676, note 3.

[3] Cf. No. 667.
[5] Cf. No. 197, note 2.

## No. 702

### Mr. Eden to Sir E. Phipps (Berlin)
### No. 301 [C 1480/4/18]

FOREIGN OFFICE, March 7, 1936

Sir,

The German Ambassador asked to see me this morning when he said that he had two communications to make. First, he wished to speak to me about the Naval Conference. The German Government had carefully considered the formula which we had submitted to them in connexion with the age of battleships,[1] and they were prepared to agree to it. The German Government were prepared to sign the Naval Agreement even without Italy on condition however that a similar agreement should be signed with the Soviet Government before the entry into force of the agreement between Great Britain and Germany, that is to say before January 1st, 1937. The only outstanding point at issue, as to which the Ambassador was confident there

[1] See No. 703 below, note 2.

would be no difficulty, was the form which the Naval Agreement between our two countries was to take. The German Government would wish this to be in the form of an exchange of notes. The Ambassador added that as I would understand from this declaration there was no longer any substantial difficulty in the way of the further Anglo-German Naval Agreement.

2. The Ambassador then went on to say that he had a communication of very great importance to make to me. He was afraid that the first part of it would not be to my taste, but the later portions contained an offer of greater importance than had been made at any time in recent history. . . .[2]

I am, &c.,

ANTHONY EDEN

[2] The remaining four paragraphs of this despatch refer to Herr Hitler's action in respect of the demilitarized zone of the Rhineland, and will be printed in a subsequent volume in this Series.

## No. 703

*Record by Mr. Craigie of a conversation with Captain Wassner*

[*A 2030/4/45*]

FOREIGN OFFICE, *March 9, 1936*

The German Naval Attaché called this morning to give me the answer of his Government to the communication made to the Ambassador in the course of the meeting with the First Lord of the Admiralty on the 4th instant.[1] The answer was to the following effect:—

1. The German Government agrees with the proposal made to them by the United Kingdom Delegation in regard to age limits for the capital ship.

The Naval Attaché agreed with a suggestion which I made that the formula communicated to them on the 4th instant[2] might be embodied in a separate exchange of communications which would be regarded as a continuation of memoranda dealing with the practical application of the Anglo-German Naval Treaty of June last. The advantage of this arrangement would be to emphasise that the matter was one which was primarily concerned not with the interpretation of the proposed qualitative treaty but with the interpretation of the Anglo-German quantitative treaty of last June.

2. The German Government are prepared, in view of the text in the safeguarding clause which has been communicated to them,[3] to sign the

[1] This meeting was held in the First Lord's room at the Admiralty at 3.45 p.m. Among those present were Admiral Chatfield and Mr. Craigie. Herr von Hoesch and Captain Wassner represented Germany. Cf. *D.G.F.P.*, Series C, vol. v, No. 46.

[2] This formula was as follows. 'It is agreed that the normal life of a capital ship should be 26 years. If, however, when the German capital ships now building or projected are approaching the age of 20 years, the German Government represent that a Power has laid down a capital ship before the date at which such ship would normally be laid down in replacement of its existing capital ship tonnage, and in consequence the retention of some or all of the German ships to the age of 26 years is an unfair restriction, no objection would be raised to their replacement at any age not less than 20 years.'

[3] See No. 691.

proposed bilateral agreement, but they nevertheless ask that the entry into force of the proposed treaty should be subject to the signature of a similar Anglo-Russian Pact.

3. The new Anglo-German Treaty would come into force on the 1st January, 1937.

4. It is suggested that six years would be a desirable period of validity.

5. The German Government consider that an exchange of notes would be an adequate method of concluding the agreement.

6. The German Government assume that they will shortly receive a draft of the proposed treaty in its final form.

I told Captain Wassner that I was sure that this answer would be received by the United Kingdom Delegation with satisfaction. The only point that worried me was that I had hoped that, in view of the scope of the safe-guarding clause, it would be possible for Germany to sign the Treaty without any reservation in regard to the signature of a similar treaty between Russia and ourselves. The laying down of the condition as to Germany's signature meant that there must be a similar condition to our signature to Germany, and this might open the door to the other countries making the entry into force of the treaty dependent on a further list of States. Perhaps at a later stage we might find such reservations very embarrassing.

R.L.C.

## No. 704

### Letter from Mr. Craigie to Mr. Davis

[*A 2171/4/45*]

*Secret*                                                         FOREIGN OFFICE, *March 9, 1936*

My dear Mr. Davis,

We have now worked out a draft text for an agreement to replace Part IV of the London Naval Treaty relative to the restriction of submarine warfare.[1] Copies of this draft are enclosed.

As you will see, we have tried to make the instrument as simple as possible and we very much hope that it will be acceptable to your Government. I should be very grateful if you would let me know as soon as possible whether you see any objection to this draft being communicated to the French and Italian Delegations and to the Japanese Embassy, not as an Anglo-American draft but purely as a U.K. draft. The French in particular are pressing for an early communication of this draft and we should like to send it to them tomorrow. Your consent to our circulating it would not of course prevent you from suggesting any amendments you wish later on, but I am anxious not to circulate the draft until I have shown it to you privately.

[1] This draft, which had been under discussion in the Foreign Office since early in January 1936, arose from the fact that the British Commonwealth, Japan, and the United States had committed themselves without limit of time to the provisions of Part IV. It was desired, therefore, to provide for the reconfirming of the commitment by those already bound by it and for its acceptance by the other naval powers.

Malkin has asked me to say that he hoped to have the opportunity of discussing the text with Mr. Flournoy[2] but that he will unfortunately be unable to do so at present, as he has to go to Paris immediately.[3]

Yours very sincerely,
R. L. CRAIGIE

ENCLOSURE IN No. 704

Whereas by their ratification of the Treaty for the Limitation and Reduction of Naval Armaments signed in London on the 22nd April, 1930, the President of the United States of America, His Majesty The King of Great Britain, Ireland and the British Dominions beyond the Seas, Emperor of India, in respect of each and all of the Members of the British Commonwealth of Nations as enumerated in the Preamble of the said Treaty, and His Imperial Majesty the Emperor of Japan have agreed to accept as established rules of international law the rules contained in Part IV of the said Treaty as to the action of submarines with regard to merchant ships, the text of which rules is annexed hereto:[4]

And whereas it is provided in Article 25 of the said Treaty that after the deposit of the ratifications of all the High Contracting Parties, the text of the said rules shall be communicated to all Powers which are not signatories of the said Treaty and that the said Powers shall be invited to accede thereto definitely and without limit of time;

And whereas it has not been possible to give effect to the foregoing provisions of Article 25 owing to the fact that the Treaty has not yet been ratified by all the High Contracting Parties;

The under-signed Plenipotentiaries, with the view of securing recognition of the said rules by as many countries as possible have agreed as follows:—

*Article 1*

It shall be open to any Power which is not a signatory of the present agreement to accede at any time to the said rules by a notification in writing addressed to His Majesty's Government in the United Kingdom of Great Britain and Northern Ireland.

The text of the said rules, as annexed hereto,[4] shall be communicated to the Governments of the said Powers with an invitation to accede thereto.

The said rules shall be binding definitely, and without limit of time, upon all Powers which have accepted them.

[2] Legal Adviser to the Department of State and a member of the United States delegation.
[3] Mr. Davis agreed to the circulation of the draft on the same day, subject to his right to suggest amendments later on. Cf. *F.R.U.S. 1936*, vol. i, p. 160.
[4] Not annexed to filed copy.

# No. 705

*Memorandum by Mr. Craigie on the Negotiation of an Anglo-German Naval Treaty*

[*A 2571/4/45*]

FOREIGN OFFICE, *March 12, 1936*

1. The Admiralty are not prepared to sign a three-Power Naval Treaty with the Washington Powers unless we sign simultaneously, or shortly afterwards, a similar treaty with Germany. They are prepared to take the risk of relying on the 'escalator' clause in the case of Japan, but not the double risk which would be involved in neither Japan nor Germany accepting the terms of the treaty.

2. Agreement has now been virtually reached with Germany for the signature of a bilateral treaty.[1] The only difficulty which remains is that Germany is making the entry into force of the bilateral treaty contingent on Soviet Russia accepting a similar bilateral treaty with us. As the attitude of Soviet Russia is doubtful, it is proposed to endeavour to induce Germany to rely in this respect on the safeguarding clause just as we rely on that clause in respect of Japan and Italy.

3. Lord Stanhope has now raised with me the question whether, in view of Germany's action in the Rhineland,[2] we should suspend negotiations for a naval treaty with Germany and, for the present at any rate, abandon the idea of concluding such an agreement. He suggests that to continue the negotiations now might perhaps embarrass the infinitely more important negotiations connected with Germany's breach of Locarno and give umbrage to France at a critical moment.

4. The First Lord of the Admiralty and the Naval Staff are strongly opposed to the suspension of negotiations with Germany. I agree with them. Apart from the fact that to break off negotiations with Germany would jeopardise the whole Naval Treaty structure which we have so laboriously built up, it seems to me that such action can only tend to embitter the controversy arising out of Germany's breach of Locarno. The First Lord quotes as an example the decision to keep Parliament in session during the general strike[3] and the tranquil[l]ising effect which this step had on public opinion in this country. He believes that, if we quietly continue our work for naval agreement, it will have a similar tranquil[l]ising effect in the international field. Moreover, action purely for the purpose of placating French feeling may prove rather quixotic, since the proposal for a bilateral agreement originally came from France, and when the present difficulties in the international situation have cleared up, France would be the first to blame us if the Naval Treaty structure had been broken up by any action on our part. A further argument in favour of continuing negotiations is that in the case

---

[1] See No. 703.
[2] German military re-occupation of the demilitarized zone had begun on the morning of March 7. Cf. No. 702, note 2.       [3] In 1926.

of Italy, who has both broken treaties and committed a flagrant act of aggression, we have been ready and anxious to sign a naval agreement; while the offence of Germany is more recent, it is also less heinous in that there is no aggression against foreign territory.

5. It is of course evident that further discussions with Germany would have to be conducted as unobtrusively as possible, and the date for the actual signature of the Treaty would have to be made dependent on the developments of the negotiations in regard to the Rhineland.

6. It may be urged that we should sign a three-Power agreement subject to a reservation that it will only come into effect when the proposed bilateral agreement with Germany comes into force. The objections to this are:—

(*a*) It opens the door to similar reservations by other signatories which may prove very embarrassing; and

(*b*) such a reservation, appearing in the Treaty at this time, would be just as unpalatable to France as would the signature of an Anglo-German Treaty, once the present tension has been eased.

7. My proposal, therefore, is that we continue unobtrusively the negotiations with Germany on the understanding that the actual signature of a Naval Agreement with that Power may have to be postponed for a few weeks—and, of course, indefinitely, if the present international situation leads to a serious deterioration in our relations with Germany.[4]

R.L.C.

[4] The reception of Mr. Craigie's proposal in the Foreign Office was unfavourable. Minutes by Mr. Wigram, Lord Stanhope, Mr. Sargent, and Sir R. Vansittart were as follows. 'I sincerely hope we shall suspend the negotiations. I cannot imagine anything more likely to add fuel to the present fire than their continuance. R.F.W. 12/3.' 'It seems to me to be quite out of the question that we should continue, however unobtrusively, negotiations with Germany for a Naval Treaty at this moment. It would not only make us look extremely ridiculous but it would convince Germany that we were quite half-hearted—if that—in objecting to her tearing up the Locarno Treaty. The effect on France would, I imagine, be deplorable. S. 12/3/36.' 'Surely it ought to be possible to employ delaying tactics in such a way as to prevent there being in fact any further negotiations with Germany during these next few critical days. By this time next week we will know where we stand ... O. G. Sargent. March 12th, 1936.' 'There can surely be no question whatever of our going on with negotiations *just* now. We cannot do it "unobtrusively". The Germans wd see to that. The Admiralty must really take some account of the immense importance to the future of what is being decided now. A sense of proportion will immediately show that the naval negotiation must take second place—for the time being anyway ... R.V. March 13.' He added 'I feel that this view may be a disappointment to Mr. Craigie, but the delay may not need to be long'. Mr. Craigie wrote, 'There can be no question of personal disappointment, for I am perfectly accustomed to this sort of thing! But, in view of the intending expansion of our naval strength, I believe the sacrifice of this naval treaty (the 3 Power treaty) will have more serious consequences for this country than the writers of the above minutes may perhaps realise. It is for this reason that I must necessarily seek to find some way round the difficulty that has arisen. ... R.L.C. 14/3.'

*Record by Mr. Craigie of a conversation with M. Cambon on March 12*
*L.N.C. (35)(U.K.) 89 [A 2195/4/45]*

I asked M. Cambon to call to-day in order to discuss with him two points of some importance in regard to the drafting of the Treaty: the first being the French reservation in regard to increasing the number of her 8″ gun cruisers, ship by ship, in the event of any other Power laying down 8″ gun cruisers during 1936; and the second the proposal of the French Delegation to link up in the escalator clause the right to build within the non-construction zone with the right to depart from the 'cruiser holiday'.

I said that both these points raised questions of some importance and that the First Lord would have wished to discuss them with M. Corbin had he not known that the Ambassador was so fully occupied at this time. It was for this reason that I had asked M. Cambon to call, but what I said might be taken as representing the views of the United Kingdom Delegation.

As regards the first point I explained to M. Cambon that our original understanding had been that the French Government would be prepared to remain at seven category A gun cruisers if Germany remained at three, (i.e., two building and one to be laid down shortly). It was true that I had told the French Delegation that I would certainly enquire whether the German Government would be prepared to remain at two Category A gun cruisers, abandoning the construction of the third, but that I had very little hope of the German Government agreeing to this. In fact, the German Embassy had made it clear that their plans definitely provided for the construction of three 8″ cruisers, but that they were prepared to abandon the construction of the other two A cruisers which they were entitled to build under the Anglo-German Naval Agreement, if the cruiser holiday were to be agreed upon between other principal naval Powers. It was thus evident that if the French Government maintained their reservation we would be signing the Treaty with the knowledge that the cruiser holiday must be broken immediately after signature. On Germany laying down her third cruiser, France would lay down her eighth, Italy her eighth: Germany would then lay down her fourth and the race in 8″ gun cruisers would thus be started before the Treaty had even come into force. Furthermore, I was sure that the only hope of inducing Japan to comply with the cruiser holiday lay in none of the other Washington Powers constructing any more of this type of cruiser. In the circumstances I expressed the hope that M. Corbin would use his influence with the French Delegation to induce them to abide by the arrangement which we understood them to have contemplated at first, namely the acceptance of three German cruisers without the further building of French cruisers. I suggested that it might suffice for French purposes if we could produce them an undertaking in writing from the German Government to the effect that, in view of the cruiser 'holiday', they would limit the number of their 8″ gun cruisers to three.

I then explained the difficulty about linking the cruiser holiday with the 'gap', stating that it struck at the root of the guiding principle of the safe-guarding clause, namely that[1] there should be no qualitative 'escalation' should take place only in respect of *qualitative* building by other Powers. Furthermore, much as we disliked the idea of a breach in the cruiser holiday, this would be less fatal to the future of qualitative limitation than building in the 'gap', which really would mean the end of all qualitative limitation other than the upper limits for the capital ship. It was therefore the earnest hope of the United Kingdom Delegation that the French Delegation would, insofar as building and the 'gap' were concerned, content themselves with the latitude accorded to them under Article A of the escalator clause.

M. Cambon promised to explain these two points to M. Corbin and to emphasise that the United Kingdom attached great importance to a separate agreement between the two Delegations with regard to them, if possible outside the proceedings of the Committee.

[1] The rest of this sentence appears to be corrupt. Possibly the four following words 'there should be no' should have been omitted.

## No. 707

*Letter from Rear-Admiral Raineri Biscia to Mr. Craigie*

[*A 2225/4/45*]

LONDON, *March 12, 1936*

Dear Mr. Craigie,

Thank you very much for your kind note dated 10th inst.[1]

After having consulted the Head of our Delegation we believe that the solution you have thought of for the extension of the provisions of Part IV of the London Naval Treaty to other Powers would be quite satisfactory for all those Powers who were not signatories to that Treaty, but could scarcely be regarded as such in the case of Italy.

We think that for our Country (and perhaps for France) the best procedure would be that the respective Governments without any official invitation should pledge themselves with a diplomatic note to the other signatories of that Treaty to observe the new rules of naval warfare for submarines.

Once this has been done then the other Powers could be invited by a document on the lines of the one you have sent us, and signed of course also by the French and Italian Governments.

Yours very sincerely,
RAINERI BISCIA

[1] Enclosing text of the draft agreement relating to submarine warfare: cf. No. 704, enclosure.

# No. 708

*Mr. Eden to Viscount Chilston (Moscow)*

*No. 35 Telegraphic [A 2230/4/45]*

FOREIGN OFFICE, *March 13, 1936, 10 p.m.*

The Soviet Counsellor was informed on the 4th March[1] that it was the hope of His Majesty's Government that, as naval agreements were almost certain to be concluded with certain Washington Treaty Powers and Germany, a bilateral treaty might also be concluded between the United Kingdom and the Soviet Union. Before, however, a formal invitation to this effect was conveyed to the Soviet Government, it was desired to ascertain unofficially whether such a proposal would be acceptable.

The Counsellor has now returned a reply to the effect that the Soviet Government, while appreciating our action in furnishing to them texts of decisions of Conference as they were agreed, had not yet been able to study the matter in detail and would like to have a draft of the proposed treaty as soon as one had been prepared. They did not feel they could reply to the above unofficial enquiry until they had formed some clearer idea as to the obligations they would be asked to assume.

Counsellor further asked whether we considered bilateral form of treaty essential or whether it would be possible for Soviet Russia to adhere to proposed three Power treaty. He was informed that three Power treaty would be open to accession only by Washington Powers and that, pending the conclusion of ultimate general treaty between all the naval Powers, bilateral agreement with the United Kingdom seemed the most appropriate form for proposed arrangements with Germany and the Soviet Union.

We are anxious for an early reply from Soviet Government on this subject and hope to communicate to the Soviet Embassy first draft of treaty this week. But Soviet Government already have all necessary material for forming an opinion on treaty and I should be glad if you would endeavour to elicit an early expression of their views.

[1] See No. 697.

# No. 709

*Note from Mr. Holman to Viscount Monsell*

*[A 2226/4/45]*

FOREIGN OFFICE, *March 16, 1936*

*The First Lord*

Mr. O'Donovan[1] rang me up at 11.15 this morning to say that the Irish Free State High Commissioner[2] had been trying to get into touch with you but had failed to do so. Mr. O'Donovan therefore asked me to communicate

[1] Secretary in the Office of the High Commissioner in London of the Irish Free State.
[2] Mr. J. W. Dulanty.

to you the following message to the effect that the Irish Free State did not propose to become a party to the new naval Treaty. The reason for this decision was as stated by the Irish Free State High Commissioner in his speech at the opening Plenary Session[3] that the problem of naval limitation was really one for naval Powers exclusively. Mr. O'Donovan added that the Treaty had no real practical application as far as the Irish Free State was concerned and that participation by it in the Treaty might entail similar participation in future naval Conferences which, in the view of the Irish Free State, should be confined to naval Powers.

A. HOLMAN

[3] See *L.N.C. 1935 Docs.*, pp. 64–65.

## No. 710

*Record by Mr. Craigie of a conversation with Captain Wassner on March 17*

[*A 2404/4/45*]

FOREIGN OFFICE, March 17, 1936

In view of the Cabinet decision that negotiations for a Naval Treaty with Germany were to be continued although the signature of the Treaty must be delayed,[1] I asked Captain Wassner to come and see me today.

2. I said that, in the course of his last interview with the Secretary of State,[2] Herr von Hoesch had intimated that the last difficulty in the way of the signature of an Anglo-German Naval Agreement was the question of the form of the agreement. The German Government preferred the form of an exchange of notes, which would harmonise with the form of the Anglo-German agreement of last June, whereas the United Kingdom representatives had appeared to prefer that the Anglo-German Agreement should be in the same form as that adopted for the three-Power Treaty, namely a Heads of States Treaty. I said that we had given careful consideration to this point; that we quite saw the force of the German argument that the two Anglo-German Treaties should be in the same form, and I was therefore glad to be able to inform him that we could agree to the method of an exchange of notes.

3. There was, however, one further difficulty which might in certain circumstances become rather serious, namely, the suggested German reserva-

[1] Lord Monsell, the First Lord of the Admiralty, told the Cabinet at its meeting on March 16 that he understood that the Foreign Office felt some doubts as to whether the negotiations with Germany for a bi-lateral naval treaty ought to go on in present conditions (cf. No. 705, note 4). 'That appeared to him a wrong view. The negotiations throughout had been kept very quiet and had attracted little public interest. We had negotiated with the Italians even while we were applying sanctions. It appeared a mistake to adopt a different course with Germany. . . .' Mr. Eden said that he did not mind the continuance of negotiations but he thought that 'the present moment would be a bad time for signing a Treaty with Germany'. The Cabinet then agreed to authorize the First Lord to continue negotiations with Germany on the understanding that there was no question of signing a treaty with Germany 'at the present time'. Cf. No. 722 below, Conclusions, section 4.

[2] See No. 702.

tion that the bilateral Treaty should not enter into force until a similar bilateral Treaty had been concluded between ourselves and Soviet Russia. We had recently been making soundings of Moscow, and I personally had no doubt that, in the fulness of time, the Soviet Government would conclude a Naval Treaty with us as proposed, but they wanted a good deal more time for consideration[3] and that might mean indefinite delay. Furthermore, there were a number of strong arguments against the inclusion in the proposed Anglo-German Treaty of a reservation such as the German Government propose. These I summarised as follows:—

(i) If the German Government insisted upon inserting such a reservation, we might have to insert a similar reservation in the three-Power Treaty, and this in turn would open the door to similar reservations by other Powers. In this way a whole network of reservations might be created, which would be likely seriously to delay the entry into force of any naval treaty, seeing that it would be possible for any one of the Powers mentioned in the reservation to stop a whole series of Treaties coming into force.

(ii) In particular, the insertion of such a reservation would place it in the power of Soviet Russia to decide not only whether the Anglo-German Naval Agreement should come into force but also whether the three-Power Naval Agreement should come into force. I felt that, if placed in such a situation, the Soviet Government must necessarily be tempted to use it for bargaining purposes. In other words we would be in a better position when it came to negotiating a Naval Treaty with Soviet Russia if such a reservation did not exist in the German Treaty.

(iii) A careful study by the German Government of the revised safeguarding clauses would, I believed, convince them that they could safely rely on the operation of these clauses, in so far as construction by Soviet Russia was concerned, supposing that Power refused to enter into a treaty with us. At all events, the United States, France and ourselves were all relying on these clauses in the event of construction by Japan and Italy. We further understood that if and when Italy acceded to the Treaty, she would do so without a reservation of this description.

(iv) It had now been definitely decided that the three-Power Treaty should only be for six years,[4] so that the Anglo-German Naval Treaty would be for a similar period. I felt sure that the German Government would agree that there was no serious danger of Soviet Russia being able, in such a period, to construct a fleet which would be embarrassing to Germany, even if the Russians had the desire to do so.

In the circumstances, we hoped the German Government would agree to sign the proposed Treaty without reservation. I asked for an early reply as we hoped to sign the three-Power Treaty next week, and we were anxious to know the German views on this point beforehand. Captain Wassner promised to enquire at once.

[3] Cf. No. 708.
[4] This decision had been taken by the First Committee on March 11, see *L.N.C. 1935 Docs.*, p. 745.

4. He then asked whether I thought that developments in the Rhineland were likely to affect our negotiations. I said I thought that we might agree to set up a demilitarised zone between St. James' Palace and Clarence House,[5] and that the two sets of negotiations could be conducted quite independently of one another. As regards signature, however, I imagined that both Governments would wish to postpone the date until the political situation had sufficiently improved to render a decision desirable in the opinion of both Governments. Captain Wassner fully agreed with the idea of a demilitarised zone, adding that the best adverb to apply to the question of the date of signature was the new expression 'alsbald'.[6]

5. As regards the various points on which an agreement had been reached between the two Governments in the recent discussion about a bilateral agreement, I suggested that we should incorporate these in a memorandum, of which we would communicate a copy to the German Government. Captain Wassner agreed that this Memorandum and the German reply to it could be regarded as a continuation of the series of memoranda relating to the application of the Anglo-German Agreement of last June, and need not appear in the exchange of notes which would bring the new Treaty into force.

R.L.C.

[5] i.e. between negotiations conducted through the normal diplomatic sources and those relating to the Naval Conference whose secretariat headquarters was at Clarence House, Westminster.                                                    [6] 'as soon as possible'.

## No. 711

*Draft*[1] *Record of a meeting of representatives of the United Kingdom Delegation on March 17, 1936, at 10.30 a.m.*[2]

*L.N.C. (35)(U.K.) 92 [A 2020/4/45]*

PRESENT: *Admiralty*: Lord Monsell, Admiral of the Fleet Sir Ernle Chatfield, Vice-Admiral Sir William James, Captain Phillips, Mr. Coxwell.

*Dominions Office*: Sir Harry Batterbee, Mr. Dixon, Mr. Holmes.
*Foreign Office*: Mr. Craigie, Mr. Holman, Mr. Gore-Booth.

(Note: A summary of the conclusions reached will be found at the end of the Record.)

### 1. *The Irish Free State and The Treaty*

MR. CRAIGIE said that from the international point of view the failure of the Irish Free State to sign the Treaty[3] would make no difference, though this would not be the case if Canada, Australia or New Zealand followed her

[1] The record here printed was identical with the final text except for the omission in the heading of the word 'Draft'.

[2] The meeting was held in the First Lord's room at the Admiralty.           [3] See No. 709.

example.[4] He had gathered, however, from a conversation with Mr. Davis on the subject, that something might depend on the terms in which Mr. Dulanty announced the Free State's intentions. If the Free State failed to express general approval of the Treaty it was just possible that action might create trouble.

SIR HARRY BATTERBEE said that the Secretary of State for Dominion Affairs had agreed that the expediency of saying something favourable to the Treaty should be suggested to Mr. Dulanty, provided that there was no question of genuflection before the Free State. It was understood that Mr. Dulanty would probably make a statement in the First Committee, if not at the Plenary Meeting.

It was agreed that the constitutional aspect of the Free State's non-accession would cause no difficulty.

## 2. Proposed United States Declaration on the subject of the Cruiser Holiday[5]

MR. CRAIGIE explained that according to a provisional arrangement arrived at after the last United Kingdom–United States meeting (see L.N.C. (35) (U.K.) 84) the intention was that the United States representatives would make a statement at a First Committee meeting, to which the United Kingdom Delegation would reply that they had no objection.

ADMIRAL CHATFIELD felt strongly that the full responsibility for the statement should be taken by the United States and that the United Kingdom Delegation should not make it appear that it was in the nature of a bilateral understanding.

MR. FITZMAURICE[6] felt that the correct interpretation of the United States action was that they would simply be stating a fact, namely that in certain circumstances they would avail themselves of the escalator clause.

ADMIRAL CHATFIELD thought that the United States statement on this point was on a par with the French unilateral reservation with regard to the German construction of 10,000 ton cruisers and should be treated as such.

MR. CRAIGIE pointed out that the United States desired to place on record the basis on which they had agreed to the cruiser holiday. There was some

[4] The position of the Union of South Africa had been explained by Mr. te Water at the first plenary meeting on December 9, 1935, when he said that: 'the national safety of the Union of South Africa does not lie in its naval armaments, for it has no fleet' (L.N.C. 1935 Docs., p. 69). In a letter of March 24, 1936, to the President of the Conference, Mr. te Water later stated that the Union Government had decided 'that the signature of His Majesty's Government in the Union of South Africa to the new Treaty is . . . rendered unnecessary by reason of the fact that it possesses no ships of war under existing category and that it contemplates no naval building whatever during the period of the present Treaty'. See also L.N.C. 1935 Docs., p. 116.

[5] Cf. No. 698, Annex and note 4. A draft of the proposed declaration (Annex to L.N.C. (35) (U.K.) 87), not printed, had been handed to Mr. Craigie by Mr. Davis on March 11. Except for minor drafting amendments, and the rewording in note 10 below, it was identical with the statement made by Mr. Davis at the sixteenth meeting of the First Committee on March 21, 1936; see L.N.C. 1935 Docs., p. 766.

[6] The name of the Third Legal Adviser to the Foreign Office appears to have been omitted in error from the list of those present at the meeting.

justice in their contention that an understanding existed in that when the cruiser holiday was first envisaged, quantitative limitation was still regarded as a possibility, and if quantitative limitation had been brought about, the British Commonwealth figure for cruisers would have been 70.

MR. CRAIGIE felt that it would be undesirable to remove the word 'understanding' from the statement since such action might re-open a controversy at a moment when it was essential to send Mr. Norman Davis and Admiral Standley home in a good frame of mind.

ADMIRAL CHATFIELD was apprehensive lest the existence of this United States statement would not result in tremendous pressure being put on his successor not to construct more than 70 cruisers, even if they might seem imperatively necessary in order that the cruiser holiday might be preserved.

LORD MONSELL said that he would have no fears about defending the acceptance of the statement and MR. CRAIGIE added that under the escalator clause as at present drafted, there was nothing in it to prevent the United States from invoking that clause even if the United Kingdom only built up to 60 cruisers. Their acceptance of a figure of 70 without any thought of counter-measures was politically a great step forward in comparison with their attitude at Geneva in 1927.

### 3. Proposed United States declaration in regard to parity[7]

LORD MONSELL thought that an explicit reaffirmation of the principle of parity between the United States and the British Commonwealth would have a very bad effect in Japan.

MR. CRAIGIE felt that it was especially undesirable for the United Kingdom to agree in any way that the needs of the British Commonwealth and the United States were the same. Mr. Norman Davis had said that some such affirmation of this kind would be an assurance against Japan, to which Mr. Craigie had replied that it seemed a pity to draw attention to the question. All that the United States Government needed was something to refer to if they were attacked in the Senate on the grounds that they had abandoned parity.

MR. CRAIGIE suggested therefore that a United Kingdom–United States meeting should be held at which the United States Delegation could say that their attitude as regards parity with the British Commonwealth had not been modified, which proposition Lord Monsell could accept on the behalf of the United Kingdom. It was important that it should be made clear that while the United States might build to the level chosen by the British Commonwealth, the latter's building was not restricted in any way by this arrangement. It might be argued that such a statement would give the impression of unrestricted competition between the United States and the United Kingdom. As had been repeatedly said, the United Kingdom envisaged no such competition, having her own absolute naval requirements; it was true, however, that the United States insisted, for prestige purposes, on keeping pace with the British Commonwealth.

[7] See Annex to No. 699.

LORD MONSELL said that he was inclined to favour a simple reaffirmation of the statement of policy quoted in the present United States draft (L.N.C. (35) (U.K.) 85).[7]

MR. CRAIGIE stated that Mr. Davis was afraid that, now that there was no quantitative limitation, there would be agitation for the United States to have the biggest navy in the world. Such a measure would affect Japan and so affect the British Commonwealth indirectly.

ADMIRAL CHATFIELD observed that the United States, realising that their desire for parity with the British Commonwealth was wrong, were trying to get the United Kingdom to recognise it as right. The Japanese fully understood the situation.

MR. CRAIGIE felt that it was politically desirable that this whole question should not be raised the moment quantitative limitation disappeared.

ADMIRAL CHATFIELD then drew attention to a formula suggested by Captain Phillips to the effect that the United States Government and His Majesty's Government in the United Kingdom 'maintain the principle of no naval rivalry nor does either country question the right of the other to parity in any category of vessel'.

### 4. Anglo-German Negotiations

LORD MONSELL said that he had raised this question at the Cabinet.[8] He had explained that the Three Power Treaty was ready for signature and that it had only been brought to this stage because the United Kingdom had consented to adopt a procedure which excluded participation by Germany. The United Kingdom Delegation were in the middle of negotiations with Germany and the Germans had proved accommodating. The signature of the Three Power Treaty by the United Kingdom depended on the certain knowledge that Germany would sign a bilateral agreement with them. The view had been put up in the Foreign Office that negotiations with the Germans could not be continued for the time being. He had argued, however, that if negotiations were continued with Italy, against whom Sanctions were being taken, there seemed no reason for not continuing them with Germany. It might even be that the continuation of negotiations would facilitate the progress of the more important negotiations with Germany. It would be a great pity if no Treaty were signed and the blame were placed on the United Kingdom.

LORD MONSELL added that Mr. Eden had seen no objection to the continuance of negotiation providing that there was no question of signature at present.

Lord Monsell felt that nothing useful would be forthcoming from the Soviet for a long time. The question now was whether to press the Germans for assent without reserves along the lines that we wanted to sign first with Germany, that Germany could rely on the safeguarding clauses, and that the Soviet Union could do little that was dangerous in six years, or whether there was any alternative.

[8] On March 16: cf. No. 710, note 1.

ADMIRAL CHATFIELD pointed out that if the Soviet Union built say seven 10,000 ton cruisers in the period of the Treaty, Germany being still bound by a 35% ratio as compared with the Commonwealth navies, would be unable to reply in kind.

MR. CRAIGIE thought that the Germans might well make a similar reservation to the French in connection with the building of 10,000 ton cruisers. They would also probably conclude with the United Kingdom an agreement to consult if anything happened which infringed the Treaty. He would propose to discuss the matter with the Germans on these lines pressing them to rely upon the safeguarding clause and on some such understanding with provision for consultation.

MR. FITZMAURICE said that it would be perfectly in order for the safeguarding clause in the Anglo-German agreement to be related to the Anglo-German quantitative agreement in such a way that the ratio set up in that agreement would be over-riding.

MR. CRAIGIE mentioned that according to the Americans the Germans might make some difficulties. He also mentioned the possibility that if Germany would not sign without the Soviet Union, the United Kingdom might sign the present Treaty with the private intention of not ratifying if no agreement was meanwhile concluded with the Germans. Such a procedure seemed justifiable since nothing but a very critical international situation was likely to prevent eventual German accession.

### 5. *Limitation in the number of Germany's 10,000 ton Cruisers*

MR. CRAIGIE said that, according to Captain Deleuze, the French were determined to reserve their position with regard to the building of 10,000 ton cruisers by any Power. Captain Deleuze had intimated, however, very privately and cautiously that France might not build another of these vessels if Germany built a third. In general the question could be dealt with under the proposed provision for mutual consultation in the event of anything occurring in 1936 contrary to the Treaty.

### 6. *Date of signature.* See CONCLUSIONS.

### 7. *Arrangements after signature*

MR. CRAIGIE said that there were various reasons for securing the eventual inclusion of other powers—for example, their nuisance value and the normal effect on Japan of such an extension of the Treaty. The use of the League of Nations machinery was suggested because, apart from practical reasons, it would keep the League authorities themselves on the right side in the matter. The League could be asked to circulate the draft Treaty to the other naval Powers, these Powers would send their observations to His Majesty's Government in the United Kingdom and a conference of the other Powers in Geneva might eventually be arranged.

LORD MONSELL said that he much preferred to deal with the matter by bilateral negotiations, since the conference procedure would encourage the small Powers to put up all kinds of objections.

MR. CRAIGIE suggested that the conference procedure was simpler in one respect, namely that the Powers were inclined to be grouped together, e.g. the Scandinavian, the small Mediterranean Powers, the Little Entente, etc. On the other hand conversations might well start bilaterally.

ADMIRAL CHATFIELD suggested that the United Kingdom Government might put the Treaty up as a basis and ask for observations or replies by a certain date. When the replies had been received, His Majesty's Government could discuss what should be done next.

CONCLUSIONS

### 1. The Irish Free State and The Treaty

It was agreed that Sir Harry Batterbee should see the Irish Free State High Commissioner in company with Mr. Craigie and suggest to him that in any statement he might wish to make announcing that the Free State would not sign the Treaty, he should, in the interests of the Free State itself, mention that his Government viewed with favour the objects aimed at by the Treaty.

### 2. Proposed United States Declaration on the subject of the Cruiser Holiday

(a) It was agreed that the United Kingdom Delegation could accept the idea that the United States should make a statement in the First Committee in the sense of the Annex to L.N.C. (U.K.) 87.[9] It should, however, first be suggested informally to the United States that the beginning of the last sentence should read 'Our acceptance of the cruiser holiday was accordingly given on the understanding etc.'[10]

(b) It was decided that the proposed statement should be shown by Sir Harry Batterbee to the Dominions Delegations and that it should be explained to them that, as it was to be purely a United States statement, it was hardly necessary to object to the incorrect terms used in describing His Majesty's Government and the navies of the Members of the Commonwealth.

### 3. Proposed United States Declaration in regard to parity

(a) It was agreed that the United States Delegation should be pressed not to insist upon any formal document recording their and the United Kingdom views on the subject of parity. It should be suggested to them rather that, at a meeting of the United States and United Kingdom Delegations, the United States should make an enquiry on the lines of the first half of the Annex to L.N.C. (35) (U.K.) 85,[11] while on behalf of the United Kingdom Delegation the First Lord would reply in the sense of the second half, the wording being changed to the effect that, 'His Majesty's Government in the United Kingdom

[9] See note 5 above.

[10] This wording was used by Mr. Davis in his statement to the First Committee. The draft text here read: 'Our acceptance of the cruiser holiday was accordingly made with the understanding that'.                                                               [11] See note 7 above.

and the United States maintain the principle of no naval rivalry, nor does either country question the right of the other to parity in any category of vessel'.

(b) It was decided that the Dominions need not be consulted in this matter, since, although parity as between the United States and the British Commonwealth as a whole was in question, the meeting was to be purely informal and the view given was to be a purely United Kingdom view.

(c) It was agreed that Mr. Dixon should first draw up a document, which from the point of view of 3 (b) would be unobjectionable in the eyes of the Dominion Office. This document would then be reviewed by the United Kingdom Delegation before a meeting was held with the United States Delegation.

## 4. *Anglo-German negotiations*

(a) It was agreed that in the light of the Cabinet decision of the 16th March, Mr. Craigie could be authorised to get into immediate touch with the German Naval Attaché with a view to continuing negotiations, on the understanding that there was no question of signature at the present time.

(b) In any conversations with the Germans, Mr. Craigie could take the line that, for various reasons, German agreement to a bilateral Treaty with the United Kingdom without any reservation in favour of the Union of Soviet Socialist Republics was much to be desired.

(c) If it was impossible to secure German agreement without a reservation in favour of the Union of Soviet Socialist Republics and if the Union of Soviet Socialist Republics held matters up for a considerable time, the Admiralty requirements, that the signature of the Three-Power Treaty should be dependent upon a similar arrangement with Germany, would not be fulfilled. It was decided, therefore, to suggest to the Secretary of State for Foreign Affairs that, in the light of this contingency, he should raise in the Cabinet the question whether, supposing Germany did not sign, His Majesty's Government would be prepared to agree to the withholding of the eventual ratification of the Three-Power Treaty.

## 5. *Limitation in the number of Germany's 10,000 ton Cruisers*

It was agreed that the United Kingdom Delegation could support the proposal that the French reservation in this matter could be dealt with under the contemplated procedure by which, if any event occurred in 1936, which appeared to be contrary to the provisions of the new Treaty, the Powers affected would agree to consult together.

## 6. *Date of signature*

It was agreed that, subject to an assurance having been obtained that Germany would come into an Agreement without waiting for the Soviet

Union, or alternatively to a Cabinet decision to the effect that United Kingdom ratification of the Treaty could be withheld pending the conclusion or assurance of an Anglo-German agreement, the signature of the proposed Treaty should be fixed, if practicable, for Tuesday, the 24th March.[12]

### 7. *Arrangements after signature*

No final conclusion was reached as to the procedure by which Other Powers should be approached and given the opportunity for making observations on the present Treaty and for adhering to a similar Treaty or similar Treaties.

[12] The Treaty was actually signed on March 25, 1936; cf. No. 718 below. Anglo-German negotiations continued until the signature in London on July 17, 1937, of the Anglo-German Agreement providing for the limitation of naval armament and the exchange of information concerning naval construction; for the text of the Agreement see *B.F.S.P.*, vol. 141, pp. 333–53. An Anglo-Soviet naval agreement was signed in London on the same day; see *ibid.*, pp. 428–33. Twelve days later, on July 29, 1937, the United Kingdom ratified the Three-Power Naval Treaty of March 25, 1936, which immediately came into force.

### No. 712

*Viscount Chilston (Moscow) to Mr. Eden (Received March 19, 7 p.m.)*
*No. 39 Telegraphic [A 2320/4/45]*

MOSCOW, *March 19, 1936, 8.10 p.m.*

Your telegram No. 35.[1]

I saw the Acting Commissar for Foreign Affairs this afternoon and enquired whether Soviet government were now in a position, as His Majesty's Government earnestly trusted would be the case, to return a reply. M. Krestinski informed me that the question had not been further considered by the Soviet government since it had been raised with the Soviet Counsellor on March 4th and the reply summarised in your telegram had been returned. Soviet government had not yet received from M. Kagan [Cahan] your answer on the possibility of accession by Soviet Union to Three Power Treaty. I therefore repeated your explanation which seemed to satisfy M. Krestinski. He stated however that the Soviet government must consider it and the first draft of the Treaty—which would be done in the most friendly spirit—before forming a definite opinion. He promised to ascertain whether any new matter had recently been received from London and in general to expedite the consideration of His Majesty's Government's suggestion.

M. Krestinski did not seem to consider it essential that the eventual naval agreement between the United Kingdom and Soviet Union should exactly coincide in time with agreements concluded with Washington Powers or Germany and I doubt very much whether the Soviet government will return an early reply.

[1] No. 708.

If the matter is urgent I suggest it might profitably be discussed with M. Litvinov[2] at this stage. He would no doubt be unable to take a decision without reference here but if he could be shown the draft treaty he would have all necessary material for forming a personal view which he could telegraph to Commissariat for Foreign Affairs. It might be advisable to emphasise the purely formal nature of reasons which exclude accession of Soviet Union to proposed three Power Treaty.

[2] M. Litvinov was in London representing the Union of Soviet Socialist Republics at the 91st (Extraordinary) session of the Council of the League of Nations held at St. James' Palace, London, March 14-24, 1936, following German action in the demilitarized zone of the Rhineland.

## No. 713

*Record by Mr. Craigie of a conversation with Mr. Fujii on March 19*
*[A 2405/4/45]*

FOREIGN OFFICE, *March 19, 1936*

Mr. Fujii called to see me to-day to enquire what was the present position in regard to the submarine warfare Protocol.[1]

I explained the difficulties that had arisen of including France and Italy as the original signatories for the proposed agreement, and said I thought that agreement had now been reached on the French draft, of which he had already received a copy. We would, however, inform him as soon as any text had definitely been agreed upon. He said that he hoped this would be done soon so that he could telegraph the text to Tokio, especially if there were to be any question of the submarine Protocol being signed at the same time as the Naval Treaty. I said that we did not wish to hurry the Japanese Government unduly in this matter, particularly as unforeseen difficulties had delayed for so long the preparation of a draft Protocol. I felt sure, however, that it would be greatly appreciated here if it did prove possible to sign the two instruments at the same time.[2]

[1] Cf. No. 704.
[2] It was not, however, found possible to do so. In a further conversation with Mr. Craigie on March 26 Mr. Fujii and Mr. Terasaki said that the Japanese Government did not much like the procès-verbal as drafted because it seemed to contemplate the granting of some new authority to France and Italy to join His Majesty's Government in communicating the submarine rules to the governments of non-signatory powers. By this time the draft, after a number of revisions, had taken virtually the form in which it was ultimately signed by representatives of the United States, Australia, Canada, France, Great Britain, India, the Irish Free State, Italy, Japan, New Zealand, and South Africa on November 6, 1936. See Treaty Series No. 29 (1936) (Cmd. 5302) *Procès-Verbal relating to the Rules of Submarine Warfare as set forth in Part IV of the London Naval Treaty of April 22, 1930* (London, November 6, 1936). Cf. *F.R.U.S. 1936*, vol. i, pp. 160-4. Germany accepted the procès-verbal on November 23, 1936, and the Soviet Union on December 27, 1936. These and 35 other accessions are listed in *B.F.S.P.*, vol. 140, p. 302.

## No. 714

*Sir E. Drummond (Rome) to Mr. Eden (Received March 23)*
*No. 84 Saving: Telegraphic [A 2343/4/45]*

ROME, *March 20, 1936*

Commenting today upon the Naval Conference, the 'Messaggero' remarks that the agreement in principle between Great Britain, the United States and France has not substantially modified the original positions and that a solution has been rendered more difficult by Japan's withdrawal and Italy's reservation. The major problems have been merely postponed and, given the present international situation, it is not possible to say how they will be solved. There are divergences on several points between the various powers, and each Power's thesis covers its own interests. If the Japanese thesis prevails, the position of Japan becomes unassailable and her hegemony in the Pacific is strengthened; if the American thesis prevails, Japan would hardly be able to bear the financial burden required to take part in the armament race; and if the British standpoint prevails, Great Britain will become, between the United States without capital ships and Japan without submarines, 'the arbiter of the Pacific'.

After returning to the points on which agreement has been reached, the 'Messagero' [*sic*] says that the results are almost insignificant; moreover they are provisional and leave the questions at issue unsolved. By adhering to the American thesis for the high tonnage limit for capital ships, Great Britain has secured for herself the possibility of increasing the number of cruisers by nearly 30 per cent. There is reason to believe that the limit of 35,000 tons for capital ships is far from contrary to her wishes. The decisions reached of late in London as regards armament will hardly please the French. The substitution of 356 mm. guns for 406 mm. guns threatens seriously to upset the French naval technique while it benefits those States which already possess units armed with 356 mm. guns.

## No. 715

*Letter from Sir E. Drummond (Rome) to Mr. Craigie (Received March 24)*
*[A 2426/4/45]*

ROME, *March 20, 1936*

My dear Craigie,

Document No. L.N.C. (35) (U.K.) 74[1] contained in the American Department's letter[2] No. A 2020/4/45 of March 14th.

We have already sent you a despatch (No. 301[3] of March 6th) about Grandi's explanations of Mussolini's conduct and very swift change of opinion about the capital ship problem, etc. I cannot say that I am convinced by his further explanations of March 2nd.

[1] No. 690 had been circulated under this reference.      [2] Not printed.
[3] No. 701.

On February 18th Mussolini certainly agreed by implication with our thesis about the size of capital ships.[4] About the 21st he shifted round completely.[5] It was not a question of a fortnight but of two or three days. I think personally that someone got at him directly after I had seen him and persuaded him that (*pace* Grandi) the Naval Conference afforded a good method of bringing pressure to bear on us about an extension of sanctions; certainly Mussolini exerted a somewhat analogous pressure on the French, utilising Locarno and the Franco-Italian military arrangements.

This does not, of course, altogether exclude other factors of the kind Grandi suggests, but the latter naturally will seek for and lay stress on explanations which are likely to be more palatable to us.

Yours ever,<br>
ERIC DRUMMOND

4 See No. 660.     5 See No. 667.


## No. 716

### Letter from Mr. Davis to Mr. Eden[1] (Received March 27)
### [A 2554/4/45]

CLARIDGE'S HOTEL, LONDON, March 24, 1936

My dear Foreign Secretary,

On the eve of the completion of the work of the Naval Conference and of our departure from London, I desire to express on behalf of the entire American Delegation appreciation for the many courtesies extended to us during our stay here. I also want to record our appreciation of the patient and untiring efforts of the United Kingdom Delegation and of their contribution of the success of the Conference in reaching the various agreements which are incorporated in the Treaty we are about to sign.

There is one thing further I should like to mention. In view of the fact that the new treaty does not provide for a continuance of quantitative limitation as established by the Washington and London Treaties, which are to expire

1 This letter and Mr. Eden's reply (No. 717 below) had been carefully drafted by the two delegations in order to satisfy the United States desire, first broached by Mr. Davis on March 4 (No. 699), for a re-affirmation of the principle of Anglo-American parity in naval matters. In a minute of March 23 Mr. Craigie remarked that the 'Admiralty—the First Sea Lord in particular—dislike the idea (1) because they have always felt the acceptance of the United States claim to parity to have been a mistake and (2) because they fear such a declaration might contain some implication of an American right to demand that we should count parity at their level, i.e., conform our strength to theirs. Having got rid of quantitative limitation, they refuse to accept even the shadow of a limitation vis-à-vis of the United States.' Mr. Craigie however did not think there was anything in these fears and he believed that it would be 'a major political blunder to appear to question America's right to parity'. On March 24 Sir R. Vansittart supported this view and Mr. Eden agreed to the exchange of letters subject to the First Lord's agreement, which was given. In the course of the discussions on this matter since March 4 Mr. Craigie had persuaded Mr. Davis to abandon the plan for a 'resounding joint declaration' (cf. No. 699, Annex) as this 'was bound to have a bad effect in Tokyo'.

at the end of this year, Admiral Standley and I have had, as you will recall, some discussion with the United Kingdom Delegation during the course of the Conference with regard to maintaining the principle of naval parity as between the fleets of the Members of the British Commonwealth and of the United States of America, which was fixed by those treaties, and which has now become a well established principle acceptable to the peoples as well as to the Governments of our respective countries. As a result of the conversations on this subject, it is our understanding that we are in agreement that there shall be no competitive naval building as between ourselves and that the principle of parity as between the fleets of the Members of the British Commonwealth and of the United States of America shall continue unchanged.

Sincerely yours,<br>
NORMAN H. DAVIS

## No. 717

*Letter from Mr. Eden to Mr. Davis*

*[A 2554/4/45]*

FOREIGN OFFICE, *March 25, 1936*

My dear Mr. Davis,

The First Lord and I very much appreciate the kind references which you make in your letter of the 24th instant[1] to the efforts of the United Kingdom Delegation to bring about a naval agreement.

I can assure you that the friendly relations which have prevailed between the United States and the United Kingdom Delegations have been a source of pleasure to all of us, and we are greatly indebted to yourself, Admiral Standley and the other members of your Delegation for your wholehearted co-operation throughout the difficult period of negotiation which now lies behind us.

I am glad, furthermore, to be able to confirm the correctness of your understanding in regard to the maintenance of the principle of parity. We are in full agreement that there must be no competitive building between our two countries and that neither country should question the right of the other to maintain parity in any category of ship. I can indeed go further than this and say that, in estimating our naval requirements, we have never taken the strength of the United States navy into account.

Yours sincerely,<br>
ANTHONY EDEN[2]

[1] No. 716.
[2] The texts of Nos. 716 and 717 are also printed in *F.R.U.S. 1936*, vol. i, p. 99.

## No. 718

### Mr. Eden to Sir R. Lindsay (Washington)[1]
### No. 102 Telegraphic [A 2519/4/45]

FOREIGN OFFICE, March 25, 1936, 7 p.m.

A Naval Treaty was signed to-day by representatives of the United States of America, France, Great Britain and Northern Ireland, Canada, Australia, New Zealand, and India.[2]

*Part I* of the Treaty consists solely of Definitions of Displacement, Categories and 'overage'.

*Part II* contains qualitative limitations which are as follows:—

Capital Ships, 35,000 tons and 14″ gun. If, however, any of the parties to the Washington Treaty fail to enter into an agreement to conform to this provision by the time the present Treaty comes into force the maximum gun calibre will be 16″.

Aircraft Carriers, 23,000 tons, 6·1″ guns.

Light Surface Vessels, 8,000 tons, with the reservation that this figure is without prejudice to any action after 1942 when the United States 10,000 ton cruisers are due for replacement.

Submarines, 2,000 tons and 5·1″ guns.

There is to be a zone of non-construction between 17,500 and 10,000 tons, and no capital ship is to be laid down whose main armament consists of guns of less than 10 inches.

*Part III* contains provision for Advance Notification and the Exchange of Information, a summary of which was given in my telegram No. 35.[3]

*Part IV* contains Safeguarding Clauses providing for escape from the limitations of the Treaty in case of war, building outside the qualitative limits by non-contracting Powers, etc.

*Part V* provides that His Majesty's Government in the United Kingdom will in the last quarter of 1940 initiate consultations with a view to the holding of a Conference to frame a new Treaty. In this consultation views are to be exchanged in order that it may be determined whether in the light of experience any reduction in the displacement or gun calibre of capital ships is possible.

The Treaty comes into force on the 1st January 1937, or as soon thereafter as it has been ratified by all signatories. It is to last for six years and to be open to the accession of any Party to the London Treaty for [? of] 1930.

A supplementary Protocol has been signed, providing (1) for consultation in case any important change of circumstances occurs before the Treaty comes into force and (2) for the provisional exchange of information during the early months of 1937 should the Treaty not be in force by that time.

[1] Identic telegrams, referring to No. 641, were sent on March 25 to Tokyo (No. 45), Paris (No. 94), Rome (No. 103), Berlin (No. 80), and Moscow (No. 48).

[2] For a brief comment on the proceedings, see *D.D.F. 1932–1939*, 2nd Series, vol. i, No. 500. [3] No. 641.

An additional protocol contains an expression of the hope that the system of advance notification and exchange of information will continue after 1942 and that it may be possible in any future treaty to achieve some further measure of reduction in naval armaments.

Copies of the text follow by bag.[3]

[3] The full English and French texts of the treaty are printed in *L.N.C. 1935 Docs.*, pp. 5–44, and in Cmd. 5136, *Miscellaneous No. 1 (1936)*; see also Cmd. 5137, *Memorandum on the London Naval Conference, December 9, 1935, to March 25, 1936.*

# APPENDIX I

# Memorandum by Sir Warren Fisher on defence requirements and naval strategy[1]

### N.C.M.(35)3 [A 4114/1938/45]

TREASURY CHAMBERS, *April 19, 1934*

### The 1935 Naval Conference

The subject matter of the Naval Staff memorandum (with comments by the Foreign Office), dated the 23rd March, 1934,[1] is of direct concern to the Treasury as the efficient preparation for war, and, if war comes, its successful conduct are only possible if Treasury policy in the sphere of finance and economics is soundly planned.

It is too generally assumed that imperial defence is a matter solely for compromise between the opinion on international affairs of the Foreign Office and the strategical and tactical conceptions of the Defence Departments: this assumption is based on a twofold illusion, as it appears to me. The first is that the resources for war which we can command are in exact proportion to the willingness of our people to subscribe paper pounds to the Exchequer, and the second is that that willingness is quite independent of the material conditions of life to which our people may have been reduced.

Of the readiness of our people—provided that they are convinced of the reality of a danger to themselves—to be taxed up to the hilt I myself have no doubt; but the translation of paper pounds into ability to secure the necessary material equipment for unlimited war is a wholly different matter. Our internal resources (apart from coal) are negligible, and we therefore must be in a position to purchase from overseas almost the whole of our requirements, whether this be food-stuffs or munitions of war. For this purpose paper pounds are, of course, useless and thus the willingness of the English taxpayer to contribute even up to 100 per cent. of his income is quite irrelevant to our capacity to conduct war indefinitely and on an indefinite scale. This disposes of illusion number one. Illusion number two, namely, our readiness to be taxed up to the hilt when our belts have been narrowed by absence of food-stuffs to vanishing point, needs no further disproof than the obvious remark that any man so situated will be ready to surrender on any terms.

The criterion applied by the Naval Staff for the security of our country seems to me to be a perfectly good one. It assumes that, even though our main fleet may be disposed for protective purposes in the Far East, there must be available in Home Waters force sufficient for the protection of essential needs until the main Fleet can be retransferred.

---

[1] This memorandum was circulated with a covering note of April 23 by the Chancellor of the Exchequer, Mr. Neville Chamberlain, referring to the memorandum of March 23, 1934, compiled by Admiral Sir Ernle Chatfield and Sir R. Vansittart on preparations for the 1935 Naval Conference (N.C.M.(35)1; cf. No. 24, note 4, and No. 566, Part I) and explaining that Sir Warren Fisher's memorandum had been prepared from the point of view of the Treasury.

The recurrent postulate in the Naval Staff's memorandum is that we could only 'accept' (*i.e.*, allow) this, that and the other position of inferiority on the part of a foreign Power or Powers as the basis of our agreement with them. No argument is adduced why the foreign Power or Powers should acquiesce in any such inferiority. The implication is presumably that we are financially in a position to threaten, in the absence on their part of such acquiescence, to outbuild them; but this is not the case. The memorandum recognises that the policy of this country has always been to disregard the strength of the United States Fleet in computing our naval requirements: this is in accordance with the self-evident fact that we could not successfully fight a country which (*a*) is twenty-five times our size; (*b*) has nearly three times our population; (*c*) has internal material resources which simply cannot be measured; and (*d*) can over-run Canada at any moment she chooses.

Apart from this fact of her material strength, it is highly improbable that the United States would initiate an attack on ourselves except in the event of our interference with her sea-borne trade in the form of a blockade by us of an enemy Power when she was a neutral.

But the inference from this decision of policy should surely be that we should settle our own conception of our own interests without reference to the United States.

From various passages in the memorandum and the Foreign Office comments included in it, it would seem that in this way and that[2] satisfaction of our own needs is regarded as almost unrealisable because it would not suit the supposed naval policy of the United States. Now—*amour-propre* apart and the exacting ideal of Rule Columbia—the risks to the safety of the United States, whether on land or in the air or at sea, from the encroachments of any foreign Power are precisely nil. She can, as already mentioned, maintain herself on her own internal resources; and the American citizen is not and never will be in the faintest danger of being physically starved. The United States likes size, particularly if she can get it 'on the cheap'; therefore she insists, or tries to, on an international agreement of limitation which provides for her having, for instance, the largest cruisers and rather more of them, though not many more, than anybody else. An agreement that includes big cruisers, though not too many, is admirably suited to the satisfaction of her vanity and, as the price of agreement, she forces us to adopt a similar policy and at the same time saves herself from having to satisfy her vanity at the cost of unlimited building.

In other words, a naval agreement between ourselves and the United States is the most complete *non sequitur* from any and every point of view, for, as already stated, 'in accordance with the policy of His Majesty's Government the strength of the United States Fleet is left out of account in computing its (that is, our own) requirements'; and, if regard be had to our own needs in the (to us) live issue of security, the last criterion we should apply is what the United States may want to force us to do. So much for the United States of America.

The Naval Staff and the Treasury are in complete agreement on the fundamental point of ensuring to the utmost limit possible the safety of our Country and Empire. But one of the principal ingredients in successful insurance is a wise disposition of our resources. The Naval Staff most pertinently observe that if 'a two-Power standard' is beyond our capacity 'we cannot simultaneously fight Japan and the strongest European naval Power'. In other words economy, properly

[2] The text here appears to be corrupt. A marginal note of interrogation was added on the filed copy.

conceived, means ability to concentrate our maximum strength on our principal danger. It will be common ground to the Admiralty and the Treasury that the British Empire, whether in Asia or elsewhere, would become defenceless if England herself were knocked out. It will probably be agreed that even at the extreme limit of her endeavour Japan by herself could not knock out England or deprive her of the essentials in food-stuffs and raw materials. That Japan could scoop not merely such outposts as Hong Kong, but the whole of our Chinese investments and trade, is hardly open to serious doubt; but given a completed Singapore—and incidentally an anti-Japanese America[3]—Japan's capacity for endangering our trade routes or India or Australasia will never assume such proportions as to lay us low.

While this is no argument for ignoring all reasonable measures to bring home to the Japanese that we are not a negligible factor, it is certainly not a reason for basing our war preparations on an encounter with Japan. For the risk which really could involve us in disaster is much nearer home; and it is highly dangerous to limit our estimate of a future German menace merely to the consideration of our present relative position *vis-à-vis* Germany in naval strength. In a recent paper, C.P. 104 (34),[4] Sir Robert Vansittart gave, in his own picturesque fashion, an appreciation of the Prussian outlook and objective. He had been preceded by a less spirited stylist. The late Chief of the Imperial General Staff, Sir George (now Lord) Milne, in a paper dated the 28th October, 1932, C.P. 362 (32),[5] came to a similar conclusion as to the ultimate policy towards which modern Germany was moving. My only comment on both papers would be that they might easily leave the impression that it was only during relatively recent times that these Teutonic impulses were given birth; as a dilettante reader of history I should, for my own part, have said that they came into being in the days of the nascent Duchy of Brandenburg.

Given the consistency of the attitude of these Teutonic tribes, who century after century have been inspired by the philosophy of brute force, we should be more than usually stupid if we assumed that the sweet reasonableness of the Treaty of Versailles had converted them to the tenets of the Sermon on the Mount; and if we want to survive we had better think most carefully how so to economise our resources as to meet the danger at its maximum point. That, at a distance of 10,000 miles, we can down the Japanese is a chimera compared with which *Alice in Wonderland* is a serious essay; that we should wish to down Japan seems to me to be worse than Don Quixote in his most idiotic moods towards a windmill; in fact we have everything to gain and nothing to lose by coming, as I believe we most easily could, to an accommodation with Japan, in substance though not in form, similar to our agreement of thirty years ago.[6]

Now the Naval Staff paper in principle does not seem to differ from this conclusion, and, from more than one talk that I have had with the Chief of the Naval Staff, I believe that he has not the least desire to get us embroiled with Japan and recognises that a mutually agreeable understanding between ourselves

[3] *Note in original*: 'I understand, however, that some agreement has recently been made between the United States and Japan, probably relating to Manchukuo and American trading interests, and possibly also to naval matters.'

[4] The memorandum of April 7, 1934, by Sir R. Vansittart, printed as Appendix III in Volume VI, was circulated to the Cabinet under this reference.

[5] Not printed.

[6] For the Anglo-Japanese Agreement signed at London on August 12, 1905, which superseded the Agreement of January 30, 1902, see *B.F.S.P.*, vol. 98, pp. 136–8.

and Japan would be a very definite increase in our security. The Naval Staff memorandum, however, as has already been mentioned, emphasises our inability to 'accept' for ourselves *vis-à-vis* the Japanese any strength that is not decisively superior to their own. Such an attitude seems to me inconsistent with any hope of resuming stable and intimate terms with the Japanese; for, apart from our complete inability to impose subordination on the Japanese, it can only have the effect of wounding their *amour-propre* and of fastening on them the conviction that we regard them as potential foes. Of course, if we could rely without question on securing and maintaining the good-will of the Americans—and by 'good-will' I mean, not high-sounding professions, but the practical assurance that if we got into difficulties anywhere we could permanently count on the effective support of the United States—I would agree that good relations between ourselves and Japan, although still most desirable, would be a less urgent problem. But the very last thing in the world that we can count on is American support;[7] and, as the policy of His Majesty's Government referred to in the Naval Staff's memorandum has been and continues to be that our naval dispositions may leave out of account the United States, I think it would be conceded that we should be singularly ill-advised to jeopardise the possibility of some friendly arrangement with the Japanese by paying any regard to the United States.

The underlying reason for our naval attitude to Japan since the end of the European War has been in no sense due to consideration of our own direct interests but to a misplaced feeling that we have got to 'keep in with' the Americans; in the result—though I am aware that the responsibility for any change is sedulously foisted on to the Dominion of Canada—we gave up a completely satisfactory treaty with Japan for a completely unsatisfactory naval Pact of Washington.[8] The natural self-respect of the Japanese was greatly mortified and although, as the memorandum of the Naval Staff points out, the material effect at the time on ourselves was not unsatisfactory, the subsequent march of events, intensified by the London Pact of 1930,[9] has been to emphasise our practical disadvantages, comprising at the same time a relative diminution in actual strength, an unsuitable type of Fleet, and a replacement in the sphere of the 'intangibles' of a thoroughly reliable good-will between Japan and ourselves for a feeling of suspicion on their part.

The Naval Staff memorandum is thus quite legitimately based on a political situation which is itself, however, fundamentally unsound if we have real regard

[7] *Note in original*: 'The late Sir John Fortescue, Librarian at Windsor Castle, in the course of the Ford Lectures at Oxford in 1911, has neatly summed up the position. The whole passage (pages 23–28) is well worth reading; I confine myself to quoting here one paragraph:— 'Now we know how the Americans—represented by their Government—have always dealt with us since they have been an independent State. They must always prevail, and never give way; they must always take and never concede; they enjoy the flouting of an older community as a proof of their superiority; and they esteem a good bargain, even if gained by dishonourable means, to mark the highest form of ability. The United States cannot engage in any form of competition with us, from athletics to diplomacy, without using foul play. They must win, if not by fair skill, then by pre-arranged trickery or violence; if not by open negotiations, then by garbled maps and forged documents. There is the fact. It may be unpleasant, but it cannot be denied.'

[8] The Treaty for the Limitation of Naval Armament signed at Washington on February 6, 1922; cf. No. 1, note 11.

[9] The Treaty for the Limitation and Reduction of Naval Armament signed at London on April 22, 1930, cf. *ibid.*, note 12.

to our own security. It is none of the Admiralty's making; though I cannot conceal from myself that some of my naval colleagues in 1922 were (not unnaturally) moved by sorrow at the possibility of 'Rule, Britannia!'—that heartening battle song of England—being degraded into 'Rule, Columbia!'

But 1922 was a mere three years or so distant in time from the complete defeat of Germany, and it is not by way of criticism of the then mentality that I say that the conclusions reached in 1922 are as remote from the realities of 1934 and future years as the North from the South Pole.

If 'we cannot simultaneously fight Japan and the strongest European naval Power'—and even the most optimistic estimate of our resources makes this self-evident—we not merely cannot afford further to alienate Japan, but it is an imperative and pressing need for us to effect a genuine and lasting reconciliation with her. And this latter we cannot do by futile insistence that we won't permit her to have such naval weapons and in such quantities as she may think necessary.

This, however, does not in the least mean that it is hopeless to imagine that we can reach some reasonable accommodation with her. If the post-War years have driven one impression home to her, it is that the English have no mind or backbone of their own, that they are ready to toe the line wherever and whenever the Americans order them, that the British Naval Forces may therefore be available at American command to support every anti-Japanese policy America may indulge —in short, that we are not merely renegades *vis-à-vis* our pre-War and War allies and friends, the Japanese themselves, but are servile adherents of the country that more than once between August 1914 and April 1917 showed a readiness to stab us in the back. This impression it is vital for us to remove; then, but not till then, can we discuss with the Japanese—not necessarily such questions as ratios, but the much wider issue of our respective needs, to be measured in the light of reciprocal friendship and the complementary nature of our Asiatic interests.

It is high time that we should analyse the true requirements of our own security; the American 'yard arm' may well get us into trouble, but will assuredly never come to our rescue.

The Treasury point of view in this matter of England's security is indistinguishable from that of the Admiralty; where it may differ is in the application of the point of view. Just as the Admiralty are the advisers of Government in regard to the technicalities of naval defence, so the Treasury are responsible to the Government for ensuring that the resources of the country—which, as I have already stated, include far more than the payment of paper pounds into the Exchequer, but embrace the whole problem of the material supplies on which a successful issue depends—are wisely developed and used for the attainment of the objective common to both Departments.

The reconciliation of any differences that there may be is, I suggest, to be found in the adoption of a national and imperial policy firmly based on the facts of the situation.

We cannot hope to secure agreement between the widely different outlooks of the various Naval Powers in any expectation that they would be prepared to subordinate their own conceptions of security to our theories of what we would wish them to do. It is simpler—and, if security be our object, more effective—for us to clear our own minds as to our own necessities and make this the touchstone of our policy.

The Report of the Defence Requirements Committee[10]—which I should like

[10] Of February 1934; cf. Introductory Note to Chapter I.

here to emphasise was quite unanimous and was not dictated by any member or members of that Committee to the rest of us—makes it clear that, as the result of some months of the closest investigation, we have no doubt whatever as to where our ultimate danger lies, *i.e.*, from Germany. It is common ground that we cannot successfully fight both Japan and Germany at the same time. The first essential, therefore, to our own safety is that we must be free to concentrate our strength where it is most needed. This implies that any German hopes of finding or getting us embroiled in a first-rate war in the Far East must well in advance be doomed to disappointment, and that the Germans themselves are left under no illusion in the matter. What, then, is the prime condition for attaining this essential object of definitely relieving ourselves of any danger of being involved in a war with Japan? I suggest that the first and, indeed, cardinal requirement for this end is the disentanglement of ourselves from the United States of America. For the Americans no question of any jeopardy to their national security can under any conceivable conditions arise. Their armed forces of all kinds are therefore in large measure a luxury. For some reason best known to themselves they view with a suspicious and, indeed, hostile eye the Japanese.[11] We, on the contrary, from the very earliest days of Japan's westernisation until the end of the European War have felt and shown a real sympathy to Japan, and have recognised that the interests of the two countries have been in the maintenance of mutual goodwill and regard; and until we threw them over in 1922 this attitude has been fully reciprocated by Japan towards ourselves. The interest of the Americans in Naval Pacts has been threefold: in the first place, such pacts have admirably played the American game in their relations *vis-à-vis* Japan, for by introducing discord between the Japanese and ourselves they have tended to diminish the international influence and potential force of Japan. Their second reason for liking these naval pacts is that the successful antagonisation of the Japanese towards the English weakens us and therefore in our turn we have lost both influence and power and are more dependent on the (non-existent) goodwill of the United States. The third motive force of the United States is vanity, for which reason alone—and for no essential need—they desire to have a fleet at least as large as ourselves; and as there is no essential need, a limiting agreement giving this result obviates the risk of the American public getting tired of paying up the vast sums which an unlimited luxury armada would entail.

Now we might tell the Americans in effect that, as our long-established policy has been to exclude them entirely from the rôle of a potential foe to England, we naturally feel quite unconcerned with the scale of their warlike preparations; whatever they may decide in this sphere is entirely a matter for their own determination, and we have no intention of trying to compete in any way with them; indeed, if they had in mind to treble or quadruple their naval strength, we should neither attempt to follow suit nor feel in the least disquieted. Our own position, as we should make clear, is wholly different from theirs, for, while we believe that we are in no danger of an attack from the United States, we cannot ignore the possibility of very serious danger from other quarters. Although our interests, of course, are by no means limited to Europe, we are an inevitable part, for geographical reasons, of the European system, and if, in the future, a further upheaval were to occur in Europe we could not help being involved sooner or later by the mere force of events. Our preparations accordingly must be related to our own position, and obviously cannot be effective for that purpose if they are to be

[11] *Note in original*: 'See footnote to page 3', i.e. note 3 above.

measured in principle or detail by purely arbitrary considerations unconnected with those needs.

Having in one way or another thus regained our freedom to consider our needs on their merits we can then make it our aim to dispose of any Japanese menace; and I, for my own part, feel no doubt that the Japanese, once they are convinced that we propose to order our own doings instead of having them ordered from Washington, will be more than ready to come to a satisfactory and lasting accommodation with ourselves. And this will be all the more likely if we, in other aspects of our relationship with Japan, show that we wish and intend to eliminate (on the basis, of course, of give and take) any serious cause of disagreement.

The result on our naval strength would be that we could have at a price which we could afford a really effective European standard, not one power but two, if the latter were considered necessary. While naturally we cannot count the French Fleet as a part of our own defensive arrangements, we know that the very last thing in the world that the French have in mind is to engage in a war against ourselves. The Naval Staff memorandum suggests, I think very fairly, that our interest in the French Fleet is that it 'provides and will provide the measure for the strength of the strongest European naval Power,' and that we have to visualise the possibility of some other European Power by no means well disposed as the French are to ourselves trying to usurp the French continental lead at sea. Here again an effort in 1935 to force on the French a limitation of their ratios just because of the possibility I have just mentioned could only result in discord, when our obvious interest, as between the French and ourselves, is goodwill; and, apart from the almost certain failure of any such effort, it is quite unnecessary if, on the lines of policy which I have sketched out above, we are in a position—fully obvious to the Germans—to prepare and mobilise naval forces of overwhelming strength to confront the latter for as long ahead as we can see.

To secure our national and imperial safety my advice therefore is (1) that we should regain our freedom to make such preparations and dispositions in regard to our Fleet as are necessitated by our own needs; (2) that we should effect a thorough and lasting accommodation with the Japanese (I am not suggesting a resumption of the alliance in its original form) in every sphere of relationship between themselves and us; and (3) that we should make it evident so that the Germans can be under no illusion—that we intend to have available for immediate concentration our maximum force in the event of their engineering any future cataclysm in Europe.

N. F. W. F.

# APPENDIX II

## Memorandum by Sir W. Malkin on the proposed Air Pact

[C 4467/55/18]

FOREIGN OFFICE, *June 1, 1935*

In accordance with the arrangements which had been made between the four Governments,[1] I discussed the question of the text of the Air Pact with my French, Belgian and Italian colleagues at Geneva in the early days of this week. I attach (Annex I) the English text of a report which we agreed that each of us should present to his Government. The first part of this report was drafted in French and the second in English; I can produce the French text of the whole if required. The French representative produced a revised version of the French draft which was handed to the Secretary of State in Paris on February 28th;[2] this revised draft is attached as Annex II,[3] in which the new passages are italicised. An English version of this text is also attached as Annex III, and the English draft which was before us is also attached for convenience of reference as Annex IV.[4]

Our instructions were not to discuss any political questions which were still outstanding, and consequently such provisions in the French draft as related to matters like the question whether the pact was to be concluded only as part of a 'general settlement', and the question of supplementary bilateral agreements, were not taken into consideration.

It soon became clear, however, that before anything in the nature of a definite text could be produced, it was essential that decisions should be reached on the question as to which of the proposed signatories were to give guarantees and which were to receive them. This is, of course, not a point which the jurists could settle, and my colleagues' information about it seemed distinctly limited. My Italian colleague had no instructions at all, and did not know of the agreement which had been reached between the United Kingdom and Italy that each of them should not give a guarantee either to or against the other.[5] Neither he nor my French colleague showed any knowledge of what the position was to be as between France and Italy as regards any guarantees going beyond those existing under Locarno. The Belgian representative intimated that he thought his Government would be willing to give a guarantee to this country against Germany, although in effect this guarantee might have to be confined to such action as Belgium could take to prevent a German air attack upon this country being made across Belgian territory; he used the expression 'barrer la route'. Both he and the French representative intimated that their countries would not be prepared to guarantee Italy against the United Kingdom or the United Kingdom against Italy. Moreover, none of us, of course, had any knowledge of the extent to which Germany was willing to give and receive guarantees to and from the other signatories.

[1] See Nos. 174 and 254.    [2] See Volume XII, Annex to No. 517.
[3] Not printed.
[4] The text here reprinted is identical with that handed to the French and Italian delegations at the Stresa Conference; see Volume XII, No. 722, pp. 912–14.
[5] See article 3 in Annex IV to this Appendix; cf. Volume XII, No. 429.

When these points have been definitely cleared up, it will be necessary to consider whether it will be possible to find a general formula covering all the guarantees to be given, or whether they will have to be dealt with separately. At present both drafts proceed on the basis of a general formula with exceptions for particular cases; this has already produced difficulties, as for instance in connexion with Article 2 of the English draft. Personally I am now disposed to think that the idea of a general formula with particular exceptions will prove impracticable, because of the number and variety of the exceptions to be made; it would be necessary to provide for quite a large number of possible combinations, including some which are outside the range of practical politics, such as an attack by Belgium upon the United Kingdom. So far as I can see at present the guarantees to be given are likely to fall into three classes: (1) those which correspond to the existing Locarno guarantees, (2) the new guarantees to be given by France and Belgium to the United Kingdom and Germany, (3) whatever new guarantees may be given as between France and Italy. I am disposed to think that each of these classes will have to be dealt with in a separate provision. This should facilitate defining the circumstances in which the guarantees in category (1) are to be given, though it would necessitate a separate definition of the circumstances in which categories (2) and (3) are to operate. Probably such a definition will have to be based on Article 2 of Locarno.

Apart from this the main difficulty which arose in our discussions related, as was to be expected, to the definition of the circumstances in which the guarantees to be given to France, Belgium and Germany (i.e. those corresponding to the existing Locarno guarantees) were to operate. This question is discussed in the first part of the report. Both the French and English drafts are based on the idea of 'unprovoked aggression'. But the French draft includes (second paragraph of Article 1) a definition under which every air attack is to be regarded as unprovoked aggression unless it falls within one of the exceptions in Article 2 of Locarno. The Belgian representative and I pointed out that the effect of this would be to bind the guarantors to intervene on the side of France in the event of an aerial counter-attack by Germany upon France after the latter had attacked Germany (in circumstances where she could legitimately do so under Article 2 of Locarno) in consequence of a German attack upon Poland or Czechoslovakia—to which the Soviet Union should now be added. The French representative made it plain that this was not the intention of his Government; his observations on this point are recorded in the second paragraph of the report, and if they may be taken as representing the view of the French Government, there is no difference of opinion between us as to the situation under Locarno in the circumstances postulated.

This being so, and since the Belgian representative and I maintained our objection to the wording of the French definition, it became apparent that one element at any rate in the definition of the circumstances in which these particular guarantees were to apply must be that the attack should constitute a violation of Article 2 of Locarno. The French jurist however then argued that if this were done there was no need to introduce in addition the idea of unprovoked aggression. Logically, I do not think that this view can be regarded as sound; for the case contemplated is only an instance of the case of 'flagrant violation of Article 2' which is contemplated in Article 4, paragraph 3, of Locarno, and under that Article the two points on which the guaranteeing Powers have to be satisfied are that the violation constitutes an unprovoked aggression and that immediate action is necessary. It is agreed that the second condition is to be regarded as fulfilled if the violation takes the form of an air attack, but the fact that the attack was made by way of the air does not necessarily make it an act of unprovoked aggression. The French representative was, however, obviously disturbed by a remark by the Belgian representative (which though probably true was perhaps, in the circumstances, rather unfortunate) that it would be necessary for the guaranteeing Powers to examine the previous policy of the State which had been attacked in order to decide whether it could be regarded as constituting provocation. Since the one thing which the French would get out of the Pact would be that in circumstances where the guarantee did apply assistance would be given immediately, this idea is naturally unwelcome to them. This question obviously involves political elements and will have to be settled between the governments concerned, and in this connexion the Germans are likely to have a good deal to say. I may add that the discussions showed that the French representative fully realised that it must be for the State whose assistance is called for to decide whether circumstances have arisen which call the guarantee into operation.

On the other points which we considered the report is, I think, sufficiently self-explanatory. The French explanation of the phrase in Article 1 of their draft, under which assistance is to be given 'aussitôt qu'elle sera demandée' (a point which had caused much anxiety here), will be noted. It will also be seen that the point about air attacks on a fleet or mercantile marine on the high seas, as to which no decision was reached at the Ministerial meeting on May 17th, was raised by the French representative; in accordance with my instructions I did not commit myself, and the point was simply left for further consideration.

I think that we should agree to the insertion of the first paragraph of Article 2 of the French draft (without the words 'ou limitée'), since it corresponds to the procedure laid down in Locarno in the case of a flagrant violation, and may be useful as emphasising the League element.

The explanation given of Article 3 of the French draft will also be noted; the questions which it raises are exclusively political, and involve the position of Holland.

WILLIAM MALKIN

ANNEX I TO APPENDIX II

*Jurists' Report*

GENEVA, *May 28, 1935*

The jurists have examined, in connexion with Article 1 of the French draft and Articles 1 and 2 of the English draft, the provisions in those drafts whose object is to determine the circumstances in which assistance is to be given against aerial aggression.

In this connexion the representative of Belgium expressed the fear that the second paragraph of Article 1 of the French draft would have the result that if France took military action against Germany in a case where the latter had attacked Czechoslovakia, and in such circumstances that the action of France was legitimate under the Treaty of Locarno, and if Germany replied to the French military action by air action, Belgium would be bound to come to the assistance of France against this German air action. The representative of France replied that this was not what the French text meant, since a state's defence against a legitimate attack directed against it could not be regarded as aggression on the part of that state.

933

With a view to appreciating the effect of the provisions proposed for determining in what cases assistance was to be given against aerial aggression, the situation as between Germany and Belgium and Germany and France was taken particularly into consideration. It appeared in this connexion that it was necessary to determine whether, as between Germany and Belgium and Germany and France, assistance was to be given in every case where the aerial aggression had been effected in violation of Article 2 of the Treaty of Locarno, or whether it was necessary to add the further condition that this aggression should be unprovoked. On the first hypothesis it would only be necessary to establish that the aerial aggression did not fall within one of the exceptions laid down in Article 2, paragraph 2, of the Treaty of Locarno; on the second hypothesis the High Contracting Parties whose assistance was called for would have to consider and decide ('apprécier') whether the state which had been attacked had provoked this attack by the policy which it had followed in regard to the aggressor state.

It is to be noted that in the case of a 'flagrant violation' where the guaranteeing states furnish their assistance without a previous decision having been taken by the Council, Article 4, paragraph 3, of the Treaty of Locarno introduces the element of non-provocation, while this element does not appear when, under paragraph 1 of this article, the Council is called upon to find that a violation of Article 2 has been committed, in which case the immediate assistance of the High Contracting Parties follows.

It is necessary to consider whether the necessity to react with particular rapidity in the case of aerial attack should lead one to the conclusion to confine oneself to the fact that the attack was effected in violation of Article 2 of the Treaty of Locarno without enquiring whether such aggression was provoked or not. But the reply to this question is not a legal matter.

Once this question has been decided as regards the relationship between Germany and Belgium and between Germany and France the solution adopted could be applied, so far as may be appropriate, to the relationships between the other signatory Powers who are to receive the guarantee provided for in the Convention.

It would then be necessary to consider whether a general formula could be found to give effect to these solutions, or whether it would be preferable to have a separate provision for each guarantee.

The Jurists also considered the following points:

### French Draft

*Article 1, first paragraph.* The representative of France explained that the phrase 'aussitôt qu'elle lui sera demandée' had been inserted with the object of preventing the guarantee from coming into operation in the case of a minor incident which the State concerned did not wish to treat seriously. It was agreed that it was desirable to achieve this result, but that the phrase employed was open to some objection, and that it would be well to find another method of dealing with the point.

*Article 1, last paragraph.* This had been inserted because of the possibility that, if Germany did not remain a member of the League, the action under Article 16 referred to in Article 2 (2) of Locarno might require to be taken under Article 17, paragraph 3. Doubts were, however, expressed as to whether it would be wise to insert this paragraph in view of the fact that no such provision exists in Locarno.

*Article 2, first paragraph.* It was pointed out that the words 'ou limitée' did not seem very appropriate in this connexion, and it was felt that they might be omitted.

*Article 2, second paragraph.* This paragraph is inconsistent with the last words of Article 4 of Locarno, under which the concurrence in the recommendations of the Council of 'the representatives of the parties which have engaged in hostilities' is not necessary. If the proposed paragraph were inserted, the position in this respect would be different according to whether the attack which led to the intervention of the guaranteeing Powers was an air attack or not. Doubts were expressed as to the wisdom of endeavouring to secure the insertion of such a provision.

*Article 3.* The representative of France explained the idea of this provision to be that neighbouring States such as Holland might be invited not to hinder, or even in certain circumstances to assist (as by allowing flying over their territory), operations undertaken in pursuance of the convention. It was felt that the questions raised by this article were exclusively of a political character.

*Articles 4 and 5.* These articles were not discussed by the jurists, since the questions raised by them were of a political character. Similarly the three Protocols attached to the French draft were not discussed.

### English Draft

*Preamble.* The United Kingdom representative explained that the paragraph beginning 'Anxious in particular to safeguard . . .' had been inserted because it was considered important to avoid any suggestion that the conclusion of the convention involved any recognition of the legitimacy of indiscriminate air attack upon the civil population; the United Kingdom Government felt that the paragraph in the French preamble beginning 'Reconnaissant que certaines méthodes' was open to objection from this point of view. The representative of France stated that this was certainly not the intention of the paragraph in question, but that there was no objection in principle to the paragraph in the English Preamble, though it might be well slightly to modify its wording, so as to avoid any suggestion that the guarantee only applied in the case of an attack upon the civil population. Apart from this point it was thought premature to discuss the wording of the Preamble.

*Article 1, first paragraph.* The French and Belgian Representatives pointed out that the phrase 'with all the air forces available for the purpose' might have an unduly limitative effect. The representative of the United Kingdom explained that the phrase had been inserted with precisely the opposite intention. It was thought that something like the phrase in the French text 'l'assistance de *ses forces aériennes*' might be employed.

*Article 1, paragraph 2.* It was pointed out that this geographical description might exclude from the operation of the guarantee air attacks upon (*e.g.*) Corsica or Sardinia. It was suggested that if it were thought desirable to confine the operation of the convention to Europe, this might be done by omitting the geographical definition and inserting the words 'in Europe' in the first paragraph of the article.

It was also pointed out by the French representative that the effect of the geographical definition, coupled with the phrase 'upon his territory', was to exclude from the operation of the guarantee an air attack upon a fleet (or upon a mercantile marine) on the high seas, or upon aircraft if not above the territory of the country to which they belonged. It was agreed that this question required investigation.

*Article* 2. Objections were suggested to the wording of this article, and it was thought that there were other ways of obtaining the object for which it had been inserted.

*Article* 3. It was observed that this article only limits the guarantees given by the United Kingdom and Italy. This involves the more general problem of determining the States who give guarantees and the States who receive them. This question of principle must be settled before seeking the appropriate formula to express the solution which is adopted.

No objections were raised to Articles 4, 5 and 6.

<h3 style="text-align:center">ANNEX III[6] TO APPENDIX II</h3>

Revised French Draft Air Convention

(*Translation*)

The President of the German Reich, His Majesty the King of the Belgians, the President of the French Republic, His Majesty the King of the United Kingdom of Great Britain and Northern Ireland, His Majesty the King of Italy:

Considering the danger to the maintenance of peace and good understanding between the nations caused by the possibility of aerial attack between Germany, Belgium, France, the United Kingdom and Italy,

Desiring to avert this danger to the greatest possible extent by assuring effective assistance to any State which could be the object of such aerial attack,

Recognising that certain methods of aerial warfare render necessary especially prompt and powerful action in the form of counter-attack and reprisals, in order to assure the effective repression of all aggression committed by way of the air,

Have resolved to conclude a treaty with this object, and have appointed as their plenipotentiaries: . . .[7]
who, having communicated their full powers, found in good and due form, have agreed as follows:—

<h3 style="text-align:center">ARTICLE 1.</h3>

In the event of one of the high contracting parties being the object of unprovoked aggression, by way of the air, on the part of one of the States named in the preamble to the present treaty, the other high contracting parties undertake, as soon as requested by the party attacked, immediately to come to its assistance with their air forces.

By 'unprovoked *aerial* aggression' in the sense of Section 1 above shall be understood all aerial attack, *whether or not accompanied by an attack by land or sea*, other than action carried out in the cases provided for in article 2 (2), paragraphs 1, 2 and 3, of the general Treaty of Locarno, or in execution either of the commitments of guarantee and assistance described in articles 1, 4 and 5 of the said treaty, or of the commitments resulting from the present convention.

*In the application of the preceding paragraph, article 16 of the Covenant of the League of Nations is understood as having the scope given to it by Article 17, paragraph 3, of the said Covenant.*

<h3 style="text-align:center">ARTICLE 2.</h3>

While the assistance rendered in accordance with Article 1 may not thereby be retarded or limited, the Council of the League of Nations shall be invited to

---

[6] For Annex II, not printed, see first paragraph of this Appendix.

[7] Omission as in the original.

936

examine the situation in order to exercise the powers conferred upon it by the Covenant of the League and the general Treaty of Locarno.

*In the calculation of the vote on the acceptance of the recommendations of the Council, the votes of the states which have rendered aerial assistance to the State attacked will be counted.*

### ARTICLE 3.

The object of the present treaty being the better assurance of the maintenance of peace, the high contracting parties will make every endeavour to obtain that other Powers may undertake not to hinder its application.

### ARTICLE 4.

The technical arrangements governing the methods by which assistance shall be rendered shall be the object of bilateral agreements between the signatory Powers.

### ARTICLE 5.

*The present convention shall be ratified and the ratifications shall be exchanged at . . .*[7] *as soon as possible.*

*It will come into force at the same time as the general agreement on the limitation of armaments contemplated in the London Declaration of February 3rd, 1935, which agreement should, so far as concerns the military status of Germany, be substituted for the provisions of Part V of the Treaty of Versailles.*

Three protocols shall be annexed to this convention:—

1. Anglo-Italian reservation.

2. Since Germany and Italy are to be parties to instruments relative to the maintenance of peace in Central Europe, the high contracting parties declare that the engagements resulting for them from the treaty of this day shall not *ipso facto* be applicable in the case of a conflict arising between Germany and Italy in consequence of their relations in that region.

3. Pending the entry into force of the convention, the signatory Powers shall recognise the right of any of them immediately to concert together, at will, by way of bilateral negotiations, in order to obtain mutual assurances of the guarantees provided by the convention for the period between its conclusion and coming into force.

### ANNEX IV TO APPENDIX II

*English Draft Air Convention*

(List of Heads of States)

Having this day concluded

Recognising that the use which might be made of modern developments in the air might lead to sudden aggression by one country upon another,

Desiring to contribute to the restoration of confidence and the prospects of peace among nations by taking steps with the object of ensuring among themselves additional security against unprovoked aggression in the form of sudden attacks from the air,

Anxious, in particular, to safeguard the civil populations of their countries against the danger of indiscriminate attacks from the air, which they recognise to be contrary to the Law of Nations,

Recalling the guarantees already given among themselves by the Treaty of Locarno,

937

Have resolved to conclude a treaty with this object and have appointed as their plenipotentiaries: . . .[7]
who, having communicated their full powers, found in good and due form, have agreed as follows:—

### ARTICLE 1.

In the event of one of the High Contracting Parties being the object of unprovoked aggression upon his territory by the air forces of another High Contracting Party, the other High Contracting Parties will, subject to the provisions of Article 3, immediately come to the assistance of the Party which has been the object of such unprovoked aggression with all the air forces available for the purpose.

For the purpose of this Article the territories of the High Contracting Parties are, respectively, Germany, the United Kingdom of Great Britain and Northern Ireland, and the territories on the Continent of Europe of Belgium, France and Italy.

### ARTICLE 2.

It is understood that the provisions of Article 1 will not be applicable if the High Contracting Party who is the object of attack has resorted to war against another State, whether a party to the present Treaty or not, in violation of his treaty obligations.

### ARTICLE 3.

The provisions of the present Treaty shall not impose any obligation upon either the United Kingdom or Italy in a case to which the obligations of that Power under Article 4 of the Treaty of Locarno would not be applicable. In particular, neither the United Kingdom nor Italy shall be under any obligation, in virtue of the present Treaty, to come to the assistance of the other.

### ARTICLE 4.

The provisions of the present Treaty are not in substitution for or qualification of any existing guarantees given by the High Contracting Parties among themselves, particularly under the Treaty of Locarno.

### ARTICLE 5.

The present Treaty, which is designed to ensure the maintenance of peace, and is in conformity with the Covenant of the League of Nations and the Pact of Paris, shall not be interpreted as restricting the duty of the League to take whatever action may be deemed wise and effectual to safeguard the peace of the world.

### ARTICLE 6.

The present Treaty shall be registered at the League of Nations in accordance with the Covenant of the League. It shall remain in force until the Council, acting on a request of one or other of the High Contracting Parties notified to the other signatory Powers three months in advance, and voting at least by a two-thirds majority, decides that the League of Nations ensures sufficient protection to the High Contracting Parties; the Treaty shall cease to have effect on the expiration of a period of one year from such decision.

### ARTICLE 7.

The present Treaty shall be ratified and the ratifications shall be deposited at . . .[7] as soon as possible. It shall come into force on . . .[7]

# APPENDIX III

## Memorandum and Correspondence on the Problem of Dominion Naval Quotas

### (a) Memorandum by the Dominions Office[1]

[A 10004/22/45]

DOMINIONS OFFICE, *November 26, 1935*

The question of the maintenance of a single quota for all the naval forces of the Commonwealth in accordance with the principle adopted in the Washington Naval Disarmament Treaty of 1922 (when inter-Imperial constitutional relations had not reached their present development) has a long history. It came up at the time of the Imperial Conference of 1926, and again in 1927, when Canada (before the Geneva Conference)[2] expressed doubts as to the desirability of its continuance.

2. Prior to the London Conference of 1930, the Dominion Governments were informed that in the Prime Minister's talks with General Dawes[3] 'it was contemplated that whatever arrangements may ultimately be arrived at would, so far as concerned the British Empire, be related to the naval forces of all parts in accordance with the Washington precedent'.[4] At the same time it was explained separately to the Canadian Government that it was thought that it would be a matter of great difficulty to persuade the United States and other Governments to proceed on any basis other than that of the single quota, and the Canadian Prime Minister indicated that he did not propose to raise any objection.

3. No comment on this aspect of the matter was received from any of the other Dominion Governments prior to the Conference, though at a meeting of Commonwealth delegates during the Conference one or two of the Dominion delegates gave indications that their Governments had not, in fact, understood that the single quota was definitely contemplated.

4. The adoption of the single quota principle did, however, give rise during the Conference to considerable difficulties in connexion with the form of the Treaty. It probably also accentuated the difficulties with regard to the representation of the Dominions at meetings of the Heads of Delegations and on committees.

5. As regards the first of these points, the drafting difficulties arising out of the desire of the Dominion delegates and Governments that the adoption of the single quota should in no way obscure the separate identities of the Dominions gave rise to prolonged discussions continuing up to the eve of the signature of the Treaty;

---

[1] A copy of this memorandum was received in the Foreign Office on November 28. A covering letter stated that it differed from an earlier version, sent to the Foreign Office on November 13, by the addition of a new paragraph (14).

[2] The reference was to the tripartite naval conference held at Geneva, June–August 1927; cf. No. 56, note 8.

[3] United States Ambassador at London, 1929–32.

[4] This assumption appears to have been taken for granted, and not directly mentioned, in the exchanges between Mr. MacDonald and General Dawes between June and December 1929; cf. Volume I of the Second Series, Nos. 35, 37, 40, 48, 146.

in fact, signature on the part of the Union of South Africa was doubtful, even when the final meeting arranged for signature began.

6. As regards the second point, the five Dominions were, of course, separately represented at the Conference by delegates furnished with Full Powers to negotiate, sign, &c., on behalf of their respective Dominions, and at plenary and other meetings of the Conference the seating arrangements and the order of speaking were alphabetical, *i.e.* United States of America, Commonwealth of Australia, Canada, France, Great Britain, and so on. The attitude of the Canadian, Union and Irish Free State delegates, which developed during the Conference, was that they could not accept anything in the nature of a 'panel' system of representation, but must be entitled to attend all operative meetings of the Conference, including formal meetings of Heads of Delegations, in order to speak on behalf of their respective Dominions. The view of the Irish Free State Government was expressed in the following passage of a telegram protesting against any other system than the full representation of the Dominions on Committees: 'The Commonwealth is a group of nations, their navies are a group of navies. No single Government has the right to speak for any other member of the group.' The general principle described above is, in fact, that followed by the Dominions at all international conferences and League meetings, and the Dominion Governments are very critical of any form of procedure which would throw any shadow of doubt on its international recognition.

7. Since 1930 the Irish Free State have made it evident that they have great objections to the form of the London Treaty, though they accepted it at the time, and it is quite clear that they could not again be induced to sign a treaty, embodying the principle of the single quota. There have been indications that some of the other Dominions share this view.

8. In this connexion it may be mentioned that discussions took place with Dominion High Commissioners in 1931 regarding certain returns required by the League of naval tonnage, effectives, &c. It was suggested by the United Kingdom Government that, as these returns were related to the Washington and London Treaties, it would be desirable that, in addition to *separate returns* for each Member of the Commonwealth the *collective figure* for all Members should in some way be sent in. All the Dominion representatives at the meeting, with the exception of the Irish Free State, agreed. The Irish Free State, however, maintained their objection to any collective figure being shown, and the Canadian and Union Governments then indicated that in the absence of unanimity they also must withdraw their agreement.

9. In June 1934 when the conversations with foreign representatives, which have led up to the forthcoming Naval Conference, were initiated, a telegram was sent to the Dominion Governments mentioning that this might be one of the points arising.[5] In that telegram two possible solutions of the question were mentioned. These were:—

(*a*) that there should be a single figure for the naval strength of all the Members of the British Commonwealth of Nations taken together;

(*b*) that there should be separate figures for each Member of the Commonwealth, and that the naval strength of foreign powers should be calculated in relation to the United Kingdom figures only.

[5] The reference was to the Dominions Office circular telegram B. No. 59 of June 18, 1934, not printed.

10. The following views were expressed by Dominion Governments after consideration of the above telegram:—

*The Commonwealth of Australia* and *New Zealand* were both very anxious for the retention of the principle of one quota for the whole British Commonwealth taken together. It was suggested in a telegram[6] from the Prime Minister of the Commonwealth of the 11th July, 1934 that an inevitable condition of the acceptance of separate figures for British Commonwealth naval strength on the part of the United States and Japan would be the complete separation of the navies of the United Kingdom and the Dominions. This might put an end to the exchange of ships and personnel and the advantages of a common training system essential to the Royal Australian Navy. In the event of any Dominion failing to maintain her quota it would not be in the United Kingdom's power to redress the balance of the total strength of the Empire.

11. The *Irish Free State* took the view that as the Treaty concerns the great naval powers exclusively, the members of the British Commonwealth other than the United Kingdom should not participate in it. This would get round any difficulty which might be met with if with all the members of the Commonwealth in the Treaty an attempt were made to calculate foreign strength on the basis of the United Kingdom alone.

12. No official expression of views from *Canada* was received, but in a discussion with Dr. Skelton, the Canadian Under Secretary of State for External Affairs, in October 1934 the suggestion was made for a single quota for those parts of the Empire which have naval forces (or special quotas with a right of transfer), the other parts of the Empire being ignored. Dr. Skelton appeared to think that the Canadian Government might be prepared to agree to such a solution with suitable safeguards of the constitutional position, e.g. a declaration to the effect that the Dominion Navies were separate naval forces, although limited in the Treaty by a single figure.

13. Although this question of quotas did not arise in connection with the Anglo-German Naval Agreement of this summer,[7] it is worth while mentioning that the Irish Free State Government took exception to the procedure adopted in that agreement, whereby the strength of the German naval forces was to be fixed in relation to the total of the naval tonnages of the Members of the British Commonwealth, on the ground that this treated the British Commonwealth as an entity and was liable to obscure the constitutional position of the Members of the Commonwealth.

14. As a matter of fact the assumption on which the telegram to Dominion Governments referred to in paragraph 9 above was sent would appear to be out of date, since it is now clear that if it is possible to secure any agreement at all on quantitative lines this will take the form of declarations as to building programmes, so that no question of quotas in reality is likely to arise. This was explained at the meeting between the First Lord and Dominion representatives which was held on the 13th November, 1935, though the point has not been made in official correspondence with Dominion Governments.

[6] Not printed.
[7] See Chapter IV in this Volume.

## (b) Letter from Mr. te Water to Mr. M. MacDonald[1]

### [A 10149/22/45]

Most secret                                    SOUTH AFRICA HOUSE, LONDON, November 25, 1935

Sir,

I have the honour, under instructions from my Government, to refer to your predecessor's telegram Circular B No. 59 of the 18th June [1934],[2] regarding the form in which limitation of the naval forces of the Members of the British Commonwealth of Nations should be expressed in any future naval treaty, and to state that this matter has recently received the further consideration of His Majesty's Government in the Union. Consideration has also been given to the question of the best method of meeting the wishes of His Majesty's Government in the United Kingdom that the figures of signatory powers should be expressed by reference to the figure assigned to the United Kingdom only instead of to those allotted to the whole British Commonwealth.

As a result, I have to state that in the view of His Majesty's Government in the Union, the contention of His Majesty's Government in the United Kingdom is perfectly legitimate, as the latter have no power of disposal over naval units of any of the Dominions. The United States of America and Japan, on the other hand, have the most complete power of disposal over the whole of the naval forces allotted to them.

The purpose which His Majesty's Government in the United Kingdom have in view could, it is felt, be achieved only if all Members of the British Commonwealth participated in any future agreement on the basis of separate figures being allotted to them, though His Majesty's Government in the Union understand that there might be some difficulty in obtaining general acceptance of this proposal.

His Majesty's Government in the Union feel, however, that, in view of the great interest which all Members of the Commonwealth have in the existence of a strong fleet in relation to other powers, an attempt should be made in other directions to achieve the object which His Majesty's Government in the United Kingdom have in view and they venture to suggest that this might best be arrived at if the Dominion Governments refrained from participation in any future agreement regarding naval forces. If this were so, the claims of His Majesty's Government in the United Kingdom would, it is felt, be unanswerable and the non-participation of the Dominions would have the additional advantage that they would be at liberty to construct their own naval forces according to their needs and without being subject to the limitations imposed by any agreement. This would have the effect, in the event of their deciding to participate in any future

[1] This letter embodied the substance of a telegram of November 21 from Pretoria received by Mr. te Water, High Commissioner in London for the Union of South Africa, on the 22nd; a paraphrased copy of this telegram reached the Dominions Office in time to be considered at an inter-departmental meeting on the 25th. Of this meeting Mr. Gore-Booth wrote on November 26: 'A meeting to discuss this tel. was held at the D.O. yesterday, as the result of which Mr. Holmes is drafting a memo. for the new S of S for Dominion Aff: [Mr. Malcolm MacDonald had succeeded Mr. J. H. Thomas as Secretary of State for Dominion Affairs on November 22] to use if necessary in his first interview with Mr. te Water. The line taken is that the proposed procedure would be even less acceptable to the foreign powers than the idea of separate figures for the Dominions, in that the Dominions being bound by no treaty wd be in a position to build any size navies they liked ... P. H. Gore-Booth. 26/11.'

[2] Cf. paragraph 9 of document (a).

war on the side of the United Kingdom that the Commonwealth would have a combined fleet larger than that of any single large naval power.

I am further instructed to state, for the information of His Majesty's Government in the United Kingdom, that under the existing agreements the figures allotted to foreign naval powers are based upon the assumption that the British Commonwealth forms a single unit for naval purposes and that when one Member is at war, all other Members participate in it with their naval forces. This assumption, in the view of my Government, has no constitutional basis whatever and is calculated unnecessarily to expose them to embarrassing criticism.

In view of the foregoing, His Majesty's Government in the Union are of the opinion that it might be preferable for all the Dominions not to take part in the forthcoming Conference and have made this suggestion to the other Members of the Commonwealth.

I have, etc.,
C. T. TE WATER

### (c) Mr. J. A. Lyons[1] to Mr. M. MacDonald
#### Paraphrase Telegram No. 89 [A 10149/22/45]

Secret                                                    CANBERRA, November 28, 1935

Reference your telegram of the 18th June 1934[2] and telegram No. 13 of the 21st November 1935 from the Minister for External Affairs, Union of South Africa.[3] The following telegram has been sent to the Union Minister for External Affairs. Begins: Secret. H.M. Government in the Commonwealth of Australia acknowledge your telegram No. 13 secret and have carefully considered your proposal(s). The subject of separate Dominion Naval quota[s] has to be considered from three aspects—naval, defence, international relations and constitutional status.

It will be recalled from my telegram of the 6th August 1934[4] that the Government of the Commonwealth of Australia are emphatically of the opinion that one Empire quota is most advantageous arrangement of Imperial Naval defence. It is to Britain that the Dominions must look to provide the main fleet that is the back-bone of naval security and there is a danger with separate defence quotas which seek to provide for ultimate strength considered necessary for naval security that the Empire may exchange a real strength for a paper one. The experience of the Commonwealth is based on 25 years of defence and naval development. The Royal Australian Navy is now at phase two of development of Empire navies under which Australia is responsible for providing manning and controlling Squadron. Australia has found this arrangement entirely satisfactory from defence and constitutional aspects.

H.M. Government in the Commonwealth of Australia consider that your suggestion for withdrawal from forthcoming Naval Conference would place on the Dominions, and on Australia and New Zealand in particular, the responsibility for any breakdown in negotiations and for a new race in naval armaments that might ensue. As the United States of America and Japan are primarily concerned

---

[1] Prime Minister of the Commonwealth of Australia.
[2] Cf. paragraph 9 of document (a).
[3] This telegram, not printed, was substantially the same as document (b).
[4] Not printed.

in questions of inclusion of Dominion naval strength in Empire quota any reactions would adversely affect relations in the Pacific Ocean and discount the recent attempt at improvement by the Latham and Debuchi mission(s).[5]

H.M. Government in the Commonwealth of Australia however feel in view of the predominant responsibility that rests on H.M. Government in the United Kingdom for Empire naval defence and conduct of naval disarmament policy that fullest weight should be given to the views of the Government of the United Kingdom in this matter. Ends. . . .[6] to South Africa, Canada, New Zealand, Irish Free State and India.

[5] In 1934 Mr. (later Sir John) Latham, the Australian Federal Attorney-General, had paid a 'goodwill' visit to Japan: the results were summed up in a report tabled in the House of Representatives at Canberra on July 6, 1934; cf. *The Times*, July 7, p. 11. In September, 1935, Mr. K. Debuchi, who had been Japanese Ambassador at Washington from 1928 to 1933, led an official Japanese mission to Melbourne and Sydney.

[6] The text was here uncertain. Presumably it should have read: 'Repeated'.

### (d) Mr. M. MacDonald to Mr. J. A. Lyons
Paraphrase Telegram No. 107[1] [A 10149/22/45]

Secret                                                DOMINIONS OFFICE, *November 29, 1935, 9.30 p.m.*

I have received from the High Commissioner for the Union of South Africa a communication[2] containing a message from His Majesty's Government in the Union of South Africa regarding the position of the Dominions in relation to the forthcoming Naval Conference in London. It is understood that a similar communication was made to the other Dominions by the Union of South Africa. The following is the text of reply which I have to-day addressed to the High Commissioner for the Union of South Africa. Begins:— We are most grateful for the suggestion of His Majesty's Government in the Union of South Africa, which we realize was made with a view to helping His Majesty's Government in the United Kingdom by ensuring that they would be in a position to maintain in all circumstances an adequate ratio with foreign Powers.

However, from a practical point of view, we fear that if, as is suggested, all or any of the Dominions were to abstain from participating in the Naval Conference, and in any Treaty negotiated there the whole Conference would be rendered abortive. The suggestion mentioned in my telegram of the 18th of June, 1934, that the Dominions should have separate quotas, and that the figures of foreign fleets should be fixed with reference to the United Kingdom figure only was mentioned tentatively to representatives of the United States in the course of the conversations last year, and met with a very unfavourable reception on their part. In fact, the reception was so unfavourable that it was considered useless to pursue the question with Japan, whose attitude would undoubtedly have been even less favourable. The suggestion now put forward that, instead of Dominion Naval forces being limited to separate quotas, there should be no Treaty limitation of Dominion Naval forces at all, would almost certainly provoke even stronger opposition on the part of foreign representatives, and we feel that if we attempt to proceed on these lines, it will make an already difficult position impossible.

[1] An identic telegram was sent to Canada (No. 94) and to New Zealand (No. 105): a copy was also sent to the Irish Free State.

[2] See document (*b*).

As you know, however, since the telegram of the 18th of June, 1934, was sent the circumstances have now completely changed. Preliminary discussions with the principal foreign countries concerned have made it clear that there is no prospect of concluding a Treaty on the lines of the Naval Treaties of Washington and London, which imposed specific limitations on the tonnages of the Contracting Powers, and the utmost that it is anticipated can be secured at the forthcoming Conference is qualitative limitation (i.e. limitation of size and gun power of the various type of vessels), accompanied possibly by some form of unilateral declaration by each of the various countries, whereby they would declare in advance their intentions as regards future naval construction. We should not contemplate that such declarations would actually form part of the Treaty, which would deal with the qualitative limitations, but that they should take the form of documents appended to it, whereby each Government would make a separate declaration that it did not intend to construct or acquire tonnage in excess of figures set out in a table.

If all or any of the Dominions, by refusing to participate in the Treaty, or to make such declarations, were to decline to accept any obligations on either of these matters, there seems no doubt that suspicion would be engendered in the minds of foreign Governments, and they might well take the line that in the circumstances they were not prepared themselves to enter into any obligations on these matters.

If the discussions should follow the lines now anticipated, it does not look as though there would be any likelihood of any constitutional difficulty arising from the proceedings of the Conference, or from any instruments negotiated thereat. But at any rate we shall continue to watch this aspect of the question with every desire, if difficulty should arise, of reaching a solution which will be satisfactory to all His Majesty's Governments.

In the circumstances, we very much hope that His Majesty's Government in the Union of South Africa will see their way to participate in the Conference.[3]

I am communicating the substance of this letter [sic] to the Governments of the other Dominions, with which I understand the Union Government communicated in similar terms. Ends.

[3] Mr. te Water participated in the Naval Conference as delegate of the Union of South Africa but abstained from signing the Agreement of March 25, 1936; cf. No. 711, note 4.

## (e) Mr. M. MacDonald to Mr. J. A. Lyons
### Paraphrase Telegram No. 108 [A 10149/22/45]

Secret                                        DOMINIONS OFFICE, November 29, 1935, 10.30 p.m.

I am much obliged for your Secret telegram No. 89[1] of the 28th November regarding the forthcoming Naval Conference in London. As will be seen from my immediately preceding telegram[2] the views of H.M. Government in the United Kingdom as to the probable effect of non-participation of Dominions in the Conference are substantially the same as those of H.M.'s Government in the Commonwealth of Australia. It will also be seen that the United Kingdom Government do not think it likely that any question of quotas, such as was contemplated when my secret telegram Circular B No. 59 of the 18th June, 1934, was sent, is likely to arise at the forthcoming Conference.

[1] Document (c).          [2] Document (d).